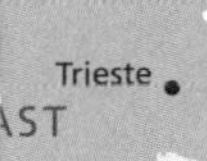

Venice

Emilia-Romagna
Pages 258–273

Trentino–Alto Adige
Pages 170–179

The Veneto and Friuli
Pages 142–169

Venice
Pages 88–141

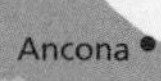

Umbria
Pages 352–367

Le Marche
Pages 368–377

Abruzzo, Molise, and Puglia
Pages 504–517

Pescara
L'Aquila
ROME
D LAZIO
Foggia
Bari
SOUTHERN ITALY
Napoli
Salerno
Potenza
Taranto

Basilicata and Calabria
Pages 518–525

Catanzaro
Palermo
Messina
Reggio di Calabria
SICILY
Catania
Agrigento

Sicily
Pages 526–547

EYEWITNESS TRAVEL

ITALY

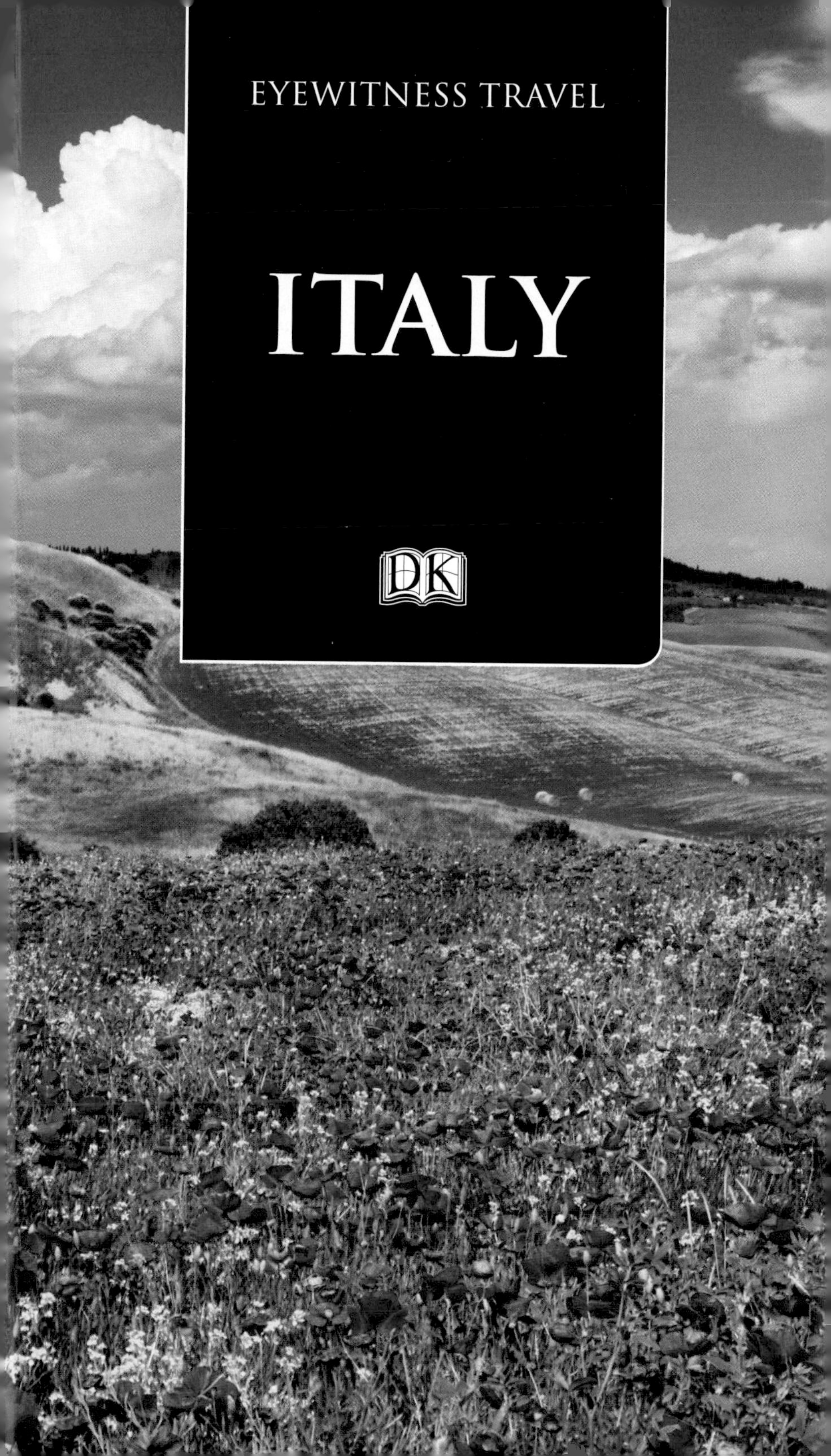
EYEWITNESS TRAVEL
ITALY
DK

LONDON, NEW YORK,
MELBOURNE, MUNICH AND DELHI
www.dk.com

Project Editor Fiona Wild
Art Editors Vanessa Courtier, Annette Jacobs
Editors Francesca Machiavelli, Sophie Martin, Helen Townsend, Nicky Tyrrell
Designers Jo Doran, Anthea Forlee, Paul Jackson, Marisa Renzullo
Main Contributors Ros Belford, Susie Boulton, Christopher Catling, Sam Cole, Paul Duncan, Olivia Ercoli, Andrew Gumbel, Tim Jepson, Ferdie McDonald, Jane Shaw

Maps
Lovell Johns Ltd., Dorling Kindersley Cartography

Photographer
John Heseltine

Illustrators
Stephen Conlin, Donati Giudici Associati srl, Stephen Gyapay, Roger Hutchins, Maltings Partnership, Simon Roulstone, Paul Weston, John Woodcock

Printed and bound by South China Printing Co. Ltd., China

First published in the UK in 1996 by Dorling Kindersley Limited
80 Strand, London WC2R 0RL

14 15 16 17 10 9 8 7 6 5 4 3 2 1

Reprinted with revisions 1997, 1999, 2000, 2001, 2002, 2003, 2004, 2005, 2006, 2007, 2008, 2009, 2010, 2011, 2012, 2013, 2014

Published in Great Britain by Dorling Kindersley Limited

A catalog record for this book is available from the Library of Congress.

ISSN 1542-1554

ISBN 978-1-46541-058-0

Floors are referred to throughout in accordance with European usage; i.e., the "first floor" is the floor above ground level.

The information in this DK Eyewitness Travel Guide is checked annually.

Every effort has been made to ensure that this book is as up-to-date as possible at the time of going to press. Some details, however, such as telephone numbers, opening hours, prices, gallery hanging arrangements, and travel information are liable to change. The publishers cannot accept responsibility for any consequences arising from the use of this book, nor for any material on third party websites, and cannot guarantee that any website address in this book will be a suitable source of travel information. We value the views and suggestions of our readers very highly. Please write to: Publisher, DK Eyewitness Travel Guides, Dorling Kindersley, 80 Strand, London WC2R 0RL, UK, or email: travelguides@uk.dk.com.

Front cover main image: Farmhouse and cypress trees, Pienza, Tuscany

◀ Rolling landscape of poppies and cypresses in San Quirico d'Orcia, Tuscany

Contents

David by Bernini, Rome

Introducing Italy

Northeast Italy

Northwest Italy

Central Italy

Gondolas weaving through the maze of canals in Venice

A traditional small shop in Volterra, Tuscany

Rome and Lazio

Southern Italy

Travelers' Needs

Survival Guide

Basilica of San Francesco in Assisi, started in 1228

HOW TO USE THIS GUIDE

This guide helps you get the most from your visit to Italy, providing expert recommendations as well as detailed practical information. *Introducing Italy* maps the whole country and sets it in its historical and cultural context. The 15 regional chapters, plus *Rome*, *Florence*, and *Venice*, describe important sights with the help of maps and images. Each section is introduced with features on regional architecture and food specialties. *Travelers' Needs* gives details of hotels and restaurants and the *Survival Guide* contains practical information on everything from transportation to personal safety.

Rome

The center of Rome has been divided into five sightseeing areas. Each area has its own chapter, which opens with a list of the sights described. All the sights are numbered and plotted on an *Area Map*. Each sight is presented in numerical order within the chapter, making it easy to locate.

All pages relating to Rome have orange thumb tabs.

1 Area Map For easy reference, the sights are numbered and located on a map. The sights are also shown on the *Street Finder* on pages 451–61.

A locator map shows where you are in relation to other areas of the city.

Sights at a Glance lists the chapter's sights by category: Churches, Museums and Galleries, Historic Buildings, Streets and Piazzas.

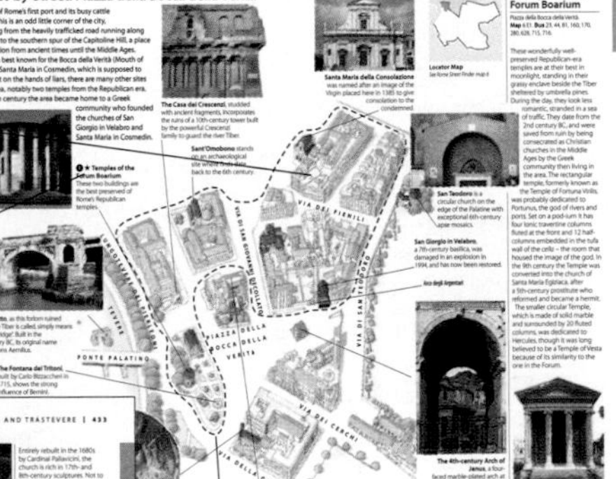

2 Street-by-Street Map This gives a bird's-eye view of the heart of each sightseeing area.

Stars indicate the sights that no visitor should miss.

A suggested route for a walk is shown in red.

3 Detailed information All the sights in Rome are described individually. Addresses and practical information are provided. The key to the symbols used in the information block is shown on the back flap.

Italy Area by Area

Apart from Rome, Florence, and Venice, Italy has been divided into 15 areas, each of which has a separate chapter. The most interesting towns and places to visit have been numbered on the section's *Regional Map*.

1 Introduction
The landscape, history, and character of each region are described here, showing how the area has developed over the centuries and what it offers to the visitor today.

Each area of Italy can be identified quickly by its color-coding, shown on the inside front cover.

2 Regional Map This shows the main road network and gives an overview of the whole region. All entries are numbered and there are also useful tips on getting around the region by car and train.

3 Detailed information
All the important towns and other places to visit are described individually. They are listed in order, following the numbering given on the *Regional Map*. Within each entry, information is given on the most important sights. The name of the provincial capital is given for smaller towns at the top of each entry.

Story boxes explore specific subjects further.

For all the top sights, a Visitors' Checklist provides the practical information you need to plan your visit.

4 Italy's top sights
These are given two or more full pages. Historic buildings are dissected to reveal their interiors; museums and galleries have color-coded floor plans to help you locate the most interesting exhibits.

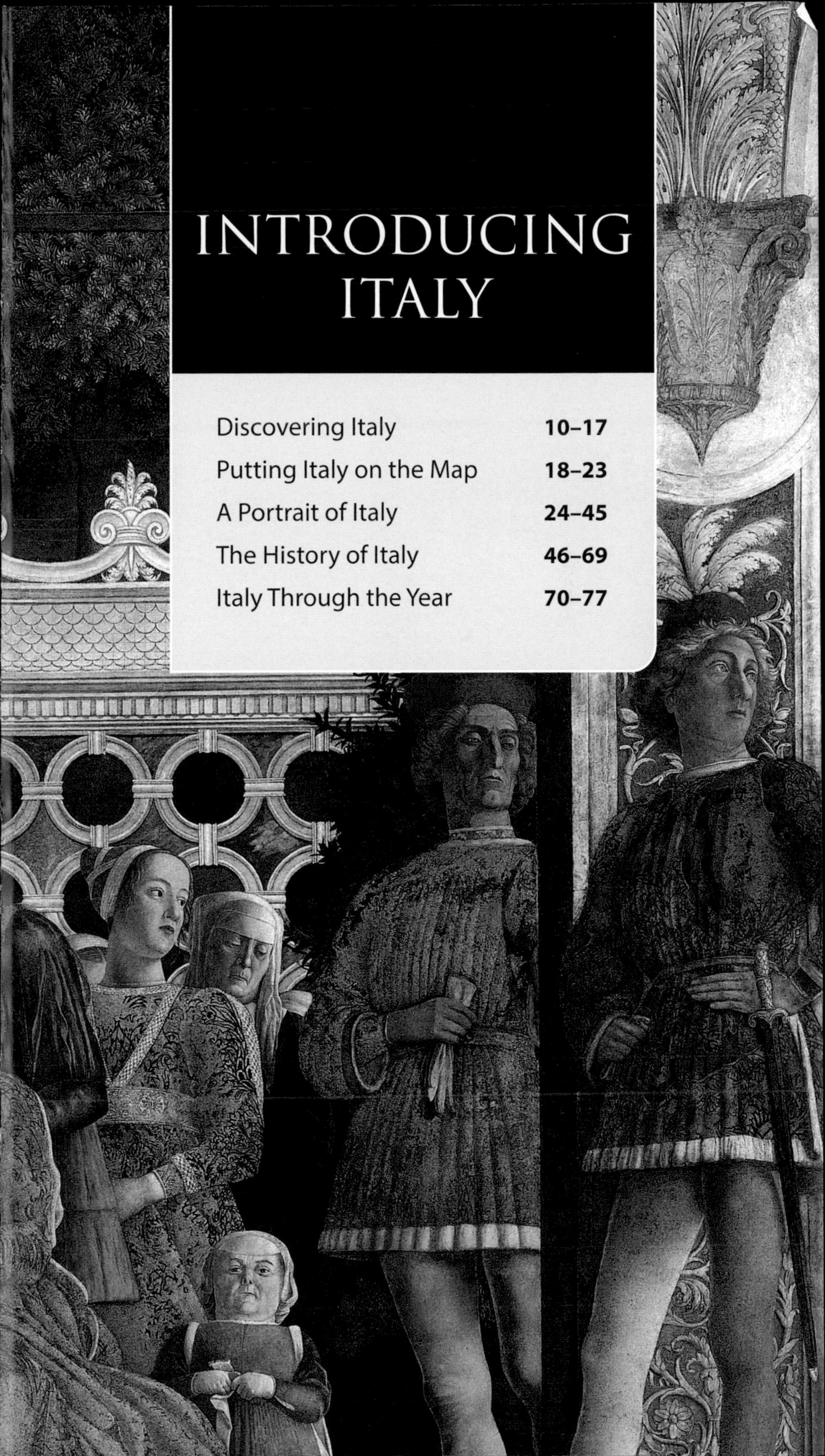

INTRODUCING ITALY

DISCOVERING ITALY

The following tours have been designed to take in as many of the country's highlights as possible, while keeping long-distance travel to a minimum. First come three 2-day tours of Italy's most glamorous cities: Rome, Florence, and Venice. These itineraries can be followed individually or combined to form a week-long tour. Extra suggestions are provided for those who want to extend their stay to 10 days.

Next come two 7-day tours, covering the north and the south of Italy. These can be combined to make a superb 2-week tour of the whole country. Finally, two themed itineraries have been designed for anyone looking to tailor their trip according to a specific interest. Pick, combine, and follow your favorite tours, or simply dip in and out and be inspired.

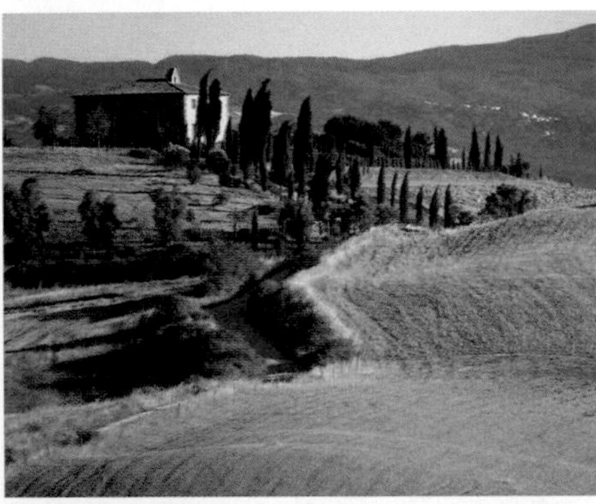

Golden fields of Tuscany
The Tuscan countryside, with its rolling hills and pencil-thin cypress trees, is a dream for artists and visitors alike.

A Week in Northern Italy

- See the artworks of the Pinoteca di Brera and shop in fashionable **Milan**.
- Take a relaxing cruise on **Lake Como** and walk in the surrounding countryside.
- Look up at Juliet's balcony in **Verona**; marvel at the architecture of **Vicenza**; admire frescoes in **Padua**.
- Enjoy a *vaporetto* ride along **Venice's** magnificent waterway, the Grand Canal.
- Take in the views of **Florence** from the Duomo and visit the city's world-famous galleries.
- Walk the dizzying pathways and hillsides of the **Cinque Terre** coastline.
- Explore the three enchanting Tuscan towns of **Lucca**, **Pisa** and **Siena**.

A Week in Southern Italy

- See treasures of the Classical World in **Rome's** museums and people-watch from the Spanish Steps.
- Marvel at sculptures and mosaics in Museo Archeologico in **Naples**; sample fantastic pizza in the city of its origin.
- Visit the evocative ruins of **Pompeii**; take a ferry to the island of **Capri**.
- Marvel at the beautiful views from the towns along the **Amalfi Coast**; enjoy the sea air at **Ravello**.
- Take a night ferry to Palermo in **Sicily** and visit the glittering Palazzo dei Normanni.
- Discover the Valley of the Temples near **Agrigento**; explore the magnificent Baroque town of **Noto**.

◀ 15th-century fresco, by Mantegna, from the Camera degli Sposi in the Palazzo Ducale

A Gourmet Tour of Central Italy

- Try fine cheeses and ham in the delightful town of **Parma**; sample vintage balsamic vinegar in **Modena**.
- Dine in style in **Bologna** and soak up the atmosphere in the city's *enoteche* (wine bars).
- Try the Tuscan specialty *Bistecca Fiorentina* in **Pisa**; enjoy *panforte* in **Siena**.
- Visit **Perugia** and stock up on the town's famous Baci chocolates; travel to **Norcia** to enjoy truffles, and pork from the region's black pigs.
- Spend a day in **Orvieto**, seeking out pecorino cheese, delicious salami, and Orvieto Classico wine.

A Tour of Etruscan Italy

- Explore fabulous museums dedicated to the Etruscan civilization in **Rome**.
- Visit the vast "city of the dead" at **Cerveteri**; marvel at the frescoed tombs in **Tarquinia**.
- See remnants of Etruscan life at the Necropoli Etrusca in **Orvieto**; spend an afternoon in the hilltop town of **Todi**.
- Travel to **Chiusi** for the fine Museo Nazionale Etrusco; visit medieval **Gubbio** to see the Eugubine Tablets.
- Spend a day in **Volterra** and see Etruscan funerary urns at the Museo Guarnacci; travel to **Florence** for the fabulous Medici Etruscan collection.

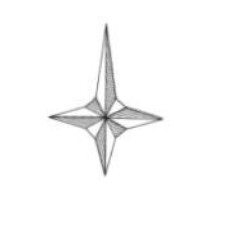

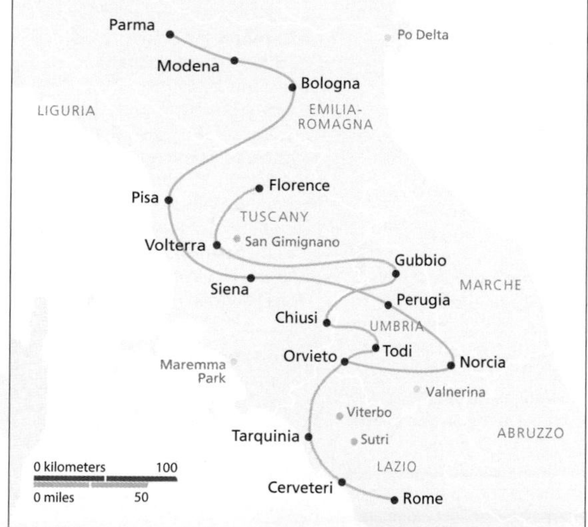

Key

- Gourmet Italy tour
- Etruscan Italy tour

Colosseum, Rome
Once the site of deadly gladiatorial combat, the Colosseum is the highlight of a trip to Rome. Tickets include access to the Forum and Palatine Museum.

Beautiful spiral staircase leading down from the Vatican Museums, Rome

2 days in Rome

The nation's capital has an overwhelming array of memorable sights, including the wonderful Vatican Museums and the Colosseum.

- **Arriving** Fiumicino (Leonardo da Vinci) is Rome's main airport, located about 18 miles (30 km) southwest of the city. The "Leonardo Express" train runs nonstop to Termini station, the city's main train station.
- **Moving on** Rome to Florence takes 1 hour 37 minutes by Eurostar.

Day 1
Morning A couple of days in **Rome** *(pp387–463)* will only scrape its surface, but do devote one day to the Vatican and St. Peter's. The fast route through the **Vatican Museums** *(pp424–31)* takes in the **Sistine Chapel** *(pp428–30)*. Don't miss Michelangelo's *Creation of Adam* on the ceiling and his dynamic altarpiece, *The Last Judgment*. The four **Raphael Rooms** *(p431)* show another Renaissance master, Raphael, at the peak of his artistic powers.
Afternoon Inside the awe-inspiring **St. Peter's** *(pp422–25)*, be sure to see Michelangelo's moving *Pietà*. Climb the dome for views, then descend to the grottoes for the papal tombs. Afterward, cross the Tiber to the *centro storico*. Look in at the **Pantheon** *(p408)*, the only ancient Roman temple to survive intact, then spend the evening among the exuberant Baroque fountains and cafés of **Piazza Navona** *(pp402–3)*.

Day 2
Morning Wander through the evocative ruins of the **Roman Forum** *(pp394–6)*, and on to the monumental **Colosseum** *(p397)*. Nearby, the church of **San Clemente** *(p439)* reveals its layers of history from pagan temple to 15th-century church.
Afternoon For great city views, head up to the **Capitoline Museums** *(pp390–91)*. The Palazzo Nuovo has a fine selection of Greek and Roman statues. For some respite, visit the pretty 17th-century pleasure gardens of **Villa Borghese** *(pp442–3)*. Visit **Piazza di Spagna** and the **Spanish Steps** *(p413)* and cast a coin in the Baroque **Trevi Fountain** *(pp414–5)*.

To extend your trip…
Take a day trip to the lovely hill town of **Tivoli** and **Hadrian's Villa** *(p472)*, about 3 miles (5 km) west of Tivoli.

View of the Vatican, with St. Peter's Basilica and Sant'Angelo bridge, Rome

2 days in Florence

Florence is the city for art lovers, with a wealth of breathtaking museums and galleries.

- **Arriving** Florence is served by two airports – Amerigo Vespucci airport, 2 miles (4 km) from the center, and Pisa airport. From Amerigo Vespucci, buses run to Florence's Santa Maria Novella train station; from Pisa, catch a direct train to Santa Maria Novella.
- **Moving on** The journey from Florence to Venice is just 2 hours by train.

The dome of Florence's Duomo, completed in 1436, designed by Brunelleschi

Day 1
Morning **Florence** *(pp274–317)*, the embodiment of the Renaissance, is much more compact than Rome. Feel the pull of Brunelleschi´s immense orange-tiled dome, which crowns the **Duomo** *(pp284–6)*. Climb the dome for stunning views, then admire Ghiberti's

Looking south from the upper terrace of the Boboli Gardens, Florence

famous bronze doors on the **Baptistry** *(pp284–6)*. A few streets away, the **Bargello** *(p287)* holds a fantastic collection of Renaissance sculpture.
Afternoon Take a stroll around **Piazza della Signoria** *(pp294–5)*, dominated by its towering city hall, the Palazzo Vecchio, and a copy of Michelangelo's *David*. Stop off at the famous Bar Vivoli Gelateria for an ice cream before tackling the **Uffizi** *(pp290–93)*. Caravaggio, Titian, Raphael – works by all the major artists of the Renaissance and beyond are on display here.

Day 2
Morning See the real statue of *David* by Michelangelo in the **Galleria dell' Accademia** *(p279)*, then visit the church of **Santa Maria Novella** *(pp300–301)* for Masaccio's *Trinity*, with its novel use of perspective.
Afternoon Visit the Gothic church of **Santa Croce** *(pp288–9)*, the final resting place of Michelangelo, Galileo, and Machiavelli. Next, cross **Ponte Vecchio** *(p289)* for the **Cappella Brancacci** *(pp302–3)* to see more frescoes by Masaccio. The fountains, grottoes, and woods of the **Boboli Gardens** *(p307)* are perfect for a picnic, and there is plenty more art in the **Palazzo Pitti** *(pp306–7)*.

To extend your trip...
Spend a day in the **Cinque Terre** *(p245)* and another exploring **Pisa** *(pp328–30)* and **Lucca** *(pp324–7)*.

2 days in Venice

This unique city on the water has romantic gondolas, magnificent churches, and wonderful art.

- **Arriving** Marco Polo airport is located at Tessera, 5 miles (8 km) north of the city. Alilaguna ferries, which stop at various points in the city, can be picked up a short walk from the airport. The travel time is around an hour. Water taxis are also available, but are expensive. Venice's main train station is Venezia Santa Lucia station.

Day 1
Morning Merely getting lost in **Venice** *(pp88–141)* will exceed expectations, as will the reality of the familiar images. To make the most of a visit to this watery city, travel by *vaporetto* or gondola along the **Grand Canal** *(pp92–5)* to **Piazza San Marco** *(pp112–13)* and the **Basilica di San Marco** *(pp114–17)*. The mosaics inside and out are ravishing, but so too are the Pala d'Oro (golden altarpiece), the jewels of the Treasury, and the four Horses of St. Mark on the balcony. Take the elevator to the top of the adjacent Campanile to be rewarded with a view stretching all the way to the Alps.
Afternoon Join a prebooked Secret Itineraries tour to get the most out of the **Palazzo Ducale** *(pp118–20)*, where the vast Sala del Maggior Consiglio, with its magnificent Tintoretto, is the highlight. Have coffee at Caffè Florian or Grancaffè Quadri on **Piazza San Marco** *(pp112–13)*, then cross the Grand Canal to the **Accademia** *(pp110–11)* for the best of the Venetian painters. If you prefer modern art, visit the **Peggy Guggenheim Collection** *(pp108–9)*, housed in the 18th-century Palazzo Venier dei Leoni.

Day 2
Morning Make for the **Rialto** *(p101)* to watch boats go by from the bridge, and stock up at the city's busiest market. Nearby is the church of **Santa Maria Gloriosa dei Frari** *(pp102–3)* with its exquisite altarpiece, a *Madonna and Child* by Bellini.
Afternoon Tour the islands of **Torcello** *(pp126–7)* for 12th- and 13th-century mosaics, **Murano** *(p125)* for the glass museum, and colorful **Burano** *(p125)* for lace. Be sure to sample some local snacks and drink an *aperitivo* in one of the many enticing bars back in Venice.

To extend your trip...
Take a day trip to **Verona** *(pp146–51)*, which has a fine Roman arena.

Stylish waiters serve drinks in refined Caffè Florian, Venice

A Week in Northern Italy

- **Airports** Arrive at Milano Malpensa airport and depart from Pisa Galileo Galilei.
- **Transportation** Trains connect the cities in 2 hours or less. Use the bus to reach Siena from Florence, and rent a car for the Cinque Terre, leaving it at La Spezia for the local train. It is easy to make day trips to Lake Como from Milan, the Veneto from Venice, and the Cinque Terre from Florence.
- **Reservations** *Milan*: Viewing of *Last Supper*; *Venice*: Basilica di San Marco; *Florence*: Accademia, Uffizi; *Pisa*: ascent of the Leaning Tower.

Day 1: Milan

If you're looking for Italian style, high fashion, art, and architecture, **Milan** *(pp196–205)*, the largest city of the north, has it all. Heading up the list of sights is Leonardo da Vinci's world-famous *Last Supper (p204)*. Visit the enormous Gothic Duomo *(p197)*, which invites a climb to its roof for the best city view. For glorious paintings from the Renaissance to the present day, don't miss the Pinacoteca di Brera *(pp202–203)*, and for those who enjoy shopping, Galleria Vittorio Emanuele II *(p198)*, with its magnificent glass dome and floor mosaics, is a must.

Day 2: Lake Como

Lake Como *(pp194–5)*, its long arms nestling between steep hillsides, is a prime example of Italy´s exquisite landscapes. Cruise the lake or take short ferry hops across the water, admiring the resplendent villas along the way. Explore Bellagio, or take a funicular up into the hills.

Day 3: Venice

Pick a day from the city itinerary on p13.

Day 4: The Veneto – Verona, Vicenza and Padua

Pick from a trio of towns, all within striking distance of Venice. Lively **Verona** *(pp146–151)* conjures up Shakespeare's *Romeo and Juliet*, and crowds still flock to see Juliet's balcony. Famous for concerts is the well-preserved Roman Arena *(p147)*, while the Romanesque church of San Zeno Maggiore *(pp150–51)* has a lovely cloister. Admirers of Palladio will appreciate **Vicenza** *(pp154–7)*, where his elegant Classical buildings surround the Piazza dei Signori. **Padua** *(pp158–63)* is known for its Cappella dei Scrovegni *(pp160–61)*, containing some wonderful frescoes by Giotto.

Day 5: Florence

Pick a day from the city itinerary on p12.

Day 6 : Cinque Terre

The five tiny villages of the **Cinque Terre** *(p245)* – Monterosso, Vernazza, Corniglia, Manarola, and Riomaggiore – are the jewels of Italy's northwest coast. Colorful houses cling to the rocky cliffs, making a hike along the connecting path a delight to the eye. You can do the whole trail (north to south is less steep) in five or six hours.

Rolling fields in Tuscany

Day 7: Tuscany – Lucca, Pisa, Siena

These three Tuscan towns are less busy than Florence, yet they offer a cultural feast with the bonus of an enchanting landscape. If time is tight, visit two. In **Lucca** *(pp324–7)*, promenade the encircling 17th-century grassy ramparts and visit the church of San Michele in Foro, its exquisite Pisan-Romanesque facade bursting with decoration. **Pisa** *(pp328–30)* is the home of the iconic 13th-century Leaning Tower, which, together with the Duomo and Baptistry, forms the Campo dei Miracoli. **Siena** *(pp342–7)* is one of Italy´s most appealing medieval towns and home to the twice-yearly Palio *(p345)*, when Piazza del Campo comes alive with spirited bareback horse racing. Within striking distance of the piazza are the Gothic Palazzo Pubblico, which contains a treasure trove of frescoes from the Middle Ages, and the magnificent Duomo *(pp346–7)*. En route from Pisa to Siena, try to catch a glimpse of the 13 medieval towers that pierce the skyline in **San Gimignano** *(pp348–9)*. The view is magical in the evening.

Pretty Bellagio, which sits on a peninsula at the top of Lake Como's two "arms"

For practical information on traveling around Italy, see pp628–35

A Week in Southern Italy

- **Airports** Arrive at Rome Fiumicino and depart from Catania airport, Sicily.
- **Transportation** Train travel from Rome to Naples is fast and easy (1 hour 10 minutes is the fastest). Take the ferry for Capri and Sicily, the bus for the coastal towns of Sorrento, Positano, Amalfi, and Ravenna, and for Agrigento from Palermo (2 hours). You will need a car to see inland Sicily: Piazza Armerina and Noto. Pompeii and Capri are easy to visit as day trips from Naples.
- **Reservations** *Rome*: Vatican Museums, Colosseum, Forum, and Palatine; *Naples*: Museo Archeologico Nazionale, Secret Cabinet Tour.

The evocative ancient temple ruins at Selinunte, Sicily

Days 1 and 2: Rome
See the city itinerary on p12.

Day 3: Naples
Naples *(pp490–97)* is chaotic, but the rewards of visiting are manifold. The main attraction is the world-renowned Museo Archeologico Nazionale *(pp494–5)* and its vast collection of Roman and Pompeiian treasures; allow at least half a day here. Reserve ahead for the Secret Cabinet tour to view the erotic works from Pompeii. Tiny Cappella Sansevero *(p491)* holds intriguing works from the 18th century, notably the virtuoso alabaster and marble *Veiled Christ* by Sammartino. Santa Chiara *(p493)* is worth seeing for its charming majolica-tiled cloisters. Don't leave without eating pizza in the city of its invention.

Day 4: Pompeii and Capri
The Circumvesuviana train skirts the base of Vesuvius from Naples to Pompeii and on to Sorrento. **Pompeii** *(pp498–9)* gives you an insight into a Roman town as it was in AD 79 before it was destroyed, most poignantly through the body casts of the people who perished here. Arrange a trip up the infamous volcano, or take a ferry from Naples or Sorrento to the idyllic island of **Capri** *(pp502–503)*, best enjoyed in the quiet of evening. Blue Grotto sea cave and Villa Jovis of Emperor Tiberius are secondary attractions to the captivating vistas you will find here.

Marina Grande on the pretty island of Capri

Day 5: Amalfi Coast
Take the hair-raising bus ride along the coast for views of a lifetime and stop off at your leisure at some of Italy's most beautiful towns. **Sorrento** *(p501)* is the most prosaic and popular, while chic **Positano** *(p501)* favors the jet set and comes with a good beach. **Amalfi** *(p501)* has a stunning 9th-century cathedral, while **Ravello** *(p501)*, set high above terraces of lemon groves, has the best of the views. Lose yourself among the bougainvillea in the lush gardens of the Villa Cimbrone or Villa Rufolo.

Days 6 and 7: Sicily
Sicily is a melting pot of Norman, Byzantine, Greek, and Arab influences and deserves at least two days' exploration. Taking the night ferry from Naples to Palermo, the island's largest town, will save you time. **Palermo** *(pp530–33)* exemplifies all these influences, notably in the Palazzo dei Normanni, whose Cappella Palatina is a glittering mix of mosaics, marble, and gold. The most famous Norman mosaics, however, are outside Palermo, at the highly ornamented Duomo of Monreale *(pp534–5)*. Seek out the intricate Norman cloisters here. To the south you can discover the ancient Greek legacy in the Valley of the Temples *(p540)*, near Agrigento, or at Selinunte *(p538)*, which has the benefit of a long and sandy beach. In the interior, the Villa Romana del Casale at **Piazza Armerina** *(p541)* sports some of Italy's liveliest mosaics, and beautiful **Noto** *(p547)*, aglow with golden stone, is a unique Baroque town rebuilt after the earthquake of l693.

A Gourmet Tour of Central Italy

- **Duration** 7 days – but extends to a 10-day tour with the extra suggestions.
- **Airports** Arrive at Milan Linate airport and depart from Rome Fiumicino airport. From Milan, travel by train or car to Parma for the first stop on the tour.
- **Transportation** This tour can be made using Italy's railroad network, but renting a car allows more flexibility.

This itinerary takes you to Italy's central regions – Emilia-Romagna, Tuscany, and Umbria – focusing on the regional food specialties along the way. If you are traveling in summer or fall, look for the copious food festivals held across the region.

Day 1: Parma
Affluent **Parma** *(p263)* is synonymous with cheese and ham – *Parmigiano Reggiano* (parmesan) and *prosciutto crudo* (Parma ham). The delicatessens here are a feast for the eyes, as are the city's main sights, which include an exquisite 12th-century baptistry and paintings by Correggio in the lovely Duomo.

Day 2: Modena
The handsome city of **Modena** *(p264)* has two main claims to fame: it is the producer of fast cars (Ferrari and Maserati) and balsamic vinegar – try the city's market for the best vintage variety. In between sampling some of the region's other specialties, such as mortadella, spicy sausage, and pig's feet, be sure to visit the very fine Romanesque Duomo and the Este collection of paintings in the Palazzo dei Musei.

Day: 3 Bologna
Dress up for dinner here – **Bologna** *(pp266–9)* has some of the country's finest restaurants and atmospheric *enoteche* (wine bars). Homemade pasta comes with the famous Bolognese (*ragù*) or cream sauce, or stuffed with ricotta, pork, or pumpkin. During the day, check out the medieval skyscrapers of the Due Torri and the Gothic church of San Petronio.

To extend your trip...
Cycle around the lagoons of the **Po Delta** *(p270–71)*, 60 miles (97 km) from Bologna.

Day 4: Pisa
Spend a day in **Pisa** *(pp328–30)*. The city's main draw is the Campo dei Miracoli, which contains the Duomo, Baptistry, and Leaning Tower. Pisa's culinary attractions include fish dishes, such as *cacciucco*, a hearty fish soup, and *baccalá alla Pisana*, salt cod with tomato sauce. Meat-eaters will love *bistecca Fiorentina* (thick charcoal-grilled steak).

The iconic Leaning Tower of Pisa

Day 5: Siena
Life in **Siena** *(pp342–7)* centers on the beautiful fan-shaped piazza of Il Campo, around which *pasticcerie* sell the city's famous *panforte* cake and *ricciarelli* (almond cookies). Admire the frescoes in the medieval Palazzo Pubblico and the treasures of the spectacular Duomo and its Museo.

To extend your trip...
Head for the coast at **Maremma Park** *(pp350–51)*, 50 miles (81 km) from Siena.

Day 6: Perugia and Norcia
Stop at **Perugia** *(pp356–7)* to stock up on Baci chocolate and see the frescoes in the Palazzo dei Priori, before traveling to the gastromic hot spot of **Norcia** *(pp366–7)*, where black truffles, salami, and pork from the local black pigs are the specialties.

To extend your trip...
Explore the mountains of the **Valnerina** *(p367)*, 30 miles (48 km) from Norcia.

Day 7: Orvieto
You can be assured of good-quality food here as **Orvieto** *(pp362–3)* is headquarters of the Città Slow movement and an advocate of slow food. Look for pecorino cheese and salami, and of course, Orvieto Classico wine. Take time to visit the Romanesque-Gothic Duomo and the 16th-century Pozzo di San Patrizio.

Atmospheric outdoor dining in Piazza della Mercanzia, Bologna

A Tour of Etruscan Italy

- **Duration** 7 days – but extends to a 10-day tour with the extra suggestions.
- **Airports** Arrive at Rome Fiumicino airport and depart from Pisa Galileo Galilei (trains from Florence to Pisa take 1 hour).
- **Transportation** This tour is most easily done by car, though Cerveteri is accessible by bus from Rome and Tarquinia and Orvieto by train.

Well-preserved "Street" of Etruscan tombs, Cerveteri

This tour focuses on the ancient Etruscan sights and museums of Lazio, Umbria, and Tuscany, as well as other interesting sights along the way. For more on Italy's first major civilization, see pp48–9.

Day 1: Rome

Be inspired by the world's best collections of Etruscan treasures in the **Etruscan Museum of the Vatican** *(p424)* and the **Museo Nazionale Etrusco** in the **Villa Giulia** *(p444)*. The tender portrayals of people on the sarcophagi, the delicate and intricate gold jewelry, and the lifelike bronze sculptures display amazing craftsmanship. Leave time for the lovely gardens of the **Villa Borghese** *(pp442–3)*.

Day 2: Cerveteri

Feel the mystery of the vast necropolis at **Cerveteri** *(p470)* as you stroll its silent streets. Here, see the tombs that were built as replicas of homes, decorated with frescoes and filled with domestic furnishings. Fifty thousand Etruscans were entombed here from the 7th to the 1st century BC in what was one of the most powerful of the 12 Etruscan cities. Visit the Museo Nazionale Cerite to see displays of objects that were buried with the bodies.

To extend your trip...
Head 40 miles (64 km) from Rome to the Etruscan amphitheater at **Sutri** *(p470)*.

Day 3: Tarquinia

Spend some time in **Tarquinia** *(p470)*, the medieval center of which was the capital of Etruria 2,500 years ago. Head uphill to the necropolis, a warren of tombs that hold lively and colorful frescoes depicting the lives of their inhabitants. For more revelations of everyday life and artistry, head for the Museo Archeologico, where, alongside the famous terra-cotta winged horses, are fine displays of jewelry, bronzes, and ceramics.

To extend your trip...
Visit the Renaissance gardens of Villa Lante at **Viterbo** *(pp468–9)*, 40 miles (64 km) from Tarquinia.

Day 4: Orvieto and Todi

You can see more Etruscan remains in **Orvieto** *(pp362–3)*, at the Museo Archeologico Faina and Museo Civico, at the Necropoli Etrusca, and even during a tour of Orvieto Underground *(www.orvietounderground.it)*. The fine, beautiful Duomo and the 16th-century Pozzo di San Patrizio add to the attractions. From here, travel to nearby **Todi** *(p363)*. This dramatic hilltop town is home to the Museo Etrusco-Romano.

Day 5: Chiusi and Gubbio

Make your way northward to **Chiusi** *(p336)* and the Museo Nazionale Etrusco for its fine display of urns and vases taken from the surrounding tombs. Then head toward the forest-clad Appenines for charming **Gubbio** *(p356)*, where the Palazzo dei Consoli houses the famous seven bronze Eugubine Tablets inscribed with Etruscan letters, and where the strange Porte della Morte, walled up doors, were once supposedly used to transport coffins.

Volterra, once an important Etruscan city

Day 6: Volterra

The city of **Volterra** *(p338)* is home to the excellent Museo Guarnacci and beautiful Etruscan funerary urns, made out of alabaster, for which the region is famous. For more alabaster, visit the Pinacoteca e Museo Civico and browse the craft shops.

To extend your trip...
A 20-mile (32-km) drive from Volterra takes you to **San Gimignano** *(pp348–9)* and its 13th-century towers.

Day 7: Florence

Finish your tour in Florence and visit the Medici Etruscan collection in the **Museo Archeologico** *(p281)*, which includes two outstanding sculptures – the Chimera and the Arringatore (Orator) bronze.

Putting Italy on the Map

Italy sits at the heart of the Mediterranean, shielded from the rest of Europe by the vast sweep of the Alps. The Po, its longest river, arcs across the industrial north, while the Apennine mountains split the boot-shaped peninsula down its length. Italy, with a population of 58 million governed from Rome, covers 116,320 sq miles (301,268 sq km) and includes Sicily and Sardinia.

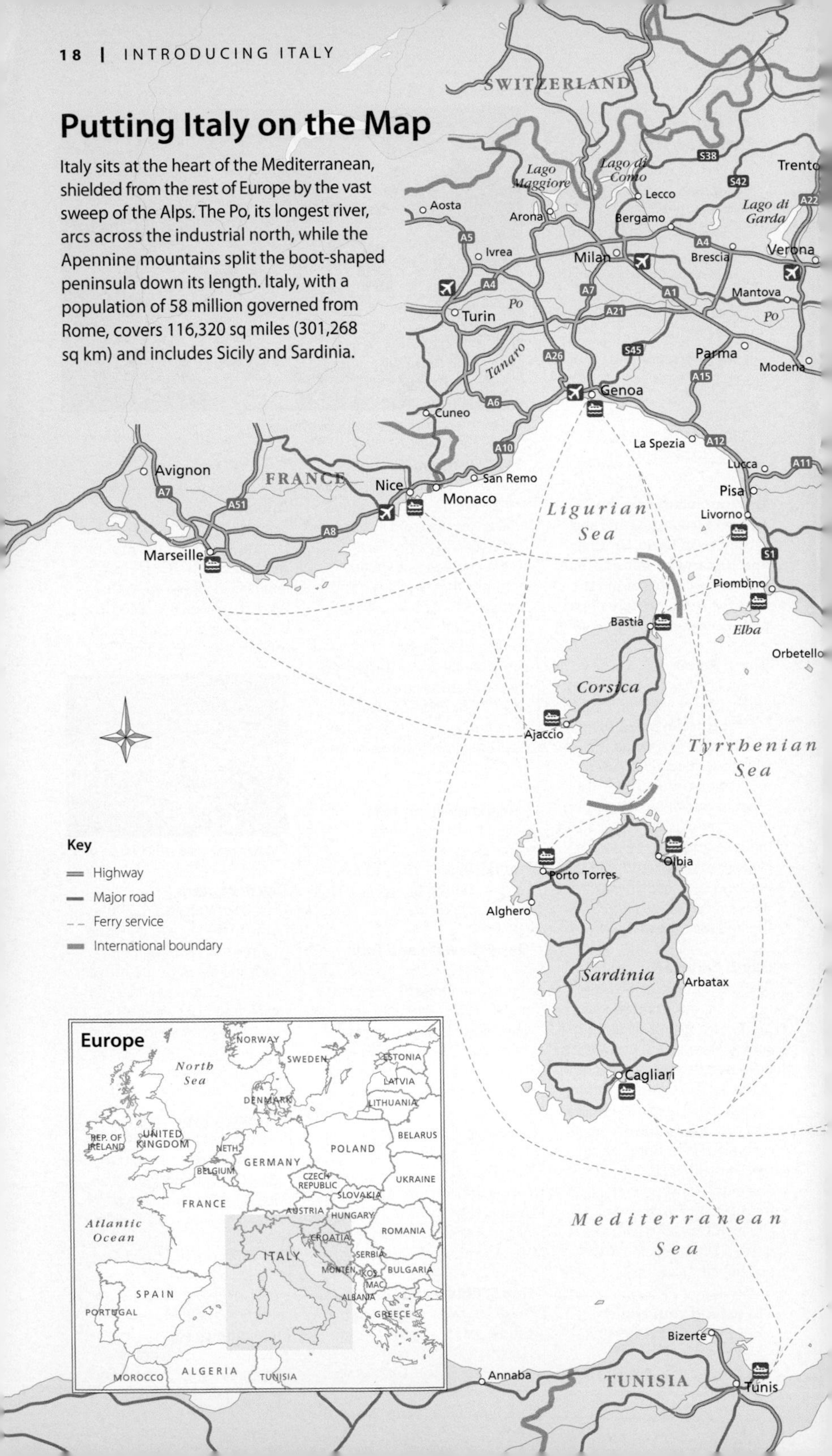

Key

- Highway
- Major road
- Ferry service
- International boundary

Europe

AUSTRIA
SLOVENIA
HUNGARY
CROATIA
BOSNIA AND HERZEGOVINA
ITALY
Adriatic Sea
Ionian Sea
Sicily
Bolzano
Cortina d'Ampezzo
Belluno
Udine
Treviso
Trieste
Vicenza
Venice
Padova
Adige
Ferrara
Bologna
Ravenna
Rimini
San Marino
Pèsaro
Florence
Ancona
Siena
Gubbio
Perugia
Ascoli Piceno
Orvieto
Terni
Viterbo
Pescara
L'Aquila
Civitavécchia
Sulmona
Rome
Anzio
Foggia
Manfredonia
Barletta
Benevento
Bari
Naples
Isola d'Ischia
Isola di Capri
Amalfi
Potenza
Matera
Taranto
Brindisi
Lecce
Lauria
Rossano
Cosenza
Crotone
Catanzaro
Vibo Valentia
Reggio di Calabria
Messina
Palermo
Trapani
Isole Egadi
Marsala
Enna
Catania
Agrigento
Gela
Siracusa
Isola di Pantelleria
Ustica
Isole Eólie o Lípari
Isole Tremiti
Klagenfurt
Dráva
Maribor
Varazdin
Ljubljana
Zagreb
Pecs
Karlovac
Rijecka
Pula
Slavonski Brod
Banja Luka
Zenica
Zadar
Sibenik
Split
Sarajevo
Mostar
Dubrovnik
Greece, Egypt
Greece
Malta
A22
S51
A23
A4
A2
A1
A3
A6
A13
A14
S71
S3
S77
A24
S4
S1
A25
S17
A16
S16
S18
S106
A20
A18
A29
A19
0 kilometers 200
0 miles 100

Northern Italy

Airline connections link the rest of Europe with Milan, Turin, Bologna, Pisa, Florence, Verona, and Venice. Major roads and railroads also provide excellent links to cities all over Europe. Transportation services are very efficient, with highways and railroads along both coasts, and across the area's main east-to-west axis at the foot of the Alps. Milan, Verona, and Bologna are the key transportation hubs, while Florence forms the focus of links to the south.

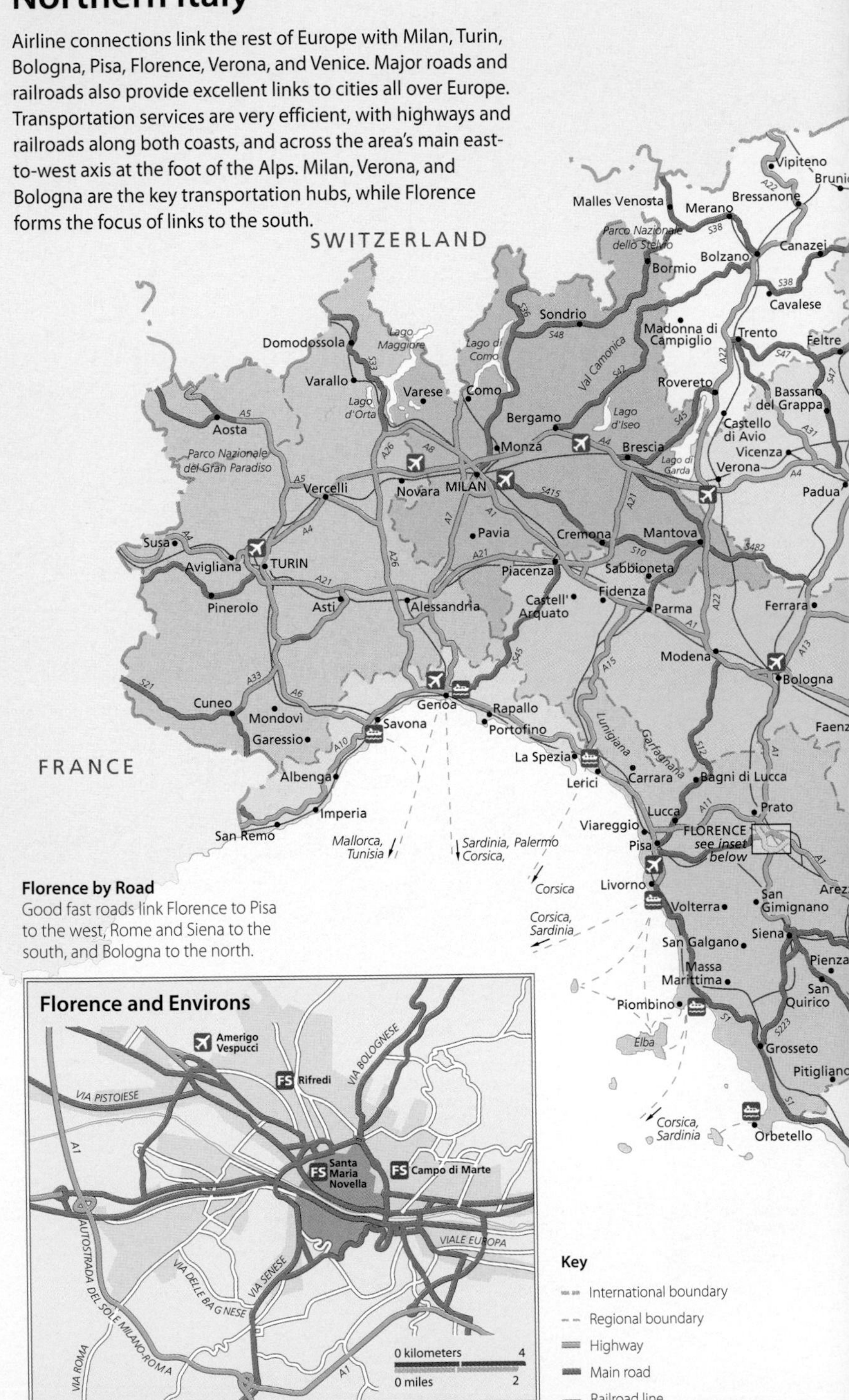

Florence by Road
Good fast roads link Florence to Pisa to the west, Rome and Siena to the south, and Bologna to the north.

For additional map symbols *see back flap*

Venice by Road
Venice is joined to the mainland by a causeway. This provides easy access to highway links with Verona and Padua.

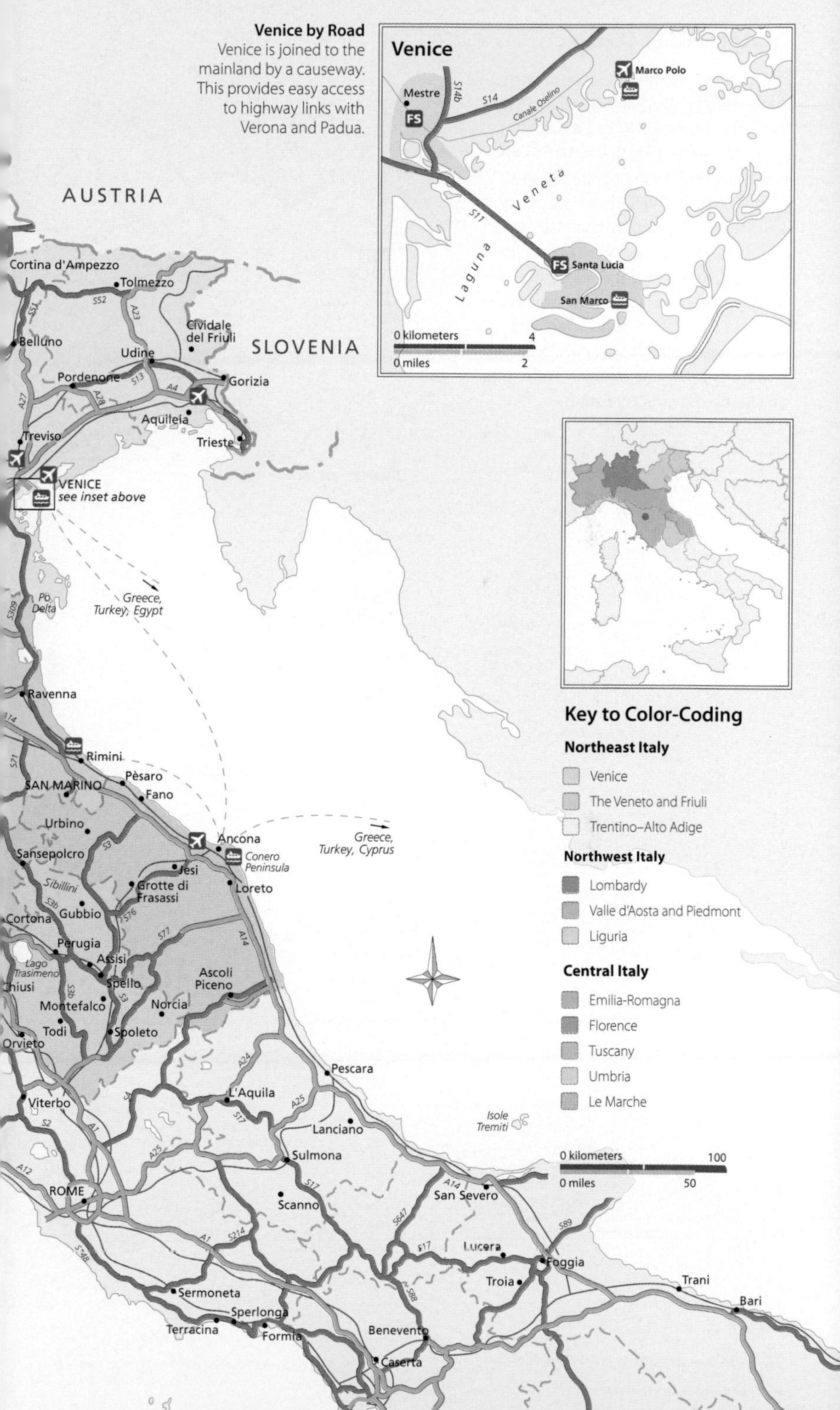

Southern Italy

International airline services operate to Rome, Naples, and Palermo in southern Italy. Transportation links within the region are generally slower than in the north, particularly inland and on the islands of Sicily and Sardinia, where buses are often a faster option than trains. Mainland coastal road and railroad links are good, however, especially those linking Rome and Naples, the region's main transportation hubs, which are connected by a high-speed train service. Two trans-Apennine highways offer the quickest cross-country routes.

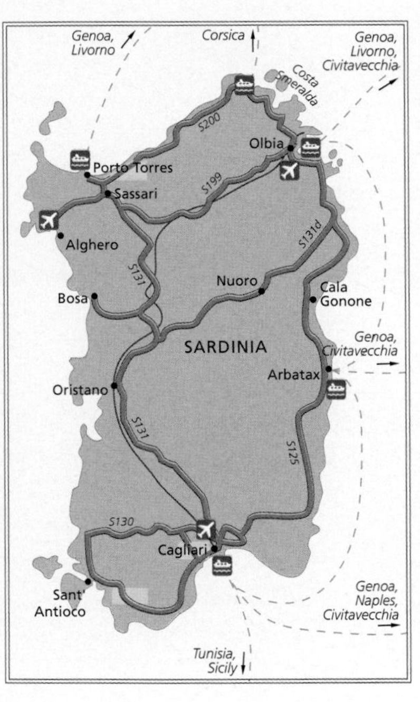

Sicily and Sardinia

Ferries operate to Sicily from Naples, Villa San Giovanni, and Reggio di Calabria. Onward connections include boats to Malta and Tunisia. Ferries run to Sardinia from several mainland ports, notably Civitavecchia, Genoa, and Livorno.

Key

- International boundary
- Regional boundary
- Highway
- Main road
- Railroad line

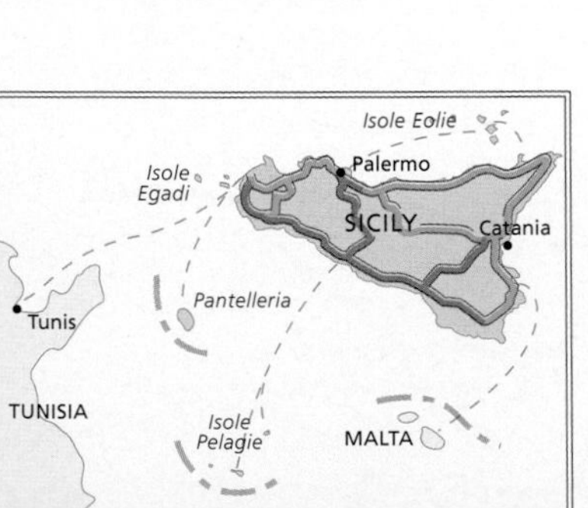

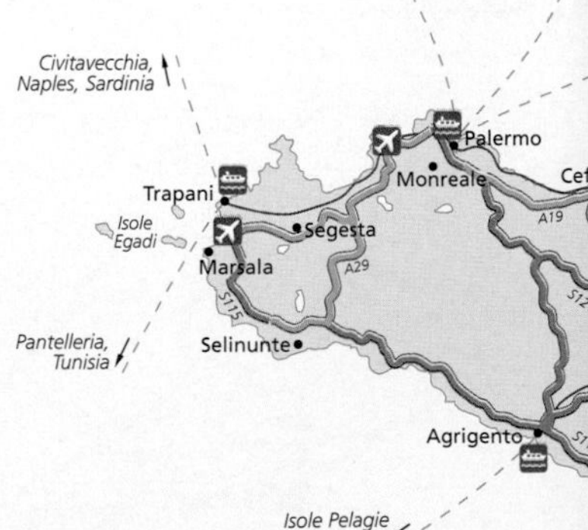

For additional map symbols *see back flap*

Rome by Road
Highway links approach Rome from Naples, Pescara, and Florence. All feed into the city's ring road, the Grande Raccordo Anulare.

Key to Color-Coding

Rome and Lazio

- Rome
- Lazio

Southern Italy

- Naples and Campania
- Abruzzo, Molise, and Puglia
- Basilicata and Calabria
- Sicily
- Sardinia

A PORTRAIT OF ITALY

Italy has drawn people in search of culture and romance for many centuries Few countries can compete with its Classical origins, its art, architecture, musical and literary traditions, its scenery or food and wine. The ambiguity of its modern image is also fascinating: since World War II Italy has climbed into the top ten world economies, yet at its heart it retains many of the customs, traditions, and regional allegiances of its agricultural heritage.

Italy has no single cultural identity. From the northern snowcapped peaks of the Alps, to the rugged southern shores of Sicily, lies a plethora of distinctive regions and peoples. Politically, Italy is a young country: it did not exist as a unified nation state until 1870, and its 20 regions have maintained their cultural individuality. Visitors to Italy are often pleasantly surprised by the diversity of its dialects, cuisines, and architecture. There is also a larger regional division. People speak of two distinct Italies: the rich industrial north and the poorer agricultural south, known as *Il Mezzogiorno* or Land of the Midday Sun. The frontier separating the two is indeterminate, lying somewhere between Rome and Naples.

The north is directly responsible for Italy's place among the world's top industrial nations. It has been the powerhouse behind the Italian economic miracle, its success achieved by internationally renowned names such as FIAT, Prada, Ferragamo, Pirelli, Olivetti, Zanussi, Alessi, and Armani. In contrast, the south, once a cradle of high culture and civilization, has been dogged by

View of the rooftops of Montalcino from the town's fortress

◀ Cobbled lane in the coastal fishing town of Cefalù, Sicily unemployment and organized crime. Some of its areas rank among the most depressed in Europe, although many southern towns did benefit from an injection of Millennium funds.

The historic divide between north and south is a powerful factor in contemporary politics. The federalist party, the Northern League, owes its popularity to this split. Those in favor of separation complain that the south is a drain on resources: Milan is seen as efficient and rich, while Naples is viewed as chaotic, dirty, and corrupt.

History and geography have both contributed to the division. The north is closer in both location and spirit to Germany and France, while the south has suffered a succession of invasions from foreign powers: Carthaginians and Greeks in ancient times, Saracens and Normans in the Middle Ages, and until the middle of the 19th century, the Bourbons from Spain held sway.

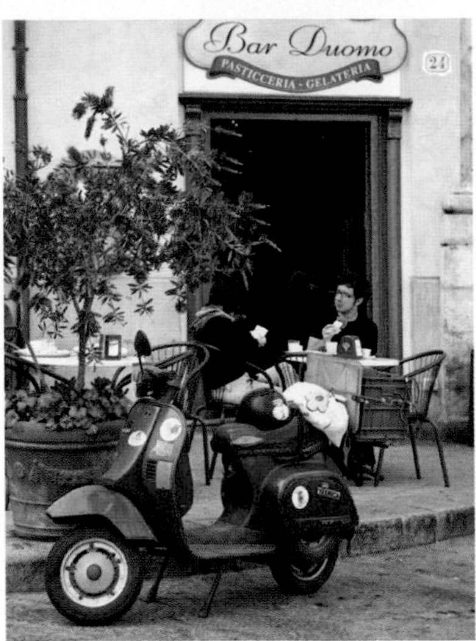

A scooter parked in front of The Bar Duomo, Piazza Duomo in Cefalù

Tradition

Distinctive variations in Italy's regions have much to do with the mountainous landscape and inaccessible valleys. Tuscan and Ligurian hill towns, for instance, have quite different silhouettes, and the farmhouses in Puglia, the famous *trulli*, are unlike those found in the landscape of Emilia-Romagna.

In southern Italy the landscape, architecture, dialects, food, and even the appearance of the people have closer affinities with the Eastern Mediterranean and North Africa than with Europe. In the far south, study of the local dialects has revealed traces of ancient Greek and old Albanian, preserved in tightly knit communities isolated by the rugged geography. Christianity and pagan ritual are closely linked; sometimes the Virgin is portrayed as a thinly disguised Demeter, the Earth goddess.

Café-goers relaxing in Marina di Pisa, Tuscany

Medieval skyscrapers emerging from the Tuscan landscape of San Gimignano

Throughout Italy, ancient techniques of husbandry endure, and many livelihoods are closely connected to the land and the seasons. Main crops include sugar beet, corn, wheat, olives, and grapes; colorful Easter celebrations *(see p70)* pay tribute to the bounty of the soil. Although some of the north's postwar economic prosperity can be attributed to industry (especially car production in and around Turin), much of it has grown from the expansion of family-owned artisan businesses and the export of handmade goods abroad. This is recognized as a distinct sector of the economy. The internationally successful retail clothes chain Prada is a good example. The "Made in Italy" label, found on goods such as clothes, shoes, and leather bags, guarantees a high standard.

Culture and Arts

The arts in Italy have had a long and glorious history and Italians are very proud of this. Given the fact that Italy has more than 100,000 monuments (archeological sites, cathedrals, churches, houses, and statues), all of which have major historical significance, it is not surprising that there is a shortage of funds to keep them in good repair. Many museums in Italy, particularly those in the south, are closed, or partially closed. You may find churches in Venice hidden behind permanent scaffolding, or those in Abruzzo shut due to earthquake damage. However, with tourism accounting for around 12 percent of Italy's Gross Domestic Product,

Bernini's 17th-century Fontana del Tritone, Rome

Roadside stall near Positano, Campania

efforts are being made to put as many buildings and collections on show as possible. The Jubilee 2000 helped matters by allocating large amounts of money for the restoration of buildings and sites belonging to the Catholic Church.

The performing arts are also underfunded, yet there are some spectacular cultural festivals. Almost every town of any size has its own opera house, and La Scala opera house in Milan stages world-class productions.

Cinema is another flourishing art form in Italy and has been so since its invention. The sets at Cinecittà, on the outskirts of Rome, have been used by many famous directors, including Fellini, Pasolini, de Sica, Visconti, and many others. Italian films such as *La Vita è Bella* and *The Son's Room* have found critical acclaim and box-office success both in Italy and abroad. In Italy the arts belong to everyone: opera is attended by people from all backgrounds, regardless of social status, as are movie theaters and galleries.

Social Customs and Politics

Italian society is still highly traditional, and Italians can be very formal. Between the generations degrees of familiarity exist: reserve *ciao* (hello or goodbye) for friends your age or younger, and greet older people with *piacere* (pleased to meet you), *buon giorno* (good day) or *buona sera* (good evening), and on parting, say *arrivederci* (goodbye). Strangers are met with a handshake, but family and friends receive a kiss.

Italian chic decrees that the clothes you wear should give the impression of wealth. If Italians wear similar outfits, it is because they are conformists in fashion as in other aspects of daily life.

Italian politics, in contrast, are not so well regulated. Governments in the postwar era were characterized by short-lived coalitions, dominated by the Christian Democrats. In 1993 Italy experienced a political crisis when an organized network of corruption was exposed, disgracing a huge number of politicians and businessmen. The investigations may have failed to eradicate corruption, but they led to the formation of two large coalitions, centre-left and centre-right. Silvio Berlusconi, leader of Forza Italia, became prime minister in 1994 but lasted a short while as he, too, was accused of corruption. In 1998 Massimo D'Alema became Italy's first left-wing Prime Minister. Recent years have seen an alternation of the two coalitions, with

Diners relaxing at a restaurant in Orta San Giulio, Piedmont

The solution to heavy traffic in Rome: motorbikes and scooters

Berlusconi dominating. Economist and academic Mario Monti became prime minister in November 2011. In April 2013 a coalition was sworn in, made up of the Democratic Party and Berlusconi's People of Freedom Party (PDL), but the PDL has split into Berlusconi's Forza Italia and the New Centre Right (NCD).

Modern Life

Food and soccer are the great constants; Italians live for both. Much time is spent on preparing food and eating. The Italian diet, particularly in the south, is among the healthiest in the world. Soccer is a national passion and inspires massive public interest and media attention, not least as a way of expressing regional loyalties.

As far as religion is concerned, the number of practicing Catholics has been in decline for some years. Although Rome lies at the center of world Catholicism, today many Italians are uninterested in religion, but still attend mass in number on saints' days or feast days. As a result of immigration, other religions are now on the increase.

The emphasis on conformity and a commitment to the institution of the family remain key factors in Italian society despite the country's low birth rate. Grandparents, children, and grandchildren often still live in family units, although this is becoming less common. Women's Liberation fought a powerful campaign in the 1970s and did much to change attitudes to women in the workplace, particularly in metropolitan areas. However, the idea that men should help with housework and the care of the children is still a fairly foreign notion among the older generation.

With the miracle of its postwar economic recovery, where industry and technology were united with design, Italy became a success story. Although the economy was dented by the worldwide recessions of recent years, the exposure of corruption in many walks of public life, and political upheaval, Italy appears unchanged to foreign visitors. Its ability to keep its regional identities and traditional values seems to allow it to ride out any changes relatively unscathed.

Medieval and Early Renaissance Art

The story of early Italian art, from the 13th century until the late 15th century, illuminates one of the richest periods in European art history. For the first time since Classical antiquity, painters and sculptors created a convincing pictorial space in which figures, modeled "in the round," were given life. Ethereal buildings were replaced by those firmly rooted in the real world, reproducing what artists actually saw. This revolution in art included the reintroduction of the fresco technique, giving artists huge surfaces for telling pictorial stories.

c. 1305 Giotto di Bondone, *The Meeting at the Golden Gate* (Cappella degli Scrovegni, Padua) Giotto broke away from the ornate Byzantine style to visualize naturalness and human emotions. His way of working would later be dubbed the Florentine style.

1235 Bonaventura Berlinghieri, *St. Francis Altarpiece* (San Francesco, Pescia)

1285 Duccio di Buoninsegna, *Rucellai Madonna*, panel (Uffizi, Florence). Duccio dominated the Sienese painting style, which combined bold linear movements with a new human intimacy.

1339 Ambrogio Lorenzetti, *Good Government Enthroned* (Sala dei Nove, Palazzo Pubblico, Siena)

1220	1240	1260	1280	1300	1320	1340
Middle Ages				Forerunners to Renaissance		
1220	1240	1260	1280	1300	1320	1340

c. 1259 Nicola Pisano, Pulpit (Baptistry, Pisa cathedral)

c. 1265 Coppo di Marcovaldo, *Madonna and Child* (Santa Monica dei Servi, Orvieto)

c. 1280 Cimabue, *Madonna Enthroned with Angels and Prophets*, also known as *Santa Trinità Madonna* (Uffizi, Florence)

c. 1291 Pietro Cavallini, *Last Judgment*, detail (Santa Cecilia, Trastevere, Rome)

c. 1316–18 Simone Martini, *Vision of St. Martin* (Lower Church of San Francesco, Assisi)

c. 1297 Giovanni Pisano, Pulpit (Sant'Andrea, Pistoia)

c. 1336 Andrea Pisano, *Baptism of St. John the Baptist*, panel on the South Doors (Baptistry, Florence cathedral)

***c.* 1425–52 Lorenzo Ghiberti**, *Gates of Paradise,* panel on the East Doors. (Baptistry, Florence cathedral). These elaborate doors mark a transition from the Gothic style to the Early Renaissance style, in Florence.

1357 Andrea Orcagna, *Enthroned Christ with Madonna and Saints* (Strozzi Altarpiece, Santa Maria Novella, Florence)

***c.* 1410 Nanni di Banco**, *Four Crowned Martyrs* (Orsanmichele, Florence)

***c.* 1435 Donatello**, *David* (Museo del Bargello, Florence)

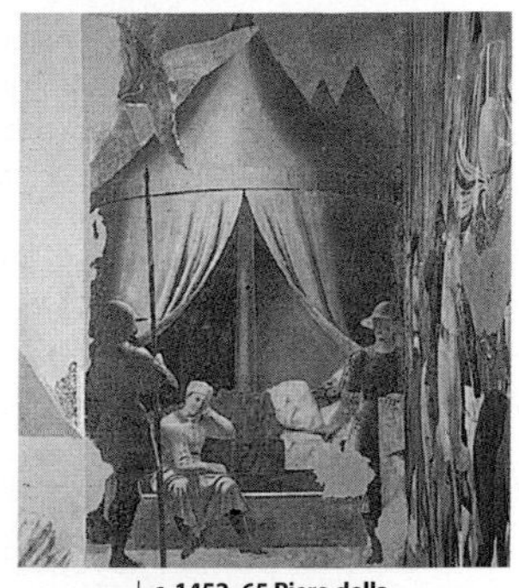

***c.* 1452–65 Piero della Francesca**, detail of *The Dream of Constantine* (San Francesco, Arezzo)

***c.* 1456 Paolo Uccello**, *Battle of San Romano* (Uffizi, Florence)

1360 | 1380 | 1400 | 1420 | 1440 | 1460

Early Renaissance

1360 | 1380 | 1400 | 1420 | 1440 | 1460

1423 Gentile da Fabriano, *Adoration of the Magi* (Uffizi, Florence)

***c.* 1440 Fra Angelico**, *Annunciation* (San Marco, Florence)

***c.* 1350 Francesco Traini**, *Triumph of Death* (Campo Santo, Pisa)

***c.* 1425–8 Masaccio**, *The Tribute Money* (Cappella Brancacci, Florence)

***c.* 1463 Piero della Francesca**, *Resurrection* (Pinacoteca, Sansepolcro)

***c.* 1465 Fra Filippo Lippi**, *Madonna with Child and Angels* (Uffizi, Florence)

***c.* 1465–74 Andrea Mantegna**, *Arrival of Cardinal Francesco Gonzaga* (Palazzo Ducale, Mantova)

***c.* 1470 Andrea del Verrocchio**, *David* (Bargello, Florence)

Fresco Technique

Fresco, meaning "fresh," refers to the technique of painting onto a thin layer of damp, freshly laid plaster. Pigments are drawn into the plaster by surface tension, and the color becomes fixed as the plaster dries. The pigments react with the lime in the plaster to produce strong, rich colors, such as those in Masaccio's *The Tribute Money.*

The Tribute Money by Masaccio (Cappella Brancacci, Florence)

High Renaissance Art

The High Renaissance in the late 15th century was marked by an increasing sense of realism in many religious works and by the technical mastery of such renowned artists as Michelangelo, Leonardo da Vinci, and Raphael. The different schools of Renaissance painting, while drawing on Classical models, produced varying styles: Florentine painting was noted for its cool clarity, while sensuous color and warm light characterized many Venetian works. By the mid-16th century, however, these styles shifted to the fanciful, contorted imagery of Mannerism.

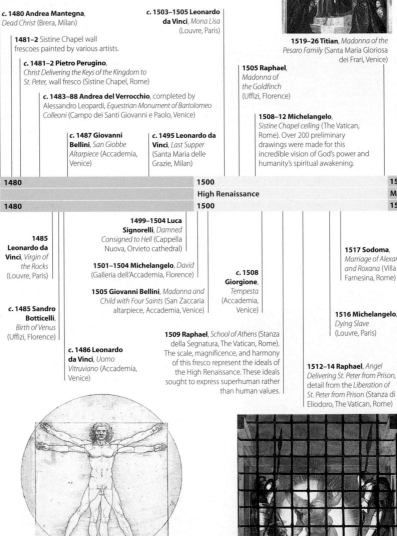

1519–26 Titian, *Madonna of the Pesaro Family* (Santa Maria Gloriosa dei Frari, Venice)

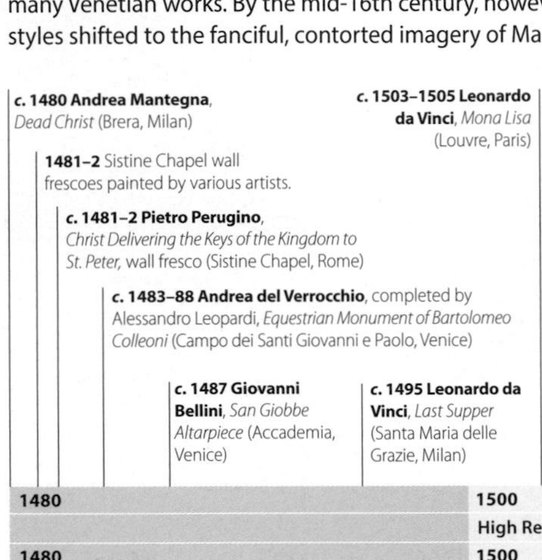

c. 1480 Andrea Mantegna, *Dead Christ* (Brera, Milan)

1481–2 Sistine Chapel wall frescoes painted by various artists.

c. 1481–2 Pietro Perugino, *Christ Delivering the Keys of the Kingdom to St. Peter*, wall fresco (Sistine Chapel, Rome)

c. 1483–88 Andrea del Verrocchio, completed by Alessandro Leopardi, *Equestrian Monument of Bartolomeo Colleoni* (Campo dei Santi Giovanni e Paolo, Venice)

c. 1487 Giovanni Bellini, *San Giobbe Altarpiece* (Accademia, Venice)

c. 1495 Leonardo da Vinci, *Last Supper* (Santa Maria delle Grazie, Milan)

c. 1503–1505 Leonardo da Vinci, *Mona Lisa* (Louvre, Paris)

1505 Raphael, *Madonna of the Goldfinch* (Uffizi, Florence)

1508–12 Michelangelo, *Sistine Chapel ceiling* (The Vatican, Rome). Over 200 preliminary drawings were made for this incredible vision of God's power and humanity's spiritual awakening.

1480	1500	1520
	High Renaissance	Manneris
1480	1500	1520

1485 Leonardo da Vinci, *Virgin of the Rocks* (Louvre, Paris)

c. 1485 Sandro Botticelli, *Birth of Venus* (Uffizi, Florence)

c. 1486 Leonardo da Vinci, *Uomo Vitruviano* (Accademia, Venice)

1499–1504 Luca Signorelli, *Damned Consigned to Hell* (Cappella Nuova, Orvieto cathedral)

1501–1504 Michelangelo, *David* (Galleria dell'Accademia, Florence)

1505 Giovanni Bellini, *Madonna and Child with Four Saints* (San Zaccaria altarpiece, Accademia, Venice)

c. 1508 Giorgione, *Tempesta* (Accademia, Venice)

1509 Raphael, *School of Athens* (Stanza della Segnatura, The Vatican, Rome). The scale, magnificence, and harmony of this fresco represent the ideals of the High Renaissance. These ideals sought to express superhuman rather than human values.

1512–14 Raphael, *Angel Delivering St. Peter from Prison*, detail from the *Liberation of St. Peter from Prison* (Stanza di Eliodoro, The Vatican, Rome)

1516 Michelangelo, *Dying Slave* (Louvre, Paris)

1517 Sodoma, *Marriage of Alexander and Roxana* (Villa Farnesina, Rome)

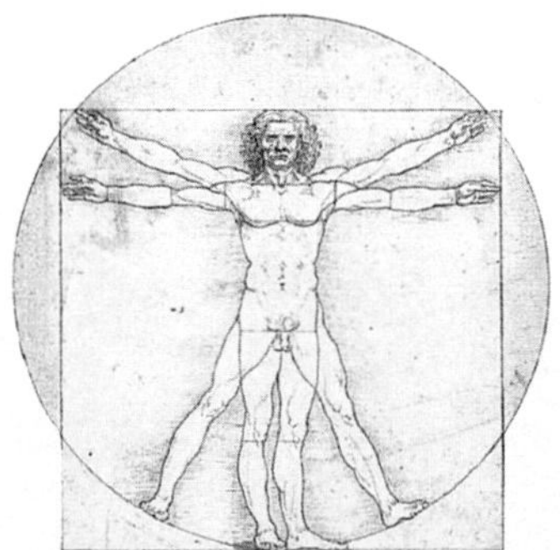

1523 Rosso Fiorentino, *Moses Defends the Daughters of Jethro* (Uffizi, Florence)

c. 1562–66 Jacopo Tintoretto, *Finding of the Body of St. Mark* (Brera, Milan)

1530–32 Giulio Romano, *Ceiling and wall frescoes* (Sala dei Giganti, Palazzo del Tè, Mantova)

c. 1532 Michelangelo, *"Blockhead" Captive* (Galleria dell' Accademia, Florence)

1534–5 Paris Bordone, *Fisherman Delivering the Ring* (Accademia, Venice)

1534–41 Michelangelo, *Last Judgment*, wall fresco (Sistine Chapel, Rome)

c. 1540–42 Titian, *David and Goliath* (Santa Maria della Salute, Venice)

c. 1550 Moretto, *Ecce Homo with Angel* (Pinacoteca Tosio Martinengo, Brescia)

1540 **1560**

1540 **1560**

1538 Titian, *Venus of Urbino* (Uffizi, Florence)

c. 1546 Titian, *Portrait of Pope Paul III Farnese with his Nephews*, (Museo di Capodimonte, Naples)

c. 1534–40 Parmigianino, *Madonna and Angels or Madonna with the Long Neck* (Uffizi, Florence). Attenuated proportions and contrasting colors make this a fine example of the Mannerist style.

c. 1540 Agnolo Bronzino, *Portrait of Lucrezia Panciatichi* (Uffizi, Florence). Elongated features, such as Lucrezia's fingers, are typical of the exaggerated Mannerist style.

1556 Veronese, *Triumph of Mordecai* (San Sebastiano, Venice)

c. 1526–30 Correggio, *Assumption of the Virgin* (Dome of Parma cathedral). Neither a Mannerist nor a High Renaissance painter, Correggio was a master of illusion, skilled at making ascending figures float convincingly, as seen in the fresco on the left.

Italian Architecture

The buildings of Italy span almost 3,000 years, drawing influences from a wide variety of sources. Etruscan and Roman buildings borrowed heavily from ancient Greece, while in later centuries Norman, Arabic, and Byzantine styles colored Italy's Romanesque and Gothic architecture. Classical ideals infused the country's Renaissance buildings, later giving way to the inspired innovations of the Baroque period.

Orvieto's Duomo displays the ornate and intricate decoration, notably sculpture, common to many Gothic cathedrals. Building stretched from the 13th to the early 17th centuries.

The Basilica di San Marco

The Basilica di San Marco (AD 832–1094) in Venice combines Classical, Romanesque, and Gothic architecture, but its key inspiration was Byzantine *(see pp114–15)*.

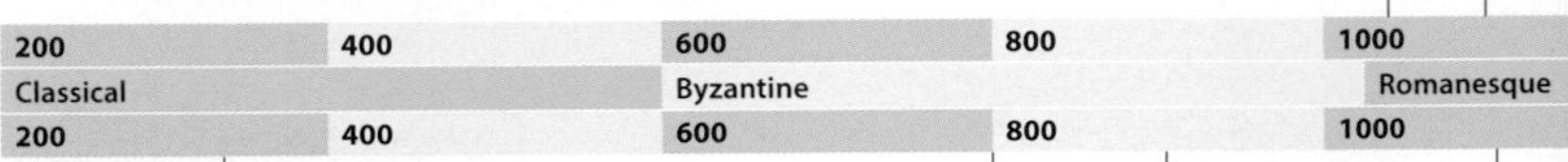

Triumphal arches such as Rome's Arch of Constantine (AD 313) were a uniquely Roman invention. Built to celebrate military victories, they were adorned with reliefs depicting episodes from successful campaigns *(see p384)*.

The round-arched Romanesque style emerged from the Dark Ages in structures such as the Duomo in Modena. The churches usually had simple interiors that derived from Roman basilicas.

The building of domes over square or rectangular spaces was a major development of the Byzantine era.

Etruscan Architecture

Virtually the only architectural memorials to the Etruscans are their necropolises (*c.* 6th century BC), found primarily in Tuscany, Lazio, and Umbria. Little else survives, probably because most day-to-day buildings were made from wood. The Etruscans' close cultural and trading ties with Greece, however, suggest that their architecture would have borrowed heavily from Greek models. Rome, in turn, looked to Etruscan architecture for inspiration, and most early Roman public buildings were probably Etruscan in style.

Model of Etruscan temple with Classical Greek portico

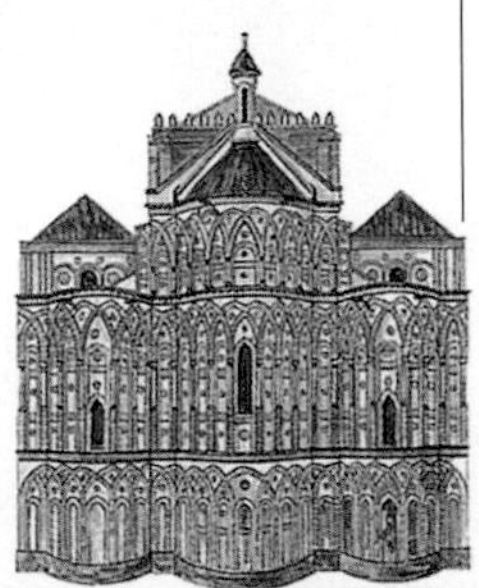

The cathedral of Monreale in Sicily, built in the 12th century, contains Norman elements blended with exotic Arabic and Byzantine decoration *(see pp534–5)*.

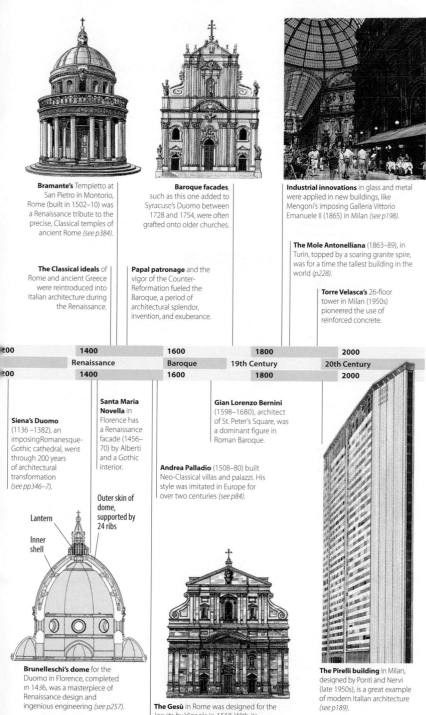

Bramante's Tempietto at San Pietro in Montorio, Rome (built in 1502–10) was a Renaissance tribute to the precise, Classical temples of ancient Rome *(see p384)*.

Baroque facades, such as this one added to Syracuse's Duomo between 1728 and 1754, were often grafted onto older churches.

Industrial innovations in glass and metal were applied in new buildings, like Mengoni's imposing Galleria Vittorio Emanuele II (1865) in Milan *(see p198)*.

The Mole Antonelliana (1863–89), in Turin, topped by a soaring granite spire, was for a time the tallest building in the world *(p228)*.

The Classical ideals of Rome and ancient Greece were reintroduced into Italian architecture during the Renaissance.

Papal patronage and the vigor of the Counter-Reformation fueled the Baroque, a period of architectural splendor, invention, and exuberance.

Torre Velasca's 26-floor tower in Milan (1950s) pioneered the use of reinforced concrete.

200	1400	1600	1800	2000
	Renaissance	Baroque	19th Century	20th Century
200	1400	1600	1800	2000

Siena's Duomo (1136 –1382), an imposingRomanesque-Gothic cathedral, went through 200 years of architectural transformation *(see pp346–7)*.

Santa Maria Novella in Florence has a Renaissance facade (1456–70) by Alberti and a Gothic interior.

Gian Lorenzo Bernini (1598–1680), architect of St. Peter's Square, was a dominant figure in Roman Baroque.

Andrea Palladio (1508–80) built Neo-Classical villas and palazzi. His style was imitated in Europe for over two centuries *(see p84)*.

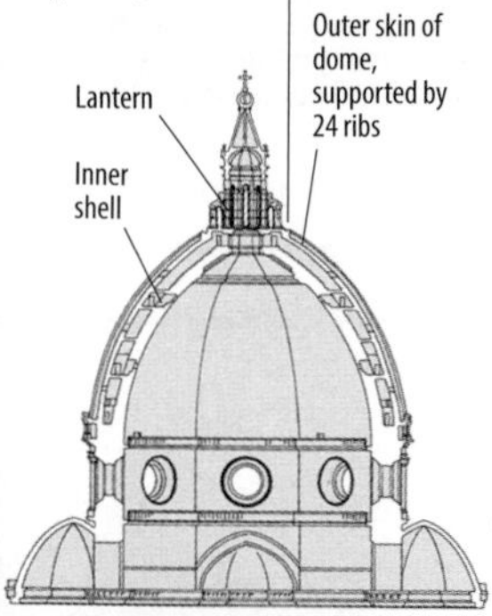

Outer skin of dome, supported by 24 ribs

Lantern

Inner shell

Brunelleschi's dome for the Duomo in Florence, completed in 1436, was a masterpiece of Renaissance design and ingenious engineering *(see p257)*.

The Gesù in Rome was designed for the Jesuits by Vignola in 1568. With its powerful facade and lavish decoration, it was the prototype for countless other Baroque churches *(see p385)*.

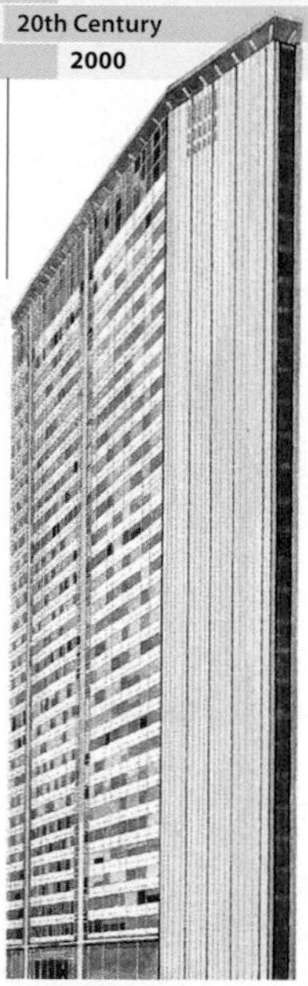

The Pirelli building in Milan, designed by Ponti and Nervi (late 1950s), is a great example of modern Italian architecture *(see p189)*.

Saints and Symbols in Italian Art

Saints and symbols are especially important in Italian art. They form part of an established visual language used by artists to narrate stories of the Bible and the Catholic church to churchgoers. Paintings of the saints were the focus for prayer and each offered assistance in a particular aspect of daily life. Patron saints protected specific cities or trades, and individuals who bore their name. Saints' days and religious festivals still play an important part in Italian life.

The Evangelists

The four evangelists, Matthew, Mark, Luke, and John, are each represented by a winged creature, standing for a divine mission.

Eagle (St. John)

St. Dominic is usually portrayed wearing the habit of his order. The lily is another of his attributes.

St. Cosmas and St. Damian are always shown together, dressed in physicians' clothing.

St. Mark the Evangelist often holds his book of the Gospels.

St. John carries a book of the Gospel bearing his name.

St. Thomas Aquinas is usually shown with a star, barely visible in this painting on his Dominican habit.

St. Lawrence carries a palm leaf as well as the gridiron on which he was roasted.

Virgin Enthroned with the Child and Saints (*c.* 1450) was painted on dry plaster by the Dominican friar Fra Angelico. It is on display at the Museo di San Marco, Florence *(see p280)*.

The Virgin, usually shown in blue robes, is depicted as Mater Amabilis – the "Mother Worthy of Love."

St. Peter Martyr, here with a palm leaf, is sometimes depicted with a head wound, carrying a sword.

Symbols

In order to identify different saints or martyrs, they were given "attributes" or symbols – particular objects to carry, or clothing to wear. These were items that played a particular role in their life story. Martyrs were known by their instruments of torture or death. Symbolism also appears in the sky, animals, flowers, colors, and numbers.

The lamb symbolizes Christ, the Lamb of God, or in early Christian art, the sinner.

The skull is a "memento mori" to remind us of death and impermanence.

Winged man (St. Matthew)

Winged lion (St. Mark)

Winged ox (St. Luke)

Giovanni Bellini's painting of *Madonna and Child with Four Saints* (see p123)

St. Peter the Apostle, the "rock" on which the Christian church was founded, carries the keys to heaven.

The Madonna, with the Christ Child, is an emblem of perfect motherly love.

St. Catherine of Alexandria is shown here with a piece of the wheel on which she was martyred.

St. Jerome is always portrayed as an old man, often a hermit, whose life was devoted to scholarship.

Detail from Madonna and Child with Four Saints, by Giovanni Bellini. The painting was produced for an altarpiece at San Zaccaria, Venice in 1505, where it is still on display.

The angel, a messenger of God to man, is portrayed in this scene as a musician of Heaven.

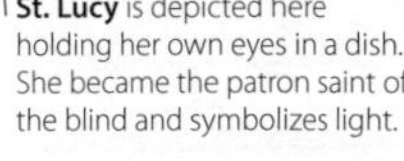

St. Lucy is depicted here holding her own eyes in a dish. She became the patron saint of the blind and symbolizes light.

The lily, flower of the Virgin, is the symbol of purity, resurrection, peace, and chastity.

The cockle shell most often represents pilgrimage. It is a particular attribute of St. Roch.

The palm represents, in Christian art, a martyr's triumph over death.

Writers, Poets, and Dramatists

Italy has produced many writers (in Latin and Italian) who have won worldwide acclaim. Each of them provides an illuminating insight into the country's turbulent past: the Classical poets Virgil, Horace, and Ovid give vivid accounts of the concerns and values of ancient Rome; medieval Florence and Tuscany are brought to life in the poetry of Dante and Petrarch and the salacious tales of Boccaccio. In less than a century these three great writers created a new literary language to rank with any in Europe. Italy's modern literature still commands international attention – Umberto Eco has to his credit one of the most widely read books of the 20th century.

Primo Levi (1919–87) gave an astonishing account of his survival of the Jewish Holocaust and World War II's aftermath in *The Truce* and *If This Is a Man.*

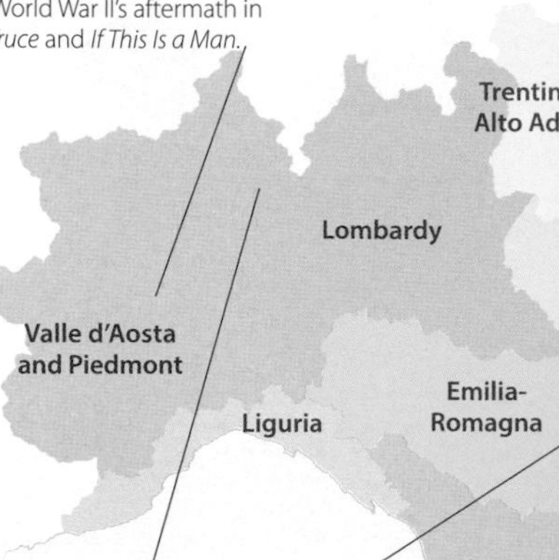

Dario Fo (born 1926) won the Nobel prize for Literature in 1997.

Umberto Eco (born 1932), a professor at the University of Bologna, wrote the novel *The Name of the Rose,* which explored his passion for the Middle Ages. The book was made into a film (above) in 1986.

Pinocchio, written by Carlo Collodi (1826–90) in 1883, is one of the world's best known children's stories. "Collodi" was Carlo Lorenzini's pseudonym, taken after his mother's birthplace in Tuscany.

Giovanni Boccaccio (1313–75) is notable for providing a fascinating social record of his era. *The Decameron*, his captivating collection of 100 short stories, is set in the plague-stricken Florence of 1348.

Dante's (1265–1321) *Divine Comedy* (*c.* 1308–21), is a journey through Hell, Purgatory, and Paradise. It includes horrific accounts of the torments suffered by the damned.

Classical Roman Writers

Texts in Latin by Classical Roman philosophers, poets, dramatists, and politicians are part of the bedrock of Western culture. Today the names Virgil *(The Aeneid)*, Ovid *(Metamorphoses)*, and Pliny *(Historia Naturalis)* are literary legends. Fascinating histories such as Livy's *Early History of Rome*, Caesar's *Gallic Wars*, Tacitus's *Annals*, and Suetonius's *The Twelve Caesars* give us an invaluable window on the distant Roman past, as do the caustic *Satires* of Juvenal. Many Latin works owe their survival to the teams of medieval monks who diligently copied and illustrated them. In the Renaissance the stories of Ovid's *Metamorphoses* were plundered by many writers and the works of Cicero had a profound influence on prose style; Seneca was seen as a master of tragedy and Plautus's *Pot of Gold* served as a model for comedies.

Detail from medieval copy of Pliny's *Historia Naturalis*

Venetian author Carlo Goldoni (1707–93) reacted against the satirical tradition of *La Commedia dell'Arte*, preferring to write more forgiving plays on contemporary Venice society.

The Veneto and Friuli

Le Marche

Umbria

Lazio

Abruzzo, Molise, and Puglia

Campania

Basilicata and Calabria

Sicily

Petrarch (1304–74), one of the earliest and greatest lyric poets, produced works which showed the first indications of Humanism.

St. Francis of Assisi (1182–1226) was the first author to write in Italian instead of formal Latin. As well as letters and sermons, he wrote poems and songs, including the popular *Canticle of the Sun*.

Roman writer Alberto Moravia (1907–90) is usually labeled a "Neo-Realist." His novels and short stories focus on the corrupt values of contemporary society. Among his best known works are *Gli Indifferenti* and *Agostino*.

The Sicilian Nobel Prize-winner Luigi Pirandello (1867–1936) was preoccupied with themes of illusion and reality. *Six Characters in Search of an Author* is his most famous work.

0 kilometers 200

0 miles 100

Music and Opera in Italy

Before Italy's unification, particularly during the 17th and 18th centuries, each major city had its own traditions of music-making. Rome, as the papal city, had musical traditions less hedonistic than elsewhere, and avoided opera. Florence had its day at the turn of the 16th century, with its celebrated *camerata* (groups set on reviving the traditions of Ancient Greek spectacle). Venice fostered church music on a grand scale, and Naples, during the 18th century, was renowned for comic opera. In the 19th century, Milan became the undisputed center of Italian opera, centered on La Scala.

The Medieval and Renaissance Periods

Through Boccaccio *(see p38)*, among others, it is known that singing, dancing, and poetry often went hand in hand in medieval and Renaissance Italy. Italy concentrated on music as part of a spectacle rather than as a pure art form.

Important contributors to the music of these periods include Guido d'Arezzo (*c.* 995–1050), a monk who perfected musical notation, and Francesco Landini (1325–97), one of the first known composers whose songs displayed a distinct concern for lyricism. The next 150 years were to be characterized by the *Ars Perfecta* style, culminating with composer Giovanni Pierluigi da Palestrina (1525–94). His vocal style subjected dissonance to strict control, and it was employed for most church music during his lifetime. Madrigals (vocal settings of poems by Petrarch and other poets) were also popular.

The early 17th century saw Italian composers such as Carlo Gesualdo da Venosa (*c.* 1561–1613) and Claudio Monteverdi challenge these traditions by introducing more declamation and more of the unexpected.

La Pietà, Venice, where Vivaldi performed

The Baroque Era

Claudio Monteverdi's music straddled the transition from the Renaissance period to 17th-century Baroque. The word "baroque" means highly ornamented, even bizarre, and embellishment was rife. Monteverdi's madrigals began as standard pieces for four voices but ended up as mini-operas. This was due to the popularity of an individual instrumental style and the development of the *basso continuo* (a supporting organ, harpsichord, or lute that unleashed the possibility for solos and duets). At this point, the beginnings of the string orchestra were in place.

A new fashion for declamation meant that various emotional states were being represented with sighs and sobs rather than just description. Monteverdi's *Vespers* followed others' in exploiting the stereophonic possibilities of San Marco in Venice by contrasting different

Major Italian Composers through the Ages

Claudio Monteverdi (1567–1643) was best known for his *Vespers* of 1610. Both his madrigals and operas are considered major landmarks in the development of music.

Antonio Vivaldi (1678–1741) wrote over 600 concertos, many of which are for the violin. *The Four Seasons,* a set of concertos, is among the best-selling classical music of all time.

Gioacchino Rossini (1792–1868) was most famous for his comic operas, like *The Barber of Seville* and *La Cenerentola.* The romantic, expressive side of his more serious works, such as *Otello*, was often overlooked.

Luciano Pavarotti performed in the most modern surroundings

forces in different parts of the building. In the 1680s, Arcangelo Corelli (1653–1713) turned to classicism. Corelli was famous for the *concerto grosso*, a style that contrasted the solo string group with the full ensemble. He was followed by Antonio Vivaldi (1678–1741), who concentrated his efforts on developing the solo form of the *concerto grosso*. He used wind and plucked instruments as well as violins.

The Emergence of Opera

Opera first emerged during the wedding celebrations of Italy's wealthy 16th-century families. Monteverdi was the first composer to establish his work firmly in the opera repertoire. During the 17th century, Alessandro Scarlatti (1660–1725) formulated a model which consisted of an orchestral overture followed by a sequence of narrative, set as *recitative*, and interrupted by *da capo* (three-part) arias. Themes for the weightier *opera seria* were largely drawn from mythology, while the lighter *opera buffa* had stock scenes that sometimes owed a large debt to the traditions of *Commedia dell'Arte*. Famous for his comic operas, such as *The Barber of Seville*, was the composer Gioacchino Rossini. Among other contributors, Vincenzo Bellini (1801–35) and Gaetano Donizetti (1797–1848) developed *bel canto* singing, a style stressing fine tone and ornamentation.

Puccini's *Tosca*, first staged in 1900

The two most prominent opera composers of the latter half of the 19th century were Giuseppe Verdi and Giacomo Puccini (1858–1924). Verdi often turned to the works of Shakespeare as well as to contemporary subjects in order to form a basis for his work, while many composers, like Puccini, turned to the new trend of *verismo* (slices of realism) – *La Bohème* is one of the most refined examples of this style.

Giuseppe Verdi (1813–1901), whose first works were for the opera house La Scala *(see p197)*, was the most important opera composer of the 19th century. His most celebrated works include *Rigoletto* and *Aida*.

The 20th Century

In the early 20th century, Puccini's *La Fanciulla del West* (The Girl of the West) brought cowboys into opera, *Turandot* looked towards the Orient, and *Tosca* brought torture and murder. Some composers have attempted to emulate French and German music, and only a few Italian pieces, such as those by Ottorino Respighi (1879–1936), have been regularly performed. The most important name in post-war Italian music was Luciano Berio (1925–2003), who developed Music Theater, an art form lying somewhere between drama and opera. In later years, however, Berio continued the tradition of Grand Opera with his elaborate production of *Un Re in Ascolto*. But it is Luciano Pavarotti (1935–2007) who must be credited with renewing an international interest in opera. In the 1990s, his televised performances with "Three Tenors" co-stars José Carreras and Placido Domingo secured a massive world audience for opera. Another star of opera and classical music is internationally renowned conductor Riccardo Muti, former director of La Scala and now the director of Rome's Teatro dell'Opera.

The illuminated interior of Rome's Teatro dell'Opera

Italian Design

Italy has had phenomenal success evolving stylish, desirable forms for everyday objects. Its 20th-century achievements can be credited to a handful of forward-thinking industrial giants, such as Olivetti, willing to entrust important product decisions to a group of inspired designers, like Ettore Sottsass. The design genius was to rethink the function of consumer objects, apply new technology, and then make the result look seductive.

The streamlined aesthetic of Italian design extends even to pasta; this Marille version was created by car designer Giorgio Giugiaro for Voiello in 1983.

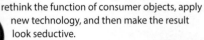

Sleek, sculptural Alessi cutlery (1988), designed by Ettore Sottsass, combines maximum utility with elegance and aesthetic integrity.

The Alessi kettle (1985), designed by Michael Graves, achieved such popularity in its first year of production that over 100,000 were sold.

One of the best known coffeemakers is Bialetti's Moka Express. Although designed in 1930, it is still enormously popular today.

Christophe Pilet's chair, designed for Giulio Cappellini's collection of contemporary furniture is a wonderful example of the 1990's aesthetic, and is still available for purchase.

The folding Cumano table, designed by Achille Castiglione for Zanotta in 1979, is still revered as a "designer object."

The Patty Difusa chair, with unusual wooden arms that curve into legs, was designed by William Sawaya for Sawaya & Moroni in Milan.

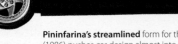

Pininfarina's streamlined form for the Ferrari Testarossa (1986) pushes car design almost into the realms of sculpture.

Light in weight, and compact in shape, Olivetti's Valentine typewriter revolutionized the role of the desk typewriter. Designed by Ettore Sottsass in 1969, its portability allowed the user to work anywhere.

Italian printer Giambattista Bodoni (1740–1813) designed the sophisticated typeface that bears his name and is still popular 200 years after its creation.

Milan's Giorgio Armani is best known for his updating of classic items such as the jacket, creating a flattering, chic, and comfortable "deconstructed" look.

Prada, the Milan-based fashion house headed by Miuccia Prada, features minimalist, cutting-edge designs and the use of innovative fabrics.

The Artemide company is renowned for combining metal and glass in many of their designs, especially lamps and lighting fixtures.

Florence has a long reputation as a producer of high-quality crafts, particularly fashion accessories such as handbags, shoes, belts, jewelry, and briefcases.

Gucci's classic items, including bags and shoes, are a revered totem for the fashion-conscious.

Piaggio's innovative Vespa scooter (1946), by Corradino d'Ascanio, provided cheap, fast, and reliable transportation at a time when few could afford the expense of a car. Hugely successful, the Vespa is still a common sight on Italy's streets.

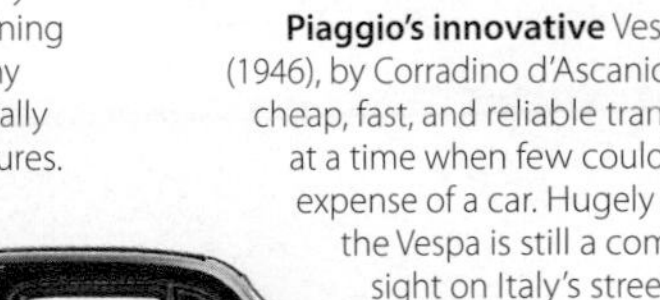

The FIAT 500 (1957), like the Vespa, became a symbol of mobility and democratization, an expression of Italy's rapid postwar recovery.

Scientists, Inventors, and Explorers

Italy has fostered a long tradition of important scientific thought and discovery, fueled in the Renaissance by such men as Galileo, who searched for a new understanding of the universe. Meanwhile, explorers such as Columbus had set off to find new worlds, a move heralded in the 13th century by Marco Polo. The spirit of scientific inquiry continued up to the 20th century, with the invention of radio and pioneering work in the field of nuclear physics.

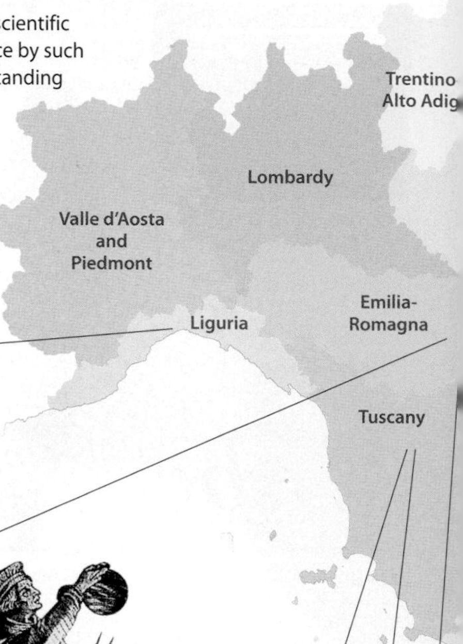

Trentino Alto Adig
Lombardy
Valle d'Aosta and Piedmont
Liguria
Emilia-Romagna
Tuscany

Genoese-born Christopher Columbus sailed west from Spain in 1492. He reached the Indies in three months, navigating with such aids as an astrolabe.

The explorer Amerigo Vespucci established that the New World was a separate land mass. A pamphlet wrongly described him as its discoverer, and so, in 1507, America acquired its name.

Guglielmo Marconi invented the first practical system for sending radio signals. In 1901, he succeeded in picking up a signal that had been sent to England from Newfoundland.

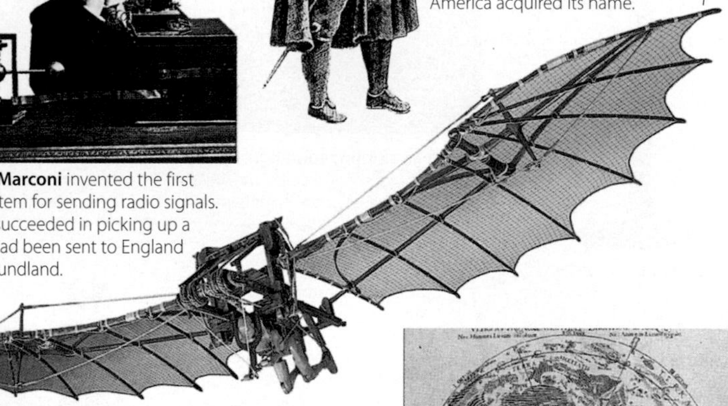

Leonardo da Vinci was the ultimate Renaissance man, accomplished in both arts and sciences. He conceived his first design for a flying machine in c.1488, more than 400 years before the first airplane took off. This model is based on one of his technical drawings.

The telescope enabled astronomers to produce accurate lunar maps. Domenico Cassini, astronomy professor at Bologna University, refined the instrument. In 1665 he traced the meridian line in the church of San Petronio.

0 kilometers 200
0 miles 100

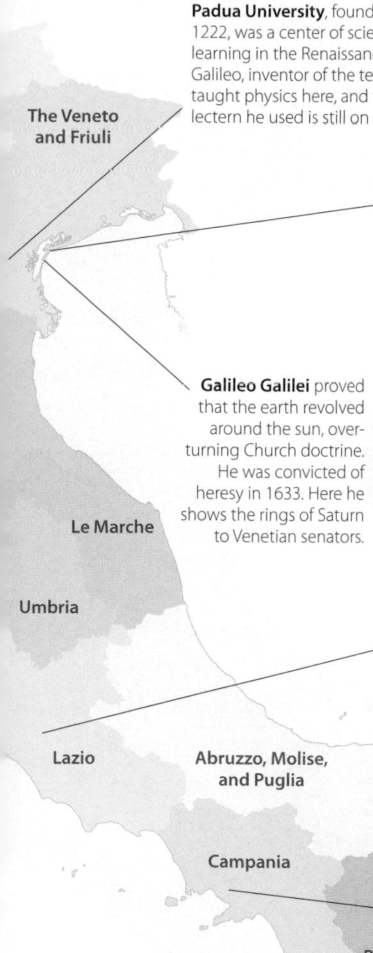

Padua University, founded in 1222, was a center of scientific learning in the Renaissance. Galileo, inventor of the telescope, taught physics here, and the lectern he used is still on view.

The Veneto and Friuli

The Venetian Marco Polo set off for the east as a youth in 1271. He stayed at the court of the Mongol emperor, Kublai Khan, for nearly two decades before returning home. He is seen here arriving at Hormuz in the Persian Gulf from India.

Galileo Galilei proved that the earth revolved around the sun, overturning Church doctrine. He was convicted of heresy in 1633. Here he shows the rings of Saturn to Venetian senators.

Le Marche

Umbria

Winner of the Nobel Prize for Physics in 1938, Enrico Fermi directed the first controlled nuclear chain reaction. He built the world's first nuclear reactor for producing power at the University of Chicago.

Lazio

Abruzzo, Molise, and Puglia

Campania

Basilicata and Calabria

Pliny the Elder wrote his catalog of human knowledge, *Natural History*, in AD 77. He died when Vesuvius erupted two years later, but his book retained its authority for 1,500 years.

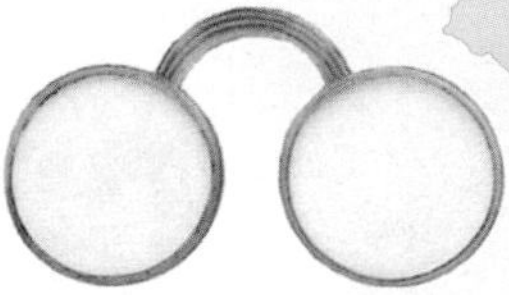

Spectacles were invented in Italy in the 13th century. They are first recorded in Venice, still an important center for glasswork today.

The mathematician Archimedes was born in c.287 BC in Syracuse, Sicily, then a Greek colony. Legend has it that he discovered the principle of specific gravity while in the bath.

Sicily

THE HISTORY OF ITALY

The concept of Italy as a geographic entity goes back to the time of the Etruscans, but Italy's history is one of discord and division. Prior to the 19th century, the only time the peninsula was united was under the Romans, who by the 2nd century BC had subdued the other Italian tribes. Rome became the capital of a huge empire, introducing its language, laws, and calendar to most of Europe before succumbing to Germanic invaders in the 5th century AD. Another important legacy of the Roman empire was Christianity and the position of the pope as head of the Catholic church. The medieval papacy summoned the Franks to drive out the Lombards and, in AD 800, crowned the Frankish king Charlemagne Holy Roman Emperor. Unfortunately, what seemed to be the dawn of a new age turned out to be anything but. For five centuries popes and emperors fought to decide which of them should be in charge of their nebulous empire.

Meanwhile, a succession of foreign invaders – Normans, Angevins, and Aragonese – took advantage of the situation to conquer Sicily and the south. The north, in contrast, saw a growth of independent city-states, the most powerful being Venice, fabulously wealthy through trade with the East. Other cities, such as Genoa, Florence, Milan, Pisa, and Siena, also had their days of glory. Northern Italy became the most prosperous and cultured region in western Europe, and it was the artists and scholars of 15th-century Florence who inspired the Renaissance. Small, fragmented states, however, could not compete with great powers. In the 16th century Italy's petty kingdoms fell prey to a foreign invader, this time to Spain, and the north subsequently came under the control of Austria.

One small kingdom that remained independent was Piedmont, but during a war between Austria and France it fell to Napoleon in 1796. In the 19th century, however, it was Piedmont that became the focus for a movement toward a united Italy, a goal that was achieved in 1870, thanks largely to the heroic military exploits of Garibaldi. In the 1920s, the Fascists seized power, and in 1946, the monarchy was abandoned for today's republic.

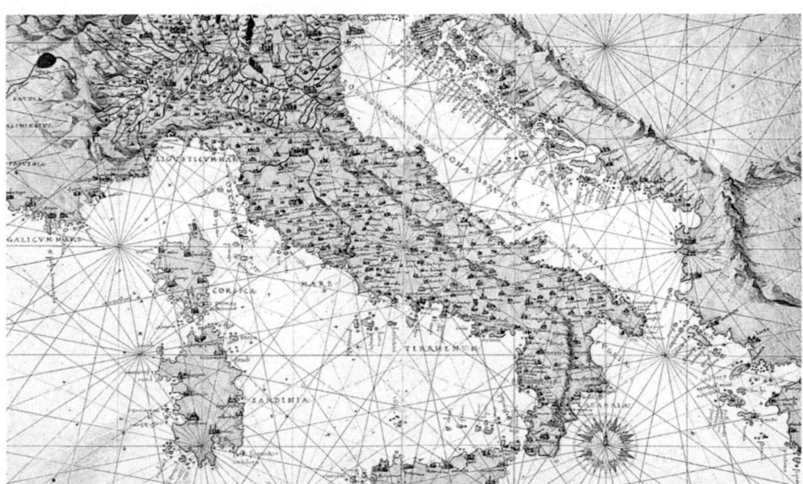

16th-century map of Italy, of the kind used by Venetian and Genoese sailors

◀ *Fall of the Rebel Angels* fresco by Giacinto Brandi on the ceiling of Sant'Ambrogio e Carlo al Corso

The Age of the Etruscans

The Etruscans were Italy's first major civilization. The frescoes, jewelry, and pottery found in their tombs are evidence of a highly artistic, cultured people. Their origin is a mystery, as is their language, but from the 9th century BC they spread through central Italy, their chief rivals being the Greeks in the south. Etruria was never a unified state, just a loose confederation of cities. In the 6th century, Etruscan kings ruled Rome, the city that would ultimately eclipse them.

Italy in 650 BC

Etruscan kingdoms

Greek colonies

The double flute was a specialty of the Etruscans. The instrument was played at festivals and funerals alike.

Terra-cotta Winged Horses
This beautiful relief of yoked horses (4th century BC) decorated the facade of the Ara della Regina temple at Tarquinia.

Bronze Sheep's Liver
The inscriptions served as a guide for telling the future from animals' entrails.

Terra-cotta Cremation Urn
The lid of the urn shows the deceased holding a writing tablet. The Etruscans introduced the alphabet to Italy.

Tomb of the Leopards
Feasts and revelry are common themes in the frescoes that decorate Etruscan tombs. These musicians are from a tomb fresco (c. 500 BC) at Tarquinia (see p470).

900 BC

c. 900 BC First traces of Iron Age in Italy; Villanovan period

9th century BC Pre-urban communities established along river valleys in Etruria

800 BC

c. 800 BC Greeks settle in Sicily and south of Italy

753 BC Legendary date of foundation of Rome by Romulus

715–673 BC Reign of the wise Numa Pompilius, second king of Rome

c. 700 BC Growth of cities in Etruria; earliest Etruscan inscriptions

700 BC

616 BC Etruscans become rulers of Rome under Tarquin the Elder

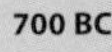

Etruscan gold earrings

A Boxing Match
Athletic competitions were held at funerals. This vase, which dates from about 500 BC, was made in Etruria, but imitates the Greek black-figure style of pottery.

The musicians and the dancer in the tomb painting are painted with a realism that indicates the influence of Greek art.

The lyre was made from a tortoise shell and played with a plectrum.

Where to see Etruscan Italy

Rock tombs like these at Sovana *(p336)* are common in the volcanic tufa of central Italy.

Tuscany, Lazio, and Umbria are rich in Etruscan remains, especially tombs. There are huge necropolises in Lazio at Cerveteri and Tarquinia *(p470)*. The latter also has an important museum. Other museums with major collections of Etruscan art and artifacts include Villa Giulia *(p444)* and the Vatican's Museo Gregoriano *(p426)* in Rome, the Museo Archeologico in Florence *(p281)*, the Museo Nazionale in Chiusi *(p336)*, and the Museo Guarnacci in Volterra *(p338)*.

Apollo of Veii
This magnificent statue of Apollo (*c.* 500 BC) shows the stylized facial features characteristic of Etruscan art.

Bronze Mirror
Wealthy Etruscans lived in great luxury. The women used polished bronze mirrors with engraved backs. This one shows Helen of Troy and the goddess Aphrodite.

Temple of Neptune
This fine temple at Paestum (5th century BC) is a legacy of Greek colonization of the south.

Mixing bowl, imported from Greece

509 BC Last Etruscan king, Tarquinius Superbus, expelled from Rome; establishment of Roman Republic

450 BC Roman law codified in the Twelve Tables

390 BC Gauls sack Rome; Capitol saved thanks to alarm sounded by cackling geese

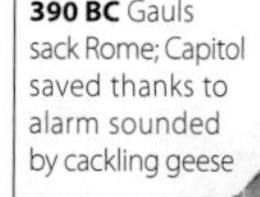

600 BC | 500 BC | 400 BC

499 BC Battle of Lake Regillus; Romans defeat alliance of Latins and Etruscans

474 BC Etruscan fleet defeated by Greeks off Cumae; blow to Etruscan naval power

c. 400 BC Gauls start to settle along valley of the Po

396 BC Veii, a major Etruscan city in present-day Lazio, falls to Rome

Relief of Capitoline geese, found in the Roman Forum

From Republic to Empire

From the scores of tribes inhabiting ancient Italy, one people, the Romans, emerged to conquer the peninsula and impose their language, customs, and laws on the rest. Rome's success was due to superb skill in military and civil organization. The state was a republic ruled by two consuls, elected each year, but as the extent of Rome's conquests grew, power passed to generals such as Julius Caesar. The Republic became unworkable and Caesar's heirs became the first Roman emperors.

Cisalpine Gaul was annexed in 202–191 BC.

Etruria was in Roman hands by 265 BC.

Julius Caesar
The great general, conqueror of Gaul, returned to Italy in 49 BC to defeat Pompey. His rise to absolute power marked the end of the Republic.

Oscan Inscription
The languages of the peoples conquered by Rome lived on for centuries before being replaced by Latin. The Oscans lived in what is now Campania.

War Elephant
In 218 BC, the great Carthaginian general Hannibal brought 37 elephants across the Alps – to spread alarm in the Roman ranks.

Roman Aqueduct
The Romans' talent for engineering found its most spectacular expression in huge aqueducts. These could be up to 50 miles (80 km) long, though for most of that distance the water ran underground.

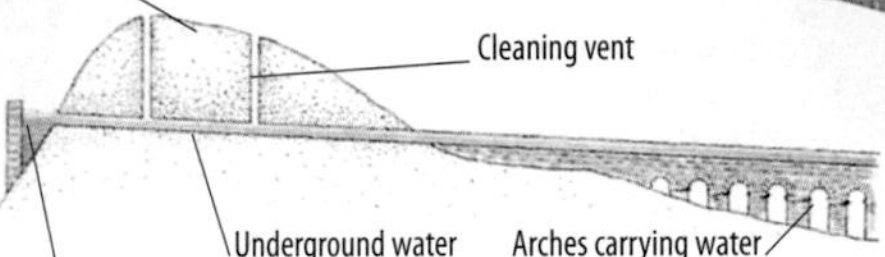

High ground
Cleaning vent
Reservoir
Underground water channel
Arches carrying water across low ground

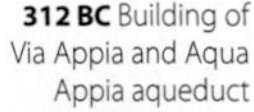

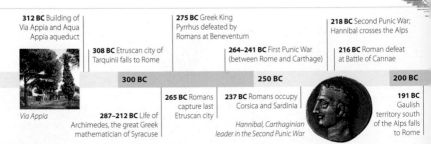

312 BC Building of Via Appia and Aqua Appia aqueduct

Via Appia

308 BC Etruscan city of Tarquinii falls to Rome

300 BC

287–212 BC Life of Archimedes, the great Greek mathematician of Syracuse

275 BC Greek King Pyrrhus defeated by Romans at Beneventum

265 BC Romans capture last Etruscan city

264–241 BC First Punic War (between Rome and Carthage)

250 BC

237 BC Romans occupy Corsica and Sardinia

Hannibal, Carthaginian leader in the Second Punic War

218 BC Second Punic War; Hannibal crosses the Alps

216 BC Roman defeat at Battle of Cannae

200 BC

191 BC Gaulish territory south of the Alps falls to Rome

Cicero Addresses the Senate
State business was debated in the Senate. The great orator Cicero (106–143 BC) argued for the Republic and against tyranny.

Where to See Italy from the Republican Era

Republican structures are very rare, most having been rebuilt under the Empire. In Rome itself, two notable exceptions are the 2nd-century BC Temples of the Forum Boarium *(p437)*. However, the legacy of the age to modern Italy is not hard to appreciate. Countless roads, such as the Via Appia Antica *(p445)*, and towns were planned originally by Roman engineers. Two striking examples of towns with original Roman street plans are Lucca *(pp324–5)* and Como *(p195)*.

These huge basalt blocks at Tharros in Sardinia *(p555)* were part of a Roman road.

Roman Legionary
This bronze shows a legionary in standard kit of helmet, breastplate, leather kilt with iron plates, greaves on his shins, and sandals.

The Via Appia was extended from Capua to Brindisi in 190 BC.

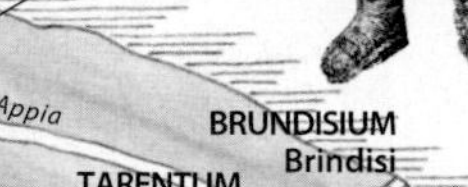

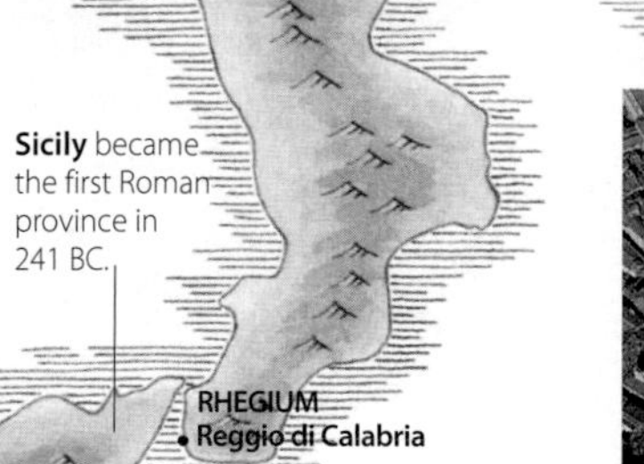

Sicily became the first Roman province in 241 BC.

Roman Roads

After conquering other tribes, the Romans imposed their authority by building roads along which legions could march rapidly to deal with any trouble. They also built towns. Many, such as Ariminum (Rimini), were "colonies," settlements for Roman citizens – often veteran legionaries.

Aerial View of Bologna
Roman street plans are still visible in city centers today. The route of the old Via Aemilia cuts straight through the center of Bologna.

168 BC End of Third Macedonian War; Romans now masters of Greece

146 BC End of Third Punic War; Carthage destroyed

150 BC

104 BC Slave revolt in Sicily

Milestone from the Via Aemilia

89 BC Social War: Rome's Italian allies granted citizenship

80 BC Building starts on the first Roman amphitheater, at Pompeii

100 BC

73–71 BC Slave revolt led by Spartacus

49 BC Caesar crosses the Rubicon and drives Pompey from Rome

50 BC

45 BC Introduction of 12-month Julian calendar

44 BC Murder of Julius Caesar; end of Roman Republic

31 BC Octavian defeats Mark Antony at Battle of Actium

30 BC Suicide of Mark Antony and Cleopatra in Egypt

The Golden Age of Rome

From the age of Augustus to the reign of Trajan, Rome's power grew until its empire stretched from Britain to the Red Sea. Despite the extravagance of emperors such as Nero, taxes and booty from military campaigns continually refilled the Imperial coffers. Under the wiser rule of Trajan, Hadrian, and Marcus Aurelius in the 2nd century AD, Roman citizens enjoyed wealth and comfort, with most of the work performed by slaves. Entertainment included visits to the baths, the theater, and the games. The town of Pompeii, buried when Vesuvius erupted in AD 79, preserves many fascinating details of everyday life.

Roman Empire in AD 117

Maximum extent of the Empire

Mosaic of Gladiators
Bloodthirsty gladiatorial combats were very popular. The gladiators were mostly slaves captured in war.

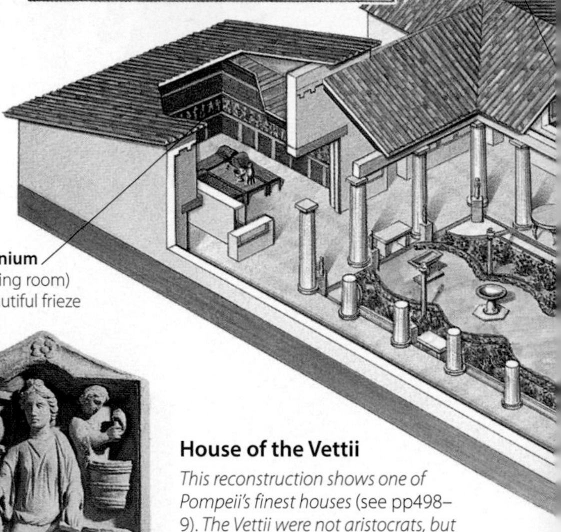

Frescoes of festoons and medallions

Trajan's Column
The carvings record Trajan's successful campaigns in Dacia (present-day Romania) in the first decade of the 2nd century AD.

The triclinium (main dining room) had a beautiful frieze of cupids.

Roman Shops
Buildings in towns were lined with small shops open to the street, like this pharmacy. The front was closed with wooden panels and locked at night.

House of the Vettii

This reconstruction shows one of Pompeii's finest houses (see pp498–9)*. The Vettii were not aristocrats, but freedmen, former slaves, who had made a fortune through trade. The rooms were richly decorated with frescoes and sculptures.*

50 BC

27 BC Augustus takes title Princeps, in effect becoming the first Roman emperor

9 BC Dedication of Ara Pacis *(see p414)* in Rome to celebrate peace after wars in Gaul and Spain

AD 1

AD 17 Tiberius fixes boundary of Empire along the Rhine and Danube

AD 37–41 Reign of Caligula

AD 43 Roman conquest of Britain in reign of Claudius

Bronze cooking pots from kitchen at Pompeii

AD 50

AD 67 Traditional date for martyrdom of St. Peter and St. Paul in Rome

AD 68 Deposition and suicide of Nero

AD 79 Eruption of Vesuvius destroys Pompeii and Herculaneum

AD 80 Inaugural games in Colosseum

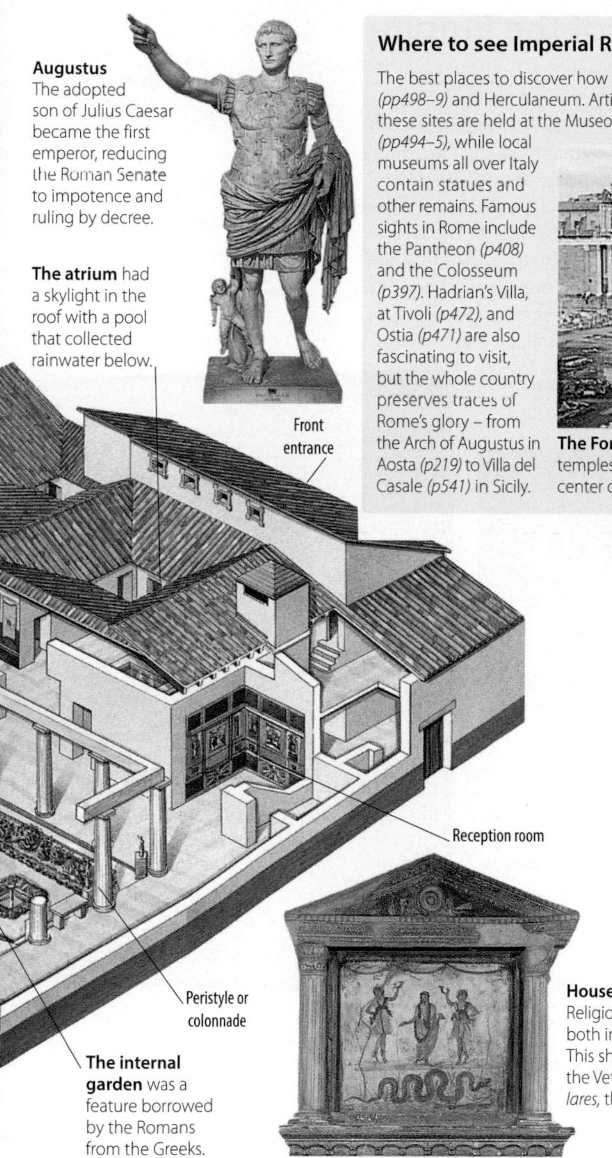

Augustus
The adopted son of Julius Caesar became the first emperor, reducing the Roman Senate to impotence and ruling by decree.

The atrium had a skylight in the roof with a pool that collected rainwater below.

The internal garden was a feature borrowed by the Romans from the Greeks.

Where to see Imperial Rome

The best places to discover how people lived are Pompeii *(pp498–9)* and Herculaneum. Artifacts and works of art from these sites are held at the Museo Archeologico in Naples *(pp494–5)*, while local museums all over Italy contain statues and other remains. Famous sights in Rome include the Pantheon *(p408)* and the Colosseum *(p397)*. Hadrian's Villa, at Tivoli *(p472)*, and Ostia *(p471)* are also fascinating to visit, but the whole country preserves traces of Rome's glory – from the Arch of Augustus in Aosta *(p219)* to Villa del Casale *(p541)* in Sicily.

The Forum *(pp394–5)*, with its temples and law courts, was the center of daily life in ancient Rome.

Mosaic of a Banquet
The Romans ate reclining on low couches. A popular accompaniment for many dishes was *garum*, a salty sauce made of dried fish.

Household Shrine
Religious rites were practiced both in public and in private. This shrine from the House of the Vettii was dedicated to the *lares*, the household gods.

AD 97 Roman Empire reaches largest extent in reign of Trajan

AD 161–180 Reign of Marcus Aurelius

AD 193–211 Reign of Septimius Severus

AD 212 Roman citizenship extended to include people from all parts of the Empire

AD 100 | **AD 150** | **AD 200**

ate 1st century AD mphitheater of Verona built

AD 125 Pantheon rebuilt by Hadrian

AD 134 Hadrian's Villa at Tivoli completed

Emperor Septimius Severus

AD 216 Baths of Caracalla completed in Rome

The Splitting of the Empire

A decisive turning point in the history of the Roman Empire came with Emperor Constantine's conversion to Christianity in AD 312 and his decision to build a new capital at Constantinople (Byzantium). By the 5th century, the Empire was split in two. Rome and the Western Empire could not stem the tide of Germanic invaders migrating southward, and Italy fell first to the Goths and later to the Lombards. The Eastern Empire retained nominal control over parts of Italy from its stronghold at Ravenna, which became the richest, most powerful city of the age, while the great palaces and arenas of Rome were reduced to ruins.

Italy in AD 600
Byzantine territories
Lombard territories

The Donation of Constantine
A medieval legend, encouraged by the papacy, tells how Constantine granted Pope Sylvester temporal power over Rome.

Belisarius (500–565) was a general who won much of Italy back from the Goths.

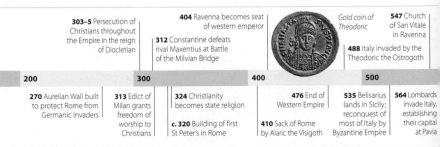

Theodolinda of the Lombards
The 6th-century queen converted her people to orthodox Catholicism. Here, gold is melted for the church she built at Monza *(see p205)*.

Justinian reigned from 527 to 565. He was a great lawgiver and one of the most powerful Byzantine emperors.

270 Aurelian Wall built to protect Rome from Germanic invaders

303–5 Persecution of Christians throughout the Empire in the reign of Diocletian

313 Edict of Milan grants freedom of worship to Christians

312 Constantine defeats rival Maxentius at Battle of the Milvian Bridge

c. 320 Building of first St Peter's in Rome

324 Christianity becomes state religion

404 Ravenna becomes seat of western emperor

410 Sack of Rome by Alaric the Visigoth

Gold coin of Theodoric

476 End of Western Empire

488 Italy invaded by the Theodoric the Ostrogoth

535 Belisarius lands in Sicily; reconquest of most of Italy by Byzantine Empire

547 Church of San Vitale in Ravenna

564 Lombards invade Italy, establishing their capital at Pavia

200 | 300 | 400 | 500

Charlemagne The King of the Franks was invited by the pope to crush the Lombards. In return, he was crowned Holy Roman Emperor in AD 800.

Saracens Besieging Messina *(843)* In the 9th century, Sicily was conquered by Muslims from Africa. Saracen raiders even reached Rome, where Pope Leo IV built a new wall to defend the Vatican.

The emperor holds a large gold paten, the dish in which the bread is placed for Mass.

Maximian, Archbishop of Ravenna

Priests

The Court of Justinian

Byzantine churches were decorated with glorious mosaics of colored glass and gold leaf. This one, from the apse of the church of San Vitale in Ravenna (see p272)*, completed in 547, depicts members of the Imperial court.*

Where to see Early Christian and Byzantine Italy

Though the fall of the Roman Empire led to war, famine, and depopulation, the continuity of the Christian religion has preserved many monuments of the late Empire and Byzantine period. Rome has the catacombs *(p446)* and great basilicas, such as Santa Maria Maggiore *(p417)*. In Ravenna, the administrative capital of the Byzantine Empire, are the churches of San Vitale and Sant'Apollinare *(pp272–3)* with their magnificent mosaics. Sicily and the south also preserve many Byzantine churches, while the finest example of late Byzantine architecture is San Marco in Venice *(pp114–15)*.

Stilo in Calabria has a beautiful Byzantine church, the Cattolica *(p524)*, dating from the 10th century.

Santa Costanza in Rome *(p445)* was built in the 4th century as the mausoleum of Constantine's daughter. Late Roman mosaics decorate the vaults.

c. 595 Lombards control two-thirds of Italy

Gregory the Great (reigned 590–604)

599 Pope Gregory negotiates peace between the Lombards and the Byzantine Empire

600

752 Lombard King Aistulf takes Byzantine stronghold of Ravenna

754 Pope appeals to Franks for help; King Pepin invades Italy and defeats Lombards

700

774 Charlemagne conquers Italy and takes Lombard crown

800 Charlemagne crowned Holy Roman Emperor in St. Peter's

800

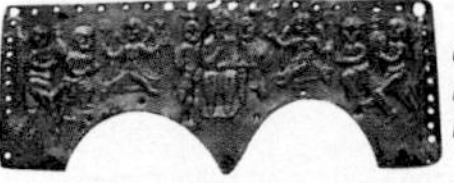

6th-century Lombard gold helmet in the Bargello museum, Florence (see p287)

878 Saracens capture city of Syracuse from Byzantine Empire and gain control of Sicily

900

The Rise of Venice

Medieval Italy saw waves of foreign invaders joining in the struggle for power between popes and emperors. In the confusion, many northern cities asserted their independence from feudal overlords. The most powerful was Venice, governed by its doge and Great Council, which grew rich through trade with the East and by shipping Crusaders to fight the Saracens in the Holy Land. Its maritime rivals on the west coast were Genoa and Pisa.

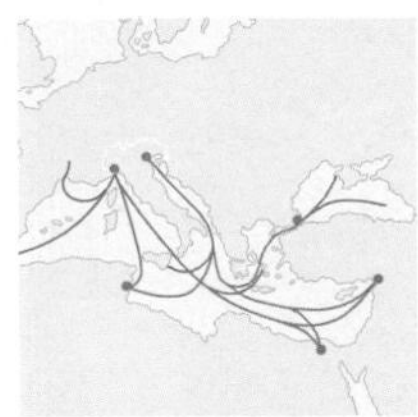

The Mediterranean (1250)

— Genoese trade routes

— Venetian trade routes

Matilda of Tuscany
Matilda, Countess of Tuscany (1046–1115) supported the radical Pope Gregory VII against the Emperor Henry IV. When she died, she left her lands to the church.

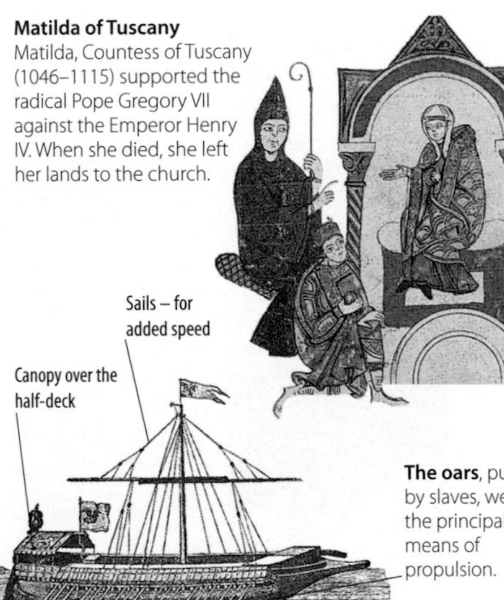

The oars, pulled by slaves, were the principal means of propulsion.

Venetian Galley
The galleys used by Venice, both as warships and for carrying cargo, were similar to ancient Greek vessels.

Basilica San Marco

Doge's Palace

The columns of San Marco and San Teodoro had been erected in the 12th century.

Marco Polo's Departure for China

Venice traded in Chinese silks and spices imported via the Middle East, but no Venetian had been to China before Marco Polo's father Nicolò. Marco Polo set off with his father in 1271, returning 25 years later with fantastic tales of his time at the court of Kublai Khan.

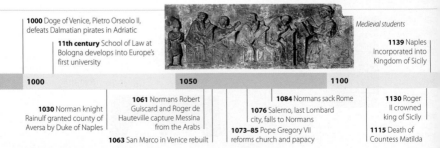

1000 Doge of Venice, Pietro Orseolo II, defeats Dalmatian pirates in Adriatic

11th century School of Law at Bologna develops into Europe's first university

Medieval students

1139 Naples incorporated into Kingdom of Sicily

1000 | **1050** | **1100**

1030 Norman knight Rainulf granted county of Aversa by Duke of Naples

1061 Normans Robert Guiscard and Roger de Hauteville capture Messina from the Arabs

1063 San Marco in Venice rebuilt

1084 Normans sack Rome

1076 Salerno, last Lombard city, falls to Normans

1073–85 Pope Gregory VII reforms church and papacy

1130 Roger II crowned king of Sicily

1115 Death of Countess Matilda

St. Francis of Assisi
(1181–1226)
In *The Dream of Pope Innocent III* by Giotto, painted around 1290–1295, St. Francis holds up the tottering edifice of the Roman church. The Franciscans' rule of poverty brought about a religious revival in reaction to the wealth of the church.

Where to See Early Medieval Italy

Of the many churches built in this period, especially fine examples are Venice's San Marco *(p114)*, Sant'Antonio *(p162)* in Padua, and the Duomo in Pisa *(p328)*. The Leaning Tower *(p330)* also dates back to the 12th century. Medieval castles include Frederick II's Castel del Monte in Puglia *(p513)* and Castello dell'Imperatore in Prato.

Castello dell' Imperatore, Prato, was built about 1240.

Monastery of Sant'Apollonia

Today's Riva degli Schiavoni

Nicolò Polo, his brother Maffeo, and son Marco prepare to embark. They sailed first to Acre in the Levant.

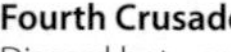

Fourth Crusade
Discord between the leaders of the crusade and Pope Innocent III culminated in the sacking of Constantinople in 1204.

Frederick II
(1194–1250) The emperor kept a court of poets and scholars in Sicily. He won Jerusalem from the Arabs by diplomacy, but was constantly at war with the pope and the cities of Lombardy.

1155 Frederick Barbarossa crowned Holy Roman Emperor

1198 Frederick II becomes king of Sicily

1204 Sacking of Constantinople

1209 Franciscan Order founded

1216 Dominican Order founded

1250 Death of Frederick II

1260 Urban IV invites Charles of Anjou to rule Naples and Sicily

1265 Birth of Dante

150 | 1200 | 1250

Frederick Barbarossa dressed as a Crusader

1220 Frederick II crowned Holy Roman Emperor

1228 Gregory IX excommunicates Frederick II; struggle between Guelphs (the papal party) and Ghibellines (supporters of the emperor)

1237 Lombard League defeats Frederick at Battle of Cortenuova

1271 Marco Polo sets off on journey to China

The Late Middle Ages

Old feuds between pope and emperor thrived throughout the 14th century, kept alive by two warring factions – the Guelphs, who backed the papacy, and the Ghibellines, who favored Imperial power. The cities of Lombardy and Tuscany used the political confusion to grow in strength. It was against this turbulent backdrop that a great new age in painting was inspired by artists such as Duccio and Giotto. Also at this time the Florentine poets Dante and Petrarch laid the foundations of Italian literature.

Italy in 1350

- Papal States
- Holy Roman Empire
- Angevin Kingdom of Naples

Medieval Town Square

Throughout central Italy, the town square was an expression of civic pride and independence. Towns, such as Perugia (see pp356–7)*, tried to overshadow their rivals in the splendor of their town halls. The center of Perugia has changed little since the 14th century when the town's main rival was Siena.*

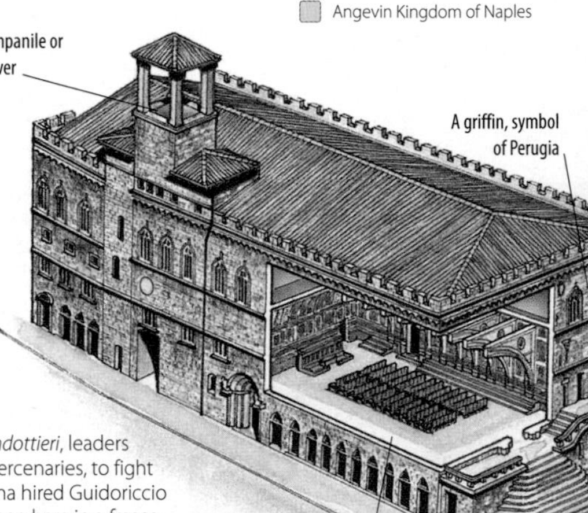

The main chamber of the town hall, the Sala dei Notari, is decorated with the coats of arms of Perugia's mayors.

The Fontana Maggiore was begun in 1275 and includes panels by Nicola Pisano. Prominently placed, it is an emblem of the town's wealth.

Condottieri
Cities paid *condottieri*, leaders of bands of mercenaries, to fight their wars. Siena hired Guidoriccio da Fogliano, seen here in a fresco by Simone Martini (1330).

Dante's Inferno
One of the harshest punishments in Dante's vision of hell is reserved for corrupt popes, such as Boniface VIII (reigned 1294–1303), who are placed upside down in fiery pits.

1275 — 1300 — 1325

1282 Sicilian Vespers; uprising against French rule in Palermo; 2,000 French soldiers killed

1282 Peter of Aragon lands at Trapani, conquers Sicily, and is crowned king in Palermo

1296 Work begins on the Duomo in Florence

1298 Marco Polo returns from China to Venice

The poet and scholar Petrarch

1304 Birth of Petrarch

1309–43 Reign of Robert the Wise of Naples

1309 Clement V moves papacy to Avignon

1310 Work begins on Palazzo Ducale in Venice

1313 Birth of Boccaccio

1321 Dante completes *La Divina Commedia* and dies the same year

1337 Death of Giotto

1339 Simon Boccanegra becomes first doge of Genoa; Giovanna I Queen of Naples

The Black Death
Bubonic plague reached Italy in 1347, carried on Genoese ships from the Black Sea. It killed over a third of the population, reducing the remainder to a state of superstitious terror.

Where to See Late Medieval Italy

Many central Italian cities and towns have public buildings from the 13th and 14th centuries; among the most impressive are Palazzo Vecchio *(p295)* in Florence and Siena's Palazzo Pubblico *(p344)*. Smaller towns that preserve much of their medieval character include Volterra *(p338)* and the walled Monteriggioni *(p338)* in Tuscany, Gubbio *(p356)* and Todi *(p363)* in Umbria, and Viterbo *(pp468–9)* in Lazio. The Duomo in Orvieto *(pp362–3)* is a fine example of a late 13th-century Gothic cathedral.

Piazza dei Priori in Volterra *(p328)* is one of the most beautiful medieval squares in Italy.

The cathedral was started in 1350 and used to include an outside pulpit in the square.

Construction of Alessandria
Almost all towns were ringed with strong walls. This fresco (1407) by Spinello Aretino is a valuable record of medieval building techniques.

Return of Pope Gregory XI to Rome *(1378)*
For 70 years the popes had lived in Avignon, protected by the French kings, while nobles and republicans fought for control of Rome.

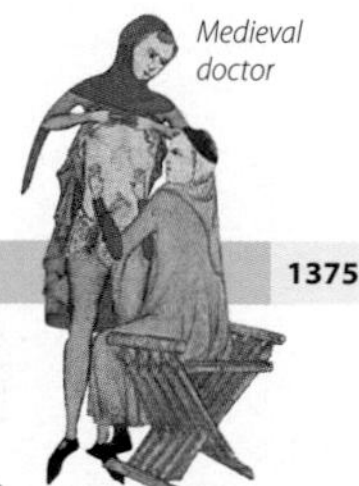

Medieval doctor

47–9 Black Death

1354 Cola di Rienzo killed in Rome

47 Cola di Rienzo tries to establish Roman Republic

350 | 1375 | 1400

1378–1415 Period of Schism, with rival popes and antipopes in Rome and Avignon

1378 Gregory XI returns from Avignon to Rome

1380 Genoese fleet surrenders to Venetians at Chioggia

1385 Gian Galeazzo Visconti becomes ruler of Milan

1406 Pisa annexed by Florence

The Renaissance

Fifteenth-century Italy saw a flowering of the arts and scholarship unmatched in Europe since the days of Greece and Rome. Architects turned from the Gothic to Classical models for inspiration, while painting, with its new understanding of perspective and anatomy, produced a generation of artists that included such giants as Leonardo da Vinci, Raphael, and Michelangelo. The patronage for this cultural "rebirth" came from the wealthy families that ruled the city states of the north, led by the Medici of Florence. In spite of intense rivalry, they oversaw a period of uneasy stability out of which the Renaissance grew.

Italy in 1492
- Republic of Florence
- Papal States
- Aragonese possessions

Handing over the Keys of St. Peter
Perugino's fresco in the Sistine Chapel *(see p430)* links the authority of the pope to the New Testament and, through the Classical buildings in the background, to ancient Rome.

Execution of Savonarola *(1498)*
Having assumed the leadership of Florence in 1494, the fanatical monk was hanged, then burned for heresy in Piazza della Signoria.

Galeazzo Maria Sforza was the son of Milan's ruler.

Piero de' Medici, Lorenzo's father, was given the nickname "the Gouty."

Self-portrait of the artist

1420 Martin V re-establishes papacy in Rome

1435 Publication of *On Painting* by Alberti, which contains the first system for the use of linear perspective

1436 Brunelleschi completes dome of Florence cathedral

1458–64 War between Houses of Aragon and Anjou over Kingdom of Naples

1469 Lorenzo the Magnificent becomes ruler of Florence

1400 | 1425 | 1450

Cosimo de' Medici

1434 Cosimo de' Medici comes to power in Florence

1442 Naples captured by Alfonso of Aragon

1444 Federico da Montefeltro becomes Duke of Urbino

1452 Birth of Leonardo da Vinci

1453 Fall of Constantinople

Filippo Brunelleschi

The Battle of Pavia *(1525)*
The French King Francis I was captured at this battle against the army of the Habsburg Emperor Charles V, who won control of Italy.

Where to See Renaissance Italy

Many cities were flourishing centers of the arts in the 15th century. None can rival Florence *(pp274–317)* with its great palazzi and the Uffizi gallery *(pp290–93)*, but Venice *(pp88–141)*, Urbino *(pp374–5)*, and Mantova *(p211)* all preserve great treasures. In Rome, do not miss the Vatican's Sistine Chapel and Raphael Rooms *(pp428–31)*.

The Spedale degli Innocenti by Brunelleschi in Florence *(p281)* shows the Classical symmetry and restraint of Renaissance architecture.

The Procession of the Magi

Benozzo Gozzoli's fresco (1459) in the Palazzo Medici-Riccardi, Florence, depicts members of the Medici family and other contemporary notables. It contains many references to a great church council held in Florence in 1439.

Lorenzo de' Medici (the Magnificent) was depicted as one of the three kings traveling to Bethlehem.

Humanism
Carpaccio's painting of St. Augustine is thought to show Cardinal Bessarion (c.1395–1472), one of the scholars who revived interest in Classical philosophy, especially Plato.

Pope Julius II
During his reign (1503–13), the worldly Julius made the papacy a major power in European politics. Raphael's portrait shows him as a shrewd old statesman.

1475 Birth of Michelangelo

1483 Sixtus IV consecrates Sistine Chapel

1483 Birth of Raphael

1487 Birth of Titian

Raphael

1494 Italy invaded by Charles VIII of France

1498 Savonarola executed; Machiavelli secretary to ruling Council in Florence

1500

1503 Giuliano della Rovere elected Pope Julius II; he proves the most powerful of the Renaissance popes

1512 Michelangelo completes Sistine Chapel ceiling

1513 Giovanni de' Medici crowned Pope Leo X

1525

1525 Francis I of France captured at Battle of Pavia

1527 Rome sacked by Imperial troops

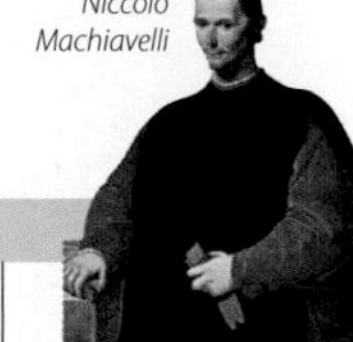

Niccolò Machiavelli

1532 Machiavelli's book *The Prince* is published, five years after his death

The Counter-Reformation

After the Sack of Rome in 1527, Italy was at the mercy of Charles V, Holy Roman Emperor and King of Spain. Pope Clement VII, who had opposed Charles, crowned him emperor in Bologna. In response to the growing threat from Protestantism, a series of reforms, known as the Counter-Reformation and backed by the Inquisition, imposed rigid orthodoxy. New religious orders, such as the Jesuits, were set up to take the battle for men's souls far overseas. The missionary spirit of the age inspired the dramatic forms of the Baroque.

Italy in 1550

Spanish possessions

States allied with Spain

Emperor Charles V and Pope Clement VII
The two former enemies settled their differences and the future destiny of Italy in the Treaty of Barcelona (1529).

Baroque Stucco Decoration

This stucco relief by Giacomo Serpotta (c. 1690) in the Oratory of Santa Zita in Palermo is a magnificent example of Late Baroque exuberance. The subject is a favorite of the period, the Battle of Lepanto, a great naval triumph for the combined forces of Christendom against the Turks (1571).

The Virgin Mary intervenes on the side of the Christians.

The center of the ingenious creation is, in effect, a framed painting in perspective.

The young boy rests his hand on a helmet, symbol of the victorious Christians.

Baroque Architecture
Guarino Guarini's decoration of the dome of the Chapel of the Holy Shroud in Turin *(see p225)* was completed in 1694.

1525 | 1550 | 1575 | 1600

1529 Charles V crowned Holy Roman Emperor in San Petronio, Bologna

1530–37 Alessandro de' Medici ruler of Florence

1540 Founding of Jesuit Order

1541 Michelangelo completes *Last Judgment* in Sistine Chapel

1542 Inquisition established in Rome

1545–63 Council of Trent sets out agenda of Counter-Reformation

Andrea Palladio

1560 San Carlo Borromeo appointed Bishop of Milan

1564 Birth of Galileo

1571 Victory over Turkish fleet at Battle of Lepanto

Giovanni Pierluigi da Palestrina

1580 Death of architect Palladio

1589 Palestrina publishes setting of the Latin Hymnal

1600 Philosopher Giordano Bruno burned for heresy in Rome

Trial of Galileo
The great astronomer was often in trouble with the Inquisition. He was summoned to Rome in 1633 and forced to deny that the Earth and planets moved round the sun.

Lepanto was the last major sea battle in which Venetian galleys played an important role.

St. Ignatius Loyola
The Spanish saint was the founder of the Jesuits – sanctioned by the pope in Rome in 1540.

Cherubs, a favorite motif in Baroque decoration

The turban, symbol of the defeated Turks

Where to see Baroque Italy

The Ecstasy of St. Teresa by Bernini *(p416)* has the dynamic theatricality characteristic of the best Baroque sculpture.

The Baroque is strongly associated with Rome and in particular with its great public spaces such as Piazza Navona *(pp402–3)* and the many churches by Borromini and Bernini. Other cities and towns with striking Baroque architecture include Lecce *(pp516–17)* in Puglia, Palermo *(pp530–33)*, Noto *(p547)*, and Syracuse *(pp546–7)* in Sicily, and Turin *(pp224–5)*.

Revolt of Masaniello *(1647)*
High taxes made Spanish rule in Naples unpopular. A proposed tax on fruit sparked off this failed revolt.

1626 New St. Peter's consecrated in Rome

1631 Duchy of Urbino absorbed by Papal States

1633 Galileo condemned by papal authorities

1642 *L'Incoronazione di Poppea* by Monteverdi

1625

1647 Revolt in Naples in response to tax on fruit

1669 Venice loses island of Crete to the Turks

1669 Major eruption of Mount Etna

1650

1674 Revolt against Spanish rule in Messina

1678 Birth of Vivaldi

1675

1693 Eastern Sicily ruined by earthquake that kills 5 percent of the island's population

1694 Andrea Pozzo completes ceiling fresco for the church of Sant'Ignazio in Rome

The Grand Tour

The treaty of Aix-la-Chapelle in 1748 marked the start of 50 years of peace. It was about this time that Italy, with its great art treasures and Classical ruins, including the newly excavated Pompeii, became Europe's first great tourist destination. Young English "milords" visited Rome, Florence, and Venice as part of a new type of pilgrimage, the Grand Tour, while artists and poets sought inspiration in Rome's glorious past. In 1800, Napoleon, who conquered and briefly united Italy, threatened to destroy the old order, but in 1815 the status quo was restored.

Charles III's Fleet at Naples *(1753)* Ruler of Naples from 1734 to 1759, when he became king of Spain, Charles attempted genuine political reforms.

Goethe in the Roman Campagna
Goethe toured Italy in the 1780s. Great poets who followed his example included the Romantics Keats, Shelley, and Byron.

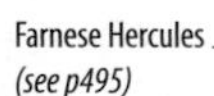

Farnese Hercules *(see p495)*

The Dying Galatian *(see p390)*

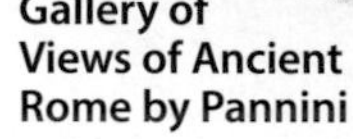

Gallery of Views of Ancient Rome by Pannini

Giovanni Pannini (1691–1765) painted views of Roman ruins for foreigners. This painting is a capriccio, an imaginary scene incorporating many well-known views and Classical statues.

Venetian Carnival
The colorful folklore of Carnival attracted many tourists, but Venice's days of greatness were over. In 1797, the proud maritime republic was ceded to Austria by Napoleon.

1700

1707 Birth of playwright Carlo Goldoni

1713 Treaty of Utrecht gives Naples and Sardinia to Austria and Sicily to Piedmont

1718 Piedmont and Sardinia united under House of Savoy; Sicily passes to Austria

1720

1725 *The Four Seasons* by Vivaldi

Medici coat of arms

1735 Peace of Vienna confirms Charles III as King of the Two Sicilies (Naples and Sicily)

1737 End of Medici dynasty in Florence; Grand Duchy of Tuscany passes to Austrian House of Lorraine

1740

1748 First excavations at Pompeii

Antonio Vivaldi, great Venetian composer

View of the Roman Forum by Piranesi
The popular series of etchings *Vedute di Roma* (Views of Rome) by Giovanni Battista Piranesi (1720–78) inspired a new interest in excavating the ruins of ancient Rome.

Where to see 18th-century Italy

The 18th century produced two of Rome's best-loved tourist attractions: the Spanish Steps *(p413)* and the Trevi Fountain *(p414)*. It was also the age of the first specially built museums, including the Vatican's Museo Pio-Clementino *(p425)*. The Neo-Classical sculpture of Antonio Canova (1757–1822) was immensely popular during this period. His tomb is in Santa Maria Gloriosa dei Frari in Venice *(pp102–3)*. Of Neo-Classical buildings, the most imposing is a vast monument to enlightened despotism: the Palazzo Reale at Caserta *(p500)*.

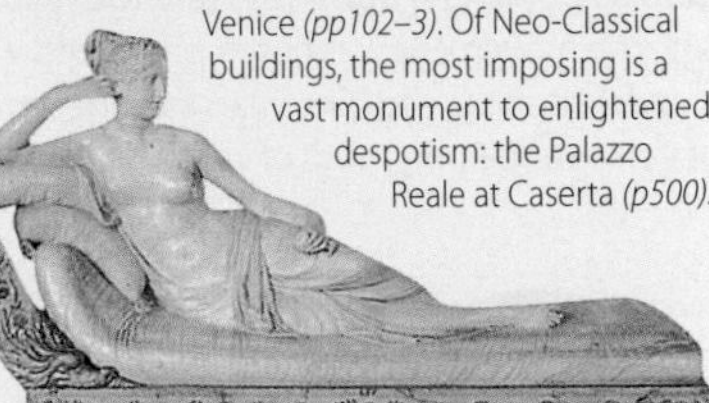

Pauline Borghese, Napoleon's sister, was the model for Antonio Canova's *Venus (1805)* in the Villa Borghese collection in Rome *(p443)*.

The Colosseum was as popular a subject in the 18th century as it is on today's picture postcards.

The Laocoön *(see p421)*

View of the Pantheon *(see p408)*

Napoleon
When Napoleon conquered Italy in 1800, he was seen by many as a liberator. The enchantment wore off as he took priceless works of art back to Paris.

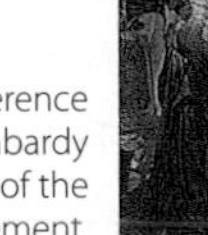

Congress of Vienna (1815) The conference decided that Austria should keep Lombardy and Venice, thereby sowing the seeds of the Italian unification movement.

La Scala Opera House, Milan (see p191)

1760

1765–90 Reign of Leopold, Grand Duke of Tuscany, who introduces enlightened reforms

1768 Corsica sold by Genoa to France

1773 Pope dissolves Jesuit Order

1778 La Scala opened in Milan

1780

1780 Joseph II succeeds to Austrian throne; minor reforms in Lombardy

1796–7 Napoleon's first campaign in northern Italy

1797 Venice given to Austria by Treaty of Campo Formio; France controls rest of northern Italy

1800

1800–1801 Napoleon conquers Italy

1806 Joseph Bonaparte becomes King of Naples

1808 Murat becomes King of Naples

1809 Pope Pius VII exiled from Rome

1815 Congress of Vienna restores status quo in Italy, though Austria keeps Venice

The Risorgimento

The word "Risorgimento" (resurgence) describes the five decades of struggle for liberation from foreign rule, culminating in the unification of Italy in 1870. In 1848, patriots rose up against the Austrians in Milan and Venice, the Bourbons in Sicily, and the pope in Rome, where a republic was declared. Garibaldi valiantly defended the republic, but all the uprisings were too localized. By 1859, the movement was better organized with Vittorio Emanuele II at its head. Two years saw the conquest of all but Venice and Rome, both of which fell within a decade.

Italy in 1861

Kingdom of Italy

Giuseppe Mazzini *(1805–72)* An exile for much of his life, Mazzini fought alongside Garibaldi to unite Italy as a republic, rather than a kingdom.

The guns were rusty, old converted flintlocks.

The red shirt was the badge of the Garibaldini.

Italian Railroads
The short railroad line from Naples to Portici was opened in 1839. Politically fragmented, Italy was slow to create an effective rail network.

Revolt of Messina
When, in 1848, Messina revolted, Ferdinand II subjected the town to a savage bombardment, earning himself the nickname King Bomba.

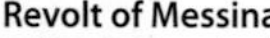

1820

1820s Carbonari secret society active in Papal States

1830

1831 Insurrection in Romagna and Le Marche against papal rule

1831 Mazzini founds *Giovine Italia* (Young Italy) movement

1840 First major railroad lines established

Daniele Manin, hero of the Venetian uprising of 1848

1840

1847 Economic crisis

1848 Revolutions throughout Italy

1849 Accession of Vittorio Emanuele II as ruler of Piedmont

1849 Republic of Rome crushed by French troops

1850

1852 Cavour becomes prime minister of Piedmont

Battle of Solferino (1859)
With the help of a French army led by Napoleon III, the Piedmontese won Milan and Lombardy from the Austrians.

Where to See Risorgimento Italy

Almost every town in Italy honors the heroes of the Risorgimento with a Via Garibaldi, a Via Cavour, a Piazza Vittorio, a Via Mazzini, and a Via XX Settembre (the date of the fall of Rome in 1870). Many cities also have Risorgimento museums. One of the best is in Turin *(p227)*.

The Victor Emmanuel Monument *(p388)* is a prominent, but largely unloved, Roman landmark.

Two old paddle steamers brought the Thousand from Quarto near Genoa.

Count Camillo di Cavour *(1810–61)*
Cavour's diplomacy as prime minister of Piedmont ensured that the House of Savoy became rulers of the new Italy. He also coined the word "Risorgimento."

The skiffs were lent by other ships moored in Marsala harbor.

Garibaldi and the Thousand

Giuseppe Garibaldi (1807–82) was a leader of courage and genius. In 1860, he landed at Marsala with 1,000 volunteers. The garrison at Palermo surrendered, Sicily fell, and he went on to conquer Naples, thus presenting Vittorio Emanuele with half a kingdom.

Giuseppe Verdi *(1813–1901)*
Composers such as Verdi, Donizetti, and Rossini made the 19th century the great era of Italian opera. Verdi's early operas inspired the Risorgimento.

1859 Battles of Magenta and Solferino; Piedmont acquires Lombardy from Austria and duchies of Parma, Modena, and Tuscany

1861 Kingdom of Italy proclaimed with capital at Turin

Pope Pius IX, who remained a virtual prisoner in the Vatican when Rome became capital of Italy

1882 Deaths of Garibaldi and Pope Pius IX

1893 Troops sent to suppress insurrection in Sicily

1860 | **1870** | **1880** | **1890**

1866 Italy wins Venice from Austria

1860 Garibaldi and the Thousand capture Kingdom of the Two Sicilies

1870 Rome falls to royalist troops and is made capital of new kingdom; Vatican announces doctrine of papal infallibility

1878 Death of Vittorio Emanuele; accession of King Umberto I

1890 Italian colony of Eritrea established by royal decree

Modern Italy

Fascism under Mussolini (1922–43) promised the Italians greatness, but delivered only humiliation. In spite of this, Italy has become one of Europe's leading economies with a standard of living undreamed of at the turn of the 20th century. This has been achieved in the face of great obstacles. Since 1946, the Republic has passed through many crises: a series of unstable coalitions, the terrorist outrages in the 1970s, and in the 1990s, corruption scandals involving numerous government ministers and officials.

1936 FIAT produces first "Topolino" car

1960 *La Dolce Vita*, Federico Fellini's film satire on Rome's decadent café society, is released

1922 Fascists march on Rome; Mussolini invited to form government

1900 Assassination of King Umberto I

1911–12 Italy conquers Libya

1918 Austrian advance halted at the river Piave, just north of Venice

1940 Italy enters World War II

1943 Allies land in Sicily; Italy signs armistice and new Badoglio government declares war on Germany

1900	1910	1920	1930	1940	1950	196

1900	1910	1920	1930	1940	1950	196

1908 Earthquake destroys many towns and villages in Calabria and eastern Sicily; Messina almost completely razed to the ground; over 150,000 die

1915 Italy enters World War I

1936 Italy conquers Abyssinia; pact with Germany, forming anti-Communist "Axis"

1943 Mussolini imprisoned, then freed by Germans

1946 Referendum in which Italy votes to become a republic; Christian Democrat party forms first of a long series of coalition governments

1920s Postwar years see continued emigration to the United States. Here, emigrants cheer as they reach New York aboard the *Giulio Cesare*

1909 In his *Futurist Manifesto*, Filippo Marinetti condemns all traditional art as too static. His idea of a new dynamic art is expressed in works such as Umberto Boccioni's bronze *Unique Forms of Continuity in Space*

1957 Treaty of Rome; Italy one of the six founder members of the European Economic Community

1960 Olympic Games held in Rome

1917 Defeat at Caporetto on Italy's northeastern border; Italian troops, such as these Alpini, retreat to defensive positions

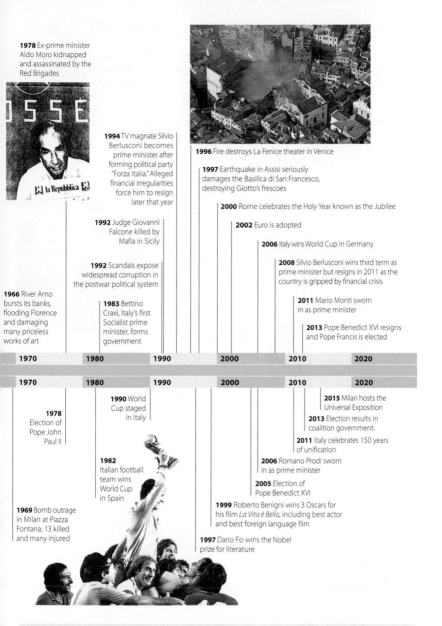

1978 Ex-prime minister Aldo Moro kidnapped and assassinated by the Red Brigades

1966 River Arno bursts its banks, flooding Florence and damaging many priceless works of art

1983 Bettino Craxi, Italy's first Socialist prime minister, forms government

1992 Scandals expose widespread corruption in the postwar political system

1992 Judge Giovanni Falcone killed by Mafia in Sicily

1994 TV magnate Silvio Berlusconi becomes prime minister after forming political party "Forza Italia." Alleged financial irregularities force him to resign later that year

1996 Fire destroys La Fenice theater in Venice

1997 Earthquake in Assisi seriously damages the Basilica di San Francesco, destroying Giotto's frescoes

2000 Rome celebrates the Holy Year known as the Jubilee

2002 Euro is adopted

2006 Italy wins World Cup in Germany

2008 Silvio Berlusconi wins third term as prime minister but resigns in 2011 as the country is gripped by financial crisis

2011 Mario Monti sworn in as prime minister

2013 Pope Benedict XVI resigns and Pope Francis is elected

1970	1980	1990	2000	2010	2020

1970	1980	1990	2000	2010	2020

1969 Bomb outrage in Milan at Piazza Fontana; 13 killed and many injured

1978 Election of Pope John Paul II

1982 Italian football team wins World Cup in Spain

1990 World Cup staged in Italy

1997 Dario Fo wins the Nobel prize for literature

1999 Roberto Benigni wins 3 Oscars for his film *La Vita è Bella,* including best actor and best foreign language film

2005 Election of Pope Benedict XVI

2006 Romano Prodi sworn in as prime minister

2011 Italy celebrates 150 years of unification

2013 Election results in coalition government.

2015 Milan hosts the Universal Exposition

Italian Cinema Since World War II

The social problems of late 1940s Italy inspired a wave of cinema known as Neo-Realism. Leading exponents included Roberto Rossellini, who made *Roma Città Aperta* (1945), Vittorio de Sica, the director of *Bicycle Thieves* (1948), Pier Paolo Pasolini, and Luchino Visconti. Since that time, the major Italian directors have cultivated their own personal styles. Visconti's later movies, such as *Death in Venice* (1971), show formal beauty and decadence, while Federico Fellini's *La Dolce Vita* (1960) and *Roma* (1972) depict life as a grotesque carnival. Italy has also produced some commercially successful movies, such as Sergio Leone's late 1960s westerns and the Oscar-winning *Cinema Paradiso* and *La Vita è Bella.*

Vittorio de Sica (1901–74)

ITALY THROUGH THE YEAR

Throughout Italy, the variety of local character and color is astonishing. This is mainly due to the survival of regionalism, particularly in the southern parts of the country. Old traditions, customs, and lifestyles are still greatly respected and there is a deep attachment to the land, which is reflected in a healthy interest in the food and produce, as well as a perseverance of seasonal religious and secular events. Annual festivals, whether in rural or urban areas, range from wine-tasting and gastronomic celebrations to elaborate commemorations of every patron saint imaginable.

Spring

The Italian spring begins early, particularly in the south. City streets and main sights are rarely overcrowded (except at Easter in Rome). The weather, however, can be unpredictable and wet in the central and northern parts of the country. Spring specialties, such as asparagus, spinach, and arugula, begin to feature on restaurant menus. This is a season of great celebration; festivals and fairs abound, especially in Sicily, and the Easter papal address always draws massive crowds to St. Peter's.

Tuscan asparagus

March

Dolomiti Ski Jazz Festival, *(mid-Mar)*, Val di Fiemme, Trentino–Alto Adige. Live jazz on the ski slopes.

Sa Sartiglia, Oristano, Sardinia. Three-day carnival ending on Shrove Tuesday.

Su e zo per i ponti *(Sun, varies)*, Venice. A lively race through the city's streets, up and down the bridges.

Procession of the Grieving Madonna on the isle of Procida

April

Procession of the Grieving Madonna *(Good Friday)*, Procida, Campania. A colorful religious procession throughout the island.

Holy Week *(Easter Week)*. Numerous Easter celebrations from Palm Sunday to Easter Sunday, throughout the country.

Papal Address *(Easter Sunday)*, Rome. The pope makes his Easter address from the Vatican.

Dance of the Devils *(Easter Sunday)*, Prizzi, Sicily. Dance recital symbolizing the attempts of evil to vanquish the forces of good.

Scoppio del Carro *(Easter Sunday)*, Florence. Firework display is lit by a mechanical dove in front of the Duomo.

Festa della Madonna che Scappa in Piazza *(Easter Sunday)*, Sulmona, Abruzzo. Re-enactment of a meeting between the Virgin and the Risen Christ.

Festa degli Aquiloni *(first Sun after Easter)*, San Miniato, Tuscany. Kite lovers perform aerial acrobatics at this festival.

Festa di San Marco *(Apr 25)*, Venice. St. Mark, the patron saint of Venice, is commemorated by a gondola race across St. Mark's Basin.

Mostra Mercato Internazionale dell'Artigianato *(last week)*, Florence. An important European exhibition of arts and crafts.

Spring strawberries

Scoppio del Carro (Explosion of the Carriage) festival in Florence

Sagra Musicale Lucchese *(dates vary)*, Lucca, Tuscany. Festival of sacred music held in Romanesque churches.

May

Festa di Sant'Efisio *(May 1)*, Cagliari, Sardinia. Paraders in traditional Sardinian costume.

Festa di San Nicola *(May 7–9)*, Bari, Puglia. A statue of St. Nicholas is taken to the sea.

Festa dei Ceri *(May 15)*, Gubbio, Umbria. Festival, including a race with four teams carrying large candles.

Festa di San Domenico Abate *(first Thu)*, Cocullo, Abruzzo. Includes a procession with a statue of St. Dominic covered with live snakes.

Festa dello Speck *(late May)*, Bolzano, Trentino–Alto Adige. A celebration of the famed ham.

Greek Drama in Theater *(May–Jun)*, Syracuse, Sicily. Festival of Greek drama.

Maggio Musicale *(May–Jun)*, Florence. This is the city's biggest arts festival, including music, drama, and dance.

Street carpeted with flowers for the Infiorata in Genzano

Summer

Summer brings the crowds to Italy, particularly the cities. Italians, however, flee and head for the coast, usually in August. The lines for tourist attractions can be long and hotels are often fully booked. Festivals vary; religious events are interspersed with those of the arts and local folklore.

June

Festa della Fragola *(Jun 1)*, Borgo San Martino, Piedmont. Musical and folkloric performances in celebration of the strawberry.

Biennale *(Jun–Sep)*, Venice. The world's biggest exhibition of contemporary art takes place during odd-numbered years only.

Infiorata *(Corpus Christi day)*, Genzano, Lazio. A procession through streets carpeted with flowers.

International Film Festival *(mid-Jun)*, Taormina, Sicily.

Festa di San Giovanni *(mid-Jun–mid-Jul)*, Turin, Piedmont. Festival in honor of the city's patron saint, John.

Calcio Storico *(Jun 24 and two other days in Jun)*, Florence. Soccer in 16th-century costumes; fireworks.

Festa di Sant'Andrea *(Jun 27)*, Amalfi, Campania. Fireworks and processions.

Festival dei Due Mondi *(late Jun–early Jul)*, Spoleto, Umbria. International festival of drama, music, and dance.

Gioco del Ponte *(last Sun)*, Pisa. "The Bridge Parade" of marchers in antique armor.

Estate Romana *(late Jun–mid-Sep)*, Rome. Outdoor movies, performances, ballet, and concerts.

July

Corsa del Palio *(Jul 2)*, Siena. Tuscany's most famous event *(see p345)* presents a medieval flag-waving exhibition and horse race.

Festa della Madonna della Bruna *(first Sun)*, Matera, Basilicata. A lively procession of clergymen and knights in costume.

Festa dei Noantri *(last two weeks Jul)*, Rome. A colorful festival in Trastevere.

Festa della Santa Maria del Carmine *(Jul 16)*, Naples. Featuring the illumination of the city's bell tower.

Umbria Jazz *(Jul)*, Perugia. World-famous jazz artists perform in various settings.

Musician from Florence's Calcio

Opera Festival *(Jul–Aug)*, Verona, Veneto. Renowned opera festival *(see p141)* overlapping with the **Shakespeare Festival**, providing music, drama, opera, and dance.

The Palio of Siena in action

August

Medieval Palio *(first weekend Aug)* Feltre, Veneto. Parades and archery competitions, medieval-style.

Festa dei Candelieri *(Aug 14)*, Sassari, Sardinia. "Festival of the Candle," dating from the 16th century.

Festa del Mare *(Aug 15)*, Diano Marina, Liguria. This "Festival of the Sea" boasts a spectacular firework display.

Corsa del Palio *(Aug 16)*, Siena, Tuscany. See July entry.

Rossini Festival *(mid-Aug)*, Pesaro, Le Marche. A celebration of the composer's work, in his birthplace.

Venice Film Festival *(late Aug–early Sep)*. International festival on the Lido.

Settimane Musicali di Stresa *(late Aug–end Sep)*, Stresa, Lombardy. Four weeks of concerts and recitals.

Sunbathers enjoying a Tuscan beach vacation

Fall

Fall is a slow, gentle season in Italy, but that doesn't mean there are fewer festivals and fairs. In addition to the various religious events at this time of year, gastronomic festivals are especially popular, commemorating such delectables as chestnuts, local cheeses, sausages, and mushrooms. Fall is the season of the *vendemmia*, the grape harvest, which is often used as an excuse for village festivities at which the latest local wines flow freely.

The climate *(see pp76–7)* in late fall is often cold and wet in the north. The south, however, can be quite warm right through October.

Advertisement for the September Palio in Asti, Piedmont

September

Festa di Santa Lucia *(first Sun)*, Lodè, Sardinia. Includes a contest where competitors improvise short poems.
Procession of the Macchina di Santa Rosa *(Sep 3)*, Viterbo, Lazio. Commemoration of the saint's body being transported to the Church of Santa Rosa in 1258.
Giostra del Saracino *(first Sun)*, Arezzo, Umbria. Joust of the Saracen and knights, dating from the 13th century.
Regata Storica *(first Sun)*, Venice. A procession of historic boats plus a colorful gondola race.
Human chess game *(second week)*, Marostica, near Vicenza. A popular costumed game held in the main square every even year.

The widely cultivated olive tree

Rassegna del Chianti Classico *(second week)*, Chianti, Tuscany. Celebration of the local wines.
Auditorium Parco della Musica Season *(Sep–Jul)*, Rome. The broad program includes classical, jazz and rock music, as well as a circus and a popular modern dance festival.
The Miracle of San Gennaro *(Sep 19)*, Naples. Reenactment of the liquefaction of the saint's blood, in a lively mass at the Duomo.
Palio *(third Sun)*, Asti, Piedmont. Includes a costumed medieval procession and bareback horse racing.

October

Amici della Musica *(Oct–Apr)*, Florence, Tuscany. The popular "Friends of Music" concert season begins.
Fiera del Tartufo *(Oct–Nov)*, Alba, Piedmont. A variety of events centered around the locally grown white truffle.
Festa di San Francesco *(Oct 4)*, Assisi, Umbria. Feast in honor of one of Italy's patron saints.
Wine festivals *(first week)*, Castelli Romani, Lazio.
Sagra del Tordo *(last Sun)* Montalcino, Tuscany. Celebration of the thrush; costumed archery contests.
Festa dell'Uva *(dates vary)*, Bolzano, Trentino–Alto Adige. Grape festival with live music and a costumed procession featuring allegoric carts.
International Festival of Cinema *(dates vary)*, Rome. A week of screenings, high-profile events, and celebrity spotting in the capital.

A roasted chestnut stall in autumn

November

Festa dei Popoli *(Nov)*, Florence, Tuscany. Film festival showing documentary films in their original languages with Italian subtitles.
Festa della Salute *(Nov 21)*, Venice. Cherished by Venetian locals, this feast gives thanks to the Virgin Mary in memory of a 1630 plague.

The human chess game in the town square of Marostica

Winter

There are fairs, markets, and religious events up and down the country at this time of year. Neapolitan Christmas cribs are famous and nearly every church has one. The Christmas holiday itself is low-key; more is made of other religious events such as the liquefaction of San Gennaro's blood in Naples and the Carnevale in Venice.

Rome during one of its rare snowfalls

December

Festa di Sant'Ambrogio *(early Dec)*, Milan. The official opening of La Scala Opera season *(see p197)*.

Festa della Madonnadi Loreto *(Dec 10)*, Loreto, Le Marche. Celebration of the Virgin's Holy House.

Mercato della Befana *(mid-Dec–Jan 6)*, Rome. Well-known Christmas fair held in Piazza Navona.

The Miracle of San Gennaro *(Dec 16)*, Naples. See September. **Christmas fair** *(mid-Dec)*, Naples. Fair selling crib figures and decorations.

Fiaccole di Natale *(Christmas Eve)*, Abbadia di San Salvatore, Tuscany. Features carols and processions in memory of the first shepherds.

Midnight Mass *(Dec 24)*, at churches all over the country.

Christmas Day *(Dec 25)*, St. Peter's Square, Rome. Public blessing by the pope.

La Befana at Piazza Navona, Rome

January

Capodanno *(Jan 1)*, all over the country. New Year's Day is celebrated with fireworks and volleys from hunters firing into the air to scare off ghosts and spirits of the old year and welcome in the new.

La Befana *(Jan 6)*, throughout Italy. Children's holiday with presents and sweets.

Pitti Immagine Uomo, Pitti Immagine Donna, Pitti Immagine Bimbo, Fortezza da Basso, Florence. Month of international fashion shows for women, men, and children.

Carnevale, Viareggio

Festa di San Sebastiano *(Sun nearest Jan 20)*, Dolceacqua, Liguria. A laurel tree covered with colorful communion hosts is carried through town.

Festa d'o'Cippo di Sant'Antonio *(Jan 17)*, Naples. A procession for St. Anthony, protector of animals.

Carnevale *(a month-long event finishing Shrove Tue)*, Viareggio, Tuscany. A carnival famous for its lively, topically themed floats.

Fair of St. Orsa *(Jan 30–31)*, Aosta, Valle d'Aosta. Exhibition of traditional arts and crafts.

February

Carnevale *(last 10 days before Lent, finishing Shrove Tuesday)*, Venice. Pre-Lent festival meaning "farewell to meat." Events are organized, but anyone can buy a mask and watch the array of gorgeous costumes on show.

Sagra delle Mandorle in Fiore *(first or second week)*, Agrigento, Sicily. Annual almond blossom celebration.

Bacanal del Gnoco *(dates vary)*, Verona. Traditional masked procession with both international and local allegorical floats. Masked balls are held in the town's squares.

Carnevale *(dates vary)*, Mamoiada, Sardinia. Processions include *mamuthones* wearing sinister black masks.

Public Holidays

New Year's Day (Jan 1)
Epiphany (Jan 6)
Easter Sunday & Monday
Liberation Day (Apr 25)
Labor Day (May 1)
Republic Day (Jun 2)
Ferragosto (Aug 15)
All Saints' Day (Nov 1)
Immaculate Conception (Dec 8)
Christmas Day (Dec 25)
Santo Stefano (Dec 26)

Carnevale revelers in Venice

The Sporting Year

Soccer is by far the most important sport in Italy, uniting the country when the national team *(Azzurri)* plays. Other sports throughout the year also attract a large following, so fans are never at a loss for varied activities. For most big sporting events, tickets can be obtained for cash at club outlets such as the venue itself. Agencies provide hard-to-get tickets at often higher prices. Beware of the inevitable scalpers at popular events, as their expensive tickets may not be valid.

Calcio Fiorentino, one of Italy's few indigenous sports, is said to be the medieval precursor of modern soccer.

The professional water polo season takes place from March through to July. The Canottieri Napoli team play consistently well through the championship.

The Giro d'Italia cycling race takes place over many stages. Ivan Basso (Italian) won the race in 2006 and 2010.

Memorial d'Aloia rowing competition, held in Umbria

Coppa Italia soccer final

January | February | March | April | May | June

Indoor Athletics Championships

Rome Marathon

International Showjumping, Rome

Rugby is becoming increasingly popular. Italy takes part in the Six Nations Championship in February and March, along with England, Scotland, Wales, Ireland, and France.

The Rome Masters, previously known as the Italian Open, takes place in Rome during May. The event is one of the most prestigious clay court tennis competitions in the world.

The Italian leg o the Circuito Mondial in Mugello. Valentin Rossi has dominate the MotoGP Worl Championship fo over a decad

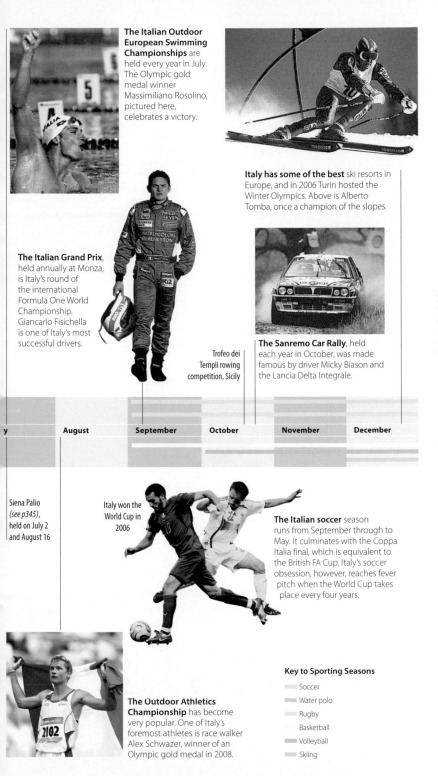

The Italian Outdoor European Swimming Championships are held every year in July. The Olympic gold medal winner Massimiliano Rosolino, pictured here, celebrates a victory.

Italy has some of the best ski resorts in Europe, and in 2006 Turin hosted the Winter Olympics. Above is Alberto Tomba, once a champion of the slopes.

The Italian Grand Prix, held annually at Monza, is Italy's round of the international Formula One World Championship. Giancarlo Fisichella is one of Italy's most successful drivers.

The Sanremo Car Rally, held each year in October, was made famous by driver Micky Biason and the Lancia Delta Integrale.

Trofeo dei Templi rowing competition, Sicily

y | August | September | October | November | December

Siena Palio *(see p345)*, held on July 2 and August 16

Italy won the World Cup in 2006

The Italian soccer season runs from September through to May. It culminates with the Coppa Italia final, which is equivalent to the British FA Cup. Italy's soccer obsession, however, reaches fever pitch when the World Cup takes place every four years.

The Outdoor Athletics Championship has become very popular. One of Italy's foremost athletes is race walker Alex Schwazer, winner of an Olympic gold medal in 2008.

Key to Sporting Seasons

- Soccer
- Water polo
- Rugby
- Basketball
- Volleyball
- Skiing

The Climate of Italy

The Italian peninsula has a varied climate falling into three distinct geographical regions. Cold Alpine winters and warm, wet summers characterize the northern regions. In the extensive Po Valley, arid summers contrast with freezing, damp winters. The rest of Italy has a pleasant climate with long, hot summers and mild winters. Cooler weather along the backbone of the Apennines can bring snow during the winter months.

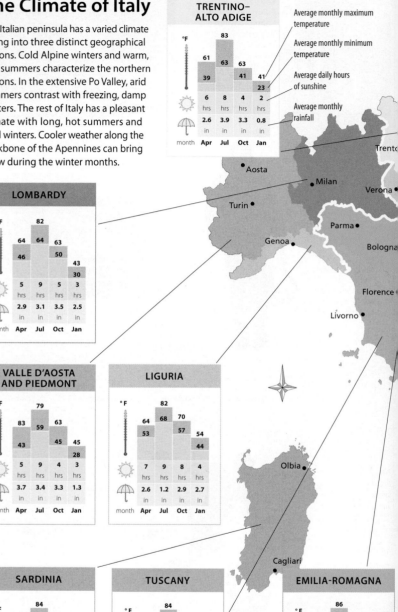

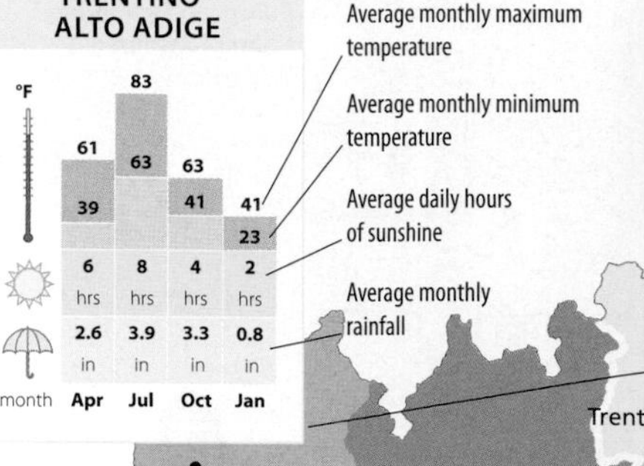

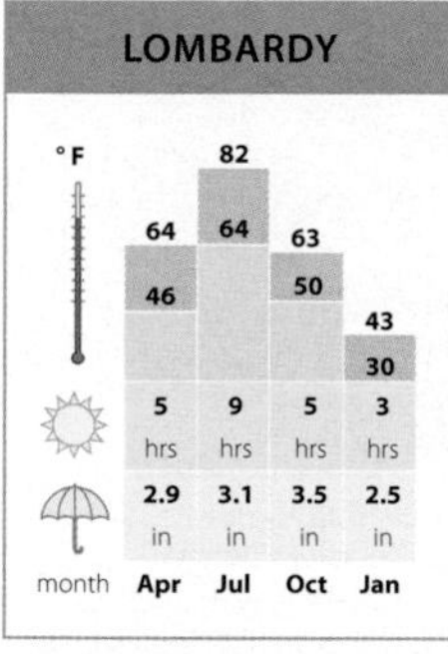

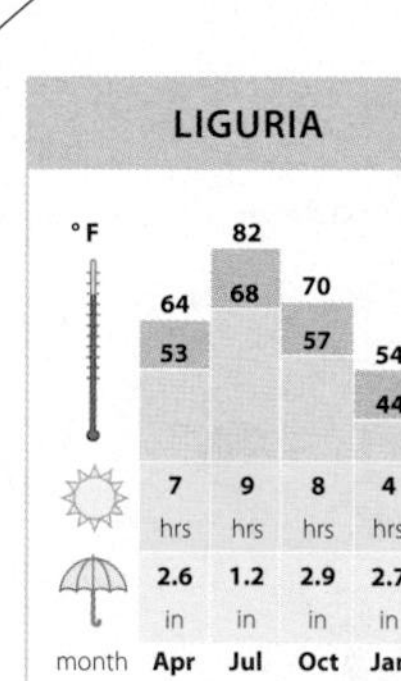

VALLE D'AOSTA AND PIEDMONT
°F
83 79 63 45
43 59 45 28
5 hrs 9 hrs 4 hrs 3 hrs
3.7 in 3.4 in 3.3 in 1.3 in
month Apr Jul Oct Jan
LIGURIA
°F
64 82 70 54
53 68 57 44
7 hrs 9 hrs 8 hrs 4 hrs
2.6 in 1.2 in 2.9 in 2.7 in
month Apr Jul Oct Jan

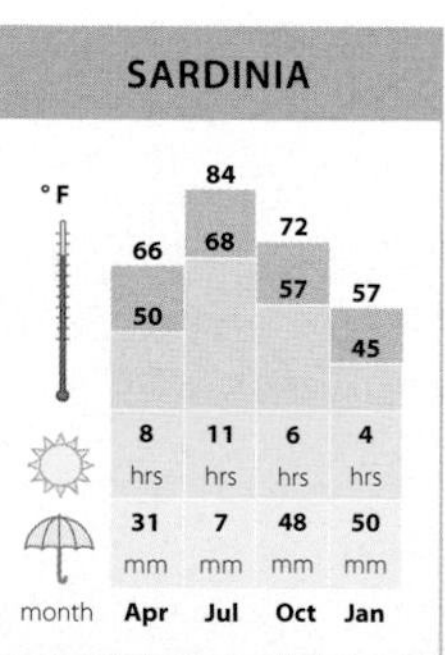

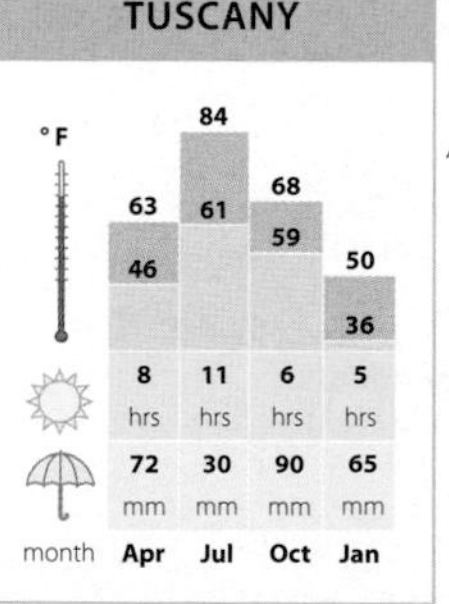

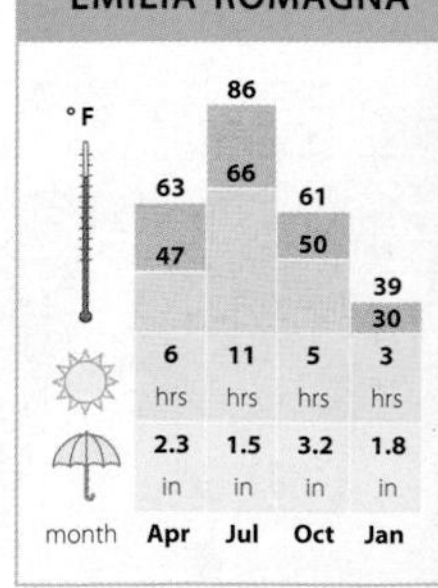

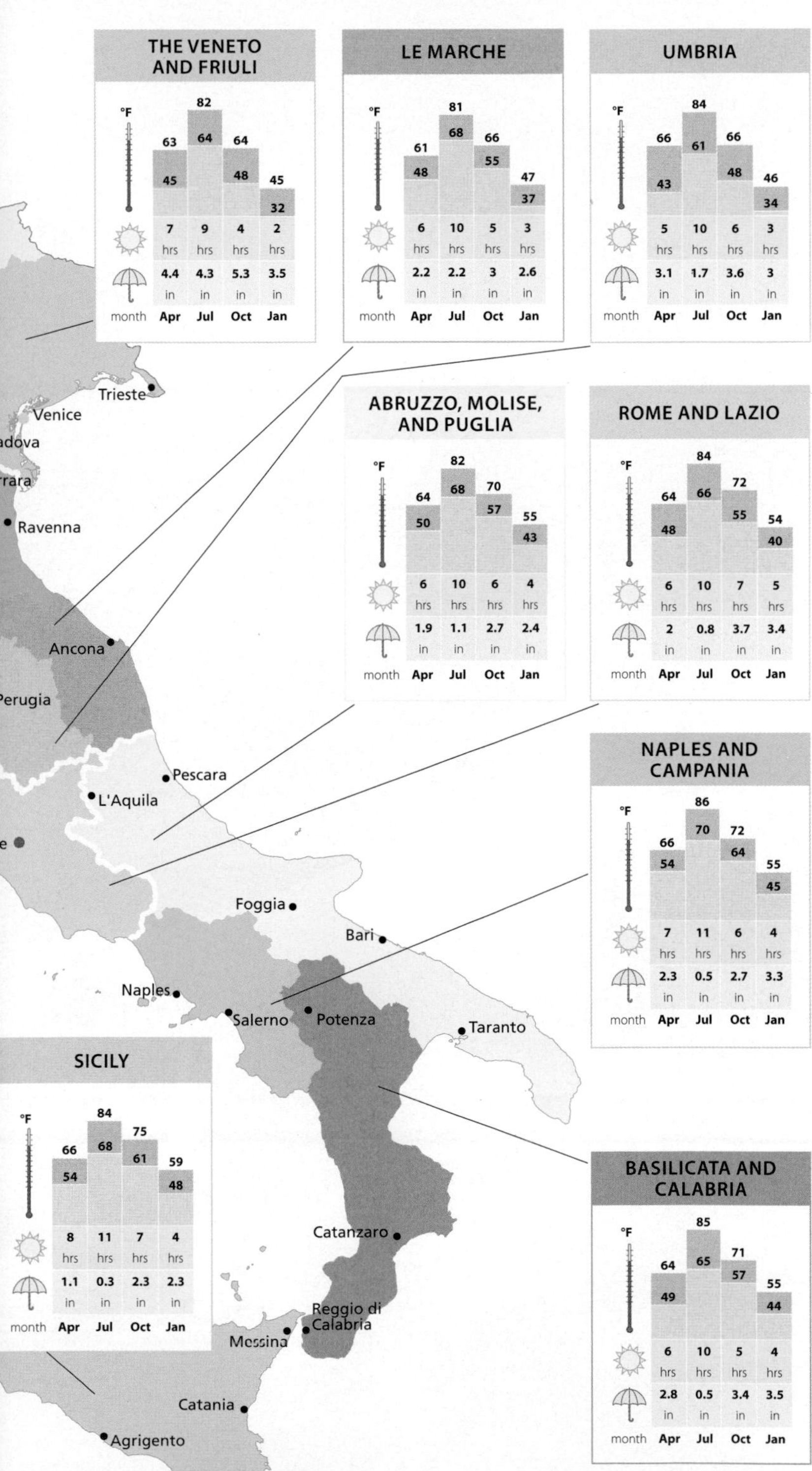
THE VENETO AND FRIULI
°F
63 45 | 82 64 | 64 48 | 45 32
7 hrs | 9 hrs | 4 hrs | 2 hrs
4.4 in | 4.3 in | 5.3 in | 3.5 in
month Apr Jul Oct Jan
LE MARCHE
°F
61 48 | 81 68 | 66 55 | 47 37
6 hrs | 10 hrs | 5 hrs | 3 hrs
2.2 in | 2.2 in | 3 in | 2.6 in
month Apr Jul Oct Jan
UMBRIA
°F
66 43 | 84 61 | 66 48 | 46 34
5 hrs | 10 hrs | 6 hrs | 3 hrs
3.1 in | 1.7 in | 3.6 in | 3 in
month Apr Jul Oct Jan
ABRUZZO, MOLISE, AND PUGLIA
°F
64 50 | 82 68 | 70 57 | 55 43
6 hrs | 10 hrs | 6 hrs | 4 hrs
1.9 in | 1.1 in | 2.7 in | 2.4 in
month Apr Jul Oct Jan
ROME AND LAZIO
°F
64 48 | 84 66 | 72 55 | 54 40
6 hrs | 10 hrs | 7 hrs | 5 hrs
2 in | 0.8 in | 3.7 in | 3.4 in
month Apr Jul Oct Jan
NAPLES AND CAMPANIA
°F
66 54 | 86 70 | 72 64 | 55 45
7 hrs | 11 hrs | 6 hrs | 4 hrs
2.3 in | 0.5 in | 2.7 in | 3.3 in
month Apr Jul Oct Jan
SICILY
°F
66 54 | 84 68 | 75 61 | 59 48
8 hrs | 11 hrs | 7 hrs | 4 hrs
1.1 in | 0.3 in | 2.3 in | 2.3 in
month Apr Jul Oct Jan
BASILICATA AND CALABRIA
°F
64 49 | 85 65 | 71 57 | 55 44
6 hrs | 10 hrs | 5 hrs | 4 hrs
2.8 in | 0.5 in | 3.4 in | 3.5 in
month Apr Jul Oct Jan
Trieste
Venice
adova
rrara
Ravenna
Ancona
Perugia
Pescara
L'Aquila
Foggia
Bari
Naples
Salerno
Potenza
Taranto
Catanzaro
Reggio di Calabria
Messina
Catania
Agrigento

NORTHEAST ITALY

Northeast Italy at a Glance

The sheer variety to be found in northeast Italy makes it a fascinating area to explore. The majestic Dolomites dominate the north, straddling Trentino-Alto Adige and the Veneto, and are dotted with medieval castles and modern ski resorts. On the plain, the cities of Verona, Vicenza, and Padua are all noted for outstanding architecture and museums, while the rural hinterland boasts beautiful villas. The incomparable and spectacular city of Venice, with its magnificent monuments, rises from the lagoon. Farther east, in Friuli, there are important Roman remains. This map pinpoints some of the highlights.

Alto Adige is a dramatic region of snow-covered mountain valleys scattered with forbidding castles and onion-domed churches in the Tyrolean style *(see pp174–5).*

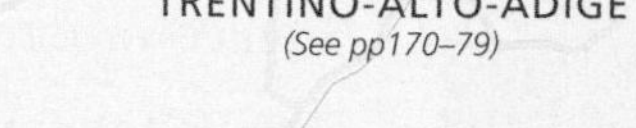

The Dolomites *(see pp86–7)* form the spectacular backdrop to many towns in northeast Italy, among them Trento, the region's capital *(see pp178–9).*

Verona is one of the loveliest cities in the Veneto, boasting the Castelvecchio and a Roman arena now used for performances of opera *(see pp146–51).*

Vicenza, a model Renaissance city, is dominated by the buildings of Palladio, such as the Palazzo della Ragione and La Rotonda *(see pp154–7).*

◀ Santa Maddalena with the Dolomites in the background

Udine in Friuli is an interesting city that centers on the elegant Piazza della Libertà. The piazza contains imposing statues, such as this colossal Hercules and the Porticato di San Giovanni *(see pp166–7).*

Locator Map

Aquileia, once a splendid Roman city, is filled with ancient remains, such as this mausoleum. Its Basilica houses early Christian mosaics *(see p168).*

Padua boasts several major sights, among them the Basilica di Sant'Antonio and the Cappella degli Scrovegni with its frescoes by Giotto *(see pp158–63).*

(see inset below)

Basilica di San Marco in Venice is one of Europe's finest Byzantine buildings, with a magnificent gilded interior *(see pp114–17).*

VENICE
(See pp88–141)

The Palazzo Ducale is a masterpiece of Venetian Gothic architecture *(see pp118–20).*

The Flavors of Northeast Italy

This diverse region is the least Italian area of Italy. Bordering on Balkan and Austro-Hungarian territory, its food reflects its rich culture and landscape. Venice's traditional trading links have given a Middle-Eastern flavor to some dishes, such as sweet and sour *saor* sauce, and spices like nutmeg, saffron, and cinnamon feature widely. While pasta is eaten, many dishes are accompanied with the more typical polenta, made from yellow corn flour, and risotto is also a favorite. Butter is sometimes used instead of olive oil. From hearty, rib-sticking fare to the most delicate and sophisticated of dishes, this is a region full of gastronomic surprises.

Saffron

Delicate, sweet fried pastries in a Trieste bakery

The Veneto & Venice

The Veneto is one of Italy's main rice-growing regions. Rice was introduced from Spain by the Arabs and is a staple ingredient for many local dishes. Creamy risottos come in many guises, including *di mare* (with seafood), in which cuttlefish ink creates a dramatic, dark appearance. The Veneto's favorite pasta is *bigoli*, a thick spaghetti.

Vegetables are plentiful, including zucchini, asparagus, bitter red radicchio (endive) from Treviso, and variegated radicchio from Castelfranco.

Venetian specialties include *cichetti* and *antipasti* – snacks and appetizers such as marinated sardines, fried artichokes (*articiochi* in the Venetian dialect), and seafood in bite-size portions, especially mussels *(peoci)*. Venetian crab *(granceola)* is highly prized, and the local fish soup *(sopa de pesse)* is deliciously hearty.

Finely sliced raw beef *(carpaccio)* had its origins here; it was created by Giuseppe Cipriani at Venice's Harry's Bar.

Delicious, traditional *tiramisù* is also said to originate from Venice, and sorbets are common too. It was the Venetians who introduced cane sugar to Europe and their sweet tooth is still evident in the rich candied fruit, sultana raisins, and pine nuts acquired from the Turks and Byzantines.

Selection of Venetian *antipasti*, the perfect appetizer

Regional Dishes and Specialties

Antipasto di frutti di mare (a mixed seafood appetizer) is a special favorite in Venice, where the ingredients come fresh from the Adriatic. From lovely Lake Garda, *anguilla del pescatore* (stewed eel), *lavarelli al vino bianco* (lake fish in white wine), and *carpione* (a type of lake trout) are all fishy delights. Another fish specialty of the region is *baccalà alla veneziana*, made with dried salt cod. Pork and salamis feature throughout the area but in Friuli goose is often used as an alternative to pork, with succulent cured meat offerings such as *salame d'oca* (goose salami). Game is also found on the menu, together with sauerkraut and filling goulash, while desserts often have an Austrian flavor too, such as *apfel strudel*. But the region is also proud of claiming as its own the decadent classic Italian dessert *tiramisù*.

Asparagus

Sarde in Saor Venetian specialty of fried sardines in a sweet and sour onion marinade, with pine nuts.

Delivering fresh vegetables on the waterways of Venice

Friuli–Venezia Giulia

A culinary crossroads, this region marks the meeting point of Slavic, Germanic, and Latin traditions and was once the poorest of the northern Italian regions. Varieties of Hungarian goulash and Austrian strudels often appear on local menus. The area produces fine sweet ham and prosciutto (including the fabled, succulent San Daniele). Goose is a staple dish, as is Istrian lamb, grazed in the open air on local herbs and grasses that impart a delicious flavor.

Trieste is famous for its Viennese pastries and sweet *gnocchi*, prune dumplings sprinkled with sugar and cinnamon. Friuli's dairy speciality is Montasio, a hard cheese made from cow's milk.

Fresh radicchio and peppers piled high in a Treviso market

Trentino & Alto Adige

Strong Austrian influences from the Alto Adige combine with hearty fare from the mountainous region of Trentino as well as more southern Italian flavors. Staple dishes include cured meats such as *speck* (smoked ham) and salamis, as well as warming soups including the classic minestrone. Bread dumplings – *canederli* in Italian but *knödel* in Alto Adige – feature more than pasta. Trentino risottos include sweet and savory variations. Especially good are those made with *finferli* mushrooms, highly prized and similar to Tuscan *porcini* in flavor and quality. Alpine trout is flavorsome, and game dishes, especially venison and rabbit, are popular in season, often served with polenta. The Trentino apple is crisp and delicious.

ON THE MENU

Carpaccio *(Venice & the Veneto)* Wafer-thin slices of raw beef in extra virgin olive oil with arugula and slivers of Parmesan cheese.

Fegato alla Veneziana Calf's liver served on a bed of onions.

Jota *(Friuli–Venezia Giulia)* A soup of barley and sauerkraut. This cheap and filling dish is often mixed with *brovada* – turnips that have been steeped in a wooden cask of grape pressings.

Strangolapreti *(Trentino–Alto Adige)* Dumplings *(gnocchi)* made with bread, spinach, or potatoes, coated with butter and cheese. Literally means "priest stranglers."

Risi e bisi Soft and moist risotto mixing rice with fresh peas, sometimes with ham and Parmesan cheese.

Polenta Cornmeal porridge served plain as a side dish, often with rabbit, or *con baccalà* (with salt cod).

Tiramisù A rich dessert of mascarpone, sponge cake, coffee, and marsala. The name means "pick me up."

Understanding Architecture in Venice and the Veneto

Trade contact with the East led medieval Venice to develop its own exotic style – known as Venetian Gothic – blending Byzantine domes and Islamic minarets with European Gothic pointed arches and quatrefoils. In the 16th century, Palladio introduced his interpretations of Classical architecture through a series of churches, public buildings, and rural villas in Venice and the Veneto. The 17th century brought the Baroque style, though its exuberance was tempered by Palladio-influenced restraint.

Andrea Palladio (1508–80)

The Architecture of Venice: Byzantine to Baroque

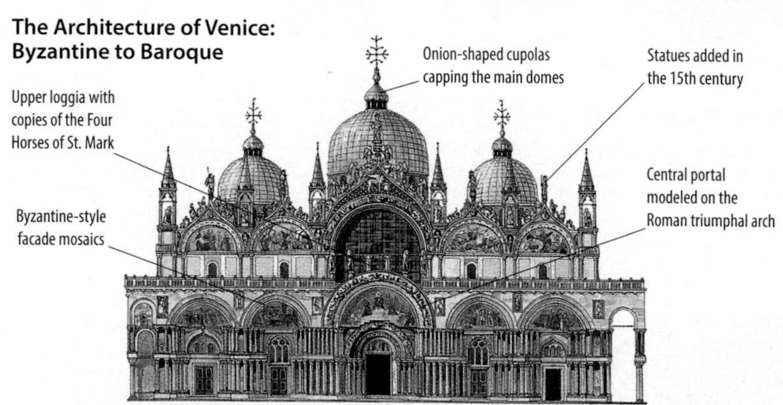

The Basilica di San Marco, western Europe's finest Byzantine church (completed 11th century), was given lavish treatment to make it a dazzling shrine for the relics of St. Mark, the Evangelist, and a fitting symbol of Venetian aspirations *(see pp114–17)*.

The Genius of Palladio

Palazzo Chiericati is a huge mansion of 1550, its simple style borrowed from the ancient Romans. It was once surrounded by water to reflect the statues of Classical deities along its roof *(see p156)*.

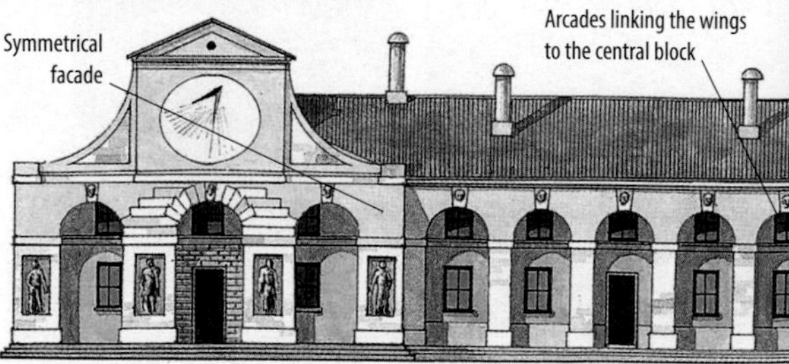

Villa Barbaro at Masèr was one of the villas designed by Palladio from the 1550s when it became fashionable for rich Venetians to acquire rural estates. This villa is typical, combining a working farm, housed in the side wings, with the elegant buildings of a country house *(see p153)*.

Where to see the Architecture

A vaporetto trip along the Grand Canal in Venice *(see pp92–5)* is a splendid way of getting an overview of Venetian architecture. Ca' d'Oro, Ca' Rezzonico, and Ca' Pesaro may also be visited for the museums they contain, and a visit to the Basilica di San Marco and the Palazzo Ducale is a must. There are numerous examples of Palladio's architecture in the Veneto, but the star is the Villa Barbaro *(see p153)*. Several of his villas line the Brenta Canal *(see p164)*, and the town of Vicenza *(see pp154–7)* is full of his buildings, including La Rotonda, his famous villa.

Typical Venetian Gothic window

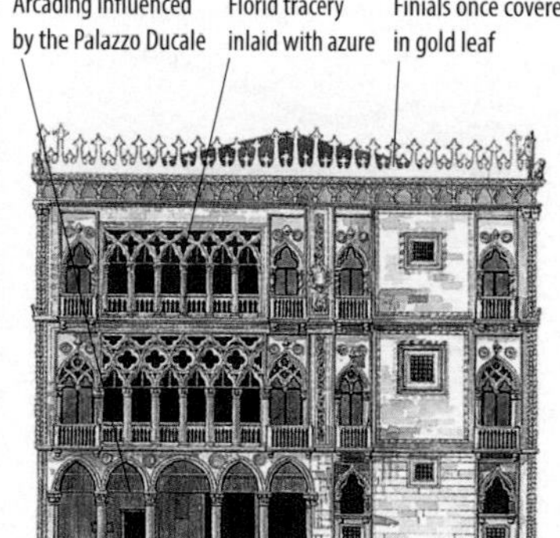

Ca d'Oro, the 15th-century "House of Gold," reveals Moorish influence in its roof finials and sinuous pointed arches *(see p98)*.

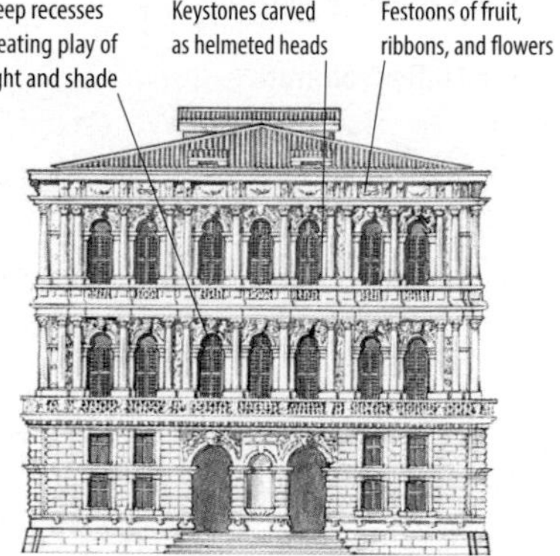

The 17th-century Ca' Pesaro typifies the Venetian Baroque style – Classical columns and rich, but subtle, ornamentation *(see p93)*.

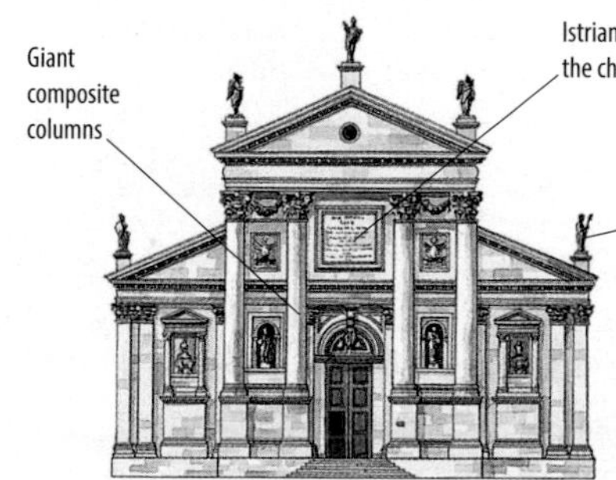

San Giorgio Maggiore, built in 1559–80, is marvelously sited at the entrance to the Venetian inner harbor. It broke from the prevailing Gothic style, introducing the clean simplicity and harmonious proportions of Classical architecture to Venice, and more resembles an ancient Roman temple than a Christian church *(see pp124–5)*.

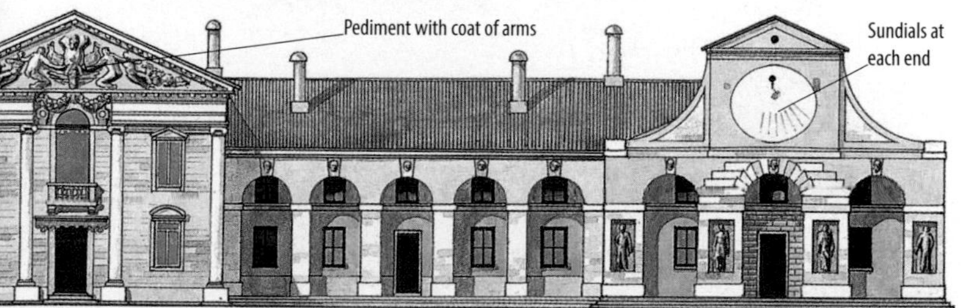

The Dolomites

The Dolomites are the most distinctive and beautiful mountains in Italy. They were formed of mineralized coral that was laid down beneath the sea during the Triassic period, and uplifted when the European and African continental plates dramatically collided 60 million years ago. Unlike the glacier-eroded saddles and ridges of the main body of the Alps, the pale rocks here have been carved by the corrosive effects of ice, sun, and rain, sculpting the cliffs, spires, and "organ pipes" that we see today. The eastern and western ranges of the Dolomites have slightly different characteristics; the eastern section is the more awe-inspiring, especially the Catinaccio (or Rosengarten) range, which is particularly beautiful, turning rose pink at sunset.

Onion dome, a common local feature

Strada Delle Dolomiti

One of the most spectacular routes through the Dolomites links Bolzano *(see p176)* with Cortina d'Ampezzo *(see p165)*. It follows the lie of the land, passing some of the greatest peaks and the most majestic landscape.

S49
Dobbiaco
Rienza
S51
TRE CIME DI LAVAREDO
Lago di Misurina
Cortina d'Ampezzo
SASSO LUNGO
S48
CINQUE TORRI
Pieve di Cadore
Bolzano
TORRI DEL VAIOLET
Canazei
MARMOLADA
Adige
S241
S12
0 kilometers 10
0 miles 5

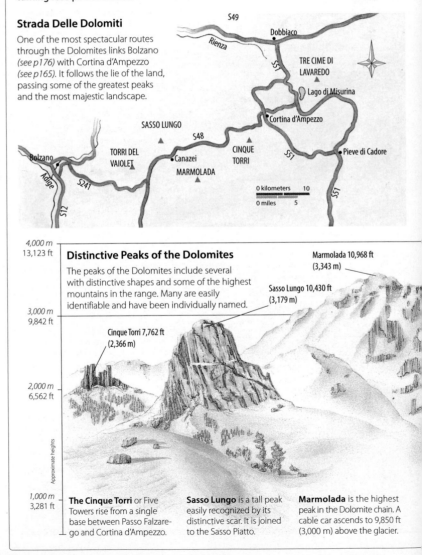

Distinctive Peaks of the Dolomites

The peaks of the Dolomites include several with distinctive shapes and some of the highest mountains in the range. Many are easily identifiable and have been individually named.

The Cinque Torri or Five Towers rise from a single base between Passo Falzarego and Cortina d'Ampezzo.

Sasso Lungo is a tall peak easily recognized by its distinctive scar. It is joined to the Sasso Piatto.

Marmolada is the highest peak in the Dolomite chain. A cable car ascends to 9,850 ft (3,000 m) above the glacier.

Lago di Misurina is a large and beautiful lake lying beside the resort of Misurina. The crystal-clear waters reflect the surrounding mountains, mirroring various peaks such as the distinctive and dramatic Sorapiss, in shimmering colors.

Outdoor activities in this area of dramatic landscapes include skiing in winter, and walking and hiking along the footpaths and to picnic sites in summer. Chairlifts from the main resorts provide easy access up into the mountains themselves, transporting you into some breathtaking scenery.

The Torri del Vaiolet is part of the beautiful Catinaccio range, known for its color.

Tre Cime di Lavaredo or Drei Zinnen dominate the valleys north of the Lago di Misurina.

Nature in the Dolomites

Forests and meadows support a breathtaking richness of wildlife in the region. Alpine plants, which flower between June and September, have evolved their miniature form to survive the harsh winds.

The Flora

Gentian roots are used to make a bitter local liqueur.

The orange mountain lily thrives on sun-baked slopes.

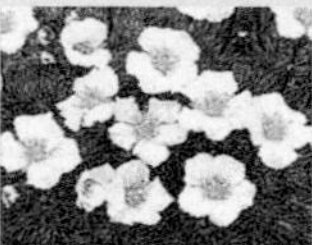

The pretty burser's saxifrage grows in clusters on rocks.

Devil's claw has distinctive pink flower heads.

The Fauna

The ptarmigan changes its plumage from mottled brown in summer to snow white in winter for effective camouflage. It feeds on mountain berries and young plant shoots.

The chamois, a shy mountain antelope prized for its soft skin, is protected in the national parks, where hunting is forbidden.

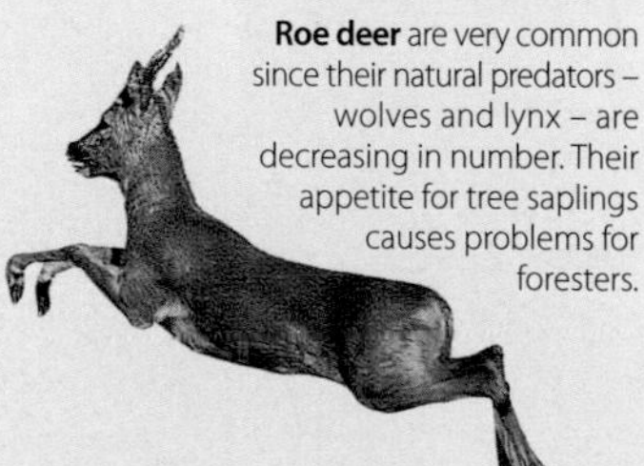

Roe deer are very common since their natural predators – wolves and lynx – are decreasing in number. Their appetite for tree saplings causes problems for foresters.

VENICE

Lying in the extreme northeast of Italy, Venice, gateway to the Orient, became an independent Byzantine province in the 10th century. Exclusive trading links with the East and victory in the Crusade of 1204 brought wealth and power, which were only gradually eroded by European and Turkish rivals. Today, Venice's ties are with the local Veneto region, which stretches from the flat river plains to the Dolomites.

Venice is one of the few cities in the world that can be truly described as unique. It survives against all the odds, built on a series of low mud banks amid the tidal waters of the Adriatic, and regularly subject to floods. During the Middle Ages, under the leadership of successive doges, Venice expanded its power and influence throughout the Mediterranean to Constantinople (modern Istanbul). The immense wealth of the city was celebrated in art and architecture throughout the city.

The riches of St. Mark's alone bear witness to Venice's position as a world power from the 12th to 14th centuries. After slowly losing ground to the new states of Europe, however, it fell to Napoleon in 1797. Finally, Venice joined the Kingdom of Italy in 1866, so bringing unity to the country for the first time in its history. Today, Venice has found a new role. Her palazzi have become museums, shops, hotels, and apartments, and her convents have been turned into centers for art restoration. Yet little of the essential fabric of Venice has altered in 200 years. The city's sounds are still those of footsteps and the cries of boatmen. The only engines are those of barges delivering supplies or waterbuses ferrying passengers between stops. The same well-worn streets are still trodden. More than 20 million visitors a year succumb to the magic of this improbable place whose "streets are full of water" and where the glories of the past are evident at every turn.

Tourists relax at cafés along a canal in Burano, Venice

◀ Dusk settles over the peaceful Venetian Lagoon, Adriatic Coast

Exploring Venice

Venice is divided into six ancient administrative districts or *sestieri*: Cannaregio, Castello, San Marco, Dorsoduro, San Polo, and Santa Croce. You can walk to most places in Venice itself, and take a ride on a waterbus to any of the islands. The Venice Card *(see p634)* covers all transportation as well as admission to most museums, such as Ca' Rezzonico, the Palazzo Ducale, and Museo Correr.

Sights at a Glance

Churches

1 Madonna dell'Orto
3 San Giovanni Grisostomo
4 Santa Maria dei Miracoli
6 San Giacomo dell'Orio
7 San Polo
8 *Santa Maria Gloriosa dei Frari pp102–3*
10 San Rocco
11 San Pantalon
13 San Nicolò dei Mendicoli
14 San Sebastiano
17 Santa Maria della Salute
19 *Basilica di San Marco pp114–15*
24 Santo Stefano
25 Santi Giovanni e Paolo
27 Santa Maria Formosa
28 San Zaccaria
30 San Giovanni in Bragora

Buildings and Monuments

5 Rialto
20 *Palazzo Ducale pp118–19*
21 Torre dell'Orologio
22 Campanile
26 Statue of Colleoni
29 Scuola di San Giorgio degli Schiavoni
31 Arsenale

Museums and Galleries

2 Ca' d'Oro
9 *Scuola Grande di San Rocco pp104–5*
12 Ca' Rezzonico
15 *Accademia pp110–11*
16 Peggy Guggenheim Collection
18 Punta della Dogana
23 Museo Correr

Lagoon

33 Murano
34 Burano
35 *Torcello pp126–7*

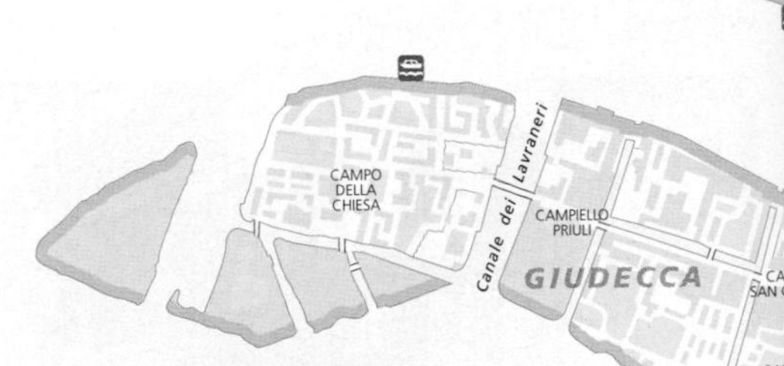

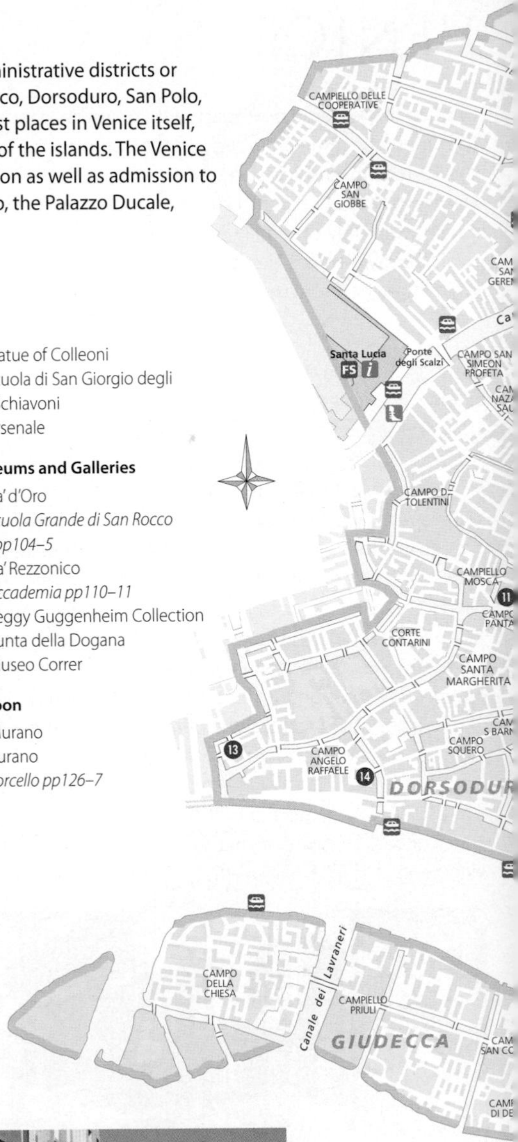

0 meters 500
0 yards 500

Santa Maria della Salute, at the mouth of the Grand Canal

For keys to symbols *see back flap*

A gondola ride along the Grand Canal

Getting Around

The only road into Venice is the S11 from Mestre, which carries you over the causeway to the Tronchetto and Piazzale Roma where there are parking lots and bus stops. Train travelers arrive at Santa Lucia station on the Grand Canal. In the city, public transportation is by *vaporetto,* or waterbus – the No.1 is best for sightseeing as it travels the length of the Grand Canal *(see pp140–1)*.

The Grand Canal: Santa Lucia to the Rialto

The best way to view the Grand Canal as it winds through the heart of the city is from a *vaporetto*, or waterbus. Two lines travel the length of the canal *(see p635)*. The palaces lining the waterway were built over a span of five centuries and present a panoramic survey of the city's history, almost all bearing the name of some once-great Venetian family.

San Marcuola
The church was rebuilt in the 18th century, but the planned new facade overlooking the canal was never completed.

San Geremia houses the relics of St. Lucy, once kept in the church of Santa Lucia where the train station now stands.

Palazzo Labia
Between 1745–50, Giambattista Tiepolo decorated the ballroom with scenes from the life of Cleopatra.

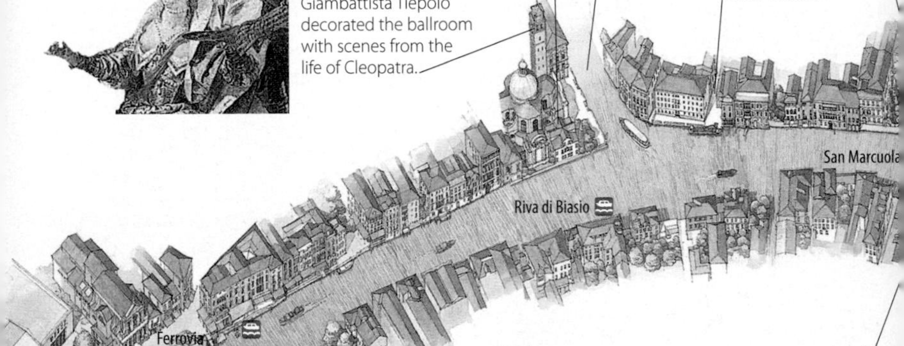

Canale di Cannaregio

Palazzo Corner-Contarini

Ferrovia

FS

Ponte degli Scalzi

Fondaco dei Turchi
A warehouse for Turkish traders in the 17th–19th centuries, this is now the Natural History Museum.

San Simeone Piccolo
This 18th-century domed church is based on the Pantheon in Rome.

The Gondolas of Venice

The gondola has been a part of Venice since the 11th century. With its slim hull and flat underside, the craft is perfectly adapted to negotiating narrow, shallow canals. There is a slight leftward curve to the prow, which counteracts the force of the oar, preventing the gondola from going around in circles.

In 1562 it was decreed that all gondolas should be black to stop people making an ostentatious show of their wealth. For special occasions they are decorated with flowers. Today, gondola rides are expensive and usually taken by tourists *(see p635)*. However, *traghetti* (gondola ferries) are a cheap, convenient way of crossing the Grand Canal.

Gondolas tied up by steps

Ca' d'Oro
The delicate Gothic tracery of the facade makes this a striking landmark. Its art collection *(see p98)* includes Bernini's model for a fountain (*c.* 1648).

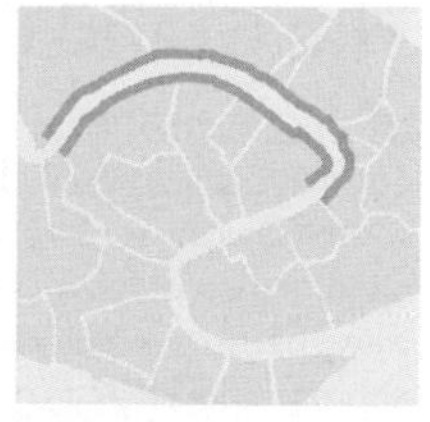

Locator Map

See Venice Street Finder maps 1, 2, 3

Palazzo Vendramin Calergi
This is one of the finest early Renaissance palaces in Venice. The German composer Richard Wagner *(left)* died here in 1883.

Palazzo Sagredo
Graceful Veneto-Byzantine and Gothic arches are both featured on the waterfront facade.

The Pescheria has been the site of a busy fish market for six centuries.

Palazzo Michiel dalle Colonne takes its name from its distinctive colonnade.

The Rialto Bridge *(see p101)* spans the canal in the commercial heart of the city.

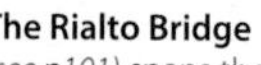

San Stae
The facade of this Baroque church is richly adorned with statues. It is a popular concert venue.

Ca' Pesaro
The huge, stately Baroque palace today houses a gallery of modern art and the Oriental Museum.

The Grand Canal: the Rialto to San Marco

After passing the Rialto, the canal doubles back on itself along a stretch known as La Volta (the bend). It then widens out and the views become more spectacular approaching San Marco. Facades may have faded and foundations crumbled with the tides, yet the canal remains, in the words of the French ambassador in 1495, "the most beautiful street in the world."

Palazzo Mocenigo
Lord Byron stayed in this huge 18th-century palace in 1818.

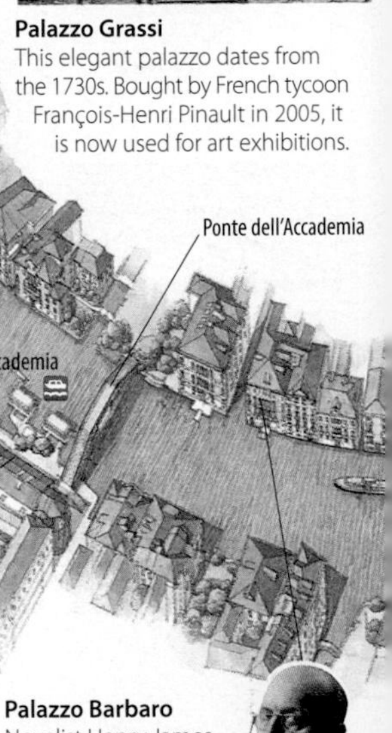

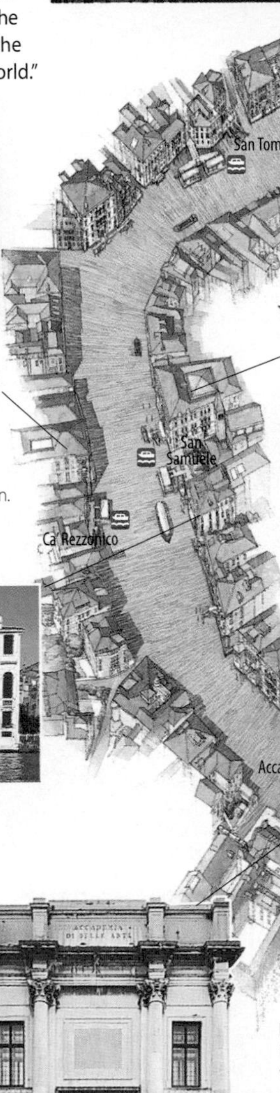

Ca' Rezzonico
Now a museum of 18th-century Venice *(see p107)*, the palace was the last home of the poet Robert Browning, seen here with his son Pen.

Palazzo Garzoni is a renovated Gothic palace, now part of the university.

Palazzo Grassi
This elegant palazzo dates from the 1730s. Bought by French tycoon François-Henri Pinault in 2005, it is now used for art exhibitions.

Palazzo Capello Malipiero
The palace was rebuilt in 1622. Beside it stands the 12th-century campanile of San Samuele.

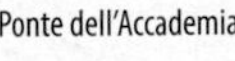

Accademia
The world's greatest collection of Venetian paintings is housed here in the former Scuola della Carità *(see pp110–11)*, which has a Baroque facade by Giorgio Massari.

Palazzo Barbaro
Novelist Henry James wrote *The Aspern Papers* here in 1888.

The Riva del Vin is the quay where wine *(vin)* used to be unloaded. It is one of the few spots where you can sit and relax on the banks of the Grand Canal.

Locator Map

See Venice Street Finder maps 6, 7

Palazzo Barzizza, rebuilt in the 17th century, preserves its early 13th-century facade.

Peggy Guggenheim Collection
A one-story palazzo houses Guggenheim's great modern art collection *(see pp108–9).*

Santa Maria della Salute
The vast weight of this Baroque church is supported by over a million timber pilings *(see p109).*

Palazzo Gritti-Pisani
The former home of the Gritti family is now the luxury Gritti Palace hotel *(see p563).*

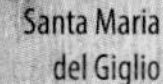

Harry's Bar, founded in 1931 by Giuseppe Cipriani, is famous for its cocktails.

Palazzo Dario
Beautiful colored marbles give the 1487 palace a highly individual facade. Legend has it the building is cursed.

The Punta della Dogana customs house, built in the 17th century, now contains the François Pinault Foundation of contemporary art. It is crowned by a golden globe topped by a weather vane *(see p109).*

Gondolas moored along the Grand Canal at sunrise ▶

Madonna dell'Orto, with 15th-century facade statues of St. Christopher and the Apostles

❶ Madonna dell'Orto

Campo Madonna dell'Orto. **Map** 2 F2. **Tel** 041 719 933. Madonna dell'Orto. **Open** 10am–5pm Mon–Sat, noon–6pm Sun. **Closed** Jan 1, Dec 25. **W madonnadellorto.org**

This lovely Gothic church, founded in the mid-14th century, was dedicated to St. Christopher, patron saint of travelers, to protect the boatmen who ferried passengers to the islands in the northern lagoon. A 15th-century statue of the saint, restored by the Venice in Peril fund, stands above the main portal. The dedication was changed and the church reconstructed in the early 15th century, after the discovery, in a nearby vegetable garden *(orto)*, of a statue of the Virgin Mary said to have miraculous powers.

The interior, faced almost entirely in brick, is large and uncluttered. On the right is a magnificent painting by Cima da Conegliano, *St. John the Baptist and Other Saints* (*c.* 1493). The vacant space in the chapel opposite belongs to Giovanni Bellini's *Madonna with Child* (*c.* 1478), stolen in 1993 for the third time.

The church's greatest remaining treasures are the works of art by Tintoretto, who was a parishioner of the church. His tomb lies with that of his children, in the chapel to the right of the chancel. The most dramatic of his works are the towering masterpieces that decorate the chancel (1562–4). On the right wall is the *Last Judgment*, whose turbulent content caused John Ruskin's wife, Effie, to flee the church in horror. In *The Adoration of the Golden Calf* on the left wall, the figure carrying the calf, fourth from the left, is believed to be a portrait of the artist. Inside the chapel of San Mauro, off the end of the right nave, stands a statue of the Madonna by Giovanni de' Santi. It was restored by the Venice in Peril fund, and inspired the rededication of the church.

❷ Ca' d'Oro

Calle Ca' d'Oro. **Map** 3 A4. **Tel** 041 520 03 45. Ca' d'Oro. **Open** 8:15am–2pm Mon, 8:15am– 7:15pm Tue–Sat (last adm: 6:45pm), 10am– 6pm Sun. **Closed** Jan 1, May 1, Dec 25; Galleria: Sun & public hols (Jan). **W cadoro.org**

In 1420 Marino Contarini, a wealthy patrician, commissioned the building of what he hoped would be the city's most magnificent palace *(see p85)*. The building's intricate carving was entrusted to a team of Venetian and Lombard craftsmen, while the facade was adorned with the most elaborate and expensive decorative finishes, including gold leaf, vermilion, and ultramarine. Over the years the palace was extensively remodeled, and by the 18th century was in a state of semi-dereliction. In 1846 it was bought by the Russian Prince Troubetzkoy for the famous ballerina Maria Taglioni. Under her direction the palace suffered barbaric restoration, losing, among other things, its staircase and much of its original stonework. It was finally rescued by Baron Giorgio Franchetti, a wealthy patron of the arts, who bequeathed both the building and his private art collection to the state in 1915.

Tullio Lombardo's Double Portrait

Pride of place on the first of the gallery's two floors goes to Andrea Mantegna's *St. Sebastian* (1506), the artist's last work, which occupies a special alcove of its own. Elsewhere, the floor's main exhibits are ranged around the *portego* (gallery). This is largely dominated by the vivid 15th-century *Double Portrait* (*c.* 1493) by the sculptor Tullio Lombardo; Sansovino's lunette of the *Madonna and Child* (*c.* 1530); and several bronze reliefs by the Paduan Andrea Briosco, "Il Riccio" (1470–1532). Rooms leading off the *portego* to the right contain numerous bronzes and medallions, with some examples by Pisanello and Gentile Bellini. Paintings here also include the famous *Madonna of the Beautiful Eyes*, attributed to Giovanni Bellini, a *Madonna and Child*, attributed to Alvise Vivarini (both late 15th century), and Carpaccio's *Annunciation* and *Death of the Virgin* (both *c.* 1504). A room to the left of the *portego* contains non-Venetian paintings, notably a *Flagellation* by Luca Signorelli (*c.* 1480). A lovely staircase leads to the second floor, which opens with a room hung with tapestries.

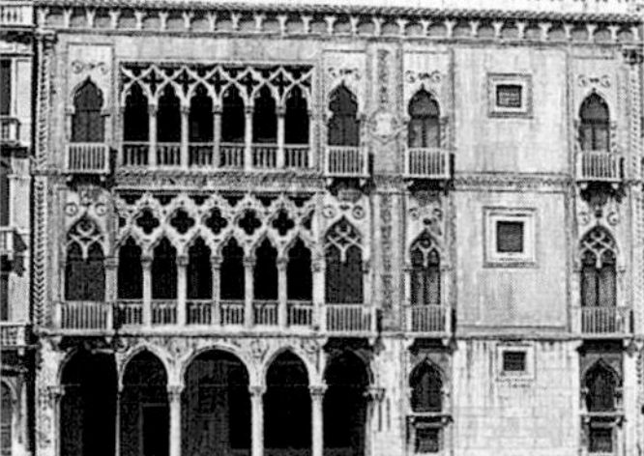
The magnificent Gothic facade of the Ca' d'Oro, or House of Gold

It has bronzes by Alessandro Vittoria and paintings by Titian and Van Dyck. The *portego* displays frescoes (*c.* 1532) by Pordenone from the cloister of Santo Stefano, while an anteroom contains damaged frescoes by Titian taken from the Fondaco dei Tedeschi.

Giovanni Bellini's 1513 altarpiece in San Giovanni Grisostomo

❸ San Giovanni Grisostomo

Campo San Giovanni Grisostomo. **Map** 3 B5. **Tel** 041 523 52 93. Rialto. **Open** 8:15am–12:15pm, 3–7pm daily. **Closed** during Mass.
sancancianovenezia.it

This terra-cotta-colored church is located near the Rialto. Built between 1479 and 1504, it is a lovely Renaissance design, the last work of Mauro Coducci.

The interior is built on a Greek-cross plan. The light meter illuminates Giovanni Bellini's *St. Jerome with Saints Christopher and Augustine* (1513) above the first altar on the right. This was most probably Bellini's last painting, executed when he was in his eighties.

Over the high altar hangs Sebastiano del Piombo's *St. John Chrysostom and Six Saints* (1509–11).

❹ Santa Maria dei Miracoli

Campo dei Miracoli. **Map** 3 B5. **Tel** 041 275 04 62. Rialto, Fondamenta Nuove. **Open** 10am–5pm Mon–Sat. **Closed** Jan 1, Dec 25.
chorusvenezia.org

An exquisite masterpiece of early Renaissance architecture, the Miracoli is the church where many Venetians like to get married. Tucked away in a maze of alleys and waterways in eastern Cannaregio, it is small and somewhat elusive.

Santa Maria dei Miracoli is decorated in various shades of marble, with some fine bas-reliefs and sculpture. It was built in 1481–9 by the architect Pietro Lombardo and his sons to enshrine *The Virgin and Child* (1408), a painting believed to have miraculous powers. The picture, by Nicoló di Pietro, can still be seen above the altar.

The interior of the church is embellished by pink, white, and gray marble. It is crowned by a barrel-vaulted ceiling (1528) that has 50 portraits of saints and prophets. The balustrade, between the nave and the chancel, is decorated by Tullio Lombardo's carved figures of St. Francis, Archangel Gabriel, the Virgin, and St. Clare.

The screen around the high altar and the medallions of the Evangelists in the cupola spandrels are also Lombardo's work. Above the main door, the choir gallery was used by the nuns from the neighboring convent, who entered the church through an overhead gallery. Santa Maria dei Miracoli has undergone a major restoration program, which was funded by the American Save Venice organization.

Decorative column from inside Santa Maria dei Miracoli

Santa Maria Dei Miracoli

This beautifully proportioned facade is composed of decorated panels and multicolored polished marble.

Carving of saint
The semicircular crowning lunette emphasizes the church's jewel-box appearance.
A false loggia is formed of Ionic arches, inset with windows. The marble used was reportedly left over from the building of San Marco.
Virgin and Child by Giorgio Lascaris
The marble panels are fixed to the bricks by metal hooks. This method prevents the build-up of damp and saltwater behind the panels, and dates from the Renaissance.

Street by Street: San Polo

The Rialto bridge and markets make this area a magnet for visitors. Traditionally the city's commercial quarter, it was here that bankers, brokers, and merchants conducted their affairs. Streets are no longer lined with stalls selling spices and fine fabrics, but the food markets and pasta shops are unmissable. Away from the bridge, streets quickly become less crowded, leading to tiny squares and quiet churches.

The Rialto Markets have existed for centuries and are renowned for their produce. The Pescheria sells fresh fish and seafood.

The 17th-century church of San Cassiano houses a carved altar (1696) and a *Crucifixion* by Tintoretto (1568).

Key

— Suggested route

0 meters 75

0 yards 75

The Frari

San Silvestro

Sant'Aponal has a facade decorated with worn Gothic reliefs. The church was founded in the 11th century, but is now deconsecrated.

San Giovanni Elemosinario is an inconspicuous church that was rebuilt in the early 16th century, although its campanile dates from the end of the 14th century. Inside it are interesting frescoes by Pordenone.

For hotels and restaurants in this region see pp562–77 and pp580–605

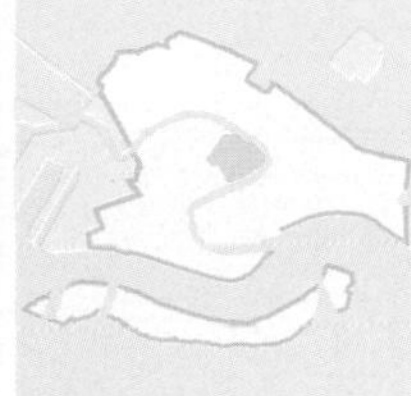

Locator Map
See Venice Street Finder maps 2, 3, 6, 7

San Giacomo di Rialto's clock face (1410), which has sadly been a poor timekeeper over the years, adorns one of Venice's oldest churches.

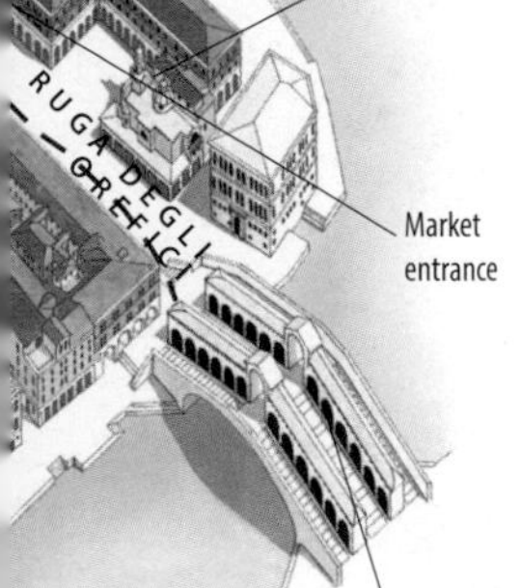

❺★ Rialto
One of Venice's most famous sights, the bridge offers fine views of the Grand Canal, and marks the heart of the city.

The lively Erberia, selling fresh fruit and vegetables

❺ Rialto

Ponte di Rialto. **Map** 7 A1. Rialto.

The Rialto takes its name from *rivo alto* (high bank) and was one of the first areas of Venice to be inhabited. A banking and then market district, it remains one of the city's busiest and most bustling areas. Locals and visitors alike jostle among the colorful stalls of the Erberia (fruit and vegetable market) and Pescheria (fish market).

Stone bridges were built in Venice as early as the 12th century, but it was not until 1588, after the collapse, decay, or sabotage of earlier wooden structures, that a solid stone bridge was designed for the Rialto. Completed in 1591, the new bridge remained the only means of crossing the Grand Canal until 1854, when the Accademia bridge was built.

Few visitors leave Venice without crossing the famous bridge. It is a wonderful place to watch and photograph the constant activity of boats on the Grand Canal below.

❻ San Giacomo dell'Orio

Campo San Giacomo dell'Orio. **Map** 2 E5. **Tel** 041 275 04 62. Riva di Biasio or San Stae. **Open** 10am–5pm Mon–Sat. **Closed** Jan 1, Dec 25. **chorusvenezia.org**

This church is a focal point of a quiet quarter of Santa Croce. The name "dell'Orio" may derive from a laurel tree *(alloro)* that once stood near the church. San Giacomo was founded in the 9th century, rebuilt in 1225, and thereafter repeatedly modified, resulting in a mixture of styles. The campanile and basilica ground plan survive from the 13th century. The ship's keel roof and the columns are Gothic, and the apses are Renaissance.

The sacristy contains a beautiful ceiling by Veronese in addition to some interesting altar paintings.

❼ San Polo

Campo San Polo. **Map** 6 F1. **Tel** 041 275 04 62. San Silvestro. **Open** 10am– 5pm Mon–Sat. **Closed** Jan 1, Dec 25. **chorusvenezia.org**

Founded in the 9th century, rebuilt in the 15th, and revamped in the early 19th in Neo-Classical style, this church is worth visiting for the lovely Gothic portal and the Romanesque lions at the foot of the 14th-century campanile – one holds a serpent between its paws, the other a human head.

Inside, follow the signs for the *Via Crucis del Tiepolo* – 14 pictures of the Stations of the Cross (1749) by the painter Giandomenico Tiepolo: many include vivid portraits of Venetian life. The church also has paintings by Veronese, Palma il Giovane (the Younger) and a dramatic *Last Supper* by Tintoretto.

A Romanesque lion at the base of San Polo's 14th-century campanile

❽ Santa Maria Gloriosa dei Frari

More commonly known as the Frari (a corruption of Frati, meaning brothers), this vast Gothic church dwarfs the eastern area of San Polo. The first church on the site was built by Franciscan friars in 1250–1338, but was replaced by a larger building completed in the mid-15th century. The airy interior is striking for its sheer size and for the quality of its works of art, including masterpieces by Titian and Giovanni Bellini, a statue by Donatello, and several grandiose tombs.

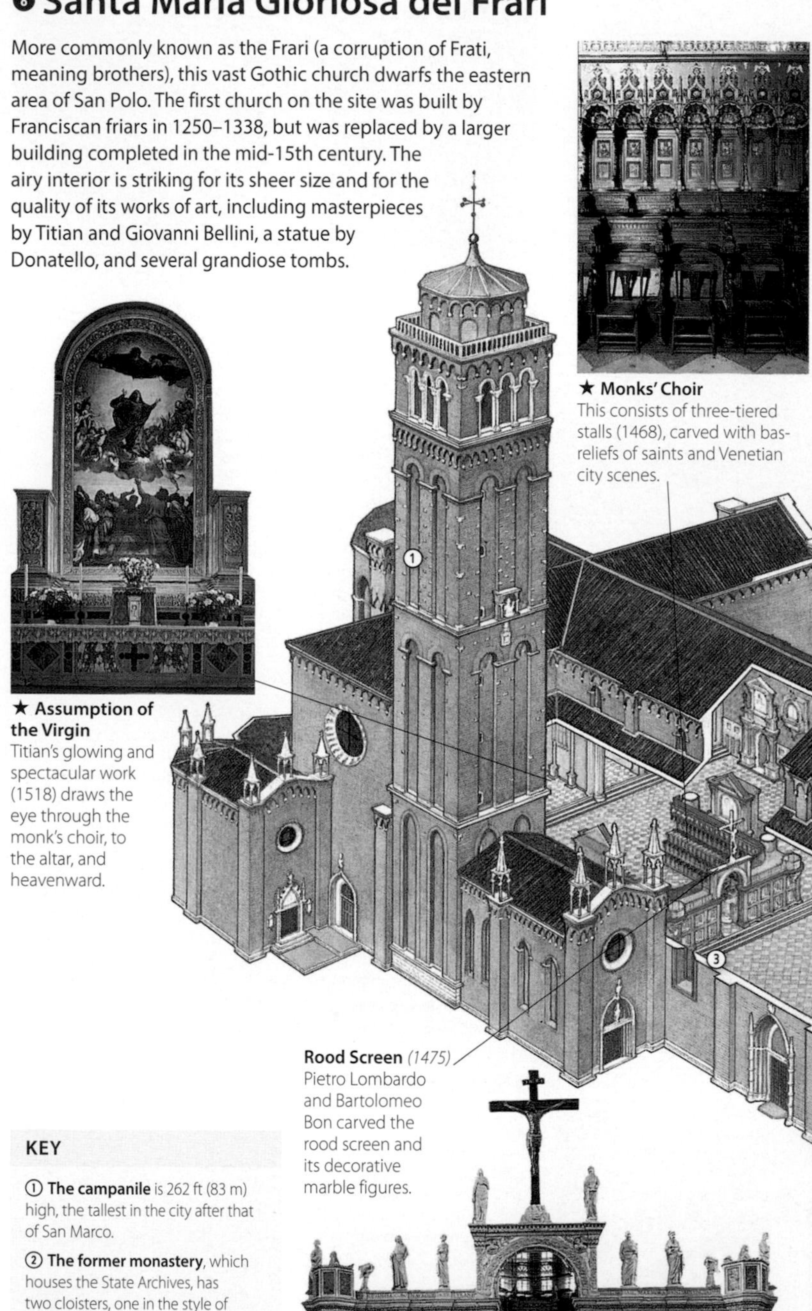

★ Monks' Choir
This consists of three-tiered stalls (1468), carved with bas-reliefs of saints and Venetian city scenes.

★ Assumption of the Virgin
Titian's glowing and spectacular work (1518) draws the eye through the monk's choir, to the altar, and heavenward.

Rood Screen *(1475)*
Pietro Lombardo and Bartolomeo Bon carved the rood screen and its decorative marble figures.

KEY

① **The campanile** is 262 ft (83 m) high, the tallest in the city after that of San Marco.

② **The former monastery**, which houses the State Archives, has two cloisters, one in the style of Sansovino, another designed by Palladio.

③ ***The Madonna di Ca' Pesaro*** (1526) shows Titian's mastery of light and color.

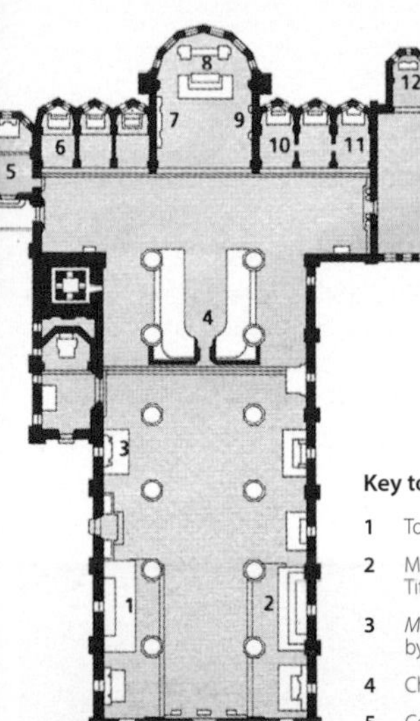

Floor Plan

The Frari's imposing cruciform interior, which is 295 ft (90 m) long, holds 12 sights that should not be missed.

VISITORS' CHECKLIST

Practical Information
Campo dei Frari. **Map** 6 D1.
Tel 041 275 04 62. **Open** 9am–6pm Mon–Sat, 1–6pm Sun & religious hols. **Closed** Jan 1, Dec 25. unless attending mass. frequent.
basilicadeifrari.it

Transportation
San Tomà.

Key to Floor Plan

1 Tomb of Canova
2 Monument to Titian
3 *Madonna di Ca' Pesaro* by Titian
4 Choir stalls
5 Corner Chapel
6 Tomb of Monteverdi
7 Tomb of Doge Nicolò Tron
8 High altar with *Assumption of the Virgin* (1518) by Titian
9 Tomb of Doge Francesco Foscari
10 *John the Baptist* (*c.* 1450) by Donatello
11 B. Vivarini's altar painting (1474), Bernardo Chapel
12 *Madonna and Child with Saints* (1488) by Bellini

★ Madonna and Child
The sacristy's altarpiece (1488) by Bellini, with its sublime use of color, is one of Venice's most beautiful Renaissance paintings.

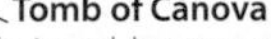

Tomb of Canova
Canova designed, but never constructed, a Neo-Classical marble pyramid like this as a monument for Titian. After Canova's death in 1822, the sculptor's pupils used a similar design for their master's tomb.

⑨ Scuola Grande di San Rocco

Restored main entrance to the Scuola di San Rocco

Founded in honor of San Rocco (St. Roch), a saint who dedicated his life to helping the sick, the Scuola started out as a charitable confraternity. Construction began in 1515 under Bartolomeo Bon and was continued by Scarpagnino until his death in 1549. The work was financed by donations from Venetians keen to invoke San Rocco's protection and the Scuola quickly became one of the wealthiest in Venice. In 1564 its members decided to commission Tintoretto to decorate its walls and ceilings. His earliest paintings, the first of over 50 works he eventually left in the Scuola, fill the small Sala dell'Albergo off the Upper Hall. His later paintings occupy the Ground Floor Hall, immediately within the entrance.

Tintoretto's magnificent *Crucifixion*, painted in 1565 for the Sala dell'Albergo in the Scuola di San Rocco

Ground Floor Hall

The ground floor cycle was executed in 1583–7, when Tintoretto was in his sixties, and consists of eight large paintings illustrating, among others, the life of Mary. The series starts with an *Annunciation* and ends with an *Assumption*.

The calm and tranquil scenes of *The Flight into Egypt*, *St. Mary Magdalene*, and *St. Mary of Egypt* are remarkable for their serenity. This is portrayed most lucidly by the repentant hermit's isolated spiritual contemplation in *St. Mary of Egypt*. In all three paintings, it is noticeable that the landscapes are rendered with rapid strokes, and are an important part of the final composition.

Detail from *The Flight into Egypt* (1582–7) by Tintoretto

Upper Hall and Sala dell'Albergo

Scarpagnino's great staircase (1544–6), with its upper flight decorated with two vast paintings commemorating the plague of 1630, leads to the Upper Hall. Here, biblical subjects decorate the ceiling and walls, painted by Tintoretto from 1575–81.

The ceiling paintings portray scenes from the Old Testament. The three large and dynamic square paintings in the center show episodes from the Book of Exodus: *Moses Strikes Water from the Rock*, *The Miracle of the Bronze Serpent*, and *The Fall of Manna in the Desert*. These all allude to the charitable aims of the Scuola in alleviating thirst, sickness, and hunger respectively. All three paintings are crowded compositions displaying much violent movement.

The vast wall paintings in the hall feature episodes from the New Testament, linking with the ceiling paintings. Two of the most striking paintings are *The Temptation of Christ*, which shows a handsome young Satan offering Christ two loaves of bread, and *The Adoration of the Shepherds*. Like *The Temptation of Christ*, *The Adoration* is composed of two halves, with a female figure, shepherds, and an ox below, and the Holy Family and onlookers above.

The breathtakingly beautiful carvings below the paintings were added in the 17th century by sculptor Francesco Pianta. The figures are allegorical and include (near the altar) a caricature of Tintoretto with his palette and brushes, representing Painting.

For hotels and restaurants in this region see pp562–77 and pp580–605

VISITORS' CHECKLIST

Practical Information
Campo San Rocco. **Map** 6 D1. **Tel** 041 523 48 64. **Open** 9:30am–5:30pm daily (ticket office closes at 5pm). **Closed** Jan 1, Easter, Dec 25. w **scuolagrandesanrocco.it**

Transportation
San Tomà.

Detail from *The Temptation of Christ* (1578–81) by Tintoretto

The easel painting *Christ Carrying the Cross* was once attributed to Giorgione, though many believe it to be by Titian.

Near the entrance to the Sala dell'Albergo is the *Annunciation* by Titian. The Sala dell'Albergo itself holds the most breathtaking of Tintoretto's works – the *Crucifixion* (1565). Henry James remarked of this painting: "No single picture contains more of human life; there is everything in it, including the most exquisite beauty." Tintoretto began the cycle of paintings in this room in 1564, when he won the commission with the ceiling painting *San Rocco in Glory*. On the wall opposite the *Crucifixion* are paintings of episodes from the Passion: *Christ before Pilate*, *The Crowning with Thorns*, and *The Ascent to Calvary*.

Key to Paintings

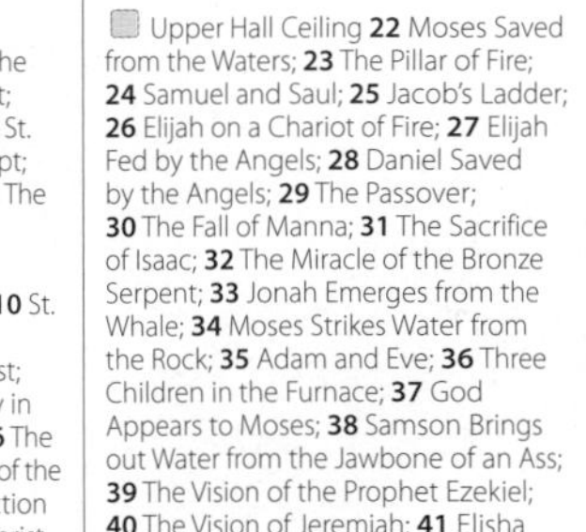

Ground Floor Hall **1** The Annunciation; **2** The Adoration of the Three Kings; **3** The Flight into Egypt; **4** The Massacre of the Innocents; **5** St. Mary Magdalene; **6** St. Mary of Egypt; **7** The Presentation in the Temple; **8** The Assumption.

Upper Hall Walls **9** San Rocco; **10** St. Sebastian; **11** The Adoration of the Shepherds; **12** The Baptism of Christ; **13** The Resurrection; **14** The Agony in the Garden; **15** The Last Supper; **16** The Vision of San Rocco; **17** The Miracle of the Loaves and Fishes; **18** The Resurrection of Lazarus; **19** The Ascension; **20** Christ Heals the Paralytic; **21** The Temptation of Christ.

Upper Hall Ceiling **22** Moses Saved from the Waters; **23** The Pillar of Fire; **24** Samuel and Saul; **25** Jacob's Ladder; **26** Elijah on a Chariot of Fire; **27** Elijah Fed by the Angels; **28** Daniel Saved by the Angels; **29** The Passover; **30** The Fall of Manna; **31** The Sacrifice of Isaac; **32** The Miracle of the Bronze Serpent; **33** Jonah Emerges from the Whale; **34** Moses Strikes Water from the Rock; **35** Adam and Eve; **36** Three Children in the Furnace; **37** God Appears to Moses; **38** Samson Brings out Water from the Jawbone of an Ass; **39** The Vision of the Prophet Ezekiel; **40** The Vision of Jeremiah; **41** Elisha Distributes Bread; **42** Abraham and Melchizedek.

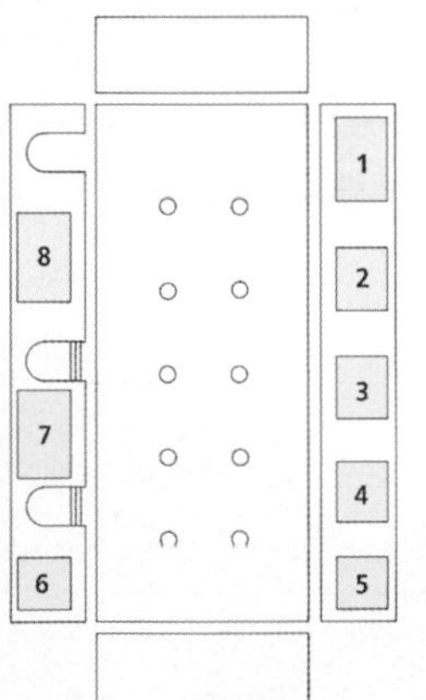

Ground Floor Hall

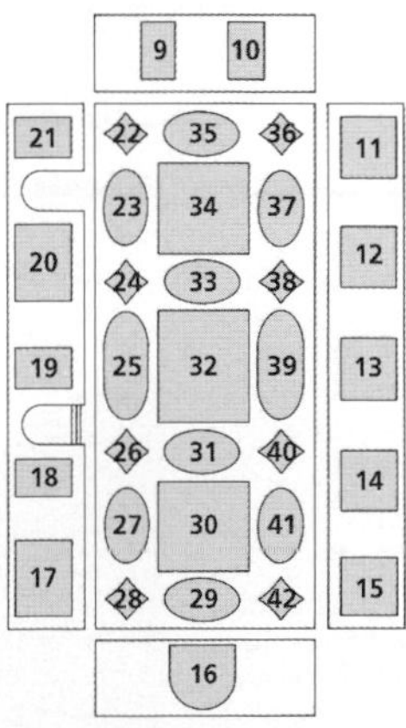

Upper Hall

⑩ San Rocco

Campo San Rocco. **Map** 6 D1. **Tel** 041 523 48 64. San Tomà. **Open** 9:30am–5:30pm daily.

On the same square as the celebrated Scuola Grande di San Rocco is the church of the same name. Designed by the sculptor and architect Bartolomeo Bon in 1489 and largely rebuilt in 1725, the exterior suffers from a mixture of styles. The facade was added in 1765–71. Inside, the chancel is decorated with a series of paintings by Tintoretto depicting scenes from the life of San Rocco.

⑪ San Pantalon

Campo San Pantalon. **Map** 6 D2. **Tel** 041 523 58 93. San Tomà, Piazzale Roma. **Open** 10am–noon, 1–3pm Mon–Sat.
w **sanpantalon.it**

Fumiani's epic ceiling painting (1680–1740) in San Pantalon

The overwhelming feature of this late 17th-century church is its vast painted ceiling, dark, awe-inspiring, and remarkable for its illusionistic effect of height. The ceiling comprises a total of 40 scenes, and admirers claim that this is the world's largest work of art on canvas.

The scenes show the martyrdom and apotheosis of the physician St. Pantalon. The artist, Gian Antonio Fumiani, took 24 years (1680–1704) to achieve the masterpiece, before allegedly falling to his death from the scaffolding.

Street-by-Street: Dorsoduro

Built on a strata of solid subsoil is the *sestiere* of Dorsoduro – the name means "hard backbone." It has as its focal point the lively Campo Santa Margherita, the largest open space in this part of Venice. The square bustles with activity, particularly in the morning when the market stands are open, and in the evening, when it is the haunt of students from nearby Ca' Foscari, now part of Venice university. The surrounding streets contain some architectural stunners, notably Ca' Rezzonico and the Scuola Grande dei Carmini, which has decorations by Tiepolo. Of the area's waterways, the delightful Rio San Barnaba is best appreciated from the Ponte dei Pugni, near the barge selling fruit and vegetables – itself a time-honored Venetian sight. Alongside the Rio Terrà Canal there are some lively cafés and a fascinating shop selling masks for Carnevale.

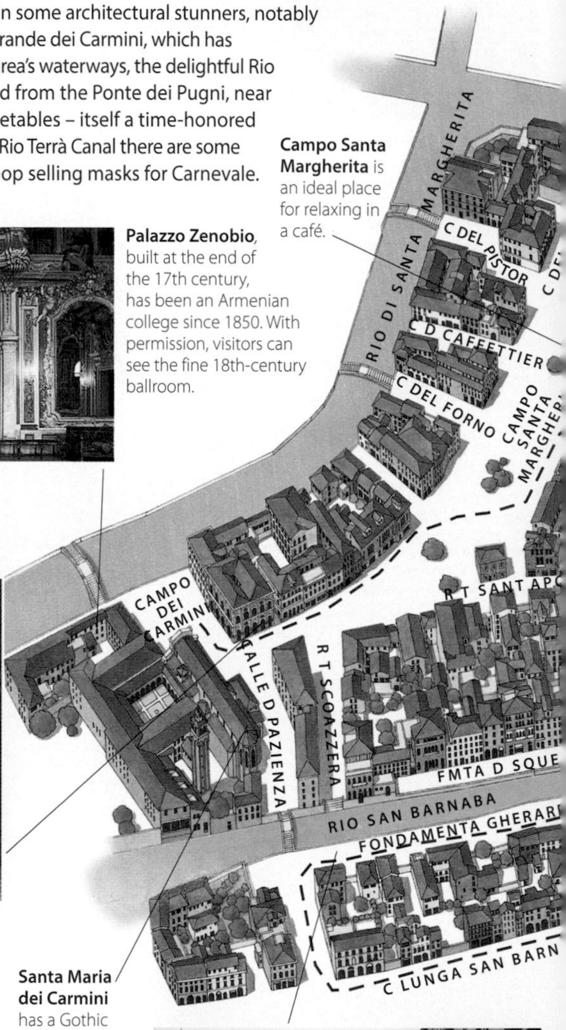

Campo Santa Margherita is an ideal place for relaxing in a café.

Palazzo Zenobio, built at the end of the 17th century, has been an Armenian college since 1850. With permission, visitors can see the fine 18th-century ballroom.

Scuola Grande dei Carmini contains nine ceiling panels (1739–44) in the hall on the upper floor, painted by Tiepolo for the Carmelite confraternity.

Santa Maria dei Carmini has a Gothic side porch carved with Byzantine reliefs.

Key

 Suggested route

0 meters 50
0 yards 50

Fondamenta Gherardini runs beside the Rio San Barnaba, one of the prettiest canals in the sestiere.

For hotels and restaurants in this region see pp562–77 and pp580–605

★ **Ca' Rezzonico** The ballroom covers the width of the palazzo once owned by Browning.

Locator Map
See Venice Street Finder maps 5, 6

Palazzo Giustinian was home to Wagner in 1858.

Ca' Foscari was completed in 1437 for Doge Francesco Foscari.

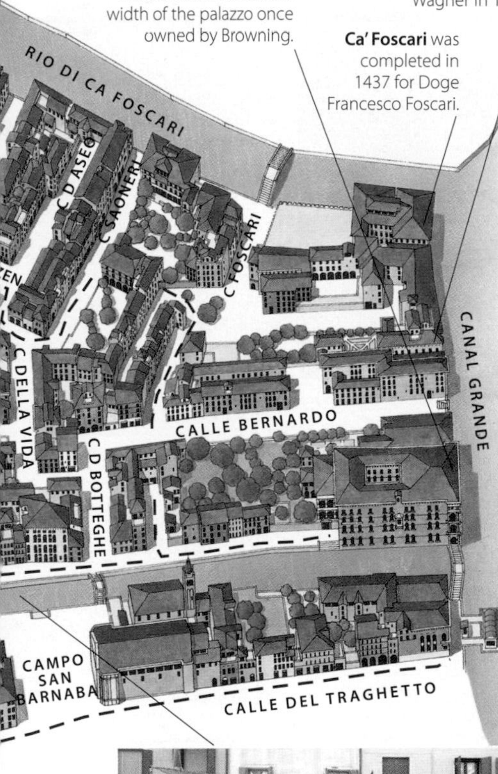

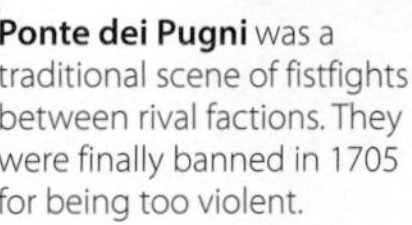

Ponte dei Pugni was a traditional scene of fistfights between rival factions. They were finally banned in 1705 for being too violent.

San Barnaba is a thriving community, with its own floating market barge crammed with fresh fruit and vegetables. It is a focal point for tourists and locals alike.

Tiepolo's *New World* fresco, part of a series in Ca' Rezzonico

⓬ Ca' Rezzonico

Fondamenta Rezzonico 3136.
Map 6 E3. **Tel** 041 241 01 00. Ca' Rezzonico. **Open** 10am–6pm Wed–Mon (Nov–Mar: to 5pm, last adm: 1 hr before closing). **Closed** Jan 1, May 1, Dec 25.
visitmuve.it

This palazzo houses the museum of 18th-century Venice, its rooms furnished with frescoes, paintings, and period pieces taken from other palaces or museums. Building began with Longhena (architect of La Salute, *see p109*) in 1667, but the funds of the Bon family, who commissioned it, ran dry before the second floor was started. In 1712 the unfinished palace was bought by the Rezzonico family of Genoa, who spent a large portion of their fortune on its completion.

The Rezzonico family sold it on, in 1888, to the famous poet Robert Browning and his son, Pen. The outstanding attraction in the palace today is Giorgio Massari's ballroom, which occupies the entire breadth of the building. It is adorned with gilded chandeliers, carved furniture by Andrea Brustolon, and a ceiling with *trompe l'oeil* frescoes. Other rooms have frescoes by Giambattista Tiepolo, including his lively *Nuptial Allegory* (1758), and one by his son, Giandomenico, originally in his villa at Zianigo. There are paintings by Longhi, Guardi, and – rare in Venice – Canaletto. On the top floor is a reconstructed 18th-century apothecary's shop and the Pinacoteca Martini.

Nave of San Nicolò dei Mendicoli, one of the oldest churches in Venice

⓭ San Nicolò dei Mendicoli

Campo San Nicolò. **Map** 5 A3. **Tel** 041 275 03 82. San Basilio. **Open** 10am–noon, 3–5:30pm Mon–Sat, 10am–noon Sun & public hols.

Contrasting with the remote and run-down area that surrounds it, this church still remains one of the most charming in Venice. Founded in the 7th century, it has been rebuilt extensively over the years. The little porch on the north flank is 15th century and once sheltered the beggars, or *mendicanti*, who gave the church its name.

Thanks to the Venice in Peril fund, in the 1970s the church underwent one of the most comprehensive restoration programs since the floods of 1966. Flooding had become such a problem that the priest often ferried himself around the church in a small wicker boat. The floor, which was 1 ft (30 cm) below the level of the canals, was rebuilt and raised slightly to prevent further flood damage. The roofs and lower walls were reconstructed, and paintings and statues restored.

The interior is delightfully embellished, particularly the nave with its 16th-century gilded wooden statues. These include the figure of San Nicolò himself. On the upper walls is a series of paintings of the life of Christ (*c.* 1553) by Alvise dal Friso and other pupils of Veronese.

Outside, a small column supports a stone lion, in a humbler echo of the Column of San Marco in the Piazzetta.

⓮ San Sebastiano

Campo San Sebastiano. **Map** 5 C3. **Tel** 041 275 04 62. San Basilio. **Open** 10am–5pm Mon–Sat. **Closed** Jan 1, Dec 25.

chorusvenezia.org

This church has one of the most homogeneous interiors in the whole of Venice. The splendor was created by Veronese, who, from 1555 to 1560 and again in the 1570s, was commissioned to decorate the sacristy ceiling, the nave ceiling, the frieze, the east end of the choir, the high altar, the doors of the organ panels, and the chancel.

The paintings feature radiant colors and rich costumes. Those on the sacristy ceiling depict the *Coronation of the Virgin* and the *Four Evangelists*.

Of the other paintings, the finest are the three that tell the story of Esther, Queen of Xerxes I of Persia, famous for securing the deliverance of the Jewish people.

Veronese is buried here. His tomb is in front of the paved chapel to the left of the chancel.

⓯ Accademia

See pp110–11.

⓰ Peggy Guggenheim Collection

Palazzo Venier dei Leoni. **Map** 6 F4. **Tel** 041 240 54 11. Accademia. **Open** 10am–6pm Wed–Mon. **Closed** Jan 9, Feb 20, Dec 25.

guggenheim-venice.it

Intended as a four-story palace, the 18th-century Palazzo Venier dei Leoni in fact never rose beyond the ground floor. In 1949 the building was bought as a home by the American

The truncated palazzo housing the Peggy Guggenheim Collection

millionaire Peggy Guggenheim (1898–1979), a collector, dealer, and patron of the arts who befriended, and then furthered the careers of, many innovative abstract and Surrealist artists. One was Max Ernst, who became her second husband. The collection consists of 200 fine paintings and sculptures, each representing the 20th century's most influential modern art movements. The dining room has notable Cubist works of art, including *The Poet* by Pablo Picasso, and an entire room is devoted to Jackson Pollock, who was "discovered" by Guggenheim.

Other artists represented are Braque, Chagall, de Chirico, Dalí, Duchamp, Léger, Kandinsky, Klee, Mondrian, Miró, Malevich, Rothko, Bacon, and Magritte, whose Surreal *Empire of Light* (1953–4) shows a night scene of a darkened house in a wooded setting with a bright day sky above. The sculpture collection, which includes Constantin Brancusi's elegant *Maiastra* (1912), is laid out in the house and garden.

Maiastra by Constantin Brancusi

Perhaps the most provocative piece is Marino Marini's *Angelo della Città* (Angel of the Citadel, 1948), located on the terrace overlooking the Grand Canal. This shows a prominently displayed man sitting on a horse, erect in all respects.

The Guggenheim is the best place in the city to see 20th-century art. Light-filled rooms and the large modern canvases provide a striking contrast to the Renaissance paintings in most Venetian churches and museums.

The garden has been paved and features an array of sculptures. Peggy Guggenheim's ashes are also preserved here. A shop and restaurant are located within the grounds. Check the website for information on temporary exhibits.

The large Baroque church of Santa Maria della Salute

⑰ Santa Maria della Salute

Campo della Salute. **Map** 7 A4. **Tel** 041 274 39 11. Salute. **Open** 9am–noon, 3–5:30pm daily. Sacristy: 10am–noon, 3–5pm daily; may be closed in the morning on religious holidays. to sacristy.

This great Baroque church standing at the entrance of the Grand Canal is one of the most imposing architectural landmarks of Venice. Henry James likened it to "some great lady on the threshold of her salon."

Santa Maria della Salute was built in thanksgiving for the city's deliverance from the plague epidemic of 1630, hence the name *Salute*, which means health and salvation.

Each November, in celebration, worshippers light candles and approach across a bridge of boats spanning the mouth of the Grand Canal for the occasion.

Baldassare Longhena started the church in 1630 at the age of 32, and worked on it for the rest of his life. It was completed in 1687, five years after his death. The interior consists of a large octagonal space below the cupola and six chapels radiating from the ambulatory. The large domed chancel and grandiose high altar dominate the view from the main door.

The altar's sculptural group by Giusto Le Corte represents the Virgin and Child giving protection to Venice from the plague. The best of the paintings are in the sacristy to the left of the altar: Titian's early altarpiece of *St. Mark Enthroned with Saints Cosmas, Damian, Roch, and Sebastian* (1511–12) and his dramatic ceiling paintings of *Cain and Abel*, *The Sacrifice of Abraham and Isaac*, and *David and Goliath* (1540–9). *The Wedding at Cana* (1551) on the wall opposite the entrance is by Jacopo Tintoretto.

⑱ Punta della Dogana

Campo della Salute. **Map** 7 A4. **Tel** 199 139 139; 041 271 90 39 from outside Italy. Salute. **Open** 10am–7pm Wed–Mon (ticket counter closes at 6pm). **Closed** Jan 1, Dec 25.
W palazzograssi.it

The magnificent 17th-century Punta della Dogana (formerly a customs house) was restored by Japanese architect Tadao Ando and opened in 2009 as a contemporary art gallery. Together with the Palazzo Grassi, it houses the French billionaire François Pinault's large collection of contemporary art. Many well-known artists are represented here, including Jeff Koons and Takeshi Murakami.

Punta della Dogana, a contemporary art museum

⓯ Accademia

The art collection in the Accademia offers a complete spectrum of the Venetian School, from the Byzantine era through the Renaissance to the Baroque and later. The basis of the collection was the Accademia di Belle Arti founded in 1750 by the painter Giovanni Battista Piazzetta. In 1807 Napoleon moved the collection to these premises, enriching it with artworks removed from churches and monasteries. The Accademia is currently undergoing extensive restoration, which may result in changes to the floor plan.

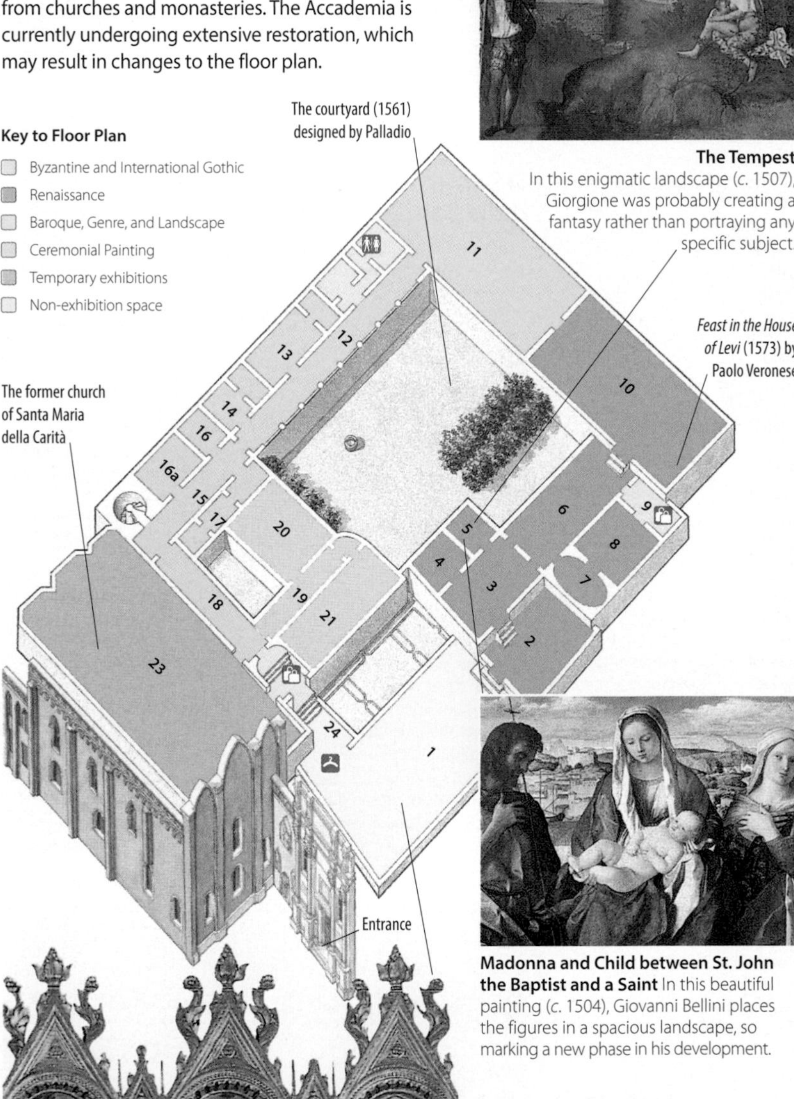

The Tempest In this enigmatic landscape (*c.* 1507), Giorgione was probably creating a fantasy rather than portraying any specific subject.

Madonna and Child between St. John the Baptist and a Saint In this beautiful painting (*c.* 1504), Giovanni Bellini places the figures in a spacious landscape, so marking a new phase in his development.

Coronation of the Virgin Paolo Veneziano's polyptych (1325) has a central image of the Virgin surrounded by a panoply of religious scenes. This detail shows episodes from the Life of St. Francis.

Healing of the Madman (*c.* 1496) by Vittore Carpaccio

VISITORS' CHECKLIST

Practical Information
Campo della Carità. **Map** 6 E3.
Tel 041 520 03 45.
Open 8:15am–7:15pm daily (to 2pm Mon, last adm: 45 min before closing). **Closed** Jan 1, May 1, Dec 25.
gallerieaccademia.org

Transportation
Accademia.

Byzantine and International Gothic

Room 1 shows the influence of Byzantine art on the early Venetian painters. In Paolo Veneziano's glowing *Coronation of the Virgin* (1325), the linear rhythms are unmistakably Gothic, but the gold background and central panel are distinctly Byzantine.

In contrast, *The Coronation of the Virgin* (1448) by Michele Giambono reveals a delicate naturalism, typical of the International Gothic style.

Renaissance

The Renaissance came late to Venice, but by the second quarter of the 15th century, it had transformed the city into a thriving art center rivaling Florence and Rome. Central to Venetian art in the 15th century was the *Sacra Conversazione*, in which the Madonna is portrayed with various saints in a harmonious composition. Giovanni Bellini's altarpiece for San Giobbe (*c.* 1487) in room 2 is one of the finest examples of this subject.

In contrast, the High Renaissance exuberance of Paolo Veronese is exemplified in the monumental *Feast in the House of Levi* (1573). The painting occupies a whole wall in room 10. Tintoretto's huge masterpiece *The Miracle of St. Mark Freeing a Slave* (1548) is also on display here.

Baroque, Genre, and Landscape

Venice lacked native Baroque painters, but a few non-Venetians kept the Venetian school alive in the 17th century. The most notable was the Genoese Bernardo Strozzi (1581–1644). The artist was a great admirer of the work of Veronese, as can be seen in his *Feast at the House of Simon* (1629) in room 11. Also represented in this room is Giambattista Tiepolo, the greatest Venetian painter of the 18th century.

The long corridor (12) and the rooms that lead from it are largely devoted to lighthearted landscape and genre paintings from the 18th century. Among them are pastoral scenes by Francesco Zuccarelli, works by Marco Ricci, scenes of Venetian society by Pietro Longhi, and a view of Venice by Canaletto (1763). This is a fine example of his sense of perspective.

Ceremonial Painting

Rooms 20 and 21 return to the Renaissance, featuring two great cycles of paintings from the late 16th century. The detail in these large-scale anecdotal canvases provides a fascinating glimpse of the life, customs, and appearance of Venice at the time.

Room 20 houses *The Stories of the Cross* by Venice's leading artists. In room 21, minutely detailed *Scenes from the Legend of St. Ursula* (1490s) by Carpaccio mix reality and imagination by linking episodes from the life of the saint to the settings and costumes of 15th-century Venice.

Feast in the House of Levi (1573) by Paolo Veronese

Street-by-Street: Piazza San Marco

Throughout its long history, Piazza San Marco has witnessed pageants, processions, political activities, and countless Carnival festivities. Visitors flock here by the thousands for two of the city's most important historic sights – the Basilica and the Palazzo Ducale. These magnificent buildings complement lesser sights, such as the Campanile, Museo Correr, and Torre dell'Orologio, not to mention the gardens of the Giardinetti Reali, open-air orchestras, elegant cafés – notably Quadri and Florian's – and numerous chic shops.

21 Torre dell'Orologio
The clock tower, with hidden clockwork figures, dates from the Renaissance.

Traditionally, gondolas have moored in the Bacino Orseolo, which is named after Doge Orseolo.

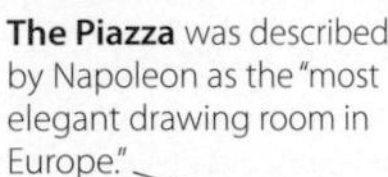

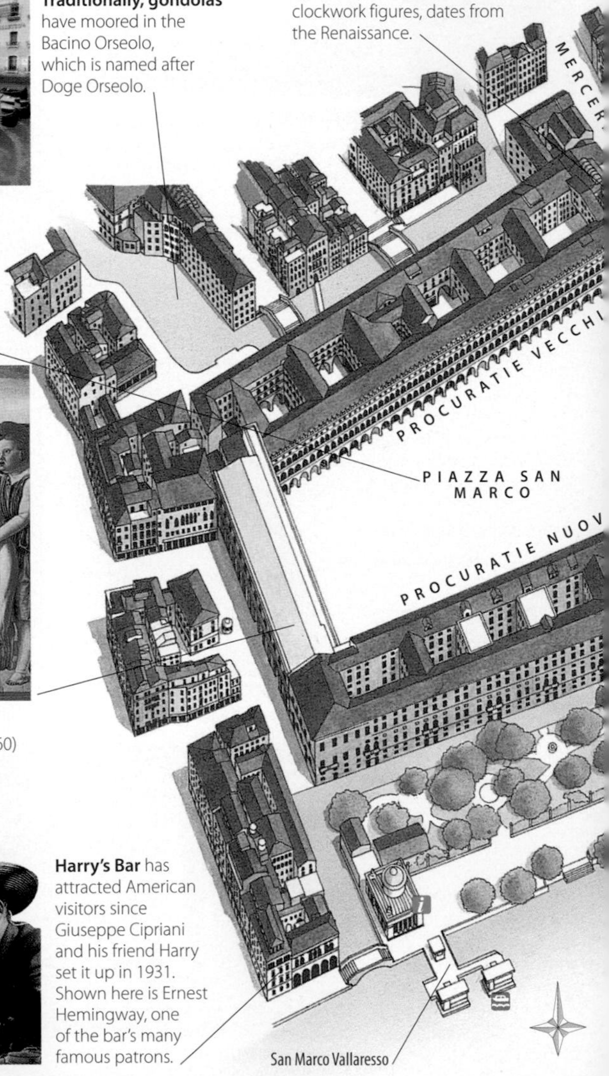

The Piazza was described by Napoleon as the "most elegant drawing room in Europe."

23 Museo Correr
Giovanni Bellini's *Pietà* (1455–60) is one of many masterpieces hanging in the galleries of the Correr.

MERCER

PROCURATIE VECCHI

PIAZZA SAN MARCO

PROCURATIE NUOV

Harry's Bar has attracted American visitors since Giuseppe Cipriani and his friend Harry set it up in 1931. Shown here is Ernest Hemingway, one of the bar's many famous patrons.

San Marco Vallaresso

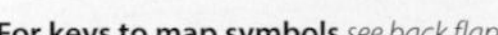

For keys to map symbols *see back flap*

⑲ ★ Basilica di San Marco
This 13th-century facade mosaic shows the body of St. Mark being carried into the basilica.

Locator Map
See Venice Street Finder map 7

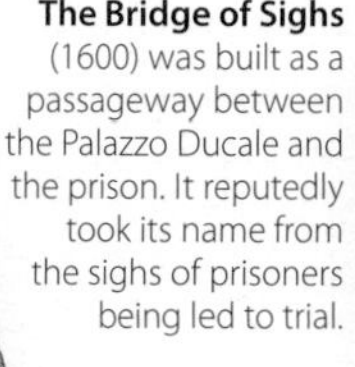

The Bridge of Sighs (1600) was built as a passageway between the Palazzo Ducale and the prison. It reputedly took its name from the sighs of prisoners being led to trial.

LARGA SAN MARCO

RIO DEL PALAZZO

PIAZZETTA

MOLO SAN MARCO

Ponte della Paglia

San Marco Giardinetti

0 meters 75

0 yards 75

⑳ ★ Palazzo Ducale
Once home to Venice's rulers, and to the offices of State, the Doges' Palace is a triumph of Gothic architecture.

㉒ The Campanile
The present Campanile replaced one that collapsed in 1902.

The vaulting of the stairway in the magnificent Libreria Sansoviniana (1588) is decorated with frescoes and gilded stucco. The national library of St. Mark is housed here.

The Zecca, designed by Sansovino and started in 1537, was the city mint until 1870, and gave its name to the *zecchino* or Venetian ducat.

For hotels and restaurants in this region see pp562–77 and pp580–605

⑲ Basilica di San Marco

Venice's famous Basilica blends the architectural and decorative styles of East and West to create one of the greatest buildings in Europe. The exterior owes its almost Oriental splendor to countless treasures from the Republic's overseas empire. Among these are copies of the famous bronze horses brought from Constantinople in 1204, and a wealth of columns, bas-reliefs, and colored marbles studded across the main facade. Mosaics from different epochs adorn the five doorways, while the main portal is framed by some of Italy's loveliest Romanesque carving (1240–65).

St. Mark and Angels
The statues crowning the central arch are additions from the early 15th century.

★ Horses of St. Mark
The four horses are replicas of the gilded bronze originals, now protected inside the Basilica's museum.

KEY

① **The elegant arches** echo those of the lower floor, forming a repeating pattern.

② **The Pentecost Dome**, showing the Descent of the Holy Ghost as a dove, was probably the first dome to be decorated with mosaics.

③ **The Ascension Dome** features a magnificent 13th-century mosaic of Christ surrounded by angels, the 12 Apostles, and the Virgin Mary.

④ **St. Mark's body**, believed lost in the fire of AD 976, supposedly reappeared when the new church was consecrated in 1094. The remains are housed in the altar.

⑤ **The Mosaic Pavement** shows beautiful pictures of birds and beasts, some of which are allegorical.

⑥ **St. Mark's Treasury**

⑦ **Romanesque carvings** adorn the arches of the main portal.

★ Facade Mosaics
A 17th-century mosaic shows the body of St. Mark being taken from Alexandria, reputedly smuggled past Muslim guards under slices of pork.

Ciborium
The fine alabaster columns of the altar canopy, or baldacchino, are adorned with scenes from the New Testament.

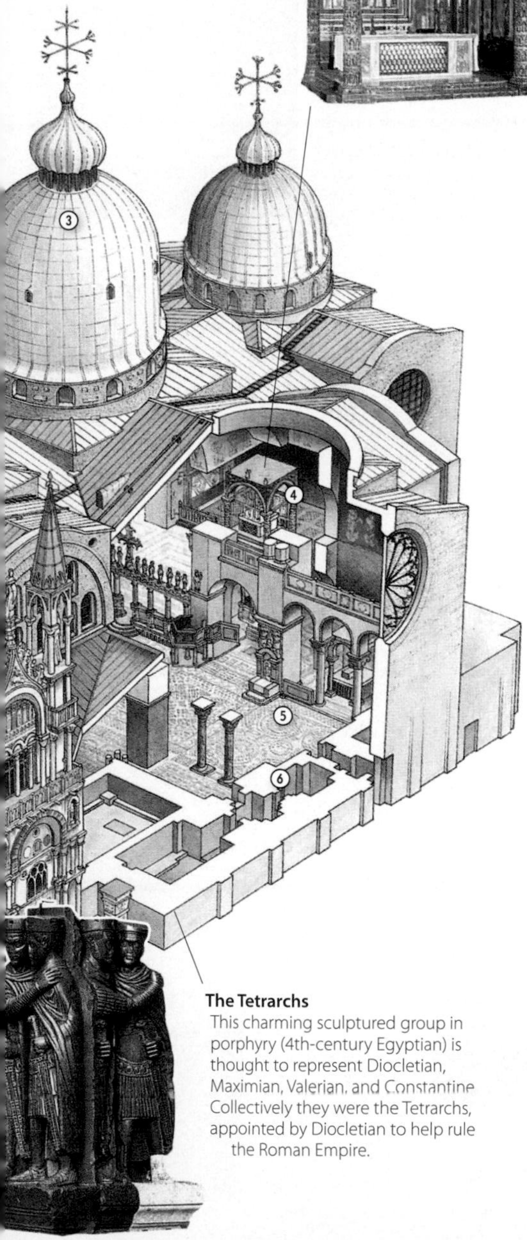

VISITORS' CHECKLIST

Practical Information
Piazza San Marco. **Map** 7 B2. **Tel** 041 270 83 11. Basilica: **Open** 9:45am–5pm Mon–Sat, 2–5pm Sun. Museum: **Open** 9:45am–5pm daily. Pala d'Oro & Treasury: **Open** 9:45am–5pm Mon–Sat, 2–5pm Sun. sightseeing limited during services. except Sun (Basilica). Treasury. **basilicasanmarco.it**

Transportation
San Marco. Pala d'Oro, Basilica, Treasury.

3

4

5

6

The Building of St. Mark's

Built on a Greek cross plan and crowned with five huge domes, this is the third church to stand on the site. The first, which enshrined the body of St. Mark in the 9th century, was destroyed by fire. The second was torn down in favor of a church reflecting Venice's growing power. The present design was inspired by the Church of the Apostles in Constantinople and was completed and decorated over the centuries. From 1075, all ships returning from abroad had, by law, to bring back a precious gift to adorn "the House of St. Mark." The mosaics inside are mostly 12th–13th century and cover 45,622 sq ft (4,240 sq m). Some were later replaced by such artists as Titian and Tintoretto. Until 1807, St. Mark's was the doge's private chapel, used for ceremonies of state, after which it succeeded San Pietro di Castello as the cathedral of Venice.

13th-century carving of a grape harvester on the main portal

The Tetrarchs
This charming sculptured group in porphyry (4th-century Egyptian) is thought to represent Diocletian, Maximian, Valerian, and Constantine. Collectively they were the Tetrarchs, appointed by Diocletian to help rule the Roman Empire.

Exploring the Basilica

St. Mark's magnificent interior is clad with dazzling mosaics, which begin in the *narthex,* or atrium, of the Basilica, and culminate in the glittering panels of the Pentecost and Ascension domes. The Genesis Cupola in the atrium has a stunning Creation of the World described in concentric circles. The *pavimento* or floor is also patterned with mosaics in marble and glass. Steps from the atrium lead to the Museo Marciano, home to the Basilica's famous horses. Other treasures include the jewel-encrusted Pala d'Oro, behind the high altar; the Nicopeia icon; and the precious hoards of silver, gold, and glassware in the Treasury.

Madonna di Nicopeia
This Byzantine icon, looted in 1204, is one of Venice's most revered images.

★ Pentecost Dome
Showing the Apostles touched by tongues of flame, the Pentecost Dome was lavishly decorated in the 12th century.

★ Ascension Dome
A mosaic of Christ in Glory decorates the enormous central dome. This masterpiece was created by 13th-century Venetian craftsmen, who were strongly influenced by the art and architecture of Byzantium.

★ Treasury
A repository for precious artifacts from both Italy and Constantinople, the treasury houses objects such as this 11th-century silver-gilt coffer.

★ Pala d'Oro
The altarpiece, created in the 10th century by medieval goldsmiths, is made up of 250 panels such as this one.

KEY

① **The columns** of the inner facade are thought to be fragments of the first basilica.

② **South side aisle**

③ **Baptistry**

④ **Cappella Zen**

⑤ **Steps to Museo Marciano**

⑥ **Atrium**

⑦ **North side aisle**

⑧ **The Porta dei Fiori** or Gate of Flowers is decorated with 13th-century reliefs.

⑨ **Cappella dei Mascoli**

⑩ **The sacristy door** has fine bronze panels by Sansovino that include portraits of himself with Titian and Aretino.

⑪ **The Altar of the Sacrament**, is decorated with mosaics of the parables and miracles of Christ dating from the late 12th or early 13th century.

Mosaics

Clothing the domes, walls, and floor of the Basilica are over 43,000 sq ft (4,000 sq m) of gleaming golden mosaics. The earliest, dating from the 12th century, were the work of mosaicists from the East. Their delicate techniques were adopted by Venetian craftsmen, who gradually took over the Basilica's decoration, combining Byzantine inspiration with Western influences. During the 16th century, many sketches by Tintoretto, Titian, Veronese, and other leading artists were reproduced in mosaic.

Among the most dazzling mosaics – many of which have been heavily restored – are those in the 13th-century central Ascension Dome and the 12th-century Pentecost Dome over the nave.

Pala d'Oro

Beyond the Cappella di San Clemente lies the entrance to the most valuable treasure of San Marco: the Pala d'Oro. This jewel-spangled altarpiece, situated behind the high altar, consists of 250 enamel paintings on gold foil, enclosed within a gilded silver Gothic frame. Originally commissioned in Byzantium in AD 976, the altarpiece was further embellished over the centuries. Napoleon stole some of the precious stones in 1797, but the screen still gleams with pearls, rubies, sapphires, and amethysts.

Museo Marciano

Steps from the atrium, signposted "Loggia dei Cavalli," take you up to the church museum, where the gallery offers a splendid view into the basilica. The gilded bronze horses, housed in a room at the far end of the museum, were stolen from the top of the Hippodrome (ancient racecourse) in Constantinople (modern Istanbul) in 1204, but their origin, either Roman or Hellenistic, remains a mystery. Also on display are mosaics, medieval manuscripts, and antique tapestries.

Baptistry and Chapels

The baptistry (closed to the public) was added by Doge Andrea Dandolo (1343–54), who is buried here, with Sansovino, who designed the font. The adjoining Cappella Zen (also closed to the public) became a funeral chapel for Cardinal Zen in 1504 in return for a bequest to the State. The left transept of the Cappella dei Mascoli is decorated with scenes from the life of Mary, while the third chapel in the same transept houses the icon of the Madonna of Nicopeia. Looted in 1204, it was once carried into battle at the head of the Byzantine army.

Noah and the Flood, atrium mosaics from the 13th century

20 Palazzo Ducale

The Palazzo Ducale (Doges' Palace) was the official residence of each Venetian ruler (doge) and was founded in the 9th century. The present palace owes its external appearance to the building work of the 14th and early 15th centuries. To create their airy Gothic masterpiece, the Venetians broke with tradition by perching the bulk of the palace (built in pink Veronese marble) on top of an apparent fretwork of loggias and arcades (built from white Istrian stone).

★ Giants' Staircase
This 15th-century staircase is crowned by Sansovino's statues of Mars and Neptune, symbols of Venice's power.

★ Porta della Carta
This 15th-century Gothic gate was once the main entrance to the palace. From it, a vaulted passageway leads to the Arco Foscari and the internal courtyard.

★ Sala del Maggior Consiglio
This vast hall was used as a meeting place for members of Venice's Great Council. Tintoretto's huge *Paradise* (1590) fills the end wall.

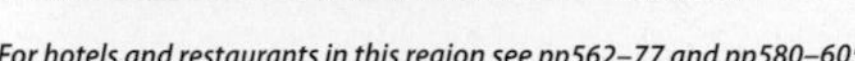

For hotels and restaurants in this region see pp562–77 and pp580–605

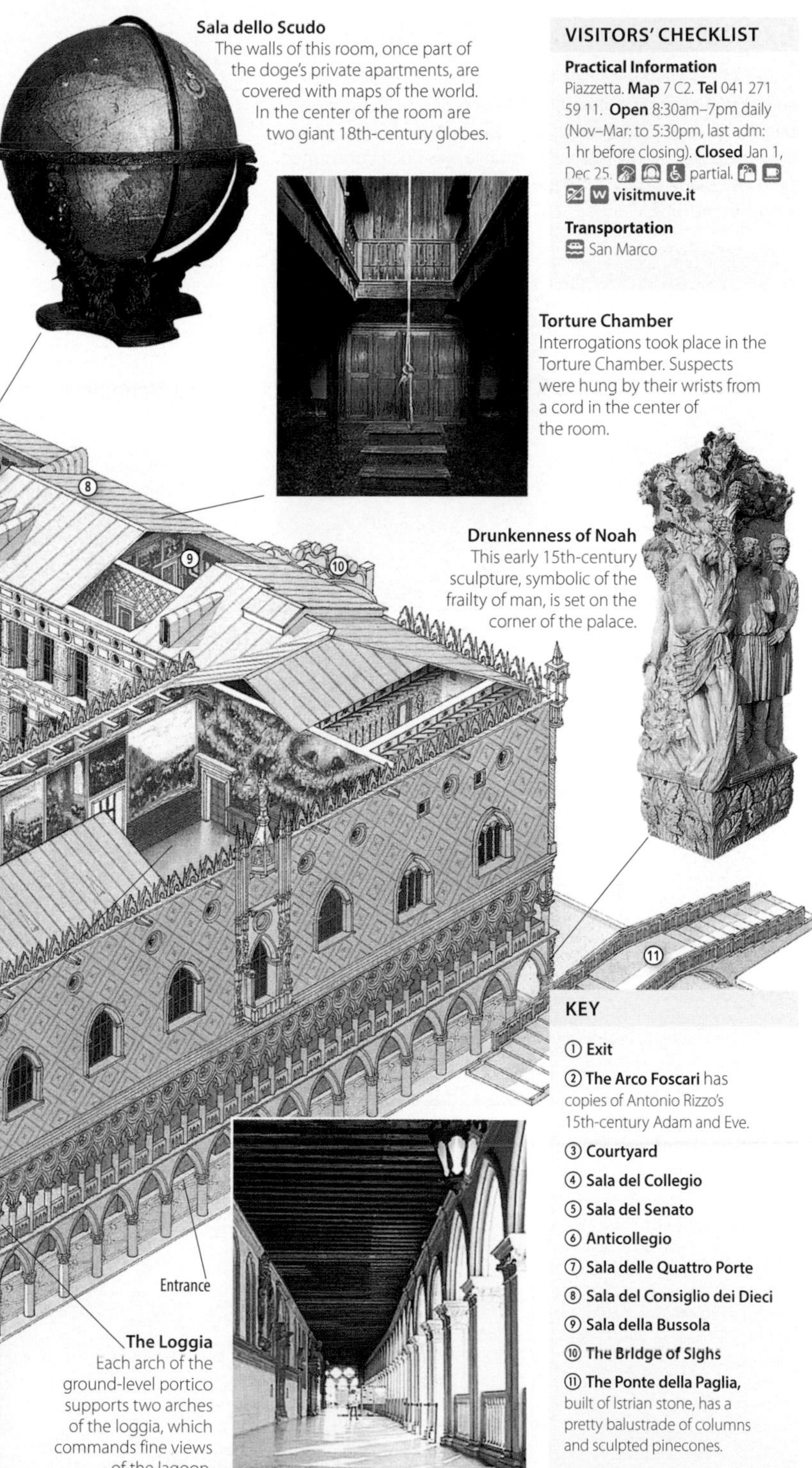

Sala dello Scudo
The walls of this room, once part of the doge's private apartments, are covered with maps of the world. In the center of the room are two giant 18th-century globes.

Torture Chamber
Interrogations took place in the Torture Chamber. Suspects were hung by their wrists from a cord in the center of the room.

Drunkenness of Noah
This early 15th-century sculpture, symbolic of the frailty of man, is set on the corner of the palace.

The Loggia
Each arch of the ground-level portico supports two arches of the loggia, which commands fine views of the lagoon.

VISITORS' CHECKLIST

Practical Information
Piazzetta. **Map** 7 C2. **Tel** 041 271 59 11. **Open** 8:30am–7pm daily (Nov–Mar: to 5:30pm, last adm: 1 hr before closing). **Closed** Jan 1, Dec 25. partial. **visitmuve.it**

Transportation
San Marco

KEY

① **Exit**

② **The Arco Foscari** has copies of Antonio Rizzo's 15th-century Adam and Eve.

③ **Courtyard**

④ **Sala del Collegio**

⑤ **Sala del Senato**

⑥ **Anticollegio**

⑦ **Sala delle Quattro Porte**

⑧ **Sala del Consiglio dei Dieci**

⑨ **Sala della Bussola**

⑩ **The Bridge of Sighs**

⑪ **The Ponte della Paglia,** built of Istrian stone, has a pretty balustrade of columns and sculpted pinecones.

Exploring the Palazzo Ducale

A tour of the Palazzo Ducale takes visitors through a succession of richly decorated chambers and halls, arranged over three floors, culminating with the Bridge of Sighs, which links the palace to the prisons. Casanova was once imprisoned here and made a daring escape from the Palazzo through a hole in the roof.

Jacopo and Domenico Tintoretto's *Paradise*, one of the world's largest paintings, in the Sala del Maggior Consiglio

Scala d'Oro and Courtyard

A passage from the Porta del Frumento opens into the palace courtyard. The ticket office and palace entrance are to the left. At the top of Antonio Rizzo's 15th-century Giants' Staircase, the new doge would be crowned with the *zogia* or dogal cap. The Scala d'Oro (golden staircase), designed by Jacopo Sansovino, leads to the palace's upper floors. It takes its name, however, from the elaborate gilt stucco vault created by Alessandro Vittoria (1554–8).

Sala delle Quattro Porte to the Sala del Senato

The second flight of the Scala d'Oro leads to the Sala delle Quattro Porte, with a ceiling designed by Palladio and frescoed by Tintoretto. The end walls of the next room, the Anticollegio, are decorated with mythological scenes by Tintoretto, while Veronese's masterly *Rape of Europa* (1580), opposite the window, is one of the palace's most dramatic works. The adjoining Sala del Collegio was where the doge and his counselors met to receive ambassadors and discuss matters of State. Embellishing the magnificent ceiling are 11 paintings by Veronese. In the next room, the Sala del Senato, the doge and some 200 senators discussed foreign affairs. The paintings are by Tintoretto and pupils.

A *bocca di leone* for denunciations

Sala del Consiglio dei Dieci to the Armeria

The Sala del Consiglio dei Dieci was the meeting room of the powerful Council of Ten, founded in 1310 to protect State security. Two fine works by Veronese adorn the ceiling: *Age and Youth* and *Juno Offering the Ducal Crown to Venice* (both 1553–4). In the Sala della Bussola, offenders awaited their fate in front of the Council of Ten. The room's *bocca di leone* (lion's mouth), was used to post secret denunciations and was just one of several in the palace. The wooden door here leads to the State Inquisitors' Room and thence to the torture chamber and prisons. The Armory – one of the finest such collections anywhere in Europe – occupies the following rooms.

Dialectic (*c*. 1577) by Veronese in the Palazzo Ducale's Sala del Collegio

Sala del Maggior Consiglio

The Scala dei Censori leads to the second floor and past the Sala del Guariento and Antonio Rizzo's statues of Adam and Eve (1480s) to the magnificent Sala del Maggior Consiglio. A vast chamber, it was used as a meeting place for the Great Council and for grand State banquets. By the mid-16th century the Great Council had around 2,000 members. Any Venetian of high birth over 25 was entitled to a seat unless he married a commoner. Tintoretto's huge *Paradise* (1587–90) occupies the eastern wall. Measuring 25 by 81 ft (7.45 by 24.65 m), it is one of the largest paintings in the world. The itinerary then continues in more somber vein, crossing the Bridge of Sighs to enter the dank world of the prisons.

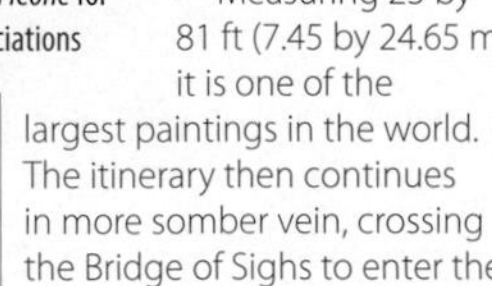

For hotels and restaurants in this region see pp562–77 and pp580–605

㉑ Torre dell'Orologio

Piazza San Marco. **Map** 7 B2. **Tel** 848 082 000 (booking). San Marco. 10 & 11am Mon–Wed, 2 & 3pm Thu–Sun (must be reserved). **Closed** Jan 1, May 1, Dec 25. **visitmuve.it**

This richly decorated clock tower on the north side of the piazza was built in the late 15th century. Mauro Coducci is thought to have worked on the design. With its display of the phases of the moon and the signs of the zodiac, the clock face was designed with seafarers in mind. According to legend, once the clock was completed, the two inventors had their eyes gouged out to prevent them from ever creating a replica.

The clock face of the Torre dell'Orologio

On the upper level, the winged lion of St. Mark stands against a star-spangled blue backdrop. At the very top the two huge bronze figures, known as the *Mori*, or Moors, strike the bell on the hour.

㉒ Campanile

Piazza San Marco. **Map** 7 B2. **Tel** 041 270 83 11. San Marco. **Open** Nov–Easter: 9:30am–3:45pm daily; Easter–Jun & Oct: 9am–7pm daily; Jul–Sep: 9am–9pm daily. **basilicasanmarco.it**

From the top of St. Mark's campanile, high above the piazza, visitors can enjoy views of the city, the lagoon, and, visibility permitting, the peaks of the Alps. It was from here that Galileo demonstrated his telescope to Doge Leonardo Donà in 1609. To do so he would have climbed the internal ramp. Access today is by elevator.

The first tower, completed in 1173, was built as a lighthouse to assist navigators in the lagoon. It took on a less benevolent role in the Middle Ages, when offenders were imprisoned – and in some cases left to die – in a cage hung near its summit. With the exception of several 16th-century renovations, the tower survived unharmed until July 1902, when, with little warning, it collapsed. The only casualties were the Loggetta at the foot of the tower and the custodian's cat. Donations flooded in, and in 1903 the foundation stone was laid for a new campanile *"dov'era e com'era"* ("where it was and as it was"). The new tower was opened on April 25 (the Feast of St. Mark) 1912. Due to small structural shifts, the foundations have been reinforced.

㉓ Museo Correr

Procuratie Nuove. Entrance in Ala Napoleonica. **Map** 7 B2. **Tel** 041 240 52 11. San Marco. **Open** Apr–Oct: 10am–7pm; Nov–Mar: 10am– 5pm (last adm: 1hr before closing). **Closed** Jan 1, Dec 25. (includes adm to Libreria Sansoviniana and Museo Archeologico). **visitmuve.it**

Teodoro Correr bequeathed his extensive collection of works of art to Venice in 1830, thus forming the core of the city's fine civic museum.

Its first rooms form a suitably Neo-Classical backdrop for early statues by Antonio Canova (1757–1822). The rest of the floor covers the history of the Venetian Republic, with maps, coins, armor, and a host of doge-related exhibits. The second floor contains a picture collection second only to that of the Accademia.

Young Man in a Red Hat (*c.* 1490) by Carpaccio in the Museo Correr

The paintings, hung chronologically, trace the evolution of Venetian painting, and show the influence of Ferrarese, Paduan, and Flemish artists.

The gallery's most famous works are by Carpaccio: *Portrait of a Young Man in a Red Hat* (*c.* 1490), and *Two Venetian Ladies* (*c.* 1507). The latter is traditionally, but probably incorrectly, known as *The Courtesans* because of the ladies' low-cut dresses. The Museo del Risorgimento on the same floor looks at the history of Venice until unification with Italy in 1866.

The ceiling of Santo Stefano, built in the form of a ship's keel

㉔ Santo Stefano

Campo Santo Stefano. **Map** 6 F2. **Tel** 041 275 04 62. Accademia or Sant'Angelo. **Open** 10am–5pm Mon–Sat. **Closed** Jan 1, Dec 25. **chorusvenezia.org**

Deconsecrated six times on account of the blood spilled within its walls, Santo Stefano – one of Venice's most beautiful churches – is now remarkably serene. Built in the 14th century, and altered in the 15th, the church has a carved portal by Bartolomeo Bon, and a campanile with a typical Venetian tilt. The interior has a splendid ship's keel ceiling, carved tie-beams, and a sacristy crammed with valuable paintings.

25 Santi Giovanni e Paolo

Known more colloquially as San Zanipolo, Santi Giovanni e Paolo vies with the Frari *(see pp102–3)* as the city's greatest Gothic church. Built by the Dominicans in the 14th century, it is striking for its vast scale and architectural austerity. Known as the Pantheon of Venice, it houses monuments to no fewer than 25 doges. Among these are several fine works of art, executed by the Lombardi family and other leading sculptors.

The Nave
The cross-vaulted interior is tied by wooden beams and supported by stone columns.

★ Tomb of Nicolò Marcello
This magnificent Renaissance monument to Doge Nicolò Marcello (died 1474) was sculpted by Pietro Lombardo.

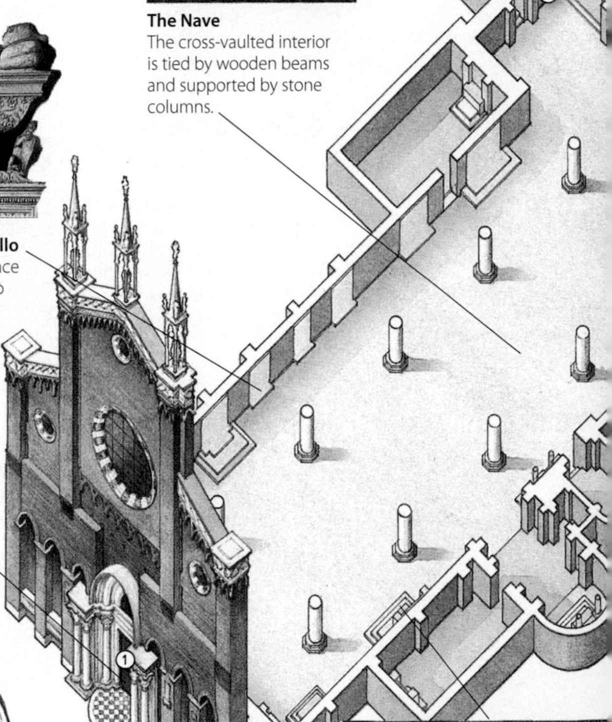

Entrance

★ Tomb of Pietro Mocenigo
Pietro Lombardo's superb tomb (1481) commemorates the doge's military pursuits when he was Grand Captain of the Venetian forces.

★ Polyptych by Bellini
This painting (*c.* 1465) shows St. Vincent Ferrer, a Spanish cleric, flanked by St. Sebastian and St. Christopher.

VISITORS' CHECKLIST

Practical Information
Campo Santi Giovanni e Paolo (also marked San Zanipolo).
Map 3 C5. **Tel** 041 523 59 13.
Open 9am–6pm daily (from noon Sun & religious hols). **Closed** Sun am (for mass).
basilicasantigiovanniepaolo.it

Transportation
Fondamente Nuove, Ospedale Civile.

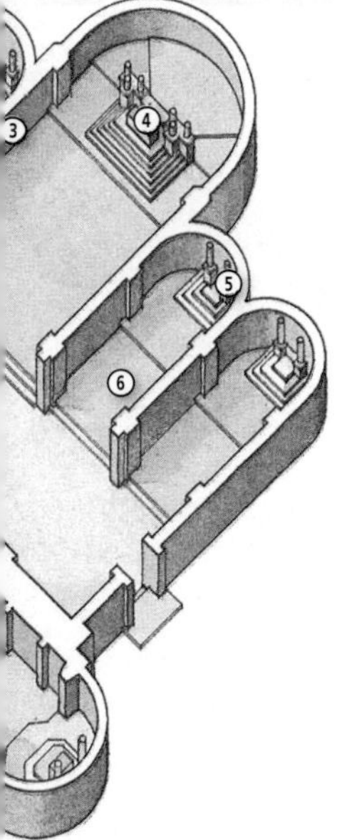

KEY

① **The doorway**, which is decorated with Byzantine reliefs and carvings by Bartolomeo Bon, is one of Venice's earliest Renaissance architectural works.

② **The bronze statue** is a monument to Doge Sebastiano Venier, who was Commander of the Fleet at Lepanto.

③ **Tomb of Andrea Vendramin**, Lombardo's masterpiece (1476–8), takes the form of a Roman triumphal arch.

④ **The Baroque high altar**, begun in 1619, is attributed to Baldassare Longhena.

⑤ **16th-century altar statues by Vittoria**

⑥ **16th-century frescoes attributed to Palma il Giovane**

㉖ Statue of Colleoni

Campo Santi Giovanni e Paolo.
Map 3 C5. Ospedale Civile.

Bartolomeo Colleoni, the famous *condottiere* or commander of mercenaries, left his fortune to the Republic on condition that his statue was placed in front of San Marco. A prominent statue in the piazza would have broken with precedent, so the Senate cunningly had Colleoni raised before the Scuola di San Marco instead of the basilica. A touchstone of early Renaissance sculpture, the equestrian statue of the proud warrior (1481–8) is by the Florentine Andrea Verrocchio, but was cast in bronze after his death by Alessandro Leopardi. The statue has a strong sense of power and movement, which arguably ranks it alongside the works of Donatello.

㉗ Santa Maria Formosa

Campo Santa Maria Formosa. **Map** 7 C1. **Tel** 041 275 04 62. Rialto.
Open 10am–5pm Mon–Sat.
Closed Jan 1, Dec 25.

chorusvenezia.org

Designed by Mauro Coducci in 1492, this church is most unusual in having two main facades – one overlooks the *campo*, the other the canal. The bell tower, or campanile, added in 1688, is noted for the grotesque face at its base.

Two paintings stand out in the interior: a triptych (1473) by Bartolomeo Vivarini, and Palma il Vecchio's *St. Barbara* (*c.* 1510).

Palma il Vecchio's *St. Barbara* (*c.* 1510) in Santa Maria Formosa

Founded in the 9th century, its facade was later rebuilt by Antonio Gambello in Gothic style. When Gambello died in 1481, Mauro Coducci completed the upper section, adding many of its Renaissance panels.

The interior's artistic highlight is Giovanni Bellini's serene and sumptuously colored *Madonna and Child with Saints* (1505) in the north aisle. A door off the right nave leads to the Chapel of St. Athanasius, which in turn leads to the Chapel of San Tarasio. The chapel contains vault frescoes (1442) by Andrea del Castagno, and polyptychs (1443–4) by Antonio Vivarini and Giovanni d'Alemagna.

㉘ San Zaccaria

Campo San Zaccaria. **Map** 8 D2.
Tel 041 522 12 57. San Zaccaria.
Open 10am–noon, 4–6pm Mon–Sat, 4–6pm Sun & public hols. chapels and crypt.

Set in a quiet square just a stone's throw from the Riva degli Schiavoni, the church of San Zaccaria is a successful blend of Flamboyant Gothic and Classical Renaissance styles.

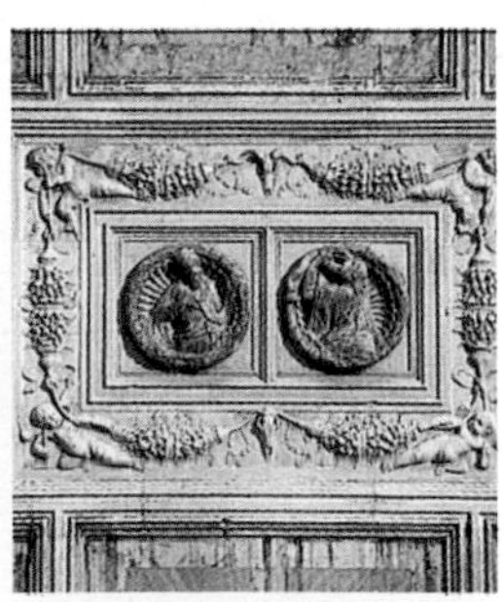

A Renaissance panel by Coducci on the facade of San Zaccaria

㉙ Scuola di San Giorgio degli Schiavoni

Calle Furlani. **Map** 8 E1. **Tel** 041 522 88 28. San Zaccaria. **Open** 9am–1pm, 2:45–6pm Tue–Sun. **Closed** Jan 1, May 1, Dec 25, and other religious hols.

Within this small gem are some of the finest paintings of Vittore Carpaccio. They were commissioned by the Schiavoni, or Dalmatian Slav community in Venice.

The Scuola was established in 1451 and rebuilt in 1551. It has changed very little since. The exquisite frieze, executed between 1502 and 1508, shows scenes from the lives of patron saints: St. George, St. Tryphone, and St. Jerome. Each episode of the narrative cycle is remarkable for its vivid coloring, minute detail, and historic record of Venetian life. Outstanding among them are *St. George Slaying the Dragon* and *St. Jerome Leading the Tamed Lion to the Monastery*.

㉚ San Giovanni in Bragora

Campo Bandiera e Moro. **Map** 8 E2. **Tel** 041 520 59 06. Arsenale. **Open** 9–11am, 3:30–5:30pm Mon–Sat, 9:30am–noon Sun.

The existing church is essentially Gothic (1475–9), and the interior contains major works of art that demonstrate the transition from Gothic to early Renaissance. Bartolomeo Vivarini's altarpiece *Madonna and Child with Saints* (1478) is unmistakably Gothic. Contrasting with this is Cima da Conegliano's *Baptism of Christ* (1492–5), on the main altar.

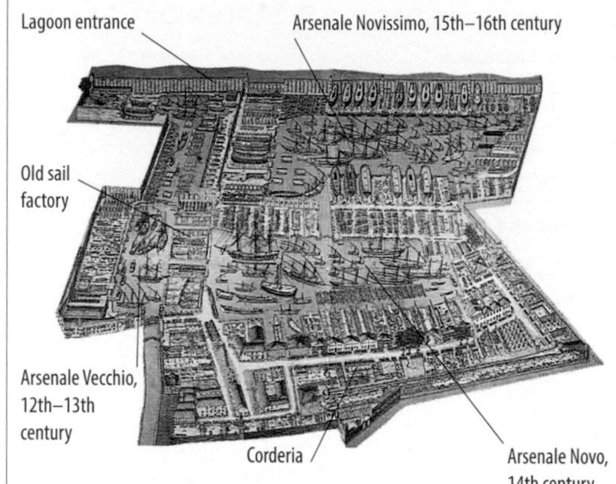

18th-century engraving of the Arsenale

㉛ Arsenale

Map 8 F1. Arsenale. Museo Storico Navale Campo San Biagio. **Map** 8 F3. **Tel** 041 244 13 99. **Open** 8:45am–1:30pm Mon–Fri; 8:45am–1pm Sat. **Closed** public hols.

The Arsenale was founded in the 12th century and by the 16th had become the greatest naval shipyard in the world, capable of constructing a whole galley in 24 hours, using an assembly-line system. Surrounded by crenellated walls, it was like a city within a city. Today the site is largely disused. Its impressive 15th-century gateway, twin towers, and guardian lions can be viewed from the *campo* or bridge outside. The gateway was built by Antonio Gambello and is often cited as Venice's first Renaissance construction.

Around the corner, in Campo San Biagio, the **Museo Storico Navale** charts Venetian naval history from the heyday of the Arsenale to the present. Exhibits include friezes from famous galleys of the past and a replica of the *Bucintoro*, the Doge's ceremonial barge.

㉜ San Giorgio Maggiore

Map 8 D4. **Tel** 041 522 78 27. San Giorgio. **Open** 9:30am–12:30pm, 2:30–5:30pm daily (to 4:30pm in winter). (Campanile). Fondazione Cini: **Tel** 041 271 04 02. **Open** 10am–4pm Sat & Sun (to 5pm Apr–Sep).

Appearing like a stage set across the water from the Piazzetta is the little island of San Giorgio Maggiore. The church and

St. George Slaying the Dragon (1502–8) by Carpaccio, in the Scuola di San Giorgio degli Schiavoni

monastery, constructed between 1559–80, are among Andrea Palladio's greatest architectural achievements. The church's temple front and the spacious interior with its perfect proportions and cool beauty are typically Palladian *(see pp84–5)*. These qualities are echoed by the church of Il Redentore on the nearby island of Giudecca, built by Palladio in 1577–92.

On the chancel walls of San Giorgio Maggiore are two fine paintings by Tintoretto: *The Last Supper* and *Gathering of the Manna* (both 1594). In the Chapel of the Dead is his last work, *The Deposition* (1592–4), finished by his son Domenico.

The top of the campanile affords superb views of the city and lagoon. You can see the monastery cloisters below, now part of the **Fondazione Cini**, a cultural center that is used to host international exhibitions.

Palladio's San Giorgio Maggiore

33 Murano

4.1 and 4.2 from Fondamente Nuove; 3 from Ferrovia and Piazzale Roma.

Much like Venice, Murano comprises a cluster of small islands, connected by bridges. It has been the center of the glassmaking industry since 1291, when the furnaces were moved here from the city because of the risk of fire and the disagreeable effects of smoke. Some of the houses on the water date from this period.

The colonnaded exterior of Murano's Basilica dei Santi Maria e Donato

Museo del Vetro

Palazzo Giustinian, Fondamenta Giustinian. **Tel** 041 73 95 86. **Open** 10am–6pm daily (Nov–Mar: to 5pm, last adm: 30 min before closing). **Closed** Jan 1, May 1, Dec 25.
visitmuve.it

In the 15th and 16th centuries Murano was the principal glass-producing center in Europe, and today most tourists visit for glass alone. The Museo del Vetro in the Palazzo Giustinian houses a collection of antique pieces. The prize exhibit is the dark blue Barovier wedding cup (1470–80), with enamel work by Angelo Barovier.

Basilica dei Santi Maria e Donato

Fondamenta Giustinian. **Tel** 041 73 90 56. **Open** 9am–noon, 3:30–7pm Mon–Sat, 3:30–7pm Sun (Nov–Mar: to 6pm daily).

With its lovely colonnaded apse, this basilica is the architectural highlight of the island. Despite major restoration, this 12th-century church still retains much of its original beauty. Note the Gothic ship's keel roof, the mosaic Madonna in the apse, and the mosaic floor dating from 1140.

Venetian glass goblet

34 Burano

12 from Fondamenta Nuove; 14 from San Zaccaria via Lido and Punta Sabbioni.

Burano is the most colorful of the lagoon islands and can be distinguished from a distance by the tilting tower of its church. In contrast with the haunting Torcello, the island is densely populated, its waterways fringed with brightly painted houses.

The main thoroughfare is Via Baldassare Galuppi, named after the Burano-born composer. It features traditional lace and linen stalls and open-air trattorias serving fresh fish.

Museo del Merletto

Piazza Baldassare Galuppi 187. **Tel** 041 73 00 34. **Open** Apr–Oct 10am–6pm Tue–Sun (Nov–Mar: to 5pm, last adm: 30 min before closing). **Closed** Jan 1, May 1, Dec 25.
visitmuve.it

The people of Burano are fishermen and lacemakers by tradition. You can still see fishermen scraping their boats or mending nets, but today lacemakers are rare. In the 16th century the local lace was the most sought-after in Europe – it was so delicate it became known as *punto in aria* ("points in the air"). After a slump in the 18th century, the industry revived, and a lace-making school was set up here in 1872. Authentic Burano lace is hard to find, but you can watch it being made at the school, now a museum, which displays fine examples of antique lace.

Brightly painted street in Burano

35 Torcello

Established between the 5th and 6th centuries, the island of Torcello boasts the oldest building in the lagoon – the cathedral of Santa Maria Assunta. Founded in AD 639, it contains some splendid ancient mosaics. The adjoining church of Santa Fosca, of pure Byzantine design, is another mark of Torcello's former glory – before it was eclipsed by Venice, the island had a population of 20,000.

★ Doomsday Mosaics
The highly decorative 12th-century mosaic of the *Last Judgment* covers the west wall.

Pulpit
The present basilica dates from 1008, but includes earlier features. The pulpit contains 7th-century fragments.

KEY

① **The exquisite Byzantine marble panels** of the iconostasis, or rood screen, are carved with peacocks, lions, and flowers.

② **The Roman sarcophagus**, below the altar, is said to contain the relics of St. Heliodorus.

③ **The 13th-century apse mosaic** of the Madonna against a gold background is one of the most beautiful in Venice.

④ **The central dome** and cross sections are supported by columns of Greek marble with Corinthian capitals.

⑤ **The Portico** of Santa Fosca, with its elegant stilted arches, is built on three sides of the church, and probably dates from the 12th century.

⑥ **The altar** was rebuilt in 1939 and stands below a 15th-century wood relief of *Santa Fosca Sleeping*.

Nave Columns
Two rows of slender marble columns, 18 in all, separate the three naves. Their finely carved capitals date from the 11th century.

For hotels and restaurants in this region see pp562–77 and pp580–605

Torcello's Last Canals
Silted canals and malaria hastened Torcello's decline. One of the remaining waterways runs from the vaporetto stop to the basilica.

VISITORS' CHECKLIST

Practical Information
Santa Maria & Campanile: **Tel** 041 241 38 17; 041 673 01 19 (Basilica). **Open** 10:30am–6pm daily (Nov–Feb: 10am–5pm). Campanile closes 30 min earlier. cathedral only. campanile only. Santa Fosca: **Open** for masses only. Museo dell'Estuario: **Tel** 041 73 07 61. **Open** 10:30am–5:30pm Tue–Sun (Nov–Feb: 10am–5pm). **Closed** public hols.

Transportation
12 from Fondamenta Nuove, then 9 from Burano

Santa Fosca
Built in the 11th and 12th centuries on a Greek cross plan, the church has a serene Byzantine interior with a central pentagonal apse.

Vaporetto boarding point →

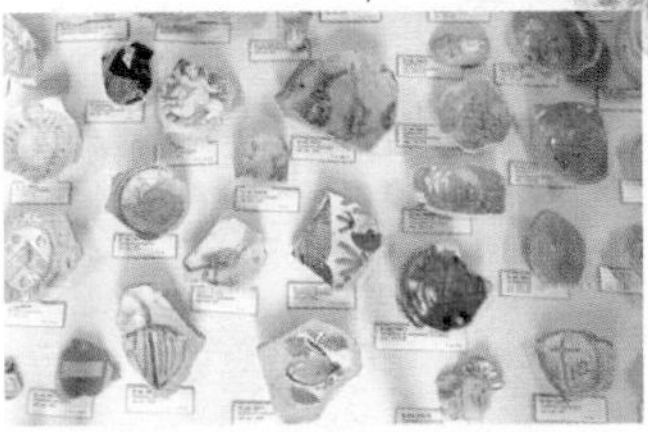

The Museo dell'Estuario houses many old church treasures.

Attila's Throne
It was said that the 5th-century king of the Huns used this marble seat as his throne.

Shopping in Venice

The attractive shop windows that line the narrow streets of Venice are an irresistible attraction for any visitor. Myriad fashion brands are available in gleaming, ultramodern stores, but the city also has a strong artisan tradition. Expert craftspeople in tiny workshops open to the public create delightful and highly original objects in glass, wood, leather, and papier-mâché. Skilled hands transform colored glass rods into playful miniature animals and exquisite flowers, while plaster molds turn out shapes destined to become ornate masks. Interior-design establishments also abound, and sleek kitchenware and fabrics make unusual purchases. Beautiful boutiques offering antique furniture and accessories are concentrated in the city center.

Where to Shop

The glittering Mercerie, which runs from Piazza San Marco to the Rialto, has been Venice's main shopping street since the Middle Ages and, along with the fashion avenue Calle Larga XXII Marzo, is still a draw for the crowds. The zigzagging Frezzeria is full of unusual shops, while across the Grand Canal, the narrow streets from the Rialto southwest toward Campo San Polo are lined with a variety of less expensive stores. The bustling Lista di Spagna, near the station, and the Strada Nova toward the Rialto cater to the everyday needs of the locals.

The islands of Murano and Burano are the places to buy traditional glass and lace.

Food and Markets

One of the delights of Venice is exploring the city's food markets and shops. Fruit and vegetable stalls sprawl to the west of the Rialto Bridge and along the Grand Canal. The Pescheria, or fish market, occupies the farthest section. The neighboring streets are full of gourmet food shops. Wine, olive oil, vinegar, and grappa in decorative bottles, as well as dried pasta in many shapes, colors, and flavors are all good purchases.

Aliani's cheese shop offers a mouthwatering selection of picnic fare, while **Drogheria Mascari** has a fine range of dried fruit, coffee, and alcohol. **Rizzo**, on the other side of the bridge, is a master pasta-maker.

Glass

The island of Murano is a good place to watch expert glass-blowing. However, for contemporary glass creations head back to Venice, around San Marco – try **Venini**'s showroom for stunning platters and huge vases, and **L'Isola** for Carlo Moretti's tumblers in rich colors.

The art of bead-making is alive and flourishing thanks to sisters **Marina e Susanna Sent**'s simple, irresistible necklaces. At **Perle e Dintorni**, customers can sort through an astonishing range of beautiful glass beads and create their own costume jewelry.

Clothing and Accessories

Promod, near San Marco, has reasonably priced fun gear for the young set. Nearby is **Benetton**'s megastore, with its trademark bright clothes, while, opposite, **Max Mara** has super-lative womenswear. Other leading names in fashion – **Armani**, **Roberto Cavalli**, **Missoni**, and **Gucci** – also have stylish shops around Piazza San Marco.

Just off San Lio, **Giovanna Zanella** can be found at her cobbler's bench crafting zany shoes and sandals. Her amazing range even includes gondola decorations.

Masks and Costumes

Mass-produced Carnival masks can be found all over the city, but a genuine one makes for a wonderful souvenir. With its striking designs, **Papier Mâché** has revived traditional mask-making. Near Campo San Polo, **Tragicomica** sells masks and costumes, as well as Commedia dell'Arte figures. You will also find these at **Leon d'Oro**, where they make string puppets too. **Ca' Macana** has a great collection of eye-catching masks. You can even participate in a mask-making workshop. Down a winding street in Cannaregio, the husband-and-wife team at **Il Pirata** make papier-mâché masks in their store. Courses are available in the decoration and history of Venetian masks.

Jewelry

Nardi, located in the arcades of Piazza San Marco, crafts an exquisite brooch with a Moor's head, among other things. A short distance away are the sparkling premises of **Bulgari**, while **Cartier**, with its beautiful collection of watches, can be found along the nearby Mercerie. Shops on the Rialto Bridge sell cheaper designs; this is a good place to find bracelets and chains, the prices of which are determined by the weight of the gold. Over the bridge, under the arcades of the ancient goldsmiths' district, is **Attombri** – two brothers who design unusual jewelry from antique Murano glass beads.

Fabric and Interior Design

Venice is famed for fine silks and velvets and sumptuous brocades, many of which are still sold at **Trois**, close to the Gritti Palace hotel. On the Grand Canal, at Sant'Angelo, **Rubelli** is fabric heaven, with a wide range of designs and rich upholstery. More down-to-earth but good-quality household linen and brilliantly colored bath accessories are sold at **TSL**, which has several stores around town.

For original kitchen items, the choice at **Epicentro** is hard to beat; or head to **Marchiol**, hidden away on a Castello backstreet, for modern light fittings and lamps.

Books and Gifts

At the Giardinetti Reali, on the San Marco waterfront, the **Venice Pavilion Bookshop** annex of the Tourist Board has an exhaustive collection of books dealing with many aspects of the city. The **Libreria Marco Polo** bookstore offers a decent English-language section, while **Mare di Carta** offers nautical books and magazines.

Alberto Valese-Ebru uses a distinctive marbling technique on fabric as well as paper. Nearby, **Paolo Olbi** has a wide range of papers and artistic books for sale. On the opposite side of the Grand Canal, at San Tomà, **Daniela Porto** has lovely old printed maps and frames, perfect as gifts, and **Signor Blum** on Campo San Barnaba has charming hand-made carved and painted wooden objects and toys.

DIRECTORY

Food and Markets

Aliani (Casa del Parmigiano)
Erberia Rialto, San Polo 214/8.
Map 3 A5.
Tel 041 520 6525.

Drogheria Mascari
Calle dei Spezieri, San Polo 381.
Map 3 A5.
Tel 041 522 9762.

Rizzo
Salizzada S. Giovanni Grisostomo, Cannaregio 5778.
Map 3 B5.
Tel 041 522 2824.

Glass

L'Isola – Carlo Moretti
Campo San Moisè, San Marco 1468.
Map 7 A3.
Tel 041 523 1973.

Marina e Susanna Sent
Campo S. Vio, Dorsoduro 669.
Map 6 F4.
Tel 041 520 81 36.

Perle e Dintorni
Calle della Mandorla, San Marco 3740.
Map 7 A2.
Tel 041 346 588 1618.

Venini
Piazzetta dei Leoncini, San Marco 314.
Map 7 B2.
Tel 041 522 4045.

Clothing and Accessories

Armani
Calle Goldoni, San Marco 4412.
Map 7 A2.
Tel 041 523 4758.

Benetton
Marzaria (Merceria) Due Aprile, San Marco 5051.
Map 7 B2.
Tel 041 296 0493.

Giovanna Zanella
Calle Carminati, Castello 5641. **Map** 7 B1.
Tel 041 523 5500.

Gucci
Calle Larga XXII Marzo, San Marco 2102.
Map 7 A3.
Tel 041 241 3968.

Max Mara
Campo San Salvador, San Marco 5033.
Map 7 A1.
Tel 041 522 6688.

Missoni
Calle Vallaresso, San Marco 1312. **Map** 7 B3.
Tel 041 520 5733.

Promod
Campo S. Bartolomeo, San Marco 5377.
Map 7 B1.
Tel 041 241 0668.

Roberto Cavalli
Calle Vallaresso, San Marco 1314.
Map 7 B3.
Tel 041 520 5733.

Masks and Costumes

Ca' Macana
Calle delle Botteghe, Dorsoduro 3172.
Map 6 D3.
Tel 041 520 32 29.

Leon d'Oro
Calle Frezzeria, San Marco 1770. **Map** 7 A2.
Tel 041 520 3375.

Il Pirata
Salizzada San Canciano, Cannaregio 5559.
Map 3 B5.
Tel 041 520 6529.

Papier Mâché
Calle Lunga Santa Maria Formosa, Castello 5175.
Map 7 C1.
Tel 041 522 9995.

Tragicomica
Calle dei Nomboli, San Polo 2800. **Map** 6 F1.
Tel 041 721 102.

Jewelry

Attombri
Sottoportego degli Orefici, San Polo 65.
Map 3 A5.
Tel 041 521 2524.

Bulgari
Calle Larga XXII Marzo, San Marco 2282.
Map 7 A3.
Tel 041 241 0553.

Cartier
Mercerie San Zulian, San Marco 606.
Map 7 B2.
Tel 041 522 2071.

Nardi
Procuratie Nuove, Piazza San Marco, San Marco 69/71.
Map 7 B2.
Tel 041 522 5733.

Fabric and Interior Design

Epicentro
Calle Frezzeria, San Marco 1728/A.
Map 7 B2.
Tel 041 523 34 92.

Marchiol
Ruga Giuffa, Castello 4920. **Map** 7 C1.
Tel 041 522 5131.

Rubelli
Campiello del Teatro, San Marco 3877.
Map 6 F2.
Tel 041 523 6110.

Trois
Campo San Maurizio, San Marco 2666.
Map 6 F3.
Tel 041 522 2905.

TSL Tessile San Leonardo
Rio Terrà San Leonardo, Cannaregio 1318.
Map 2 D3.
Tel 041 718 524.

Books and Gifts

Alberto Valese-Ebru
Campiello Santo Stefano, San Marco 3471.
Map 6 F3.
Tel 041 523 8830.

Daniela Porto
Rio Terrà dei Nomboli, San Polo 2753.
Map 6 E1.
Tel 041 523 1368.

Libreria Marco Polo
Calle del Teatro Malibran, Cannaregio 5886/a.
Map 3 B5.
Tel 041 522 63 43.

Mare di Carta
Fondamenta dei Tolentini, Santa Croce 222.
Map 5 C1.
Tel 041 716 304.

Paolo Olbi
Calle della Mandola, San Marco 3653.
Map 6 F2.
Tel 041 528 5025.

Signor Blum
Campo San Barnaba, Dorsoduro 2840.
Map 6 D3.
Tel 041 522 6367.

Venice Pavilion Bookshop
Palazzetto Selva, Giardinetti Reali, San Marco 2.
Map 7 B3.
Tel 041 522 5150.

VENICE STREET FINDER

All the map references given for sights, hotels, and restaurants in Venice refer to this section of the book. The key map below shows which areas of the city are covered by the Street Finder. The first figure of the map reference indicates which map to turn to, and the letter and number that follow are for the grid reference. Standard Italian spelling has been used on all the maps in this book, but when exploring Venice you will find that the names on many street signs are written in Venetian dialect. Mostly this means only a slight variation in spelling (as in the word Sottoportico/Sotoportego below), but some names look totally different. For example, the church of Santi Giovanni e Paolo *(see map 3)*, is frequently signposted as "San Zanipolo." A further map showing the vaporetto routes follows the street maps.

Recognizing Street Names

The signs for street *(calle)*, canal *(rio)*, and square *(campo)* will soon become familiar, but the Venetians have a colorful vocabulary for the maze of alleys that makes up the city. When exploring, the following may help.

FONDAMENTA S.SEVERO

Fondamenta is a street that runs alongside a canal, often named after the canal it follows.

RIO TERRA GESUATI

Rio Terrà is a filled-in canal. Similar to a *rio terrà* is a *piscina*, which often forms a square.

SOTOPORTEGO E PONTE S.CRISTOFORO

Sottoportico or Sotoportego means a covered passageway.

SALIZADA PIO X

Salizzada is a main street (formerly a paved street).

RIVA DEI PARTIGIANI

Riva is a wide *fondamenta,* often facing the lagoon.

RUGAGIUFFA

Ruga is a street lined with shops.

CORTE DEI DO POZZI

Corte means a courtyard.

RIO MENUO O DE LA VERONA

Many streets and canals in Venice have more than one name: *o* means "or."

0 meters 500
0 yards 500

Key to Street Finder

- Major sight
- Place of interest
- Train station
- Vaparetto boarding point
- Traghetto crossing
- Gondola mooring
- Bus terminus
- Tourist information
- Hospital with emergency room
- Police station
- Church
- Synagogue
- Train line

Scale of map pages

0 meters 150

0 yards 150

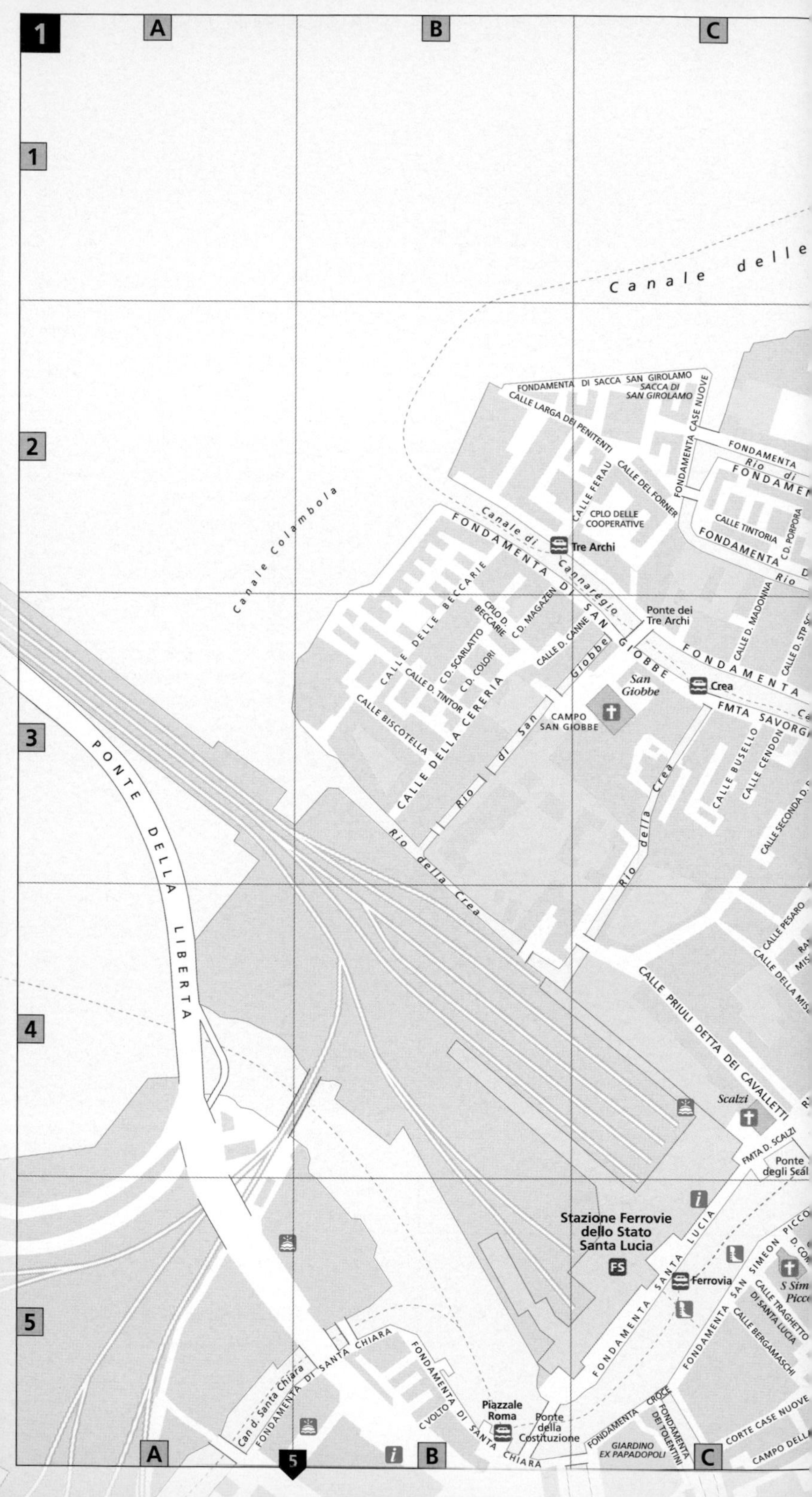
1
A
B
C
Canale delle
Canale Colambola
FONDAMENTA DI SACCA SAN GIROLAMO
SACCA DI SAN GIROLAMO
CALLE LARGA DEI PENITENTI
FONDAMENTA CASE NUOVE
CALLE FERAU
CALLE DEL FORNER
CPLO DELLE COOPERATIVE
CALLE TINTORIA
C.D. PORPORA
Canale di Cannaregio
Tre Archi
FONDAMENTA DI SAN GIOBBE
CALLE DELLE BECCARIE
CPLO D. BECCARIE
C.D. MAGAZEN
CALLE D. CANNE
C.D. SCARLATTO
C.D. COLORI
CALLE D. TINTOR
CALLE BISCOTELLA
CALLE DELLA CERERIA
Ponte dei Tre Archi
CALLE D. MADONNA
San Giobbe
CAMPO SAN GIOBBE
Crea
FMTA SAVORGNAN
Rio di San Giobbe
Rio della Crea
CALLE BUSELLO
CALLE CENDON
PONTE DELLA LIBERTA
CALLE PESARO
CALLE DELLA MISERICORDIA
CALLE PRIULI DETTA DEI CAVALLETTI
Scalzi
FMTA D. SCALZI
Ponte degli Scalzi
Stazione Ferrovie dello Stato Santa Lucia
FS
FONDAMENTA SANTA LUCIA
Ferrovia
FONDAMENTA SAN SIMEON PICCOLO
CALLE TRAGHETTO DI SANTA LUCIA
CALLE BERGAMASCHI
Can d. Santa Chiara
FONDAMENTA DI SANTA CHIARA
C VOLTO
Piazzale Roma
Ponte della Costituzione
FONDAMENTA CROCE
FONDAMENTA DEI TOLENTINI
GIARDINO EX PAPADOPOLI
CORTE CASE NUOVE
CAMPO DELLE
2
3
4
5
5

D
E
F
2
1
2
3
4
5
3
3
6
Sacche
Sant'Alvise
Orto
CANNAREGIO
SANTA CROCE
Canal Grande
Sant' Alvise
Palazzo Michiel
Madonna dell'Orto
Palazzo Mastelli
Casa del Tintoretto
Museo Ebraico
Sinagoga
Guglie
Ponte delle Guglie
Palazzo Làbia
San Geremia
San Marcuola
Palazzo Vendramin Calergi
Palazzo Belloni Battagia
Fóndaco dei Turchi
Riva di Biasio
Palazzo Donà Balbi
San Zan Degolà
San Stae
Ca' Pésaro
Ca' Corner della Regina
Ca' Mocenigo
Sta Maria Mater Domini
San Giácomo dell'Orio
S Simeone Grande
San Cassiano
San Marziale
Parco Groggia
Fondamenta dei Riformati
Fondamenta della Sensa
Fondamenta degli Ormesini
Fondamenta della Misericordia
Fondamenta Madonna dell'Orto
Rio Terra San Leonardo
Rio Terra Farsetti
Via Vittorio Emanuele
Strada Nova
Campo San Leonardo
Campo Ghetto Nuovo
Campo San Geremia
Campo San Marcuola
Campo San Stae
Campo San Cassiano
Campo Nazario Sauro
Corte Barbaro
Campiello Piave
Campo dei Mori

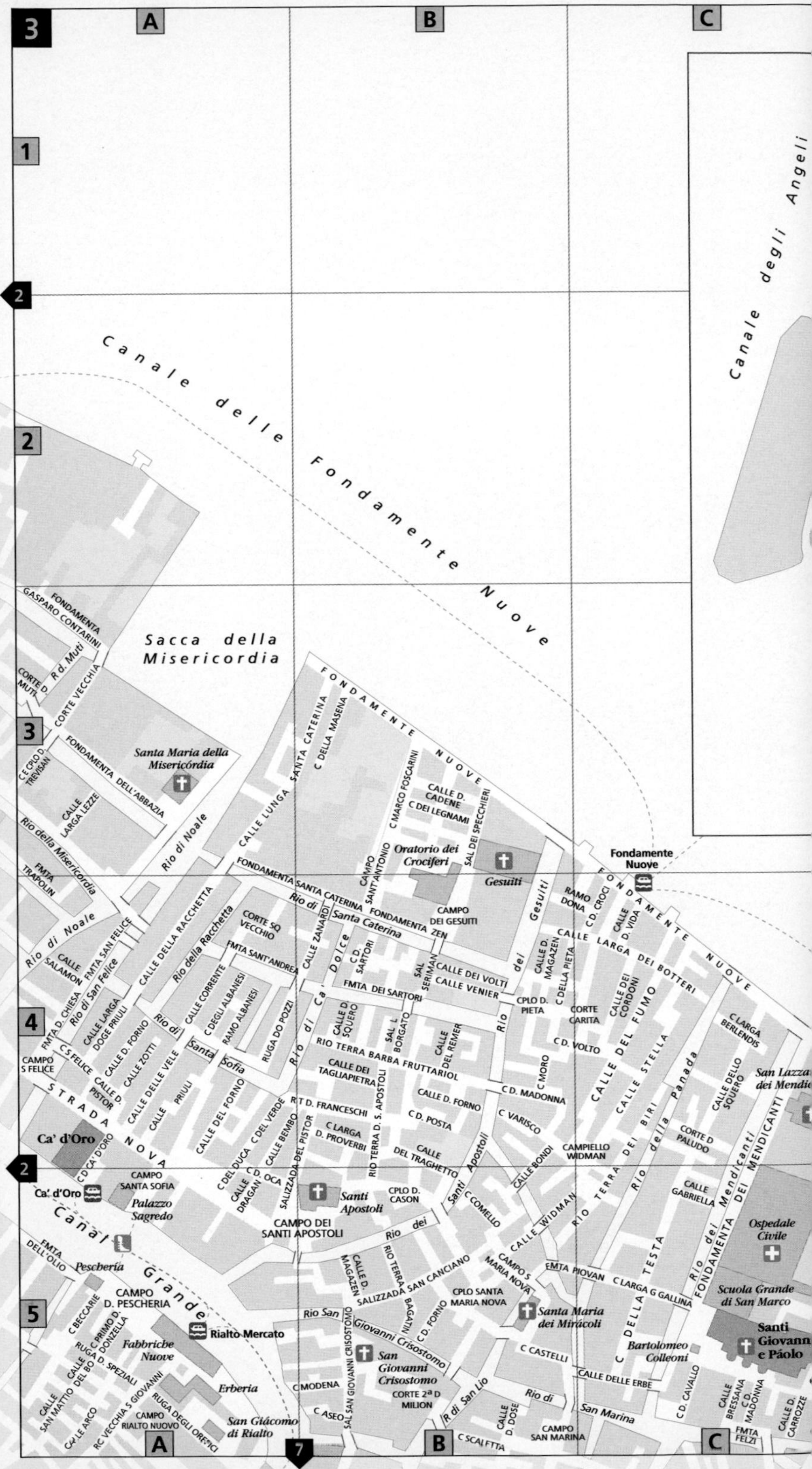

3
A
B
C
1
2
3
4
5
2
7
Canale delle Fondamente Nuove
Canale degli Angeli
Sacca della Misericordia
Santa Maria della Misericórdia
Oratorio dei Crociferi
Gesuiti
Fondamente Nuove
FONDAMENTE NUOVE
Ca' d'Oro
Palazzo Sagredo
Santi Apostoli
CAMPO DEI SANTI APOSTOLI
Canal Grande
Pescheria
CAMPO D. PESCHERIA
Rialto Mercato
Fabbriche Nuove
Erberia
San Giácomo di Rialto
CAMPO RIALTO NUOVO
San Giovanni Crisostomo
Santa Maria dei Miràcoli
Bartolomeo Colleoni
Scuola Grande di San Marco
Santi Giovanni e Páolo
Ospedale Civile
San Lazzaro dei Mendicanti
STRADA NOVA
CAMPO SANTA SOFIA
CAMPO S FELICE
Rio della Misericordia
Rio di Noale
Rio della Racchetta
Rio di San Felice
Rio di Santa Sofia
Rio di Santa Caterina
Rio di Ca' Dolce
Rio dei Gesuiti
Rio dei Santi Apostoli
Rio San Giovanni Crisostomo
Rio di San Lio
Rio di San Marina
Rio della Panada
Rio dei Mendicanti
FONDAMENTA DEI MENDICANTI
FONDAMENTA SANTA CATERINA
FONDAMENTA ZEN
FONDAMENTA DELL'ABBAZIA
FONDAMENTA GASPARO CONTARINI
CALLE LUNGA SANTA CATERINA
CALLE DELLA RACCHETTA
CALLE LARGA DEI BOTTERI
CALLE DEL FUMO
CALLE STELLA
RIO TERRA BARBA FRUTTARIOL
RIO TERRA DEI BIRI
SALIZZADA SAN CANCIANO
SALIZZADA DEL PISTOR
CAMPO DEI GESUITI
CAMPIELLO WIDMAN
CORTE CARITA
CALLE DELLE ERBE
CAMPO SAN MARINA

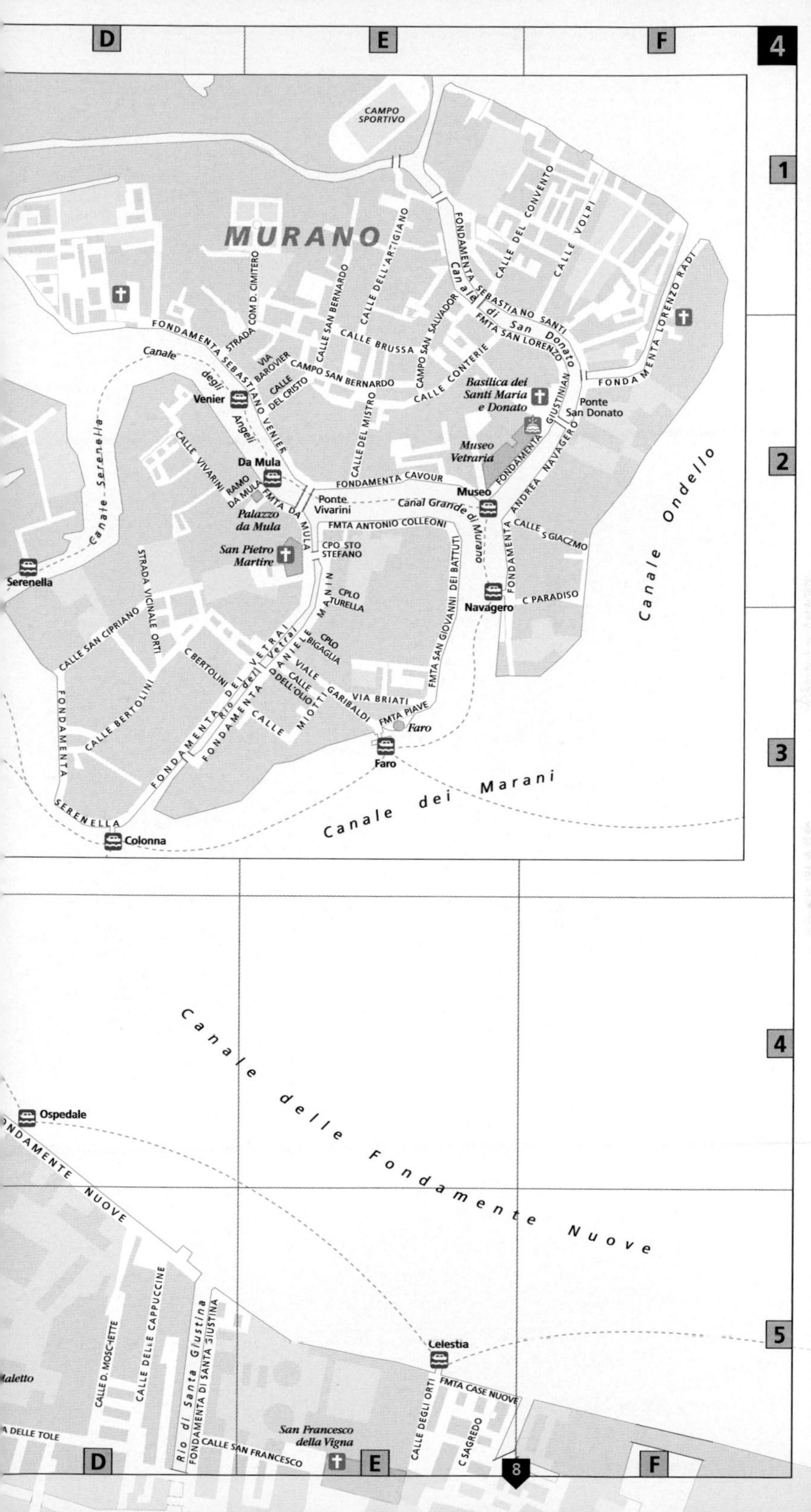

D
E
F
4
1
2
3
4
5
MURANO
CAMPO SPORTIVO
Canale di San Donato
Canal Grande di Murano
Canale degli Angeli
Canale Serenella
Canale Ondello
Canale dei Marani
Canale delle Fondamente Nuove
Basilica dei Santi Maria e Donato
Museo Vetraria
Palazzo da Mula
San Pietro Martire
Ponte Vivarini
Ponte San Donato
Faro
Venier
Da Mula
Museo
Navagero
Serenella
Colonna
Ospedale
Celestia
FONDAMENTA SEBASTIANO VENIER
FONDAMENTA SEBASTIANO SANTI
FMTA SAN LORENZO
FONDAMENTA LORENZO RADI
FONDAMENTA GIUSTINIAN
FONDAMENTA ANDREA NAVAGERO
FONDAMENTA CAVOUR
FMTA ANTONIO COLLEONI
FMTA DA MULA
FONDAMENTA DEI VETRAI
FONDAMENTA DANIELE MANIN
FMTA SAN GIOVANNI DEI BATTUTI
FMTA PIAVE
FONDAMENTA SERENELLA
CALLE DEL CONVENTO
CALLE VOLPI
STRADA COM D. CIMITERO
CALLE DELL'ARTIGIANO
CALLE SAN BERNARDO
CALLE BRUSSA
CAMPO SAN SALVADOR
CALLE CONTERIE
CAMPO SAN BERNARDO
VIA BAROVIER
CALLE DEL CRISTO
CALLE DEL MISTRO
CALLE VIVARINI
RAMO DA MULA
CPO STO STEFANO
CPLO TURELLA
CPLO BIGAGLIA
CALLE S GIACZMO
C PARADISO
STRADA VICINALE ORTI
CALLE SAN CIPRIANO
C BERTOLINI
CALLE BERTOLINI
VIALE GARIBALDI
CALLE DELL'OLIO
CALLE MIOTTI
VIA BRIATI
Rio dei Vetrai
FONDAMENTE NUOVE
CALLE D. MOSCHETTE
CALLE DELLE CAPPUCCINE
Rio di Santa Giustina
FONDAMENTA DI SANTA GIUSTINA
CALLE SAN FRANCESCO
San Francesco della Vigna
CALLE DEGLI ORTI
FMTA CASE NUOVE
C SAGREDO
DELLE TOLE
8

5
A
B
C
1
2
3
4
5
SANTA CROCE
DORSO
GIUDECCA
Piazzale Roma
PIAZZALE ROMA
CAMPO SANT'ANDREA
GIARDINO EX PAPADOPOLI
San Nicolò da Tolentino
Canale Scomenzera
Canale di Santa Chiara
Canale di Santa Maria Maggiore
FONDAMENTA SANT'ANDREA
RIO TERRA DEI PENSIERI
Rio della Cazziola
Rio Nuovo
Rio del Malcanton
Rio del Tintor
Rio Briati
Rio dei Carmini
Rio dell'Arziere
Rio delle Terese
Rio di San Nicolò
Rio dell'Angelo Raffaele
Rio di San Sebastiano
Rio dell'Avogaria
Santa Maria dei Carmini
Collegio Armeno
San Nicolò dei Mendicoli
Angelo Raffaele
San Sebastiano
Stazione Marittima
BANCHINA DEL PORTO COMMERCIALE
BANCHINA DI SAN BASEGIO
FMTA ZATTERE PONTE
San Basilio
Canale di Fusina
Sacca Fisola
FONDAMENTA BEATA GIULIANA
CALLE DELLA SACCA
CALLE LARGA DEI LAVRANERI
Canale dei Lavraneri
Hilton Mulino Stucky
Rio di San Biagio
Rio delle Convertite
CAMPO DELLA CHIESA
CAMPIELLO PRIULI
FMTA SAN GERARDO SAGREDO
Can Sacca Fisola
San Biagio

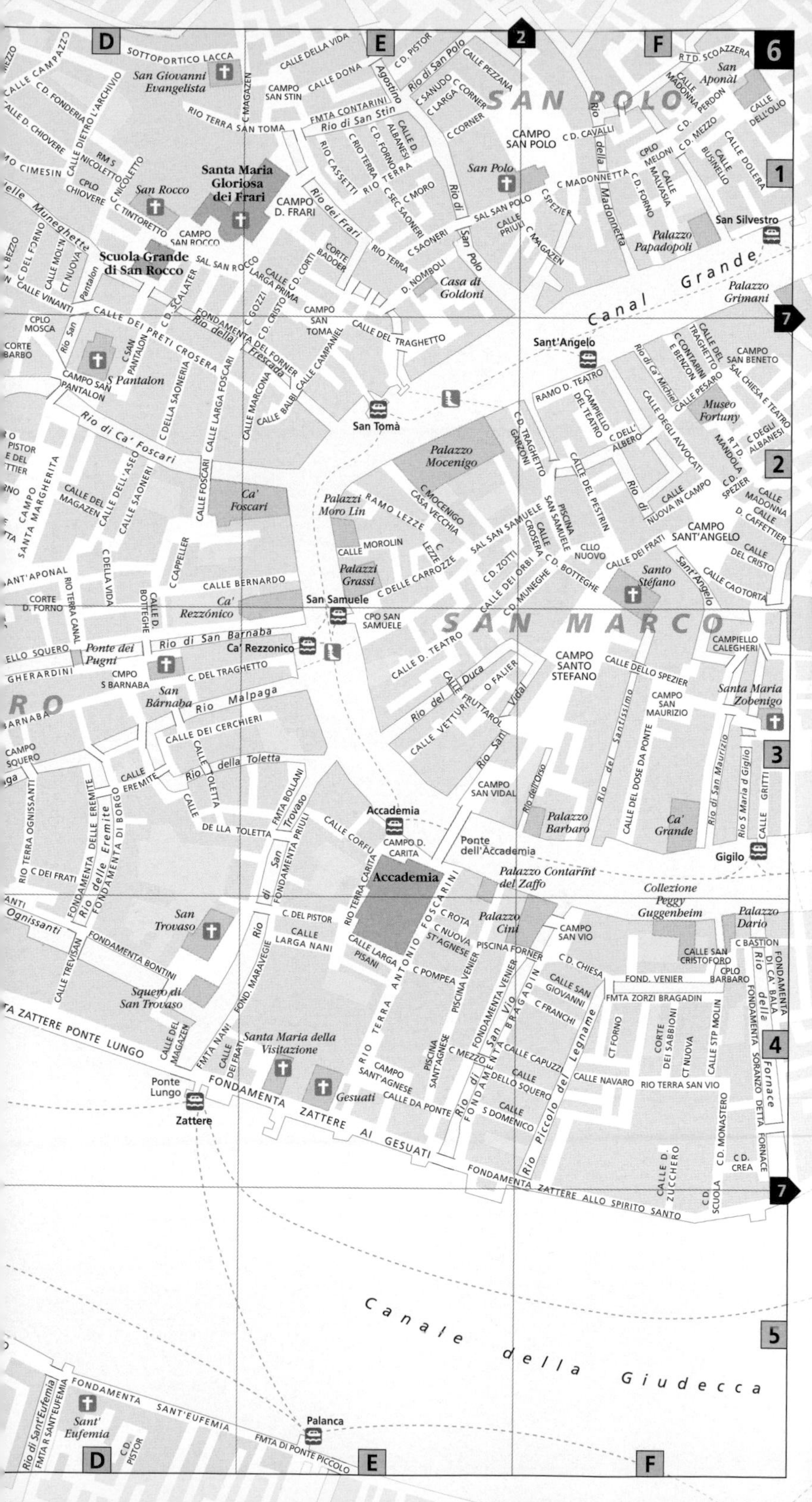

D
E
F
2
6
1
2
3
4
5
7
SAN POLO
SAN MARCO
Canal Grande
Canale della Giudecca
San Giovanni Evangelista
Santa Maria Gloriosa dei Frari
San Rocco
Scuola Grande di San Rocco
Campo San Polo
San Polo
San Aponal
San Silvestro
Palazzo Papadopoli
Palazzo Grimani
Casa di Goldoni
Campo San Tomà
San Tomà
Sant'Angelo
Museo Fortuny
Palazzo Mocenigo
S Pantalon
Ca' Foscari
Palazzi Moro Lin
Palazzi Grassi
Campo Sant'Angelo
Santo Stéfano
Ca' Rezzónico
San Samuele
Ca' Rezzonico
Ponte dei Pugni
San Bárnaba
Campo Santo Stefano
Santa Maria Zobenigo
Campo San Vidal
Accademia
Ponte dell'Accademia
Palazzo Barbaro
Ca' Grande
Gigilo
Palazzo Contarini del Zaffo
Collezione Peggy Guggenheim
Palazzo Dario
Palazzo Cini
San Trovaso
Squero di San Trovaso
Santa Maria della Visitazione
Gesuati
Ponte Lungo
Zattere
Fondamenta Zattere ai Gesuati
Fondamenta Zattere allo Spirito Santo
Sant' Eufemia
Fondamenta Sant'Eufemia
Palanca

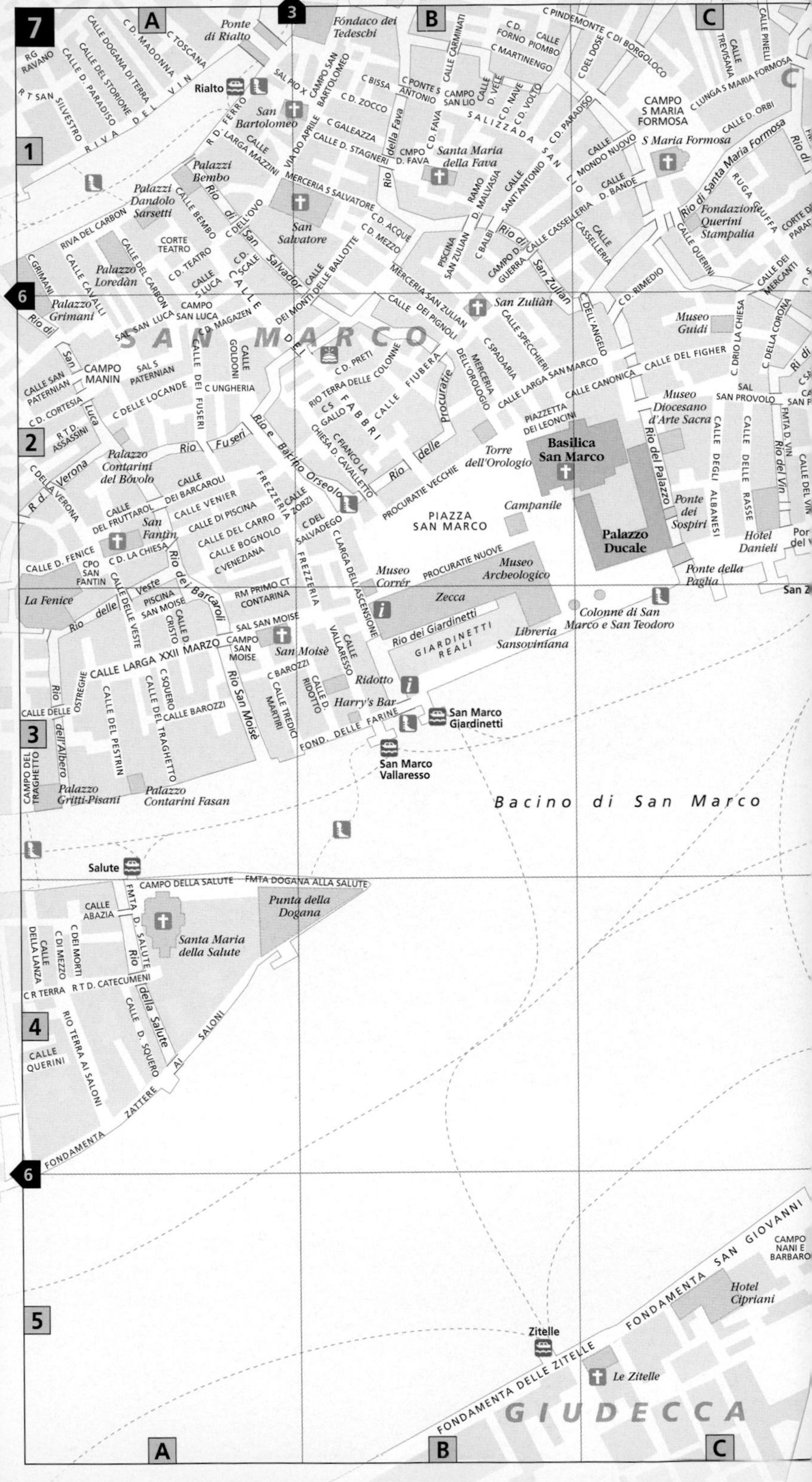
7
A
B
C
1
2
3
4
5
Ponte di Rialto
Fóndaco dei Tedeschi
Rialto
San Bartolomeo
Santa Maria della Fava
S Maria Formosa
Fondazione Querini Stampalia
Palazzi Bembo
Palazzi Dandolo Sarsetti
San Salvatore
Palazzo Loredàn
Palazzo Grimani
San Zulian
Museo Guidi
SAN MARCO
CAMPO MANIN
Museo Diocesano d'Arte Sacra
Palazzo Contarini del Bòvolo
Torre dell'Orologio
Basilica San Marco
Campanile
PIAZZA SAN MARCO
Palazzo Ducale
Ponte dei Sospiri
Hotel Danieli
San Fantin
La Fenice
Museo Corrér
Museo Archeologico
Ponte della Paglia
Zecca
Colonne di San Marco e San Teodoro
Libreria Sansoviniana
San Moisè
Ridotto
Harry's Bar
San Marco Giardinetti
San Marco Vallaresso
Palazzo Gritti-Pisani
Palazzo Contarini Fasan
Bacino di San Marco
Salute
Punta della Dogana
Santa Maria della Salute
Hotel Cipriani
Zitelle
Le Zitelle
GIUDECCA

8
D
E
F
4
1
2
3
4
5
ARSENALE
SAN GIORGIO MAGGIORE
Canale di San Marco
Arsenale
San Francesco della Vigna
San Lorenzo
Scuola di S Giorgio d. Schiavoni
San Giorgio dei Greci
La Pietà
San Giovanni in Brágora
San Martino
Museo Stórico Navale
Dársena Grande
Arsenale Vecchio
Canale delle Galeazze
San Giorgio Maggiore
Teatro Verde
RIVA DEGLI SCHIAVONI
RIVA CA' DI DIO
RIVA SAN BIAGIO
RIVA DEI SETTE MARTIRI
VIA GIUSEPPE GARIBALDI
CAMPO DELLA TANA
CAMPO BANDIERA E MORO
CAMPO ARSENALE
CAMPO SAN BIAGIO
CAMPO SAN GIORGIO
CAMPO SAN LORENZO
CAMPO DELLA CONFRATERNITA
Rio di San Francesco
Rio della Celestia
Rio di Santa Ternita
Rio delle Gorne
Rio di San Martino
Rio Ca' di Dio
Rio dell'Arsenale
Rio della Tana
Rio della Pietà
Rio dei Greci
Rio di San Lorenzo
CALLE DEL LION
CALLE DEI FURLANI
SALIZZADA SANT'ANTONIN
CALLE DIETRO LA PIETA
CORTE NUOVA
della Grazia

Aer
Mar

Venice Vaporetto Routes

The ACTV network runs regular scheduled routes around the city and out to most of the islands. Some routes are circular; others are extended during the peak season. There are also additional lines during the summer months. More details of the different types of *vaporetti* and how to use them are given on pages 634–5.

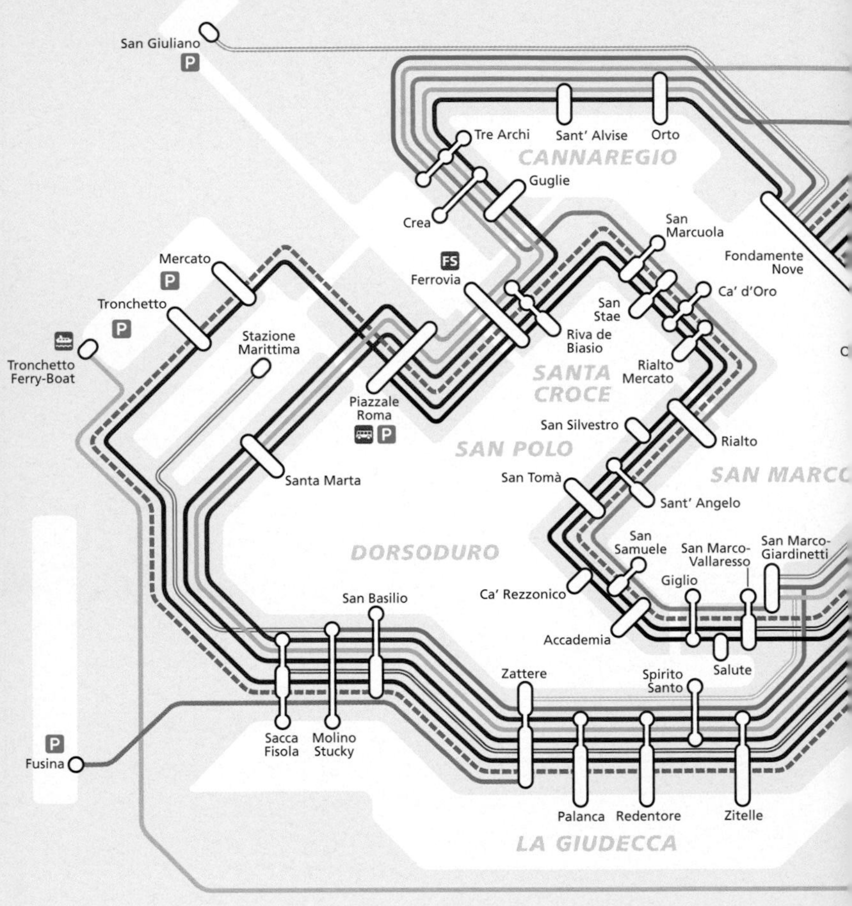

Key

Airport	City center route 1	City center route 5.2 (clockwise)
Train station	City center route 2 (part seasonal)	City center route 6
Car ferry	City center route 3	City center route 7 (seasonal)
Car parking lot	City center route 4.1 (counterclockwise)	City center route 8 (seasonal)
Main bus terminal	City center route 4.2 (clockwise)	City center route 10 (part season
Waterbus stop	City center route 5.1 (counterclockwise)	Night service N

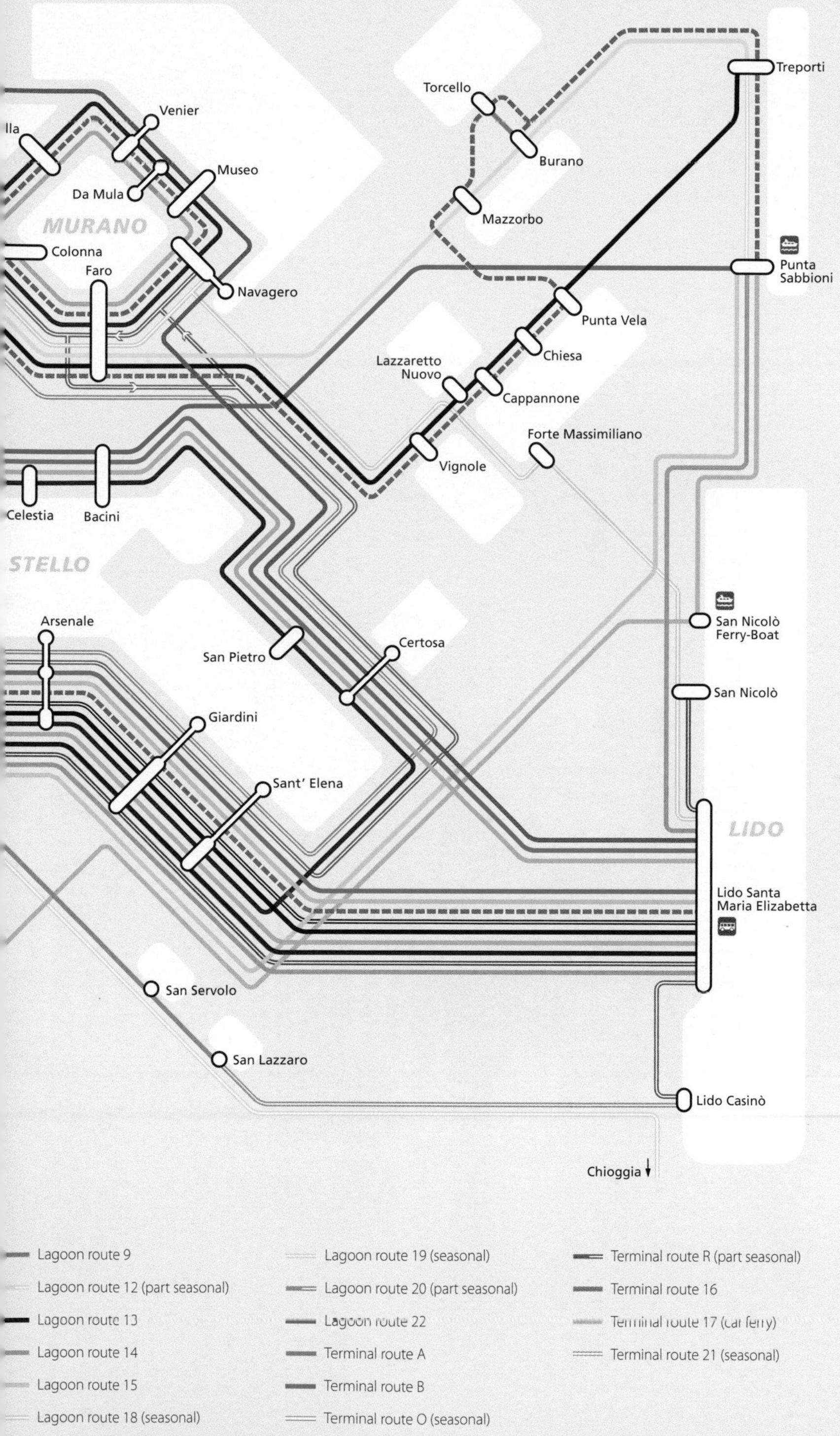

Lagoon route 9
Lagoon route 12 (part seasonal)
Lagoon route 13
Lagoon route 14
Lagoon route 15
Lagoon route 18 (seasonal)
Lagoon route 19 (seasonal)
Lagoon route 20 (part seasonal)
Lagoon route 22
Terminal route A
Terminal route B
Terminal route O (seasonal)
Terminal route R (part seasonal)
Terminal route 16
Terminal route 17 (car ferry)
Terminal route 21 (seasonal)

THE VENETO AND FRIULI

The Veneto is a region of tremendous contrasts, encompassing the breathtaking natural beauty of the Dolomites, Lake Garda (Italy's largest lake), and the rolling Euganean Hills, and the man-made delights of magnificent ancient cities such as Verona, Vicenza, and Padua. Neighboring Friuli–Venezia Giulia lines the border with Slovenia to the east, taking in the Carnic Hills in the north, the Roman town of Aquileia, and the bustling Adriatic port of Trieste.

The Romans built frontier posts on this fertile land of silt deposits, and these survive today as the cities of Vicenza, Padua, Verona, and Treviso. Strategically placed at the hub of the empire's road network, the cities prospered under Roman rule, but suffered in the wave of Germanic invasions of the 5th century AD.

The region's fortunes revived under the benign rule of the Venetian empire. The medieval cities of the Veneto lay on important trade routes such as the Serenissima, the road connecting the flourishing port cities of Venice and Genoa, and the Brenner Pass, used by commercial travelers crossing the Alps from northern Europe. Wealth from agriculture, commerce, and the spoils of war paid for the beautification of these cities through the building of Renaissance palaces and public buildings, many designed by the Veneto's great architect, Andrea Palladio. His palazzi and villas are telling symbols of the leisured existence once enjoyed by the area's aristocrats.

Today the Veneto is a thriving wine exporter, textile producer, and agricultural center, and Friuli is a focus for new technology, while remaining largely agricultural. Both regions are popular tourist destinations, despite lying a little in the shadow of Venice, and boast an abundant and enchanting variety of attractions.

A leisurely *passeggiata* in one of Verona's ancient streets

◀ The Renaissance Alpini Bridge by Palladio at Bassano del Grappa in the Veneto

Exploring the Veneto and Friuli

The flat landscape of the Veneto plain is dramatically offset by the spectacular Dolomite mountains, which form the northwestern border of the Veneto. Friuli, Italy's most northeasterly region, lies tucked up against Austria to the north and Slovenia to the east. Both the Veneto and Friuli are bordered to the south by the Adriatic, with its beaches and ports, which provide a contrast with the area's gently rolling countryside, the vast stretch of Lake Garda, and the many attractive resorts and ancient towns.

View of Verona from the Teatro Romano

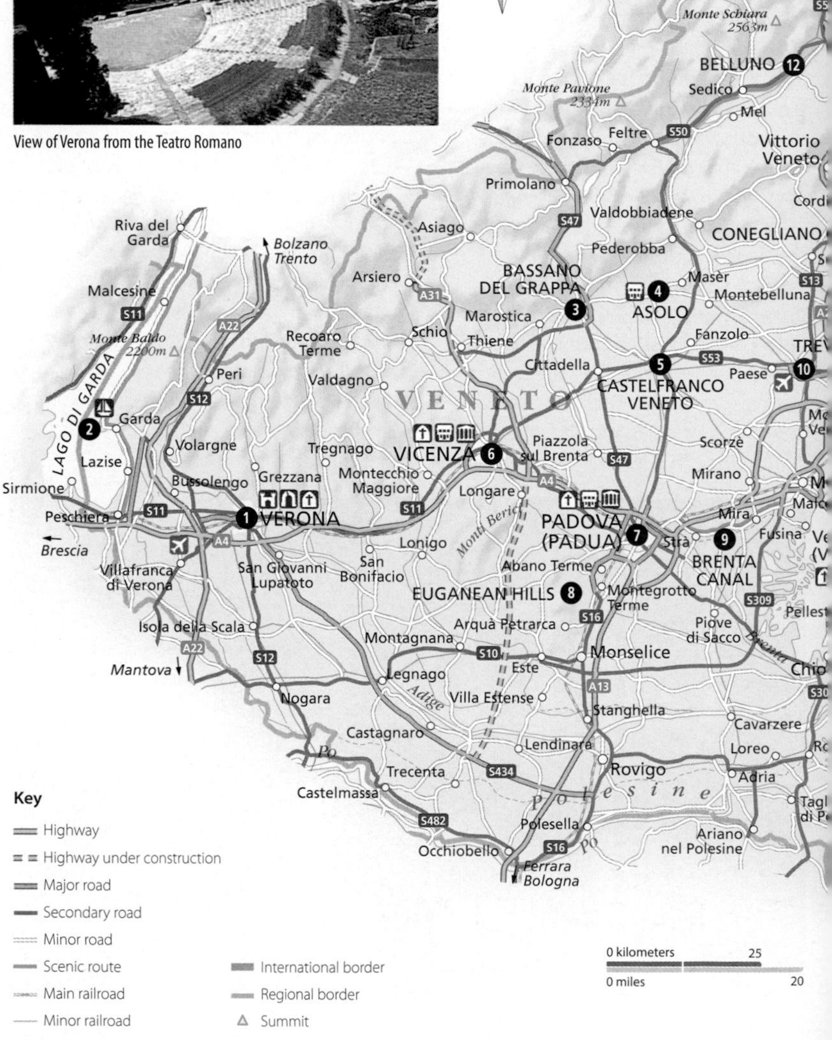

Key

- Highway
- Highway under construction
- Major road
- Secondary road
- Minor road
- Scenic route
- Main railroad
- Minor railroad
- International border
- Regional border
- Summit

0 kilometers 25

0 miles 20

For additional map symbols *see back flap*

Getting Around

An extensive railroad network and good bus services make this region easy to explore by public transportation, though only buses operate around Lake Garda. Highways and main roads provide good links between the main cities. The Venice Simplon-Orient-Express train, which operates from London to Venice, offers a novel approach to the area.

The bridge at Cividale del Friuli

Sights at a Glance

1. *Verona pp146–51*
2. Lago di Garda
3. Bassano del Grappa
4. Asolo
5. Castelfranco Veneto
6. *Vicenza pp154–7*
7. *Padua (Padova) pp158–61*
8. Euganean Hills
9. Brenta Canal
10. Treviso
11. Conegliano
12. Belluno
13. Cortina d'Ampezzo
14. Tolmezzo
15. Pordenone
16. Udine
17. Cividale del Friuli
18. Gorizia
19. Aquileia
20. Trieste

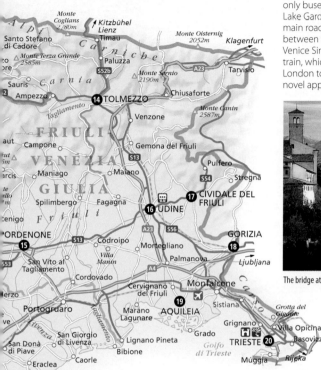

Venice pp88–141

A mountain chalet in Cortina d'Ampezzo

❶ Verona

Verona is a vibrant trading center, the second biggest city in the Veneto region (after Venice), and one of the most prosperous in northern Italy. Its ancient center boasts many magnificent Roman ruins, second only to those of Rome itself, and fine palazzi built of *rosso di Verona*, the local pink-tinged limestone, by the city's medieval rulers. Verona has two main focal points: the massive 1st-century AD Arena, which is still the setting for major events including a large opera festival, and Piazza Erbe with its colorful market. One of the main attractions, however, is the church of San Zeno Maggiore *(see pp154–5)*, which boasts unusual medieval bronze door panels: they are carved with extraordinary scenes, some biblical, others on the life of San Zeno.

View of Verona from the Museo Archeologico

Verona's Rulers

In 1263 the Scaligeri began their 124-year rule of Verona. They used ruthless tactics in their rise to power, but once established, the Scaligeri family brought peace to the city. They proved to be relatively just and cultured rulers – the poet Dante was welcomed to their court in 1301, and he dedicated the final part of his epic *Divine Comedy* to the ruling Cangrande I. Today their legacy remains in their ornate tombs and in Castelvecchio.

In 1387 Verona fell to the Visconti of Milan, and a succession of outsiders – Venice, France, and Austria – then ruled the city until the Veneto was united with Italy in 1866.

Castelvecchio

Corso Castelvecchio 2. **Tel** 045 592 985. **Open** 8:30am–7:30pm daily (from 1:30pm Mon, last adm: 45 mins before closing). **Closed** Jan 1, Dec 25 & 26.

This impressive castle, built by Cangrande II between 1355 and 1375, houses one of the finest art galleries in the Veneto outside Venice.

The first section contains late Roman and early Christian items. The section on medieval and early Renaissance art demonstrates the influence of northern art on local painters: the emphasis is on brutal

Verona's enormous Roman Arena seen from Piazza Brà

Ponte Scaligero, part of the old defense system of Castelvecchio

realism as opposed to serene idealism. The late Renaissance works include a fine collection of 15th-century Madonnas.

Jewelry, armor, swords, and Veronese's *Deposition* (1565) are also on display.

A walkway offers views of the river Adige, the Ponte Scaligero, and the 14th-century statue of Cangrande I from his tomb *(see p152)*.

Sights at a Glance

① *San Zeno Maggiore (pp154–5)*
② Castelvecchio
③ Ponte Scaligero
④ San Lorenzo
⑤ Arena
⑥ Tomba di Giulietta
⑦ San Fermo Maggiore
⑧ Casa di Giulietta
⑨ Piazza Erbe
⑩ Piazza dei Signori
⑪ Tombs of the Scaligeri
⑫ Sant'Anastasia
⑬ Duomo
⑭ San Giorgio in Braida
⑮ Teatro Romano
⑯ Museo Archeologico
⑰ Giardino Giusti

For keys to symbols *see back flap*

Ponte Scaligero

This medieval bridge was built by Cangrande II between 1354 and 1376. Such is the Veronese affection for the bridge that it was rebuilt after the retreating Germans blew it up in 1945, an operation that involved dredging the river to salvage the masonry. The bridge leads from Castelvecchio to the Arsenal on the north bank, fronted by public gardens.

San Lorenzo

Corso Cavour. **Tel** 045 59 28 13.
Open daily.

San Lorenzo is one of Verona's lesser-known churches, but is one of the city's most beautiful. Built in 1117 on the remains of a paleo-Christian basilica, the Romanesque exterior, with alternate strips of stone and bricks, is typical of Veronese churches. The bell tower dates to the 15th century, and inside there are some 13th-century frescoes. The church features two unusual cylindrical towers.

Arena

Piazza Brà. **Tel** 045 800 51 51.
Open 8:30am–7:30pm daily (from 1:30pm Mon, last adm: 1 hr before closing. **Closed** Jan 1, Dec 25 & 26; Jun–Aug: from mid-afternoon on performance days. partial.

Completed in AD 30, this is the world's third-largest Roman amphitheater, after Rome's Colosseum and the amphitheater at Santa Maria Capua Vetere, near Naples. It could hold almost the entire population of Roman Verona, and visitors came from across the Veneto to watch gladiatorial combats. Since then, the arena has seen executions, fairs, bullfights, and opera productions.

VISITORS' CHECKLIST

Practical Information
261,000. Via degli Alpini 9 (045 806 86 80). daily. combined churches ticket. Apr: Vinltaly wine fair; Jun–Aug: Estate Teatrale Veronese; Nov: International Horse Fair.
turismoverona.eu

Transportation
Villafranca 9 miles (14 km) SW. FS Piazzale 25 Aprile.

San Fermo Maggiore

Stradone San Fermo. **Tel** 045 59 28 13.
Open daily.

San Fermo Maggiore is not one but two churches: this is most clearly seen from the outside, where the apse has pointed Gothic elements rising above a sturdy Romanesque base. The lower church, begun in 1065 by Benedictine monks on the site of an earlier sanctuary, has frescoes on the simple arcades.

The more impressive upper church dates from 1313 and is covered with a splendid ship's keel roof. The interior also boasts much medieval fresco work, including a 14th-century section by Stefano da Zevio. Nearby is the Brenzoni mausoleum (*c.* 1440) by Giovanni di Bartolo, and above it a 1426 fresco of the Annunciation by Pisanello (1377–1455).

The 11th-century apse of the lower church of San Fermo Maggiore

Exploring Verona

Since the days of the Roman Empire, Piazza Erbe – built on the site of the ancient Roman forum – has been the center of Verona. Many of the city's fine palazzi, churches, and monuments are nearly as ancient, several dating from the medieval period.

The fountain, erected in the 14th century at the center of Piazza Erbe

Piazza Erbe

Piazza Erbe is named after the city's old herb market. Today's stands, shaded by umbrellas, sell everything from herb-flavored roast suckling pig in bread rolls to succulent fresh-picked fruit and delicious wild mushrooms.

At the northern end of the square is the Baroque **Palazzo Maffei** (1668), surmounted by statues. In front of it rises a column supporting the **Venetian lion** marking Verona's absorption into the Venetian empire (1405). On the west side is the **Casa dei Mercanti**, a largely 17th-century building that dates originally from 1301. Opposite, wall frescoes are still visible above the cafés.

The **fountain** in the middle of the piazza is often over-shadowed by the market stands, though the statue at its center dates from Roman times. It serves as a reminder that this piazza has been used as a marketplace for 2,000 years.

Piazza dei Signori

Torre dei Lamberti. **Tel** 045 927 30 27. **Open** 8:30am–7:30pm daily (Jun–Sep: to 8:30pm Sat–Thu, to 11pm Fri).

In the center of the square is a 19th-century **statue of Dante**, whose gaze seems fixed on the forbidding **Palazzo del Capitano**, once the home of Verona's military commanders. Beside it is the equally intimidating **Palazzo della Ragione**, the palace of Reason, or law court; both were built in the 14th century. The courtyard of the law court has a handsome external stone staircase, added in 1446–50. Stunning views of the Alps can be enjoyed from atop the 275-ft (84-m) **Torre dei Lamberti**, which rises from the western side of the courtyard.

Behind the statue of Dante is the **Loggia del Consiglio** (1493), the council chamber. The building is topped by statues of Roman worthies born in Verona: they include Pliny the Elder, the natural historian, and Vitruvius, the architectural theorist.

The square is linked to Piazza Erbe by the Arco della Costa, or the Arch of the Rib, named after the whale rib long ago hung beneath it.

The frescoed Renaissance facade of the Loggia del Consiglio on Piazza dei Signori

Tombs of the Scaligeri

Via Arche Scaligeri.

Beside the entrance to the tiny Romanesque church of **Santa Maria Antica**, once the parish church of the powerful Scaligeri family, lie a profusion of bizarre tombs of the one-time rulers of Verona.

Over the entrance to the church is the impressive tomb of Cangrande I (died 1329), surmounted by an equestrian statue of the ruler, a copy of the original which is now in Castelvecchio *(see p147)*.

The other Scaligeri tombs are next to the church, behind a wrought-iron fence that incorporates the ladder emblem of the family's original name *(della Scala*, meaning "of the steps"). Towering above the fence are the tombs of Mastino II (died 1351) and Cansignorio (died 1375), splendidly decorated with a profusion of tiny Gothic spires. Other members of the Scaligeri family lie within a series of plainer tombs that stand closer to the church wall.

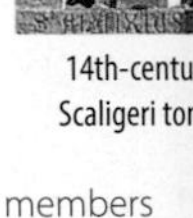

14th-centu[ry] Scaligeri to[mb]

Sant'Anastasia

Piazza Sant'Anastasia. **Tel** 045 59 28 13. **Open** daily.

The huge and lofty church of Sant'Anastasia was begun in 1290. Faded 15th-century frescoes and carved scenes from the life of St. Peter Martyr adorn its Gothic portal.

Inside, there are two holy-water stoups, supported on figures of beggars, known as *i gobbi* (the hunchbacks). These figures were carved a century apart: the earlier one (on the left) dates from 1495. The sacristy, off the north aisle, is home to a fine (but damaged) fresco by Pisanello: *St. George and the Princess* (1433–8).

The so-called Casa di Giulietta

Romeo and Juliet

The tragic story of Romeo and Juliet, two young lovers from rival families, was written by Luigi da Porto of Vicenza in the 1520s and has inspired countless dramas, movies, and ballets.

At the **Casa di Giulietta** (Juliet's house), No. 23 Via Cappello, Romeo is said to have climbed to Juliet's balcony; in reality this is a restored 13th-century inn. Crowds throng to see the simple facade and stand on the small marble balcony. The run-down **Casa di Romeo** is a few streets away, in Via Arche Scaligeri.

The so-called **Tomba di Giulietta** is displayed in a crypt below the cloister of San Francesco al Corso on Via del Pontiere. The stone sarcophagus lies in an extremely atmospheric setting.

Both the Casa and the Tomba di Giulietta are open daily (on Mondays in the afternoon only). There is an admission charge.

Duomo

Piazza Duomo. **Tel** 045 59 28 13. **Open** daily.

Verona's cathedral was begun in 1139 and is fronted by a magnificent Romanesque portal carved by Nicolò, one of the two master masons responsible for the facade of San Zeno *(see pp150–51)*. Here he sculpted the sword-bearing figures of Oliver and Roland, two of Charlemagne's knights, whose exploits were much celebrated in medieval poetry. Alongside them stand evangelists and saints with wide eyes and flowing beards. To the south there is a second Romanesque portal carved with Jonah and the Whale and with comically grotesque caryatids.

The highlight of the interior is Titian's lovely *Assumption* (1535–40), and outside there is a Romanesque cloister in which the excavated ruins of earlier churches are visible. The 8th-century baptistry, or San Giovanni in Fonte (St. John of the Spring), was built from Roman masonry; the marble font was carved in 1200.

Teatro Romano
Museo Archeologico

Regaste Redentore 2. **Tel** 045 800 03 60. **Open** 1:30–7:30pm Mon (all day if pub hol); 8:30am–7:30pm Tue–Sun. The theater closes early in the afternoon on performance days. **Closed** Jan 1, Dec 25 & 26.

This Roman theater was built in the 1st century BC; little survives of the stage area, but the semicircular seating area is largely intact. It offers great views over Verona: in the foreground is the only one of three Roman bridges to have survived, though it was rebuilt after World War II.

An elevator takes visitors from the Teatro Romano up the cliffs to the monastery above, now an archaeological museum. The exhibits around the tiny cloister and in the old monks' cells include mosaics, pottery, and glass. There is also a fine bronze bust of the first Roman emperor, Augustus (63 BC–AD 14), who in 31 BC overcame his opponents, including Mark Antony and Cleopatra, to become the sole ruler of the Roman world.

The imposing facade of Verona's Duomo, Santa Maria Matricolare

Statuary and formal hedges in the Renaissance Giardino Giusti

Giardino Giusti

Via Giardino Giusti 2. **Tel** 045 803 40 29. **Open** 9am–8pm daily (Oct–Mar: to 7pm). **Closed** Dec 25.

This fine Renaissance garden was laid out in 1580. As with other gardens of the period, there is a deliberate juxtaposition of nature and artifice: the formal lower garden of clipped box-wood hedges, gravel walks, and potted plants contrasts with wilder, natural woods above.

John Evelyn, the English author and diarist who visited Verona in 1661, thought this the finest garden in Europe.

San Giorgio in Braida

Lungadige San Giorgio. **Tel** 045 834 02 32. **Open** daily. **Closed** during mass.

This lovely domed Renaissance church was begun in about 1530 by Michele Sanmicheli. The altar includes the famous *Martyrdom of St. George* (1566) by Veronese, and above the west door is the *Baptism of Christ*, usually attributed to Tintoretto (1518–94).

Verona: San Zeno Maggiore

San Zeno, built in 1120–38 to house the shrine of Verona's patron saint, is the most ornate Romanesque church in northern Italy. The facade is adorned with an impressive rose window, marble reliefs, and a graceful porch canopy. The highlight, however, is the fascinating 11th- and 12th-century bronze door panels. A squat tower just north of San Zeno is said to cover the tomb of King Pepin of Italy (777–810).

Nave Ceiling
The nave has a magnificent example of a ship's keel ceiling, so called because it resembles the inside of an upturned boat. This ceiling was constructed in 1386 when the apse was rebuilt.

Altarpiece by Mantegna
The Madonna's halo in Andrea Mantegna's altarpiece of the Virgin and Child with saints (1457–59) echoes the shape of the church's rose window.

VISITORS' CHECKLIST

Practical Information
P. San Zeno. **Tel** 045 59 28 13. **Open** 8:30am–6pm Mon–Sat, 12:30–6pm Sun (Nov–Feb: 10am–1pm, 1:30–5pm Tue–Sat, 12:30–5pm Sun). **Closed** for mass. times vary.
basilicasanzeno.it

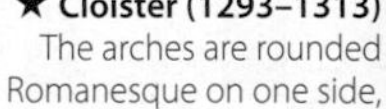

★ Cloister (1293–1313)
The arches are rounded Romanesque on one side, pointed Gothic on another.

For hotels and restaurants in this region see pp562–77 and pp580–605

Bronze Door Panels

The 48 bronze panels of the west doors are primitive but forceful in their depiction of biblical stories and scenes from the life of San Zeno. Those on the left date from 1030 and survive from an earlier church on the site; those on the right were made after the earthquake in 1137. The panels are the work of three separate craftsmen and are linked with masks. Huge staring eyes and Ottoman-style hats, armor, and architecture feature prominently. Among the scenes, some of which are unclear, are Adam and Eve, Salome dancing for the head of John the Baptist, and a startling Descent into Limbo.

Descent into Limbo | Christ in Glory | Human head

KEY

① **Former washroom**

② **The bell tower**, started in 1045, reached its present height of 236 ft (72 m) in 1173.

③ **The rose window**, dating from the early 12th century, symbolizes the Wheel of Fortune: figures on the rim show the rise and fall of human luck.

④ **The Romanesque porch** is one of the finest examples of the style in northern Italy. Since 1138 it has shielded biblical bas-reliefs, above the west doors, from the elements.

⑤ **Marble side panels**, which were carved in 1140, depict events from the Life of Christ (to the left of the doors) and scenes from the Book of Genesis (to the right).

⑥ **Striped brickwork** is typical of Romanesque buildings in Verona. Courses of local pink brick are alternated with ivory-colored tufa.

⑦ **The Crypt** has a vaulted crypt that contains the tomb of San Zeno, appointed eighth bishop of Verona in AD 362, who died in AD 380.

Nave and Main Altar
The plan of the church is modeled on an ancient Roman basilica, the Hall of Justice. The main altar is situated in the raised sanctuary where the judge's throne would have stood.

★ West Doors
Each of the wooden doors has 24 bronze plates nailed on to make the doors look like solid metal. A multicolored bas-relief above them depicts San Zeno, flanked by the people of Verona, vanquishing the devil.

❷ Lago di Garda

Garda, the largest and easternmost of the Italian lakes, borders three regions: Trentino to the north, Lombardy to the west and south, and the Veneto to the south and east. The low-lying countryside around the southern stretches becomes increasingly dramatic farther north, until impressive rocky cliffs, sometimes swathed in pines, hug the shoreline of the northern tip. The numerous sporting facilities, many sights, and splendid scenery of snow-capped mountains help make the lake a favorite summer playground.

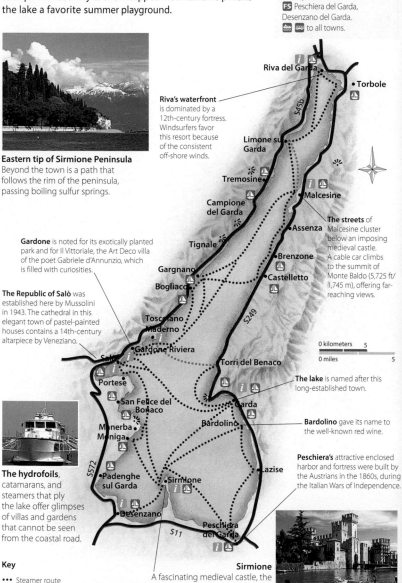

VISITORS' CHECKLIST

Practical Information
Brescia, Verona & Trento. Viale Marconi 8, Sirmione (030 91 61 14). Il Vittoriale: Gardone. **Tel** 0365 29 65 11. **Open** daily. Rocca Scaligera: Sirmione. **Tel** 030 91 64 68. **Open** Tue–Sun. **sirmionebs.it**

Transportation
FS Peschiera del Garda, Desenzano del Garda. to all towns.

Eastern tip of Sirmione Peninsula
Beyond the town is a path that follows the rim of the peninsula, passing boiling sulfur springs.

Riva's waterfront is dominated by a 12th-century fortress. Windsurfers favor this resort because of the consistent off-shore winds.

Gardone is noted for its exotically planted park and for Il Vittoriale, the Art Deco villa of the poet Gabriele d'Annunzio, which is filled with curiosities.

The Republic of Salò was established here by Mussolini in 1943. The cathedral in this elegant town of pastel-painted houses contains a 14th-century altarpiece by Veneziano.

The streets of Malcesine cluster below an imposing medieval castle. A cable car climbs to the summit of Monte Baldo (5,725 ft/ 1,745 m), offering far-reaching views.

The lake is named after this long-established town.

Bardolino gave its name to the well-known red wine.

Peschiera's attractive enclosed harbor and fortress were built by the Austrians in the 1860s, during the Italian Wars of Independence.

The hydrofoils, catamarans, and steamers that ply the lake offer glimpses of villas and gardens that cannot be seen from the coastal road.

Sirmione
A fascinating medieval castle, the Rocca Scaligera dominates the town of Sirmione. At the tip of the peninsula lie Roman ruins.

Key

- Steamer route
- Car ferry

The 16th-century wooden bridge by Palladio at Bassano del Grappa

❸ Bassano del Grappa

Vicenza. 39,000. FS Largo Corona d'Italia 35 (0424 52 43 51). Thu & Sat am.

This peaceful town lies at the foot of Monte Grappa. The river Brenta is straddled by the graceful Ponte degli Alpini, which was designed in 1569 by Palladio. It is built of timber to allow it to flex when hit by the spring meltwaters. Bassano is well known for its majolica (decorated and glazed earthenware), some of which is on display in the **Palazzo Sturm**. The town is also synonymous with the popular Italian after-dinner drink, the clear spirit known as *grappa*. It is produced from the lees *(graspa)* left over from wine production; information about the process is given in the **Museo degli Alpini**.

Palazzo Sturm
Via Schiavonetti. **Tel** 0424 52 49 33. **Open** Tue–Sun.

Museo degli Alpini
Via Angarano 2. **Tel** 0424 50 36 62. **Open** Tue–Sun. **museibassano.it**

❹ Asolo

Treviso. 2,000. Piazza Garibaldi 73 (0423 52 90 46). Sat. **asolo.it**

Asolo is beautifully sited among the cypress-clad foothills of the Dolomites. This tiny walled town was once ruled by Queen Caterina Cornaro (1454–1510), the Venetian wife of the King of Cyprus, who poisoned her husband so that Venice would gain Cyprus. Cardinal Pietro Bembo, a poet, coined the verb *asolare* to describe the bittersweet life of enforced idleness she endured in exile here. Among others who fell in love with the narrow streets and grand houses was poet Robert Browning, who named a volume of poems *Asolanda* (1889) after Asolo.

Environs
At Maser, 6 miles (10 km) east of the town, stands the magnificent **Villa Barbaro** *(see pp84-5)*. It was designed by Palladio in about 1555, in conjunction with the artist Veronese, and perfectly blends symmetry and light, airy rooms with sumptuous *trompe l'oeil* frescoes.

Villa Barbaro
Maser. **Tel** 0423 92 30 04. **Open** opening times vary; check website for details. **Closed** Jan 1, Easter Sun, Dec 25. **villadimaser.it**

Fresco (*c.* 1561) by Veronese adorning the Villa Barbaro near Asolo

❺ Castelfranco Veneto

Treviso. 30,000. FS Via Francesco M Preti 66 (0423 49 50 00). Tue am & Fri am.

Fortified in 1199 by rulers of Treviso as a defense against the neighboring Paduans, the historic core of this town lies within well-preserved walls. In the **Casa di Giorgione**, said to be the birthplace of the painter Giorgione (1478–1511), about whom little is known, there is a museum devoted to his life. Giorgione innovatively used landscape to create mood, adding figures to intensify the atmosphere – for instance, in his most famous work, the broodingly mysterious but evocative *The Tempest* *(see p110)*. Another of his few directly attributable works hangs here in the **Duomo**: the *Madonna and Child with Saints Liberal and Francis* (1504).

Environs
About 5 miles (8 km) northeast of the town, at Fanzolo, lies the **Villa Emo** (*c.* 1555). Designed by Palladio, it is a typical example of his work: a cube flanked by two symmetrical wings. Inside there are lavish frescoes by Zelotti.

Casa di Giorgione
Piazza San Liberale. **Tel** 0423 72 50 22. **Open** Tue–Sun. **Closed** pub hols.

Villa Emo
Via Stazione 5, Fanzolo. **Tel** 0423 47 63 34. **Open** May–Oct: daily (pm only Mon–Sat); Nov–Apr: daily. **Closed** Jan 1, Dec 25, 26 & 31.

6 Street by Street: Vicenza

Vicenza is known as the adoptive city of Andrea Palladio (1508–80), who started out as a stonemason and became the most influential architect of his time. The evolution of his distinctive style is visible all around the city. In the center is the monumental basilica he adapted to serve as the town hall, nearby is the Teatro Olimpico, and all around are the palaces he built for Vicenza's wealthy citizens.

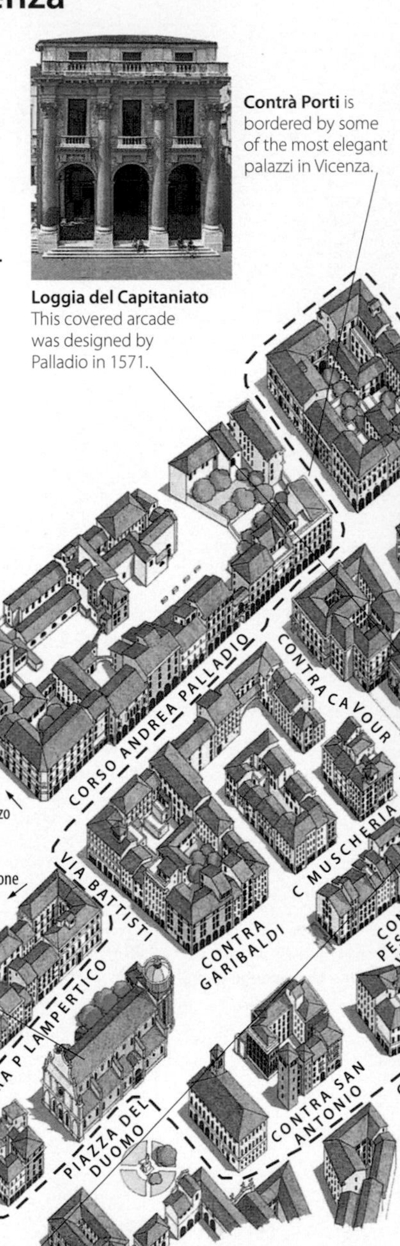

Contrà Porti is bordered by some of the most elegant palazzi in Vicenza.

Loggia del Capitaniato
This covered arcade was designed by Palladio in 1571.

Palazzo Valmarana Braga
Palladio's impressive building of 1566 is decorated with giant pilasters and sculpted scenes. It was not completed until 1680, 100 years after the architect's death.

Duomo
Vicenza's cathedral was rebuilt after bomb damage during World War II left only the facade and choir entirely intact.

Andrea Palladio
This memorial to Vicenza's most famous citizen is usually surrounded by market stalls.

Key

— Suggested route

VISITORS' CHECKLIST

Practical Information
116,000. Piazza Matteotti 12 (0444 32 08 54). Tue & Thu. May–Jun: concert season; Sep–Oct: theater season; end Jun–early Jul: Concerti in Villa.
vicenzae.org

Transportation
FS Piazza Stazione.

A large hall is all that remains of the 15th-century Palazzo della Ragione.

Torre di Piazza, built in the 12th century, is an impressive 269 ft (82 m) high.

Santa Corona

Teatro Olimpico Museo Civico

COVNTRA S BARBARA

PIAZZA DELLE BIADE

CONTRA CATENA

C GAZZOLE

CONTRA PIANCOLI

CONTRA SAN PAOLO

CONTRA PONTE SAN MICHELE

RETRONE

PESCARIA

La Rotonda Monte Berico Villa Valmarana ai Nani

★ Piazza dei Signori
Palladio's elegant buildings flank the Piazza dei Signori, including the majestic two-tier colonnades of the 16th-century "Basilica," built around the old Palazzo della Ragione.

The Quartiere delle Barche contains numerous attractive palaces built in the 14th-century Venetian Gothic style.

Ponte San Michele
This elegant stone bridge, built in 1620, provides lovely views of the surrounding town.

Piazza delle Erbe, the city's market square, is overlooked by a 13th-century prison tower.

Casa Pigafetta
This striking15th-century house was the birthplace of Antonio Pigafetta, who in 1519 set sail around the world with Magellan.

The lion of St. Mark gazing down on Piazza dei Signori

Piazza dei Signori

Basilica: **Tel** 0444 32 36 81. **Open** for exhibitions only, when it is possible to walk along the balustrade and visit the loggia (call tourist office for schedule).

This square at the heart of Vicenza is dominated by the Palazzo della Ragione, often referred to as the **Basilica**. Its green, copper-clad roof is shaped like an upturned boat with a balustrade bristling with the statues of Greek and Roman gods. The colonnades were designed by Palladio in 1549 as a facing to support the city's 15th-century town hall, which had begun to subside. The Basilica is now used as an exhibition space. Beside it stands the 12th-century Torre di Piazza.

The **Loggia del Capitaniato**, to the northwest, was built by Palladio in 1571: the Loggia's upper rooms contain the city's council chamber.

Contrà Porti

Contrà (an abbreviation of *contrada*, or district) is the Vicenza dialect word for street. On one side of the Contrà is a series of pretty Gothic buildings with painted windows and ornate balconies, reminiscent of Venice and a reminder that Vicenza was once part of the Venetian empire.

Several elegant Palladian palazzi stand on this street. Palazzo Porto Barbarano (No. 11), Palazzo Thiene (No. 12), and Palazzo Iseppo da Porto (No. 21) illustrate the variety of Palladio's style – all share Classical elements but each is unique. An intriguing detail is that Palazzo Thiene appears to be of stone, but it is in fact built of cheap brick, rendered to look like masonry.

Exploring Vicenza

Vicenza, the great Palladian city and one of the wealthiest cities in the Veneto, is celebrated the world over for its splendid and varied architecture; it also offers the visitor elegant shops and cafés to visit.

Brusazorzi's ceiling fresco in the large entrance hall of the Museo Civico

Museo Civico

Piazza Matteotti 37–39.
Tel 0444 22 28 11.
Open 9am–5pm Tue–Sun.
museicivicivicenza.it

This museum is housed in **Palazzo Chiericati** *(see p84)* by Palladio. Inside is a fresco by Domenico Brusazorzi of a naked charioteer, representing the Sun, who seems to fly over the entrance hall. Among the Gothic altarpieces from churches in Vicenza is Hans Memling's *Crucifixion* (1468–70), the central panel from a triptych whose side panels are now in New York.

Other rooms contain works by the local artist Bartolomeo Montagna (*c.* 1450–1523).

Santa Corona

Contrà Santa Corona.
Tel 0444 32 36 44. **Open** Tue–Sun.

This Gothic church was built in 1261 to house a thorn donated by Louis IX of France and said to be from Christ's Crown of Thorns. The Cappella Porto houses the tomb of Luigi da Porto, author of *Giulietta e Romeo*, on which Shakespeare based his famous play. Notable paintings include Giovanni Bellini's *Baptism of Christ* (*c.* 1500) and the *Adoration of the Magi* (1573) by Paolo Veronese.

Teatro Olimpico

Piazza Matteotti 11. **Tel** 0444 22 28 00.
Open 9am–5pm Tue–Sun. **Closed** during performances, Jan 1, Dec 25.
teatrolimpicovicenza.it

Europe's oldest surviving indoor theater is a remarkable structure, largely made of wood and plaster, and painted to look like marble. Palladio began work on the design in 1579, but he died the year after. His pupil Vincenzo Scamozzi took over the project, completing the theater in time for its opening performance of Sophocles' tragic drama *Oedipus Rex* on March 3, 1585.

Odeon Frescoes
The gods of Mount Olympus, after which the theater is named, decorate the Odeon, a room used for music recitals.

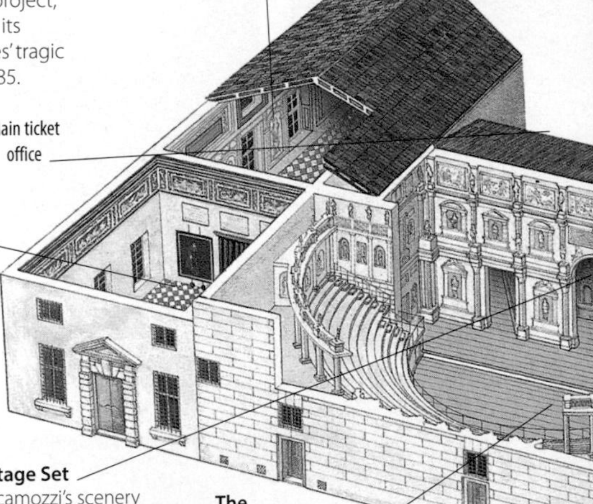

The Anteodeon contains frescoes depicting the theater's opening performance and oil lamps from the original stage set.

Main ticket office

Stage Set
Scamozzi's scenery represents the Greek city of Thebes. The streets are cleverly painted in perspective and rise at a steep angle to give the illusion of great length.

The Auditorium was designed by Palladio to resemble the outdoor theaters of ancient Greece and Rome, such as the Arena at Verona *(see p147)*, with a semicircle of "stone" benches and a ceiling painted to portray the sky.

San Lorenzo

Piazza San Lorenzo. **Open** daily.

The portal of this church is a magnificent example of Gothic stone carving, richly decorated with the figures of the Virgin and Child, and St. Francis and St. Clare. Inside there are fine tombs and damaged frescoes. The lovely cloister, north of the church, is an attractive, flower-filled haven of calm.

Monte Berico

Basilica di Monte Berico. **Tel** 0444 55 94 11. **Open** daily (Sun pm only).

Monte Berico is the green, cypress-clad hill to the south of Vicenza to which wealthy residents once escaped, in the heat of summer, to enjoy the cooler air and pastoral charms of their country estates. Today, shady *portici*, or colonnades, adorned with shrines, line the wide avenue linking central Vicenza to the basilica on top of the hill. The domed basilica itself, built in the 15th century and enlarged in the 18th, is dedicated to the Virgin, who appeared here during the 1426–8 plague to announce that Vicenza would be spared.

The ornate interior contains a moving *Pietà* fresco (1500) by Bartolomeo Montagna, a fossil collection in the cloister, and Veronese's fine painting *The Supper of St. Gregory the Great* (1572) in the refectory.

La Rotonda (1550–52), most famous of all Palladio's works

The Baroque hilltop church, the Basilica di Monte Berico

Villa Valmarana ai Nani

Via dei Nani 8. **Tel** 0444 32 18 03. **Open** 10am–12:30pm, 3–6pm Tue–Sun. **Closed** Nov 5–Mar 9.
villavalmarana.com

The wall alongside the Villa Valmarana, built in 1688 by Antonio Muttoni, is topped by figures of dwarfs (*nani*) which give the building its name.

Inside, the walls are covered with frescoes by Tiepolo, in which the gods of Mount Olympus float about on clouds watching scenes from the epics of Homer and Virgil. In the separate Foresteria (guesthouse), the 18th-century frescoes depicting peasant life and the seasons, painted by Tiepolo's son Giandomenico, are imbued with an earthy realism.

The villa can be reached by a 10-minute walk from the basilica on Monte Berico. Head downhill along Via Massimo d'Azeglio to the high-walled convent on the right where the road ends, then take Via San Bastiano.

La Rotonda

Via Rotonda 45. **Tel** 0444 32 17 93. Villa: **Open** Mar 13–Nov 4: Wed & Sat. Garden: **Open** Tue–Sun.
villalarotonda.it

With its perfectly regular, symmetrical forms, this villa, also known as the Villa Capra Valmarana, is the epitome of Palladio's architecture *(see pp84–5)* of which there are several fine examples throughout the Veneto. The design, consisting of a dome rising above a cube, received immediate acclaim for the way it blends perfectly with its surroundings. A pleasant contrast exists between the terracotta roof tiles, the white walls, and the green lawns.

The villa, built in 1550–52, has inspired many copies in cities as far away as London, St. Petersburg, and Delhi. Fans of *Don Giovanni* will enjoy spotting locations used in Joseph Losey's 1979 film.

La Rotonda can be reached by bus from town, or on foot, following the path alongside the Villa Valmarana ai Nani.

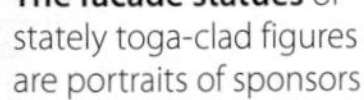

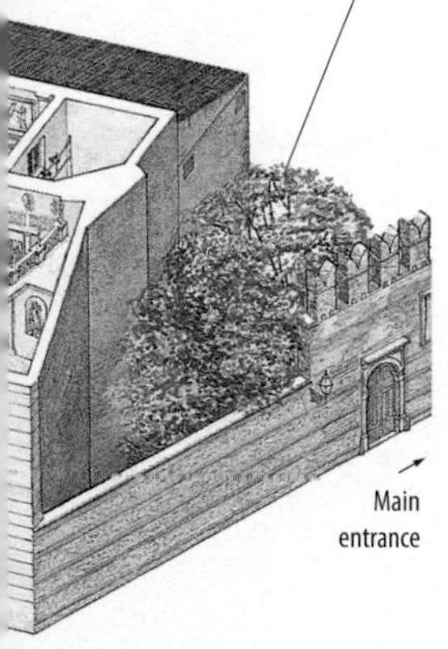

The facade statues of stately toga-clad figures are portraits of sponsors who paid for the theater's construction.
The courtyard giving access to the Teatro is decorated with ancient sculptures. These were donated by members of the Olympic Academy, the learned body that built the theater.
Main entrance

❼ Street-by-Street: Padua

Padua (Padova) is an old university town with an illustrious academic history. Rich in art and architecture, it has two particularly outstanding sights. The magnificent Cappella degli Scrovegni *(see pp160–61)*, north of the city center, is famous for Giotto's lyrical frescoes. Close to the train station, it forms part of the complex incorporating the Eremitani church and museums. The Basilica di Sant'Antonio, which forms the focal point in the southern part of the city, is one of the most popular pilgrimage destinations in Italy.

Palazzo del Capitanio
Built between 1599 and 1605 for the head of the city's militia, the tower incorporates an astronomical clock made in 1344.

Corte Capitaniato, a 14th-century arts faculty (open for concerts), contains frescoes that include a rare portrait of the poet Petrarch.

Loggia della Gran Guardia
This fine Renaissance building dating from 1523 once housed the Council of Nobles. It is now used as a conference center.

★ Duomo and Baptistry
The 12th-century baptistry of the Duomo contains one of the most complete medieval fresco cycles to survive in Italy, painted by Giusto de' Menabuoi in 1378.

Piazza dei Signori is bordered by attractive arcades that house small specialty shops, cafés, and old-fashioned wine bars.

The Palazzo del Monte di Pietà has 16th-century arcades and statues enclosing a medieval building.

Key

— Suggested route

0 meters 75

0 yards 75

Caffè Pedrocchi
Built like a Classical temple, the Caffè Pedrocchi has been a famous meeting place for students and intellectuals since it opened in 1831.

VISITORS' CHECKLIST

Practical Information
220,000. Mon–Sat, Piazza delle Erbe. Jun–Sep: Cultural Festival. **turismopadova.it**

Transport
Piazzale della Stazione 13A (049 875 20 77). Piazza Boschetti.

A bronze statue of a woman (1973) by Emilio Greco stands at the center of this largely pedestrianized square.

Stazione Chiesa Degli Eremitiani Cappella Degli Scrovegni Museo Civico

PIAZZA CAVOUR

VIA GORIZIA

PIAZZA DELLE FRUTTA

VIA OBERDAN

VIA VIII FEBBRAIO

PITTA GARZERIA

PIAZZA DELLE ERBE

V SAN CANZIANO

Basilica di Sant'Antonio Orto Botanico

Padua University
Founded in 1222, this is Italy's second oldest university. Elena Piscopia was the first woman graduate, in 1678.

alazzo della Ragione, he medieval court of justice, ontains magnificent frescoes.

Piazza delle Erbe
There are some excellent views over the marketplace from the 15th-century loggia that runs alongside the 13th-century Palazzo della Ragione.

Duomo and Baptistry

Piazza Duomo. Baptistry: **Tel** 049 65 69 14. **Open** 10am–6pm daily. **Closed** Jan 1, Easter, Dec 25.

The Duomo was built in 1552 to plans partly by Michelangelo, on the site of an earlier 14th-century cathedral. Beside it stands a domed baptistry (*c.* 1200). The interior is entirely decorated with vibrant frescoes painted by Giusto de' Menabuoi, dating from around 1378. The frescoes depict episodes from the Bible, including scenes of the Creation, the Miracles, the Passion, the Crucifixion, and the Resurrection of Christ.

Palazzo della Ragione

Piazza delle Erbe (entrance via the town hall). **Tel** 049 820 50 06. **Open** 9am–7pm Tue–Sun (Nov–Jan: to 6pm). **Closed** Jan 1, May 1, Dec 25 & 26.

The "Palace of Reason" was built in 1218 to serve as Padua's law court and council chamber. The vast main hall was originally decorated with frescoes by Giotto, but fire destroyed his work in 1420. The Salone is breathtaking in its sheer size. It is the largest undivided medieval hall in Europe, 260 ft (80 m) long, 90 ft (27 m) wide, and 90 ft (27 m) high. Frescoes painted in 1420–25 by Nicola Miretto cover its walls: the 333 panels depict the months of the year, with appropriate gods, signs of the zodiac, and seasonal activities.

A 1466 copy of the huge Gattamelata statue (*see p162*) by Donatello stands at one end of the hall.

Caffè Pedrocchi

Via VIII Febbraio 15. **Tel** 049 878 12 31. **Open** daily. **Closed** Aug. Museum: **Open** Tue–Sun.

Caffè Pedrocchi opened in 1831 and became famous as the café that never closed its doors. Today people come as much to talk, play cards, or watch the world go by as to eat or drink. The upstairs rooms, decorated in Moorish, Egyptian and other styles, house a museum documenting modern Italian history.

Padua: Cappella degli Scrovegni

Enrico Scrovegni built this chapel in 1303, hoping thereby to spare his dead father, a usurer, from the eternal damnation in hell described by the poet Dante in his *Inferno*. The interior of the chapel is entirely covered with beautiful frescoes of scenes from the life of Christ, painted by Giotto between 1303 and 1305. As works of great narrative force, they exerted a powerful influence on the development of European art.

The Nativity
The naturalism of the Virgin's pose marks a departure from Byzantine stylization, as does the use of natural blue for the sky, in place of celestial gold.

Expulsion of the Merchants
Christ's physical rage, the cowering merchant, and the child hiding his face show an animation that is characteristic of Giotto's style.

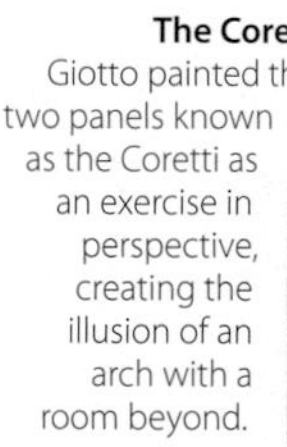

The Coretti
Giotto painted the two panels known as the Coretti as an exercise in perspective, creating the illusion of an arch with a room beyond.

View toward altar

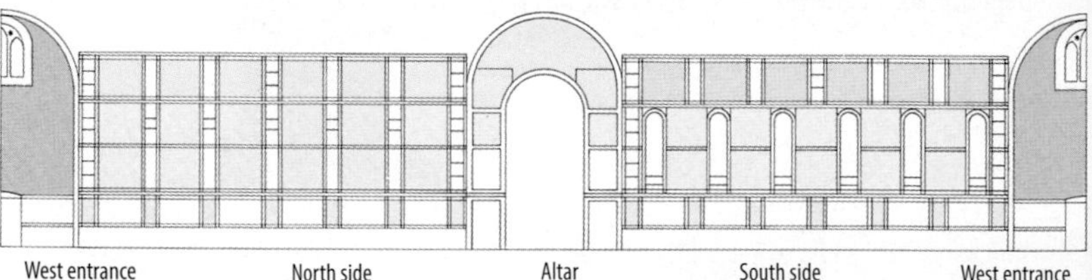

Gallery Guide

Due to the Cappella degli Scrovegni's small size, the number of visitors allowed in at any one time is strictly limited. Prior to entering, visitors are required to spend 15 minutes in a decontamination chamber, where multimedia and multilingual information on the chapel is provided. The visit itself is also restricted to 15 minutes. Advance booking is required, either by phone (049 201 00 20) or online (www. cappelladegliscrovegni.it), with a credit card payment.

Key

- Episodes of Joachim and Anna
- Episodes from the Life of Mary
- Episodes from the Life and Death of Christ
- The Virtues and Vices
- The Last Judgment

The Last Judgment
This scene fills the entire west wall of the chapel. Its formal composition is closer to Byzantine tradition than some of the other frescoes, with parts probably painted by assistants. A model of the chapel is shown (center left, at the bottom) being offered to the Virgin by Scrovegni.

VISITORS' CHECKLIST

Practical Information
Piazza Eremitani. **Tel** 049 201 00 20. **Open** 9am–7pm daily; Mar–Jun: 7–10pm Tue–Sun (call 049 296 37 20 for reservations). **Closed** main public hols. Advance reservations required (see opposite).
cappelladegliscrovegni.it

Transportation
to Piazzale Boschetti.

View toward entrance

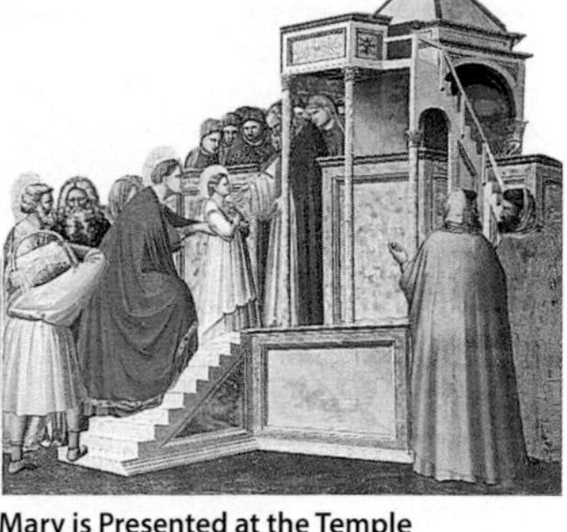

Mary is Presented at the Temple
Giotto sets many scenes against an architectural background, using the laws of perspective to give a sense of three dimensions.

Injustice
The Vices and Virtues are painted in monochrome. Here Injustice is symbolized by scenes of war, murder, and robbery.

Lament over the Dead Christ
Giotto's figures express their grief in different ways: some huddle together, another gestures wildly.

Giotto

The Florentine artist Giotto (1266–1337) is regarded as the father of the Renaissance, the great revival in the Classical traditions of Western art. His work, with its sense of pictorial space, naturalism, and narrative drama, marks a decisive break with the Byzantine tradition of the preceding 1,000 years. Although he was regarded in his lifetime as a great artist, few of the works attributed to him are fully documented. Some may have been painted by others, but his authorship of the frescoes in the Scrovegni Chapel need not be doubted.

Exploring Padua

Padua is a city of many attractions, with a rich history: this is reflected in the major museum complex that occupies a group of 14th-century monastic buildings attached to the church of the Eremitani, a reclusive Augustinian order. Next door is the Cappella degli Scrovegni *(see pp160–1)*. Padua is, in addition, the setting for one of Italy's most important churches – the splendid Basilica di Sant'Antonio – and for one of the earliest universities to be founded in Italy.

15th-century *Angels in Armor* by Guariento, Museo Civico Eremitani

Chiesa degli Eremitani and Museo Civico Eremitani

Piazza Eremitani 8. **Tel** 049 820 45 50. Museum: **Open** Tue–Sun.

The Eremitani church, built from 1276 to 1306, contains magnificent roof and wall tombs. Among them is that of Marco Benavides (1489–1582), a professor of law at the city university, whose Renaissance tomb was the work of Florentine architect Ammannati (1511–92). Celebrated frescoes (1454–7) by Mantegna, portraying scenes from the lives of St. James and St. Christopher, were destroyed during a World War II bombing raid in 1944. Two scenes from this magnificent series survive in the Cappella Ovetari, to the south of the sanctuary: *The Martyrdom of St. James* and *The Martyrdom of St. Christopher*.

The Museo Civico Eremitani comprises a coin collection (which includes rare Roman medallions and an almost complete set of Venetian coinage), an archaeological section, and an art gallery.

The rich archaeological collection contains interesting Roman tombs, fine mosaics, and impressive life-size statues. Renaissance bronzes include the comical *Drinking Satyr* by Il Riccio (1470–1532).

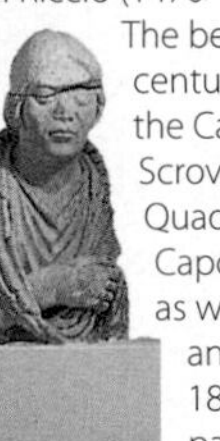

A 1st-century AD tomb in the archaeological collection

The beautiful 14th-century Crucifix from the Cappella degli Scrovegni is in the Quadreria Emo Capodilista, as well as works by Giotto and 15th- to 18th-century paintings from the Venetian and Flemish schools.

Basilica di Sant'Antonio

Piazza del Santo. **Tel** 049 822 56 52. **Open** 7am–7:30pm daily.

This exotic church, with its minaret-like spires and Byzantine domes, is also known as Il Santo. It was built from 1232 to house the remains of St. Anthony of Padua, a preacher who modeled himself on St. Francis of Assisi. Although he was a simple man who rejected worldly wealth, the citizens of Padua built a lavish church to serve as his shrine.

The influence of Byzantine architecture is clearly visible in the basilica's outline: a cone-shaped central dome rises above seven encircling domes; the facade combines Gothic and Romanesque elements.

Inside, the high altar features Donatello's magnificent reliefs (1444–5) on the miracles of St. Anthony, and his statues of the Crucifixion, the Virgin, and Paduan saints. The tomb of St. Anthony, hung with offerings, lies in the north transept; large marble reliefs depicting the saint's life, carved in 1505–77 by various artists, adorn the walls around it. A lively fresco scene of the Crucifixion by Altichiero da Zevio (1380s) adorns the south transept.

The Basilica di Sant'Antonio, and Donatello's statue of Gattamelata

Statue of Gattamelata

Beside the entrance to the basilica stands one of the great works of the Renaissance: a statue of the mercenary soldier Gattamelata. This gritty portrait was created in 1443–52, in honor of a man who during his life did great service to the Venetian Republic. The artist Donatello won fame for the monument, the first equestrian statue made on such a large scale since Roman times.

Scuola del Santo and Oratorio di San Giorgio
Piazza del Santo 11. **Tel** 049 822 56 52. **Open** daily.

Five excellent frescoes, including the earliest documented paintings by Titian, are to be found in these two buildings. The Scuola del Santo contains two scenes from the life of St. Anthony, which were painted by Titian in 1511. The works in the San Giorgio oratory are by Altichiero da Zevio and Jacopo Avenzo, who painted them in 1378–84.

Orto Botanico
Via Orto Botanico 15. **Tel** 049 827 21 19. **Open** daily (Nov–Mar: Mon–Sat). **ortobotanico.unipd.it**

Padua's botanical garden, one of the oldest in Europe (1545), still retains much of its original appearance. The gardens and hothouses were used to cultivate the first lilac trees (1568), sunflowers (1568), and potatoes (1590) to be grown in Italy.

Palazzo del Bo
Via VIII Febbraio 2. **Tel** 049 827 51 11. **Open** for guided tours only. Tue, Thu, Sat am, Mon, Wed, Fri pm. Times vary: call in advance. **unipd.it**

The historic main university building originally housed the medical faculty, renowned throughout Europe. Among its famous teachers and students was Gabriele Fallopio (1523–62), after whom the Fallopian tubes are named.

Guided tours include the pulpit Galileo used when he taught physics here from 1592 until 1610 and the wooden anatomy theater, built in 1594 and now the oldest surviving medical lecture theater in the world.

The 16th-century anatomy theater in the old medical faculty of the university's Palazzo del Bo, Padua

The Euganean Hills, formed by ancient volcanic activity

8 Euganean Hills

FS to Terme Euganee, Montegrotto Terme. Viale Stazione 60, Montegrotto Terme (049 892 83 11). **turismopadova.it**

The conical Euganean Hills, remnants of long-extinct volcanoes, rise abruptly out of the surrounding plain. Hot water springs bubble up out of the ground at Abano Terme and Montegrotto Terme, where scores of establishments offer thermal treatments, ranging from mud baths to immersion in the hot sulfurated waters. Spa cures originated in Roman times; remains of the original baths and theater are still visible at Montegrotto Terme.

Abbazia di Praglia
Via Abbazia di Praglia 16, Bresseo di Teolo. **Tel** 049 999 93 00. **Open** Tue–Sun (pm only). **Closed** religious holidays. Donations welcome. **praglia.it**

The Benedictine monastery at Praglia, 4 miles (6 km) west of Abano Terme, is a peaceful haven in the hills where the monks grow herbs and restore manuscripts. They lead guided tours of parts of the abbey and the church (1490–1548), noted for its beautiful cloister. There are also richly carved stalls in both the choir and the refectory, and paintings and frescoes by Zelotti, a 16th-century painter from Verona.

Casa di Petrarca
Via Valleselle 4, Arquà Petrarca. **Tel** 0429 71 82 94. **Open** Tue–Sun (also Mon if public hol). **Closed** public hols.

The picturesque town of Arquà Petrarca, on the southern edge of the Euganean Hills, is named after Francesco Petrarca (1304–74). This medieval poet, known in English as Petrarch, spent the final years of his life here, in a house frescoed with scenes from his lyrical poems, overlooking a landscape of olive groves and vineyards. He lies buried in a simple sarcophagus in front of the church.

The Casa di Petrarca (part 14th century) in Arquà Petrarca

Villa Barbarigo
Valsanzibio. **Tel** 049 805 92 24. **Open** Mar–Nov: 10am–1pm, 2pm–sunset daily.

This 18th-century villa north of Arquà boasts one of the finest Baroque gardens in the Veneto, planned by Antonio Barbarigo in 1669. The gardens are a grandiose mix of statuary, fountains, a maze, formal parterres, lakes, and avenues of cypress trees.

The 16th-century Villa Foscari at Malcontenta, beside the Brenta Canal

9 Brenta Canal

Padua and Venice. FS Venezia Mestre, Dolo, Mira. to Mira, Dolo, and Strà. Canal trips on Il Burchiello: Venice. **Tel** 041 241 32 96. **Closed** Jan 25–Feb 7. **ilburchiello.it**

Over the centuries, in order to prevent the Venetian lagoon silting up, the rivers flowing into it were diverted. The river Brenta was canalized in two sections: the older branch, between Padua and Fusina (just west of Venice), dates back to the 1500s and flows for 22 miles (36 km). Its potential as a transportation route was quickly realized and fine villas were built along its length. Many of these elegant buildings can still be admired today – the S11 road runs alongside most of the canal's length – and several of them are open to the public.

The 18th-century **Villa Pisani** at Strà has an extravagant frescoed ceiling by Tiepolo. The **Barchessa Valmarana** at Mira (a pretty village) boasts 18th-century decorations. In the village of Malcontenta is **Villa Foscari**, or Villa Malcontenta, one of Palladio's loveliest villas *(see pp84–5)*. It was built in 1560 and the interior decorated with magnificent frescoes by Zelotti. These villas may also be visited as part of an indulgent 8.5-hour guided tour from Padua, traveling to Venice (or, on alternate days, from Venice to Padua) along the river in a leisurely fashion on board the *Burchiello* motor launch – the cost, however, is fairly prohibitive.

Barchessa Valmarana
Via Valmarana 11, Mira. **Tel** 041 426 63 87. **Open** Apr–Oct: 10am–6pm Tue–Sun; Nov–Feb: Sat & Sun, groups by appt only.

Villa Pisani
Via Pisani, Strà. **Tel** 049 50 20 74. **Open** Tue–Sun. **Closed** Jan 1, May 1, Dec 25. Fri–Sun (in Italian).

Villa Foscari
Via dei Turisti 9, Malcontenta. **Tel** 041 547 00 12. **Open** Tue & Sat am. **Closed** Nov–Mar.

The houses of the medieval town of Treviso overlooking ancient canals

10 Treviso

81,700. FS Piazzale Duca D'Aosta 25 (0422 54 76 32). Tue & Sat am. **turismo.provincia.treviso.it**

Despite comparisons with Venice, the lovely fortified city of Treviso has its own very distinctive character.

A good place to start a tour of the streets, some lined with attractive balconied houses, is **Calmaggiore**. The street links the Duomo with the Palazzo dei Trecento, the rebuilt 13th-century town hall. The **Duomo** was founded in the 1100s but rebuilt several times. Inside, Titian's *Annunciation* (1570) vies for attention with the striking *Adoration of the Magi* fresco (1520) by Titian's archrival, Il Pordenone. More paintings by Titian and other artists of the Renaissance may be seen in the **Museo Civico**.

The fish market, which dates from medieval times, is held on an island in the middle of Treviso's river Sile; this allows the remains of the day's trading to be flushed away.

The Dominican church of **San Nicolò**, nestling by the 16th-century city wall, contains interesting tombs and frescoes, including, on a wall of the chapter house, the first-ever depiction of spectacles in art. A magnificent tomb (1500) by Antonio Rizzo is framed by a fresco of pageboys by Lorenzo Lotto.

Museo Civico
Chiesa di Santa Caterina, Piazzeta Mario Botter 1. **Tel** 0422 54 48 64. **Open** Tue–Sun. **Closed** public hols.

The facade and entrance to the Renaissance Palazzo dei Rettori in Belluno

⓫ Conegliano

Treviso. 35,000. FS Via XX Settembre 61 (0438 212 30). Fri.

Conegliano lies among Prosecco-producing vineyards, and wine makers from all over Italy learn their craft at Conegliano's renowned wine school. Via XX Settembre, the arcaded main street, is lined with fine 15th- to 18th-century palazzi, many in the Venetian Gothic style or decorated with fading frescoes. The **Duomo** contains the town's one great work of art, an altarpiece painted by local artist Cima da Conegliano (1460–1518) depicting the *Virgin and Child with Saints* (1493).

Reproductions of Cima's most famous works are on show in the **Casa di Cima**, the artist's birthplace. The detailed landscapes in the background of his paintings were based on the hills around the town; the same views can still be seen from the gardens surrounding the Castelvecchio (old castle).

A mythical statue on Conegliano's theater

Casa di Cima
Via Cima 24. **Tel** 0438 21 660.
Open Sat & Sun, pm only and during temporary exhibitions.

⓬ Belluno

36,000. FS Piazza Duomo 2 (0437 94 00 83). Sat.
infodolomiti.it

Picturesque Belluno, capital of Belluno province, serves as a bridge between the two different parts of the Veneto, with the flat plains to the south and the Dolomite peaks to the north. Both are encapsulated in the views to be seen from the 12th-century **Porta Rugo** at the southern end of Via Mezzaterra, the main street of the old town. More spectacular still are the views from the bell tower of the 16th-century **Duomo** (subsequently rebuilt). The nearby baptistry houses a font cover with the figure of John the Baptist carved by Andrea Brustolon (1662–1732). Brustolon's works also grace the churches of San Pietro (on Via San Pietro) and Santo Stefano (Piazza Santo Stefano). North of Piazza del Duomo stands the elegant **Palazzo dei Rettori** (1491) – once home to the town's Venetian rulers – and the 12th-century **Torre Civica**, all that now survives of a medieval castle.

The **Museo Civico** contains paintings by Bartolomeo Montagna (1450–1523) and Sebastiano Ricci (1659–1734), and a notable archaeological section. North of the museum is Belluno's finest square, the **Piazza del Mercato**, with its arcaded Renaissance palaces and its fountain of 1410.

South of the town are the ski resorts of the Alpe del Nevegal; in the summer a chairlift operates from Faverghera up the flank of the mountain to a height of 5,250 ft (1,600 m), offering extensive views.

Museo Civico
Piazza Duomo 16. **Tel** 0437 94 48 36.
Open Tue–Sun. Closed Wed, Thu, Sat & Sun pm.

⓭ Cortina d'Ampezzo

Belluno. 6,800. Piazzetta San Francesco 8 (0436 32 31). Tue am & Fri am. **infodolomiti.it**

Italy's top ski resort, much favored by the smart set from Turin and Milan, is well supplied with restaurants and bars. Cortina is set amid the extremely dramatic scenery of the Dolomites *(see pp86–7)*, which explains part of the resort's attraction: all around, crags and spires thrust their distinctive weather-beaten shapes above the trees.

Cortina benefits from better-than-average sports facilities, thanks to hosting the 1956 Winter Olympics. In addition to downhill and cross-country skiing, there is also a ski jump and a bobsled run for those who favor something more adventurous than usual, as well as an Olympic ice stadium, several swimming pools, tennis courts, and riding facilities.

During the summer months, Cortina becomes an excellent base for walkers. Useful information on trails and guided walks is available from the tourist office or, during the summer, from the Guides' office opposite.

Corso Italia in Cortina d'Ampezzo, Italy's most important ski resort

Traditional copper pans on display in the Museo Carnico in Tolmezzo

⓮ Tolmezzo

10,000. Via della Vittoria 4 (0433 448 98). Mon am.
turismofvg.it

Tolmezzo is the capital of the Carnia region, named after the Celtic tribe that inhabited the area around the 4th century BC. The town is surrounded by the high peaks of the Carnic Alps, including the pyramidal Monte Amariana (6,253 ft/1,906 m) to the east. The best place to begin a tour of the region is the **Museo delle Arti Popolari**, which has displays of local costumes, crafts, textiles, and agriculture.

Southwest of the town, a scenic road climbs 9 miles (14 km) to the ski resort of **Sella Chianzutan**, a good base for walking in the summer. More resorts line the road, west of Tolmezzo, to **Ampezzo**, at which point a minor road heads north through the gorge of the River Lumiei. Following this road to the Ponte di Buso bridge and the **Lago di Sauris** is an excellent introduction to the majestic Carnic Alps.

Above this point the road is often impassable in winter, but in summer there are flower-filled meadows all along the road up to Sella di Razzo, and then back along the **Pesarina Valley**, via Comeglians and Ravascletto. Returning south, **Zuglio** was once the Roman town of Forum Iulii Carnicum, guarding the road over the pass. Today it is worth a detour for the remains of its Roman basilica, baths, and forum.

Museo delle Arti Popolari
Via della Vittoria 2. **Tel** 0433 432 33. **Open** Tue–Sun (Aug: daily). **Closed** Jan 1, Dec 25.

⓯ Pordenone

49,000. FS Via Damiani 2/c (0434 52 03 81). Sat am & Wed.
turismofvg.it

Old Pordenone consists of one long street, the **Corso Vittorio Emanuele**, lined with pretty arcaded houses of pink brick, some with the faded traces of decorative frescoes on their facades. The 13th-century **Palazzo Comunale** forms a striking conclusion to the street, with its eccentrically shaped roofline of curves and minaret-like side towers, and its 16th-century clock tower. Opposite is the **Museo d'Arte**, housed in the 17th-century Palazzo Ricchieri, where works by the local artist Il Pordenone (1484–1539) are on display.

Around the corner stands the **Duomo**, which contains the lovely altar painting of the *Madonna della Misericordia* (1515) by Il Pordenone. The bell tower beside the Duomo is a fine example of Romanesque decorative brickwork.

Museo d'Arte
Corso Vittorio Emanuele II 51. **Tel** 0434 39 29 35. **Open** Tue–Sun (pm only Tue–Sat).

Lago di Sauris, an artificial lake lying in the Carnic Alps above Tolmezzo

⓰ Udine

99,000. FS Piazza I Maggio 7 (0432 29 59 72). Sat.

Udine is a city of varied and surprising architecture. In the center lies **Piazza della Libertà**, where the Loggia del Lionello (1448–56), built of pink stone in Venetian Gothic style, stands beside the Art Deco Caffè Contarena. Opposite, the Renaissance symmetry of the Porticato di San Giovanni is interrupted by the Torre dell'Orologio (Clock Tower, 1527), crowned by two bronze Moors who strike the hours. Note also the fountain of 1542, the two 18th-century statues, and the column supporting the Lion of St. Mark.

Beyond the **Arco Bollani**, a gateway designed by Palladio in 1556, steps lead up to a 85-ft (26-m) hill that offers sweeping views over the city. On the hill is the 16th-century castle, now the **Musei Civici e Galleria di Storia e Arte Antica**, which houses fine art and archaeology collections.

Southeast of Piazza Matteotti, at the end of Via Savorgnana where a small market is held, stands the **Oratorio della Purità**, and the **Duomo** with its octagonal bell tower. Both contain important paintings and frescoes by Giambattista Tiepolo (1696–1770). More of Tiepolo's work can be seen in the **Museo Diocesano e Galleria Tiepolo**, formerly the Palazzo Arcivescovile, which the artist decorated with frescoes.

The arcaded Porticato di San Giovanni on Piazza della Libertà, Udine

Environs

Outside Codroipo, 15 miles (24 km) west, rises the imposing **Villa Manin**. A road passes through the villa's grounds, so it can be seen even when the house – once the retreat of Ludovico Manin, the last doge of Venice (1725–1802) – and its gardens are closed to the public.

Musei Civici e Galleria di Storia e Arte Antica
Castello di Udine. **Tel** 0432 27 15 91. **Open** Tue–Sun. **Closed** Jan 1, Easter, May 1, Dec 25.

Museo Diocesano e Galleria Tiepolo
Piazza Patriarcato 1. **Tel** 0432 298 056. **Open** Wed–Sun. **Closed** Jan 1, Easter, Dec 25.

Villa Manin
Passariano. **Tel** 0432 821 210. **Open** daily. **Closed** Jan 1, Dec 25. for exhibitions only.

⓱ Cividale del Friuli

11,000. FS Piazza Paolo Diacono 10 (0432 71 04 60). Sat.
cividale.net

A gate in the medieval walls of Cividale leads down the main street and straight to the dramatic ravine of the River Natisone, which is spanned by the arch of the **Ponte del Diavolo** (Devil's Bridge).

Above the river's north bank stands the **Tempietto Longobardo** (Lombardic Chapel), a very rare example of an 8th-century church decorated with reliefs of saints, modeled in stucco. The town's history is traced in the excellent **Museo Archeologico Nazionale**, which contains the excavated remains of buildings from a Roman town, and a collection of Lombardic items including jewelry, ivory, and weapons.

Next door is the **Duomo**, rebuilt in 1453 after a fire, with its beautiful silver altarpiece (13th century). The **Museo Cristiano**, off the south aisle, contains sculptures from the original church: of particular interest is the altar donated by Ratchis, the Lombardic Duke of Friuli and later King of Italy (737–44), which is finely carved with scenes from the Life of Christ. There is in addition the unusual baptismal font of Patriarch Callisto (737–56): this octagonal structure, with a roof supported by pillars, is decorated with symbols of the Evangelists.

The Lion of Venice above the entrance to Gorizia's castle

Tempietto Longobardo
Via Monastero Maggiore 34. **Tel** 0432 70 08 67. **Open** daily.

Interior view of the Tempietto Longobardo in Cividale del Friuli

Museo Archeologico Nazionale
Palazzo dei Provveditori Veneti, P.za del Duomo 13. **Tel** 0432 70 07 00. **Open** 9am–2pm Mon, 8:30am–7:30pm Tue–Sun. **Closed** Jan 1, Dec 25.

Museo Cristiano
Via Condotti 1. **Tel** 0432 73 04 03. **Open** Jun–Sep daily, Oct–May Wed–Sun. **Closed** Jan 1, Dec 25.

⓲ Gorizia

37,000. FS Corso Italia 9 (0481 53 57 64). Thu, Fri.
turismofvg.it

Gorizia was at the center of fierce fighting during both world wars and was split in two by the 1947 Treaty of Paris, leaving part in Italy, part in Yugoslavia (now Slovenia).

The town's arcaded streets and pastel-painted houses have been carefully restored following substantial damage during World War II. The modern Museo Provinciale della Grande Guerra (Museum of the Great War), housed in the basement of the **Museo Provinciale**, provides a fascinating introduction to the realities of war. Videos, photographs, and life-size mock-ups of trenches, latrines, and gun emplacements are used to show the waste, squalor, and heroism of war.

Rooms on the upper floor of the museum house temporary exhibitions and items from the town's art collection, which includes works by local artists.

On a mound nearby rises the castle, encircled by 16th-century fortifications. From here there are extensive views stretching over the town.

Environs

Southwest of Gorizia, scenic country roads pass through the foothills of the **Carso**, a limestone plateau stretching down to Trieste. The plateau is dotted with fields enclosed by drystone walls and gouged with tunnels, caves, and underground rivers.

Museo Provinciale
Borgo Castello 13. **Tel** 0481 53 39 26. **Open** Tue–Sun. **Closed** Dec 25.

The attractive harborside at Grado, along the coast south of Aquileia

⓳ Aquileia

3,300. Piazza Capitolo 4 (0431 91 087). Tue.
turismofvg.it

Aquileia, now little more than a village but encircled by the ruins of palatial villas, baths, temples, and market buildings, provides a poignant reminder of the lost splendor of the Roman Empire.

It was here that Emperor Augustus received Herod the Great, King of Judea, in 10 BC, and it was here too, in AD 381, that the early Christian church held a major council attended by the learned saints Ambrose and Jerome to settle doctrinal issues. In the 5th century, however, the town was abandoned following several sackings. Fortunately, substantial parts of the early Christian basilica have survived. These contain the town's particular treasure: ornate floor mosaics.

Basilica

Piazza Capitolo. **Tel** 0431 919 719. **Open** daily. **Closed** during Mass. Crypt

The basilica was founded in about AD 313 and much of the original structure still survives, including the magnificent floor mosaics of the nave and **Cripta degli Scavi** below. The designs are a mixture of geometric patterns, biblical stories, and scenes from everyday life in ancient Aquileia. There is a lively portrayal of the tale of Jonah, who was swallowed by an extraordinary sea monster: the fishing boats are also surrounded by a rich array of creatures from the deep, including wide-eyed dolphins and squid.

Museo Archeologico Nazionale

Via Roma 1. **Tel** 0431 910 16. **Open** 8:30am–7:30pm Tue–Sun. **museoarcheo-aquileia.it**

The mosaics in the basilica demonstrate a tradition of craftsmanship that flourished in the city from the 2nd century AD. Additional examples of mosaics and stone carvings from the Classical era (1st to 3rd centuries) are on display in this museum, together with glass, amber, and a collection of flies, beautifully worked in gold, that formed the adornment of a Roman matron's veil.

Museo Paleocristiano

Località Monastero. **Tel** 0431 911 31. **Open** 8:30am–1:45pm Tue–Sun. **Closed** Jan 1, May 1, Dec 25.

This museum, which stands not far from Aquileia's ancient harbor beside the once-navigable Natissa River, focuses on the development of art during the early Christian era.

Environs

South of Udine, **Palmanova** is worth a visit for its remarkable octagonal layout and intact walls. The town was built in 1593 by the Venetians to commemorate the Battle of Lepanto.

Grado sits on a group of low islands in the middle of the Adriatic lagoon, attached to the mainland by a narrow causeway. The town grew into a port for Aquileia in the 2nd century and was used as a haven by Aquileia's citizens during the barbarian invasions. Today, Grado is a popular seaside resort. At the center of the old town is the **Duomo**, which contains 6th-century frescoes in the apse, similar to those on the vaults of San Marco in Venice *(see pp114–17)*. Nearby, in the church of **Santa Maria delle Grazie**, there are more 6th-century mosaics.

Symbolism in Early Christian Art

Christians were persecuted until their religion was granted official status by Constantine the Great in AD 313. Prior to this they had developed a language of secret symbols to express their beliefs, many of which can be seen in the mosaics and marble tomb chests of Aquileia. Many of these and other symbols later found their way into popular bestiaries and folk art.

Part of the 4th-century floor mosaic in the basilica at Aquileia

The winged figure of Victory holding a laurel wreath was a Classical symbol of triumph and holiness. Later, it came to represent Christ's resurrection, and more generally, victory over death.

⑳ Trieste

218,000. Piazza Unità d'Italia 4/b (040 347 83 12). Tue–Sat. **turismofvg.it**

Trieste is an atmospheric city, tucked up next to Slovenia, with a long, bustling harbor lined with handsome buildings and lapped by the waves of the Adriatic Sea.

Acquario Marino

Molo Pescheria 2, Riva Nazario Sauro 1. **Tel** 040 30 62 01. **Open** 9am–7pm Tue–Sun (Nov–Mar: to 1pm).

The aquarium, one of Trieste's most popular attractions, contains examples of the fascinating marine life in the Adriatic.

Castello di San Giusto

P.za Cattedrale 3. **Tel** 040 30 93 62. **Open** daily. Castle: 9am–6pm (Nov–Mar: to 5pm); museums: 9am–1pm.

Up above the harbor stands a hilltop castle built by Trieste's Venetian governors from 1368. It is set on a terrace that offers sweeping views over the Gulf of Trieste. The castle houses two museums containing Roman mosaics, and a collection of weapons and armor.

Basilica Paleocristiana

Via Madonna del Mare 11. **Tel** 040 4362. **Open** 10am–noon Wed; other times by appointment only.

Beside the castle lie the substantial ruins of the Roman basilica or law court built around AD 100. Note the stone magistrates' bench and throne.

Duomo

P.za Cattedrale 2. **Tel** 040 30 96 66. **Open** daily.

In the church of **San Giusto**, the city's Duomo, magistrates' bench, and throne of the Roman basilica were reinterpreted to become the seat of the bishop and clergy. Because the building was formed in the 14th century by linking two 5th-century churches that stood side by side, there are two thrones and benches here. The two apses are decorated with very fine 13th-century mosaics in the Venetian style.

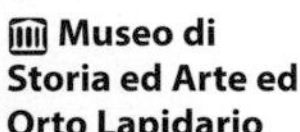

Museo di Storia ed Arte ed Orto Lapidario

Piazza della Cattedrale 1. **Tel** 040 31 05 00. **Open** 10am–5pm Tue–Sun. **Closed** public hols.

The important archaeological collection here provides fascinating evidence of Trieste's extensive trade links with the ancient Greek world.

The Castello di Miramare on the bay of Trieste

13th-century mosaics in the apse of San Giusto, Trieste's Duomo

Environs

From **Villa Opicina**, just north of Trieste, sweeping views may be had over the city, the bay, and south down the coast of Slovenia. A little beyond, at Borgo Grotta Gigante, lies the **Grotta del Gigante**, a huge cavern filled with stunning "organ pipe" formations and tall columns of stalagmites.

At Grignano, 5 miles (8 km) northwest of the city, stands the **Castello di Miramare**, a white castle set in lush green gardens beside the sparkling blue Adriatic. It was built by the Habsburg Archduke Maximilian in 1856–60 as his summer retreat, a few years before he was assassinated in Mexico. It is still furnished in contemporary style.

Grotta del Gigante
Borgo Grotta Gigante 42a. **Tel** 040 32 73 12. **Open** Tue–Sun (Jul & Aug: daily).

Castello di Miramare
Viale Miramare, Grignano. **Tel** 040 22 41 43. **Open** daily. (castle).

The tortoise hiding in his shell represented darkness and ignorance, while the cockerel, who crows at dawn, signified light and enlightenment.

ICHTHUS, or fish, was an acronym for Iesous CHristos THeou Uios Soter – Jesus Christ, Son of God, Savior, in ancient Greek.

Colorful birds, such as peacocks, symbolized immortality and the glorious transformation of the soul when it arrives in Heaven.

TRENTINO-ALTO ADIGE

The Italian-speaking Trentino – named after Trento, the regional capital – and the German-speaking Alto Adige or Südtirol (South Tyrol, the region bordering the upper reaches of the River Adige) differ dramatically in culture. However, they do have one feature in common: the majestic Dolomites that form the backdrop to every town and village, covered in snow for three months of every year and carpeted with exquisite Alpine plants for another three.

The region's mountains have been cut by glaciers into a series of deep, broad valleys. Many of these face south, so it remains unusually warm and sunny, even in winter. Travelers have passed up and down these valleys for generations – as confirmed by the extraordinary discovery, in 1991, of a 5,000-year-old man's body found emerging from the surface of a melting glacier in Alto Adige. The frozen corpse wore leather boots, stuffed with hay for warmth, and was armed with a copper ice pick.

The paths that Neolithic man once trod became major road networks under the Romans, when many of the region's cities were founded. By the Middle Ages, Alto Adige had established its very own distinctive culture under the Counts of Tyrol, whose land (later appropriated by the Habsburgs) straddled both sides of today's Italian/Austrian border. The Tyrolean nobility built the castles that still line the valleys and the mountain passes, in order to protect travelers from brigands.

Another ancient legacy is the tradition of hospitality to be found in the numerous guesthouses along the valleys. Many of these are built in the distinctive Tyrolean style, with beautiful timber balconies for making the most of the winter sun, and overhanging roof eaves to keep snow at a distance. Cozy in winter, with log fires and warming food, and offering marvelous views, they make the ideal base for enjoying the region's mountain footpaths and ski slopes.

Skiers enjoying the slopes around Monte Spinale, near Madonna di Campiglio, in Trentino

◀ Hikers climbing the glowing peaks of the Rosengarten mountain range in the Dolomites, South Tyrol

Exploring Trentino–Alto Adige

Trentino–Alto Adige is a region where unspoiled nature is complemented by a wealth of sporting opportunities. The tributary valleys feeding into the Adige valley contain lakes, rivers, and streams, and also woodland, vineyards, and Alpine pasture full of butterflies, birds, and flowers. Southeast of the region rise the distinctive limestone peaks of the Dolomites, while further north the area becomes more mountainous still, enclosed finally by the splendid heights of the Alps.

Via Ponte Aquila in Bressanone

Sights at a Glance

1. Malles Venosta (Mals im Vinschgau)
2. Merano (Meran)
3. Vipiteno (Sterzing)
4. Brunico (Bruneck)
5. Bressanone (Brixen)
6. Bolzano (Bozen)
7. Ortisei (Sankt Ulrich)
8. Canazei
9. Cavalese
10. San Martino di Castrozza
11. Cembra
12. Madonna di Campiglio
13. Trento
14. Rovereto
15. Castello di Avio

Key

- Highway
- Major road
- Secondary road
- Minor road
- Scenic route
- Main railroad
- Minor railroad
- International border
- Regional border
- △ Summit

0 kilometers 25

0 miles 10

For additional map symbols *see back flap*

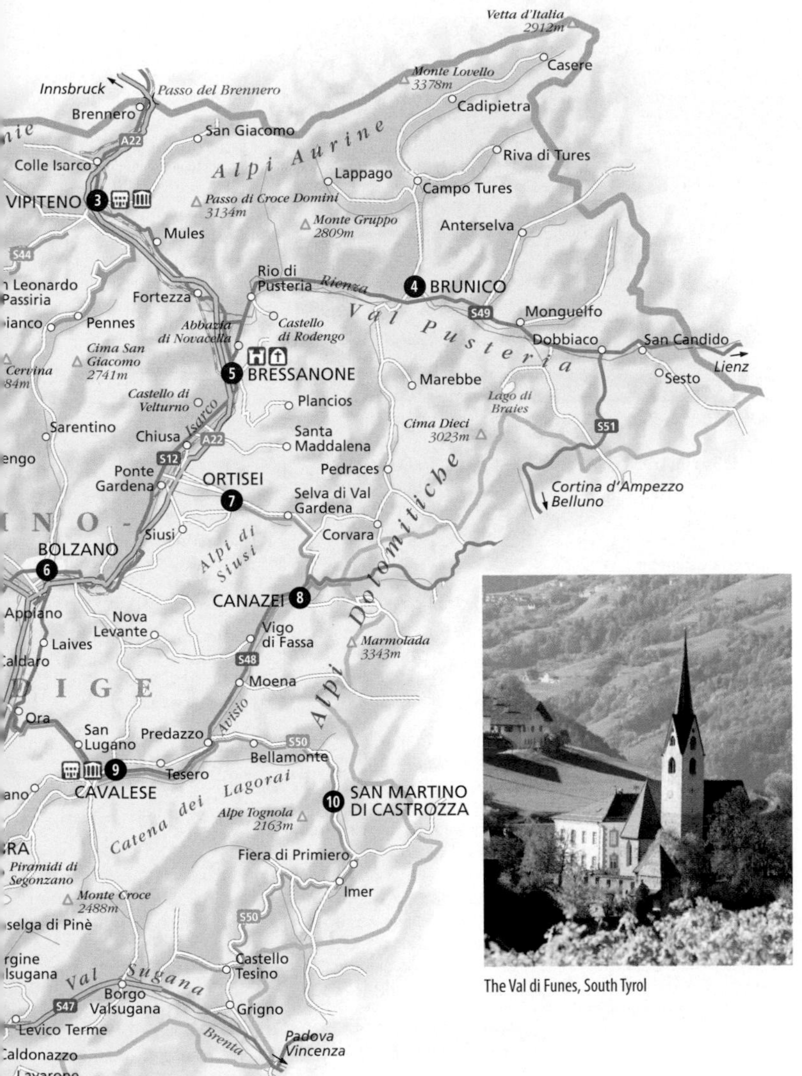

The Val di Funes, South Tyrol

View of the Dolomites from Madonna di Campiglio

Getting Around

The region's main artery is the Brenner Pass road: it runs from Austria in the north, following the River Adige from Bolzano to Trento, and southward on to Verona. Both the highway and the main road beside it are among the busiest in Europe, and the valley roads can also be congested during the ski season. Winter driving can be hazardous, requiring special tires and snow chains. An excellent railroad and bus network serves the whole area.

Abbazia di Monte Maria, founded in the 12th century, near Malles Venosta

❶ Malles Venosta

Mals Im Vinschgau

4,600. FS Via San Benedetto 1 (0473 83 11 90). Wed. **altavenosta-vacanze.it**

Malles Venosta sits in high border country, close to Switzerland and Austria, and was a customs point during the Middle Ages. The town has several Gothic churches, whose spires and towers give an appealing skyline, mirroring the jagged peaks that rise all around. The oldest is the tiny church of **San Benedetto**, a 9th-century Carolingian building on Via San Benedetto, with frescoes of its patrons.

Environs

The medieval **Castel Coira** (Churburg) rises at Sluderno (Schluderns), 2.5 miles (4 km) southeast of Malles. It contains an excellent collection of weapons and armor.

Clinging to the mountainside above the town of Burgusio (Burgeis), 3 miles (5 km) north of Malles, is the Benedictine **Abbazia di Monte Maria** (Marienberg), founded in the 12th century but enlarged in the 18th and 19th. The church's crypt shelters an outstanding series of 12th-century frescoes.

The glorious medieval town of **Glorenza** lies just 1 mile (2 km) south of Malles.

Castel Coira
Churburg, Sluderno. **Tel** 0473 61 52 41. **Open** 20 Mar–Oct: Tue–Sun (& Mon if pub hol). compulsory.

Abbazia di Monte Maria
Tel 0473 83 13 06. **Open** Apr–Oct: Mon–Sat; Nov–Apr: groups by appt only. **Closed** public hols.

❷ Merano

Meran

35,000. FS Corso della Libertà 45 (0473 27 20 00). Tue, Fri. **meran.eu**

Merano is an attractive spa town popular with Austrians, Germans, and Italians. On Corso Libertà, a street of chic shops and hotels, stands the **Kurhaus**, or Spa Hall, built in 1914, now a concert venue. Furnished in period style, the 15th-century **Castello Principesco** was home to the Habsburg Archduke Sigismund. Inviting gardens line the Passirio River, which winds its way through the town. The Passeggiata Lungo Passirio d'Inverno (Winter Walk) follows the north bank to the Roman bridge, Ponte Romano; the Passeggiata d'Estate (Summer Walk) on the south bank leads to the medieval Ponte Passirio.

The Art Nouveau facade of the Kurhaus in Merano

Environs

The romantic 12th-century **Castel Tirolo** lies 2.5 miles (4 km) to the north. It hosts a museum of Tyrolean history.

The grounds of **Castel Trauttmansdorff** house a fascinating botanical garden.

Castello Principesco
Via Galilei. **Tel** 3290 18 63 90. **Open** Tue–Sun & public hols. **Closed** Jan–Feb.

Castel Tirolo
Via Castello 24, Tirolo. **Tel** 0473 22 02 21. **Open** mid Mar–10 Dec: Tue–Sun. **Closed** Dec–mid-Mar.

Castel Trauttmansdorff
Via S. Valentino 51a. **Tel** 0473 27 01 72. **Open** Apr 1–Nov 15: daily. **touriseum.it**

❸ Vipiteno

Sterzing

5,600. FS Piazza Città 3 (0472 76 53 25). daily.

Surrounded by mineral-rich valleys, Vipiteno is very Tyrolean in feel. On Via Città Nuova, lined with fine mansions, rise the Gothic **Palazzo Comunale**, containing Renaissance sculpture and paintings, and the Torre dei Dodici, the symbol of the town. Wood carvings in the **Museo Multscher** are by Hans Multscher; the Bavarian sculptor came to Vipiteno in 1456–8 to carve the altar for the parish **church**, which lies just south of the town.

To the west, the charming **Val di Racines** includes waterfalls and a natural rock bridge.

Palazzo Comunale
Via Città Nuova 21. **Tel** 0472 72 37 00. **Open** Mon–Fri. **Closed** Fri pm & public hols.

Museo Multscher
Via della Commenda 11. **Tel** 0472 76 64 64. **Open** Apr–Oct: Tue–Sat. **Closed** public hols.

For hotels and restaurants in this region see pp562–77 and pp580–605

The medieval castle dominating the town of Brunico

4 Brunico

Bruneck

13,000. FS Piazza Municipio 7 (0474 55 57 22). Wed. **bruneck.com**

This attractive town, overlooked by the imposing form of its medieval **castle**, retains 14th-century fortifications and a network of narrow streets that can only be explored on foot. The church of **St. Ursula**, to the northwest of St. Ursula's Gate, holds a series of outstanding mid-15th-century altar reliefs of the Nativity. The **Museo Etnografico di Teodone** offers displays of traditional agricultural life and local costumes; this folklore museum also provides an ideal opportunity to visit a 16th-century farmhouse and barn.

St Ursula's Gate sundial, Brunico

Museo Etnografico di Teodone
Via Duca Teodone 24, Teodone. **Tel** 0474 55 20 87. **Open** Easter–Oct: Tue–Sat, Sun and public hols pm (Aug: also Mon).

5 Bressanone

Brixen

18,000. FS Via Ratisbona 9 (0472 83 64 01). Mon. **brixen.org**

The narrow medieval alleys of Bressanone cluster around the cathedral and the palace of the prince-bishops who ruled the town for much of its history. The **Duomo**, on Piazza del Duomo, was rebuilt in the 18th century but retains its 12th-century cloister, decorated with superb 15th-century frescoes. The lavish interiors of Palazzo Vescovile, the bishops' Renaissance palace, house the **Museo Diocesano**. It contains precious items from the Middle Ages, as well as the **Museo dei Presepi**, with its collection of wooden crib figures that are carved locally.

Environs

At Velturno (Feldthurns), 5 miles (8 km) southwest, stands the Renaissance **Castello di Velturno**, the summer retreat of the rulers of Bressanone, noted for its frescoed rooms. A little over 2 miles (3 km) north of Bressanone lies the **Abbazia di Novacella**, a picturesque group of fortified monastic buildings with an outstanding series of cloister frescoes. Farther north up the valley, at **Rio di Pusteria** (Mühlbach), the remains of a 16th-century fortified barrier can be seen to the east of the town. The barrier funneled ancient travelers through the customs post that divided Tyrol from the Görz district.

High above Rio di Pusteria, to the southeast, looms the massive outline of the **Castello di Rodengo** (Rodeneck). The castle contains wonderful 13th-century frescoes showing battle scenes, the Last Judgment, and courtly episodes from the *Iwein* romance by Hartmann von Aue, the medieval poet.

Museo Diocesano & Museo dei Presepi
Piazza Palazzo Vescovile 2. **Tel** 0472 83 05 05. Museo Diocesano: **Open** 10am–6pm Tue–Sun (Jul–Sep: 7pm–midnight). **Closed** Nov–mid-Mar. Museo dei Presepi: **Open** mid-Mar–Oct: 10am–6pm Tue–Sun (Dec–Jan 6: to 5pm). **Closed** Dec 24 & 25.

Castello di Velturno
Velturno. **Tel** 0472 85 55 25. **Open** Mar–Nov: Tue–Sun. only.

Abbazia di Novacella
Via Abbazia 1/2b, Varna. **Tel** 0472 83 61 89. **Open** Mon–Sat. **Closed** Mon (Jan–Mar) & pub hols. only.

Castello di Rodengo
Rodengo. **Tel** 0472 45 40 56. **Open** May–mid-Oct: Sun–Fri.

The cloisters of Bressanone Duomo with their 15th-century frescoes

The Baroque interior of the church of St. Ulrich in Ortisei

❻ Bolzano

Bozen

98,000. FS i Piazza Walther 8 (0471 30 70 00). Sat.
bolzano-bozen.it

Bolzano, the capital of the Alto Adige, is the gateway between the Italian-speaking Trentino region and the German-speaking Alto Adige, or Südtirol, and has a marked Tyrolean atmosphere. The old center, **Piazza Walther**, is dominated by the 15th-century Gothic **Duomo**, with its multicolored mosaic-patterned roof and elaborate spire. The "wine door" inside the Duomo is carved with figures at work among vines and reflects the importance of wine to the local economy. In the middle of Piazza Walther is a statue of Walther von der Vogelweide, the 13th-century troubadour – born, according to legend, in this area. North of the square, the streets are lined with houses adorned with intricate gables, balconies, and oriel windows. The outdoor market, starting at Piazza Grano, forms an inviting array of local produce that continues along the arcaded Via dei Portici. The modern **Museo Archeologico** houses impressive finds from the Stone Age, the Bronze Age, the Iron Age, Roman times, and the time of Charlemagne. A key exhibit is Ötzi, the famous 5,000-year-old "Iceman." The **Chiesa dei Domenicani** (Dominican church), on Piazza Domenicani, has 14th-century *Triumph of Death* frescoes and a frescoed cloister.

The Duomo spire, Bolzano

Museo Archeologico
Via Museo 43. **Tel** 0471 32 01 00.
Open Tue–Sun (Jul, Aug & Dec: daily).
Closed Jan 1, May 1, Dec 25.
iceman.it

❼ Ortisei

Sankt Ulrich

4,500. i Via Rezia 1 (0471 77 76 00). Fri. **valgardena.it**

Ortisei is the prosperous main resort for the pretty Val Gardena and Alpe di Siusi region, and a major center for woodcarving; examples of local craftsmanship may be seen in local shops, in the **Museo della Val Gardena** (which also focuses on local archaeology), and in the church of **St. Ulrich**.

To the south is the **Alpe di Siusi** (Seiser Alm) region, noted for its Alpine meadows, balconied farmsteads, and onion-domed churches. The best way to explore this beautiful area is by cableway from Ortisei: to the northeast another cable car runs to 8,260-ft- (2,518-m-) high Monte Seceda, and walks from here lead into the Odle Dolomites.

Museo della Val Gardena
Via Rezia 83. **Tel** 0471 79 75 54.
Open Jan–Mar: Tue–Fri; mid-May–Oct: Mon–Fri; Jul & Aug: Mon–Sat.
museumgherdeina.it

❽ Canazei

1,800. i Piazza Marconi 5 (0462 60 96 00). Sat (Jul–Sep).
fassa.com

Located at the base of some of the highest and most awe-inspiring groups of peaks, Canazei is a good base for exploring the Dolomites. In summer, chair lifts climb to viewpoints where the beauty of the encircling mountains can be appreciated to the fullest. The most popular viewpoints are Pecol and Col dei Rossi, reached by the Belvedere cableway from Via Pareda in Canazei: the cliffs of the Sella group are visible to the north, with Sasso Lungo to the west and Marmolada, the highest of the Dolomites at 10,965 ft (3,343 m), to the south.

Skiers enjoying views of the Dolomites above Canazei

For hotels and restaurants in this region see pp562–77 and pp580–605

Environs

At **Vigo di Fassa**, 8 miles (13 km) southwest, the **Museo Ladino** focuses on the Ladin-speaking people of some of the valleys. Ladin – a Rhaeto-Romance language – is taught in local schools and the ancient traditions still thrive.

Museo Ladino
Località San Giovanni, Vigo di Fassa. **Tel** 0462 76 01 82. **Open** Tue–Sat pm (late Jun–mid-Sep & Dec 20–Jan 6: daily). **istladin.net**

The frescoed facade of the Palazzo della Magnifica Comunità

9 Cavalese

3,600. Via Fratelli Bronzetti 60 (0462 24 11 11). last Tue of month (not Jul). **visitfiemme.it**

Cavalese is the chief town in the Val di Fiemme, a pretty region of flower-filled aromatic pastures, delightful wooded valleys, and Tyrolean architecture. At the center of the town stands the **Palazzo della Magnifica Comunità**. Originally built in the 13th century, this was the seat of the medieval governing council that ruled the area as a semiautonomous region. Today the paneled interiors contain medieval paintings by local artists, and an archaeology collection. Most visitors come for the excellent summer and winter resort facilities, and to climb, by cable car, to the 7,311-ft (2,229-m) top of **Alpe Cermis**, the mountain that rises to the south of the town.

Environs

The church in **Tesero**, the next village east, bears a 15th-century fresco by an unknown painter depicting Sabbath-breakers. The church itself, dating back to

Vines growing on the terraced slopes of the Cembra valley

1450, has a flurry of Gothic vaulting, and a modern representation of the Crucifixion painted against a background of the village.

At **Predazzo**, about 8 miles (13 km) east, the **Museo di Geologia e Etnografia** explains the local geology.

Palazzo della Magnifica Comunità
Piazza Cesare Battisti 2. **Tel** 0462 34 03 65. **Open** Tue–Sun. **palazzomagnifica.eu**

Museo di Geologia e Etnografia
Via Cesare Battisti 4. **Tel** 0462 50 23 92. **Open** 10am–noon & 5–7pm Mon–Sat (mid-Sep–Feb by appt).

10 San Martino di Castrozza

470. Via Passo Rolle 165 (0439 76 88 67). **sanmartino.com**

The resort of San Martino occupies one of the most scenic and accessible valleys in the southern Dolomites, making it very popular with walkers and skiers. Cable cars rise to the peak of **Alpe Tognola** (7,095 ft/ 2,163 m), southwest of the town, and up the **Cima della Rosetta** (8,557 ft/ 2,609 m) to the east. Both offer fabulous views of the Pale di San Martino peaks, a stirring sight as the massive rock peaks, split by glaciers, rise above a sea of green meadows and woodland.

Piramidi di Segonzano, near Cembra

San Martino is almost entirely surrounded by forest, which once supplied the Venetian Republic with timber for ships. The forest is now protected, and as a result it is possible to see Alpine flowers, mushrooms, birds, and other wildlife with relative ease.

11 Cembra

2,500. Piazza San Rocco 10 (0461 68 31 10). Wed am.

The wine-producing town of Cembra nestles on the terraced slopes of a scenic valley of flower-filled villages. Some 4 miles (6 km) east of Cembra stand the **Piramidi di Segonzano**, a rare series of erosion pillars, some over 100 ft (30 m) high, each topped by a rock. The footpath to the pillars is well signposted, with informative noticeboards along the way explaining the formation of the bizarre columns, which are similar in appearance to giant termites' nests. Their setting amid bird-filled woodland makes the steep climb up to the site well worthwhile. A further reward is the fine view, from the top of the hill, along the Cembra valley and westward as far as the Brenta group of Dolomites.

Piramidi di Segonzano
Strada Statale 612 to Cavalese. **Open** daily.

The impressive falls of the Cascate di Nardis, Madonna di Campiglio

⓬ Madonna di Campiglio

1,300. Via Pradalago 4 (0465 44 75 01). Jul–Aug: Tue & Thu. **campigliodolomiti.it**

Madonna di Campiglio is the chief resort in the Val Meledrio. Nestling between the Brenta and Adamello groups of peaks, it makes the perfect base for walking or skiing amid the magnificent mountain terrain. Cableways radiate out from the town in every direction, giving easy access to the peaks.

Environs

The church at **Pinzolo**, 9 miles (14 km) south, has a well-preserved fresco depicting a *Dance of Death* (1539). The inevitable march of the figures, both rich and poor, is underlined by a text written in local dialect.

North of Pinzolo, the road west from Carisolo leads to the verdant and popular, yet unspoiled, **Val Genova**. About 2 miles (4 km) along the valley is the spectacular **Cascate di Nardis**, a waterfall that plunges down 300 ft (90 m). The two masses of rock at the bottom are said to be the forms of petrified demons.

⓭ Trento

105,000. FS Via Manci 2 (0461 21 60 00). Thu am.

Trento, the capital of the region to which it gave its name, is also the most attractive town in Trentino: it has a fine Romanesque cathedral, a richly decorated castle, and streets lined with handsome Renaissance mansions. Trento is noted as the venue for the **Council of Trent** (1545–63), set up by the Catholic Church to consider reforms that might encourage breakaway groups, in particular the German Protestants, to return to the fold. The reforms, which ushered in the period of the Counter-Reformation, were only partly successful.

The **Duomo**, site of some of the Council meetings, was built in robust Romanesque style from the 13th century. It was three centuries before it was completed, in 1515, but the builders maintained architectural harmony by ignoring Gothic and Renaissance styles entirely. The result is a church of unusual integrity. The Duomo stands on **Piazza Duomo**, the city's main square, first laid out by the Romans as their central marketplace or forum. Trento's Roman name, Tridentum, is commemorated in the figure of Neptune who stands holding his trident at the top of the fountain, which stands in the middle of the main square.

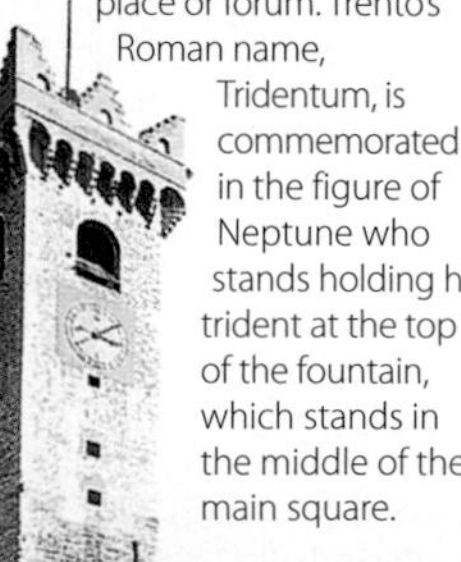

Museo Diocesano Tridentino

Piazza Duomo 18. **Tel** 0461 23 44 19. **Open** Wed–Mon. **Closed** Jan 1, Dec 25. **museodiocesanotridentino.it**

This museum is housed in the **Palazzo Pretorio**, an imposing medieval building that stands on the eastern side of Piazza Duomo. Its contents include early ivory reliquaries, Flemish tapestries, and paintings depicting the Council of Trent.

Castello del Buonconsiglio

Via Bernardo Clesio 5. **Tel** 0461 23 37 70. **Open** Tue–Sun. **Closed** Jan 1, Dec 25. **buonconsiglio.it**

Inner courtyard of the Magno Palazzo

This large castle, built in the 13th century and later enlarged with additional buildings, is part of the defenses of the town. Trento was an important frontier on the main road linking Italy to northern Europe, and thick walls still encircle the town.

The southern section of the castle consists of the magnificent **Magno Palazzo** (1530), built for the ruling prince-bishops of Trento, who were given extensive powers by the Holy Roman Emperor to foster loyalty and discourage defection to the pope. The lavish decoration (including frescoes of virile satyrs and nymphs by Gerolamo Romanino, 1531–2) speaks of huge wealth and a luxurious lifestyle. The palazzo houses the **Museo Provinciale**, with paintings, ceramics, and 15th-century wood carvings, and prehistoric, Etruscan and Roman items. The **Torre dell' Aquila** (Eagle Tower)

Palazzo Pretorio and the Duomo in Trento's main square

The commanding form of the Ossario del Castel Dante in Rovereto

nearby contains frescoes painted around 1400 that depict the months of the year.

Environs
Immediately to the west of Trento, a scenic round-trip along a winding road leads up the north flank of **Monte Bondone** and back, via **Vezzano**, down the western slopes. The views along the route are magnificent, in particular from Vaneze and Vason. East of Trento, Pergine marks the start of the **Val Sugana**, a broad valley with lakes. In the hills north of Lake Levico lies the spa town of **Levico Terme**, distinguished by elegant Neo-Classical buildings set amid beautifully wooded parkland.

⓮ Rovereto

33,000. FS. Corso Rosmini 6 (0464 43 03 63). Tue.
W **visitrovereto.it**

Rovereto was at the center of fierce fighting during World War I, after which the Venetian castle (built in 1416) that dominates the town was transformed into the **Museo Storico Italiano della Guerra**, a war museum. The displays include sections on wartime humor, propaganda, and spying. Near the museum entrance, stairs lead out onto the castle roof for a view of the imposing **Ossario del Castel Dante.**

Some distance away is the **Campana dei Caduti** (Bell of the Fallen), which was cast from melted-down cannons at the end of World War II and mounted in an imposing building above the town; it is rung daily at sunset. Below the war museum is the **Museo Civico**, with its collections on archaeology, art, natural history, and folklore. Another branch of the museo, in Corso Bettini, houses a collection of sculpture by Carlo Fait. The Mario Botta–designed **Museo di Arte Contemporanea di Trento e Rovereto (MART)** showcases 20th-century Italian art. A second site, in Via Portici, holds Italian Futurist art.

Environs
A little over 5 miles (8 km) north of Rovereto is **Castel Beseno**, rising on a hill to the east. This enormous castle was built and rebuilt from the 12th century to the 18th to guard the junction of the three valleys.

Three miles (5 km) south of Rovereto, the main road passes through a valley littered with massive boulders created by landslides: these are known as Lavini di Marco or **Ruina Dantesca**, because they are mentioned in Dante's *Inferno* (XII, 4–9). Fossilized dinosaur footprints have been discovered there.

Museo Storico Italiano della Guerra
Via Castelbarco 7. **Tel** 0464 43 81 00. **Open** Tue–Sun. **Closed** Jan 1, Dec 24, 25, & 31.

Museo Civico
Borgo Santa Caterina 41. **Tel** 0464 45 28 00; Palazzo Alberti, Corso Bettini 41. **Tel** 0464 45 28 30. **Open** Tue–Sun. **Closed** Jan 1, Aug 5, Nov 1, Dec 25.
W **museocivico.rovereto.tn.it**

MART
Corso Bettini 43. **Tel** 0464 43 88 87; Casa d'Arte Futurista Depero, Via Portici 38. Tel 0464 43 18 13. **Open** Tue–Sun.

Castel Beseno
Besenello. **Tel** 0464 83 46 00. **Open** Mar–Oct: Tue–Sun (Mon if public hol); Nov–Feb: Sat & Sun.

Castello di Avio in its lush setting

⓯ Castello di Avio

Via Castello, Sabbionara d'Avio. **Tel** 0464 68 44 53. FS to Vo, then 2-mile (3-km) walk. **Open** Mar–Sep: 10am–6pm Wed–Sun (open Tue in Aug); Oct–Nov: 10am–5pm Tue–Sun. **Closed** Dec–Feb.

Castles line the Adige valley all the way to the Brenner Pass, but few are as accessible as the Castello di Avio. It was founded in the 11th century, extended in the 13th, and today offers visitors far-reaching views. Among the numerous frescoes is a rare series in the Casa delle Guardie (the Sentry House) depicting 13th-century battle scenes.

The extensive walls enclosing Castel Beseno above Rovereto

NORTHWEST ITALY

Northwest Italy at a Glance

The northwest of Italy is made up of three very different geological characteristics: the jagged Alps, the flat plain, and the undulating shoreline of the Mediterranean. Within this varied landscape, some of it still wild and unspoiled, lie extremely rich and diverse vestiges of the area's substantial cultural heritage. The major sights, in the regions of Valle d'Aosta and Piedmont, Liguria and Lombardy, are shown on this map.

The Parco Nazionale del Gran Paradiso is a beautiful wilderness, and the habitat of rare Alpine fauna and flora *(see pp220–21).*

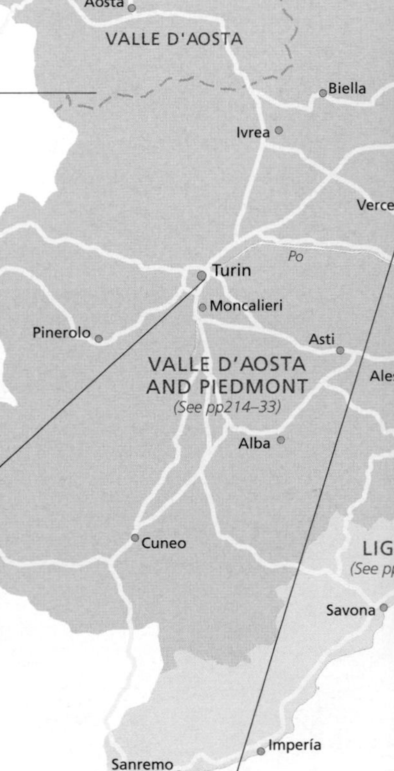

The capital of Piedmont is Turin, an elegant and bustling city of splendid Baroque architecture. Its skyline is dramatically dominated by the Mole Antonelliana *(see p228).*

Sanremo is a typical Riviera resort, with palm trees and a casino. The onion-domed outline of the Russian church adds an exotic flavor to the town *(see p238).*

The Basilica di Sant'Andrea in Vercelli is an important Romanesque building, one of the earliest to use Gothic elements *(see p232).*

◀ The picturesque Isola San Giulio in the center of Lake Orta, Valle d'Aosta

Isola Bella is an enchanting island on romantic Lake Maggiore. Nearby lies beautiful Lake Como *(see pp194–95)*.

Milan's Duomo, with its distinctive bristling spires, is one of the many architectural gems in this stylish city *(see p197)*.

Portofino is one of Italy's most exclusive resorts. Nestling in a creek, its pretty pastel-colored houses surround a yacht-filled harbor *(see p244)*.

The Certosa di Pavia, a charming Carthusian monastery, includes a richly decorated Gothic church with a magnificent Renaissance facade, and a series of attractive cloisters *(see pp208–9)*.

The Flavors of Northwest Italy

From Mediterranean Liguria to the Alps, the Lombardy plain, and Piedmont, this diverse area is characterized by its rich yet hearty cuisine. Along with the Veneto, Lombardy and Piedmont are Italy's main rice-growing areas and risotto features widely, especially delicious when made with local wild mushrooms. The white truffles of Alba are the "white gold" of Piedmont, while lush pastures produce some of the country's best meat and many of Italy's finest cheeses. The mild Ligurian climate favors olives and herbs – especially basil, used in pesto sauce. And fish teem in the sparkling Mediterranean.

Fresh basil

A precious haul of aromatic Piedmontese truffles

Lombardy

This is the home of dishes prepared *alla Milanese*, rich in butter, *ossobuco* (shin of veal), vegetable soups, and boiled meats *(bollito misto)*. From veal to beef and from pork to poultry, Lombardy produces some of the country's finest meat, but it is also associated with *cucina povera* (the cuisine of the poor), in which polenta (corn porridge) still features from its days as the staple diet of impoverished country folk. The other staple food, the short-grained rice that is used in risotto, grows abundantly in the area around Pavia. Lombardy is one of Italy's largest cheese-making regions, the most famous including Gorgonzola, Mascarpone, Bitto, and Grana Padano.

Piedmont & Valle d'Aosta

The "Slow Food" movement was born in Piedmont in 1986. Its mission is "to defend biodiversity in our food supply, spread taste education, and connect producers of excellent food." The movement now has more than 100,000 members in more than 50 countries. Piedmontese flavors are robust,

Mouthwatering range of northwest Italy's finest cheeses

Regional Dishes and Specialties

Gianduiotti

Veal is especially popular in Lombardy and Piedmont, and a great favorite with the Milanese is *ossobuco*. Another classic Piedmontese dish, *vitello tonnato* is a surprisingly delicious blend of cold roast veal served with a sauce made with mayonnaise, tuna, gherkins, and capers. As well as pesto, a traditional dish from Genoa is *buridda alla Genovese* – a delicious fish soup or stew containing mussels, shrimps, octopus, squid, and clams. Shavings of truffle in dishes such as risotto and *fagiano tartufato* (pheasant stuffed with white truffle and pork fat) give a taste of sheer luxury, and fortunately, a little of this very expensive delicacy goes a long way. And, for those with a sweet tooth, *panettone* is a soft Christmas cake studded with dried and candied fruit, another Milanese specialty.

Bagna Caôda From Piedmont; a warm mix of olive oil, anchovies, and garlic into which raw vegetables are dipped.

Boxes of fresh fish are unloaded onto a Ligurian quayside

rich, and earthy, and laced with French flair, reflecting a history of French rule and influence.

The paddy fields of Vercelli are the rice capital of Europe and truffle risotto, especially when flavored using the prized white variety from Alba, is truly memorable fare.

The mountains are famous for cow's milk cheese, especially the semisoft Fontina from the Valle d'Aosta, cured meats, salamis, terrines, and game. Piedmont also produces Italy's greatest red wines, and the prized Barolo and Barbaresco often feature as a marinade in beef dishes.

The Turinese are passionate about chocolate, echoing Turin's tradition of chocolate-making originating in the 17th century. Most famous are the sublime ingot-shaped *gianduiotti*, filled with a rich chocolate-hazelnut cream. The city is also the birthplace of *grissini*, crisp breadsticks that grace every restaurant table. The tradition of the *aperitivo* also originates in Turin. The spread that accompanies a glass of Prosecco or a cocktail in bars throughout the city between 6pm and 8pm is substantial.

Delicious foccacia bread made with Ligurian olive oil

Liguria

The Mediterranean climate is perfect for growing herbs, fruits and vegetables, nuts, and olives. Ligurian olive oil is of the highest quality and is used in the preparation of many dishes. To accompany pasta, pesto is the signature sauce, made from basil, pine nuts, garlic, and olive oil, as well as a mix of Pecorino and Parmesan. This use of aromatic herbs is typical of Ligurian cuisine in general.

Not surprisingly, fish and seafood are as common as meat and dairy in this region, where the vast majority of people live on the coast.

ON THE MENU

Agnolotti Piedmont pasta specialty – crescent-shaped ravioli stuffed with meat or vegetables. Served with *ragù* or a creamy sauce.

Brasato al Barolo Braised beef cooked gently with vegetables in Barolo wine.

Lumache Piedmontese snails, the best of which come from Cherasco, served either in garlic and butter or in a sauce of olive oil, tomatoes, and garlic.

Oca alla Piemontese Goose preserved in fat.

Risotto alla Milanese Rich, saffron-scented dish of rice with white wine, onion, and Parmesan cheese.

Trenette con pesto A Ligurian dish of flat noodles with a sauce of basil, garlic, pine nuts, and olive oil.

Ossobuco Milanese shin of veal, braised slowly in white wine. The bone marrow is considered a delicacy.

Zabaione A frothy dessert of egg yolks, sugar, and Marsala, *zabaione* is a specialty of the Piedmont region.

The Wines of Northwest Italy

Grapes are grown throughout the northwest – from the cliffs of Liguria to the steep mountainsides of Valle d'Aosta. The best wines, however, come from Piedmont, in particular the Langhe hills southwest of Turin, source of two of Italy's finest reds: the rich, powerful, long-lived Barolo and Barbaresco. Both of these are now showing the benefits of modern techniques and a renewed interest in high-quality wine making. Lighter, everyday red wines that go well with the local cuisine include Dolcetto and the popular Barbera. Another Piedmont specialty is sparkling *spumante*, Italians' instinctive choice whenever there is something around to celebrate.

Castiglione Falletto in the heart of Piedmont

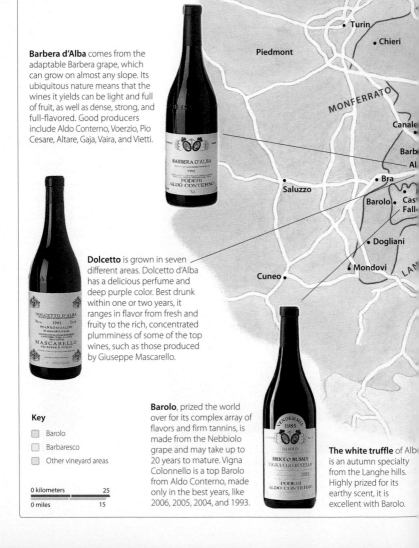

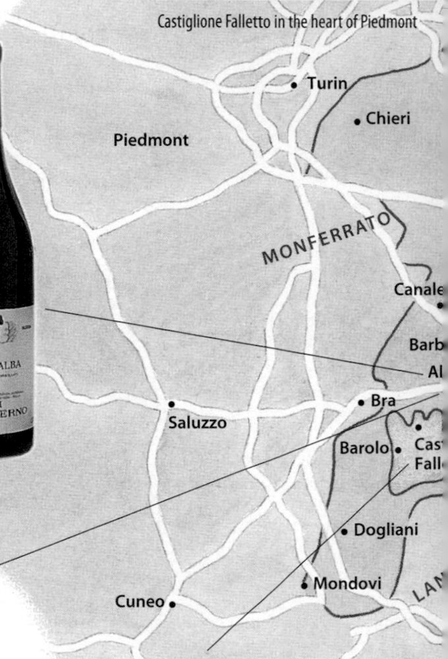

Turin
Chieri
Piedmont
MONFERRATO
Saluzzo
Bra
Barolo
Dogliani
Mondovi
Cuneo

Barbera d'Alba comes from the adaptable Barbera grape, which can grow on almost any slope. Its ubiquitous nature means that the wines it yields can be light and full of fruit, as well as dense, strong, and full-flavored. Good producers include Aldo Conterno, Voerzio, Pio Cesare, Altare, Gaja, Vaira, and Vietti.

Dolcetto is grown in seven different areas. Dolcetto d'Alba has a delicious perfume and deep purple color. Best drunk within one or two years, it ranges in flavor from fresh and fruity to the rich, concentrated plumminess of some of the top wines, such as those produced by Giuseppe Mascarello.

Key

- Barolo
- Barbaresco
- Other vineyard areas

0 kilometers 25

0 miles 15

Barolo, prized the world over for its complex array of flavors and firm tannins, is made from the Nebbiolo grape and may take up to 20 years to mature. Vigna Colonnello is a top Barolo from Aldo Conterno, made only in the best years, like 2006, 2005, 2004, and 1993.

The white truffle of Alba is an autumn specialty from the Langhe hills. Highly prized for its earthy scent, it is excellent with Barolo.

Moscato d'Asti is an excellent *aperitivo* or light dessert wine made from the aromatic, fruity Moscato grape. It is light in alcohol with a gently sweet finish and may have a slight sparkle. Ideal for refreshing the palate after a hearty Piedmontese meal, Araldica's versatile Moscato is delicious when served well chilled.

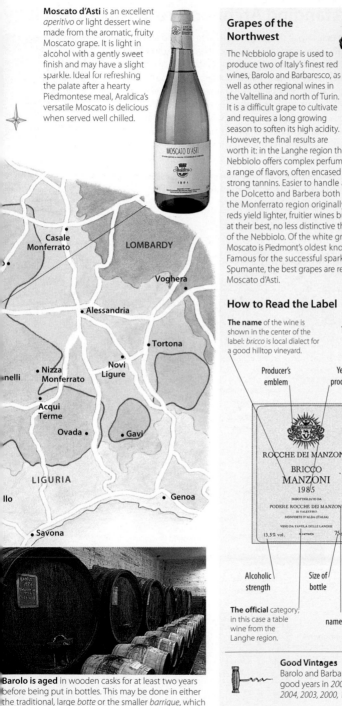

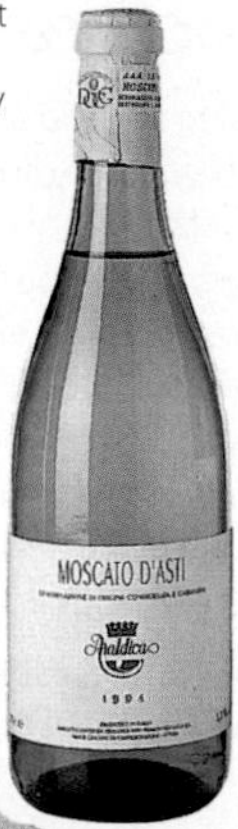

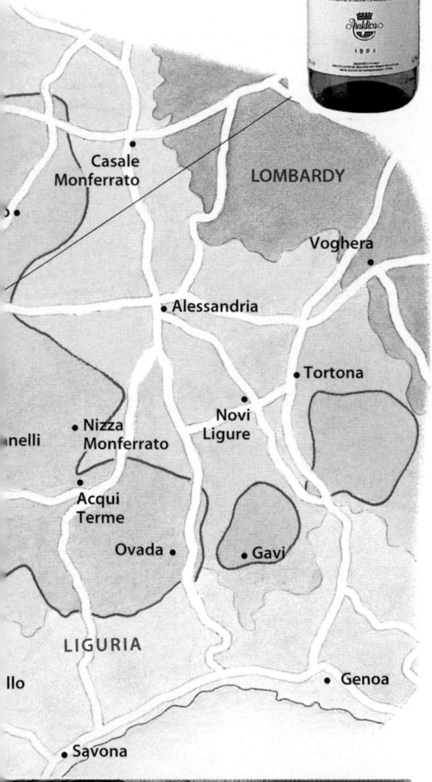

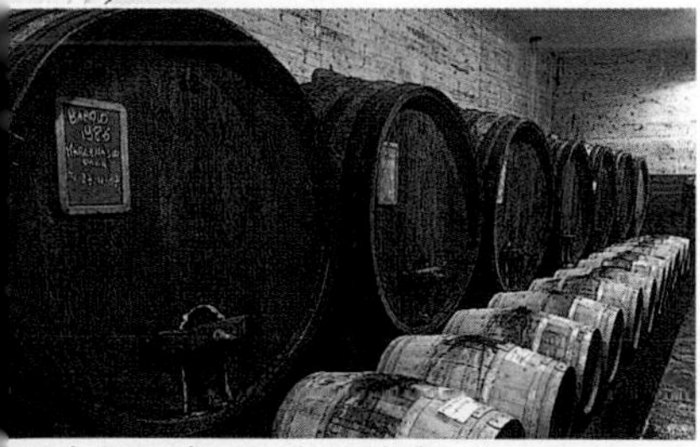

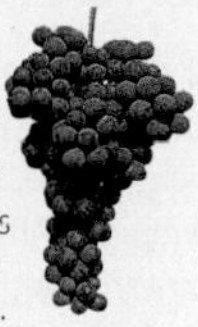

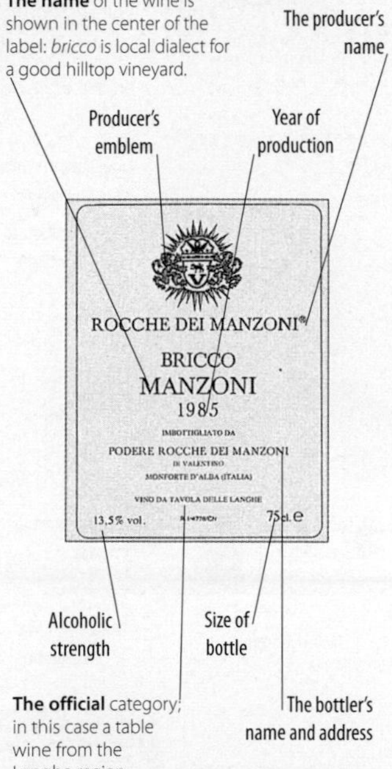

Barolo is aged in wooden casks for at least two years before being put in bottles. This may be done in either the traditional, large *botte* or the smaller *barrique*, which imparts a strong oaky flavor to the wine.

Grapes of the Northwest

Nebbiolo grapes

The Nebbiolo grape is used to produce two of Italy's finest red wines, Barolo and Barbaresco, as well as other regional wines in the Valtellina and north of Turin. It is a difficult grape to cultivate and requires a long growing season to soften its high acidity. However, the final results are worth it: in the Langhe region the Nebbiolo offers complex perfumes and a range of flavors, often encased within strong tannins. Easier to handle and lighter, the Dolcetto and Barbera both came from the Monferrato region originally. These reds yield lighter, fruitier wines but, when at their best, no less distinctive than those of the Nebbiolo. Of the white grapes, the Moscato is Piedmont's oldest known variety. Famous for the successful sparkling Asti Spumante, the best grapes are reserved for Moscato d'Asti.

How to Read the Label

The name of the wine is shown in the center of the label: *bricco* is local dialect for a good hilltop vineyard.

The producer's name

Producer's emblem

Year of production

Alcoholic strength

Size of bottle

The official category; in this case a table wine from the Langhe region.

The bottler's name and address

Good Vintages

Barolo and Barbaresco had good years in *2006, 2005, 2004, 2003, 2000, 1998, 1997.*

Understanding Architecture in Northwest Italy

Although the buildings of the northwest tend to be solid and imposing – a result partly of the more severe climate – there is no distinctive architectural stamp as there is around Venice, Florence, or even Rome. Instead, a variety of buildings in different styles, many borrowed or reinterpreted from elsewhere, are dotted across the area: enchanting medieval castles, outstanding Romanesque and Gothic buildings, unusual Baroque structures. The northwest is also rich in modern architecture – in terms of both design and materials – influenced by the region's industrial developments and its strong flair for innovative design, which also often draws its inspiration from earlier architectural styles.

Castello Sforzesco, 1451–66 *(see p192)*

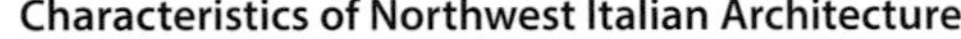

Characteristics of Northwest Italian Architecture

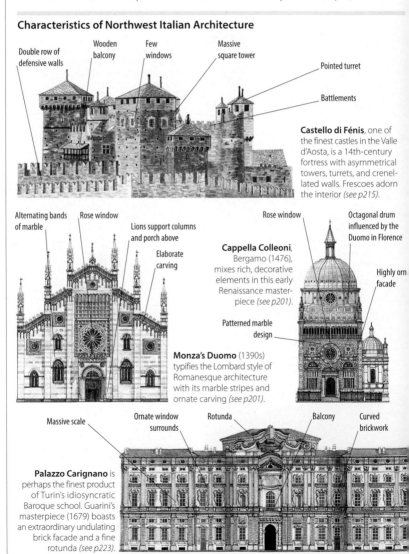

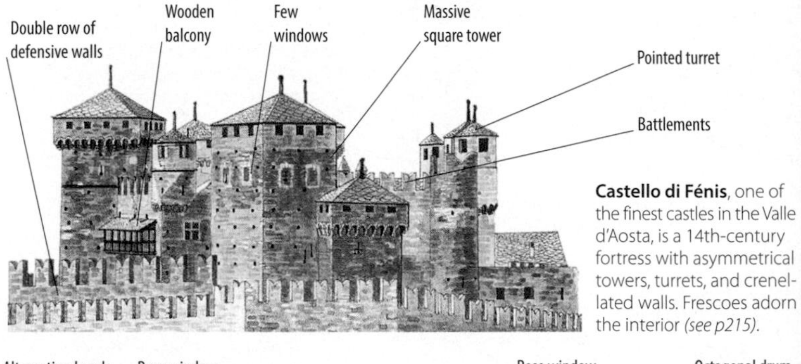

Castello di Fénis, one of the finest castles in the Valle d'Aosta, is a 14th-century fortress with asymmetrical towers, turrets, and crenellated walls. Frescoes adorn the interior *(see p215)*.

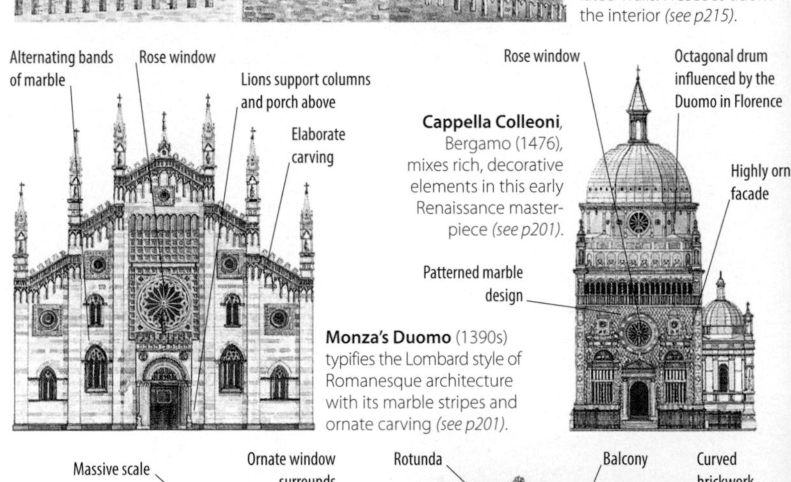

Cappella Colleoni, Bergamo (1476), mixes rich, decorative elements in this early Renaissance masterpiece *(see p201)*.

Monza's Duomo (1390s) typifies the Lombard style of Romanesque architecture with its marble stripes and ornate carving *(see p201)*.

Palazzo Carignano is perhaps the finest product of Turin's idiosyncratic Baroque school. Guarini's masterpiece (1679) boasts an extraordinary undulating brick facade and a fine rotunda *(see p223)*.

Where to see the Architecture

The road to Aosta is flanked by numerous medieval castles *(see p214)* while inspirational Romanesque and Gothic churches are found in Lombardy – at Monza *(p201)*, Pavia *(p203)*, Milan *(pp192–201)*, and Como *(pp190–91)*. The 15th-century Certosa di Pavia *(pp204–5)* is a must, as well as the charming city of Mantua *(p207)*. Turin *(pp220–24)* is famous for its unique Baroque school, and Bergamo for its exuberance. Architecture from the last two centuries is best represented in Milan and Turin, and in Genoa some exciting redevelopment projects are taking place.

Renzo Piano's mast structure (1992) in Genoa's redeveloped port

19th–20th Century Architecture

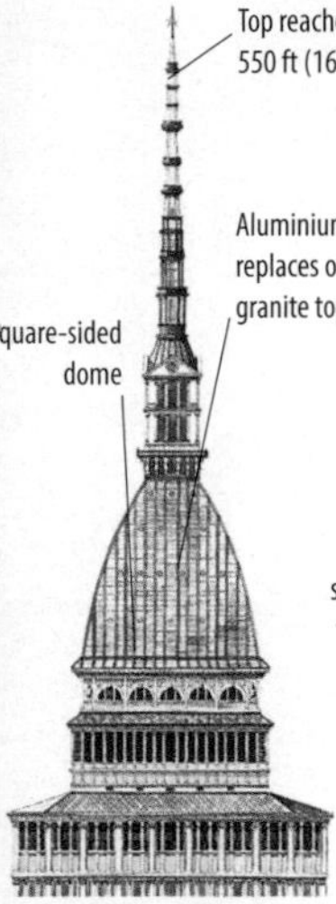

Top reaches 550 ft (167 m)

Aluminium replaces original granite top

quare-sided dome

The Mole Antonelliana (1863–97), designed by Antonelli, was the tallest building in the world when it was built *(see p224)*.

Glass balcony

Overhanging upper stories

Struts support the top

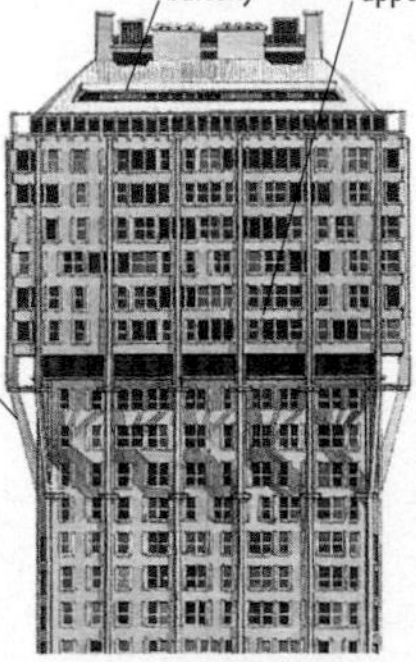

Torre Velasca, Milan, is a 26-floor tower south of the Duomo. The design, from the 1950s, was influenced by medieval castles such as the Castello Sforzesco.

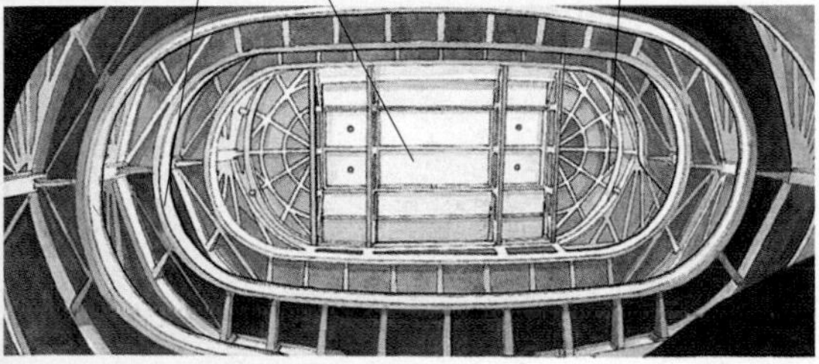

Central dome

Mosaics

Galleria Vittorio Emanuele II in Milan, designed by Mengoni in 1865, was the first Italian building to use glass and iron structurally *(see p194)*.

Spiral ramps up to roof

Roof served as test track

Reinforced concrete

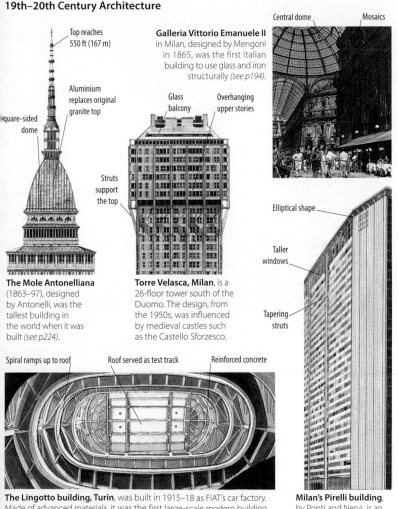

The Lingotto building, Turin, was built in 1915–18 as FIAT's car factory. Made of advanced materials, it was the first large-scale modern building in Italy. The structure of the ramps up to the roof is similar to the interior of Guarini's Baroque dome for San Lorenzo in Turin.

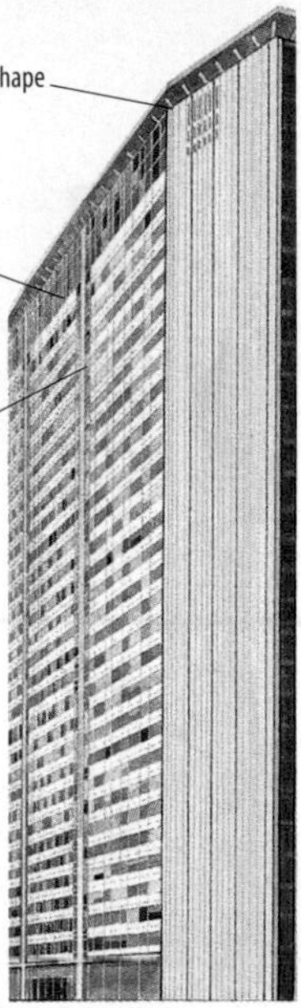

Elliptical shape

Taller windows

Tapering struts

Milan's Pirelli building, by Ponti and Nervi, is an elegant and innovative skyscraper built in 1959.

LOMBARDY

The region of Lombardy stretches from the Alps, on the border with Switzerland, down through the romantic lakes of Como and Maggiore to the broad, flat plain of the River Po. It is an area of lakeside villas with azalea-filled gardens, of wealthy towns with imposing palazzi and highly decorated churches, and of efficient, modern industry and large-scale agriculture, the financial heart of Italy. At its center stands Milan, the style-conscious capital of Lombardy.

The region was named after the Lombards or Longobards, a Germanic tribe that invaded Italy in the 6th century AD. During the Middle Ages, Lombardy was part of the Holy Roman Empire, but not always loyal to its German emperors. The Lombards, who had a talent for banking and commerce, resented any outside interference with their prosperity.

The 12th century saw the rise of the Lega Lombarda, or Lombard League, a band of forceful separatists founded to counter the brutal imperialism of Frederick Barbarossa (their most modern incarnation being the Lega Nord political party). Power was seized by the region's great families, most notably the Visconti and the Sforza of Milan, from the 14th to the early 16th century. These dynasties also became great patrons of the arts, commissioning exquisite palaces, churches, and artworks, many of which can still be seen. Bergamo, Mantua, and Cremona – not to mention Milan itself – contain a remarkably rich array of art treasures. Here are such pinnacles of European civilization as the charterhouse at Pavia, Leonardo da Vinci's *Last Supper*, and the magnificent paintings of the Pinacoteca di Brera in Milan.

Lombardy – famous as the birthplace of Virgil, Monteverdi, Stradivarius, and Donizetti – today offers visitors the contrasting pleasures of lyrical lakeside landscapes (resorts on lakes Como and Maggiore have attracted poets, aristocrats, and gamblers for centuries) and beautiful, bustling cities.

Strolling through Milan's enormous Galleria Vittorio Emanuele II

◀ The village of Corenno Plinio on the peaceful eastern shores of the beautiful Lake Como

Exploring Lombardy

The enormous plain of the River Po runs through much of Lombardy, providing a landscape that is flat and perfectly suited to the consequent expansion of industry in the region. This is, however, also a region of great contrasts. To the north, in a still unspoiled setting in the foothills of the mountains, lie the lakes Como and Maggiore, as well as the dramatic valleys and peaks of the Parco Nazionale dello Stelvio around Bormio, Sondrio, and Val Camonica. Further south, busy industrialized areas give way to huge tracts of agriculture dotted with towns of great beauty such as Cremona, Mantua, and Pavia, which offer a rich and splendid array of artistic pleasures.

A view of Isola Bella on Lake Maggiore

Sights at a Glance

1. Lago di Como
2. Lago Maggiore
3. *Milan (Milano) pp196–205*
4. Monza
5. Bergamo
6. Parco Nazionale dello Stelvio
7. Val Camonica
8. Lago d'Iseo
9. Brescia
10. Lodi
11. Pavia
12. *Certosa di Pavia pp208–9*
13. Cremona
14. Sabbioneta
15. Mantua

The colorful facade of the Cappella Colleoni in Bergamo

For additional map symbols *see back flap*

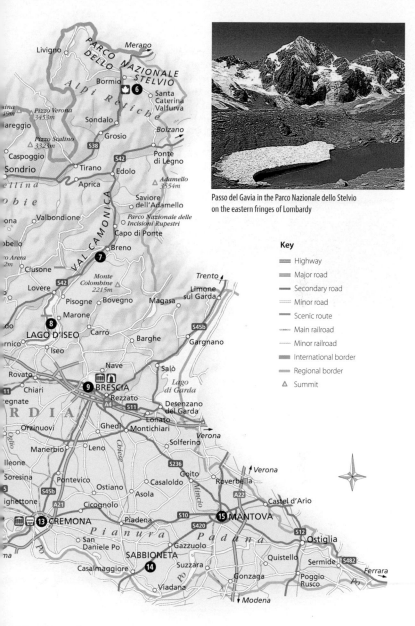

Passo del Gavia in the Parco Nazionale dello Stelvio on the eastern fringes of Lombardy

Key

- Highway
- Major road
- Secondary road
- Minor road
- Scenic route
- Main railroad
- Minor railroad
- International border
- Regional border
- △ Summit

Getting Around

Milan has three international airports, which are obvious gateways into northern Italy, and the vast and flat Lombard plain has its advantages when it comes to transport: roads and railway lines crisscross it and make trips between the larger towns very easy. The lakes, however, are better visited by car: only two main towns are served by trains, though there are bus and boat services around the shores. The Parco Nazionale dello Stelvio and the mountains are more remote still, but offer good tourist facilities.

❶ Lago di Como

Set in an idyllic landscape of mountains and rugged hillsides, Lake Como has for centuries attracted visitors who come here to go boating, for walks in the hills, or for relaxation and inspiration. The northern stretches, in particular, are shrouded in an almost eerie calm. The long and narrow lake, shaped into a wishbone by glacial erosion, offers fine views up to the Alps and down to the towns of Como and Lecco.

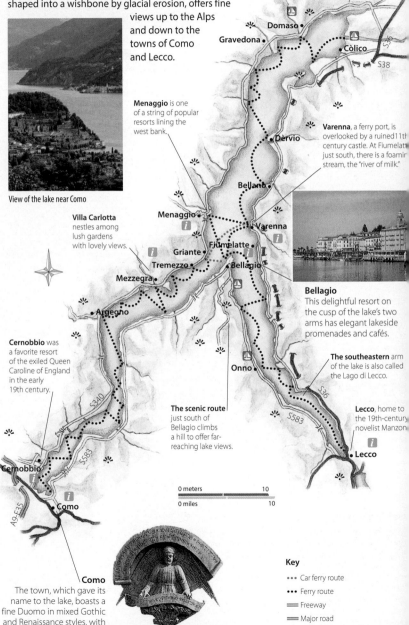

View of the lake near Como

The northern stretches are wilder and less populated than the southern part, offering visitors great tranquility.

Menaggio is one of a string of popular resorts lining the west bank.

Varenna, a ferry port, is overlooked by a ruined11th century castle. At Fiumelatte just south, there is a foaming stream, the "river of milk."

Villa Carlotta nestles among lush gardens with lovely views.

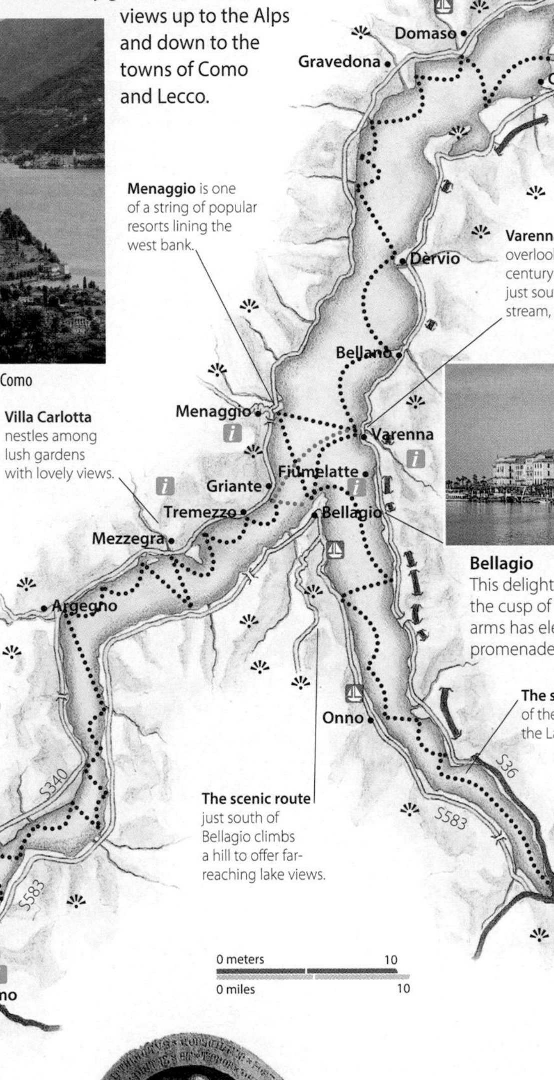

Bellagio
This delightful resort on the cusp of the lake's two arms has elegant lakeside promenades and cafés.

Cernobbio was a favorite resort of the exiled Queen Caroline of England in the early 19th century.

The southeastern arm of the lake is also called the Lago di Lecco.

The scenic route just south of Bellagio climbs a hill to offer far-reaching lake views.

Lecco, home to the 19th-century novelist Manzoni

Domaso
Gravedona
Còlico
S36
S38
Dèrvio
Bellano
Menaggio
Varenna
Fiumelatte
Griante
Tremezzo
Bellagio
Mezzegra
Argegno
Onno
S340
S583
S36
S583
Lecco
Cernobbio
Como
A9-E35

0 meters 10
0 miles 10

Como
The town, which gave its name to the lake, boasts a fine Duomo in mixed Gothic and Renaissance styles, with carvings on its facade.

Key

- Car ferry route
- Ferry route
- Freeway
- Major road
- Minor road

For hotels and restaurants in this region see pp562–77 and pp580–605

VISITORS' CHECKLIST

Practical Information
P.za Cavour 17, Como (031 26 97 12); Via Sauro 6, Lecco (0341 29 57 20). **lakecomo.org.uk**

Transportation
Como, Lecco.

all towns.

Tadoline's copy (1834) of Canova's *Cupid and Psyche* in Villa Carlotta

Exploring Lago di Como

In the heart of **Como** lies the elegant Piazza Cavour. Nearby rises the beautiful 14th-century **Duomo**, with its 15th- and 16th-century reliefs and paintings, and fine tombs. The 18th-century dome is by Turin's famous Baroque architect, Juvarra. Next to the Duomo stand the 13th-century Broletto (town hall), charmingly striped in white, pink, and gray, and the tall Torre del Comune. At Tremezzo, **Villa Carlotta** is an elegant 18th-century summer-house known for its gardens. In springtime, all sorts of flowers burst into color in this pretty setting. The villa houses a collection of sculptures.

Lecco, a small industrial town lying to the south of the lake's eastern arm, was home to Alessandro Manzoni (1785–1873). The writer's childhood home, the **Villa Manzoni**, is devoted to memorabilia of his life and works. A monument in Piazza Manzoni depicts scenes from his most famous novel, *I Promessi Sposi (The Betrothed)* – set in 17th-century Lecco and Milan.

Villa Carlotta
Via Regina 2b, Tremezzo. **Tel** 0344 404 05. **Open** Apr–mid-Oct: 9am–6pm daily (mid-Mar–end Mar & mid Oct early-Nov: 10am–5pm daily).

Villa Manzoni
Via Guanella 1, Lecco. **Tel** 0341 48 12 47. **Open** 9.30am–5:30pm Tue–Sun. **Closed** Jan 1, Easter, May 1, Aug 15, Dec 25.

❷ Lago Maggiore

Verbania. Stresa, Verbania, Baveno & the islands. Piazza Marconi 16, Stresa (0323 301 50). **distrettolaghi.it**

Lake Maggiore, the second largest Italian lake after Lake Garda, is a long expanse of water nestling right against the mountains and stretching into Alpine Switzerland; it is warmer in atmosphere and more romantic than Lake Como. The gently sloping shores are dotted with camellias, azaleas, and verbena – from which the ancient lake derived its Roman name, Verbanus.

A huge copper statue of Cardinal San Carlo Borromeo, the chief patron of the lake, stands in **Arona**, the town where he was born in 1538. It is possible to climb up and look out over the lake through his eyes and ears. Arona also boasts a ruined castle and a chapel, Santa Maria, dedicated to the Borromeo family.

Farther up the western coast of the lake is **Stresa**, the chief resort and main jumping-off point for visits to the islands; the town boasts many grand hotels, handsome villas, and pleasant gardens. Behind Stresa, a cable car ride away, rises Monte Mottarone, a snow-capped peak offering spectacular panoramic views of the surrounding mountains, including Monte Rosa.

The statue of Carlo Borromeo in Arona

The **Borromean islands**, at the center of the lake near Stresa, are small jewels of natural beauty augmented by artificial grottoes, architectural follies, and landscaped gardens. **Isola Bella** is home to the 17th-century **Palazzo Borromeo** and its splendid gardens, while Isola Madre is largely given over to a botanical garden. The only island inhabited year-round is Isola dei Pescatori, with a population of 50. The private Isola di San Giovanni is the smallest of the isles, with a villa that once belonged to the great conductor Arturo Toscanini (1867–1957).

The lake becomes quieter toward the Swiss border, but continues to be lined with attractive villas. The **Villa Taranto**, located on the outskirts of Verbania, houses a fine exotic botanical collection.

About 2 miles (3 km) west of **Cannobio**, a market town near Switzerland, is the dramatic gorge and tumbling waterfall of Orrido di Sant'Anna, which can be reached by boat.

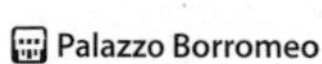

Palazzo Borromeo
Isola Bella. from Stresa. **Tel** 0323 305 56. **Open** mid-Mar–mid-Nov: daily. **borromeoturismo.it**

Villa Taranto
Via Vittorio Veneto 111, Verbania, Pallanza. **Tel** 0323 55 66 67. **Open** mid-Mar–Oct: daily.

Isola Bella's 17th-century Palazzo Borromeo and garden on Lago Maggiore

❸ Milan

Center of fashion, business, and finance, Milan has a bustling, businesslike feel about it. It is stylish rather than attractive – a city of wealth as opposed to imagination, and the heartland of the Italian economy. Its name is thought to come from a composite of the Latin words *medio* and *planum*, meaning "middle of the plain." It has long been an important trading center at the junction of trans-Alpine routes, and a prize for powerful dynasties. Today, it is the best place to see Italy at its most cosmopolitan and stylish.

Portrait of a Young Woman by Pollaiuolo, Museo Poldi-Pezzoli

Castello Sforzesco

Piazza Castello. **Tel** 02 88 46 37 00. Castello: **Open** daily. Musei del Castello: **Open** 9am–5:30pm Tue–Sun. **Closed** public hols.
milanocastello.it

The first castle on this site was built by the Visconti family, but demolished when their reign ended in the mid-15th century. Milan's new ruler, Francesco Sforza, built in its place this Renaissance palace. The castle is based on a series of courtyards, the most beautiful of which, the Cortile della Rocchetta, is a graceful arcaded square designed by Bramante and Filarete. The palace now contains, together with sections on Applied Arts, Archaeology, and Coins, the **Musei del Castello**. This fine collection of furniture, antiquities, and paintings includes Michelangelo's unfinished sculpture known as the *Rondanini Pietà*. The canvases in the picture collection, dating from the Renaissance to the 18th century, are particularly impressive.

Michelangelo's *Rondanini Pietà* (c. 1564) in the Castello Sforzesco

Museo Poldi-Pezzoli

Via Alessandro Manzoni 12. **Tel** 02 79 48 89. **Open** 10am–6pm Wed–Mon.
museopoldipezzoli.it

Giacomo Poldi-Pezzoli was a wealthy nobleman who, on his death in 1879, bequeathed his magnificent art collection to the state. Its most famous painting is the 15th-century Renaissance *Portrait of a Young Woman* by Antonio Pollaiuolo, though there are also works by Piero della Francesca, Botticelli, and Mantegna, among others. The applied arts section is richly endowed with fascinating items ranging from rugs and lace to glass, enamels, and porcelain, as well as sculpture, jewelry, and sundials.

Sights at a Glance

① Castello Sforzesco
② *Pinacoteca di Brera pp202–203*
③ Museo Poldi-Pezzoli
④ Teatro alla Scala
⑤ Galleria Vittorio Emanuele II
⑥ Duomo)
⑦ Palazzo Reale (Museo della Reggia)
⑧ San Satiro
⑨ Pinacoteca Ambrosiana
⑩ Sant'Ambrogio
⑪ San Lorenzo Maggiore
⑫ Civico Museo Archeologico
⑬ Parco Sempione

Teatro alla Scala

P.za della Scala. **Tel** 02 887 91. Box Office **Tel** 02 72 00 37 44. Museo Teatrale Largo Ghiringhelli 1 (Piazza Scala). **Tel** 02 88 79 24 73. **Open** 9am–noon, 1:30–5pm daily.
teatroallascala.org

This Neo-Classical theater opened in 1778 and is one of the world's most prestigious opera houses. It has one of the largest stages in Europe and hosts sumptuous productions. Two hours before each performance the box office opens to sell tickets at discount prices. The **Museo Teatrale** houses sets and costumes of past productions and theatrical items dating back to Roman times. There is also a good view of the auditorium, with its gilded box galleries, *trompe-l'oeil* effects, and huge chandelier.

The facade of the world-famous Teatro alla Scala

VISITORS' CHECKLIST

Practical Information
1,325,000. P. del Duomo 19 (02 77 40 43 43); Stazione Centrale (02 77 40 43 19). daily. Dec 7: Sant'Ambrogio.
visitamilano.it

Transportation
Malpensa 31 miles (50 km) NW; Linate 5 miles (8 km) E. Stazione Centrale, P.za Duca d'Aosta. P.za Freud.

Duomo

Piazza del Duomo. **Tel** 02 72 02 26 56. **Open** 7am–6:45pm daily. Baptistry digs: **Open** 10am–5:30pm. Treasury: **Open** 9:30am–5:30pm Mon–Fri (to 5pm Sat), 1:30–3:30pm Sun & public hols. Roof: **Open** 9am–6:10pm (to 7pm Nov–Feb). for roof.
duomomilano.it

Milan's cathedral is one of the largest Gothic churches in the world. It was begun in the 14th century under Prince Gian Galeazzo Visconti but not completed until more than 500 years later. The building's most startling feature is the extraordinary roof, with its 135 spires and innumerable statues and gargoyles, and from which, on a clear day, there are views of the Alps. Below, the facade boasts an assortment of styles from Gothic through to Renaissance and Neo-Classical. The bronze doors are faced with bas-reliefs recounting episodes from the life of the Virgin and of Sant'Ambrogio, and scenes retelling the history of Milan.

The aisles are divided by 52 giant pillars and well lit by stained-glass windows. Look out for the Visconti family symbol – a serpent swallowing a man – in the fine tracery of the apse windows. Among the many statues is a depiction of the flayed San Bartolomeo carrying his own skin. The treasury, beneath the main altar, contains much medieval gold and silverwork, and the remains of a 4th-century baptistry.

The Gothic Duomo, crowned with spires

For keys to map symbols *see back flap*

Exploring Milan

In addition to the great monuments in Milan, such as the cathedral and the castle, there is a host of varied and interesting museums, churches, and civic buildings that provide an enthralling mix of old and new. This chic and busy metropolis offers plenty of opportunities for cultural activities, gastronomic adventures, designer-fashion shopping, or just strolling about, Milan-style.

The glass ceiling and dome covering the Galleria Vittorio Emanuele II

Galleria Vittorio Emanuele II

Main entrances on Piazza del Duomo and Piazza della Scala.

This ornate shopping arcade, known as *il Salotto di Milano* (Milan's drawing room), was designed by the architect Giuseppe Mengoni in 1865. The galleria had a tragic start, however, as Mengoni fell to his death from the scaffolding not long before its inauguration in 1877 (a year before the arcade was actually finished). Tourists are nevertheless attracted to its stylish shops and cafés, as well as Savini, one of Milan's historic restaurants.

The galleria itself has a floorplan in the shape of a Latin cross, with an octagonal center adorned with mosaics representing four continents (Europe, America, Africa, and Asia), together with others representing Art, Agriculture, Science, and Industry. Its finest feature is its metal and glass roof, crowned with a magnificent central dome. The roof was the first structure in Italy to use metal and glass in a structural way, rather than just decoratively. The floors are decorated with mosaics of the signs of the zodiac; tourists may be seen stepping on the genitals of Taurus the Bull, which is said to bring good luck.

Palazzo Reale

Piazza del Duomo. **Tel** 02 88 46 52 36. **Open** Museo della Reggia.

The former royal palace, for centuries home to the Visconti and other rulers of Milan, houses the **Museo della Reggia**. It displays the sumptuous interiors of the building and showcases the four historic phases of the palace including the Neo-Classical era and the Restoration. Palazzo Reale is also a prestigious venue for temporary art exhibitions. The building abutting it to the west (the Arengario) has been transformed into a Modern Art museum, the **Museo del Novecento**, and many Italian artworks from the 20th century are displayed here.

Villa Belgiojoso Bonaparte and Galleria d'Arte Moderna

Villa Belgiojoso Bonaparte, Via Palestro 16. **Tel** 02 88 44 59 47. **Open** 9am–1pm, 2–5:30pm Tue–Sun. **gam-milano.com**

Milan's 19th-century and Modern Art collections are housed in a Neo-Classical villa built by Leopold Pollack in 1790 for Count Ludovico Barbiano di Belgiojoso. It was lived in by Napoleon in 1802 and later by Marshal Radetzky. The villa houses 19th-century Italian art, showing all the major art movements, as well as the Grassi and Vismara collections of 19th- and 20th-century Italian and foreign artists and the Marino Marini Museum. Of particular note are works by Giorgio Morandi (1890–1964) and Carlo Carrà (1881–1966), as well as by Modigliani (1884–1920) and De Chirico (1888–1978). Non-Italian artists include Van Gogh, Cézanne, Gauguin, Picasso, Matisse, Klee, Mondrian, and Kandinsky.

Still Life (1920) by Giorgio Morandi in the Galleria d'Arte Moderna

Fruit Basket (c. 1596) by Caravaggio in the Pinacoteca Ambrosiana

Pinacoteca Ambrosiana

Piazza Pio XI 2. **Tel** 02 80 69 21. **Open** 10am–6pm Tue–Sun. **ambrosiana.eu**

The Ambrosiana is home to Cardinal Federico Borromeo's magnificent library of 36,000 manuscripts. These include a 5th-century illustrated *Iliad*, early manuscripts of Dante's *Divine Comedy* (1353), and the *Atlantic Codex* (1478–1519) by Leonardo da Vinci. In order to exhibit as much of the *Atlantic Codex* as possible, the pages on display are changed every three months.

The building also houses an art gallery, bequeathed by Borromeo in 1618. The collection ranges from 14th-century pieces to works of the early 19th century. Among the canvases are *Portrait of a Musician* by Leonardo, the *Madonna of the Canopy* by Botticelli (15th century), a cartoon version of Raphael's Vatican fresco, *The School of Athens* (16th century), and Caravaggio's *Fruit Basket*. There is also a strong collection of Venetian art, with paintings by Giorgione, Titian, Bassano, and Tiepolo, and panel paintings by the late-15th-century Lombard painter Bergognone.

San Satiro

Via Speronari 3. **Tel** 02 87 46 83. **Open** 7:30am–noon, 3–6:30pm Mon–Fri; 3:30–7pm Sat; 8:30am 12:30pm, 3:30–7pm Sun.

The church of Santa Maria presso San Satiro is one of the most beautiful Renaissance buildings in Milan. It was built on the site of a 9th-century sanctuary, little of which remains apart from the Cappella della Pietà, beside an 11th-century bell tower.

The interior seems to be in the shape of a Greek cross, but this is an illusion created by *trompe-l'oeil* effects, since space restrictions led Bramante to choose a T-shaped plan. Above the altar is a 13th-century fresco. An octagonal baptistry lies off the right aisle. The church's facade was finished in the 19th century.

Civico Museo Archeologico

Corso Magenta 15. **Tel** 02 88 44 52 08. 1, 2 Cadorna. 16, 19, 27. 50, 58, 94. **Open** 9am–5:30pm Tue–Sun. (phone ahead).

At the entrance to this museum is a model of Roman Milan, which illustrates urban planning and architecture in Milan from the 1st to the 4th century AD. The exhibition begins in a hall on the right, containing clay objects and Roman sculpture. At the end of this room is a huge fragment of a torso of Hercules and 3rd-century AD floor mosaics. Also in this room are two of the most important works in the museum: the Parabiago Patera and the Diatreta Cup. The Patera is a gilded silver plate with a relief of the goddess Cybele (4th century AD). The Diatreta Cup, dating from the same period, is a single piece of colored glass, with finely wrought, intricate decoration.

Parco Sempione

Piazza Castello–Piazza Sempione. 1 Cadorna, Cairoli, 2 Lanza, Cadorna. Ferrovie Nord, Cadorna. 1, 2, 4, 12, 14, 19, 27. 43, 57, 61, 94. **Open** May: 6:30am–10pm; Jun–Sep: 6:30am–11:30pm; Oct–Apr: 6:30am–9pm.

Although it covers an area of about 116 acres (47 ha), this park occupies only a part of the old Visconti ducal garden, enlarged by the Sforza in the 15th century to make a 740-acre (300-ha) hunting reserve.

The present-day layout was designed by Emilio Alemagna between 1890–93.

Among the trees are monuments to Napoleon III by Francesco Barzaghi, De Chirico's *Mysterious Baths*, the sulfur water fountain, and the Torre Branca, a tower of steel tubes made in 1932 to a design by Gio Ponti.

Gallerie d'Italia

Via Manzoni 10. **Tel** 800 16 76 19. **Open** 9:30am–7:30pm Tue–Sun (to 10:30pm Thu). **gallerieditalia.com**

Housed in the Palazzo Anguissola Antona Traversi and Palazzo Brentani, Gallerie d'Italia has around 200 works of art from the 1800s. This collection offers a fascinating journey through one century of Italian art, with pieces by such artists as Antonio Canova, Angelo Inganni, and Umberto Boccioni.

View of the Parco Sempione with the Arco della Pace in the background

Shopping in Milan

In Milan, one of the most affluent cities in Italy, shopping is synonymous with buying designer apparel. High-fashion flagship stores here are invariably smart and stylish, especially in the city center, and looking is almost as satisfying as making a purchase. However, Milan also has many independent boutiques with a range of styles to suit all tastes. If you are looking for gifts to take home, there are some excellent *pasticcerie* (pastry shops), where you can buy authentic delicacies and traditional local confectionery. Alternatively, a cutting-edge object of design will make for an impressive souvenir of your trip to the city.

Where to Shop

All leading fashion designers have shops in the area between Via Montenapoleone, Via della Spiga, Via Manzoni, and Via Sant'Andrea, the so-called "fashion quadrilateral."

Those interested in interior design will enjoy Via Durini, while lovers of antiques should head to Brera or the Navigli, where antiques markets are held monthly.

If time is of the essence, call ahead to check on opening hours. In Milan generally, non-food shops are closed on Monday mornings, and food shops are closed on Monday afternoons. The largest shops tend to stay open throughout the day, but sometimes a lunch break is taken. Shops are closed on Sundays, except for the run-up to Christmas and during the main fashion shows.

Designer Fashion

Milan is renowned as a world capital of fashion, and most national and international designers have a flagship store here. As well as the designers that you would expect to find in a fashion center, such as **Dolce & Gabbana**, **Giorgio Armani**, **Gucci**, **Prada**, and **Hugo Boss**, there are many smaller designer stores. For an overview of what's new, check out multibrand boutiques such as **Banner**, which features a selection of the best from a wide array of names. For the latest on what the younger set is wearing, go to **Amedeo D** or to the Corso di Porta Ticinese area.

Up-and-coming designers are gathering in the areas around Corso Garibaldi and Corso Como. As well as of-the-moment clothes and accessories, **10 Corso Como** offers a bookstore, record store, art gallery, café, and restaurant, and even a top-class B&B. The **Gianfranco Ferrè** boutique, on the other hand, has a spa attached.

Most designers carry men's as well as women's apparel. Specialized men's stores include **Pal Zileri**, **Ermenegildo Zegna**, and **Corneliani**.

Regular Clothing

Designer outlets sell samples, seconds, and last season's goods at a discount. Among Milan's longest-established outlets are **Salvagente** and **DMagazine**. Many designers also have their own outlets: fans of Max Mara, for example, should head for **Diffusione Tessile**.

Milan's main department stores are **La Rinascente** and **Coin**. The former carries many leading-edge fashion designers, while the latter features smaller fashion labels, handbags, costume jewelry, and housewares. There is more to Milan than upmarket, cutting-edge designer fashion, though. For good-value casualwear for the whole family, try **Oviesse**.

Many fashion shoppers also scour the stalls at the Saturday market at Viale Papiniano, at the Piazza Sant'Agostino end, which starts at 8:30am and goes on until 5pm. Corso Vercelli is also recommended.

Accessories

Handbags, shoes, hats, and jewelry, real or otherwise, are also worth seeking out. Chains such as **Furla** and **Coccinelle** offer a wide array of bags, while those looking for shoes can head to **René Caovilla** for a pair of stylish heels, or purchase comfortable shoes with a twist from **Tod's** and **Hogan**. **Garlando** carries a number of classic styles in a wide array of colors and sizes, while **Ghigodonna** has elegant shoes in larger sizes. **Borsalino** is synonymous with stylish headwear.

The "fashion quadrilateral" also features many jewelers, such as **Federico Buccellati**, **Bulgari**, and **Pianegonda**.

Food and Wine

Gourmands will have a great time in Milan. **Peck** consists of three floors of the best that Italy can offer, in terms of both food and wine. **Giovanni Galli Marroni e Canditi** offers a different take on chocolate-coated delicacies.

For those who like a hands-on approach to their food, **High Tech** is a gold mine for kitchen tools, including all the top names such as Alessi, as well as plates and cutlery.

Design, Books, and Gifts

Milan is the cradle of designer furniture. Several top stores are around Piazza San Babila. A stroll down Via Durini will reveal, among others, **Cassina** and **B&B**. For lighting, see **Flos** and **Artemide**. Those interested in 20th-century design could visit **Spazio 900**.

If an item of furniture is not an option, the next best thing might be a book on design or architecture. Visit the bookstore of the **Triennale** or that of the art-catalogue publisher **Skira** for the best on the market.

Fabriano, the company that developed the first paper mill in the 1200s, has a store selling handsome writing paper, envelopes, and gift items.

DIRECTORY

Designer Fashion

10 Corso Como
Corso Como 10.
Tel 02 2900 2674.
Tel 02 626 163 (B&B).
Tel 02 2901 3581 (bar & restaurant).
Tel 02 653 531 (gallery).
W 10corsocomo.it

Amedeo D
Corso Vercelli 23.
Tel 02 4800 4048.
W amedeod.it

Banner
Via Sant'Andrea 8.
Tel 02 7600 4609.
W biffi.com

Corneliani
Via Montenapoleone 26.
Tel 02 7631 7955.
W corneliani.com

Dolce & Gabbana
Via della Spiga 26 (women).
Tel 02 7600 1155.
Corso Venezia 15 (men).
Tel 02 7602 8485.
Via della Spiga 2 (women's accessories).
Tel 02 795 747.
Corso Venezia 7 (D&G).
Tel 02 7600 4091.
W dolcegabbana.it

Ermenegildo Zegna
Via Montenapoleone 27.
Tel 02 7600 6437.
W zegna.com

Gianfranco Ferrè
Via Sant'Andrea 15.
Tel 02 7601 7526 (spa and beauty parlor).
W gianfrancoferre.com

Giorgio Armani
Via Sant'Andrea 9.
Tel 02 7600 3234.
Via Manzoni 31 (megastore).
Tel 02 7231 8600.
Via Montenapoleone 2 (Collezioni).
Tel 02 7639 0068.
Via Montenapoleone 10 (Armani Junior).
Tel 02 783 196. Via Manzoni 37 (Armani Casa).
Tel 02 657 2401. Corso di Porta Ticinese 60 (Armani Jeans).
Tel 02 8324 1924.
W armani.com

Gucci
Via Montenapoleone 5–7.
Tel 02 771 271.
Galleria Vittorio Emanuele II 11 (accessories).
Tel 02 859 7991.
W gucci.com

Hugo Boss
Corso Matteotti 11 (men).
Tel 02 7639 4667.
Corso Matteotti 8 (women).
Tel 02 7601 3266.
W hugoboss.com

Pal Zileri
Via Manzoni 20.
Tel 02 7639 4680.
W palzileri.com

Prada
Galleria Vittorio Emanuele 63–65.
Tel 02 876 979.
Via Montenapoleone 8 (women).
Tel 02 777 1771.
Via Montenapoleone 6 (men).
Tel 02 7602 0273.
Via della Spiga 18 (accessories).
Tel 02 780 455.
W prada.com

Regular Clothing

Coin
Piazza Cinque Giornate.
Tel 02 5519 2083.
Corso Vercelli 30.
Tel 02 4399 0001.
Piazza Cantore 12.
Tel 02 5810 4385.
W coin.it

Diffusione Tessile
Galleria San Carlo 6.
Tel 02 7600 0829.

DMagazine
Via Montenapoleone 26.
Tel 02 7600 6027.

Oviesse
Galleria Passarella 2.
Tel 02 7628 1677.
Corso Garibaldi 72.
Tel 02 655 1649.
Corso Buenos Aires 35.
Tel 02 20 40 48 01.
W oviesse.it

La Rinascente
Piazza del Duomo.
Tel 02 88 521.
W rinascente.it

Salvagente
Via Fratelli Bronzetti 16.
Tel 02 7611 0328.
W salvagentemilano.it

Accessories

Borsalino
Galleria Vittorio Emanuele II 92.
Tel 02 8901 5436.
W borsalino.com

Bulgari
Via Montenapoleone 2.
Tel 02 777 001.
W bulgari.com

Coccinelle
Via Manzoni 26.
Tel 02 7602 8161.
Corso Buenos Aires 16.
Tel 02 2040 4755.

Federico Buccellati
Via della Spiga 2.
Tel 02 7600 3867.
W federicobuccellati.it

Furla
Piazza Duomo 31.
Tel 02 8909 6794.
Corso Vercelli 11.
Tel 02 4801 4189.
W furla.com

Garlando
Via Madonnina 2.
Tel 02 874 665.
W alfonsogarlando.it

Ghigodonna
Viale Tunisia 2.
Tel 02 2940 8414.
W ghigocalzature.com

Hogan
Via Montenapoleone 23.
Tel 02 7601 1174.
W hogan.com

Pianegonda
Via Montenapoleone 6.
Tel 02 7600 3038.
W pianegonda.com

René Caovilla
Via Bagutta 28.
Tel 02 7631 9049.
W renecaovilla.com

Tod's
Via della Spiga 22.
Tel 02 7600 2423.
Galleria Vittorio Emanuele.
Tel 02 877 997.
W todsgroup.com

Food and Wine

Giovanni Galli Marroni e Canditi
Via Victor Hugo 2.
Tel 02 8646 4833.

High Tech
Piazza XXV Aprile 12.
Tel 02 624 1101.

Peck
Via Spadari 9.
Tel 02 802 3161.
W peck.it

Design, Books, and Gifts

Artemide
Corso Monforte 19.
Tel 02 7600 6930.
W artemide.com

B&B
Via Durini 14.
Tel 02 764 4411.
W bebitalia.it

Cassina
Via Durini 16.
Tel 02 7602 0745.
W cassina.it

Fabriano
Via Ponte Vetero 17.
Tel 02 7631 8754.
W cartierefabriano.it

Flos
Corso Monforte 7.
Tel 02 794 559.
W flos.net

Skira
Via Torino 61.
Tel 02 724 441.
W skira.it

Spazio 900
Viale Campania 51.
Tel 02 7012 5737.
Corso Garibaldi 42.
Tel 02 7200 1775.
W spazio900.net

Triennale
Viale Alemagna 6.
Tel 02 724 341.
W triennale.it

Milan: Pinacoteca di Brera

Milan's finest art collection is held in an imposing 17th-century building, the Palazzo di Brera. This is where, in the 18th century, the Accademia di Belle Arti was founded; the picture collection developed alongside the academy. Inside the Brera hang some of the finest examples of Italian Renaissance and Baroque painting, including works by Piero della Francesca, Mantegna, Canaletto, Bellini, Raphael, Tintoretto, Veronese, and Caravaggio. The collection also includes 20th-century works by some of Italy's most famous modern artists.

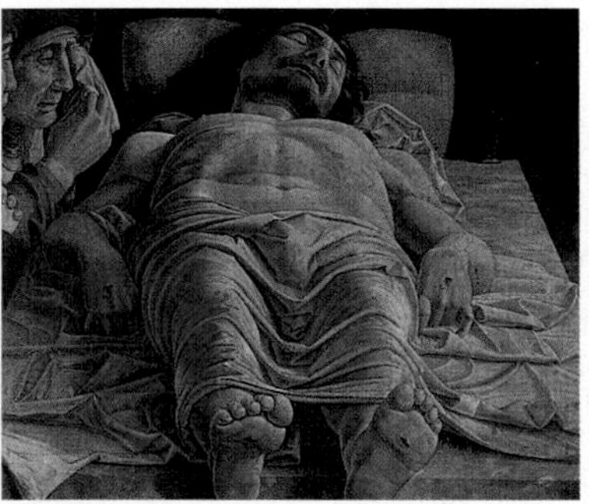

★ Dead Christ by Mantegna
The subtle lighting and dramatic perspective of this lamentation by Mantegna (1430–1506) make it one of his greatest masterpieces.

Gallery Guide

The collection is displayed in 38 rooms, and was first built up by paintings from churches, later from acquisitions. Not all of it is permanently on view – this is due to restoration work and research.

Twin staircases lead up to the first-floor entrance of the Pinacoteca.

The Kiss *(1859)*
Francesco Hayez's painting is one of the most reproduced works of Italian 19th-century art. Patriotic and sentimental, it became a symbol of the optimism surrounding the unification of Italy.

The bronze statue (1809) by Canova depicts Napoleon as a demigod with Victory wings in his hand.

Key to Floor Plan

- 15th- to 16th-century Italian painting
- 16th- to 17th-century Dutch and Flemish painting
- 17th-century Italian painting
- 18th- to 19th-century Italian painting
- 20th-century Italian painting and sculpture and Jesi Collection
- Nonexhibition space

Works by Rubens and Van Dyck represent some of the non-Italian artists on show.

For hotels and restaurants in this region see pp562–77 and pp580–605

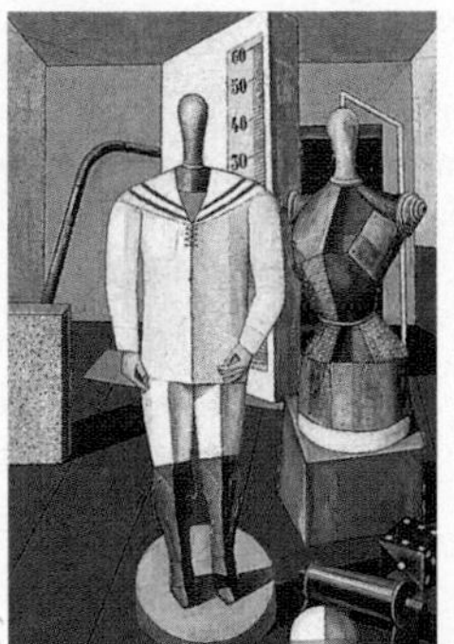

Mother and Son *(1917)*
The metaphysical paintings of Carlo Carrà show a dream world full of strange and obscure symbols.

VISITORS' CHECKLIST

Practical Information
Via Brera 28. **Tel** 02 72 26 32 64; 02 72 26 32 29. **Open** 8:30am–7:15pm Tue–Sun (last adm: 45 min before closing). **Closed** Jan 1, May 1, Dec 25.
brera.beniculturali.it

Transportation
Lanza, Montenapoleone, & Duomo. 61, 97.

Portrait of Moisè Kisling
Modigliani's angular portrait of 1915 reflects his interest in African sculpture.

Madonna della Candeletta *(c. 1490)*
This painting by Carlo Crivelli was the central part of a polyptych. It is richly detailed with much distinctive ornamentation.

Twinned columns support the arcades in the courtyard.

The stone facade presents a regular and slightly austere appearance.

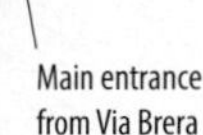

Main entrance from Via Brera

★ Marriage of the Virgin by Raphael
This graceful altarpiece was painted in 1504. The circular temple is signed with the artist's name.

Milan: Southwest of the Center

Some of Milan's finest treasures are to be found in its religious buildings: the ancient monasteries and churches make up some very fine architectural ensembles in themselves, as well as incorporating important ruins and relics dating back to Roman times. It is also in Milan that one of the most famous images in the world is to be found: Leonardo's evocative masterpiece, *The Last Supper.*

The entrance to Sant'Ambrogio, flanked by unequal bell towers

Sant'Ambrogio

Piazza Sant'Ambrogio 15. **Tel** 02 86 45 08 95. Basilica: **Open** 10am–noon, 2:30–6pm Mon–Sat, 3–5pm Sun. Museum: **Open** 9:30am–noon, 2:30–6pm Mon–Sat, 3–5pm Sun. **basilicasantambrogio.it**

Sant'Ambrogio, or St. Ambrose, Milan's patron saint and its bishop in the 4th century, was so eloquent that bees were said to fly into his mouth, attracted by his honey tongue. This is the basilica that he began in AD 379, though today most of it is 10th-century Romanesque. A gateway leads to the bronze doors of the entrance, flanked by two bell towers. Inside, note the fine rib vaulting and pulpit, and the 9th-century altar decorated with gold, silver, and gems. In a chapel off the south aisle, fine mosaics line a stunning cupola. In the crypt lies the tomb of Sant'Ambrogio himself.

Above the portico, a small museum contains architectural fragments, tapestries, and paintings relating to the church.

San Lorenzo Maggiore

Corso di Porta Ticinese 39. **Tel** 02 89 40 41 29. **Open** 7:30am–6:45pm Mon–Sat, 9am–7pm Sun. Cappella Sant'Aquilino: **Open** 9am– 6:30pm daily. for the Cappella. **sanlorenzomaggiore.com**

This church contains a vast collection of Roman and early Christian remains. The octagonal basilica was built in the 4th century, above what was probably a Roman amphitheater, and rebuilt in the 12th and 16th centuries.

In front of the church stands a row of 16 Roman columns and a statue of Emperor Constantine. Fine 4th-century mosaics adorn the Cappella di Sant'Aquilino, a Romanesque chapel, with two early Christian sarcophagi. Other Roman architectural elements of this church are in a chamber below the chapel.

San Lorenzo Maggiore viewed from the northeast

Santa Maria delle Grazie

Piazza Santa Maria delle Grazie 2. **Tel** 02 46 76 111. Cenacolo: **Tel** 02 92 80 03 60 (reservations required – up to 60 days in advance). **Open** 8:15am–6:45pm Tue–Sun. **Closed** public hols. **cenacolovinciano.org**

This beautiful 15th-century Renaissance convent, its lovely apse and calm small cloister designed by Bramante, contains one of the key images of western civilization: the *Cenacolo (The Last Supper)* by Leonardo da Vinci. The image captures the moment at which Christ tells his disciples that one of them will betray him. The Christ figure is unfinished: Leonardo did not consider himself worthy enough to complete it.

The artist also spurned the standard fresco technique of painting on wet plaster, applying tempera to the dry wall instead. The result has deteriorated badly: the paint is flaking off, and restoration has proved difficult. The painting is now protected by a filtration system.

Leonardo da Vinci's *Last Supper* (1494–7) adorning the refectory wall of Santa Maria delle Grazie

For hotels and restaurants in this region see pp562–77 and pp580–605

4 Monza

Monza. 120,000. FS P.za Carducci 2 (039 32 32 22). **Open** 9am–noon, 3–6pm daily. Thu & Sat.

These days Monza is mostly famous for its international Formula One **Autodromo**, which lies inside a vast park that also has an elegant Rococo hunting lodge, the Villa Reale, and a golf course. At one time, however, Monza was one of the most important towns in Lombardy. Theodolinda, the 6th-century Lombard queen, built its first cathedral and bequeathed her treasure to the town.

In the town center is the **Duomo**, with its notable green and white 14th-century facade and beautiful 15th-century frescoes portraying Theodolinda's life. Behind the high altar is the small Iron Crown, believed to have belonged to Emperor Constantine: it is prized for the iron strip, said to have been one of the nails from the cross of Christ. More local treasures may be found in the Duomo's **Museo e Tesoro del Duomo**, including a silver hen standing over seven tiny chicks (which symbolize Lombardy and the seven provinces it ruled) and a relic said to be John the Baptist's tooth.

Autodromo
Parco di Monza. **Tel** 039 248 21. **Open** daily. **Closed** public hols.

Duomo
Piazza Duomo. **Tel** 039 38 94 20. Museo e Tesoro del Duomo: **Open** 9am–1pm, 2–6pm Tue–Sun.

Leonello d'Este (*c.* 1440) by Pisanello in the Accademia Carrara, Bergamo

5 Bergamo

120,000. FS Via Gombito 13 (035 24 22 26). **Open** 9am–5:30pm daily. Mon.
W **turismo.bergamo.it**

Bergamo owes much of its artistic inspiration and architectural splendor to the influence of Venice, which ruled it from the 15th to the late 18th century. The town is divided into two distinct parts: Bergamo Alta, crowning the hill with its cluster of attractive medieval and Renaissance buildings, and the more modern Bergamo Bassa below.

The jewel of the upper town is **Piazza Vecchia**, containing one of the most appealing architectural ensembles in the region. Its buildings include the 12th-century Torre del Comune with its fine clock and curfew bell that rings daily at 10pm, the late 16th-century Biblioteca Civica, and the attractive 12th-century Palazzo della Ragione, or law courts, adorned with a bas-relief of the Lion of Venice.

The arcades of the Palazzo della Ragione lead to Piazza del Duomo, the square of the Neo-Classical Duomo. The square is dominated by the **Cappella Colleoni** *(see p184)*, a chapel built in 1476 to house the tomb of Bergamo's famous political leader, Bartolomeo Colleoni. It is flanked by two 14th-century buildings: an octagonal baptistry and the porch leading to the Romanesque basilica of Santa Maria Maggiore. The basilica's austere exterior contrasts with its Baroque interior, which contains the tomb of Bergamoborn composer Gaetano Donizetti (1797–1848).

The collection from the **Galleria dell' Accademia Carrara**, a major picture gallery with works by Venetian masters and local artists, as well as masterpieces from the rest of Italy, is housed temporarily in **Palazzo della Ragione** while the building is being restored. It includes 15th- and 16th-century works by Pisanello, Crivelli, Mantegna, Giovanni Bellini, Botticelli, Titian, Raphael, and Perugino, and 18th-century canvases by Tiepolo, Guardi, and Canaletto, as well as paintings by Holbein, Dürer, Bruegel, and Velázquez.

Palazzo della Ragione
Città Alta. **Tel** 035 39 96 77. **Open** Jun–Sep: 10am–9pm Tue–Sun (to 11pm Sat); Oct–May: 9:30am–5:30pm Tue–Fri, 10am–6pm Sat–Sun.

Emperor Constantine

The Edict of Milan

Milan was colonized by the Romans in 222 BC and quickly grew to be an important city at the junction of various trading routes. As the Roman Empire grew and then split in two, the emperors began to neglect Rome for the better-placed Mediolanum (literally, city in the middle of the plain). It was here that Emperor Constantine declared his edict of AD 313, in which Christianity was recognized as one of the permitted religions of the empire, ending centuries of persecution. The emperor is said to have converted following a vision, but by the 4th century adopting Christianity was also one way to unite the disparate empire.

Detail from the Cappella Colleoni

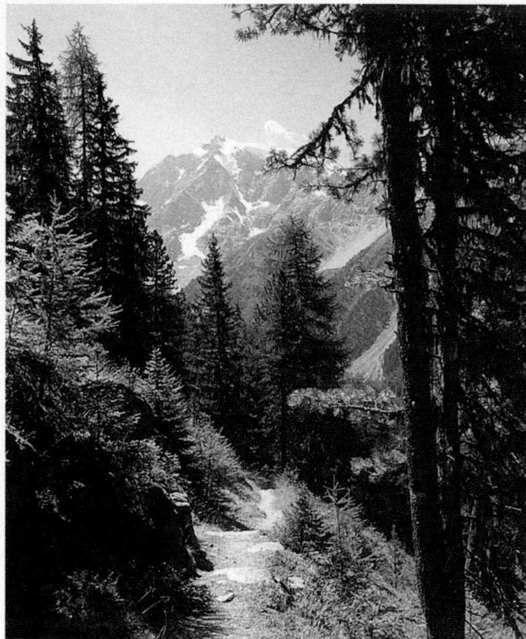

A leafy pathway through the Parco Nazionale dello Stelvio

6 Parco Nazionale dello Stelvio

Trento, Bolzano, Sondrio, & Brescia. from Bormio to Santa Caterina Valfurva & Madonna dei Monti. Via de Simoni 42, Bormio (0342 90 08 11). **stelviopark.it**

The Stelvio, Italy's largest national park, is the gateway from Lombardy to the glacier-strewn Dolomite mountains stretching into Trentino–Alto Adige. The glaciers are dotted with more than 50 lakes, and dominated by craggy peaks such as Gran Zebrù, Cevedale, and Ortles – the tallest mountain here at 12,811 ft (3,905 m).

For walkers, the area offers excellent hiking, and access to remote areas populated by ibexes, marmots, chamois, and eagles. The only real population center in the Lombardy part of the park is at **Bormio**, which boasts plenty of winter and summer sports facilities, and is a good base from which to explore the area. The town's **Giardino Botanico**, a 0.6 mile (1 km) walk from the center, displays some of the species of mountain plants found in the region.

Giardino Botanico Alpino Rezia
Via Sertorelli, Loc. Rovinaccia, Bormio. **Tel** 0342 90 08 55. **Open** May–mid-Sep: daily. **stelviopark.it**

7 Val Camonica

Brescia. FS Capo di Ponte. Via Briscioli 42, Capo di Ponte (0364 420 80). **proloco.capo-di-ponte.bs.it**

This attractive broad valley formed by a glacier is the setting for an extraordinary series of prehistoric rock carvings. These form an astonishing outdoor mural from the Lago d'Iseo to Capo di Ponte and beyond, and the valley is a UNESCO cultural protection zone. More than 180,000 engravings from the Neolithic era until early Roman times have been discovered; the best are in the **Parco Nazionale delle Incisioni Rupestri**. Do not miss the Naquane rock, carved with nearly 1,000 figures from the Ice Age. The **Centro Camuno** focuses on the Roman settlement in the valley.

Centro Camuno di Studi Preistorici
Via Marconi 7, Capo di Ponte. **Tel** 0364 420 91. **Closed** to tourists.

Parco Nazionale delle Incisioni Rupestri
Capo di Ponte. **Tel** 0364 421 40. **Open** 8:30am–7:30pm Tue–Sun (mid-Oct–Feb to 4:30pm). **Closed** Jan 1, May 1, Dec 25.

8 Lago d'Iseo

Bergamo & Brescia. FS Iseo. Lungolago Marconi 2, Iseo (030 98 02 09). **lagodiseo.org**

This glaciated lake is surrounded by tall mountains and waterfalls and boasts a mini-mountain of its own, in the form of the island of Monte Isola. Along the shores of the lake are a clutch of fishing villages such as Sale Marasino and Iseo itself. From Marone, on the east bank of the lake, a road leads to the village of **Cislano**, about 3 miles (5 km) away. Here, extraordinary spire-like rock formations rise from the ground, each spire topped by a boulder. These distinctive erosion pillars, one of the strangest natural wonders in Lombardy, are known as the "Fairies of the Forest."

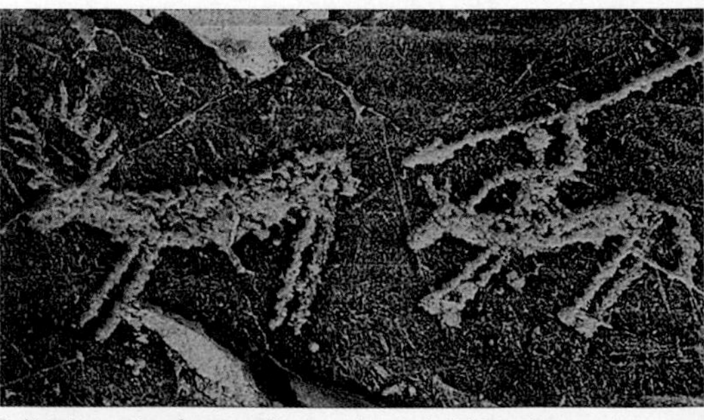

Prehistoric engraving of a mounted hunter and stag in the Val Camonica

For hotels and restaurants in this region see pp562–77 and pp580–605

The partly Renaissance Ponte Coperto, straddling the River Ticino at Pavia

9 Brescia

195,000. FS i Via Musei 32 (030 374 96 16). Sat.

Lombardy's second city after Milan boasts a rich artistic heritage, ranging from Roman temples to the triumphalist Mussolini-era architecture of Piazza Vittoriale. The major sights include the Roman ruins around Piazza del Foro, consisting of the **Tempio Capitolino** – a three-part temple incorporating the **Museo di Santa Giulia**, Brescia's main gallery – and a theater. The **Pinacoteca Civica Tosio Martinengo** has masterpieces by Raphael, Lorenzo Lotto, and Tintoretto; it is currently closed for restoration, but important paintings are on display at the Museo di Santa Giulia. The **Duomo** on Piazza Paolo VI, with its 11th-century core and 17th-century exterior, is another main attraction. One of the relics in the Duomo is the banner from the *Carroccio*, or sacred ox cart, which served as a symbol for the medieval Lega Lombarda. **Piazza della Loggia**, where the market is held, is named after the Renaissance loggia, built in Palladian style. The 18th-century church of San Nazaro e San Celso on Via Bronzoni contains an altarpiece by Titian.

Tempio Capitolino
Via Musei 57a. **Open** 11am–4pm Tue–Sun.

Museo di Santa Giulia
Via Musei 81b.
Tel 030 297 78 34
Open Tue–Sun.

Pinacoteca Civica Tosio Martinengo
Via Martinengo da Barcol.
Tel 030 377 49 99.
Closed for restoration.

10 Lodi

Lodi. 44,000. FS i Via Fanfulla 14 (0371 44 27 11). Tue, Thu, Sat, & Sun. W **turismo.provincia.lodi.it**

This is a charming medieval town of pastel-colored houses, pretty courtyards, and gardens. Just off Piazza della Vittoria, the arcaded square on which the 12th-century Duomo stands, is the fine Renaissance church of the **Incoronata**. The magnificent octagonal interior is entirely decorated with wall paintings and gilding, and crowned with a dome. One of the chapels has 15th-century works by Bergognone.

11 Pavia

71,000. FS i Palazzo del Broletto, Piazza della Vittoria (0382 07 99 43). Wed & Sat. W **turismo.provincia.pv.it**

During Pavia's golden age, the city was the Lombards' capital, and later witnessed coronations of Charlemagne and Frederick Barbarossa. Even after it lost its status to Milan in 1359, Pavia remained an important city, and great Romanesque churches, tall towers, and other monuments still reflect this.

As well as the Charterhouse (Certosa) *(see pp204–5)*, there is the sandstone **Basilica di San Michele** off Corso Garibaldi. The building was founded in the 7th century but largely rebuilt in the 12th. Its facade is decorated with symbols and friezes of fantastic animals, and inside there are intricate carvings on the columns; a chapel to the right of the main altar contains a 7th-century silver crucifix.

In the town center, around Piazza della Vittoria, are several ancient monuments, such as the medieval **Broletto** (town hall), with its 16th-century facade, and the **Duomo**, originally begun in 1488 and worked on in turn by Amadeo, Leonardo, and Bramante. The dome was added in the 1880s. The 11th-century tower that stood next to it collapsed suddenly in 1989. Crossing the river is the **Ponte Coperto**, a Renaissance covered bridge with a consecrated chapel halfway along it. The bridge was rebuilt after World War II.

Pavia is also the site of one of Europe's oldest (1361) and most respected universities, now residing around a series of Neo-Classical courtyards off Strada Nuova. This road continues northward to the 14th-century castle, now home to the **Museo Civico**.

Northwest of Piazza Castello is the 12th-century church **San Pietro in Ciel d'Oro**. It no longer boasts the fine gilded ceiling after which it is named, but does still contain a magnificent shrine to St. Augustine, whose bones were allegedly brought to Pavia in the 8th century. The body of the philosopher Boëthius (*c.* 480–524) is buried down in the crypt.

The Roman Tempio Capitolino in Brescia

Museo Civico
Castello Visconteo, Viale XI Febbraio 35.
Tel 0382 338 53. **Open** 10am–5:50pm Tue–Sun (Jan, Jul, Aug, & Dec: 9am–1:30pm). **Closed** public hols.

⑫ Certosa di Pavia

The Charterhouse 5 miles (8 km) north of Pavia is the pinnacle of Renaissance architecture in Lombardy, a gloriously decorated Carthusian monastery built over 200 years. Conceived as a monument to Gian Galeazzo Visconti, the Milanese ruler who founded the complex in 1396, this shrine was created by the great 15th-century craftsman Giovanni Antonio Amadeo, among others, who used innovative techniques of relief work and multicolored decoration. The Certosa is still home to Carthusian monks, who are under a strict vow of silence.

Pietra Dura Altar
Several of the 17th-century altars in the chapels have lavish designs worked in semiprecious stones ("pietra dura").

KEY

① **The side chapels** are richly decorated with marble, *trompe l'oeil* frescoes, and ornate altars and altarpieces.

② **The interior** of the church is largely Gothic.

③ **The grilles** date from *c.* 1660.

④ **The choir stalls** (15th century) are deeply carved and inlaid with intricate marquetry.

⑤ **The tomb** of Gian Galeazzo Visconti (1351–1402) is in the south transept.

⑥ **The New Sacristy** is painted with colorful ceiling frescoes.

⑦ **Monk's cell**

⑧ **This delightful**, arcaded Small Cloister, with fine terra-cotta ornamentation, contains a small garden, planted in formal designs.

⑨ **Main entrance** to the Certosa.

Tomb of Ludovico il Moro and Beatrice d'Este
This realistic marble portrait of Ludovico and his child bride was begun by Cristoforo Solari in 1497, some 11 years before Ludovico's death.

★ **Frescoes by Bergognone** *(c. 1488–93)*
This striking portrait of Christ is one of several frescoes by Bergognone in the transept and chapels, together with an altar painting of Sant'Ambrogio.

Great Cloister
This huge cloister is reached through the Small Cloister. It is framed on three sides by the two-story monks' cells, each backed by a small garden. A hatch beside the door permits food to be delivered without any communication.

VISITORS' CHECKLIST

Practical Information
Viale del Monumento 4, Pavia. **Tel** 0382 92 56 13. from Pavia & Milan. **Open** 9–11:30am, 2:30–4:30pm Tue–Sun & pub hols (Mar, Oct: to 5pm; Apr, Sep: to 5:30pm; May–Aug: to 6pm). (Last adm: 30 mins before closing.) Donation to guide.

Transportation
FS Certosa. Followed by 0.5 mile (1 km) walk.

★ Altarpiece by Perugino
The six-panel altarpiece was painted in 1499, but now only one panel – that depicting God the Father – is original; it is flanked by two paintings by Bergognone.

★ Renaissance Facade
The 15th-century lower part of the facade is profusely decorated with statues and carvings of Roman emperors, saints (here St. Peter), apostles, and prophets. The upper part dates from 1500.

The Duomo on Piazza del Comune, Cremona

⓭ Cremona

72,000. FS i Piazza del Comune 5 (0372 40 63 91). Wed & Sat. W **turismocremona.it**

Cremona, a major agricultural market, is most famous for music, thanks to native sons such as the composer Claudio Monteverdi (1567–1643) and the violin-maker Stradivarius (1644–1737). The town itself is dominated by the beautiful Piazza del Comune.

The main attraction is the exuberant part-Romanesque **Duomo** and its bell tower – said to be the tallest medieval tower in Italy – known as the **Torrazzo**; the two are linked by a Renaissance loggia. The wonderful facade is dominated by the large 13th-century rose window and by a number of intricate touches, including a small portico with statues of the Virgin and saints. Inside, the Duomo is sumptuously decorated with magnificent early 16th-century frescoes and Flemish tapestries, as well as paintings in the side chapels. The top of the Torrazzo offers sweeping views. Outside the Duomo, note the pulpit where itinerant preachers, including San Bernardino of Siena, spoke.

Next to the Duomo stands an octagonal 12th-century baptistry, while on the other side of the piazza rise the arcades of the late 13th-century **Loggia dei Militi** where the town's lords once met, now a war memorial.

The **Palazzo del Comune** is the other major building on the square. It was rebuilt in the 1200s and houses the Stradivari family collection of violins and masterpieces by Amati and Guarnieri.

The **Museo Civico**, in a 16th-century palazzo, houses the Pinacoteca, containing paintings, wood carvings, the cathedral's treasure, and ceramics. The **Museo di Violino** has a large display of important historic instruments. It also tells in detail the history of the violin and the importance of Cremona in the history of violin-making.

On the eastern outskirts of the town, on the road to Casalmaggiore, lies the Renaissance church of **San Sigismondo** (closed at lunchtime). It was here in a small chapel that Francesco Sforza married Bianca Visconti in 1441. The interior is richly decorated with 16th-century paintings, altarpieces, and frescoes by artists of the Cremona school (Campi family, Gatti, and Boccaccino).

Torrazzo
P. del Comune. **Tel** 0372 49 50 29.
Open 10am–1pm, 2:30–6pm Tue–Sun.

Palazzo del Comune
Piazza del Comune. **Tel** 0372 80 36 18.
Open 9am–6pm Tue–Sat; 10am– 6pm Sun. **Closed** public hols.

Museo Civico
Via Ugolani Dati 4. **Tel** 0372 80 36 22.
Open 10am–5pm Tue–Sun.
Closed public hols.

Museo di Violino
Piazza Marconi 5. **Tel** 0372 80 18 01.
Open 10am–6pm Tue–Sun.
Closed public hols.

⓮ Sabbioneta

Mantua. 4,400. from Mantua. i Piazza d'Armi 1 (0375 520 39). Wed am. apply at tourist office. W **iatsabbioneta.org**

Sabbioneta is the result of a delightful experiment in the theory of Renaissance architecture. It was built by Vespasiano Gonzaga Colonna (1531–91) as an ideal city, and within its hexagonal walls is a perfect gridwork arrangement of streets and buildings designed on a human scale. The finest buildings include the splendid Teatro All'Antica designed by Scamozzi, the Palazzo Ducale, and the frescoed Palazzo del Giardino, which may be visited as part of a tour of the town.

Antonio Stradivari and His Violins

19th-century engraving of Antonio Stradivari

The city of Cremona has been synonymous with violin-making since the 1530s, when Andrea Amati's instruments became sought after at the royal courts throughout Europe because of their superior tone to the medieval fiddle.

However, it was Antonio Stradivari, known as Stradivarius (1644–1737) – the pupil of Andrea Amati's grandson Niccolò – who raised the level of violin craftsmanship to genius. He went walking in the forests of the Dolomites in search of the perfect wood for his instruments. Stradivarius produced more than 1,100 violins in his workshop, of which more than 400 exist today. The main stopping-off points on a Stradivarius tour of Cremona are the Museo di Violino in the Museo Civico, the string collection in the Palazzo del Comune, and the great man's tombstone in the public gardens in Piazza Roma.

For hotels and restaurants in this region see pp562–77 and pp580–605

The ceiling of the Camera degli Sposi, by Mantegna, in the Palazzo Ducale

⑮ Mantua

49,000. FS i Piazza Andrea Mantegna 6 (0376 43 24 32). Thu. **turismo.mantova.it**

Mantua (Mantova in Italian) is a striking place of fine squares and aristocratic architecture, bordered on three sides by lakes formed by the River Mincio. The climate can be humid as a result, but the city makes up for it with its cultural history: it was the birthplace of the poet Virgil and the playground of the Gonzaga dukes for three centuries. It was also the refuge where Shakespeare sent Romeo into exile from Verona, and the setting for Verdi's opera *Rigoletto*. These links are all celebrated in street names, signposts, and monuments around the town. The theatrical connections are enhanced by the 18th-century **Teatro Accademico Bibiena**, on Via Accademia, which Mozart's father claimed was the finest he had ever seen.

Mantua is focused on three attractive main squares: Piazza delle Erbe, Piazza Broletto, named after the 13th-century building adorned with a statue of the poet Virgil, and the cobbled Piazza Sordello. On one side of Piazza Sordello is the **Duomo**, with an 18th-century facade and fine interior stuccoes by Giulio Romano (*c*. 1492–1546); on another side, the forbidding facade of the Palazzo Bonacolsi, with its tall prison tower. Piazza delle Erbe is dominated by the **Basilica di Sant'Andrea** (15th century), designed largely by Leon Battista Alberti, the early Renaissance architect and theorist, and now flanked by an arcade of shops. The square is also notable for the appealing 11th-century Rotonda di San Lorenzo, and the part-13th-century Palazzo della Ragione with its 15th-century clock tower.

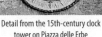

Detail from the 15th-century clock tower on Piazza delle Erbe

Palazzo Ducale

Piazza Sordello 40. **Tel** 0412 41 18 97. **Open** 8:15am–7:15pm (last adm: 6pm) Tue–Sun. **Closed** Jan 1, May 1, Dec 25. **Camera degli Sposi** Make advance reservations at **Tel** 041 241 18 97 or **ducalemantova.org**

The vast, 500-room home of the Gonzaga family covers the northeastern corner of t he town and incorporates Castello San Giorgio (a 14th-century fortress), a basilica, and the palace proper. The many works of art include an unfinished series of 15th-century frescoes by Pisanello, retelling episodes from the Arthurian legends; a large portrait by Rubens (17th century) of the ducal family in the Salone degli Arcieri; and – most absorbing of all – the frescoes by Mantegna in the **Camera degli Sposi** (1465–74). These portray Lodovico Gonzaga and members of his family and court in all their magnificence *(pp208–9)*. The entire room is decorated with images of people, animals, and fantastic landscapes, and is completed by a lighthearted *trompe l'oeil* ceiling of figures, *putti*, and a blue sky.

Palazzo Tè

Viale Tè. **Tel** 0376 32 32 66. **Open** 1–6pm Mon, 9am–6pm Tue–Sun. **Closed** Jan 1, May 1, Dec 25. **palazzote.it**

At the other end of town stands the early 16th-century Palazzo Tè, built by Giulio Romano for the Gonzaga family as a base from which they could go horseback riding. Here the artworks conspire with the architecture to produce striking effects: in the **Sala dei Giganti**, for instance, the frescoed Titans seem to be tearing down the very pillars of the room. Also remarkable is the **Sala di Amore e Psiche**, decorated with erotic scenes from Apuleius' *Golden Ass* and said to celebrate Federico II's love for his mistress. Other rooms are lavishly painted with horses and signs of the Zodiac.

The 13th-century facade of Palazzo Ducale overlooking Piazza Sordello

Late Renaissance fresco, by Romano, in the Duomo di Mantua, Mantua ▶

VALLE D'AOSTA AND PIEDMONT

Piedmont and the neighboring Valle d'Aosta are – apart from Turin and its cultural splendors – essentially countryside. To the north lie the Alps, with ski resorts such as Courmayeur, and the wild stretches of the Parco Nazionale del Gran Paradiso. To the south lie the vineyard-clad hills around Barolo, and seemingly endless fields of grain and rice, used in the local dish, risotto.

The northwest is also rich in culture. From the 11th century to the 18th, both the verdant Valle d'Aosta and Piedmont were part of the French-speaking principality of Savoy and enjoyed the influences of both sides of the Alpine divide. Even today, French and dialectal variants are still spoken in the remote valleys of Piedmont and in much of the Valle d'Aosta. It was only under Duke Emanuele Filiberto in the 16th century that the region was brought definitively into the Italian sphere of influence, and later it was to play the key role in the Risorgimento *(see pp66–7)*, the ambitious movement that united Italy under a king from Piedmont. The vestiges of this history are to be found in the medieval castles of the Valle d'Aosta and the clusters of chapels known as *sacri monti* (sacred mountains) built into the foothills of the Alps. Piedmont also spawned a school of painting, which is in evidence in the small parish churches and excellent fine art collections in the region. The most impressive architecture in the northwest, however, is undoubtedly to be found in Turin, a much underrated and surprisingly elegant Baroque city that boasts, among other things, one of the best Egyptian museums in the world. Piedmont is also known for its industry – FIAT in Turin, Olivetti in Ivrea, Ferrero in Alba – but it has not forgotten its agricultural roots, and food and drink play an important role in the life of the region: the hills of southern Piedmont produce many of the great Italian red wines.

Traditional sidewalk café in the heart of Turin

◀ Banners hanging outside of the Gothic Duomo in Asti, Piedmont

Exploring Valle d'Aosta and Piedmont

The vast flat plain of the Po, covered with the watery expanse of rice fields around Vercelli and Novara, eventually gives way, in the west, to the majestic heights of the Alps. Turin, the largest city in the area and the capital of Piedmont, stands at the edge of the plain, nestling almost in the shadow of the mountains. Further northwest, attractive Alpine valleys headed by dramatic peaks provide the setting for the traditional villages, ancient towns, and castles around Aosta. The Parco Nazionale del Gran Paradiso is an unspoiled tract of breathtaking scenery.

Rice fields around Vercelli

Sights at a Glance

1. Monte Bianco
2. Colle del Gran San Bernardo
3. Monte Cervino
4. Monte Rosa
5. Aosta
6. *Parco Nazionale del Gran Paradiso pp220–21*
7. Ceresole Reale
8. Via Lattea
9. Susa
10. Sacra di San Michele
11. Avigliana
12. Pinerolo
13. *Turin (Torino) pp224–9*
14. Palazzina di Caccia Stupinigi
15. Basilica di Superga
16. Venaria Reale
17. Santuario d'Oropa
18. Domodossola
19. Varallo
20. Lago d'Orta
21. Novara
22. Vercelli
23. Asti
24. Cuneo
25. Bossea Caves
26. Garessio

For additional map symbols *see back flap*

Turin, the capital of Piedmont, in the valley of the Po

Getting Around

The Fréjus Pass and the Mont Blanc Tunnel link France with northwest Italy, while the tunnel under the Simplon or Sempione Pass provides a direct rail route from Switzerland. From the rest of Italy there are excellent highway connections across the plain to Turin and up to Aosta. The region is well served with railroad links, and buses connect the main towns and outlying resorts. Getting around the mountains is more difficult, making the car the best method of transportation.

St. Pierre castle in the Valle d'Aosta

0 kilometers 25

0 miles 20

vona

nasco

RESSIO

Key

- Highway
- Major road
- Secondary road
- Minor road
- Scenic route
- Main railroad
- Minor railroad
- International border
- Regional border
- Summit

❶ Monte Bianco

Aosta. FS Pré-St-Didier. 🚌 Courmayeur. *i* Piazzale Monte Bianco 13, Courmayeur (0165 84 20 60).

Monte Bianco (Mont Blanc), the tallest mountain in the Alps at 15,780 ft (4,810 m), dominates the western Aosta valley and its attractive all-year resort, **Courmayeur**. A series of cable car rides from Entrèves, 3 miles (5 km) further north, leads to Chamonix. Passing its highest point (12,606 ft, 3,842 m) at Aiguille du Midi, it offers a spectacular view. From Pré-St-Didier, below Courmayeur, the **Little St. Bernard Pass**, with its small glaciers, forests, and ravines, can be explored.

❷ Colle del Gran San Bernardo

Aosta. FS 🚌 Aosta. *i* Strada Nazionale Gran San Bernardo 13, Etroubles (0165 785 59). **Open** daily.

The Great St. Bernard pass is synonymous with the hardy mountain rescue dogs that have been trained locally by Catholic monks since the 11th century.

The **Monks' Hospice,** founded around 1050 by St. Bernard of Aosta, lies just over the Swiss border (bring your passport), on the shores of a lovely lake; the dogs are still being trained here. The pretty Great St. Bernard valley itself includes the town of Etroubles, set in a forest of conifers, the hamlet of St-Oyen with its pretty parish church, and the resort of St-Rhémy-en-Bosses.

A St. Bernard dog

Monks' Hospice
Colle San Bernardo, Switzerland.
Tel 00 41 277 87 12 36. **Open** daily.

❸ Monte Cervino

Aosta. FS 🚌 Breuil-Cervinia. *i* Piazza Rey Guido, Breuil-Cervinia (0166 94 91 36).

The distinctive triangular peak of Monte Cervino (the Matterhorn) rises to 14,691 ft (4,478 m) and is easily recognizable. Below the mountain lies a scattering of attractive villages like Antey-St-André, Valtournanche (which gave its name to the valley), and the resort of **Breuil-Cervinia**. From Breuil a cable car rises to the Plateau Rosa (11,418 ft, 3,480 m), offering dramatic views of the surrounding mountains. This entire area is a paradise for both skiers and walkers.

❹ Monte Rosa

Aosta. FS Verrès. 🚌 St-Jacques. *i* Route Varasc, Champoluc/Ayas (0125 30 71 13).

Monte Rosa, Italy's second-highest mountain, overlooks the picturesque Ayas and Gressoney valleys. The rolling lower Ayas valley is dominated by the ruins of the 11th-century **Castello di Graines**. Higher up, the resort of Champoluc has a cable car connection with the striking **Testa Grigia** (10,877 ft/3,315 m). The Gressoney valley is home to the Walser people, who speak a German dialect. At the bottom of the valley, north of Pont-St-Martin, lies **Issime**: the 16th-century church here has a fresco of the Last Judgment on its facade.

Castello di Graines
Graines, Strada Statale 506.

Medieval Castles and Forts in the Valle d'Aosta

The mountains alone provided insufficient protection to the fragmented fiefs that covered the Valle d'Aosta in the Middle Ages. The medieval lords, who ruled ruthlessly over their small domains, built castles to enforce their often fragile power. Of the many built, 70 castles survive in some form to this day. You will pass a number of them if you drive into Italy by the Mont Blanc tunnel; they stretch from Aosta to Pont-St-Martin.

Originally, Aosta castles were designed to be defensive and threatening, such as the looming tower of **Montmayer**, perched high on a huge rock by the Valgrisenche valley. Nearby, the equally forbidding dark tower of **Ussel** throws a melancholy, brooding watchfulness over the valley.

Fénis and **Verrès** represent an important shift in the function of the feudal castle. Both Fénis, a splendid 14th-century showpiece *(see p184)*, and Verrès were not just important military outposts but also examples of palatial opulence and good living. **Issogne** too furthered this luxurious trend with its elaborate frescoes, loggias, and fountains. Decoration was also important to Vittorio Emanuele II, owner of **Sarre**, who turned the halls of his fortress into a plush hunting lodge. The owners of **Châtelard**, set in some of the highest vineyards in Europe, placed fine wine production alongside military aims.

The strategically sited 14th-century castle at Verrès

The 12th-century cloister, with 40 carved columns of darkened marble, in Sant'Orso

❺ Aosta

35,000. FS Porta Pretoria 3 (0165 23 66 27). Tue. **lovevda.it**

Lying on a plain surrounded by dramatic mountains, the town of Aosta provides a remarkable mixture of ancient culture and spectacular scenery. The Romans captured it from the Salassian Gauls in 25 BC, and Aosta is still dotted with fine Roman architecture built in honor of Emperor Augustus – indeed the town was once called *Augusta Praetoria*, its name only evolving into Aosta over the centuries. The medieval town was later fortified by the Challant family and then by the Dukes of Aosta, who added towers to the old Roman walls.

Modern Aosta is a bustling crossroads for local industries and tourists on their way to the mountains. The center, however, still consists of a delightful grid of large squares and surprising architectural treasures, which justify Aosta's nickname of "Rome of the Alps."

Roman Ruins

Roman Theater, Via Baillage. **Open** 9am–8pm daily (to 7pm Sep–Mar, to 6:30pm Oct & Feb, to 5pm Nov–Jan). **Roman Forum**, Piazza Giovanni XXIII. **Open** daily.

In Roman times, entry to Aosta was over the **bridge** to the east of the town (beyond the modern bridge) and through the **Arch of Augustus**. This triumphal arch is today marred by a roof added in the 18th century. Ahead stands the **Porta Pretoria**, its double row of stone arches flanked by a medieval tower; the gateway originally stood about 8 ft (2.5 m) higher than at present. Also worth a look is the 65-ft (20-m) high facade of the **Roman Theater**. A little to the north is the elliptical amphitheater, although this is buried apart from three columns that form part of the convent of San Giuseppe. In the old town, next to the cathedral, lies the **Roman Forum**, or marketplace, with its huge cryptoporticus: the function of this impressive underground gallery remains the subject of speculation.

Detail of a medieval mosaic on the floor of Aosta's Cattedrale

Cattedrale

Piazza Giovanni XXIII. **Open** 6:30am–12:30pm, 2–7:30pm Mon–Fri, 7am–noon, 2–6pm Sat & Sun (early Sep–Easter: 6:30am–noon, 3–7pm). **Museo del Tesoro Tel** 0165 404 13. **Open** 3–5:30pm Sat & Sun. **Closed** during religious services.

This relatively modest shrine to St. John the Baptist was first built in the 12th century, but has been altered many times since. The interior is Gothic, with finely carved 15th-century choir stalls and floor mosaics. Next door, the **Museo del Tesoro** contains a rich collection of statuettes and reliquaries, and a number of impressive medieval tombs.

Sant'Orso

Via Sant'Orso. **Open** daily.

East of the town walls is the architectural highlight of Aosta: a medieval complex of church buildings. Sant'Orso itself has an unusual Gothic facade with a narrow, tall portal. The interior has 11th-century frescoes, a crypt holding the tomb of St. Orso, patron saint of Aosta, and a beautiful **cloister** with carved columns and capitals.

Environs

The castle at **Fénis** *(see p218)*, 8 miles (12 km) east, is one of the few castles in the Aosta valley with a well-preserved interior, including beautiful frescoes and wooden galleries. **Issogne**, 23 miles (38 km) south-east, is the setting for another highly decorated castle, remodeled around 1490. It has many frescoes and decorative motifs, including an octagonal fountain with a centerpiece in the shape of a pomegranate tree.

Castello di Fénis

Fénis. **Tel** 0165 76 42 63. **Open** daily. **Closed** Tue (Nov–Feb); Jan 1, Dec 25.

Castello di Issogne

Issogne. **Tel** 0125 92 93 73. **Open** daily. **Closed** Wed (Nov–Feb); Jan 1, Dec 25.

Some of the impressive ruins standing in the Roman Forum in Aosta

❻ Parco Nazionale del Gran Paradiso

A breathtaking wilderness of dramatic mountains and lush meadows, the Gran Paradiso is Italy's foremost national park, created in 1922 from part of a former royal hunting reserve of the House of Savoy. It is mainly a summer resort for walkers due to its unspoiled scenery, rare wildlife, and unusual Alpine flowers, though there is also cross-country skiing during the winter months. The king of the park is the ibex, a relative of the goat family all but extinct in the rest of Europe. The park is also prized by naturalists for its chamois, ptarmigan, golden eagles, rare butterflies, and marmots.

Castello di Aymavilles
The 18th-century core of this castle is framed by medieval corner towers.

Val di Rhêmes-Notre-Dame
This peaceful and broad valley offers magnificent scenery with waterfalls and fast-flowing streams running from the glacier at its head.

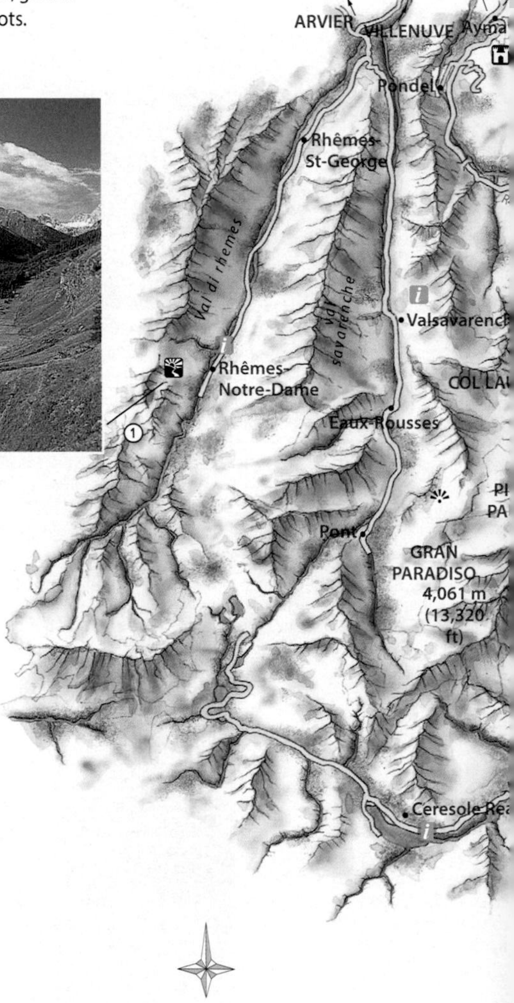

ARVIER
VILLENUVE
Pondel
Rhêmes-St-George
Val di rhemes
Val savarenche
Rhêmes-Notre-Dame
Eaux Rousses
Pont
GRAN PARADISO 4,061 m (13,320 ft)
Ceresole

KEY

① **Goletta Waterfall** is an impressive cascade near the Lago di Goletta.

② **Cogne** is the main resort and a good base from which to explore the park. Maps of the park's routes and hiking trails are available here.

③ **Lillaz** is sedate and off the beaten track, while Valnontey and Cogne are two of the busiest resorts.

★ Paradisia Alpine Garden
The botanic garden contains a collection of Alpine plants, including the delicate "twinflower."

Cascata di Lillaz
This tall, dramatic waterfall, situated a little to the east of the rustic village of Lillaz, is best observed after the spring snowmelt.

VISITORS' CHECKLIST

Practical Information
Piemonte and Valle d'Aosta.
Segreteria Turistica, Cheriettes Aymavilles (0165 90 26 93); Centro Visitatori Parco Nazionale del Gran Paradiso, Ceresole Reale, (0124 95 31 66).
Paradisia Alpine Garden: Valnontey, Cogne. **Tel** 0165 741 47. **Open** mid-Jun–mid-Sep: daily. **pngp.it**
parks.it

Transportation
FS Aosta & Pont Canavese.
from Aosta or Pont Canavese to the different valleys.

★ Valnontey
This lovely valley, after which the resort is named, provides dramatic views of glaciers and easy access to various hiking trails.

Key
═ Main road

0 kilometers 5
0 miles 5

Male Ibex
The ibex lives largely above the tree line. Groups are often seen around Col Lauson at dawn and dusk, and also around Pont in June.

The small resort of Ceresole Reale under winter snow

❼ Ceresole Reale

Turin. 🚌 to Ceresole Reale. ℹ Palazzo Comunale, Ceresole Reale (0124 95 32 00). W **turismotorino.org**

On the southern, Piedmont side of the extensive Parco Nazionale del Gran Paradiso *(see pp216–17)* lies the small resort of Ceresole Reale. The route from Cuorgnè traverses rolling countryside and follows the S460 along a narrow gorge with a cascading stream. At **Noasca**, a spectacular waterfall may be seen high above the houses.

Ceresole Reale lies in a basin surrounded by meadows and forests of larch, and framed by mountains – the Gran Paradiso range to the north, Levanna to the southwest – which are reflected in the clear waters of a spectacular artificial mountain lake, which is actually a dammed reservoir, providing energy to supply Turin with electricity. This nevertheless unspoiled corner of the country is a good base for walking, climbing, and hiking, and also offers facilities for skiing during the winter.

❽ Alta Val Susa

Turin. FS Oulx. 🚌 to Sauze d'Oulx. ℹ Via Louset, Sestriere (0122 75 54 44). W **vialattea.it**

The closest ring of mountain resorts to Turin, and as a consequence popular for weekend excursions, is also known colloquially as the Via Lattea or "Milky Way." Villages such as **Bardonecchia** and **Sauze d'Oulx** preserve traditional old stone and wood buildings that have been a feature of the region for centuries. The small church in Bardonecchia has, in addition, a fine 15th-century carved choir. In contrast, the supermodern complex at **Sestriere** was purpose-built to accommodate skiers in winter and hikers in summer.

From Bardonecchia a chairlift operates some of the way up **Punta Colomion**, which rises immediately to the south of the resort. The summit, at 6,738 ft (2,054 m), offers fine views, and numerous hiking and walking possibilities.

❾ Susa

Turin. 👥 6,500. FS 🚌 ℹ Corso Inghilterra 39 (0122 62 24 47). 🛍 Tue. W **turismotorino.org**

This attractive mountain town flourished in Roman times: the **Arch of Augustus**, built in 8 BC, commemorates the alliance between the local Gaulish

The impressive part-Roman gateway, Porta Savoia, in Susa

chieftain and the Emperor Augustus. Other relics from the Roman period include two arches of an aqueduct, sections of an amphitheater, and traces of the old town walls. **Porta Savoia**, an imposing Roman gateway dating from the 4th century, was remodeled in the Middle Ages.

Most of the historic center of the town is medieval, including the castle of Countess Adelaide and the **Duomo**, both originally 11th century. The Duomo, much altered since then, houses a polyptych (*c.* 1500) attributed to Bergognone, and a copy of a precious 14th-century Flemish triptych portraying the *Virgin and Saints*. South of the town lies the Gothic church of **San Francesco**, surrounded by an area of early medieval houses.

A street in the traditional village of Bardonecchia, in Alta Val Susa

Carved capitals on the Porta dello Zodiaco at the Sacra di San Michele

⑩ Sacra di San Michele

Strada Sacra San Michele. **Tel** 011 93 91 30. May–Sep: Sun pm from Avigliana & Turin. **Open** 9:30am–noon, 2:30–6pm Tue–Sun (mid-Oct–mid-Mar: to 5pm). Call ahead to arrange group visits. **sacradisanmichele.com**

This somewhat forbidding abbey complex is perched on a ridge halfway up Monte Pirchiriano, at 3,156 ft (962 m). Its monastic community was founded around the year 1000, possibly on the site of a previous sanctuary, though the exterior looks every bit as much a fortress as the spiritual refuge that it was for 600 years.

During its prime, the abbey attracted pilgrims on their way to Rome, and as a result it grew enormously wealthy and powerful, controlling over 100 other abbeys in Italy, France, and Spain. It was subsequently looted several times, despite being fortified, before falling into decline and eventually being suppressed in 1662.

The sanctuary is reached by climbing 154 steep steps hewn out of the rock, which offer wonderful views over the surrounding countryside and up to the Alps. At the very top of this stairway, known as the Scalone dei Morti (Stairway of the Dead), is the Romanesque Porta dello Zodiaco, a doorway carved with creatures and symbols relating to the signs of the Zodiac. Beyond the doorway a few more steps lead into the church itself, which dates from the 12th–13th centuries and incorporates traces of an earlier building. The interior houses 15th- and 16th-century paintings and frescoes, and a 16th-century triptych by the Piedmontese artist Defendente Ferrari. The crypt holds the tombs of the early dukes and princes of the House of Savoy-Carignano.

⑪ Avigliana

Turin. 12,000. FS Piazza Conte Rosso 17 (011 97 69 111). Thu. **comune.avigliana.to.it**

On a fine day, this small town perched beside two glacier-fed lakes and encircled by tall mountains looks breathtakingly beautiful. Avigliana is overlooked by a castle, first erected in the mid-10th century but now in ruins, which was once the home of the Counts of Savoy. Until the early 15th century the town was one of their favorite bases.

The medieval houses here are largely unspoiled, particularly in the two main *piazzas,* Santa Maria and Conte Rosso. Other buildings of note are the Casa della Porta Ferrata and the 15th-century Casa dei Savoia, both on Via XX Settembre. The church of San Giovanni (13th–14th century) contains early 16th-century paintings by Defendente Ferrari.

⑫ Pinerolo

Turin. 36,000. FS Viale Giolitti 7/9 (0121 79 55 89). Wed & Sat. **turismotorino.org**

Pinerolo lies in an attractive setting beside hills at the confluence of the Lemina and Chisone valleys. The town was the capital of the Acaia family, a branch of the House of Savoy, and in the 14th and 15th centuries it was known for the cultural atmosphere that prevailed here under the family's patronage. However, the town enjoyed none of the stability of Turin: it was occupied by the French five times between the 15th and 18th centuries. During the 17th century the French demolished many of the town's ancient buildings in order to make Pinerolo a defensive stronghold; among the political prisoners allegedly held here was the notorious "Man in the Iron Mask." Today the town is a busy center of commerce.

A number of monumental buildings do remain, however. The **Duomo**, at the center of the town, was remodeled in Gothic style in the 15th–16th centuries and has a fine portal and an impressive bell tower. Via Principi d'Acaia climbs up to the 14th-century palace of the Princes of Acaia, and to the 15th-century church of **San Maurizio**, where the Acaia princes are buried; beside it rises a 14th-century bell tower.

The medieval arcades surrounding Piazza Conte Rosso in Avigliana

Turin ⓭

Mention Turin (Torino) and most people will think of industry and prosperity. It is certainly an economic powerhouse, but it is also a town of grace and charm, with superb Baroque architecture, elegant arcades of shops, and excellent museums, set against the dramatic scenery of the foothills of the Alps. Turin is also, of course, home to the famous Turin Shroud, the FIAT car company, and the Juventus soccer team.

Exploring Turin

Though settled by the Romans (**Porta Palatina** is an impressive 1st-century AD relic), and the seat of a university since the Middle Ages, Turin came into its own only after 1563, when Emanuele Filiberto of Savoy moved his capital here. Three centuries of prosperity ensued. Turin then became the base for Italy's unification movement and, from 1861 to 1865, the first capital of the newly united country. Subsequently its main power was economic. In 1899 the Agnelli family created the car company **FIAT** (Fabbrica Italiana Automobili Torino), which grew to be one of the biggest in Europe. After World War II, Turin attracted thousands of poor Italians from the south who came to work in its factories. Though there have been social conflicts and labor disputes as a result, managers and workers unite over soccer: the Juventus team is owned by the Agnelli family.

The FIAT car factory logo

Statue of Emperor Augustus in front of the Roman Porta Palatina

Duomo

Piazza San Giovanni. **Tel** 011 436 15 40. **Open** daily.

The cathedral, which was built in 1491–8 and dedicated to St. John the Baptist, is the only

Turin Town Center

1. Porta Palatina
2. Duomo
3. San Lorenzo
4. Palazzo Reale
5. Armeria Reale
6. Palazzo Madama
7. Museo Egizio and Galleria Sabauda
8. Palazzo Carignano
9. Mole Antonelliana

0 meters 500

0 yards 500

For keys to map symbols *see back flap*

The 15th-century Duomo, with the Cappella della Sacra Sindone beyond

example of Renaissance architecture in Turin. The sober square bell tower, which pre-dates the rest of the church by 30 years, stands in refreshing contrast to Turin's sumptuous Baroque buildings; its top was designed by Filippo Juvarra in 1720. Inside, the Duomo is heavy with statuary and paintings. On the right side of the church is the **Cappella della Sacra Sindone** (Chapel of the Holy Shroud), which is incorporated into the Palazzo Reale *(see p224)*. The chapel is a remarkable feat, designed by Guarino Guarini (1624–83), with an extraordinary meshlike cupola; the exterior view is equally eccentric.

Palazzo Madama

Piazza Castello. **Tel** 011.443.3501. **Open** 10am–6pm Tue–Sat, 10am–7pm Sun (last adm: 1 hour before closing). **palazzomadamatorino.it**

Turin's main square once contained a medieval castle that incorporated elements of the original Roman city walls. The castle was later enlarged and remodeled, and a new facade by Juvarra was added, at the request of a royal widow, in the 18th century. The Palazzo Madama – as it was renamed – sits in the center of the square with a stately facade. The interior, with its grand staircase and first floor, both designed by Juvarra, houses the **Museo Civico d'Arte Antica**. This collection contains treasures ranging from the Graeco-Roman era to the 19th century. The display includes *Portrait of an Unknown Man* by Antonello da Messina (15th century) among the paintings and sculptures, and reproductions of the Duc de Berry's *Book of Hours* from *c.* 1420. Glass, jewelry, textiles, and furniture are also on display.

The facade of the Palazzo Madama, designed by Filippo Juvarra in 1718–21

VISITORS' CHECKLIST

Practical Information

910,000. Piazza Castello 161 *(011 53 51 81)*, also at Stazione Porta Nuova. Sat. Jun 24: Festa di San Giovanni. **turismotorino.org**

Transportation

Caselle 9 miles (15 km) N. Porta Nuova, Piazza Carlo-Felice. Porta Susa, Piazza XVIII Dicembre. Corso Vittorio Emanuele II 131.

Detail of the mysterious 12th-century Holy Shroud

The Holy Shroud

The most famous – and most dubious – holy relic of them all is kept in Turin's Duomo. The Shroud, said to be the winding-sheet in which the body of Christ was wrapped after his crucifixion, owes its fame to the fact that the Shroud bears the imprint of a crucified man with a wound in his side, and bruises from what might have been a crown of thorns.

The Shroud is one of the most famous medieval relics. Its early history is unclear, but the House of Savoy was in possession of it around 1450, and had it displayed in Guarini's chapel from 1694. The "original" Shroud – which sits in a silver casket inside an iron box within a marble coffer – is not on display, though a replica is, together with a welter of scientific explanations as to the Shroud's possible origins. In 1988, however, the myth of the Shroud was exploded: a carbon-dating test showed that it dates back no further than the 12th century. The Shroud nevertheless remains an object of religious veneration.

Exploring Turin

The city of Turin is blessed with numerous interesting museums, which are housed in splendid palazzi and civic buildings. The center itself is relatively small, with broad, straight streets, often bordered with historic cafés and shops, which are pleasant places to stroll along. The city is also famous for its innovative cuisine and boasts some of the country's finest restaurants.

Granite statue of Ramses II (13th century BC) in the Museo Egizio

Museo Egizio

Via Accademia delle Scienze 6. **Tel** 011 561 77 76. **Open** 8:30am–7:30pm Tue–Sun (last adm: 6:30pm).
W museoegizio.it

Turin owes its magnificent Egyptian Museum – one of the most important in the world – largely to the Piedmont-born Bernardo Drovetti, who was stationed in Egypt as French Consul General at the time of the Napoleonic Wars. It was the booty he brought back that formed the basis of this very fine collection of Egyptian artifacts.

On the ground floor, items on display include monumental sculptures and reconstructed temples; upstairs, there are collections of papyrus and everyday objects. Among the most impressive sculptures are a black granite Ramses II (13th century BC, or 19th dynasty), the slightly earlier Amenophis II, and the basalt figure of Gemenef-Har-Bak, a vizier from the 26th dynasty. The Sala della Nubia contains a reconstruction of the 15th-century BC **Rock Temple of Ellesija**.

Extraordinary wall and tomb paintings are displayed on the upper floor, together with items of daily use such as the tools used for measuring, weaving, fishing, and hunting. The 14th-century BC Tomb of Kha and Merit, complete with the food, tools, and ornaments buried with them for the afterlife, is particularly fascinating. The papyrus collection is beautiful and of enormous interest to scholars: these documents have been vital to modern understanding of Egyptian language, customs, and history – one document, the *Papiro dei Re* (Royal Papyrus), lists all the pharaohs up to the 17th dynasty, with their dates.

Detail from an 18th-dynasty papyrus Book of the Dead, Museo Egizio

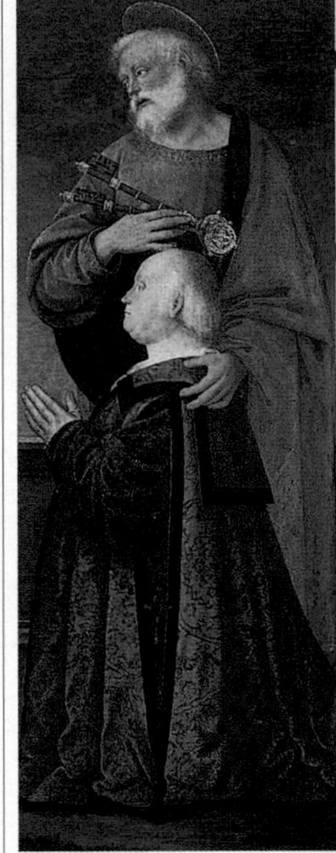

G. Ferrari's *St. Peter and a Donor* (16th century), Galleria Sabauda

Galleria Sabauda

Via Accademia delle Scienze 6.
Tel 011 56 41 749. **Open** 8:30am–7:30pm Tue–Sun.
W artito.arti.beniculturali.it

The Palazzo dell'Accademia delle Scienze, the building by Guarini in which the Egyptian Museum is housed, is also home to the House of Savoy's main painting collection. The top two floors are the setting for a stunning array of works by Italian, French, Flemish, and Dutch masters.

The collection was originally begun in the mid- to late-1400s, and has been expanded over the centuries. It is grouped in regional schools. The Piedmontese section includes masterpieces by Gaudenzio Ferrari (*c*. 1480–1546) and two early 16th-century paintings by Defendente Ferrari. Among works of particular interest from other Italian schools are Antonio and Piero Pollaiolo's 15th-century *Tobias and the*

For hotels and restaurants in this region see pp562–77 and pp580–605

Spacious arcades on Turin's Via Roma

Archangel Raphael, and the *Ritratto di Gentiluomo* by Bronzino. Bellini, Mantegna, and Veronese are among other Italian artists represented.

The section on Dutch and Flemish art includes important works such as Jan Van Eyck's *St. Francis* (15th century) and Rembrandt's *Old Man Sleeping* (17th-century), as well as several portraits by Van Dyck, which include his *Principe Tommaso di Savoia-Carignano* (1634). Among the French works here are 17th-century landscape paintings by Claude Lorrain and Poussin. Plans are underway to move the Galleria Sabauda collection to the Palazzo Reale by 2015.

Palazzo Carignano

Via Accademia delle Scienze 5. **Tel** 011 562 11 47. **Open** 9am–7pm Tue–Sun.

This Baroque palazzo is not only Guarini's masterpiece, it is arguably the finest building in Turin, with its magnificent facade and ornate rotunda. It was built in 1679 for the Carignano family – an offshoot of the main House of Savoy and ancestors of the Italian kings – but came into its own in the 1800s. The first king of Italy, Vittorio Emanuele II, was born here in 1829. After Italy was unified in 1861 by a series of referenda, the former royal residence was used as the first national parliament building.

The palazzo is home to the **Museo Nazionale del Risorgimento**, which, through paintings and a collection of artifacts (housed in the rooms where history was made), tells the story of unification. It introduces Mazzini, Cavour, and Garibaldi – key figures in the Risorgimento *(see pp66–7)*.

Via Roma

Running through the historic center, Turin's main street Via Roma leads from Piazza Castello (north) through Piazza San Carlo to the distinctive arched facade of Stazione Porta Nuova (south). Via Roma is a magnificent concourse lined with stylish shops and shaded arcades, interrupted only by cobbled squares. A grid pattern of side streets branches off either side of Via Roma, revealing additional shopping arcades.

Piazza San Carlo

The ensemble of Baroque architecture on this square, now a pedestrian zone, has earned it the nickname of "Turin's drawing room." At its southern end are the twin churches of Santa Cristina and San Carlo; both were built in the 1630s, though **Santa Cristina** has a Baroque facade, crowned with statues, which was designed by Juvarra in the early 18th century.

At the center of the square stands a 19th-century statue of Duke Emanuele Filiberto. The work, by Carlo Marocchetti, has become an emblem of the city. At the corners of the square, frescoes depict the Holy Shroud. The **Galleria San Federico**, in the square's northwestern corner, is a stylish shopping arcade.

Piazza San Carlo is known for its society cafés. In one such establishment, in 1786, Antonio Benedetto Carpano invented the drink known as vermouth, which is still very popular all over Italy today.

Pinacoteca Giovanni e Marella Agnelli

Lingotto, Via Nizza 230. **Tel** 011 00 62 713. **Open** 10am–7pm Tue–Sun (last adm: 6:15pm).

pinacoteca-agnelli.it

Located on the roof of the former FIAT factory redesigned by architect Renzo Piano, this museum holds paintings by Modigliani and Canaletto, as well as two statues by Canova.

Parco del Valentino

Corso Massimo D'Azeglio. **Open** daily. Borgo Medioevale: Viale Virgilio 107. **Tel** 011 443 17 01. **Open** 9am–7pm daily (to 8pm Apr–Oct). Orto Botanico: **Tel** 011 670 59 85. **Open** Apr–Sep: Sat & Sun.

borgomedievaletorino.it

This park contains the **Borgo Medioevale**, a complex of medieval buildings erected for an exhibition in the late 1880s. The edifices show different types of design and construction, based on traditional houses and castles found throughout the region.

The **Orto Botanico**, beside the medieval complex, is an impressive botanical garden in a pleasant setting.

Looking south across the elegant Piazza San Carlo, "Turin's drawing room"

Turin: Symbols of the City

Turin's architecture mirrors the city's transition from monarchic power to industrial power. Witness the ostentation of the Baroque apartments of the Savoy family in Palazzo Reale, and contrast them with the futuristic Mole Antonelliana, a tall structure that heralded the dawn of the modern industrial age. Much of Turin's history in the 20th century has been dominated by the automobile: FIAT is synonymous with Turin. For the curious, the city's extensive motor museum is worth a visit, since it maps out the history of Italian car design.

Mole Antonelliana

Via Montebello 20. **Tel** 011 813 85 61. Panoramic elevator **Open** 10am–8pm Tue–Sun (to 11pm Sat). Museo del Cinema: **Tel** 011 813 85 64. **Open** 9am–8pm Tue–Sun (to 11pm Sat) (last adm: 45 mins before closing).
museocinema.it

This building is the Turin equivalent of the Eiffel Tower in Paris: an unmissably tall landmark that is a signature for the city. It looks like a glorified lightning conductor: indeed in 1954 an electric storm struck down the top 155 ft (47 m), which was later replaced. The 550-ft (167-m) Mole, by Alessandro Antonelli (1798–1888), was meant to be a synagogue, but upon its completion in 1897, the city used it to house the Risorgimento museum. The Mole ("massive structure") – for a time the world's tallest brick building – provides panoramic views from its elevator and now houses the Cinema Museum.

Palazzo Reale

Piazzetta Reale. **Tel** 011 436 14 55. **Open** 8:30am–7:30pm Tue–Sun (last adm: 6:20pm).
piemonte.beniculturali.it

The interior of San Lorenzo's dome

This palace was the seat of the Savoy royal family from 1660 until the unification of Italy in 1861. Behind the austere facade, designed by Amedeo di Castellamonte, lie richly decorated state apartments; the ceilings were painted by Morello, Miel, and Seyter in the 17th century. The many splendid furnishings, tapestries, and ornaments date from the 17th to the 19th centuries; they include the elaborate Chinese Cabinet, the Alcove Room, the lavishly decorated Throne Room, and the innovative Scala delle Forbici, or Scissor Stairs, created by Juvarra in 1720. Behind the palace are extensive gardens, which extend northward.

To the left of the main entrance is the church of **San Lorenzo**. This fine Baroque building, begun in 1634, is by architect Guarino Guarini, its ornate interior boasting another of his extraordinary, geometric domes.

A lavishly decorated gallery in the 17th-century Palazzo Reale, a royal residence until unification

The 19th-century tower, Mole Antonelliana, dominating Turin

Armeria Reale

Piazza Castello 191. **Tel** 011 54 38 89. **Open** 8:30am–7:30pm Tue–Sun (last adm: 30 mins before closing). **Closed** Jan 1, Dec 25.
artito.arti.beniculturali.it

One wing of the Palazzo Reale, on the northern side of the main square, provides the splendid setting for one of the most extensive and breathtaking collections of arms and armory in the world.

Opened to the public in 1837, the armory originally belonged to the House of Savoy. The fine rooms, such as the splendid Galleria Beaumont, designed by Juvarra in 1733, hold treasures ranging from Roman and Etruscan times to the 1800s. The collection has magnificent medieval and Renaissance items from some of the world's greatest armorers and gunsmiths, including a pistol that belonged to Emperor Charles V. One section is devoted largely to Oriental arms and armor.

The Royal Library contains a collection of drawings, including a self-portrait by Leonardo da Vinci on display during special exhibitions only.

Environs

About 2 miles (3 km) out of the city center is the vast **MAUTO – Museo dell'Automobile di Torino**. Founded in 1933, and since renovated by the architect Cino Zucchi, it now houses over 150 veteran, vintage, and classic cars. The collection includes glorious Bugattis, Maseratis, Lancias, FIATs, and some fine foreign cars. The first gas-driven car made in Italy (1896) is kept here, as well as the first FIAT (1899) and the 1929 Isotta Fraschini *coupé de ville* used to transport Gloria Swanson in the film *Sunset Boulevard*. Note also that a large number of the sports cars from the 1950s are right-hand drive in deference to the great British car-makers such as Aston Martin.

MAUTO – Museo dell'Automobile di Torino
Corso Unità d'Italia 40. **Tel** 011 67 76 66. **Open** daily.
W **museoauto.it**

An interior view of the 18th-century Palazzina di Caccia di Stupinigi

Designs from 1949 for the Ferrari 166 MM

14 Palazzina di Caccia di Stupinigi

Piazza Principe Amedeo 7, Stupinigi. **Tel** 011 358 12 20. 4 to Piazza Caio Mario, then 41. **Open** times vary, so call ahead.

In 1729–30 the architect Filippo Juvarra (1676–1736) designed a magnificent hunting lodge at Stupinigi, a beautiful location 5 miles (9 km) southwest of Turin. Known as the Palazzina di Caccia di Stupinigi, the building was created for Duke Vittorio Amedeo II of Savoy and is one of the very finest hunting lodges, built on an impressive scale, reminiscent of the palace of Versailles in France.

The dynamic and complex plan incorporates semicircles and an octagon, with the main block consisting of a dome rising above a circular building from which wings jut out, not unlike the arms of a windmill.

The mass of the central section is lightened by balustrading topped with urns and figures, while the dome is crowned with an 18th-century bronze figure of a stag.

The huge interior includes rooms sumptuously decorated with *trompe l'oeil* paintings and frescoes on a hunting theme – the 18th-century *Triumph of Diana*, for instance, in the main *salone*. About 40 of those rooms house the interesting **Museo d'Arte e di Ammobiliamento**, a museum specializing in 17th- and 18th-century furniture and furnishings. Many of the ornate items on display in these rooms were originally kept in other former royal residences.

Outside there are extensive grounds, which feature an elegant combination of spectacular broad avenues, parkland, and colorful formal parterres.

15 Basilica di Superga

Strada Basilica di Superga 75, Comune di Torino. 15, 61, 68 from city center. **Open** daily. **Closed** Sep 8. Tombs **Tel** 011 899 74 56. **Open** daily; times vary so call ahead. **Closed** public hols. **W** **basilicadisuperga.com**

On a hill to the east of Turin, accessible by car, Tram-Track, and bus 79, stands the superb Baroque Basilica of Superga, built by Juvarra in 1717–31. The commission came from Duke Vittorio Amedeo II, in fulfillment of a vow made to the Virgin Mary in 1706 while the French were besieging the duke and his army in Turin.

The beautiful yellow and white facade is dominated by a large portico designed like a Classical temple, with a 213-ft (65-m) high dome immediately beyond. It is flanked by twin bell towers. The interior is magnificent, decorated in light blue and yellow, and contains fine paintings and carvings.

Underneath the Basilica lies the great mausoleum that houses the tombs of the kings, princes, and princesses of Savoy from the 18th and 19th centuries. The victims of the 1949 aircrash, including the Turin soccer team, are commemorated on a plaque behind the Basilica.

One other benefit of visiting the basilica is seeing the views over Turin.

The imposing facade of the 18th-century Baroque Basilica di Superga designed by Filippo Juvarra

The 17th-century Basilica dell'Assunta dominating Sacro Monte, Varallo

⓰ Venaria Reale

Piazza della Repubblica 4. **Tel** 011 499 23 33. FS 🚌 **Open** 9am–6pm Tue–Sun (to 8pm Sat & Sun). W **lavenaria.it**

This grandiose complex dates from the mid-17th century, when Charles Emanuel II of Savoy decided to build a royal hunting lodge on the site of the existing town of Altessano Superiore. Venaria Reale incorporates the **Reggia di Diana**, a formal palace and garden built between 1660 and 1671, as well as **La Mandria**, the 3,000-hectare (7,413-acre) park surrounding it.

Venaria's historical center was designed by Amadeo di Castellamonte between 1667 and 1690; its focal point is the Piazza dell'Annunziata, with statues depicting the Angel Gabriel and the Virgin Mary.

⓱ Santuario d'Oropa

Via Santuario d'Oropa 480, Comune di Biella. **Tel** 015 255 512 00. FS Biella. 🚌 from Biella. ♿ **Basilica Antica Open** 7:30am–7pm daily. **Basilica Superiore Open** 8:30am–4:30pm daily. W **santuariodioropa.it**

Perched above the wool town of Biella stands the tranquil church and hospice complex of Oropa, comprised of a series of three squares surrounded by pale buildings with stone-shingled roofs, cut into the hillside. The sanctuary was founded in the 4th century by Sant'Eusebio, Bishop of Vercelli. It was intended as a hospice for the poor, and to honor the "Black Madonna," which he had brought back from the Holy Land. The Madonna, said to be the work of St. Luke himself, is the object of some of the most important pilgrimages in the region.

The statue of the Madonna is kept in the restored **Basilica Antica** (Old Church). Beyond it, at the top of the complex, is the imposing Neo-Classical **Basilica Superiore** (Upper Church), which was begun in 1885 but completed only in 1960.

⓲ Domodossola

Verbania. 19,000. FS 🚌 i Stazione entrance, P.za Matteotti 24 (0324 24 82 65). Sat. W **prodomodossola.it**

At the center of this pretty mountain town of Roman origin lies the **Piazza Mercato**, or market square, framed by attractive arcades and houses from the 15th and 16th centuries. The Ossola valley, where the town lies, sits in an Alpine landscape of pasture and forest sliced by rivers and streams. Pretty villages north of the town include **Crodo**, with its cold-water mineral spas, and **Baceno**, where the 14th–16th-century church contains fine frescoes and wood carvings.

⓳ Varallo

Vercelli. 7,500. FS 🚌 i Corso Roma 38 (0163 56 44 04). Tue. W **atlvalsesiavercelli.it**

The small town and tourist resort of Varallo lies halfway up the attractive Sesia valley, and boasts a remarkable church, **Santa Maria delle Grazie**. The late 15th-century church is notable for its beautiful frescoed wall depicting the Life of Christ and *trompe l'oeil* architectural elements; the paintings are the work of Gaudenzio Ferrari (1484–1546).

A long stairway behind the church (and also a cableway) climbs up to the extraordinary **Sacro Monte**, a religious community built at an altitude of about 2,000 ft (610 m). This "Sacred Mount" was founded as a sanctuary of the New Jerusalem in 1486 under the patronage of the Archbishop of Milan, San Carlo Borromeo.

The Basilica dell'Assunta, with a 19th-century facade, is set in a tranquil courtyard with palm trees and a fountain; the interior is a riot of ornate Baroque architecture. Dotted around it are over 40 chapels representing the sacred sites of Jerusalem, with statues and painted figures positioned in front of frescoed backdrops painted by Gaudenzio Ferrari, Tanzio da Varallo, and others.

Christ Condemned (16th century) in a chapel at Varallo's Sacro Monte

For hotels and restaurants in this region see pp562–77 and pp580–605

The interior of the church of San Giulio in the center of Lago d'Orta

⑳ Lago d'Orta

Novara. FS 🚌 ⛴ Orta. ℹ Via Panoramica, Orta San Giulio (0322 90 56 14). W **distrettolaghi.it**

Lago d'Orta is one of Italy's least visited lakes – unjustly, as it is delightfully set among the foothills of the Alps.

The lake's main resort is **Orta San Giulio**, a small town containing handsome palazzi, and houses decorated with wrought iron balconies. In the lakeside **Piazza Principale** stands the Palazzo della Comunità, a frescoed building of 1582 resting on arcades. A cobbled pathway leads up to the 15th-century church of **Santa Maria Assunta** (rebuilt in the 17th century), with a Romanesque doorway and an interior that is richly decorated with 17th-century frescoes and paintings.

Above Orta San Giulio is the sanctuary of **Sacro Monte**, a UNESCO World Heritage site built from 1591 to 1770 and dedicated to St. Francis of Assisi. A winding path, offering lovely views of the lake, climbs to the church. The path is lined by 21 chapels, most of them Baroque, in which frescoes and life-size figure groups by various artists depict scenes from the life of St. Francis.

In the center of the lake rises the picturesque **Isola San Giulio**. The island was said to have been liberated from snakes and monsters by the 4th-century Christian preacher Julius, from whom the island's name derives. The basilica here is notable for its 12th-century black marble pulpit and for the 15th-century frescoes – including one attributed to Gaudenzio Ferrari, of the *Virgin and Child Enthroned*.

View across Lago d'Orta to the Isola San Giulio

Fresco detail of a horseman (17th century) by Morazzone in San Gaudenzio, Novara

㉑ Novara

105,000. FS 🚌 ℹ Baluardo Quintino Sella 40 (0321 39 40 59). Mon, Thu, & Sat. W **turismonovara.it**

Novara has distant origins as the Roman city of Nubliaria – meaning "surrounded in mist." Nowadays its delightful arcaded streets and squares, and historic buildings, exude a quiet affluence. Many of the most important buildings stand around Piazza della Repubblica. They include the beautiful Renaissance courtyard of the **Broletto** (town hall), with its graceful 15th-century red-brick arcades and covered stairway.

Across the piazza rises the **Duomo**, rebuilt by the architect Alessandro Antonelli in around 1865 in Neo-Classical style, with a huge central doorway. The interior contains dramatic Renaissance paintings of the Vercelli school and Flemish tapestries, as well as the remains of an earlier sanctuary on this site: these include the frescoed 12th-century chapel of San Siro and the 15th-century cloisters. The octagonal **Baptistry** next door dates in part from the 5th century and is painted with medieval scenes of the Apocalypse. The **Museo della Canonica del Duomo** beside the Duomo has tombstones and inscriptions from the Roman and early Christian eras.

A few streets away stands the **Basilica di San Gaudenzio**. It is strikingly crowned by an elongated four-tiered dome and spire. Designed by Antonelli, it is reminiscent of his Mole Antonelliana in Turin *(224)*. At the top of the spire, which is 400 ft (121 m) high, is a statue of San Gaudenzio himself. Inside, the late 16th-century church contains a fine collection of Renaissance and Baroque paintings by artists from Piedmont: these include a notable 17th-century battle scene by Tanzio da Varallo, a 16th-century altarpiece by Gaudenzio Ferrari, and a fresco painting by Pier Francesco Morazzone (*c.* 1572–1626).

Baptistry
Piazza della Repubblica. **Tel** 0321 66 16 35. **Open** to book visit the Curia Arcivescovile.

Museo della Canonica del Duomo
Vicolo della Canonica 9. **Tel** 0321 66 16 35. **Open** 3–6pm Sat–Sun.

㉒ Vercelli

47,000. FS Viale Garibaldi 90 (0161 58 002). Tue & Fri.
atlvalsesiavercelli.it

Vercelli is the rice capital of Europe, set in a vast plain of paddy fields that provide a sight of shimmering sheets of water stretching far into the distance. Vercelli itself also developed its own school of painting in the 16th century, and has one major architectural treasure, the 13th-century **Basilica di Sant'Andrea**.

The Basilica, standing just across from the train station, is famous as the first example of Italian architecture to be influenced by the Gothic style of northern France – note the beautiful vaulted nave and the flying buttresses, typical Gothic elements. Overall, however, the Basilica remains a stunning achievement in Romanesque architecture, built from 1219 to 1227 as part of an abbey for the papal legate Cardinal Guala Bicheri. The facade, curiously, changes color halfway up, the blue-gray of the lower part turning to red and white in the twin towers; these are linked by a double arcade. A carving attributed to Antelami (12th century) adorns the central lunette.

The three-aisled interior is gently illuminated through rose windows. The muted decoration is largely focused on the vaulting, which is supported by tall, slender shafts. Off the north side is the simple 13th-century cloister, beautifully framed by arcades rising from clustered columns.

Vercelli's other important historic buildings are not far away, including the imposing 16th-century **Duomo**, the church of **San Cristoforo**, with frescoes and a particularly fine Madonna degli Aranci (both *c.* 1529) painted by Gaudenzio Ferrari, and the **Piazza Cavour** with its medieval arcades. The **Museo Borgogna** is the best place to admire the masterpieces of the Vercelli school. The main shopping street, Corso Libertà, has a handful of attractive 15th-century houses and courtyards.

Detail of the carving on the 15th-century porch at the entrance to the Duomo in Asti

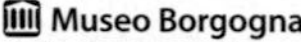

Museo Borgogna
Via A. Borgogna 4/6. **Tel** 0161 25 27 76. **Open** Tue–Fri pm, Sat am, Sun am & pm. **Closed** Jan 1, Aug 15, Nov 1, Dec 25. **museoborgogna.it**

The 13th-century cloisters of the Basilica di Sant'Andrea in Vercelli

㉓ Asti

77,000. FS Piazza Alfieri 29 (0141 53 03 57). Wed & Sat.
astiturismo.it

Renowned for its *spumante* (sparkling) wine, Asti is at the center of Italy's most prestigious wine region *(see pp186–7)* and is also a tranquil and noble city of medieval towers, elegant churches, and warm red roofs.

Just north of the main train station lies the Piazza del Campo del Palio, the largest square in Asti and formerly the site of its annual horse race, now in Piazza Alfieri. The race, held on the third Sunday of September to coincide with the local wine fair, rivals the Palio in Siena *(see p345)* for outrageous horsemanship and medieval pageantry.

Beyond this square lies the triangular-shaped **Piazza Alfieri**. A statue here commemorates the local poet and dramatist Vittorio Alfieri (1749–1803), in whose honor both this square and the main street were renamed.

Corso Alfieri runs the entire length of the old city center. At its eastern end stands the 15th-century church of **San Pietro in Consavia**, with its terracotta decoration, 17th-century frescoes, and attractive cloister. Beside it is the circular Romanesque **baptistry** which dates from the 10th–12th centuries; it was once the church of the knights of the Order of St. John of Jerusalem, who had their headquarters here.

West of Piazza Alfieri is the **Collegiata di San Secondo** (13th–15th century), named after Asti's patron saint, which houses a Renaissance polyptych by Gandolfino d'Asti and 15th-century frescoes. The area around the western section of Corso Alfieri contains a few of the medieval towers for which the town was once famous; they include the Torre dei Comentini, the very elegant

The watery expanses of the rice fields around Vercelli

Torre Troyana, and, at the far end, the Torre Ropa. This was built on the ruins of a tower in which San Secondo, a Roman soldier, was held. The nearby 14th-century Gothic **Duomo** has a 15th-century porch and, inside, 18th-century frescoes and two 12th- to 13th-century carvings on the west corner of the transept.

The Castello di Casotto in the hills above the resort of Garessio

㉔ Cuneo

55,000. FS Via Amedeo II 8a (0171 69 02 17). Tue, Fri.
cuneoholiday.com

"Cuneo" in Italian means wedge-shaped, and this perfectly describes the sliver of land that the town occupies at the confluence of two rivers, the Gesso and the Stura di Demonte. In early November the town hosts the regional cheese fair, with unusual local cheese varieties.

The town centers on a large square, **Piazza Galimberti**, with its old arcades, where the traders come to hawk their wares every Tuesday. Much of the town was rebuilt in the 18th and 19th centuries, providing Cuneo with wide, tree-lined boulevards, though the impressive viaduct that takes the railroad line into town dates from the 1930s. The deconsecrated 13th-century church of **San Francesco** has a fine 15th-century portal. The 18th-century church of **Santa Croce** has a concave facade by Francesco Gallo.

Cuneo is a good base for exploring the pretty local valleys, such as the Valle Stura, where rare flowers grow.

Market day in the enormous Piazza Galimberti at the center of Cuneo

㉕ Bossea Caves

Località Bossea, Comune Frabosa Soprana. **Tel** 0174 34 92 40. FS Mondovì. from Mondovì. **Open** daily for guided tours only.
grottadibossea.com

Some 16 miles (25 km) south of Mondovì, near the end of a scenic route that follows the valley of the Torrente Corsaglia up into the Maritime Alps, are the caves of Bossea, some of the finest in Italy. The series of caves contains remarkable stalactite columns and shapes that have formed over many hundreds of thousands of years. Guided tours lead through different chambers – some of them surprisingly vast – following the underground rivers and lakes. The skeleton of a prehistoric bear, *Ursus spelaeus*, which was discovered here, is also on display.

Bring a sweater – the temperature rarely rises above 50°F (9°C).

㉖ Garessio

Cuneo. 3,400. FS Corso Statuto 1 (0174 80 31 45). Fri.
garessio.net

One of the prettier resorts of the Maritime Alps, Garessio is no more than a sprinkling of houses spread out over the hills, surrounded by woods of chestnut trees. It is also a popular spa.

According to legend, the waters here have miraculous powers: in about AD 980 an octogenarian nobleman found instant relief from his kidney and circulatory problems by drinking the mineral-rich water. Since then, the waters have been drunk for their remedial properties – linked in particular with the relief of diuretic and digestive problems – and for their refreshing taste.

Environs

About 4 miles (10 km) west of Garessio stands the **Castello di Casotto**, the dramatically sited summer palace used by the House of Savoy. The royal family used to come here to enjoy the local mineral water, the attractive scenery and the exceptionally pure air of the hills.

The town of **Ormea**, 7 miles (12 km) southwest, is interesting for its ruined 11th-century castle, its church with late 14th-century Gothic frescoes, and its attractive houses.

Castello di Casotto
Garessio. **Tel** 0174 80 31 45. **Open** call ahead for opening times.

LIGURIA

Liguria is a long, thin coastal strip nestling at the foot of vine-covered mountains. Here pastel-colored houses bask in the Mediterranean sun, while their gardens, flourishing in the mild climate, are a riot of colorful plants. In contrast with resorts like Portofino and even Sanremo, the bustling city of Genoa, for centuries a trading port of immense power, is the only major population center.

Genoa has a long history as a seafaring power, achieving greatness first as a trading post with ancient Greece and Phoenicia, and later as the capital of a small commercial empire that at one stage eclipsed even Venice. The great sea admiral Andrea Doria came from Genoa, as did the 15th-century explorer of the Americas, Christopher Columbus.

Genoa's rise began in the 12th century, when it succeeded in beating the Saracen pirates who plagued the Ligurian coast. Thereafter, the maritime republic prospered, profiting from the Crusades to set up trading posts in the Middle East and marshaling its naval might to humble its rivals. The golden age lasted from the 16th to the mid-17th century, and included the glorious reign of Andrea Doria, who enriched the city by financing the wars of Genoa's European allies through the offices of the city's bank. Factionalism among the ruling aristocracy, however, and foreign conquest, by the French in 1668 and the Austrians in 1734, led to the region's decline. It was only in the early 19th century, with unification fervor spreading thanks to native son Giuseppe Mazzini and the revolutionary Garibaldi, that Liguria ever recaptured a glimpse of its former prominence. Today, sheltered by the steep slopes that rise from the sea, faded, elegant mansions lie along the coast, particularly in Sanremo, where aristocrats came to spend the winter at the end of the 19th century.

Green shutters and rich ocher walls characterize the houses of Portofino

◀ The sunlit harbor of Riomaggiore, one of the Cinque Terre

Exploring Liguria

Liguria divides neatly into two parts. The western coastline, known as the Riviera Ponente, is a thin strip of coastal plain stretching across to the French border, while the eastern coastline, or Riviera Levante, is more rugged and picturesque, descending directly into the sea. Between the two lengths of coast lies the region's capital and biggest port, Genoa (Genova). The faded elegance of the tranquil coastal villages contrasts with this cramped and busy port that snakes along the coast, hemmed in between the sea and the mountains rising steeply behind it.

Stag motif of the city of Cervo, above the cathedral doors

Genoese street market selling fruit and vegetables

Sights at a Glance

1 Balzi Rossi
2 Villa Hanbury
3 Dolceacqua
4 Sanremo
5 Bussana Vecchia
6 Cervo
7 Albenga
8 Grotte di Toirano
9 *Genoa (Genova) pp240–41*
10 Camogli
11 Portofino Peninsula
12 Rapallo
13 Cinque Terre
14 Portovenere
15 Lerici

Key

- Highway
- Major road
- Secondary road
- Minor road
- Scenic route
- Main railroad
- Minor railroad
- International border
- Regional border
- △ Summit

For additional map symbols *see back flap*

The stylish resort of Sanremo on the Riviera Ponente, west of Genoa

Getting Around

If you keep to the coast, transportation in Liguria is straightforward. Both the A10–E80 highway, becoming the A12–E80 at Genoa, and a mainline railroad hug the shore from the French border to Tuscany. The main stations along the route are at Ventimiglia, Sanremo, Imperia, Savona, Genoa, and La Spezia. There are good road and railroad links between Genoa and Milan and Turin. Access to inland Liguria is harder because of the mountains. Bus services link many of the coastal towns with the prettiest hill villages. You can explore some of the countryside by car by following the smaller routes, such as the S28 from Imperia toward Garessio in Piedmont, the S334 from Albisola, or the S456 from Voltri toward Milan.

Houses wedged into the cliffs in Riomaggiore, Cinque Terre

The spectacular gardens of the Villa Hanbury near Ventimiglia

❶ Balzi Rossi

Imperia. FS Ventimiglia & Menton. Bus from Ventimiglia to Ponte San Luigi, then a 10-minute walk. W **archeoge.arti.beniculturali.it**

An unassuming promontory is the setting for some of the most important caves in northern Italy. Guided tours lead through the traces of the cave-dwelling civilization of pre–Iron Age Liguria. The caves contain excavated burial sites where the dead were adorned with seashells. The **Museo Nazionale dei Balzi Rossi** contains tools, weapons, and stone-etched female figures dating from 100,000 years ago. There is also a reproduction of an etching of a horse.

Museo Nazionale dei Balzi Rossi
Via Balzi Rossi 9. **Tel** 0184 381 13. **Open** Tue–Sun. **Closed** Jan 1, May 1, Dec 25.

❷ Villa Hanbury

Corso Monte Carlo 43, Località La Mortola. **Tel** 0184 22 95 07. FS Ventimiglia. Bus from Ventimiglia. **Open** 9:30am–5pm (Mar–mid-Jun & mid-Sep–mid-Oct: to 5pm; mid-Jun–mid-Sep: to 6pm; mid-Oct–Feb: to 4pm) daily. **Closed** Mon Nov–Feb. W **giardinihanbury.com**

In 1867 the English botanist Sir Thomas Hanbury and his brother bought this villa on the Mortola promontory. They took full advantage of the exceptionally mild Ligurian climate to establish a garden of exotic plants along the sloping pathways of the seaside villa.

The collection, gathered by Hanbury on trips to Africa and Asia, has grown to number more than 3,000 varieties of tropical flora, including rubber trees, palms, and wild cacti.

The garden is now run by the state and is one of the most impressive botanical gardens in Italy, even during the winter.

❸ Dolceacqua

Imperia. 2,000. FS Bus i Via Barberis Colomba 3 (0184 20 66 66). Thu. W **dolceacqua.it**

This pretty village, 5 miles (8 km) north of Ventimiglia, is built on either side of the churning Nervia River, its two halves joined by an arching 108-ft (33-m) medieval stone bridge. The highlight is the ruined 12th- to 15th-century **castle**, inhabited for a while in the 16th century by the powerful Doria family from Genoa. The two square towers at the front dominate the village. The terraced vineyards in the surrounding hills produce grapes for general consumption as well as for a robust red wine known as Rossese or vino di Dolceacqua.

The village of Dolceacqua with its medieval bridge and ruined castle

The Casinò Municipale in Sanremo, completed in 1906

❹ Sanremo

Imperia. 57,000. FS Bus i Largo Nuvoloni 1 (0184 590 59). Tue & Sat am. W **visitrivieradeifiori.it**

Sanremo is a pleasant resort of faded elegance. The composer Tchaikovsky, Alfred Nobel (the father of modern explosives), and the nonsense poet Edward Lear all stayed in the stuccoed mansions of the palm-lined seafront avenue, the Corso Imperatrice. The focus of the town, then as now, is the Casino. A little farther down the Corso stands the ornate Russian Orthodox church of San Borilio.

The old town, La Pigna ("fir cone"), is a huddle of narrow lanes with medieval houses and pastel-colored shutters. A coach service goes from Sanremo to San Romolo, a small village 2,579 ft (786 m) above sea level that offers beautiful views of the area.

A delightful flower market is held in Valle Armea (5–7am, Jun–Oct, by appt, 0184 517 11), while the Italian Song Festival takes place here in February.

❺ Bussana Vecchia

Imperia. Off Sanremo–Arma di Taggia road.

Bussana Vecchia is a marvelously atmospheric ghost town. In February 1887 an earthquake shook the village, reducing its Baroque church and

For hotels and restaurants in this region see p562–77 and pp580–605

surrounding houses to ruins. (One survivor, Giovanni Torre del Merlo, went on to invent the ice-cream cone.)

The town was rebuilt closer to the sea, and since then the original village has been taken over by artists, who have restored some interiors, providing a venue for summer concerts and exhibitions.

6 Cervo

Imperia. 1,200. FS Piazza Santa Caterina 2 (0183 40 81 97). Thu. **cervo.com**

Cervo is the prettiest of the many old seafront villages just east of Imperia, with a narrow complex of streets and houses rising dramatically up from the pebble beach. At the top of the village stands the concave Baroque facade of **San Giovanni Battista**. Charming chamber orchestra performances are held in front of the church in July and August. The church is also known as the *"dei corallini,"* after the coral fishing which once brought prosperity to the local people. Now Cervo is an unassuming but characteristic Ligurian vacation resort, with unspoiled hotels near the beach.

San Giovanni Battista at Cervo

Spectacular rock formations in the grottoes of Toirano

7 Albenga

Savona. 24,000. FS Piazza del Popolo (0182 55 84 44). Wed. **inforiviera.it**

Until the Middle Ages, the Roman port of Albium Ingaunum played an important maritime role. The sea, however, gradually moved farther out, leaving the town, now called Albenga, stranded on the Centa River. Most striking now is its Romanesque brick architecture, in particular the three 13th-century towers clustered around the cathedral of **San Michele**. The cathedral's interior was restored to its medieval form in the late 1960s. To the south is an intriguing 5th-century **Baptistry** with a ten-sided exterior and octagonal interior. Inside, the original 5th-century blue and white mosaics of doves represent the 12 apostles. To the north of the cathedral is the small Piazza dei Leoni, named after its three stone lions imported from Rome.

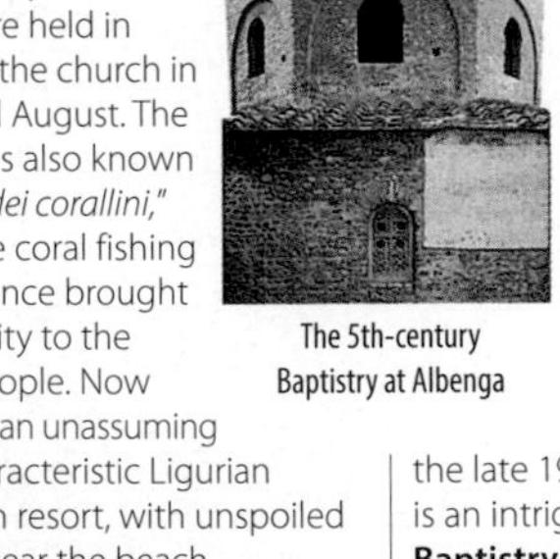

The 5th-century Baptistry at Albenga

In a 14th-century palace on Piazza San Michele is the **Museo Navale Romano**, founded in 1950 following the salvage of a Roman ship that had sunk in the 1st century BC. The museum contains ancient amphorae as well as exhibits salvaged from more recent shipwrecks.

Baptistry
Piazza San Michele. **Tel** 0182 502 88. **Open** 10am–noon, 3–6pm Tue–Sun. **Closed** Jan 1, Easter, Dec 25.

Museo Navale Romano
Piazza San Michele 12. **Tel** 0182 512 15. **Open** 10am–12:30pm, 2:30–6pm Tue–Sun. **Closed** Jan 1, Easter, Dec 25.

8 Grotte di Toirano

Piazzale delle Grotte, Toirano. **Tel** 0182 980 62. from Albenga to Borghetto Santo Spirito. FS to Borghetto Santo Spirito or Loano. **Open** 9:30am–12:30pm, 2–5pm daily. **Closed** Dec 25–Jan 1. times vary (book ahead). **toiranogrotte.it**

Beneath the delightful medieval town of Toirano lies a series of caves containing relics of Paleolithic life dating from 100,000 years ago.

The **Grotta della Basura** (Witch's Cave) has remarkable prehistoric human and animal footprints, and a collection of ancient bear bones and teeth in the "bear cemetery." The **Grotta di Santa Lucia** reveals the full beauty of the yellow and gray stalactites and stalagmites that have formed here over hundreds of thousands of years.

The **Museo Etnografico della Val Varatella**, housed in the 16th century stables of the Palazzo del Marchese, has a collection of agricultural and domestic tools from the 17th to the early 20th century.

Museo Etnografico della Val Varatella
Via Giuseppe Polla, Toirano. **Tel** 0182 98 99 68. **Open** 10am–1pm, 3–8pm daily.

❾ Street-by-Street: Genoa

There is something refreshingly rough-edged about Genoa (Genova in Italian), Italy's most important commercial port. In contrast to the genteel resorts along the neighboring coast, the narrow streets of the old town are the haunts of sailors and streetwalkers.

With its natural harbor and the mountains to protect it, Genoa rose to prominence as a sea-based power. During the 16th century, Andrea Doria cemented Genoa's importance, and also proved an astute patron of the arts.

Piazza San Matteo
The houses and church of San Matteo were built by the Doria family in 1278. Palazzo Quartara has a bas-relief of St. George above the doorway.

Musei di Strada Nuova

PIAZZA CAMPETTO

PIAZZA SAN MATTEO

SALITA SAN

VIA DI SCURRERIA

VIA ARCHIVESCOVATO

The port and Palazzo Reale

VIA SAN LORENZO

PIAZZA MATTEOTTI

SALITA POLLAIUOLI

PIAZZA ERBE

VICO DEI TRE RE MAGI

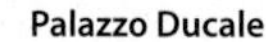

San Lorenzo
The black and white striped Gothic facade of the Duomo dates from the early 13th century.

Palazzo Ducale
Once the seat of the doges of Genoa, this elegant building with its two fine 16th-century courtyards and arcades now contains a major arts and cultural center.

San Donato has a splendid 12th-century octagonal bell tower.

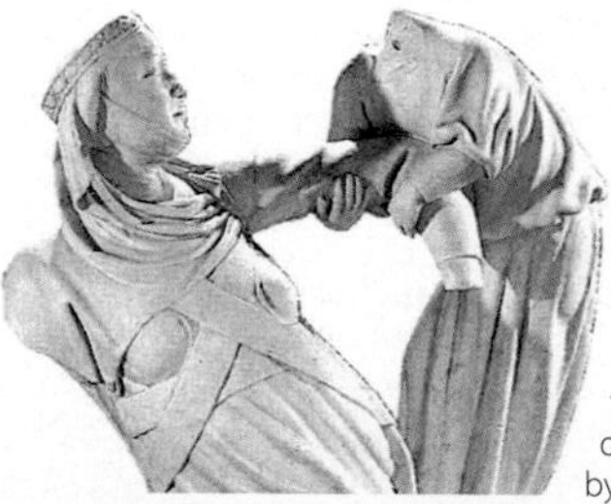

Sant'Agostino
The 13th-century church and convent were bombed during World War II, but the bell tower remains. The cloisters now house sculpture like this fragment from the tomb of Margaret of Brabant by Pisano (1312).

Key

– Suggested route

0 meters 100

0 yards 100

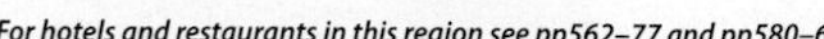

Church of Gesù
This Baroque church, built between 1589 and 1606, is also known as the church of Santi Ambrogio e Andrea.

VISITORS' CHECKLIST

Practical Information
610,000. Aeroporto Cristoforo Colombo (010 601 52 47); Stazione Principe (010 246 26 33). Mon, Wed & Thu. 24 Jun: San Giovanni Battista; Jul: Ballet Festival; Oct: Fiera Nautica.
turismoinliguria.it

Transportation
Cristoforo Colombo 4 miles (6 km) W. FS Stazione Principe, Piazza Acquaverde. Stazione Marittima, Ponte dei Mille.

Piazza De Ferrari is the site of the Neo-Classical Banco di Roma and the Accademia, as well as the restored Teatro Carlo Felice.

The bronze fountain in Piazza De Ferrari was constructed in 1936.

Porta Soprana
The eastern gateway to the city has curved outer walls and stands close to the site of Christopher Columbus's house.

Sant'Andrea
The 12th-century cloisters standing in a small garden are all that remain of the convent that once stood here.

San Lorenzo (Duomo)

Piazza San Lorenzo. **Tel** 010 254 12 50. **Open** daily. Museo del Tesoro: **Tel** 010 254 12 50. **Open** 9am–noon, 3–6pm Mon–Sat.

The Duomo, with its black and white striped exterior, blends many architectural styles, from the 12th-century Romanesque side portal of San Giovanni to the Baroque touches of some of its side chapels. The three portals at the west end are in French Gothic style.

The most sumptuous of the chapels is dedicated to St. John the Baptist, patron saint of the city; it includes a 13th-century sarcophagus that once held the venerated saint's relics.

Steps lead down from the sacristy to the **Museo del Tesoro di San Lorenzo**. It houses such treasures as the Roman green glass dish said to have been used at the Last Supper, and a blue chalcedony plate on which the head of John the Baptist was allegedly served up to Salome.

The Port

Aquarium Ponte Spinola. **Tel** 010 234 56 78. **Open** 9:30am–7:30pm daily (to 8:30pm Sat, Sun & hols); Jul & Aug: 8:30am–10pm daily. Last adm: 90 min before closing.
acquariodigenova.it

The port is the heart of Genoa and the origin of its power as a seafaring city-state in the 11th and 12th centuries. A workaday place, it is ringed by busy roads and 1960s buildings.

Among the vestiges of its medieval glory is the **Lanterna** lighthouse (restored in 1543) near the Stazione Marittima. In the old days, fires would be lit at the top of the Lanterna to guide ships into port. Today, regeneration of the port is in part due to the Renzo Piano–designed conference center *(see p189)* and the **Aquarium**, one of the largest in Europe and an ideal place to sample the richness of marine life.

Exploring Genoa

Visitors are well rewarded when they explore Genoa – a city proud of its history and legends. The palazzi of Via Balbi and Via Garibaldi, and the paintings and sculptures dotted around the city in churches and museums, are among the finest in northwestern Italy. The environs, too, provide scenic and relaxing locations for excursions along the coast or in the steep hills behind.

The courtyard of the University on Via Balbi

Sant'Agostino

Piazza Sarzano 35. **Tel** 010 251 12 63. Museo di Architettura e Scultura Ligure: **Tel** 010 251 12 63. **Open** 9am–7pm Tue–Fri, 10am–7pm Sat & Sun. **Closed** public hols.

This Gothic church was begun in 1260, but it was bombed to pieces in World War II. It is now deconsecrated and all that remains of the original building is the fine Gothic bell tower, decorated with colored tiles. The monastery, of which the church of Sant'Agostino was once a part, was also bombed. What remained were two ruined cloisters – one of which forms the only triangular building in Genoa. The cloisters have been reconstructed and converted into the **Museo di Architettura e Scultura Ligure**. The museum contains the city's collection of architectural pieces, some dating back to the Roman era, along with fragments of sculpture and frescoes – all salvaged from Genoa's other destroyed churches. The finest piece is a magnificent fragment from the tomb of Margaret of Brabant, who died in 1311. She was the wife of Emperor Henry VII who invaded Italy in 1310. Carved by Giovanni Pisano around 1313, the sculptures from her tomb were restored and repositioned in 1987. The figures, whose garments are arranged in simple folds, seem to be helping Margaret to lie down to rest.

Palazzo Reale

Via Balbi 10. **Tel** 010 271 02 36. **Open** 9am–1:30pm Tue & Wed, 9am–7pm Thu–Sun (last adm: 30 mins before closing). **Closed** Jan 1, May 1, Dec 25.

This austere-looking residence, used by the Kings of Savoy from the 17th century onward, has a highly ornate Rococo interior – notably its ballroom and its Hall of Mirrors. Among the paintings is a *Crucifixion* by Van Dyck. The garden, which slopes down toward the old port, includes an intriguing cobblestone mosaic around the central fountain, depicting houses and animals.

Opposite the palace is the old **University** (1634) designed by the architect Bartolomeo Bianco, as was much of Via Balbi. The large building brilliantly overcomes Genoa's hilly topography, and is constructed on four levels.

Palazzo Bianco

Via Garibaldi 11. **Tel** 010 557 21 93. **Open** 9am–7pm Tue–Fri (from 10am Sat & Sun). **Palazzo Rosso Tel** 010 557 49 72. **Open** as for Palazzo Bianco. **Palazzo Tursi Tel** 010 557 21 93. **Open** as for Palazzo Bianco.

The Palazzo Bianco is situated on Genoa's most beautiful street, **Via Garibaldi**, where there are numerous fine 16th-century mansions and palazzi. The Palazzo Bianco contains the city's prime collection of paintings, including the works of many Genoese artists such as Luca Cambiaso, Bernardo Strozzi

Christopher Columbus in Genoa

A portrait of Columbus, Villa Doria at Pegli

The name of Cristoforo Colombo, or Christopher Columbus, as English speakers know him, is in evidence all over Genoa. A statue of the explorer of the New World greets you as soon as you emerge in Piazza Acquaverde from the Porta Principe train station; various public buildings bear his name; even the airport is named after him. In the 17th-century Palazzo Belimbau, built on top of the old city walls, is a series of frescoes by the local artist Tavarone celebrating the explorer's life, and you can see three of his letters in the Sala del Sindaco in Palazzo Tursi (the city hall) on Via Garibaldi. It is not certain whether Columbus (*c.* 1451–1506) was born in Genoa, in Savona 9 miles (15 km) to the west, or even outside Italy. However, city registers mention his father, a weaver, and various family homes within the city. The small ivy-clad house adjacent to Porta Soprana may have been Columbus's childhood home, where he first discovered his passion for the sea.

The house where Columbus may have lived

The romantic gardens at Villa Durazzo-Pallavicini in Pegli

Domenico Piola, and Giovanni Benedetto Castiglione. Better-known artists include Filippino Lippi Van Dyck, Veronese, and Rubens. At number 9 Via Garibaldi, **Palazzo Tursi** hosts the Lord Mayor's boardrooms, as well as an extension of the Palazzo Bianco Gallery. Across the street in the **Palazzo Rosso** are more paintings, including works by Dürer and Caravaggio, as well as ceramics and furniture.

Fine tomb architecture from the huge Staglieno Cemetery

Staglieno Cemetery

Piazzale Resasco, Staglieno. **Tel** 010 87 01 84. **Open** daily. **Closed** pub hols.

This grandiose cemetery, just over the hills northeast of Genoa along the Bisagno River, is so big (81.5 acres/33 ha) that it has its own internal bus system. Founded in 1844, its tombs and monuments make up an eerie city of miniature cathedrals, Egyptian temples, and Art Nouveau palaces. Its most famous resident is Giuseppe Mazzini, the Genoese revolutionary who died near Pisa in 1872.

Environs

Until World War II, **Pegli**, 4 miles (6 km) west of the city center, was a popular weekend retreat for rich Genoese. Now it forms part of the city, but maintains an air of tranquility thanks to its parks and two villas, the 19th-century **Villa Durazzo-Pallavicini** and the 16th-century **Villa Doria, Museo Navale**. The latter is a naval history museum celebrating Genoa's glorious past: you can see compasses, astrolabes, globes, model ships, and a portrait of Columbus, ascribed to Ghirlandaio, probably dating from 1525. An archaeological museum in the Villa Durazzo-Pallavicini relates the pre-Roman history of the Ligurian coast. The villa's garden is landscaped with romantic grottoes, pavilions, and fountains.

Nervi, 5 miles (8 km) to the east of the city, is another former resort town, famous for its seafront promenade, the **Passeggiata Anita Garibaldi** (named after Garibaldi's wife). The walk follows a route that has been cut into the rock face, giving panoramic views of the coast. The lush **Parco Municipale** is another feature of Nervi. It once formed the grounds of two aristocratic villas – the Villa Serra and the Villa Gropallo. The former, on Via Capolungo, now houses the **Galleria d'Arte Moderna** featuring modern Italian painting. The **Villa Luxoro** on Via Aurelia is notable for its collection of clocks, fabrics, furniture, and lace. The area is also famous as Garibaldi's departure point when he set off for Sicily with his *Mille* (the famous "Thousand" men) to help bring about the unification of Italy. A large monument at Quarto dei Mille, about 2 miles (3 km) back toward the city, marks the place where the volunteers met in May 1860 to follow the intrepid revolutionary *(see p66–7)*. **Villa Grimaldi** houses an art and sculpture collection showing late 18th- and early 19th-century works by Fattori, Boldi, and Messina.

Galleria d'Arte Moderna
Villa Serra, Via Capolungo 3, Nervi. **Tel** 010 372 60 25. **Open** Tue–Sun.

Villa Doria, Museo Navale
Piazza Bonavino 7, Pegli. **Tel** 010 696 98 85. **Open** Tue–Sun. **Closed** public hols.

Villa Durazzo-Pallavicini
Via Pallavicini 11, Pegli. **Tel** 010 698 10 48. **Open** 9am–7pm Tue–Fri (from 10am Sat–Sun). **Closed** public hols.

Villa Grimaldi
Via Capolungo 9, Nervi. **Tel** 010 32 23 96. **Open** Tue–Sun.

Villa Luxoro
Via Mafalda di Savoia 3, Nervi. **Tel** 010 32 26 73. **Open** Tue–Sat. **Closed** public hols.

Pini (*c.* 1920) by Rubaldo Merello in the Galleria d'Arte Moderna at Nervi

Pastel-colored houses near the pebbly beach at Camogli

⑩ Camogli

Genoa. 5,500. FS Via XX Settembre 33 (0185 77 10 66). Wed. **camogli.it**

Built on a pine-wooded slope, Camogli is a fishing village where seashells adorn the pastel-painted house walls, and the smell of frying fish wafts out from the small restaurants into the streets. Near the pebble beach and fishing port is the medieval Castello della Dragonara.

Camogli celebrates its famous festival of the Blessing of the Fish on the second Sunday of May when sardines are fried in a huge pan 13 ft (4 m) in diameter. The fish is distributed free to all comers.

⑪ Portofino Peninsula

Genoa. Portofino. Via Roma 35 (0185 26 90 24). **turismoinliguria.it**

Portofino is the most exclusive harbor and resort town in Italy, crammed with the yachts of the wealthy. You can reach Portofino by road (although cars are not allowed into the village), or by boat, from the resort of Santa Margherita Ligure. Above the town are the church of **San Giorgio**, containing relics said to be those of the dragon-slayer, and a castle.

On the other side of the peninsula, which you have to reach on foot (a two-hour walk) or by boat, is the **Abbazia di San Fruttuoso**, named after a 3rd-century saint whose followers were shipwrecked here and, according to legend, protected by three lions. The white abbey buildings, set among pines and olive trees, date mostly from the 11th century, although the imposing Torre dei Doria was added 500 years later. You can take a boat to try to locate the **Cristo degli Abissi**, a bronze statue of Christ that sits on the sea bed near San Fruttuoso, protecting sailors. Further west along the coast is Punta Chiappa, a rocky promontory famous for the changing colors of the surrounding sea.

Abbazia di San Fruttuoso
San Fruttuoso. **Tel** 0185 77 27 03. **Open** Mar–Oct: daily; Nov–Jan: Tue–Sun. **Closed** Feb.

⑫ Rapallo

Genoa. 31,000. FS Lungomare Vittorio Veneto 7 (0185 23 03 46). Thu. Cable car **Tel** 0185 52 41. **turismoinliguria.it**

Historians know Rapallo as the place where two post-World War I treaties were signed, while film buffs might recognize it from the 1954 movie *The Barefoot Contessa*, which was shot here. Rapallo was also a haven for writers such as D.H. Lawrence and Ezra Pound. Its villas still have a patrician feel to them, as do the riding stables, golf course, and tennis courts. The palm-lined esplanade ends in a small 16th-century **castle**, in which art exhibitions are occasionally held. A cable ca from the center of the town lead to the 16th-century **Santuario c Montallegro**, which houses a Byzantine icon said to possess miraculous powers.

The 16th-century castle jutting into Rapallo harbor

Santuario di Montallegro
Montallegro. Tel 0185 23 90 00. **Open** daily (**closed** noon–2:30pm).

Large yachts moored in Portofino's famous harbor

For hotels and restaurants in this region see pp562–77 and pp580–605

The dramatic coastline near Corniglia in the Cinque Terre

⓭ Cinque Terre

La Spezia. FS to all towns.
⛴ Monterosso, Vernazza.
i Via Fegina 40, Monterosso (0187 81 70 59) (summer only); Piazza Rio Finale 26, Riomaggiore (0187 92 06 33).
W parconazionale5terre.it

The Cinque Terre are five self-contained villages – Monterosso al Mare, Vernazza, Corniglia, Manarola, and Riomaggiore – located on the rocky coastline of the Riviera di Levante. Clinging dramatically to the steep cliffs, these villages are linked only by an ancient footpath known as the Sentiero Azzurro (Blue Path), which offers spectacular views of the rocky coastlines and terraced vineyards that produce the local dry white Cinque Terre wines. The footpath also provides access to secluded beaches.

These days the five villages suffer from some depopulation. The largest, **Monterosso al Mare**, on the northwestern edge of the Cinque Terre, overlooks a wide bay with its own sandy beach. **Vernazza**, further down the coast, has streets linked by steep steps or *arpaie*. **Corniglia**, perched at the pinnacle of rocky terraces, seems untouched by the passage of time, as does **Manarola**, which is linked by the famous Via dell'Amore, or Lovers' Lane, to **Riomaggiore**, a 15-minute walk away.

The best way to visit the villages is by boat (from La Spezia, Lerici or Porto Venere) or by train (La Spezia–Genoa railroad line).

⓮ Portovenere

La Spezia. 3,900. *i* Piazza Bastreri 1 (0187 79 06 91). Mon.
W portovenere.it

Named after the goddess Venus, Portovenere is one of the most romantic villages on the Ligurian coast with its cluster of narrow streets lined with pastel-colored houses. In the upper part of the village is the 12th-century church of **San Lorenzo**. A sculpture over the doorway here depicts the martyrdom of the saint who was roasted alive on a grill. On the stone promontory that curls out into the sea is the small, black-and-white 13th-century church of **San Pietro**. From here, or from the 16th-century castle on the cliffs on the northwestern side of the village, there are superb views of the Cinque Terre and the small island of Palmaria, about 435 yards (400 m) offshore.

Above the doorway of San Lorenzo in Portovenere

⓯ Lerici

La Spezia. 10,500. *i* Via Biagini 6, Località Venere Azzurra (0187 96 73 46). Sat am.
W parconazionale5terre.it

This stretch of coast, along the Gulf of La Spezia or Poets' Gulf, was once popular with such literati as Yeats and D.H. Lawrence. The village of San Terenzo, across the bay from Lerici, was where the poet Shelley spent the last four years of his life. It was from his home, the Casa Magni, that he set out in 1822 on a voyage to meet Leigh Hunt in Livorno. Tragically, he was shipwrecked near Viareggio and drowned.

The popular resort of Lerici sits on the edge of a beautiful bay overlooked by pastel-colored houses. The forbidding medieval **Castello di Lerici** (13th century), built by the Pisans and later passed to the Genoese, dominates the vacation villas below. Today it houses a museum of geo-paleontology and hosts art exhibitions and concerts.

Castello di Lerici
Piazza San Giorgio. **Tel** 0187 96 90 42.
Open Tue–Sun. **Closed** Dec 9–26.
W castellodilerici.it

The harbor of Vernazza in the Cinque Terre

Brightly painted buildings in Manarola, one of the villages that make up the Cinque Terre ▶

CENTRAL ITALY

Central Italy at a Glance

The central regions of Italy are popular with visitors because they offer a range of beautiful landscapes and towns rich in culture and history, including outstanding churches, towers, and palaces. Emilia-Romagna is home to the impressive Po Delta that provides a haven for wildlife. Tuscany is dominated by Florence, one of Italy's most celebrated centers. Umbria and Le Marche offer gentle pastoral countryside and picturesque hill towns. The major sights of this rewarding area are shown here.

The Leaning Tower of Pisa and the Duomo *(see pp328–30)*, splendid examples of 12th- and 13th-century architecture, are decorated with Arabic-inspired, complex geometric patterns.

Florence

(See pp274–317)

The Duomo and the Baptistry, set in the heart of Florence, dominate the city *(see pp284–6)*. The dome dwarfs many surrounding buildings.

The Uffizi contains a superb collection of Florentine art from Gothic to High Renaissance and beyond *(see pp290–93)*.

The Palazzo Pitti, begun in 1457 for the banker Luca Pitti, became the main residence of the Medici. It now houses their treasures *(see pp306–7)*.

◀ Sun setting over a tranquil vineyard in Tuscany

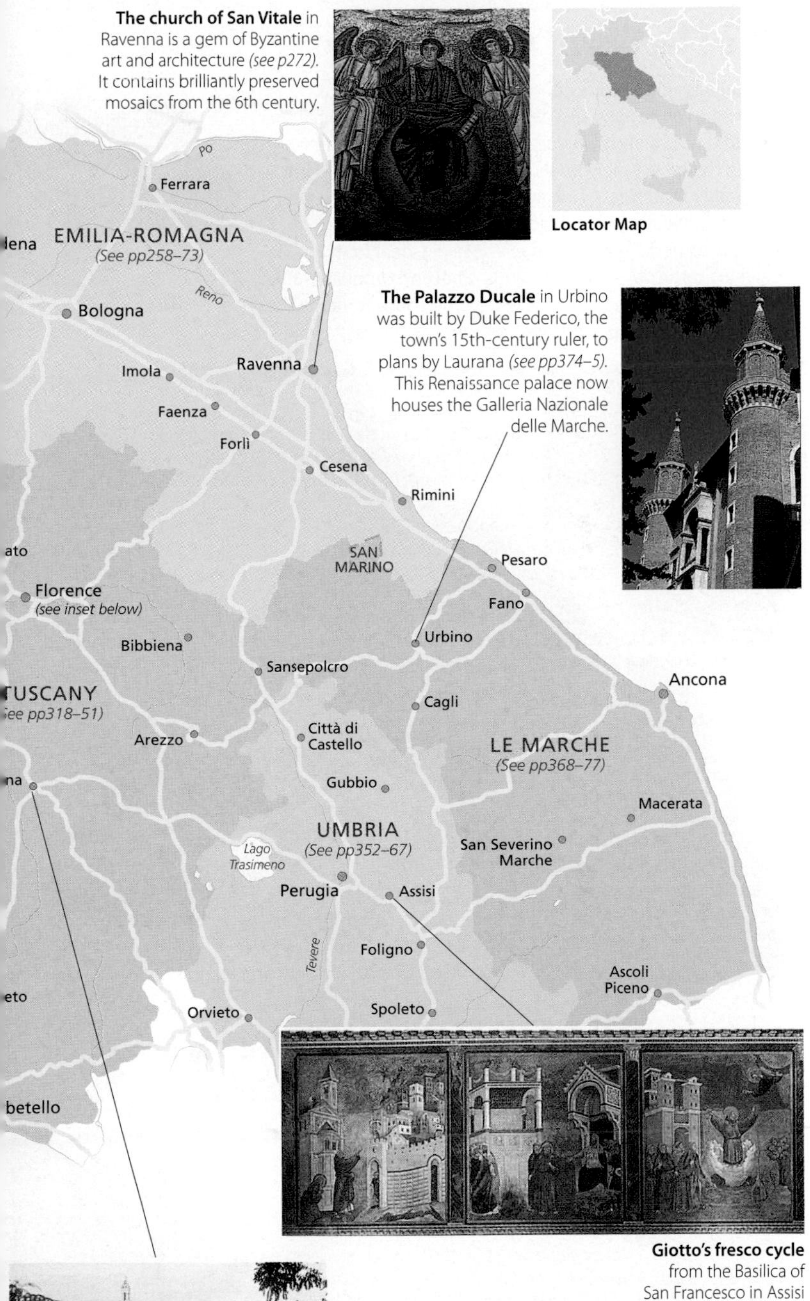

The church of San Vitale in Ravenna is a gem of Byzantine art and architecture *(see p272)*. It contains brilliantly preserved mosaics from the 6th century.

The Palazzo Ducale in Urbino was built by Duke Federico, the town's 15th-century ruler, to plans by Laurana *(see pp374–5)*. This Renaissance palace now houses the Galleria Nazionale delle Marche.

Giotto's fresco cycle from the Basilica of San Francesco in Assisi was executed in the 13th century *(see pp358–61)*. The church is visited by thousands of pilgrims each year.

Siena, a medieval town steeped in tradition, centers around the Campo, the large piazza shaped like a scallop shell *(see pp342–7)*. The lively horse race, the Corsa del Palio, is held here in July and August.

The Flavors of Central Italy

Emilia-Romagna is Italy's gourmet capital, and home to Parmesan, Parma ham, and balsamic vinegar. Bologna has earned the epithet *La Grassa* ("the fat") for rich dishes in which butter, cheese, and velvety sauces feature strongly. The lush lands and rolling hills of Tuscany, Umbria, and Le Marche tend to offer simpler flavors and more rustic, peasant cuisine. Top-quality pork from the Cinta Senese pig, beef from the Chianina cattle of Tuscany, fabulous *fungi* and Umbrian truffles, superb wild boar, and saffron-scented fish soups from the coast of Le Marche are all gastronomic delights of Central Italy.

Italian tomatoes

Tray of perfect, freshly made tortellini pasta

Emilia-Romagna

Not only is this rich, fertile land the home of many of Italy's most classic ingredients, but it has also given the world *bolognese* sauce (*ragù*). The authentic sauce contains some 20 ingredients and is usually served with tagliatelle – never spaghetti. Pasta is an art form here. Legend has it that tagliatelle was invented in honor of Lucrezia Borgia's golden hair, while tortellini pasta is said to be modelled on the shape of Venus's navel.

The region's pork butchers are the most famous in Italy, making excellent sausages, *salumi*, and mortadella, and using every part of the animal including the feet, which are stuffed to form the local specialty *zamponi*. Emilia and coastal Romagna were once two provinces, and there is still a culinary distinction between them. While Emilia's gastronomy is liberally laced with butter, cheese, and mushrooms, Romagna's keynotes tend to be olive oil, garlic, and onions – and fish. The Adriatic in this region teems with life and is an especially good catching ground for turbot (*rombo*) – the "pheasant of the sea."

Selection of the finest Italian salumi and other cooked meats

Regional Dishes and Specialties

Tuscan olive oil is outstanding in quality. It has many uses and is an integral part of *crostini*, slices of toasted bread smeared with olive oil on which different toppings are spread, such as chicken livers in *crostini alla Toscana*. *Salumi* producers are a great feature of the region and *prosciutto di cinghiale* (wild boar ham) is a rich, gamey delicacy. As well as *tagliatelle al ragù* in Bologna, other very popular pastas include tortellini and tortelloni (the latter being larger than the former), often filled with cheese, butter, and herbs. *Panforte* is the Italian Christmas specialty – a delicious confection of fruits, nuts, honey, sugar, and spices originating in Siena. Try also *ricciarelli*, diamond-shaped almond biscuits, and *torta di riso* – a rich, golden cake made with rice.

Crostini alla Toscana

Cacciucco A fish and seafood soup from Livorno, flavored with herbs and tomatoes and ladled over garlicky toast.

Just part of a gigantic wheel of Parmigiano-Reggiano, or Parmesan

Tuscany

Tuscany is the orchard and vegetable garden of Italy. It is also famous for red meat, especially from the prized Valdichiana cattle, from south of Arezzo. Pork is also excellent, and the Tuscan passion for hunting ensures that hare, pheasant, and wild boar, often served with local chestnuts, feature prominently on menus.

If there is one staple Tuscan ingredient it is fruity olive oil, liberally used in cooking and for seasoning everything from bread to salads, vegetables, stews and soups.

Broths and soups are very popular, often made with beans, especially white cannellini beans. Not for nothing are Tuscans known as *toscani mangiafagioli* (Tuscan bean-eaters).

Umbria & Le Marche

Umbria, "the green heart of Italy," is the only area outside Piedmont where truffles are found in such high concentration. Norcia is the capital of the black truffle, and shops everywhere sell truffle paste and truffle oils. Norcia is also famous for its pigs, and a favorite dish is *porchetta* – whole roast suckling pig stuffed with herbs. Wild mushrooms are plentiful in season, in particular *porcini*. Game features too, usually in the form of pheasant, guinea fowl, or pigeon, with the odd songbird thrown in, although it is now illegal to catch wild songbirds. The rural interior of Le Marche also features *porchetta*; lamb and rabbit are popular, too. The long coastline yields a bounty of fish, often made into fish broths, and a specialty of Ancona, *zuppa di pesce*, fish soup with saffron.

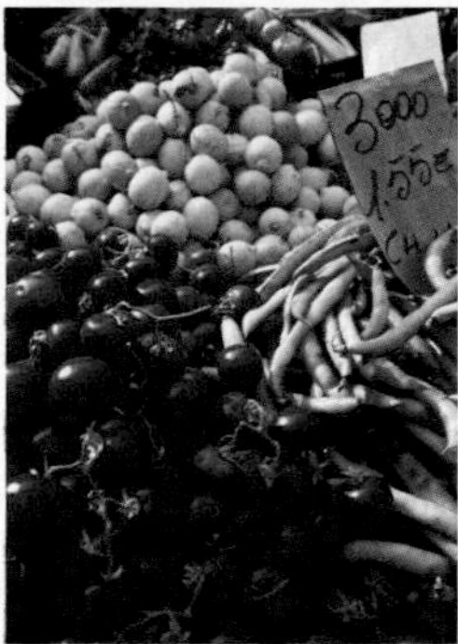

Tuscan market stall piled high with fresh, ripe vegetables

ON THE MENU

Baci From Perugia, these are chocolate-coated hazelnuts, their name literally meaning "kisses" in Italian.

Bistecca alla Fiorentina Steak, marinated in herbs, garlic, and finest extra virgin olive oil, rapidly grilled over wood coals. The best meat for this is Chianina beef.

Cinghiale in Umido Traditional Tuscan wild boar stew with red wine, tomatoes, garlic, and vegetables. Usually served with polenta.

Vincisgrassi A baked, layered dish from Le Marche of ham, pasta, and béchamel sauce, sprinkled with truffle shavings.

Tagliatelle al ragù Flat strips of pasta are tossed with the quintessential Italian meat sauce from Bologna.

Arista alla Fiorentina Pork loin is roasted in the oven with garlic and rosemary, a specialty of Florence.

Zuccotto A Tuscan specialty of light sponge cake filled with hazelnuts, almonds, chocolate, and cream.

The Wines of Central Italy

Vineyards are seen everywhere in Central Italy, from the rolling cypress-fringed hills of Tuscany to the flatter, Lambrusco-producing plains of Emilia-Romagna. The finest red wines are made in the hills of southeastern Tuscany: Chianti Classico, Brunello di Montalcino, and Vino Nobile di Montepulciano. Today's innovative mix of modern and traditional techniques is steadily improving the quality of much of the region's wine.

Chianti Classico is the heart of the Chianti zone. Chianti may be light and fruity or dense and long-lived – price is the usual guide. Rocca delle Macie is very reasonably priced.

Vernaccia di San Gimignano is a Tuscan white wine with a long, distinguished history. Traditionally a golden, often oxidized wine, it is now also produced in a fresher style, for early drinking. Teruzzi e Puthod make consistently good Vernaccia.

Vino Nobile di Montepulciano is made from the same grapes as Chianti. It can be of superior quality, hence its claim to be a "noble wine." The vineyards are set around the delightful hilltop village of Montepulciano.

Brunello di Montalcino is made from Sangiovese, Brunello being its local name. Its firm tannins may need up to 10 years to soften before the rich, spicy flavors are revealed. Rosso di Montalcino, on the other hand, can be enjoyed much younger.

0 kilometers 50

0 miles 25

Super-Tuscans

During the 1970s, innovative wine makers set out to create new, individual wines, even though under the existing rules they would be labeled as simple table wine. A trend which started with Antinori's Tignanello (a Sangiovese–Cabernet Sauvignon blend), this approach has reinvigorated Tuscan wine, to produce some exciting variations.

Sassicaia, a red wine made from the Cabernet Sauvignon grape

Chianti estate at Badia a Passignano in Tuscany

Key

- Chianti
- Chianti Classico
- Vernaccia di San Gimignano
- Brunello di Montalcino
- Vino Nobile di Montepulciano
- Orvieto Classico
- Orvieto
- Verdicchio dei Castelli di Jesi
- Lambrusco

Verdicchio is a dry white wine from Le Marche with a crisp, slightly salty taste. The single-vineyard Verdicchio, such as Umani Ronchi's CaSal di Serra, is winning much acclaim.

Orvieto Classico is a popular Umbrian white wine. This fresh, dry *(Secco)* version from the Antinori estate is a good example of a modern-style Orvieto. The wine also comes in a sweeter form, known as *Abboccato*.

Grapes of Central Italy

Sangiovese grapes

The versatile Sangiovese grape dominates wine making in Central Italy. It is the main grape in Chianti, in Vino Nobile di Montepulciano, in Brunello di Montalcino, and in many of the Super-Tuscan wines. Of the established whites, Trebbiano and Malvasia head the list. Imported varieties such as Chardonnay and Cabernet Sauvignon play a role, often being used to complement and enhance native varieties, of which there has been a resurgence.

How to Read the Label

The DOCG name guarantees the origin of the wine.

Producer's name

Year of production

The bottler's name and address are given so the region of production is clear.

Alcoholic content

Good Wine Producers

Chianti: Antinori, Badia a Coltibuono, Brolio, Castello di Ama, Castello di Rampolla, Fattoria Selvapiana, Felsina Berardenga, Il Palazzino, Isole e Olena, Monte Vertine, Riecine, Rocca delle Macie, Ruffino, Tenuta Fontodi.

Brunello di Montalcino: Argiano, Altesino, Caparzo, Castelgiocondo, Costanti, Il Poggione, Villa Banfi.

Vino Nobile di Montepulciano: Avignonesi, Le Casalte, Poliziano.

In **Umbria**: Adanti, Lungarotti.

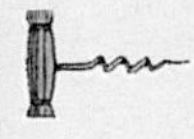

Good Chianti Vintages
2008, 2007, 2004, 2003, 2001, 2000, 1999, 1997, 1995, 1993, 1990, 1988.

Understanding Architecture in Central Italy

Central Italy has countless fine Renaissance buildings, many of them concentrated in and around Florence. Their clear lines, elegant simplicity, and harmonious proportions came out of a re-evaluation of the past. Turning their backs on the Gothic style, the architects of the Renaissance returned to Classical Rome for inspiration. Most of the large buildings had been started by the late 15th century, paid for by the Catholic Church or by powerful noble families, such as the Medici of Florence.

The Palazzo Ducale in Urbino (begun 1465)

Religious Buildings

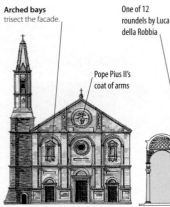

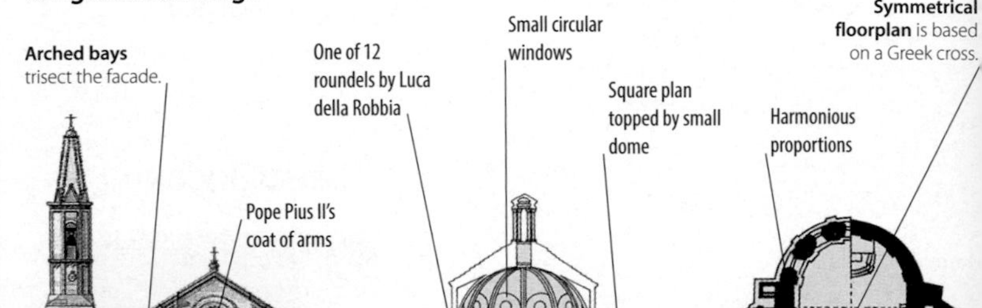
Arched bays trisect the facade.
Pope Pius II's coat of arms
One of 12 roundels by Luca della Robbia
Small circular windows
Square plan topped by small dome
Harmonious proportions
Symmetrical floorplan is based on a Greek cross.

Pienza's Duomo was built by Bernardo Rossellino in *1459* for Pope Pius II as part of his vision of the ideal Renaissance city *(see p337)*.

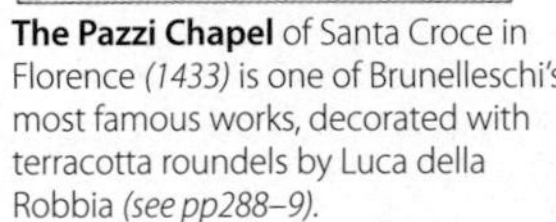

The Pazzi Chapel of Santa Croce in Florence *(1433)* is one of Brunelleschi's most famous works, decorated with terracotta roundels by Luca della Robbia *(see pp288–9)*.

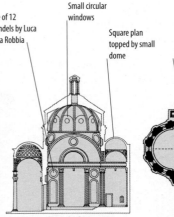

Santa Maria della Consolazione in Todi, begun in *1508*, owes much to the ideas of the architect Bramante *(see p363)*.

Town and Country Houses

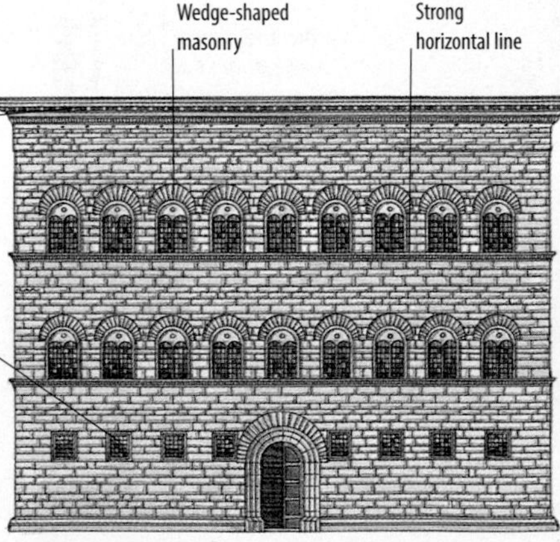
Wedge-shaped masonry
Strong horizontal line
The cornice was designed to cast a shadow over the face of the palace around midday.
Square windows are found only on the ground floor.

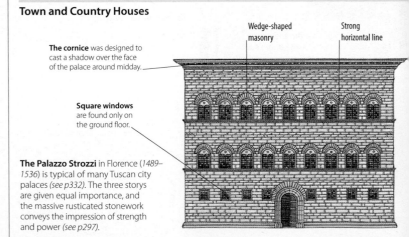

The Palazzo Strozzi in Florence (*1489–1536*) is typical of many Tuscan city palaces *(see p332)*. The three storys are given equal importance, and the massive rusticated stonework conveys the impression of strength and power *(see p297)*.

Where to see the Architecture

The simple canons of the Renaissance were interpreted differently away from the hotbed of artistic thought and cultural endeavor of Florence, which has the greatest number of churches and palaces. Alberti's Tempio Malatestiano at Rimini *(see p270)* evokes the sobriety of ancient Roman architecture yet seeks to reinterpret it in his own unique fashion. Urbino's Palazzo Ducale *(pp374–5)* perfects the grace and polish of the era and is a truly noble period residence. On a smaller scale are the planned Renaissance centers of elegant towns such as Ferrara *(p265)*, Pienza *(p337)*, and Urbania *(p373)*. All three centers are examples of enlightened patronage, and pay homage to the art of antiquity.

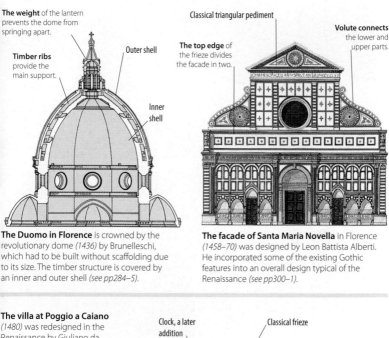

Vista in the Boboli Gardens, Florence

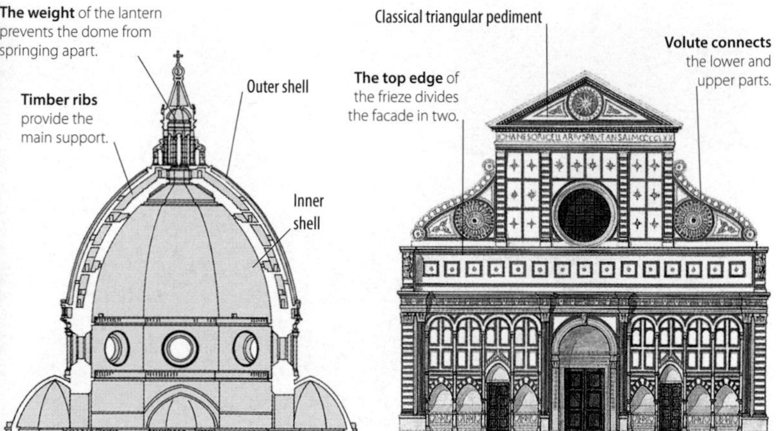
The weight of the lantern prevents the dome from springing apart.
Timber ribs provide the main support.
Outer shell
Inner shell
Classical triangular pediment
Volute connects the lower and upper parts.
The top edge of the frieze divides the facade in two.

The Duomo in Florence is crowned by the revolutionary dome *(1436)* by Brunelleschi, which had to be built without scaffolding due to its size. The timber structure is covered by an inner and outer shell *(see pp284–5)*.

The facade of Santa Maria Novella in Florence *(1458–70)* was designed by Leon Battista Alberti. He incorporated some of the existing Gothic features into an overall design typical of the Renaissance *(see pp300–1)*.

The villa at Poggio a Caiano *(1480)* was redesigned in the Renaissance by Giuliano da Sangallo *(see p332)*. The graceful, curved staircase was added around *1802*.

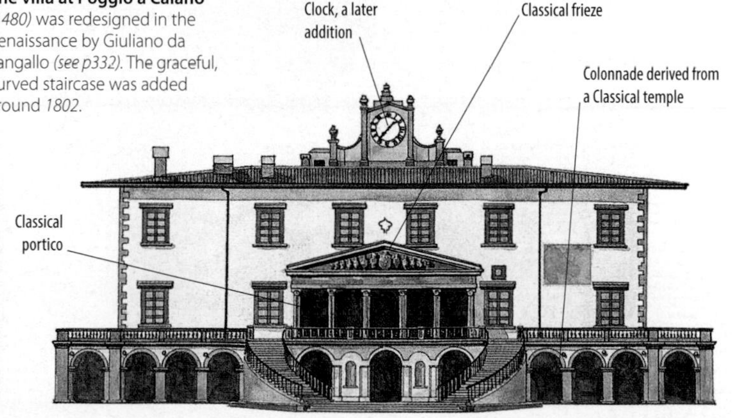
Clock, a later addition
Classical frieze
Colonnade derived from a Classical temple
Classical portico

PRIMA DEL MEZZ
AGRA
GOA
TOBOLSK
ISPAHAN
MOSKOW
ZZODÌ
23 DIC.
1907
2006

EMILIA-ROMAGNA

Emilia-Romagna is the heartland of central Italy, a broad corridor through the hills and plains of the Po Valley that marks the watershed between the cold north of the Alps and the hot Mediterranean south. With its rich agricultural land, historical cities, and thriving industry, it is one of the most prosperous areas in Italy.

Most of the major towns in Emilia-Romagna lie near the Via Aemilia, a Roman road built in 187 BC that linked Rimini on the Adriatic coast with the garrison town of Piacenza. Prior to the Romans, the Etruscans had ruled from their capital, Felsina, located on the site of present-day Bologna. After the fall of Rome, the region's focus moved to Ravenna, which became a principal part of the Byzantine Empire administered from Constantinople.

During the Middle Ages, pilgrims heading for Rome continued to use the Via Aemilia. Political power, however, passed to influential noble families – the Malatesta in Rimini, the Bentivoglio in Bologna, the d'Este in Ferrara and Modena, and the Farnese in Parma and Piacenza. Great courts grew up around the families, attracting poets such as Dante and Ariosto, as well as painters, sculptors, and architects whose works still grace the medieval centers of these towns. Cobbled together from separate Papal States in 1860, modern Emilia-Romagna was given its present borders in 1947. Emilia, the western part of the region, is traditionally associated with a more northern outlook and a tendency toward the left in politics. Romagna, on the other hand, has witnessed an increase in the support for right-wing parties calling for political independence from Rome.

The entire region has a reputation as a great gastronomic center. Agriculture has long thrived on the Po's alluvial fringes, earning the Pianura Padana (Po Plain) epithets such as the "bread basket" and "fruit bowl" of Italy. Pigs still outnumber humans in many areas, and some of the country's most famous staples – Parma ham and Parmesan cheese – originate here.

he medieval Palazzo del Comune in Ferrara

◀ The statue of Garibaldi that stands in front of the Palazzo del Governatore, Parma

Exploring Emilia-Romagna

Emilia-Romagna is a checkerboard of fields and plains between the Po river to the north and the forest-covered Apennine mountain slopes to the south. The best place to begin a tour of the region is centrally situated Bologna. Modena, its longtime rival, boasts one of the country's loveliest Romanesque cathedrals. Parma has a more provincial feel and Ferrara, too, has an easygoing air. Castell'Arquato offers a taste of the smaller villages that dot the hills south of the Po.

Piazza Cavalli, Piacenza's central square

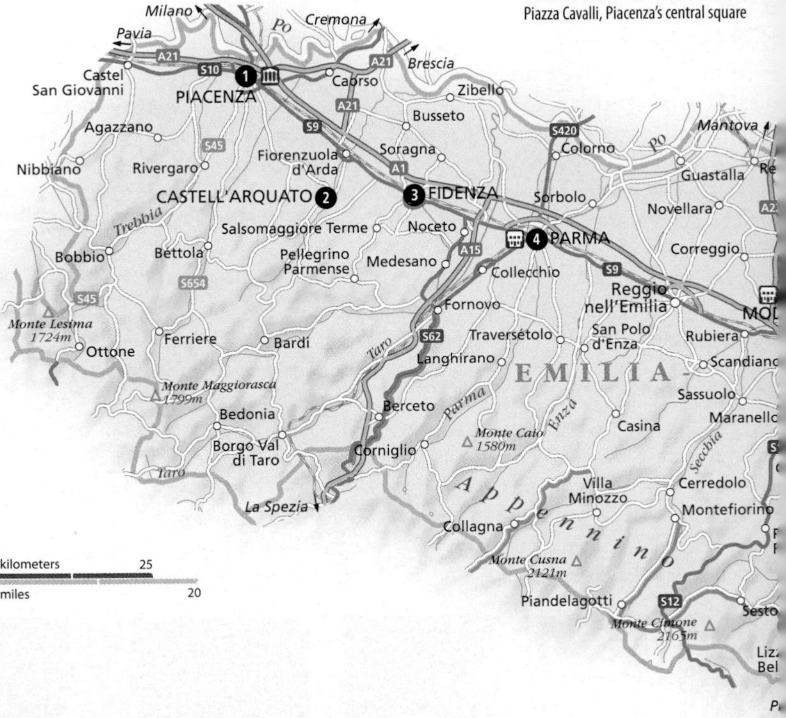

Reed-lined shores along the Po Delta

Sights at a Glance

1. Piacenza
2. Castell'Arquato
3. Fidenza
4. Parma
5. Modena
6. Ferrara
7. *Bologna pp266–9*
8. Faenza
9. Rimini
10. Po Delta
11. *Ravenna pp271–3*

For additional map symbols *see back flap*

Getting Around

Excellent road and railroad links, aided by mostly flat terrain, make this region quick and easy to get around. Bologna is connected by the A1–E35 to Florence and by the A13 to Ferrara and Venice. The busy A1–E35 links Bologna to Milan via Piacenza, Fidenza, and Parma. The A15–E31 connects Parma with La Spezia, and the A21–E70 joins Piacenza and Cremona. Fast, frequent train services run along almost parallel routes.

The beach at Cesenatico, north of Rimini on the Adriatic coast

Padova
Mesola
Bosco della Mesola
10 PO DELTA
Copparo
Po
Padova
Bondeno
Pontelagoscuro
Codigoro
6 FERRARA
Volano
Panaro
Migliarino
Lagosanto
Poggio Renatico
RA8
Ostellato
Lido di Pomposa
Cento
Comacchio
Lido degli Scacchi
A13
Altedo
S16
Valli di Comacchio
San Giovanni in Persiceto
S64
Molinella
Argenta
Lido di Spina
Menata
S309
Budrio
Reno
Marina Romea
7 BOLOGNA
Sillaro
Alfonsine
Medicina
Mezzano
MAR ADRIATICO
San Lazzaro di Savena
Bagnacavallo
11 RAVENNA
A14
S610
Lugo
Pianoro
Russi
Imola
Felisio
Lido di Classe
S9
Idice
FAENZA 8
S67
S71
S65
S610
Casemurate
Cervia
Monghidoro
Brisighella
Forlì
Cesenatico
A1
Castel del Rio
Forlimpopoli
Gatteo a Mare
S302
Bertinoro
S16
Igea Marina
Dovadola
Cesena
Viserba
Predappio
S9
Tredozio
S67
Savignano sul Rubicone
9 RIMINI
Borello
A14
Riccione
Galeata
S71
Verucchio
Mercato Saraceno
Pesaro
Sarsina
Morciano di Romagna
Corniolo
Campigna
Verghereto
Monte Fumaiolo 1407m

Key

- Highway
- Major road
- Secondary road
- Minor road
- Scenic route
- Main railroad
- Minor railroad
- International border
- Regional border
- Summit

The 13th-century Palazzo Pretorio in Castell'Arquato

❶ Piacenza

105,000. FS Piazza Cavalli 7 (0523 32 93 24). Wed & Sat.

Piacenza traces its history back to Roman times. Located near the Po, it served as a fortified camp protecting the Emilian plain from invasion. The center is still based on the Roman plan.

Piacenza has a pleasantly understated old center full of fine medieval and Renaissance buildings. Pride of place goes to two bronze equestrian **statues** in the central Piazza Cavalli, the work of the 17th-century sculptor Francesco Mochi, a pupil of Giambologna. Lauded as masterpieces of Baroque sculpture, the statues represent Alessandro Farnese, a soldier of fortune, and his son, Ranuccio: both were rulers of 16th-century Piacenza.

Behind the statues is the red-brick **Palazzo del Comune**, also known as "Il Gotico," an evocatively battlemented Lombard-Gothic palace begun at the end of the 13th century. It is one of Italy's most beautiful medieval buildings. The **Duomo**, at the end of Via XX Settembre, has a rather leaden Lombard-Romanesque exterior (begun in 1122) and a 14th-century campanile. The interior features Guercino's painted cupola and medieval frescoes. There are also frescoed saints near the main door, painted to resemble members of the congregation.

The **Museo Civico** offers an eclectic mixture of sculpture and paintings – the star among these is the *Madonna and Child with John the Baptist* by Botticelli (1444–1510). There is also an armory and archaeology section. The highlight here is the so-called *Fegato di Piacenza*, an Etruscan bronze representation of the sheep livers once used by priests for divination, inscribed with deities' names.

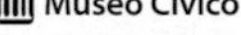

Museo Civico
Palazzo Farnese, Piazza Cittadella. **Tel** 0523 49 26 61. **Open** Tue–Sun (Tue–Thu am only). **Closed** public hols.

❷ Castell'Arquato

Piacenza. 4,500. Piazza Municipio 1 (0523 80 32 15). Mon.

Tucked into the folded hills between Fidenza and Piacenza, Castell'Arquato is one of the prettiest villages in the countryside south of the Po. Day visitors come at the weekends to escape Emilia's larger cities, thronging the restaurants and bars around the beautiful **Piazza Matteotti**. The best medieval building on the piazza is the 13th-century **Palazzo Pretorio**, a Romanesque basilica. The impressive **Rocca Viscontea** (14th century), a former fortress, is on Piazza del Municipio. The village's hilltop site offers good views, particularly over the verdant Arda Valley to the east.

❸ Fidenza

Parma. 25,000. FS Piazza Duomo 16 (0524 833 77). Wed & Sat.

Like many towns hugging the line of the Po, Fidenza owed its early prominence to the Via Aemilia (the old Roman road). The town assumed greater importance as a medieval way station for pilgrims en route to Rome. Today Fidenza is visited for its superb **Duomo** on Piazza Duomo (13th century), a composite piece of architecture that embraces Lombard, Gothic, and transitional Romanesque elements. The most immediately eye-catching feature is the opulent facade, most probably created by the craftsmen who worked with Benedetto Antelami on Parma's Duomo. Inside, the walls are dotted with fragments of medieval frescoes, while the crypt contains the relics of San Donnino, the Duomo's patron.

Detail from facade of Duomo in Fidenza

For hotels and restaurants in this region see pp562–77 and pp580–605

Interior of Parma Baptistry

❹ Parma

190,000. FS i Via Melloni 1a (0521 21 88 89). Wed & Sat; Thu (flea market). **turismo.comune.parma.it**

Few Italian towns are as prosperous as Parma, not only a byword for fine food and good living but also a treasure trove of excellent paintings, superlative sculpture, and fine medieval buildings. It boasts one of Italy's top opera houses and a panoply of elegant shops and first-rate bars and restaurants.

The Lombard-Romanesque **Duomo** on Piazza Duomo, among the greatest in northern Italy, is renowned for the painting that fills its main cupola, the *Assumption* (1526–30) by Antonio da Correggio. The nave is adorned with the work of Correggio's pupils. The south transept features a carved frieze of *The Deposition* (1178) by Benedetto Antelami, who was also responsible for much of the exquisite **Baptistry** (1196) just south of the cathedral. The reliefs inside and outside the latter – particularly those describing the months of the year – are among the most important of their age in Italy.

East of the Duomo is the church of **San Giovanni Evangelista** (rebuilt 1498–1510) whose dome features a fresco (*c.* 1520) of the *Vision of St. John at Patmos* by Correggio. Frescoes by Parmigianino can be seen here and in the 16th-century church of **Madonna della Steccata** on Via Dante.

Palazzo Pilotta

Piazzale della Pilotta 15. Galleria: **Tel** 0521 23 36 17. **Open** Tue–Sun am. Museo: **Tel** 0521 23 37 18. **Open** Tue–Sat am, Sun pm.

This vast palace was built for the Farnese family during the 1500s and rebuilt after bomb damage from World War II. It comprises several parts, including the **Teatro Farnese** (1628), a copy of Palladio's ravishing theater in Vicenza, built entirely of wood.

Both Correggio and Parmigianino are represented in the palace's **Galleria Nazionale**, which also houses works by Fra Angelico, El Greco, and Bronzino, and two paintings by Ludovico Carracci: the *Apostles at the Sepulchre* and the *Funeral of the Virgin* (both late 16th century).

The **Museo Archeologico Nazionale**, on the lower floor, has exhibits from Velleia, an Etruscan necropolis, and from prehistoric sites in the hills around Parma.

Camera di Correggio

Via Melloni. **Tel** 0521 23 33 09. **Open** Tue–Sun (am only).

Originally the refectory of the Benedictine convent of San Paolo, this room was frescoed by Correggio in 1518 with mythological scenes.

Campanile and Baptistry in Parma

The Making of Parmesan Cheese and Parma Ham

No cheese is as famous or as vital to Italy's cuisine as Parmesan *(Parmigiano)*. There are two types: the superior Parmigiano-Reggiano and the lower-quality Grana. The cheese is made using techniques that have barely altered in centuries. Partially skimmed milk is added to whey, to promote fermentation, and rennet is used to curdle the milk. The cheese is then salted and shaped. Parmesan is not only used in cooking but is delicious eaten on its own, or with pears – an Italian specialty. Parma ham owes its excellence to techniques perfected over many years and to the special conditions in which it is cured. It is made from pigs fattened on whey left over from the making of Parmesan cheese. The meat has a character that requires little more than salt and pepper to produce the famous *prosciutto crudo*. The breezy hills of Langhirino, south of Parma, are ideal for curing the hams, which are aged for up to ten months. Each ham is branded with the five-pointed crown of the old Duchy of Parma.

Shop selling Parmesan cheese and Parma ham

Flora by Carlo Cignani (1628–1719) in the Galleria Estense in Modena

5 Modena

185,000. FS Piazza Grande 14 (059 203 26 60). Mon.
turismo.comune.modena.it

To most Italians Modena means fast cars, for both Ferrari and Maserati have factories in its industrial outskirts, and opera, since this is the birthplace of Luciano Pavarotti. Monuments to an earlier age, however, make this one of Emilia's most enticing historic destinations. A thriving colony since Roman times, the city rose to medieval prominence on the back of its broad agricultural hinterland and the arrival in 1598 of the d'Este nobles from Ferrara. This family continued to rule the city until the 18th century.

Duomo

Corso Duomo. **Tel** 059 21 60 78. **Open** daily. Torre Ghirlandina: **Open** Apr–Oct: 9:30am–12:30pm, 3–7pm Sun. **Closed** Aug.

Modena's superlative **Duomo** rises alongside the old Roman Via Emilia. One of the region's greatest Romanesque buildings, it was founded by Countess Matilda of Tuscany, ruler of Modena in the 11th century. It was designed by Lanfranco and dedicated to San Geminiano, the city's patron saint, whose stone coffin lies under the choir. Its most noticeable feature is the **Torre Ghirlandina**, a perilously leaning tower begun at the same time as the Duomo and completed two centuries later. It once housed the *Secchia*, a wooden bucket whose 1325 theft from Bologna allegedly sparked a war between the two cities. It also inspired Tassoni's 17th-century mock epic poem *La Secchia Rapita* (The Stolen Bucket), and became the symbol of a rivalry between the cities.

The large reliefs on the Duomo's main (west) facade are the work of the 12th-century sculptor Wiligelmus. The highlight of the rather severe interior is a large carved *tribuna* (rood screen) decorated with 12th-century scenes from the Passion.

Palazzo dei Musei

Largo di Porta Sant'Agostino 337. Galleria Estense: **Tel** 059 439 57 11. **Open** Call for opening times. Biblioteca Estense: **Tel** 059 22 22 48. **Open** Tue–Thu (Mon, Fri, & Sat am). **Closed** public hols.

Northwest of the Duomo, and reached through an attractive warren of old streets, is the Palazzo dei Musei. Formerly an arsenal and workhouse, it is now home to the city's best museums and galleries. Its finest section is the **Galleria Estense**, given over to the d'Este private art collection, which was transferred here when the city of Ferrara, the family's former dominion, became part of the Papal States. Most of the paintings are by Emilian and Ferrarese artists (notably Reni and the Carracci) but there are also works by Velázquez, Tintoretto, Bernini, and Veronese.

Among the permanent displays in the **Biblioteca Estense**, the d'Este Library, are a 1481 edition of Dante's *Divine Comedy* and dozens of fascinating maps and diplomatic letters, many dating back centuries. A map dated 1501 was among the first to show the 1492 voyage by Columbus to the New World. The jewel of the collection is the magnificent illuminated Borso d'Este Bible, with gloriously decorated pages containing over 1,200 miniatures by 15th-century artists of the Ferrara school, most notably Taddeo Crivelli and Franco Russi Certain sections of the museum are closed due to damage caused by an earthquake, but are due to reopen in late 2013.

Environs

The **Ferrari** factory, 12 miles (20 km) to the south, was founded by Enzo Ferrari in 1945. The FIAT-owned manufacturer now produces around 2,500 cars annually. The **Galleria Ferrari** has an excellent exhibition featuring memorabilia, classic engines, and many vintage cars.

Galleria Ferrari

Via Dino Ferrari 43, Maranello. **Tel** 0536 94 97 13. **Open** 9:30am–6pm daily (to 7pm summer). **Closed** Jan 1, Dec 25.

6 Ferrara

135,000. FS Castello Estense, Largo Castello (0532 20 93 70). Mon & Fri.

The d'Este Dynasty has left an indelible mark on Ferrara, one of the region's greatest walled towns. The noble family took control of the town under Nicolò II in the late 13th century, holding power until 1598, when the family was forced by the papacy to move to Modena.

Ferrari 250 SWB, produced between 1959 and 1962

For hotels and restaurants in this region see pp562–77 and pp580–605

Castello Estense

.argo Castello. **Tel** 0532 29 92 33. **)pen** Tue–Sun (Mar–May: daily). **:losed** public hols.

Nith its towers and battlements, he Este family's dynastic seat begun 1385) looms over the own center. Ferrante and Giulio 1'Este were incarcerated in its dungeons for plotting to overthrow Alfonso I d'Este. Parisina d'Este, wife of Nicolò III, was executed here for having in affair with Ugo, her llegitimate stepson.

Palazzo del comune

'iazza Municipale.

3ronze statues of Nicolò III ind Borso d'Este, one of Vicolò's reputed 27 children, adorn this medieval palace begun 1243). Both are copies of the 15th-century originals by Leon Battista Alberti.

he impressive medieval Castello stense in Ferrara

Facade of the Duomo in Ferrara

Museo della Cattedrale

Via San Romano. **Tel** 0532 76 12 99. **Open** Tue–Sun. **Closed** Jan 1 & 6, Easter, Dec 25 & 26.

Ferrara's 12th-century Duomo is a Romanesque-Gothic hybrid designed by Wiligelmus, who is widely regarded as the first great Italian sculptor. Fine reliefs on the facade depict scenes from the Last Judgment. The excellent **museum** (in a deconsecrated church opposite the cathedral) contains a fine set of marble reliefs of the *Labors of the Months* (late 1100s), two painted organ shutters (1469) of *St. George* and the *Annunciation* by Cosmè Tura, and the *Madonna of the Pomegranate* (1408) by Jacopo della Quercia.

The d'Este Family Dynasty

During their medieval heyday, the d'Este family presided over one of Europe's leading courts, combining the roles of blood-crazed despots with enlightened Renaissance patrons. Nicolò III, for example, had his wife and her lover brutally murdered. Alfonso I (1503–34) married Lucrezia Borgia, descendant of one of Italy's most notorious families, while Ercole I (1407–1505) attempted to poison a nephew who tried to usurp him (and eventually had him executed). At the same time the d'Este court attracted writers like Petrarch, Tasso, and Ariosto, and painters such as Mantegna, Titian, and Bellini. Ercole I also rebuilt Ferrara, creating one of Europe's finest Renaissance cities.

Portrait of Alfonso I d'Este by Titian (c. 1485–1576)

Palazzo Schifanoia

Via Scandiana 23. **Tel** 0532 24 49 49. **Open** Tue–Sun. **Closed** public hols.

Building work in the d'Este summer retreat begun in 1385. The estate is famous for its Salone dei Mesi (Room of the Months), decorated with beautiful 15th-century murals by Tura and other Ferrarese painters with detailed scenes depicting the different months of the year.

Museo Archeologico Nazionale

Palazzo di Ludovico il Moro, Via XX Settembre 122. **Tel** 0532 662 99. **Open** 9:30am–5pm Tue–Sun. **Closed** May 1, Dec 25.

The most interesting exhibits in the Museo Archeologico Nazionale are artifacts that were excavated from Spina, a Greco-Etruscan trading post near Comacchio on the Po Delta.

Palazzo dei Diamanti

Corso Ercole d'Este 21. **Tel** 0532 24 49 49. **Open** 9am–7pm daily.

Named after the diamond motifs on its facade, the Palazzo dei Diamanti houses a modern art gallery, an interesting museum devoted to the Risorgimento, and the Pinacoteca Nazionale, which contains works from leading exponents of the local Renaissance school.

❼ Street by Street: Bologna

The historic city center of Bologna is a handsome ensemble of brick buildings and charming porticoed streets. Medieval palaces are clustered around the two central squares, Piazza Maggiore and Piazza del Nettuno, flanked to the south by the churches of San Petronio and San Domenico. The university of Bologna is the oldest in Europe and the venerable Archiginnasio was its first official building. Further afield, the skyline is etched by the Asinelli and Garisenda towers, and by the campanile of Santo Stefano.

Fontana di Nettuno
The famous Neptune fountain (1566) was designed by Tommaso Laureti and decorated with magnificent bronze figures by Giambologna.

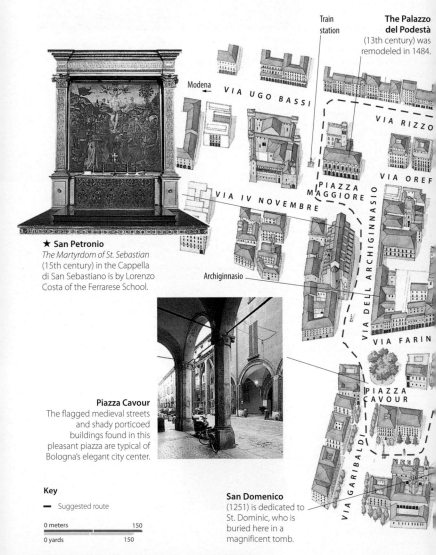

Train station

The Palazzo del Podestà
(13th century) was remodeled in 1484.

Modena

VIA UGO BASSI
VIA RIZZO
VIA OREF
PIAZZA MAGGIORE
VIA IV NOVEMBRE
VIA DELL ARCHIGINNASIO
VIA FARIN
PIAZZA CAVOUR
VIA GARIBALDI

★ San Petronio
The Martyrdom of St. Sebastian (15th century) in the Cappella di San Sebastiano is by Lorenzo Costa of the Ferrarese School.

Archiginnasio

Piazza Cavour
The flagged medieval streets and shady porticoed buildings found in this pleasant piazza are typical of Bologna's elegant city center.

San Domenico
(1251) is dedicated to St. Dominic, who is buried here in a magnificent tomb.

Key

— Suggested route

0 meters 150

0 yards 150

San Giacomo Maggiore
The *Triumph of Death* fresco by Costa (1483–6) adorns the Cappella Bentivoglio.

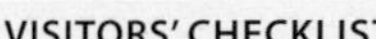

VISITORS' CHECKLIST

Practical Information
380,000. Airport; Piazza Maggiore 1/A; Stazione Centrale (051 23 96 60). Fri & Sat. Mar–Jun: Bologna Music Festival.
bolognawelcome.com

Transportation
Marconi 5 miles (9 km) NW.
Piazza Medaglia d'Oro.
Piazza XX Settembre.

Pinacoteca Nazionale
Museo di Anatomia
Umana Normale

VIA ZAMBONI

VIA SAN VITALE

Ravenna

STRADA MAGGIORE

ZZA DI PORTA GNANA

VIA SANTO STEFANO

VIA CASTIGLIONE

Firenze

Torri degli Asinelli e Garisenda
The colossal towers are two of the few remaining towers begun by Bologna's important families in the 12th century.

San Giacomo Maggiore

Piazza Rossini. **Open** daily.

This Romanesque-Gothic church, begun in 1267 but altered substantially since, is visited mainly for the Cappella Bentivoglio, a superb family chapel founded by Annibale Bentivoglio in 1445 and consecrated in 1486. Pride of place naturally goes to a portrait with subtle characterization of the patrons by Lorenzo Costa (1460–1535), who was also responsible for the frescoes of the *Apocalypse*, the *Madonna Enthroned*, and the *Triumph of Death*. The chapel's altarpiece, depicting the *Virgin and Saints with Two Angel Musicians* (1488), is the work of Francesco Francia. The Bentivoglio family is further glorified in the tomb of Anton Galeazzo Bentivoglio (1435) opposite the chapel. It was among the last works of the noted Sienese sculptor, Jacopo della Quercia. The Oratory of Santa Cecilia features frescoes on the lives of Santa Cecilia and San Valeriano by Costa and Francesco Francia (1504–6).

The Bentivoglio tomb (1435) by Jacopo della Quercia

Abbazia di Santo Stefano
The Fontana di Pilato, or Pilate's fountain, in the courtyard features a basin with Lombard inscriptions from the 8th century.

Exploring Bologna

Monuments to Bologna's rich cultural heritage are scattered across the city, from the leaning towers and the church of San Petronio in the old center to the Pinacoteca Nazionale in the university district.

Torri degli Asinelli e Garisenda

Piazza di Porta Ravegnana. Torre degli Asinelli: **Open** daily.

The famous leaning towers – Torre degli Asinelli and Torre Garisenda – are among the few survivors of the original 200 that once formed the skyline of Bologna. Both were begun in the 12th century, though there were probably earlier towers on the site – Dante mentioned a pair of towers here in his *Inferno*. Torre Garisenda was shortened as a safety measure within only a few years of its construction, and still leans some 10 ft (3 m) from the vertical. At 318 ft (97 m) tall, Torre Asinelli is the fourth highest tower in Italy after those in Cremona, Siena, and Venice. Its 500-step ascent offers fine views over the city's rooftops to the hills beyond.

Abbazia di Santo Stefano

Via Santo Stefano 24. **Tel** 051 22 32 56. **Open** 9am–noon, 3:30–6:30pm daily.

Santo Stefano is a curious collection of four medieval churches (originally seven) jumbled together under one roof. The 11th-century church of the Crocifisso provides little more than a corridor to

Exterior of the Abbazia di Santo Stefano

San Petronio

Piazza Maggiore. **Tel** 051 23 14 15. **Open** daily.

Dedicated to the city's 5th-century bishop, this church ranks among the greatest of Italy's brick-built medieval buildings. Founded in 1390, it was originally intended to be larger than St. Peter's in Rome, but its size was scaled down when the church authorities diverted funds to the nearby Palazzo Archiginnasio. The resulting financial shortfall left the church decidedly lopsided, with a row of columns on its eastern flank that were intended to support an additional internal aisle. The project's financial profligacy, nonetheless, was said to have been instrumental in turning Martin Luther against Catholicism.

The altarpiece of the *Martyrdom of St. Sebastian* is from the late Ferrarese School.

The pink and white interior adds to the overall light and airy effect.

The canopied main portal features beautiful biblical reliefs (1425–38) by Jacopo della Quercia.

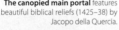

Gothic Interior

The interior is airy, with graceful pillars supporting the roof. Twenty-two chapels, shielded by screens, open off the nave. In 1547 the Council of Trent (174) was temporarily moved here due to the plague.

Entrance

Unfinished upper facade

The meridian line was traced in 1655 by the astronomer Gian Domenico Cassini. It is 219 ft (67 m) long.

The stained-glass windows (1464–6) in this chapel are by Jacob of Ulm.

For hotels and restaurants in this region see pp562–77 and pp580–605

polygonal San Sepolcro, the most appealing of the quartet. Also dating from the 11th century, its centerpiece is the tomb of St. Petronius, a marvelously overstated affair modeled on the Holy Sepulchre of Jerusalem. The courtyard contains the so-called Fontana di Pilato, an 8th-century basin.

The 5th-century Santi Vitale e Agricola is the oldest church in the city. It was rebuilt in the 8th and 11th centuries. Inside are the sarcophagi of Saints Vitalis and Agricola, martyred in the 4th century. Santa Trinità features a small museum of minor paintings and religious artifacts, including wooden statues of the *Adoration of the Magi* painted by Simone dei Crocifissi (c.1370).

Choir Stalls The exquisite inlaid choir stalls of the Chapel of the Holy Sacrament were made by Raffaello da Brescia in 1521.

Pinacoteca Nazionale

Via delle Belle Arti 56. **Tel** 051 420 94 11. **Open** Tue–Sat. **Closed** Jan 1, May 1, Aug 15 Dec, 25.

Bologna's principal art gallery, and one of northern Italy's most important collections, stands on the edge of the city's university district, a bustling area of bars, bookstores, and cheap restaurants. The gallery is mainly dedicated to work by Bolognese painters, notably Vitale da Bologna, Guido Reni, Guercino, and the Carracci family. Members of the Ferrarese School are also represented, in particular Francesco del Cossa and Ercole de' Roberti. The two highlights are Perugino's *Madonna in Glory* (*c.* 1491) and Raphael's famous *Ecstasy of St. Cecilia*, painted around 1515, both artists having worked in Bologna.

The Ecstasy of St. Cecilia (c.1515) by Raphael in Bologna's Pinacoteca Nazionale

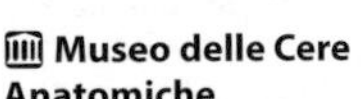

Museo delle Cere Anatomiche

Via Irnerio 48. **Tel** 051 209 15 33/ 209 15 56. **Open** 9am–1pm, 2–4pm Mon–Fri. **Closed** Jan 1, Easter, May 1, Dec 25, public hols.

The Museum of Anatomical Waxworks is one of the more memorable of Bologna's smaller museums, featuring occasionally gruesome visceral waxworks and numerous models of organs, limbs, and flayed bodies. Sculpted rather than made from casts, they have an artistic as well as scientific appeal. The models were used as medical teaching aids until the 19th century. Exhibits from the 18th century are in Palazzo Poggi, which also contains the Museo Cartageographica.

San Domenico

Piazza di San Domenico 13. **Tel** 051 640 04 11. **Open** daily.

Bologna's San Domenico can lay claim to being the most important of Italy's many Dominican churches. Begun in 1221, after St. Dominic's death, it was built to house the body of the saint, who died here and lies buried in a tomb known as the Arca di San Domenico. A magnificent composite work, the tomb's statues were executed by Nicola Pisano; the reliefs of scenes from the *Life of St. Dominic* were the work of Nicola Pisano and his assistants; the canopy (1473) is attributed to Nicola di Bari; while the figures of the angels and Saints Proculus and Petronius are early works by Michelangelo. The reliquary (1383) behind the sarcophagus contains St. Dominic's head.

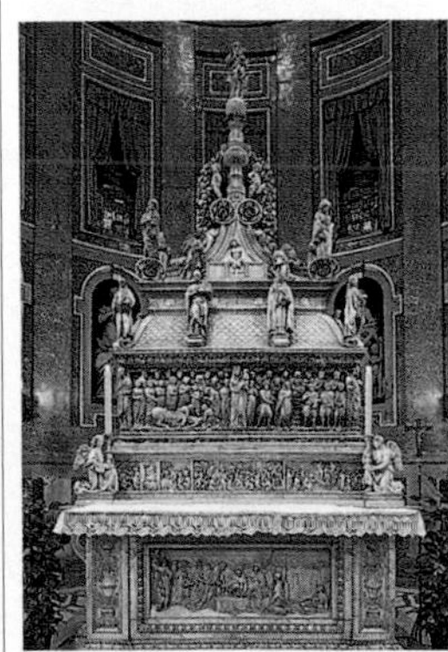

Arca di San Domenico in the Basilica di San Domenico

Fresco of Malatesta and St. Sigismund (1451) by Piero della Francesca in the Tempio Malatestiano, Rimini

❽ Faenza

Ravenna. 54,000. FS
Voltone Molinella 2 (0546 252 31).
Tue, Thu & Sat.

Faenza is synonymous with the *faïence* ceramic-ware to which it gave its name. Renowned across Europe for over 500 years, the pottery, with its distinctive blue and ocher coloring, is still made in countless small factories around the town.

The highlight of Faenza is the **Museo Internazionale delle Ceramiche**, one of the largest ceramic collections in Italy. Its exhibits feature not only examples of local ware, but also pottery from other countries and other periods, including Roman ceramics and medieval majolica. There is also a section devoted to the modern ceramic art of Picasso, Matisse, and Chagall.

Museo Internazionale delle Ceramiche
Viale Baccarini 19. **Tel** 0546 69 73 11. **Open** Apr–Oct: Tue–Sun; Nov–Mar: Tue–Sun (Tue–Thu am only). **Closed** Jan 1, May 1, Aug 15, Dec 25.

❾ Rimini

140,000. FS Piazzale Fellini 3 (0541 70 45 87). Wed & Sat.
riminiturismo.it

Rimini was once a quaint sea side resort, whose charms were celebrated in the early films of Federico Fellini (1920–93), the director born and raised here. Today it is the largest beach resort in Europe. The seafront, which stretches unbroken for almost 9 miles (15 km), is lined with clubs, bars, and restaurants. The crowded beaches are clean and well groomed, though entrance fees are charged at private beaches.

The town's old quarter, by contrast, is pleasantly quiet. Its charming cobbled streets gather around **Piazza Cavour**, dominated by the 14th-century **Palazzo del Podestà**. Rimini's finest building is the **Tempio Malatestiano**, built as a Franciscan church but converted in 1450 by Leon Battista Alberti, the great Florentine architect, into one of Italy's great Renaissance monuments. The work was commissioned by Sigismondo Malatesta (1417–68), a descendant of Rimini's ruling medieval family, and reputedly one of the most evil and debauched men of his time. Ostensibly designed as a chapel, the Tempio became little more than a monument to Malatesta. Inside are sculptures by Agostino di Duccio and a fresco (1451) by Piero della Francesca of Malatesta kneeling before St. Sigismund (1451).

The entwined initials of Malatesta and his fourth wife, Isotta degli Atti, provide a recurring decorative motif, and there are reliefs depicting scenes of bacchanalian excess and oddities such as strangely posed elephants (a Malatesta family emblem). All this led Pope Pius II to condemn the building as "a temple of devil-worshippers," and to burn Malatesta's effigy for acts of "murder, violation, adultery, incest, sacrilege, and perjury."

Environs
Farther along the coast, the resorts become relatively quieter. **Cesenatico**, 11 miles (18 km) north, offers all the usual facilities yet the beaches are less crowded.

Tempio Malatestiano
Via IV Novembre. **Tel** 0541 511 30. **Open** 8:30am–12:30pm, 3:30–7pm daily (9am–1pm, 3:30–7pm Sun).

❿ Po Delta

Ferrara. FS Ferrara Ostellata. to Goro or Gorino. from Porto Garibaldi, Goro & Gorino. Via Mazzini 4, Comacchio (0533 31 41 54). Parco Delta del Po: **Tel** 0533 31 40 03.
parcodeltapo.it

The Po is Italy's longest river. Its vast basin covers some 15 percent of the country and supports

Facade of the Renaissance Tempio Malatestiano in Rimini

For hotels and restaurants in this region see pp562–77 and pp580–605

around a third of the nation's population. Although ravaged in many places by Industrial pollution, at its finest it offers beautifully subtle landscapes – rows of poplar trees across misty fields and vistas over the shifting sands of its vast delta, an estuary of marshes, dunes, and islands.

The immense **Parco Delta del Po** is a national park stretching for 234 sq miles (600 sq km), all the way to the Veneto. Wetland areas such as the **Valli di Comacchio** north of Ravenna have long been nature reserves, a winter home to thousands of breeding and migrating birds. Ornithologists gather here to see gulls, coots, bean geese, and black terns, and far rarer species such as the white egret, hen harrier, and pygmy cormorant. **Comacchio**, the nearest settlement, comprises 13 tiny islands connected by bridges. It is one of several fishing villages in the area, and its most famous catch is eels, often caught using methods, like water gates, that date back as far as Roman times.

Hen harrier, found in the Po Delta

Other nature reserves include the **Bosco della Mesola**, a tract of ancient woodland planted by the Etruscans and cared for by generations of monks. You can either walk or cycle through it, with excellent opportunities for seeing large herds of deer.

For a good look at the entire region, follow the S309 – part of the old Via Romea pilgrimage trail to Rome – that runs north to south through 60 miles (100 km) of the park. A number of smaller lanes branch off into the wilderness. There are also boat trips to some of the delta's remote corners: key departure points include the villages of Ca'Tiepolo, Ca'Vernier, and Taglio di Po. Most areas also offer the possibility of renting bicycles. The 78-mile (125-km) ride along the right bank of the Po is very popular with cyclists.

Piazza del Popolo, Ravenna's central square

⓫ Ravenna

160,000. FS Via Salara 8–12 (0544 357 55/354 04). Wed & Sat; antiques on 3rd weekend of each month. **turismo.ravenna.it**

Most people visit Ravenna for its superb mosaics from the Byzantine period *(see p22–3)*, but the town itself is a surprisingly pleasant medley of old streets, fine shops, and peaceful piazzas. The **Museo Nazionale** has a wide range of icons, paintings, and archaeological displays. The best place to take a break from sightseeing is Piazza del Popolo, a lovely ensemble of medieval buildings.

Museo Nazionale
Via Fiandrini. **Tel** 0544 21 56 18.
Open Tue–Sun. **Closed** Jan 1, May 1, Dec 25.

The peaceful landscape along the banks of the river in the Po Delta

A Tour of Ravenna

Ravenna rose to power in the 1st century BC under the Emperor Augustus, who built a port and naval base at nearby Classe, currently the site of a major excavation project. As Rome's power declined, Ravenna was made the capital of the Western Empire (AD 402), a role it retained during the Ostrogoth and Byzantine rule in the 5th and 6th centuries. Ravenna is renowned for its early Christian mosaics – the town had converted to Christianity in the 2nd century AD. The mosaics span the years of Roman and Byzantine rule, offering comparisons between Classically inspired designs and later Byzantine motifs.

② The Good Shepherd
This mosaic adorns the tiny Mausoleo di Galla Placidia. Begun in 430, this exquisite building probably never received the remains of Placidia, wife of a barbarian emperor.

① San Vitale
San Vitale's apse mosaics (526–547) show Christ, San Vitale (being handed a martyr's crown), two angels, and Bishop Ecclesius, who began the church *(see pp54–5)*.

③ Baptism of Jesus
The 5th-century Battistero Neoniano (Neonian Baptistry) is named after the bishop who may have commissioned its decoration, including this beautiful mosaic. It was built near the remains of a Roman bathhouse and is Ravenna's oldest monument.

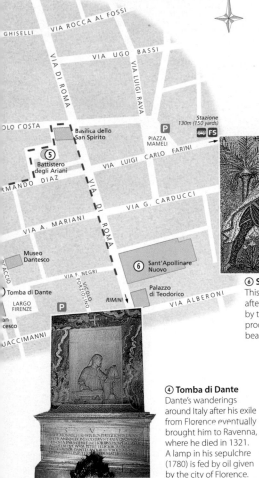

⑤ **Battistero degli Ariani**
The cupola of this late 5th-century baptistry has a mosaic showing the Apostles ringed around a centerpiece depicting the Baptism of Christ.

VISITORS' CHECKLIST

Practical Information
San Vitale & Mausoleo di Galla Placidia: Via Fiandrini. **Tel** 0544 54 16 88. **Open** Apr–Sep: 9am–7pm daily; Nov–Feb: 9:30am–5pm; Mar & Oct: 9am–5:30pm (last adm: 15 mins before closing). **Closed** Jan 1, Dec 25. Battistero Neoniano, Via Battistero. **Tel** 0544 54 16 88. **Open & Closed** as above, except Nov–Feb: 10am–5pm.
Sant'Apollinare Nuovo: Via di Roma. **Tel** 0544 54 16 88. **Open** & **Closed** as above.
Tomba di Dante: Via Dante Alighieri. **Tel** 0544 336 62. **Open** Apr–Sep: 9:30am–6:30pm daily; Oct–Mar: 10am–4pm daily. **Closed** Jan 1, Dec 25.
Battistero degli Ariani: Via degli Ariani. **Tel** 0544 54 37 11. **Open** 8:30am–7:30pm daily (last adm: 15 mins before closing). **Closed** Jan 1, May 1.
A combined ticket is available. For reservations (mandatory for Mausoleo di Galla Placidia): **Tel** 800 303 999, 0544 54 16 88.
turismo.ravenna.it

⑥ **Sant'Apollinare Nuovo**
This glorious 6th-century church, named after Ravenna's first bishop, is dominated by two rows of mosaics. Both show processions of martyrs and virgins bearing gifts for Christ and the Virgin.

④ **Tomba di Dante**
Dante's wanderings around Italy after his exile from Florence eventually brought him to Ravenna, where he died in 1321. A lamp in his sepulchre (1780) is fed by oil given by the city of Florence.

Key
— Suggested route

0 meters 200
0 yards 200

For additional map symbols *see back flap*

FLORENCE

Florence is a vast and beautiful monument to the Renaissance, the artistic and cultural reawakening of the 15th century. Writers such as Dante, Petrarch, and Machiavelli contributed to its proud literary heritage, though it was the paintings and sculptures of artists such as Botticelli, Michelangelo, and Donatello that turned the city into one of the world's greatest artistic capitals.

While the Etruscans had long settled the hills around Fiesole, Florence first sprang to life as a Roman colony in 59 BC. Captured by the Lombards in the 6th century, the city later emerged from the Dark Ages as an independent city-state. By the 13th century a burgeoning trade in wool and textiles, backed by a powerful banking sector, had turned the city into one of Italy's leading powers. Political control was wielded first by the guilds, and later by the Florentine Republic. In time, power passed to leading noble families, of which the most influential were the Medici, a hugely wealthy banking dynasty. Florence, and later Tuscany, remained under the family's almost unbroken sway for three centuries. During this time the city was at the cultural and intellectual heart of Europe, its cosmopolitan atmosphere and wealthy patrons providing the impetus for a period of unparalleled artistic growth. Artists, sculptors, and architects flocked to the city, filling its streets, churches, and palaces with some of the world's greatest Renaissance works. By 1737 the Medici had died out, leaving the city under Austrian (and briefly Napoleonic) control until Italian Unification in 1860. Between 1865 and 1871 Florence was the capital of the new Kingdom of Italy. The historic streets and artistic heritage were ravaged by the Arno floods of November 1966.

Florentines strolling in front of Ponte Vecchio (1345), the old bridge lined with shops spanning the Arno

◀ A replica of Michelangelo's *David* in Piazza della Signoria

Exploring Florence

Historic Florence is a surprisingly compact area, and the majority of the sights described on the following pages can easily be reached on foot. Most visitors head for the Duomo, the city's geographical and historical focus, ideally placed to explore the Campanile, Baptistry, and Museo dell'Opera del Duomo. To the south is Piazza della Signoria, long the city's political heart, flanked by the Palazzo Vecchio, Florence's town hall, and the Uffizi, one of Italy's leading art galleries. To the east lies the church of Santa Croce, home to frescoes by Giotto and the tombs of some of Florence's greatest men. To the west stands Santa Maria Novella, the city's other great church, also adorned with fresco-filled chapels. Across the Ponte Vecchio and the Arno – the river that bisects the city – is the district of Oltrarno, dominated by Santo Spirito and the vast Pitti Palace, containing galleries with works by great Renaissance artists including Raphael and Titian.

Getting Around

Florence has excellent bus service. Three streetcar lines operate in the city; one links the city center to the outskirts. The compact city center, a restricted traffic area, is best negotiated on foot.

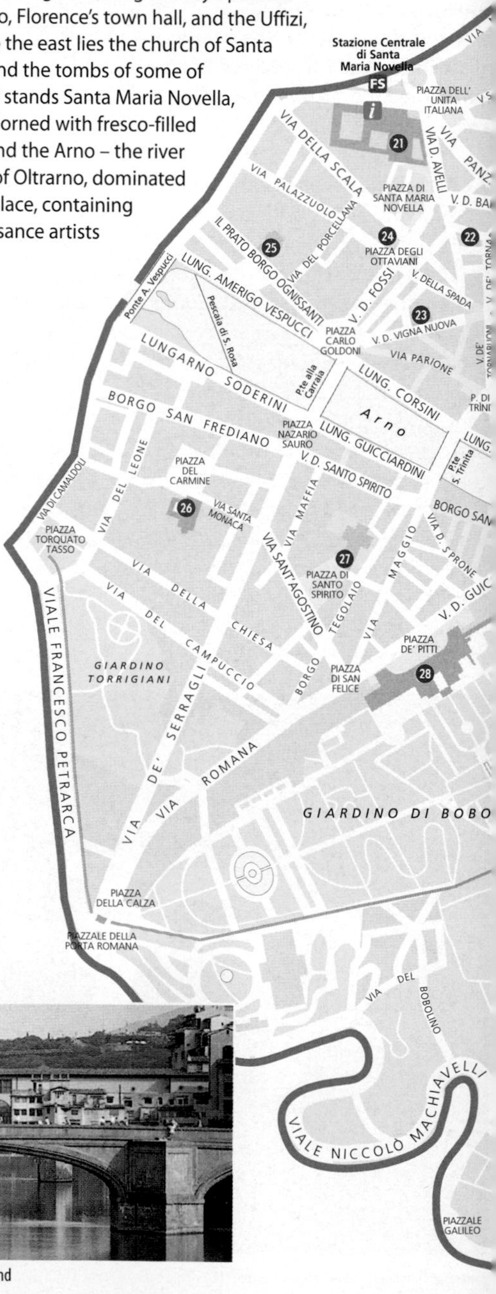

Key

- Major sight
- Place of interest
- Pedestrian street
- City walls

Ponte Vecchio with Ponte Santa Trinità in the foreground

For additional map symbols *see back flap*

Sights at a Glance

Churches

- 2 Convento di San Marco
- 3 Santissima Annunziata
- 7 *Duomo and Baptistry pp280–82*
- 8 Orsanmichele
- 10 Santa Croceg Ognissanti
- 18 San Lorenzo
- 19 Cappelle Medicee
- 21 Santa Maria Novella
- 25 *Ognissanti*
- 26 *Cappella Brancacci pp298–9*
- 27 Santo Spirito
- 29 Santa Felìcita
- 31 San Miniato al Monte

Buildings, Monuments, and Squares

- 5 Spedale degli Innocenti
- 12 Ponte Vecchio
- 14 Piazza della Signoria
- 15 Palazzo Vecchio
- 16 Palazzo Davanzati
- 17 Palazzo Strozzi
- 20 Mercato Centrale
- 22 Palazzo Antinori
- 23 Palazzo Rucellai
- 30 Piazzale Michelangelo

Museums and Galleries

- 1 Galleria dell'Accademia
- 4 Museo Archeologico
- 6 Museo dell'Opera del Duomo
- 9 Bargello
- 11 Museo Galileo
- 13 *Uffizi pp286–9*
- 24 Museo Nazionale Alinari della Fotografia
- 28 *Palazzo Pitti pp302–3*

Bell tower, Palazzo Vecchio

0 meters 500
0 yards 500

Street by Street: Around San Marco

The buildings in this part of Florence once stood on the fringes of the city, serving as stables and barracks. The Medici menagerie of lions, elephants, and giraffes was housed here. Today it is a student quarter and the streets are often busy with young people attending the university or the Accademia di Belle Arti, the world's oldest art school, founded in 1563.

3 Santissima Annunziata
This Renaissance church has an opulent Baroque interior.

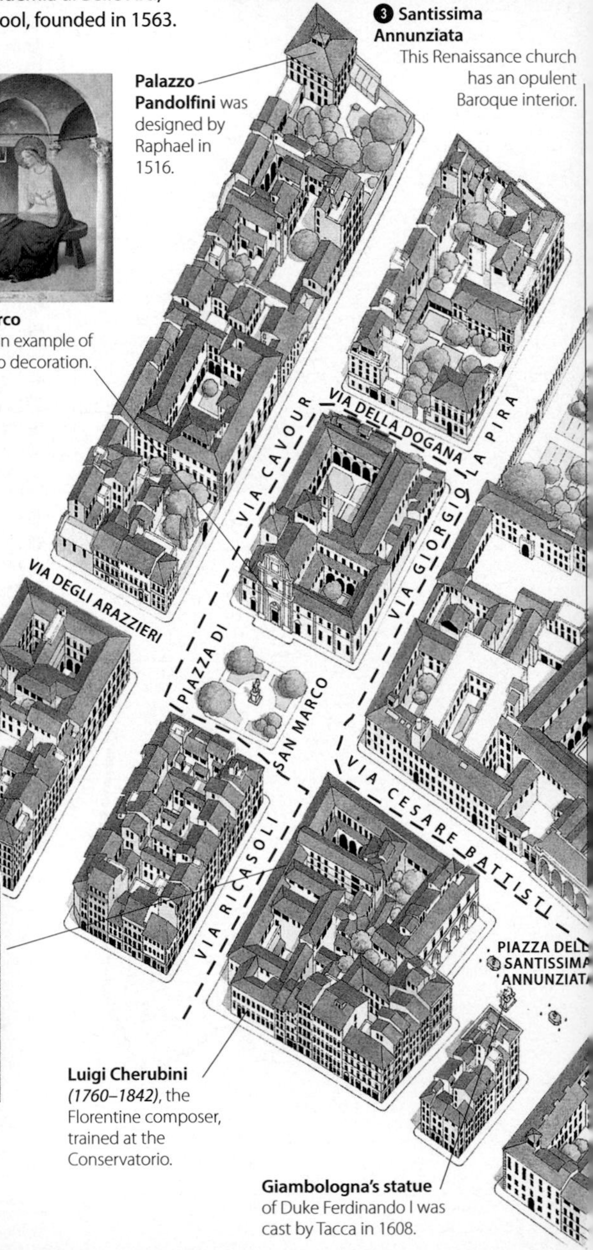

Palazzo Pandolfini was designed by Raphael in 1516.

2 ★ Convento di San Marco
The Annunciation (*c.* 1445) is an example of Fra Angelico's exquisite fresco decoration.

Sant'Apollonia features a fresco of the *Cenacolo* (Last Supper) by Andrea del Castagno (1450).

1 ★ Galleria dell'Accademia
This detail is from a 14th-century altarpiece, the *Madonna and Saints*, by an unnamed master.

Luigi Cherubini *(1760–1842)*, the Florentine composer, trained at the Conservatorio.

Giambologna's statue of Duke Ferdinando I was cast by Tacca in 1608.

For hotels and restaurants in this region see pp562–77 and pp580–605

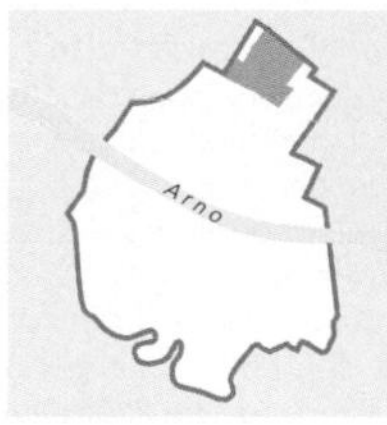

Locator Map
See Florence Street Finder map 2

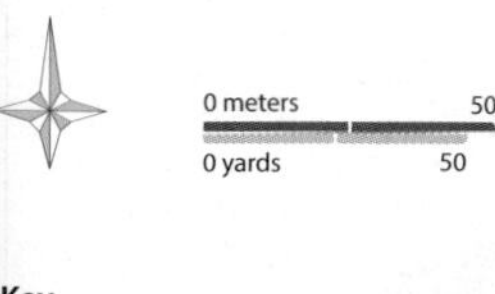

Key

— Suggested route

The Giardino dei Semplici was opened in 1543.

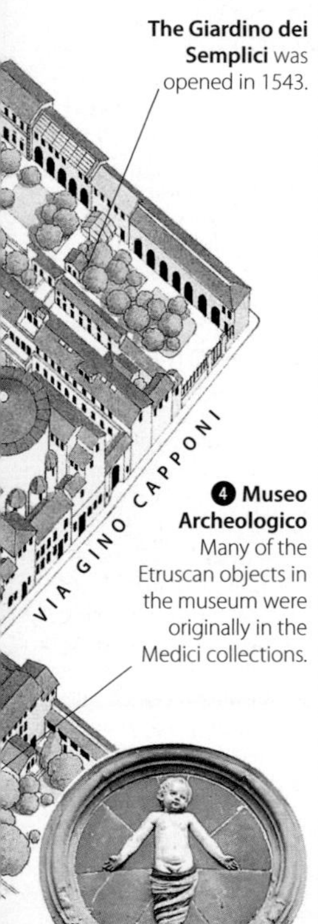

4 Museo Archeologico Many of the Etruscan objects in the museum were originally in the Medici collections.

5 Spedale degli Innocenti Opened in 1444, the city orphanage by Brunelleschi was decorated with cameos by Andrea della Robbia.

Part of the 15th-century *Cassone Adimari* by Lo Scheggia in the Accademia

1 Galleria dell'Accademia

Via Ricasoli 60. **Map** 2 D4. **Tel** 055 238 86 12 (information); 055 29 48 83 (reservations). **Open** 8:15am– 6:50pm Tue–Sun (occasional extended hours in the summer). **Closed** public hols.

The Academy of Fine Arts, founded in 1563, was the first school established in Europe specifically to teach the techniques of drawing, painting, and sculpture. The art collection displayed here was formed in 1784 to provide material for students to study and copy.

The most famous work is Michelangelo's *David* (1504), a colossal (17 ft/5.2 m) nude of the biblical hero who killed the giant Goliath. The sculpture was commissioned by the city for Piazza della Signoria, but it was moved to the Accademia for safe-keeping in 1873. One copy now stands in its original position *(see pp294–5)* and a second is on Piazzale Michelangelo. The *David* established Michelangelo, at the age of 29, as the foremost sculptor of his time.

Michelangelo's other master-pieces in the Accademia include the *Quattro Prigionieri* (the Four Prisoners), sculpted between 1521 and 1523 and intended to adorn the tomb of Pope Julius II. The muscular figures struggling to free themselves from the stone are among the most dramatic of Michelangelo's works. The statues were presented to the Medici family in 1564 by the artist's nephew, Leonardo. They were then moved to the Grotta Grande in the Boboli Gardens, where casts of the originals can now be seen.

The Accademia also contains an important collection of paintings by 15th- and 16th-century Florentine artists, among them Filippino Lippi, Fra Bartolomeo, Bronzino, and Ridolfo del Ghirlandaio. The major works include the *Madonna del Mare* (Madonna of the Sea), attributed to Botticelli (1445–1510), and *Venus and Cupid* by Jacopo Pontormo (1494–1556), based on a preparatory drawing by Michelangelo. Also here is an elaborately painted wooden chest, the *Cassone Adimari* (1440–45) by Lo Scheggia, the step-brother of Masaccio. Originally part of a wealthy bride's trousseau, it is decorated with details of Florentine life, clothing and architecture. A scene of the bridal party appears on the chest in front of the Baptistry.

Michelangelo's *David*

The Salone della Toscana (Tuscany Room) features modest paintings and sculptures by 19th-century members of the Accademia and plaster models by sculptor Lorenzo Bartolini.

The light and airy former library, designed by Michelozzo

❷ Convento di San Marco

Piazza di San Marco. **Map** 2 D4. **Tel** 055 28 76 28 (information). **Open** 7am–noon, 4–8pm. ✝ Museo di San Marco: **Tel** 055 238 86 08 (reservations). **Open** 8:15am–1:50pm (to 4:50pm Sat, Sun). **Closed** Jan 1, May 1, Dec 25, 2nd & 4th Mon and 1st, 3rd, & 5th Sun of each month.

The Convent of San Marco was founded in the 13th century and enlarged in 1437 when Dominican monks from nearby Fiesole moved there at the invitation of Cosimo il Vecchio. He paid a considerable sum to have the convent rebuilt by his favorite architect, Michelozzo, whose simple cloisters and cells provide the setting for a remarkable series of devotional frescoes (*c.* 1438–45) by Florentine painter and Dominican friar Fra Angelico. The convent and art collections form the **Museo di San Marco**.

Michelozzo's magnificent **Chiostro di Sant'Antonino** was named after the convent's first prior, Antonino Pierozzi (1389–1459), who later became the Archbishop of Florence. Most of the faded frescoes in this cloister describe scenes from the saint's life by Bernardino Poccetti. The panels in the corner are by Fra Angelico. A door in the right side of the cloister leads to the **Ospizio dei Pellegrini** (Pilgrims' Hospice). Today it houses the museum's free-standing paintings, including two famous masterpieces: Fra Angelico's moving *Deposition* (*c.* 1435–40), an altarpiece painted for the church of Santa Trinità, and the *Madonna dei Linaiuoli*, commissioned by the Linaiuoli (flaxworkers' guild) in 1433.

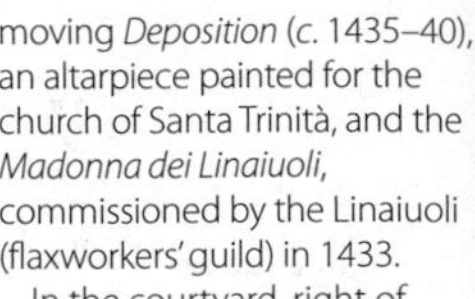

A detail from Fra Angelico's poignant *Deposition* (*c.* 1440)

In the courtyard, right of the convent's former bell, is the vaulted **Sala Capitolare** (Chapter House), decorated with a noted but over-restored *Crucifixion and Saints* (1440) painted by Fra Angelico.

Covering one wall of the small **Refettorio** (refectory) is a fresco of the *Last Supper* (*c.* 1480) by Domenico Ghirlandaio. Stairs from the courtyard lead to the first floor, where you suddenly see Fra Angelico's *Annunciation* (*c.* 1440), thought by many to be among the city's most beautiful Renaissance paintings.

Beyond, ranged around three sides of the cloister, are the **Dormitory Cells**. These 44 tiny monastic cells are frescoed with scenes from *The Life of Christ* by Fra Angelico and assistants (1439–45). The cells numbered 1 to 11 are generally attributed to Fra Angelico personally, as is the lovely fresco of the *Madonna and Saints* on the right of the corridor *(see p36)*.

Cells 12–14 were once occupied by Savonarola, the zealous Dominican monk who became Prior of San Marco in 1491. Among other deeds, Savonarola incited Florentines to rebel against the Medici and was responsible for the burning of many works of art. Denounced as a heretic, he was burned at the stake in Piazza della Signoria in 1498.

Along the third corridor lies an airy colonnaded hall, formerly a public **library** designed by Michelozzo in 1441 for Cosimo il Vecchio. Beyond it lie two cells (38 and 39) which were used by Cosimo when he went on retreat here. Each is decorated with two frescoes (the other cells have only one), and they are both larger than any of the neighboring rooms.

Fra Angelico's allegorical fresco, the *Mocking of Christ* (*c.* 1442), showing Jesus blindfolded and being struck by a Roman guard

The Birth of the Virgin (1514) by del Sarto in Santissima Annunziata

❸ Santissima Annunziata

Piazza della Santissima Annunziata. **Map** 2 E4. **Tel** 055 26 61 81. **Open** 7:30am–12:30pm, 4pm–6:30pm daily.

Founded by the Servite order in 1250, the church of the Holy Annunciation was later rebuilt by Michelozzo between 1444 and 1481. Its atrium contains frescoes by the Mannerist artists Rosso Fiorentino, Andrea del Sarto, and Jacopo Pontormo. Perhaps the finest of its panels are *The Journey of the Magi* (1511) and *The Birth of the Virgin* (1514) by Andrea del Sarto.

The heavily decorated, dark interior has a frescoed ceiling completed by Pietro Giambelli in 1669. Here is one of the city's most revered shrines, a painting of the Virgin Mary begun by a monk in 1252 but miraculously completed by an angel, according to devout Florentines. Newlywed couples traditionally visit the shrine (on the left as you enter the church) to present a bouquet of flowers to the Virgin and to pray for a long, fruitful, and fecund marriage.

A door from the north transept leads to the **Chiostrino dei Morti** (Cloister of the Dead), so called because it was originally used as a burial ground. Today it is best known for del Sarto's beautiful fresco, *The Madonna del Sacco* (1525). The church is situated on the northern flank of **Piazza della Santissima Annunziata**, one of the finest Renaissance squares in Florence. Designed by Brunelleschi, the delicate nine-bay arcade fronts the Spedale degli Innocenti to its right, while at the center of the square stands a bronze equestrian statue of Duke Ferdinando I. Started by Giambologna, it was finished in 1608 by his assistant Pietro Tacca (who designed the square's bronze fountains).

❹ Museo Archeologico

Via della Colonna 36. **Map** 2 E4. **Tel** 055 235 75. **Open** 8:30am–7pm Tue–Fri, 8:30am–2pm Sat & Sun. **Closed** Jan 1, May 1, Dec 25.

The Archaeological Museum in Florence is in a palazzo built by Giulio Parigi for the Princess Maria Maddalena de' Medici in 1620. It now exhibits an outstanding collection of Etruscan, Greek, Roman, and Egyptian artifacts, although parts of the collection are being restored following the flood in 1966.

The first floor contains a splendid series of Etruscan bronzes as well as the famous *Chimera* (4th century BC), a mythical lion with a goat's head imposed on its body and a serpent for a tail.

Etruscan warrior, Museo Archeologico

Equally impressive is the 1st-century *Arringatore* bronze found near Lake Trasimeno in Umbria. It is inscribed with the name of Aulus Metellus.

A large section on the second floor is dedicated to Greek vases, notably the famed François Vase, found in an Etruscan tomb near Chiusi.

❺ Spedale degli Innocenti

Piazza della Santissima Annunziata 12. **Map** 2 E4. **Tel** 055 203 73 08. **Open** 8:30am–7pm daily. **Closed** Jan 1, Easter, Dec 25.

Named after Herod's biblical Massacre of the Innocents, the "Hospital" opened in 1444 as Europe's first orphanage. Part of the building is still used for this purpose. Brunelleschi's arcaded loggia is decorated with glazed terracotta roundels, added by Andrea della Robbia around 1498, showing babies wrapped in swaddling bands. At the left end of the portico you can see the *rota*, a rotating stone cylinder on which anonymous mothers could place their unwanted children and ring the bell for them to be admitted to the orphanage.

Within the building lie two elegant cloisters: the **Chiostro degli Uomini** (Men's Cloister), built between 1422 and 1445 and decorated with *sgraffito* roosters and cherubs, and the smaller Women's Cloister (1438). A small upstairs gallery contains a handful of fine works, including terracottas by della Robbia and pictures by Botticelli, Piero di Cosimo, and Domenico Ghirlandaio.

Part of Brunelleschi's arcaded loggia, Spedale degli Innocenti

Street by Street: Around the Duomo

While much of Florence was rebuilt during the Renaissance, the eastern part of the city retains a distinctly medieval feel. With its maze of tiny alleys, it is an area that would still be familiar to Dante (1265–1321), whose birthplace allegedly lay somewhere among these lanes. The poet would recognize the church of Santa Maria de' Cerchi, where he first glimpsed Beatrice, as well as the gaunt outlines of the Bargello. He would also be familiar with the Baptistry, one of the city's oldest buildings, though he would not know the Campanile nor the Duomo, whose foundations were laid in the poet's old age.

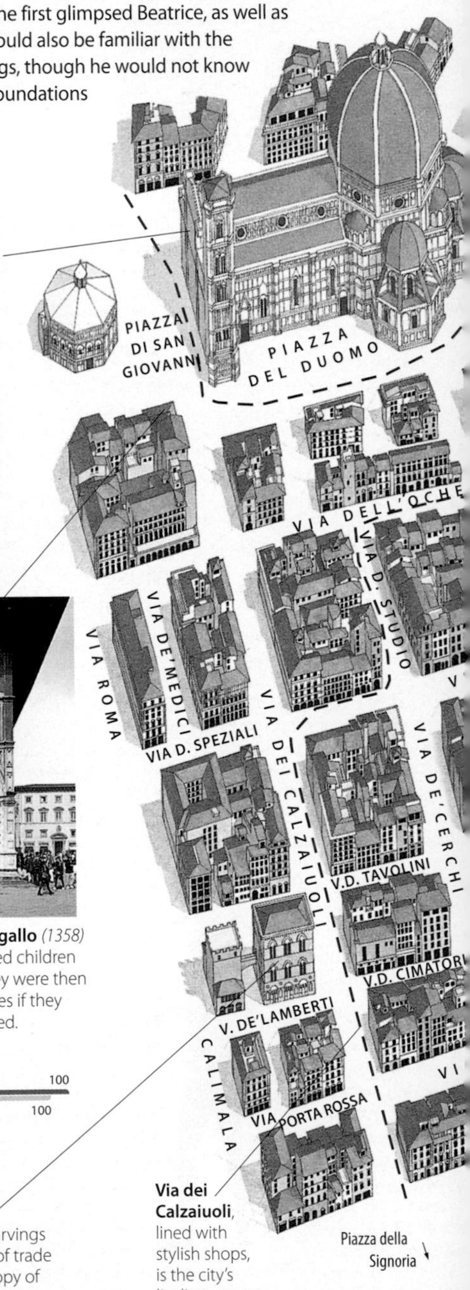

7 ★ Duomo and Baptistry
The exteriors of the Duomo and Baptistry are richly decorated with marbles and reliefs, such as this detail from the Duomo's façade.

The Loggia del Bigallo *(1358)* is where abandoned children were once left. They were then sent to foster homes if they remained unclaimed.

Key

— Suggested route

0 meters 100

0 yards 100

8 Orsanmichele
The church's niche carvings depict patron saints of trade guilds, such as this copy of Donatello's *St. George.*

Via dei Calzaiuoli, lined with stylish shops, is the city's liveliest street.

Piazza della Signoria

❻ **Museo dell'Opera del Duomo**
Works from the Duomo, Campanile, and Baptistry are displayed in this museum.

Locator Map
See Florence Street Finder map 6

Pegna sells a range of fine wines, oil, and honey.

Badia Fiorentina, the abbey church founded in 978, is home to *The Virgin Appearing to St. Bernard* (1485) by Filippino Lippi.

Casa di Dante, a restored medieval house, is reputedly Dante's birthplace.

❾ ★ **Bargello**
The city's old prison is home to a rich collection of applied arts and sculpture, including this figure of *Mercury* by Giambologna (1564).

Carving from Luca della Robbia's choir loft in the Museo dell'Opera

❻ Museo dell'Opera del Duomo

Piazza del Duomo **Map** 2 D5 (6 E2). **Tel** 055 230 28 85. **Open** 9am–7:30pm daily (to 1:40pm Sun & public hols) (last adm: 40 mins before closing). **Closed** Jan 1, Easter, Dec 25.

The Cathedral Works Museum has reopened after extensive remodeling, and now a series of rooms is dedicated to the history of the Duomo. The main ground-floor room holds statues from Arnolfo di Cambio's workshop that were once placed in the cathedral's niches. Nearby is Donatello's *St. John*. Another room contains 14th- and 15th-century religious paintings and reliquaries.

Michelangelo's *Pietà* has pride of place on the staircase. The hooded figure of Nicodemus is widely believed to be a self-portrait.

The first room on the upper floor contains two choir lofts, dating to the 1430s, by Luca della Robbia and Donatello. Carved in crisp white marble and decorated with colored glass and mosaic, both depict children playing musical instruments and dancing. Other works by Donatello in this room are his statue of *La Maddalena* (1455) and several Old Testament figures.

The room to the left contains an exhibition of the tablets that used to decorate the bell tower. A lower level houses examples of the tools used by Brunelleschi's workmen and a copy of di Cambio's original cathedral façade.

❼ Duomo and Baptistry

Rising above the heart of the city, the richly-decorated Duomo – Santa Maria del Fiore – and its orange-tiled dome have become Florence's most famous symbols. Typical of the Florentine determination to lead in all things, the cathedral is Europe's fourth-largest church, and to this day it remains the city's tallest building. The Baptistry, with its celebrated bronze doors, may date back to the 4th century, making it one of Florence's oldest buildings. The Campanile, designed by Giotto in 1334, was completed in 1359, 22 years after his death.

Campanile
At 276 ft (85 m) the Campanile is 20 ft (6 m) shorter than the dome. It is clad in white, green, and pink Tuscan marble.

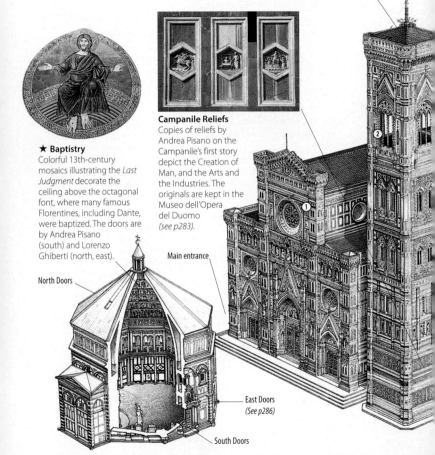

★ Baptistry
Colorful 13th-century mosaics illustrating the *Last Judgment* decorate the ceiling above the octagonal font, where many famous Florentines, including Dante, were baptized. The doors are by Andrea Pisano (south) and Lorenzo Ghiberti (north, east).

Campanile Reliefs
Copies of reliefs by Andrea Pisano on the Campanile's first story depict the Creation of Man, and the Arts and the Industries. The originals are kept in the Museo dell'Opera del Duomo *(see p283)*.

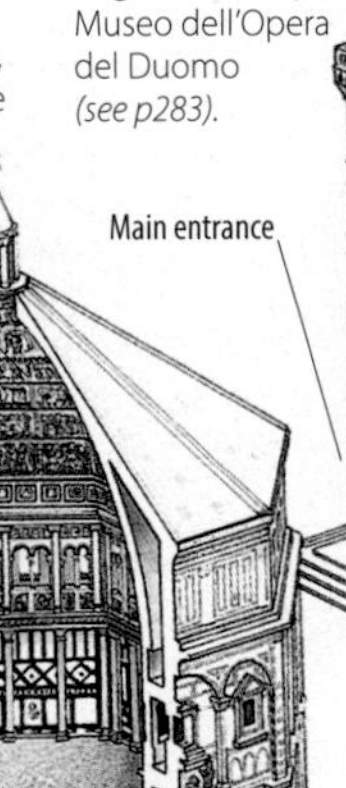

KEY

① **The Neo-Gothic marble facade** echoes the style of Giotto's Campanile, but was only added in 1871–87.

② **Gothic windows**

③ **The top of the dome** offers spectacular views over the city.

④ **The *Last Judgment*** frescoes (1572–4) by Vasari were completed by Zuccari.

⑤ **Bricks were set** between marble ribs in a self-supporting herringbone pattern – a technique Brunelleschi copied from the Pantheon in Rome.

⑥ **The marble sanctuary** around the High Altar was created by Bacci Bandinelli in 1555.

★ Dome by Brunelleschi
Brunelleschi's dome, finished in 1463, was the largest of its time to be built without scaffolding. The outer shell is supported by a thicker inner shell that acts as a platform for it.

3

4

5

6

Entrance leading to the dome

VISITORS' CHECKLIST

Practical Information
Piazza del Duomo.
Map 2 D5 (6 E2).
Tel 055 230 28 85.
Cathedral: **Open** 10am–5pm Mon–Sat (4:30pm Thu, 4:45pm Sat), 1:30–4:45pm Sun. Crypt: **Open** 10am–5pm Mon–Sat (4:45pm Sat). Baptistry: **Open** 12:15–7pm Mon–Sat, 8:30am–2pm Sun. Dome: **Open** 8:30am–7pm Mon–Sat (5:40pm Sat). Campanile: **Open** 8:30am– 7:30pm daily. All buildings: **Closed** Jan 1, Easter, Aug 15, Sep 8, Dec 25.
operaduomo.firenze.it

Transportation
1, 6, 14, 17, 23

Chapels at the East End
The three apses, crowned by smaller copies of the dome, have five chapels each. The 15th-century stained glass is by Ghiberti.

rble Pavement
e colorful, intricately inlaid pavement
th century) was designed in part by Baccio
gnolo and Francesco da Sangallo.

Dante Explaining the Divine Comedy *(1465)*
This painting by Michelino shows the poet outside Florence against a backdrop of Purgatory, Hell, and Paradise.

The East Doors of the Baptistry

Lorenzo Ghiberti's famous bronze Baptistry doors were commissioned in 1401 to mark the city's deliverance from the plague. Ghiberti was chosen to make a set of new doors after a competition that involved seven leading artists, including Donatello, Jacopo della Quercia, and Brunelleschi. The trial panels by Ghiberti and Brunelleschi are so different from Florentine Gothic art of the time, notably in the use of perspective and individuality of figures, that they are often regarded as the first works of the Renaissance.

Ghiberti's winning panel

"Gate of Paradise"
Having spent 21 years working on the North Doors, Ghiberti was commissioned to make the East Doors (1424–1452). Michelangelo enthusiastically dubbed them the "Gate of Paradise." The original 10 relief panels showing scriptural subjects are now exhibited in the Museo dell'Opera del Duomo *(see p283)*; those on the Baptistry are copies.

Abraham and the Sacrifice of Isaac
The jagged modeled rocks symbolizing Abraham's pain are carefully arranged to emphasize the sacrificial act.

Joseph Sold into Slavery
Ghiberti, a master of perspective, formed the architectural elements in shallower relief behind the figures to create the illusion of depth in the scene.

Key to the East Doors

1	2
3	4
5	6
7	8
9	10

1 Adam and Eve Are Expelled from Eden
2 Cain Murders His Brother, Abel
3 The Drunkenness of Noah and His Sacrifice
4 Abraham and the Sacrifice of Isaac
5 Esau and Jacob
6 Joseph Sold into Slavery
7 Moses Receives the Ten Commandments
8 The Fall of Jericho
9 The Battle with the Philistines
10 Solomon and the Queen of Sheba

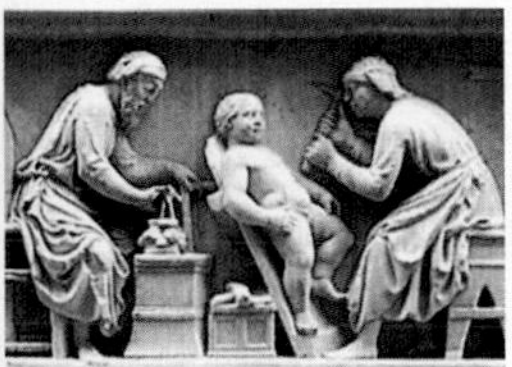

Detail of carvings by Donatello on the wall of Orsanmichele

❽ Orsanmichele

Via dell'Arte della Lana. **Map** 3 C1 (6 D3). **Tel** 055 28 49 44. **Open** 10am–5pm daily. **Closed** Jan 1, May 1, Mon in Aug, Dec 25.

Built in 1337 as a grain market, Orsanmichele was later converted into a church which took its name from *Orto di San Michele*, a monastic garden long since vanished. The arcades of the market became windows, which are today bricked in, but the original Gothic tracery can still be seen. The decoration was entrusted to Florence's major *Arti* (guilds). Over 60 years they commissioned sculptures of their patron saints to adorn the 14 exterior niches; however today many of the figures are copies. Among the sculptors were Lorenzo Ghiberti, Donatello, and Verrocchio.

The beautifully tranquil interior contains an opulent 14th-century altar by Andrea Orcagna, a *Virgin and Child* by Bernardo Daddi (1348), and a statue of the *Madonna and Child with St. Anne* by Francesco da Sangallo (1522).

Brunelleschi's *Sacrifice of Isaac* (1402) in the Bargello

❾ Bargello

Via del Proconsolo 4. **Map** 4 D1 (6 E3). **Tel** 055 29 48 83. 14, A. **Open** 8:15am–5pm daily. **Closed** 2nd & 4th Mon of each month; Jan 1, May 1, Dec 25.

Florence's second-ranking museum after the Uffizi, the Bargello contains a wonderful medley of applied arts and Italy's finest collection of Renaissance sculpture. Begun in 1255, the fortresslike building was initially the town hall (making it the oldest seat of government in the city), but later became a prison and home to the chief of police (the *Bargello*). It also became known for its executions, which took place in the main courtyard until 1786, when the death sentence was abolished by Grand Duke Pietro Leopoldo. Following extensive renovation, the building opened as one of Italy's first national museums in 1865.

The key exhibits range over three floors, beginning with the Michelangelo Room, superbly redesigned after extensive damage during the 1966 flood. Three contrasting works by Michelangelo lie dotted around the room, the most famous a tipsy-looking *Bacchus* (1497), the sculptor's first large freestanding work. Close by is a powerful bust of *Brutus* (1539–40), the only known portrait bust by Michelangelo, and a beautifully delicate circular relief depicting the *Madonna and Child* (1503–5). Countless works by other sculptors occupy the same room. Among them is an exquisite *Mercury* (1564) by the Mannerist genius, Giambologna, as well as several virtuoso bronzes by the sculptor and goldsmith Benvenuto Cellini (1500–71).

Across the courtyard, full of fragments and the coats of arms of the Bargello's various incumbents, two more rooms contain exterior sculptures removed from sites around the city. The courtyard's external staircase leads to the first floor, which opens with a wonderfully eccentric bronze menagerie by Giambologna. To the right is the Salone del Consiglio Generale, a cavernous former courtroom that contains the cream of the museum's Early Renaissance sculpture. Foremost among its highlights is Donatello's heroic *St. George* (1416) – the epitome of "youth, courage, and valor of arms" in the words of Vasari. Commissioned by the Armorers' Guild, the statue was brought here from Orsanmichele in 1892. At the center of the room, in direct contrast, is Donatello's androgynous *David* (c.1430), famous as the first freestanding nude by a Western artist since antiquity. Among the room's more easily missed works, tucked away on the right wall, are two reliefs depicting *The Sacrifice of Isaac* (1402). Created by Brunelleschi and Lorenzo Ghiberti respectively, both were entries in the competition to design the Baptistry doors.

Donatello's *David* (c.1430) in the Bargello

Beyond the Salone, the Bargello's emphasis shifts to the applied arts, with room after room devoted to rugs, ceramics, silverware, and a host of other beautiful *objets d'art*. The most celebrated of these rooms is the Salone del Camino on the second floor, which features the finest collection of small bronzes in Italy. Some are reproductions of antique models, others are small copies of Renaissance statues. Giambologna, Cellini, and Antonio del Pollaiuolo are among those represented.

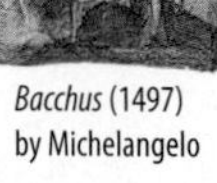

Bacchus (1497) by Michelangelo

⑩ Santa Croce

Work began around 1294 on the Gothic church of Santa Croce, which contains tombs and monuments of famous Florentines, such as Michelangelo, Galileo, and Machiavelli, as well as radiant early 14th-century frescoes by Giotto and his pupil Taddeo Gaddi. In the cloister alongside the church stands the Cappella de' Pazzi (Pazzi Chapel), a Renaissance masterpiece designed by Filippo Brunelleschi.

★ Cappella de' Pazzi
Brunelleschi's domed chapel with Classical proportions was begun in 1443. The roundels (*c.* 1442–52) are by Luca della Robbia.

Tomb of Leonardo Bruni (1447)
Rossellino's effigy of this great humanist was unusual in its sensitive realism and lack of monumental pomp.

Cimabue's Crucifixion
Badly damaged in the flood of 1966, this 13th-century masterpiece is among the highlights of the collection, as is Taddeo Gaddi's magnificent *Last Supper* (*c.* 1355–60).

Ticket booth and entrance

Exit

KEY

① **Refectory**

② ***Tree of Life*** **by Taddeo Gaddi**

③ **Vasari's Tomb of Michelangio** is decorated with figures representing sculpture and architecture.

④ **The Neo-Gothic facade** by Niccolò Matas was added in 1863.

⑤ **Tomb of Galileo**

⑥ **Tomb of Machiavelli**

⑦ ***Annunciation*** **by Donatello (15th century)**

⑧ **The Cappella Baroncelli**, frescoed by Taddeo Gaddi between 1332 and 1338, contains the first true night scene in Western art.

⑨ **Sacristy**

⑩ **The Neo-Gothic campanile** was added in 1842, after the original was destroyed in 1512 by lightning.

VISITORS' CHECKLIST

Practical Information
Piazza di Santa Croce. **Map** 4 E1 (6 F4). **Tel** 055 246 61 05. Basilica: **Open** 9:30am–5:30pm daily (from 2pm Sun). Ticket office closes at 5pm. **Closed** during mass. (includes visit to the Museo.) Museo, Cloister & Cappella de' Pazzi: **Open** as above. **Closed** Jan 1, Easter, Jun 13, Oct 4, Dec 25 & 26. (includes visit to the Basilica.)

Transportation
C2, C3.

★ **Cappella Bardi Frescoes**
Giotto frescoed the Bardi and Peruzzi chapels to the right of the high altar between 1315 and 1330. This touching scene from the left-hand wall of the chapel shows *The Death of St. Francis* (1317).

⓫ Museo Galileo

Piazza de' Giudici 1. **Map** 4 D1 (6 E4). **Tel** 055 26 53 11. **Open** 9:30am–6pm daily (to 1pm Tue). **Closed** 1 & 6 Jan, May 1, Easter, Jun 24, Aug 13, Nov 1 & 8, Dec 25 & 26.

This lively and superbly presented museum devotes two floors to various scientific themes, illustrating each with countless fine displays and a panoply of old and beautifully made scientific instruments. It is also something of a shrine to the Pisa-born scientist Galileo Galilei (1564–1642), and houses the only surviving instruments he designed and built, including two telescopes and the objective lens from the telescope with which he discovered Jupiter's moons.

Astrolabe, Museo Galileo

A number of rooms are devoted to astronomical, mathematical, and navigational instruments, with galleries concentrating on Galileo, telescopes, and optical games. The museum also houses the scientific collections of the two dynasties that once ruled Florence: the Medici and the House of Lorraine.

Some of the best exhibits on display are early maps, globes and astrolabes, antique microscopes, thermometers, and barometers. There are also some fine old clocks, mathematical instruments, calculators, a horrifying collection of 19th-century surgical instruments, and some graphic anatomical models. The museum has installed a large bronze sundial outside the entrance that can be used to read the hour and the date.

⓬ Ponte Vecchio

Map 4 D1 (6 E4).

Ponte Vecchio, the oldest surviving bridge in the city, was built in 1345, the last in a succession of bridges and fords on the site that dated back to Roman times. Designed by Giotto's pupil Taddeo Gaddi, it was originally the domain of blacksmiths, butchers, and tanners (who used the river for disposing of waste). They were reviled for their noise and stench and were evicted in 1593 by Duke Ferdinando I and replaced by jewelers and goldsmiths. The elevated Corridoio Vasariano runs along the eastern side of the bridge, above the shops. Giorgio Vasari designed the corridor in 1565 to allow the Medici family to move about their residences without having to mix with the public. This was the city's only bridge to escape destruction during World War II and visitors today come as much to admire the views as to browse among the antique shops and specialty jewelry stores. A bust of the famous goldsmith Benvenuto Cellini stands in the middle of the bridge.

Ponte Vecchio viewed from the Ponte Santa Trinità

⓭ Uffizi

The Uffizi, Italy's greatest art gallery, was built in 1560–80 to house offices *(uffici)* for Duke Cosimo I. The architect Vasari used iron as reinforcement, enabling his successor, Buontalenti, to create an almost continuous wall of glass on the upper story. This was used as a gallery for Francesco I to display the Medici art treasures. In the 19th century the collection's ancient objects were moved to the archaeological museum and sculpture to the Bargello, leaving a priceless collection of paintings. Continuing renovations may mean some room closures; check the website for details.

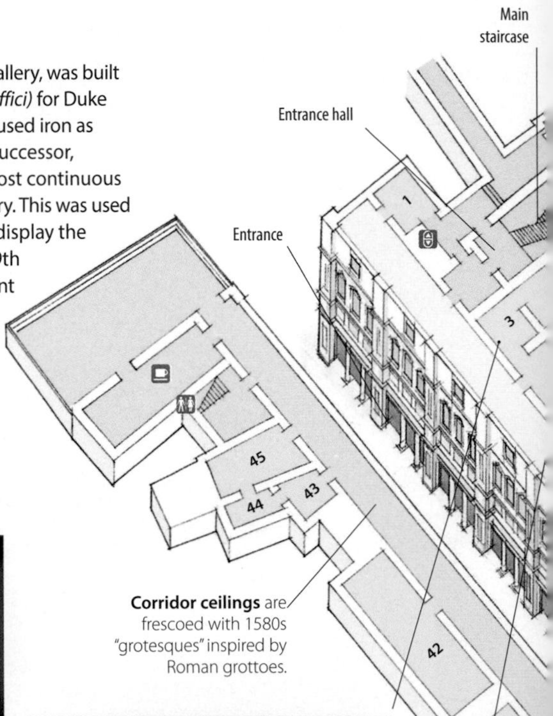

Main staircase

Entrance hall

Entrance

1

3

45

44

43

42

41

38

31

Corridor ceilings are frescoed with 1580s "grotesques" inspired by Roman grottoes.

Buontalenti staircase

Bacchus *(c. 1589)*
Caravaggio's early work depicting the god of wine can be found in the first floor exhibition rooms. The mood of dissipation is echoed in the foreground in the decaying fruit.

Annunciation *(1333)*
The Sienese painter Simone Martini was strongly influenced by French Gothic art, and this is one of his masterpieces. The two saints are by Martini's pupil and brother-in-law, Lippo Memmi.

Ognissanti Madonna *(c. 1310)*
Giotto's grasp of spatial depth and substance in this altarpiece was a milestone in the mastery of perspective.

Gallery Guide

Ancient Greek and Roman sculptures are in the second floor corridor around the inner side of the horseshoe-shaped building. The paintings are hung in a series of rooms off the main corridor, in chronological order, to show the development of Florentine art from Gothic to Renaissance and beyond. Many well-known paintings are in rooms 7–18. Restoration work may result in some exhibits being moved around the gallery and some being loaned to other galleries.

Key to Floor Plan

- East Corridor
- West Corridor
- Arno Corridor
- Gallery rooms 1–45
- Nonexhibition space

For hotels and restaurants in this region see pp562–77 and pp580–605

The Duke and Duchess of Urbino *(c. 1465–70)*
Piero della Francesca's portraits of Federico da Montefeltro and his wife Battista Sforza were painted after Battista died at age 26. Her portrait was probably based on her death mask.

VISITORS' CHECKLIST

Practical Information
Piazzale degli Uffizi 6. **Map** 4 D1 (6 D4). **Tel** 055 238 86 51 (info); 055 29 48 83 (reservations; book in advance to avoid the lines). **Open** 8:15am–6:50pm Tue–Sun (occasional extended hours in summer). Last adm: 45 mins before closing. **Closed** Jan 1, May 1, Dec 25.
uffizi.firenze.it

Transportation
B, 23.

The Tribune, decorated in red and gold, contains the works most valued by the Medici.

The Birth of Venus *(c. 1485)*
Botticelli shows the goddess of love flanked by Zephyrus, god of the west wind, who blows the risen Venus to shore on a half-shell. The myth may symbolize the birth of beauty through the divine fertilization of matter.

The Holy Family *(1507)*
Michelangelo's painting, the first to break with the convention of showing Christ on the Virgin's lap, inspired Mannerist artists through its expressive handling of color and posture.

Vasari's Classical Arno facade (begun 1560)

The Venus of Urbino *(1538)*
Titian's sensuous nude, inspired by Giorgione's *Sleeping Venus*, may in fact be a portrait of a courtesan deemed sufficiently beautiful to represent a goddess.

The Vasari Corridor is a passageway across the Arno to the Pitti Palace.

Exploring the Uffizi

The Uffizi offers not only the chance to see the world's greatest collection of Italian Renaissance paintings, but also the opportunity to enjoy masterpieces from as far afield as Holland, Spain, and Germany. Accumulated over the centuries by the Medici, the collection was first housed in the Uffizi in 1581, and eventually bequeathed to the Florentine people by Anna Maria Lodovica, the last of the Medici.

Madonna and Child with Angels (1455–66) by Fra Filippo Lippi

Gothic Art

Past the statues and antiquities of room 1, the Uffizi proper opens in style with three altarpieces of the *Maestà*, or Madonna Enthroned, by Giotto, Duccio, and Cimabue, some of Italy's greatest 13th-century painters. Each work marks a stage in the development of Italian painting away from the stilted conventions of Byzantium to the livelier traditions of Gothic and Renaissance art. The shift is best expressed in Giotto's version of the subject (known as the *Ognissanti Madonna*), where new feeling for depth and naturalistic detail is shown in the range of emotion displayed by the saints and angels, and by the carefully evoked three-dimensionality of the Virgin's throne.

Giotto's naturalistic influence can also be seen among the paintings of room 4, which is devoted to the 14th-century Florentine School, an interesting counterpoint to the Sienese paintings of Duccio and his followers in room 3. Among the many fine paintings here are works by Ambrogio and Pietro Lorenzetti, and Simone Martini's *Annunciation.*

Room 6 is devoted to International Gothic, a highly decorative style that represented the height of Gothic expression. It is exemplified by Gentile da Fabriano's exquisite, glittering *Adoration of the Magi* painted in 1423.

Early Renaissance

A new understanding of geometry and perspective during the 15th century increasingly allowed artists to explore the complexities of space and depth. None became more obsessed with these new compositional possibilities than Paolo Uccello (1397–1475), whose picture of *The Battle of San Romano* (1456) in room 7 is one of the gallery's most fevered creations.

Room 7 also contains two panels from 1460 by Piero della Francesca, another artist preoccupied with the art of perspective. The panels, which are among the earliest Renaissance portraits, depict the Duke and Duchess of Urbino on one side and representations of their virtues on the other.

While such works can seem coldly experimental, Fra Filippo Lippi's *Madonna and Child with Angels* (1455–66), in room 8, is a masterpiece of warmth and humanity. Like many Renaissance artists, Lippi uses

Sandro Botticelli's allegorical painting, *Primavera* (1480)

For hotels and restaurants in this region see pp562–77 and pp580–605

a religious subject to celebrate earthly delights such as landscape and feminine beauty. A similar approach is apparent in the works of Botticelli, whose famous paintings in rooms 10–14 are for many the highlight of the gallery. In *The Birth of Venus*, for example, Venus takes the place of the Virgin, expressing a fascination with Classical mythology common to many Renaissance artists. The same is true of the *Primavera* (1480), which breaks with Christian religious painting by illustrating a pagan rite of spring.

Detail from *The Annunciation* (1472–5) by Leonardo da Vinci

High Renaissance and Mannerism

Room 15 features works attributed to the young Leonardo da Vinci, notably a sublime *Annunciation* (1472–5), which reveals hints of his still emerging style, and the *Adoration of the Magi* (1481), which remained unfinished when he left Florence for Milan to paint *The Last Supper* (1495–8).

Room 18, better known as the Tribune, was designed in 1584 by Buontalenti in order to accommodate the best-loved pieces of the Medici collection. Its most famous work is the so-called Medici Venus (1st century BC), a Roman copy of a Greek statue deemed to be the most erotic in the ancient world. The copy proved equally salacious and was removed from Rome's Villa Medici by Cosimo III to keep it from corrupting the city's art students. Other highlights in room 18 include Agnolo Bronzino's portraits of *Cosimo I* and *Eleonora di Toledo*, both painted around 1545, and Pontormo's *Charity* (1530) and the portrait of *Cosimo il Vecchio* (1517).

Rooms 19 to 23 depart from the gallery's Florentine bias, demonstrating how rapidly Renaissance ideas and techniques spread beyond Tuscany. Painters from the German and Flemish schools are well represented, together with painters from Umbria like Perugino, but perhaps the most captivating works are the paintings by Venetian and northern Italian artists such as Mantegna, Carpaccio, Correggio, and Bellini.

Room 25, which returns to the Tuscan mainstream, is dominated by Michelangelo's *Holy Family* or Doni Tondo (1456), notable for its vibrant colors and the Virgin's unusually twisted pose. The gallery's only work by Michelangelo, it was to prove immensely influential with the next generation of painters, especially Bronzino (1503–72), Pontormo (1494–1556), and Parmigianino (1503–40). The last of these was responsible for the *Madonna of the Long Neck* (c.1534) in room 29. With its contorted anatomy, unnatural colors and strange composition, this painting is a masterpiece of the style that came to be called Mannerism. Earlier, but no less remarkable masterpieces in rooms 26 and 28 include

Madonna of the Goldfinch (1506) by Raphael

Madonna of the Long Neck (c. 1534) by Parmigianino

Raphael's sublime *Madonna of the Goldfinch* (1506) and Titian's notorious *Venus of Urbino* (1538), censured by Mark Twain as the "foulest, the vilest, the obscenest picture the world possesses." Others hold it to be one of the most beautiful nudes ever painted.

Later Paintings

Visitors, already sated by a surfeit of outstanding paintings, are often tempted to skim through the Uffizi's final rooms. The paintings in rooms 30 to 35 – which are mainly from the Veneto and Emilia-Romagna – are mostly unexceptional, but the gallery's last rooms (41–45) contain important paintings. Rooms 41 and 42 have works by Rubens and Van Dyck. Room 44, dedicated to Rembrandt and northern European painting, features Rembrandt's *Portrait of an Old Man* (1665) and two self-portraits of the artist as a young and old man (painted in 1634 and 1664, respectively). Rooms on the first floor hold works by Caravaggio. These include *Medusa* (1596–8), painted for a Roman cardinal; *Bacchus* (c.1589), one of the artist's earliest works; and the *Sacrifice of Isaac* (c.1590), whose violent subject is belied by the painting's gentle background landscape. These rooms also hold works by Guido Reni.

⓮ Piazza della Signoria

Piazza della Signoria and Palazzo Vecchio have been at the heart of Florence's political and social life for centuries. The great bell once used to summon citizens to *parlamento* (public meetings) here, and the square has long been a popular promenade for both visitors and Florentines. The piazza's statues (some are copies) commemorate the city's major historical events, though its most famous episode is celebrated by a simple sidewalk plaque near the loggia: the execution of the religious leader Girolamo Savonarola, who was burned at the stake.

David
This copy of the famous Michelangelo statue symbolizes triumph over tyranny. The original *(see p279)* stood in the piazza until 1873.

Heraldic Frieze
The crossed keys on this shield represent Medici papal rule.

KEY

① **The Fontana di Nettuno**, created by Ammannati (1575), is of the Roman sea god surrounded by water nymphs and commemorates Tuscan naval victories.

② **Sala dei Gigli**

③ **The Uffizi**

④ **The Loggia dei Lanzi**, designed by Orcagna (1382), is named after the Lancers, the bodyguards of Cosimo I who were billeted here.

⑤ **Roman statues**, possibly of emperors, line the Loggia.

⑥ **The Marzocco** is a copy of the heraldic lion of Florence carved by Donatello in 1420. The original is in the Bargello *(see p287)*.

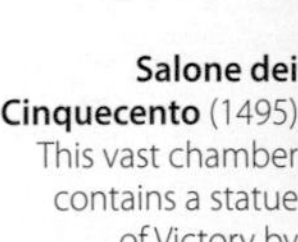

Salone dei Cinquecento (1495)
This vast chamber contains a statue of Victory by Michelangelo and frescoes by Vasari describing Florentine triumphs over Pisa and Siena.

★ **Palazzo Vecchio** (completed 1332)
his Republican frieze over the palace entrance is nscribed with the words, "Christ is King," implying hat no mortal ruler has absolute power.

★ **The Rape of the Sabine Women by Giambologna** (1583)
The writhing figures in Giambologna's famous statue were carved from a single block of flawed marble.

★ **Perseus by Cellini**
This bronze statue (1554) of Perseus beheading Medusa was intended to warn Cosimo I's enemies of their probable fate.

⓯ Palazzo Vecchio

Piazza della Signoria (entrance on via della Ninna). **Map** 4 D1 (6 D3). **Tel** 055 276 83 25. A, B. **Open** Apr–Sep: 9am–midnight (to 2pm Thu); Oct–Mar: 9am–7pm (to 2pm Thu). **Closed** Jan 1, Easter, May 1, Aug 15, Dec 25. Secret Itineraries & Children's Museum (by reservation only). **Tel** 055 276 83 25.

The "Old Palace" still fulfills its original role as town hall. It was completed in 1322 when a huge bell, used to call citizens to meetings or warn of fire, flood, or enemy attack, was hauled to the top of the imposing bell tower. While retaining much of its medieval appearance, the interior was remodeled for Duke Cosimo I in 1540. The redecoration was undertaken by Vasari, who incorporated bombastic frescoes (1563–5) of Florentine achievements. Michelangelo's *Victory* statue (1525) graces the Salone dei Cinquecento, which also has a tiny study decorated by Florence's leading Mannerist painters in 1569–1573.

Other highlights include the Cappella di Eleonora, painted by Bronzino (1540–45); the loggia, with its views over the city; the Sala dei Gigli (Room of Lilies) with Donatello's *Judith and Holofernes* (c. 1455); and frescoes of Roman heroes by Ghirlandaio (1485); as well as the excellent museum for children and the secret rooms and passageways.

A copy of Verrocchio's Putto fountain in Vasari's courtyard

Street by Street: Around Piazza della Repubblica

Underlying the street plan of modern Florence is the far older pattern of the ancient Roman city. Nowhere is this more evident than in the grid of narrow streets around Piazza della Repubblica, site of the old Roman forum. This pivotal square housed the city's main food market until the 1860s, when redevelopment tidied up the area, and added the triumphal arch that now stands in today's café-filled square.

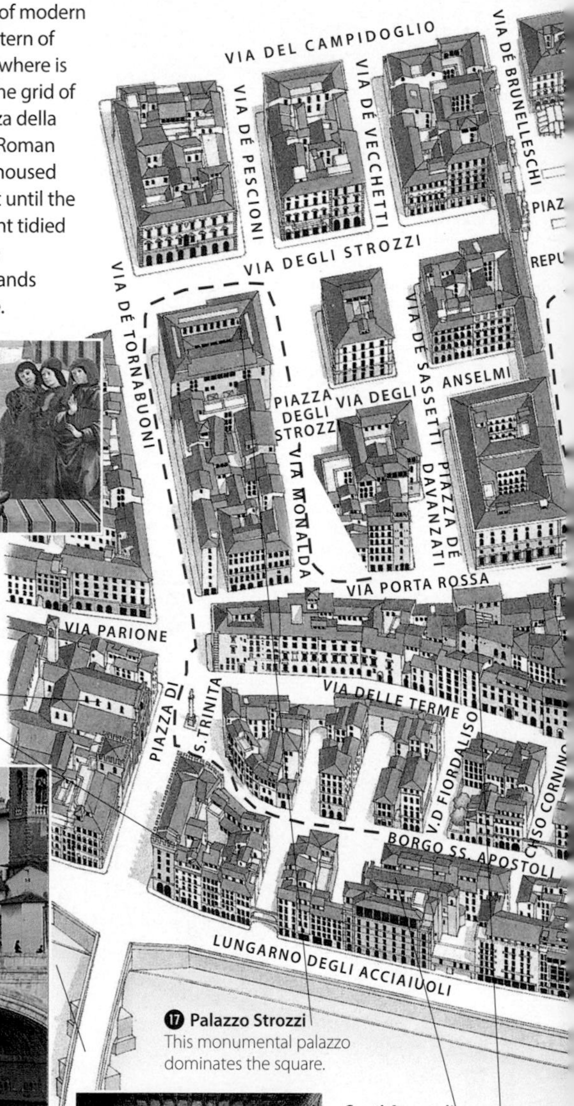

Santa Trìnita has frescoes by Ghirlandaio on the Life of St. Francis (1486), depicting events that took place in this area. Here, a child is revived after falling from the Palazzo Spini-Ferroni.

Palazzo Spini-Ferroni

Ponte Santa Trìnita was built in wood in 1290 and then rebuilt by Ammannati in 1567 to celebrate the defeat of Siena.

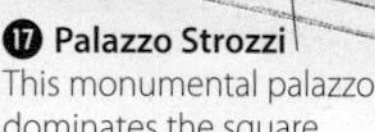

17 Palazzo Strozzi
This monumental palazzo dominates the square.

Santi Apostoli was reputedly founded by Charlemagne.

16 Palazzo Davanzati
Frescoes with exotic birds decorate the Sala dei Pappagalli, which was once the dining room of this 14th-century palazzo.

Key

— Suggested route

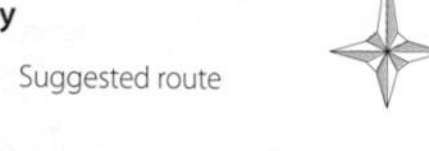

Locator Map
See Florence Street Finder maps 5, 6

Piazza della Repubblica, which dates from the 19th century, is lined by some of Florence's oldest and best known cafés.

Mercato Nuovo, the "New Market" (1547), now deals mainly in souvenirs.

VIA POR SANTA MARIA

Palazzo di Parte Guelfa was the headquarters of the Guelphs, the dominant political party of medieval Florence.

Ponte Vecchio
(See p289)

Detail of a frieze illustrating a medieval romance in Palazzo Davanzati

⓰ Palazzo Davanzati

Via Porta Rossa 13. **Map** 3 C1 (5 C3). **Tel** 055 238 86 10. **Open** 8:15am–1:50pm daily. **Closed** 1st, 3rd, & 5th Mon and 2nd and 4th Sun of the month, Jan 1, May 1, Dec 25. 10am, 11am, noon (2nd floor only).

This wonderful museum, also known as the Museo dell'Antica Casa Fiorentina, uses original fittings and furniture to recreate a typical well-to-do 14th-century town house. Among the highlights are the Salone Madornale, where large gatherings would have been held, and the Sala dei Pappagalli (Parrots Room), with its frescoes and rich tapestries.

Pelting holes in the vaulted ceiling of the entrance courtyard were for dropping missiles on unwanted visitors. In one corner of the inner courtyard is a well and a pulley system to raise pails of water to each floor – a real luxury since most medieval households had to fetch water from a public fountain.

⓱ Palazzo Strozzi

Piazza degli Strozzi. **Map** 3 C1 (5 C3). **Tel** 055 264 51 55. **Open** 9am–8pm daily (to 11pm Thu) for exhibitions. **W palazzostrozzi.org**

Sheer size accounts for the impact of the Palazzo Strozzi, and although it is only three stories high, each floor exceeds the height of a normal palazzo. It was commissioned by the wealthy banker Filippo Strozzi, who had 15 buildings demolished to make way for the palazzo. He hoped it would rival the Medici palaces elsewhere in the city. Strozzi died in 1491, just two years after the first stone was laid.

Work on the building continued until 1536, with three major architects contributing to its design – Giuliano da Sangallo, Benedetto da Maiano, and Simone del Pollaiuolo (also known as Cronaca). The exterior, built of huge rusticated masonry blocks, remains unspoiled. Look out for the original Renaissance torch-holders and lamps and the rings for tethering horses that still adorn the corners and facades. The palace is now primarily used as an exhibition venue, when visitors can also access "La Strozzina," a vaulted gallery space in the basement, where small temporary exhibitions are held.

Exterior of Palazzo Strozzi, with masonry block rustication

⑱ San Lorenzo

San Lorenzo was the parish church of the Medici family, and in 1419 Brunelleschi was commissioned to rebuild it in the Classical style of the Renaissance. Almost a century later, Michelangelo submitted some plans for the facade and began work on the Medici tombs in the Sagrestia Nuova (the Old Sacristy). He also designed a library, the Biblioteca Mediceo-Laurenziana, to house the family's collection of manuscripts. The lavish family mausoleum, the Cappella dei Principi, was started in 1604.

Cappella dei Principi
The Medici mausoleum, behind the high altar, was begun in 1604 by Matteo Nigetti, and forms part of the Cappelle Medicee.

Biblioteca Staircase
Michelangelo's Mannerist staircase, one of the artist's most innovative designs, was built by Ammannati in 1559.

KEY

① **St. Joseph and Christ in the Workshop**, a striking work showing the young Christ with his father, is by Pietro Annigoni (1910–88), one of the few modern artists whose work is seen in Florence.

② **The cloister garden** is planted with boxwood hedges and pomegranate and orange trees.

③ **Michelangelo** designed the desks and ceiling of the Biblioteca, where exhibitions of Medici manuscripts are often held.

④ **The Old Sacristy** was designed by Brunelleschi and decorated by Donatello.

⑤ **The huge dome** by Buontalenti echoes that of the Duomo *(see pp284–6)*.

⑥ **Campanile**

⑦ **The Cappelle Medicee** complex comprises the Cappella dei Principi and its crypt, the Sagrestia Nuova *(see p299)*.

⑧ **A simple stone** slab marks the unostentatious grave of Cosimo il Vecchio (1389–1464), founder of the Medici dynasty.

⑨ **Michelangelo** submitted several designs for the facade of San Lorenzo, but it remains unfinished.

The Martyrdom of St. Lawrence

Entrance to church

VISITORS' CHECKLIST

Practical Information
Piazza San Lorenzo 9. **Map** 1 C5 (6 D1). Basilica: **Tel** 055 21 40 42. **Open** 10am–5pm Mon–Sat (Mar–Oct: also Sun pm), 1:30–5pm holidays. Biblioteca: **Tel** 055 21 07 60. **Open** only to scholars.

Transportation
C1, C2

Pulpits by Donatello
The bronze pulpits in the nave were Donatello's last works. Completed by his pupils in 1460, the reliefs capture the flinching pain of Christ's Passion and the glory of the Resurrection.

The Martyrdom of St. Lawrence
Bronzino's vast Mannerist fresco of 1569 is a bravura, choreographed study of the human form, rather than a reverential response to the agony of the saint.

9

The Tomb of the Duke of Nemours (1520–34) by Michelangelo in the Cappelle Medicee's New Sacristy

⓳ Cappelle Medicee

Piazza di Madonna degli Aldobrandini. **Map** 1 C5 (6 D1). **Tel** 055 29 48 83. (reservations). many routes. **Open** 8:15am–5pm daily (Nov & Dec: 8:15am–1:50pm daily). Last adm: 30 mins before closing. **Closed** 1st, 3rd, & 5th Mon of each month, 2nd & 4th Sun, Jan 1, May 1, Dec 25.

The Medici Chapels divide into three distinct areas. Beyond the entrance hall lies a low-vaulted crypt, a suitably subdued space for the brass-railed tombs of many lesser members of the Medici family. From here, steps lead to the octagonal **Cappella dei Principi** (Chapel of Princes), a vast family mausoleum begun by Cosimo I in 1604. The ceiling is garishly frescoed and the walls are smothered in huge swaths of semiprecious *pietre dure* (inlaid stone). Spaced around the walls are the tombs of six Medici Grand Dukes.

A corridor leads to Michelangelo's **New Sacristy**, designed as a counterpoint to Brunelleschi's Old Sacristy in San Lorenzo. Three groups of statues, all carved by Michelangelo between 1520 and 1534, stand around the walls: that on the near left-hand wall is *The Tomb of the Duke of Urbino* (grandson of Lorenzo the Magnificent). Opposite is *The Tomb of the Duke of Nemours* (Lorenzo's third son). Close to the unfinished *Madonna and Child* (1521) is the simple tomb containing Lorenzo the Magnificent and his murdered brother, Giuliano (died 1478).

⓴ Mercato Centrale

Piazza del Mercato Centrale. **Map** 1 C4 (5 C1). **Open** 7am–2pm Mon–Sat.

At the heart of the San Lorenzo street market is the bustling Mercato Centrale, Florence's busiest food market. It is housed in a vast two-story building of cast iron and glass, built in 1874 by Giuseppe Mengoni.

The ground floor stands sell meat, poultry, fish, hams, cheeses, and olive oils. There are also Tuscan take-out foods such as *porchetta* (roast suckling pig), *lampredotto* (pig's intestines), and *trippa* (tripe). Fresh fruit, vegetables, and flowers are sold on the top floor: look for wild mushrooms and truffles in the fall, and fava beans and baby artichokes in early spring.

Yellow zucchini flowers and other vegetables in the Mercato Centrale

㉑ Santa Maria Novella

The Church of Santa Maria Novella was built by the Dominicans between 1279 and 1357. The lower Romanesque part of its facade was incorporated into one based on Classical proportions by the pioneering Renaissance architect Leon Battista Alberti in 1456–70. The Gothic interior contains superb frescoes, including Masaccio's powerful Trinity. The famous Green Cloister, frescoed with perspective scenes by Paolo Uccello, and the dramatically decorated Spanish Chapel now form a museum.

The Nave
The piers of the nave are spaced closer together at the altar end. This trick of perspective creates the illusion of an exceptionally long church.

Trinity by Masaccio
This pioneering fresco (*c.* 1428) is renowned as a masterpiece of perspective and portraiture. The kneeling figures flanking the arch are the painting's sponsors, judge Lorenzo Lenzi and his wife.

Main door

Entrance to museum

Entrance (via courtyard)

KEY

① **Chiostro Verde** takes its name from the green base used in Uccello's frescoes, which were sadly damaged by the 1966 floods.

② **Cappellone degli Spagnuoli**, the chapel used by the Spanish courtiers of Eleonora of Toledo, has frescoes of salvation and damnation.

③ **Monastic buildings**

④ **The arcade arches** are emphasized by gray and white banding.

⑤ **The Strozzi Tomb** is by Benedetto da Maiano (1493).

⑥ **Cappella di Filippo Strozzi** features Filippino Lippi's frescoes of St. John raising Drusiana from the dead and St. Philip slaying a dragon.

Cappella Strozzi
The 14th-century frescoes by Nardo di Cione and his brother Andrea Orcagna were inspired by Dante's epic poem, *The Divine Comedy.*

VISITORS' CHECKLIST

Practical Information
Piazza di Santa Maria Novella.
Map 1 B5 (5 B1).
Church: **Tel** 055 21 92 57.
Open 9am–5:30pm daily (from 11am Fri, from noon Sun).
Museo: **Tel** 055 28 21 87.
Open 9am–5pm Mon–Thu & Sat, 9am–2pm Sun. Last adm: 30 mins before closing.
Closed Jan 1, Easter, May 1, Aug 15, Dec 8 & 25.

Transportation
C2, D.

Ghirlandaio's *Madonna della Misericordia* (1472) in Ognissanti

22 Palazzo Antinori

Piazza Antinori 3. **Map** 1 C5 (5 C2). **Closed** to the public. Cantinetta Antinori: **Tel** 055 29 22 34. **Open** 12:30–2:30pm, 7–10:30pm Mon–Fri.

Palazzo Antinori was built in 1461–6 and is one of the finest small Renaissance palazzi in Florence. It was acquired by the Antinoris in 1506 and has remained with the family ever since. The dynasty produces a range of wines, oils, and liqueurs that can be sampled – along with fine Tuscan dishes – in the Cantinetta Antinori, the wine bar off the main courtyard.

23 Palazzo Rucellai

Via della Vigna Nuova 16. **Map** 1 C5 (5 B2). **Closed** to the public.

Built in 1446–51, this is one of the most ornate Renaissance palaces in the city. It was commissioned by Giovanni Rucellai, whose enormous wealth derived from the import of a rare and costly red dye made from lichen found only on the Spanish island of Majorca. The precious dye was called *oricello*, from which the name Rucellai is derived. Giovanni commissioned several buildings from the architect Leon Battista Alberti, who designed this palace as a virtual textbook illustration of the major Classical orders. The palazzo used to house the Museo Alinari but the collection has now moved to Piazza Santa Maria Novella.

Cappella Tornabuoni
Ghirlandaio's famous fresco cycle, *The Life of John the Baptist* (1485), peoples the biblical episodes with Florentine aristocrats in contemporary dress.

24 Museo Nazionale Alinari della Fotografia

Piazza Santa Maria Novella 14ar. **Map** 1 B5 (5 B2). **Tel** 055 21 63 10. **Open** 10am–6:30pm Thu–Tue. **mnaf.it**

The Alinari brothers began taking pictures of Florence in the 1840s. They supplied high-quality postcards and prints to visitors to Florence in the 19th century. The exhibits offer a vivid insight into the social history of Florence at that time. The museum also houses a collection of cameras, documents, and objects that illustrate the history of photography.

25 Ognissanti

Borgo Ognissanti 42. **Map** 1 B5 (5 A2). **Tel** 055 239 87 00. Church: **Open** 7am–12:30pm, 4–8pm daily. Ghirlandaio's The Last Supper **Open** 9am–noon Mon, Tue, Sat.

Ognissanti, or All Saints, was the parish church of the Vespucci, one of whose members, the 15th-century navigator Amerigo, gave his name to the New World. The young Amerigo is depicted in Ghirlandaio's fresco of the *Madonna della Misericordia* (1472) in the second chapel on the right; Ghirlandaio's *The Last Supper* (1480) can be seen in the convent next door.

In a chapel to the left of the transept hangs the 14th-century, 16 ft- (5 m-) high Ognissanti Crucifix by Giotto di Bondone.

26 Cappella Brancacci

The Church of Santa Maria del Carmine is famous for the Brancacci Chapel, which contains frescoes on *The Life of St. Peter* commissioned by the Florentine merchant Felice Brancacci around 1424. Although the paintings were begun by Masolino in 1425, many of the scenes are by his pupil, Masaccio (who died before completing the cycle) and by Filippino Lippi, who completed the work in 1480. Masaccio's revolutionary use of perspective, his narrative drama, and the tragic realism of his figures placed him in the vanguard of Renaissance painting. Many great artists, including Michelangelo, later visited the chapel to study his pioneering work.

St. Peter Healing the Sick
Masaccio's realistic portrayal of cripples and beggars was revolutionary in his time.

KEY

① **Masaccio's simple style** allows us to focus on the figures central to the frescoes without distracting detail.

② **The grouping** of stylized figures in Masaccio's frescoes reflects his interest in the sculpture of Donatello.

③ **In every scene**, St. Peter is distinguished from the crowds as the figure in the orange cloak.

④ **St. Peter** is depicted against a background of Florentine buildings.

⑤ **Masolino's Temptation of Adam and Eve** is gentle and decorous, in contrast with the emotional force of Masaccio's painting on the opposite wall.

Expulsion of Adam and Eve
Masaccio's ability to express emotion is well illustrated by his harrowing portrait of Adam and Eve being driven out of the Garden of Eden, their faces wracked by misery, shame, and the burden of self-knowledge.

Key to the Frescoes: Artists and Subjects

Masolino
Masaccio
Lippi

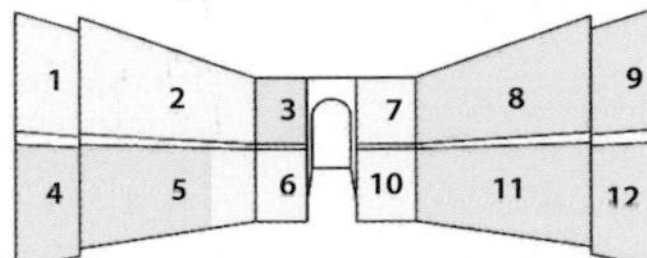

Expulsion of Adam and Eve
The Tribute Money
St. Peter Preaching
St. Peter Visited by St. Paul
Raising the Emperor's Son; St. Peter Enthroned
St. Peter Healing the Sick
7 St. Peter Baptizing the Converts
8 St. Peter Healing the Cripple; Raising Tabitha
9 Temptation of Adam and Eve
10 St. Peter and St. John Giving Alms
11 Crucifixion; Before the Proconsul
12 The Release of St. Peter

VISITORS' CHECKLIST

Practical Information
Piazza del Carmine.
Map 3 A1 (5 A4).
Tel 055 238 21 95 (reservation required).
Open 10am–5pm Mon, Wed–Sat; 1–5pm Sun.
Closed pub hols.

Transportation
D.

Woman in a Turban
The freshness of Masaccio's original colors is seen in this rediscovered roundel, hidden behind the altar for 500 years.

4

5

Two Figures
Masolino's work tends to be more formal, less naturalistic, and less animated than that of Masaccio.

Before the Proconsul
Filippino Lippi was called in to complete the cycle of frescoes in 1480. He added this emotional scene showing the Proconsul sentencing St. Peter to death.

Street-by-Street: Oltrarno

For the most part, the Oltrarno is an appealing area of small houses, quiet squares, and shops selling antiques, bric-a-brac, and foodstuffs. The Via Maggio, a busy thoroughfare, breaks this pattern, but step into the side streets and you escape the bustle to discover a corner of old-world Florence. The restaurants serve authentic, reasonably priced food, and the area is full of studios and workshops restoring antique furniture. Among the things to see are Santo Spirito and Palazzo Pitti, one of the city's largest palaces, whose medley of museums contains an art collection second only to that of the Uffizi.

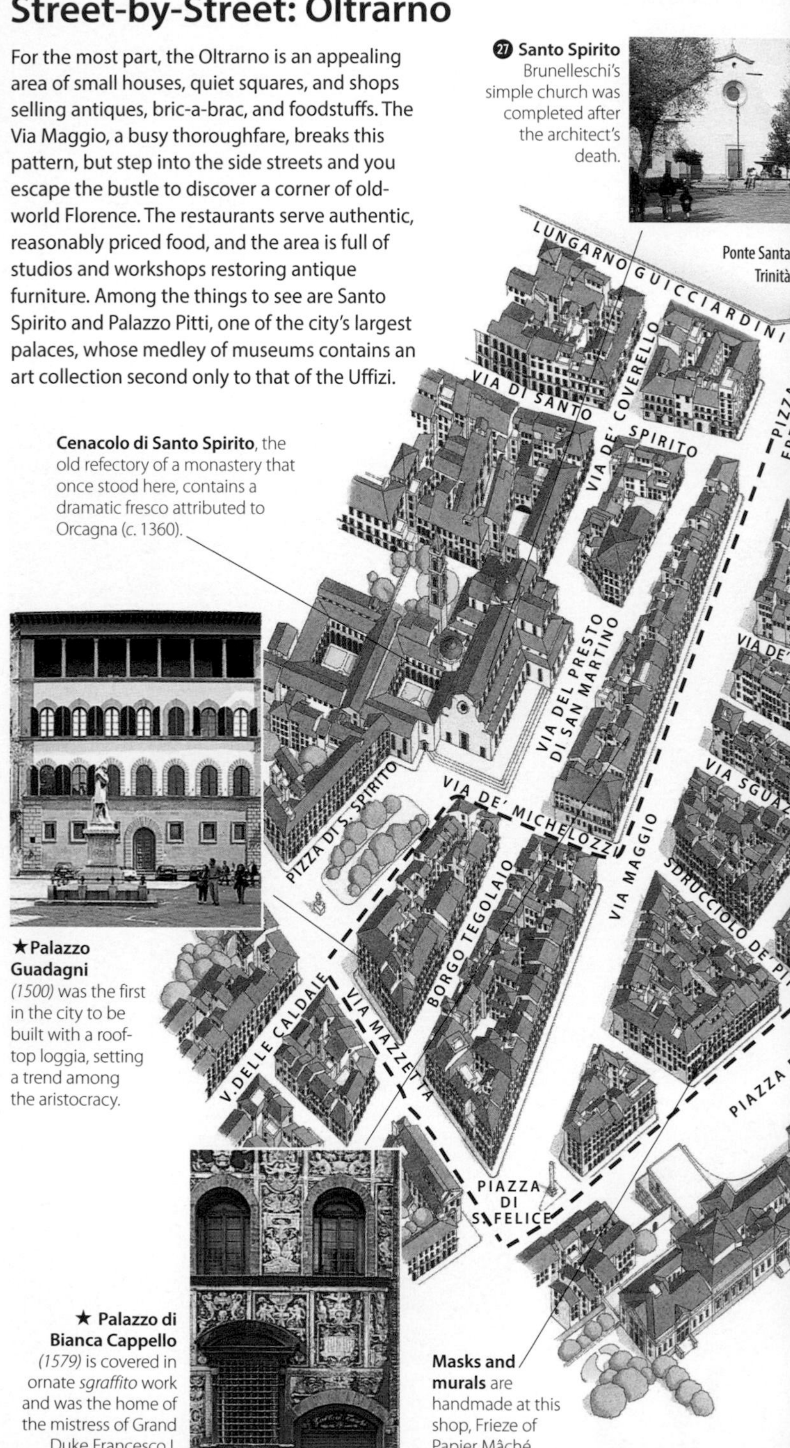

27 Santo Spirito Brunelleschi's simple church was completed after the architect's death.

Cenacolo di Santo Spirito, the old refectory of a monastery that once stood here, contains a dramatic fresco attributed to Orcagna (*c*. 1360).

★ Palazzo Guadagni *(1500)* was the first in the city to be built with a roof-top loggia, setting a trend among the aristocracy.

★ Palazzo di Bianca Cappello *(1579)* is covered in ornate *sgraffito* work and was the home of the mistress of Grand Duke Francesco I.

Masks and murals are handmade at this shop, Frieze of Papier Mâché.

The 16th-century fountain and gargoyle in Piazza de' Frescobaldi were designed by Buontalenti, as was the facade (1593–4) of the nearby church of Santa Trinità.

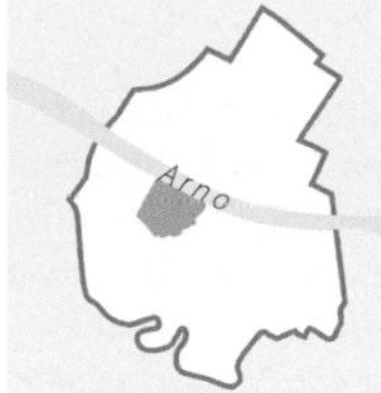

Locator Map
See Florence Street Finder maps 3, 5

Ponte Vecchio
(see p289)

Palazzo Guicciardini was the birthplace of historian Francesco Guicciardini.

28 ★ Palazzo Pitti
Several museums are contained in this massive palazzo, including an outstanding collection of paintings. This painting of Palazzo Pitti was made by Giusto Utens in 1599.

Key

— Suggested route

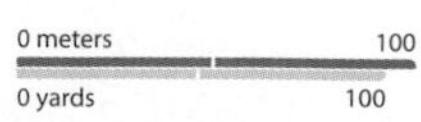

27 Santo Spirito

Piazza di Santo Spirito 30. **Map** 3 B2 (5 B4). D. **Tel** 055 21 00 30. **Open** 9:30am–12:30pm, 4–5:30pm Mon–Sat; 11:30am–12:30pm & 4–5:30pm Sun. **Closed** Wed.

The Augustinian foundation of this church dates from 1250. The present building, dominating the northern end of the pretty Piazza di Santo Spirito, was designed by the architect Brunelleschi in 1435, but not completed until the late 15th century. The unfinished, modest facade was added in the 18th century.

Inside, the harmony of the proportions has been somewhat spoiled by the elaborate Baroque baldacchino and the High Altar, which was finished in 1607 by Giovanni Caccini. The church has 38 side altars, decorated with 15th- and 16th-century Renaissance paintings and sculpture, among them works by Cosimo Rosselli, Domenico Ghirlandaio, and Filippino Lippi. The latter painted a magnificent *Madonna and Child* (1466) for the Nerli Chapel in the south transept.

In the north aisle, a door beneath the organ leads to a vestibule with an ornate coffered ceiling. It was designed by Simone del Pollaiuolo, more commonly known as Cronaca, in 1491. The sacristy adjoining the vestibule, in which 12 huge columns are crammed into a tiny space, was designed by Giuliano da Sangallo in 1489.

Interior of Santo Spirito with colonnaded aisle

㉘ Palazzo Pitti

The Palazzo Pitti was originally built for the banker Luca Pitti. The huge scale of the building, begun in 1457 and attributed to Brunelleschi, illustrated Pitti's determination to outrival the Medici family through its display of wealth and power. Ironically, the Medici later purchased the palazzo when building costs bankrupted Pitti's heirs. In 1550 it became the main residence of the Medici, and subsequently all the rulers of the city lived here. Today the richly decorated rooms exhibit countless treasures from the Medici collections.

Judith (1620–30) by Artemisia Gentileschi

The Three Ages of Man (c.1510), attributed to Giorgione

Galleria Palatina

The Palatine Gallery, which forms the heart of the Pitti museum complex, contains countless masterpieces by artists such as Botticelli, Titian, Perugino, Andrea del Sarto, Tintoretto, Veronese, Giorgione, and Gentileschi. The works of art, accumulated by the Medici family and the house of Habsburg-Lorraine, are still hung much as the grand dukes wished, regardless of subject or chronology. The gallery consists of 11 main salons, the first 5 of which are painted with allegorical ceiling frescoes glorifying the Medici. Begun by Pietro da Cortona in 1641, they were completed in 1665 by his pupil Ciro Ferri. Room 1 (Sala di Venere) contains Antonio Canova's statue of the *Venus Italica* (1810), commissioned by Napoleon to replace the *Venus de' Medici* (which was to be taken to Paris). Room 2 (Sala di Apollo) features Titian's *Portrait of a Gentleman* (1540), perhaps the finest of several paintings by the artist in the gallery. Still finer pictures adorn rooms 4 and 5, including some by Perugino and Andrea del Sarto and a host of paintings by Raphael. The most beautiful of the last group are Raphael's High Renaissance *Madonna della Seggiola* or Madonna of the Chair (c.1514–15) and the *Donna Velata* or Veiled Woman (c.1516), whose model was reputedly the artist's mistress. Other paintings in the remaining gallery rooms include Fra Filippo Lippi's lovely *Madonna and Child*, painted in the mid-15th century, and Caravaggio's *The Sleeping Cupid* (1608).

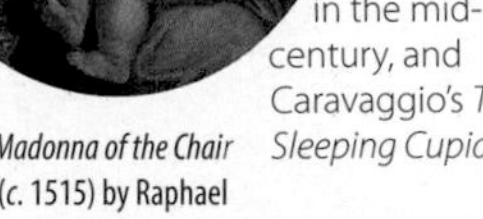

Madonna of the Chair (*c.* 1515) by Raphael

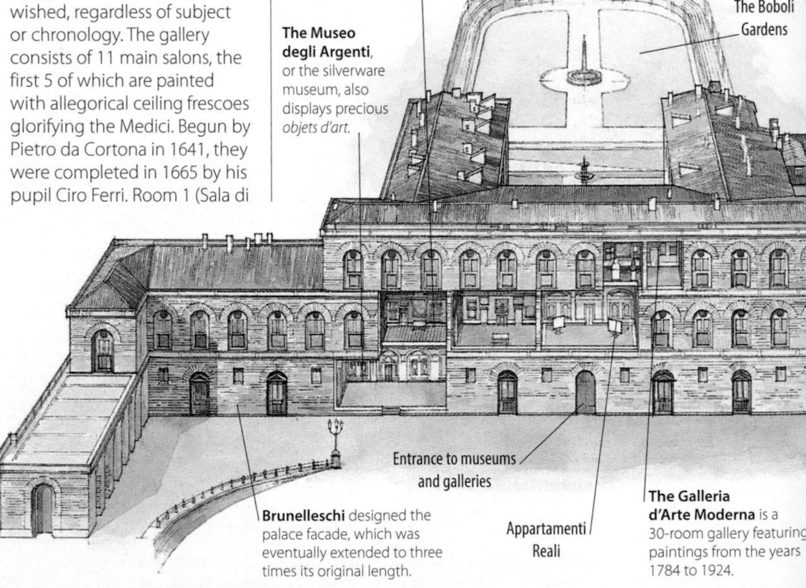

Galleria Palatina
The Boboli Gardens
The Museo degli Argenti, or the silverware museum, also displays precious *objets d'art*.
Entrance to museums and galleries
Brunelleschi designed the palace facade, which was eventually extended to three times its original length.
Appartamenti Reali
The Galleria d'Arte Moderna is a 30-room gallery featuring paintings from the years 1784 to 1924.

The Palmieri Rotonda by Giovanni Fattori (1825–1908)

Appartamenti Reali

The Royal Apartments on the first floor of the south wing of the palazzo were built in the 17th century. They are decorated with frescoes by various Florentine artists, a series of portraits of the Medici by the Flemish painter Justus Sustermans, who worked at the court between 1619 and 1681, and a group of 18th-century Gobelins tapestries. In the late 18th and early 19th centuries, the apartments were revamped in Neo-Classical style by the Dukes of Lorraine when they succeeded the Medici dynasty as the rulers of Florence.

The apartments are lavishly appointed with ornate gold and white stuccoed ceilings and rich decoration, notably the walls of the Parrot Room, which are covered with an opulent crimson fabric detailed with a bird design. The Tapestry Rooms are hung with 17th- and 18th-century tapestries of French, Belgian, and Italian manufacture. The apartments reflect the tastes of three distinct historical periods.

The Throne Room of the Appartamenti Reali

Other Collections

The Museo degli Argenti (Silverware Museum) is housed in rooms formerly used by the Medici as summer apartments. The family's lavish taste is reflected in the vast array of precious objects on display. These embrace beautiful examples of Roman glassware, ivory, carpets, crystal, amber, and fine works by Florentine and German goldsmiths. Pride of place goes to 16 *pietre dure* vases (decorated with hard or semiprecious inlaid stones), once owned by Lorenzo the Magnificent.

The Galleria del Costume, which opened in 1983, reflects the changing taste in the courtly fashion of the late 18th century up to the 1920s.

The highlights of the Galleria d'Arte Moderna (Modern Art Gallery) are the wonderful paintings of the *Macchiaioli* (spot-makers), who were a group of Tuscan artists with a style very similar to that of the French Impressionists.

Piazza della Signoria depicted in precious stones

VISITORS' CHECKLIST

Practical Information
Piazza de' Pitti.
Map 3 C2 (5 B5).
Tel 055 29 48 83 (info & booking).
Galleria Palatina & Royal Apartments: **Open** 8:15am–6:50pm Tue–Sun.
Closed Jan 1, May 1, Dec 25.
Boboli Gardens: **Open** 8:15am–6:30pm daily (Mar: to 5:30pm; Jun–Aug: to 7:30pm; Nov–Feb: to 4:30pm).
Closed 1st & last Mon.
Other collections:
Open & **Closed** same as Boboli Gardens.

Transportation
D.

A copy of Giambologna's *Oceanus Fountain* (1576)

The Boboli Gardens

The Boboli Gardens, a lovely place to escape the rigors of sightseeing, were laid out for the Medici after they bought the Palazzo Pitti in 1549. An excellent example of stylized Renaissance gardening, they were opened to the public in 1766. The more formal parts of the garden, nearest the palazzo, consist of box hedges clipped into symmetrical geometric patterns. These lead to wilder groves of ilex and cypress trees, planted to create a contrast between artifice and nature. Countless statues adorn the gardens, particularly along the Viottolone, an avenue of cypress trees planted in 1637. High above the gardens stands the Forte di Belvedere, designed by Buontalenti in 1590 for the Medici Grand Dukes.

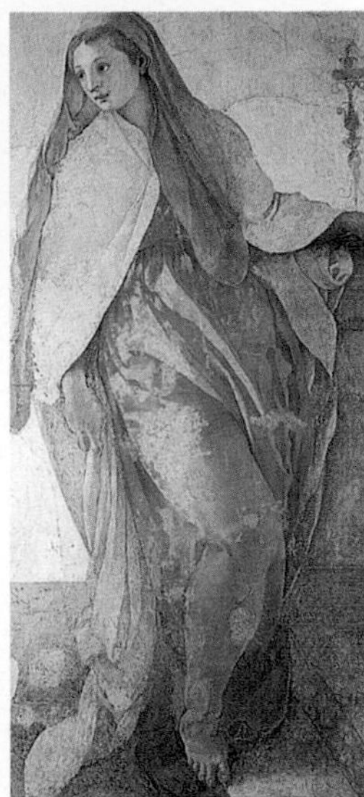
The Virgin from *The Annunciation* (1528) by Pontormo

㉙ Santa Felicità

Piazza di Santa Felicita. **Map** 3 C2 (5 C5). D. **Tel** 055 21 30 18.
Open 9:30am–noon, 3:30–5:30pm daily (only am Sun).

There has been a church on this site since the 4th century. The present structure, begun in the 11th century, was remodeled in 1736–9 by Ferdinando Ruggieri, who retained Vasari's earlier porch (added in 1564) as well as many of the church's original Gothic features.

The Capponi family chapel to the right of the entrance contains two works by Jacopo da Pontormo: *The Deposition* and *The Annunciation* (1525–28). Their strange composition and remarkable coloring make them two of Mannerism's greatest masterpieces.

㉚ Piazzale Michelangelo

Piazzale Michelangelo. **Map** 4 E3. 12, 13.

Of all the great Florentine viewpoints – such as the Duomo and Campanile – none offers such a magnificent panorama of the city as Piazzale Michelangelo. Laid out in the 1860s by Giuseppe Poggi, and dotted with copies of Michelangelo's statues, its balconies attract many visitors and the inevitable massed ranks of souvenir sellers. However, this square remains an evocative spot, especially when the sun sets over the Arno and distant Tuscan hills.

㉛ San Miniato al Monte

Via del Monte alle Croci. **Map** 4 E3. **Tel** 055 234 27 31. 12, 13.
Open 8am–1pm, 3:30–7pm daily.
Closed public hols.

San Miniato is one of the most beautiful Romanesque churches in Italy. Begun in 1018, it was built over the shrine of San Miniato (St. Minias), a rich Armenian merchant beheaded for his beliefs in the 3rd century. The facade, begun around 1090, has the geometric marble patterning typical of Pisan-Romanesque architecture. The statue on the gable shows an eagle carrying a bale of cloth, the symbol of the powerful Arte di Calimala (guild of wool importers), who financed the church in the Middle Ages. The 13th-century mosaic shows Christ, the Virgin, and St. Minias. The same protagonists appear in the apse mosaic inside the church, which sits above a crypt supported by columns salvaged from ancient Roman buildings. The floor of the nave is covered with seven mosaic panels of animals and signs of the Zodiac. These mosaics date back to 1207.

The facade of the church of San Miniato al Monte

Other highlights include Michelozzo's freestanding Cappella del Crocifisso (1448) and the Renaissance Cappella del Cardinale del Portogallo (1480) with terracotta roundels (1461) on the ceiling by Luca della Robbia. There is a fresco cycle of *Scenes from the Life of St. Benedict* by Spinello Aretino in the sacristy, which was completed in 1387.

Ponte Vecchio and the Arno from the heights of Piazzale Michelangelo

Shopping in Florence

Few cities of comparable size can boast such a profusion and variety of high-quality shops as Florence. As you wander through its medieval streets, you will find all the big names in Italian fashion and jewelry alongside artisan workshops and family-run businesses. The city has translated its reputation as a center of artistic excellence into a wealth of antiques and fine-art shops. Tuscan tanneries are justifiably renowned, and there is nowhere better than Florence to buy shoes, bags, and other leather goods. Those searching for unusual gifts and souvenirs – from handmade stationery to delicious foodstuffs – will also be spoiled for choice.

Where to Shop

The center of Florence is packed with all sorts of shops, from fashion designer flagships to secondhand bookstores. The tiny jewelry shops on the Ponte Vecchio sell both antique items and high-quality new gold pieces. Antiques shops are mostly clustered around Via dei Fossi, Via dei Serragli, and Via Maggio. The best bargains can be found in the January and July sales.

Clothing

Most leading Italian designer names – **Gucci**, **Armani**, **Versace**, and **Prada**, for example – can be found on Via de' Tornabuoni. Opposite Palazzo Strozzi is **Louis Vuitton**, with its collections of footwear, clothing, and luggage. **Dolce & Gabbana** is nearby, as is **Patrizia Peppe**, while **Valentino** is in Via dei Tosinghi. **La Perla**, specializing in sophisticated lingerie, is located in Via della Vigna Nuova, but more affordable lingerie styles can be found at **Intimissimi**.

Most department stores sell clothing. For mid-range fashion, try **Coin**. The more upmarket **La Rinascente** has designer clothing, lingerie, and a great rooftop bar.

For discounts on designer fashion, visit **The Mall** or **Barberino Designer Outlet**, both about 30 minutes away from Florence.

There are fine silks and handwoven fabrics at **Casa dei Tessuti**.

Shoes and Leather Goods

The main meccas for fans of designer Italian shoes are **Ferragamo**, **Gucci**, and **Prada**. For more classic styles, head to **Quercioli**, which stocks handmade leather footwear. The mid-priced range is well represented by **Peppe Peluso** and the chain store **Bata**.

The streets around Piazza di Santa Croce are filled with leather shops. Inside the cloisters of the church itself is the **Scuola del Cuoio**, where customers can watch the leather craftsmen at work.

Classic leather bags are sold at **Il Bisonte** and **Beltrami**; for more contemporary styles head to **Coccinelle** and **Furla**.

Bound leather books, leather boxes, and leather-covered wooden desk objects are sold at **Scriptorium**.

Jewelry

Florence has always been noted for its gold- and silversmiths. Visit **Torrini**, whose family has produced jewelry for six centuries, and **Pomellato**'s stunning shop for its chunky white gold rings with huge semi-precious gems. **Bulgari** is on the same street, and so is **Parenti**, which has unique antique jewels. Try **Aprosio & Co** for decorative jewelry made from precious metals and tiny glass stones.

Art and Antiques

Galleria Romanelli has bronze statuary and works encrusted in semiprecious stones. The gallery also stocks marble sculptures and statues. It was established in 1860 and is still run by the same founding family. For lovers of Art Nouveau and Art Deco, there is **Galleria Tornabuoni**, while **Ugo Poggi** has a selection of elegant porcelain. **Ugolini** and **Mosaico di Pitti** create tables and framed pictures using the age-old technique of marble inlay.

Books and Gifts

Feltrinelli International and **Edison** sell publications in several languages, while **Paperback Exchange** has a wide selection of new and secondhand books in English.

Typical Florentine crafts include bookbinding and handmade marbled paper, used to decorate a variety of objects. These are available at **Il Torchio** and **Il Papiro**.

For terracotta and ceramics, try **Sbigoli Terracotte**; for chandeliers and decorative glass objects head to **La Bottega dei Cristalli**.

Signum sells postcards, posters, and prints, while **Mandragora** has a wide range of gifts based on famous artworks in the city.

Food and Markets

Florence's main food market is the covered **Mercato Centrale** (*see p295*), but fruit and vegetable stalls can also be found at the **Mercato di Sant'Ambrogio**. On Tuesday mornings, there is a large market at the **Parco delle Cascine** with food, affordable clothing, and shoes.

Pegna is a mini-supermarket that stocks fresh foods, as well as a range of gourmet items. The **Bottega dell'Olio** sells extra virgin Tuscan olive oils, and **Grom** is famous for its artisan gelato.

Dolceforte sells chocolate souvenirs in the shape of the Duomo and the statue of *David*. Biscuits and chocolates fill the front half of **Alessi**, while at the back are fine wines, spirits, and liqueurs. At **Procacci**, you can stop for a glass of Italian wine while choosing between pots of black or white truffles and other delicacies to buy.

DIRECTORY

Clothing

Armani
Via de'Tornabuoni 48–50r.
Map 1 C5 & 5 C2.
Tel 055 21 90 41.

Barberino Designer Outlet
A1 Firenze-Bologna, Exit Barberino di Mugello.
Tel 055 84 21 61.

Casa dei Tessuti
Via dei Pecori 20–24r.
Map 1 C5 & 6 D2.
Tel 055 21 59 61.

Coin
Via dei Calzaiuoli 56r.
Map 6 D3.
Tel 055 28 05 31.

Dolce & Gabbana
Via dei Strozzi 12–18r.
Map 1 C5 & 5 C3.
Tel 055 28 10 03.

Gucci
Via de'Tornabuoni 73r.
Map 1 C5 & 5 C2.
Tel 055 26 40 11.

Intimissimi
Via dei Calzaiuoli 99r.
Map 3 C1 & 6 D3.
Tel 055 230 26 09.

Louis Vuitton
Piazza degli Strozzi 1.
Map 1 C5 & 5 C3.
Tel 055 26 69 81.

The Mall
Via Europa 8, Leccio Reggello.
Tel 055 865 77 75.

Patrizia Peppe
Via degli Strozzi 11/19r.
Map 3 C1 & 6 D2.
Tel 055 230 25 18.

La Perla
Via Strozzi 24r.
Map 1 C5 & 5 C3.
Tel 055 21 52 42.

Prada
Via de'Tornabuoni 67r.
Map 1 C5 & 5 C2.
Tel 055 26 74 71.

La Rinascente
Piazza della Repubblica 1.
Map 1 C5 & 6 D3.
Tel 055 21 91 13.

Valentino
Via dei Tosinghi 52r.
Map 1 C5 & 6 D2.
Tel 055 29 31 42.

Versace
Via de'Tornabuoni 13–15r.
Map 1 C5 & 5 C2.
Tel 055 28 26 38.

Shoes and Leather Goods

Bata
Via dei Calzaiuoli 110r.
Map 3 C1 & 6 D2.
Tel 055 21 16 24.

Beltrami
Via della Vigna Nuova 70r.
Map 1 C5 & 5 C2.
Tel 055 28 77 79.

Il Bisonte
Via del Parione 31r.
Map 1 C5 & 5 C3.
Tel 055 21 57 22.

Coccinelle
Via Por Santa Maria 49r.
Map 3 C1 & 6 D4.
Tel 055 239 87 82.

Ferragamo
Via de'Tornabuoni 14r.
Map 1 C5 & 5 C2.
Tel 055 29 21 23.

Furla
Via de'Calzaiuoli 47r.
Map 3 C1 & 6 D3.
Tel 055 23.8 28 83.

Peppe Peluso
Via del Corso 5–6r.
Map 3 C1 & 6 D3.
Tel 055 26 82 83.

Quercioli
Via Calzaiuoli 18/20r.
Map 3 C1 & 6 D2.
Tel 055 21 39 41.

Scriptorium
Via dei Servi 5–7r.
Map 2 D5 & 6 E2.
Tel 055 21 18 04.

Scuola del Cuoio
Piazza di Santa Croce 16.
Map 3 C1 & 6 F4.
Tel 055 24 45 33.

Jewelry

Aprosio & Co
Via della Spada 38/r.
Map 3 B1 & 5 B4.
Tel 055 265 40 77.

Bulgari
Via de'Tornabuoni 61r.
Map 1 C5 & 5 C3.
Tel 055 239 67 86.

Parenti
Via de'Tornabuoni 93r.
Map 1 C5 & 5 C2.
Tel 055 21 44 38.

Pomellato
Via de'Tornabuoni 89–91r.
Map 1 C5 & 5 C2.
Tel 055 28 85 30.

Torrini
Piazza del Duomo 10r.
Map 2 D5 & 6 D2.
Tel 055 230 24 01.

Art and Antiques

Galleria Romanelli
Borgo San Frediano 70.
Map 3 C1 & 5 C4.
Tel 055 239 60 47.

Galleria Tornabuoni
Borgo San Jacopo 53r.
Map 3 C1 & 5 C4.
Tel 055 28 47 20.

Mosaico di Pitti
Piazza de' Pitti 16–18r.
Map 3 B2 & 5 B5.
Tel 055 28 21 27.

Ugo Poggi
Via degli Strozzi 26r.
Map 1 C5 & 5 C3.
Tel 055 21 67 41.

Ugolini
Lungarno degli Acciaiuoli 66–70r.
Map 3 C1 & 5 C4.
Tel 055 28 49 69.

Books and Gifts

La Bottega dei Cristalli
Via dei Benci 51r.
Map 3 C1 & 6 F4.
Tel 055 234 48 91.

Edison
Piazza della Repubblica 27r.
Map 1 C5 & 6 D3.
Tel 055 21 31 10.

Feltrinelli International
Via dè Cerretani 30/32r.
Map 2 D4.
Tel 055 238 26 52.

Mandragora
Piazza del Duomo 9r.
Map 2 D5 & 6 D2.
Tel 055 29 25 59.

Paperback Exchange
Via delle Oche 4r.
Map 2 D5 & 6 E2.
Tel 055 29 34 60.

Il Papiro
Piazza del Duomo 24r.
Map 2 D5 & 6 D2.
Tel 055 649 91 51.

Sbigoli Terracotte
Via Sant'Egidio 4r.
Map 6 F2.
Tel 055 247 97 13.

Signum
Borgo dei Greci 40r.
Map 3 C1 & 6 E4.
Tel 055 28 06 21.

Il Torchio
Via de' Bardi 17.
Map 3 C2 & 6 D5.
Tel 055 234 28 62.

Food and Markets

Alessi
Via delle Oche 27r.
Map 3 C1 & 6 D2.
Tel 055 21 49 66.

Bottega dell'Olio
Piazza del Limbo 2r.
Map 3 C1 & 6 D4.
Tel 055 267 04 68.

Dolceforte
Via della Scala 21.
Map 1 C5 & 5 B2.
Tel 055 21 91 16.

Grom
Via del Campanile (on the corner of Via delle Oche).
Map 2 D5 & 6 D2.
Tel 055 21 61 58.

Mercato Centrale
Via dell'Ariento 10–14.
Map 1 C4 & 5 C1.

Mercato di Sant'Ambrogio
Piazza Sant'Ambrogio.
Map 4 F1. **Open** 7am–2pm Mon–Sat.

Parco delle Cascine
Piazza Vittorio Veneto.
Open 8am–2pm Tue.

Pegna
Via dello Studio 26r.
Map 6 E2.
Tel 055 28 27 01.

Procacci
Via de'Tornabuoni 64r.
Map 1 C5 & 5 C2.
Tel 055 21 16 56.

FLORENCE STREET FINDER

Map references given for sights in the Florence section refer to the maps on the following pages. Where two references are provided, the one in brackets relates to the large-scale maps, 5 and 6. References are also given for Florence hotels *(see pp562–77)* and restaurants *(see pp580–605)*, and for useful addresses in the *Travelers' Needs* and *Survival Guide* sections at the back of the book. The map below shows the area of Florence covered by the *Street Finder*. The symbols used for sights and other features on the *Florence Street Finder* maps are listed below. Streets in Florence have double sets of numbers: red numbers are for businesses, and black or blue for domestic residences.

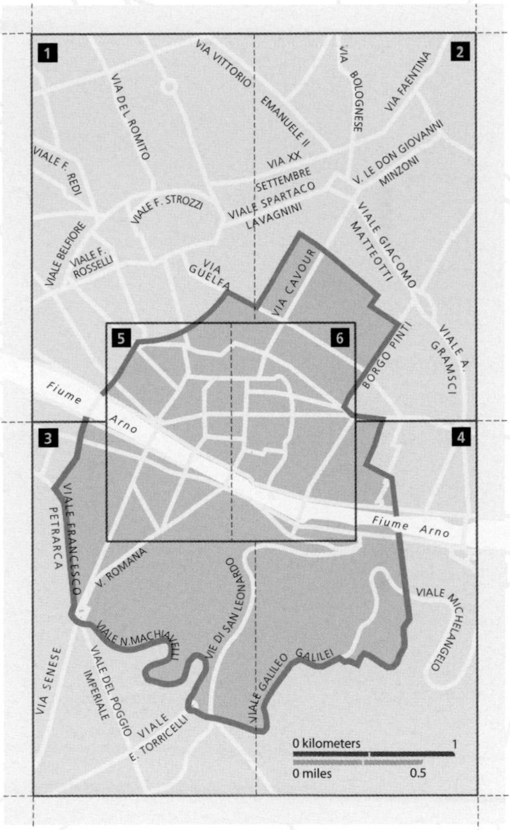

Scale of Maps 1–2 & 3–4

0 meters 200

0 yards 200

1:11,000

Scale of Maps 5–6

0 meters 125

0 yards 125

1:6000

0 kilometers 1

0 miles 0.5

Key to Street Finder

Major sight

Place of interest

Train station

Bus station

Streetcar stop

Tourist information

Hospital with emergency room

Police station

Synagogue

Church

Railroad line

City walls

Pedestrianized street

1
A
B
C
1
2
3
4
5
A
B
C
3
VIA DELL'ARCOVATA
V. CIRCONDARIA
VIALE CORSICA
VIA PIERO CIRONI
VIA FILIPPO CORRIDONI
VIA MARCO LASTRI
VIA ANTONIO LOCATELLI
VIA SCIPIO SLATAPER
VIA SCIPIO SIGHELE
VIA DEL PALAZZO BRUCIATO
V. RIGUCCIO GALLUZZI
PIAZZA PIETRO LEOPOLDO
V. SALLUSTIO BANDINI
V. POMPEO NERI
PIAZZA BERNARDO TANUCCI
VIA ENRICO MAYER
VIA SCIPIONE DE' RICCI
V. FRANCESCO GIANNI
VIA ATTO VANNUCCI
VIA ALFREDO ORIANI
VIA CELESTINO BIANCHI
VIA GIOVANNI FABRONI
VIA GIANFRANCESCO PAGNINI
VIA GASPERO BARBERA
VIA RAFFAELLO LAMBRUSCHINI
PIAZZA GIAMPIETRO VIESSEUX
VIA GAETANO MILANESI
V. ANTONIO ZOBI
VIA FRANCESCO BONAINI
VIA ANGELO MARIA BANDINI
V. LUIGI PASSERINI
V. CESARE GUASTI
V. FRANCESCO MARUCELLI
VIA FERDINANDO PAOLETTI
V. GIOVANNI LORENZONI
VIA EGISTO FABBRI
PIAZZA LUDOVICO ANTONIO MURATORI
VIALE GIOVANNI
VIA GIUSEPPE RICHA
VIALE DEL ROMITO
V. LUIGI GORDIGIANI
VIA ONOFRI OZEFFIRINI
VIALE FRANCESCO REDI
VIALE DEI
VIA DELLO STATUTO
VIA DELLE CINQUE GIORNATE
VIA DELLA
VIA FRANCESCO PUCCINOTTI
VIA VENTIQUATTRO MAGGIO
PIAZZA FILIPPO BALDINUCCI
VIA CRIMEA
VIA COSSERIA
PIAZZA DELLA COSTITUZIONE
V. GIOVANNI TARGIONI TOZZETTI
VIA DEL PONTE ALL'ASSE
VIA SAN JACOPINO
V. MARAGLIANO
V. GASPARE LUIGI SPONTINI
PIAZZA DI S. JACOPINO
VIA ALFREDO CATALANI
V. FRANCESCO LANDINI
VIA CASSIA
V. B. CRISTOFORI
CIMAROSA
V. DOMENICO
V. GIOACCHINO ROSSINI
V. BENEDETTO MARCELLO
VIA GUIDO SPADOLINI
VIALE FILIPPO STROZZI
PIAZZALE CADUTI NEI LAGER
Fortezza da Basso
VIALE BELFIORE
VIA DELLA CITTADELLA
VIA DELLE GHIACCIAIE
V. GUIDO MONACO
VIA I. PERI
PIAZZALE MONTELUNGO
VIA PIER LUIGI DA PALESTRINA
VIA DELLE PORTE NUOVE
V. GIUSEPPE DOLFI
VIA COSIMO RIDOLFI
VIA DI BARBANO
VIA DEL PRATELLO
VIA DELLA FORTEZZA
V. FAUSTO DIONISI
PIAZZA DELL'INDIPENDENZA
PIAZZA DEL CROCIFISSO
VIA GIUSEPPE MONTANELLI
VIALE FRATELLI ROSSELLI
VIA LUIGI ALAMANNI
V. DEL PONTE ALLE MOSSE
PIAZZALE DELLA PORTA AL PRATO
VIA IACOPO DA DIACCETO
PIAZZA ADUA
V. BERNARDO CENNINI
VIA VALFONDA
VIA FIUME
VIA FAENZA
VIA NAZIONALE
V. CHIARA
VIA DELL'ARIENTO
VIA PANICALE
PIAZZA MERCATO CENTRALE
Mercato Centrale
Stazione Centrale di Santa Maria Novella
FS
i
5
VIA DELLA SCALA
VIA ORICELLARI
V. BERNARDO RUCELLAI
VIA MAGENTA
VIA IL PRATO
VIA SOLFERINO
VIA GIUSEPPE GARIBALDI
VIA MONTEBELLO
VIA DEGLI ORTI ORICELLARI
Autostazione Sita
LARGO FRATELLI ALINARI
PIAZZA DELLA STAZIONE
VIA SANT'ANTONINO
Cappelle Medicee
PIAZZA DELL'UNITÀ ITALIANA
PIAZZA DI MADONNA DEGLI ALDOBRANDINI
San Lorenzo
Santa Maria Novella
VIA D. AVELLI
VIA PANZANI
VIA DEL GIGLIO
V. DELL' ALLORO
CORSO ITALIA
VIA PALESTRO
VIA DI SANTA LUCIA
BORGO OGNISSANTI
VIA CURTATONE
V. M. FINIGUERRA
V. DELL'ALBERO
VIA DE' CANACCI
V. BENEDETTA
VIA PALAZZUOLO
PIAZZA DI SANTA MARIA NOVELLA
Museo Nazionale Alinari della Fotografia
VIA DEI BANCHI
Santa Maria Maggiore
V. LUNGARNO AMERIGO VESPUCCI
V. MELEGNANO
Ognissanti
VIA DEL PORCELLANA
PIAZZA DI SAN PAOLINO
Palazzo Antinori
VIA D. BELLE DONNE
VIA TEATINA
VIA D. AGLI
VIA DE' PECORI
Arno
LUNGARNO DI S. ROSA
Ponte A. Vespucci
SEE PAGES 5–6 FOR ENLARGEMENT OF THIS AREA
PIAZZA DEGLI OTTAVIANI
V. DEL SOLE
Museo Marino Marini (San Pancrazio)
V. D. FOSSI
Palazzo Rucellai
V. DE' TORNABUONI
VIA DE' PESCIONI
VIA DE' VECCHIETTI
VIA DE' BRUNELLESCHI
PIAZZA DELLA REPUBBLICA
VIA DEGLI STROZZI

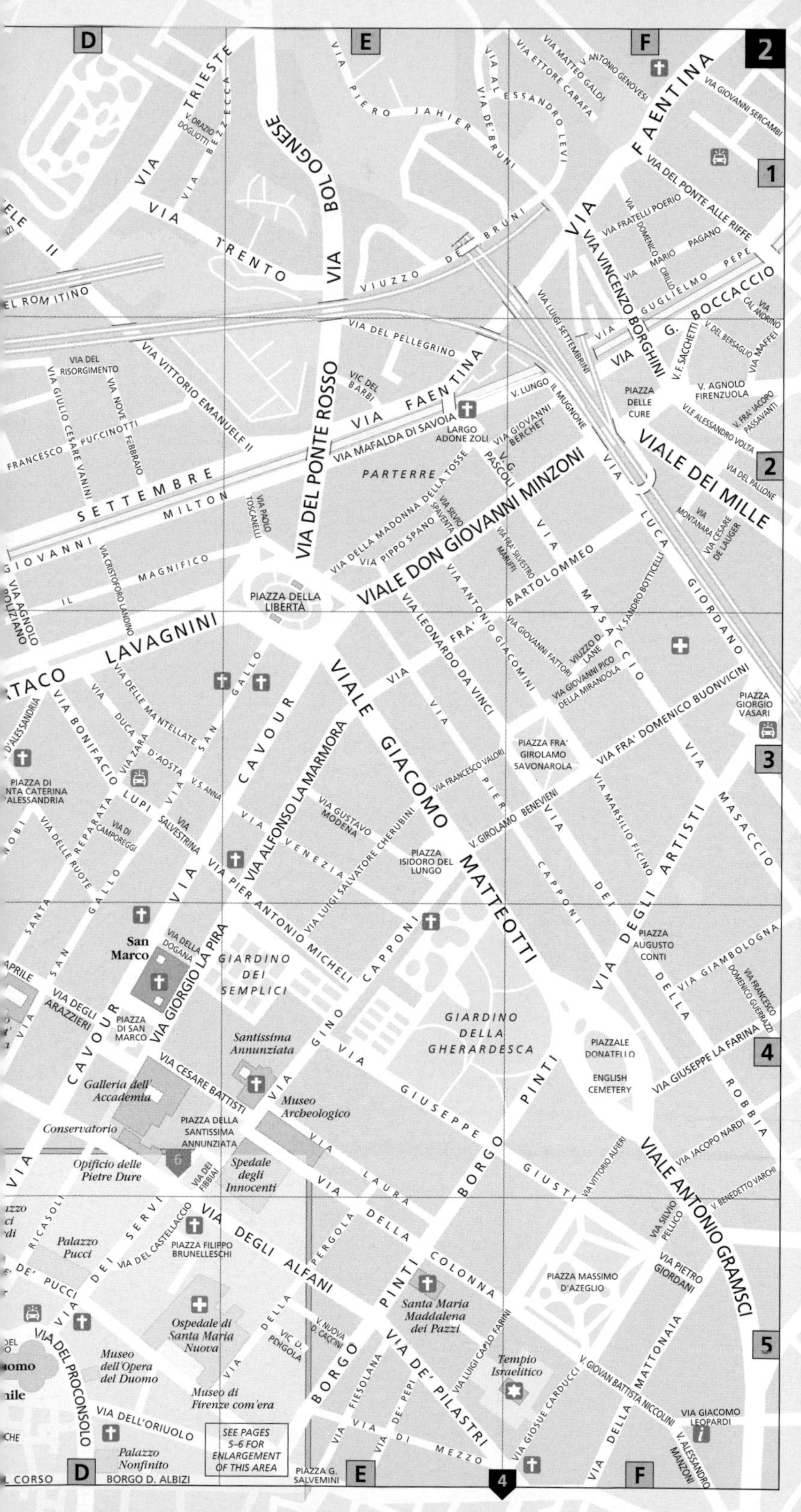
D
E
F
2
1
2
3
4
5
VIA TRIESTE
V. ORAZIO DOGLIOTTI
VIA BEZZECCA
VIA TRENTO
VIA BOLOGNESE
VIA PIERO JAHIER
VIA AL ESSANDRO LEVI
VIA DE' BRUNI
VIA ETTORE CARAFA
VIA MATTEO GALDI
V. ANTONIO GENOVESI
VIA FAENTINA
VIA GIOVANNI SERCAMBI
VIA DEL PONTE ALLE RIFFE
VIA FRATELLI POERIO
VIA DOMENICO CIRILLO
VIA MARIO PAGANO
VIA GUGLIELMO PEPE
VIA VINCENZO BORGHINI
VIA G. BOCCACCIO
VIA CAL ANDRINO
VIUZZO DE' BRUNI
VIA DEL ROMITINO
VIA DEL PELLEGRINO
VIA LUIGI SETTEMBRINI
V. F. SACCHETTI
V. DEL BERSAGLIO
VIA MAFFEI
VIA DEL RISORGIMENTO
VIA GIULIO CESARE VANINI
VIA NOVE FEBBRAIO
VIA VITTORIO EMANUELE II
VIC DEL BARBI
VIA FAENTINA
V. LUNGO IL MUGNONE
PIAZZA DELLE CURE
V. AGNOLO FIRENZUOLA
V.LE ALESSANDRO VOLTA
V. FRA' IACOPO PASSAVANTI
FRANCESCO PUCCINOTTI
VIA MAFALDA DI SAVOIA
LARGO ADONE ZOLI
VIA GIOVANNI BERCHET
V. G. PASCOLI
VIALE DEI MILLE
VIA DEL PALLONE
SETTEMBRE
MILTON
VIA PAOLO TOSCANELLI
VIA DEL PONTE ROSSO
PARTERRE
VIA DELLA MADONNA DELLA TOSSE
VIA SILVIO SPAVENTA
VIALE DON GIOVANNI MINZONI
VIA MONTANARA
VIA CESARE DE LAUGER
GIOVANNI
VIA CRISTOFORO LANDINO
IL MAGNIFICO
VIA PIPPO SPANO
VIA FRA' SILVESTRO MARUFFI
VIA LUCA GIORDANO
VIA AGNOLO POLIZIANO
PIAZZA DELLA LIBERTÀ
VIA FRA' BARTOLOMMEO
VIA MASACCIO
V. SANDRO BOTTICELLI
LAVAGNINI
VIA LEONARDO DA VINCI
VIA ANTONIO GIACOMINI
VIA GIOVANNI FATTORI
VIUZZO D. LANE
VIA GIOVANNI PICO DELLA MIRANDOLA
SPARTACO
VIA DELLE MANTELLATE
VIA SAN GALLO
VIALE GIACOMO MATTEOTTI
VIA FRA' DOMENICO BUONVICINI
PIAZZA GIORGIO VASARI
VIA D'ALESSANDRIA
VIA BONIFACIO LUPI
VIA DUCA D'AOSTA
VIA ZARA
CAVOUR
VIA ALFONSO LA MARMORA
PIAZZA FRA' GIROLAMO SAVONAROLA
VIA FRANCESCO VALORI
VIA PIER CAPPONI
PIAZZA DI SANTA CATERINA D'ALESSANDRIA
V. S. ANNA
VIA SALVESTRINA
VIA GUSTAVO MODENA
V. GIROLAMO BENEVIENI
VIA MARSILIO FICINO
VIA DEGLI ARTISTI
VIA DELLE RUOTE
REPARATA
VIA DI CAMPOREGGI
VIA VENEZIA
VIA LUIGI SALVATORE CHERUBINI
PIAZZA ISIDORO DEL LUNGO
VIA PIER ANTONIO MICHELI
SANTA
SAN GALLO
San Marco
VIA DELLA DOGANA
VIA GIORGIO LA PIRA
GIARDINO DEI SEMPLICI
CAPPONI
PIAZZA AUGUSTO CONTI
VIA DELLA ROBBIA
VIA GIAMBOLOGNA
VIA FRANCESCO DOMENICO GUERRAZZI
APRILE
VIA DEGLI ARAZZIERI
PIAZZA DI SAN MARCO
Santissima Annunziata
VIA GINO CAPPONI
GIARDINO DELLA GHERARDESCA
PINTI
PIAZZALE DONATELLO
ENGLISH CEMETERY
VIA GIUSEPPE LA FARINA
Galleria dell' Accademia
VIA CESARE BATTISTI
Museo Archeologico
VIA GIUSEPPE GIUSTI
Conservatorio
PIAZZA DELLA SANTISSIMA ANNUNZIATA
VIA LAURA
BORGO
VIA VITTORIO ALFIERI
VIALE ANTONIO GRAMSCI
VIA JACOPO NARDI
VIA BENEDETTO VARCHI
6
Opificio delle Pietre Dure
VIA DEI FIBBIAI
Spedale degli Innocenti
VIA RICASOLI
VIA DEI SERVI
VIA DEL CASTELLACCIO
VIA DEGLI ALFANI
VIA DELLA PERGOLA
VIA DELLA COLONNA
V. SILVIO PELLICO
V. BENEDETTO VARCHI
Palazzo Pucci
PIAZZA FILIPPO BRUNELLESCHI
PIAZZA MASSIMO D'AZEGLIO
VIA PIETRO GIORDANI
DE' PUCCI
Santa Maria Maddalena dei Pazzi
Ospedale di Santa Maria Nuova
VIC. D. PERGOLA
V. NUOVA D. CACCINI
VIA LUIGI CARLO FARINI
VIA DELLA MATTONAIA
Duomo
VIA DEL PROCONSOLO
Museo dell'Opera del Duomo
Tempio Israelitico
V. GIOVAN BATTISTA NICCOLINI
Museo di Firenze com'era
BORGO PINTI
VIA FIESOLANA
VIA DE' PEPI
VIA DE' PILASTRI
VIA GIOSUE CARDUCCI
VIA GIACOMO LEOPARDI
V. ALESSANDRO MANZONI
VIA DELL'ORIUOLO
SEE PAGES 5–6 FOR ENLARGEMENT OF THIS AREA
Palazzo Nonfinito
VIA DI MEZZO
CORSO
BORGO D. ALBIZI
PIAZZA G. SALVEMINI
4

3
A
B
C
1
2
3
4
5
SEE PAGES 5–6 FOR ENLARGEMENT OF THIS AREA
LUNGARNO SODERINI
BORGO SAN FREDIANO
PIAZZA DI VERZAIA
PIAZZA DEL TIRATOIO
PIAZZA DI CESTELLO
San Frediano in Cestello
PIAZZA DE' NERLI
PIAZZA CARLO GOLDONI
V. D. VIGNA NUOVA
Palazzo Corsini
LUNGARNO CORSINI
Palazzo Strozzi
PIAZZA DEGLI STROZZI
V. D. ANSELMI
PIAZZA REPUBBLICA
Santa Trìnita
V. P.TA ROSSA
Palazzo Davanzati
Palazzo Spini-Ferroni
Palazzo Bartolini-Salimbeni
Palazzo Parte Guelfa
Santi Apostoli
PIAZZA NAZARIO SAURO
LUNGARNO GUICCIARDINI
LUNG. D. ACCIAIUOLI
VIA DI SANTO SPIRITO
PIAZZA DE' FRESCOBALDI
BORGO SAN JACOPO
PIAZZA DEL CARMINE
BORGO DELLA STELLA
PIAZZA PIATTELLINA
Cappella Brancacci (Santa Maria del Carmine)
PIAZZA TORQUATO TASSO
Santo Spirito
Cenacolo di Santo Spirito
PIAZZA DI SANTO SPIRITO
PIAZZA DI S. FELICITA
Santa Felìcita
V. D. GUICCIARDINI
VIA DE' SERRAGLI
VIA DELLA CHIESA
VIA DEL CAMPUCCIO
VIA MAGGIO
PIAZZA DE' PITTI
Palazzo Pitti
VIA ROMANA
Museo La Specola
GIARDINO TORRIGIANI
VIALE FRANCESCO PETRARCA
VIA DEL CASONE
GIARDINO DI BOBOLI
Forte di Belvedere
PIAZZA DELLA CALZA
PIAZZALE DELLA PORTA ROMANA
VIA UGO FOSCOLO
VIA PIETRO METASTASIO
VIALE NICCOLÒ MACHIAVELLI
VIA SENESE
VIALE DEL POGGIO IMPERIALE
VIA DANTE DA CASTIGLIONE
VIA BENEDETTO DA FOIANO
PIAZZALE GALILEO
V.LE EVANGELISTICA TORRICELLI
VIA DI SAN LEONARDO
VIA LORENZO BELLINI
VIA BENEDETTO CASTELLI
VIALE LORENZO MAGALOTTI
VIA DEL GELSOMINO
VIA LEONARDO XIMENES
VIA V. VIVIANI
VIA GUGLIELMO RIGHINI
VIA GIOVANNI ALFONSO BORELLI

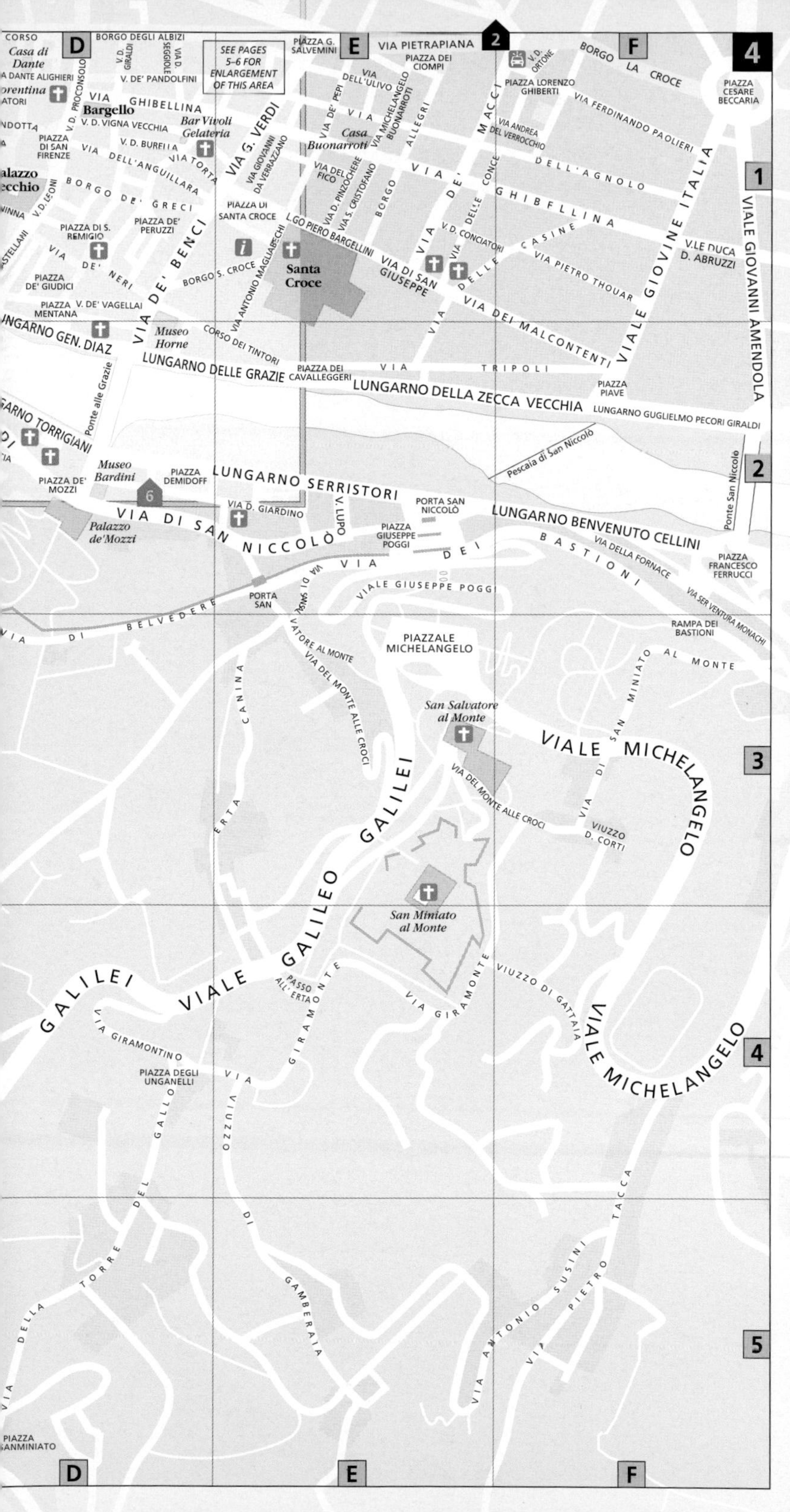

SEE PAGES 5–6 FOR ENLARGEMENT OF THIS AREA
Casa di Dante
Bargello
Bar Vivoli Gelateria
Casa Buonarroti
Santa Croce
Museo Horne
Museo Bardini
Palazzo de'Mozzi
PIAZZALE MICHELANGELO
San Salvatore al Monte
San Miniato al Monte
VIA GHIBELLINA
VIA G. VERDI
VIA DE' BENCI
VIA PIETRAPIANA
BORGO LA CROCE
VIALE GIOVINE ITALIA
VIALE GIOVANNI AMENDOLA
LUNGARNO GEN. DIAZ
LUNGARNO DELLE GRAZIE
LUNGARNO DELLA ZECCA VECCHIA
LUNGARNO SERRISTORI
LUNGARNO BENVENUTO CELLINI
VIA DI SAN NICCOLÒ
VIA DI BELVEDERE
VIA DEI BASTIONI
VIALE GIUSEPPE POGGI
VIALE MICHELANGELO
VIALE GALILEO GALILEI
VIA GIRAMONTE
VIA DEL MONTE ALLE CROCI
VIA DI SAN MINIATO AL MONTE
VIA DEL GALLO
VIA DELLA TORRE DEL GALLO
VIUZZO DI GAMBERAIA
VIA ANTONIO SUSINI
VIA PIETRO TACCA
PIAZZA SANMINIATO

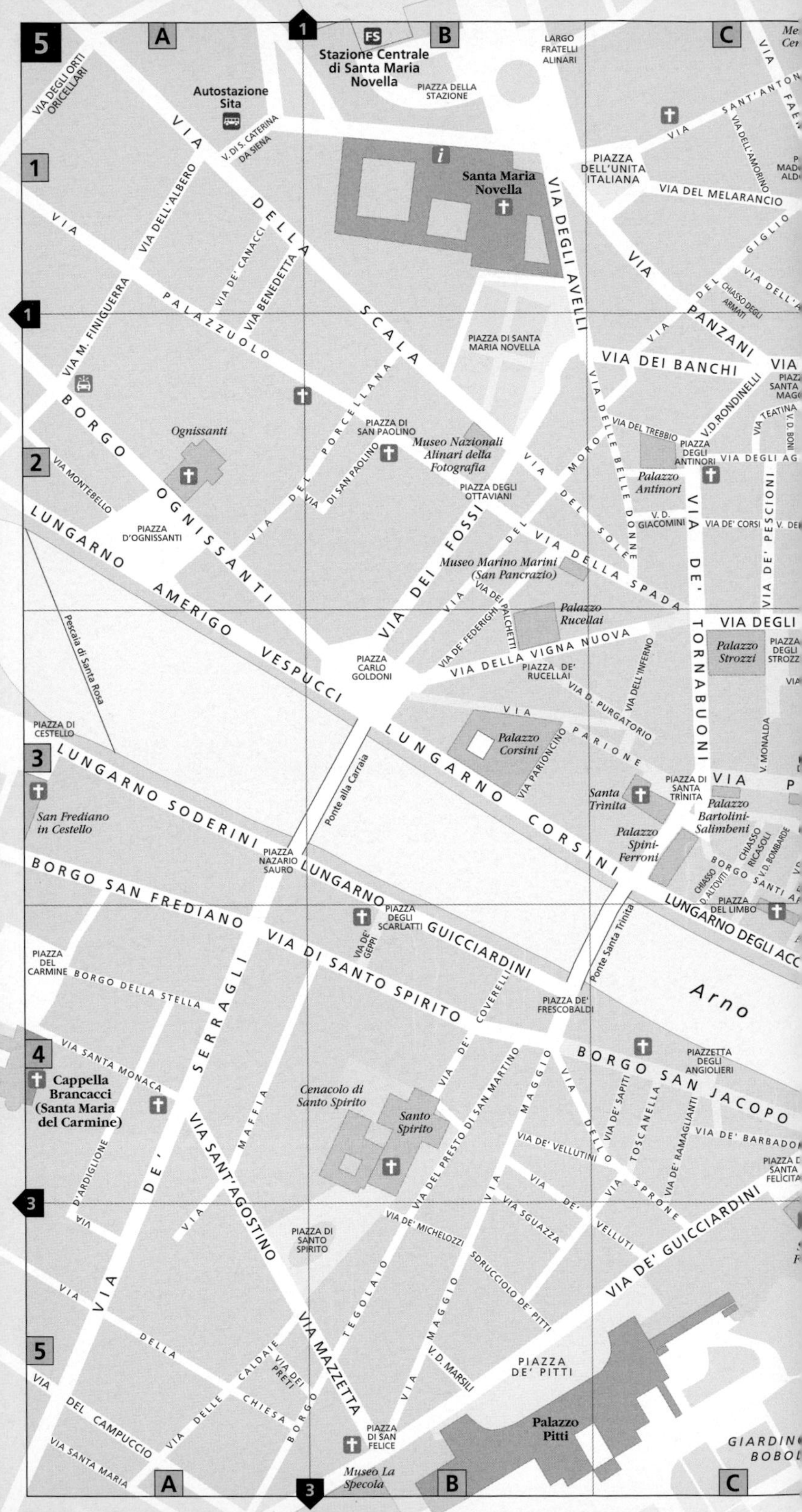

5
A
B
C
1
2
3
4
5
Stazione Centrale di Santa Maria Novella
Autostazione Sita
Santa Maria Novella
Ognissanti
Museo Nazionali Alinari della Fotografia
Museo Marino Marini (San Pancrazio)
Palazzo Rucellai
Palazzo Strozzi
Palazzo Antinori
Palazzo Corsini
Santa Trinita
Palazzo Bartolini-Salimbeni
Palazzo Spini-Ferroni
San Frediano in Cestello
Cappella Brancacci (Santa Maria del Carmine)
Cenacolo di Santo Spirito
Santo Spirito
Palazzo Pitti
Museo La Specola
Arno
PIAZZA DELLA STAZIONE
LARGO FRATELLI ALINARI
PIAZZA DELL'UNITA ITALIANA
PIAZZA DI SANTA MARIA NOVELLA
PIAZZA DI SAN PAOLINO
PIAZZA DEGLI OTTAVIANI
PIAZZA D'OGNISSANTI
PIAZZA CARLO GOLDONI
PIAZZA DE' RUCELLAI
PIAZZA DEGLI ANTINORI
PIAZZA DEGLI STROZZI
PIAZZA DI SANTA TRINITA
PIAZZA DEL LIMBO
PIAZZA DI CESTELLO
PIAZZA NAZARIO SAURO
PIAZZA DEGLI SCARLATTI
PIAZZA DEL CARMINE
PIAZZA DE' FRESCOBALDI
PIAZZETTA DEGLI ANGIOLIERI
PIAZZA DI SANTO SPIRITO
PIAZZA DE' PITTI
PIAZZA DI SAN FELICE
VIA DEGLI ORTI ORICELLARI
V. DI S. CATERINA DA SIENA
VIA DELLA SCALA
VIA DELL'ALBERO
VIA DE' CANACCI
VIA BENEDETTA
VIA PALAZZUOLO
VIA M. FINIGUERRA
BORGO OGNISSANTI
VIA MONTEBELLO
VIA DEL PORCELLANA
VIA DI SAN PAOLINO
VIA DEGLI AVELLI
VIA DEI FOSSI
VIA DEL MORO
VIA DEL SOLE
VIA DELLA SPADA
VIA DELLE BELLE DONNE
VIA DEL TREBBIO
V. D. GIACOMINI
VIA DE' CORSI
VIA DE' TORNABUONI
VIA DE' PESCIONI
VIA DEI BANCHI
VIA PANZANI
VIA DEL GIGLIO
VIA DEL MELARANCIO
VIA DELL'AMORINO
VIA SANT'ANTONINO
CHIASSO DEGLI ARMATI
V.D. RONDINELLI
VIA TEATINA
VIA DEGLI AGLI
VIA DE' FEDERIGHI
VIA DEI PALCHETTI
VIA DELLA VIGNA NUOVA
VIA DELL'INFERNO
VIA D. PURGATORIO
VIA PARIONE
VIA PARIONCINO
V. MONALDA
LUNGARNO AMERIGO VESPUCCI
Pescaia di Santa Rosa
LUNGARNO CORSINI
LUNGARNO SODERINI
Ponte alla Carraia
Ponte Santa Trinita
BORGO SAN FREDIANO
LUNGARNO GUICCIARDINI
LUNGARNO DEGLI ACC
VIA DE' GEPPI
VIA DI SANTO SPIRITO
VIA DE' COVERELLI
BORGO DELLA STELLA
VIA DEL SERRAGLI
VIA SANTA MONACA
VIA MAFFIA
VIA SANT'AGOSTINO
VIA D'ARDIGLIONE
VIA DE' SERRAGLI
VIA DEL PRESTO DI SAN MARTINO
VIA MAGGIO
VIA DELLO SPRONE
VIA DE' SAPITI
VIA TOSCANELLA
VIA DE' RAMAGLIANTI
BORGO SAN JACOPO
VIA DE' BARBADORI
VIA DE' VELLUTINI
VIA DE' VELLUTI
VIA SGUAZZA
VIA DE' MICHELOZZI
SDRUCCIOLO DE' PITTI
VIA DE' GUICCIARDINI
VIA TEGOLAIO
V. D. MARSILI
VIA MAZZETTA
BORGO TEGOLAIO
VIA DELLA CHIESA
VIA DEI PRETI
VIA DELLE CALDAIE
VIA DEL CAMPUCCIO
VIA SANTA MARIA
CHIASSO RICASOLI
V.D. BOMBARDE
BORGO SANTI APOSTOLI
CHIASSO D. ALTOVITI
GIARDINO BOBOLI

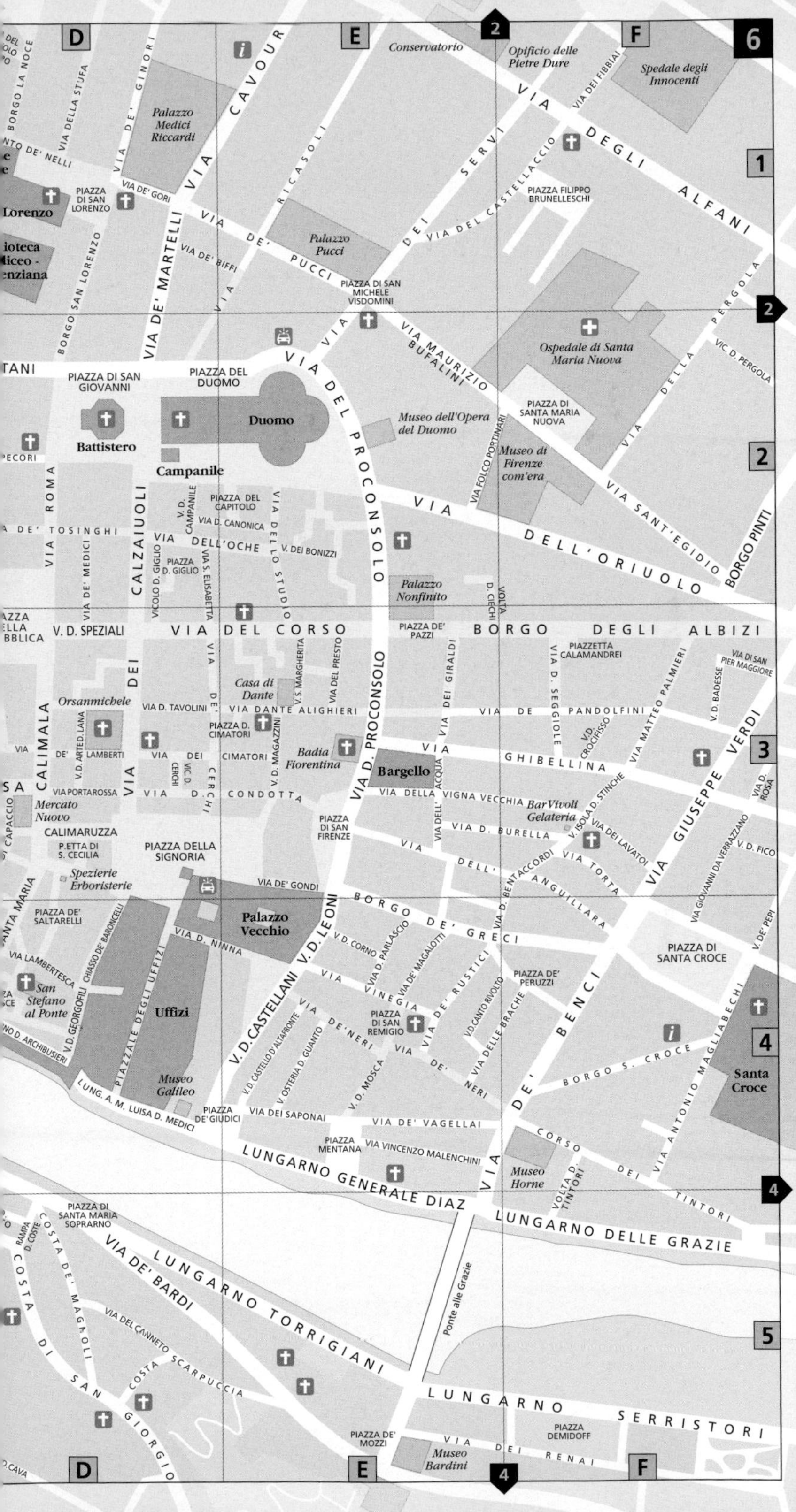
6
D
E
F
2
4
1
2
3
4
5
Conservatorio
Opificio delle Pietre Dure
Spedale degli Innocenti
Palazzo Medici Riccardi
Palazzo Pucci
Piazza Filippo Brunelleschi
Piazza di San Lorenzo
Lorenzo
Piazza di San Michele Visdomini
Ospedale di Santa Maria Nuova
Piazza di Santa Maria Nuova
Piazza di San Giovanni
Piazza del Duomo
Battistero
Duomo
Campanile
Museo dell'Opera del Duomo
Museo di Firenze com'era
Piazza del Capitolo
Piazza D. Giglio
Palazzo Nonfinito
Piazza de' Pazzi
Piazzetta Calamandrei
Casa di Dante
Piazza D. Cimatori
Orsanmichele
Badia Fiorentina
Bargello
Bar Vivoli Gelateria
Mercato Nuovo
Calimaruzza
P.etta di S. Cecilia
Piazza della Signoria
Piazza di San Firenze
Spezierie Erboristerie
Palazzo Vecchio
Piazza de' Saltarelli
San Stefano al Ponte
Uffizi
Museo Galileo
Piazza de' Peruzzi
Piazza di Santa Croce
Piazza di San Remigio
Santa Croce
Piazza de' Giudici
Piazza Mentana
Museo Horne
Piazza di Santa Maria Soprarno
Ponte alle Grazie
Piazza de' Mozzi
Museo Bardini
Piazza Demidoff
Via Cavour
Via de' Ginori
Via della Stufa
Borgo la Noce
Via dei Servi
Via degli Alfani
Via dei Fibbiai
Via del Castellaccio
Via Ricasoli
Via de' Gori
Via de' Pucci
Via de' Martelli
Via de' Biffi
Borgo San Lorenzo
Via Maurizio Bufalini
Via della Pergola
Vic. d. Pergola
Via del Proconsolo
Via Folco Portinari
Via Sant'Egidio
Borgo Pinti
Via dell'Oriuolo
Via Roma
Via de' Tosinghi
Via dei Calzaiuoli
Via dell'Oche
V. dei Bonizzi
Via dello Studio
Via D. Canonica
Via de' Medici
Borgo degli Albizi
Via del Corso
V. D. Speziali
Volta d. Ciechi
Via dei Giraldi
Via D. Seggiole
Via Matteo Palmieri
Via di San Pier Maggiore
Via Dante Alighieri
Via D. Tavolini
Via de' Pandolfini
Via Ghibellina
Via Giuseppe Verdi
Calimala
Via de' Lamberti
Via dei Cimatori
Via Portarossa
Via d. Condotta
Via della Vigna Vecchia
Via D. Burella
Via dell'Anguillara
Via Torta
Via dei Lavatoi
Via Giovanni da Verrazzano
Via de' Gondi
Borgo de' Greci
Via D. Ninna
Via Lambertesca
Chiasso de' Baroncelli
Piazzale degli Uffizi
V. D. Castellani
V. D. Leoni
Via Vinegia
Via de' Neri
Via de' Benci
Borgo S. Croce
Via Antonio Magliabechi
Lung. A. M. Luisa D. Medici
Via dei Saponai
Via de' Vagellai
Via Vincenzo Malenchini
Corso dei Tintori
Lungarno Generale Diaz
Lungarno delle Grazie
Via de' Bardi
Lungarno Torrigiani
Costa de' Magnoli
Costa di San Giorgio
Via del Canneto
Costa Scarpuccia
Lungarno Serristori
Via dei Renai

TUSCANY

Renowned for its art, history, and evocative landscape, Tuscany is a region where the past and present merge in pleasant harmony. Hill towns gaze across the countryside from on high, many encircled by Etruscan walls and slender cypress trees. Handsome palaces testify to the region's wealth while medieval town halls indicate a long-standing tradition of democracy and self-government.

In the countryside, among the vineyards and olive groves, there are hamlets and farmhouses, as well as fortified villas and castles that symbolize the violence and intercommunal strife that tore Tuscany apart during the Middle Ages. Several imposing castles and villas were built for the Medici family, the great patrons of the Renaissance who supported eminent scientists, such as Galileo.

Northern Tuscany, and the heavily populated plain between Florence and Lucca, is dominated by industry, with intensively cultivated land between the cities and the wild mountainous areas.

The area centerd around Livorno and Pisa is now the region's economic hub. Pisa, at the height of its powers, dominated the western Mediterranean from the 11th to the 13th centuries. Its navy opened up extensive trading routes with North Africa, and brought to Italy the benefits of Arabic scientific and artistic achievement. During the 16th century the Arno estuary began to silt up, ending Pisan power.

At the heart of central Tuscany lies Siena, which was involved in a long feud with Florence. Its finest hour came with its victory in the Battle of Montaperti in 1260, but it was devastated by the Black Death in the 14th century and finally suffered a crushing defeat by Florence in the siege of 1554–5.

Northeastern Tuscany, with its mountain peaks and woodland, provided refuge for hermits and saints, while the east was home to Piero della Francesca, the early Renaissance painter whose timeless and serene works are imbued with an almost religious perfection.

A timeless view and way of life in Casole d'Elsa, near San Gimignano in central Tuscany

◀ The picturesque farmlands of Pienza in Tuscany

Exploring Tuscany

Tuscan cities such as Florence, Siena, and Pisa, together with smaller towns like Lucca, Cortona, and Arezzo, contain some of Italy's most famous artistic treasures. Medieval villages such as San Gimignano, with its famous towers, or Pienza, a tiny Renaissance jewel, sit at the heart of the glorious pastoral countryside for which the region is equally renowned. Elsewhere landscapes range from the spectacular mountains of the Alpi Apuane to the gentle hills of Chianti.

Sights at a Glance

View of Cortona in eastern Tuscany

For additional map symbols *see back flap*

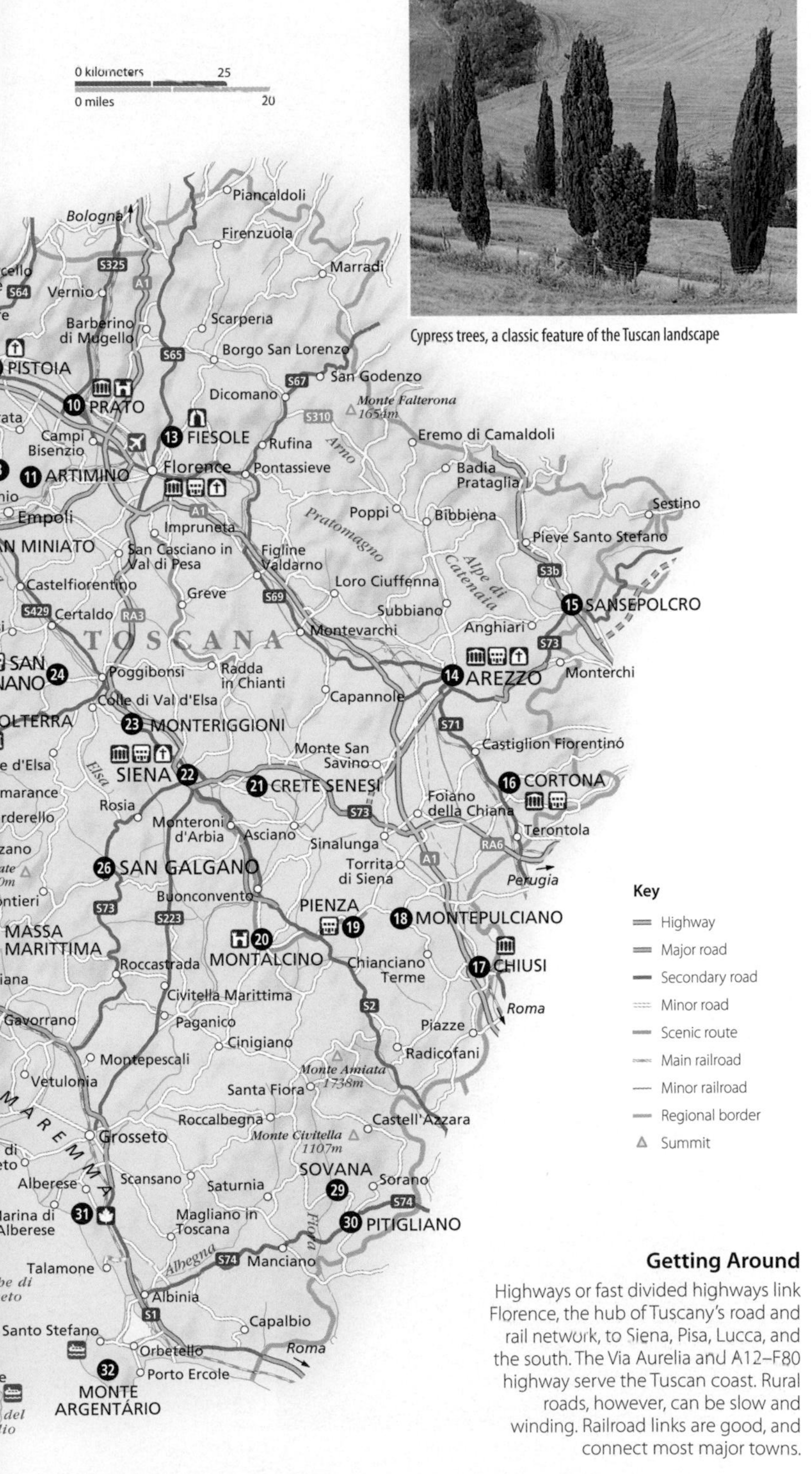

Cypress trees, a classic feature of the Tuscan landscape

Getting Around

Highways or fast divided highways link Florence, the hub of Tuscany's road and rail network, to Siena, Pisa, Lucca, and the south. The Via Aurelia and A12–E80 highway serve the Tuscan coast. Rural roads, however, can be slow and winding. Railroad links are good, and connect most major towns.

❶ Carrara

Massa Carrara. 200,000. FS
Lungomare Vespucci 24 (0585 24 00 63). Mon.

Internationally renowned for its marble quarries, Carrara's almost flawless white stone has been prized for centuries by famous sculptors from Michelangelo to Henry Moore (the stone for Michelangelo's *David* came from Carrara). The region's 300 or more quarries date back to Roman times, making this one of the oldest industrial sites in continuous use in the world. Many of the town's marble-sawing mills and workshops welcome visitors, offering them the chance to see the ways in which marble and quartz are worked. These techniques – along with marble artifacts old and new – can be seen at the **Museo Civico del Marmo**.

Local marble is put to good use in the town's **Duomo** in Piazza del Duomo, particularly in the fine Pisan-Romanesque facade with its delicate rose window. The cathedral square also contains Michelangelo's house, used by the sculptor during his visits to select blocks of marble. The town has some lovely corners to explore, in particular the elegant Piazza Alberica. Most visitors head for the stone quarries that are open to the public at nearby **Colonnata** and at **Fantiscritti** (take one of the regular town buses or follow the signs to the "Cave di Marmo"). The latter features a small museum with displays of various marble quarrying techniques.

A quarry in the marble-bearing hills around Carrara

Museo Civico del Marmo
Viale XX Settembre. **Tel** 0585 84 57 46. **Open** Mon–Sat.

The Parco Naturale delle Alpi Apuane on the edge of the Garfagnana

❷ Garfagnana

Lucca. FS Castelnuovo di Garfagnana. Piazza delle Erbe, Castelnuovo di Garfagnana (0583 651 69).

A verdant, silent valley wedged between the Orecchiella Mountains and the Alpi Apuane, the Garfagnana region can be explored from **Seravezza**, **Barga**, or **Castelnuovo di Garfagnana**. While the town of Barga makes the prettiest base, thanks to its tawny stone cathedral and charming streets, Castelnuovo is more convenient for drives and walks in the surrounding mountains. **San Pellegrino in Alpe** in the Orecchiella has a fascinating folklore museum, the **Museo Etnografico**. It is easily seen in conjunction with the **Orto Botanico Pania di Corfino** at the headquarters of the **Parco dell'Orecchiella** at Pania di Corfino, with its collection of local Alpine trees.

To the west is the Parco Naturale delle Alpi Apuane, an area whose spectacular jagged peaks and wooded valleys are crisscrossed by hiking trails and scenic mountain roads.

Museo Etnografico
Via del Voltone 15, San Pellegrino in Alpe. **Tel** 0583 64 90 72. **Open** Tue–Sun (Jul–Aug: daily).

Parco dell'Orecchiella
Centro Visitatori, Orecchiella. **Tel** 0583 61 90 02. **Open** Jun & Sep: 10am–5pm daily; Jul & Aug: 9am–7pm daily.

Orto Botanico Pania di Corfino
Parco dell'Orecchiella. **Tel** 0583 64 49 11. **Open** May–Sep: daily.

For hotels and restaurants in this region see pp562–77 and pp580–605

One of many seaside cafés lining the waterfront in the popular beach resort of Viareggio

3 Bagni di Lucca

Lucca. 7,400. Via E. Wipple c/o Chiesa Inglese (0583 80 57 45). Sat.

All over Tuscany there are hot springs of volcanic origin, like Bagni di Lucca. The Romans first exploited the springs and built bath complexes where army veterans who settled in the area could relax. More spas came into prominence in the Middle Ages and the Renaissance, and they have continued to be recommended for relieving a variety of ailments, such as arthritis.

Tuscan spas really came into their own in the early 19th century when Bagni di Lucca reached its heyday as one of Europe's most fashionable spas, frequented by emperors, kings, and aristocrats. Visitors came not only for thermal cures, but also for the **Casino** (1837), one of Europe's first licensed gambling houses. These days the town is rather sleepy, and its main sights are the 19th-century monuments, including the Neo-Gothic **English Church** (1839) on Via Crawford and the **Cimitero Anglicano** (Protestant Cemetery) on Via Letizia.

Environs

Southeast of Bagni di Lucca lies another popular spa town, **Montecatini Terme**. Developed in the 18th century, this town is one of the most interesting with a wide range of spa architecture, from Neo-Classical to Art Nouveau spa establishments.

4 Viareggio

Lucca. 65,000. FS Viale Carducci 10 (0584 96 22 33). Thu.

Known for its carnival, held in January and early February, this is also the most popular of the resorts on the Versilia coast. Its famous "Liberty" (Art Nouveau) style of architecture can be seen in the grand hotels, villas, and cafés built in the 1920s after the resort's original boardwalk and timber chalets went up in flames in 1917. The finest example of the architecture is the **Gran Caffè Margherita** at the end of Passeggiata Margherita, designed by the prolific father of Italian Art Nouveau, Galileo Chini.

5 Torre del Lago Puccini

Lucca. 11,000. FS Viale Kennedy 2 (0584 35 98 93). Fri.

A glorious avenue of linden trees, the Via dei Tigli, connects Viareggio with Torre del Lago Puccini, once the home of the opera composer Giacomo Puccini (1858–1924). He and his wife are buried in their former home, now the **Museo Villa Puccini**, a small museum that features the piano on which the maestro composed many of his works. Equal prominence is given to the villa's original fixtures, including the gun room that housed Puccini's hunting rifle. **Lago Massaciuccoli**, a nature reserve for rare and migrant birds, provides a pretty backdrop for open-air performances of Puccini's works.

Museo Villa Puccini
Piazzale Belvedere Puccini 226.
Tel 0584 34 14 45. **Open** Tue–Sun.
Closed Nov, Dec 25.

Near Puccini's lakeside home at Torre del Lago Puccini

❻ Street by Street: Lucca

Lucca's regular grid of streets still follows the pattern of the former Roman colony founded in 180 BC. Great, solid ramparts, built in the 16th to 17th century, help to shut out traffic, making the city a pleasant place to explore on foot. San Michele in Foro – one of the town's many fine Pisan-Romanesque churches – stands on the site of the Roman forum *(foro)*, the city's main square laid out in ancient times. It is still Lucca's main square today.

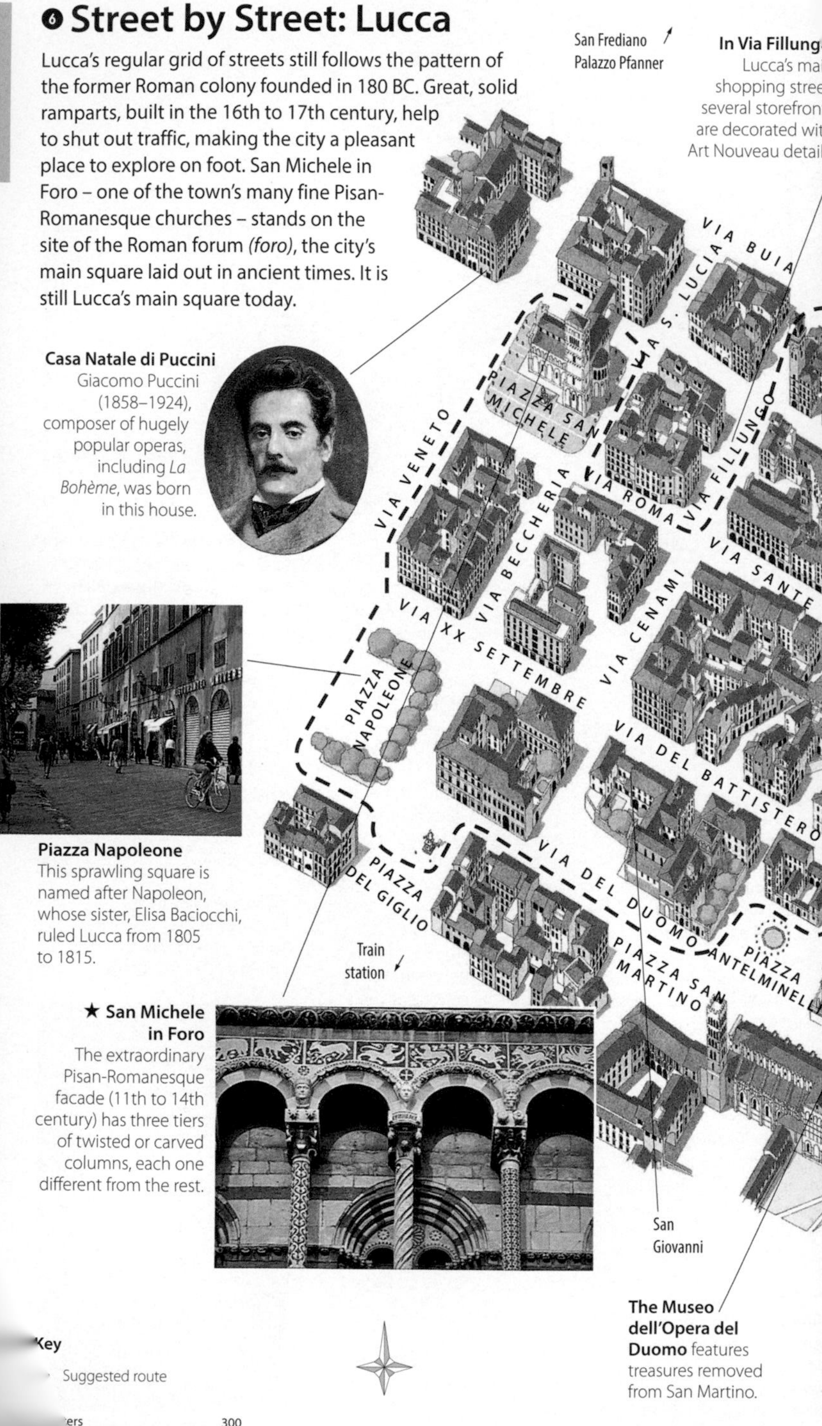

In Via Fillung
Lucca's mai shopping street, several storefronts are decorated with Art Nouveau details.

Casa Natale di Puccini
Giacomo Puccini (1858–1924), composer of hugely popular operas, including *La Bohème*, was born in this house.

Piazza Napoleone
This sprawling square is named after Napoleon, whose sister, Elisa Baciocchi, ruled Lucca from 1805 to 1815.

★ San Michele in Foro
The extraordinary Pisan-Romanesque facade (11th to 14th century) has three tiers of twisted or carved columns, each one different from the rest.

The Museo dell'Opera del Duomo features treasures removed from San Martino.

Key

Suggested route

ers 300

300

VISITORS' CHECKLIST

Practical Information
85,000. Piazza Santa Maria 35 (0583 91 99 31). 3rd Sun of month (antiques), Wed, Sat. Jul 12: Palio della Balestra; Jul: Lucca Summer Festival; Sep 13: Luminara di Santa Croce.
luccaturismo.it

Transportation
Piazza Ricasoli.
Piazzale Verdi.

an Martino
a's beautiful 11th-century mo is one of the outstanding nples of the exuberant Pisan-anesque style.

Apostles from the mosaic on the facade of San Frediano in Lucca

San Frediano

Piazza San Frediano. **Open** daily.

San Frediano's striking facade features a colorful 13th-century mosaic, *The Ascension*, a fine prelude to the church's wonderfully atmospheric interior. Pride of place goes to a splendid Romanesque font on the right, its sides carved with scenes from the Life of Christ and the story of Moses. Note the scene of Moses and his followers (dressed as medieval knights) as they pass through the divided Red Sea. In the second chapel in the north aisle, Aspertini's frescoes (1508–9) tell the story of Lucca's precious relic, the Volto Santo – a carving said to date from the time of the Crucifixion. The fine altarpiece (1422) in the fourth chapel of San Frediano's north aisle is by Jacopo della Quercia.

San Michele in Foro

Piazza San Michele. **Open** daily.

Built on the site of the old Roman forum *(foro)*, San Michele's rich mixture of twisted marble columns and Cosmati work (inlaid marble) adorns one of the most exuberant Pisan-Romanesque facades in Tuscany. Built between the 11th and 14th centuries, its decoration is overwhelmingly pagan. Only the huge winged figure of St. Michael on the pediment marks this out as a church. The interior has little of interest except for the beautiful painting of *Saints Helena, Jerome, Sebastian, and Roch* by Filippino Lippi (1457–1504).

Casa Natale di Puccini

Corte San Lorenzo 9. **Tel** 0583 58 40 28. **Open** Apr–Oct: 10am–6pm daily; Nov–Mar: 11am–5pm. **Closed** Tue, Jan 1, Dec 25.

The fine 15th-century house in which Giacomo Puccini (1858–1924) was born is now a shrine to the great opera composer. It contains portraits of Puccini, costume designs for his operas, and the piano he used when composing his last opera, *Turandot*.

Via Fillungo

Lucca's principal shopping street winds its way through the heart of the city toward the Anfiteatro Romano. Its northern end has several shops with Art Nouveau ironwork; halfway down lies the deconsecrated church of San Cristoforo, built in the 13th century, with a lovely interior.

One of the many bars and shops along Via Fillungo

Exploring Lucca

Lucca's peaceful narrow lanes wind among the medieval buildings, opening suddenly to reveal churches, tiny piazzas, and many other reminders of the city's long history, including a Roman amphitheater.

Medieval buildings mark the outline of Lucca's old Roman amphitheater

Anfiteatro Romano

Piazza del Mercato.

Roman *Luca* was founded in 180 BC, and stones from the ancient Roman amphitheater have been ransacked over the centuries to build churches and palaces, leaving only a handful of original fragments studded into today's arena-shaped Piazza del Mercato. Slum housing clogged the piazza until 1830, when it was cleared on the orders of Marie Louise, the city's Bourbon ruler of that time. It was then that the amphitheater's original shape was revealed, a graphic and evocative reminder of Lucca's rich Roman heritage. Low archways at the piazza's cardinal points mark the gates through which beasts and gladiators would once have entered the arena.

Museo dell'Opera del Duomo

Piazza Antelminelli 5. **Tel** 0583 49 05 30. **Open** daily. **Closed** Jan 1, Easter (am), Dec 25.

The museum, housed in the former Archbishop's Palace (14th century), displays the treasures of the Duomo of San Martino. These include the 11th-century carved stone head of a king and a rare

San Martino

Piazza San Martino. **Tel** 0583 95 70 68. **Open** daily. for sacristy.

Lucca's cathedral was built after the campanile, hence the facade's cramped and asymmetric appearance. The main portals contain remarkable 13th-century carvings by Nicola Pisano and Guidetto da Como. The Tempietto inside houses a painting by Tintoretto and the Volto Santo, a revered 13th-century effigy once believed to have been carved at the time of the Crucifixion.

Facade
The cathedral facade is decorated with Romanesque sculptures and colonnading (1204).

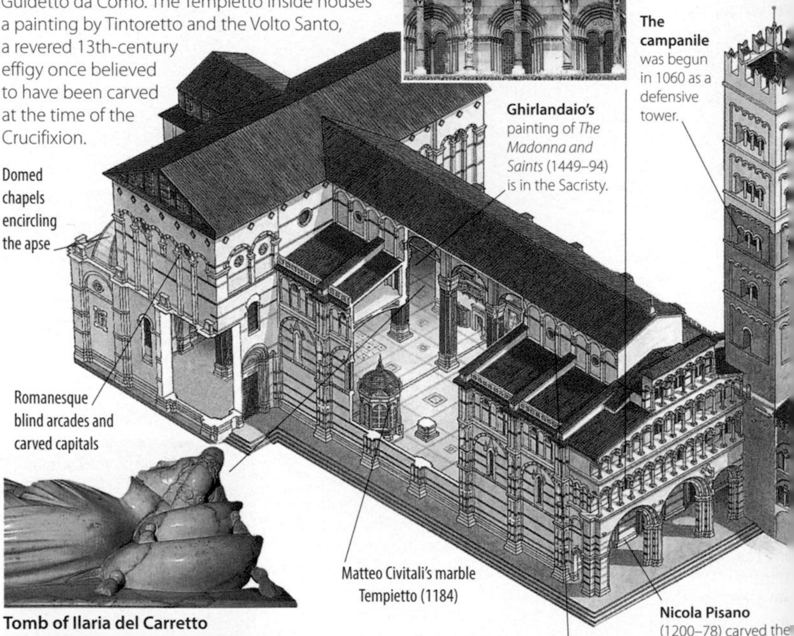

The campanile was begun in 1060 as a defensive tower.

Ghirlandaio's painting of *The Madonna and Saints* (1449–94) is in the Sacristy.

Domed chapels encircling the apse

Romanesque blind arcades and carved capitals

Matteo Civitali's marble Tempietto (1184)

Tomb of Ilaria del Carretto
This beautiful portrait in marble by Jacopo della Quercia (1405–6) is of the youthful bride of Paolo Guinigi.

Circular clerestory windows, in the nave and above the aisle roof, illuminate the church's unusually tall nave.

Nicola Pisano (1200–78) carved the *Journey of the Magi* and *Deposition* on the left portal.

aroque gods and goddesses in the garden of the Palazzo Pfanner

2th-century Limoges casket, ›ossibly created for a relic of St. homas à Becket. The Croce dei 'isani, made by Vincenzo di Aichele in 1411, is a sublime nasterpiece of the goldsmith's rt. It shows Christ on the Tree f Redemption, surrounded by ngels, the Virgin, St. John, and he other Evangelists.

Palazzo Pfanner

ia degli Asili 33. **Tel** 0583 954 029. **pen** Apr–Oct: 10am–6pm; Nov 1–15: 1am–4pm; rest of year: by appt.

his elegant, imposing house 1667) has a beautiful outside taircase. It also boasts one f Tuscany's most delightful ormal gardens. Laid out in he 18th century, the garden's entral avenue is lined with aroque statues of the gods nd goddesses of ancient oman mythology. The garden an also be viewed while valking along the ramparts.

The house itself contains n interesting collection f furniture, antiques, and nedical instruments.

Ramparts

)ne of the pleasures of visiting ucca is strolling along the amparts – the magnificent ity walls, whose tree-lined romenade offers some ntrancing views of the city. Vork on the ramparts began around 1500, when advances in military technology made the old medieval defenses ineffective. On their completion in 1645, the walls were some of the most advanced of their time. One of their most curious features was the open space that lay beyond them, and which survives to this day, cleared to prevent the enemy taking cover in trees and undergrowth. Ironically, the walls never actually had to be defended, and they were eventually converted into a public park in the early 19th century.

Part of the imposing 17th-century ramparts that encircle Lucca

Santa Maria Forisportam

Piazza di Santa Maria Forisportam. **Open** daily.

This church was built at the end of the 12th century, beyond the Roman walls of Lucca. Its name, Forisportam, means "outside the gate." The unfinished marble facade, in Pisan-Romanesque style, has blind arcading. Above the central portal is a relief of the *Coronation of the Virgin* (17th century). The interior was redesigned in the early 16th century, resulting in the nave and transepts being raised. The fourth altar of the south aisle contains a painting of *St. Lucy,* and the north transept has an *Assumption,* both by Guercino (1591–1666).

Museo Nazionale di Villa Guinigi

Via della Quarquonia. **Tel** 0583 49 60 33. **Open** 8:30am–7pm Tue–Sat. **Closed** Jan 1, May 1, Dec 25.

This massive Renaissance villa was built in 1418 for Paolo Guinigi, leading light of the noble family who ruled Lucca in the early 15th century. A familiar landmark of the city is the battlemented tower, the Torre dei Guinigi, with oak trees growing at the top. It offers good views over the city and the Apuan Alps. The garden features traces of a Roman mosaic, together with a pride of Romanesque lions removed from the city's walls.

Romanesque lion in the Museo Nazionale Guinigi

Inside, the museum's first floor is devoted to sculptures and archaeological displays. The highlights are works by Matteo Civitali and Jacopo della Quercia and fine Romanesque reliefs removed from several of Lucca's churches. Most of the paintings in the gallery on the floor above are by minor local artists, with the exception of two by Fra Bartolomeo (*c.* 1472–1517): *God the Father with Saints Catherine and Mary Magdalene* and the *Madonna della Misericordia.* The floor also has furnishings, church vestments, and choir stalls from Lucca's cathedral, inlaid with marque views of the city carved in 1

7 Pisa

For much of the Middle Ages, Pisa's powerful navy ensured its dominance of the western Mediterranean. Trading links with Spain and North Africa in the 12th century brought vast mercantile wealth and formed the basis of a cultural revolution that is still reflected in Pisa's splendid buildings – especially the Duomo, Baptistry, and Campanile (Leaning Tower). Pisa's decline began in 1284, with its defeat by Genoa, and was hastened by the silting up of the harbor. The city fell to the Florentines in 1406, but suffered its worst crisis in 1944 when it fell victim to Allied bombing.

The Baptistry, Duomo, and Leaning Tower in Pisa's Campo dei Miracoli

Leaning Tower

See p330. **Tel** 050 83 50 11/12. **Open** daily. Visits last 30 min. No children under 8 allowed. **opapisa.it** (reservations).

Duomo and Baptistry

Piazza Duomo. **Tel** 050 83 50 11. **Open** daily (Duomo: pm only on Sun). **opapisa.it**

Pisa's famous Leaning Tower is now the best-known building in the Campo dei Miracoli (Field of Miracles). Originally, however, it was intended as a ...mpanile to complement the ...omo, which was begun by ...cheto in 1064. Today the Duomo stands as one of the finest Pisan-Romanesque buildings in Tuscany, its wonderful four-tiered facade a medley of creamy colonnades and intricate blind arcades. Buscheto's tomb is in the left arch of the facade. Other important features of the exterior include the Portale di San Ranieri (leading to the south transept) and the bronze doors (1180), decorated with reliefs cast by Bonanno Pisano, the first architect of the Leaning Tower. Inside, the highlights are the carved pulpit (1302–11) by Giovanni Pisano, the *Tomb of Emperor Henry VII* (1315) by Tino

A detail from the Duomo pulpit

da Camaino, and a mosaic of *Christ in Majesty* in the apse, completed by Cimabue in 1302.

The circular Baptistry was begun in 1152 along Romanesque lines, and finished a century later (the delay caused by a shortage of money) in a more ornate Gothic style by Nicola and Giovanni Pisano. The former was responsible for the marble pulpit (1260) in the interior, carved with reliefs of the *Nativity*, the *Adoration of the Magi*, the *Presentation*, the *Crucifixion*, and the *Last Judgmen*... The pillars that support the pulp... feature statues of the Virtues. The inlaid marble font (1246) is by Guido da Como.

Camposanto

Piazza dei Miracoli. **Tel** 050 83 50 11. **Open** daily. **Closed** Jan 1, Dec 25.

The Camposanto (cemetery) is the fourth element in the Camp... dei Miracoli's lovely ensemble. Begun in 1278 by Giovanni di Simone, the vast marble arcade of this long, rectangular building are said to enclose soil from the Holy Land. Bombs in World War II all but destroyed it once famous frescoes, leaving only traces of *The Triumph of Death* (1360–80). Nearby is the Orto Botanico, one of Europe's oldest botanical gardens.

A fresco from the *Triumph of Death* cycle in the Camposanto

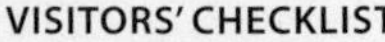

Santa Maria della Spina alongside the River Arno in Pisa

VISITORS' CHECKLIST

Practical Information
90,000. Pza Duomo (050 56 04 64); Pza Vittorio Emanuele 16 (050 422 91). Wed & Sat. 17 Jun: Regata di San Ranieri; last Sun in Jun: Gioco del Ponte.
pisaunicaterra.it

Transportation
Galileo Galilei 3 miles (5 km) S. Pisa Centrale, Pza della Stazione. Pza Sant'

Museo dell'Opera del Duomo

Piazza del Duomo 6. **Tel** 050 83 10 11. **Open** daily.

Housed in the cathedral's 13th-century former Chapter House, this excellent modern museum displays exhibits removed over the years from the Duomo, Baptistry, and Camposanto. Among the highlights is an imposing 10th-century hippogriff (half horse, half griffin). Cast in bronze by Moorish craftsmen, this statue was looted by Pisan adventurers during the wars against the Saracens. There are also works by both Nicola and Giovanni Pisano, notably Giovanni's ivory *Virgin and Child* (1300), carved for the Duomo's high altar. Other exhibits include paintings, Roman and Etruscan remains, and ecclesiastical treasures.

10th-century bronze hippogriff

Museo Nazionale di San Matteo

Lungarno Mediceo, Piazza San Matteo 1. **Tel** 050 54 18 65. **Open** 9am–7pm Tue–Sun (Sun: am only).

This museum is located on the banks of the Arno in San Matteo, an elegantly fronted medieval convent that in the 1800s also served as a prison. Much of the building has been closed for years – several of the rooms have no numbers and some of the exhibits are poorly labeled. Nevertheless, the museum presents a unique opportunity to examine the complete sweep of Pisan and Florentine art from the 12th to the 17th centuries.

The first rooms are devoted to sculpture and early Tuscan paintings. The best exhibits include a 14th-century polyptych by Francesco Traini of *Scenes from the Life of St. Dominic*, Simone Martini's fine polyptych of *The Madonna and Saints* (1321), and a 14th-century statue of the *Madonna del Latte* attributed to Andrea Pisano, another member of Pisa's talented school of medieval sculptors. The half-length statue, in gilded marble, shows Christ feeding at his mother's breast. In room 6 are some of the highlights of the museum, including Masaccio's *St. Paul* (1426), Gentile da Fabriano's radiant 15th-century *Madonna of Humility*, and Donatello's reliquary bust of *San Rossore* (1424–7). Additional rooms contain paintings by Guido Reni, Benozzo Gozzoli, and Rosso Fiorentino, and an important picture of *Christ* attributed to Fra Angelico (*c.* 1395–1455).

Santa Maria della Spina

Lungarno Gambacorti. **Tel** 055 12 19 19. **Open** Tue–Sun.

The roofline of this tiny church, located just beyond the Ponte Solferino, bristles with spiky Gothic pinnacles, spires, and niches sheltering statues of apostles and saints. The decoration reflects the history of the church, which was built between 1230 and 1323 to house a thorn *(spina)* from Christ's Crown of Thorns, the gift of a Pisan merchant. The church was once even closer to the Arno, but was rebuilt on the present site in 1871 to protect it from flooding.

Piazza dei Cavalieri

The huge building on the north side of this square is the Palazzo dei Cavalieri, home to one of Pisa University's most prestigious colleges: the Scuola Normale Superiore. Designed by Vasari in 1562, the building, which is covered in exuberant black and white *sgraffito* decoration (designs scratched into wet plaster), served as the headquarters of the Cavalieri di Santo Stefano, an order of knights created by Cosimo I in 1561.

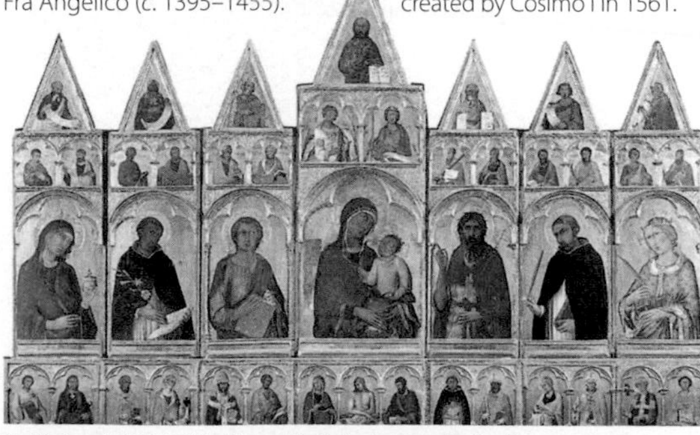

The Virgin and Child (1321) by Simone Martini in the Museo Nazionale

The Leaning Tower of Pisa

Begun in 1173 on sandy silt subsoil, the Leaning Tower (Torre Pendente) started to tilt even before the third story was finished in 1274. Despite the shallow foundations, construction continued, and the structure was completed in 1350. The tower's apparent flouting of the laws of gravity has attracted many visitors over the centuries, including the Pisan scientist Galileo, who climbed to the top to conduct his experiments on the velocity of falling objects. After several engineering interventions that decreased the lean by 14 inches (38 cm), the tower is once again safe and open to the public.

Galileo Galilei (1564–1642)

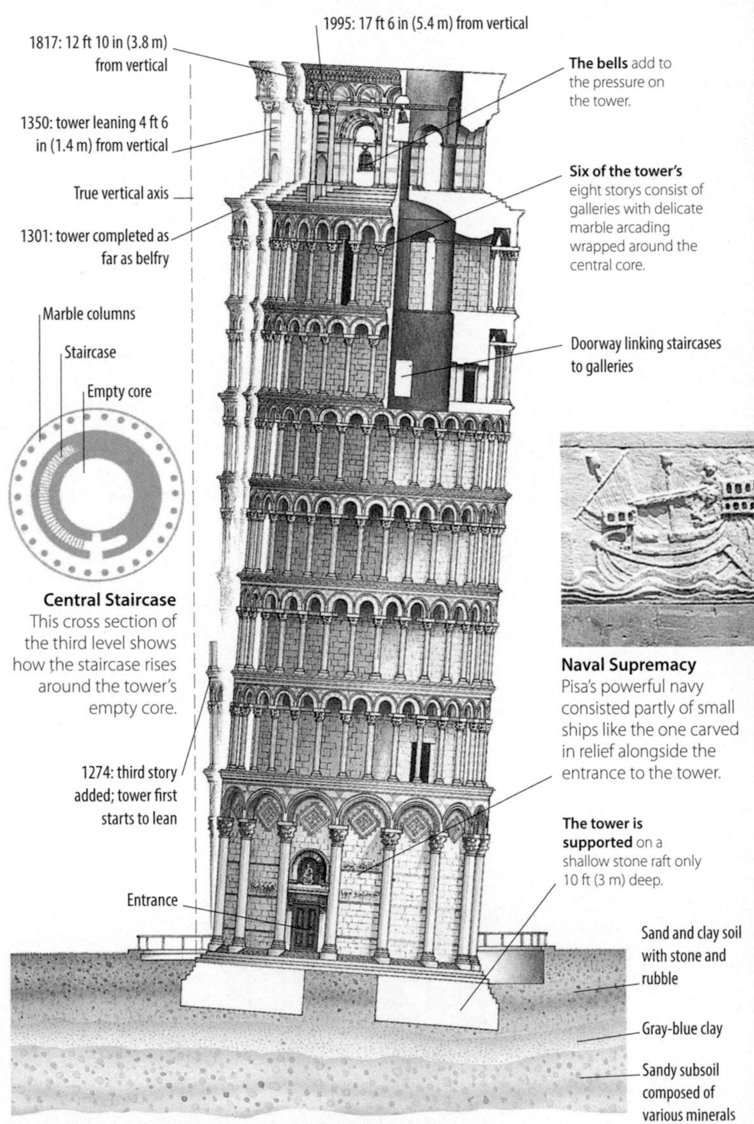

The bells add to the pressure on the tower.

Six of the tower's eight storys consist of galleries with delicate marble arcading wrapped around the central core.

Central Staircase
This cross section of the third level shows how the staircase rises around the tower's empty core.

Naval Supremacy
Pisa's powerful navy consisted partly of small ships like the one carved in relief alongside the entrance to the tower.

The tower is supported on a shallow stone raft only 10 ft (3 m) deep.

8 Vinci

Florence. 15,000. Wed.

Famous as the birthplace of Leonardo da Vinci (1452–1519), this hilltop town celebrates the genius in the **Museo Leonardiano**, housed in the 13th-century castle. Among the displays are wooden models of Leonardo's machines and inventions – most are based on drawings from his notebooks, copies of which are shown alongside. These include a bicycle, his conception of a car, an armored tank, and even a machine gun.

Museo Leonardiano

Castello dei Conti Guidi. **Tel** 0571 93 32 51. **Open** daily.

Model bicycle based on designs by Leonardo, Museo Leonardiano

9 Pistoia

93,000. FS Palazzo dei Vescovi, Piazza del Duomo (0573 216 22). Wed & Sat.

Pistoia's citizens were once known for violence and intrigue, a reputation grounded in the medieval disputes between the city's rival factions, the Bianchi and Neri (Whites and Blacks). Their favored weapon was a tiny, locally made dagger known as a *pistola*. Long a center of metalwork, everything from buses to mattress springs are now made here. In the center, several fine historic buildings are preserved.

Duomo

Piazza del Duomo. **Open** daily.

Piazza del Duomo, Pistoia's main square, is dominated by the Duomo (San Zeno) and its bulky 12th-century campanile, originally built as a watchtower in the city walls. The interior of the Duomo is rich in funerary monuments. The finest of these, in the south aisle, is the tomb of Cino da Pistoia. He was a friend of Dante and fellow poet, and is depicted in a relief (1337) lecturing to a class of young boys.

Nearby is the chapel of St. James and its extraordinary silver altar decorated with more than 600 statues and reliefs. Although the earliest of these dates from 1287, the altar was not completed until 1456. One of the craftsmen involved was Brunelleschi, who began his career as a silversmith before turning to architecture. Also in the Piazza del Duomo is the octagonal Baptistry, completed in 1359.

Detail of frieze (1514–25) by Giovanni della Robbia, Ospedale del Ceppo

Ospedale del Ceppo

Piazza Giovanni XXIII.

This hospital and orphanage, founded in 1277, was named after the *ceppo* (hollowed-out tree trunk) that was used to collect donations for its work. The main facade features colored terra-cotta panels (1514–25) by Giovanni della Robbia illustrating the *Seven Works of Mercy*. The portico is by Michelozzo.

The Pisan-Romanesque facade of Pistoia's Duomo (San Zeno)

Cappella del Tau

Corso Silvano Fedi 70. **Tel** 0573 322 04. **Open** 8:30am–1:30pm Mon–Sat.

The Cappella del Tau (1360) is so called because the monks who built it wore on their cloaks the letter T (*tau* in Greek), symbolizing a crutch and their work with the sick and disabled. Inside there are frescoes by Niccolò di Tommaso on *The Creation* and the *Life of St. Anthony Abbot* (1370). Two doors down, the **Palazzo Tau** has work by Marino Marini, Pistoia's best-known 20th-century artist.

The Fall (1372) by Niccolò di Tommaso in the Cappella del Tau

San Giovanni Fuorcivitas

Via Cavour. **Open** daily.

Built in the 12th to 14th centuries, the striking church of San Giovanni Fuorcivitas (literally "St. John Outside the City") once stood beyond the city walls. Its north flank is clad in banded marble and there is a Romanesque relief of the Last Supper over the portal. Inside, the holy water stoup, carved in marble with figures of the Virtues, is by Giovanni Pisano (1245–1320). A masterly pulpit, carved in 1270 with scenes from the New Testament, is by Guglielmo da Pisa. Both are among the finest works of this period, when artists were reviving the art of carving.

⑩ Prato

190,000. Piazza Buonamici 7 (0574 241 12). Mon.

While textile factories gird its outskirts, the center of Prato retains several important churches and museums. The **Duomo** (begun 1211) is flanked by the Pulpit of the Holy Girdle (1434–8), designed by Donatello and Michelozzo, used once a year to display a girdle reputedly given to Thomas the Apostle before the Assumption of the Virgin. Inside the Duomo is *The Life of John the Baptist* (1452–66) by Fra Filippo Lippi, and a fresco cycle (1392–5) by Agnolo Gaddi.

Other sights include the **Museo Civico**, **Santa Maria delle Carceri**, a Renaissance church in Piazza delle Carceri; the **Castello dell' Imperatore**, a fortress built by Emperor Frederick II in 1237; the **Centro per l'Arte Contemporanea Pecci**; and the **Museo del Tessuto**, which traces the history of Prato's textile industry.

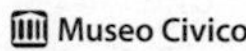

Museo Civico
Palazzo Pretorio, Piazza del Comune. **Tel** 0574 183 61. **Closed** for restoration.

Castello dell'Imperatore
Piazza delle Carceri. **Open** Wed–Mon.

Centro per l'Arte Contemporanea Pecci
Viale della Repubblica 277. **Tel** 0574 53 17. **Open** Wed–Mon.

Museo del Tessuto
Via Puccetti 3. **Tel** 0574 61 15 03. **Open** Tue–Sun. free Sun.

Madonna del Ceppo by Fra Filippo Lippi in Prato's Museo Civico

Buontalenti's Villa di Artimino, or "Villa of a Hundred Chimneys"

⑪ Artimino

Prato. 400.

A small fortified hamlet, Artimino is remarkable for the unspoiled Romanesque church of **San Leonardo**. Outside the walls lies the **Villa di Artimino**, designed by Buontalenti in 1594 for Grand Duke Ferdinando I. Also known as the "Villa of a Hundred Chimneys" – after the chimney pots crowding the roofline – it houses the **Museo Archeologico Etrusco**, a collection of beautiful archaeogical exhibits.

Environs
Lovers of Pontormo's paintings, should visit the church of **San Michele** in Carmignano, 3 miles (5 km) north of Artimino, because it contains *The Visitation* (1530). East of here lies the villa of **Poggio a Caiano**. Built in 1480 by Giuliano da Sangallo for Lorenzo de' Medici *(see p257)*, it was the first Italian villa to be designed in the Renaissance style.

Villa di Artimino
Viale Papa Giovanni 23. Villa: **Tel** 055 875 14 27. **Open** Tue am by appt. Museum: **Tel** 055 871 81 24. **Open** 9:30am–1:30pm daily. **Closed** Wed.

Poggio a Caiano
Piazza Medici. **Tel** 055 87 70 12. **Open** Tue–Sun; also 1st & 4th Mon of month.

⑫ San Miniato

Pisa. 3,900. Piazza del Popolo (0571 427 45). Tue.

This hilltop town manages to remain aloof from the vast industrial sprawl of the Arno valley. Its key building is the semiderelict Rocca (castle), built for Frederick II, German Holy Roman Emperor, in the 13th century. Close by stands the **Museo Diocesano**, which is home to a *Crucifixion* (*c.* 1430) attributed to Filippo Lippi, a terra-cotta bust of Christ attributed to Verrocchio (1435–88), and the *Virgin of the Holy Girdle* by Andrea del Castagno (*c.* 1417–57). Next door, the red-brick Romanesque facade of the **Duomo** dates from the 12th century. Its strange inset majolica plates, evidence of trade with Spain or North Africa, probably represent the North Star and the constellations of Ursa Major and Minor (all three were key points of reference for early navigators).

Museo Diocesano
Piazza Duomo. **Tel** 0571 41 80 71. **Open** 10am–1pm, 2–5pm Thu–Sun (Apr–Sep: 10am–6pm).

Facade of the Duomo in San Miniato

⑬ Fiesole

Florence. 15,000. Via Portigiani 3 (055 596 13 23). Sat.

Fiesole stands in rolling hilly countryside 5 miles (8 km) north of Florence. Idyllically situated among olive groves, it is a popular retreat from the city thanks to its hilltop position, which brings cool breezes. Founded in the 7th century BC, the original Etruscan colony was a powerful force in central Italy,

A view over the hills and rooftops of Fiesole from Via di San Francesco

only surrendering its supremacy after the foundation of Florence (1st century BC).

The restored **Duomo** of San Romolo in Piazza Mino da Fiesole was begun in 1028. It has a massive bell tower and a bare Romanesque interior. Behind the Duomo, an archaeological area contains the remains of a 1st-century BC **Roman theater**, traces of **Etruscan walls** from the 4th century BC, and the **Museo Faesulanum**, with a collection of bronzes, ceramics, and jewelry dating from the Bronze Age.

Via di San Francesco, a steep lane offering lovely views, leads to the Franciscan friary of **San Francesco** (14th century) and the interesting 9th-century church of **Sant'Alessandro**, with a Neo-Classical facade.

Via Vecchia Fiesolana leads to the hamlet of **San Domenico**, where the 15th-century church of the same name contains a painting of the *Madonna with Angels and Saints* (*c.* 1430) by Fra Angelico and the Chapter House contains a fresco of *The Crucifixion* (*c.* 1430), also by him. Close by, on the Via della Badia dei Roccettini, is the **Badia Fiesolana**, a pretty Romanesque church with a striped marble facade and interior of local gray sandstone, *pietra serena*.

Museo Faesulanum
Via Portigiani 1. **Tel** 055 596 12 93.
Open daily (Oct–Mar: Wed–Mon).

⓮ Arezzo

100,000. Piazza della Repubblica 28 (0575 268 50). Sat.

Arezzo is one of Tuscany's wealthiest cities, its prosperity based on a thriving jewelry industry. Although much of its medieval center was destroyed during World War II, resulting in extensive rebuilding and many medieval alleys being replaced by broad avenues, the city preserves some outstanding sights: foremost are Piero della Francesca's famous frescoes in the church of **San Francesco** *(see pp334–5)*. Close to the church on Corso Italia, the main street, stands the **Pieve di Santa Maria**, which boasts one of the most ornate Romanesque facades in the region. To its rear stretches the steeply sloping **Piazza Grande**, flanked by an arcade (1573) designed by Vasari, and by the **Palazzo della Fraternità dei Laici** (1377–1552). The latter features a *Madonna* relief by Bernardo Rossellino. The huge **Duomo** to the north is best known for its 16th-century stained glass and a small fresco of *Mary Magdalene* by Piero della Francesca (1416–92). The **Museo Diocesano (Mudas)** features three wooden crucifixes, dating from the 12th and 13th centuries, a bas-relief of *The Annunciation* (1434) by Rossellino, and paintings by Vasari. More works by Vasari can be seen in the **Casa di Vasari**, a house built by the artist in 1540. Still more frescoes by him are displayed in the **Museo d'Arte Medioevale e Moderna**, a museum that is famed for its excellent collection of majolica pottery.

The **Fortezza Medicea**, a ruined Medici castle built by Antonio da Sangallo during the 16th century, has fine views.

Museo Diocesano (Mudas)
Piazzetta Dietro il Duomo 12.
Tel 0575 402 72 68. **Open** daily.

Casa di Vasari
Via XX Settembre 55. **Tel** 0575 40 90 40. **Open** Wed–Mon.

Museo d'Arte Medioevale e Moderna
Via di San Lorentino 8.
Tel 0575 40 90 50. **Open** Tue–Sun.

Fortezza Medicea
Parco il Prato. **Tel** 0575 37 76 78.
Open daily.

The monthly antique market held in Arezzo's Piazza Grande

Arezzo: San Francesco

The 13th-century Church of San Francesco houses one of Italy's greatest fresco cycles, the *Legend of the True Cross* (1452–66), Piero della Francesca's masterpiece. The scenes, on the walls of the choir, are now visible again after a long restoration. They describe the history of the Cross used to crucify Christ, from sprig to Tree of Knowledge, to its use as a bridge during the reign of Solomon, and ultimately its discovery by Helena, mother of Constantine, the first Christian emperor.

A Group of Onlookers
These figures kneel in wonder while Heraclius returns the True Cross to Jerusalem.

Excavation of the Cross
The town, meant to be Jerusalem, gives a fair representation of 15th-century Arezzo.

KEY

① **The Defeat of Chosroes** depicts the defeat of a Persian king who had stolen the Cross.

② **The Cross** returns to Jerusalem.

③ **Judas reveals** where the Cross is hidden.

④ **The 13th-century Crucifix** forms the focal point of the fresco cycle. The figure at the foot of the Cross represents St. Francis, to whom the church is dedicated.

⑤ **The prophets** appear to play no part in the narrative cycle; their presence may be for purely decorative reasons.

⑥ **The wood** of the Cross is buried in a pit.

⑦ **The Queen of Sheba** recognizes the wood of the Cross.

⑧ **The buildings** in the fresco reflect the newly fashionable styles of Renaissance architecture.

⑨ **Constantine dreams** of the Cross on the eve of battle against rival emperor Maxentius.

⑩ **Constantine leads** his cavalry into battle.

Key to Frescoes

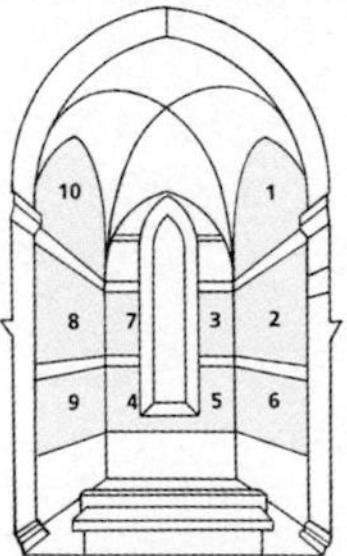

1 The Death of Adam; a sprig from the Tree of Knowledge is planted over his grave.

2 The Queen of Sheba visits Solomon and foresees that a bridge made from the Tree will be used to crucify the greatest king in the world.

3 Solomon, assuming he is the greatest king in the world, orders the bridge to be buried.

4 The Annunciation: Christ's death is foreshadowed in the panel's cruciform structure.

The Death of Adam
Piero's vivid portrayal of Adam and Eve in old age shows an adept treatment of anatomy. He was one of the first Renaissance artists to paint nude figures.

VISITORS' CHECKLIST

Practical Information
P. San Francesco. **Tel** 0575 35 27 27 (booking mandatory).
Open 9am–6:30pm Mon–Fri, 9am–5:30pm Sat, 1–5:30pm Sun.
Closed Jan 1, Dec 25.

5 Constantine has a vision of the Cross and hears a voice saying, "In this sign you shall conquer."
6 Constantine defeats his rival Maxentius.
7 The Levite Judas is tortured and reveals the location of the True Cross.
8 Three crosses are dug up; Constantine's mother Helena recognizes the True Cross.
9 The Persian king Chosroes is defeated after stealing the Cross.
10 The True Cross is returned to Jerusalem.

Solomon's Handshake
The handshake between the Queen of Sheba and Solomon, King of Israel, portrays 15th-century hopes for a union between the Orthodox and Western churches.

Piero's *The Resurrection* (1463) in Sansepolcro

⓯ Sansepolcro

Arezzo. 16,000. Via Matteotti 8 (0575 74 05 36). Tue, Sat.

Sansepolcro is the birthplace of Piero della Francesca (1410–92). The town's **Museo Civico** contains two of his masterpieces: *The Resurrection* (1463) and the *Madonna della Misericordia* (1462). It also has a 15th-century *Crucifixion* by Luca Signorelli. In the church of **San Lorenzo** on Via Santa Croce there is a *Deposition* in the Mannerist style by Rosso Fiorentino (1494–1541).

Another renowned painting by Piero della Francesca, the *Madonna del Parto* (1460), can be seen at Via Reglia 1 in Monterchi, 8 miles (13 km) southwest of Sansepolcro.

Museo Civico
Via Aggiunti 65. **Tel** 0575 73 22 18. **Open** daily. **Closed** public hols.

⓰ Cortona

Arezzo. 23,000. FS Piazza Signorelli 9 (0575 63 72 23). Sat.

Cortona was founded by the Etruscans and apart from being one of the oldest hill towns in Tuscany, it is also one of the most scenic. A major power in the Middle Ages, it was able to hold its own against Siena and Arezzo. Today it is a charming maze of old streets and medieval buildings, like the **Palazzo Comunale** on Piazza della Repubblica. The town's early history is traced in the **Museo dell'Accademia Etrusca**, which contains Etruscan artifacts and a wide variety of Egyptian and Roman remains. The small **Museo Diocesano** features several fine paintings, in particular a *Crucifixion* by the Renaissance artist Pietro Lorenzetti, a *Deposition* (1502) by Luca Signorelli, and a sublime *Annunciation* (c. 1434) by Fra Angelico. Signorelli, born in Cortona, is buried in the church of **San Francesco** (built in 1245), which contains an *Annunciation* painted in Baroque style by Pietro da Cortona, another native artist. The **Madonna del Calcinaio** (1485), a gem of Renaissance architecture, is located on the southern outskirts of town.

The 13th-century Palazzo Comunale in Cortona

Museo dell'Accademia Etrusca
Palazzo Casali, Piazza Signorelli 9. **Tel** 0575 63 72 35. **Open** daily (Tue–Sun in winter).

Museo Diocesano
Piazza del Duomo 1. **Tel** 0575 628 30. **Open** daily (Tue–Sun in winter).

⓱ Chiusi

Siena. 10,000. FS Via Porsenna 79 (0578 22 76 67). Tue.

Chiusi is now a largely modern town, but in the past it was one of the most powerful cities in the Etruscan league, reaching the height of its influence in the 7th and 6th centuries BC *(see p48–49)*. Numerous Etruscan tombs lie dotted in the surrounding countryside, the source of the exhibits in the town's **Museo Nazionale Etrusco**. Founded in 1871, the museum is packed with cremation urns, vases decorated with black figures, and Bucchero ware, burnished to resemble bronze.

The Romanesque **Duomo** in Piazza del Duomo incorporates recycled Roman pillars and capitals. The wall decorations in the nave, resembling frescoes, were painted by Arturo Viligiardi in 1887. There is a Roman mosaic underneath the high altar. Visits can be made to several Etruscan tombs under the town from the **Museo della Cattedrale**, a museum in the cloister of the Duomo that has displays of Roman, Lombardic, and medieval sculpture.

Museo Nazionale Etrusco
Via Porsenna 93. **Tel** 0578 201 77. **Open** 9am–8pm daily (to 2pm Sun & public hols).

Museo della Cattedrale
P. del Duomo. **Tel** 0578 22 64 90. **Open** daily (Jan–Mar: Tue, Thu, Sat, Sun).

Etruscan frieze in the Museo Nazionale Etrusco in Chiusi

ienza's Piazza Pio II, designed by Bernardo Rossellino (1459)

3 Montepulciano

iena. 14,000. Piazza Don Ainzoni 1 (0578 75 73 41). Thu.
W prolocomontepulciano.it

'his is one of Tuscany's highest ill towns, its walls and ortifications offering broad iews over Umbria and outhern Tuscany, and the ineyards providing the Vino Jobile wine that has made its ame famous. The streets are rimming with Renaissance alazzi. The main street, the Corso, climbs to the **Duomo** 1592–1630), the setting for ne of the masterpieces of the ienese School, the *Assumption* 1401) by Taddeo di Bartolo. 'he High Renaissance church, **'empio di San Biagio** (1518–4), lies off the road to Pienza.

Pienza

iena. 2,300. Piazza Dante lighieri 18 (0578 74 83 59). Fri.

'ienza is a delightful village vhose intimate little center was lmost completely redesigned n the 15th century by Pope Pius . Born as Aeneas Sylvius 'iccolomini in 1405, when the illage was known as Corsignano, he became a eading Humanist scholar and hilosopher. Elected pope in 458, he decided to rebuild his irthplace, renaming it Pienza in is own honor. The Florentine rchitect and sculptor Bernardo Rossellino was commissioned to uild a cathedral, papal palace, nd town hall (all completed in the three years from 1459 to 1462), but the grander scheme for a planned model Renaissance town was never realized. Some idea of what might have been, however, can still be gained from the **Palazzo Piccolomini**, the former papal palace, which continued to be inhabited by Pius's descendants until 1968. The rooms open to the public include Pius's bedroom and library, though the highlight of a visit is the superb panorama from the loggia and arcaded courtyard at the palace's rear.

Pleasant walks and more great views can be had from the village walls. The airy **Duomo** *(see p256)* next door contains six altarpieces of the *Madonna and Child*, each commissioned from the leading Sienese painters of the day. Rossellino was forced to build the Duomo on a cramped site with poor foundations, and cracks appeared in the building before it was even completed. Today the church's eastern end suffers from severe subsidence.

Palazzo Piccolomini
Piazza Pio II. **Tel** 0577 28 63 00. **Open** 10am–6:30pm Tue–Sun (to 4:30pm mid-Oct–mid-Mar). **Closed** Jan–mid-Feb, mid–end Nov.

20 Montalcino

Siena. 5,100. Costa del Municipio 1 (0577 84 93 31). Fri.

Hilltop Montalcino sits at the heart of vineyards that produce Brunello, one of Italy's finest red wines. It can be sampled in the Enoteca (wine shop) situated in the 14th-century **Fortezza** with its impressive ramparts. The town's timeless streets are a pleasure to wander, and there are some buildings of interest. On the way from the fortress into town is the monastery of Sant' Agostino and its 14th-century church, and, just beyond, the Palazzo Vescovile. On Piazza del Popolo the slim tower of the Palazzo Communale, constructed in the 13th and 14th centuries, stands tall above the town.

Fortezza
Piazzale della Fortezza. **Tel** 0577 84 92 11. for ramparts. Enoteca: **Open** 9am–8pm daily (Nov–Mar: 9am–6pm Tue–Sun).

The Tempio di San Biagio on the outskirts of Montepulciano

The landscape of the Crete Senesi

㉑ Crete Senesi

Asciano. FS 🚌 i Via delle Fonti (0577 71 88 11).

To the south of Siena and central Tuscany is the area known as the Crete Senesi, which is characterized by round clay hillocks eroded by heavy rain over the centuries. Dubbed the "Tuscan desert," it is almost completely barren. Cypress and pine trees, planted to provide windbreaks along roads and around isolated farm houses, are an important feature in this empty, primeval landscape. Shepherds tend flocks of sheep here; the milk is used to produce the strongly flavored *pecorino* cheese that is popular throughout Tuscany.

㉒ Siena

See pp342–7.

㉓ Monteriggioni

Siena. 99,000. 🚌 i Piazza Roma (0577 30 48 34).
W **monteriggioniturismo.it**

Monteriggioni is a gem of a medieval hilltop town. It was built in 1203 and ten years later became a garrison town. It is completely encircled by high walls with 14 heavily fortified towers, built to guard the northern borders of Siena's territory against invasion by Florentine armies.

Dante used Monteriggioni as a simile for the deepest abyss at the heart of his *Inferno*, which compares the town's "ring-shaped citadel… crowned with towers" with giants standing in a moat. The perfectly preserved walls are best viewed from the Colle di Val d'Elsa road. Within the walls, the sleepy town consists of a large piazza, a pretty Romanesque church (on the piazza), a few houses, a couple of craft shops, restaurants, and shops selling many of the locally produced Castello di Monteriggioni wines.

Environs
West of Monteriggioni by 2 miles (3 km) lies the former Cistercian Abbey of **Abbadia dell' Isola** (12th century). This Romanesque church was largely rebuilt in the 18th century, after the cupola fell apart. It contains frescoes by Taddeo di Bartolo and Vincenzo Tamagni.

Detail from the pulpit in Volterra's Duomo

㉔ San Gimignano

See pp348–9.

㉕ Volterra

Pisa. 13,000. 🚌 i Piazza dei Priori 20 (0588 872 57). Sat.
W **volterratur.it**

Like many Etruscan cities, Volterra is situated on a high plateau, offering fine views over the surrounding hills. In many places the ancient Etruscan walls still survive. The **Museo Guarnacci** contains one of the best collections of Etruscan artifacts in Italy. Of special interest is the group of over 600 cinerary urns, made from alabaster or terra-cotta, many of which were gathered from local tombs.

The **Palazzo dei Priori**, the medieval seat of government on Piazza dei Priori, is the oldes of its kind in Tuscany. It was begun in 1208 and there are 14th-century frescoes inside. The Pisan-Romanesque **Duomo**, located on Piazza San Giovanni, has a fine 13th-century pulpit with sculpted panels.

Volterra's excellent art gallery and museum, the **Pinacoteca e Museo Civico**, features works by Florentine artists. *Christ in Majesty* (1492) by Ghirlandaio shows Christ hovering above an idealized Tuscan landscape. Luca Signorelli's *Virgin and Chil with Saints* (1491) states his deb to Roman art through the relief on the base of the Virgin's thron Painted in the same year, his *Annunciation* is a beautifully balanced composition. Anothe highlight is Rosso Fiorentino's Mannerist painting, *The Deposition* (1521).

The city is famous for its craftsmen, who have been

The beautifully preserved walls of Monteriggioni in central Tuscany

The ruined abbey at San Galgano, surrounded by dense woodland

carving elaborate statues and *objets d'art* from locally mined alabaster for 2,500 years.

Museo Guarnacci
Via Don Minzoni 15. **Tel** 0588 863 47. **Open** daily. **Closed** Jan 1, Dec 25.

Pinacoteca e Museo Civico
Via dei Sarti 1. **Tel** 0588 875 80. **Open** daily. **Closed** Jan 1, Dec 25.

26 San Galgano

Siena. from Siena. Abbey & oratory: **Open** daily.
sangalgano.org

The remote Cistercian abbey at San Galgano lies in a superb setting. San Galgano (1148–81) was a brave but dissolute knight who turned to God, renouncing the material world. When he tried to break his sword against a rock as a symbol of his rejection of war, it was swallowed by the stone. This he interpreted as a sign of God's approval. He built a hut on a hill above the abbey (the site of today's beehive-shaped chapel at **Montesiepi**, built *c.* 1185). Here he later died a hermit. Pope Urban III declared him a saint.

The abbey, begun in 1218, is Gothic in style, reflecting the French origins of the Cistercian monks who designed it. They avoided contact with the outside world and divided their lives between prayer and labor. Despite an emphasis on poverty, the monks became wealthy from the sale of wood, and by the middle of the 14th century the abbey was corruptly administered and gradually fell into decline.

In the late 14th century, the English mercenary Sir John Hawkwood sacked the abbey, and by 1397 the abbot was its sole occupant. It was eventually dissolved in 1652.

St. Galgano's sword stands embedded in a stone just inside the door of the circular **oratory**. The 14th-century stone walls of the side chapel are covered with worn frescoes showing scenes from Galgano's life by Ambrogio Lorenzetti (1344).

27 Massa Marittima

Grosseto. 9,500. Amatur, Via Todini 3–5 (0566 90 27 56). Wed.

Set in the Colline Metallifere (metal-bearing hills) where lead, copper, and silver ores were mined as early as Etruscan times, Massa Marittima is far from being a grimy industrial town. Examples of Romanesque architecture survive from the time when the town became an independent republic (1225–1335). The Romanesque-Gothic **Duomo** in Piazza Garibaldi is dedicated to St. Cerbone, a 6th-century saint whose story is sculpted in stone above the main portal. Inside the building, the *Maestà* is attributed to Duccio (*c.* 1316).

The **Museo della Miniera** (museum of mining) is located partially inside a former mine shaft and has exhibits that explain mining techniques, tools, and minerals.

The **Museo Archeologico e Museo d'Arte Sacra** has material from Paleolithic to Roman times. Other attractions are the Fortezza Senese and the Torre della Candeliera.

Museo della Miniera
Via Corridoni. **Tel** 0566 90 22 89. **Open** Tue–Sun. compulsory.

Museo Archeologico e Museo d'Arte Sacra
Palazzo del Podestà, P.za Garibaldi. **Tel** 0566 90 22 89. **Open** Tue–Sun.

View across the rooftops of Massa Marittima

The Gothic Palazzo Pubblico (town hall) in Siena ▶

22 Street by Street: Siena

Siena's principal sights cluster in the maze of narrow streets and alleys around the fan-shaped Piazza del Campo. One of Europe's greatest medieval squares, the piazza sits at the heart of the city's 17 *contrade*, a series of parishes whose ancient rivalries are still acted out in the twice-yearly Palio *(see p345)*. Loyalty to the *contrada* of one's birth is fierce, and as you wander the streets you will see the parishes' animal symbols repeated on flags, plaques, and carvings. Siena's hilly position also means that city walks offer delightful hidden corners and countless sudden views.

The Duomo dominating Siena's skyline

Bus station

Train station

Via della Galluzza leads to the house of St. Catherine.

The Baptistry has fine frescoes and a font with reliefs by Donatello, Jacopo della Quercia, and Ghiberti.

VIA D. GALLUZZA

PIAZZA INDIPENDENZA

VIA DI FONTEBRANDA

VIA DI DIACCETO

VIA DI CITTÀ

VIA FRANCIOSA

PIAZZA SAN GIOVANNI

VIA DEI PELLEGRINI

VIC. D. CAMPANE

VIA DEL FUSARI

VIA DEL POGGIO

PIAZZA DEL DUOMO

VIA DEL CAPITANO

★ Duomo
Striped black and white marble pillars, surmounted by a carved frieze of the popes, support the Duomo's vaulted ceiling, painted blue with gold stars to resemble the night sky.

Each tier of the Duomo's bell tower has one more window than the floor below.

Museo dell'Opera del Duomo
Duccio's *Maestà*, one of the greatest Sienese paintings, was paraded around Siena's streets on its completion in 1311, and influenced the city's painters for decades to come.

Key

▬ Suggested route

0 meters 300

0 yards 300

oggia della Mercanzia
uilt in 1417, the arcade is where iena's medieval merchants and noney dealers carried out their usiness.

VISITORS' CHECKLIST

Practical Information
60,000 Piazza del Campo 56 (0577 28 05 51). Wed. 2 Jul, 16 Aug: Palio; Jul: Settimana Musicale Chigiana (classical music).
terresiena.it

Transportation
FS Piazzale Rosselli.
Piazza S. Domenico.

The Logge del Papa, or Pope's colonnade, was built in honor of Pius II in 1462.

Tourist information

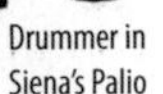

Drummer in Siena's Palio

Fonte Gaia
These reliefs are 19th-century copies of originals by Jacopo della Quercia.

Piazza del Campo

Italy's loveliest piazza occupies the site of the old Roman forum, and for much of Siena's early history was the city's principal marketplace. It began to assume its present shape in 1293, when the Council of Nine, Siena's ruling body at the time, began to acquire land with a view to creating a grand civic piazza. The red brick paving was begun in 1327 and completed in 1349, its distinctive nine segments designed to reflect the authority of the Council of Nine and to symbolize the protective folds of the Madonna's cloak. The piazza has been the focus of city life ever since, a setting for executions, bullfights, and the twice-yearly drama of the Palio *(see p341)*, a festival centered around a bareback horse race. Cafés, restaurants, and fine medieval palazzi now line the Campo's fringes, dominated by the **Palazzo Pubblico** (1297–1342) and **Torre del Mangia**, built in 1348 *(see p340)*. This imposing ensemble tends to overshadow the little **Fonte Gaia** on the piazza's northern edge. The fountain is a 19th-century copy of an original carved by Jacopo della Quercia in 1409–19. Its reliefs depict the *Virtues*, *Adam and Eve*, and the *Madonna and Child* (the originals are on the rear loggia of the Palazzo Pubblico). The fountain's water is still supplied by a 500-year-old aqueduct.

★ Palazzo Pubblico
The graceful Gothic town hall was completed in 1342. At 330 ft (102 m), the bell tower, Torre del Mangia, is the second highest medieval tower ever built in Italy.

The Piazza del Campo and Fonte Gaia from the Torre del Mangia

Exploring Siena

Once a capital to rival Florence, Siena is Italy's prettiest medieval town, still endowed with the grandeur of the age in which it was at its peak (1260–1348). Begin an exploration of its historic center in Piazza del Campo and the surrounding maze of medieval alleys.

Lorenzetti's *Allegory of Good Government* (1338), Palazzo Pubblico

Palazzo Pubblico

Piazza del Campo 1. **Tel** 0577 29 22 26/ 29 22 23. Museo Civico & Torre del Mangia: **Open** Mid-Mar–end Oct: 10am–7pm daily; Nov–mid-Mar: to 6pm daily.

Although it continues in its ancient role as Siena's town hall, the Palazzo Pubblico's medieval rooms, some decorated with paintings of the Sienese School, are open to the public. The **Museo Civico** is housed here. The main council chamber, or Sala del Mappamondo, is named after a map of the world painted by Ambrogio Lorenzetti in the early 14th century. One wall is covered by Simone Martini's fresco of the *Maestà* (1315), which depicts the Virgin in Majesty as the Queen of Heaven, attended by the Apostles, saints, and angels. Opposite is a fresco (attributed to Simone Martini, but possibly later) of the mercenary *Guidoriccio da Fogliano* (1330). The walls of the chapel are covered with frescoes of the *Life of the Virgin* (1407) by Taddeo di Bartolo, and the choir stalls (1428) are decorated with wooden panels inlaid with biblical scenes. The Sala della Pace contains the famous *Allegory of Good and Bad Government* (1338–40), a pair of frescoes by Ambrogio Lorenzetti. They form one of the most important series of secular paintings from the Middle Ages. In the *Good Government* fresco, civic life flourishes, while the *Bad Government*, presided over by a demon, reveals garbage-strewn streets and ruins.

The Sala del Risorgimento is covered with late 19th-century frescoes illustrating the events leading up to the unification of Italy under King Vittorio Emanuele II.

In the palace courtyard is the entrance to the magnificent **Torre del Mangia**, the palace's huge bell tower. Rising 330 ft (102 m), it is a prominent feature of Siena's skyline. Built by the brothers Muccio and Francesco di Rinaldo between 1338 and 134[illegible] it was named after the first bell-ringer, whose idleness led to the nickname *Mangiaguadagni* (literally "eat the profits"). There are 505 steps to the top, which has wonderful views.

Santuario e Casa di Santa Caterina

Costa di Sant'Antonio. **Tel** 0577 28 81 75. **Open** daily.

Siena's patron saint, Catherine Benincasa (1347–80), was the daughter of a tradesman. At the age of eight she devoted herself to God and had many visions, as well as later receiving the stigmata (wounds of Christ). Like her namesake, St. Catherine of Alexandria, she was believed to have been betrothed to the Christ child in a vision – a scene that inspired many artists. Her eloquence persuaded Pope Gregory XI to return the seat of the papacy to Rome in 1376, after 67 years of exile in Avignon. St. Catherine died in Rome and was canonized in 1461.

Today Catherine's house is surrounded by chapels and cloisters. Among them is the Church of the Crucifixion, which was built in 1623 in her orchard to house the late 12th-century Crucifixion in front of which she received the stigmata in 1375. The house is decorated with paintings of events from her life by artists including her contemporaries Francesco Vanni and Pietro Sorri.

Cloister of Santuario e Casa di Santa Caterina, birthplace of Siena's patron saint

Palazzo Piccolomini

Piazza Pio II. **Tel** 0577 28 63 00. **Open** 10am–6:30pm Tue–Sun (to 4:30pm Oct–Mar). **Closed** Jan 7–Feb 14, Nov 16–30.

Siena's most imposing private palazzo was built for the wealthy Piccolomini family in the 1460s by the Florentine architect and sculptor Bernardo Rossellino. It now contains the Sienese state archives, account books, and taxation documents dating back to the 13th century. Some of the leading artists of the day were employed to paint the wooden bindings used to enclose the tax and account records. The paintings, now on display in the Sala di Congresso, often show scenes of Siena itself or episodes from the city's past.

Other records include a will attributed to Boccaccio, and the council's contract with Jacopo della Quercia for the Fonte Gaia *(see p343)*.

A detail from Martini's *Blessed Agostino Novello* (*c.* 1330)

Pinacoteca Nazionale

Via San Pietro 29. **Tel** 0577 28 61 43. **Open** daily (Sun & Mon am only). **Closed** Jan 1, May 1, Dec 25.

This fine gallery, which is housed in the 14th-century Palazzo Buonsignori, contains an unsurpassed collection of paintings by artists of the Sienese School. Arranged in chronological order, from the 13th century through to the Mannerist period (1520–1600), highlights include Duccio's *Madonna dei Francescani* (1285) and Simone Martini's masterpiece *The Blessed Agostino Novello and Four of His Miracles* (*c.* 1330). Pietro Lorenzetti's *Two Views,* from the 14th century, are early examples of landscape painting, and Pietro da Domenico's *Adoration of the Shepherds* (1510) shows how the art of Siena remained visibly influenced by its Byzantine roots long after the naturalism of the Renaissance had reached across the rest of Europe.

The austere exterior of the church of San Domenico (begun 1226)

San Domenico

Piazza San Domenico. **Open** daily.

The preserved head of the city's patroness, St. Catherine of Siena (1347–80), can be seen in a gilded tabernacle on the altar of a chapel dedicated to her in the huge, barnlike Gothic church of San Domenico (begun 1226). The chapel itself was built in 1460 for this purpose and is dominated by Sodoma's frescoes (1526), to the right and left of the altar, which show Catherine in states of religious fervor and her early life. The church has the only portrait of St. Catherine considered authentic, painted by her friend Andrea Vanni. The fresco by Vanni can be found in the Chapel of the Vaults.

The Palio of Siena

The Palio is Tuscany's most celebrated festival, and it occurs in the Campo each year on July 2 and August 16 at 7pm. This special event is a bareback horse race first recorded in 1283, but it may have had its origins in Roman military training. The jockeys represent 10 of Siena's 17 *contrade* (districts); the horses are chosen by the drawing of lots and are blessed at the local *contrada* churches. Preceded by days of colorful pageantry, costume processions, and heavy betting, the races themselves last only 90 seconds each. Thousands of spectators crowd into the piazza to watch the race, and rivalry between competitors is intense. The winner is rewarded with a silk *palio* (banner). Festivities for the winners can last for weeks.

A *contrada* symbol

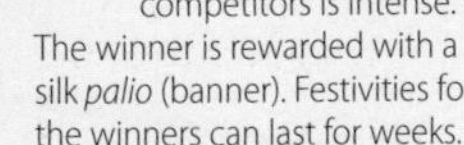

The Sienese displaying their flag-throwing skills before the Palio

Siena: Duomo

Siena's Duomo (1136–1382) is one of Italy's greatest cathedrals, a spectacular mixture of sculpture, paintings, and Pisan-influenced Romanesque-Gothic architecture. Had 14th-century plans to create a new nave come to fruition, the building would have become the largest church in Christendom. In the end, the plan came to nothing, abandoned when the plague of 1348 virtually halved the city's population. Among the Duomo's treasures are sculptural masterpieces by Nicola Pisano, Donatello and Michelangelo, a fine inlaid pavement, and a magnificent fresco cycle by Pinturicchio.

Baptismal Font
This Renaissance font by della Quercia, Ghiberti, and Donatello stands in the Baptistry.

Pulpit Panels
Carved in 1265–8 by Nicola Pisano, with help from Arnolfo di Cambio and his son Giovanni, the panels on the octagonal pulpit depict scenes from the *Life of Christ.*

KEY

① **In the nave** black and white marble pillars support the vault.

② **The Campanile** was added in 1313.

③ **Archway** leading to the Baptistry.

④ **The Museo dell'Opera del Duomo** occupies the side aisle of the unfinished nave, which was roofed over to house the museum.

⑤ **The facade** gives an indication of the planned size of the nave.

⑥ **The unfinished nave**, if completed, would have measured 162 ft (50 m) in length and 97 ft (30 m) in breadth.

⑦ **The doors** were built in 1284–97, the rest of the facade a century later.

⑧ **The north aisle** contains sculptures by Michelangelo of Saints Peter, Pius, Gregory and Paul (1501–4).

⑨ **Chapel of St. John the Baptist**

Piccolomini Library
Pinturicchio's frescoes (1509) portray the life of the Piccolomini Pope, Pius II. Here he presides at the betrothal of Frederick III to Eleonora of Portugal.

Inlaid Marble Floor
The Massacre of the Innocents is one of a series of scenes in the inlaid marble floor. The marble is usually uncovered during September each year.

Facade Statues
Many facade statues have been replaced by copies; the originals are in the Museo dell'Opera del Duomo.

VISITORS' CHECKLIST

Practical Information
Piazza del Duomo. **Tel** 0577 28 63 00. Duomo & Library:
Open Mar–Nov: 10:30am–7pm (Duomo: 1:30–6pm Sun); Nov–Feb: 10:30am–5:30pm (Duomo: 1:30–5:30pm Sun).
operaduomo.siena.it

Transportation
Pollicino.

Museo dell'Opera del Duomo

Piazza del Duomo 8. **Tel** 0577 28 63 00.
Open daily; call for opening times.

Part of this museum is devoted to items removed from the Duomo, including a tondo of a *Madonna and Child*, probably by Donatello, as well as several badly eroded Gothic statues by Giovanni Pisano and Jacopo della Quercia. The highlight is Duccio's huge *Maestà* (1308–11), one of the Sienese School's finest works. It depicts the Madonna and Child on one side, and scenes from the Life of Christ on the other. It was originally placed on the Duomo's high altar, where it replaced the striking *Madonna of the Large Eyes* (1220–30) by an anonymous Sienese painter, also in the museum.

Statues from the Duomo now on display in the Museo dell'Opera

Fortezza Medicea

Piazza Libertà 1 **Open** daily.
Enoteca: **Tel** 0577 22 88 43.
Open noon–1am Mon–Sat.

This huge red-brick fortress was built for Cosimo I by Baldassarre Lanci in 1560, following Siena's defeat by the Florentines in the 1554–5 war. After an 18-month siege, during which more than 8,000 Sienese died, the town's banking and wool industries were suppressed by the Florentine masters and all major building work ended.

The fortress now houses the Enoteca Italica, offering visitors the chance both to taste and to buy quality wines from all over Italy. There is also a restaurant on the site.

24 Street by Street: San Gimignano

The 13 towers that dominate San Gimignano's skyline were built by noble families in the 12th and 13th centuries, when the town's position – on the main pilgrim route from northern Europe to Rome – brought it great prosperity. The plague of 1348, and the diversion of the pilgrim route, led to its decline as well as its preservation. Today only one of the towers, the Torre Grossa, is open. San Gimignano is rich in works of art as well as good shops and restaurants, although many close from November to March.

San Gimignano's famous skyline, almost unchanged since the Middle Ages

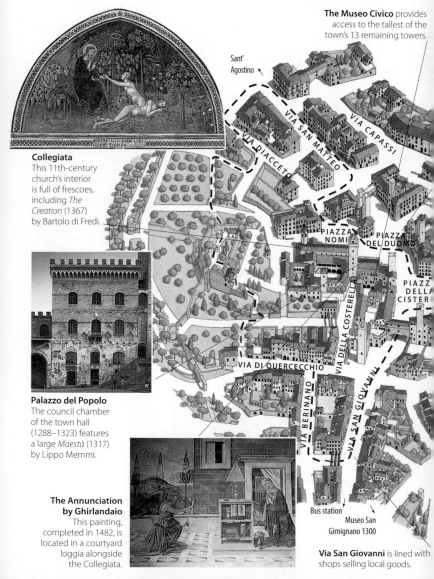

The Museo Civico provides access to the tallest of the town's 13 remaining towers.

Sant' Agostino

Collegiata
This 11th-century church's interior is full of frescoes, including *The Creation* (1367) by Bartolo di Fredi.

Palazzo del Popolo
The council chamber of the town hall (1288–1323) features a large *Maestà* (1317) by Lippo Memmi.

The Annunciation by Ghirlandaio
This painting, completed in 1482, is located in a courtyard loggia alongside the Collegiata.

Bus station

Museo San Gimignano 1300

Via San Giovanni is lined with shops selling local goods.

For hotels and restaurants in this region see pp562–77 and pp580–605

VISITORS' CHECKLIST

Practical Information
Siena. 7,000. Piazza del Duomo 1 (0577 94 00 08). Thu. Patron saints' festivals: Jan 31 San Gimignano & Mar 12 Santa Fina; varying dates in Feb: Carnival; 1st Sun in Aug: Fiera di Santa Fina; Aug 29: Fiera di Sant'Agostino; Sep 8: Festa della Madonna di Panacole.
sangimignano.com

Transportation
Porta San Giovanni.

Among the Piazza del Duomo's historic buildings is the Palazzo Vecchio del Podestà (1239), whose tower is probably the town's oldest.

Piazza della Cisterna This square is named after the well at its center and is the heart of the old town.

Key
— Suggested route

0 meters 250
0 yards 250

Museo Civico

Palazzo del Popolo, Piazza del Duomo. **Tel** 0577 99 03 12. Museum & tower: **Open** Apr 1–Sep 30: 9:30am–7pm daily; Oct 1–Mar 31: 11am–5:30pm daily. **Closed** Dec 25.

Frescoes in the courtyard of this museum feature the coats of arms of city mayors, as well as a 14th-century *Virgin and Child* by Taddeo di Bartolo.

The first room is the Sala di Dante, where an inscription recalls a visit by the poet in 1300. The floor above has an art collection, which includes excellent works by Pinturicchio, Bartolo di Fredi, Benozzo Gozzoli, and Filippino Lippi. The famous *Wedding Scene* frescoes by Memmo di Filippucci (early 14th century) show a couple sharing a bath and going to bed – an unusual record of life in 14th-century Tuscany.

Collegiata

Piazza del Duomo. **Open** daily.

This 12th-century Romanesque church contains a feast of frescoes. In the north aisle the frescoes comprise 26 episodes from the Old Testament (1367) by Bartolo di Fredi. The opposite wall features scenes from the *Life of Christ* (1333–41) by Lippo Memmi, while at the back of the church there are scenes from the *Last Judgment* painted by Taddeo di Bartolo.

Bartolo di Fredi's *Christ*, Sant'Agostino

The ceiling of the Collegiata, painted with gold stars

Sant'Agostino

Piazza Sant'Agostino. **Open** daily.

Consecrated in 1298, this church has a simple facade, contrasting markedly with the heavily decorated Rococo interior (*c.* 1740) by Vanvitelli. Above the main altar is the *Coronation of the Virgin* by Piero del Pollaiuolo, dated 1483. The choir is covered in a cycle of frescoes of *The Life of St. Augustine* (1465) executed by the Florentine artist Benozzo Gozzoli.

Museo San Gimignano 1300

Via San Giovanni 50. **Tel** 327 439 5165. **Open** 10am–7pm daily.

This museum houses a reconstruction of San Gimignano as it was during the 13th and 14th centuries. The exhibits have been made entirely by hand and include 72 "tower houses," symbols of the city's power during the Middle Ages.

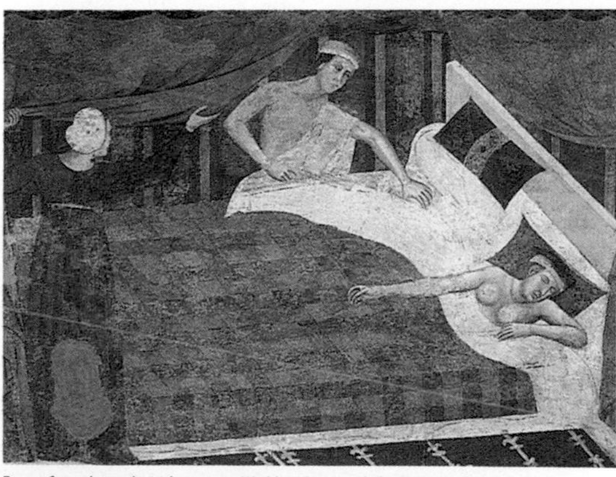

Fresco from the early 14th-century *Wedding Scene* cycle by Memmo di Filippucci in the Museo Civico

㉘ Elba

Livorno. 30,000. Portoferraio. Calata Italia 26 (0565 91 46 71). Portoferraio: Fri.

Elba's most famous resident was Napoleon, who spent nine months here after the fall of Paris in 1814. Today Italy's third largest island is mainly populated by vacationers, who come by ferry from Piombino, 6 miles (10 km) away on the mainland. The main town is Portoferraio, with an old port and a modern seafront of hotels and fish restaurants.

The landscape of the island is varied. On the west coast, which tends to be a little quieter, there are sandy beaches suitable for all water sports. The east coast, centered on the town of Porto Azzurro, the island's second port, is more rugged, with high cliffs and stony beaches. Inland, olive groves and vineyards line hillsides, and vegetation covers the mountains. A good way to see the interior is to take the road from Marciana Marina to the old medieval village of Marciana Alta. Close by, a minor road leads to a cable car that runs to Monte Capanne (3,300 ft/1,018 m), a magnificent viewpoint.

Marciana Marina on Elba

㉙ Sovana

Grosseto. 100. Piazza Busatti 8 (0564 63 30 99).

Sovana is one of southern Tuscany's prettiest villages. Its single little street ends in Piazza del Pretorio, home to the ancient church of Santa Maria, which contains frescoes and a 9th-century altar canopy. A lane beyond leads through olive groves to the Romanesque Duomo, filled with reliefs and carvings from an earlier church on the site. Some fine Etruscan tombs lie in the surrounding countryside, many of them clearly marked and easily visited from the village.

View over Pitigliano and the town's dramatic cliffs and caves

㉚ Pitigliano

Grosseto. 4,400. Piazza Garibaldi 51 (0564 61 71 11). Wed.

Pitigliano is spectacularly situated high above the cave-riddled cliffs of the Lente valley. Its maze of tiny medieval streets includes a small Jewish ghetto, formed in the 17th century by Jews fleeing from Catholic persecution.

㉛ Maremma

Grosseto. Viale Monterosa 206, Grosetto (0564 46 26 11). to entrances from Alberese. **Open** daily. Inner Park Areas: from Alberese to tour departure point. **Open** 8:30am–2pm daily. **parcomaremma.it**

The Etruscans, followed by the Romans, were the first to cultivate the marshes and low hills of the Maremma. Following the collapse of the Roman Empire, however, the area fell prey to flooding and malaria, twin scourges that left it virtually uninhabited until the 18th century. The land has since been reclaimed, the irrigation canals unblocked, and farming developed on the fertile soil. The stunning Parco Naturale della Maremma was set up in 1975 to preserve the area's native flora and fauna, and to prevent development on one of Italy's few pristine stretches of coastline. Entrance to much of the park is restricted to access on foot or by a park bus from Alberese. Other areas more on the borders of the park, however, such as the excellent beach at Marina di Alberese and the countryside around Talamone in the south, are easier to see.

The Ombrone estuary is a mixture of pines, marsh, and dunes and is home to birds such as the flamingo, sea eagle, roller, and bee-eater.

Key

- Roads
- Paths
- Canals and rivers
- Itineraries

0 kilometers 2

0 miles 1

The **Palazzo Orsini** has its water supply brought in by an impressive aqueduct, built in 1545. It houses the **Museo di Palazzo Orsini** with its exhibit of painted, engraved, and sculptured works dating from the 14th century. Within the display are pieces by local artist Francesco Zuccarelli (1702–88). He also painted two of the altarpieces in the **Duomo** in Piazza San Gregorio. The **Museo Etrusco** contains finds from ancient local settlements.

Museo di Palazzo Orsini
Piazza della Fortezza Orsini 4. **Tel** 0564 78 85 20. **Open** 10am–1pm, 3–7pm Tue–Fri (to 5pm in winter).

Museo Etrusco
Piazza della Fortezza Orsini 59. **Tel** 0564 61 40 67. **Open** 10am–6pm daily (call for winter times).

32 Monte Argentario

Grosseto. 13,000. Piazzale Sant'Andrea, Porto Santo Stefano (0564 81 42 08). Tue.

Monte Argentario was an island until the early 1700s, when the shallow waters separating it from the mainland began to silt up, creating two sandy spits of land, known as *tomboli*, which enclose the Orbetello lagoon. Today the lagoon hosts a beautiful nature reserve. **Orbetello** itself, a lively and relatively unspoiled little town, was linked to the island in 1842, when a dyke was constructed from the mainland. The harbor towns of **Porto Ercole** and **Porto Santo Stefano** are upmarket resorts, busy with visitors in summer. Interior roads – notably the Strada Panoramica – offer peaceful drives past rocky coves and bays.

Porto Ercole, Monte Argentario

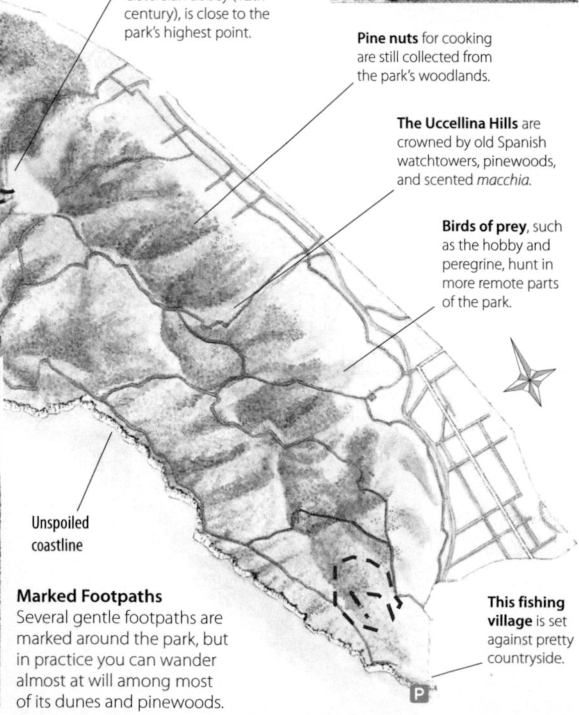

Entry tickets are sold at Alberese's park headquarters.

Wild Boar
The most impressive of the Maremma's many wild animals is the indigenous wild boar, a smaller creature than the Eastern European boar found elsewhere in Tuscany.

San Rabano, a ruined Cistercian abbey (12th century), is close to the park's highest point.

Pine nuts for cooking are still collected from the park's woodlands.

The Uccellina Hills are crowned by old Spanish watchtowers, pinewoods, and scented *macchia.*

Birds of prey, such as the hobby and peregrine, hunt in more remote parts of the park.

Unspoiled coastline

Marked Footpaths
Several gentle footpaths are marked around the park, but in practice you can wander almost at will among most of its dunes and pinewoods.

This fishing village is set against pretty countryside.

For additional map symbols *see back flap*

UMBRIA

Long dismissed as Tuscany's "gentler sister," Umbria has finally emerged from the shadow of its more famous western neighbor. Forming an expanse of gentle pastoral countryside and high mountain wilderness, the picturesque region has been dubbed the "Green Heart of Italy." Umbria is also well-known for the beauty and profusion of its medieval hill towns.

The region was inhabited in the 8th century BC by the Umbrians, a peaceable farming tribe, and later colonized by the Etruscans and Romans. In the Middle Ages, the Lombards established a dukedom centered around Spoleto. By the 13th century much of the region was scattered with independent city-states, most of them eventually absorbed by the Papal States, where they remained until Italian unification in 1860.

Today the old towns are Umbria's chief glory. In Perugia, the region's capital, and the smaller centers of Gubbio, Montefalco, and Todi, there are numerous Romanesque churches, civic palaces, vivid fresco cycles, and endless medieval nooks and crannies. Spoleto, renowned for its summer arts festival, blends grandiose medieval monuments with Roman remains and some of Italy's oldest churches. The surrounding Vale of Spoleto is a checkerboard of agricultural countryside and fascinating traditional villages.

Assisi, the birthplace of St. Francis, contains the Basilica di San Francesco, frescoed in part by Giotto. At Orvieto, magnificently situated on its volcanic crag, there are Etruscan remains and one of Italy's finest Romanesque-Gothic cathedrals.

Umbria's oak woods, ice-clear streams, and rich soils yield many delicacies. Chief among these are trout and truffles, olive oils to rival those of Tuscany, prized lentils from Castelluccio, cured meats from Norcia, and tangy mountain cheeses. A variety of well-regarded wines are produced from the vineyards of Torgiano and Montefalco.

shop in Norcia selling a selection of Italy's finest hams, sausages, and salamis

◀ One of the ceilings in the Palazzo Pianetti, a flamboyant building in the town of Jesi

Exploring Umbria

Assisi and Spoleto, Umbria's loveliest towns, are the most convenient and charming bases for exploring the region. Both these medieval gems are unmissable, as is the old center of Perugia, the region's capital, and the alluring hill towns of Orvieto, Gubbio, Spello, Montefalco, and Todi. Umbria's landscapes are as compelling as its towns, from the eerie wastes of the Piano Grande and the mountain splendor of the Monti Sibillini national park (best reached from Norcia) to the gentler countryside of the Valnerina and the beach-fringed shores of Lake Trasimeno.

Sights at a Glance

1. Gubbio
2. *Assisi pp358–9*
3. Perugia
4. Lake Trasimeno
5. Orvieto
6. Todi
7. Spoleto
8. Montefalco
9. Spello
10. Monti Sibillini
11. Norcia
12. Valnerina

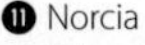
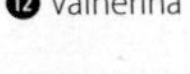

Olive harvest in the Umbrian countryside near Orvieto

Getting Around

Excellent road, railroad, and bus links exist in the region. The A1 from Florence passes Orvieto, which is linked to Todi by the S448. The S75 connects Perugia, Assisi, and Spello, then the S3 continues to Trevi, Spoleto, and Terni. Rome–Florence trains serve Orvieto, and Rome–Ancona trains serve Spoleto, with branch lines connecting Perugia, Spello, and Assisi.

For additional map symbols *see back flap*

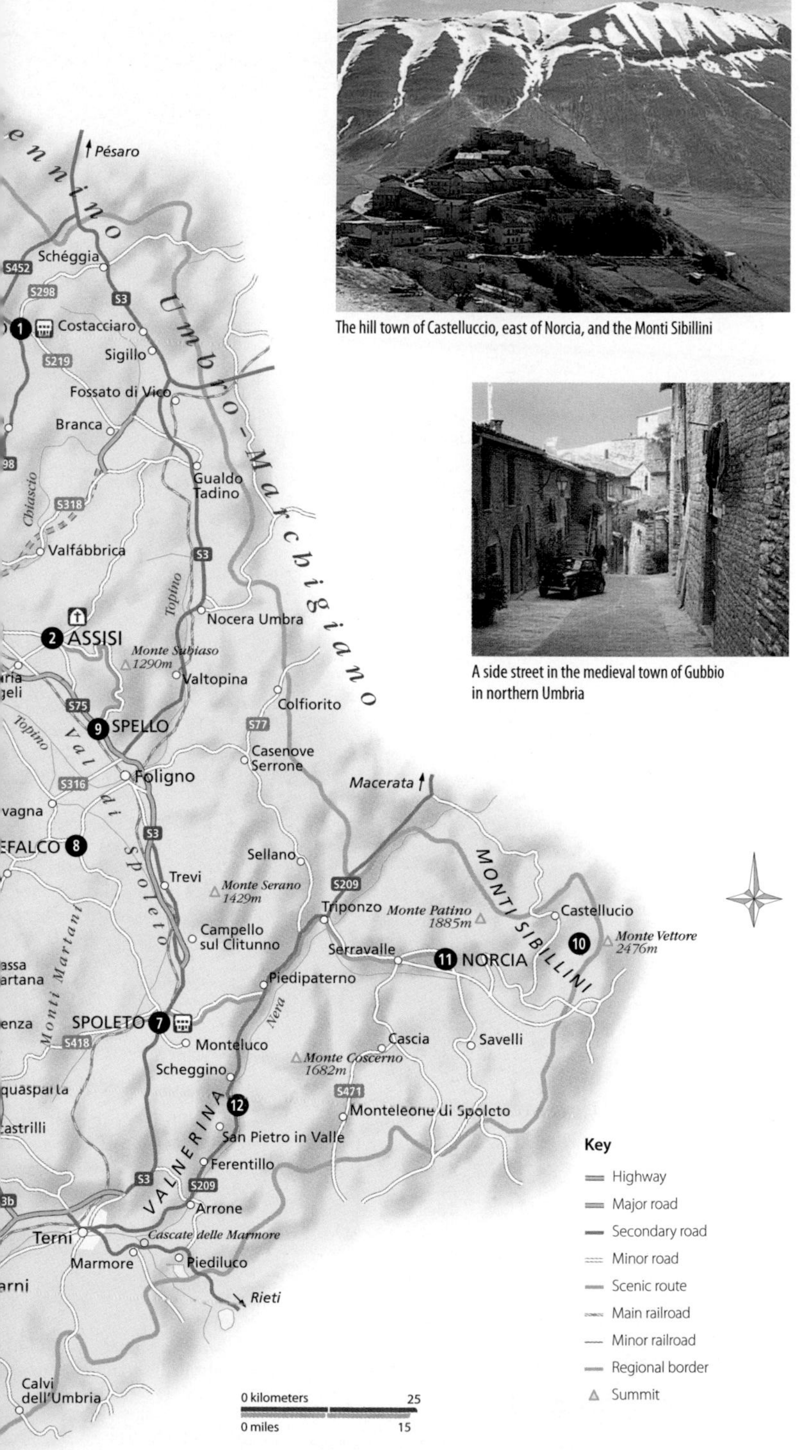

The hill town of Castelluccio, east of Norcia, and the Monti Sibillini

A side street in the medieval town of Gubbio in northern Umbria

❶ Gubbio

Perugia. 33,000. FS Fossato di Vico-Gubbio. Via della Repubblica 15 (075 922 06 93). Tue.

Gubbio vies with Assisi for the title of Umbria's most medieval town. The beauty of its twisting streets and terra-cotta-tiled houses is enhanced by the forest-swathed Apennines. Founded by the Umbrians in the 3rd century BC as Tota Ikuvina, it assumed greater prominence in the 1st century AD as a Roman colony (Eugubium). It emerged as an independent commune in the 11th century, having spread up the slopes of Monte Ingino. From 1387 to 1508 Gubbio was ruled from Urbino by the Dukes of Montefeltro.

The 13th-century **Duomo** is distinguished by a wagon-vaulted ceiling whose curved arches symbolize hands in prayer. Medieval Via dei Consoli leads to the 13th-century **Palazzo del Bargello** – a stone-faced building formerly the headquarters of the chief of police. Also here is the **Fontana dei Matti** (Fountain of the Mad), named after the tradition that anyone who walks around it three times will go insane.

Macabre legends surround the walled-up **Porte della Morte** (Doors of Death) that can be seen in Via dei Consoli and elsewhere in the town. Reputedly used for the passage of coffins from houses, the doors, once tainted, were sealed and never used again. Their purpose was probably defensive. In the lower town, the church of **San Francesco** (1259–82) is known for 17 faded frescoes showing scenes from the *Life of the Virgin* (1408–13) by Ottaviano Nelli. Opposite is the **Tiratoio** (Weavers' Loggia). Wool was stretched out to dry in its shady arcade. West of here are the ruins of a 1st-century AD Roman amphitheater.

The interior of Perugia's San Pietro, rebuilt in the 15th century

Palazzo dei Consoli

Piazza Grande. **Tel** 075 927 42 98. **Open** 10am–1pm, 3–6pm daily (Nov–Mar: 10am–1pm, 2:30–5:30pm). **Closed** Jan 1, May 13–15, Dec 25.

Dominating the skyline of Gubbio is this mighty civic palace, begun in 1332 by Gattapone. Its Salone dell'Arengo houses the Museo Civico, best known for the Eugubine Tablets (250–150 BC). Discovered in 1444, the seven bronze slabs are inscribed with Etruscan and Roman characters, probably a phonetic translation of prayers and rituals from the ancient Umbrian and Etruscan languages. Upstairs a small art gallery contains works by local painters.

One of the Eugubine Tablets in Gubbio

Facade of the Palazzo dei Consoli in Gubbio

Palazzo Ducale

Via Federico da Montefeltro. **Tel** 075 927 58 72. **Open** 8:30am–7pm Tue–Sun. **Closed** Jan 1, Dec 25.

Attributed to Francesco di Giorgio Martini, this palace was built in 1470 for the Montefeltro as a copy of the family home in Urbino *(see pp374–5)*. It also has a pretty Renaissance courtyard.

❷ Assisi

See pp358–9.

❸ Perugia

160,000. FS Piazza Vittorio Veneto. Piazza Matteotti 18 (075 573 64 58). Tue, Sat. W turismo.comune.perugia.it

Perugia's old center hinges around the pedestrianized Corso Vannucci, named after the local painter Pietro Vannucci (Perugino). At its northern end is Piazza IV Novembre, dominated by the **Fontana Maggiore**, a 13th-century fountain by Nicola and Giovanni Pisano. To the rear rises the 15th-century **Duomo**, its entrance flanked by a statue of Pope Julius II (1555) and a pulpit built for Siena's San Bernardino (1425). Its Cappella del Santo Anello contains the Virgin's "wedding ring," a weighty piece of agate said to change color according to the character of the person wearing it. The third pillar in the south nave holds a Renaissance painting of the *Madonna delle Grazie* by Gian Nicola di Paolo. The figure is credited with miraculous powers, and mothers bring newly baptized children to kneel before it. Buried in the transepts are popes Urban IV and Martin IV.

Away from the Corso is the **Oratorio di San Bernardino** (1457–61) on Piazza San Francesco, with a colorful facade by Agostino di Duccio.

ɜeyond the old city walls on ɜorgo XX Giugno stands **San ʼietro**. Founded in the 10th entury and rebuilt in 1463, the ɔest feature of the fine interior is he wooden choir (1526).

Piazza Giordano Bruno is ɪome to **San Domenico** (1305–632), Umbria's largest church, vhich is known for the Gothic omb of Benedict XI (*c.* 1304) nd decoration by Agostino i Duccio.

Museo Archeologico ɬazionale dell'Umbria

an Domenico, Piazza Giordano Bruno 0. **Tel** 075 572 71 41. **Open** daily. **:losed** Jan 1, May 1, Dec 25.

ɬoused in the cloisters of San)omenico, this museum ›xhibits prehistoric, Etruscan, nd Roman artifacts.

Palazzo dei Priori

:orso Vannucci 19. **Tel** 075 573 64 58. **)pen** daily (Sun: am ɪnly). **Closed** Jan 1, ɬay 1, Dec 25 & 1st Mon ach month. Collegio el Cambio: **Open** daily.

'he monumental valls and bristling renellations of this ɔalace mark it as Jmbria's finest public ɔuilding *(see pp58–9)*. ɩmong its fine rooms ; the Sala dei Notari :. 1295), the former lawyers' ɪall, vividly frescoed with scenes 'om the Old Testament – the vork of a follower of Pietro :avallini. The doorway is guarded ɔy a pair of large bronzes made ɪ 1274: a Guelph lion and a ɪriffin, the medieval emblem of Perugia. The Sala di Udienza del Collegio della Mercanzia, built around 1390, was formerly used by the Merchants' Guild. This room is late Gothic in style, with exquisite panelling and 15th-century inlaid wood.

Also in the palace is the **Collegio del Cambio**, Perugia's former money exchange, which was begun in 1452. This room was used by the Bankers' Guild. Its walls are covered with superlative frescoes (1498–1500) by Perugino, works devoted to Classical and religious scenes. A glum self-portrait scowls down from the center of the left wall, while the hand of Perugino's pupil Raphael may be evident in some panels on the right wall.

Medieval street in Perugia

Entrance of Palazzo dei Priori, Perugia

Colorful facade of Perugia's Oratorio di San Bernardino

Galleria Nazionale dell'Umbria

Palazzo dei Priori, Corso Vannucci 19. **Tel** 075 58 66 84 10. **Open** Tue–Sun. **Closed** Jan 1, May 1, Dec 25.

Umbria's greatest collection of paintings is displayed here on the third floor of the palace. Most of the works are 13th- to 18th-century paintings by local artists, but the highlights are altarpieces by Piero della Francesca and Fra Angelico.

❹ Lake Trasimeno

Perugia. FS Castiglione del Lago. i Piazza Mazzini 10, Castiglione del Lago (075 965 24 84). **W regioneumbria.eu**

Edged with low hills, this is Italy's fourth-largest lake. Its miles of placid water and reed-lined shores have a tranquil, melancholy beauty.

Drainage of the lake began under the Romans, but today the lake is gently drying up of its own accord. The town of **Castiglione del Lago**, jutting out on a fortified promontory, has an easygoing atmosphere and small sandy beaches. The 16th-century **castle** is used for summer concerts. The church of **Santa Maria Maddalena**, begun in 1836, has a fine *Madonna and Child* (*c.* 1500) by Eusebio di San Giorgio.

Like Castiglione, **Passignano sul Trasimeno** offers boat trips to **Isola Maggiore**. The island's charming village is known for lacemaking.

The Battle of Lake Trasimeno

In 217 BC the Romans suffered one of their worst-ever military defeats on the shores of Lake Trasimeno. The Carthaginian general, Hannibal, lured the Romans (who were led by the consul Flaminius) into a masterful ambush close to present-day Ossaia (Place of Bones) and Sanguineto (Place of Blood). Some 16,000 legionaries perished, hacked down on the lake's marshy fringes. Hannibal, by contrast, lost only 1,500 men. Today you can explore the battlefield, which includes over 100 mass graves found near Tuoro sul Trasimeno.

19th-century engraving of General Hannibal

Assisi: Basilica di San Francesco

The burial place of St. Francis, this basilica was begun in 1228, two years after the saint's death. Over the next century its Upper and Lower Churches were decorated by the foremost artists of their day, among them Cimabue, Simone Martini, Pietro Lorenzetti, and Giotto, whose frescoes on the *Life of St. Francis* are some of the most renowned in Italy. The basilica, which dominates Assisi, is one of the great Christian shrines and receives vast numbers of pilgrims throughout the year.

Lower Church
Side chapels were created here in the 13th century to accommodate the growing number of pilgrims.

St. Francis
Cimabue's simple painting (*c.* 1280) captures the humility of the revered saint, who stood for poverty, chastity, and obedience.

KEY

① **The crypt** contains the tomb of St. Francis.

② **Steps to the Treasury**

③ **The choir** (1501) features a 13th-century stone papal throne.

④ **The campanile** was built in 1239.

⑤ **Faded paintings** by Roman artists line the walls above Giotto's Life of St. Francis.

⑥ **The facade** and its rose window are early examples of Italian Gothic.

★ Frescoes by Lorenzet
The bold composition of Pietro Lorenzetti's fresc entitled *The Deposition* (1323), is based around th truncated Cross, focusing attention on th twisted figure of Chris

VISITORS' CHECKLIST

Practical Information
Piazza San Francesco. **Tel** 075 819 00 84. **Open** 6am–5:45pm daily (Lower Church: from 8:30am). Longer hours Sun & summer.
w **sanfrancescoassisi.org**

Transportation
FS

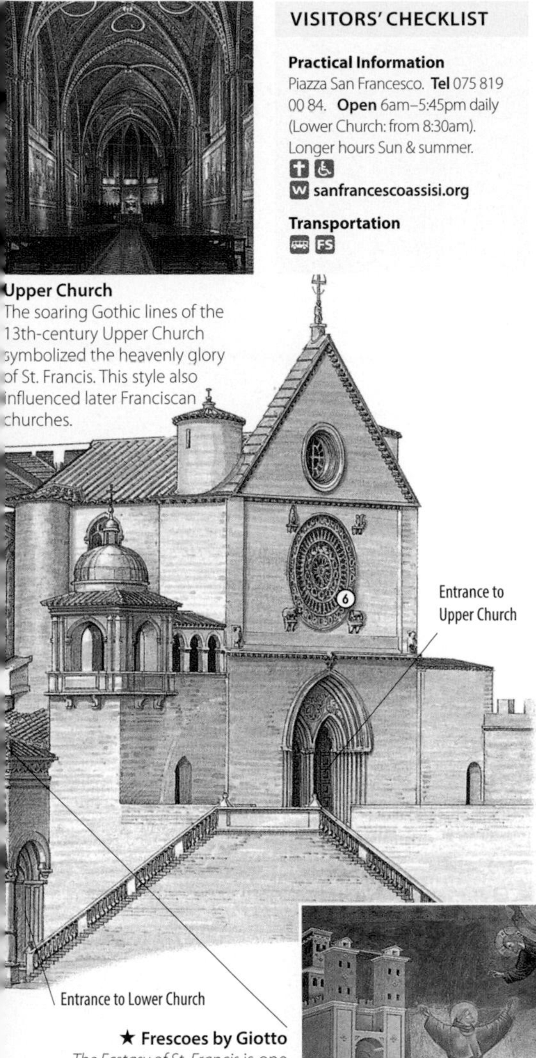

Upper Church
The soaring Gothic lines of the 13th-century Upper Church symbolized the heavenly glory of St. Francis. This style also influenced later Franciscan churches.

★ Frescoes by Giotto
The Ecstasy of St. Francis is one of 28 panels that make up Giotto's cycle on the *Life of St. Francis* (*c.* 1290–95).

★ Cappella di San Martino
The frescoes in this chapel on the *Life of St. Martin* (1315) are by the Sienese painter Simone Martini. This panel shows the *Death of the Saint.* Martini was also responsible for the fine stained glass in the chapel.

❷ Assisi

Perugia. 25,000. FS *i* Piazza del Comune 22 (075 81 25 34). Sat. **w** **conoscerelumbria.regioneumbria.eu**

This beautiful medieval town, with its geranium-hung streets, lovely views, and fountain-splashed piazzas, is heir to the legacy of St. Francis (*c.* 1181–1226), who is buried in the **Basilica di San Francesco**. The town suffered serious damage during the earthquake of September 1997, but restoration was relatively swift – completed in approximately two years. The tourist office can give information on which sights are open to visitors.

Piazza del Comune, Assisi's main square, is dominated by the columns of the **Tempio di Minerva**, a Roman temple-front from the Augustan age. The Palazzo Comunale, opposite, is home to the **Pinacoteca Comunale**, an art gallery with works by local medieval artists.

Down Corso Mazzini lies the **Basilica di Santa Chiara**, the burial place of St. Clare – Francis's companion and the founder of the Poor Clares (an order of nuns). One of its chapels contains the crucifix that is said to have bowed its head and ordered Francis to "Repair God's church." It came from **San Damiano**, a sublime church set amid olive groves south of the Porta Nuova.

The **Duomo (San Rufino)**, built during the 12th and 13th centuries, has a superb Romanesque facade. Inside is a small museum of paintings, and there are archaeological items in the crypt. From the Duomo, Via Maria delle Rose leads to the **Rocca Maggiore** (rebuilt in 1367), an evocative if much-restored castle.

Thirteenth-century **San Pietro**, on Piazza San Pietro, is a simple and carefully restored Romanesque church. The nearby **Oratorio dei Pellegrini**, a 15th-century pilgrims' hospice, contains well-preserved frescoes by Matteo da Gualdo.

Giotto's fresco, *St. Francis Appearing to the Friars at Arles* (*c.* 1295), in the Basilica di San Francesco, Assisi ▶

❺ Orvieto

Terni. 22,000. FS *i* Piazza Duomo 24 (0763 34 17 72). Thu & Sat. **W** **orvietoonline.com**

Perched on a 984-ft (300-m) plateau, Orvieto looks down over a vineyard-spotted plain. Visitors flood into the town to admire the **Duomo**, among the greatest of Italy's Romanesque-Gothic cathedrals.

The tiny 14th-century church of **San Lorenzo in Arari** is at the end of Via Scalza. Its walls feature frescoes describing the martyrdom of St. Lawrence, who was grilled to death. The altar is made from an Etruscan sacrificial slab. Via Malabranca leads to **San Giovenale** at Orvieto's western tip, a church that is beautifully and almost completely covered in detailed frescoes from the 15th and 16th centuries. It offers broad views over the surrounding countryside. **Sant'Andrea**, in Piazza della Repubblica, is distinguished by a curious 12-sided campanile, part of the original 12th-century building.

Museo dell' Opera del Duomo & Museo d'Arte Moderna "Emilio Greco"

Piazza Duomo. **Tel** 0763 34 35 92. **Open** Apr–Sep: 9:30am–7pm daily; Nov–Feb: 9:30am–1pm, 2:30–5pm daily; Mar & Oct: 9:30am–6pm daily. **W** **opsm.it**

The Museo dell'Opera del Duomo is an interesting little museum containing an eclectic collection of treasures given to the Duomo. Among the highlights are paintings by Lorenzo Maitani (died 1330) and sculptures by Andrea Pisano (*c.* 1270–1348).

The "Emilio Greco" museum is devoted to the modern Sicilian sculptor Emilio Greco, who made the bronze doors (1964–70) of the Duomo in Orvieto.

View into the Pozzo di San Patrizio in Orvieto

Museo Archeologico Faina & Museo Civico

Piazza Duomo 29. **Tel** 0763 34 10 39. **Open** 8:30am–7:30pm daily. **Closed** Jan 1, May 1, Dec 25.

The first of these two museums has a well-known, low-key collection of Etruscan remains including many Greek vases that were found in Etruscan tombs in the surrounding area. The Museo Civico contains ancient Greek artifacts and Etruscan copies of Greek works.

Duomo of Orvieto

Piazza Duomo. **Tel** 0763 34 11 67. **Open** daily.

Some 300 years in the building, Orvieto's Duomo (begun 1290), with its breathtaking facade, is one of Italy's greatest cathedrals. It was inspired by the Miracle of Bolsena in which real blood from a consecrated host supposedly fell on the altar cloth of a church in nearby Bolsena.

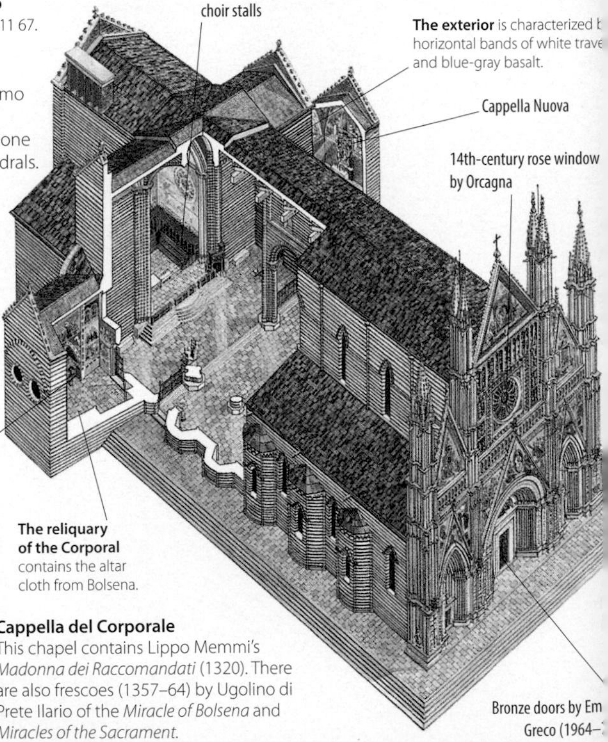

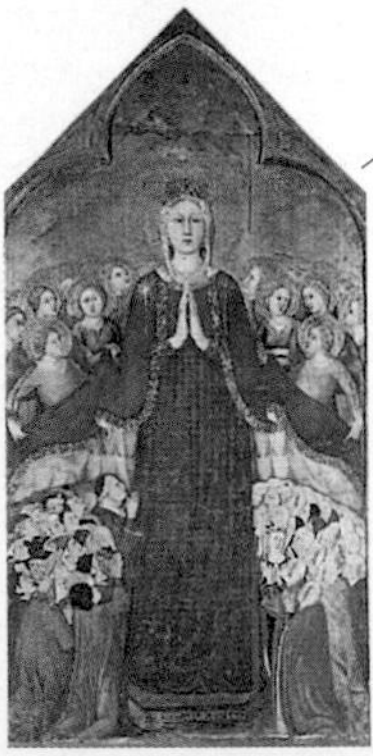

Carved choir stalls

The exterior is characterized b horizontal bands of white trave and blue-gray basalt.

Cappella Nuova

14th-century rose window by Orcagna

The reliquary of the Corporal contains the altar cloth from Bolsena.

Cappella del Corporale

This chapel contains Lippo Memmi's *Madonna dei Raccomandati* (1320). There are also frescoes (1357–64) by Ugolino di Prete Ilario of the *Miracle of Bolsena* and *Miracles of the Sacrament.*

Bronze doors by Em Greco (1964–

Pozzo di San Patrizio
'iale San Gallo. **Tel** 0763 34 37 68. **)pen** daily. allows entry at Museo l'Arte Moderna.

'his well was commissioned in 527 by Pope Clement VII and lesigned by the Florentine ırchitect Antonio da Sangallo to ɔrovide the town with a water upply in case of attack. Two !48-step staircases drop into its lank interior, cleverly arranged ıs a double helix (spiral) so as ıot to intersect. The 203-ft (62-m) haft took ten years to complete.

Necropoli Etrusca – :rocefisso del Tufo
trada Statale 71 to Orvieto Scalo, km ,600. **Tel** 0763 34 36 11. **Open** :30am–7pm (Oct–Mar: to 5pm) daily. **:losed** Jan 1, May 1, Dec 25.

'his Etruscan necropolis from he 6th century BC has burial hambers built of blocks of tufa. truscan letters, thought to be he names of the deceased, are ıscribed on the tombs.

'appella Nuova
.uca Signorelli's great fresco cycle f the *Last Judgment* (1499–1504) ɜatures prominently in this chapel. 'a Angelico and Benozzo Gozzoli vorked here before Signorelli.

'he Facade
ɪere are detailed carvings . 1320–30) at the base of its four ıain pilasters. By Lorenzo Maitani, ıey depict scenes from the Old ıd New Testaments, including ell and damnation.

View of the hill-town of Todi in southern Umbria

6 Todi

Perugia. 17,000. FS Piazza del Popolo 38 (075 894 54 16). Sat.

Looking down over the Tiber valley from its hilltop eyrie, Todi is one of the most strikingly situated of Umbria's famous hill towns. An ancient Etruscan and then Roman settlement, it still preserves an uncorrupted medieval air, with several tiny churches, three austere public palaces, and many sleepy corners.

Most people are drawn here by the **Piazza del Popolo**, the main square, flanked by the lovely plain-faced **Duomo**. Built in the 13th century on the site of a Roman temple to Apollo, it has a dusky interior and one of Umbria's finest choirs (1521–30). Note Ferraù da Faenza's huge painting (1596) on the rear wall, a less than totally successful copy of Michelangelo's *Last Judgment*, and the altarpiece at the end of the right aisle by Giannicola di Paolo (a follower of Perugino).

Also flanking the piazza are the **Palazzo dei Priori** (1293–1337) and the linked **Palazzo del Capitano** (1290) and **Palazzo del Popolo** (1213). In the Palazzo del Capitano, distinguished by its redoubtable medieval interior, lies the **Museo Etrusco-Romano**. The museum contains a collection of local Etruscan and Roman artifacts. There are altarpieces and sacred objects in the **Pinacoteca Comunale**, also housed in the palace.

A few steps from the piazza rises **San Fortunato** (1292–1462), named after Todi's first bishop, with a florid Gothic doorway (1415–58). The high vaulted plan is based on German Gothic "hall" churches and the "barn" churches of Tuscany, characterized by a low-pitched vault, polygonal apse, and naves and aisles of equal height. The choir (1590) is superb, but the church's most famous work is a *Madonna and Child* (1432) by Masolino da Panicale (fourth chapel on the right). The crypt contains the tomb of Jacopone da Todi (*c.* 1228–1306), a noted medieval poet and mystic.

To the right of the church are some shady gardens, from which a path (past the tiny castle) drops through the trees to emerge in front of **Santa Maria della Consolazione** (1508–1607), near the N79. One of central Italy's finest Renaissance churches, and based on a Greek cross, it may have been built to a plan by Bramante. The stark, chill interior is overshadowed by the harmonious exterior.

Museo Etrusco-Romano and Pinacoteca Comunale
Piazza del Popolo 29/30. **Tel** 075 894 41 48. **Open** Tue–Sun.

Santa Maria della Consolazione in Todi

7 Spoleto

Perugia. 38,000. FS Piazza della Libertà 7 (0743 21 86 20 or 21 86 21). Fri. regioneumbria.eu

Founded by the Umbrians, Spoleto was one of central Italy's most important Roman colonies, a prominence maintained by the Lombards, who in the 7th century made it the capital of one of their three Italian dukedoms. After a spell as an independent city-state, in 1354 Spoleto fell to the papacy.

Spoleto, within its wooded setting, is the loveliest of the Umbrian hill towns. Its urbane atmosphere is enhanced by its superb monuments and by the Festival dei Due Mondi, one of Europe's leading arts festivals held annually in June and July.

At the southern end of Piazza del Mercato is the **Arco di Druso**, a 1st-century AD Roman arch. It is flanked by the church of **Sant'Ansano**, whose crypt is covered in frescoes that may date from the 6th century. Via Aurelio Saffi, at the piazza's northern end, leads to **Sant'Eufemia**. This utterly simple 10th-century Romanesque church is known for its matroneum (women's gallery), once used to segregate the congregation.

A short way beyond, the fan-shaped Piazza del Duomo opens out to reveal Spoleto's 12th-century **Duomo**, graced with an elegant Romanesque facade. Filling the apse of the Baroque interior is a great fresco cycle. The final work of Fra Lippo Lippi, 1467–9, it describes episodes from the *Life of the Virgin*. The Cappella Erioli is adorned with Pinturicchio's unfinished *Madonna and Child* (1497).

Ponte delle Torri, Spoleto

The best of the exceptional churches in the lower town is 4th-century **San Salvatore**, located in the main cemetery, a spot suited to the church's eerie sense of antiquity. Nearby stands **San Ponziano**, fronted by a captivating three-tiered Romanesque facade typical of Umbria.

Facade of San Pietro in Spoleto

It has a 10th-century crypt, supported by odd little columns and decorated with Byzantine frescoes.

Romanesque **San Gregorio** in Piazza Garibaldi dates from 1069, but its cramped facade and stolid campanile incorporate fragments of Roman buildings. Inside is a raised presbytery and a lovely multi-columned crypt. Well-preserved patches of fresco dot the walls. Some 10,000 Christian martyrs are supposedly buried near the church. They were reputedly slaughtered in the town's Roman **amphitheater**, traces of which can be seen in the barracks on Via del Anfiteatro.

Ponte delle Torri

This magnificent 14th-century aqueduct, the "bridge of towers" is 262 ft (80 m) high. Designed by Gattapone (from Gubbio), it is the town's single most famous monument.

Romanesque Churches in Umbria

Umbria's church-building tradition had its roots in ancient Roman basilicas and in the chapels built over the shrines of its many saints and martyrs. The region's Romanesque facades are usually divided into three tiers, often with three rose windows arranged above a trio of arched portals. The three doors usually correspond to the interior's nave and two aisles, which derive from the simple barnlike plan of Roman basilicas. Inside, the presbytery is often raised in order to allow for the building of a crypt, which usually contained the relics of a saint or martyr. Many of the churches took centuries to build, or were repeatedly modified over time, often acquiring elements of Gothic, Baroque or Renaissance styles.

San Lorenzo di Arari in Orvieto takes its name from an Etruscan altar *(arari)*. This 14th-century church has a very simple facade *(see p362)*.

Spoleto's Duomo (1198) has eight rose windows, a mosaic (1207), and a Renaissance portico (1491). The tower was built from old Roman ruins.

'rom the bridge, there are views ɔf the bastions of the **Rocca Albornoz**, a huge papal fortress built in 1359–64, also by Gattapone. Across the bridge, a path leads to the Strada di Monteluco and the church of **San Pietro**, famous for the fascinating 12th-century carvings on its facade.

Rocca Albornoz
Piazza Campello 1. **Tel** 0743 22 49 52. **Open** daily. compulsory.

Museo del Tessile e del Costume
Via delle Terme. **Tel** 0743 459 40. **Open** 3:30–7:30pm Sat & Sun. **Closed** Jan 1, Dec 25.

Among the exhibits in this exquisite collection are sacred vestments complete with headgear, ties, and gold chains, and a series of 17th-century tapestries that once belonged to Queen Christina of Sweden.

8 Montefalco

Perugia. 4,900. Mon.

Montefalco, whose name (Falcon's Mount) draws inspiration from its lofty position and sweeping views, is the best of the fascinating villages in the Vale of Spoleto. Crisscrossed by streets almost too narrow for cars, it takes less than five minutes to walk through the village. Yet you might happily spend a morning here, most of it in the polished **Museo Civico** housed in the former church of San Francesco. Its highlight is Benozzo Gozzoli's *Life of St. Francis* (1452), a radiant fresco cycle that borrows heavily from Giotto's cycle in Assisi *(see pp358–61)*. Other painters represented here are Perugino, Tiberio d'Assisi, and Nicolò Alunno, all leading medieval Umbrian artists.

The simple Gothic church of **Sant'Agostino** (begun 1279) on Corso Mameli is dotted with frescoes from the 14th–16th centuries. The church also contains three mummies.

In the main square, local wines for sale include the rich red Sagrantino di Montefalco. Just outside the town walls, the church of **Sant'Illuminata** is covered with charming frescoes, the work of the local 16th-century artist Francesco Melanzio. About 1 mile (2 km) beyond, the prettily situated church of **San Fortunato** is decorated with frescoes by Gozzoli and Tiberio d'Assisi.

A panel from Gozzoli's fresco cycle (1452) in Montefalco's Museo Civico

Environs
The village in the Vale of Spoleto with the most spectacular setting is **Trevi**. The churches of **San Martino** (16th century), on Passeggiata di San Martino, and **Madonna delle Lacrime** (1487–1522), south of Trevi on the road into the village, contain paintings by Perugino and Tiberio d'Assisi, among others.

Museo Civico di San Francesco
Via Ringhiera Umbra 9. **Tel** 0742 37 95 98. **Open** daily (Nov–Feb: Tue–Sun). **Closed** Jan 1, Dec 25.

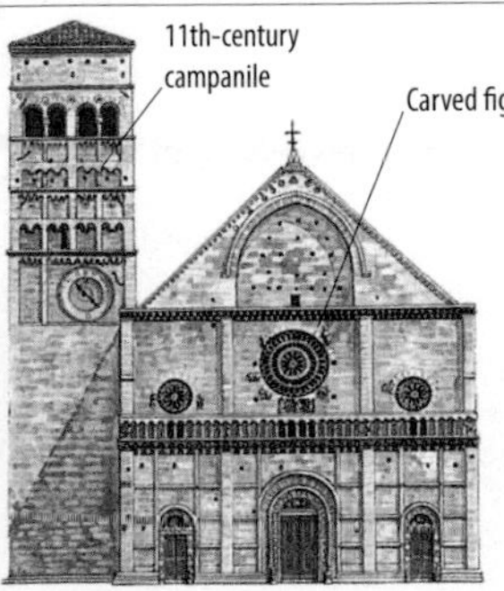

The Duomo (1253) in Assisi is a fine example of the three-tiered facades found across central Italy *(see p359)*. It has a pointed arch and a row of arcading.

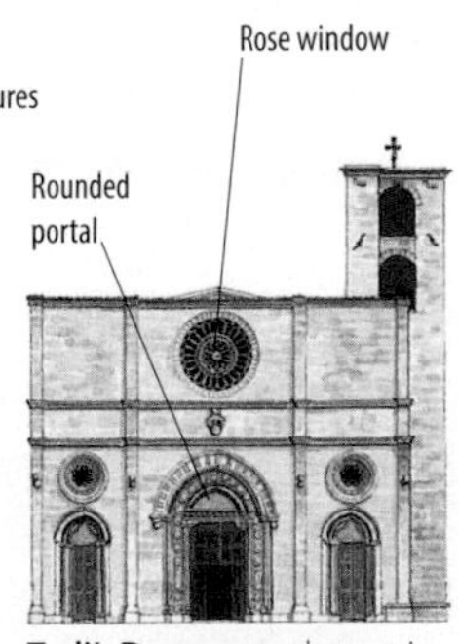

Todi's Duomo was begun in the 12th century, but work on its windows and portals continued until the 17th century *(see p363)*.

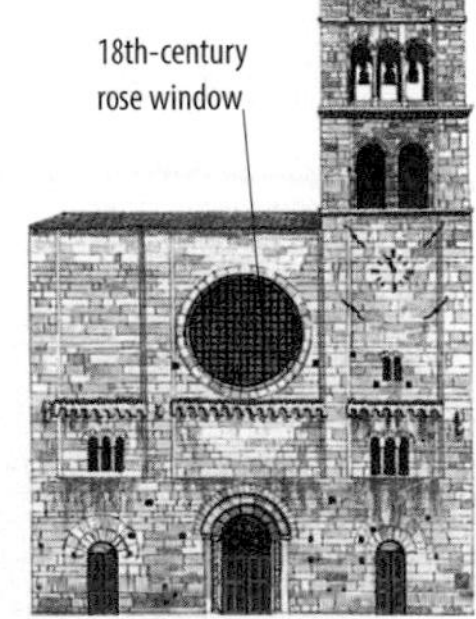

San Michele (*c.* 1195) in Bevagna has a beautiful portal that combines both Romanesque and old Roman fragments *(see p366)*.

❾ Spello

Perugia. 8,000. FS Piazza Matteotti 3 (0742 30 10 09). Wed.

Spello is one of the better known villages in the Vale of Spoleto. It is renowned for a fresco cycle by Pinturicchio in the Cappella Baglioni of the church of **Santa Maria Maggiore** (12th–13th century) on Via Consolare. Executed around 1500, the frescoes depict scenes from the New Testament. Toward the center of the village is the Gothic church of **Sant'Andrea** (13th century) on Via Cavour. This road becomes Via Garibaldi, which leads to **San Lorenzo**, a Baroque gem of a church dating from the 12th century.

Spello also boasts Roman ruins from the age of Augustus: the **Porta Consolare** at the end of Via Consolare, and the twin-towered **Porta Venere** by Via Torri di Properzio.

The road to Assisi over **Monte Subasio** offers stunning views from the top of the mountain above Spello.

Environs

The least known village in the Vale of Spoleto is **Bevagna**. Like Spello, it sprang to life as a way station on the Via Flaminia (the Roman road that ran through this part of Umbria). The medieval Piazza Silvestri is the setting for two Romanesque churches.

The lofty peaks of the Monti Sibillini in eastern Umbria

San Silvestro (1195) is the more atmospheric of the pair, thanks to its shadowy interior and ancient crypt, but **San Michele** (late 12th century) has an elegant portal, famed for the little gargoyles on either side. Both churches are the work of Maestro Binello.

❿ Monti Sibillini

Macerata. FS Spoleto. Visso. Piazza del Forno 1, Visso (0737 97 27 11). **sibillini.net**

The national park of the Monti Sibillini in eastern Umbria provides the region's wildest and most spectacular scenery. A range 25 miles (40 km) long, the mountains form part of the Apennines, a chain that runs the length of the Italian peninsula. **Monte Vettore** is the loftiest point, and the peninsula's third highest; it stands at 8,123 ft (2,476 m), a great whale-backed peak close to the cave of the mythical sybil that gave the region its name.

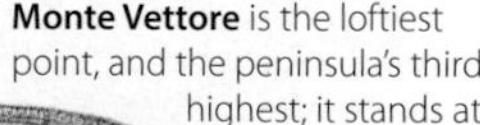

Good maps and trails make this a superb walking area, while drivers can follow hairpin roads to some of Italy's most magical landscapes. Chief of these is the **Piano Grande**, a huge upland plain surrounded by a vast amphitheater of mountains. Bare but for flocks of sheep and bedraggled haystacks, the plain blazes with wildflowers in spring and with lentils later in the year. The only habitation is **Castelluccio**, a beautiful, neglected mountain village now being restored. It can be reached by road from Norcia and Arquata del Tronto.

Shop front in Norcia displaying the town's varied meats

⓫ Norcia

Perugia. 4,700. Piazza San Benedetto (0743 82 49 11). Thu.

The birthplace of St. Benedict, Norcia is a robust mountain town and an excellent base for exploring Valnerina and Monti Sibillini. One of Italy's culinary capitals, it is renowned for truffles and for some of Italy's best hams, sausages, and salamis. Indeed, the Italian word for a pork butcher (*norcineria*) derives from the name of the town.

Norcia's main sights are in **Piazza San Benedetto**. On the eastern flank, the church of **San Benedetto** has a 14th-century portal adorned with statues of Benedict and his sister (Santa Scolastica). Legend claims that the church marks the site of Benedict's birth, and there are remains of a 5th-century building in the crypt. However,

Pinturicchio's *Annunciation* (c. 1500) in Spello's Santa Maria Maggiore

The 8th-century monastery of San Pietro in Valle, set in the beautiful Valnerina

the church was more likely to have been built over the site of an old Roman temple, since the forum of the Roman colony of Nursia once occupied this spot.

Left of the church stands the **Palazzo Comunale**, a monument to the town's period as a free commune during the 13th and 14th centuries. On the opposite side of the square rises the **Castellina** (1554), a blunt papal fortress designed by Vignola to help impose order on an unruly mountain district. The **Duomo** (1560), to the left of the Castellina, has been ravaged by earthquakes over the centuries. Indeed, Norcia has been the victim of successive earthquakes and its houses are low and heavily buttressed with thick walls to protect them from further damage. **Sant'Agostino** on Via Anicia features a range of good 16th-century frescoes. A little way beyond, the **Oratorio di Sant'Agostinaccio** in Piazza Palatina contains a superb 17th-century ceiling. Via Umberto shelters the **Edicola** (1354), a strange tabernacle believed to have been carved for a Holy Week procession.

⓬ Valnerina

Perugia. FS Spoleto, then bus. i Piazza Garibaldi 1, Cascia (0743 711 47).

The Valnerina (Little Valley of the Nera River) curves through a broad swath of eastern Umbria, draining the mountains around Norcia and the Sibillini before emptying into the Tiber. It is edged with craggy, tree-covered slopes and dotted with upland villages and fortified hamlets.

The high spot is **San Pietro in Valle**, an idyllically situated monastery in the hills above the village of Colleponte. Founded in the 8th century, it is one of the few surviving memorials to the Lombards, whose central Italian duchy had its capital in Spoleto. The main body of the monastery church dates from this period, as does the high altar. The nave walls are covered in a wealth of 12th-century frescoes. Some of the best Romanesque carvings in Umbria can be found here.

More popular than the monastery are the **Cascate delle Marmore** near Terni, among Europe's highest waterfalls at 541 ft (165 m). Created by the Romans during drainage work, their waters are now diverted to produce hydroelectric power on all but a few special days. You can view the falls from Marmore village or the S209.

Piazza San Benedetto and the church of San Benedetto in Norcia

San Pietro in Valle
Località Ferentillo, Terni. **Tel** 0744 78 01 29. **Open** daily (Sat & Sun in winter).

Cascate delle Marmore
4 miles (7 km) along S209 Valnerina, Terni. **Open** daily. Visit the website for opening hours. W **marmorefalls.it**

LE MARCHE

Tucked away in a remote corner between the Adriatic Sea and the Apennine mountains, Le Marche (the Marches) is an enchanting rural patchwork of old towns, hill country, and long, sandy beaches. In pre-Christian times the area was settled by the Piceni, a tribe eventually assimilated by the Romans.

In the 4th century BC, exiles from Magna Graecia colonized much of the region. The most notable town was Ancona, also the northernmost point of Greek influence on the Italian peninsula. During the early Middle Ages the region marked the edge of the Holy Roman Empire, giving rise to its present name (*march* meant border area).

The region's historical peak was reached in the 15th century under Federico da Montefeltro, whose court at Urbino became one of Europe's leading cultural centers. Much of Urbino's former grandeur survives, particularly in Federico's magnificent Renaissance Palazzo Ducale, now home to a regional art collection. Ascoli Piceno is almost as enchanting as Urbino, its central Piazza del Popolo among the most evocative old squares in Italy. Smaller towns like San Leo and Urbania and the republic of San Marino also boast fine medieval monuments.

Today probably as many people come to Le Marche for its beaches and towns as for its hilly, unspoiled interior. Especially beautiful are the snowcapped peaks of the Monti Sibillini, situated in magnificent walking and skiing country.

Regional cuisine encompasses the truffles and robust cheeses of the mountains, tender hams and salamis, *olive ascolane* (olives stuffed with meat and herbs), and *brodetto*, fish soup made in several versions up and down the coast. Dry, white Verdicchio is the best known wine, although more unusual names, such as Bianchello del Metauro, are gaining in popularity.

A field of poppies and olive trees in the heart of Le Marche's countryside

◀ A view of the Piazza del Popolo, built in traventine marble, in the town of Ascoli Piceno

Exploring Le Marche

The medieval towns of Urbino and Ascoli Piceno are the highlights of the region, but the rolling hills of the interior contain an abundance of smaller towns and all but undiscovered villages. San Leo, with its dramatic fortress, is one of the best. Most of the countryside is a pretty mixture of woods and remote hills, rising in the west to the majestic Monti Sibillini. Ancona and the attractive town of Pèsaro are the pivotal points of the vast coastline.

Rimini
Gabicce Mare
SAN MARINO 2
Cesena
San Marino
Novafeltria
1 SAN LEO
Mercatino Conca
Montecchio
Sant'Agata Feltria
Montefeltro
Foglia
Macerata Feltria
Mombaroccio
Casteldelci
Sassocorvaro
Carpegna
S423
Calcinelli
Lunano
5 URBINO
Belforte all' Isauro
S73b
Fossombrone
Fermignano
Mercatello sul Metauro
URBANIA 6
Acqualagna
S73b
San Lorenzo in Campo
Piobbico
Pergola
Apecchio
Monte Nerone 1525m
Cagli
Arezzo
S3
Monte Petrano 1162m
Appennino Umbro-Marchigiano
Cantiano
Monte Catria 1701m
Sassoferrato
GROTTE DI FRASASSI
Fabriano
Foligno
S77

Key

Freeway

Major road

Secondary road

Minor road

Scenic route

Main train line

Minor train line

International border

Regional border

Summit

Rolling countryside between Loreto and Ascoli Piceno

View of Ascoli Piceno, one of the prettiest towns in Le Marche

For additional map symbols *see back flap*

Sights at a Glance

1. San Leo
2. San Marino
3. Pèsaro
4. Fano
5. *Urbino pp374–5*
6. Urbania
7. Grotte di Frasassi
8. Jesi
9. Ancona
10. Conero Peninsula
11. Loreto
12. Ascoli Piceno

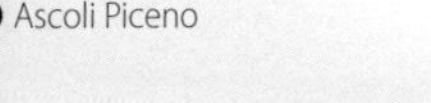

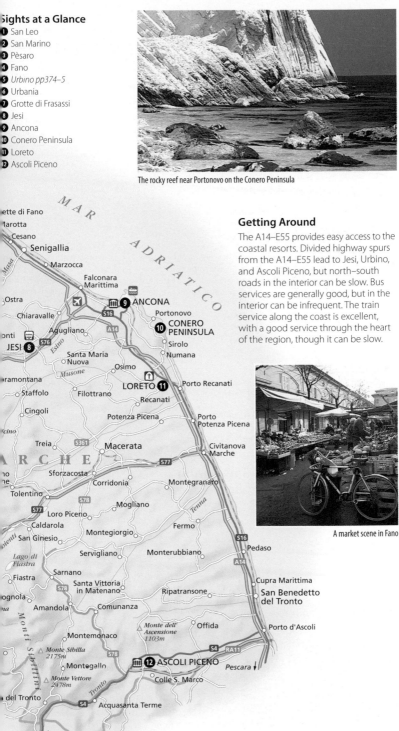

The rocky reef near Portonovo on the Conero Peninsula

Getting Around

The A14–E55 provides easy access to the coastal resorts. Divided highway spurs from the A14–E55 lead to Jesi, Urbino, and Ascoli Piceno, but north–south roads in the interior can be slow. Bus services are generally good, but in the interior can be infrequent. The train service along the coast is excellent, with a good service through the heart of the region, though it can be slow.

A market scene in Fano

The bell tower of the Duomo rising above the village of San Leo

❶ San Leo

Pèsaro. 3,000. Piazza Dante Alighieri 14 (0541 91 63 06). from Rimini, change at Villanova. **san-leo.it**

Few castles are as impressive as the great **fortress** that towers over the village of San Leo. Dante used this crag-top site as a model for the landscapes of *Purgatorio*, while Machiavelli considered the citadel to be the finest piece of military architecture in Italy. Its rocky ramparts once contained the Mons Feretrius, a Roman temple dedicated to Jupiter.

An earlier Roman fortress on the site became a papal prison in the 18th century. Its most famous inmate was the larger-than-life Conte di Cagliostro. A swindler, womanizer, necromancer, quack, and alchemist, Cagliostro was imprisoned for heresy in the 1790s. His cell was specially built so that its window faced the village's two churches. It is still visible, together with a small picture gallery, state rooms, and the majestic Renaissance ramparts, built by Francesco di Giorgio Martini for the dukes of Montefeltro in the 15th century.

The captivating village has a quaint cobbled square with a superb 9th-century **Pieve** (parish church). Built partly with stone from the ruined Mons Feretrius, the church was raised over the site of a 6th-century chapel.

Just behind is the 12th-century **Duomo**, a fine Romanesque building with Corinthian capitals and Roman columns from the Mons Feretrius. The lid of St. Leo's sarcophagus is in the crypt. Ancient pagan carvings can be seen on the wall behind the altar.

Fortress
Via Leopardi. **Tel** 0541 91 63 06.
Open daily. **Closed** lunch Oct–Mar.

❷ San Marino

26,000. San Marino Città (fr Rimini). Contrada Omagnano (0549 88 29 14). **visitsanmarino.com**

Europe's oldest republic, tiny San Marino was reputedly founded by St. Marinus, a 4th-century monk and stonemason forced to flee the religious persecution of the Emperor Diocletian. With him was St. Leo, founder of the nearby town of San Leo. Situated on the slopes of Monte Titano, the country has its own mint, stamps, soccer team – even its own 1,000-strong army. It is also famous for Formula One racing. There are no customs formalities in this country, whose borders are just 7 miles (12 km) apart at the widest point. The capital, **San Marino**, is overrun with visitors and souvenir stands through the year. Garibaldi sought shelter here after fleeing Venice in 1849 and is honored by a monument in Piazza Garibaldi. The town of **Borgomaggiore** lies at the foot of Monte Titano, with a cable car to the capital above.

Duty-free shop in San Marino

❸ Pèsaro

110,000. FS Viale Trieste 164 (0721 693 41). Tue & 1st Thu of month.

One of the Adriatic's larger seaside resorts, Pèsaro has managed to retain a stylish air. Behind the promenade and the wall of white stucco hotels is a lively, attractive medieval area.

The art gallery of the **Musei Civici** contains Giovanni Bellini's sumptuous polyptych, the *Coronation of the Virgin* (*c*. 1470). The museum also features Renaissance ceramics.

The **Museo Archeologico Oliveriano** presents historical displays from Roman remains to Iron Age artifacts from the necropolis of nearby Novilara.

The best of the town's churches is **Sant'Agostino** on Corso XI Settembre, remarkable for its choir stalls, each a patchwork of inlaid landscapes and narrative scenes.

Pèsaro is also a point of musical pilgrimage because the composer Gioacchino Rossini was born here in 1792. His home, **Casa Rossini**, contains memorabilia, while his piano and some

Detail of the *Coronation of the Virgin* by Bellini (*c*. 1470) in the Musei Civici

original manuscripts lie in the **Conservatorio Rossini**. His operas are performed in **Teatro Rossini** in Piazza Lazzarini during the annual August music festival.

Musei Civici
Pza Mosca 29. **Tel** 0721 38 72 95. **Open** Tue–Sun. **Closed** Jan 1, Dec 25.

Museo Archeologico Oliveriano
Via Mazza 97. **Tel** 0721 333 44. **Open** Mon–Sat.

Casa Rossini
Via Rossini 34. **Tel** 0721 38 73 57. **Open** Tue & Wed am, Thu–Sun.

Conservatorio Rossini
Piazza Olivieri 5. **Tel** 0721 336 71. **Open** Mon–Sat, but phone first to arrange. **Closed** public hols.

4 Fano

Pèsaro. 65,000. FS Via Cesare Battisti 10 (0721 80 35 34). Wed & Sat.

Ancient Fano stands out from the string of beach resorts south of Pèsaro, thanks to its fine old center and historic monuments. Named after Fanum Fortunae, a pagan temple to the goddess Fortuna, it became the terminus of the Via Flaminia (an important consular road from Rome) and the largest Roman colony on the Adriatic coast. The **Arco d'Augusto** (AD 2), on Via Arco d'Augusto, is Fano's most significant ancient monument, having narrowly escaped destruction at the hands of Federico da Montefeltro in 1463. He destroyed its upper section while besieging the town as a papal *condottiere*.

The 16th-century **Fontana della Fortuna**, in Piazza XX Settembre, is dedicated to the goddess Fortuna. The large **Palazzo Malatesta** that rises up to its rear was built around 1420 and enlarged in 1544 for Fano's rulers, the Rimini-based Malatesta family. Inside is the small **Museo Civico** and the **Pinacoteca Malatestiana**, with works by Guercino, Guido Reni, and the Venetian artist Michele Giambono.

Museo Civico and Pinacoteca Malatestiana
Piazza XX Settembre. **Tel** 0721 82 83 62. **Open** Tue–Sun. **Closed** Jan 1, Dec 25 & 26.

Fontana della Fortuna in Fano

Entrance to the Palazzo Ducale in Urbania

5 Urbino

See pp374–5.

6 Urbania

Pèsaro. 7,200. Corso Vittorio Emanuele 21 (0722 31 31 40). Thu.

Urbania, with its elegant arcaded center, takes its name from Pope Urban VIII (1623–44), who entertained the notion of converting the old medieval village known as Castel Durante into a model Renaissance town.

Its chief attraction is a monument from an earlier age, the huge **Palazzo Ducale**, built by the dukes of Montefeltro as one of several residential alternatives to the Palazzo Ducale in nearby Urbino. It was begun in the 13th century, and then rebuilt in the 15th and 16th centuries. Beautifully situated alongside the Metauro River, it houses a small art gallery, a modest museum, old maps and globes, and the remnants of Duke Federico's famous library.

Palazzo Ducale
Palazzo Ducale. **Tel** 0722 31 31 51. **Open** Tue–Sun. **Closed** public hols.

Urbino: Palazzo Ducale

Italy's most beautiful Renaissance palace was built for Duke Federico da Montefeltro, ruler of Urbino (1444–82). He was a soldier, but also a man of the arts, and his palace, with its library, paintings, and refined architecture, is a tribute to courtly life and to the artistic and intellectual ideals of the Renaissance. The Palazzo Ducale houses the Galleria Nazionale delle Marche.

★ The Flagellation by Piero della Francesca
Dramatic perspective creates an unsettling effect in this 15th-century painting of the scourging of Christ.

The palace rising above Urbino

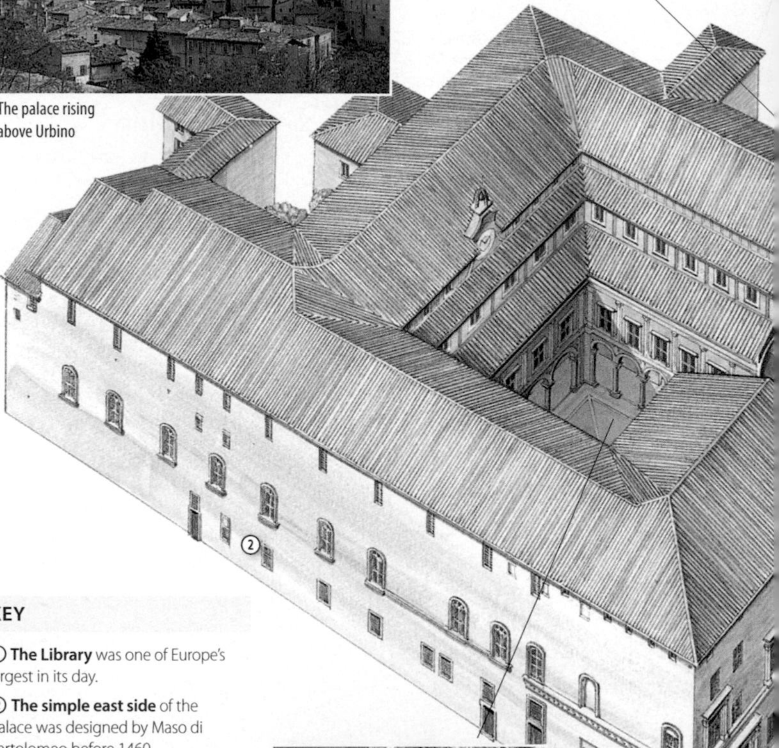

②

KEY

① **The Library** was one of Europe's largest in its day.

② **The simple east side** of the palace was designed by Maso di Bartolomeo before 1460.

③ **Towers attributed to Laurana**

④ **The Ideal City**, attributed to Luciano Laurana, is a 15th-century painting of an imaginary Renaissance city. The piece is notable for its measured perspective and lack of people.

⑤ **Hanging garden**

⑥ **The rooms** in this wing are known as the Appartamento della Duchessa.

Cortile d'Onore
This early Renaissance courtyard was designed by the Dalmatian-born artist Luciano Laurana (1420–79).

★ **Studiolo**
The former study of Federico da Montefeltro is decorated with intarsia (inlaid wood), some of it designed by Botticelli.

Duke Federico by Pedro Berruguete
The duke, shown here with his son in this 15th-century painting, was always portrayed in left profile after an injury to his face.

Main entrance

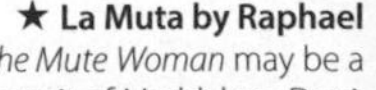

★ **La Muta by Raphael**
The Mute Woman may be a portrait of Maddalena Doni, a Florentine noblewoman.

VISITORS' CHECKLIST

Practical Information
Piazza Duca Federico 13.
Tel 1991 511 23.
turismo.marche.it
Open 8:30am–2pm Mon, 8:30am–7:15pm Tue–Sun. Last adm: 60 mins before closing.
Closed Jan 1, Dec 25.

Transportation
Piazza del Mercatale.

5 Urbino

Pèsaro. 16,000. Piazza Rinascimento (0722 26 13). Sat.
turismo.pesarourbino.it

Amid Urbino's tangle of medieval and Renaissance streets stands the Neo-Classical **Duomo**, on Piazza Federico, built in 1789. Of special interest is the painting of the *Last Supper* by Federico Barocci (*c.* 1535–1612). The **Museo Diocesano** contains a collection of ceramics, glass, and religious artifacts.

Urbino's famous son, the painter Raphael (1483–1520), lived in the **Casa Natale di Raffaello**. It has a highly evocative interior, especially the kitchen and courtyard.

In Via Barocci is the medieval **Oratorio di San Giuseppe**, known for its *presepio* (Christmas crib), and the 14th-century **Oratorio di San Giovanni Battista**, whose interior is smothered in 15th-century frescoes of the *Crucifixion* and the *Life of John the Baptist* by Giacomo and Lorenzo Salimbeni.

The 15th-century **Fortezza dell'Albornoz** on Viale Bruno Buozzi is the defensive focus of Urbino's surviving 16th-century walls and bastions.

Museo Diocesano
Piazza Pascoli 2. **Tel** 0722 48 18. **Open** 9:30am–1pm, 2:30–6:30pm daily.

Casa Natale di Raffaello
Via di Raffaello 57. **Tel** 0722 32 01 05. **Open** 9am–2pm daily (Sun am only). **Closed** Jan 1, Dec 25.

A street scene in the medieval town of Urbino

Fresh seafood and fishing boats in the harbor at Ancona

7 Grotte di Frasassi

Ancona. **Tel** 0732 97 21 66. FS Genga San Vittore Terme. **Open** daily. Guided tours only (70 mins). **Closed** Jan 1, Jan 10–30, Dec 4, Dec 25. W **frasassi.com**

Some of Europe's largest publicly accessible caverns lie in the cave network gouged out by the River Sentino southwest of Jesi. Of the vast network of 11 miles (18 km), an area of about 3,281 ft (1,000 m) is open to the public. The colossal **Grotta del Vento** is large enough to contain Milan cathedral – its ceiling extends to a height of 787 ft (240 m). This cavern has been used for a range of experiments, from sensory deprivation to an exploration of the social consequences of leaving a group of people alone in its depths for long periods.

8 Jesi

Ancona. 41,000. FS i Piazza della Repubblica 11 (0731 53 84 20). Wed & Sat. W **comune.jesi.an.it**

Perched on a long, rocky ridge, Jesi lies in the heart of the verdant hill country where Verdicchio is produced. A crisp, white wine, Verdicchio is bottled in unique containers – glass models of the terra-cotta amphorae once used to export the wine to ancient Greece. There are many vineyards in the surrounding countryside.

Housed in the town's 18th-century Palazzo Pianetti is the **Pinacoteca e Musei Civici**, which contains fine late-period paintings by Lorenzo Lotto. Almost as alluring as the gallery's paintings, however, is the great central salon – an orgy of Rococo decoration that once formed the centerpiece of the Palazzo Pianetti. The nearby **Palazzo della Signoria** features an interesting collection of archaeological finds, while beyond the old town's Renaissance walls stands the 14th-century church of **San Marco**, known for its collection of well-preserved Giottesque frescoes.

Pinacoteca e Musei Civici
Via XV Settembre. **Tel** 0731 53 83 42. **Open** Tue–Sun.

Palazzo della Signoria
Piazza Colocci. **Tel** 0731 53 83 45. **Open** Mon–Sat. **Closed** Mon am & Sat pm.

9 Ancona

98,000. FS i Via della Loggia 50 (071 35 89 91). Tue & Fri. W **turismo.marche.it**

The capital of Le Marche and its largest port (with ferries to and from Greece and Croatia), Ancona dates back to at least the 5th century BC, when it was settled by Greek exiles from Siracusa. Its name derives from *ankon* (Greek for elbow), a reference to the rocky spur that juts into the sea to form the town's fine natural harbor.

Heavy bombing during World War II destroyed much of the medieval town. The 15th-century **Loggia dei Mercanti** (merchants' exchange) on Via della Loggia survives as a monument to the town's medieval heyday.

Just north of the loggia is the Romanesque church of **Santa Maria della Piazza**, with a lovely facade. The nearby **Pinacoteca Comunale F Podesti e Galleria d'Arte Moderna** includes canvases by Titian and Lorenzo Lotto. In the **Museo Archeologico Nazionale delle Marche** there are displays of Greek, Gallic, and Roman art. The **Arco di Traiano**, by the harbor, was erected in AD 115 and is one of Italy's better preserved Roman arches.

An impressive cavern in the cave system of the Grotte di Frasassi

For hotels and restaurants in this region see pp562–77 and pp580–605

'he beach at the village of Sirolo on the Conero Peninsula

Pinacoteca Comunale F
odesti e Galleria d'Arte Moderna
'ia Pizzecolli 17. **Tel** 071 222 50 41.
)pen Tue–Sat daily (Sun pm).
:losed public hols.

Museo Archeologico
lazionale delle Marche
'ia Ferretti 1. **Tel** 071 20 26 02.
)pen 8:30am–7pm Tue–Sun. **Closed**
an 1, May 1, Aug 15, Dec 25.

10 Conero Peninsula

ncona. FS Ancona. from
ncona to Sirolo or Numana. Via
ella Loggia 50, Ancona (071 35 89 91).
parcodelconero.eu

'he beautiful, cliff-edged Conero 'eninsula is the only natural eature to disturb the almost ınbroken line of beaches along he coast of Le Marche. Easily ccessible from Ancona to the ıorth, it is a semi-wild area nown for its scenery, its wines notably Rosso del Conero), nd for a collection of coves, beaches, and little resorts.

The best of these resorts is **'ortonovo**, above whose beach stands **Santa Maria li Portonovo**, a pretty 1th-century Romanesque hurch mentioned by Dante in Canto XXI of *Paradiso*. **Sirolo** and **lumana** are busier and more ommercialized, but you can scape the crowds by hiking the ower-swathed slopes of Monte Conero, which stands at 1,877 ft 572 m), or by taking a boat trip o the smaller beaches beyond he resorts.

11 Loreto

Ancona. 11,000. FS Via Solari 3 (071 97 02 76). Fri.

Legend has it that in 1294, the house of the Virgin Mary (**Santa Casa**) miraculously uprooted itself from the Holy Land and was brought by angels to a laurel grove *(loreto)* south of Ancona. Each year several million pilgrims visit the **Santa Casa** in Loreto and its **Basilica**. Begun in 1468, the latter was designed and built in part by Renaissance architects Bramante, Sansovino, and Giuliano da Sangallo. Its paintings include works by Luca Signorelli. The **Museo-Pinacoteca** has 16th-century paintings by Lorenzo Lotto.

Santa Casa in Loreto

Basilica and Santa Casa
Piazza Santuario. **Tel** 071 97 01 04.
Open daily.

Museo-Pinacoteca
Palazzo Apostolico. **Tel** 071 974 71 98.
Open Apr–Oct: Tue–Sun; Nov–Mar: Fri–Sun.

12 Ascoli Piceno

54,000. Palazzo Comunale, Piazza Arringo (0736 25 30 45). Wed & Sat.

This alluring town takes its name from the Piceni, a tribe eventually conquered by the Romans in 89 BC. The gridiron plan of Roman Asculum Picenum is visible in the streets today, but it is the town's medieval heritage that attracts most visitors.

The enchanting **Piazza del Popolo** is dominated by the 13th-century **Palazzo dei Capitani del Popolo**, whose facade was designed by Cola dell'Amatrice, and the church of **San Francesco**, a large and faintly austere Gothic ensemble built between 1262 and 1549.

Via del Trivio leads north to a medieval district overlooking the River Tronto. Along Via Cairoli lies the 13th-century church of **San Pietro Martire**. Opposite is the church of **Santi Vincenzo e Anastasio** (11th century), with an ancient crypt built over a spring said to cure leprosy.

Around Piazza dell'Arringo is the 12th-century **Duomo**, spoiled by a Baroque overlay. Its Cappella del Sacramento contains a polyptych by the 15th-century artist Carlo Crivelli. The **Pinacoteca Civica** has more works by Crivelli and by Guido Reni, Titian, and Alemanno. The **Museo Archeologico** contains Roman, Piceni, and Lombard artifacts.

Pinacoteca Civica
Palazzo Comunale, Piazza Arringo.
Tel 0736 29 82 13. **Open** Tue–Sun.

Museo Archeologico
Palazzo Panighi, Piazza Arringo.
Tel 0736 25 35 62. **Open** Tue–Sun.
Closed Jan 1, May 1, Dec 25.

A view of the medieval town of Ascoli Piceno

GLYPHIS TA
NI CVLTV AB
IVSSV CLEMENTIS·XIII·PONT·MAX·OPVS

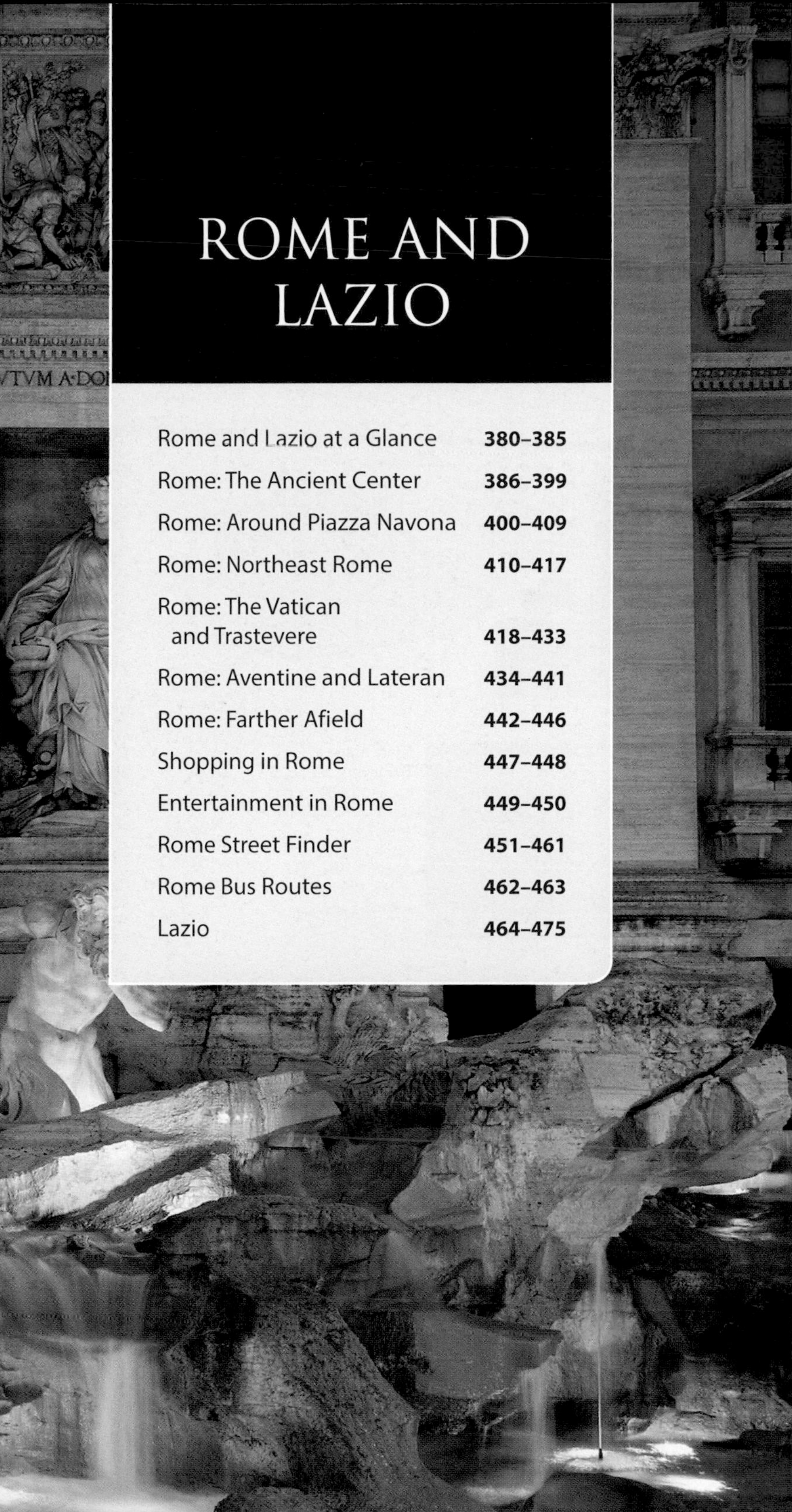

ROME AND LAZIO

Rome and Lazio at a Glance

The first settlements in the region can be traced back to the early Etruscan civilization in northern Lazio. Rome grew to rule a vast empire and, as the empire began to divide, the region became the center of the Christian world. Artists and architects flocked to work for the popes and their families, notably in the Renaissance and Baroque periods, when some magnificent architectural works were created. The legacy of this uninterrupted history can be seen all over the city and the surrounding area.

St. Peter's, with its majestic dome by Michelangelo, is a magnificent and sumptuous 16th-century basilica *(see pp422–3)*.

Piazza Navona, flanked by cafés, contains three Baroque fountains, including the colossal Fontana dei Quattro Fiumi, one of Bernini's finest works *(see p403)*.

PIA
NAV
(See p

THE VATICAN AND TRASTEVERE
(See pp418–33)

Santa Maria in Trastevere, probably the first Christian church in Rome, holds some remarkable mosaics such as this detail from Cavallini's *Life of the Virgin*, which dates from 1291 *(see p432)*.

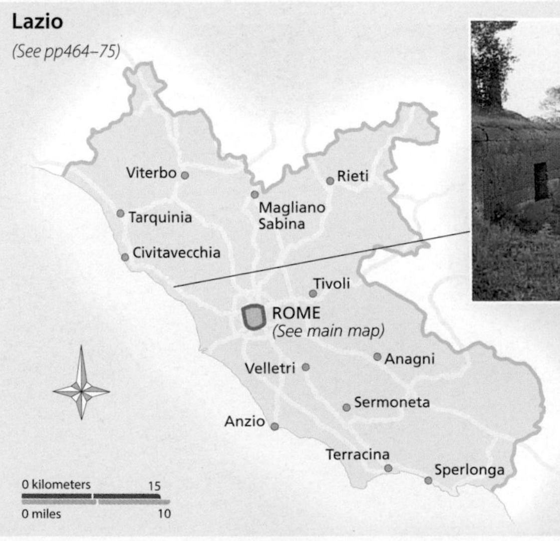

Cerveteri is one of the many necropolises left by the Etruscan civilization in northern Lazio. The larger tumulus tombs often contained frescoes and utensils useful in the afterlife *(see p470)*.

◀ The famous Trevi Fountain, designed by Nicola Salvi

The Pantheon, built between AD 118 and 125, is a marvel of Roman engineering with its huge dome hidden behind the Classical portico *(see p408)*.

Locator Map

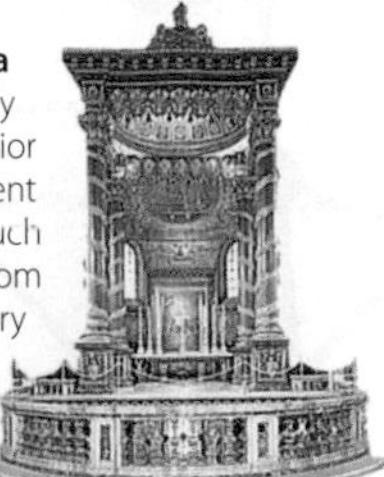

Santa Maria Maggiore's richly decorated interior blends different architectural styles, such as this baldacchino from the 18th century *(see p417)*.

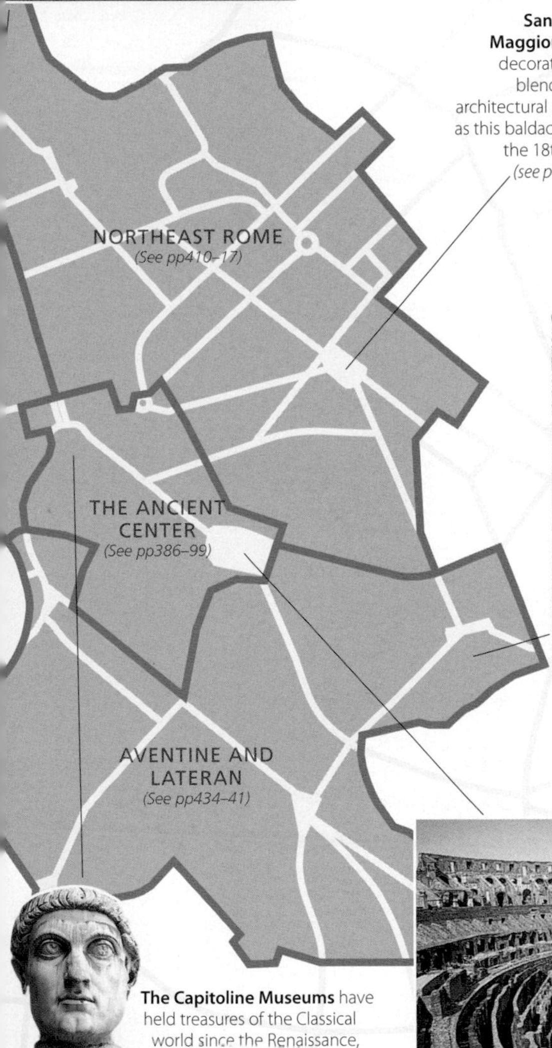

NORTHEAST ROME
(See pp410–17)

THE ANCIENT CENTER
(See pp386–99)

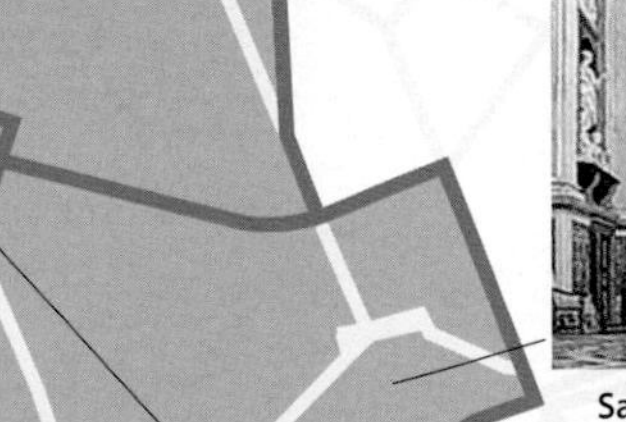

San Giovanni in Laterano, the Cathedral of Rome, incorporates the elaborate Corsini Chapel, built in the 1730s *(see p440)*.

AVENTINE AND LATERAN
(See pp434–41)

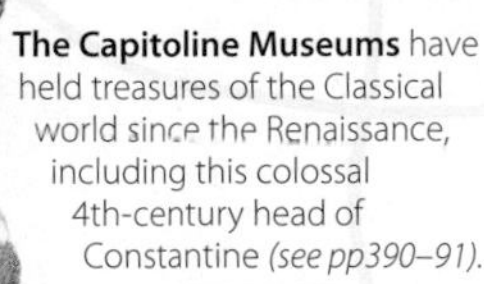

The Capitoline Museums have held treasures of the Classical world since the Renaissance, including this colossal 4th-century head of Constantine *(see pp390–91)*.

0 meters 750
0 yards 750

The Colosseum was constructed in AD 80 by Emperor Vespasian. His aim was to gain popularity by staging deadly gladiatorial combats and wild animal fights for public viewing *(see p397)*.

The Flavors of Rome and Lazio

The countryside of Lazio varies from gently rolling hills to mountains to shimmering coast. Olive groves and vineyards cloak this fertile area, where wild boar roam and many other kinds of game find their way onto the table. But authentic Roman cuisine takes its origins from organ meats, and slow, inventive cooking transforms these traditionally "poor" cuts into flavorsome dishes. Pasta is still the vital ingredient in any meal, and several well-known dishes originate from Rome. Many of the capital's top restaurants are dedicated to fish and seafood and, as home of *la dolce vita*, there is a long tradition of delicious pastries, cakes, and ice cream.

Globe artichokes

A stand of Lazio vegetables, fresh from field to market

Traditional Roman cuisine originated in the Testaccio area, near the old slaughterhouse whose butchers *(vaccinari)* were paid partly in meat, usually organ meat. The "fifth quarter" *(quinto quarto)* included head, trotters, tail, intestines, brain, and other bits of the beast not for the squeamish, but which, when cooked slowly and richly flavored with herbs and spices, became a culinary delight. These robust dishes, such as the signature dish *coda alla vaccinara* (literally, oxtail in the style of the slaughterhouse butcher) still feature on many menus.

Cucina Romana

Authentic *cucina romana* also has its roots in Jewish cuisine of the atmospheric Ghetto area, whose origins date back over 400 years. Plump, locally grown globe artichokes are fried whole in olive oil *(carciofi alla giudia)* or served *alla romana*, with oil, garlic and Roman mint. Just as popular are salt cod fillets *(filetti di baccalà)* deep fried, Jewish-style.

Seafood and fish restaurants are among the best in Rome and, while not cheap, many are temples of gastronomy. It was in response to the launch of

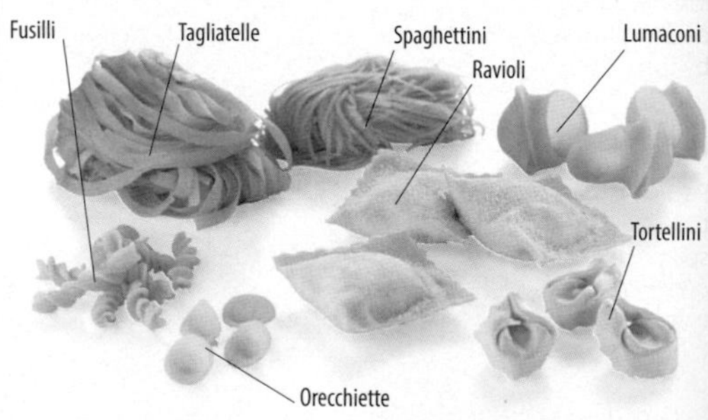

Just a few of the hundreds of types of pasta available in Italy

Regional Dishes and Specialties

Crispy fried vegetables, especially artichokes and zucchini flowers, are often served as an *antipasto*. For the *primo* course, pasta dishes include *bucatini all'amatriciana* – long, thin pasta tubes in a delicious spicy tomato and bacon sauce, sprinkled with grated Pecorino cheese made from tangy ewe's milk. Veal is a great favorite and features on many restaurant menus; look for *rigatoni alla pajata* (pasta with milk-fed veal intestines). Lamb is also very popular, with dishes such as *abbacchio al forno* (roasted milk-fed lamb) or *alla cacciatore* ("huntsman's style" with anchovy sauce). Organ meats are very common in traditional *trattorie*, and delicacies include *cervelle* (calves' brains), *ossobuco* (beef shins with marrow jelly), *pajata* (veal intestines), and *trippa* (tripe).

Bruschetta

Gnocchi alla romana Little dumplings, made with semolina flour, are usually served with a tomato or meat *ragù*.

Sumptuous Roman pizzas, sizzling hot from the wood-fired oven

the first McDonald's in Rome in 1986 that the Slow Food Movement started in Piedmont *(see p178)*, but more typical Roman fast food includes *bruschetta* ("lightly burned bread" in Roman dialect) rubbed with garlic, sea salt, and olive oil and topped with a selection of intense flavors. There's also authentic thin and crispy *pizza romana* from wood-fired ovens, often served *al taglio* – by the slice.

Pasta, Pasta

Pasta is still the mainstay of the Roman meal, especially spaghetti. *Spaghetti alla carbonara*, made with *pancetta* (cured bacon) or *guanciale* (pig's cheek), egg yolks, and cheese, is a classic Roman dish, as is *spaghetti alle vongole*, with garlic and clams. At a conservative estimate, there is one type of pasta for every day of the year. Many varieties have wonderfully descriptive or poetic names, such as *capelli d'angelo* (angel's hair) or *ziti* (bridegrooms), whose shape is best left to the imagination.

An array of mouthwatering *gelati* in a Roman ice-cream parlor

La Dolce Vita

For those with a taste for "the sweet life," nuts, fruits and versatile ricotta cheese are often combined in mouth-wateringly delicious sweets.

Ice cream is an art form in Rome, where some parlors offer over 100 flavors of homemade *gelati*. Types vary from the classic *crema* and *frutta* to *grattachecca* (water ice), from *semifreddo* (a half-frozen sponge pudding, similar to *tiramisù* in consistency) to *granità* (ice shavings flavored with fruit syrups). Glorious *gelato* is one of the great pleasures here, to be enjoyed at any time of the day – or night.

ON THE MENU

Abbacchio alla cacciatore Lamb cooked with anchovies, garlic, Castelli Romani wine, rosemary, and olive oil.

Coda alla vaccinara Oxtail braised in herbs, tomatoes, and celery.

Fave al guanciale Young spring fava beans simmered in olive oil with pig's cheek and onion.

Filetti di baccalà Salt cod fillets in batter – once a Jewish specialty, now a feature of Roman cuisine.

Spigola alla romana Sea bass with *porcini* mushrooms (ceps), Roman-style.

Spaghetti alle vongole The classic Italian pasta is here served with a sauce made of baby clams and tomatoes.

Saltimbocca alla romana Veal slices are rolled with prosciutto and sage. Saltimbocca means "jump in the mouth."

Torta di ricotta Ricotta cheese is baked in a tart with sugar, lemon, brandy, eggs, and cinnamon.

Understanding Architecture in Rome and Lazio

The architecture of Imperial Rome, a combination of Etruscan and Classical Greek styles, gradually developed new and uniquely Roman forms based on the arch, the vault, and the dome. During the early Christian period, simple, rectangular basilicas were built, forms that by the 12th century had been incorporated into the stark Romanesque style. The Renaissance, inspired by the example of Florence, saw a return to Classical ideals of simplicity and harmonious proportions, though it was in the flamboyance of the 17th-century Baroque that Rome once again found great architectural expression.

The extravagant Baroque style of the Fontana di Trevi, Rome

From Etruscan to Classical Rome

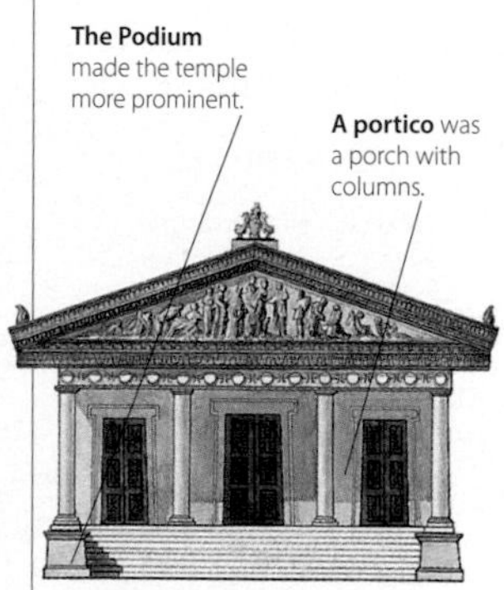
The Podium made the temple more prominent.
A portico was a porch with columns.

Etruscan temples, based on Greek models, inspired early Roman architecture. A front portico was the only entrance.

The arch became a feature of Roman architecture.
Reliefs were scavenged from earlier monuments.

The Arch of Constantine (AD 315) is typical of triumphant Imperial Roman architecture *(see p393)*. It stands at a colossal 82 ft (25 m).

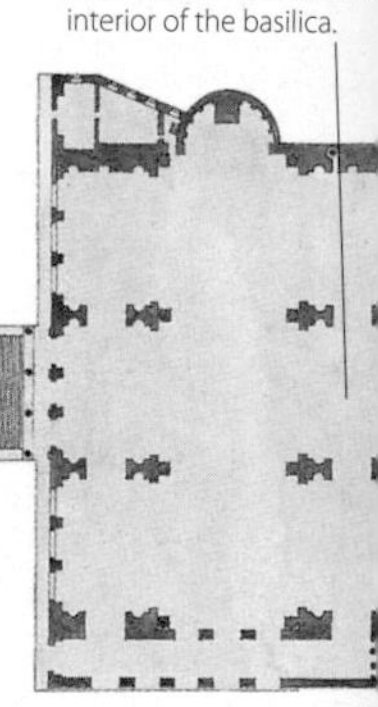
Three naves divided the interior of the basilica.

Early Christian basilicas (4th century) were based on a rectangular floor plan.

From Renaissance to Baroque

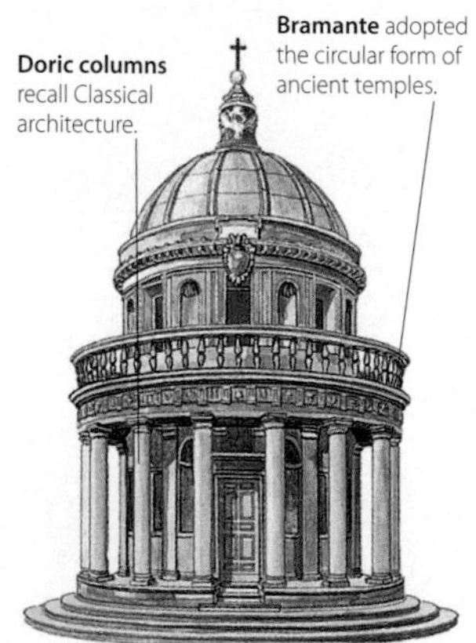
Doric columns recall Classical architecture.
Bramante adopted the circular form of ancient temples.

The Tempietto at San Pietro in Montorio, Rome (1502) is a model of Renaissance architecture: simple and perfectly proportioned *(see p433)*.

Rustication, massive blocks divided by deep joints, was used for palazzi.

Ionic pilasters lend an air of elegance to the imposing upper stories.

The elliptical staircase was a typical feature of Mannerist houses.

Palazzo Farnese at Caprarola, a pentagonal building completed in 1575 *(see p469)*, combines some Mannerist tricks of architecture with the strict geometric proportions characteristic of the Renaissance.

Where to see the Architecture

A walk through the back streets of the center of Rome will reveal masterpieces of virtually every architectural age. The most ancient treasures are seven obelisks stolen from Egypt. One stands on the back of Bernini's elephant *(see p408)*. Highlights from ancient Rome include triumphal arches and temples such as the Pantheon *(see p408)*. Romanesque elements survive in the church of San Clemente *(see p439)*, while the Renaissance finds expression in the dome of St. Peter's *(see pp422–3)*. Magnificent Baroque treasures dot the entire city, in particular flamboyant fountains that adorn the squares. Outside the city, the outstanding sights are the late Renaissance villas such as Caprarola *(see p469)*.

Part of Bernini's elephant supporting an ancient Egyptian obelisk

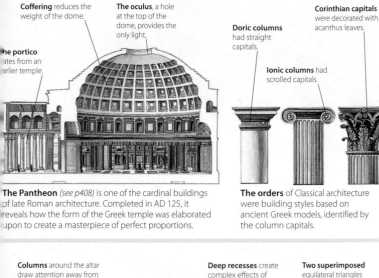

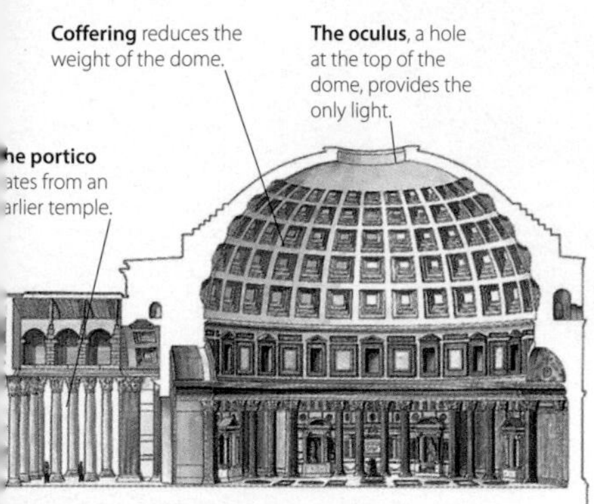

Coffering reduces the weight of the dome.
The oculus, a hole at the top of the dome, provides the only light.
he portico ates from an arlier temple.

The Pantheon *(see p408)* is one of the cardinal buildings of late Roman architecture. Completed in AD 125, it reveals how the form of the Greek temple was elaborated upon to create a masterpiece of perfect proportions.

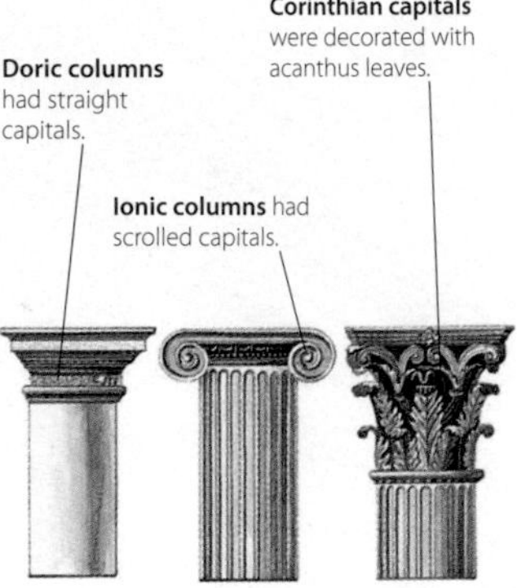

Doric columns had straight capitals.
Corinthian capitals were decorated with acanthus leaves.
Ionic columns had scrolled capitals.

The orders of Classical architecture were building styles based on ancient Greek models, identified by the column capitals.

Columns around the altar draw attention away from the prominent lateral axis.
concave ortico reflects ie oval body f the church.

he oval floor plan of the aroque Sant'Andrea al Quirinale *ee p415)* makes ingenious use f restricted space.

Engaged pillars replace the flat pilasters of the Renaissance.
Deep recesses create complex effects of light and shade.

The Gesù facade (1584) epitomizes Counter-Reformation architecture and has been imitated throughout the Catholic world *(see p407)*.

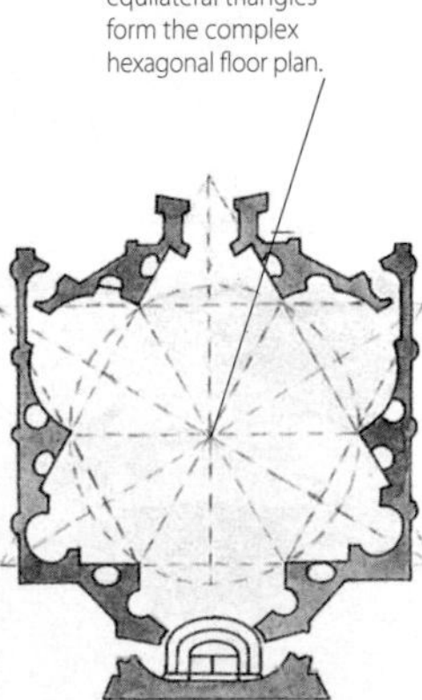

Two superimposed equilateral triangles form the complex hexagonal floor plan.

Sant'Ivo alla Sapienza's floor plan (1642) favored grandiose design over Classical form *(see p404)*.

THE ANCIENT CENTER

The Capitol, the southern summit of the Capitoline Hill, was the symbolic center of the Roman world and home to the city's three most important temples. These were dedicated to the god Jupiter Optimus Maximus, protector of Rome; Minerva, goddess of wisdom and war; and Juno Moneta, a guardian goddess. Below the Capitol lies the Forum, once the focus of political, social, legal, and commercial life; the Imperial Fora, built when Rome's population grew; and the Colosseum, the center of entertainment. Overlooking the Forum is the Palatine Hill, where Romulus is said to have founded Rome in the 8th century BC and emperors made their home for over 400 years.

Sights at a Glance

Churches

3 Santa Maria in Aracoeli

Museums and Galleries

1 *Capitoline Museums pp390–91*

Historic Piazzas

2 Piazza del Campidoglio

Ancient Sites and Buildings

4 Trajan's Forum and Markets
5 Forum of Augustus
6 Mamertine Prison
7 Forum of Caesar
8 *Roman Forum pp394–5*
9 *Colosseum p397*
10 Arch of Constantine
11 *Palatine pp398–9*

VIA IV NOVEMBRE
V.D. PLEBISCITO
PIAZZA VENEZIA
VIA S. EUFEMIA
VIA NAZIONALE
V. MAZZARINO
VIA DEI SERPENTI
VIA PANISPERNA
V. S. AGATA DEI GOTI
PIAZZA S. MARCO
V. S. MARCO
VIA ALESSANDRINA
VIA TOR DE CONTI
VIA BACCINA
VIA MADONNA D. MONTI
VIA CAVOUR
VIA DI SAN PIETRO IN CARCERE
VIA DEI FORI IMPERIALI
VIA D. TEATRO DI MARCELLO
LARGO CORRADO RICCI
VIA FRANGIPANE
VIA CARDELLO
VIA DEGLI ANNIBALDI
VIA CURIA
VIA DEL COLOSSEO
VIA DI VILLA CAFFARELLI
V.DEL TEMPIO DI GIOVE
FORO ROMANO
VIA SACRA
V. D. CONSOLAZIONE
V. DEL FORO ROMANO
Colosseo
VIA N. SALVI
PIAZZA DEL COLOSSEO
V. DEI FIENILI
CAMPITELLI
VIA DI S. TEODORO
V. CELIO VIBENNA
PALATINE
VIA DI S. GREGORIO
VIA DEI CERCHI
PIAZZA DI PORTA CAPENA
0 meters 250
0 yards 250

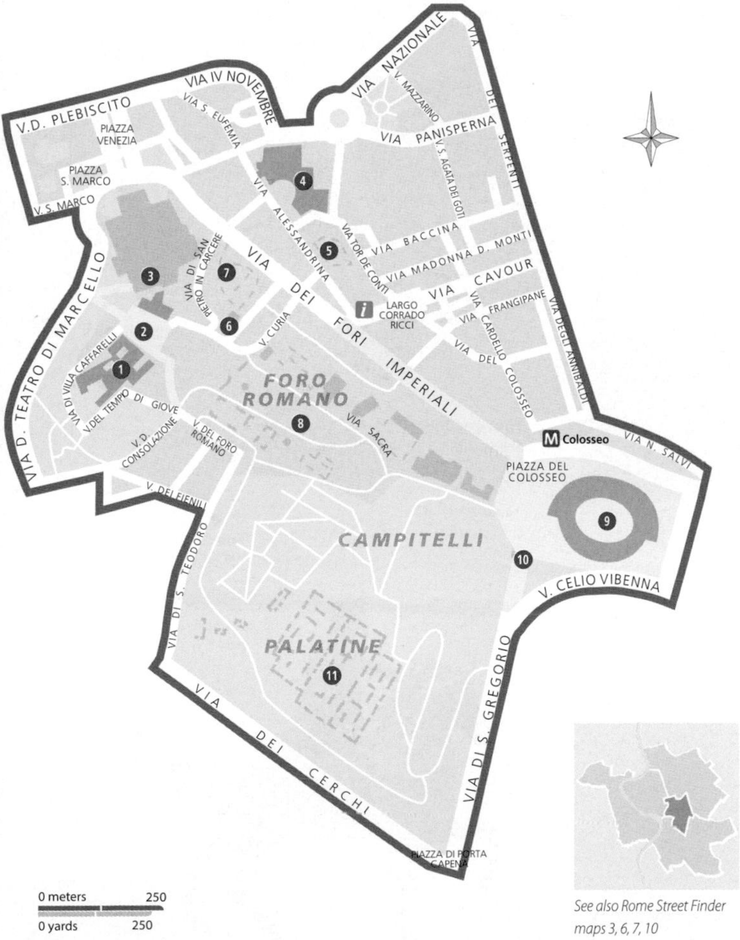

See also Rome Street Finder maps 3, 6, 7, 10

◀ View of the Colosseum's Ionic and Corinthian tiers

Street by Street: The Capitoline Hill

The Capitol, citadel of ancient Rome, was redesigned by Michelangelo in the 16th century. He was responsible for the trapezoid Piazza del Campidoglio as well as the Cordonata, the broad flight of steps leading up to it. The piazza is flanked by Palazzo Nuovo and Palazzo dei Conservatori, housing the Capitoline Museums, with their fine collections of sculpture and paintings. It is also well worth walking behind the museums to the Tarpeian Rock, for a fine view of the Forum lying below.

The Victor Emmanuel Monument was begun in 1885 and inaugurated in 1911 in honor of Victor Emmanuel II, the first king of unified Italy.

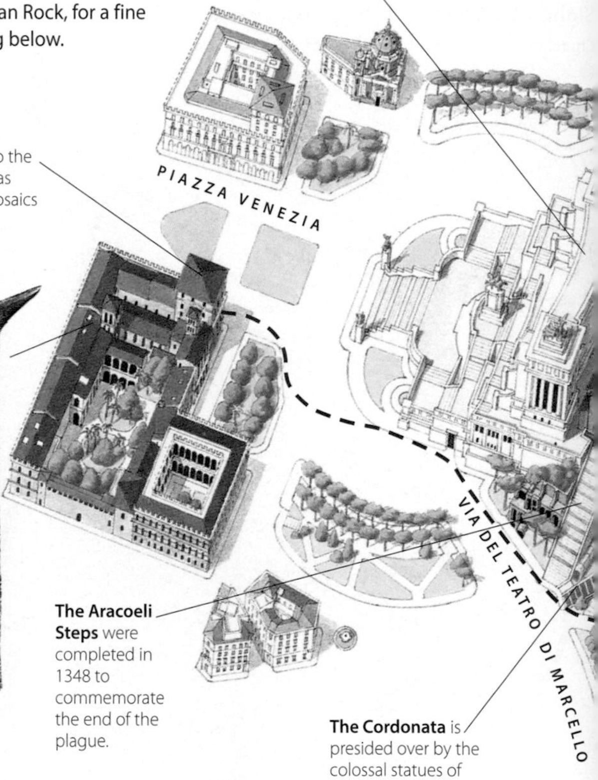

San Marco, dedicated to the patron saint of Venice, has splendid 9th-century mosaics in the apse.

Palazzo Venezia, once the home of Mussolini, now holds a museum of fine and decorative arts. Exhibits include this medieval gilt and enamel angel.

The Aracoeli Steps were completed in 1348 to commemorate the end of the plague.

The Cordonata is presided over by the colossal statues of Castor and Pollux.

❶ ★ Capitoline Museums
The collections of art and ancient sculpture include this statue of the Emperor Marcus Aurelius, a replica of which stands in the center of the piazza.

Key

— Suggested route

0 meters 75
0 yards 75

3 Santa Maria in Aracoeli
The brick facade hides treasures such as this 15th-century fresco of *The Funeral of San Bernardino* by Pinturicchio.

Locator Map
See Rome Street Finder map 3

Palazzo Nuovo was made into a public museum in 1734.

Palazzo Senatorio, the splendid Renaissance seat of the city government, is built on the ruins of the ancient Tabularium.

2 Piazza del Campidoglio
Michelangelo designed the geometric paving and the facades of the buildings.

Palazzo dei Conservatori

The Temple of Jupiter, represented on this coin, was dedicated to Jupiter Optimus Maximus, the most important of the Roman gods. He was believed to have the power to protect or destroy the city.

The Tarpeian Rock is a cliff from which traitors were believed to have been thrown to their death in ancient Rome.

Steps to the Capitoline

1 Capitoline Museums

See pp390–91.

2 Piazza del Campidoglio

Map 3 A5. 🚌 40, 63, 70, 81.

When Emperor Charles V announced he was to visit Rome in 1536, Pope Paul III Farnese asked Michelangelo to give the Capitoline a facelift. He redesigned the piazza, renovated the facades of its palaces, and built a new flight of steps, the Cordonata. This gently rising ramp is now crowned with the massive statues of Castor and Pollux.

3 Santa Maria in Aracoeli

Piazza d'Aracoeli. **Map** 3 A5. **Tel** 06 69 76 38 39. 🚌 63, 70, 81. **Open** 9am–6:30pm daily (9:30am–5:30pm in winter).

This church stands on the site of the temple of Juno on the northern summit of the Capitoline Hill, and dates back at least to the 6th century. The church is famous for its ornate gilded ceiling and a very fine series of frescoes by Pinturicchio, dating from the 1480s. They depict scenes from the life of San Bernardino of Siena. The miracle-working *Santo Bambino* figure, stolen in 1994, has been replaced by a replica.

The marble steps and austere facade of Santa Maria in Aracoeli

❶ Capitoline Museums: Palazzo Nuovo

A collection of Classical sculptures has been kept on the Capitoline Hill since Pope Sixtus IV donated a group of bronze statues to the city in 1471. Paintings as well as sculpture are now housed in two palaces designed by Michelangelo. The Palazzo Nuovo contains a fine selection of Greek and Roman sculptures. Access is via the Palazzo dei Conservatori *(opposite)*.

Locator Map
See Rome Street Finder map 10

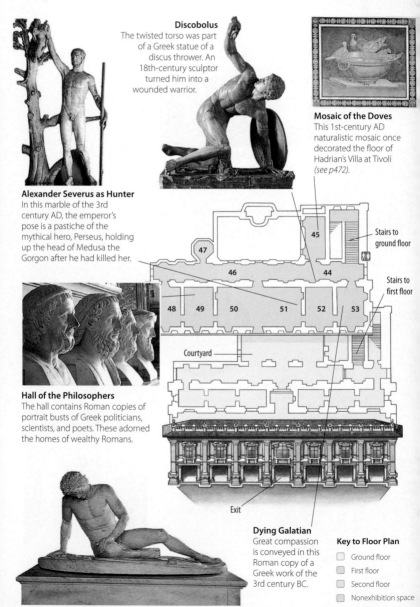

Discobolus
The twisted torso was part of a Greek statue of a discus thrower. An 18th-century sculptor turned him into a wounded warrior.

Mosaic of the Doves
This 1st-century AD naturalistic mosaic once decorated the floor of Hadrian's Villa at Tivoli *(see p472)*.

Alexander Severus as Hunter
In this marble of the 3rd century AD, the emperor's pose is a pastiche of the mythical hero, Perseus, holding up the head of Medusa the Gorgon after he had killed her.

45
Stairs to ground floor
47
46
44
Stairs to first floor
48
49
50
51
52
53
Courtyard
Exit

Hall of the Philosophers
The hall contains Roman copies of portrait busts of Greek politicians, scientists, and poets. These adorned the homes of wealthy Romans.

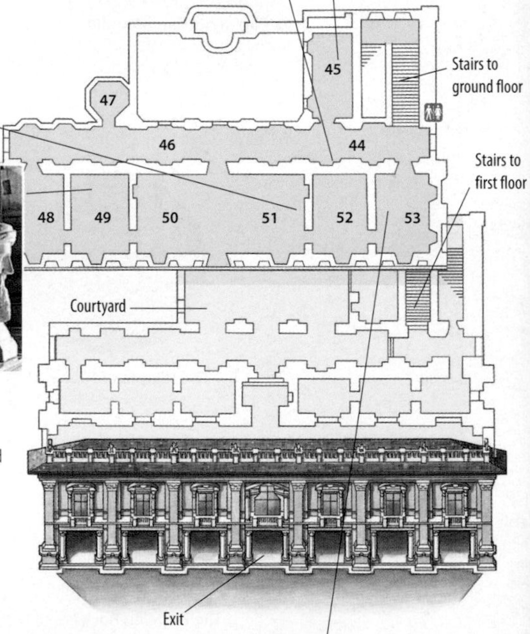

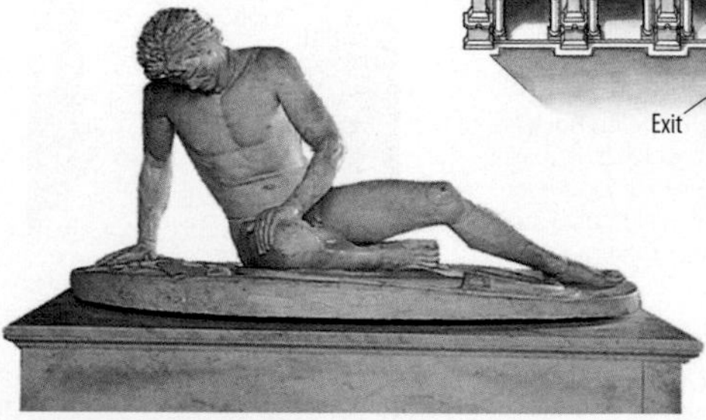

Dying Galatian
Great compassion is conveyed in this Roman copy of a Greek work of the 3rd century BC.

Key to Floor Plan
- Ground floor
- First floor
- Second floor
- Nonexhibition space

Palazzo dei Conservatori

The Palazzo dei Conservatori was the seat of the city's magistrates during the late Middle Ages. Its frescoed halls are still used occasionally for political meetings and the ground floor houses the municipal registry office. While much of the palazzo is given over to sculpture, including fragments of a huge sculpture of Constantine, the art galleries on the second floor hold works by Veronese, Tintoretto, Caravaggio, Van Dyck, and Titian.

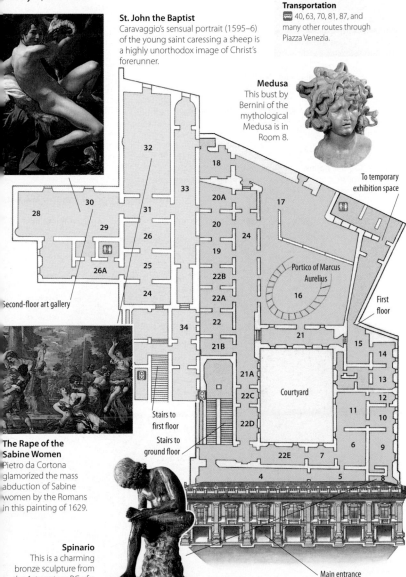

VISITORS' CHECKLIST

Practical Information
Musei Capitolini, Piazza del Campidoglio.
Map 3 A5. **Tel** 06 06 08.
museicapitolini.org
Open 9am–8pm Tue–Sun.
Closed Jan 1, May 1, Dec 25.
Entrance ticket is valid for both museums.

Transportation
40, 63, 70, 81, 87, and many other routes through Piazza Venezia.

St. John the Baptist
Caravaggio's sensual portrait (1595–6) of the young saint caressing a sheep is a highly unorthodox image of Christ's forerunner.

Medusa
This bust by Bernini of the mythological Medusa is in Room 8.

The Rape of the Sabine Women
Pietro da Cortona glamorized the mass abduction of Sabine women by the Romans in this painting of 1629.

Spinario
This is a charming bronze sculpture from the 1st century BC of a boy trying to remove a thorn from his foot.

Second-floor art gallery

Stairs to first floor

Stairs to ground floor

Portico of Marcus Aurelius

Courtyard

To temporary exhibition space

First floor

Main entrance

❹ Trajan's Forum and Markets

Map 3 B4. Trajan's Forum, Via dei Fori Imperiali. **Closed** to the public. Trajan's Markets, Via IV Novembre. **Tel** 06 06 08. **Open** 9am–7pm Tue–Sun (last adm: 6pm).

Trajan began to build his forum in AD 107 to commemorate his final conquest of Dacia (present day Romania) after successful campaigns in AD 101–2 and 105–6. His new forum was the most ambitious yet, with a vast colonnaded open space centering on an equestrian statue of the emperor, a huge basilica, and two big libraries. Dominating the ruins today is **Trajan's Column**, which originally stood between the two libraries.

Trajan's Column

Spiraling up its 98 ft (30 m) high stem are minutely detailed scenes from the Dacian campaigns, beginning with the Romans preparing for war and ending with the Dacians being ousted from their homeland. The subtly modeled reliefs were designed to be seen from viewing platforms on the libraries, and are consequently difficult to interpret from ground level. If you want to examine the scenes in detail there are casts in the Museo della Civiltà Romana *(see p446)*.

The **market** complex, which is situated directly behind the forum, was begun slightly earlier. Like the forum it was probably designed by Apollodorus of Damascus, and was the ancient Roman equivalent of the modern shopping center. There were around 150 shops selling everything from oriental silks and spices to fruit, fresh fish, and flowers. It was also here that the *annone*, or corn dole, was distributed. This was a free ration of corn given to Roman men, a practice that was introduced in the Republic by politicians who wanted to buy votes and prevent unrest during periods of famine.

Via Biberatica, the main street through Trajan's Markets

Reconstruction of Trajan's Markets

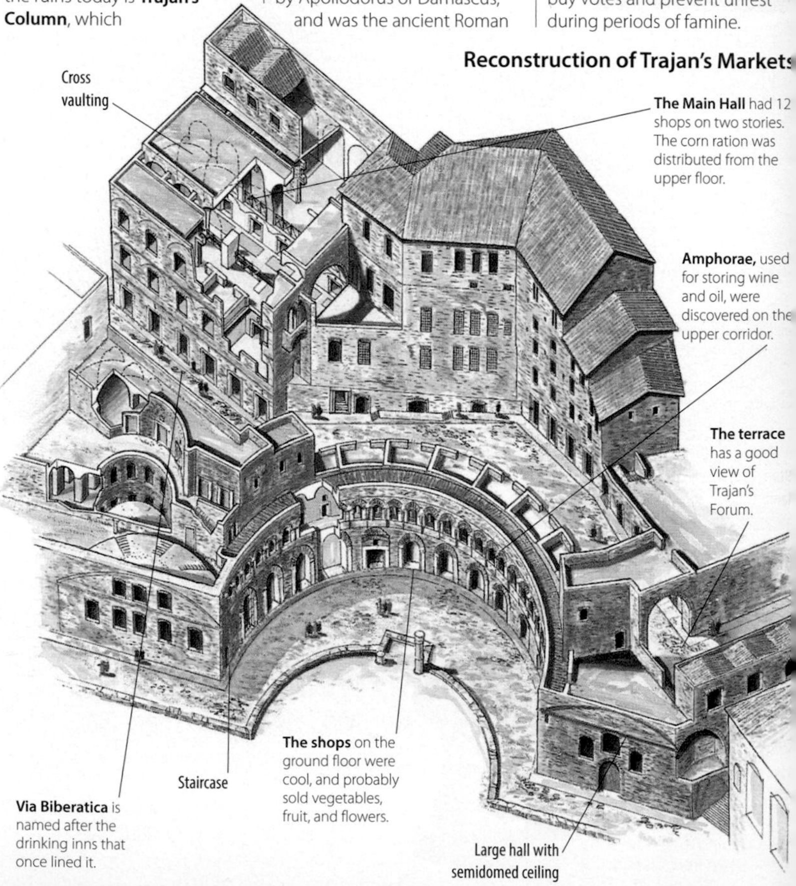

Cross vaulting

The Main Hall had 12 shops on two stories. The corn ration was distributed from the upper floor.

Amphorae, used for storing wine and oil, were discovered on the upper corridor.

The terrace has a good view of Trajan's Forum.

Large hall with semidomed ceiling

The shops on the ground floor were cool, and probably sold vegetables, fruit, and flowers.

Staircase

Via Biberatica is named after the drinking inns that once lined it.

Forum of ugustus

iazza del Grillo 1. **Map** 3 B5. **Tel** 06 06 8. 87, 186. **Open** to research cholars by appt.

he Forum of Augustus, which nce stretched from the foot f sleazy Suburra to the edge f Caesar's Forum, was built to elebrate Augustus's victory in 1 BC over Brutus and Cassius, he assassins of Julius Caesar. onsequentially, the temple in s center was dedicated to Mars the Avenger. The temple, vith its cracked steps and four orinthian columns, is easily dentified. Originally it had a tatue of Mars that looked very ke Augustus, but in case anyone ailed to notice the resemblance, colossal statue of the emperor imself was placed against the vall of the Suburra quarter.

9th-century engraving of the lamertine Prison

Mamertine rison

livo Argentario 1. **Map** 3 A5. el 06 69 89 61. 80, 85, 87, 175, 86. **Open** 9am–7pm daily (to 5pm in vinter). every 20 mins.

elow the 16th-century church f San Giuseppe dei Falegnami s a dank dungeon in which, ccording to Christian legend, t. Peter and St. Paul were imprioned. They are said to have aused a spring to bubble up into the cell, and to have used the water to baptize two prison guards. The prison was in an old cistern with access to the city's main sewer (the Cloaca Maxima). The lower cell was used for executions, and corpses were thrown into the sewer. However, the inmates, who received no food, often died of starvation.

Podium of the Temple of Mars the Avenger, Forum of Augustus

7 Forum of Caesar

Via del Carcere Tulliano. **Map** 3 A5. **Tel** 06 06 08. 80, 85, 87, 175, 186, 810. **Open** to research scholars by appt only.

The first of Rome's Imperial fora was built by Julius Caesar to relieve congestion in the Roman Forum when Rome's population boomed. He spent a fortune – most of it booty from his recent conquest of Gaul – buying up and demolishing houses on the site. Pride of place went to a temple dedicated in 46 BC to Venus Genetrix (Venus the Ancestor), as Caesar claimed to be descended from the goddess. The temple contained statues of Caesar and Cleopatra as well as of Venus, but all that remains today is a platform and three Corinthian columns. The forum was once enclosed by a double colonnade, under which was sheltered a row of shops. However, this burned down in AD 80 and was rebuilt by Domitian and Trajan. The latter also added the Basilica Argentaria – which became an important financial exchange – as well as shops and a heated public lavatory.

8 Roman Forum

See pp394–5.

9 Colosseum

See p397.

10 Arch of Constantine

Between Via di San Gregorio and Piazza del Colosseo. **Map** 6 F1. 75, 85, 87, 175, 673, 810. 3. M Colosseo.

This triumphal arch is one of Imperial Rome's last monuments, built in AD 315, a few years before Constantine moved the capital of the Empire to Byzantium. It was built to celebrate Constantine's victory in AD 312 over his co-emperor Maxentius at the Battle of the Milvian Bridge. Constantine attributed the victory to a dream in which he was told to mark his men's shields with *chi-rho*, the first two Greek letters of Christ's name. Christian tradition prefers a version in which the emperor has a vision of the Cross, mid-battle. There is nothing Christian about the arch: most of the reliefs were from earlier pagan monuments.

11 Palatine

See pp398–9.

The north side of the Arch of Constantine

❽ Roman Forum

In the early Republic, the Forum was a chaotic place, containing food stands and brothels as well as temples and the Senate House. By the 2nd century BC it was decided that Rome required a more salubrious center, and the food stores were replaced by business centers and law courts. The Forum remained the ceremonial center of the city under the Empire, with emperors renovating old buildings and erecting new temples and monuments.

Arch of Septimius Severus
This triumphal arch was erected in AD 203, the 10th anniversary of Emperor Septimius Severus' accession.

The Temple Antoninus a Faustina is n incorporat into the church San Loren in Miran

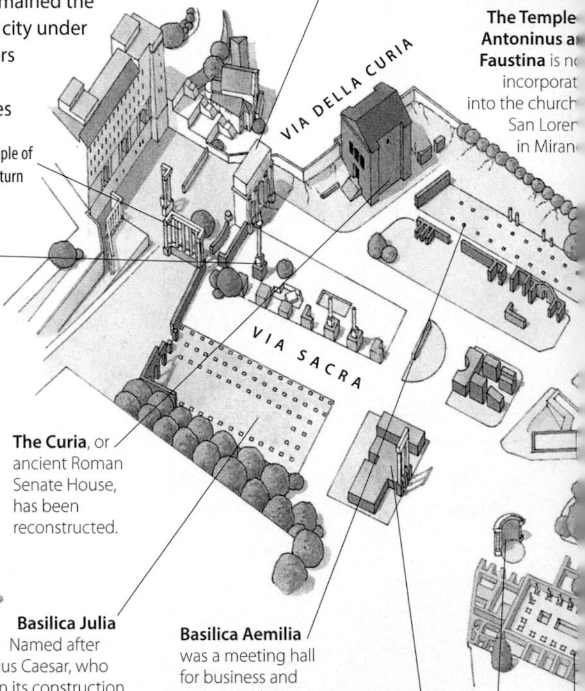

VIA DELLA CURIA

Temple of Saturn

The Rostra was the orator's tribune from which speeches were made.

VIA SACRA

The Curia, or ancient Roman Senate House, has been reconstructed.

Basilica Julia
Named after Julius Caesar, who began its construction in 54 BC, this was the seat of the civil magistrates court.

Basilica Aemilia was a meeting hall for business and money exchange.

Temple of Vesta

Temple of Castor and Pollux
Although there has been a temple here since the 5th century BC, the columns and elaborate cornice date from AD 6, when the temple was rebuilt.

★ House of the Vestal Virgins
The priestesses who tended the sacred flame in the Temple of Vesta lived here. The house was a large rectangular building around a central garden.

0 meters 500
0 yards 500

★ Basilica of Constantine and Maxentius
The basilica's three vast barrel vaults are all that remain of the Forum's largest building. Like other basilicas, it was used for the administration of justice and conducting business.

VISITORS' CHECKLIST

Practical Information
Entrance: Via della Salara Vecchia 5/6.
Map 3 B5. **Tel** 06 39 96 77 00.
Open 8:30am–one hour before sunset. **Closed** Jan 1, Dec 25.
Includes entry to the Colosseum and the Palatine.

Transportation
85, 87, 117, 175, 186, 810.
M Colosseo. 3.

The Temple of Romulus, now part of the church of Santi Cosma e Damiano, which stands behind it, retains its original 4th-century bronze doors.

Arch of Titus
This arch was erected by Emperor Domitian in AD 81 to commemorate the sack of Jerusalem by his father Vespasian and brother Titus, 13 years earlier.

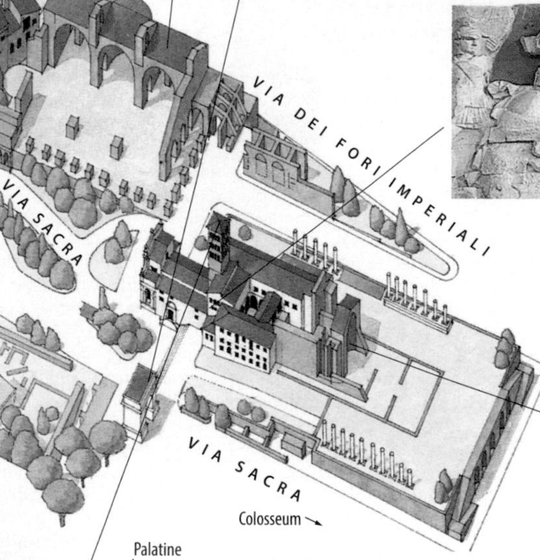

Antiquarium Forense
This small museum contains finds from the Forum. Exhibits range from Iron Age burial urns to this frieze of Aeneas from the Basilica Aemilia.

The Temple of Venus and Rome was built in AD 135, and was largely designed by Hadrian.

Santa Francesca Romana
The Romanesque bell tower of Santa Francesca Romana towers over one of a number of churches built among the ruins of the Forum.

The Vestal Virgins

The cult of Vesta, the goddess of fire, dates back to at least the 8th century BC. Romulus and Remus were allegedly born of the Vestal priestess Rhea and the god Mars. Six virgins kept the sacred flame of Vesta burning in her circular temple. The girls, who came from noble families, were selected when they were between 6 and 10 years old, and served for 30 years. They had high status and financial security, but were buried alive if they lost their virginity and whipped by the high priest if the sacred flame died out. Although they were permitted to marry after finishing their service, few did so.

Honorary statue of a Vestal Virgin

Exploring the Roman Forum

To appreciate the layout of the Roman Forum before wandering through its confusing patchwork of ruined temples, triumphal arches, and basilicas, it is best to view the whole area from the Capitoline Hill above. From there you can make out the more substantial ruins, and the course of the Via Sacra (Sacred Way), the route followed through the Forum by religious and triumphal processions making their way up to the Capitol to give thanks at the Temple of Jupiter *(see p389)*.

Corinthian columns of the Temple of Castor and Pollux

The Main Sights

The first building you come to on entering the Forum is the **Basilica Aemilia**. A rectangular hall built in 179 BC, it was a meeting place for moneylenders, businessmen, and tax collectors. Although little more remains of it than a pastel marble sidewalk fringed with column stumps, you can still find splashes of verdigrised bronze, reputedly the remains of coins that melted when the Visigoths invaded Rome and burned down the basilica in the 5th century.

Inside the Curia – the stark brick building next to the basilica – are the **Plutei of Trajan**, relief panels commissioned by either Trajan or Hadrian to decorate the Rostra, the public oratory platform. On one panel are piles of books holding tax records, which Trajan had destroyed in order to free citizens from debts. The **Arch of Septimius Severus** is the best preserved of the Forum's monuments. The marble relief panels depict the military triumphs of the emperor in Parthia (modern-day Iran and Iraq) and Arabia. The **Temple of Saturn** was the focus of the annual Saturnalia celebrations, when, for up to a week in December, schools closed, slaves dined with their masters, presents were exchanged, and a fair and market were held.

Soaring above the remains of the Basilica Julia are three delicately fluted columns and a finely carved slab of entablature taken from the **Temple of Castor and Pollux**. This striking relic is dedicated to the twin brothers of Helen of Troy, who were supposed to have appeared at the battle of Lake Regillus in 499 BC, aiding the Romans in their defeat of the Etruscans.

Restored section of Temple of Vesta

The elegant circular **Temple of Vesta** was one of ancient Rome's most sacred shrines and was dedicated to the goddess of the hearth. The flame, kept alive by the Vestal Virgins, symbolized the perpetuity of the state and its extinction prophesied doom for the city. The building was partly reconstructed in 1930, but the circular form goes back to the Latin mud huts that originally occupied the site.

Just behind is the **House of the Vestal Virgins**, the living quarters of the priestess and the Vestals. This enormous complex of 50 rooms was once annexed to the Temple. Best preserved are the rooms overlooking a pretty courtyard, ornamented with statues of Vestals, ponds of waterlilies, and rose trees.

On the other side of the Forum lie the impressive remains of the **Basilica of Constantine**. It was begun in AD 308 by Maxentius, and is therefore also known as the Basilica of Maxentius. Constantine completed it after he defeated his rival at the battle of Milvio in AD 312. The stark remains of the huge arches and ceilings give an indication of the original scale and grandeur of the forum's public buildings. Three enormous coffered vaults remain; these originally measured up to 115 ft (35 m) and were faced with marble. The interior walls, which held niches for statues, were also covered with marble below and stucco above. Remains of a spiral staircase that once led to the roof can be found scattered on the ground.

The basilica's apse and hexagonal arches were often used as models by Renaissance architects striving to recreate a Classical symmetry and nobility in their work. They include Michelangelo, who allegedly studied the basilica's architecture when working on the dome of St. Peter's.

Central courtyard of the House of the Vestal Virgins

9 Colosseum

Rome's greatest amphitheater was commissioned by Emperor Vespasian in AD 72. Deadly gladiatorial combats and wild animal fights were staged by emperors and wealthy citizens, largely to gain popularity. Slaughter was on a huge scale: at the inaugural games in AD 80, over 9,000 wild animals were killed. The Colosseum could hold up to 55,000 people, who were seated according to rank.

VISITORS' CHECKLIST

Practical Information
Piazza del Colosseo.
Map 7 A1.
Tel 06 39 96 77 00. .
Open 8:30am–one hour before sunset.
Closed Jan 1, Dec 25. includes entry to the Forum and Palatine. limited.

Transportation
75, 80, 85, 87, 117, 175, 810.
M Colosseo. 3 to Piazza del Colosseo.

Internal Corridors
These allowed the large and often unruly crowd to move freely and be seated quickly.

The Velarium, a huge sailcloth awning that sheltered spectators from the sun, was supported by poles on the upper story.

The Colossus of Nero
This gilt bronze statue from Nero's palace, over which the Colosseum was built, may have given the amphitheater its name.

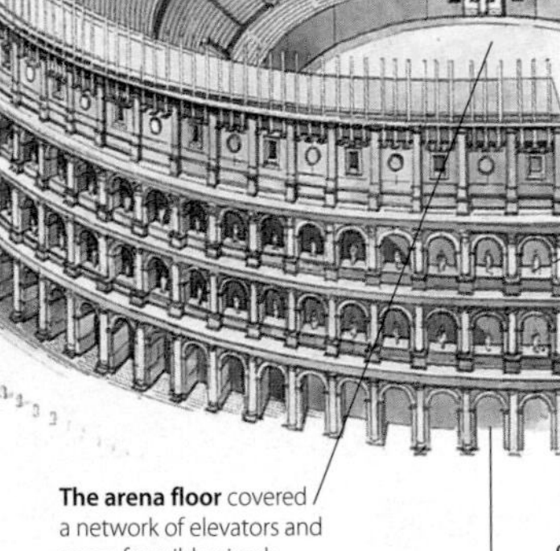

Entry routes and stairs led to seats at the various levels. The emperor and consul had their own, separate entrances.

Corinthian columns

Ionic columns

Doric columns

Entrances

The arena floor covered a network of elevators and cages for wild animals.

Doric, Ionic, and Corinthian Tiers
The tiers inspired many Renaissance architects, who also plundered the building, using its travertine to build palaces and part of St. Peter's.

Roman Gladiators
These were originally soldiers in training. Their combat became a sport, and slaves, prisoners of war, or criminals were forced to fight men or wild animals to the death.

Emperor Vespasian
He ordered the Colosseum to be built on the site of Nero's palace, to dissociate himself from the hated tyrant.

⓫ Palatine

The Palatine, once the residence of emperors and aristocrats, is the most pleasant of Rome's ancient sites. The ruins range from the simple house in which Augustus is thought to have lived, to the Domus Flavia and Domus Augustana, the public and private wings of a luxurious palace built by Domitian.

Cryptoporticus

★ House of Augustus
This building boasts four rooms with magnificent frescoes.

★ House of Livia
Many of the wall paintings have survived in the private quarters of the house where Augustus is believed to have lived with his wife Livia.

KEY

① **Domus Augustana** was the private home of the emperors.

② **The Huts of Romulus**, indicated by holes left by the supporting posts, were reputedly founded by Romulus in the 9th century BC.

③ **Temple of Cybele, goddess of fertility**

④ **The courtyard** of the Domus Flavia was lined by Domitian with mirrorlike marble, so he could spot would-be assassins.

⑤ **The exedra** of the stadium may have housed a balcony.

★ Domus Flavia
The courtyard of the Domus Flavia was lavishly paved with colored marble. The Roman poets praised this villa as the most splendid.

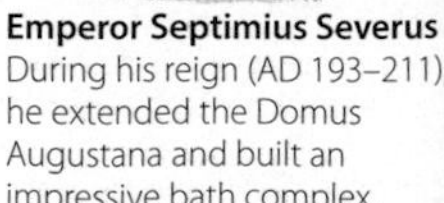

Emperor Septimius Severus
During his reign (AD 193–211), he extended the Domus Augustana and built an impressive bath complex.

Cryptoporticus
This underground gallery, elaborately decorated with stuccoed walls, was built by Emperor Nero.

VISITORS' CHECKLIST

Practical Information
Via di San Gregorio 30.
Map 6 F1.
Tel 06 39 96 77 00.
Open 8:30am– one hour before sunset.
Closed Jan 1, Dec 25.
includes entry to the Forum, the Colosseum, and the Palatine Museum.

Transportation
75, 80, 81, 175, 673, 850.
M Colosseo. 3.

Forum entrance

The Palace of Septimius Severus
This extension of the Domus Augustana projected beyond the hillside, supported on giant arches.

0 meters 75
0 yards 75

Stadium
Part of the Imperial palace, this enclosure may have been used by the emperors as a private garden.

A History of the Palatine Hill

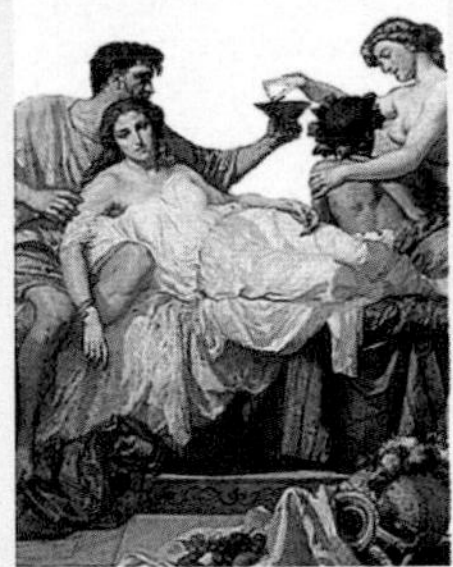

Romans of the Decadence by Thomas Couture (1815–79)

The Founding of Rome
According to legend, the twins Romulus and Remus were brought up on the Palatine by a wolf. Here Romulus, having killed his brother, is said to have founded the village that was destined to become Rome. Traces of mud huts dating back to the 8th century BC have been found on the hill, lending archaeological support to the legend.

The Republic
By the 1st century BC the Palatine was the most desirable address in Rome and home to the leading citizens of the Republic. Its residents, including the erotic poet Catullus and the orator Cicero, were notoriously indulgent, and their villas were magnificent dwellings with doors of ivory, floors of bronze, and frescoed walls.

The Empire
Augustus was born on the Palatine in 63 BC, and lived there in a modest house after becoming emperor. The hill was therefore an obvious choice of abode for future emperors. Domitian's ambitious house, the Domus Flavia (1st century AD), and its private quarters, the Domus Augustana, remained the official residence of future emperors (who were referred to as *Augustus*) for more than 300 years.

AROUND PIAZZA NAVONA

The area around Piazza Navona, known as the *centro storico*, has been inhabited for at least 2,000 years. Piazza Navona stands above an ancient stadium; the Pantheon has been a temple since AD 27; and the Theater of Marcellus in the Ghetto has been converted into exclusive apartments.

The area's heyday began in the 15th century, when the papacy returned to Rome. Throughout the Renaissance and Baroque eras, princes, popes, and cardinals settled here, as did the artists and artisans they commissioned to build and adorn lavish palaces, churches, and fountains.

Sights at a Glance

Churches and Temples

2 Sant'Ivo alla Sapienza
3 San Luigi dei Francesi
5 Santa Maria della Pace
6 Chiesa Nuova
13 Gesù
15 Santa Maria sopra Minerva
17 Sant'Ignazio di Loyola
20 La Maddalena

Ancient Sites and Buildings

4 Palazzo Altemps
7 Palazzo della Cancelleria
9 Palazzo Farnese
12 Area Sacra di Largo Argentina
16 Pantheon
22 Historic Building

Museums and Galleries

10 Palazzo Spada
14 Palazzo Doria Pamphilj

Historic Piazzas and Areas

1 Piazza Navona
8 Campo de' Fiori
11 Ghetto and Tiber Island
18 Piazza Colonna
19 Piazza di Montecitorio

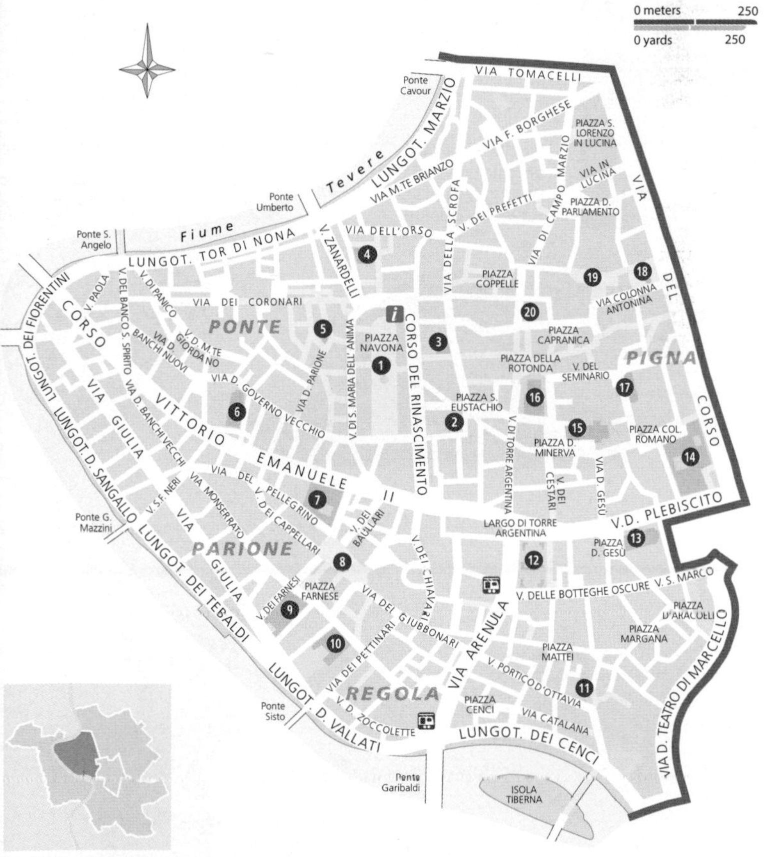

See also Rome Street Finder maps 9, 10

◀ The starry blue vault of the nave in Santa Maria sopra Minerva, Piazza della Minerva

For keys to symbols see back flap

Street-by-Street: Around Piazza Navona

No other piazza in Rome can rival the theatricality of Piazza Navona. The luxurious cafés are the social center of the city, and day and night there is always something going on in the pedestrian area around the three flamboyant Baroque fountains. The Baroque is also represented in many of the area's churches. To discover an older Rome, walk along Via del Governo Vecchio to admire the facades of Renaissance buildings, browse in the fascinating antique shops, and eat lunch in one of the many trattorias.

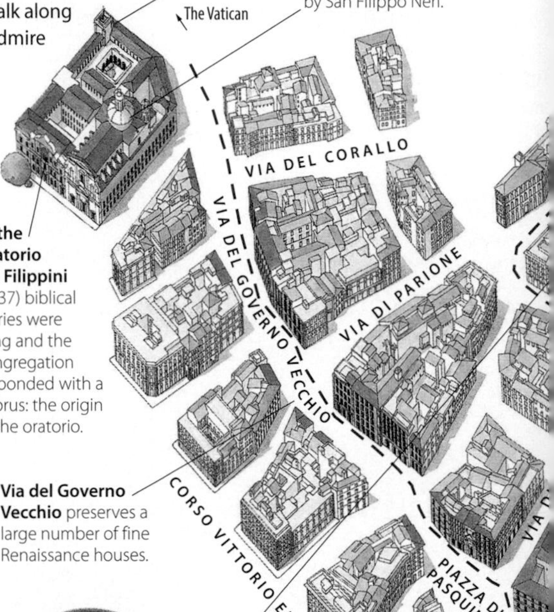

The Torre dell'Orologio by Borromini (1648) formed part c the Oratorio dei Filippini.

6 Chiesa Nuova
This church was rebuilt in 1575 for the order founded by San Filippo Neri.

The Vatican

At the Oratorio dei Filippini (1637) biblical stories were sung and the congregation responded with a chorus: the origin of the oratorio.

Via del Governo Vecchio preserves a large number of fine Renaissance houses.

5 Santa Maria della Pace
This Renaissance church has frescoes of the Four Sibyls by Raphael and a refined courtyard by Bramante. The Baroque portico is by Pietro da Cortona.

Pasquino is a 3rd-century BC Hellenistic statue of Menelaus. Romans have been hanging satirical verses at its feet since the 16th century.

Palazzo Braschi, a late-18th-century building designed by Cosimo Morelli, has a splendid balcony overlooking the piazza.

Palazzo Pamphilj

Fontana del Moro

Campo de' Fiori

Key

Suggested route

Sant'Andrea della Valle, begun in 1591, has a flamboyant Baroque facade flanked by angels with outstretched wings by Ercole Ferrata. The church is the setting of the first act of Puccini's *Tosca*.

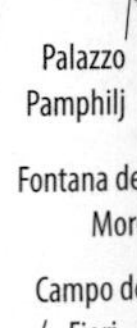

For hotels and restaurants in this region see pp562–77 and pp580–605

Sant'Agnese in Agone by Borromini (1657) is allegedly built on the site where, in AD 304, the young St. Agnes was publicly stripped to force her to renounce her faith.

AROUND PIAZZA NAVONA
Tevere
VATICAN AND TRASTEVERE

Locator Map
See Rome Street Finder map 2

Fontana dei Quattro Fiumi

❸ **San Luigi dei Francesi**
This church, which was completed in 1589, is best known for three paintings by Caravaggio.

VIA DEL SALVATORE
CORSIA AGONALE
PIAZZA NAVONA
CORSO DEL RINASCIMENTO
VIA DEGLI STADERARI
VIA DEI SEDIARI
S. ANDREA DELLA VALLE

Palazzo Madama, the seat of the Italian Senate, was originally built for the Medici family in the 16th century, on the site of one of their banks.

❷ **Sant'Ivo alla Sapienza**
This tiny domed church is one of Borromini's most original creations. He worked on it between 1642 and 1650.

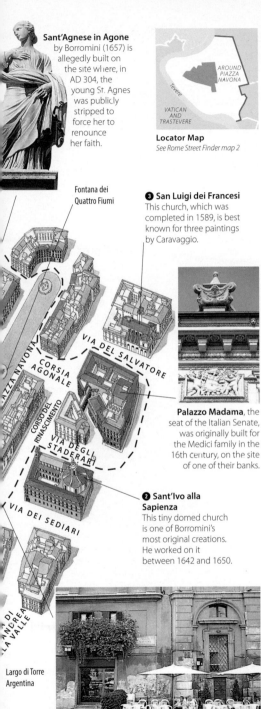

Largo di Torre Argentina

❶ ★ **Piazza Navona**
The piazza is lined with palaces and sidewalk cafés, and punctuated by flamboyant Baroque fountains.

❶ Piazza Navona

Map 2 E4. 🚌 30, 70, 81, 87, 130, 186, 492, 628.

Rome's most beautiful Baroque piazza follows the shape of a 1st-century AD stadium built by Domitian, which was used for athletic contests *(agones)*, chariot races, and other sports. Traces of the stadium are still visible below the church of Sant'Agnese in Agone, which is dedicated to a virgin martyred on the site for refusing to marry a pagan.

The piazza began to take on its present appearance in the 17th century, when Pope Innocent X, whose family palazzo was on the piazza, commissioned a new church, palace, and fountain. The fountain, the Fontana dei Quattro Fiumi, is Bernini's most magnificent, with statues of the four great rivers of the world at that time (the Nile, the Plate, the Ganges, and the Danube) sitting on rocks below an obelisk. Bernini also designed the musclebound Moor in the Fontana del Moro, though the present statue is a copy. Until the 19th century, the piazza was flooded in August by stopping the fountain outlets. The rich would splash around in carriages, while street urchins paddled. Even today the piazza remains the social center of the city.

Symbolic figure of the Nile River on Bernini's Fontana dei Quattro Fiumi

❷ Sant'Ivo alla Sapienza

Corso del Rinascimento 40. **Map** 2 F4. **Tel** 06 361 25 62. 30, 70, 81, 87, 116, 186, 492, 628. **Open** 9am–noon Sun.

Hidden in the courtyard of Palazzo della Sapienza, seat of the old University of Rome, Sant'Ivo's spiral belfry is nevertheless a distinctive landmark on Rome's skyline. Built by Borromini in 1642–60, the church is astonishingly complex, an ingenious combination of concave and convex surfaces. The work spanned the reigns of three popes, and incorporated in the design are their emblems: Urban VIII's bee, Innocent X's dove and olive branch, and the star and hills of Alexander VII.

❸ San Luigi dei Francesi

Piazza di San Luigi de' Francesi 5. **Map** 2 F4 & 12 D2. **Tel** 06 68 82 71. 70, 81, 87, 116, 186, 492, 628. **Open** 10am–12:30pm, 3–7pm daily. **Closed** Thu pm.

The French national church in Rome, San Luigi is a 16th-century building, best known for three magnificent canvases by Caravaggio in the Cerasi chapel. Painted between 1597 and 1602, these were Caravaggio's first significant religious works: *The Calling of St. Matthew*, *Martyrdom of St. Matthew*, and *St. Matthew and the Angel*. The first version of this last was initially rejected because it depicted the saint as an old man with dirty feet.

Detail from Caravaggio's *The Calling of St. Matthew* (1597–1602) in San Luigi dei Francesi

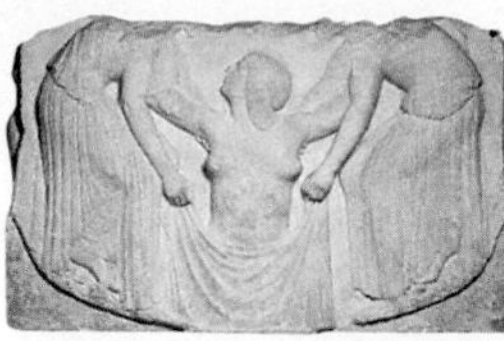

Side relief of the Ludovisi Throne, on display in the Palazzo Altemps

❹ Palazzo Altemps

Via di Sant'Apollinare 46. **Map** 2 E3. **Tel** 06 39 96 77 00. 70, 81, 87, 115, 280, 628. **Open** 9am–7:45pm Tue–Sun. **Closed** Jan 1, Dec 25.

An extraordinary collection of Classical sculpture is housed in this branch of the Museo Nazionale Romano (*see p416*). Restored as a museum during the 1990s, the palazzo was originally built for Girolamo Riario, nephew of Pope Sixtus IV, in 1480. In the popular uprising that followed the pope's death in 1484, the building was sacked and Girolamo fled the city. In 1568 Cardinal Marco Sittico Altemps bought the palazzo; it was renovated in the 1570s by Martino Longhi the Elder, who added the obelisk-crowned belvedere and marble unicorn.

The Altemps family were avid collectors; the courtyard and its staircase are lined with ancient sculptures, which complement the Ludovisi sculptures. One of the highlights is the marble statue *Galata's Suicide*, a copy of the original, in the Salone del Camino. On the first floor is the Greek, 5th-century BC Ludovisi Throne, a carved relief shows Aphrodite.

Galata's Suicide in the Palazzo Altemps

❺ Santa Maria della Pace

Vicolo del Arco della Pace 5. **Map** 2 E3. **Tel** 06 686 11 56. 70, 81, 87, 116, 492, 628. **Open** 9am–noon Mon, Wed, Sat.

Named by Pope Sixtus IV to celebrate the peace he hoped to bring to Italy, this church dates from the 1480s and contains a beautiful fresco by Raphael. Bramante's refined cloister was added in 1504, while the facade was designed in 1656 by Pietro da Cortona.

❻ Chiesa Nuova

Piazza della Chiesa Nuova. **Map** 2 E4. **Tel** 06 687 52 89. 46, 64. **Open** 7:30am–noon, 4:30–7:30pm daily.

San Filippo Neri commissioned this church in 1575 to replace the dilapidated one given to his Order by Pope Gregory XIII. Neri required his followers to humble themselves, and set aristocratic young men to work as laborers on the church.

Against his wishes, the nave, apse, and dome were richly frescoed after his death by Pietro da Cortona. There are three paintings by Rubens around the altar. The first versions were rejected, so Rubens repainted them on slate, placing the originals above his mother's tomb.

❼ Palazzo della Cancelleria

Piazza della Cancelleria. **Map** 2 E4. **Tel** 06 69 88 75 66. 46, 62, 64, 116, 916. **Open** 7:30am–2pm, 4–8pm. **Closed** Sun.

A supreme example of the confident delicacy of early Renaissance architecture, this palazzo was begun in 1485, and was allegedly financed by the ambling proceeds of Raffaele iario, a nephew of Pope Sixtus I. 1478 Riario was involved in he Pazzi conspiracy against the Medici, and when Giovanni de' Medici became Pope Leo XIII in 513, he took belated revenge, eizing the palace and turning it nto the papal chancellery.

Tiber Island, with Ponte Cestio, built in 46 BC, linking it to Trastevere

8 Campo de' Fiori

Map 2 E4. 116 & routes to Corso ittorio Emanuele II.

ampo de' Fiori (field of flowers) vas one of the liveliest and oughest areas of medieval and enaissance Rome. Cardinals nd nobles mingled with ishmongers and foreigners in he piazza's market; Caravaggio illed his opponent after losing game of tennis on the square; nd the goldsmith Cellini nurdered a business rival earby. Today, the area ontinues to be a hub of secular ctivity. The colorful market, rattorias, and down-to-earth ars retain the original nimated atmosphere.

In the Renaissance the piazza vas surrounded by inns, many of which were owned by the 5th-century courtesan annozza Catanei, mistress of Pope Alexander VI.

The square was also a place of execution. The statue in its enter is the philosopher iordano Bruno, burned at the stake for heresy on this spot in 1600 for suggesting the earth moved around the sun.

9 Palazzo Farnese

Piazza Farnese. **Map** 2 E5. Tel 06 68 60 11. 23, 116, 280 & routes to Corso Vittorio Emanuele II. only (3pm, 4pm & 5pm on Mon, Wed & Fri. Book in advance. **www.ambafrance.org**

Originally constructed for Cardinal Alessandro Farnese, who became Pope Paul III in 1534, this palazzo was started by Antonio da Sangallo the Younger, and continued after his death by Michelangelo, who created the cornice on the facade and the courtyard's third story.

The palace, now the French Embassy, is closed to the public, but when the chandeliers are lit at night you may be able to glimpse the ceiling of the Galleria, an illusionistic masterpiece (1597–1603) by Annibale Carracci based on Ovid's *Metamorphoses*.

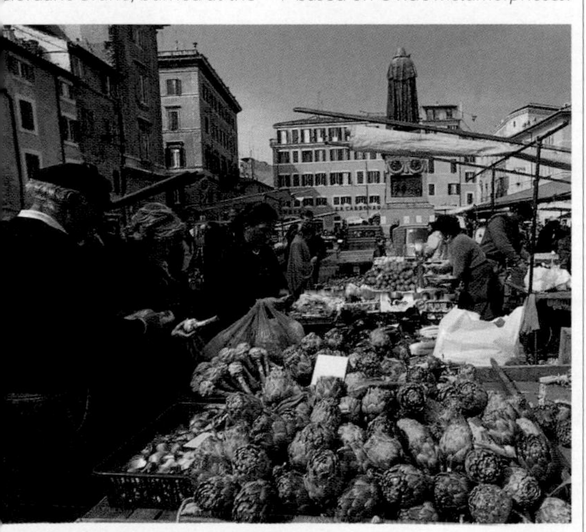

ruit stalls at Campo de' Fiori's lively morning market

10 Palazzo Spada

Piazza Capo di Ferro 13. **Map** 2 E5. **Tel** 06 686 11 58 (Palazzo) and 06 683 24 09 (Galleria). 23, 116, 280, & routes to Largo di Torre Argentina. **Open** 8:30am–7:30pm Tue–Sun (last adm: 7pm). **Closed** Jan 1, Dec 25.

A stucco extravaganza studded with reliefs of illustrious Romans, this palazzo was built in 1550, but bought in 1637 by Cardinal Bernardino Spada. A patron of the arts, he commissioned Borromini to create an illusionistic tunnel that appears four times longer than it is. The cardinal's art collection, in the Galleria Spada, includes works by Guercino, Dürer, and Artemisia Gentileschi.

11 Ghetto and Tiber Island

Map 2 F5 & 6 D1. 23, 63, 280, 780 and routes to Largo di Torre Argentina.

The first Jews came to Rome as traders in the 2nd century BC and were greatly appreciated for their financial and medical skills during the Roman Empire. Persecution began in the 16th century, when Pope Paul IV forced all of the Jews to live within a walled enclosure, an area later to form the hub of the present-day Ghetto.

Today Via del Portico d'Ottavia, the district's main street, leads to Rome's central synagogue, passing restaurants and shops selling Roman Jewish food. Ponte Fabricio links the Ghetto with Tiber Island, a center of healing since 293 BC when a Temple to Aesculapius was founded. The island is now home to a hospital.

Street-by-Street: Around the Pantheon

The maze of narrow streets around the Pantheon is a mixture of lively restaurants and cafés, and some of Rome's finest sights. This is also the city's financial and political district, home to Parliament, government offices, and the stock exchange. The Pantheon itself, with its awe-inspiring domed interior, has long been a symbol of the city.

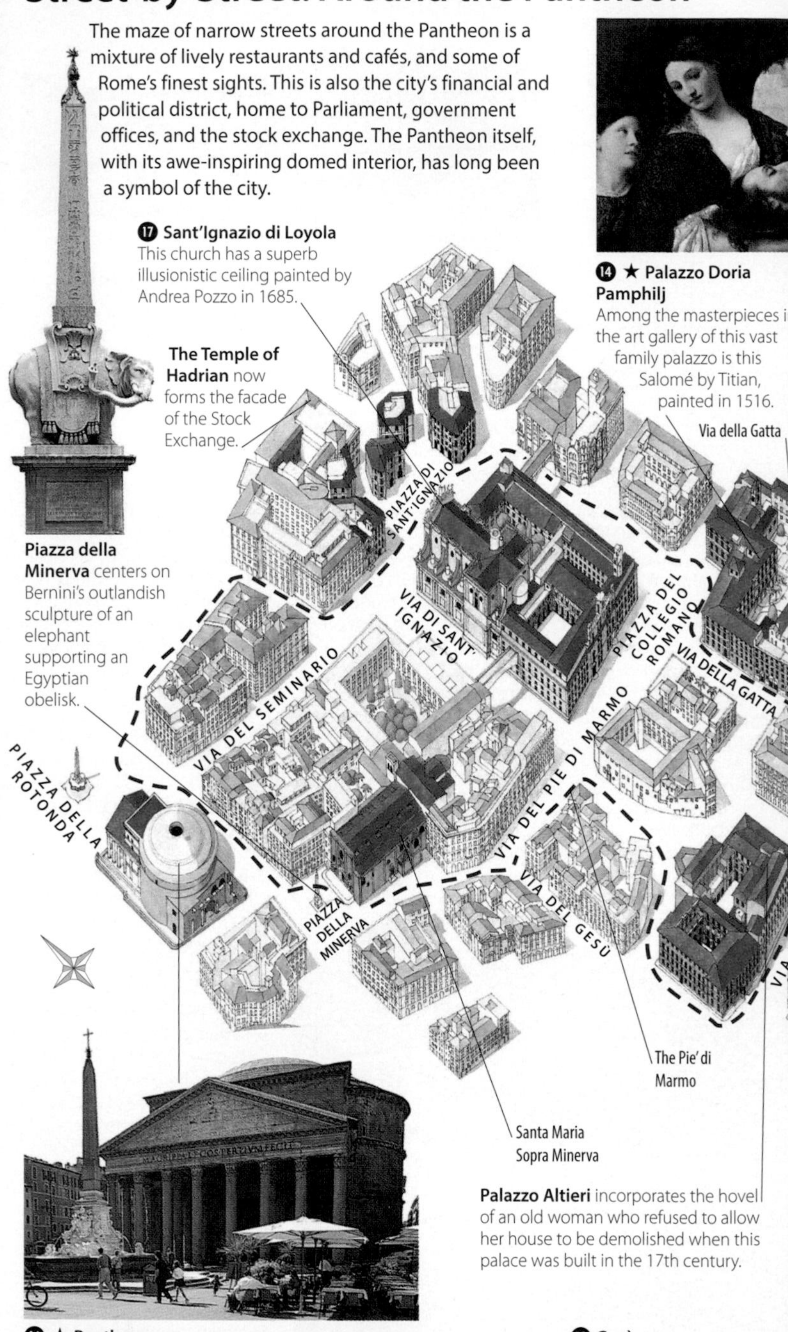

17 Sant'Ignazio di Loyola
This church has a superb illusionistic ceiling painted by Andrea Pozzo in 1685.

The Temple of Hadrian now forms the facade of the Stock Exchange.

Piazza della Minerva centers on Bernini's outlandish sculpture of an elephant supporting an Egyptian obelisk.

14 ★ Palazzo Doria Pamphilj
Among the masterpieces in the art gallery of this vast family palazzo is this Salomé by Titian, painted in 1516.

Palazzo Altieri incorporates the hovel of an old woman who refused to allow her house to be demolished when this palace was built in the 17th century.

16 ★ Pantheon
The Pantheon, a temple to "all the gods," is Rome's best-preserved ancient building. It was built in the 1st century AD, probably to a design by Emperor Hadrian.

13 Gesù
Built in the late 16th century, this Jesuit church served as a model for the Order's churches throughout the world.

For hotels and restaurants in this region see pp562–77 and pp580–605

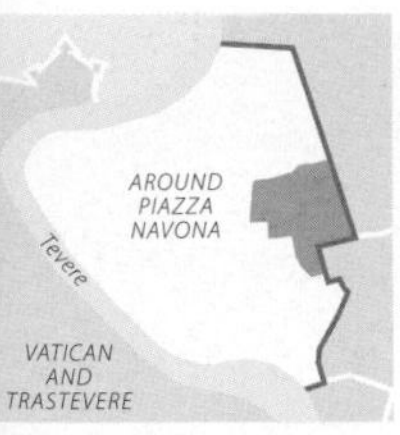

Locator Map
See Rome Street Finder map 3

Via della Gatta is overlooked by this marble statue of a cat *(gatta)* that gives the narrow street its name.

The Pie' di Marmo, an ancient marble foot, is probably part of a giant statue from the temple to the Egyptian goddess Isis.

⓯ Santa Maria sopra Minerva
This is one of Rome's few Gothic churches, with works by Michelangelo, Bernini, and Filippino Lippi.

Key

▬ Suggested route

0 meters 75
0 yards 75

⓬ Area Sacra di Largo Argentina

Largo di Torre Argentina. **Map** 2 F5. 🚌 40, 46, 62, 64, 70, 81, 87, 186, 492. **Closed** to the public.

The remains of four temples were discovered in the 1920s at the center of Largo Argentina, now a busy bus terminal and traffic intersection. They date from the era of the Republic, and are among the oldest found in Rome. For the purpose of identification, they are known as A, B, C, and D. The oldest (temple C) dates from the early 3rd century BC. It was placed on a high platform preceded by an altar and is typical of Italic temple plans as opposed to the Greek model. Temple A is from the 3rd century BC, but in medieval times the small church of San Nicola di Cesarini was built over its podium and the remains of its two apses are still visible. The column stumps to the north belonged to a great portico, known as the Hecatostylum (portico of 100 columns). In Imperial times two marble latrines were built here – the remains of one are visible behind temple A. Behind temples B and C, near Via di Torre Argentina, are the remains of a great platform of tufa blocks. These have been identified as part of the Curia of Pompey, a rectangular building where the Senate met, and where Julius Caesar was assassinated by Brutus, Cassius and their followers on March 15, 44 BC.

Area Sacra, with the ruins of circular temple B

Baroque *Triumph of Faith over Idolatry* by Pierre Legros, Gesù

⓭ Gesù

Piazza del Gesù. **Map** 3 A4. **Tel** 06 69 70 01. 🚌 H, 46, 62, 64, 70, 81, 87, 186, 492, 628 & other routes. **Open** 7am–12:30pm, 4–7:45pm daily.

Built between 1568 and 1584, the Gesù was Rome's first Jesuit church. The Jesuit order was founded in Rome in 1537 by a Basque soldier, Ignatius Loyola, who became a Christian after he was wounded in battle. The order was austere, intellectual, and heavily engaged in missionary activity and religious wars.

The much-imitated design of the Gesù typifies Counter-Reformation architecture, with a large nave with side pulpits for preaching to crowds, and a main altar as the centerpiece for the mass. The illusionistic decoration on the nave ceiling and dome was added by Il Baciccia in the 17th century.

The nave depicts the *Triumph of the Name of Jesus* and its message is clear: faithful Catholic worshippers will be joyfully uplifted to heaven while Protestants and heretics are flung into the fires of hell. The message is reiterated in the Cappella di Sant'Ignazio, a rich display of lapis lazuli, serpentine, silver, and gold. The Baroque marble by Legros, *Triumph of Faith over Idolatry*, shows a female "Religion" trampling on the head of the serpent Idolatry, while in Théudon's *Barbarians Adoring the Faith*, an angel aims a kick toward a decrepit old barbarian couple entangled with a snake.

⓮ Palazzo Doria Pamphilj

Via del Corso 305. **Map** 3 A4. **Tel** 06 679 73 23. 64, 81, 119, 492. **Open** 9am–7pm daily. **Closed** Jan 1, Easter Sun, May 1, Dec 25. by appt for private apartments.

Palazzo Doria Pamphilj is a vast edifice whose oldest parts date from 1435. When the Pamphilj family took over in 1647, they built a new wing, a splendid chapel, and a theater.

The family art collection has over 400 paintings dating from the 15th–18th centuries, including a portrait of Pope Innocent X by Velázquez and works by Titian, Guercino, Caravaggio, and Claude Lorrain. The opulent rooms of the private apartments retain many of their original furnishings, including Brussels and Gobelins tapestries, Murano chandeliers, and a gilded crib.

Velázquez's *Pope Innocent X* (1650)

⓯ Santa Maria sopra Minerva

Piazza della Minerva 42. **Map** 2 F4. **Tel** 06 679 39 26. 116 & many other routes. **Open** 7:10am–7pm Mon–Sat, 8am–noon, 2–7pm Sun.

One of Rome's rare Gothic buildings, this church was built in the 13th century over what were thought to be the ruins of a Temple of Minerva. It was a stronghold of the Dominicans, who produced some of the Church's most infamous inquisitors, and who tried the scientist Galileo in the adjoining monastery.

Inside, the church has a superb collection of art and sculpture, ranging from 13th-century Cosmatesque tombs to a bust by Bernini. Highlights include Antoniazzo Romano's *Annunciation* featuring Cardinal Juan de Torquemada, uncle of the vicious Spanish Inquisitor, and the Carafa Chapel's frescoes by Filippino Lippi.

In the Aldobrandini Chapel are the tombs of the 16th-century Medici popes, Leo X and his cousin Clement VII, and near the steps of the choir is a stocky *Risen Christ*, begun by Michelangelo.

The church also contains the tombs of many famous Italians, such as St. Catherine of Siena, who died in 1380 and Fra Angelico, the Dominican friar and painter, who died in 1455. Outside, Bernini's spectacular sculpture of an elephant holds an obelisk on its back.

Interior of the Pantheon, burial place for Italian monarchs

Simple vaulted nave of Santa Maria sopra Minerva

⓰ Pantheon

Piazza della Rotonda. **Map** 2 F4. **Tel** 06 68 30 02 30. 116 & many routes. **Open** 8:30am–7:30pm daily (9am–6pm Sun). **Closed** Jan 1, May 1, Dec 25.

The Pantheon, the Roman "temple of all the gods," is the most extraordinary and best preserved ancient building in Rome. The first temple on the site was a conventional rectangular affair erected by Agrippa between 27 and 25 BC; the present structure was built and possibly designed by Emperor Hadrian in AD 118.

The temple is fronted by a massive pedimented portico screening what appears to be a cylinder fused to a shallow dome. Only from the inside can the true scale and beauty of this building be appreciated: a vast hemispherical dome equal in radius to the height of the cylinder, giving perfectly harmonious proportions to the building. A circular opening, the *oculus*, lets in the only light.

In the 7th century, Christians claimed to be plagued by demons as they passed by, and permission was given to make the Pantheon a church. Today it is lined with tombs, ranging from a restrained monument to Raphael to huge marble and porphyry sarcophagi holding the bodies of Italian monarchs.

⑰ Sant'Ignazio di Loyola

Piazza di Sant'Ignazio. **Map** 2 F4. **Tel** 06 679 44 06. 117, 119, 492. **Open** 7:30am–12:30pm, 3pm–7:20pm daily (from 9am Sun).

This church was built by Pope Gregory XV in 1626 in honor of St. Ignatius of Loyola, founder of the Society of Jesus (Jesuits) and the man who most embodied the zeal of the Counter-Reformation.

Together with the Gesù *(see p407)*, Sant'Ignazio forms the nucleus of the Jesuit area of Rome. It is one of the most extravagant Baroque churches, and its vast interior is plated with precious stones, marble, stucco, and gilt, creating a thrilling sense of theater. The church has a Latin cross plan, with an apse and many side chapels. A cupola was planned but never built, as the nuns from a nearby convent objected that it would obscure the view from their roof garden. Instead, the space was filled by a perspective painting of a dome on a flat disc.

Even more striking is the illusionistic ceiling created by the Jesuit artist Andrea Pozzo in 1685, a propagandist extravaganza extolling the success of Jesuit missionaries throughout the world. Above four women, representing Asia, Europe, America, and Africa, lithe angels and beautiful youths are sucked into a heaven of fluffy clouds.

Detail from the AD 180 Column of Marcus Aurelius, Piazza Colonna

⑱ Piazza Colonna

Map 3 A3. 116, 117, 492.

Home to Palazzo Chigi, official residence of the prime minister, Piazza Colonna is dominated by and named after the majestic Column of Marcus Aurelius. This was erected after the death of Marcus Aurelius in AD 180 to commemorate his victories over the barbarian tribes of the Danube. It is clearly an imitation of Trajan's Column *(see p392)* with scenes from the emperor's wars spiraling in reliefs up the column. The 80-year lapse between the two works produced a great artistic change: the wars of Marcus Aurelius are rendered with simplified pictures in stronger relief, sacrificing Classical proportions for the sake of clarity and immediacy.

Baroque illusionistic ceiling by Andrea Pozzo in Sant'Ignazio di Loyola

⑲ Piazza di Montecitorio

Map 2 F3. Palazzo di Montecitorio **Tel** 06 676 01. 116. **Open** 10am–3:30pm 1st Sun of month.

The obelisk in the center of Piazza di Montecitorio formed the spine of a giant sundial brought back from Egypt by Augustus. It vanished in the 9th century, and was rediscovered under medieval houses during the reign of Julius II (1503–13).

The piazza is dominated by the rugged facade of Palazzo di Montecitorio, designed by Bernini and completed in 1697, after his death, by Carlo Fontana. It has been the seat of Italy's Chamber of Deputies since the late 19th century.

La Maddalena's stuccoed facade

⑳ La Maddalena

Piazza della Maddalena. **Map** 2 F3. **Tel** 06 899 281. 116 & many other routes. **Open** 8:30–11:30am, 5–6:30pm daily (Sat am only).

Situated in a small piazza near the Pantheon, the Maddalena's Rococo facade, built in 1735, epitomizes the love of light and movement of the late Baroque. The facade has been restored, despite the protests of Neo-Classicists who dismissed its painted stucco as icing sugar.

The diminutive dimensions of the church did not deter 17th- and 18th-century decorators from filling the interior with paintings and ornaments from the floor to the top of the elegant cupola.

NORTHEAST ROME

This area stretches from the exclusive shopping streets around Piazza di Spagna to the Esquiline Hill, once bourgeois, but now a poor, often seedy area full of early Christian churches. The Piazza di Spagna and Piazza del Popolo district grew up in the 16th century, when the increase in the influx of pilgrims was such that a road was built to channel them as quickly as possible to the Vatican. About the same time, the Quirinal Hill became the site of a papal palace. When Rome became capital of Italy in 1870, Via Veneto became a lavish residential area, and the Esquiline was covered with apartments for the new civil servants.

Sights at a Glance

Churches

3 Santa Maria del Popolo
7 Sant'Andrea al Quirinale
8 San Carlo alle Quattro Fontane
10 Santa Maria della Concezione
11 Santa Maria della Vittoria
13 Santa Prassede
14 San Pietro in Vincoli
15 Santa Maria Maggiore

Museums and Galleries

9 Galleria Nazionale di Arte Antica: Palazzo Barberini
12 Museo Nazionale Romano Palazzo Massimo

Ancient Sites and Buildings

4 Ara Pacis
5 Mausoleum of Augustus

Historic Buildings

2 Villa Medici

Piazzas and Fountains

1 Piazza di Spagna and the Spanish Steps
6 Trevi Fountain

See also Rome Street Finder maps 2, 3, 4, 7

◀ The Spanish Steps leading up to the church of the Santissima Trinità dei Monti

Street-by-Street: Piazza di Spagna

The network of narrow streets around Piazza di Spagna forms one of the most exclusive areas in Rome, drawing droves of tourists and Romans to the elegant shops around Via Condotti. The square and its nearby coffee houses have long attracted those who want to see and be seen. In the 18th century the area was full of hotels for frivolous aristocrats doing the Grand Tour, as well as artists, writers, and composers, who took the city's history and culture more seriously.

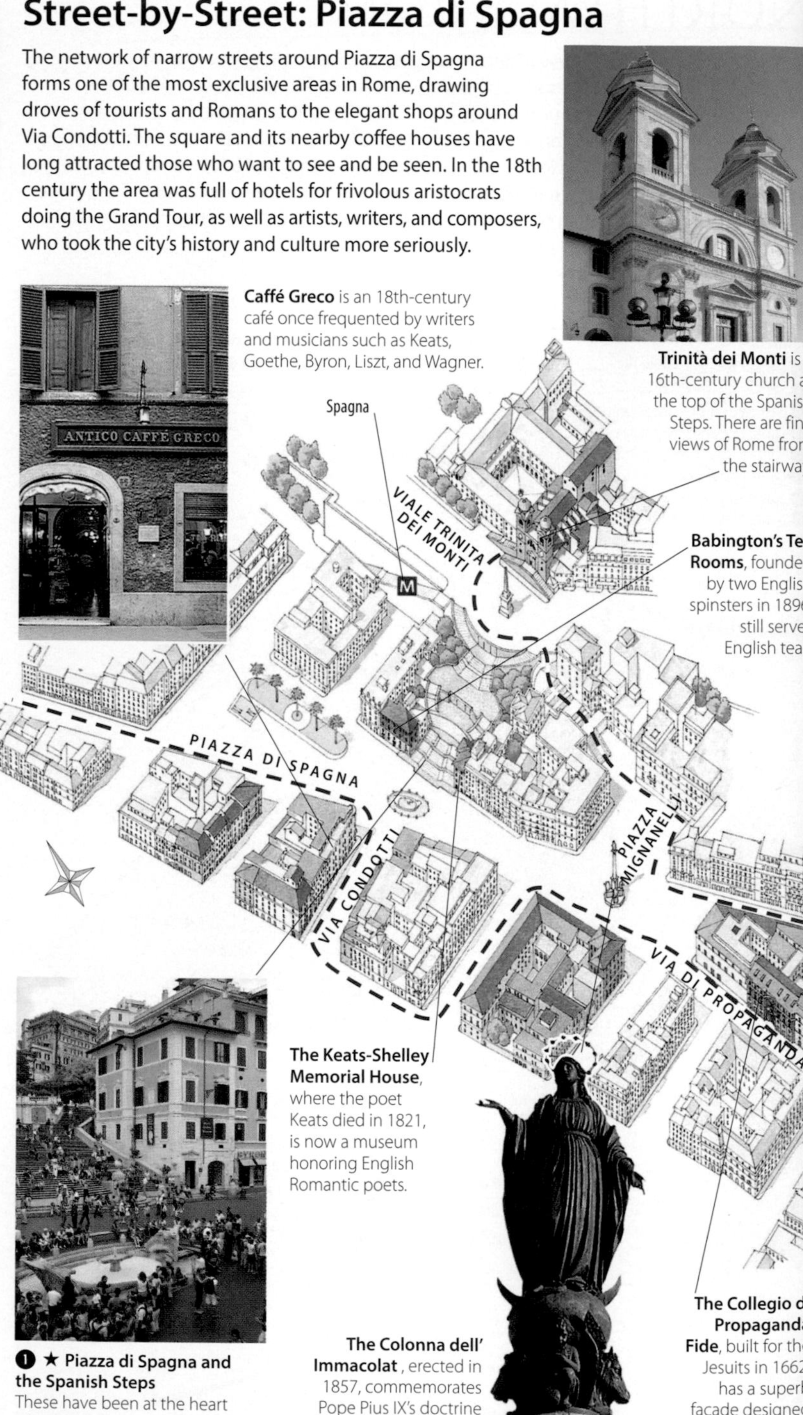

Caffè Greco is an 18th-century café once frequented by writers and musicians such as Keats, Goethe, Byron, Liszt, and Wagner.

Trinità dei Monti is a 16th-century church at the top of the Spanish Steps. There are fine views of Rome from the stairway.

Babington's Tea Rooms, founded by two English spinsters in 1896, still serves English teas.

The Keats-Shelley Memorial House, where the poet Keats died in 1821, is now a museum honoring English Romantic poets.

1 ★ Piazza di Spagna and the Spanish Steps
These have been at the heart of tourist Rome since the 18th century.

The Colonna dell' Immacolat, erected in 1857, commemorates Pope Pius IX's doctrine of the Immaculate Conception.

The Collegio di Propaganda Fide, built for the Jesuits in 1662, has a superb facade designed by Francesco Borromini.

For hotels and restaurants in this region see pp562–77 and pp580–605

Locator Map

See Rome Street Finder map 3

Sant'Andrea delle Fratte contains two angels by Bernini (1669) made for Ponte Sant'Angelo, which Pope Clement X thought too lovely to expose to the weather.

LE CASE

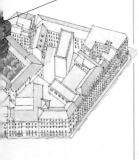

0 meters 75

0 yards 75

Key

▬ Suggested route

The Fontana della Barcaccia at the foot of the Spanish Steps

❶ Piazza di Spagna and the Spanish Steps

Map 3 A2. 🚌 116, 117. Ⓜ Spagna.

Shaped like a crooked bow tie, and surrounded by muted, shuttered facades, Piazza di Spagna is crowded all day and (in summer) most of the night. The most famous square in Rome, it takes its name from the Palazzo di Spagna, built in the 17th century to house the Spanish Embassy to the Holy See.

The piazza has long been the haunt of foreign visitors and expatriates. In the 18th and 19th centuries the square stood at the heart of the city's main hotel district. Some of the travelers came in search of knowledge and inspiration, although most were more interested in collecting statues to adorn their family homes.

When the Victorian novelist Charles Dickens visited, he reported that the Spanish Steps were crowded with models dressed as Madonnas, saints, and emperors, hoping to attract the attention of foreign artists.

The steps were built in the 1720s to link the square with the French church of Trinità dei Monti above. The French wanted to place a statue of Louis XIV at the top, but the pope objected, and it was not until the 1720s that the Italian architect Francesco de Sanctis produced the voluptuous Rococo design that satisfied both camps. The Fontana Barcaccia, sunk into the paving at the foot of the steps due to low water pressure, was designed by Bernini's less famous father, Pietro.

❷ Villa Medici

Accademia di Francia a Roma, Viale Trinità dei Monti 1. **Map** 3 A2. **Tel** 06 67 611. 🚌 117. Ⓜ Spagna. **Open** garden visits: 11am–noon, 2:30–4:30pm Tue–Sun (Cardinal's apartments: Wed only). only (at noon in English).

Superbly positioned on the Pincio Hill, this 16th-century villa has retained the name that it assumed when Cardinal Ferdinando de' Medici bought it in 1576. It is now home to the French Academy, founded in 1666 to give artists the chance to study in Rome. From 1803, musicians were also allowed to study here: both Berlioz and Debussy were students.

The villa is only open for exhibitions, but the formal gardens, with a gorgeously frescoed pavilion and copies of ancient statues, can be visited in certain months.

19th-century engraving of the inner facade of the Villa Medici

Pinturicchio's fresco of the *Delphic Sibyl* (1509) in Santa Maria del Popolo

❸ Santa Maria del Popolo

Piazza del Popolo 12. **Map** 2 F1. **Tel** 06 361 08 36. 117, 119, 490, 495, 926. Ⓜ Flaminio. **Open** 7am–noon, 4–7pm Mon–Sat; 7:30am–1:30pm, 4:30–7:30pm Sun.

Santa Maria del Popolo was one of the first Renaissance churches in Rome, commissioned by Pope Sixtus IV della Rovere in 1472. Lavish endowments by Sixtus's descendants and other powerful families have made it one of Rome's greatest artistic treasures.

Shortly after Sixtus died in 1484, Pinturicchio and his pupils frescoed two chapels (first and third right) for the della Rovere family. On the altar of the first chapel there is a lovely *Nativity* from 1490 that depicts a stable at the foot of a Classical column.

In 1503 Sixtus IV's nephew Giuliano became Pope Julius II and had Bramante build a new apse. Pinturicchio was called in again to paint its vaults with Sibyls and Apostles framed in an intricate tracery of freakish beasts.

In 1513 Raphael created the Chigi chapel (second left) for the wealthy banker Agostino Chigi. The design is an audacious Renaissance fusion of the sacred and profane; there are pyramid-like tombs and a ceiling mosaic of God holding the signs of the zodiac describing Chigi's horoscope. Raphael died before the chapel was finished, and it was completed by Bernini, who added the dynamic statues of Daniel and Habakkuk. In the Cerasi chapel, left of the altar, there are two realistic works painted by Caravaggio in 1601: the *Conversion of St. Paul* and the *Crucifixion of St. Peter*. The artist uses daringly exaggerated lighting effects and foreshortening techniques to intensify the dramatic effect.

Detail of the Ara Pacis frieze

❹ Ara Pacis

Lungotevere in Augusta. **Map** 2 F2. **Tel** 06 06 08. 70, 81, 117, 119, 186, 628. **Open** 9am–7pm Tue–Sun (last adm: 6pm). **Closed** Jan 1, Dec 25. **W arapacis.it**

Painstakingly reconstructed over many years from scattered fragments, the exquisitely carved Ara Pacis (Altar of Peace) celebrates the peace created by Emperor Augustus throughout the Mediterranean. Commissioned by the Senate in 13 BC and completed four years later, the altar stands in a square enclosure of Carrara marble, carved with realistic reliefs of such quality that experts think the craftsmen may have been Greek.

The reliefs on the north and south walls depict a procession that took place on July 4, 13 BC, in which the members of the emperor's family can be identified, including Augustus's grandson, Lucius, clutching at the skirt of his mother, Antonia. The site is housed in a building by architect Richard Meier.

❺ Mausoleum of Augustus

Piazza Augusto Imperatore. **Map** 2 F2. **Tel** 06 06 08. 81, 117, 492, 628, 926. **Closed** for restoration.

Now just a weedy mound ringed with cypresses and strewn with litter, this was once the most prestigious burial place in Rome. Augustus had the mausoleum built in 28 BC, the year before he became sole ruler, as a tomb for himself and his descendants. The circular building was 270 ft (87 m) in diameter with two obelisks (now in Piazza del Quirinale and Piazza dell' Esquilino) at the entrance. Inside were four concentric passageways linked by corridors where urns holding the ashes of the Imperial family were placed, including those of Augustus, who died in AD 14.

❻ Trevi Fountain

Piazza di Trevi. **Map** 3 B3. 116 & many other routes.

Nicola Salvi's theatrical design for Rome's largest and most famous fountain was completed in 1762. The central figures are Neptune, flanked by two Tritons, one trying to master an unruly "sea horse," the other leading

Rome's largest and most famous fountain, the Trevi

For hotels and restaurants in this region see pp562–77 and pp580–605

a quieter beast, symbolizing the two contrasting moods of the sea.

The site originally marked the terminal of the Aqua Virgo aqueduct, built by Augustus' right-hand man and son-in-law, Agrippa, in 19 BC to channel water to Rome's new bath complexes. One of the reliefs on the first story shows a young girl, Trivia, after whom the fountain may have been named. She is said to have first shown the spring, 14 miles (22 km) from the city, to thirsty Roman soldiers.

Interior, Sant'Andrea al Quirinale

7 Sant'Andrea al Quirinale

Via del Quirinale 29. **Map** 3 B3. **Tel** 06 474 08 07. 116, 117. **Open** 8:30am–noon, 3:30–7pm Mon–Sat; 9am–noon, 4–7pm Sun.

Sant'Andrea was designed for the Jesuits by Bernini and executed by his assistants between 1658 and 1670. The site was wide but shallow, so Bernini took the radical step of pointing the long axis of his oval plan toward the sides, and leading the eye around to the altar by means of a strong horizontal cornice. At the altar he combined sculpture and painting to create a theatrical crucifixion of Sant'Andrea (St. Andrew); the diagonally crucified saint on the altarpiece looks up at a stucco effigy of himself ascending to the lantern, where the Holy Spirit and cherubs await him in heaven.

The dome of San Carlo alle Quattro Fontane, by Borromini

8 San Carlo alle Quattro Fontane

Via del Quirinale 23. **Map** 3 B3. **Tel** 06 488 31 09. 116 & routes to Piazza Barberini. M Barberini. **Open** 10am–1pm, 3–6pm daily (only am Sat & Sun).

In 1638, Borromini was commissioned by the Trinitarians to design a church and convent on a tiny cramped site at the Quattro Fontane crossroads. The church, so small that it is said it would fit inside one of the piers of St. Peter's, is designed with bold, fluid curves on both facade and interior to give light and life to the diminutive building. The dome, with its concealed windows, illusionistic coffering, and tiny lantern designed to make it look higher than it really is, is a clever feature.

Ceiling fresco detail in Palazzo Barberini (1633)

9 Galleria Nazionale di Arte Antica Palazzo Barberini

Via delle Quattro Fontane 13. **Map** 3 B3. **Tel** 06 482 41 84. 52, 53, 61, 62, 63, 80, 116, 175, 492, 590. M Barberini. **Open** 8:30am–7pm Tue–Sun (last adm: 6:30pm). **Closed** Jan 1, Dec 25. (elevator). **W galleriabarberini.beniculturali.it**

When Maffei Barberini became Pope Urban VIII in 1623, he decided to build a grand family palazzo. Designed by Carlo Maderno as a typical country villa on the fringes of the city, it now overlooks Piazza Barberini, where traffic hurtles around Bernini's Triton fountain. Maderno died shortly after the foundations had been laid, and Bernini and Borromini took over. The most dazzling room is the Gran Salone, with an illusionistic ceiling frescoed by Pietro da Cortona in 1633–9. The palazzo also houses part of the Galleria Nazionale d'Arte Antica with works by Titian, Filippo Lippi, Caravaggio, and Artemisia Gentileschi. The most famous is a portrait of a courtesan, reputedly Raphael's lover, *La Fornarina*, although not painted by the artist himself.

10 Santa Maria della Concezione

Via Veneto 27. **Map** 3 B2. **Tel** 06 487 11 85. 52, 53, 61, 62, 63, 80, 116, 175. M Barberini. Crypt and museum: **Open** 9am–7pm daily.

Below this unassuming church on Via Veneto is a crypt decked with the dismembered skeletons of 4,000 Capuchin monks. They form a macabre reminder of the transience of life, with vertebrae wired together to make sacred hearts and crowns of thorns, and, in one chapel, the poignant skeleton of a tiny Barberini princess.

⓫ Santa Maria della Vittoria

Via XX Settembre 17. **Map** 3 C2. **Tel** 06 42 74 05 71. 61, 62, 175, 910. M Repubblica. **Open** 8:30am–noon, 3:30–7pm daily.

Santa Daria della Vittoria is an intimate Baroque church with a lavish, candlelit interior. Inside the Cornaro chapel is one of Bernini's most ambitious sculptures, the *Ecstasy of St. Teresa* (1646). The physical nature of St. Teresa's ecstasy is apparent as she appears collapsed on a cloud with her mouth half open and eyes closed, struck by the arrow of a smiling angel. Ecclesiastical members, past and present, of the Venetian Cornaro family, who commissioned the chapel, sit in boxes as if watching and discussing the scene being played out in front of them.

Bernini's *Ecstasy of St. Teresa* in Santa Maria della Vittoria

⓬ Museo Nazionale Romano Palazzo Massimo

Palazzo Massimo, Largo di Villa Peretti 1 (1 of 5 sites). **Map** 4 D3. **Tel** 06 39 96 77 00. all routes to Termini. M Repubblica. **Open** 9am–7:45pm Tue–Sun. ticket valid for all sites.

Founded in 1899, the Museo Nazionale Romano – one of the world's leading museums of Classical art – houses most of the antiquities found in Rome since 1870, as well as important older collections. During the 1990s it underwent a major reorganization and now has five branches: the Palazzo Altemps *(see p404)*; the Baths of Diocletian; the Aula Ottagona, the Crypta; Balbi, and the Palazzo Massimo. In the latter, exhibits dating from the 2nd century BC to the late 4th century AD are displayed in a series of rooms over three floors. Highlights include the *Quattro Aurighe* mosaics from a villa in northern Rome, the breathtaking series of frescoes from Livia's summer villa, and the famous statue of her husband, the Emperor Augustus.

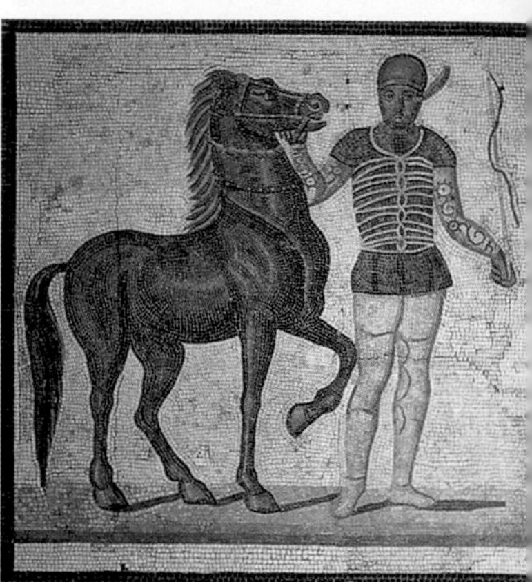

One of the finely detailed Quattro Aurighe mosaics on display at the Museo Nazionale Romano Palazzo Massimo

⓭ Santa Prassede

Via Santa Prassede 9a. **Map** 4 D4. **Tel** 06 488 24 56. 16, 70, 71, 75, 714. M Vittorio Emanuele. **Open** 7:30am–noon, 4–6:30pm daily (from 8am Sun).

The church was founded by Pope Paschal II in the 9th century and decorated by Byzantine artists with the most important, glittering mosaics in Rome. In the apse Christ stands between Santa Prassede and her sister, dressed as Byzantine empresses, among white-robed elders, lambs, feather-mop palms, and bright red poppies. The Cappella di San Zeno is even lovelier, a jewel box of a mausoleum, built by Pope Paschal II for his mother, Theodora. Her square halo shows that she was still alive when the mosaic was created.

9th-century mosaic, Santa Prassede

⓮ San Pietro in Vincoli

Piazza di San Pietro in Vincoli. **Map** 3 C5. **Tel** 06 97 84 49 50. 75, 85, 117. M Colosseo. **Open** 8am–12:30pm, 3–7pm daily (Oct–Mar: to 6pm).

The church's name means St. Peter in Chains, so called because it houses what are said to be the chains with which St. Peter was shackled in the Mamertine Prison *(see p393)*. According to tradition, one set of chains was sent to Constantinople by Empress Eudoxia; when it was returned to Rome some years later it miraculously fused with its partner.

San Pietro is now best known for the Tomb of Julius II, commissioned from Michelangelo by the pope in 1505. Much to the artist's chagrin, Julius soon became more interested in the building of a new St. Peter's, and the tomb project was laid to one side. After the pope died in 1513, Michelangelo resumed work on the tomb, but had only completed the statues of the *Dying Slaves* (now found in Paris and Florence) and *Moses* when he was called away to paint the *Last Judgment* in the Sistine Chapel.

⑮ Santa Maria Maggiore

A confident blend of architectural styles, ranging from Early Christian to late Baroque, Santa Maria is also famous for its superb mosaics. Founded in about AD 420, it retains the original colonnaded triple nave, lined with panels of rare 5th-century mosaics. The Cosmatesque marble floor and bell tower are medieval, as are the spectacular mosaics on the triumphal arch and in the loggia. The lavish coffered ceiling is Renaissance; the facades, domes, and chapels Baroque.

VISITORS' CHECKLIST

Practical Information
Piazza di Santa Maria Maggiore.
Map 4 D4.
Tel 06 69 88 68 00.
Open 7am–6:45pm daily.

Transportation
16, 70, 71, 714. 14. Termini, Cavour.

Coronation of the Virgin
This is one of the wonderful 13th-century mosaics in the apse by Jacopo Torriti.

Tomb of Cardinal Rodriguez
This Gothic tomb, which dates from 1299, contains magnificent marblework by the Cosmati.

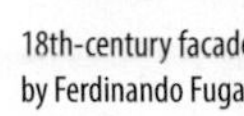

Cappella Paolina
Flaminio Ponzio, architect of the Villa Borghese, designed this sumptuous chapel in 1611 for Pope Paul V, who is buried here.

Column in Piazza Santa Maria Maggiore
In 1611 a bronze of the Virgin and Child was added to this ancient marble column, which came from the Basilica of Constantine.

Cappella Sistina
This chapel was built for Pope Sixtus V (1584–7) by Domenico Fontana and was opulently covered with ancient marble. It houses the pope's tomb.

THE VATICAN AND TRASTEVERE

Vatican City, the world capital of Catholicism, is the world's smallest state. It occupies 106 acres (43 ha) within high walls watched over by the Vatican guard. It was the site where St. Peter was martyred (*c.* AD 64) and buried, and it became the residence of the popes who succeeded him. The papal palaces, next to the great basilica of St. Peter's, are home to the Sistine Chapel and the eclectic collections of the Vatican Museums, as well as being the residence of the pope. Neighboring Trastevere is quite different, a picturesque old quarter whose inhabitants consider themselves to be the only true Romans. The proletarian identity of the place is in danger of being destroyed by the proliferation of trendy restaurants, clubs, and shops.

Sights at a Glance

Churches

2 *St. Peter's pp422–3*
7 Santa Maria in Trastevere
8 Santa Cecilia in Trastevere
9 San Francesco a Ripa
10 San Pietro in Montorio and the Tempietto

Museums and Galleries

3 *Vatican Museums pp424–31*
5 Palazzo Corsini and Galleria Nazionale d'Arte Antica

Historic Buildings

1 Castel Sant'Angelo
4 Villa Farnesina

Parks and Gardens

6 Botanical Gardens

See Rome Street Finder maps 1, 2, 5, 6, 9

◀ View of St. Peter's with the Ponte Sant'Angelo in the foreground

For keys to symbols *see back flap*

A Tour of the Vatican

The Vatican, a sovereign state since February 1929, is ruled by the pope, Europe's only absolute monarch. About 500 people live here and, as well as accommodation for staff and ecclesiasts, the city has its own post office, banks, currency, judicial system, radio station, shops, and a daily newspaper, *L'Osservatore Romano*.

★ St. Peter's
Most of the great architects of the Renaissance and Baroque had a hand in the design of the Basilica of St. Peter's, the most famous church in Christendom *(see pp422–3)*.

★ Sistine Chapel
Michelangelo frescoed the ceiling with scenes from Genesis (1508–12), and the altar wall with the *Last Judgment* (1534–41). The chapel is used by cardinals when electing a new pope *(see p428)*.

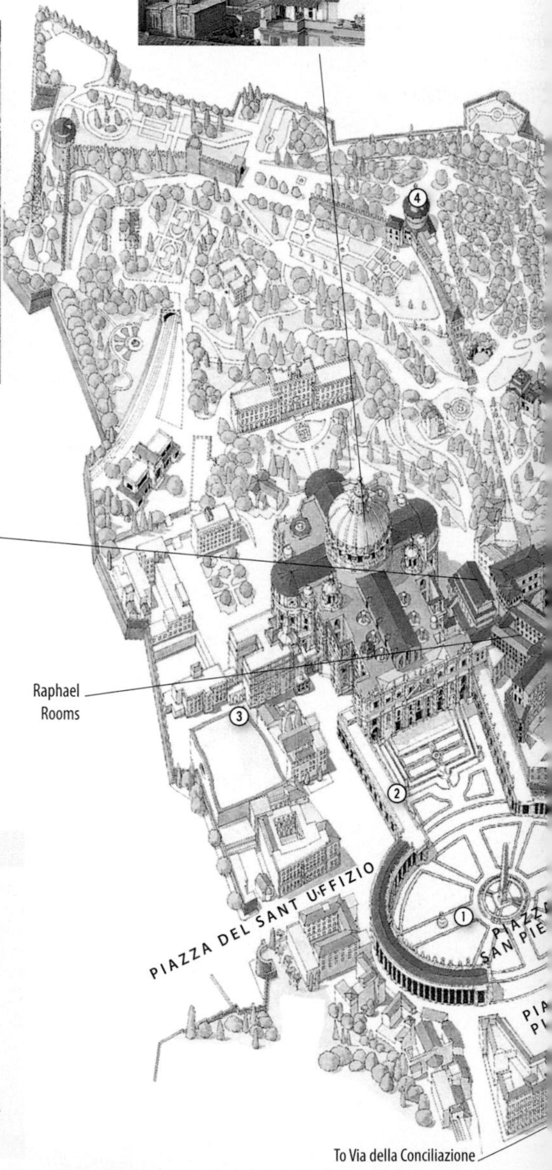

Raphael Rooms

0 meters 75
0 yards 75

PIAZZA DEL SANT UFFIZIO

To Via della Conciliazione

KEY

① **Piazza San Pietro** was laid out by Bernini between 1656 and 1667.

② **Information office**

③ **The Papal Audience Chamber**

④ **Vatican Radio** broadcasts throughout the world in 20 languages from this tower, part of the 9th-century Leonine Wall.

⑤ **The Vatican Gardens**, open for guided tours, make up a third of the Vatican's territory.

Locator Map
See Rome Street Finder map 1

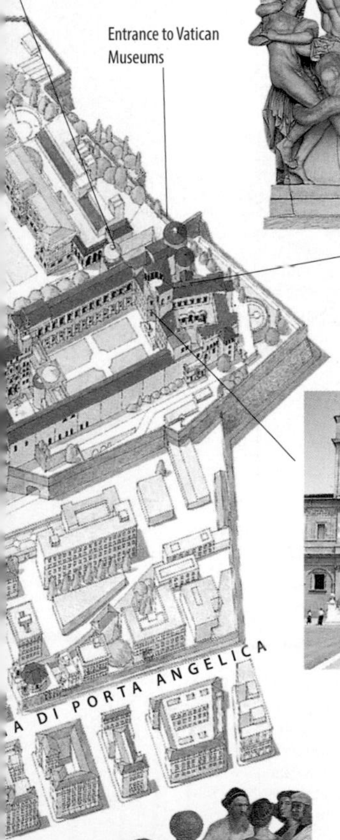

This staircase leading down from the museums, designed in 1932 by Giuseppe Momo, is in the form of a double helix, consisting of two spirals: one to walk up and one to walk down.

Entrance to Vatican Museums

★ Vatican Museums
The marble group of the *Laocoön* (AD 1) is one of many prestigious works of art in the Vatican *(see p426)*.

The Cortile della Pigna is named after a bronze pine cone from an ancient fountain.

★ Raphael Rooms
Raphael frescoed this suite in the early 16th century. Works like *The School of Athens* established his reputation, to equal that of his contemporary Michelangelo *(see p431)*.

❶ Castel Sant'Angelo

Lungotevere Castello. **Map** 2 D3. **Tel** 06 681 91 11. 🚌 34, 280. **Open** 9am–7:30pm Tue–Sun (last entry 6:30pm). **Closed** Jan 1, Dec 25.
castelsantangelo.beniculturali.it

This massive fortress takes its name from the vision of the Archangel Michael by Pope Gregory the Great in the 6th century as he led a procession across the bridge, praying for the end of the plague.

The castle began life in AD 139 as the Emperor Hadrian's mausoleum. Since then it has been a bridgehead in the Emperor Aurelian's city wall, a medieval citadel and prison, and a place of safety for popes during times of political unrest. A corridor links it with the Vatican Palace, providing an escape route for the Pope. From dank cells to fine apartments of Renaissance popes, the museums cover all aspects of the castle's history, including the Sala Paolina, with illusionistic frescoes (1546–8) by Pellegrino Tibaldi and Perin del Vaga and the Courtyard of Honor.

Illusionistic frescoes by Pellegrino Tibaldi

View of Castel Sant'Angelo from the Ponte Sant'Angelo

❷ St. Peter's

Catholicism's most sacred shrine, the sumptuous, marble-caked basilica of St. Peter's draws pilgrims and tourists from all over the world. It holds hundreds of precious works of art, some salvaged from the original 4th-century basilica built by Constantine, others commissioned from Renaissance and Baroque artists. The dominant tone is set by Bernini, who created the baldacchino twisting up below Michelangelo's huge dome. He also created the Cathedra in the apse, with four saints supporting a throne that contains fragments once thought to be relics of the chair from which St. Peter delivered his first sermon.

Dome of St. Peter's
The 448-ft- (136.5-m-) high dome, designed by Michelangelo, was not completed in his lifetime.

KEY

① **Entrance to Historical Artistic Museum and Sacristy**

② **The Monument to Pope Alexander VII** was Bernini's last work in St. Peter's. Completed in 1678, it shows the Chigi Pope among figures of Truth, Justice, Charity, and Prudence.

③ **A staircase** of 537 steps leads to the summit of the dome.

④ **The Baldacchino** was commissioned by Pope Urban VIII in 1624; Bernini's extravagant Baroque canopy stands above St. Peter's tomb.

⑤ **The Papal Altar** stands over the crypt where St. Peter is reputedly buried.

⑥ **The church** is 615 ft (186 m) long.

⑦ **The foot of St. Peter**, sculpted by Arnolfo di Cambio in the 13th century, has worn thin from the touch of pilgrims over the centuries.

⑧ **Two minor cupolas by Vignola (1507–73)**

⑨ **Markings on** the floor of the nave show how other churches compare in length.

⑩ **Facade by Carlo Maderno (1614)**

⑪ **From this Library window** the Pope blesses the faithful gathered in the piazza below.

⑫ **The Holy Door** is used only in Holy Years.

⑬ **Atrium by Carlo Maderno**

Historical Plan of the Basilica of St. Peter's

St. Peter was buried in AD 64 in a necropolis near the site of his crucifixion in the Circus of Nero. In AD 324 Constantine constructed a basilica over the tomb. The old church was rebuilt in the 15th century, and throughout the 16th and 17th centuries various architects developed the existing structure. The new church was inaugurated in 1626.

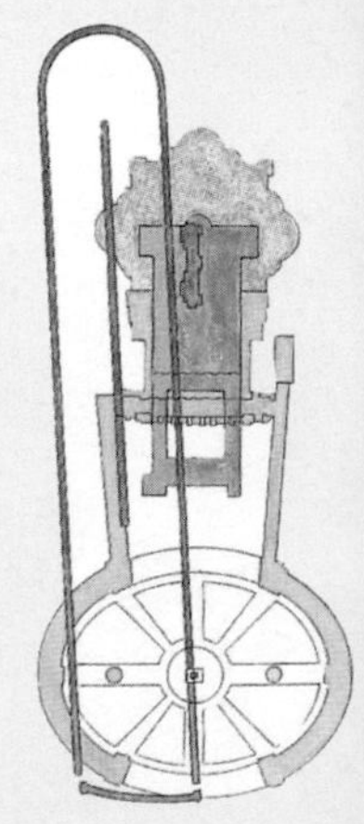

Key

- Circus of Nero
- Constantinian
- Renaissance
- Baroque

The Grottoes
A fragment of this 13th-century mosaic by Giotto, salvaged from the old basilica, Is now in the Grottoes, where many popes are buried.

Michelangelo's Pietà
Protected by glass since an attack in 1972, the Pietà was created in 1499 when Michelangelo was only 25.

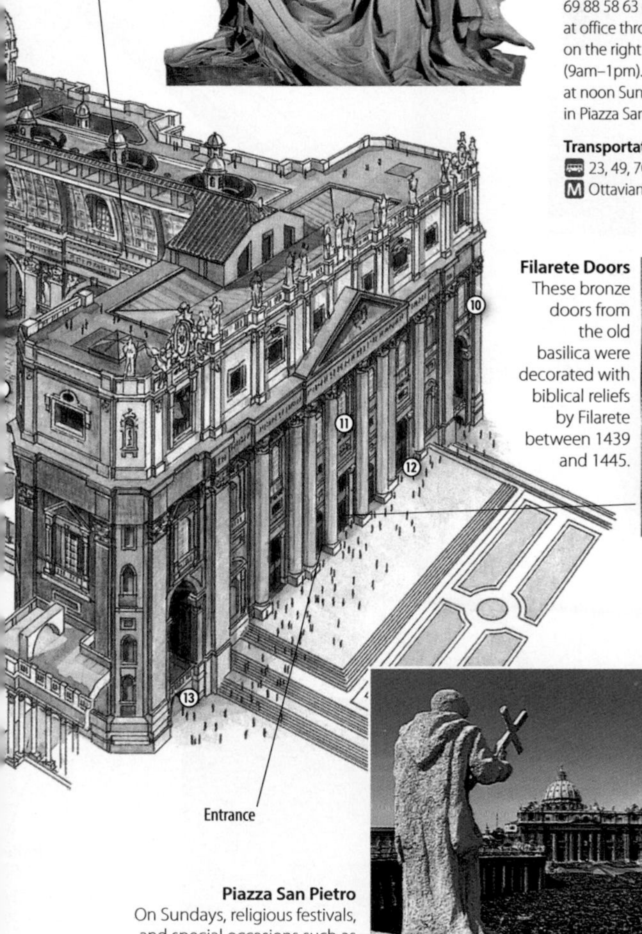

Filarete Doors
These bronze doors from the old basilica were decorated with biblical reliefs by Filarete between 1439 and 1445.

10

11

12

13

Entrance

Piazza San Pietro
On Sundays, religious festivals, and special occasions such as canonizations, the Pope blesses the crowds from a balcony.

VISITORS' CHECKLIST

Practical Information
Piazza San Pietro.
Map 1 B3.
Tel 06 69 88 37 12 (sacristy); 06 69 88 16 62 (tourist info).
Basilica: **Open** Apr–Sep: 7am–7pm daily (mid-Oct–Mar: to 6:30pm).
Treasury: **Open** Apr–Sep: 8am–7pm daily (Oct–Mar: to 6pm).
Grottoes: **Open** Apr–Sep: 7am–7pm daily (Oct–Mar: 6pm).
Dome: **Open** 8am–6pm daily (Oct–Mar: to 5pm).
Papal audiences: Usually Wed at 10:30am in Piazza San Pietro or in the Papal Audience Chamber Tickets (free) from Prefecture of the Pontifical Household. Call 06 69 88 58 63 or check availability at office through the bronze doors on the right of the colonnade (9am–1pm). The Pope appears at noon Sun to bless the crowd in Piazza San Pietro.

Transportation
23, 49, 70, 180, 492.
M Ottaviano San Pietro.

❸ Vatican Museums

Home to the Sistine Chapel and Raphael Rooms as well as to one of the world's most important art collections, the Vatican Museums are housed in palaces originally built for Renaissance popes Julius II, Innocent VIII, and Sixtus IV. Most of the later additions were made in the 18th century, when priceless works of art accumulated by earlier popes were first put on display.

Etruscan Museum
The Etruscan collection includes a woman's gold clasp *(fibula)* from the 7th-century-BC Regolini-Galassi tomb at Cerveteri, north of Rome.

Gallery of Maps
The *Siege of Malta* is one of 40 maps of the Church's territories, frescoed by the 16th-century cartographer Ignazio Danti on the gallery's walls.

Gallery of the Candelabra

Raphael Rooms
This is a detail of the *Expulsion of Heliodorus from the Temple*, one of many frescoes painted by Raphael and his pupils for Julius II's private apartments *(see p431)*.

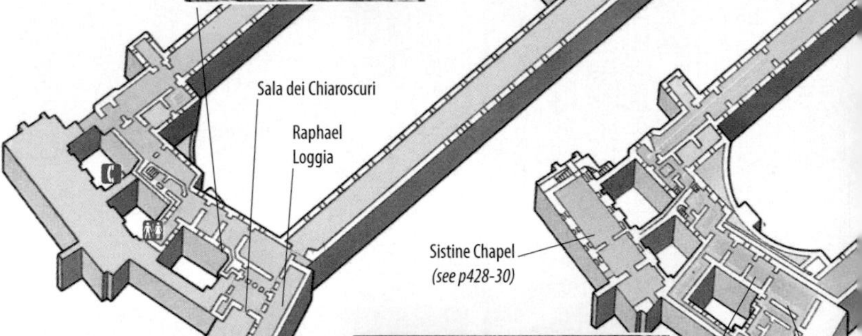

Gallery of Tapestries

St
dc

Upper floor

Sala dei Chiaroscuri

Raphael Loggia

Sistine Chapel *(see p428-30)*

Gallery Guide

The museum complex is vast: the Sistine Chapel is 20–30 minutes' walk from the entrance, so allow plenty of time. There is a strict one-way system, and it is best to be selective or choose one of four color-coded itineraries, which vary from 90 minutes to a 5-hour marathon.

Borgia Apartment
Pinturicchio and his assistants frescoed these rooms for Alexander VI in 1492–5.

Modern religiou **art** on view here was sent to the popes by artist worldwide, suc as Bacon, Erns and Carrà

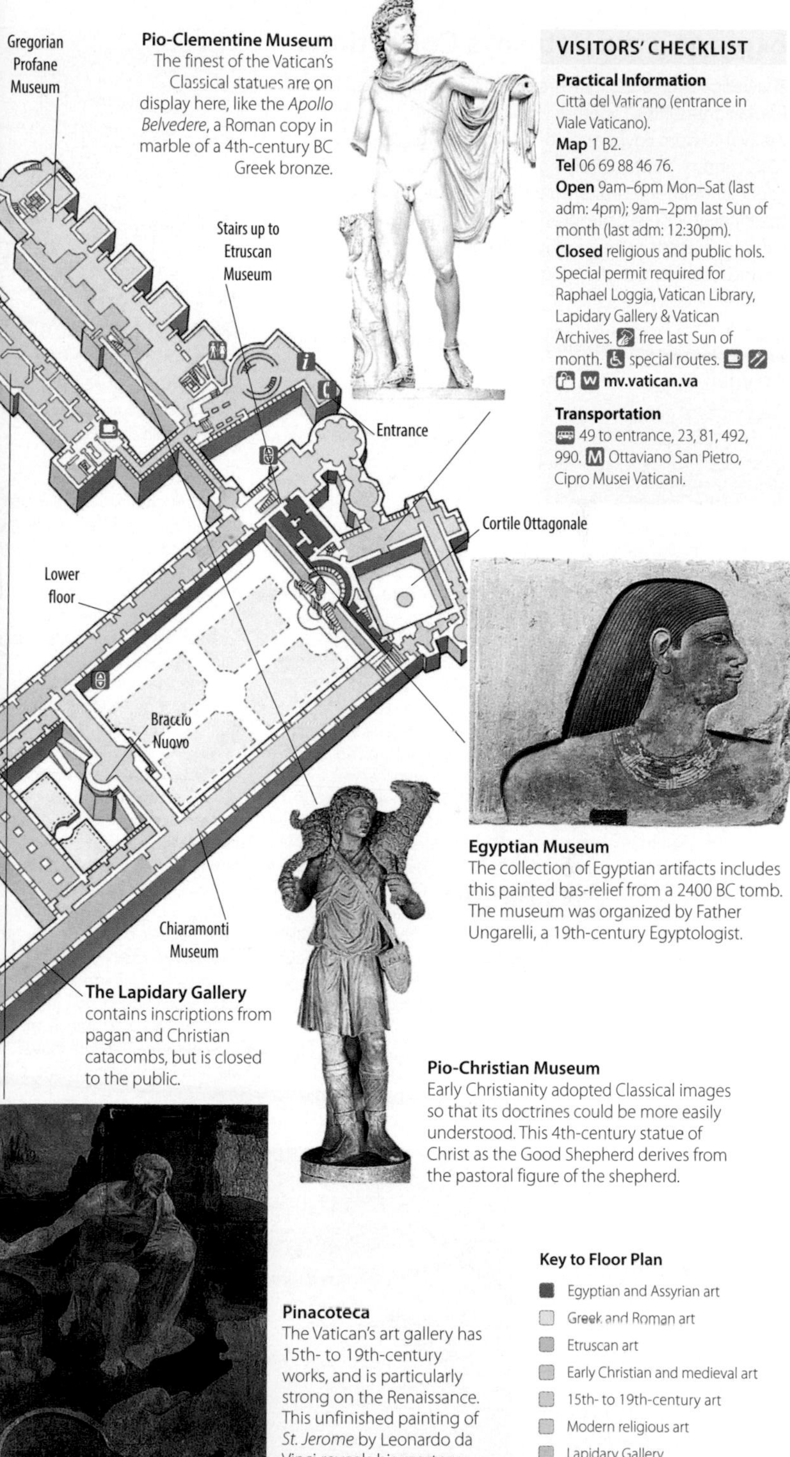

Pio-Clementine Museum The finest of the Vatican's Classical statues are on display here, like the *Apollo Belvedere*, a Roman copy in marble of a 4th-century BC Greek bronze.

Egyptian Museum The collection of Egyptian artifacts includes this painted bas-relief from a 2400 BC tomb. The museum was organized by Father Ungarelli, a 19th-century Egyptologist.

The Lapidary Gallery contains inscriptions from pagan and Christian catacombs, but is closed to the public.

Pio-Christian Museum Early Christianity adopted Classical images so that its doctrines could be more easily understood. This 4th-century statue of Christ as the Good Shepherd derives from the pastoral figure of the shepherd.

Pinacoteca The Vatican's art gallery has 15th- to 19th-century works, and is particularly strong on the Renaissance. This unfinished painting of *St. Jerome* by Leonardo da Vinci reveals his mastery of anatomy.

VISITORS' CHECKLIST

Practical Information
Città del Vaticano (entrance in Viale Vaticano).
Map 1 B2.
Tel 06 69 88 46 76.
Open 9am–6pm Mon–Sat (last adm: 4pm); 9am–2pm last Sun of month (last adm: 12:30pm).
Closed religious and public hols. Special permit required for Raphael Loggia, Vatican Library, Lapidary Gallery & Vatican Archives. free last Sun of month. special routes. **mv.vatican.va**

Transportation
49 to entrance, 23, 81, 492, 990. Ottaviano San Pietro, Cipro Musei Vaticani.

Key to Floor Plan

- Egyptian and Assyrian art
- Greek and Roman art
- Etruscan art
- Early Christian and medieval art
- 15th- to 19th-century art
- Modern religious art
- Lapidary Gallery
- Nonexhibition space

Exploring the Vatican's Collections

The Vatican's greatest treasures are its superlative Greek and Roman antiquities, together with the magnificent artifacts excavated from Egyptian and Etruscan tombs during the 19th century. Some of Italy's greatest artists, such as Raphael, Michelangelo, and Leonardo da Vinci, are represented in the Pinacoteca (art gallery) and parts of the former palaces, where the artists were employed by popes to decorate sumptuous apartments and galleries.

Head of an athlete in mosaic from the Baths of Caracalla, AD 217

Egyptian and Assyrian Art

The Egyptian collection contains finds from 19th- and 20th-century excavations in Egypt, as well as statues that were brought to Rome in Imperial times. There are also Roman imitations of Egyptian art from Hadrian's Villa *(see p472)* and from temples in Rome devoted to Egyptian gods and goddesses, such as Isis and Serapis.

The genuine Egyptian works, displayed on the lower floor next to the Pio-Clementine Museum, include statues, mummies, mummy cases, and a Book of the Dead. One of the main treasures is a colossal 13th-century granite statue of Queen Mutuy, the mother of Rameses II, which was found on the site of the Horti Sallustiani gardens near Via Veneto. Also noteworthy are the head of a statue of Montuhotep IV (20th century BC), the beautiful mummy case of Queen Hetepheres, and the tomb of Iri, who was the guardian of the Pyramid of Cheops. This dates back to the 22nd century BC.

Greek, Etruscan, and Roman Art

The greater part of the Vatican Museums is dedicated to Greek and Roman art. However, the Etruscan Museum houses a superb collection of Etruscan *(see p48)* and pre-Roman artifacts from Etruria and the Greek colonies of southern Italy. Here, the most famous exhibits are the gold jewelry and bronze throne, bed, and funeral cart, found in the 650 BC Regolini-Galassi tomb in Cerveteri *(see p470)*.

Prize Greek and Roman pieces form the nucleus of the Pio-Clementine Museum. These include high-quality Roman copies of 4th-century BC Greek statues, such as the *Apoxyomenos* (an athlete wiping his body after a race) and the *Apollo del Belvedere*. The splendid *Laocoön* (1st century AD), originally from Rhodes, was found in 1506 in the ruins of Nero's Golden House. Works such as these inspired Michelangelo and other Renaissance artists.

Roman copy of the Greek *Doryphoros*

The much smaller Chiaramonti Museum is lined with ancient busts, and its extension, the Braccio Nuovo, has a 1st-century BC statue of Augustus from the villa of his wife Livia. It is based on the *Doryphoros* (spear-carrier) by the 5th-century BC Greek sculptor Polyclitus. There is also a Roman copy of this on display opposite. The Gregorian Profane Museum, housed in a separate wing, follows the evolution of Roman art from reliance on Greek models to a recognizably Roman style.

In this museum, original Greek works include large marble fragments from the Parthenon in Athens. Among the Roman pieces are two reliefs, the *Rilievi della Cancelleria*, commissioned by Domitian in AD 81 to glorify the military parades of his father, Emperor Vespasian. There are also fine Roman floor mosaics, two from the Baths of Caracalla *(see p441)*, and one, in the Round Room, dated 3rd century AD, from the Baths of Otricoli in Umbria.

In the Vatican Library is the 1st-century AD *Aldobrandini Wedding*, a beautiful Roman fresco depicting a bride being prepared for her marriage.

Roman mosaic from the Baths of Otricoli, Umbria, in the Round Room

arly Christian and ledieval Art

he main collection of early hristian antiquities is in the io-Christian Museum, which ontains inscriptions and culpture from catacombs and arly Christian basilicas. The culpture consists chiefly of eliefs from sarcophagi, though ne most striking work is a eestanding 4th-century tatue of the *Good Shepherd*. he sculpture's chief interest es in the way it blends iblical episodes with pagan ythology. The idealized astoral figure of the shepherd ecame Christ himself, while earded philosophers turned nto the Apostles.

The first two rooms of the inacoteca are dedicated to late edieval art, mostly wooden tarpieces painted in tempera. he outstanding work is Giotto's *tefaneschi Triptych* of about 300 which decorated the main ltar of the old St. Peter's.

The Vatican Library has a umber of medieval treasures ncluding reliquaries, textiles, namels, and icons.

etail of Giotto's *Stefaneschi Triptych* 330) in the Pinacoteca

5th- to 19th- entury Art

Pietà (c.1471–4) by the Venetian artist Giovanni Bellini in the Pinacoteca

lany Renaissance popes were onnoisseurs of the arts who onsidered it their duty to ponsor the leading painters, culptors, and goldsmiths of the age. The galleries around the Cortile del Belvedere were decorated by great artists between the 16th and the 19th centuries.

The Gallery of Tapestries is hung with tapestries woven in Brussels to designs by students of Raphael. The Apartment of Pope Pius V has beautiful 15th-century Flemish tapestries, and the Gallery of Maps is frescoed with 16th-century maps of ancient and contemporary Italy.

Alongside the Raphael Rooms *(see p431)* are the Room of the Chiaroscuri and Pope Nicholas V's private chapel. This was frescoed between 1447 and 1451 by Fra Angelico. Also worth seeing is the Borgia Apartment, decorated in the 1490s by Pinturicchio and his pupils for the Borgia Pope, Alexander VI. Another set of fascinating frescoes can be found in the Loggia of Raphael, but a visit here requires special permission.

Pinturicchio's *Adoration of the Magi* (1490), Borgia Apartment

The Pinacoteca has many important Renaissance works. Highlights from the 15th century are a fine *Pietà* by Giovanni Bellini, part of his *Coronation of the Virgin* altarpiece in Pèsaro *(see p372)*; and Leonardo da Vinci's unfinished *St. Jerome*, discovered, after being long lost, in two halves. One was being used as a coffer lid in an antique shop, the other as the seat of a stool in a shoemaker's. Exceptional pieces from the 16th century include eight tapestry cartoons, the *Transfiguration*, and *Madonna of Foligno* by Raphael, in a room devoted to the artist; a *Deposition* by Caravaggio; an altarpiece by Titian; and *St. Helen* by Veronese, which shows the saint as a gorgeously dressed aristocrat.

Sistine Chapel: The Ceiling

Michelangelo frescoed the ceiling for Pope Julius II between 1508 and 1512, working on specially designed scaffolding. The main panels, which chart the Creation of the World and Fall of Man, are surrounded by subjects from the Old and New Testaments – except for the Classical Sibyls who are said to have foreseen the birth of Christ. In the 1980s the ceiling was restored, revealing colors of an unsuspected vibrancy.

Libyan Sibyl
The pagan prophetess reaches for the Book of Knowledge. Like most female figures Michelangelo painted, the beautiful Libyan Sibyl was probably modeled on a man.

Creation of the Sun and Moon

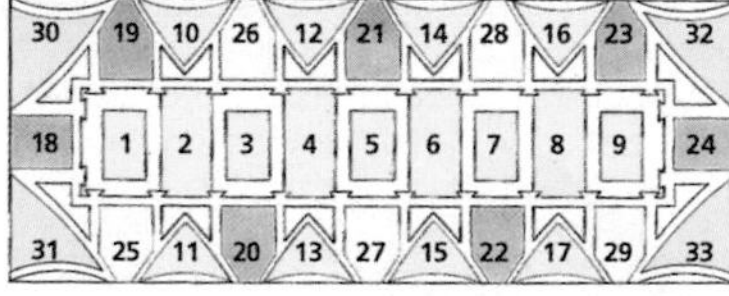

Key to Ceiling Panels

Genesis: 1 God Dividing Light from Darkness; **2** Creation of the Sun and Moon; **3** Separating Waters from Land; **4** Creation of Adam; **5** Creation of Eve; **6** Original Sin; **7** Sacrifice of Noah; **8** The Deluge; **9** Drunkenness of Noah.

Ancestors of Christ: 10 Solomon with his Mother; **11** Parents of Jesse; **12** Rehoboam with Mother; **13** Asa with Parents; **14** Uzziah with Parents; **15** Hezekiah with Parents; **16** Zerubbabel with Parents; **17** Josiah with Parents.

Prophets: 18 Jonah; **19** Jeremiah; **20** Daniel; **21** Ezekie **22** Isaiah; **23** Joel; **24** Zechariah.

Sibyls: 25 Libyan Sibyl; **26** Persian Sibyl; **27** Cumaean Sibyl; **28** Erythrean Sibyl; **29** Delphic Sibyl.

Old testament scenes of salvation: 30 Punishment c Haman; **31** Moses and the Brazen Serpent; **32** David and Goliath; **33** Judith and Holofernes.

KEY

① **Illusionistic architecture**

② **The lunettes** are devoted to frescoes of the ancestors of Christ, like Hezekiah.

③ **The Ignudi** are athletic male nudes whose significance is uncertain.

riginal Sin
his shows Adam and Eve tasting the forbidden fruit from he Tree of Knowledge, and their expulsion from Paradise. ichelangelo represents Satan as a snake with the body f a woman.

Creation of the Sun and Moon
Michelangelo depicts God as a dynamic but terrifying figure commanding the sun to shed light on the earth.

Restoration of the Sistine Ceiling

The restorers of the Sistine Chapel used computers, photography, and spectrum technology to analyze the fresco before cleaning began. They separated Michelangelo's work from that of later restorers and discovered that the restorers had attempted to clean the ceiling with materials ranging from bread to retsina wine. The new restoration revealed the familiarly dusky, eggshell-cracked figures to have creamy skins, lustrous hair, and brightly colored, luscious robes: "a Benetton Michelangelo," mocked one critic, claiming that a layer of varnish that the artist had added to darken the colors had been removed. However, after examining the work, most experts agreed that the new colors probably matched those painted by Michelangelo.

A restorer cleaning the Libyan Sibyl

Sistine Chapel: The Walls

The massive walls of the Sistine Chapel, the main chapel in the Vatican Palace, were frescoed by some of the finest artists of the 15th and 16th centuries. The 12 paintings on the side walls, by artists including Perugino, Ghirlandaio, Botticelli, and Signorelli, show parallel episodes from the lives of Moses and Christ. The decoration of the chapel walls was completed between 1534 and 1541 by Michelangelo, who added the great altar wall fresco, the *Last Judgment*.

Key to the Frescoes: Artists and Subjects

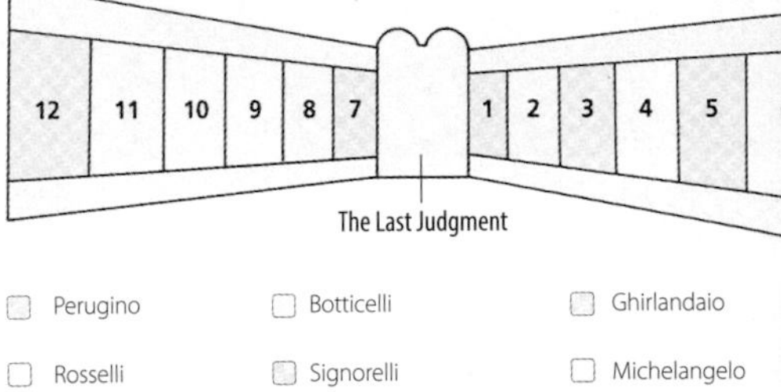

Perugino | Botticelli | Ghirlandaio

Rosselli | Signorelli | Michelangelo

1 Baptism of Christ in the Jordan
2 Temptations of Christ
3 Calling of St. Peter and St. Andrew
4 Sermon on the Mount
5 Handing over the Keys to St. Peter
6 Last Supper
7 Moses's Journey into Egypt
8 Moses Receiving the Call
9 Crossing of the Red Sea
10 Adoration of the Golden Calf
11 Punishment of the Rebels
12 Last Days of Moses

The Last Judgment by Michelangelo

Revealed in 1993 after a year's restoration, the *Last Judgment* is considered to be the masterpiece of Michelangelo's mature years. It was commissioned by Pope Paul III Farnese, and required the removal of some earlier frescoes and two windows over the altar. A new wall was erected, slanting inward to stop dust from settling on it. Michelangelo worked alone on the fresco for seven years, until its completion in 1541.

The painting depicts the souls of the dead rising up to face the wrath of God, a subject that is rarely used for an altar decoration. The Pope chose it as a warning to Catholics to adhere to their faith in the turmoil of the Reformation. In fact, the work conveys the artist's own tormented attitude to his faith. It offers neither the certainties of Christian orthodoxy nor the ordered view of Classicism.

In a dynamic, emotional composition, the figures are caught in a vortex of motion. The dead are torn from their graves and hauled up to face Christ the Judge, whose athletic, muscular figure is the focus of all the painting's movement.

Christ shows little sympathy for the agitated saints around him, clutching the instruments of their martyrdom. Neither is any pity shown for the damned, hurled down to the demons in hell. Here Charon, pushing people off his boat into the depths of Hades, and the infernal judge Minos, are taken from Dante's *Inferno*. Minos has ass's ears, and is a portrait of courtier Biagio da Cesena, who had objected to the nude figures in the fresco. Michelangelo's self-portrait is on the skin held by the martyr St. Bartholomew.

Souls meeting the wrath of Christ in Michelangelo's *Last Judgment*

Raphael Rooms

ope Julius II's private apartments were built above those f his hated predecessor, Alexander VI, who died in 1503. ulius was impressed with Raphael's work and chose him o redecorate the four rooms *(stanze)*. Raphael and his upils began in 1508, replacing works by better-known rtists, including Raphael's teacher, Perugino. The new rescoes quickly established the young artist's reputation n Rome, but the project took 16 years to complete and he lied before it was finished.

etail from Raphael's *The Mass of Bolsena* 1512)

Hall of Constantine

he frescoes in this room were tarted in 1517 and completed 1525, five years after Raphael's eath, and are largely the work f the artist's pupils. The theme f the decoration is the triumph f Christianity over paganism, nd the four major frescoes how scenes from the life of onstantine, the first Christian mperor. These include the *ision of the Cross* and the mperor's victory over his rival, laxentius, at *The Battle of the ilvian Bridge*, for which aphael had provided a reparatory sketch.

Room of Heliodorus

aphael decorated this private ntechamber between 1512 nd 1514. The main frescoes all ontain thinly veiled references the protective powers of the apacy. The room's name refers the fresco on the right, *The xpulsion of Heliodorus from the Temple*, showing Heliodorus felled by a horseman as he tries to rob the Temple in Jerusalem. It alludes to Pope Julius II's victory over foreign armies in Italy. *The Mass of Bolsena* on the left wall refers to a miracle that occurred in 1263, in which a priest who doubted the doctrine of the Holy Host was said to have seen blood issue from it at the moment of sacrifice.

Room of the Segnatura

Completed between 1508 and 1511, the frescoes here are the most harmonious in the series. The scheme followed by Raphael, dictated by Pope Julius II, reflected the Humanist belief that there could be perfect harmony between Classical culture and Christianity in the search for truth. The most famous work, *The School of Athens*, centers on the debate about truth between the Greek philosophers Plato and Aristotle. Raphael depicted some of his contemporaries as philosophers, including Leonardo da Vinci, Bramante, and Michelangelo.

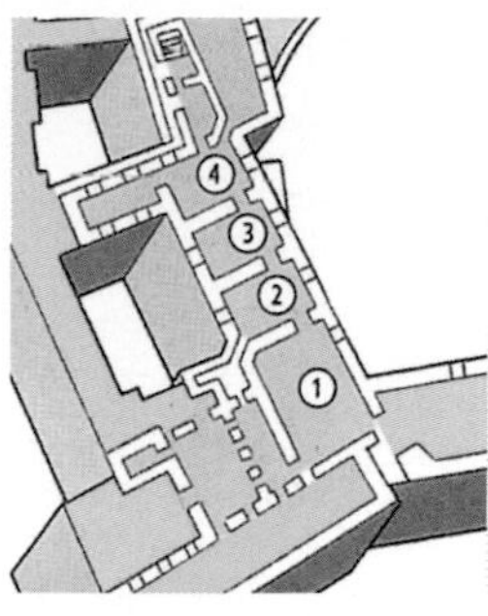

Key to Floor Plan

① Hall of Constantine
② Room of Heliodorus
③ Room of the Segnatura
④ Room of the Fire in the Borgo

Room of the Fire in The Borgo

This was originally the dining room, but when the decoration was completed under Pope Leo X, it became a music room. All the frescoes exalt the reigning pope by depicting events in the lives of his 9th-century namesakes, Leo III and IV. The main frescoes were designed by Raphael, but finished by his assistants between 1514 and 1517. The most famous, *The Fire in the Borgo*, shows a miracle of 847, when Pope Leo IV put out a fire by making the sign of the cross. Raphael draws a parallel between this and the legendary flight of Aeneas from Troy, recounted by Virgil. Aeneas appears in the foreground, carrying his father Anchises on his back.

The School of Athens (1511) showing philosophers and scholars

❹ Villa Farnesina

Via della Lungara 230. **Map** 2 E5. **Tel** 06 68 02 72 68. 23, 280. **Open** 9am–2pm Mon–Sat and every second Mon of the month.

The fabulously wealthy Sienese banker Agostino Chigi commissioned this villa in 1508 from his fellow Sienese Baldassare Peruzzi. Chigi's main home was across the Tiber, and the villa was designed purely for lavish banquets. Artists, poets, cardinals, princes, and the pope himself were entertained here in magnificent style. Chigi also used the villa for sojourns with the courtesan Imperia, who allegedly inspired one of the *Three Graces* painted by Raphael in the Loggia of Cupid and Psyche.

The simple, harmonious design of the Farnesina, with a central block and projecting wings, made it one of the first true villas of the Renaissance. Peruzzi decorated some of the interiors himself, such as the Sala della Prospettiva upstairs, in which the illusionistic frescoes create the impression of looking out over 16th-century Rome through a marble colonnade.

Other frescoes, by Sebastiano del Piombo and Raphael and his pupils, illustrate Classical myths, while the vault of the main hall, the Sala di Galatea, is adorned with astrological scenes showing the position of the stars at the time of Chigi's birth. After his death the business collapsed, and in 1577 the villa was sold off to the Farnese family.

Raphael's *Three Graces* in the Villa Farnesina

Queen Christina of Sweden's bedroom in the Palazzo Corsini

❺ Palazzo Corsini and Galleria Nazionale d'Arte Antica

Via della Lungara 10. **Map** 2 D5. **Tel** 06 68 80 23 23. 23, 280. **Open** 8:30am–7:30pm Tue–Sun. **Closed** Jan 1, Dec 25 & 31.
galleriacorsini. beniculturali.it

Built for Cardinal Domenico Riario in 1510–12, the Palazzo Corsini has numbered Bramante, the young Michelangelo, Erasmus, and the mother of Napoleon among its guests. Queen Christina of Sweden died here in 1689. The palazzo was rebuilt by Ferdinando Fuga, who planned the facade to be viewed from an angle, as Via della Lungara is too narrow for a full frontal view.

When the palazzo was bought by the state in 1893, the Corsini family donated their collection of paintings, which formed the core of the national art collection and was soon augmented. The collection is now split between Palazzo Barberini and Palazzo Corsini. Although the best works are in the Barberini, there are paintings by Van Dyck, Rubens, Murillo, and, notably, an androgynous *St. John the Baptist* (*c.* 1604) by Caravaggio and a *Salome* (1638) by Reni. The strangest work is a portrait of the rotund Queen Christina as the goddess Diana by J. Van Egmont.

❻ Botanical Gardens

Largo Cristina di Svezia 24. **Map** 2 D5. **Tel** 06 49 91 71 08. 23, 280. **Open** 9:30am–6:30pm (Oct–Mar: 5:30pm) Mon–Sat. **Closed** public hols.

Sequoias, palm trees, orchids, and bromeliads are among the 7,000 plants from all over the world represented in the Botanical Gardens (Orto Botanico). Indigenous and exotic species are grouped to illustrate their botanical families and their adaptation to different climates and ecosystems. There are also some curious plants like the ginkgo that have survived almost unchanged from earlier eras.

Palm trees in the Botanical Gardens, Trastevere

❼ Santa Maria in Trastevere

Piazza Santa Maria in Trastevere. **Map** 5 C1. **Tel** 06 581 94 43. H, 23, 280. **Open** 7:30am–9pm daily.

Santa Maria in Trastevere was probably the first Christian place of worship in Rome, founded by Pope Callixtus I in the 3rd century, when emperors were still pagan and Christianity a minority cult. According to legend, it was built on the site where a fountain of oil had miraculously sprung up on the day that Christ was born. The basilica became the focus of devotion to the Madonna, and although today's church, and its remarkable mosaics, date largely from the 12th and 13th centuries, images of the Virgin continue to dominate. The facade mosaics probably date

Apse mosaic of the *Coronation of the Virgin*, Santa Maria in Trastevere

from the 12th century, and show Mary, Christ, and ten lamp-bearing women. Inside in the apse is a stylized 12th-century *Coronation of the Virgin*, and below, a series of realistic scenes from the life of the Virgin by the 13th-century artist Pietro Cavallini. The oldest image of the Virgin is a 7th-century icon, the *Madonna di Clemenza*, which depicts her as a Byzantine empress flanked by a guard of angels. It sits above the altar in the Cappella Altemps.

❽ Santa Cecilia in Trastevere

Piazza di Santa Cecilia. **Map** 6 D1. **Tel** 06 589 92 89. 🚌 H, 23, 44, 280. **Open** 9:30am–1pm, 4–6:30pm daily. Cavallini fresco **Open** 10am–12:30pm Mon–Fri.

St. Cecilia, aristocrat and patron saint of music, was martyred here in AD 230. After an unsuccessful attempt to suffocate her by locking her in the hot steam bath of her house for three days, she was beheaded. A church was built, possibly in the 4th century, on the site of her house (still to be seen beneath the church, along with the remains of a tannery). Her body was lost, but it turned up again in the Catacombs of San Callisto *(see p446)*. In the 9th century it was reburied here by Pope Paschal I, who rebuilt the church.

A fine apse mosaic survives from this period. The altar canopy by Arnolfo di Cambio and the fresco of *The Last Judgment* by Pietro Cavallini can be reached through the adjoining convent; they date from the 13th century, one of the few periods when Rome had a distinctive artistic style.

In front of the altar is a delicate statue of St. Cecilia by Stefano Maderno, which is based on sketches made of her perfectly preserved relics when they were briefly disinterred in 1599.

❾ San Francesco a Ripa

Piazza San Francesco d'Assisi 88. **Map** 5 C2. **Tel** 06 581 90 20. 🚌 H, 23, 44, 75, 280. **Open** 7:30am–1pm, 2–7:30pm daily. ♿

St. Francis of Assisi lived here in a hospice when he visited Rome in 1219, and his stone pillow and crucifix are preserved in his cell. The church was built by a follower, a local nobleman called Rodolfo Anguillara, who is portrayed on his tombstone wearing the Franciscan habit.

Entirely rebuilt in the 1680s by Cardinal Pallavicini, the church is rich in 17th- and 18th-century sculptures. Not to be missed in the Altieri chapel (fourth left, along the nave) is Bernini's exquisite late work, the *Ecstasy of Beata Ludovica Albertoni* (1674).

Bramante's circular Tempietto at San Pietro in Montorio

❿ San Pietro in Montorio and the Tempietto

Piazza San Pietro in Montorio 2. **Map** 5 B1. **Tel** 06 581 39 40. 🚌 44, 75, 115. **Open** 8:30am–noon daily, 3–4pm Mon–Fri. Tempietto **Open** 9:30am–12:30pm, 2–4:30pm Tue–Sat.

The Tempietto, a diminutive masterpiece of Renaissance architecture completed by Bramante in 1502, stands in the courtyard of San Pietro in Montorio. The name means "little temple," and its circular shape echoes early Christian *martyria*, chapels built on the site of a saint's martyrdom. This was erroneously thought to be the spot in Nero's Circus where St. Peter was crucified. Bramante ringed the chapel with Doric columns, a Classical frieze, and a fine balustrade.

Bernini's *Ecstasy of Beata Ludovica Albertoni*, San Francesco a Ripa

AVENTINE AND LATERAN

This is one of the greenest parts of the city, taking in the Celian and Aventine Hills as well as the very congested area around San Giovanni in Laterano. The Celian, now scattered with churches, was a fashionable place to live in Imperial Rome. Some of the era's splendor is still apparent in the ruins of the Baths of Caracalla. Behind the Baths rises the Aventine Hill, a peaceful, leafy area, with the superb basilica of Santa Sabina, and lovely views across the river to Trastevere and St. Peter's. In the valley below, cars and Vespas skim around the Circus Maximus, following the ancient charioteering track, while to the south lies Testaccio, a lively working-class district.

Sights at a Glance

Churches

2 Santa Maria in Cosmedin
3 Santa Maria in Domnica
4 Santo Stefano Rotondo
5 Santi Quattro Coronati
6 *San Clemente see p439*
7 San Giovanni in Laterano
11 Santa Sabina

Ancient Sites and Building

1 Temples of the Forum Boarium
8 Baths of Caracalla

Monuments and Tombs

9 Pyramid of Caius Cestius
10 Protestant Cemetery

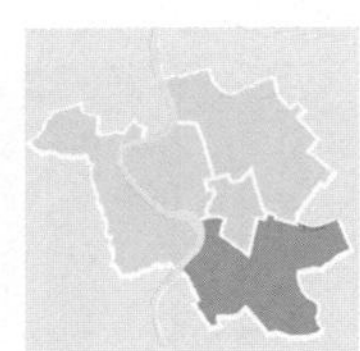

See Rome Street Finder maps 6, 7, 8

◀ One of the mosaics in the Baths of Caracalla

For keys to symbols *see back flap*

Street-by-Street: Piazza della Bocca della Verità

The site of Rome's first port and its busy cattle market, this is an odd little corner of the city, stretching from the heavily trafficked road running along the Tiber to the southern spur of the Capitoline Hill, a place of execution from ancient times until the Middle Ages. Although best known for the Bocca della Verità (Mouth of Truth) in Santa Maria in Cosmedin, which is supposed to snap shut on the hands of liars, there are many other sites in the area, notably two temples from the Republican era. In the 6th century the area became home to a Greek community that founded the churches of San Giorgio in Velabro and Santa Maria in Cosmedin.

The Casa dei Crescenzi, studded with ancient fragments, incorporates the ruins of a 10th-century tower built by the powerful Crescenzi family to guard the Tiber River.

Sant'Omobono stands on an archaeological site where finds date back to the 6th century.

1 ★ Temples of the Forum Boarium
These two buildings are the best preserved of Rome's Republican temples.

Ponte Rotto, as this forlorn ruined arch in the Tiber is called, simply means "broken bridge." Built in the 2nd century BC, its original name was the Pons Aemilius.

LUNGOTEVERE DEI PIERLEONI

VIA DI SAN GIOVANNI DECOLL...

TEVERE

PIAZZA DELLA BOCCA DELLA VERITÀ

PONTE PALATINO

The Fontana dei Tritoni, built by Carlo Bizzaccheri in 1715, shows the strong influence of Bernini.

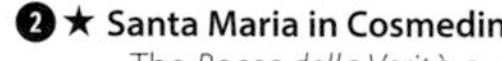

2 ★ Santa Maria in Cosmedin
The *Bocca della Verità*, a medieval drain cover, is set into the portico.

VIA DELLA

San Giovanni Decollat... belonged to a confraternity tha... encouraged condemne... prisoners to repen...

Key

 Suggested route

0 meters 75

0 yards 75

Santa Maria della Consolazione was named after an image of the Virgin placed here in 1385 to give consolation to the condemned.

Locator Map
See Rome Street Finder map 6

❶ Temples of the Forum Boarium

Piazza della Bocca della Verità. **Map** 6 E1. 🚌 23, 44, 81, 160, 170, 280, 628, 715, 716.

These wonderfully well-preserved Republican-era temples are at their best in moonlight, standing in their grassy enclave beside the Tiber, sheltered by umbrella pines. During the day, they look less romantic, stranded in a sea of traffic. They date from the 2nd century BC, and were saved from ruin by being consecrated as Christian churches in the Middle Ages by the Greek community then living in the area. The rectangular temple, formerly known as the Temple of Fortuna Virilis, was probably dedicated to Portunus, the god of rivers and ports. Set on a podium, it has four Ionic travertine columns fluted at the front and 12 half-columns embedded in the tufa wall of the *cella* – the room that housed the image of the god. In the 9th century the Temple was converted into the church of Santa Maria Egiziaca, after a 5th-century prostitute who reformed and became a hermit.

The smaller circular Temple, which is made of solid marble and surrounded by 20 fluted columns, was dedicated to Hercules, though it was long believed to be a Temple of Vesta because of its similarity to the one in the Forum.

San Teodoro is a circular church on the edge of the Palatine with exceptional 6th-century apse mosaics.

San Giorgio in Velabro, a 7th-century basilica, was damaged in an explosion in 1994, and has now been restored.

Arco degli Argentari

The 4th-century Arch of Janus, a four-faced marble-plated arch at the edge of the Forum Boarium market, was an ideal place for merchants and customers to do business in the shade.

The Ionic facade of the Republican era Temple of Portunus

Apse mosaic from the 9th century of the Virgin and Child in Santa Maria in Domnica

❷ Santa Maria in Cosmedin

Piazza della Bocca della Verità. **Map** 6 E1. **Tel** 06 678 77 59. 23, 44, 81, 160, 170, 280, 628, 715, 716. **Open** 9:30am–6pm daily (5pm in winter).

This beautiful church was built in the 6th century on the site of the ancient city's food market. The Romanesque bell tower and portico were added during the 12th century. In the 19th century a Baroque facade was removed and the church was restored to its original simplicity. It contains many fine examples of Cosmati work, in particular the mosaic sidewalk, the raised choir, the bishop's throne, and the canopy over the main altar.

Set into the wall of the portico is the Bocca della Verità (Mouth of Truth), a grotesque marble face, thought to have been an ancient drain cover. Medieval tradition had it that the jaws would snap shut on liars – a useful way of testing the faithfulness of spouses.

The nave of Santa Maria in Cosmedin with its Cosmati floor

❸ Santa Maria in Domnica

Piazza della Navicella 12. **Map** 7 A2. **Tel** 06 772 02 685. 81, 117, 673. M Colosseo. **Open** 9am–noon, 3:30–7pm daily (until 6pm in winter).

Santa Maria in Domnica was probably founded in the 7th century, and renovated in the 9th century. By this time the Romans had lost the art of making mosaics, so Pope Paschal I imported mosaicists from Byzantium. They created an exquisite apse mosaic showing the Virgin, Child, and angels in a delicate garden of paradise. Paschal I is kneeling at the Virgin's feet wear ing a square halo, indicating that he was alive when it was made.

In 1513 Andrea Sansovino added a portico decorated with lions' heads, a punning homage to Pope Leo X.

❹ Santo Stefano Rotondo

Via di Santo Stefano Rotondo 7. **Map** 7 B2. **Tel** 06 42 11 99. 81, 117, 673. **Open** 9:30am–12:30pm, 3–6pm (2–5pm in winter) Tue–Sun.

Santo Stefano Rotondo was built between 468 and 483 on a circular plan with four chapels in a cruciform shape. Its circular inner area is enclosed by two concentric corridors. A third, outer corridor was demolished on the orders of Leon Battista Alberti in 1453. In the 1500s Niccolò Pomarancio, Antonio Tempesta, and others covered the walls with 34 frescoes detailing the martyrdoms of saints.

Cloister of Santi Quattro Coronati

❺ Santi Quattro Coronati

Via dei Santi Quattro Coronati 20. **Map** 7 B1. **Tel** 06 70 47 54 27. 85, 117, 810. 3. **Open** 6:30am–12:45pm, 3–7:45pm daily. Cloister & Chapel of St. Sylvester **Open** 10–11:45am, 4–5:45pm daily.

This fortified convent was built in the 4th century to house the relics of four Persian stonemasons, martyred after they refused to make a statue of the pagan god Aesculapius. It was rebuilt after invading Normans set fire to it in 1084.

Highlights are a delightful garden cloister and the Chapel of St. Sylvester, where 12th-century frescoes recount the legend of Emperor Constantine's conversion to Christianity.

6 San Clemente

In 1857 Father Mullooly, the Irish Dominican prior of San Clemente, began excavations beneath the existing 12th-century basilica. Directly underneath, he and his successors discovered a 4th-century church, and below that a number of ancient Roman buildings. Both basilicas are dedicated to St. Clement, the fourth Pope. On the lowest level is a temple devoted to the cult of Mithras, a mystical all-male religion imported from Persia which rivaled Christianity for popularity.

VISITORS' CHECKLIST

Practical Information
Via di San Giovanni in Laterano.
Map 7 B1. **Tel** 06 774 00 21.
Open 9am–12:30pm, 3–6pm Mon–Sat (from noon Sun & public hols). Last adm: 20 mins before closing. excavations.

Transportation
85, 87, 117, 186, 810.
M Colosseo. 3.

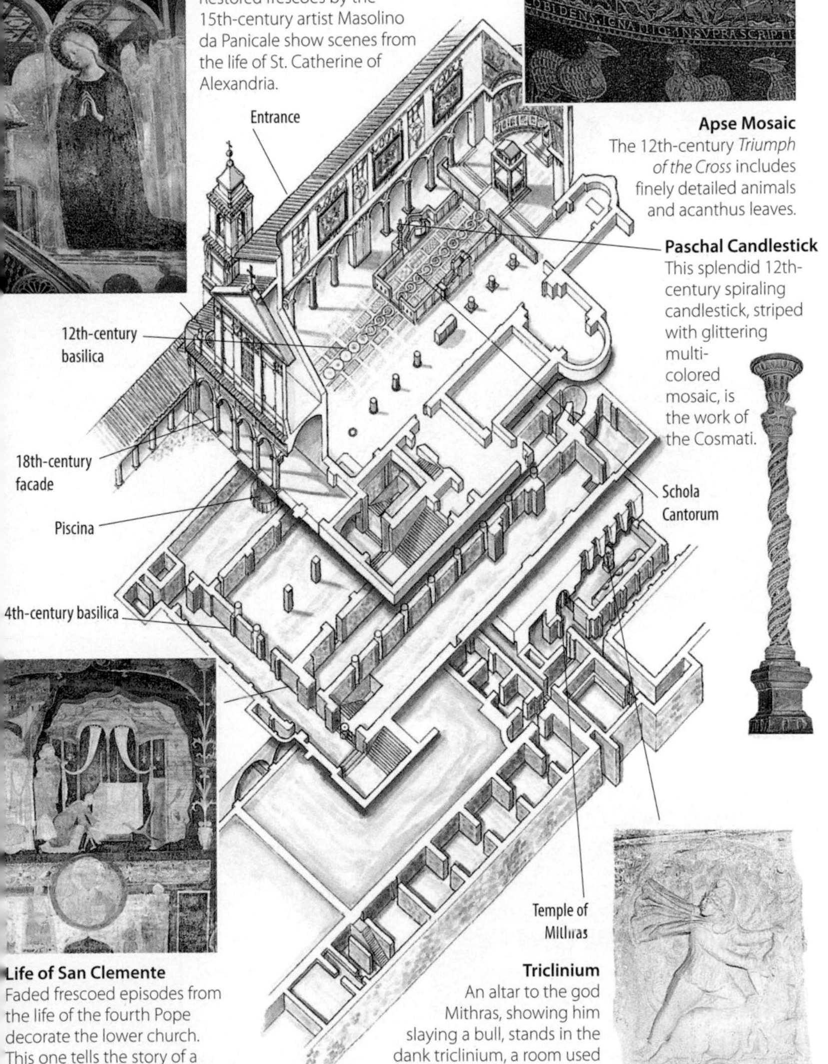

Cappella di Santa Caterina
Restored frescoes by the 15th-century artist Masolino da Panicale show scenes from the life of St. Catherine of Alexandria.

Apse Mosaic
The 12th-century *Triumph of the Cross* includes finely detailed animals and acanthus leaves.

Paschal Candlestick
This splendid 12th-century spiraling candlestick, striped with glittering multi-colored mosaic, is the work of the Cosmati.

Life of San Clemente
Faded frescoed episodes from the life of the fourth Pope decorate the lower church. This one tells the story of a boy found alive in his tomb under the sea.

Triclinium
An altar to the god Mithras, showing him slaying a bull, stands in the dank triclinium, a room used for ritual banquets by cult members.

❼ San Giovanni in Laterano

San Giovanni, the cathedral of Rome, was founded by Emperor Constantine in the early 4th century. It has been rebuilt several times, notably in 1646 when Borromini restyled the interior, but retains its original basilica form. Before the papacy moved to Avignon in 1309, the adjoining Lateran Palace was the official papal residence. The present structure dates from 1589, but older parts survive, like the Scala Santa (Holy Staircase), which Christ is said to have climbed at his trial.

VISITORS' CHECKLIST

Practical Information
Piazza di San Giovanni in Laterano. **Map** 8 D2. **Tel** 06 69 88 64 93. Cathedral: **Open** 7am–6:30pm daily. Cloisters: **Open** 9am–6pm daily. Museum: **Open** 10am–5:30pm daily. Baptistry: **Open** 7am–12:30pm, 4–6:30pm daily.

Transportation
16, 81, 85, 87, 650. 3. M San Giovanni.

Baptistry
Though much restored, the octagonal baptistry contains some beautiful 5th-century mosaics.

North facade

East Facade
The main entrance, on the east facade (1735), is adorned with statues of Christ and the Apostles.

Museum entrance

Apse

Lateran Palace

Papal Altar
The Gothic baldacchino, which rises over the papal altar, is decorated with 14th-century frescoes.

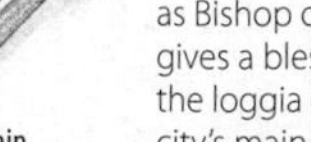

On Maundy Thursday the
as Bishop of Rc
gives a blessin
the loggia of th
city's main cath

Main entrance

The Corsini Chapel was built in the 1730s for Pope Clement XII Corsini, who lies buried in a porphyry tomb from the Pantheon.

Cloisters
Built by the Vassalletto family in about 1220, the cloisters are remarkable for their twisted columns and inlaid marble mosaics.

Boniface VIII Fresco
Possibly by Giotto, this fragment shows the Pope announcing the Holy Year of 1300, which attracted around two million pilgrims.

Part of one of the gymnasia in the Baths of Caracalla

❽ Baths of Caracalla

Viale delle Terme di Caracalla 52. **Map** 7 A3. **Tel** 06 39 96 77 00. 160, 628. 3. **Open** 9am–1 hr before sunset Tue–Sun, 9am–2pm Mon. **Closed** Jan 1, Dec 25.

Rearing up at the foot of the Aventine Hill are the monolithic red-brick ruins of the Baths of Caracalla. Begun by Emperor Septimius Severus in AD 206, and completed by his son Caracalla in AD 217, they remained in use until the 6th century, when the Goths sabotaged the city's aqueducts.

Going for a bath was one of the social events of the day in ancient Rome. Large complexes such as Caracalla, with a capacity for 1,600 bathers, were not simply places to have a chat and get washed, but also areas which offered an impressive array of facilities: art galleries, gymnasia, gardens, libraries, conference rooms, lecture rooms, and shops selling food and drink.

A Roman bath was a long and complicated business, beginning with a form of Turkish bath, followed by a spell in the *caldarium*, a large hot room with pools of water to moisten the atmosphere. Then came the lukewarm *tepidarium*, followed by a visit to the large central meeting place known as the *frigidarium*, and finally a plunge into the *natatio*, an outdoor swimming pool. For the rich, this was followed by a rubdown with scented woolen cloth.

Most of the rich marble decorations of the baths were scavenged by the Farnese family in the 16th century to adorn the rooms of Palazzo Farnese *(see p405)*. There are, however, statues and mosaics from the Baths in the Museo Nazionale Archeologico in Naples *(see pp494–5)* and in the Vatican's Gregorian Profane Museum *(see p426)*.

So dramatic is the setting that it is the regular venue for the outdoor opera season in summer.

❾ Pyramid of Caius Cestius

Piazzale Ostiense. **Map** 6 E4. 23, 280. 3. Ⓜ Piramide. only.

Caius Cestius was a wealthy but unimportant 1st-century BC *praetor*, or senior magistrate. At the time, inspired by the Cleopatra scandals, there was a craze for all things Egyptian, and Caius decided to commission himself a pyramid as a tomb. Set into the Aurelian Wall near Porta San Paolo, it is built of brick and faced with white marble; according to an inscription, it took just 330 days to build in 12 BC.

The Pyramid of Caius Cestius on Piazzale Ostiense

❿ Protestant Cemetery

Cimitero Acattolico, Via di Caio Cestio. **Map** 6 D4. **Tel** 06 574 19 00. 23, 280. 3. **Open** 9am–5pm Mon–Sat, 9am–1pm Sun. Last adm: 30 mins before closing. Donation.

Non-Catholics have been buried in this cemetery behind the Aurelian Wall since 1738. In the oldest part (on the left as you enter) is the grave of the poet John Keats, who died in 1821 in a house on Piazza di Spagna *(see p412)*. He wrote his own epitaph: "Here lies one whose name was writ in water." Close by rest the ashes of Percy Bysshe Shelley, who drowned in 1822.

The interior of Santa Sabina

⓫ Santa Sabina

Piazza Pietro d'Illiria 1. **Map** 6 D2. **Tel** 06 57 94 01. 23, 44, 170, 781. **Open** 8:15am–12:30pm, 3:30–6pm daily.

High on the Aventine stands an early Christian basilica, founded by Peter of Illyria in AD 425 and later given to the Dominican order. It was restored to its original simplicity in the early 20th century. Light filters through 9th-century windows onto a nave framed by pale Corinthian columns. Above the main door is a blue and gold 5th-century mosaic inscription to Peter. In the side portico outside is a 5th-century paneled door carved with biblical scenes, notably one of the oldest images of the Crucifixion (top left-hand corner).

Farther Afield

It is well worth making the effort to see some of Rome's outlying sights. Highlights are the Villa Giulia, home to a magnificent Etruscan museum, and the Museo Borghese on the splendid Villa Borghese estate, with its extraordinary collection of virtuoso statues by Bernini. Other sights range from ancient churches and catacombs to the more modern suburb of EUR, a strange architectural medley begun by Mussolini in the 1930s.

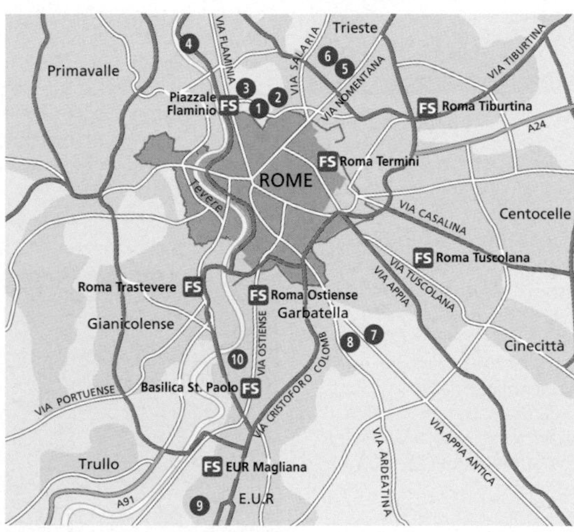

Sights at a Glance

Churches and Temples

5 Sant'Agnese fuori le Mura
6 Santa Costanza
10 San Paolo fuori le Mura

Museums and Galleries

2 Museo e Galleria Borghese
3 Villa Giulia
4 MAXXI

Parks and Gardens

1 Villa Borghese

Ancient Roads and Sites

7 Via Appia Antica
8 Catacombs

City Districts

9 EUR

Key

Central Rome
Suburbs
Freeway
Major road
Minor road
City walls

0 kilometers 3
0 miles 3

1 Villa Borghese

Map 3 B1. 52, 53, 88, 116, 490. 3, 19. Park **Open** dawn–sunset daily.

The villa and its park were designed in 1605 for Cardinal Scipione Borghese, the sybaritic nephew of Pope Paul V. An extravagant patron of the arts, he amassed one of Europe's finest collections of paintings, statues, and antiquities, many of which are still displayed in the villa that he built especially to house his antique sculptures.

The **park** was one of the first of its kind in Rome, its formal gardens divided by avenues and graced with statues. It contained 400 newly planted trees, garden sculpture by Bernini's father, Pietro, along with many ingenious fountains, "secret" flower gardens, enclosures of exotic animals and birds, and even a grotto with artificial rain. There was also a speaking robot and a trick chair, which trapped anyone who sat in it. At first the grounds were open to the public, but after a visitor was shocked by the collection of erotic paintings, Paul V decided to keep the park private.

In 1773, work began on redesigning the park in the wilder, Romantic style made fashionable by landscape artists like Claude Lorrain and Poussin. Over the next few years, mock-Classical temples, fountains, and *casine* (summer houses) were added. In 1901, the park and villa were acquired by the state, and in 1911 the area was chosen as the site for the International Exhibition. Pavilions were built by many of the world's nations, the most impressive of which is the **British School at Rome** by Edwin Lutyens. In the northeastern corner of the park lie the Museo Zoologico and a small redeveloped zoo, known as the Bioparco, where the emphasis is on conservation. Today the estates of the Villa Borghese, Villa Giulia, and the Pincio gardens form one vast park, with the **Giardino del Lago**, at its center, named after an artificial boating lake. Its main entrance is marked by an 18th-century copy of the Arch of Septimius Severus, while on the lake's island is a fake Ionic temple to the Greek god of health, Aesculapius, designed by the 18th-century architect Antonis Aspurucci.

Temple of Aesculapius, an 18th-century folly, at the Villa Borghese

For hotels and restaurants in this region see pp562–77 and pp580–605

A circular Temple of Diana folly lies between the Porta Pinciana, at the top of Via Veneto, and Piazza di Siena, a grassy amphitheater that hosts Rome's international horse show in May. Its umbrella pines inspired the composer Ottorino Respighi to write *The Pines of Rome* (1924). The open-air opera season is also held in the park.

To the northwest of the park is the Galleria Nazionale d'Arte Moderna, and the Orangery is now home to the Carlo Bilotti museum.

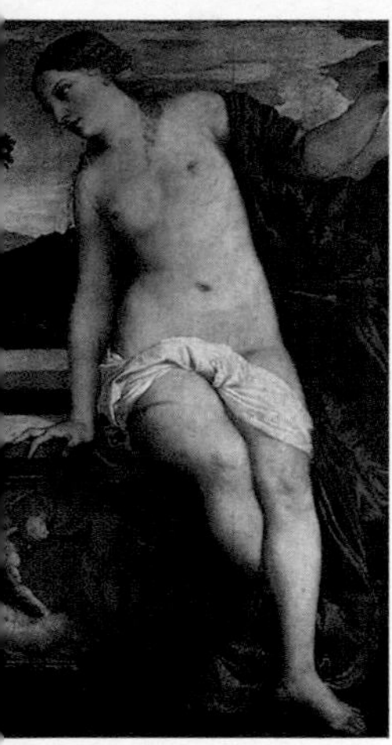

Sacred and Profane Love by Titian (1514), in the Galleria Borghese

❷ Museo e Galleria Borghese

Villa Borghese, Piazzale Scipione Borghese 5. **Tel** 06 328 10. 52, 53, 116, 910. 3, 19. **Open** 8:30am–7pm Tue–Sun (reservations advised; essential on weekends). **Closed** Jan 1, Dec 25.
galleriaborghese.it

Cardinal Scipione Borghese's villa was designed in 1605 as a typical Roman country house, with its wings projecting into the surrounding gardens. It was built by Flaminio Ponzio, Pope Paul V's architect, and was used by Scipione for entertaining guests and for displaying his impressive collection of paintings and sculpture. Between 1801 and 1809, Prince Camillo Borghese, husband to Napoleon's sister Pauline, unfortunately sold many of the family paintings to his brother-in-law, and swapped 200 of Scipione's Classical statues for an estate in Piedmont. These statues are still in the Louvre and, as a consequence, the remaining antique Classical collection is less interesting than it might once have been. However, the hedonistic cardinal was an enthusiastic patron of the arts and the sculptures he commissioned from artists such as the young Bernini now rank among their most famous works.

The eight rooms of the ground floor of the Villa Borghese are set around a central hall, the Salone. The most famous statue is one of Bernini's finest works, *Apollo and Daphne* (1624) in room 3, which shows the nymph Daphne with bay leaves sprouting from her outstretched fingers, roots growing from her toes and rough bark enfolding her smooth body, as she begins to metamorphose into a laurel tree to escape being abducted by the god Apollo. Abduction is also the theme of *The Rape of Proserpina,* again by Bernini, in room 4. Depicting Pluto, the god of the underworld, carrying Proserpina, daughter of Ceres, off to be his bride, the sculpture is a virtuoso piece in which Bernini contrasts the taut musculature of Pluto with the soft yielding flesh of Proserpina, whose thigh dimples in his iron grip.

The third famous Bernini piece, which dates from 1623, is *David* in room 2. The artist captures the tensed, grimacing youth the moment before he releases the stone that slew Goliath. It is said that Pope Urban VIII held a mirror up to Bernini so that the sculptor could model David's face on his own. In the next alcove is the Villa Borghese's most infamous work – a sculpture, executed in 1805 by Canova, of Pauline Borghese as *Venus Victrix* (Venus the Conqueror). The semi-naked Pauline reclining on a chaise longue shocked those who saw it, and Pauline's husband kept the statue locked away, even denying Canova access to it. The next room holds a selection of antiquities, notably a Roman copy of a plump *Bacchus* by the 4th-century BC Greek sculptor Praxiteles, and fragments of a 3rd-century AD mosaic found on one of the Borghese estates in Torrenova, showing gladiators battling with wild animals.

Bernini's *Apollo and Daphne* (1624)

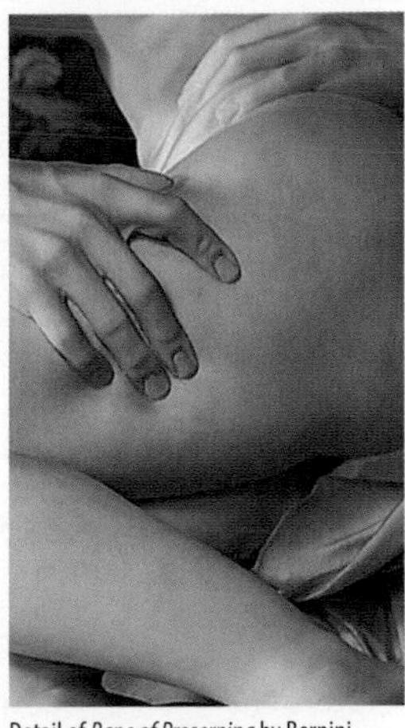

Detail of *Rape of Proserpina* by Bernini (1622), Museo Borghese

The Galleria Borghese, on the upper floor, houses some magnificent Baroque and Renaissance paintings. Works on display here include Raphael's masterpiece, the *Deposition,* various works by Caravaggio, the graceful *Danäe* by the 16th-century artist Correggio, and works by Pinturicchio, Barocci, Rubens, and Titian.

❸ Villa Giulia

This villa was built in 1550 as a country retreat for Pope Julius III. Designed by Vignola and Ammannati, with contributions by Michelangelo and Vasari, it was intended for entertaining guests of the Vatican, such as Queen Christina of Sweden, rather than as a permanent home. The gardens were planted with 36,000 trees and peppered with pavilions and fountains. Villa Giulia also used to house an outstanding collection of sculptures: 160 boats filled with statues and ornaments were sent to the Vatican after the death of Pope Julius III in 1555.

Since 1889 the villa has been home to the Museo Nazionale Etrusco, an impressive collection of pre-Roman antiquities from central Italy.

VISITORS' CHECKLIST

Practical Information
Piazzale di Villa Giulia 9.
Tel 06 322 65 71.
Open 8:30am–7:30pm Tue–Sun (last adm: 6:30pm).
Closed Jan 1, Dec 25. with seven days' notice.

Transportation
52. 3, 19.

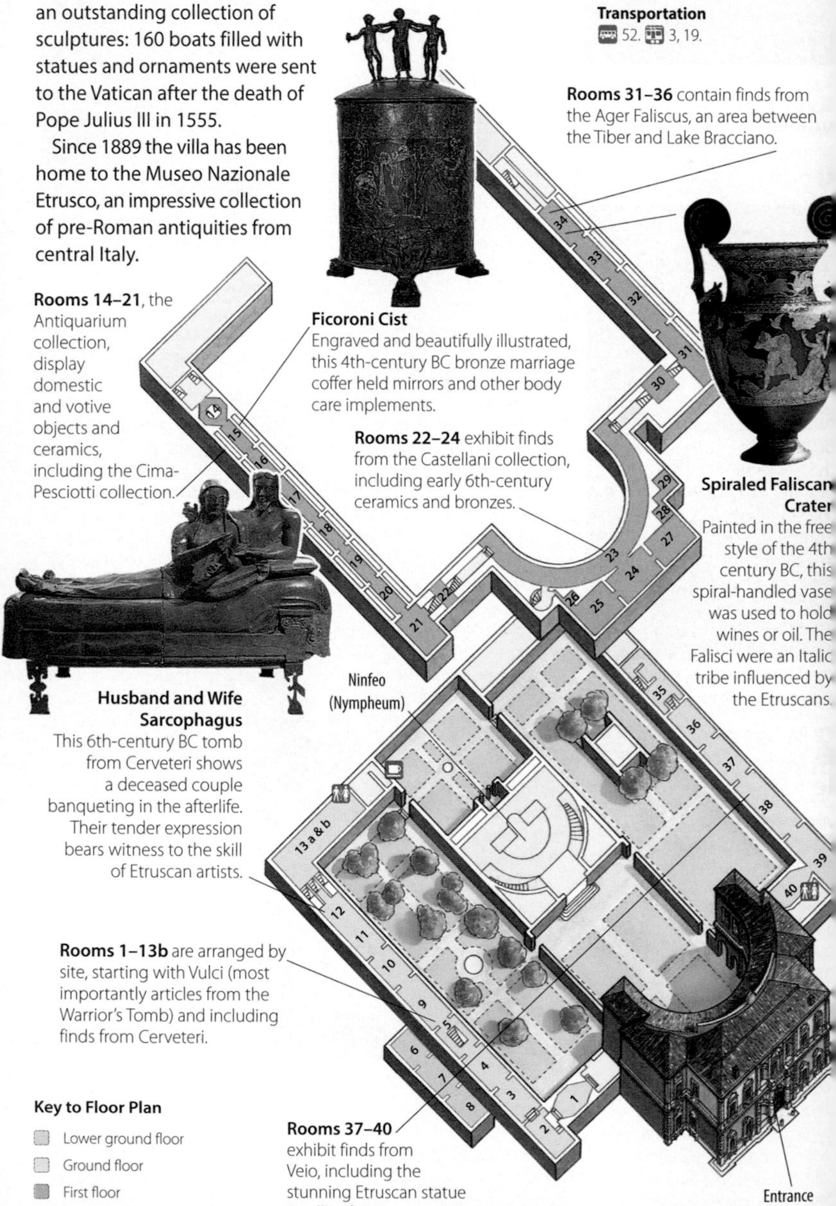

Rooms 31–36 contain finds from the Ager Faliscus, an area between the Tiber and Lake Bracciano.

Rooms 14–21, the Antiquarium collection, display domestic and votive objects and ceramics, including the Cima-Pesciotti collection.

Ficoroni Cist
Engraved and beautifully illustrated, this 4th-century BC bronze marriage coffer held mirrors and other body care implements.

Rooms 22–24 exhibit finds from the Castellani collection, including early 6th-century ceramics and bronzes.

Spiraled Faliscan Crater
Painted in the free style of the 4th century BC, this spiral-handled vase was used to hold wines or oil. The Falisci were an Italic tribe influenced by the Etruscans.

Husband and Wife Sarcophagus
This 6th-century BC tomb from Cerveteri shows a deceased couple banqueting in the afterlife. Their tender expression bears witness to the skill of Etruscan artists.

Ninfeo (Nympheum)

Rooms 1–13b are arranged by site, starting with Vulci (most importantly articles from the Warrior's Tomb) and including finds from Cerveteri.

Rooms 37–40 exhibit finds from Veio, including the stunning Etruscan statue Apollo of Veii.

Entrance

Key to Floor Plan
- Lower ground floor
- Ground floor
- First floor
- Nonexhibition space

MAXXI, the National Museum of 21st Century Arts, designed by Zaha Hadid

4 MAXXI (National Museum of 21st Century Arts)

Villa Guido Reni 4A. **Tel** 06 399 673 50. 53, 217, 910. 2. **Open** 11am–7pm Tue–Sun (11am–10pm Sat). **Closed** May 1, Dec 25. (free up to age 14). **W fondazionemaxxi.it**

Along with the nearby Parco della Musica *(see p449)*, MAXXI, the National Museum of 21st Century Arts, has put Rome on the contemporary arts map. Completed in 2009, it is located in a stunning building designed by architect Zaha Hadid. The museum showcases emerging Italian and international artists. An impressive amount of space is also given over to architecture.

5 Sant'Agnese fuori le Mura

Via Nomentana 349. **Tel** 06 862 054 56. 60, 82, 90. **Open** 7:30am–noon, 4–7:30pm daily. **Closed** late Oct–late Nov. to catacombs.

Sant'Agnese fuori le Mura was built in the 4th century above the crypt of the 13-year-old martyr St. Agnes, and although much altered, it retains the form of the original basilica. According to legend it was founded by Constantine's daughter Constantia, who was cured from leprosy after sleeping beside Agnes's tomb.

In the 7th-century apse mosaic, St. Agnes appears as a bejeweled Byzantine empress in a stole of gold and a violet robe. Tradition has it that she appeared like this eight days after her death, holding a white lamb. On January 21, two lambs are blessed in the church and a vestment called a *pallium* is woven from their wool, to be given to a new archbishop.

Apse mosaic in Sant'Agnese, showing the saint flanked by popes

6 Santa Costanza

Via Nomentana 349. **Tel** 06 862 054 56. 60, 82, 90. **Open** 9am–noon, 4–6pm daily (Sun pm only). **Closed** late Oct–late Nov.

This circular church was built in the early 4th century as a mausoleum for Emperor Constantine's daughters, Constantia and Helena. The dome and its drum are supported by an arcade that rests on 12 magnificent pairs of granite columns. The encircling ambulatory has a barrel-vaulted ceiling decorated with the world's earliest surviving Christian mosaics, which date from the 4th century.

In a niche on the far side of the church is a replica of Constantia's ornate porphyry sarcophagus, carved with cherubs crushing grapes. The original was moved to the Vatican Museums in 1790.

The sanctity of Constantia is somewhat debatable. Described by the historian Marcellinus as a fury incarnate, constantly goading her equally unpleasant husband, Hannibalianus, to violence, her canonization was probably the result of some confusion with a saintly nun of the same name.

7 Via Appia Antica

118, 218.

The first part of the Via Appia was built in 312 BC by Appius Claudius Caecus. In 190 BC, when it was extended to the ports of Taranto and Brindisi, the road became Rome's link with its empire in the East. It was the route taken by the funeral processions of the dictator Sulla (78 BC) and Emperor Augustus (AD 14), and it was along this road that St. Paul was led as a prisoner to Rome in AD 56. The church of Domine Quo Vadis? marks the spot where St. Peter is said to have met Christ when fleeing Rome. The road is lined with ruined family tombs, decaying monuments, and collective burial places *(columbaria)*. Beneath the fields on either side lies a maze of catacombs, including those of San Callisto and San Sebastiano.

Cypresses lining the Roman road, Via Appia

8 Catacombs

Via Appia Antica 126. 118, 218. San Callisto **Tel** 06 513 01 580. **Open** 9am–noon, 2–5pm Thu–Tue. **Closed** Jan 1, late Jan–late Feb, Easter Sun, Dec 25.

In burying their dead in underground cemeteries outside the city walls, the early Christians were simply obeying the laws of the time. They were not forced to use them because of persecution, as later popular myth has suggested. Many saints were buried here, and the catacombs later became shrines and places of pilgrimage.

Today several catacombs are open to the public. The vast Catacombs of San Callisto, hewn from volcanic tufa, contain niches, or *loculi*, which held two or three bodies, as well as the burial places of several early popes. Close by, walls in the Catacombs of San Sebastiano are covered in graffiti invoking St. Peter and St. Paul, whose remains may once have been moved here.

Engraving of Christian ceremony in Catacombs of San Callisto (AD 50)

9 EUR

170, 671, 714. M EUR Fermi, EUR Palasport. Museo della Civiltà Romana Piazza G. Agnelli 10. **Tel** 06 06 08. **Open** 9am–2pm Tue–Sun. Last adm 1 hr before closing. **Closed** Jan 1, May 1, Dec 25.

The Esposizione Universale di Roma (EUR), a suburb to the south of the city, was originally built for an international exhibition, a kind of "Work Olympics," that was planned

EUR's Palazzo della Civiltà del Lavoro, the "Square Colosseum"

for 1942, but never took place because of the outbreak of war. The architecture was intended to glorify Fascism, and as a result the bombastic style of the buildings can look overblown and rhetorical to modern eyes. Of all the buildings the best known is probably the Palazzo della Civiltà del Lavoro (the Palace of the Civilization of Work), an unmistakable landmark for people arriving from Fiumicino airport.

The scheme was eventually completed in the 1950s. Despite the area's dubious architecture, EUR has been a planning success, and people are still keen to live here. As well as residential housing, the vast marble halls along the wide boulevards are also home to a number of government offices and museums. Best among the latter is the Museo della Civiltà Romana, famous for its casts of the reliefs from the Column of Trajan, and for a large-scale model depicting 4th-century Rome with all the buildings which then stood within the Aurelian walls. The south of the suburb features a lake and shady park, and the huge domed Palazzo dello Sport, built for the 1960 Olympics.

10 San Paolo fuori le Mura

Via Ostiense 186. 23, 128, 170, 670, 761, 766, 769. M San Paolo. **Tel** 06 698 80 800. **Open** 7am–6:30pm daily. Cloister **Open** 9am–6pm daily.

Today's church is a faithful if soulless reconstruction of the great 4th-century basilica destroyed by fire in 1823. Only a few fragments of the earlier church survived, most notably the cloister (1241), with its pairs of colorful inlaid columns, considered one of the most beautiful in Rome.

Elsewhere, the church's triumphal arch is decorated on one side with heavily restored 5th-century mosaics, and on the other with mosaics by Pietro Cavallini originally on the facade. The equally fine mosaics (1220) in the apse represent the figures of Christ with St. Peter, St. Andrew, St. Paul, and St. Luke.

The single most outstanding work of art is the fine marble canopy over the high altar, the work of Arnolfo di Cambio (1285), with the possible assistance of Pietro Cavallini. Below the altar is the *confessio* where it is alleged St. Paul was once buried. To its right is an impressive Paschal candlestick dating from the 12th century by Nicolò di Angelo and Pietro Vassalletto.

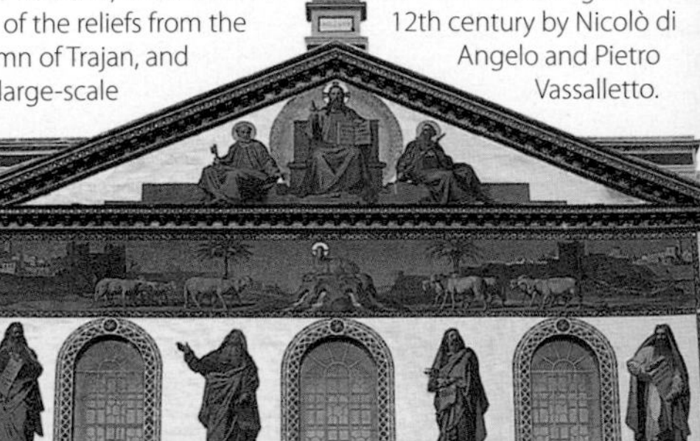

19th-century mosaic on facade of San Paolo fuori le Mura

Shopping in Rome

Rome has always been a thriving center for design and shopping. In ancient times, the finest craftsmen were drawn to the city, and artifacts and products of all kinds, including gold, furs, and wine, were imported from far-flung corners of the Empire to satisfy the needs of the wealthy local population. Shopping in Rome today in many ways reflects this diverse tradition. Italian designers have a well-deserved reputation for their luxuriously chic style in fashion, knitwear, and leather goods (especially shoes and handbags), as well as in interior design, fabrics, ceramics, and glass. The artisan tradition is strong, and the love of good design filters through into the smallest items. Rome is not a city for bargains (although it is often better value than Florence or Milan), but the joys of window shopping here will offer plenty of compensation.

Fashion

Italy is one of the leading lights in high fashion, or *alta moda*. Many famous designers may be based in Milan, but Rome is home to a cluster of sophisticated and internationally distinguished fashion houses. The most notable among them are probably **Fendi**, **Laura Biagiotti**, **Prada**, and **Valentino**, whose studio dominates Piazza Mignanelli.

But even for those unable to splash out on genuine designer gear, much fun can be gained from a stroll down the streets that radiate out from the Piazza di Spagna: some of the window displays here are truly spectacular.

Rome is not a good place to buy everyday wear, since there is a distinct lack of mid-price shops bridging the gap between the dazzlingly priced *alta moda* designer exclusives and the ultracheap goods sold in markets. However, at **Discount dell'Alta Moda** you can find end-of-season designer labels at 50 percent less than the boutique prices.

Books and Gifts

Rome offers huge scope for gift buying, both in the well-established tourist stores in the historic center and in smaller shops located in less frequented parts of the city that might not feature in your planned itinerary.

The central Via del Pellegrino is a street crammed with small specialist outlets, such as **Le Tre Ghinee**, which sells ceramics and glass objects. If you are more interested in contemporary design, visit the **Palazzo delle Esposizioni**, where a wide range of objects by famous designers is available.

The **Feltrinelli International** bookstore has an excellent range of foreign-language fiction, as well as nonfiction covering various subjects, including Italian art and architecture, cooking, travel, and history. It also stocks some superb photographic, art, and film posters. For cut-price deals on books try the secondhand stalls in Via delle Terme di Diocleziano and in Largo della Fontanella di Borghese.

Near the Pantheon, the Florentine **Il Papiro** sells a great range of illustrious paper-based products, including diaries, notebooks, envelopes, and beautiful seal-and-wax sets that make ideal gifts.

Religious artifacts are readily available in bookstores near the main basilicas, such as the **Libreria Belardetti** near St. Peter's. Other shops specialize in religious items for both the clergy and the layperson. Facing the Vatican gates, in Via di Porta Angelica, there are several shops, including **Al Pellegrino Cattolico**, that sell mementos to visiting pilgrims.

Food and Drink

If you are tempted to take home some irresistible Italian delicacies, such as pecorino romano cheese, Parma ham, extra virgin olive oil, dried porcini mushrooms, sun-dried tomatoes, olives, and grappa, as well as superb wines from Lazio and elsewhere, then the traditional food stores, *alimentari*, are a great place to start. Try the well-stocked **Fratelli Fabbi**, near Piazza di Spagna, with its exceptional selection of delicious cold meats and cheeses from every corner of Italy, as well as quality wines and champagnes. A few doors down on the same street is **Focacci**, with its wonderful array of Italian delicacies. The historic but expensive **Volpetti** in Testaccio is synonymous with great service and uncompromising quality. Aside from specializing in unusual cheeses, olive oils, vinegars, and a fabulous selection of food baskets, Volpetti also stocks a variety of Italian lard and caviar – you can even try before you buy.

In Pinciano, **Casa dei Latticini Micocci** sells a comprehensive range of cheeses from even the most remote regions of Italy, while in Trastevere, the family-run **Antica Caciara Trasteverina** has a vast assortment of local and regional dairy products, which include sheep's ricotta and the Piedmontese *toma del fen*. More local, reasonably priced cheeses are available at **Cisternino**.

If cakes and chocolate feature on your list, then there is plenty of opportunity to satisfy those cravings too. **Chocolat**, in the historic center, sells brand-name and homemade chocolate and organizes occasional tastings and dinners for connoisseurs, while **Moriondo e Gariglio** specializes in chocolate delights made to traditional Piedmontese recipes. **La Delizlosa**, near Piazza Navona, offers a great range of Italian desserts and cakes; the ricotta-based variety deserves a special mention.

Bear in mind that customs restrictions can apply to certain foodstuffs.

Markets

Rome's outdoor markets are quintessential examples of the bubbling exuberance and earthiness for which Romans are renowned. They are wonderfully vivid experiences, too, since Italian stallholders have raised the display of even the humblest vegetable to an art form.

The city is dotted with small local food markets, and there are several fascinating well-established markets near the center. These include **Campo de' Fiori** for foodstuffs, the **Mercato delle Stampe** for old prints, books, and magazines, and the **Nuovo Mercato Esquilino** for international foods.

Trastevere's famous flea market, **Porta Portese**, was established shortly after the end of World War II and is said to have grown out of the thriving black market that operated at Tor di Nona, opposite Castel Sant'Angelo, during those lean years. Anything and everything seems to be for sale, piled high on stalls in carefully arranged disorder – clothes, shoes, bags, linen, luggage, camping equipment, towels, pots, pans, kitchen utensils, plants, pets, cassettes and CDs, old LPs, and 78s.

If you are looking for a traditional food market in the heart of the old city, Rome's most picturesque market is also its most historical. Its name, Campo de' Fiori *(see p405)*, which translates as "field of flowers," sometimes misleads people into expecting a flower market. In fact, the name is said to derive from *Campus Florae* (Flora's square) – Flora being the lover of the great Roman general Pompey. A market has been held in this beautiful central piazza for many centuries. Every morning, except Sunday, the piazza is transformed by an array of stalls selling fruit and vegetables, meat, poultry, and fish. One or two stalls also specialize in legumes, rice, and dried fruits and nuts.

Throughout the year Rome also plays host to many street fairs. If they coincide with your visit, these are fun to go to, because they normally sell a good variety of local produce, handicrafts, and clothes. Seasonal fairs also occur, especially around Christmas; among them is **Mercatino di Natale** in Piazza Navona, where you can stock up on toys and Nativity figurines.

Be sure to keep your wits about you at markets: pick-pockets work with lightning speed in the bustling crowds.

DIRECTORY

Fashion

Discount dell'Alta Moda
Via di Gesù e Maria 14 & 16A. **Map** 2 F2.
Tel 06 322 37 96.

Fendi
Largo Goldoni 419.
Map 10 E3.
Tel 06 33 45 01.

Laura Biagiotti
Via Mario de' Fiori 26.
Map 10 F1.
Tel 06 679 12 05.

Prada
Via Condotti 92–95.
Map 3 A2.
Tel 06 679 08 97.

Valentino
Via Condotti 15.
Map 3 A2.
Tel 06 673 94 20.

Books and Gifts

Al Pellegrino Cattolico
Via di Porta Angelica 83.
Map 1 C2.
Tel 06 68 80 23 51.

Feltrinelli International
Via VE Orlando 84–86.
Map 3 C3.
Tel 06 487 01 71.

Libreria Belardetti
Via della Conciliazione 4A.
Map 1 C3.
Tel 06 686 55 02.

Palazzo delle Esposizioni
Via Milano 15–17.
Map 3 B4.
Tel 06 48 91 33 61.

Il Papiro
Via del Pantheon 50 (leading to Via degli Orfani).
Map 10 D2.
Tel 06 679 55 97.

Le Tre Ghinee
Via del Pellegrino 90.
Map 2 E4.
Tel 06 687 27 39.

Food and Drink

Antica Caciara Trasteverina
Via San Francesco a Ripa 140A/B.
Map 5 C1.
Tel 06 581 28 15.

Casa dei Latticini Micocci
Via Collina 14. **Map** 4 D2.
Tel 06 474 17 84.

Chocolat
Via del Teatro Valle 54.
Map 10 D3.
Tel 06 68 13 55 45.

Cisternino
Vicolo del Gallo 18–19.
Map 9 C4.
Tel 06 687 28 75.

La Deliziosa
Vicolo Savelli 50.
Map 9 B3.
Tel 06 68 80 31 55.

Focacci
Via della Croce 43.
Map 2 F2.
Tel 06 679 12 28.

Fratelli Fabbi
Via della Croce 28.
Map 2 F2.
Tel 06 679 06 12.

Moriondo e Gariglio
Via del Piè di Marmo 21.
Map 10 E3.
Tel 06 699 08 56.

Volpetti
Via Marmorata 47.
Map 6 D2.
Tel 06 574 23 52.

Markets

Campo de' Fiori
Piazza Campo de' Fiori.
Map 2 E4 & 9 C4.
Open 7am–1:30pm Mon–Sat.

Mercatino di Natale
Piazza Navona.
Map 9 C4.
Open end Nov–early Jan: daily.

Mercato delle Stampe
Largo della Fontanella di Borghese.
Map 2 F3 & 10 D1.
Open 9am–1pm Mon–Sat.

Nuovo Mercato Esquilino
Via Principe Amedeo.
Map 4 E4.
Open 9am–2pm Mon–Fri.

Porta Portese
Via Portuense & Via Ippolito Nievo.
Map 5 C3.
Open 6:30am–2pm Sun.

Entertainment in Rome

There's a particular excitement attached to entertainment in Rome. Soccer and opera, for example, are worth experiencing for sheer atmosphere alone, whether or not you are a fan. There is also a good jazz scene, with international stars appearing alongside local talent. Unexpectedly, given the general shutdown among shops and restaurants, the summer is Rome's liveliest time in terms of entertainment and cultural events, with the city's Renaissance squares, vast parks, villa gardens, Classical ruins, and other open spaces hosting various arts festivals. Concerts and films take on an added dimension when performances take place beneath the stars in the many outdoor arenas across the city. Rome also has plenty of nightclubs to choose from.

Practical Information

Good sources of information about what's happening are the listings magazine *WHERE Rome* and *Trovaroma*, the weekly Thursday supplement to *La Repubblica* newspaper. Also worth getting hold of is *L'Evento*, available from the Rome Tourist Office *(see p617)*, which gives details in English for cultural events in the city.

Buying Tickets

Among the ticket agencies that will book seats for some performances for you (for a small fee) are **Orbis** and **Box Office**. Many theaters do not accept telephone reservations – you have to visit the box office in person. They will charge you a *prevendita* supplement (about 10 percent of the normal price) for any tickets sold in advance. The **Teatro dell'Opera** box office handles sales for both summer and winter seasons. Tickets for most big rock and jazz events can be bought at Orbis and at larger record stores, such as **Ricordi Media Store**. Look out for *due per uno* coupons in local bars – these allow two people entrance for the price of one.

Outdoor Entertainment

Outdoor opera, movies, classical music, and jazz concerts fill the Roman calendar from late June until the end of September. Both the **Cineporto**, a festival held along the Tiber, at the Ponte Milvio, and the **Festival di Massenzio**, at the Forum, offer films, live music, food, and small exhibitions in July and August. The summer months also bring excellent outdoor rock, jazz, and world-music festivals, while Rome's main autumn performing-arts festival, **RomaEuropa**, has occasional performances on the grounds of the Villa Medici. Theater also moves outside in the summer months, and some movie theaters roll back their ceilings for open-air screenings.

More traditional is Trastevere's community festival, the **Festa de Noantri** *(see p71)*, with music, processions, and fireworks. This religious festival begins on the Saturday after July 16, and celebrations continue until the end of the month.

Classical Music and Dance

Classical concerts take place in a surprising number of venues. Tickets for opera premieres may be hard to find, but soloists, groups, or orchestras playing in gardens, churches, villas, or ancient ruins are more accessible.

World-renowned soloists and orchestras make appearances throughout the year in venues such as the Renzo Piano–designed **Parco della Musica** and the **Accademia Filarmonica Romana**. Past visitors have included Luciano Pavarotti and Placido Domingo, the Berlin Philharmonic, and prima ballerina Sylvie Guillem. One of the most innovative programs of classical and contemporary music is provided by the **Aula Magna dell'Università La Sapienza**. The opera season starts late at the **Teatro dell'Opera**, between November and January. The great ballet classics are also staged at this venue. The **Equilibrio Festival** in February brings contemporary dance to the city; performances take place mainly at the Parco della Musica.

Rock, Jazz, and World Music

Rome's nonclassical music scene is unpredictable and subject to vast seasonal changes. However, there is a huge variety of music at the many clubs and stadiums, such as the **Palalottomatica** and the **Stadio Olimpico**, which attract foreign and homegrown stars. The best jazz musicians play at the splendid **Casa del Jazz**, and at **Alexanderplatz**. Trastevere's **Big Mama** is one of the city's legendary addresses for important jazz names, while world music is well served at the aptly named **Villaggio Globale**.

For smaller venues you might need to buy a monthly or annual membership card (between €2 and €11), which often includes the entrance fee for smaller bands.

Film and Theater

Moviegoing is a popular pastime in Rome, with around 40 films showing on an average weekday. Most Roman movie theaters are *prima visione* (first run) and show the latest international films in dubbed versions. The best theaters for decor and comfort are the **Fiamma** (two screens) and the **Barberini** (three screens). Films in their original language are often shown at the excellent **Casa del Cinema** and at the **Nuovo Olimpia**. Smaller art cinemas, such as the **Azzurro Scipioni**, are more likely to show subtitled versions of foreign films.

Theater productions are performed in Italian whether the plays are national classics or by foreign playwrights. The main theaters – **Teatro Argentina**, **Teatro Quirino**, and the **Eliseo** – offer a selection by great Italian playwrights. There are also performances of traditional cabaret, dance, and avant-garde theater at the **Teatro India**. Theater tickets cost between €8 and €50 and can generally be booked only in advance, by visiting the theater box office in person or through agencies such as Box Office.

Nightlife

Rome's nightlife has never been as vibrant as it is today, with a sharp rise in the number of bars and clubs, all catering for an ever more demanding clientele. Once the choice was limited to a few well-established bars in the center and the hugely popular clubs in the Ostiense area and in San Lorenzo, such as the unashamedly commercial **Goa** or the more cutting-edge **Locanda Atlantide**, which hosts a whole range of DJs from funk to reggae. Now, though, the capital offers a wide range of options designed to satisfy all tastes and budgets.

Head first to a stylish pre-clubbing venue such as **'Gusto**, where you can rub shoulders with out-on-the-town locals taking advantage of the range of facilities – on three sites there is a restaurant, a pizzeria, a wine bar, and live music. Alternatively, for a more leisurely start to your evening, simply relax in a wine bar in one of the historic center's breathtaking squares.

If you are looking for a gay venue, **Coming Out**, near the Colosseum, attracts both gay and straight drinkers, and **Planet Roma** just off Via Ostiense regularly hosts gay nights.

For an alternative edge to Rome's vivacious nightlife, try out the *centri sociali*, illegally occupied buildings that have been converted into arts and entertainment centers. Top billing goes to **Brancaleone**, which features Italian and international DJs for the best in electronic and house tunes.

A night out in Rome can be expensive – you can be charged as much as €10 for a cocktail in the bars around the central parts of Rome. For a cheaper alternative, visit one of the many bars in the area around San Lorenzo.

DIRECTORY

Buying Tickets

Box Office
Largo Argentina 11 (inside Feltrinelli bookshop). **Map** 10 D4. **Tel** 06 68 30 85 96.

Orbis
Piazza dell'Esquilino 37. **Map** 4 D4. **Tel** 06 482 74 03.

Ticketeria
W ticketeria.it

Classical Music and Dance

Accademia Filarmonica Romana
Via Flaminia 118. **Tel** 06 320 17 52. **W filarmonicaromana.org**

Aula Magna dell'Università La Sapienza
Piazzale Aldo Moro 5. **Map** 4 F3. **Tel** 06 361 00 51. **W concertiiuc.it**

Parco della Musica
Viale de Coubertin 30. **Tel** 06 80 24 12 81 (info); 89 29 82 (credit card sales). **W auditorium.com**

RomaEuropa
Via dei Magazzini Generali 20a. **Tel** 06 45 55 30 50. **W romaeuropa.net**

Teatro dell'Opera
Piazza Beniamino Gigli 1. **Map** 3 C3. **Tel** 06 48 16 01. **W operaroma.it**

Rock, Jazz, and World Music

Alexanderplatz
Via Ostia 9. **Map** 1 B1. **Tel** 06 39 74 21 71.

Big Mama
Vicolo San Francesco a Ripa 18. **Map** 5 C2. **Tel** 06 581 25 51.

Casa del Jazz
Viale di Porta Ardeatina 55. **Map** 7 A4. **Tel** 06 70 47 31. **W casajazz.it**

Palalottomatica
Piazzale dello Sport. **Tel** 06 54 09 01.

Stadio Olimpico
Viale dei Gladiatori (north-west of city center, across the Tiber by Monte Mario).

Villaggio Globale
Ex-Mattatoio, Lungotevere Testaccio 1. **Map** 6 D4. **Tel** 347 413 12 05.

Film and Theater

Azzurro Scipioni
Via degli Scipioni 82. **Map** 1 C2. **Tel** 06 39 73 71 61.

Barberini
Piazza Barberini 24. **Map** 3 B3. **Tel** 06 86 39 13 61.

Casa del Cinema
Largo Mastroianni 1. **Map** 3 B1. **Tel** 06 06 08. **W casadelcinema.it**

Eliseo
Via Nazionale 183. **Map** 3 B4. **Tel** 06 488 21 14.

Fiamma
Via Bissolati 47. **Map** 3 C2. **Tel** 06 48 55 26.

Nuovo Olimpia
Via in Lucina 16. **Map** 10 E1. **Tel** 06 686 10 68.

Teatro Argentina
Largo Argentina 56. **Map** 2 F4. **Tel** 06 684 00 03 11. **W teatrodiroma.net**

Teatro India
Via L Pierantoni 6. **Map** 5 C5. **Tel** 06 684 00 03 11.

Teatro Quirino
Via delle Vergini 7. **Map** 3 B3 & 10 F2. **Tel** 06 679 45 85. **W teatroquirino.it**

Nightlife

Brancaleone
Via Levanna 13 (in Montesacro). **Tel** 06 82 00 43 82.

Coming Out
Via San Giovanni in Laterano 8. **Map** 7 B1. **Tel** 06 700 98 71.

Goa
Via Libetta 13 (in Ostiense) **Tel** 06 574 82 77.

'Gusto
Piazza Augusto Imperatore 9. **Map** 2 F2. **Tel** 06 322 62 73.

Locanda Atlantide
Via dei Lucani 22b (San Lorenzo district). **Tel** 06 96 04 58 75.

Planet Roma
Via del Commercio 36–8. **Map** 8 D5. **Tel** 06 574 78 26.

ROME STREET FINDER

Map references given with sights described n the Rome chapters relate to the maps on he following pages. Map references are lso given for hotels *(see pp562–77)* and estaurants *(see pp580–605)* and for useful ddresses in the *Travelers' Needs* and *Survival Guide* sections at the back of the book. The irst figure in the map reference tells you which Street Finder map to turn to, and the letter and number that follow refer to the grid reference on that map. The small map below shows the area of Rome covered by each of the eight maps, and the corresponding map number is given in black. All the major sights are sketched out on the maps, and symbols, listed in the key below, are used to indicate the location of other important buildings.

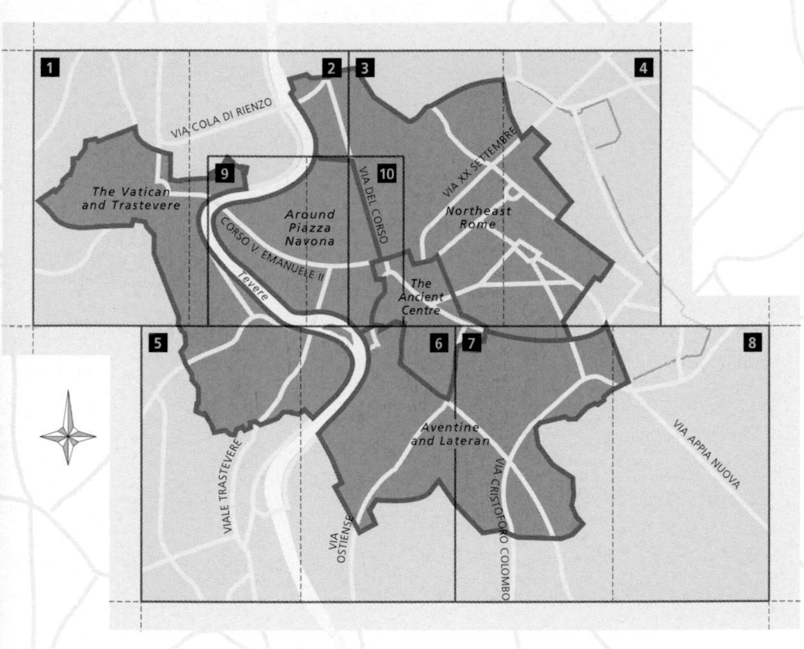

ey and Scale for Street Finder Pages

- Major sight
- Place of interest
- Train station
- Metro station
- Streetcar stop
- Tourist information
- Hospital with emergency room
- Police station
- Church
- Synagogue
- Railroad line
- City walls
- Pedestrian street

Scale of Maps 1–8

0 meters 250
0 yards 250
1:12,000

Scale of Maps 9–10

0 meters 150
0 yards 150
1:7600

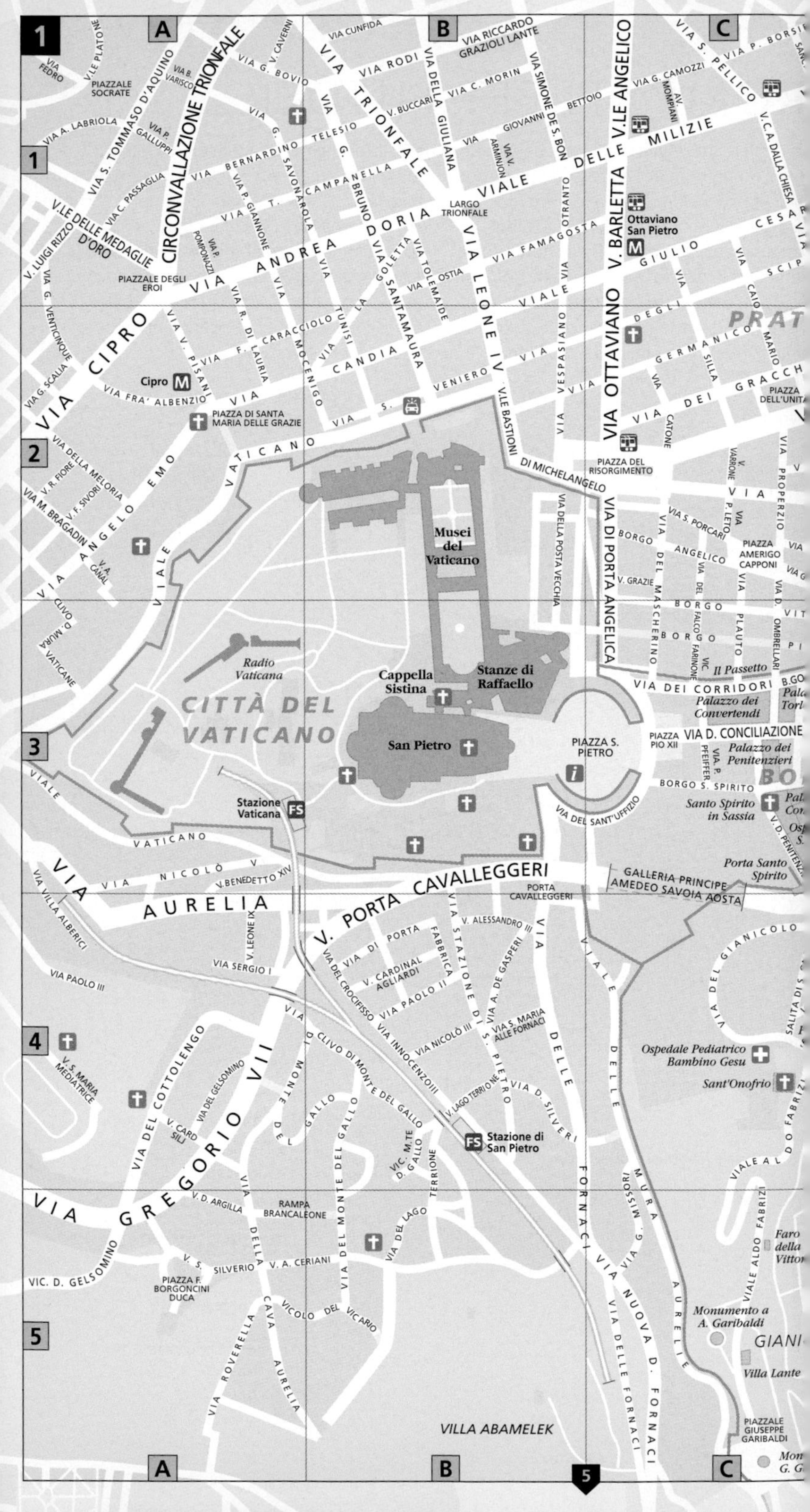

1
A
B
C
1
2
3
4
5
CIRCONVALLAZIONE TRIONFALE
VIA TRIONFALE
VIA DELLA GIULIANA
VIA SIMONE DE S. BON
V.LE ANGELICO
VIA S. PELLICO
VIA P. BORSI
VIA RICCARDO GRAZIOLI LANTE
VIA CUNFIDA
VIA RODI
VIA C. MORIN
VIA G. CAMOZZI
VIA G. BOVIO
VIA S. TOMMASO D'AQUINO
VIA B. VARISCO
VIA V. CAVERNI
VIA FEDRO
V.LE PLATONE
PIAZZALE SOCRATE
VIA A. LABRIOLA
VIA P. GALLUPPI
VIA BERNARDINO TELESIO
V. BUCCARI
VIA GIOVANNI BETTOLO
VIA ARMINJON
VIA V. ARMINJON
VIA G. SAVONAROLA
VIA G. BRUNO
VIA T. CAMPANELLA
VIA C. PASSAGLIA
VIA P. GIANNONE
VIALE DELLE MILIZIE
V.C.A. DALLA CHIESA
V.LE DELLE MEDAGLIE D'ORO
V. LUIGI RIZZO
VIA P. POMPONAZZI
VIA ANDREA DORIA
LARGO TRIONFALE
VIA LEONE IV
VIA DELLA GOLETTA
VIA TOLEMAIDE
VIA OSTIA
VIA SANTAMAURA
VIA FAMAGOSTA
VIA OTRANTO
V. BARLETTA
Ottaviano San Pietro
VIA CESARE
VIA GIULIO
VIA SCIPIONI
VIA CAIO MARIO
PIAZZALE DEGLI EROI
VIA G. VENTICINQUE
VIA CIPRO
VIA V. PISANI
VIA R. DI LAURIA
VIA F. CARACCIOLO
VIA MOCENIGO
VIA TUNISI
VIA CANDIA
VIALE GIULIO CESARE
VIA DEGLI SCIPIONI
VIA OTTAVIANO
VIA GERMANICO
VIA SILLA
PRATI
Cipro
VIA G. SCALIA
VIA FRA' ALBENZIO
VIA S. VENIERO
VIA VESPASIANO
V.LE BASTIONI DI MICHELANGELO
VIA DEI GRACCHI
PIAZZA DELL'UNITÀ
VIA CATONE
PIAZZA DI SANTA MARIA DELLE GRAZIE
VIALE VATICANO
VIA DELLA MELORIA
V. R. FIORE
V. F. SIVORI
VIA M. BRAGADIN
VIA ANGELO EMO
V. A. CANAL
CLIVO D. MURA VATICANE
PIAZZA DEL RISORGIMENTO
V. VARRONE
VIA P. LETO
VIA PROPERZIO
VIA S. PORCARI
BORGO ANGELICO
PIAZZA AMERIGO CAPPONI
VIA DELLA POSTA VECCHIA
VIA DI PORTA ANGELICA
Musei del Vaticano
V. GRAZIE
VIA DEL MASCHERINO
VIA DEL FALCO
VIC. FARINONE
BORGO VITTORIO
BORGO PIO
VIA PLAUTO
VIA D. OMBRELLARI
Il Passetto
Radio Vaticana
Cappella Sistina
Stanze di Raffaello
VIA DEI CORRIDORI
Palazzo dei Convertendi
CITTÀ DEL VATICANO
San Pietro
PIAZZA S. PIETRO
PIAZZA PIO XII
VIA D. CONCILIAZIONE
Palazzo dei Penitenzieri
VIA P. PFEIFFER
BORGO S. SPIRITO
Santo Spirito in Sassia
Stazione Vaticana
VIA DEL SANT'UFFIZIO
V.D. PENITENZA
VIA AURELIA
VIA NICOLÒ V
V. BENEDETTO XIV
V. PORTA CAVALLEGGERI
PORTA CAVALLEGGERI
GALLERIA PRINCIPE AMEDEO SAVOIA AOSTA
Porta Santo Spirito
VIA VILLA ALBERICI
V. LEONE IX
VIA SERGIO I
VIA PAOLO III
VIA DI PORTA FABBRICA
V. CARDINAL AGLIARDI
VIA PAOLO II
VIA STAZIONE DI S. PIETRO
V. ALESSANDRO III
VIA A. DE GASPERI
VIA S. MARIA ALLE FORNACI
VIA NICOLÒ III
VIA DEL CROCIFISSO
VIA INNOCENZO III
VIA DEL GIANICOLO
SALITA DI S. ONOFRIO
Ospedale Pediatrico Bambino Gesu
Sant'Onofrio
V. S. MARIA MEDIATRICE
VIA DEL COTTOLENGO
VIA DEL GELSOMINO
V. CARD. SILJ
VIA GREGORIO VII
VIA DI MONTE DEL GALLO
CLIVO DI MONTE DEL GALLO
V. LAGO TERRIONE
VIA D. SILVERI
Stazione di San Pietro
VIC. M.TE D. GALLO
TERRIONE
VIA DEL MONTE DEL GALLO
VIALE DELLE FORNACI
VIALE ALDO FABRIZI
V. D. ARGILLA
RAMPA BRANCALEONE
VIA DEL LAGO
VIA DELLA CAVA AURELIA
VIA G. MISSORI
MURA AURELIE
Faro della Vittoria
V. S. SILVERIO
V. A. CERIANI
VIC. D. GELSOMINO
PIAZZA F. BORGONCINI DUCA
VICOLO DEL VICARIO
VIA NUOVA D. FORNACI
VIA DELLE FORNACI
Monumento a A. Garibaldi
GIANICOLO
Villa Lante
VIA ROVERELLA
VILLA ABAMELEK
PIAZZALE GIUSEPPE GARIBALDI
5

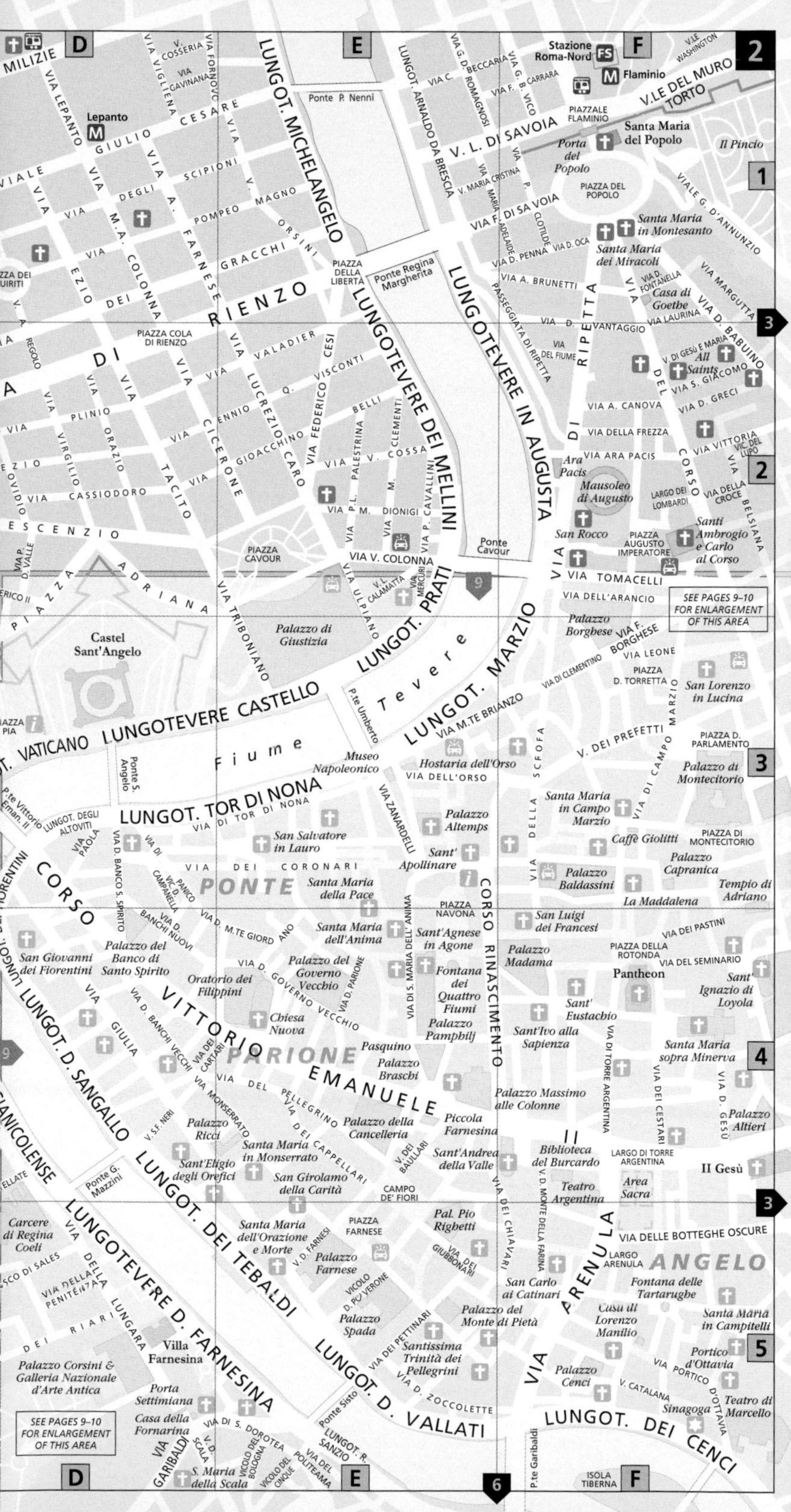

D
E
F
2
1
2
3
3
4
3
5
6
9
9
Stazione Roma-Nord
FS
Flaminio
M
Lepanto
M
MILIZIE
VIA LEPANTO
V. COSSERIA
VIA GAVINANA
VIA VIGLIENA
VIA FORNOVO
LUNGOT. MICHELANGELO
Ponte P. Nenni
LUNGOT. ARNALDO DA BRESCIA
VIA G. D. ROMAGNOSI
VIA C. BECCARIA
VIA F. CARRARA
VIA G. B. VICO
V.LE WASHINGTON
V.LE DEL MURO TORTO
PIAZZALE FLAMINIO
Santa Maria del Popolo
Il Pincio
Porta del Popolo
PIAZZA DEL POPOLO
V. L. DI SAVOIA
V. MARIA CRISTINA
VIA F. DI SA VOIA
VIALE G. D'ANNUNZIO
Santa Maria in Montesanto
Santa Maria dei Miracoli
VIA D. PENNA
VIA D. OCA
CLOTILDE
VIA A. BRUNETTI
VIA D. FONTANELLA
Casa di Goethe
VIA MARGUTTA
VIA LAURINA
VIA D. BABUINO
VIA D. VANTAGGIO
VIALE GIULIO CESARE
VIA SCIPIONI
VIA POMPEO MAGNO
VIA DEGLI GRACCHI
VIA ORSINI
VIA M. A. COLONNA
VIA FARNESE
VIA EZIO
VIA COLA DI RIENZO
PIAZZA DELLA LIBERTÀ
Ponte Regina Margherita
LUNGOTEVERE DEI MELLINI
LUNGOTEVERE IN AUGUSTA
PASSEGGIATA DI RIPETTA
VIA DI RIPETTA
VIA DEL FIUME
PIAZZA DEI QUIRITI
PIAZZA COLA DI RIENZO
VIA REGOLO
VIA VALADIER
VIA FEDERICO CESI
VIA Q. VISCONTI
VIA LUCREZIO CARO
VIA PLINIO
VIA ORAZIO
VIA VIRGILIO
VIA ENNIO
VIA CICERONE
VIA GIOACCHINO BELLI
VIA PALESTRINA
VIA V. COSSA
VIA CLEMENTI
VIA M. DIONIGI
VIA P. L.
VIA P. CAVALLINI
VIA CASSIODORO
VIA TACITO
VIA OVIDIO
VIA CRESCENZIO
VIA P. D. VALLE
PIAZZA CAVOUR
VIA V. COLONNA
Ponte Cavour
V. DI GESÙ E MARIA
All Saints
VIA S. GIACOMO
VIA A. CANOVA
VIA D. GRECI
VIA DELLA FREZZA
VIA VITTORIA
VIC. DEL LUPO
VIA ARA PACIS
Ara Pacis
Mausoleo di Augusto
LARGO DEI LOMBARDI
VIA DELLA CROCE
VIA BELSIANA
VIA DEL CORSO
San Rocco
PIAZZA AUGUSTO IMPERATORE
Santi Ambrogio e Carlo al Corso
VIA TOMACELLI
VIA DELL'ARANCIO
SEE PAGES 9–10 FOR ENLARGEMENT OF THIS AREA
Palazzo Borghese
VIA F. BORGHESE
VIA LEONE
PIAZZA D. TORRETTA
VIA DI CLEMENTINO
San Lorenzo in Lucina
PIAZZA ADRIANA
Castel Sant'Angelo
VIA TRIBONIANO
Palazzo di Giustizia
VIA ULPIANO
V. L. CALAMATTA
VIA MERCURI
LUNGOT. PRATI
LUNGOT. MARZIO
Tevere
P.te Umberto
Fiume
PIAZZA PIA
LUNGOTEVERE CASTELLO
LUNGOT. VATICANO
Ponte S. Angelo
VIA M.TE BRIANZO
Museo Napoleonico
Hostaria dell'Orso
VIA DELL'ORSO
V. DEI PREFETTI
PIAZZA D. PARLAMENTO
Palazzo di Montecitorio
VIA DI CAMPO MARZIO
VIA DELLA SCROFA
LUNGOT. TOR DI NONA
VIA DI TOR DI NONA
P.te Vittorio Eman. II
LUNGOT. DEGLI ALTOVITI
VIA PAOLA
VIA D. BANCO S. SPIRITO
San Salvatore in Lauro
VIA ZANARDELLI
Palazzo Altemps
Santa Maria in Campo Marzio
Caffè Giolitti
PIAZZA DI MONTECITORIO
Sant' Apollinare
VIA DEI CORONARI
PONTE
Santa Maria della Pace
CORSO RINASCIMENTO
Palazzo Baldassini
Palazzo Capranica
Tempio di Adriano
La Maddalena
CORSO VITTORIO EMANUELE II
VIA D. BANCHI NUOVI
VIA D. M.TE GIORDANO
PIAZZA NAVONA
San Luigi dei Francesi
VIA DEI PASTINI
Santa Maria dell'Anima
Sant'Agnese in Agone
Palazzo Madama
PIAZZA DELLA ROTONDA
VIA DEL SEMINARIO
San Giovanni dei Fiorentini
Palazzo del Banco di Santo Spirito
Palazzo del Governo Vecchio
VIA D. PARIONE
VIA DI S. MARIA DELL'ANIMA
Fontana dei Quattro Fiumi
Pantheon
Sant' Ignazio di Loyola
Oratorio dei Filippini
VIA D. GOVERNO VECCHIO
Palazzo Pamphilj
Sant' Eustachio
Chiesa Nuova
VIA GIULIA
VIA D. BANCHI VECCHI
VIA DEI CARTARI
PARIONE
Pasquino
Sant'Ivo alla Sapienza
Santa Maria sopra Minerva
Palazzo Braschi
VIA DI TORRE ARGENTINA
VIA DEI CESTARI
LUNGOT. D. SANGALLO
VIA MONSERRATO
VIA DEL PELLEGRINO
Palazzo Massimo alle Colonne
VIA D. GESÙ
Palazzo Altieri
Palazzo Ricci
V. S.F. NERI
Palazzo della Cancelleria
Piccola Farnesina
VIA DEI CAPPELLARI
Santa Maria in Monserrato
V. DEI BAULLARI
Sant'Andrea della Valle
Biblioteca del Burcardo
LARGO DI TORRE ARGENTINA
Il Gesù
Sant'Eligio degli Orefici
San Girolamo della Carità
CAMPO DE' FIORI
Teatro Argentina
Area Sacra
Ponte G. Mazzini
VIA GIANICOLENSE
LUNGOT. DEI TEBALDI
VIA DEI CHIAVARI
V.D. MONTE DELLA FARINA
Carcere di Regina Coeli
Santa Maria dell'Orazione e Morte
PIAZZA FARNESE
Pal. Pio Righetti
VIA ARENULA
VIA DELLE BOTTEGHE OSCURE
LUNGOTEVERE D. FARNESINA
VIA DELLA LUNGARA
VIA DELLA PENITENZA
VIA D. FARNESI
Palazzo Farnese
VIA DEI GIUBBONARI
LARGO ARENULA
ANGELO
San Carlo ai Catinari
Fontana delle Tartarughe
VICOLO D. POLVERONE
Palazzo Spada
Palazzo del Monte di Pietà
Casa di Lorenzo Manilio
Santa Maria in Campitelli
VIA DEI RIARI
VIA DEI PETTINARI
Villa Farnesina
Santissima Trinità dei Pellegrini
Portico d'Ottavia
VIA PORTICO D'OTTAVIA
Palazzo Corsini & Galleria Nazionale d'Arte Antica
LUNGOT. D. VALLATI
Palazzo Cenci
V. CATALANA
Sinagoga
Teatro di Marcello
Porta Settimiana
VIA D. ZOCCOLETTE
Casa della Fornarina
Ponte Sisto
LUNGOT. DEI CENCI
VIA DI S. DOROTEA
LUNGOT. R. SANZIO
VIA GARIBALDI
V. D. SCALA
VICOLO DEL BOLOGNA
VICOLO DEL CINQUE
VIA DEL POLITEAMA
S. Maria della Scala
P.te Garibaldi
ISOLA TIBERINA

3
A
B
C
VILLA BORGHESE
V.LE DEI PUPAZZI
VIALE DEI CAVALLI MARINI
VIALE DELLE MAGNOLIE
VIALE S. PAOLO DEL BRASILE
VIALE GOETHE
VIALE DELLA PINETA
VIALE DEL MUSEO BORGHESE
GALOPPATOIO
VIALE DEL GALOPPATOIO
VIALE DEL MURO TORTO
PORTA PINCIANA
VIA PINCIANA
CORSO D'ITALIA
VIA CAMPANIA
LUDOVISI
VIA G. PUCCINI
VIA PO
VIA DI S. TERESA
VIA SARDEGNA
VIA ABRUZZI
VIA ROMAGNA
VIA SICILIA
VIA PUGLIE
VIA BONCOMPAGNI
VIALE TRINITÀ DEI MONTI
Villa Medici
VIA MARGUTTA
V. DEL BABUINO
VIA ALIBERT
CAMPO MARZIO
Spagna
VIA DI PORTA PINCIANA
VIA LAZIO
VIA VITTORIO VENETO
VIA MARCHE
VIA TOSCANA
VIA PIEMONTE
VIA QUINTINO SELLA
VIA LOMBARDIA
VIA AURORA
VIA EMILIA
SALLUSTIANO
VIA LUCULLO
VIA SALLUSTIANA
VIA FRIULI
Casino dell'Aurora
VIA LUDOVISI
V. CADORE
Palazzo Margherita
VIA LIGURIA
VIA UMBRIA
VIA G. CARDUCCI
VIA PAGANO
VIA SALANDRA
Ministero dell'Agricoltura e delle Foreste
Santa Maria della Vittoria
VIA L. BISSOLATI
VIA D. CROCE
PIAZZA DI SPAGNA
Babington's Tea Rooms
Trinità dei Monti
Scalinata della Trinità dei Monti
V. DELLE CARROZZE
VIA BOCCA DI LEONE
VIA CONDOTTI
Caffè Greco
Museo Keats-Shelley
PIAZZA MIGNANELLI
VIA D. ARTISTI
V. S. ISIDORO
VIA VITTORIO VENETO
VIA MOLISE
V. VERSILIA
SALITA DI S. NICOLA DA TOLENTINO
VIA FRANCESCO CRISPI
VIA PURIFICAZIONE
Santa Maria della Concezione
Fontana delle Api
VIA S. NICOLA DA TOLENTINO
VIA BARBERINI
Santa Susanna
Fontana del Mosè
VIA MARIO DE' FIORI
10
Colonna dell'Immacolata
VIA FRATTINA
VIA GREGORIANA
VIA DUE MACELLI
VIA SISTINA
Barberini
SEE PAGES 9–10 FOR ENLARGEMENT OF THIS AREA
VIA CAPO LE CASE
VIA D. MERCEDE
Sant'Andrea delle Fratte
VIA ZUCCHELLI
PIAZZA BARBERINI
Fontana del Tritone
Palazzo Barberini
PIAZZA S. BERNARDO
V. V.E. ORLANDO
San Bernardo alle Terme
VIA DEL TRITONE
V. D. AVIGNONESI
VIA D. BOCCACCIO
VIA DELLE QUATTRO FONTANE
VIA XX SETTEMBRE
Ministero della Difesa Esercito
PIAZZA SAN SILVESTRO
VIA DEL POZZETTO
TREVI
VIA POLI
VIA DEL TRAFORO
VIA DEI MARONITI
VIA RASELLA
VIA D. GIARDINI
VIA S. CLAUDIO
LARGO CHIGI
VIA IN ARCIONE
VIA D. SCUDERIE
GIARDINI DEL QUIRINALE
Le Quattro Fontane
VIA MODENA
Teatro dell'Opera
Palazzo Chigi
VIA S. M. IN VIA
VIA D. STAMPERIA
Accademia di San Luca
VIA D. PANETTERIA
(TRAFORO UMBERTO I)
VIA DEL QUIRINALE
San Carlo alle Quattro Fontane
VIA FIRENZE
PIAZZA COLONNA
Santa Maria in Trivio
Fontana di Trevi
V. SAN VINCENZO
Santi Vincenzo e Anastasio
VIA PIACENZA
VIA GENOVA
VIA S. VITALE
VIA NAZIONALE
GALL. REG. MARGHERITA
VIA NAPOLI
Colonna di Marco Aurelio
VIA D. MURATTE
Palazzo del Quirinale
Sant'Andrea al Quirinale
VIA A. DEPRETIS
PIAZZA D. VIMINALE
VIA DEL CORSO
VIA MINGHETTI
V. DEI LUCCHESI
VIA D. DATARIA
PIAZZA DEL QUIRINALE
VIA PALERMO
PIGNA
VIA DELL'UMILTÀ
Università Gregoriana
Castore e Polluce
VIA D. CONSULTA
VIA PARMA
Palazzo delle Esposizioni
San Marcello al Corso
V. S. MARCELLO
PIAZZA D. PILOTTA
SS. Apostoli
VIA XXIV MAGGIO
VIA CESARE BALBO
MONTI
Palazzo del Collegio Romano
Palazzo Odescalchi
Palazzo Colonna
V. D. PILOTTA
VIA MILANO
Santa Pudenziana
PIAZZA COLLEGIO ROMANO
Palazzo Doria Pamphilj
PIAZZA DEI SS. APOSTOLI
4
V. IV NOVEMBRE
VIA NAZIONALE
Banca d'Italia
VIA MAZZARINO
Sant'Agata dei Goti
VIA DEI SERPENTI
VIA DEL BOSCHETTO
VIA PANISPERNA
VIA CIMARRA
VIA S. M. MAGGIORE
VIA CIANCALEONI
VIA CAPOCCI
VIA URBANA
V. CLEMENTINA
VIA DELLA GATTA
V.D. PLEBISCITO
PIAZZA VENEZIA
Villa Aldobrandini
Palazzo Venezia
San Marco
Gesù
Colonna Traiana
VIA ALESSANDRINA
Torre delle Milizie
Santi Domenico e Sisto
V. S. AGATA DEI GOTI
Santa Maria dei Monti
VIA D. ZINGARI
Cavour
Mercati Traianei
VIA S. MARCO
PIAZZA S. MARCO
Il Vittoriano
VIA DEI FORI IMPERIALI
Casa dei Cavalieri di Rodi
VIA LEONINA
VIA GIOVANNI LANZA
LARGO VENOSTA
PIAZZA D'ARACOELI
Santa Maria in Aracoeli
Foro di Augusto
VIA TOR DE CONTI
VIA BACCINA
VIA MADONNA D. MONTI
VIA CAVOUR
Foro di Cesare
Foro di Nerva
Palazzo Nuovo
Carcere Mamertino
LARGO CORRADO RICCI
VIA FRANGIPANE
VIA DEGLI ANNIBALDI
VIA EUDOSSIANA
San Pietro in Vincoli
VIA D. SERPENTI
PIAZZA DEL CAMPIDOGLIO
5
Musei Capitolini
Palazzo Senatorio
VIA CURIA
Curia
VIA CARDELLO
VIA DEL COLOSSEO
Basilica Aemilia
Palazzo dei Conservatori
Colonna di Foca
VIA D. TEATRO DI MARCELLO
Tempio di Saturno
Basilica Giulia
Tempio di Antonino e Faustina
Tempio di Romolo
Basilica di Costantino e Massenzio
V. TERME DI TITO
VIALE
Tempio di Giove
V.D. CONSOLAZIONE
Rupe Tarpea
Tempio di Castore e Polluce
Tempio di Vesta
Foro Romano
S. Francesca Romana
L.GO G. AGNESI
Colosseo
VIA N. SALVI
Antiquarium Forense
PIAZZA DEL COLOSSEO
S. M. della Consolazione
Casa delle Vestali
Tempio di Venere e Roma
Colosseo
6
2
1

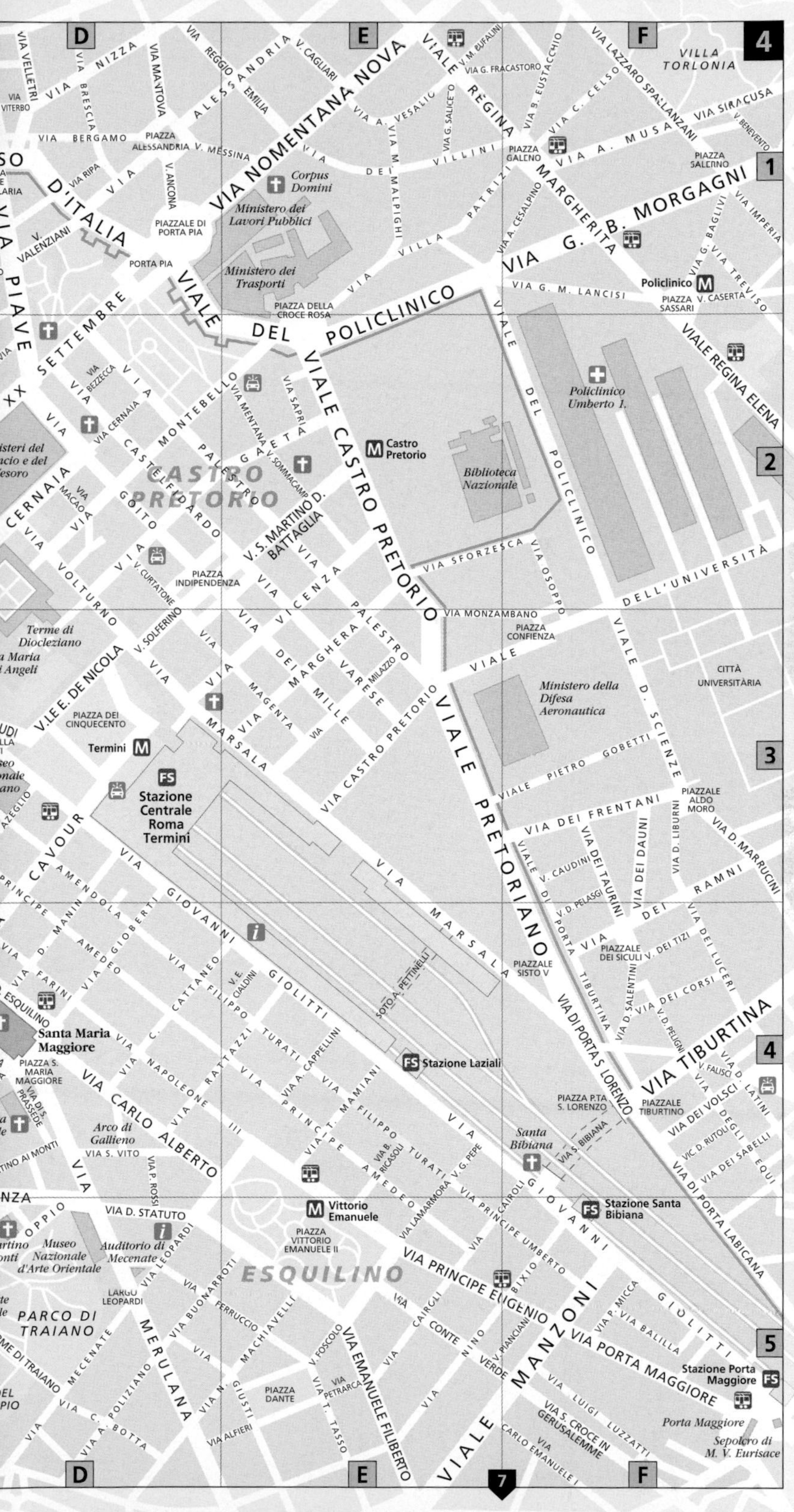
D
E
F
4
VILLA TORLONIA
1
2
3
4
5
D
E
F
7
VIA VELLETRI
VIA NIZZA
VIA BRESCIA
VIA VITERBO
VIA BERGAMO
VIA MANTOVA
PIAZZA ALESSANDRIA
V. MESSINA
VIA ALESSANDRIA
VIA REGGIO EMILIA
V. CAGLIARI
VIA NOMENTANA NOVA
V. M. BUFALINI
VIALE REGINA MARGHERITA
VIA G. FRACASTORO
VIA B. EUSTACCHIO
VIA LAZZARO SPALLANZANI
VIA C. CELSO
VIA SIRACUSA
V. BENEVENTO
VIA A. VESALIO
VIA G. SALICETO
VIA M. MALPIGHI
VIA DEI VILLINI
PIAZZA GALENO
VIA A. MUSA
PIAZZA SALERNO
VIA G. B. MORGAGNI
VIA IMPERIA
VIA G. BAGLIVI
VIA TREVISO
CORSO D'ITALIA
VIA RIPA
V. ANCONA
Corpus Domini
Ministero dei Lavori Pubblici
PIAZZALE DI PORTA PIA
V. VALENZIANI
VIA PIAVE
PORTA PIA
Ministero dei Trasporti
VIA A. CESALPINO
VIA PATRIZI
VIA VILLA
VIA G. M. LANCISI
Policlinico
PIAZZA SASSARI
V. CASERTA
VIALE REGINA ELENA
VIA XX SETTEMBRE
VIALE DEL POLICLINICO
PIAZZA DELLA CROCE ROSA
VIALE CASTRO PRETORIO
VIA MONTEBELLO
VIA MENTANA
VIA SAPRI
VIA BEZZECCA
VIA CERNAIA
VIA GAETA
VIA PALESTRO
VIA CASTELFIDARDO
V. SOMMACAMPAGNA
Castro Pretorio
Policlinico Umberto I.
Biblioteca Nazionale
CASTRO PRETORIO
VIA MACAO
VIA GOITO
V. S. MARTINO D. BATTAGLIA
VIA SFORZESCA
VIA OSOPPO
VIALE DELL'UNIVERSITÀ
VIA VOLTURNO
V. CURTATONE
PIAZZA INDIPENDENZA
VIA VICENZA
VIA MONZAMBANO
PIAZZA CONFIENZA
Terme di Diocleziano
V. SOLFERINO
VIA DEI MILLE
VIA MAGHERA
VIA VARESE
VIA MILAZZO
VIALE CASTRO PRETORIO
CITTÀ UNIVERSITÀRIA
V. LE E. DE NICOLA
VIA MAGENTA
Ministero della Difesa Aeronautica
VIALE D. SCIENZE
PIAZZA DEI CINQUECENTO
VIA MARSALA
VIA CASTRO PRETORIO
VIALE PIETRO GOBETTI
Termini
Stazione Centrale Roma Termini
VIALE PRETORIANO
PIAZZALE ALDO MORO
VIA DEI FRENTANI
VIA D. LIBURNI
VIA D. MARRUCINI
VIA CAVOUR
VIA AMENDOLA
VIA DEI DAUNI
VIA DEI TAURINI
V. CAUDINI
VIALE DI PORTA TIBURTINA
V. D. PELASGI
VIA DEI RAMNI
VIA PRINCIPE
VIA D. MANIN
VIA GIOBERTI
VIA GIOVANNI GIOLITTI
VIA MARSALA
PIAZZALE DEI SICULI
V. DEI TIZI
VIA DEI LUCERI
VIA FARINI
VIA CATTANEO
V. E. CIALDINI
SOTO. A. PETTINELLI
PIAZZALE SISTO V
VIA DEI CORSI
V. D. SALENTINI
V. D. PELIGNI
V. ESQUILINO
VIA FILIPPO TURATI
VIA TIBURTINA
Santa Maria Maggiore
VIA C. NAPOLEONE III
VIA RATTAZZI
VIA A. CAPPELLINI
Stazione Laziali
VIA DI PORTA S LORENZO
PIAZZA S. MARIA MAGGIORE
VIA CARLO ALBERTO
VIA T. MAMIANI
PIAZZA P.TA S. LORENZO
PIAZZALE TIBURTINO
V. FALISCI
VIA D. LATINI
VIA DEI VOLSCI
VIA DI S. PRASSEDE
Arco di Gallieno
VIA PRINCIPE AMEDEO
VIA B. RICASOLI
Santa Bibiana
VIA S. BIBIANA
VIA DEGLI EQUI
VIC. D. RUTOLI
VIA DEI SABELLI
VIA S. VITO
VIA P. ROSSI
VIA LAMARMORA
V. G. PEPE
VIA PRINCIPE UMBERTO
VIA CAIROLI
Stazione Santa Bibiana
VIA DI PORTA LABICANA
VIA D. STATUTO
Vittorio Emanuele
PIAZZA VITTORIO EMANUELE II
Museo Nazionale d'Arte Orientale
Auditorio di Mecenate
VIA LEOPARDI
VIA OPPIO
VIA PRINCIPE EUGENIO
VIA BIXIO
ESQUILINO
LARGO LEOPARDI
PARCO DI TRAIANO
VIA BUONARROTI
VIA FERRUCCIO
VIA MACHIAVELLI
VIA CONTE VERDE
VIA NINO BIXIO
V. PIANCIANI
VIA P. MICCA
VIA BALILLA
VIA PORTA MAGGIORE
Stazione Porta Maggiore
VIA MERULANA
VIA MECENATE
VIA N. GIUSTI
V. FOSCOLO
VIA EMANUELE FILIBERTO
VIA PETRARCA
PIAZZA DANTE
VIA T. TASSO
VIA ALFIERI
VIALE MANZONI
VIA LUIGI LUZZATTI
VIA S. CROCE IN GERUSALEMME
Porta Maggiore
Sepolcro di M. V. Eurisace
VIA CARLO EMANUELE I
VIA A. POLIZIANO
VIA C. BOTTA

5
Santa Maria dei Sette Dolori
S. Egidio
Museo de Roma in Trastevere
Santa Maria in Trastevere
Tempietto di San Pietro in Montorio
Fontana dell' Acqua Paola
Accademia d'America
Ministero della Pubblica Istruzione
VILLA SCIARRA
Stazione Quattro Venti
Stazione Trastevere
Fiume Tevere
Ospedale San Camillo
VIA G. GARIBALDI
VIA DI S. PANCRAZIO
VIALE DI TRASTEVERE
CIRCONVALL. GIANICOLENSE
VIA A. PACINOTTI
VIA PORTUENSE
VIA ETTORE ROLLI
VIA ALESSANDRO POERIO
VIALE DEI QUATTRO VENTI
VIA LUCIANO MANARA
Ponte Testaccio
Ponte dell'Industria

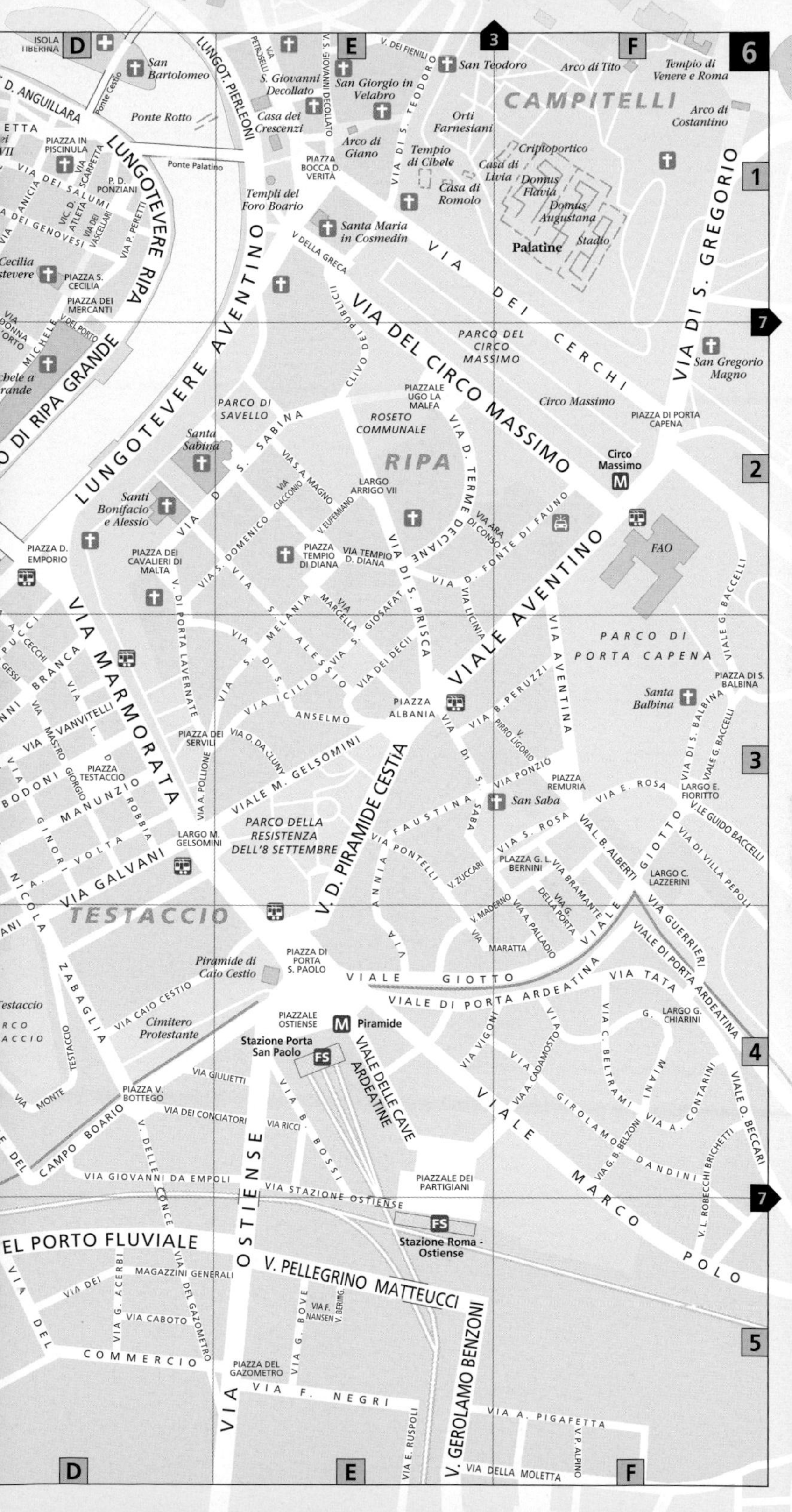

D
E
F
3
6
1
2
3
4
5
7
CAMPITELLI
RIPA
TESTACCIO
San Bartolomeo
Ponte Rotto
Ponte Palatino
LUNGOT. PIERLEONI
S. Giovanni Decollato
San Giorgio in Velabro
San Teodoro
Arco di Tito
Tempio di Venere e Roma
Arco di Costantino
Orti Farnesiani
Casa dei Crescenzi
Arco di Giano
Tempio di Cibele
Criptoportico
Casa di Livia
Domus Flavia
Domus Augustana
Casa di Romolo
Stadio
Palatine
Templi del Foro Boario
Santa Maria in Cosmedin
PIAZZA BOCCA D. VERITÀ
VIA DEI CERCHI
VIA DI S. GREGORIO
San Gregorio Magno
PARCO DEL CIRCO MASSIMO
Circo Massimo
PIAZZA DI PORTA CAPENA
VIA DEL CIRCO MASSIMO
LUNGOTEVERE AVENTINO
LUNGOTEVERE RIPA
PIAZZA IN PISCINULA
PIAZZA S. CECILIA
PIAZZA DEI MERCANTI
PARCO DI SAVELLO
Santa Sabina
Santi Bonifacio e Alessio
PIAZZALE UGO LA MALFA
ROSETO COMMUNALE
LARGO ARRIGO VII
PIAZZA TEMPIO DI DIANA
PIAZZA D. EMPORIO
PIAZZA DEI CAVALIERI DI MALTA
FAO
VIALE AVENTINO
PARCO DI PORTA CAPENA
Santa Balbina
PIAZZA DI S. BALBINA
PIAZZA ALBANIA
San Saba
PIAZZA REMURIA
LARGO E. FIORITTO
VIA MARMORATA
PIAZZA TESTACCIO
PIAZZA DEI SERVILI
VIALE M. GELSOMINI
PARCO DELLA RESISTENZA DELL'8 SETTEMBRE
V. D. PIRAMIDE CESTIA
LARGO M. GELSOMINI
VIA GALVANI
PIAZZA G. L. BERNINI
LARGO C. LAZZERINI
Piramide di Caio Cestio
PIAZZA DI PORTA S. PAOLO
VIALE GIOTTO
VIALE DI PORTA ARDEATINA
Cimitero Protestante
PIAZZALE OSTIENSE
Piramide
Stazione Porta San Paolo
VIALE DELLE CAVE ARDEATINE
LARGO G. CHIARINI
VIALE MARCO POLO
PIAZZA V. BOTTEGO
VIA DEI CONCIATORI
VIA GIOVANNI DA EMPOLI
VIA OSTIENSE
VIA STAZIONE OSTIENSE
PIAZZALE DEI PARTIGIANI
Stazione Roma - Ostiense
VIA DEL PORTO FLUVIALE
MAGAZZINI GENERALI
V. PELLEGRINO MATTEUCCI
VIA DEL COMMERCIO
PIAZZA DEL GAZOMETRO
VIA F. NEGRI
V. GEROLAMO BENZONI
VIA A. PIGAFETTA
VIA DELLA MOLETTA

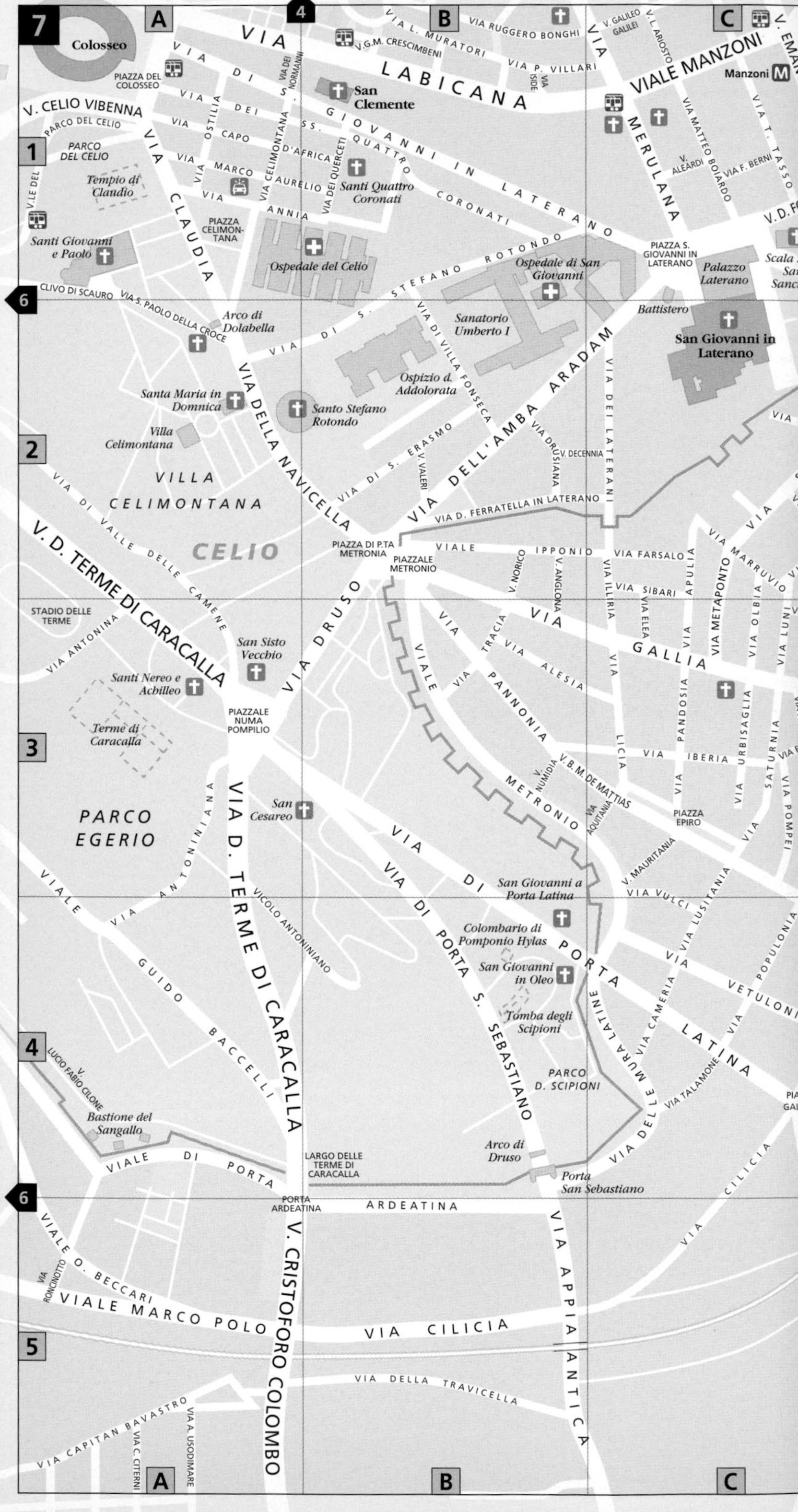

7
Colosseo
San Clemente
Santi Quattro Coronati
Ospedale del Celio
Santi Giovanni e Paolo
Tempio di Claudio
PARCO DEL CELIO
Ospedale di San Giovanni
Sanatorio Umberto I
San Giovanni in Laterano
Palazzo Laterano
Battistero
Arco di Dolabella
Santa Maria in Domnica
Santo Stefano Rotondo
Ospizio d. Addolorata
Villa Celimontana
VILLA CELIMONTANA
CELIO
San Sisto Vecchio
Santi Nereo e Achilleo
Terme di Caracalla
PARCO EGERIO
San Cesareo
San Giovanni a Porta Latina
Colombario di Pomponio Hylas
San Giovanni in Oleo
Tomba degli Scipioni
PARCO D. SCIPIONI
Arco di Druso
Porta San Sebastiano
Bastione del Sangallo
Manzoni
VIA LABICANA
VIALE MANZONI
VIA MERULANA
VIA DI S. GIOVANNI IN LATERANO
VIA CLAUDIA
VIA DELLA NAVICELLA
VIA DELL'AMBA ARADAM
VIA DRUSO
V. D. TERME DI CARACALLA
VIA D. TERME DI CARACALLA
V. CRISTOFORO COLOMBO
VIA DI PORTA LATINA
VIA DI PORTA S. SEBASTIANO
VIA APPIA ANTICA
VIA GALLIA
VIALE MARCO POLO
VIA CILICIA

8
D
E
F
1
2
3
4
5
Sepolcri Repubblicani
Museo degli Strumenti Musicali
Santa Croce in Gerusalemme
Anfiteatro Castrense
PIAZZA S. CROCE IN GERUSALEMME
Stazione Ponte Casilino
PIAZZA DEL PIGNETO
VIA CASILINA
V. GALLARATE
VIA TERAMO
VIALE CASTRENSE
VIA LA SPEZIA
PIAZZA LODI
PIAZZA DI VILLA FIORELLI
VIA TARANTO
VIA APPIA NUOVA
Re di Roma
PIAZZA DEI RE DI ROMA
VIA TUSCOLANA
PIAZZA LUGO
PIAZZA RAGUSA
PIAZZALE STAZIONE TUSCOLANA
Stazione Tuscolana
PIAZZA S. DONÀ DI PIAVE
Ponte Lungo
VIA ETRURIA
VIA ALBENGA
PIAZZA DI PONTE LUNGO
PIAZZA FINOCCHIARO APRILE
PIAZZA D. ALBERONE
PIAZZA ZAMA
VIA CIRCONVALLAZIONE APPIA
Furio Camillo
VIALE FURIO CAMILLO
VIA LATINA
PIAZZA S. AMMIRATO
LARGO GREGOROVIUS
PIAZZA C. BARONIO
VIA CESARE BARONIO
VILLA LAZZARONI
VIA CARLO DENINA
VIA MACEDONIA

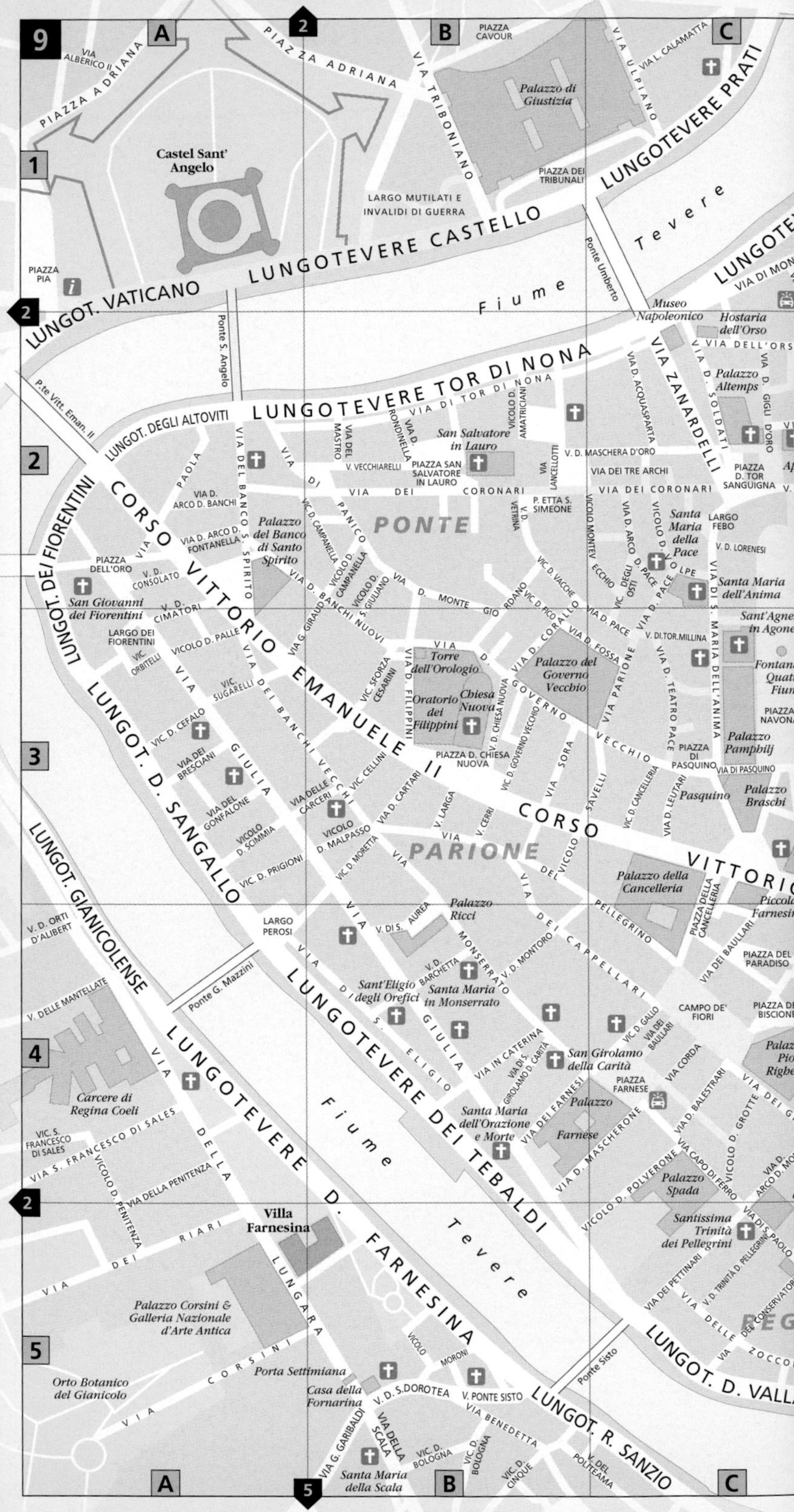

9
A
B
C
1
2
3
4
5
Castel Sant' Angelo
Palazzo di Giustizia
Piazza Cavour
Piazza Adriana
Via Alberico II
Via Triboniano
Via Ulpiano
Via L. Calamatta
Lungotevere Prati
Piazza dei Tribunali
Largo Mutilati e Invalidi di Guerra
Lungotevere Castello
Lungot. Vaticano
Piazza Pia
Fiume Tevere
Ponte Umberto
Ponte S. Angelo
Museo Napoleonico
Hostaria dell'Orso
Via di Monte Brianzo
Via dell'Orso
Lungotevere Tor di Nona
Via di Tor di Nona
Via Zanardelli
Via d. Soldati
Via d. Gigli d'Oro
Palazzo Altemps
Via d. Acquasparta
Vicolo d. Amatriciani
P.te Vitt. Eman. II
Lungot. degli Altoviti
Via del Mastro
Via d. Rondinella
San Salvatore in Lauro
Piazza San Salvatore in Lauro
V. Vecchiarelli
Via Lancellotti
V. d. Maschera d'Oro
Via dei Tre Archi
Via dei Coronari
Piazza d. Tor Sanguigna
Via Paola
Via d. Arco d. Banchi
Via del Banco S. Spirito
Via di Panico
P. etta S. Simeone
V. d. Vetrina
Vicolo Montevecchio
Via d. Arco d. Pace
Vicolo d. Volpe
Santa Maria della Pace
Largo Febo
V. d. Lorenesi
Ponte
Lungot. dei Fiorentini
Corso Vittorio Emanuele II
Via d. Arco d. Fontanella
Palazzo del Banco di Santo Spirito
Vic. d. Campanella
Vicolo d. Campanella
Vicolo d. S. Giuliano
Piazza dell'Oro
V. d. Consolato
San Giovanni dei Fiorentini
V. d. Cimatori
Via d. Banchi Nuovi
Via d. Monte Giordano
Vic. d. Vacche
Vic. d. Fico
Via d. Pace
Degli Osti
Via d. Pace
Santa Maria dell'Anima
Via di S. Maria dell'Anima
Sant'Agnese in Agone
Largo dei Fiorentini
Vicolo d. Palle
Vic. Orbitelli
Via G. Giraud
Via d. Governo Vecchio
Via d. Coronari
Via d. Fossa
V. di Tor Millina
Torre dell'Orologio
Oratorio dei Filippini
Chiesa Nuova
Palazzo del Governo Vecchio
Via Parione
Via d. Teatro Pace
Fontana dei Quattro Fiumi
Piazza Navona
Vic. Sugarelli
Vic. Sforza Cesarini
Via d. Filippini
Via d. Chiesa Nuova
Vic. d. Governo Vecchio
Palazzo Pamphilj
Lungot. d. Sangallo
Vic. d. Cefalo
Via dei Bresciani
Via Giulia
Via dei Banchi Vecchi
Vic. Cellini
Via delle Carceri
Via d. Cartari
Piazza d. Chiesa Nuova
Via Sora
Savelli
Vic. d. Cancelleria
Via d. Leutari
Piazza di Pasquino
Via di Pasquino
Pasquino
Palazzo Braschi
Via del Gonfalone
Vicolo d. Scimmia
Vicolo d. Malpasso
V. Larga
V. Cerri
Corso Vittorio
Vic. d. Prigioni
Vic. d. Moretta
Via Parione
Via del Pellegrino
Palazzo della Cancelleria
Piazza della Cancelleria
Piccola Farnesina
Lungot. Gianicolense
V. d. Orti d'Alibert
Largo Perosi
V. di S. Aurea
Palazzo Ricci
Via Monserrato
Via dei Cappellari
Via dei Baullari
Piazza del Paradiso
V. delle Mantellate
Ponte G. Mazzini
Lungotevere dei Tebaldi
Sant'Eligio degli Orefici
V. d. Barchetta
Santa Maria in Monserrato
V. d. Montoro
Campo de' Fiori
Piazza de Biscione
Via di S. Eligio
Vic. d. Gallo
Via in Caterina
Via di S. Girolamo d. Carità
San Girolamo della Carità
Via Corda
Palazzo Pio Righetti
Carcere di Regina Coeli
Lungotevere della Farnesina
Piazza Farnese
Palazzo Farnese
Via dei Farnesi
Santa Maria dell'Orazione e Morte
Via d. Mascherone
Via d. Balestrari
Vicolo d. Grotte
Vic. S. Francesco di Sales
Via S. Francesco di Sales
Via della Penitenza
Vicolo d. Penitenza
Via d. Polverone
Via Capo di Ferro
Palazzo Spada
Via d. Arco d. Monte
Villa Farnesina
Via dei Riari
Via della Lungara
Santissima Trinità dei Pellegrini
Via di S. Paolo
Via dei Pettinari
V. d. Trinità d. Pellegrini
Via delle Zoccolette
Via dei Conservatori
Palazzo Corsini & Galleria Nazionale d'Arte Antica
Vicolo Moroni
Ponte Sisto
Lungot. d. Vallati
Via Corsini
Orto Botanico del Gianicolo
Porta Settimiana
Casa della Fornarina
V. d. S. Dorotea
V. Ponte Sisto
Via Benedetta
Lungot. R. Sanzio
Via G. Garibaldi
Via della Scala
Vic. d. Bologna
Vic. d. Cinque
V. del Politeama
Santa Maria della Scala

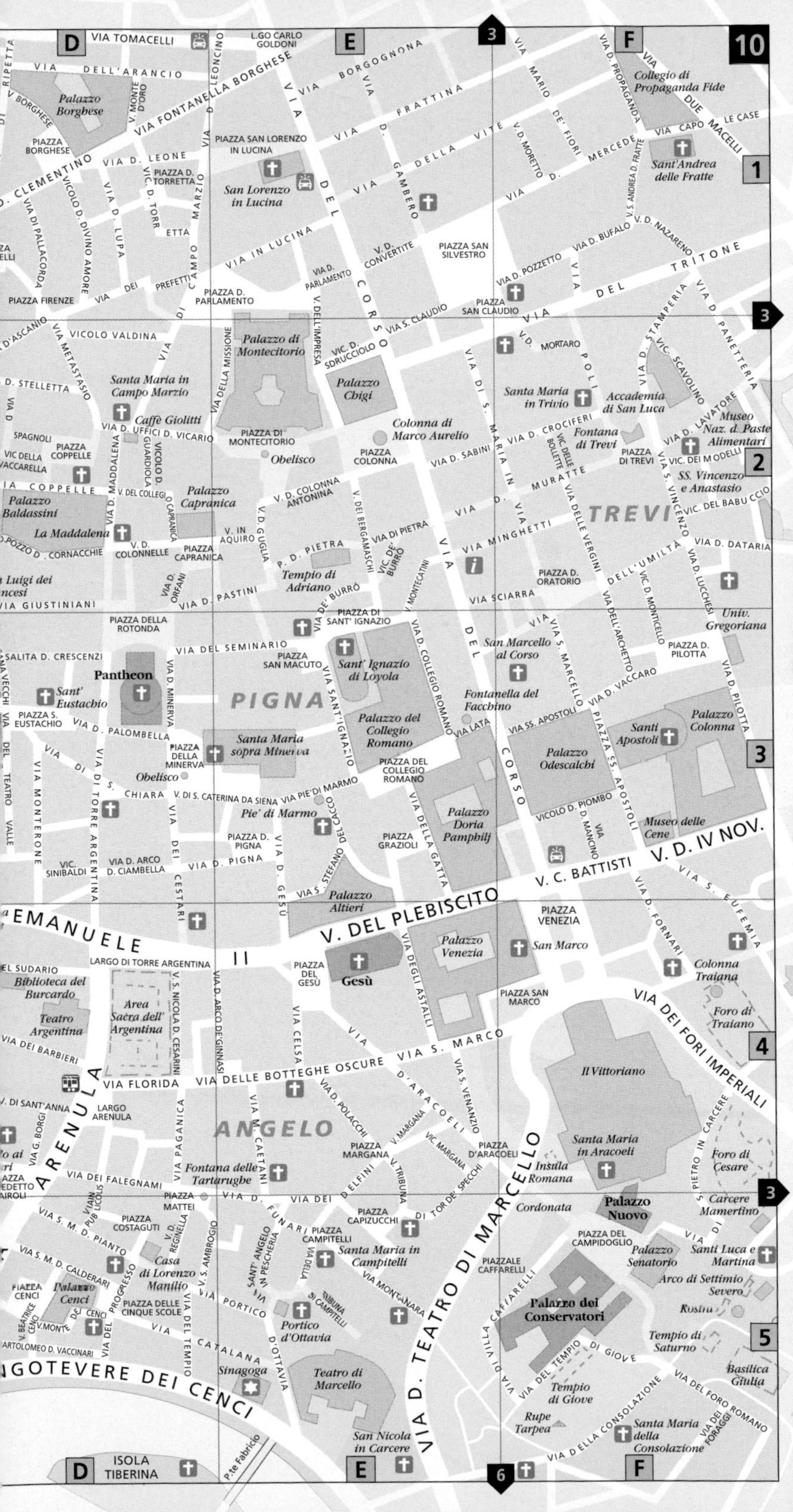
10
D
E
F
1
2
3
4
5
3
6
VIA TOMACELLI
L.GO CARLO GOLDONI
VIA DELL'ARANCIO
VIA FONTANELLA BORGHESE
VIA BORGOGNONA
VIA FRATTINA
VIA DELLA VITE
VIA MARIO DE' FIORI
VIA D. PROPAGANDA
VIA DUE MACELLI
VIA CAPO LE CASE
Collegio di Propaganda Fide
Palazzo Borghese
PIAZZA BORGHESE
V. MONTE D'ORO
PIAZZA SAN LORENZO IN LUCINA
San Lorenzo in Lucina
VIA D. LEONE
PIAZZA D. TORRETTA
VIC. D. TORRETTA
VIA CLEMENTINO
VICOLO D. DIVINO AMORE
VIA D. LUPA
VIA DI PALLACORDA
VIA DEL CORSO
VIA D. GAMBERO
V.D. MORETTO
VIA D. MERCEDE
V. S. ANDREA D. FRATTE
Sant'Andrea delle Fratte
VIA IN LUCINA
V. D. CONVERTITE
PIAZZA SAN SILVESTRO
VIA D. BUFALO
V. D. NAZARENO
VIA DEL TRITONE
PIAZZA FIRENZE
VIA DEI PREFETTI
VIA DI CAMPO MARZIO
PIAZZA D. PARLAMENTO
VIA D. PARLAMENTO
VIA D. POZZETTO
PIAZZA SAN CLAUDIO
VIA S. CLAUDIO
VIA D'ASCANIO
VICOLO VALDINA
VIA METASTASIO
VIA DELLA MISSIONE
Palazzo di Montecitorio
V. DELL'IMPRESA
VIC. D. SDRUCCIOLO
V. D. MORTARO
VIA POLI
VIA D. STAMPERIA
VIC. SCAVOLINO
VIA D. PANETTERIA
D. STELLETTA
Santa Maria in Campo Marzio
Palazzo Chigi
Santa Maria in Trivio
Accademia di San Luca
Caffè Giolitti
VIA D. UFFICI D. VICARIO
PIAZZA DI MONTECITORIO
Obelisco
Colonna di Marco Aurelio
PIAZZA COLONNA
VIA D. SABINI
VIA D. CROCIFERI
Fontana di Trevi
VIC. DELLE BOLLETTE
PIAZZA DI TREVI
VIA D. LAVATORE
Museo Naz. d. Paste Alimentari
VIC. DEI MODELLI
SPAGNOLI
PIAZZA COPPELLE
VIC DELLA VACCARELLA
VIA COPPELLE
VIA D. MADDALENA
V. DEL COLLEGIO
VICOLO D. GUARDIOLA
Palazzo Capranica
V. D. COLONNA ANTONINA
V. DEI BERGAMASCHI
VIA D. MURATTE
VIA DELLE VERGINI
TREVI
SS. Vincenzo e Anastasio
VIA S. VINCENZO
VIC. DEL BABUCCIO
Palazzo Baldassini
La Maddalena
V. D. COLONNELLE
V. IN AQUIRO
V. D. GUGLIA
PIAZZA CAPRANICA
VIA DI PIETRA
P. D. PIETRA
VIC. DE' BURRO
VIA MINGHETTI
VIA D. DATARIA
POZZO D. CORNACCHIE
Tempio di Adriano
V. MONTECATINI
PIAZZA D. ORATORIO
VIA DELL'UMILTÀ
VIC. D. MONTICELLO
VIA D. LUCCHESI
San Luigi dei Francesi
VIA D. ORFANI
VIA D. PASTINI
VIA DE' BURRO
VIA SCIARRA
VIA GIUSTINIANI
PIAZZA DELLA ROTONDA
PIAZZA DI SANT' IGNAZIO
Univ. Gregoriana
VIA DELL'ARCHETTO
SALITA D. CRESCENZI
VIA DEL SEMINARIO
PIAZZA SAN MACUTO
Sant' Ignazio di Loyola
VIA D. COLLEGIO ROMANO
San Marcello al Corso
VIA S. MARCELLO
PIAZZA D. PILOTTA
Pantheon
VIA D. MINERVA
PIGNA
Fontanella del Facchino
VIA D. VACCARO
VIA D. PILOTTA
Sant' Eustachio
PIAZZA S. EUSTACHIO
VIA D. PALOMBELLA
VIA SANT'IGNAZIO
Palazzo del Collegio Romano
VIA LATA
VIA SS. APOSTOLI
Santi Apostoli
Palazzo Colonna
PIAZZA DELLA MINERVA
Santa Maria sopra Minerva
Palazzo Odescalchi
PIAZZA SS. APOSTOLI
Obelisco
VIA DI S. CHIARA
V. DI S. CATERINA DA SIENA
VIA PIE' DI MARMO
PIAZZA DEL COLLEGIO ROMANO
VIA MONTERONE
VIA DI TORRE ARGENTINA
VIA DEL TEATRO VALLE
Pie' di Marmo
VIA DEL CACCO
Palazzo Doria Pamphilj
VICOLO D. PIOMBO
VIA D. MANCINO
Museo delle Cere
PIAZZA D. PIGNA
PIAZZA GRAZIOLI
VIA DELLA GATTA
V. C. BATTISTI
V. D. IV NOV.
VIC. SINIBALDI
VIA D. ARCO D. CIAMBELLA
VIA D. PIGNA
VIA DEI CESTARI
VIA D. GESÙ
VIA S. STEFANO DEL CACCO
Palazzo Altieri
VIA S. EUFEMIA
VIA D. FORNARI
EMANUELE II
V. DEL PLEBISCITO
PIAZZA VENEZIA
Palazzo Venezia
San Marco
Colonna Traiana
EL SUDARIO
LARGO DI TORRE ARGENTINA
PIAZZA DEL GESÙ
Gesù
VIA DEGLI ASTALLI
PIAZZA SAN MARCO
Foro di Traiano
Biblioteca del Burcardo
Area Sacra dell' Argentina
V. S. NICOLA D. CESARINI
VIA D. ARCO DE'GINNASI
VIA CELSA
VIA DEI FORI IMPERIALI
Teatro Argentina
VIA DEI BARBIERI
VIA S. MARCO
Il Vittoriano
VIA FLORIDA
VIA DELLE BOTTEGHE OSCURE
VIA D'ARACOELI
VIA S. VENANZIO
ARENULA
V. DI SANT'ANNA
LARGO ARENULA
VIA PAGANICA
VIA M. CAETANI
ANGELO
VIA D. POLACCHI
V. MARGANA
VIC. MARGANA
Santa Maria in Aracoeli
VIA S. PIETRO IN CARCERE
VIA G. BORGHI
PIAZZA MARGANA
PIAZZA D'ARACOELI
Foro di Cesare
Fontana delle Tartarughe
VIA D. DELFINI
V. TRIBUNA
VIA D. TEATRO DI MARCELLO
Insula Romana
VIA DEI FALEGNAMI
VIA DI TOR DE' SPECCHI
PIAZZA MATTEI
VIA D. FUNARI
PIAZZA CAPIZUCCHI
Cordonata
Palazzo Nuovo
Carcere Mamertino
VIA IN PUBLICOLIS
VIA S. M. D. PIANTO
PIAZZA COSTAGUTI
V. D. REGINELLA
VIA S. AMBROGIO
SANT' ANGELO IN PESCHERIA
PIAZZA CAMPITELLI
Santa Maria in Campitelli
PIAZZA DEL CAMPIDOGLIO
Palazzo Senatorio
Santi Luca e Martina
VIA S. M. D. CALDERARI
Casa di Lorenzo Manilio
VIA DELLA TRIBUNA DI CAMPITELLI
VIA MONTANARA
PIAZZALE CAFFARELLI
Arco di Settimio Severo
PIAZZA CENCI
Palazzo Cenci
VIA DEL PROGRESSO
PIAZZA DELLE CINQUE SCOLE
VIA DEL PORTICO D'OTTAVIA
Portico d'Ottavia
VIA DI VILLA CAFFARELLI
Palazzo dei Conservatori
Rostra
V. BEATRICE CENCI
V. MONTE DEI CENCI
VIA DEL TEMPIO
VIA CATALANA
Tempio di Saturno
BARTOLOMEO D. VACCINARI
VIA DEL TEMPIO DI GIOVE
LUNGOTEVERE DEI CENCI
Sinagoga
Teatro di Marcello
Basilica Giulia
Tempio di Giove
VIA DELLA CONSOLAZIONE
VIA DEL FORO ROMANO
VIA DEI FORAGGI
Rupe Tarpea
San Nicola in Carcere
Santa Maria della Consolazione
ISOLA TIBERINA
P.te Fabricio

Rome Bus Routes
Key to Bus Map
Bus route
Start/end of bus route (capolinea)
Direction
Streetcar route
Start/end of streetcar route (capolinea)
Metro station
Train station
Major sight
0 meters 500
0 yards 500
PRATI
CITTÀ DEL VATICANO
BORGO
PONTE
PARIONE
TRASTEVERE
Gianicolo
Musei Vaticani
Cappella Sistina
San Pietro
Castel Sant'Angelo
Pantheon
Villa Farnesina
Santa Maria in Trastevere
Villa Doria Pamphilj
Stazione di San Pietro
Stazione Trastevere
Stazione Roma-Nord
Villa Giulia
Santa Maria del Popolo
Flaminio
Lepanto
Ottaviano
Tevere
VIALE DELLE MILIZIE
VIA COLA DI RIENZO
VIA CRESCENZIO
VIA CICERONE
PIAZZA DEL RISORGIMENTO
PIAZZA SAN PIETRO
BORGO S. ANGELO
V. D. CONCILIAZONE
VIA D. PORTA CAVALLEGGERI
CORSO VITTORIO EMANUELE II
CORSO D. RINASCIMENTO
PIAZZA D. ROTONDA
L.GO TORRE ARGENTINA
VIA ARENULA
VIA DEL CORSO
VIA DEL BABUINO
VIA D. RIPETTA
VIA TOMACELLI
V.CONDOTTI
PIAZZA D. POPOLO
P.ZA CAVOUR
Ponte Cavour
Ponte Umberto
Ponte Pr. Amedeo
Ponte Mazzini
Ponte Sisto
Ponte Garibaldi
Ponte Palatino
Ponte Sublicio
Ponte Testaccio
LT. TEBALDI
LT. D. FARNESINA
LT. D. VALLATI
LT. D. CENCI
LT.D. ANGUILLARA
LUNGOTEVERE AVENTINO
VIALE ALDO FABRIZI
V. D. STAZIONE DI S. PIETRO
V. DI TRASTEVERE
VIALE DI TRASTEVERE
VIA D'ANDOLO
VIA MANUZIO
VIA MARMORATA
VIA ZABAGLIA
TESTACCIO
Gesù

Galleria Borghese
LUDOVISI
SALLUSTIANO
CASTRO PRETORIO
ESQUILINO
CELIO
VIA PINCIANA
VIA SALARIA
VIA NIZZA
VIA NOMENTANA
VIA REGINA ELENA
CORSO D'ITALIA
VIA XX SETTEMBRE
VIA LE D. POLICLINICO
VIALE D. POLICLINICO
VIA GOITO
V. VOLTURNO
M Policlinico
M Castro Pretorio
M Repubblica
PIAZZA D. REPUBBLICA
PIAZZA DEI CINQUECENTO
H-M-38-40-64-86-90-92-105-170-175-217-310-714-910
M Termini
Stazione Termini
VIA G. GIOLITTI
VIALE PRETORIANO
VIA DEI RAMNI
VIA TIBURTINA
VIA DEPRETIS
VIA NAZIONALE
VIA CAVOUR
Santa Maria Maggiore
VIA TURATI
V. NAPOLEONE III
M Vittorio Emanuele
M Cavour
Mercati Traianei
Colosseo
M Colosseo
Parco Oppio
VIA DI PORTA MAGGIORE
PIAZZA PORTA MAGGIORE
V. S. CROCE IN GERUSALEMME
M Manzoni
VIA LABICANA
San Clemente
VIA S. GIOVANNI IN LATERANO
VIA D. SAN GREGORIO
VIA CLAUDIA
Villa Celimontana
VIA DELL' AMBA ARADAM
San Giovanni in Laterano
M San Giovanni
VIA MAGNA GRECIA
VIA CERVETERI
M Re di Roma
VIA GALLIA
VIA ETRURIA
VIA PANNONIA
M Circo Massimo
VIALE DELLE TERME DI CARACALLA
Parco Egerio
PIAZZA ZAMA

LAZIO

Lying between the Apennines and the Tyrrhenian Sea, Lazio is a varied region of volcanic lakes, mountains, ravines, vineyards, and olive groves. Before the rise of Rome, it was populated by the Etruscans and various Italic tribes, including the Latins, after whom the region is named. Besides rich archaeological sites, Lazio also offers skiing and swimming and water sports in the lakes and sea.

Lazio was inhabited at least 60,000 years ago, although the first signs of a substantial civilization date back to the 10th century BC. By the 7th century BC, a flourishing Etruscan and Sabine civilization based on trade and agriculture existed in the north, while the region's southern margins were colonized by the Latins, Volsci, and Hernici. History mingles with myth in the writings of Virgil, who describes how Aeneas landed in Lazio, where he married the daughter of the king of the Latins. Romulus and Remus (legendary founders of Rome) were descendants of this alliance.

With the rise of Rome as a power, the Etruscan and Latin peoples were, in time, overwhelmed, and the focus of the region turned to the city of Rome. Great roads and aqueducts extended out of the city like spokes of a wheel, and wealthy patricians built lavish villas in the surrounding countryside.

The early Middle Ages saw the rise of the Church's temporal power, and with the foundation of monasteries at Subiaco and Montecassino, Lazio became the cradle of western monasticism, and eventually part of the Papal States. In the 16th and 17th centuries, wealthy papal families competed with one another to build luxurious villas and gardens, hiring some of the best architects of the Renaissance and Baroque.

Throughout its history, however, Lazio has been eclipsed and neglected by Rome. The Pontine marshes were a malaria-ridden swamp until the 1920s, when Mussolini had them drained and brought new roads and agricultural improvements to the area.

Looking out over Caprarola during the early evening *passeggiata*

◀ View of Civita di Bagnoregio a small hilltown in Viterbo

Exploring Lazio

Much of Lazio's landscape was formed by the eruption of four volcanoes that showered the area with lava. Lakes formed in the craters, and the soil, rendered fertile by the lava, nourished vines, olives, and fruit and nut trees. The volcanic activity also left Lazio with hot springs, notably around Tivoli, Viterbo, and Fiuggi. Rome dominates the area, dividing the wooded hills of the north from the reclaimed Pontine marshes in the south. Swimming and sailing are possible in lakes Bracciano, Bolsena, and Albano, while Lazio's best beaches lie between Gaeta and Sabaudia in the Parco Nazionale del Circeo.

Sights at a Glance

1. Tuscania
2. Viterbo
3. Montefiascone
4. Bomarzo
5. Caprarola
6. Tarquinia
7. Cerveteri
8. Lake Bracciano
9. Ostia Antica
10. Frascati and the Castelli Romani
11. Tivoli
12. Palestrina
13. Subiaco
14. Montecassino
15. Anagni
16. Sermoneta and Ninfa
17. Terracina
18. Sperlonga
19. Gaeta

ROME pp387–463

The Tolfa hills southwest of Lake Bracciano

Key

- Highway
- Major road
- Road under construction
- Secondary road
- Minor road
- Scenic route
- Main railroad
- Minor railroad
- Regional border
- △ Summit

For additional map symbols *see back flap*

The old quarter overlooking the beach at Sperlonga

Getting Around

Rome's two international airports at Fiumicino and Ciampino serve the region. The main highways are the *Autostrada del Sole* Firenze–Roma (A1) and Roma–Napoli (A1–E45), and the Roma–L'Aquila (A24–E80). Rome's beltway *(raccordo anulare)* connects the highways and main roads.

The Lazio bus service, COTRAL, serves all the main towns with transfer points for the smaller locations in Rome and at Latina, Frosinone, Viterbo, and Rieti. Train routes into the region from other Italian cities are efficient, although within Lazio the services are slower and less frequent.

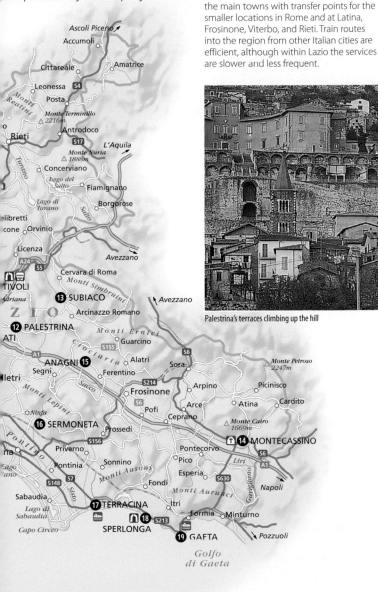

Palestrina's terraces climbing up the hill

Carved loggia of the Palazzo Papale, Viterbo

❶ Tuscania

Viterbo. 8,200. Piazzale Trieste (0761 43 63 71). Fri am.

Tuscania's trim walls and towers are visible from afar on the empty low-lying plains between Viterbo and Tarquinia. Although shaken by an earthquake in 1971, its medieval and Renaissance buildings have since been carefully reconstructed. Just outside the city walls, on the rocky Colle San Pietro, two remarkable churches dating from the Lombard-Romanesque period occupy the site of Tuscana, a major Etruscan center conquered by Rome in 300 BC.

Santa Maria Maggiore, at the foot of the hill, has a typically Lombard-Romanesque asymmetric facade with blind arcades and a bold rose window. Over the central door is a simple marble Madonna and Child, framed by abstract motifs and biblical scenes. Inside, a rare 12th-century full-immersion baptism font stands in the aisle. The Lombard-Romanesque church of **San Pietro**, on top of the hill, is a striking building of ocher-hued tufa and white marble details. It stands on a grassy piazza, along with two medieval towers and a bishop's palace. The facade features an intricately inlaid rose window flanked by strange reliefs, including three-headed bearded demons. The interior is true to its 8th-century form, with squat columns, toothed arches, capitals carved with stylized plants, and a Cosmati floor. Below the church lies a strange mosque-like crypt.

Facade of San Pietro, Tuscania

❷ Viterbo

63,000. FS Via Ascenzi 4 (0761 32 59 92). Sat.

Viterbo was an important Etruscan center before falling to the Romans in the 4th century BC. Its heyday, however, came in the 13th century when it briefly became the papal seat (1257–81). During World War II it was devastated, but the austere gray stone medieval core, still encircled by walls, and many of the town's churches, have been carefully restored.

In **San Pellegrino**, Viterbo's oldest and best preserved quarter, medieval houses with towers, arches, and external staircases line narrow streets running between little piazzas decorated with fountains.

On Piazza San Lorenzo the 12th-century **Duomo** boasts an elegant black and white striped bell tower, a solemn 16th-century facade, and a stark Romanesque interior. The adjacent 13th-century **Palazzo Papale**, with a finely carved loggia, was built for popes on their visits to the city.

The town's civic buildings border the main square, Piazza del Plebiscito. The most interesting is the 15th-century **Palazzo dei Priori**, frescoed inside by Baldassare Croce with scenes from the town's history and mythological past.

Outside the city walls, on Viale Capocci, the Romanesque **Santa Maria della Verità** has wonderful 15th-century frescoes by Lorenzo da Viterbo.

Villa Lante's small but splendid Renaissance gardens, considered Vignola's masterpiece

For hotels and restaurants in this region see pp562–77 and pp580–605

Environs
The **Villa Lante**, northeast of Viterbo, was begun in 1562 by Vignola for Cardinal Gambara. The main attractions are the outstanding Renaissance gardens and fountains. Be careful not to be a victim of a 16th-century practical joke: many of the fountains will sprinkle people without warning.

Palazzo dei Priori
Piazza Plebiscito. **Tel** 0761 30 47 95. **Open** daily.

Villa Lante
Bagnaia. **Tel** 0761 28 80 08. **Open** 8:30am–one hour before sunset Tue–Sun. **Closed** Jan 1, May 1, Dec 25. to gardens.

Carved 11th-century capital in San Flaviano, Montefiascone

❸ Montefiascone

Viterbo. 13,000. FS Piazza V. Emanuele (0761 83 20 60). Wed.

This pretty town is perched on the edge of a defunct volcanic crater between the shores of Lake Bolsena, over which there are splendid views, and the Via Cassia. It is dominated by the octagonal bulk of its cathedral, **Santa Margherita**, whose dome, created in the 1670s by Carlo Fontana, is second in size only to St. Peter's.

On the town's outskirts, along the Via Cassia toward Orvieto, lies **San Flaviano**, a lovely double decker building with a 12th-century church oriented east over an 11th-century church pointing west. Inside are some fine 14th-century frescoes and freely carved capitals, thought to have been inspired by the traditions of Etruscan art.

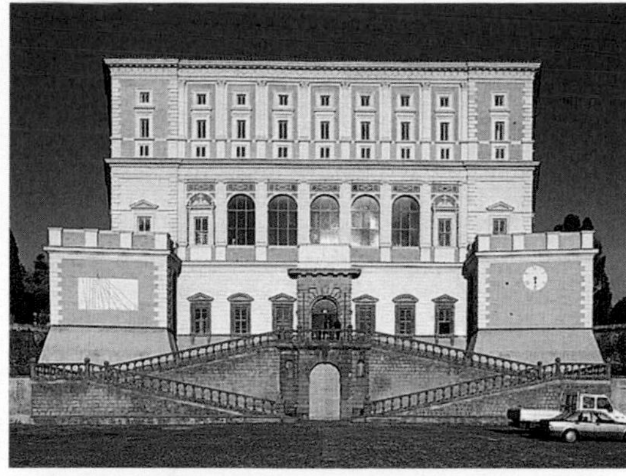

The main facade of the pentagonal Palazzo Farnese at Caprarola

Environs
The popular lakeside beach resort of **Bolsena**, 9 miles (15 km) north on Lake Bolsena, has a medieval castle, as well as boats to the islands of Bisentina and Martana.

❹ Bomarzo

Parco dei Mostri, Bomarzo. **Tel** 0761 92 40 29. FS to Viterbo. from Viterbo (not Sun or public hols).
Open 8:30am–sunset in winter (8:30am–7pm in summer).
W **parcodeimostri.com**

The Sacro Bosco beneath the town of Bomarzo was created between 1522 and 1580 by Duke Vicino Orsini as a bizarre memorial to his late wife. Far from a simple monument, Orsini embraced the artificiality and distortion of the Mannerist period by creating lopsided buildings and sculpting huge boulders of stone into fantastic creatures and vast allegorical monsters.

One of the bizarre stone monsters in Bomarzo's Sacro Bosco

❺ Caprarola

Viterbo. 5,700. Via Filippo Nicolai 2 (0761 64 61 57). Tue.

Perhaps the grandest of the country villas created during the 17th century by the wealthy families of Rome, **Palazzo Farnese** *(see p384)* is the focal point of the medieval village of Caprarola. Designed by Vignola, it was built between 1559 and 1575 and takes its star shape from the foundations of a large pentagonal fortress designed by Antonio da Sangallo the Younger half a century earlier. On the main floor, reached by an elaborately stuccoed spiral staircase, the rooms were frescoed, largely by the Zuccari brothers in 1560, with scenes depicting heroic episodes from the life of Hercules and the Farnese family.

Environs
Created, according to legend, by the god Hercules ramming his club into the ground, **Lago di Vico**, 3 miles (4 km) west of Caprarola, in fact occupies the remnants of a volcanic crater. An idyllic enclave, the lake is encircled by the wooded slopes of the Cimini Hills (much of which is a nature reserve). A scenic road runs around the lake, and the best place for swimming is on the southeast shore.

Palazzo Farnese
Caprarola. **Tel** 0761 64 60 52. **Open** Tue–Sun. **Closed** Jan 1, Dec 25.

Etruscan tumulus tombs from the necropolis at Cerveteri

6 Tarquinia

Viterbo. 15,000. FS Barriera di San Giusto (0766 84 92 82). Wed.

Ancient Tarquinia (Tarxuna) was one of Etruria's most important centers. It occupied a strategic position to the northeast of the present town, on a ridge dominating the coastal plain, until the 4th century BC when it fell to Rome.

Tarquinia itself is worth a wander for its crumbling medieval churches and spacious main square, though the main reason to visit is the **Museo Archeologico e Necropoli**, which has one of Italy's better collections of Etruscan finds. Reclining statues of the deceased adorn the sarcophagi on the ground floor, but the star attraction is a group of terra-cotta winged horses dating from the 4th century BC.

On a hilltop 1 mile (2 km) southeast of town are the frescoed tombs of the **necropolis** dug into the soft volcanic tufa. There are almost 6,000 tombs, but only about 15 can be visited at a time. The frescoes that decorate them, designed to remind the dead of life, range from frenetic dancing figures in the Tomba delle Leonesse to the diners reclining in the Tomba dei Leopardi.

Museo Archeologico e Necropoli
Piazza Cavour. **Tel** 0766 85 60 36; 85 63 08 (necropolis). **Open** Tue–Sun. **Closed** Jan 1, May 1, Dec 25.

7 Cerveteri

Roma. 36,000. FS P.za Risorgimento 19 (06 99 55 19 71). Fri.

In the 6th century BC Cerveteri (ancient Kysry) was one of the largest and most culturally rich towns of the Mediterranean, trading with Greece and controlling a large area along the coast. The **necropolis**, a city of the dead 1 mile (2 km) outside town, is a network of streets lined with tombs dating from the 7th to the 1st century BC. Some of the larger tumulus tombs, like the Tomba degli Scudi e delle Sedie, are arranged like houses, with rooms, doors, and corridors. The Tomba dei Rilievi is decorated with plaster reliefs of tools, pets, and mythological figures. Although the best finds from the necropolis are in museums such as the Vatican Museums, Villa Giulia, and the British Museum in London, some can be seen in the small **Museo Nazionale Cerite** in the center of town.

Dancers from the 4th-century-BC frescoed Tomba del Triclinio in the Museo Archeologico, Tarquinia

Environs
There are more traces of the Etruscans to be seen at **Norchia**, where the tombs are carved out of a rock face, and **Sutri**, whose amphitheater is one of the few relics of the living Etruscans.

Necropolis
Via Necropoli. **Tel** 06 994 00 01. **Open** Tue–Sun. **Closed** some pub hols.

Museo Nazionale Cerite
Piazza Santa Maria. **Tel** 06 994 13 54. **Open** Tue–Sun. **Closed** pub hols.

Medieval Anguillara on Lake Bracciano

8 Lake Bracciano

Roma. FS Bracciano. Piazza Mazzini 5, Bracciano (06 99 81 62 62).

Bracciano is a large lake famous for its fish and popular for water sports and lakeside lunches.

Medieval **Anguillara**, to the south, is the prettiest of the lakeside towns, with romantic views over the water. The main town, **Bracciano**, on the east shore, is dominated by the Orsini-Odescalchi fortress, a pentagonal 15th-century structure with frescoes by Antoniazzo Romano and other Tuscan and Umbrian artists.

Castello Orsini-Odescalchi
P.za Mazzini 14. **Tel** 06 99 80 43 48. **Open** Tue–Sun. **Closed** Jan 1, Dec 25.

For hotels and restaurants in this region see pp562–77 and pp580–605

9 Ostia Antica

Viale dei Romagnoli 717, Ostia. **Tel** 06 56 35 80 03. M Piramide, then FS from Porta San Paolo to Ostia Antica. Excavations & Museum: **Open** 8:30am–7:30pm Tue–Sun. **Closed** Jan 1, May 1, Dec 25.

For over 600 years Ostia was Rome's main port and a busy trading center, until the 5th century AD, when a disastrous combination of malaria and commercial competition brought the town into decline. Silt preserved its buildings, and it now lies 3 miles (5 km) inland.

The ruins of Ostia give a vivid idea of life in Classical times. The main thoroughfare, the **Decumanus Maximus**, runs through the Forum, which houses Ostia's largest temple, the **Capitol**, and past the restored **theater**, still used for open-air concerts in summer. The road is lined with baths, shops, and multi-story buildings. There is even a **Thermopolium**, or bar, with a marble counter and paintings advertising food and drink.

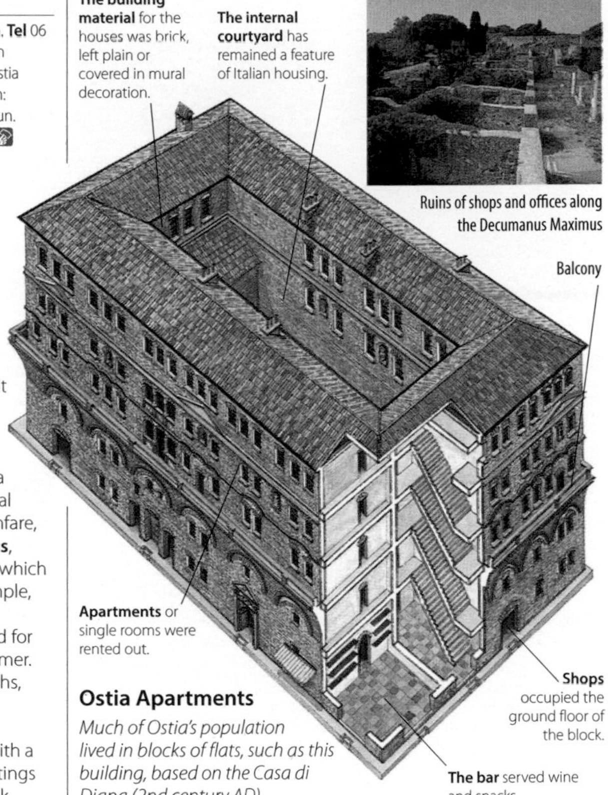
The building material for the houses was brick, left plain or covered in mural decoration.
The internal courtyard has remained a feature of Italian housing.
Balcony
Apartments or single rooms were rented out.
Shops occupied the ground floor of the block.
The bar served wine and snacks.

Ruins of shops and offices along the Decumanus Maximus

Ostia Apartments

Much of Ostia's population lived in blocks of flats, such as this building, based on the Casa di Diana (2nd century AD).

10 Frascati and the Castelli Romani

Roma. FS Frascati. Villa Aldobrandini Gardens: **Tel** 06 942 14 34. **Open** Mon–Fri.

The Alban hills have long been a country retreat for Romans. In Classical times they were scattered with villas; in the Middle Ages with fortified castles (hence the name); and in the 16th and 17th centuries with luxurious residences and their spectacular parks. During World War II, German defenses were based in the Alban hills and many Castelli towns were damaged by Allied bombs. Although partly protected by a nature preserve, the hilltop towns are popular day-trip destinations as well as being famous for their white wine. **Frascati**'s central piazza is a belvedere overlooked by the Villa Aldobrandini, a majestic 17th-century building set in a splendid park of secret grottoes, fountains, and statues.

The fortified Abbazia di San Nilo in **Grottaferrata**, 2 miles (3 km) south, was founded in 1004 and contains some lovely 17th-century frescoes by Domenichino in the chapel. Overlooking Lake Albano, 4 miles (6 km) south, **Castel Gandolfo** is the site of the pope's summer palace. When in residence, the pope addresses the crowd from the balcony.

Gathered around a sturdy 9th-century castle, and famed for its strawberries, **Nemi**, 6 miles (10 km) southeast, looks down onto the glassy dark blue waters of Lake Nemi.

The forested shores around the small, volcanic Lake Nemi

Tivoli, a favorite place to escape the heat of the Roman summer

⓫ Tivoli

Roma. 57,000. FS Piazzale Nazioni Unite (0774 31 35 36). Wed.

Hill town Tivoli, a popular excursion from Rome, was once a favored resort of the ancient Romans, attracted by its fresh water and sulfur springs and its beautiful countryside. The temples that once covered Tivoli's hilltop are still visible in places. Some are half buried in medieval buildings; others, such as the Temples of Sibyl and Vesta, inside the gardens of the Sibilla restaurant (on Via Sibilla), are relatively intact.

The town's most famous sight is the **Villa d'Este**, a sumptuous country residence created in the 16th century by Pirro Ligorio for Cardinal Ippolito d'Este from the shell of a Benedictine monastery. It is known primarily for its gardens, steeply raked on terraces, and studded with spectacular, if somewhat faded and moss-hung, fountains. Although suffering from reduced water pressure and polluted water due to centuries of neglect, the gardens give a vivid impression of the frivolous luxury enjoyed by the papal families. Highlights include the Viale delle Cento Fontane and the Fontana dell'Organo Idraulico, which, thanks to a hydraulic system, can play music. At the other end of town, the **Villa Gregoriana**, now a hotel, is set in a lush wooded valley where paths wind down into a deep ravine.

Splendors from around the world reproduced in Hadrian's Villa

Environs

About 3 miles (5 km) west of Tivoli are the ruins of **Hadrian's Villa**. Easily seen in conjunction with a visit to the town, this is one of the largest and most spectacular villas ever built in the Roman Empire (it once covered an area greater than the center of Imperial Rome).

Hadrian was an inveterate traveler and his aim in creating the villa was to reproduce some of the wonders he had seen around the world. The Stoa Poikile, for example, a walkway around a rectangular pool and garden, recalls the painted colonnade of the Stoic philosophers in Athens, while the Canopus evokes the grand sanctuary of Serapis in Alexandria. There are also ruins of two bath complexes, a Latin and a Greek library, a Greek theater, and a private study on a little island known as the Teatro Marittimo.

Today the rambling ruins, full of shady nooks and hidden corners, make a lovely place to relax, picnic, or explore.

Villa d'Este
Pza Trento 1. **Tel** 0774 31 20 70. **Open** Tue–Sun. **Closed** Jan 1, Dec 25.

Villa Gregoriana
Largo Sant'Angelo. **Tel** 06 39 96 77 01. **Open** Tue–Sun. **Closed** Dec–Feb.

Hadrian's Villa
Tel 0774 53 02 03. **Closed** pub hols.

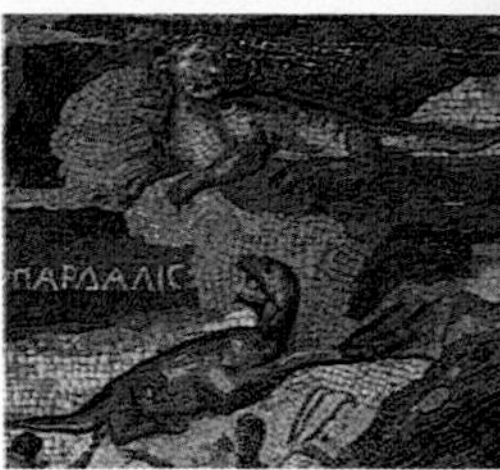

Mosaic fragment of Nile in flood, Museo Nazionale Prenestino, Palestrina

⓬ Palestrina

Roma. 18,000. Piazza Santa Maria degli Angeli 2 (06 957 31 76). Sat.

Medieval Palestrina grew up over the terraces of a huge temple dedicated to the goddess Fortuna Primigenia, the mother of all gods. The temple, founded in the 8th century BC and rebuilt in the 2nd century BC by Sulla, housed one of the most important oracles of ancient times. The terraces of the sanctuary, littered with fragments of columns and porticoes, lead up to the curved **Palazzo Barberini**. Built over the site of a circular temple, it now houses the **Museo Nazionale Prenestino**, best known for a 1st-century BC mosaic of the Nile in flood and a famous sculpture of the Capitoline Triad.

Museo Nazionale Prenestino
Via Barberini. **Tel** 06 953 81 00. **Open** daily. **Closed** Jan 1, May 1, Dec 25.

For hotels and restaurants in this region see pp562–77 and pp580–605

⓭ Subiaco

Roma. 9,000. Town Library, Viale della Repubblica 26 (0774 81 64 07). Sat.

In the 6th century, weary of the decadence of Rome, St. Benedict left the city to become a hermit in a cave above Subiaco. Others joined him, and eventually there were 12 monasteries in the area.

Only two now survive: **Santa Scolastica**, dedicated to Benedict's sister, is organized around three cloisters, one Renaissance, one early Gothic, and the third Cosmatesque. Higher up, the 12th-century **San Benedetto** is a more rewarding destination. Overhanging a deep gorge, it comprises two churches built on top of each other. The upper is decorated with 14th-century Sienese frescoes; the lower, built over several levels, incorporates the original cave where Benedict spent three years after fleeing Rome.

Santa Scolastica
2 miles (3 km) E of Subiaco.
Tel 0774 824 21. **Open** daily.

San Benedetto
2 miles (3 km) E of Subiaco.
Tel 0774 850 39. **Open** daily.
(upper church only).

⓮ Montecassino

Cassino. **Tel** 0776 31 15 29. FS Cassino then bus. **Open** 9am–12:30pm, 3:30–6pm daily (Nov–Mar: to 5pm).

The Abbey of Montecassino, mother church of the Benedictine order and a center of medieval art, was founded in 529 by St. Benedict. By the 8th century it was an important center of learning, and by the 11th century it had become one of the richest monasteries in Europe.

In 1944 it was a German stronghold and a target for Allied bombs. Most of the complex was devastated, including the lavish Baroque church, but the walls remained intact and the abbey stood for three months before falling to the Allies. The adjoining war cemeteries commemorate the 30,000 soldiers killed.

The Monasteries of Lazio

Rose window, Fossanova

St. Benedict founded the Abbey of Montecassino around 529 and there wrote his famous Rule. Based on the principles of prayer, study, and manual labor, it became the fundamental monastic code of western Europe. The Cistercian Order, an offshoot of the Benedictines, came to Italy from Burgundy in the 12th century. The Cistercians were followers of St. Bernard, whose creed was based on austerity and self-sufficiency, qualities that were reflected in the simple, early Gothic architecture of their monasteries. Their first abbey was at Fossanova. Other Cistercian abbeys in Lazio include Valvisciolo (northeast of Sermoneta) and San Martino in Cimino (near Lago di Vico).

The Abbey of Montecassino, destroyed during World War II, was rebuilt as a replica of its 17th-century predecessor.

The Abbey of San Benedetto, Subiaco, was founded in the 11th century over St. Benedict's cave. A staircase carved in the rock leads to the grotto where he preached to shepherds.

The Abbey of Casamari, 8 miles (14 km) east of Frosinone, was founded by Benedictine monks in 1035 and handed over to the Cistercians, who rebuilt it in 1203.

The abandoned medieval village of Ninfa, now a beautiful garden

⓯ Anagni

Frosinone. 20,000. FS
Piazza Innocenzo III (0775 72 78 52). Wed.

According to legend, Saturn founded five towns in southeast Lazio, including Anagni, Alatri, and Arpino. This area is now known as La Ciociaria, from *ciocie*, the bark clogs worn in the area until about 30 years ago.

Before the Romans conquered this part of Lazio, it was inhabited by several different tribes: the Volsci, the Sanniti, and the Hernici. Little is known of them, apart from the extra-ordinary walls with which they protected their settlements. In later years these were believed to have been built by the Cyclops, a mythical giant, which gave them their present name of Cyclopean walls.

Anagni was the most sacred Hernician center until its destruction by the Romans in 306 BC. In the Middle Ages it was the birthplace and family seat of several popes, an era from which many buildings survive, most notably Boniface VIII's 13th-century mullion-windowed palace.

The beautiful Romanesque **Duomo**, Santa Maria, built over the ancient Hernician acropolis, boasts a fine Cosmati mosaic floor from the 13th century as well as 14th-century Sienese frescoes. The crypt of San Magno is frescoed with one of the most complete surviving cycles of the 12th and 13th centuries.

Environs

Alatri, perched on an olive-covered slope 17 miles (28 km) east of Anagni, was an important Hernician town. It preserves an impressive double set of Cyclopean walls, 1 mile (2 km) long and 10 ft (3 m) high, from its 7th-century BC acropolis. In the medieval town below the walls is the Romanesque church of Santa Maria Maggiore, greatly restored in the 13th century.

Arpino, 25 miles (40 km) east of Alatri, is a bustling town with a medieval core, and was the birthplace of the Roman orator Cicero. About 2 miles (3 km) above Arpino, at the site of the ancient town of Civitavecchia, is a tremendous stretch of Cyclopean walls that includes a rare gateway with a pointed arch.

An unusual pointed arch in the Cyclopean walls at Arpino

⓰ Sermoneta and Ninfa

Latina. FS Latina Scalo. from Latina. Via Duca di Mare 19, Latina (0773 69 54 04). Ninfa **Tel** 0773 35 42 41(call for group reservations). **Open** Apr–Oct: 1st Sat & Sun of the month.

Sermoneta is a lovely hilltop town overlooking the Pontine Plains, with narrow cobbled streets winding around medieval houses, palaces, and churches. The **Duomo** has a fine 15th-century panel by Benozzo Gozzoli showing the Virgin cradling Sermoneta in her hands. At the top of the town rises the moated fairy-tale Castello Caetani, frescoed with mythological scenes by a pupil of Pinturicchio.

In the valley below lies the abandoned medieval village of **Ninfa**, converted into lush gardens by the Caetani family in 1921. Streams and waterfalls punctuate the picturesque garden laid out among the crumbling buildings.

17 Terracina

Latina. 44,000. FS i Viale Europa 204 (0773 70 77 02). Thu.

Roman Terracina was an important commercial center on the Via Appia (the Appian Way). Today it is a popular seaside resort, with a fascinating collage of medieval buildings and Roman ruins in its historic center, perched on the slopes of the Ausonian Hills. The more modern part of town by the sea is full of restaurants, bars, and hotels.

Bombing during World War II uncovered many of the town's ancient structures, notably a stretch of the Appian Way and the original paving of the Roman Forum in Piazza del Municipio. The 11th-century **Duomo** was built in the shell of a Roman temple, and is still entered by the temple's steps. The medieval portico is adorned with a lovely 12th-century mosaic and the interior preserves the 13th-century mosaic pavement. Next door, the modern town hall houses the **Museo Archeologico**, devoted to local Greek and Roman finds.

Duomo at Terracina with original Roman steps

About 2 miles (3 km) above the town are the podium and foundations that once supported the Temple of Jove Anxur, dating back to the 1st century BC. This huge arcaded platform is illuminated at night and offers vertiginous views of Terracina and its bay.

Museo Archeologico
P Municipio. **Tel** 0773 70 73 13. **Open** daily. **Closed** Mon pm, some pub hols.

18 Sperlonga

Latina. 4,000. i Corso San Leone 22 (0771 55 70 00). Sat.

Sperlonga is a seaside resort surrounded by sandy beaches. The old town sits on a rocky promontory, a picturesque labyrinth of whitewashed buildings, narrow alleyways, piazzettas, and balconies offering an occasional glimpse of the sea below. It is now full of bars, restaurants, and boutiques. The modern part of town lies down on the seafront.

The area around Sperlonga was a favorite retreat for the ancient Romans during the summer months. They built villas along the coast, and converted the natural caves in the nearby cliffs into places to dine and relax.

In 1957 archaeologists excavating the complex of Tiberius's luxury villa, half a mile (1 km) on the southern outskirts of town, found some marvelous 2nd-century BC Hellenistic sculptures in a large cave open to the sea. These sculptures, representing incidents from Homer's *Odyssey*, are thought to be by the same artists from Rhodes (where the Emperor Tiberius once lived) who were responsible for the Laocoön *(see p421)*. They are displayed, along with other local finds, in the **Museo Archeologico Nazionale**, which is part of the archaeological zone.

12th-century bell tower at Gaeta

Zona Archeologica
Via Flacca. **Tel** 0771 54 80 28. **Open** daily. **Closed** Jan 1, Dec 25.

19 Gaeta

Latina. 22,000. i Via Serapide 26 (0771 45 25 18). Wed.

According to Virgil, Gaeta was named after Aeneas's wet nurse Caieta, who was allegedly buried here. The town sits on the southern headland of the gulf of Gaeta, under Monte Orlando. The historic center is dominated by a mighty Aragonese castle and the pinnacles of mock-Gothic San Francesco. To the north, the modern quarter links Gaeta to the bay of Serapo, a picturesque beach resort.

Gaeta's most beautiful feature is the **Duomo**'s elegant late Romanesque bell tower, its lofty summit topped by a roof of colored ceramic tiles. On the seafront lies the tiny 10th-century church of **San Giovanni a Mare**, with faded frescoes, a hemispherical dome, and a sloping floor to let the sea flow out after flooding.

Stretches of sandy beach along the coast between Gaeta and Terracina

SOUTHERN ITALY

Southern Italy at a Glance

Visitors to southern Italy find a rich array of archaeological remains. Although those of the Romans at Pompeii are high on everyone's list, Greek ruins are found in Sicily and the southern coast, and there are mysterious ancient structures, called *nuraghe*, in Sardinia. Campania, Puglia, and Sicily are admired for their architecture, while across the south there are magnificent landscapes, abundant wildlife, and endless opportunities for outdoor activities. The cuisine alone, with its eclectic heritage and diversity of tastes, provides the excuse to dawdle on the coast or in the mountain villages.

The Parco Nazionale d'Abruzzo, a vast, unspoiled wilderness, is home to wolves, bears, and many species of birds *(see pp506–7)*.

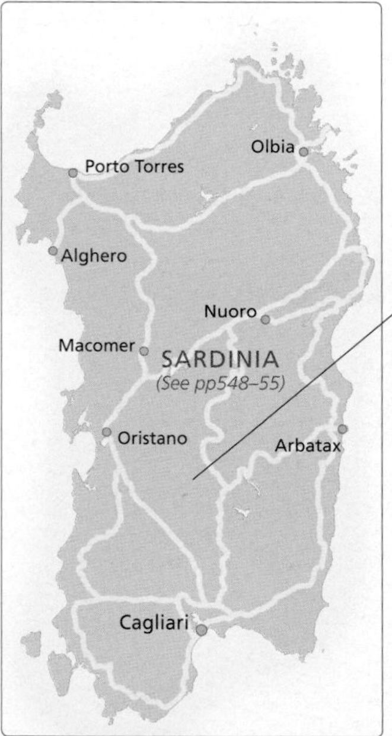

Su Nuraxi at Barumini, built around 1500 BC, is the most celebrated of Sardinia's mysterious stone *nuraghe* sites *(see p549)*.

The cloister decoration at Monreale cathedral is a legacy of Sicily's Arabic past, with elaborate columns adorned with fine mosaics and splendid sculpted capitals *(see pp530–31)*.

Sicily's Valley of the Temples at Agrigento contains some of the best-preserved Greek ruins outside Greece. Mostly Doric in style, they date from the 5th and 6th centuries BC *(see p536)*.

◀ Colorful terraced villas scaling down to the beach in Positano on the Amalfi Coast

The Museo Archeologico Nazionale in Naples is one of Italy's most important museums. It houses the treasures of Pompeii, including sculptures, vases, and everyday artifacts that provide a detailed glimpse of Roman life *(see pp490–91)*.

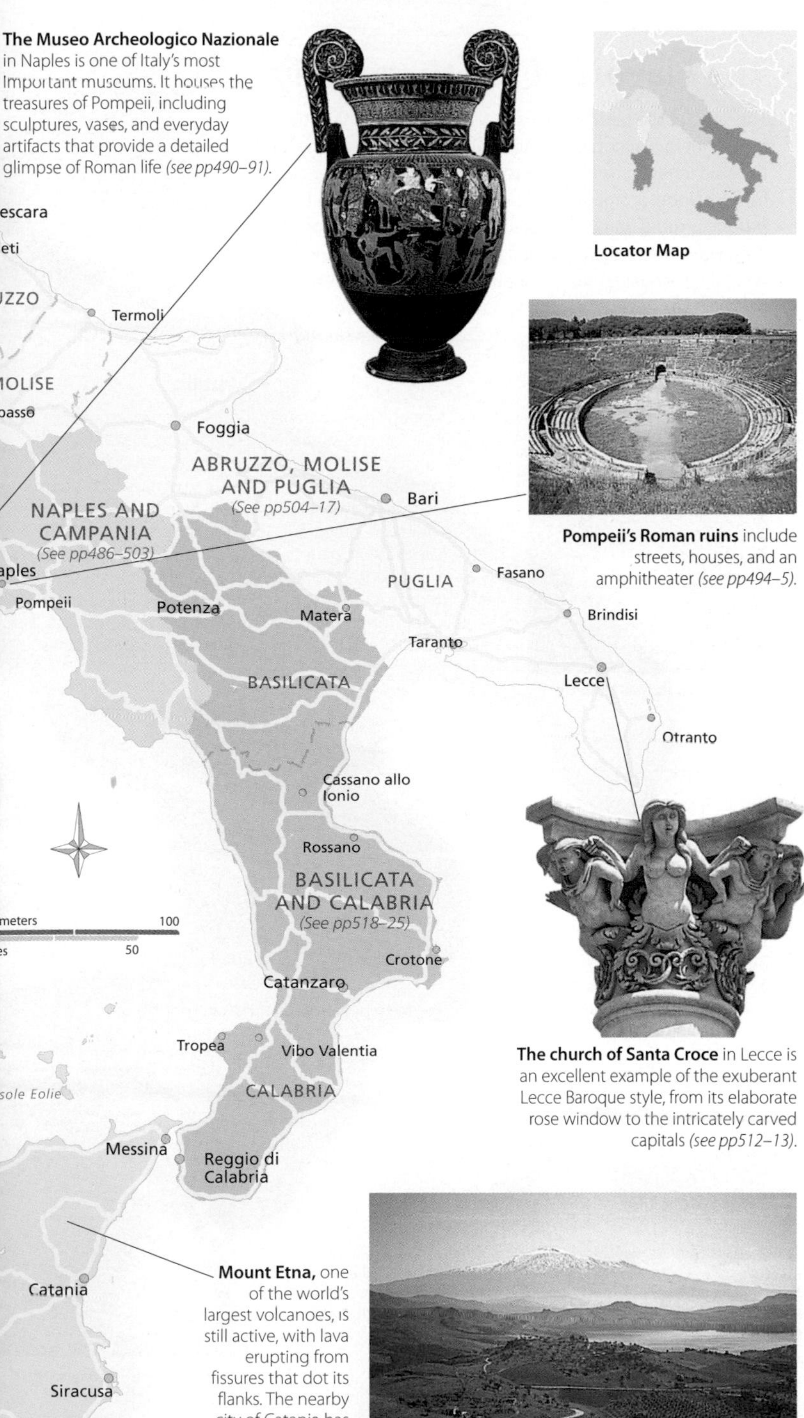

Pompeii's Roman ruins include streets, houses, and an amphitheater *(see pp494–5)*.

The church of Santa Croce in Lecce is an excellent example of the exuberant Lecce Baroque style, from its elaborate rose window to the intricately carved capitals *(see pp512–13)*.

Mount Etna, one of the world's largest volcanoes, is still active, with lava erupting from fissures that dot its flanks. The nearby city of Catania has suffered repeatedly from volcanic damage *(see p539)*.

The Flavors of Southern Italy

The "land of the midday sun," the *Mezzogiorno* is majestic and fertile, yet in places barren and achingly poor. This is the land of the Mediterranean diet, which relies heavily on bright vegetables, fresh seafood, aromatic herbs, and fruity olive oil. Puglia produces more grapes and olives than any other region in Italy, while the fertile volcanic soil around Vesuvius and Etna is ideal for growing plump vegetables, juicy fruits, and vines. Naples is the birthplace of the pizza, and the region of Campania also produces the best buffalo mozzarella in the country.

Mixed herbs

Sicilian cheesemaker with a basket of fresh ricotta

Campania

Naples is famous for pizza, but it's also the home of the tomato-based pasta sauce. Especially prized are the distinctive long, tapered tomatoes from San Marzano in Salerno. The tradition of combining mozzarella and tomato originates here. Pasta is generally tubular (in the north it tends to be ribbonlike). Other staple Campanian ingredients are olive oil, garlic, basil, chilies, and lemons. Excellent seafood includes octopus and squid, anchovies, mussels, and clams, most of which are prepared simply, using lemon, garlic, and pepper. Lamb, kid, and buffalo are the most popular meats. There is also a long tradition of making pastries and ice cream.

Puglia

This region is responsible for producing 80 percent of Italy's pasta, as well as being the source of most of the country's fish. As in the rest of Southern Italy, meats such as poultry, pork, and kid are often roasted over aromatic herbs. The distinctive local ear-shaped pasta, *orecchiette*, is popular, and fruits and vegetables,

Display of the superb seafood caught along the coastline of the south

Regional Dishes and Specialties

Figs

Some of Italy's classic sauces originated in the South, such as the powerful *puttanesca* with tomatoes, anchovies, chilies, capers, and olives. Along the Campanian coast, *zuppa di cozze* (mussels in hot pepper sauce) is a specialty. Octopus is particularly good served in dishes such as *polpo alla luciana*, where it is gently cooked in tomatoes and olive oil with parsley and garlic. *Orecchiette con cime di rapa* (ear-shaped pasta with turnip tops) is a signature dish from Puglia, as is *agnello allo squero* – lamb, spit-roasted over a fire scented with thyme and herbs. For those with a sweet tooth, mouthwatering *cassata Siciliana* is a rich sponge cake layered with ricotta cheese, liqueur, candied fruits, and pistachio nuts.

Maccheroncini con le sarde
Sicilian macaroni with sardines, fennel, pine nuts, raisins, breadcrumbs, and saffron.

resses of vine-ripened tomatoes hanging on a southern market stall

specially figs and quinces, are bundant.

A bounty of fish and shellfish caught along the 250-mile 400-km) coastline. As well s mozzarella, other good heeses include ricotta, goat's, nd smoked cheeses.

icily

he island's long list of nvasions is reflected in its aried cuisine. Greek colonists n the 8th century BC were mazed at the fertility of he volcanic soil. Rice was ntroduced to the area by the rabs, while the influence of orth African cuisine is shown n *cuscusu* (couscous) and ther Arab flavors that appear n sweet and spicy dishes.

The lamb and pork raised in nountain pastures and oak forests is exceptional. Fish is excellent, especially sardines, tuna, anchovies, and swordfish. Vegetables are plump and delicious and eggplant (aubergine) is a firm favorite. Sheep's milk ricotta cheese features in many delicious pastries and puddings, such as the sinfully rich Sicilian *cassata*.

Newly harvested olives, ready to be pressed into olive oil

Other Regions

Mountainous Abruzzo and Molise are good sheep-rearing territory, so lamb is a specialty here, as is guitar-shaped pasta *(maccheroni alla chitarra)*. Food in Calabria and Basilicata is strong on spices, especially chili peppers, which are considered a cure-all. Sardinia bakes wafer-thin unleavened bread – *carta da musica* (music paper). Honey, wild boar ham, and thrushes are popular, as is *torrone*, a delicious almond nougat.

ON THE MENU

Arancini Sicilian rice balls, usually stuffed with a meat, cheese, or vegetable filling.

Caciocavallo Spun cow's milk cheese, especially good from Avellino in Campania.

Insalata caprese Salad from Campania with mozzarella, tomato, basil, olives, and oregano.

Maccheroni di fuoco Pasta dish from Basilicata with large quantities of garlic and chili.

Seadas A kind of doughnut from Sardinia, fried and covered with honey.

Soppressata A spicy, dry-cured salami from Calabria.

izza Napoletana This thin-rusted pizza is topped simply ith tomato, garlic, oregano, asil, and anchovies.

Pesce spada In Campania, Puglia, Calabria, and Sicily, swordfish steak is grilled with lemon and oregano.

Sfogliatella Paper-thin layers of pastry ooze with butter, sugar, cinnamon, orange peel, and ricotta.

Understanding the Architecture of Southern Italy

The Romanesque style of southern Italy owes much to the Normans, who in the 11th century brought from France both form and style in architecture and sculpture. In the southeast, the style has hefty Byzantine overtones; in Sicily it is characterized by strong traditional Islamic motifs and a love of rich color, pattern, and ornamentation. These elements surface later in Sicily's Baroque style and are allied to a dynamism that originates in the Baroque of Rome – though in Sicily it is more vivacious. Neapolitan Baroque is more sophisticated and displays a greater interest in the creative use of space.

Baroque carving on Bagheria's Villa Palagonia

Byzantine and Romanesque Features

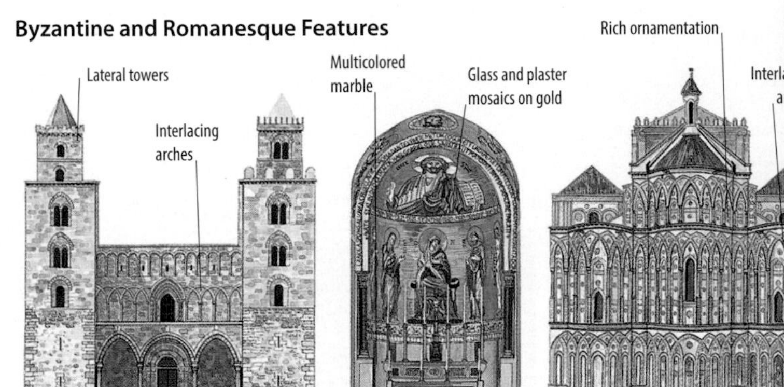

Cefalù, begun in 1131 by Roger II, is one of Sicily's great Norman cathedrals *(see p539)*. Its west front exhibits many northern Romanesque features, such as the massive towers.

Christ Pantocrator, a Byzantine apse mosaic (*c.* 1132), adorns the Cappella Palatina *(see p530)*.

The east end of the Norman cathedral of Monreale, founded ir 1172 by William II, is built of multicolored materials with interlacing arches *(see pp534–5)*.

Baroque Features

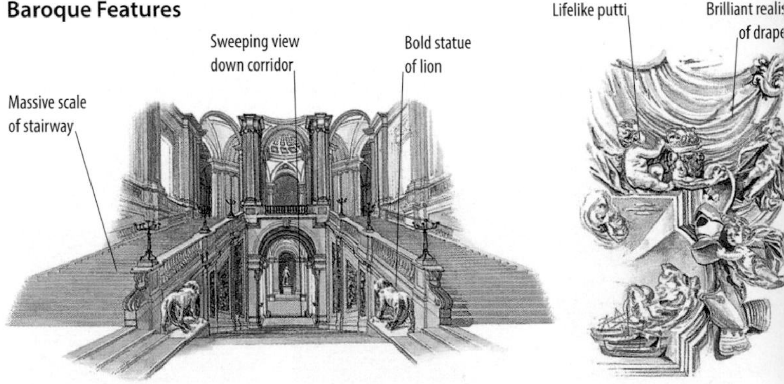

Caserta's Palazzo Reale, a sumptuous royal palace begun by Charles III in 1752, is characterized by its monumental scale *(see p500)*. The richly decorated interior is prefaced by several huge entrances and impressive staircases offering views. The enormous building was designed by Luigi Vanvitelli.

Giacomo Serpotta's stucco reliefs (*c.* 1690) in Palermo's Oratorio di Santa Zita illustrat Sicilians' love of exuberant decoration *(see p533)*.

Where to see the Architecture

The best places to see Romanesque architecture are Puglia and the cathedral cities of northwestern Sicily. Puglia's best churches are those at Trani *(see p513)* and nearby Canosa, Molfetta, and Bitonto; Ruvo di Puglia *(p514)*, San Leonardo di Siponto on the Gargano Peninsula, and Martina Franca, near Alberobello. The Baroque style of the south is epitomized by the villas, palaces, and churches of Naples and Sicily, and by the deeply encrusted ornamentation found on church facades in Lecce *(pp516–17)*, in Puglia. In Sicily, the Baroque of Palermo *(pp530–31)*, Bagheria *(p536)*, Noto, Modica, and Ragusa *(p547)* and Siracusa *(pp546–7)* is well known. Less so are churches at Piazza Armerina *(p541)*, Trapani *(p536)*, Palazzolo Acreide, close to Siracusa, and Acireale, near Catania.

The Duomo portal in Ruvo di Puglia

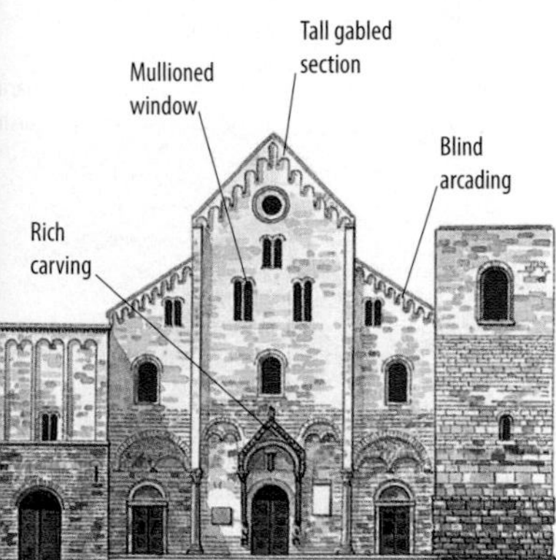

Bari's Basilica di San Nicola *(founded 1087)* was the model for subsequent churches in Puglia *(see p514)*. Based on Norman architecture, its facade is flanked by towers and divided vertically into three, reflecting the tripartite nature of its plan.

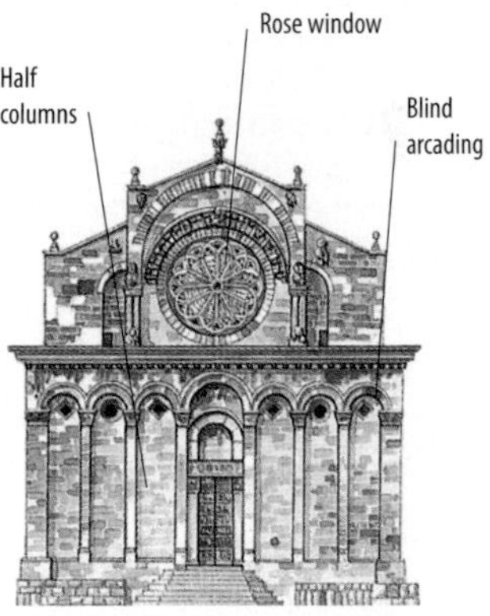

The facade of Troia cathedral *(1093 –1125)* owes its design to Pisan architecture and its rich ornamentation to Byzantine and Arab models *(see pp512–13)*.

The facade of Siracusa's Duomo, begun in 1728 by Andrea Palma, is animated by broken or curved elements *(see pp546–7)*.

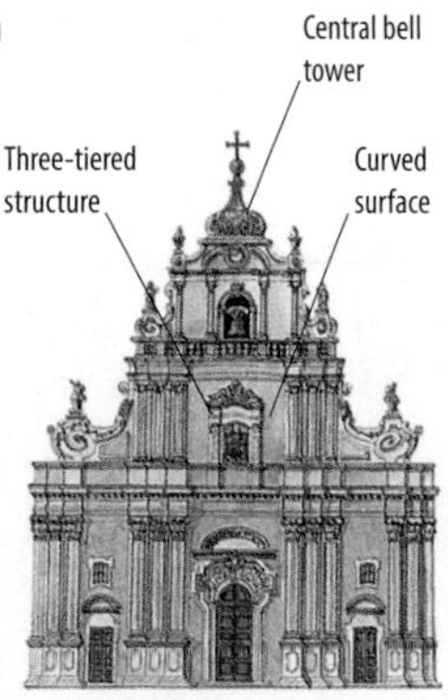

San Giorgio in Ragusa *(1744)* has a facade by Gagliardi with layers of ornamentation culminating in the tower *(see p547)*.

Lecce's Chiesa del Rosario *(begun 1691)* was built by Lo Zingarello of soft local sandstone in the Lecce Baroque style of profuse carving *(see pp516–17)*.

The Ancient Greeks in Southern Italy

Some of the best ruins of the ancient Greek world are in Southern Italy. Syracuse, Selinunte, Segesta, and Gela are among the better known Sicilian sites, while those on the mainland include Crotone, Locri, and Paestum. Magna Graecia is the collective name given to these scattered colonies of ancient Greece, the earliest of which were founded in the Naples area between the 8th and 6th centuries BC. Many great figures of the age – including Pythagoras, Archimedes, and Aeschylus – lived in these settlements, and it was here that wine making flourished. Artifacts from this age are exhibited in the excellent archaeological museums of Naples, Syracuse, and Taranto.

Ancient Herakleia (Herculaneum) was named after its patron deity, the mighty Hercules. It was buried by the eruption of Mount Vesuvius in AD 79 *(see p499)*.

Poseidonia (today's Paestum), was the city of Poseidon, God of the Sea. Its ruins, dating from the 6th century BC, include the hulks of two of the finest Doric temples in Europe *(see pp502–3)*.

Mount Etna was believed to be the forge of Hephaistos (Vulcan) – God of Fire – and the Cyclops, the one-eyed giant *(see p543)*.

Tyndaris was one of the last Greek cities founded on Sicily.

Eryx, founder of the town, was the son of Aphrodite and Poseidon.

The legendary founder of Agrigento was Daedalus, who created wings for himself and his son, Icarus, so they could fly.

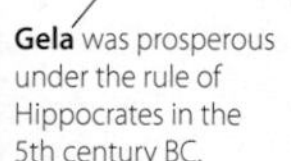

Gela was prosperous under the rule of Hippocrates in the 5th century BC.

Egesta (built 426–416 BC) was colonized by the Elymians, who may have originated at Troy. Among the ruins of this town are a half-completed temple and a theater *(see p538)*. Ancient Greeks used theaters for plays and cultural entertainment rather than combat.

Aeschylus, the dramatist, died in Gela in 456. Considered the father of Greek tragedy, his plays include *Seven Against Thebes*, *Women of Aetna*, and *Prometheus Bound*.

0 kilometers 100

0 miles 50

Metapontion (Metapontum) was home to Pythagoras after his expulsion from Crotone. Its ruins include Doric temples, the Tavole Palatine, and a theater *(see p523)*.

Taras was home to the philosopher and scientist Archytas, and to Aristoxenes, author of the earliest treatise on music.

Founded by Spartan Greeks (8th century BC), Taras was a rich and powerful city.

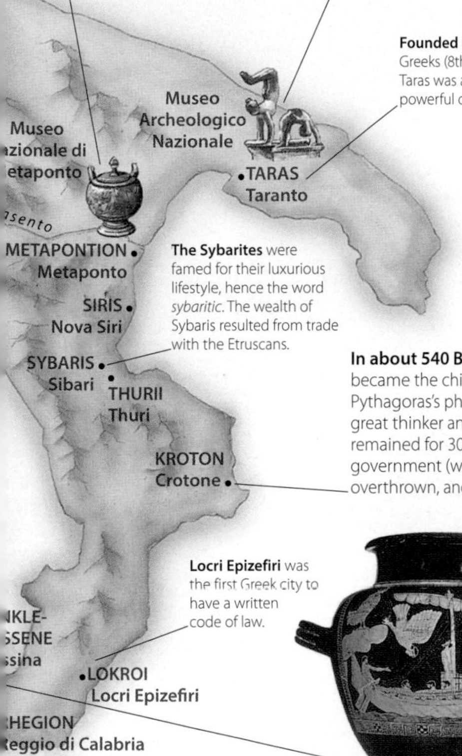

Museo Archeologico Nazionale

Museo Nazionale di Metaponto

TARAS Taranto

METAPONTION Metaponto

SIRIS Nova Siri

SYBARIS Sibari

THURII Thuri

KROTON Crotone

LOKROI Locri Epizefiri

RHEGION Reggio di Calabria

Naxos

Greece and its Colonies

7th–5th century BC

The Sybarites were famed for their luxurious lifestyle, hence the word *sybaritic*. The wealth of Sybaris resulted from trade with the Etruscans.

In about 540 BC Crotone became the chief school of Pythagoras's philosophy. Here the great thinker and mathematician remained for 30 years until the government (which he supported) was overthrown, and he was expelled.

Locri Epizefiri was the first Greek city to have a written code of law.

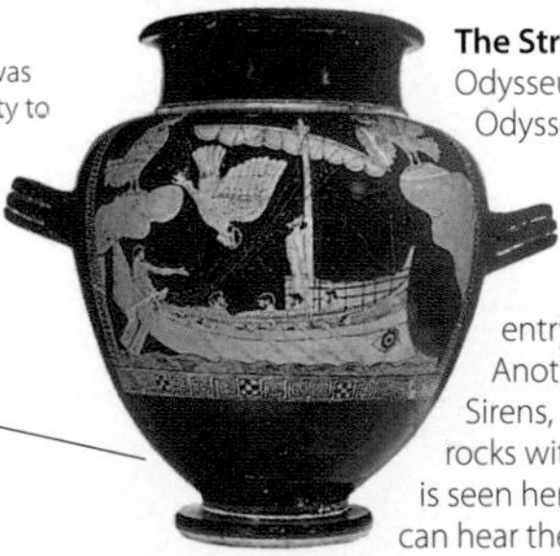

The Straits of Messina vexed Odysseus, the hero of Homer's Odyssey. Here at the meeting of two seas the currents created a "whirlpool" – Charybdis – which posed a threat to safe entry of Messina *(see p542)*. Another threat were the Sirens, who lured voyagers onto rocks with their singing. Odysseus is seen here tied to a mast, so he can hear their song, but resist its call.

Plato the philosopher visited Syracuse and advised the ruler, Dionysius II, how to govern.

The mathematician and inventor Archimedes was born in Syracuse *c.* 287 BC. His inventions included the famous Archimedean screw, and various weapons to stave off the Romans *(see pp546–7)*.

Demeter and Persephone

The complex web of Greek mythology was part of the daily life of the ancients. Enna was once the seat of the cult of Demeter, the earth goddess, and between 480 and 460 BC a temple was erected there in her honor. According to the legend, Persephone, the daughter of Demeter and Zeus, was abducted in the nearby fields by Hades, who carried her off into the Underworld. Demeter then left Olympus and wandered the world searching in vain for her daughter. Discovering that Zeus had allowed the abduction to happen, Demeter put a blight on Sicily: it would remain barren until Persephone returned. Finally Hades allowed her return from the Underworld, but only for a few months of each year – from spring to fall. Demeter, satisfied with the result, ensured that Sicily became the most fertile place on earth.

Sculpture of Persephone

NAPLES AND CAMPANIA

The capital of Campania, Naples is one of the few European cities of the ancient world that has never been completely extinguished. Founded by Greeks, it was embellished and enlarged by the Romans and in subsequent centuries was the much-prized booty of foreign invaders and Imperialists – most prominently the Normans, Hohenstaufen, French, and Spanish.

Naples today is a chaotic yet spectacular metropolis sprawling noisily and dirtily around the edge of the Bay of Naples. To one side is Mount Vesuvius; facing from the sea are the islands of Capri, Ischia, and Procida. Pompeii and Herculaneum, lying in the shadow of the volcano that destroyed them, contain the most revealing Roman ruins in Italy.

For centuries Naples dominated the Italian south, or *Mezzogiorno* (land of the midday sun). Unemployment and crime are a problem – the Camorra is as deep-seated here as the Mafia is in Sicily – but there is also an attractive, rough ebullience to the city.

The ancient history of Campania is linked to the Etruscans and the Greeks, whose massive ruins can be seen at Paestum. Next came a time of great prosperity under the Romans; archaeological evidence of this still exists at Benevento, Santa Maria Capua Vetere, and Pozzuoli.

The hinterland, with its rich, well-cultivated plains, is eclipsed by the Amalfi coastline, with its breathtaking views, and the terrific seaboard of the Cilento. The mountainous interior, remote and unvisited, contains small towns that were settled by the Greeks, developed by the Romans, and often abandoned in the wake of malaria and Saracen attacks.

A glimpse into the narrow streets of Naples' Quartieri Spagnoli (Spanish Quarter)

◀ Picturesque beach and town of Amalfi, the largest town on the Amalfi Coast

Exploring Naples and Campania

The main center from which to explore Campania is the city of Naples (Napoli). To the north, verdant plains sweep down to Santa Maria Capua Vetere. To the east, the mountainous province of Benevento overlooks the valley, while earthquake-ravaged Avellino and its province lurk on a plain beyond Vesuvius. The Campi Flegrei area, west of Naples, is famous for the Roman ruins at Cuma. Farther south is the splendid, rugged Amalfi Coast. Clean sandy beaches lie beyond the tip of the Sorrentine Peninsula and along the Cilento coast as well as on Capri, Ischia, and Procida in the Gulf of Naples.

Sights at a Glance

1. *Naples (Napoli) pp490–97*
2. *Pompeii pp498–9*
3. Santa Maria Capua Vetere
4. Caserta
5. Benevento
6. Amalfi Coast
7. Salerno
8. Paestum
9. Capri
10. Ischia and Procida

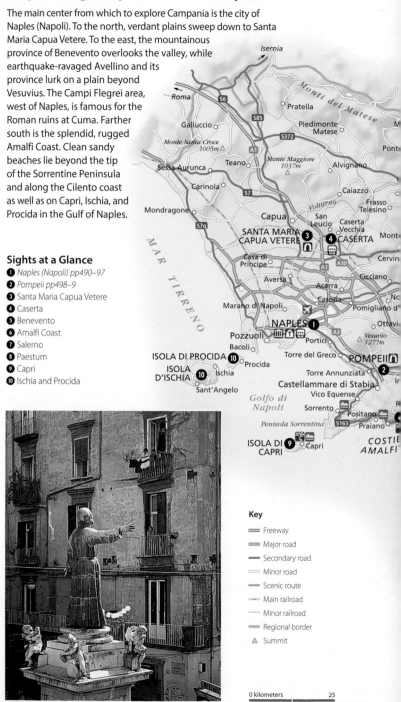

Typical Naples street viewed from Santa Maria Maggiore

Key

- Freeway
- Major road
- Secondary road
- Minor road
- Scenic route
- Main railroad
- Minor railroad
- Regional border
- △ Summit

0 kilometers 25
0 miles 20

For additional map symbols *see back flap*

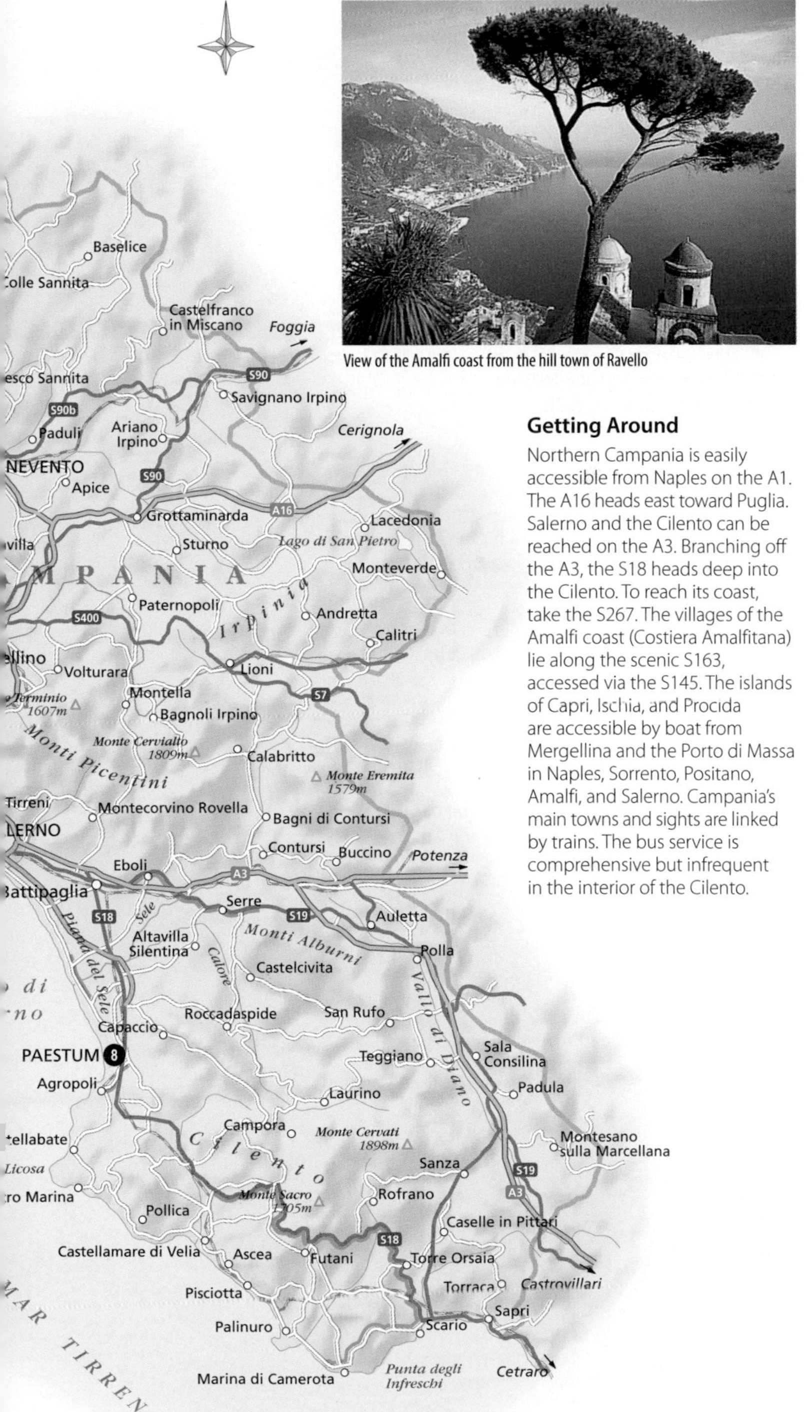

View of the Amalfi coast from the hill town of Ravello

Getting Around

Northern Campania is easily accessible from Naples on the A1. The A16 heads east toward Puglia. Salerno and the Cilento can be reached on the A3. Branching off the A3, the S18 heads deep into the Cilento. To reach its coast, take the S267. The villages of the Amalfi coast (Costiera Amalfitana) lie along the scenic S163, accessed via the S145. The islands of Capri, Ischia, and Procida are accessible by boat from Mergellina and the Porto di Massa in Naples, Sorrento, Positano, Amalfi, and Salerno. Campania's main towns and sights are linked by trains. The bus service is comprehensive but infrequent in the interior of the Cilento.

❶ Naples

The compact center of Naples, filled with palaces, churches, convents, and monasteries, revolves around just a few streets. From the Piazza del Plebiscito, Via Toledo (also called Via Roma) proceeds north toward Piazza Dante. To the east, narrow Via dei Tribunali and Via San Biagio dei Librai penetrate the historic and noisy heart of the city, the *Spaccanapoli* (split Naples). South of Palazzo Reale is the Santa Lucia district. To the west is the port of Mergellina, and overlooking the city is the Vomero district.

View of the Bay of Naples and Mount Vesuvius

Exploring Northeast Naples

Much of the city's most interesting art and architecture can be found here, including the Museo Archeologico Nazionale and its Roman treasures from Herculaneum and Pompeii. The buildings provide a wide range of architectural styles from the French-Gothic of the Duomo to the Florentine-Renaissance style of the Porta Capuana.

MADRE

Via Settembrini 79. **Tel** 081 193 13 016. **Open** 10am–7pm Mon, Wed–Sun. (free Mon).
museomadre.it

Opened in 2005, the Museo d'Arte Contemporanea Donna Regina Napoli (MADRE) is located in the Palazzo Donnaregina, from which it gets its name. The museum houses a remarkable collection by well-known artists such as Andy Warhol, Robert Rauschenberg, Mimmo Paladino, Claes Oldenburg, Robert Mapplethorpe, and Roy Lichtenstein, among others. On the first floor is a library and a children's area, while the third floor is used for temporary exhibitions. The museum often hosts special events such as movie screenings, concerts, and theatrical performances. The church of Santa Maria Donnaregina, at the back of the museum, provides additional exhibition space in a beautiful setting.

The beautiful Renaissance gate of Porta Capuana

Castel Capuano and Porta Capuana

Piazza Enrico de Nicola.

Begun by Norman King William I and completed by Frederick II, Castel Capuano was a royal palace until 1540, when it became the Court of Justice. Today it is a courthouse.

Nearby, between the Aragonese towers of the Capua Gate and facing a market, is a rare sculpture in the Florentine-Renaissance manner. Created by Giuliano da Maiano (and finished in 1490 by Luca Fancelli) as a defensive gate, Porta Capuana is perhaps Italy's finest Renaissance gateway.

For hotels and restaurants in this region see pp562–77 and pp580–605

Sights at a Glance

1. *Museo Archeologico Nazionale pp494–5*
2. MADRE
3. Castel Capuano and Porta Capuana
4. Duomo
5. Pio Monte della Misericordia
6. Cappella Sansevero
7. San Lorenzo Maggiore

8. San Gregorio Armeno
9. Museo Filangieri
10. Sant'Angelo a Nilo
11. San Domenico Maggiore
12. Santa Chiara
13. Gesù Nuovo
14. Sant'Anna e San Bartolomeo dei Lombardi
15. Castel Nuovo
16. Quartieri Spagnoli
17. Galleria Umberto I and Teatro San Carlo
18. Palazzo Reale

Interior of the Duomo

Duomo

Via Duomo 147. **Tel** 081 44 90 97. **Open** 8am–12:30pm, 4:40–7pm Mon–Sat; 8am–1:30pm, 5–7:30pm Sun. **Closed** public hols.

Built between 1294 and 1323, the Cattedrale di Santa Maria Assunta, or Duomo, lies behind a mostly 19th-century facade. The nave is lined with ancient columns, and there is an array of monuments to past rulers, along with paintings by Lanfranco and Domenichino.

The Duomo houses the relics of San Gennaro, Naples' patron saint (martyred AD 305). The Cappella San Gennaro holds vials of his congealed blood, which miraculously liquefies three times a year (the Saturday before the first Sunday in May, Sep 19, and Dec 16). The Cappella Carafa, a Renaissance masterpiece built from 1497 to 1506, contains the saint's tomb.

Accessible from the Duomo's north aisle is the Cappella di Santa Restituta, founded in the 4th century on the site of a former Temple of Apollo, and rebuilt in the 1300s. It has ceiling paintings by Luca Giordano (1632–1705) and a 5th-century baptistry. The nearby Museo del Tesoro di San Gennaro (Tel: 081 29 49 80) exhibits a range of gold, silverware, jewels, statues, and art.

VISITORS' CHECKLIST

Practical Information

1,300,000. P. del Gesù Nuovo (081 551 27 01), Via San Carlo (081 40 23 94). daily. San Gennaro: 19 Sep. **inaples.it**

Transportation

Capodichino 2.5 miles (4 km) NW. Centrale, P. Garibaldi. P. Garibaldi. Stazione Marittima, Molo Beverello & Mergellina.

Pio Monte della Misericordia

Via dei Tribunali 253. **Tel** 081 44 69 44. Church & gallery **Open** 9am–2:30pm Mon–Tue, Thu–Sun. **Closed** public hols. Gallery only.

The octagonal church belonging to this charitable foundation houses Caravaggio's *Seven Acts of Mercy* (1607). The art gallery has paintings by Luca Giordano and Mattia Preti.

Cappella Sansevero

Via F. de Santis 19. **Tel** 081 551 84 70. **Open** 10am–5:40pm Wed–Mon (to 1:10pm Sun & public hols). (church). **museosansevero.it**

This tiny 16th-century chapel is the burial sepulchre of the Princes of Sangro di Sansevero. Featuring both Christian and Masonic symbolism, the chapel has an unusual character.

Remarkable 18th-century sculpture fills the chapel. *The Resurrection of the Prince*, by an unknown artist, is mirrored by that of Christ, above the altar. Giuseppe Sammartino's *Veiled Christ* is an alabaster figure beneath a marble veil, and is a work of technical virtuosity.

Prince Raimondo, an 18th-century alchemist, is associated with the chapel. He performed gruesome experiments on human bodies, for which he was excommunicated. The results of some of his experiments can be seen in the crypt.

Sammartino's Veiled Christ (1753) in the Cappella Sansevero

For keys to symbols *see back flap*

Exploring Central Naples

The part of Santa Lucia bordered by Via Duomo to the east, Via Tribunali to the north, Via Toledo (Roma) to the west, and the water to the south is the old heart of Naples. Especially rich in 14th- and 15th-century churches, the area offers visitors an abundance of sights.

Interior of San Gregorio Armeno

San Lorenzo Maggiore

Via dei Tribunali 316. **Tel** 081 45 49 48. Church & Excavations: **Open** 9:30am–5:30pm daily (to 1:30pm Sun). excavations. church.

This mainly 14th-century Franciscan church (with an 18th-century facade) was built during the reign of Robert the Wise of Anjou. The storyteller Giovanni Boccaccio (1313–75) reputedly based the character Fiammetta on King Robert's daughter Maria, whom he saw here on Easter Eve, 1334. For Naples, San Lorenzo Maggiore is a rare Gothic edifice. Its nave and the apse ambulatory have a magnificent period simplicity. The church houses medieval tombs including the Gothic tomb of Catherine of Austria, who died in 1323, by a pupil of Giovanni Pisano. Excavations in the monastic cloister, where the lyric poet and scholar Petrarch *(see p163)* once stayed, have found the remains of a Roman basilica. There are also important Greek and medieval excavations.

The simple Gothic interior of San Lorenzo Maggiore, looking down the nave to the apse

San Gregorio Armeno

Piazza San Gaetano 1. **Tel** 081 551 70 76. **Open** am daily. cloister.

Benedictine nuns still preside over this church. The convent attached to it earned a reputation for luxury since the nuns, traditionally from noble families, were accustomed to lavish living, which continued here.

The sumptuous Baroque interior of the church sports frescoes by Luca Giordano. Via San Gregorio Armeno is lined with the workshops of vendors of Nativity figures *(presepi)*.

Museo Filangieri

Palazzo Cuomo, Via Duomo 288. **Tel** 081 20 31 75. **Open** 9:30am–2pm, 3:30–7pm Mon–Sat; 9:30am–1:30pm Sun and public hols.

The 15th-century Renaissance Palazzo Cuomo houses the Museo Filangieri. Founded in 1881, the original museum collections put together by Prince Gaetano Filangieri were destroyed during World War II. The current collection contains interesting and varied objects, including porcelain, embroidery, manuscripts, Italian and Spanish arms, objects from local archaeological excavations, and paintings by such artists as Luca Giordano, Ribera, and Mattia Preti. There is also an important bust by Antonio Canova.

Renaissance tomb of Cardinal Brancaccio, Sant'Angelo a Nilo

Sant'Angelo a Nilo

Piazzetta Nilo. **Tel** 081 211 08 60. **Open** 8am–1pm, 4:30–7:30pm daily.

This 14th-century church contains a fine work of Renaissance sculpture: the Tomb of Cardinal Rinaldo Brancaccio. Designed by Michelozzo, it was sculpted in Pisa, and then shipped to Naples upon completion in 1428. Donatello reputedly carved the right-hand angel drawing back the curtain, the shallow relief Assumption, and the cardinal's head.

San Domenico Maggiore

Piazza San Domenico Maggiore. **Tel** 081 45 91 88. **Open** 8:30am–1pm, 4–7pm Tue–Sun. Treasury: **Open** same as church.

This Gothic church (1289–1324) contains some of the finest Renaissance monuments and sculpture in Naples. The tomb slab of John of Durazzo (died 1335), by Tino da Camaino, is in the south transept. In the sacristy are the *Apotheosis of Faith* ceiling frescoes by Solimena (18th century). The choir features a paschal candlestick (1585) supported by figures by da Camaino. The Cappellone del Crocifisso contains a medieval painting of the *Crucifixion*, which supposedly spoke to St. Thomas Aquinas. The grand Brancaccio tomb by Jacopo della Pila (1492) is in the Chiesa Antica.

Detail of the embossed facade of Gesù Nuovo

Santa Chiara

Via Benedetto Croce. Church: **Tel** 081 797 12 31. **Open** 7am–1pm, 4:30–8pm daily. Cloister: **Tel** 081 797 12 24. **Open** 9:30am–5:30pm Mon–Sat, 10am–2:30pm Sun & public hols.

This 14th-century church was bombed in World War II, but a reconstruction uncovered the original Provençal-Gothic structure. The tombs of the Angevin monarchs are housed here. The tomb of Robert the Wise (died 1343) is by Giovanni and Pacio Bertini; that of Robert's son, Charles of Calabria (died 1328), is by Tino da Camaino; and the tomb of Charles's wife, Mary of Valois (died 1331), is by da Camaino and his followers. Adjacent is a convent with a cloister designed by Vaccaro (1742). There is also a museum and a Roman bath house (AD 1).

Gesù Nuovo

Piazza del Gesù Nuovo 2. **Tel** 081 557 81 11. **Open** daily.

The 16th-century Jesuit church was constructed by Valeriano (and later Fanzago and Fuga) from the Severini palace (15th century), of which only a facade survives. The ebullient decoration of the interior (1600s) is fully in accordance with the needs of the Jesuits, who used drama and direct appeal to the emotions to draw the faithful. It is resplendent with colored marble and paintings, including works by Ribera and Solimena. In 1688 an earthquake destroyed the dome – the present one is 18th-century.

Sant'Anna e San Bartolomeo dei Lombardi

Via Monteoliveto. **Tel** 081 551 33 33. **Open** 9am–noon Tue–Sat.

Mazzoni's *Pietà* (1492) in Sant'Anna e San Bartolomeo dei Lombardi

Also known as Santa Maria di Monteoliveto, this church was built in 1411 and restored after World War II. It is a repository of Renaissance art. Entering, past the tomb (1627) of Domenico Fontana (who completed the dome of St. Peter's in Rome after Michelangelo's death), the richness of the interior unfolds.

The Cappella Mastrogiudice contains an *Annunciation* panel by Florentine sculptor Benedetto da Maiano (1489) and the Cappella Piccolomini contains Antonio Rossellino's monument (c.1475) to Maria d'Aragona (completed by da Maiano). The Cappella del Santo Sepolcro houses a *Pietà* by Guido Mazzoni (1492). Its eight terra-cotta figures are considered life-size portraits of the artist's contemporaries. The old Sacristy, frescoed by Vasari (1544), has inlaid stalls by Giovanni da Verona (1510).

Majolica tiles decorated with scenes of rural life in the cloisters of Santa Chiara

Naples: Museo Archeologico Nazionale

This building, housing one of the world's most important archaeological museums, started life in the late 1500s as the home of the royal cavalry and was rebuilt in the early 17th century as the seat of Naples university. In 1777, when Ferdinand IV transferred the university to the former monastery of Gesù Vecchio, the building was again adapted to house the Real Museo Borbonico and library. In 1860 it became public property. The 1980 earthquake caused much damage to the collections. Major restoration and reorganization of exhibits continue but most areas of the museum are open on Sundays.

Spring Fresco
The fresco removed from the Villa Stabia in the Varano plain is a masterpiece of grace and elegance; the female figure rendered with soft, delicate colors.

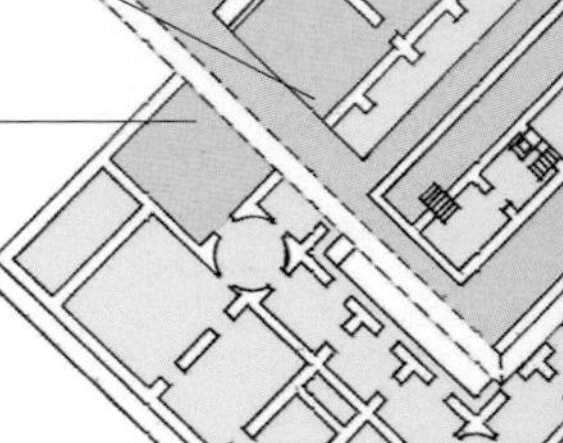

Villa of the Papyri

Bust of "Seneca"
Found in the Villa dei Papiri in Herculaneum, this 1st-century BC bronze head was long thought to represent the philosopher Seneca the Elder (*c.* 55 BC–AD 39). Today, however, its identity is less certain.

★ The Battle of Alexander
The splendid mosaic from the House of the Faun in Pompeii *(see p498)* depicts Alexander the Great's victory over Persian emperor Darius III (333 BC).

Key to Floor Plan

- Epigraphs
- Egyptian collection
- Engraved gems
- Sculptures
- Mosaics
- Numismatics
- Didactics
- Herculaneum & Pompeii
- Hall of the Sundial
- Prehistoric, Greek, and Etruscan collections
- Nonexhibition space

The Secret Cabinet
The erotic works from Pompeii and Herculaneum housed here caused embarrassment at the time of the Bourbons. Today, however, they are available for public viewing (book ahead).

Blue Vase
This wine vessel found in a Pompeii tomb was made with the so-called glass-cameo technique: a layer of opaque white paste was placed over colored glass and then engraved with decorative motifs.

VISITORS' CHECKLIST

Practical Information
Piazza Museo Nazionale 19.
Tel 081 44 22 149.
Open 9am–7:30pm Wed–Mon.
museo archeologiconazionale. campaniabeniculturali.it

Transportation
M Piazza Cavour-Museo. C64, C83, E1, R1, R4, 24, 47, 110, 135.

Temple of Isis

Sacrifice of Iphigenia
In this Pompeiian fresco, Iphigenia, daughter of Agamemnon, is about to be sacrificed to Artemis, who saves her by taking a deer instead.

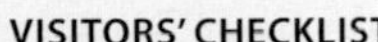

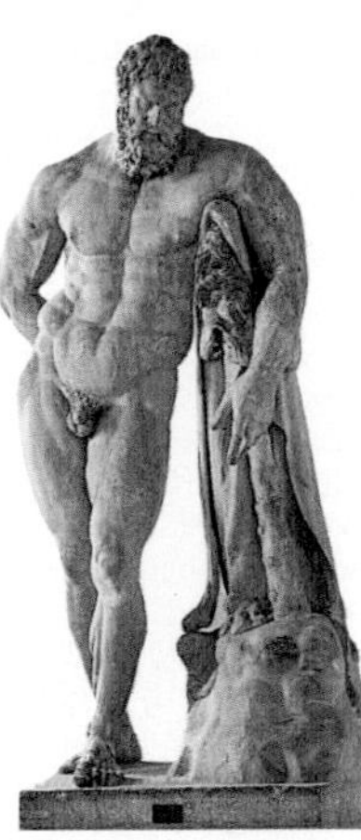

★ Farnese Hercules
Made by Glykon of Athens, this statue is an enlarged copy of a sculpture by the Greek master Lysippus. Napoleon is said to have regretted leaving it behind when he removed his booty from Italy in 1797.

Entrance

Stairs down to Egyptian Collection

★ Farnese Bull
Excavated in the Baths of Caracalla in Rome *(see p441)*, this is the largest sculptural group (*c.* 150 BC) to have survived from antiquity. The best-known piece in the Farnese Collection, it shows the punishment of Dirce who, having ill-treated Antiope, was tied to an enraged bull by the latter's sons.

Exploring Southeast Naples

The area south of Via A. Diaz is home to Naples' castles and royal palace as well as the densely populated Spanish Quarter. On the outskirts of the old town are a number of museums in historic buildings.

Castel Nuovo

Piazza Municipio. **Tel** 081 795 58 77/ 081 420 13 42. **Open** 9am– 8pm Mon–Sat. Last adm: 7pm. **Closed** some public hols. Museo Civico: **Tel** 081 795 58 77. **Open** 9am–6pm Mon–Sat.

Also known as the Maschio Angioino, this Angevin fortress was built for Charles of Anjou in 1279–82. However, apart from the squat towers and the Cappella Palatina (with Francesco Laurana's *Madonna* of 1474 above the portal), most of the structure is Aragonese.

The castle was the main royal residence. In the Sala dei Baroni, Ferdinand I of Aragon brutally suppressed the ringleaders of the Baron's revolt of 1486. The Aragonese were capable of violence, but they were also patrons of the arts.

The triumphal arch of the castle's entrance (begun 1454) is theirs. Commemorating Alfonso of Aragon's entry to Naples in 1443, this ingenious application of the ancient triumphal arch design was worked on, in part, by Laurana. The original bronze doors by Guillaume le Moine (1468) are in the Palazzo Reale. Part of the castle houses the **Museo Civico**.

The colorful and compact Quartieri Spagnoli

Quartieri Spagnoli

Via Toledo (Roma) to Via Chiaia.

The Spanish Quarter – the neighborhood west of Via Toledo, sloping up to San Martino and Vomero – is one of the city's most densely populated areas. It was named after the Spanish troops who laid out its grid of narrow streets in the 17th century. This is where the archetypal Neapolitan scene comes to life, in which laundry hung above the streets crowds out the sun. This area is lively by day, sinister by night.

Museo Nazionale di San Martino

Largo di San Martino 5. **Tel** 081 229 45 02/ 081 558 64 08. Museo: **Open** 8:30am–7:30pm Thu–Tue. Castel Sant'Elmo: **Open** 8:30am–6:30pm Wed–Mon.

High above Santa Lucia, the Baroque Certosa di San Martino, founded in the 1300s as a Carthusian monastery, has great views of the Bay of Naples. It houses a museum featuring a variety of *presepi*, Christmas cribs of Neapolitan tradition. The cloister was completed in 1623–9 by Cosimo Fanzago (the creator of Neapolitan Baroque) to the 16th-century designs of Dosio. The church and choir are other examples of his virtuosity.

Next to the Certosa, **Castel Sant'Elmo**, built from 1329–43 and rebuilt in the 1500s, offers stunning views over the bay.

Museo Diego di Aragona Pignatelli Cortes

Riviera di Chiaia 200. **Tel** 081 66 96 75. **Open** 9am–1pm, 4–7:30pm Tue–Sun. **Closed** Jan 1, May 1, 15 Aug.

The Neo-Classical Villa Pignatelli, once home to the Rothschilds, houses this museum and its interesting collection of porcelain, period furniture, paintings, and sculpture.

The bold Castel Nuovo, with the triumphal arch entrance

For hotels and restaurants in this region see pp562–77 and pp580–605

Galleria Umberto I

Via Toledo. **Open** daily. Teatro San Carlo: **Tel** 081 797 23 31. **Open** Aug, rehearsals and performances. 9am–5:30pm daily (081 66 45 45 to book). **teatrosancarlo.it**

Once a focus for fashionable Neapolitans, the handsome arcades of the Galleria Umberto I were built in 1887 and rebuilt after World War II. They face Italy's largest and oldest opera house: the **Teatro San Carlo**. Built for Charles of Bourbon in 1737, and later rebuilt, its fine auditorium once aroused envy in the courts of Europe.

Danaë and the Shower of Gold by Titian in the Museo di Capodimonte

Magnificent glass-roofed interior of the Galleria Umberto I

Palazzo Reale

Piazza Plebiscito. Museo: **Tel** 081 40 05 47. **Open** 9am–8pm Thu–Tue (last adm: 1 hr before closing). **Closed** Jan 1, May 1, Dec 25. Biblioteca: **Tel** 081 781 92 31. **Open** 8:30am–7:30pm Mon–Fri (to 1:30pm Sat). Bring ID.

Begun by Domenico Fontana for the Spanish Viceroys in 1600, and expanded by subsequent residents, Naples' royal palace is a handsome edifice with great halls filled with furniture, tapestries, paintings, and porcelain. The small private Teatro di Corte (1768) was built by Ferdinando Fuga. The building houses the riches of the Biblioteca Nazionale (library). The exterior of the palace has been partly restored and the huge Piazza del Plebiscito facing it has been cleaned up. The great colonnades sweep toward 19th-century **San Francesco di Paola**, modeled on Rome's Pantheon.

The facade of the Palazzo Reale, Naples' royal palace

Villa Floridiana

Via Aniello Falcone 171. **Tel** 081 578 84 18. **Open** 8:30am–4pm Wed–Mon. Park: **Open** daily. **Closed** Jan 1, May 1, Aug 15, Dec 25. Museum: **Open** 8:30am–2pm Wed–Mon.

Set in handsome gardens, this Neo-Classical villa houses the **Museo Nazionale della Ceramica Duca di Martina**, famous for its ceramics collection, including porcelain and majolica.

Museo di Capodimonte

Parco di Capodimonte. **Tel** 081 749 91 11. **Open** 8:30am–7:30pm Thu–Tue. **museo-capodimonte.it**

Begun in 1738 by the Bourbon king Charles III as a hunting lodge, the **Palazzo Reale di Capodimonte** houses this museum and its magnificent collections of Italian paintings. Included are works by Titian, Botticelli, Raphael, and Perugino, much of it originating in the Farnese family collections. There is also a gallery of 19th-century art, largely from southern Italy.

Catacombs of San Gennaro

Via di Capodimonte 13. **Tel** 081 744 37 14. **Open** 10am–7pm daily (to 1pm Sun). call to arrange visit.

These catacombs – the original burial place of San Gennaro – are located near the church of San Gennaro in Moenia. The small church was founded in the 8th century, and is adjoined by a 17th-century workhouse. Two tiers of catacombs dating from the 2nd century penetrate the tufa, and there are mosaics and early Christian frescoes. Farther along the street, the Catacombs of San Gaudioso commemorate the 5th-century saint who founded a monastery on the spot. Above is the 17th-century church of Santa Maria della Sanità.

Castel dell'Ovo

Borgo Marinari. **Tel** 081 795 45 93. **Open** 9am–5:30pm daily (to 2pm Sun & hols). for exhibitions.

This castle, begun in 1154, occupies a small island facing, and joining, the Santa Lucia district – once the site of the city's shellfish market. A royal residence under the Normans and Hohenstaufen, today it belongs to the army. Interesting exhibitions are held here.

Beneath its ramparts, tiny Porta Santa Lucia is filled with seafood restaurants, and the Via Partenope running past it is a lovely promenade.

❷ Pompeii

An earthquake in AD 62, which shook Pompeii and damaged many buildings, was merely a prelude to the tragic day in AD 79 when Mount Vesuvius erupted, burying the town in 20 ft (6 m) of pumice and ash. Although it was discovered in the 16th century, serious excavation began only in 1748, revealing a city petrified in time. In some buildings paintings and sculpture have survived, and graffiti is still visible on street walls.

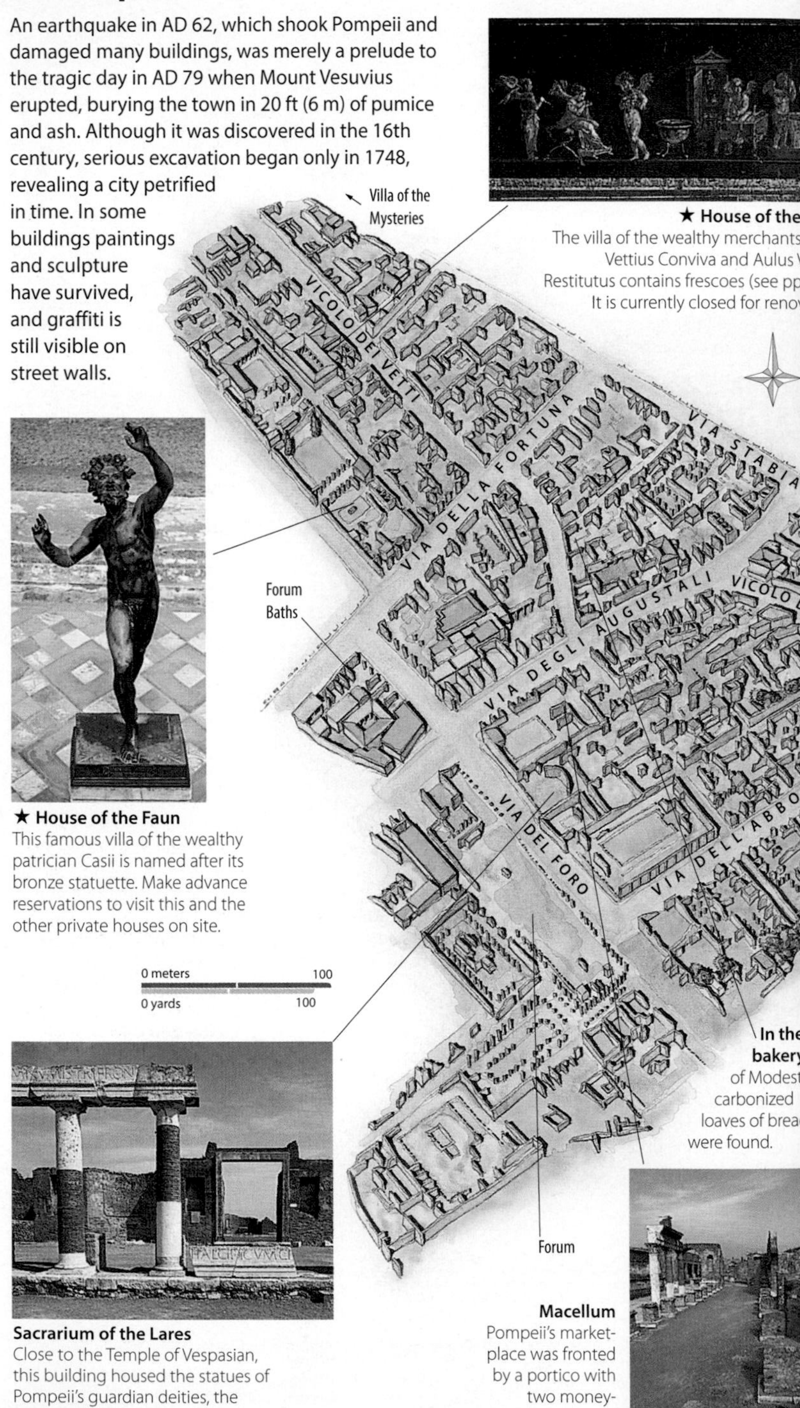

★ House of the V
The villa of the wealthy merchants A Vettius Conviva and Aulus Ve Restitutus contains frescoes (see pp4 It is currently closed for renova

★ House of the Faun
This famous villa of the wealthy patrician Casii is named after its bronze statuette. Make advance reservations to visit this and the other private houses on site.

In the bakery of Modestu carbonized loaves of bread were found.

Sacrarium of the Lares
Close to the Temple of Vespasian, this building housed the statues of Pompeii's guardian deities, the Lares Publici.

Macellum
Pompeii's market-place was fronted by a portico with two money-changers' kiosks.

Plan of Pompeii

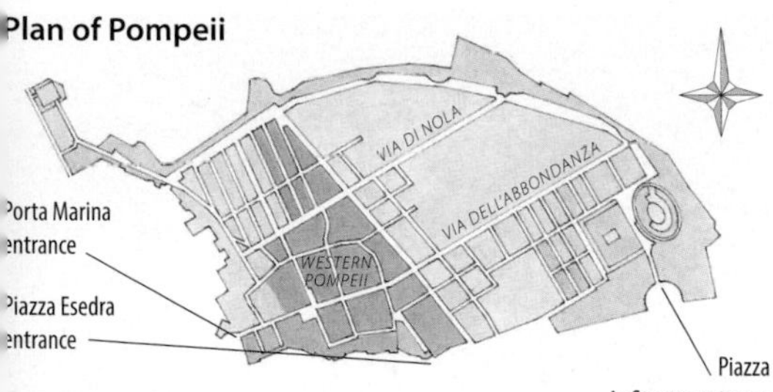

Area illustrated below

VISITORS' CHECKLIST

Practical Information
Piazza Esedra 5. **Tel** *081 857 53 47*. **Open** 8:30am–7:30pm (last adm: 6pm) (Nov–Mar: to 5pm, last adm: 3:30). **Closed** Jan 1, Dec 25. **pompeiisites.org** **ticket4art.it**

Transportation
FS Naples–Salerno: station Pompei Scavi; Circumvesuviana Naples–Sorrento: station Pompei Villa dei Misteri.

Western Pompeii

This detailed illustration is of the western area, where the most impressive and intact Roman ruins are located. There are several large patrician villas in the eastern section, as wealthy residents built their homes outside the town center. However, much of eastern Pompeii awaits excavation.

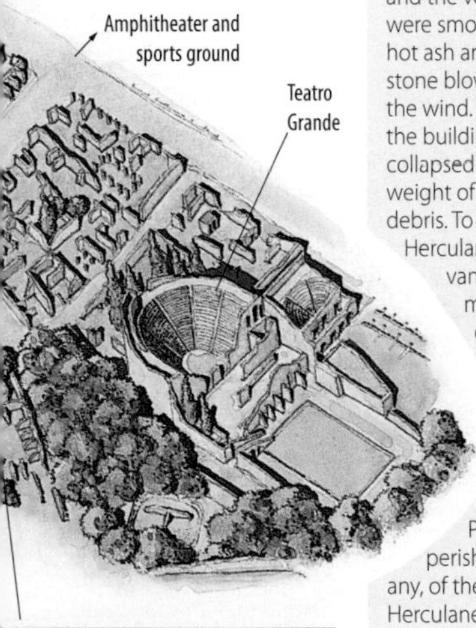

Via dell'Abbondanza
This was one of the original and most important roads through ancient Pompeii. Many inns lined the route.

Vesuvius and the Campanian Towns

Nearly 2,000 years after the eruption of Mount Vesuvius, the Roman towns in its shadow are still being released from the petrification that engulfed them. Both Pompeii and Stabiae (Castellammare di Stabia), to the southeast of Naples and the volcano, were smothered by hot ash and pumice stone blown there by the wind. The roofs of the buildings collapsed under the weight of the volcanic debris. To the west, Herculaneum (Ercolano) vanished under a sea of mud. A large number of its buildings have survived, their roofs intact, and many domestic items were preserved by the mud. In all, about 2,000 Pompeiians perished but few, if any, of the residents of Herculaneum died.

In AD 79 Pliny the Elder, the Roman soldier, writer, and naturalist, was the commander of a fleet stationed off Misenum (present-day Miseno, west of Naples), and with his nephew Pliny the Younger observed the impending eruption from afar. Eager to see this natural catastrophe closer at hand, Pliny the Elder proceeded to Stabiae, but was overcome by fumes and died. Based on reports by survivors, Pliny the Younger related the first hours of the eruption and his uncle's death in detail in two letters to the Roman historian Tacitus.

Pompeiian vase in Museo Nazionale Archeologico

Much of our knowledge of the daily lives of the ancient Romans derives from the excavations of Pompeii and Herculaneum. Most of the artifacts from them as well as Stabiae are now in Naples' Museo Archeologico Nazionale *(see pp494–5)*, creating an outstanding collection.

Mount Vesuvius has not erupted since 1944, but occasional rumbles have caused minor earthquakes. Visitors can reach it by train to Castellammare di Stabia, or by car. A useful website is www.guidevesuvio.it.

Casts of a dying mother and child seen at Pompeii

❸ Santa Maria Capua Vetere

Caserta. 34,000. FS i Palazzo Reale, Caserta (0823 32 22 33). Thu & Sun.

This town boasts a 1st-century AD Roman **amphitheater**, once Italy's largest after the Colosseum, with well-preserved tunnels beneath it. The town occupies the site of ancient Capua, an Etruscan city and then a flourishing center during the Roman Empire. It was the scene of the revolt of the gladiators, led by Spartacus in 73 BC. The on-site **Gladiator Museum** re-creates the history of the gladiators. Nearby is a **Mithraeum** (2nd–3rd century) with well-preserved frescoes. Finds from the sites are shown in the **Museo Archeologico dell'Antica Capua** in Capua.

Amphitheater
P.za 1 Ottobre. **Tel** 0823 79 88 64. **Open** 9am–1 hr before sunset Tue–Sun. valid for Mithraeum:. **Open** Tue–Sun.

Museo Archeologico dell'Antica Capua
Via Roberto d'Angio 48, Capua. **Tel** 0823 84 42 06. **Open** 9am–7pm Tue–Sun.

Tunnels under the amphitheater in Santa Maria Capua Vetere

❹ Caserta

79,000. FS i Palazzo Reale (0823 32 22 33). Wed & Sat. W **casertaturismo.it**

Magnificently opulent, the vast **Palazzo Reale** dominates Caserta. Built for the Bourbon King Charles III, Italy's largest royal palace boasts over 1,000 rooms, grand staircases, and richly adorned apartments. It was designed by Luigi Vanvitelli and construction started in 1752. The surrounding park boasts fountains, ornamental waterworks, statuary, and an English Garden. Sound and light shows, in English and Italian, take place in summer.

A fountain in the gardens of the Palazzo Reale at Caserta

Environs

The medieval town of **Caserta Vecchia** lies 6 miles (10 km) to the northeast. Its 12th-century cathedral is a fine example of southern Norman architecture. **San Leucio**, 2 miles (3 km) northwest of Caserta, is a model town built by Ferdinand IV, who also founded its silk industry.

Palazzo Reale
Piazza Carlo III. **Tel** 0823 44 80 84. **Open** 8:30am–7:30pm Wed–Mon. **Closed** public hols. Park: **Open** 8:30am–1 hr before sunset daily.

❺ Benevento

62,000. FS i Via Sala 31 (0824 31 99 11/38). Mon & Wed–Sat. W **comune.benevento.it**

Benevento, set in a lonely, mountainous province, is home to one of southern Italy's most interesting ancient Roman monuments: the **Arch of Trajan** on Via Traiano. The Roman city, Beneventum, was an important center. It stood at the end of the first extension of the Via Appia from Capua, and the Arch was erected across the old road in honor of Trajan. Built from AD 114–166 of marble, it is extremely well preserved. The relief sculpture adorning it – scenes from the life of Trajan and mythological subjects – is in excellent condition.

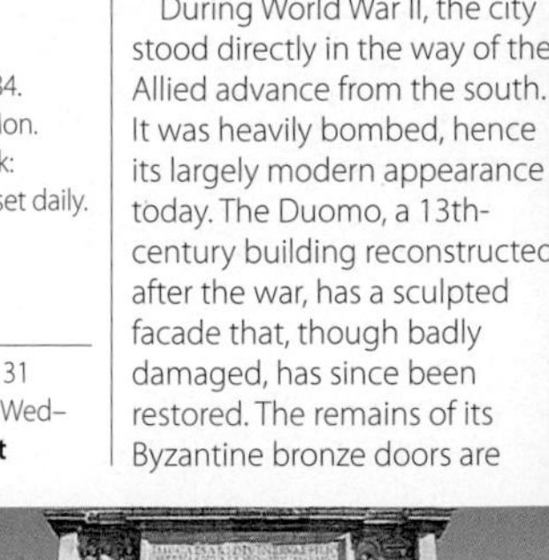

Elsewhere, evidence of the Romans is to be found in the ruined **Roman theater**, built during Hadrian's reign, and in the **Museo del Sannio**, which contains artifacts from the region, from ancient Greek finds to modern art.

During World War II, the city stood directly in the way of the Allied advance from the south. It was heavily bombed, hence its largely modern appearance today. The Duomo, a 13th-century building reconstructed after the war, has a sculpted facade that, though badly damaged, has since been restored. The remains of its Byzantine bronze doors are

The ornate 2nd-century Roman arch in Benevento, built to honor Trajan

within. The town has centuries-old associations with pagan worship, and a liqueur called *Strega* (witch) is made here.

Roman Theater
Piazza Caio Ponzio Telesino. **Tel** 0824 47 213. **Open** 9am–1 hr before sunset daily. **Closed** public hols.

Museo del Sannio
Piazza Santa Sofia. **Tel** 0824 218 18. **Open** 9am–7pm Tue–Sun. **Closed** Jan 1, Dec 25.

6 The Amalfi Coast

Salerno. Amalfi. Corso delle Repubbliche Marinare 27, Amalfi (089 87 11 07). **amalfitourist office.it**; **ravellotime.it**; **aziendaturismopositano.it**

The small town of Atrani on the Amalfi Coast

The most enchanting route in Campania is that skirting the southern flank of Sorrento's peninsula: the Amalfi Coast (Costiera Amalfitana). Popular pleasures here include dining on grilled fish and sipping Lacrima Christi from the vineyards on the slopes of Vesuvius, beach-hopping, and trips to coastal summits to admire the breathtaking views.

From **Sorrento**, a well-developed holiday resort, the road winds down to **Positano**, a village clambering down a vertiginous slope to the sea. A top spot for the jet set, it is nonetheless a good place to swim, or to catch the hydrofoil or ferry to Capri. Further on, **Praiano** is just as fashionable.

Amalfi is the coast's largest town and a popular resort. It was a maritime power before being subdued in 1131 by King Roger of Naples. The world's oldest maritime code, the *Tavole Amalfitane*, originated here. The 13th-century Chiostro del Paradiso flanks the Duomo, a magnificent 9th-century structure fronted by a rich 13th-century facade, and facing the town from the top of a long flight of steps. The style is Lombard-Norman, though the cloisters have a Saracenic-inspired appearance.

Ravello has the best views on this coast, the prime vantage points being the gardens of Villa Cimbrone and Villa Rufolo. Views from the latter provided inspiration for Wagner's *Parsifal*. The 11th-century Duomo has entrance doors by Barisano da Trani (1179) and an ornate 13th-century ambo (pulpit) held aloft by six spiral columns. The chapel of San Pantalcone contains the blood of its 4th-century namesake, which liquefies annually in May and August.

Beyond **Atrani**, the ruins of a Roman villa at **Minori** show that this coastline has always been a popular holiday spot.

A breathtaking view of the steep village of Positano on the Amalfi Coast

7 Salerno

Salerno. FS Salerno. Piazza Vittorio Veneto 1 (089 23 14 32); Lungomare Trieste (089 22 47 44).

Salerno is a big, busy port. Here the Allies landed in 1943, leaving in their wake a much-bombed city. Once famous for its School of Medicine (12th century), it is visited today for its **Duomo**, an 11th-century structure built on an earlier foundation. Its best feature is the Atrium, whose columns came from nearby Paestum. In the crypt is the Tomb of St. Matthew, brought here in 954.

The **Museo Diocesano** is home to most of the cathedral treasures, including an 11th-century ivory altar-front called the Paliotto. Before wandering off down the bustling Corso Vittorio Emanuele, visit the **Museo Provinciale** for local archaeological finds.

Environs

The **Cilento** is a mountainous region south of Salerno with a remote interior and a lovely, quiet coastline that is only slightly more populous. Among the towns along the coast, **Agropoli** is a busy little seaside resort 25 miles (42 km) south of Salerno. Outside Castellammare di Velia, a further 17 miles (28 km) to the southeast, are the ruins of the Greek town of **Elea** (founded 6th century BC). It was much visited by the Romans – Cicero was here, and Horace came on his doctor's orders to undergo a treatment of sea bathing. Excavations have revealed a magnificent 4th-century Roman gateway: the Porta Rosa, Roman baths, the foundations of a temple, and the remains of the acropolis.

The busy port of Salerno

The Temple of Hera I (left) and the Temple of Neptune at Paestum

Museo Diocesano
Largo Plebiscito. **Tel** 089 23 91 26. **Open** 9am–1pm Mon–Sat, 3–7pm Sun.

Museo Provinciale
Via San Benedetto. **Tel** 089 23 11 35. **Open** 9am–7pm Tue–Sat.

8 Paestum

Zona Archeologica. Via Magna Grecia 887. **Tel** 0828 81 10 16. from Salerno. FS Paestum. **Open** 9am–1hr before sunset daily. Museum: **Tel** 0828 81 10 23. **Open** 9am–7pm Tue–Sun. **Closed** 1st & 3rd Mon of month, Jan 1, Dec 25.

This is the most important ancient Greek site south of Naples in Campania. The Greeks founded this city on the edge of the Piana

9 Capri

Napoli. Capri. Piazza Umberto I, Capri (081 837 06 86). Grotta Azzurra from Marina Grande; from Anacapri. **Open** in calm sea. Certosa: Via Certosa, Capri. **Tel** 081 837 62 18. **Open** 9am–2pm Tue–Sun. Villa Jovis: Via Tiberio. **Open** daily.
capritourism.com

Capri's reputation as a sybaritic paradise is nearly eclipsed by its notoriety as a tourist trap. However, the views are unmarred by the throng.

The home of emperors, seat of monasteries, place of exile, its fortunes changed during the 19th century when English and German expatriates discovered its charms. Today it barely has a "low season"; farmers run little hotels, and fishermen rent pleasure boats. Capri enjoys its well-deserved reputation as a Garden of Eden.

The Grotta Azzurra, or the Blue Grotto, is a cave bathed in iridescent blue light, which can be reached by tour boat from Marina Grande.

Anacapri is Capri's second town.

0 kilometers 1
0 miles 0.5

del Sele in the 6th century BC and called it Poseidonia, the City of Poseidon. The Romans renamed it in 273 BC. It fell into decline and was abandoned in the 9th century due to malaria and a Saracen assault and was rediscovered in the 18th century.

Paestum has three massive Doric temples in an excellent state of repair: the **Basilica** or **Temple of Hera I** (mid-6th century BC); the **Temple of Neptune** (5th century BC), the largest and most complete at Paestum; and the **Temple of Ceres**, thought to date between its two neighbors.

Excavations have revealed the remains of the ancient city, its public and religious buildings, roads and protective walls. A **museum** contains the extensive finds from the site, including tomb paintings, tomb treasures, some terra-cotta votive offerings, architectural fragments, and sculpture.

A view from the highest point of Procida, called Terra Murata

⑩ Ischia and Procida

Napoli. Ischia & Procida. Via Sogliuzzo 72, Ischia (081 507 42 11); Via V. Emanuele 168 (081 810 19 68). La Mortella: **Tel** 081 98 62 20. **Open** Apr–Oct: 9am–7pm Tue, Thu, Sat–Sun. **infoischiaprocida.it**

Ischia is the biggest island in the Bay of Naples and, with its beach resorts, thermal springs, and therapeutic mud baths, it is nearly as popular as Capri. Ferries dock at **Ischia Porto**, the harbor and modern part of the main town, **Ischia. Ischia Ponte**, the older part, is a short walk away. The northern and western shores are developed; the southern flank of the island is the quietest. Here, the village of **Sant' Angelo** is dominated by a long-extinct volcano, **Monte Epomeo**, whose summit of 2,585 ft (788 m) offers terrific views across the bay. Also worth a visit are the gardens of **La Mortella** in Forio.

The tiny, picturesque island of Procida is less visited and very tranquil. The swimming is good at **Chiaiolella**, and as at Ischia, there are inexpensive places to stay. The main town, also called **Procida**, is home to the main ferry port – the **Marina Grande**.

There are views toward Vesuvius and the Bay of Naples from the north of the island.
Capri is the main town on the island.
Marina Piccola is reached by dramatic Via Krupp.
I Faraglioni

Marina Grande
This is Capri's main port of call for ferries from Naples and other ports on the Tyrrhenian coast. An array of colorful houses overlooks the harbor.

Villa Jovis
Covering an enormous area, this was the Imperial villa from which Tiberius ruled the Roman Empire during his final years.

Certosa di San Giacomo
Founded in 1371 on the site of one of Tiberius's villas, this Carthusian monastery was suppressed in 1808 and is now in part a school. The distant rocks are I Faraglioni.

ABRUZZO, MOLISE, AND PUGLIA

ᴾuglia is the "heel" of the Italian boot, the Gargano ᴾeninsula is its "spur," and Abruzzo and Molise together ᶠorm the "ankle." Hugging the southeastern seaboard of taly and looking toward the Balkans, the mountainous 'egions of Abruzzo and Molise, united until 1963, differ :onsiderably from Puglia, the richest of the three.

\bruzzo and Molise are sparsely populated, quiet places where the wild landscape exerts a strong influence. Settled by various Apennine tribes in the Middle Bronze Age, the areas were later subdued by the Romans, united under the Normans n the 12th century, and thereafter ruled by a succession of dynasties based in Naples. Abruzzo, dominated by the Apennines, is a brooding, introspective land of shepherds. Vertiginous drops preface the ascent to ramshackle hill towns clinging to the sides of high mountains, semi-abandoned and poor. Molise's landscape is ess dramatic. Legends of witches persist in both regions, as do strange fertility rites and ituals celebrating the changing seasons.

Puglia's advantage over its poverty-tricken neighbors is that it is nearly all flat and highly fertile. It produces the largest amount of olive oil in Italy, and its big cities – Lecce, Bari, and Taranto – are lively commercial centers. The region experienced a long-lasting Greek influence, though the golden age of Puglia's past was under the rule of the Normans, followed by Frederick II, who, between his return from Germany as emperor in 1220 and his death 30 years later, spent only four years away from here.

Puglia has glorious architecture, particularly in the churches and castles of the north. The curious *trulli* houses in central Puglia, the florid Baroque of Lecce, and the Levantine atmosphere of its merchant cities complete the picture of an ancient land subject to more influences from outside the Italian peninsula than from within it.

'aditional dress worn in the town of Scanno in Abruzzo

◀ A row of *trulli* houses in the town of Alberobello, Puglia

Exploring Abruzzo, Molise, and Puglia

Dominated by the Apennine mountain range, the hinterland of Abruzzo and Molise forms one of Italy's last wildernesses. At 9,554 ft (2,912 m), the highest peak is the Gran Sasso. Parts of Abruzzo are covered in tracts of forest, while Molise features high plains, gentle valleys, and lonely peaks. The coastline of the Gargano Peninsula in Puglia (Apulia) is packed with cliffs, caves, and islets. Reaching south is the fertile Tavoliere Plain, and farther south a series of upland plateaux (the Murge) descends toward the dry Salentine Peninsula and the Adriatic.

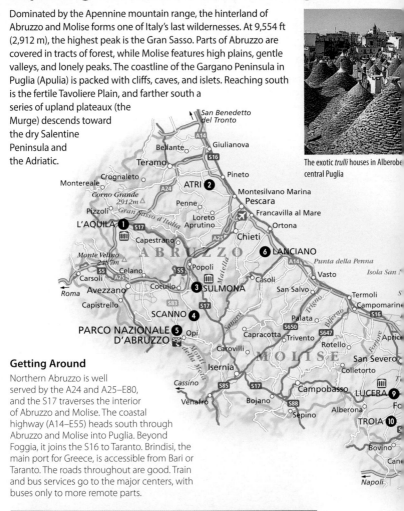

The exotic *trulli* houses in Alberobe central Puglia

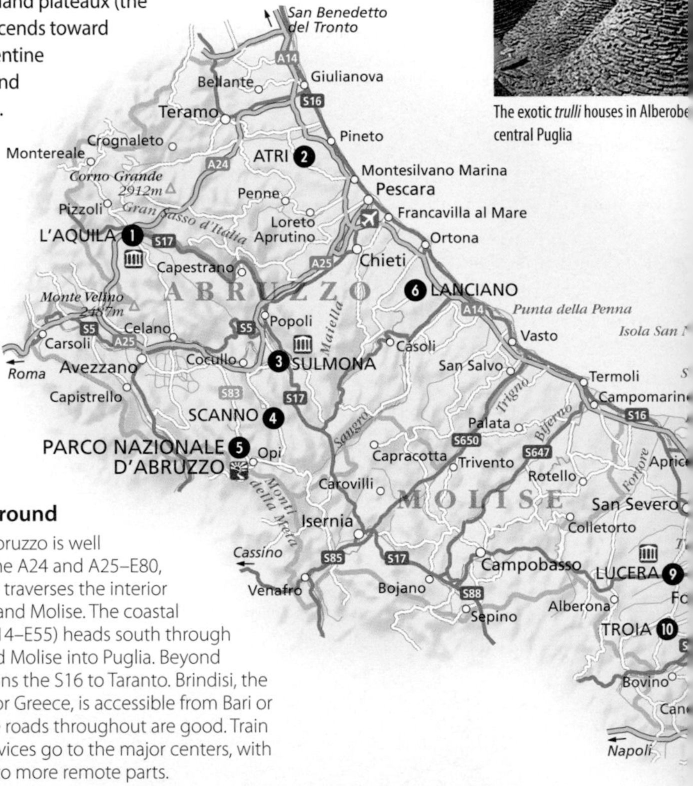

Getting Around

Northern Abruzzo is well served by the A24 and A25–E80, and the S17 traverses the interior of Abruzzo and Molise. The coastal highway (A14–E55) heads south through Abruzzo and Molise into Puglia. Beyond Foggia, it joins the S16 to Taranto. Brindisi, the main port for Greece, is accessible from Bari or Taranto. The roads throughout are good. Train and bus services go to the major centers, with buses only to more remote parts.

The coast at Vieste on the beautiful Gargano Peninsula in Puglia

Key

- Freeway
- Major road
- Secondary road
- Road under construction
- Minor road
- Scenic route
- Main railroad
- Minor railroad
- Regional border
- Summit

For additional map symbols *see back flap*

Sights at a Glance

1. L'Aquila
2. Atri
3. Sulmona
4. Scanno
5. *Parco Nazionale d'Abruzzo, Lazio e Molise pp510–11*
6. Lanciano
7. Isole Tremiti
8. Gargano Peninsula
9. Lucera
10. Troia
11. Trani
12. Castel del Monte
13. Ruvo di Puglia
14. Bari
15. Alberobello
16. Taranto
17. *Lecce pp516–17*
18. Galatina
19. Otranto

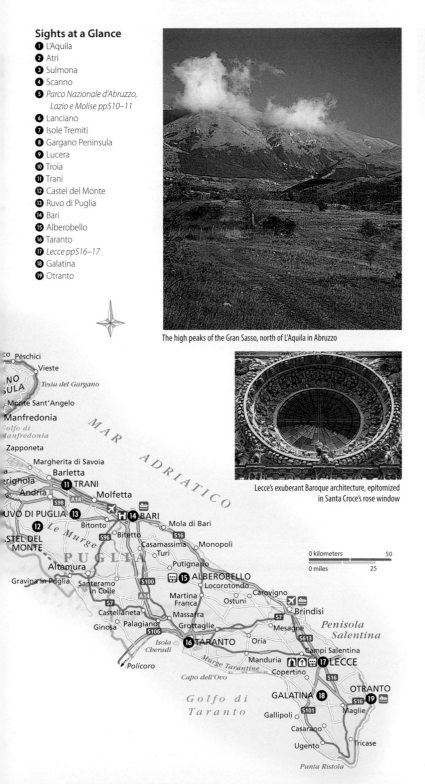

The high peaks of the Gran Sasso, north of L'Aquila in Abruzzo

Lecce's exuberant Baroque architecture, epitomized in Santa Croce's rose window

The pink and white stone facade of Santa Maria di Collemaggio in L'Aquila

❶ L'Aquila

73,000. FS Via XX Settembre 10 (0862 223 06). daily.
abruzzoturismo.it

Abruzzo's capital lies at the foot of the **Gran Sasso**, at 9,554 ft (2,912 m) the highest point of the Italian mainland south of the Alps (and good for skiing). Its ancient streets are peppered with churches. In April 2009 an earthquake, measuring 6.3 in magnitude, struck central Italy with the epicenter close to L'Aquila. Many of the historical churches and buildings described below have been seriously damaged by the quake. Restoration work is being carried out on many buildings, so do check with the tourist office before visiting.

The domed **Santa Giusta** (1257), off Via Santa Giusta, has a rose window and a *Martyrdom of St. Stephen* (1615) by Cavalier d'Arpino. **Santa Maria di Paganica**, off Via Paganica, has a 14th-century facade and a carved portal. The **Duomo** (1257) in Piazza del Duomo was rebuilt in the 18th century. The massive church of **Santa Maria di Collemaggio**, on Piazza di Collemaggio, has a facade of pink and white stone. It was built in the 13th century by Pietro dal Morrone, who later became Pope Celestine V.

Detail of Fontanelle delle Novantanove Cannelle in L'Aquila

San Bernardino, on Via di San Bernardino, houses the tomb (1505) of San Bernardino of Siena. The church (built 1454–1472), has a facade (1527) by Cola dell'Amatrice and an 18th-century carved ceiling by Ferdinando Mosca. The bell tower collapsed in the 2009 earthquake. The second chapel in the south aisle has an altarpiece by Andrea della Robbia, the Renaissance artist.

The medieval **Fontanelle delle Novantanove Cannelle** at the end of Via San Iacopo is a fountain commemorating the 99 villages that Frederick II supposedly united when he founded L'Aquila in 1240.

The **Museo Nazionale d'Abruzzo**, in the 16th-century castle, contains the remains of a prehistoric elephant, Roman artifacts, and religious works.

Museo Nazionale d'Abruzzo
Castello Cinquecentesco. **Tel** 0862 63 32 29. **Closed** for restoration – call for details.

❷ Atri

Teramo. 12,000.
0861 24 42 22. Mon.
comune.atri.te.it

The prettiest in a series of small hill towns in Abruzzo, Atri is a warren of stepped streets, alleys, and passages bound by mostly brick and stone churches and houses. The 13th-century **Duomo** occupies the site of a Roman bath; the crypt was once a swimming pool; and fragments of the original mosaic floor are visible in the apse. Also in the apse is Andrea Delitio's beautifu 15th-century fresco cycle, in which he combined landscape and architecture in a variety of religious scenes from the Old and New Testaments. The cloister has views of the 15th-century brick campanile.

Environs
South of Atri is the hill town of **Penne**, with its homogeneous buildings of reddish brick, which give it a wonderful, warm glow. East of Atri, **Loreto Aprutino** is known for the *Last Judgment* fresco (14th century) in Santa Maria in Piano.

Detail from 15th-century fresco by Andrea Delitio in Atri's Duomo

❸ Sulmona

L'Aquila. 26,000. FS Corso Ovidio 208 (0864 532 76). Wed & Sat. Sep: International Exhibition c Contemporary Art. **sulmona.org**

This town is famous as the hom of both Ovid and *confetti* (sugared almonds). After a wedding, guests are given *confetti* as a good luck token. Sulmona is filled with ancient buildings, especially along medieval **Via dell'Ospedale**. Th **Palazzo dell'Annunziata** was founded in 1320 and combines Gothic and Renaissance styles.

For hotels and restaurants in this region see pp562–77 and pp580–605

The **Museo Civico** holds a collection of local antiquities, costumes, paintings, and the work of goldsmiths formerly housed in the palace. The adjacent church of the **Annunziata**, with a Baroque facade, was rebuilt in the 18th century. Behind the church are 1 BC–AD 2 ruins of a Roman house.

At the end of Viale Matteotti is the cathedral of **San Panfilo**, built over a Roman temple. **San Francesco della Scarpa**, in Piazza del Carmine, has a 13th-century portal. Winding past it to the **Fontana del Vecchio** (1474) is an aqueduct that once fueled local industry.

Environs

East of Sulmona is the Maiella National Park, a massif of 61 peaks and forested valleys offering walking, bird-watching, climbing, and skiing. To the west, Cocullo hosts the May Processione dei Serpari (Festival of Snakes) in which a statue of the patron saint, Domenico Abate, is draped with snakes and carried through the town. In the 11th century he is said to have rid the area of venomous snakes.

Museo Civico
Palazzo dell'Annunziata, Corso Ovidio.
Tel 0864 21 02 16. **Open** 9am–7pm Mon–Fri, 9am–1pm Sat & Sun.

Ovid, the Latin Poet

Born in 43 BC, Ovid (Publius Ovidius Naso) was Sulmona's most illustrious son. Not much survives here to remind you of his presence, however, apart from a **Corso Ovidio**, a 20th-century statue of him in Piazza XX Settembre, and, just outside the town, a ruin traditionally known as **Ovid's Villa**. Known as one of the greatest poets of Classical Rome, his subjects included love *(Ars Amatoria)* and mythology *(Metamorphoses)*. In AD 8 he was banished into exile on the Black Sea, the far edge of the Roman Empire, after being implicated in a scandal of adultery with Julia, the granddaughter of Emperor Augustus *(see pp52–3)*. Ovid continued to write of his hardships, and died in exile in AD 17.

4 Scanno

L'Aquila. 2,400. Piazza Santa Maria della Valle 12 (0864 743 17). Tue. **scanno.org**

Wonderfully well-preserved, this medieval hill town set in beautiful, wild countryside is one of Abruzzo's most popular attractions. There are alleys and narrow flights of steps, oddly-shaped courtyards into which small churches have been pressed, and ancient mansions in whose windows women can be seen making lace or embroidering.

Traditional costume still worn in Scanno

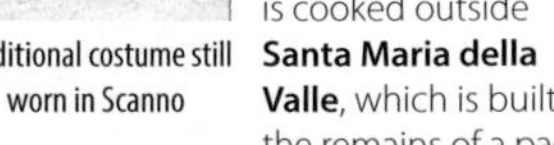

In the shadow of Apennine peaks and beside lovely **Lago di Scanno**, the town is also a favored stop on the way to the Parco Nazionale d'Abruzzo *(see pp510–11)*. The summer months are the busiest, with a variety of activities from riding, boating, and camping by the lake, to the August classical music festival. During the January Festa di Sant' Antonio Abate, a large lasagna is cooked outside **Santa Maria della Valle**, which is built on the remains of a pagan temple. The food is doled out on a first-come, first-served basis.

High Apennine peaks looming above the medieval hill town of Scanno in Abruzzo

❺ Parco Nazionale d'Abruzzo, Lazio, e Molise

This vast park, inaugurated in 1922, has a rich landscape of high peaks, rivers, lakes, and forests, and is one of Europe's most important nature reserves. Part of a royal hunting reserve until 1877, today it provides refuge for 66 species of mammal, 52 types of reptile, amphibian, and fish, and 230 species of bird, including the golden eagle and white-backed woodpecker, as well as over 2,000 varieties of flora. The park offers an extensive network of paths, and there are opportunities for riding, trekking, and climbing.

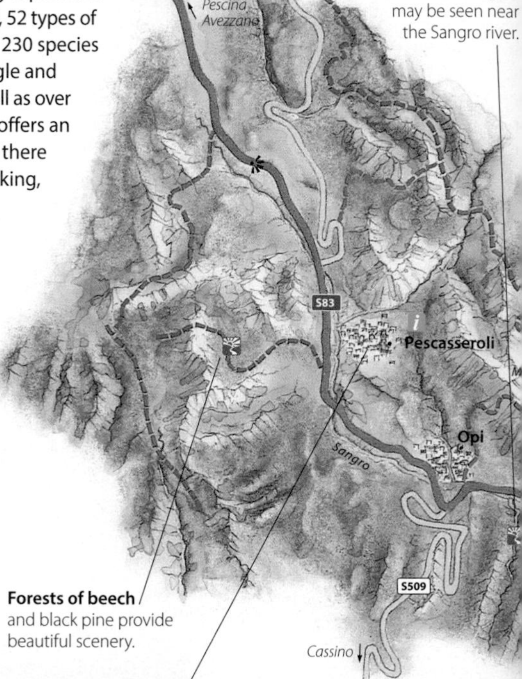

Golden eagles may be seen near the Sangro river.

Young Chamois
Dense forests of beech and maple hide the Apennine chamois. There are also red and roe deer in the park.

Forests of beech and black pine provide beautiful scenery.

Pescasseroli
This town is a major center for information on the area. It has good tourist facilities and a small zoological garden with animals living in the region, such as bears and wolves.

Apennine Wolves
The park guarantees protection for the Apennine wolf, and about 60 wolves survive here. The chances of seeing one, however, are fairly remote.

Marsican Brown Bear
Once hunted almost to extinction, between 80 and 100 brown bears now roam in the park.

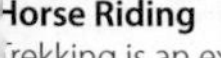

Horse Riding
Trekking is an excellent way to explore more remote areas of the park.

VISITORS' CHECKLIST

Practical Information
L'Aquila. i Nature Center: Pescasseroli (0863 911 32 21); visit the website for opening hours.
W **parcoabruzzo.it**

Transportation
FS Avezzano or Castel di Sangro, then to Pescasseroli.

Lake Barrea
Created by the artificial damming of the River Sangro, this lake is surrounded by valleys and forests offering walking and pony trekking.

Dense Forests
Beech and maple forests, dotted with black hornbeam, ash, hawthorn, cherry, wild apple, and pear, protect the once persecuted bears and wolves.

The Camosciara is a spectacular area, home to many wild animals.

Key
- Major road
- Minor road
- Walking path

0 kilometers 5
0 miles 5

❻ Lanciano

Chieti. 35,000. FS i Piazza Plebiscito 50 (0872 71 91 27). Wed & Sat. W **lanciano.it**

Large parts of Lanciano's old nucleus remain from the Middle Ages. In the crumbling Civitanova quarter is the 13th-century church of **Santa Maria Maggiore**, with a magnificent 14th-century portal and a silver processional cross (1422). Also in this area is the now disused **San Biagio** (begun *c.* 1059), near the 11th-century **Porta San Biagio** – a rare surviving town gate. The **Duomo** stands on the remains of a Roman bridge dating from the time of Diocletian. An underground passage links the bridge to the **Sanctuary of the Eucharistic Miracle**, where a host and wine that turned into live Flesh and Blood in the 8th century are kept. The Ripa Sacca (Jewish ghetto) was a busy commercial center in the Middle Ages – the period of Lanciano's greatest prosperity. The hefty walls of the **Torri Montanara** were built then by the Aragonese as a bulwark against attack.

❼ Isole Tremiti

Foggia. 400. San Nicola. i Via Perrone 17, Foggia (0881 72 31 41); Via Sant'Antonio Abate 21, Monte Sant'Angelo (0884 56 89 11).
W **lecinqueisole.it**

Off the Gargano coast, the Tremiti are the Italian islands least visited by foreigners. **San Domino** is the largest, with a sandy beach and coves. Julia, granddaughter of Augustus, was exiled here for adultery from AD 8 until her death in AD 28. The poet Ovid was allegedly involved *(see p509)*.

Santa Maria a Mare, in **San Nicola**, the administrative center of the islands, is an abbey fortress founded in the 8th century. It was turned into a prison in the late 1700s, a role it maintained until 1945.

Both the islands of San Domino and Santa Maria a Mare are popular with Italians. The swimming is good, though the coastline of San Nicola is rocky.

The coast near Peschici on the Gargano Peninsula

❽ Gargano Peninsula

Foggia. FS 🚌 ℹ Piazza del Popolo 10, Manfredonia (0884 58 19 98); Via Sant'Antonio Abate 21, Monte Sant'Angelo (0884 56 89 11).
W parcogargano.it

A rocky spur jutting into the Adriatic Sea, the Gargano is dotted with coves and cliffs. Its coastal towns of **Manfredonia**, **Rodi Garganico**, **Peschici**, and **Vieste** are popular with vacationers. To the east lies the **Foresta Umbra**, a vast woodland of beech, oak, yew, and pine, and to the north the salt lakes of **Lesina** and **Varano**, havens for waterfowl. Plunging through the Gargano is an old pilgrim route (S272) from **San Severo** in the west to the shrine at **Monte Sant'Angelo** in the east. The first stop is **San Marco in Lamis**, dominated by a huge 16th-century convent. Farther along, **San Giovanni Rotondo** is a focus for pilgrims visiting the tomb of Padre Pio (1887–1968), a beatified miracle-worker. The last stop is **Monte Sant'Angelo** with its grotto where the Archangel Michael is said to have appeared to the Bishop of Sipontum in 493.

To the south of Manfredonia, beside the ruins of ancient Siponto, is the oriental-inspired 12th-century church of **Santa Maria di Siponto**.

Typical street scene in the town of Vieste on the Gargano Peninsula

❾ Lucera

Foggia. 👥 35,000. 🚌 ℹ Piazza Nocelli 6 (0881 52 27 62). Wed.
W comune.lucera.fg.it

On the northeast edge of town, once a prosperous Roman colony, are the ruins of a Roman **amphitheater**. Lucera was rebuilt in the 13th century by Frederick II, who peopled it with 20,000 Sicilian Muslims. It became one of the strongest fortresses in southern Italy, and its **castle** is one of Puglia's most magnificent. Built in 1233 by Frederick II, and enlarged after 1269, its fortified wall of 2,953 ft (900 m) is interspersed with 24 towers. Of Frederick's origina palace, only the base and some vaulting remains.

In 1300 Charles II, who killed most of Lucera's Muslim population, began the **Duomo** on the site of their main mosque. The high, soaring nave is filled with 15th- and 16th-century frescoes and carvings.

The **Museo Civico Fiorelli** has displays of episodes from throughout Lucera's history.

Museo Civico Fiorelli
Via de Nicastri 44. **Tel** 0881 54 70 41. **Open** 10am–1pm Tue–Sun (also 4–7pm Tue, Wed, Sat).

The remains of Lucera castle

❿ Troia

Foggia. 👥 33,000. 🚌 ℹ 0881 97 82 41. 1st & 3rd Sat of month.
W comune.troia.fg.it

Founded in 1017 as a Byzantine fortress against the Lombards, Troia fell to the Normans in 1066. Until Frederick II destroyec it in 1229, the town had been ruled by a succession of powerful bishops who were responsible for producing many remarkable buildings, including Troia's **Duomo** *(see pp482–3)*.

Begun in 1093 and constructec over the following 30 years, it exhibits an extraordinary diversity of styles. It successfully blends elements of Lombard, Saracenic, and Byzantine style with that of the Pisan-Romanesque.

Elegant blind arcading distinguishes the Duomo's lower story. The upper sections are characterized by powerfully carved sculpture – projecting lions and bulls. The upper facade displays a rose window with Saracenic-style detailing.

The main entrance, with bronze doors by Oderisio da Beneventano (1119), is dominated by carved capitals and an architrave, both Byzantine in style. Within the Duomo is a Romanesque pulpit (1169).

⓫ Trani

Bari. 55,000. FS Piazza Sacra Regia Udienza II (0883 58 88 30). Tue. **traniweb.it**

During the Middle Ages this small, lively whitewashed port of Jewish origin bustled with mercantile activity and was filled with merchants and traders from Genoa, Amalfi, and Pisa. It reached its peak of prosperity under Frederick II.

Today it is visited for its Norman **Duomo** in Piazza Duomo, built mainly from 1159 to 1186 over an earlier church whose predecessor, the Ipogei di San Leucio, dates from the 7th century. It is dedicated to St. Nicholas the Pilgrim, a little-remembered miracle worker (died 1094) who was canonized as an act of rivalry against the town of Bari, which possessed the bones of another, more memorable St. Nicholas. The Duomo's most notable external features are its sculptures, particularly surrounding the rose window and the arched window below it, and the entrance portal with bronze doors (1175–9) by Barisano da Trani. The vigor of the interior has been revealed following restoration.

The facade of Trani's Duomo

Next to the Duomo is the **castle** (1233–49) founded by Frederick II. Rebuilt in the 14th and 15th centuries, it is a well-preserved edifice with one wall dropping sheer into the sea.

The 15th-century Gothic-Renaissance **Palazzo Caccetta**, in Piazza Trieste, is a rare survivor. Nearby, on Via Ognissanti, the 12th-century Romanesque church of the **Ognissanti**, the chapel of the Knights Templar erected in the courtyard of their hospital, is notable for its original portico. Other churches worth a visit are Santa Teresa and the monastery of La Colonna.

⓬ Castel del Monte

Località Andria, Bari. Beni Culturali (0883 56 99 97). **Open** Mar–Sep: 10:15am–7:45pm daily; Oct–Feb: 9am–6pm daily. **Closed** Jan 1, Dec 25. **casteldel monte.beniculturali.it**

Frederick II

Remote in the endless plains near Ruvo di Puglia, Castel del Monte, built in the mid-13th century, outclasses every other castle associated with Frederick II. It is also one of the most sophisticated secular buildings of the Middle Ages. The emperor had broad intellectual interests, and he used his castles as hunting lodges where he could retire from court life with his falcons and books. Inside there are two floors, each with eight rib-vaulted rooms, some still lined with marble. This, and the marble moldings on the entrance and the upper floor, as well as sophisticated lavatory arrangements, mark the castle as a palace.

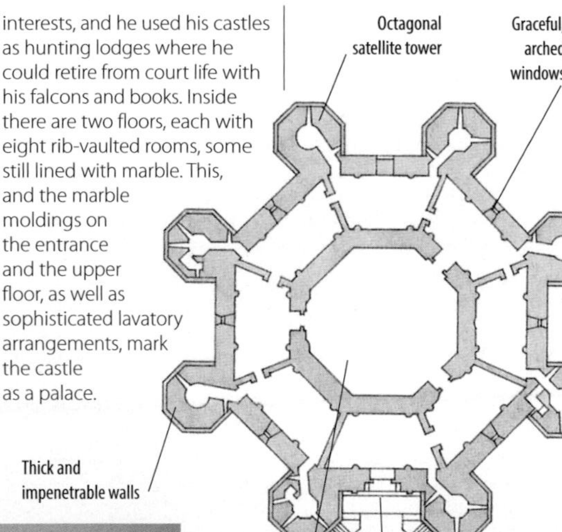

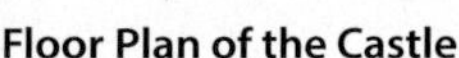
The main entrance portal is in the style of a Roman triumphal arch.

The castle standing alone on the summit of a low hill

Floor Plan of the Castle

The building is a harmonious geometrical study with two stories of eight rooms each. The reasons for such precise planning of this giant octagon remain a mystery to this day.

⓭ Ruvo di Puglia

Bari. 24,000. FS Piazza Matteotti 31 (080 950 71 11). Sat.
W **ruvodipugliaweb.it**

Once celebrated for its vases, Ruvo di Puglia's ceramics industry, producing "Apulian" ware, flourished until the 2nd century BC. The style was inspired by the striking red and black colors of Attic and Corinthian models. The **Museo Archeologico Nazionale Jatta** has a good overview.

The 13th-century **Cattedrale** is a bold example of the Apulian-Romanesque style with a portal that blends Byzantine, Saracenic, and Classical motifs.

Museo Archeologico Nazionale Jatta
Piazza Bovio 35. **Tel** 080 361 28 48. **Open** 8:30am–1:30pm daily (to 7:30pm Thu–Sat). **Closed** Jan 1, May 1, Dec 25.
W **palazzojatta.org**

Portal detail of Ruvo di Puglia's Duomo

⓮ Bari

321,000. FS
Piazza Aldo Moro 33a (080 524 23 61). daily.
W **comune.bari.it**

Roman Barium was simply a commercial center, but the city became the regional capital under the Saracens in 847, and was later the seat of the *catapan*, the Byzantine governor of southern Italy. Under the Normans, to whom it fell in 1071, Bari became a center of maritime significance. Today it is Puglia's lively capital and an important port with ferries to and from Croatia and Greece.

The **Basilica di San Nicola**, one of Puglia's first great Norman churches (begun 1087), has a plain exterior with a tall gabled section flanked by towers. The Apulian-Romanesque portal has carving on the doorjambs and arch in Arabic, Byzantine, and Classical styles. Beyond the choir screen is a fine 12th-century altar canopy and an episcopal throne (*c.* 11th century). The relics of St. Nicholas – patron saint of the city (and also of Russia) – are buried in the crypt.

Sculpture at Bari castle

The late 12th-century Apulian-Romanesque **Cattedrale** is based on San Nicola, with a dome and one surviving tower (the other one collapsed in 1613). The Baroque portals on the facade incorporate 12th-century doorways. The interior has been restored to its medieval simplicity. The canopy over the high altar, the pulpit, and the episcopal throne are reconstructions from fragments of the originals. The sacristy, built as a baptistry, is known as the *Trulla*. The crypt houses the remains of San Sabino, Bari's original patron saint.

The city's **castle**, founded by Roger II, was adapted by Frederick II in 1233–9. In the vaulted hall is a collection of plaster casts of sculpture and architectural fragments from various Romanesque monuments in the region.

Bari castle, in the old district known as Città Vecchia, where most of the town's sights are clustered

15 Alberobello

Bari. 11,000. FS to Alberobello & Ostuni. Piazza Ferdinando IV (080 432 51 71). in English, French, and German offered by Trulli e Natura (080 432 38 29). Oct/Nov: Frantoi Aperti (visits to the major olive-pressing factories). **alberobello.net**

Whitewashed and sun-baked *trulli* in Alberobello

The parched landscape of the **Murge dei Trulli** features olive groves, vineyards, and *trulli*. Strange circular buildings with conical roofs and domed within, *trulli* are built from local limestone stacked without using mortar. The walls and openings are generally whitewashed, while the stone roof tiles often have religious, pagan, or magical symbols painted on them. The origins of *trulli* are obscure, though the name is traditionally applied to ancient round tombs found in the Roman countryside. Most *trulli* are souvenir shops.

Alberobello is a UNESCO World Heritage site and the *trulli* capital. Here the strange white buildings crowd the narrow streets, and there are *trulli* restaurants, shops, and even a *trulli* cathedral.

Environs

The pretty whitewashed hill town of **Locorotondo** is an important wine center. The elegant streets of **Martina Franca** are enlivened by Rococo balconies. The spectacular **Grotte di Castellana** are caves estimated to be 50 million years old.

16 Taranto

200,000. FS Corso Umberto I (099 453 23 92). Wed, Fri, & Sat. **comune.taranto.it**

Little remains of the old city of Taras, founded by Spartans in 708 BC and at its most prosperous in the mid-4th century BC. The **Museo Archeologico Nazionale**, founded in 1887, has artifacts that shed light on the region's history. The museum has since been expanded to allow for a growing collection of historically significant pieces. Taranto was heavily bombed in World War II and is garlanded by factories. The picturesque **Città Vecchia**, an island dividing the Mare Grande from the Mare Piccolo, was the site of the Roman citadel of Tarentum. A lively fish market offering the shellfish for which the city is famous, is housed in an Art Nouveau building. Here, too, is the **Duomo**. Founded in 1071, it has been the object of subsequent rebuilding. The most interesting features include the catacomb-like crypt, with its sarcophagi and fragmented frescoes, and the antique marble columns of the nave. Behind it is the 11th-century **San Domenico Maggiore**, which later gained a high double-approach Baroque staircase. The huge **castle** built by Frederick of Aragon (15th century) covers the eastern corner of the Città Vecchia. Now a military area, the castle is strictly off limits.

Aphrodite in museum in Taranto

Museo Archeologico Nazionale
Via Cavour 10. **Tel** 0994 53 21 12.
Open 8:30am–7:30pm daily.

The Tarantella

Italy's lively and graceful folk dance, the Tarantella, grew out of tarantism – the hysteria that appeared in 15th- to 17th-century Italy, and was prevalent in Galatina *(see p517)*. Alleged victims of the tarantula spider's bite could supposedly cure themselves through frenzied dancing, which sweated out the poison. The dance is characterized by light, quick steps and a "teasing" flirt. The strange, private ritual takes place annually on June 29 at 6am at the celebrations for the Feast of Saints Peter and Paul in Galatina, the only place on the Salentine Peninsula where tarantism has survived.

⑰ Street by Street: Lecce

Lecce was the site of the Greek Messapi settlement. It became an important center of the Roman Empire, and in the Middle Ages developed a strong tradition of scholarship. Much of the architecture is in the highly decorative Lecce Baroque style, which flourished in the 1600s and earned the city the name of Florence of the South. This style was possible due to the *pietra di Lecce*, an easily carved stone. Giuseppe Zimbalo (Lo Zingarello) was its greatest master. Lecce is also famed for its papier-mâché workshops.

★ Palazzo Vescovile and Duomo
The bishop's palace (rebuilt in 1632), the adjoining Duomo by Lo Zingarello (after 1659), and a seminary (1709) enclose the Piazza Duomo.

Tourist information

Key

— — — Suggested route

0 meters 100

0 yards 100

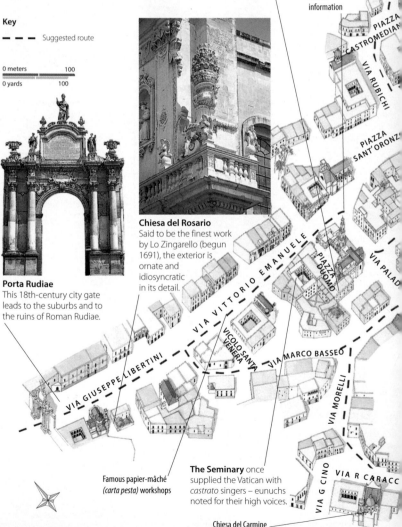

Chiesa del Rosario
Said to be the finest work by Lo Zingarello (begun 1691), the exterior is ornate and idiosyncratic in its detail.

Porta Rudiae
This 18th-century city gate leads to the suburbs and to the ruins of Roman Rudiae.

Famous papier-mâché *(carta pesta)* workshops

The Seminary once supplied the Vatican with *castrato* singers – eunuchs noted for their high voices.

Chiesa del Carmine

★ Santa Croce
Built 1549–1679, this church was begun by Gabriele Riccardi; the rose window is by Lo Zingarello. Next door is the ex-convent of the Celestines.

VISITORS' CHECKLIST

Practical Information
105,000. Via Vittorio Emanuele 23 (0832 33 24 63), Via Monte San Michele 20 (0832 31 41 17). Aug 24–26: Sant' Oronzo; Dec 13–24: Fiera dei Pupi e Pastori. **pugliaturismo.it**

Transportation
FS Viale Oronzo Quarta.
Via Boito & Via Adua.

The 16th-century Castello
lies between ancient city and modern suburbs. A 12th-century construction is enclosed by a wall built later by Charles V. Only one floor is open to the public.

Colonna di Sant'Oronzo
St. Oronzo was appointed Bishop of Lecce by St. Paul in AD 57, and later martyred by the Roman emperor Nero. This bronze statue dates from 1739.

Church of San Matteo

A Roman theater
was excavated virtually intact with its orchestra and seats.

Roman Amphitheater
Excavated in 1938, only part of this 1st-century BC amphitheater is visible.

Detail of a 15th-century fresco in Santa Caterina d'Alessandria

⓲ Galatina

Lecce. 28,000. FS Sala dell'Orologio (0836 56 99 84). Thu. Jun 29: Feast of Saints Peter & Paul. **comune.galatina.le.it**

An important Greek colony in the Middle Ages, this *città d'arte* (city of art, a status given by the region) retains its Greek flavor. It is the center of one of Puglia's chief wine-producing regions, although it is more famous for the ritual of tarantism *(see p515)*.

The Gothic church of **Santa Caterina d'Alessandria** (begun 1384) on Piazza Orsini contains early 15th-century frescoes with scenes from the Old and New Testaments that glorify the Orsini, who were feudal lords.

⓳ Otranto

Lecce. 5,500. FS Piazza Castello (0836 84 14 36). Wed. **comune.otranto.le.it**

Otranto was one of Republican Rome's leading ports for trade with Asia Minor and Greece, and under the Byzantines was an important toehold of the Eastern Empire in Italy. In 1070 it fell to the Normans. Turks attacked in 1480 and slaughtered its inhabitants. The 800 survivors were promised their lives if they renounced Christianity: all refused.

The Norman **Duomo** (founded 1080) on Via Duomo houses the bones of the martyrs. There is a 12th-century mosaic floor and a fine crypt. A **castle** (1485–98) built by the Aragonese at the center of town adds to Otranto's charm and there are some fine beaches close by.

BASILICATA AND CALABRIA

Remote and wild, Basilicata is one of the poorest regions in Italy. It is underdeveloped and undervisited, and rural areas remain unspoiled. Neighboring Calabria has been immortalized in the drawings of Edward Lear, who, traveling through on a donkey in 1847, was transfixed by the "horror and magnificence" of its savage landscape.

Today these regions are distinctly separate, but they share a common history and, along with Sicily and Puglia, were part of Magna Graecia. Ancient Metaponto in Basilicata was an important center, as were Crotone and Locri Epizephiri in Calabria. Their ruins evoke an illustrious past.

After the Greeks came the Romans, followed by Basilian monks. These were members of the Greek-Byzantine church who were fleeing their territories that had been invaded by Muslims. Their religious establishments make up a core of interesting monuments, such as the Cattolica at Stilo and Matera, where the monks took refuge in caves.

Many of the historic remains are Norman, but sporadic evidence of Swabian, Angevin, Aragonese, and Spanish occupation still exists.

Centuries of rule by Naples led to the marginalization of Basilicata and Calabria. Nowadays Calabria has an infamous reputation due to the *'ndrangheta*, the ferocious first cousin to the Mafia, whose activities are a constant menace. Banditry exists, but the sensible traveler should have little to fear.

Owing to emigration, Basilicata and Calabria are sparsely populated and have as much to offer in unspoiled countryside as in historic centers. The vast coastline boasts fine beaches, while the interior features the Aspromonte and Sila mountain ranges.

The remote landscape has kept change at bay. Isolated Pentedattilo, for example, preserves customs of Byzantine origin, while around San Giorgio Albanese there live close-knit communities of Albanians, descended from 15th-century refugees.

Sparsely populated, rugged countryside surrounding Stilo in southern Calabria

◀ Traditional white houses nestled among the hills of il Dirupo, Pisticci

Exploring Basilicata and Calabria

Mostly upland country, Basilicata (or Lucania, as it is also known) is scattered with Greek ruins (like those at Metaponto), medieval abbeys, and Norman castles (such as Melfi's). Matera, its most interesting city, stands amid an arid lunar landscape of denuded valleys. Calabria is often described as the land between two seas. The lovely beaches and virgin landscape between Tropea and Maratea attract many visitors. The Ionian coast's chief attractions are its Greek ruins, such as Locri Epizephiri, and the hill towns, like Stilo and Gerace.

Repairing nets in the town of Pizzo, northeast of Tropea

Key

- Highway
- Major road
- Secondary road
- Minor road
- Scenic route
- Main railroad
- Minor railroad
- Regional border
- △ Summit

The picturesque hill town of Rivello, north of Maratea in Basilicata

Sights at a Glance

1. Melfi
2. Venosa
3. Lagopesole
4. Matera
5. Metaponto
6. Maratea
7. Rossano
8. Tropea
9. Stilo
10. Gerace
11. Reggio di Calabria

For additional map symbols *see back flap*

The port of Maratea on the Tyrrhenian coast of Basilicata

Getting Around

Calabria's Tyrrhenian coast is well served by the A3–E45, a spur of which extends to Potenza in Basilicata. To reach the Ionian coast, it is best to skirt the Aspromonte via the S106–E90 from Reggio to Basilicata. Although the mountains can be crossed, namely on the S280–E848 to Catanzaro, the roads are narrow and pass through isolated countryside. Much of Basilicata is even less accessible, and Matera is more easily reached from Puglia. There are airports at Reggio di Calabria, Lamezia Terme (west of Catanzaro), Crotone, Bari, and Brindisi (Puglia). Trains connect the bigger centers and country buses serve the small towns.

The countryside near Miglionico, south of Matera

The impressive castle at Melfi, showing evidence of both Angevin and later construction

❶ Melfi

Potenza. 18,000. FS i Piazza Umberto I (0972 23 97 51). Wed & Sat. W **aptbasilicata.it**

A brooding and now almost deserted medieval town, Melfi is crowned by the **castle** where Pope Nicholas II conducted Robert Guiscard's investiture in 1059, thus legitimizing the Normans in the south. Melfi later became the Norman capital. Here Frederick II proclaimed his *Constitutiones Augustales* (1231), which unified his kingdom as a state. In the castle is the **Museo Nazionale del Melfese**, with its collection of Byzantine jewelry. The **Duomo**, off Via Vittorio Emanuele, was begun in 1155 by William the Bad but rebuilt in the 18th century. Only the campanile survives.

Museo Archeologico Nazionale del Melfese
Castello di Melfi, Via Castello. **Tel** 0972 23 87 26. **Open** 9am–8pm Tue–Sat (to 2pm Sun). **Closed** Mon am, Jan 1, Dec 25. (Sat & Sun).

❷ Venosa

Potenza. 12,200. FS i Piazza Castello 47 (0972 316 09). 1st & 3rd Thu of month. W **comune.venosa.pz.it**

Venosa was one of the most important Roman colonies around 290 BC, and remains of **baths** and an **amphitheater** survive in the archaeological zone along Via Vittorio Emanuele. It was also the birthplace of the Latin poet Horace (65–8 BC) and the site where the Roman general Marcellus died at the hands of Hannibal in 208 BC. Marcellus' reputed **tomb** is in Via Melfi. For more treasures, visit the **Museo Archeologico Nazionale**.

The **Duomo**, also on Via Vittorio Emanuele, and the huge **castle** in Piazza Umberto I date from the 16th century.

An abbey complex formed by an older, possibly early Christian (5th–6th century) church, **La Trinità** is backed by an unfinished 11th-century construction, in which Robert Guiscard (died 1085) was buried with his half-brothers and Alberada, his first wife. Only her tomb has survived.

Museo Archeologico Nazionale
P.za Castello. **Tel** 0972 360 95. **Open** 9am–8pm Wed–Mon.

❸ Lagopesole

Potenza. **Tel** 0971 860 83. FS to Lagopesole Scalo then bus to town. **Open** 9:30am–1pm, 4–7pm daily (3–5pm in winter). W **aptbasilicata.it**

Rising dramatically on a hill, Lagopesole's **castle** (1242–50) was the last castle built by Frederick II. The interesting carved heads above the portal of the keep are said to represent Frederick Barbarossa (grandfather of Frederick II) and Barbarossa's wife, Beatrice. Inside, the royal apartments and chapel can be visited.

The Sassi district of Matera

❹ Matera

56,900. FS i Via de Viti de Marco 9 (0835 33 19 83). 0835 31 94 58. Sat. W **materaturismo.it**

Perched on the edge of a deep ravine, this town consists of the bustling upper district and the silent, lower **Sassi** (caves) district, divided into the Sasso Barisano and the more picturesque Sasso Caveoso. The people of Matera once lived here in dwellings scooped out of the rock. The two parts are odd neighbors, making Matera a truly fascinating city.

For the best overview, walk along the **Strada Panoramica dei Sassi** and look down into the caves. From the 8th to the

13th centuries, such caves probably provided refuge for monks from the Byzantine empire. Many chapels, gouged out of the rock, were taken over in the 15th century by peasants. Later, a cave-dwelling Matera evolved and by the 18th century some buildings fronting the caves had become fairly grand mansions and convents. By the 1950s and '60s the Sassi were overtaken by squalor and poverty, and the inhabitants forcibly rehoused. Carlo Levi (1912–75) drew attention to their living conditions in his book *Christ Stopped at Eboli*, comparing the Sassi to Dante's *Inferno*. The area was made a UNESCO World Heritage site in 1993.

Of the 120 *chiese rupestri* (rock-cut churches; www.parco murgia.it) in the Sassi and the Agri district outside the town, **Santa Maria di Idris** in the Monte Errone area and **Santa Lucia alle Malve** in the Albanian quarter both contain 13th-century frescoes.

The **Museo della Tortura** (torture), in Via San Biagio, has exhibits dating back to the time of the Inquisition, while the **Museo Nazionale Ridola** provides a background to Matera and the Sassi. The artifacts from many Neolithic trench villages, necropolises, and other ancient sites are displayed here.

Church of San Francesco in Matera

The Apulian-Romanesque **Duomo** (13th century) in Piazza Duomo has a 12th-century painting of the *Madonna della Bruna*, the patroness of Matera. Via Duomo leads toward **San Francesco d'Assisi** (13th century with Baroque overlay). Other churches to visit are **San Domenico** and **San Giovanni Battista** on Via San Biagio (both 13th century), and the **Purgatorio** (1770) on Via Ridola.

Matera is where Mel Gibson's *The Passion of the Christ* (2004) was largely filmed.

Museo Nazionale Ridola
Via Ridola 24. **Tel** 0835 31 00 58. **Open** 9am–8pm daily (from 2pm Mon). **Closed** Jan 1, Dec 25.

The Tavole Palatine in Metaponto

❺ Metaponto

Metaponto Borgo. FS to Metaponto. Via Apollo Licio (0835 74 52 20). **Open** 9am–1 hr before sunset daily. **Closed** Mon am, Jan 1, Easter, Dec 25. **aptbasilicata.it**

Founded in the 7th century BC, ancient Metapontum was once the center of a wealthy city-state with a philosophical tradition expounded by Pythagoras, who settled here after his expulsion from Croton. Its ruins include the **Tavole Palatine** (6th century BC) at the Bradano River bridge, 15 columns that are part of a Doric temple, probably dedicated to Hera. The **Museo Nazionale di Metaponto** displays artifacts from the site. The ruins of a theater and the Doric **Temple of Apollo Lycius** (6th century BC) are in the **Archaeological Zone**. Farther south, modern **Policoro** occupies the site of ancient Heracleia (founded 7th– 5th century BC). Its **Museo Nazionale della Siritide** has finds from this and other sites.

Museo Nazionale di Metaponto
Via Aristea 21. **Tel** 0835 74 53 27. **Open** 9am–8pm daily. **Closed** Mon am, pub hols. includes Archaeological Zone.

Museo Nazionale della Siritide
Via Colombo 8, Policoro. **Tel** 0835 97 21 54. **Open** 9am–7pm daily. **Closed** Tue am, Jan 1, May 1, Dec 25.

❻ Maratea

Potenza. 5,200. FS Piazza del Gesù 32 (0973 87 69 08). 1st & 3rd Sat of month.

A tiny stretch of Basilicata meets the Tyrrhenian Sea in the Gulf of Policastro. This unblemished coast is home to Maratea. Its small port (Maratea Inferiore) is beneath the old center (Maratea Superiore), which straddles the flank of a hill. From here the road climbs Monte Biagio to a summit with breathtaking views where a huge statue of the **Redeemer** stands.

Environs
Dramatically sited **Rivello**, 14 miles (23 km) to the north, once had a largely Greek population. Byzantine influences can be seen in the churches of **Santa Maria del Poggio** and **Santa Barbara**.

The small port of Marina di Maratea with fishing boats

A page from the precious *Codex Purpureus Rossanensis*

❼ Rossano

Cosenza. 39,000. FS Piazza Matteotti (0983 52 09 08). 2nd & 4th Fri of month.

This pretty hill town was one of the main centers of Byzantine civilization in Calabria. It assumed power when Reggio di Calabria fell to the Saracens (9th–11th centuries). The **Museo Diocesano** houses the *Codex Purpureus Rossanensis*, a rare 6th-century Greek Gospel with silver lettering and splendidly detailed miniatures.

The Baroque **cathedral** contains the *Madonna Acheropita* fresco, a much-venerated Byzantine relic of the 8th or 9th century.

Environs
On a hilltop to the southeast is the five-domed Greek church of **San Marco** (10th century). The 12th-century **Panaghia**, another Greek church, lies off Via Archivescovado. Both contain fragments of early frescoes.

Santa Maria del Patirion, on a hilltop 11 miles (18 km) to the west, is magnificently adorned with colored brickwork, tile, and stone. It offers great views over the Piana di Sibari (Plain of Sibari), the alleged location of the fabled city of Sybaris, destroyed in 510 BC.

Museo Diocesano
Palazzo Arcivescovile, Via Arcivescovado 5. **Tel** 0983 52 52 63. **Open** 9:30am–noon, 3–5pm Tue–Sun; 10am–noon, 4–6pm public hols.

❽ Tropea

Vibo Valentia. 6,700. FS Piazza Ercole (0963 614 75). Sat. **tropea.biz**

One of the most picturesque towns on Calabria's largely built-up Tyrrhenian coast, Tropea offers superb views of the sea and beaches. The old town hangs on to a cliffside facing a large rock, formerly an island. The rock is topped by **Santa Maria dell'Isola**, a former medieval Benedictine sanctuary. The **cathedral** at the end of Via Roma is of Norman origin, although it has been rebuilt several times. Inside is a 14th-century painting, the *Madonna di Romania*, by an unknown artist.

Casa Trampo (14th century) and **Palazzo Cesareo** (early 20th century) in Vicolo Manco are the most interesting of the small palaces in Tropea. The latter has a splendid balcony adorned with carvings.

Below the town are pretty beaches and a good choice of places to eat. Other seaside towns to visit are **Scilla** to the south and **Pizzo** to the north.

❾ Stilo

Reggio di Calabria. 3,000. Town hall (0964 77 60 06). Tue.

A short distance from the coast, Stilo is an earthquake-damaged town clamped to the side of Monte Consolino. Standing on a ledge looking out over the olive trees is the **Cattolica**, which has made Stilo a focus of pilgrimage for lovers of Byzantine architecture. Built in the 10th-century by Basilian monks, the brick building with its terra-cotta-tiled roof is based on a Greek cross-in-a-square plan. Four antique, mismatched marble columns divide the interior into nine quadrants. The capitals are placed at the base of the columns, instead of on top, to indicate the triumph of Christianity over paganism. The frescoes within, discovered and restored in 1927, date from the 11th century.

The Cattolica dominates the town, but on Via Tommaso Campanella there is a medieval **Duomo** as well as the 17th-century ruins of the **Convent of San Domenico**, where the philosopher and Dominican friar Tommaso Campanella (1568–1639) lived. The church of **San Francesco**, built around 1400, has an ornate carved wooden altar and a lovely 16th-century painting of the *Madonna del Borgo* (unknown origin). Bivongi, northwest of Stilo, has two churches dedicated to St. John: the Byzantine-Norman **San Giovanni Theresti**, and the Norman **San Giovanni Vecchio**.

Cattolica
1 mile (2 km) above Stilo on Via Cattolica. **Tel** 0965 81 22 56. **Open** Mon–Sat.

The beautiful and unspoiled coastline at Tropea

The distinctive five-domed Cattolica in Stilo

⑩ Gerace

Reggio di Calabria. 3,000.
Pro Loco, Via Regina Margherita 77, Locri (0964 23 27 60). **comune.gerace.rc.it**

Occupying a crag on the north-eastern flank of the Aspromonte, Gerace was founded by refugees from **Locri Epizephiri** who fled in the 9th century to escape Saracen attack. Its defensive character is reinforced by the medieval town walls and the remains of the castle.

Apart from the slow pace of life here – where you are as likely to meet a flock of sheep in an alley as a Fiat 500 – the main attraction is Calabria's grandest **Duomo**. This large structure indicates the significance of Gerace at least up to the time of the Normans. Constructed around the early 12th century, rebuilt in the 13th century, and restored in the 18th century, the crypt is its chief treasure. Both crypt and church are simple, adorned by a series of antique colored marble and granite columns probably stolen from the site of ancient Locri Epizephiri. At the end of Via Cavour is 12th-century **San Giovanello**, part Byzantine and part Norman. Nearby is the Gothic church of **San Francesco d'Assisi** which contains a Baroque marble altar (1615) and the Pisan-style tomb of Niccolò Ruffo (died 1372), a member of a prominent Calabrian family.

Environs

The vast site of **Locri Epizephiri**, the first Greek city to have a written code of law (660 BC), was a famous center of the cult of Persephone. There are remains of **temples**, a **theater**, and Greek and Roman **tombs**. The **Museo Nazionale** displays a ground plan of the site, as well as Greek and Roman votive statues, coins, and sculptural fragments.

Locri Epizephiri
Southwest of Locri on the SS 106, Contrada Marasà. **Open** 9am–7pm Tue–Sun. **locriantica.it**

Museo Nazionale
Contrada Marasà, SS 106.
Tel 0964 39 00 23. **Open** Tue–Sun.

⑪ Reggio di Calabria

183,000. FS
Station. Fri. **turismo.reggiocal.it**

One reason to visit Reggio di Calabria, which was heavily rebuilt after a major earthquake in 1908, is the **Museo Nazionale della Magna Grecia**. It houses a fine collection of artifacts from ancient Rhegion – a Greek city on the site of the present town – and from other Greek sites.

Chief among its treasures are the Greek bronzes, larger-than-life statues of warriors dredged from the sea off Riace Marina in 1972. Statue A (460 BC) is thought to be by Phidias, the Athenian sculptor and chief exponent of the idealizing, Classical style. If true, it is a rare survivor because his works were hitherto known to us only from Roman copies. Statue B (430 BC) has been attributed to Polyclitus. It is possible that the statues originated from an Athenian shrine at Delphi built to celebrate the victory of Marathon.

Museo Nazionale della Magna Grecia
Piazza de Nava 26. **Tel** 0965 81 22 55. **Closed** for renovations; call 800 98 51 64 to visit Riace bronzes at the Palazzo della Regione.
museonazionalerc.it

Riace Bronzes (6th and 5th century BC) in Reggio's Museo Nazionale

SICILY

On a crossroads in the Mediterranean, part of Europe and Africa, yet belonging to neither, Sicily was tramped across by half the ancient civilized world. As conquerors came and went, they left behind a rich and varied cultural deposit. This has resulted in a quirky mixture in almost every aspect of the local vernacular from language, customs, and cooking to art and, most notably, the architecture of the island.

During the 6th and 5th centuries BC, there cannot have been much difference between Athens and the Greek cities of Sicily. Their ruins are among the most spectacular of the ancient Greek world. The Romans took over in the 3rd century BC, followed by the Vandals, Ostrogoths, and Byzantines. Not much that is tangible has survived from the days of the Arabs, who ruled from the 9th to 11th centuries, though Palermo's Vucciria is more souk than market. The Norman era, beginning in 1061, spawned brilliant artistic achievements, such as the cathedrals of Monreale and Cefalù, while the eclecticism of that period's architecture is best seen at Santi Pietro e Paolo outside Taormina.

The Sicilian Baroque of the 17th and 18th centuries is just as individual. The palaces and churches of Palermo, reflecting the elaborate ritual of the Spanish Viceregal court, tend toward extravagant display. At Noto, Ragusa, Modica, Siracusa, and Catania the buildings are a useful vehicle for the Sicilians' love of ornamentation, itself a remnant from the island's early fling with the Arab world. The style is an expression of the nature of Sicilians, whose sense of pomp and pageantry is both magnificent and extreme.

Sicily is a curiosity, and the legacy of the past is redolent everywhere. The fact that it is an island has intensified the cultural impact of each successive occupier. They say that today there's less Italian blood in Sicilian veins than there is Phoenician, Greek, Arabic, Norman, Spanish, or French. The resulting mixture – exotic, spicy, and highly inflammable – has created a separate nation at the foot of Italy.

Detail of a 12th-century mosaic from the Palazzo dei Normanni in Palermo

◀ The fishing harbor in the town of Cefalù on a clear summer evening

Exploring Sicily

The vast coastline of Sicily (Sicilia) provides hundreds of long, sandy beaches, particularly at Taormina and the Golfo di Castellammare by San Vito Lo Capo – part of a large nature reserve. Sicily's varied interior is characterized by remote hill towns and plains punctuated by mountain ranges known for spring flowers and wildlife. Among the most famous sights is Mount Etna, an active volcano whose lava flows over the centuries have fertilized the land, which supports an abundance of walnut trees, citrus groves, and vineyards.

Fishermen at work in their boats at Siracusa

Sights at a Glance

1. *Palermo pp530–33*
2. *Monreale pp534–5*
3. Bagheria
4. Trapani
5. Erice
6. Marsala
7. Segesta
8. Selinunte
9. Cefalù
10. Agrigento
11. Piazza Armerina
12. Enna
13. Tindari
14. Messina
15. Taormina
16. Mount Etna
17. Catania
18. Pantalica
19. Siracusa
20. Noto

Getting Around

The A19–E932 links Palermo and Catania, the A18–E45 Catania and Messina, and the A20–E90 Palermo and Messina. The west is accessible from Palermo on the A29–E90. Ferry routes run from Messina to Reggio di Calabria, and from Palermo to Genoa or Naples. Between the larger towns, train services are efficient, but for smaller towns the buses are better. Catania, Palermo, and Trapani have international airports.

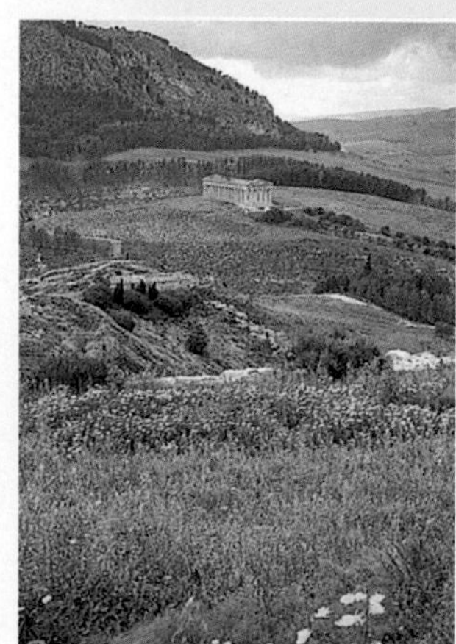
The magnificent temple at Segesta

For keys to symbols *see back flap*

The Norman Duomo in Palermo

❶ Palermo

Nestling on the protective flank of Monte Pellegrino, with Monte Alfano to the east, Palermo lies in a natural amphitheater called the Conca d'Oro (Golden Shell). The city is an eclectic mix of Oriental and old European influences, and it features architectural styles that range from Arabic to Norman, Baroque, and Art Nouveau. This cultural infusion is unmatched in Italy, making this exotic city an exciting place to explore.

Gesù

Piazza Casa Professa 21. **Tel** 091 607 62 23. **Open** 7–11:30am, 5–6:30pm daily (to 12:30pm Sun; Aug: 7–10am only). **Closed** for Mass.

This Baroque church (1564–1633) is also known as the church of the Casa Professa. The interior is an example of the skill of Sicilian craftsmen in the treatment of marble carving and inlay. The oldest Jesuit church in Sicily, it was restored after World War II.

Ruined cloister with the red domes of San Giovanni degli Eremiti behind

San Giovanni degli Eremiti

Via dei Benedettini. **Tel** 091 651 50 19. **Open** 9am–7pm Tue–Sun.

Reflecting Islamic architectural tradition with bulbous domes, corner arches, and filigreed windows, this deconsecrated Norman church (1132–48) was built in the grounds of a mosque. Beyond church and mosque, a ruined cloister from a 13th-century monastery encloses a pretty garden.

Palazzo dei Normanni

Piazza Indipendenza. **Tel** 091 626 28 33. **Open** 8:30am–5pm daily (to 12:30pm Sun & hols). Last adm: 45 mins before closing. Cappella Palatina **Open** 8:30am–noon, 2:30–5pm Mon–Sat; 8:30am–2pm Sun. **Closed** for Mass; Easter, Apr 25, May 1, Dec 26. Sun.

This site has been the focus of power since the days of Byzantine rule and is now home to Sicily's regional government. The nucleus of the present building was constructed by the Arabs, but after the Norman conquest of the city in 1072, it was enlarged for the Norman court. See the luxurious royal apartments, especially the Sala di Ruggero, and the splendid Cappella Palatina. Built by Roger II (1132–40), this dazzling chapel blends Byzantine, Islamic, and Norman styles. It is lavishly adorned with fine mosaics and marble inlaid with gold. Next to the palace is the eccentrically decorated Porta Nuova (1535).

Sumptuous interior of the Cappella Palatina, Palazzo dei Normanni

Duomo's exterior displaying a mixture of styles

VISITORS' CHECKLIST

Practical Information
654,000. P. Castelnuovo 35 (091 605 81 11). Mon–Sat. Jul 10–15: U Festinu for the city's patron saint, Santa Rosalia; Sep 4: Pilgrimage to Santa Rosalia's grotto; Easter: Byzantine Catholic celebrations in La Martorana.
palermotourism.com

Transportation
Punta Raisi 20 miles (32 km) W. FS Stazione Centrale, Piazza Giulio Cesare. Via Balsamo. Stazione Marittima, Molo Vittorio Veneto.

Sights at a Glance

① San Giovanni degli Eremiti
② Palazzo dei Normanni
③ Gesù
④ Duomo
⑤ Santa Caterina
⑥ La Martorana
⑦ Vucciria
⑧ Oratorio del Rosario di San Domenico
⑨ San Domenico
⑩ Museo Archeologico Regionale
⑪ Oratorio di Santa Zita
⑫ Oratorio di San Lorenzo
⑬ Palazzo Abatellis and Galleria Regionale di Sicilia
⑭ La Magione
⑮ Villa Giulia

Duomo

Corso Vittorio Emanuele. **Tel** 091 33 43 73. **Open** 7am–7pm Mon–Sat, 9am–5:30pm Sun & hols. **Closed** during Mass. Treasury **Open** 9:30am–1:30pm, 2:30–5:30pm daily. **cattedrale.palermo.it**

Founded in 1184, the Duomo displays many architectural styles. The exterior shows the development of the Gothic style from the 13th–14th centuries. The south porch (1453) is a masterpiece of the Catalan style, and at the apse end, sturdy Norman work can be seen through an Islamic-inspired overlay. The dome is 18th century. Within the much-altered interior are the tombs of Sicily's kings. Squeezed into an enclosure by the south porch are the remains of Emperor Frederick II; his wife, Constance of Aragon; his mother, Constance, daughter of Roger II (also entombed here); and his father, Henry VI. The Treasury houses the 12th-century Imperial Diadem of Constance of Aragon, which was removed from her tomb in the 18th century.

Santa Caterina

Piazza Bellini. **Tel** 091 616 24 88. **Open** 9:30am–1pm daily (summer: also 5–7pm Mon–Sat).

Although begun in 1580, most of the internal decoration of this unique church dates from the 17th and 18th centuries. A powerful example of the Palermitan Baroque, it boasts sculpture, marble inlay, and illusionistic ceiling frescoes (18th century) – by Filippo Randazzo in the nave and by Vito d'Anna in the dome.

The church is flanked by Piazza Pretorio, which is dominated by the huge Mannerist Fontana Pretoria (1544).

Fontana Pretoria with Santa Caterina in the background

For keys to symbols *see back flap*

Exploring Palermo

East of the Quattro Canti, where Via Maqueda and Corso Vittorio Emanuele meet, the city is sprinkled with ornate palaces and more churches. Squeezed behind them are labyrinthine medieval quarters where ancient, crumbling buildings still stand.

La Martorana

Piazza Bellini. **Tel** 345 828 82 31. **Open** 8:30am–1pm, 3:30–5:30pm Mon–Sat; 8:30am–1pm Sun & hols (to 7pm in summer).

Also called Santa Maria dell' Ammiraglio, this church was built around 1140 by George of Antioch, Roger II's admiral. The design derives from Norman and Islamic traditions with mosaics possibly by Greek artisans. In the right aisle, King Roger receives the Imperial Diadem from Christ; in the left aisle, George of Antioch is portrayed.

A nearby convent, founded by Eloisa Martorana in 1193, was the site where the Sicilian Parliament met in 1295 and decided to hand the crown of Sicily to Frederick of Aragon. The church was presented to the convent in 1433.

Mosaic of Christ with Four Angels in the dome of La Martorana

Vucciria

Via Roma. **Open** daily.

Nowhere is Palermo's Arabic past more apparent than in this medieval casbah-style market that burrows through the ruinous Loggia district below Via Roma. Merchants, hawkers, shoppers, and pickpockets crowd an area once the haunt of artisans. The alleys all around are named after their professions, such as silversmiths, dyers, and keymakers. This busy market, the largest in Palermo, offers the usual market wares, from household items to junk, as well as a wide selection of fresh fruit, vegetables, fish, and meat.

Stuccoed interior of the Oratorio del Rosario di San Domenico

Oratorio del Rosario di San Domenico

Via dei Bambinai 2. **Open** 9am–1pm daily.

The interior of this tiny 16th-century chapel displays elegant Baroque decoration by the master of stucco, Giacomo Serpotta. Created around 1720–30, this was possibly his finest work. Serpotta's technical virtuosity, not to mention the sensory indulgence and whimsical fantasy in evidence here, is remarkable. The altarpiece is the famous *Madonna of the Rosary* (1624–8) by Anthony Van Dyck, and there are wall paintings by Luca Giordano and Pietro Novelli.

San Domenico

P.za San Domenico. **Tel** 091 32 95 88. **Open** 9–11:30am Tue–Sat (also 5–7pm Sat & Sun). Cloister: **Open** call to check. Museo del Risorgimento: **Tel** 091 58 27 74. **Open** 9am–1pm Mon, Wed & Fri. **Closed** Aug. **storiapatria.it**

Although the present building was begun in 1640, there has been a Dominican church on the site since the 14th century. Tommaso Maria Napoli, one of the masters of Sicilian Baroque, created the exuberant church facade (1726) and square in front (1724).

Within, the most interesting feature is Antonello Gagini's bas-relief of *Santa Caterina* (1528) in the third chapel on the left. Next to the church is a 14th-century cloister that gives access to the Museo del Risorgimento.

Museo Archeologico Regionale

P.za Olivella 24. **Tel** 091 68 06 07. **Closed** closed for repairs. End date not known; call ahead before visiting.

Housed in a former monastery of the Filippini, Sicily's most important museum contains sculpture, architectural fragments and ceramics, bronzes, glassware, jewelry, weapons, and terracottas. The collection is taken from the island's Phoenician, Greek, and Roman sites of antiquity – Tindari, Termini Imerese, Agrigento, Siracusa, Selinunte, and Mozia. The highlights are sculptures from the friezes of the ancient Greek temples at Selinunte.

Palermo's noisy, bustling Vucciria market, east of Via Roma

Oratorio del Rosario di Santa Cita

Via Valverde 3. **Tel** 091 843 16 05 or 091 609 03 08 (to book). **Open** Apr–Oct: 9am–6pm Mon–Fri, 9am–3pm Sat; Nov–Mar: 9am–3pm Mon–Sat.

This small chapel is dedicated to the Virgin of the Rosary after her miraculous intervention at the Battle of Lepanto *(see pp62–3)*. The stucco relief decoration is the work of Giacomo Serpotta (after 1688): the panel on the rear wall depicts the battle, and other reliefs show scenes from the New Testament. The neighboring 16th-century church of Santa Zita, from which the oratory takes its name, is filled with sculptures (1517–27) by Antonello Gagini.

Ornate interior of the Oratorio di Santa Cita

Oratorio di San Lorenzo

Via Immacolatella 5. **Tel** 091 611 81 68. **Open** 10am–6pm daily.

Lining the walls of this tiny oratory are incredible stucco scenes from the lives of St. Francis and St. Lawrence, and allegorical figures and putti by Giacomo Serpotta (1699–1706). These remarkable works exhibit the virtuosity of their creator in the handling of his medium. Caravaggio's *Nativity with St. Francis and St. Lawrence* (1609) was stolen from above the altar in 1969. The oratory lies hidden next to the 13th-century church of San Francesco d'Assisi, which brims with great sculpture. The highlight of the church is the triumphal arch (1468) by Pietro da Bonitate and Francesco Laurana in the Cappella Mastrantonio.

The Palazzina Cinese (*c.* 1799), set in the Parco della Favorita

Palazzo Abatellis and Galleria Regionale di Sicilia

Via Alloro 4. **Tel** 091 623 00 11. **Open** 9am–6pm Tue–Fri, 9am–1pm Sat.

Matteo Carnelivari built this palace combining Spanish late-Gothic and Italian Renaissance styles in the 15th century. It is home to the Galleria Regionale di Sicilia, which houses Antonello da Messina's *Vergine Annunziata* (1476) and Francesco Laurana's marble head of Eleanor of Aragon (15th century). Nearby, the 15th-century church of Santa Maria degli Angeli (or La Gancia) contains works by Antonello Gagini and Giacomo Serpotta.

Vergine Annunziata (1476) by da Messina in the Galleria Regionale

La Magione

Via Magione 44. **Tel** 091 617 05 96 or 339 377 41 37 (mobile). **Open** 8:45–11:45am, 3–6pm Mon–Sat; 8:45am–12:30pm Sun.

W basilicalamagione.diocesipia.it

Restorations have revealed the ancient structure of this church founded in 1191 by Roger II's chancellor, Matteo d'Aiello. A highlight of Norman architecture, it has a simple nave flanked by fine Gothic columns.

Villa Giulia

Via Abramo Lincoln. **Open** 9am–5pm daily. Orto Botanico: **Tel** 091 740 40 28. **Open** Nov–Mar: 8am–5pm daily (to 2pm Sun); longer opening hours in the summer. **Closed** pub hols.

The villa's formal gardens were established in the 1700s. Once, with their statues and fountains, they evoked the antique world. Nowadays, their tropical flora and faded grandeur make them delightful for walks. There are splendid tropical plants in the adjacent Orto Botanico (botanical gardens), and plant specimens can be examined in Léon Dufourny's Neo-Classical Gymnasium (1789). Palermo's only central park, Villa Giulia has good children's facilities.

Parco della Favorita

Entrance on Piazza Leoni & Piazza Generale Cascino. **Open** daily. Museo Etnografico Siciliano Pitré: Via Duca degli Abruzzi 1. **Tel** 091 740 48 90. **Open** 8:30am–7:30pm Sat–Thu. **Closed** pub hols.

This park, laid out as a hunting ground in 1799 by the Bourbon Ferdinand IV, was surrounded by the nobles' summer villas. One of these, the Palazzina Cinese (*c.* 1799), was built in a Chinese style for Ferdinand III and Maria Carolina, the sister of Marie Antoinette. The Museo Etnografico Siciliano Pitré, in the stables of the Palazzina Cinese, has a fine collection of Sicilian objects.

❷ Monreale

Magnificently adorned, and with a splendid view of the Conca d'Oro, the Duomo at Monreale is one of the great sights of Norman Sicily. Founded in 1172 by the Norman King William II, it flanks a monastery of the Benedictine Order. The interior of the cathedral glitters with mosaics carried out by Sicilian and Byzantine artists – the inspiration of a king who wanted to rival the power of the Archbishop of Palermo. Like Cefalù, and later Palermo, it was to serve as a royal sepulchre.

★ Christ Pantocrator
The cathedral's Latin-cross plan focuses on the imposing mosaic of the all-powerful Christ (12th–13th century).

Apse Exterior
With their rich multicolored ornamentation in tufa and marble, the three apses represent the apogee of Norman decoration.

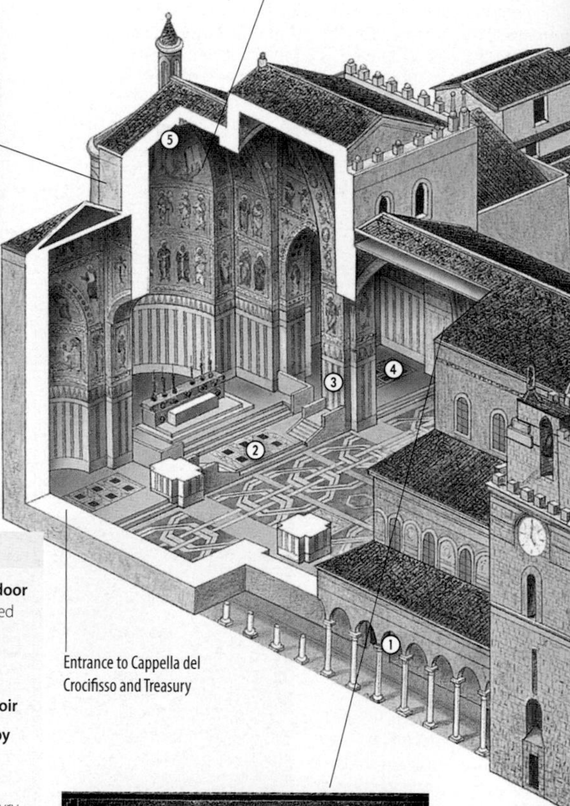

Entrance to Cappella del Crocifisso and Treasury

KEY

① **Barisano da Trani's bronze door** (1179) on the north side is shielded by a portico designed by Gian Domenico and Fazio Gagini (1547–69).

② **Original Cosmati floor in choir**

③ **Nave and aisles separated by Roman columns**

④ **The royal tomb** of William II, in white marble, flanks the porphyry tomb of William I in the corner of the transept.

⑤ **Magnificent gilded wood ceiling**

⑥ **The south wall and cloisters** survive as elements from the Benedictine monastery.

⑦ **Small Oriental-inspired fountain**

⑧ **The 18th-century porch** is surrounded by two squat towers.

★ Mosaic Cycle
Completed in 118[illegible] the rich mosaics show scenes from the Old Testament (nave), Teachings of Christ (aisles, choir, and transepts) and the Gospels (side apses). The story of Noah's Ark is depicted here.

For hotels and restaurants in this region see pp562–77 and pp580–605

★ Cloisters
A masterpiece of Norman artistic expression from the time of William II, the columns – plain, carved or inlaid with richly lustered tiles – support elaborate capitals from which spring Saracenic-style arches.

VISITORS' CHECKLIST

Practical Information
Piazza Duomo.
duomo monreale.it
Church: **Tel** 091 640 44 13. **Open** Mar–Oct: 8:30am–12:45pm, 2:30–5pm daily; Nov–Feb: 8am–12:30pm, 3:30–6pm daily. Cloister: **Tel** 091 640 44 03. **Open** 9am–1pm Mon–Sat. Treasury: **Open** same as the church.

Transportation
389, 809, 8/9 and many others going west.

6

7

8

Column Detail
Craftsmen from Campania, Puglia, Lombardy, and Sicily worked on the cloister columns. The detail here shows Adam and Eve.

Bronze Door Panel
Bonanno da Pisa's fine bronze door (1185), signed by him, depicts 42 scenes from the Bible, set within elaborate borders. The lion and griffin are symbols of the Norman kingdom.

❸ Bagheria

Palermo. 50,000. FS Corso Umberto I (091 90 90 20). Wed.
W **comune.bagheria.pa.it**

Today Bagheria is almost a suburb of Palermo, though open countryside with olive and orange groves once separated them. In the 17th century, Giuseppe Branciforte, Prince of Butera, built a summer retreat here, starting a fashion that was quickly followed by other Palermitan aristocrats. The town's core is sprinkled with their Baroque and Neo-Classical villas.

The **Villa Palagonia** was designed in 1705 by the architect Tommaso Maria Napoli for Ferdinando Gravina, the Prince of Palagonia. It has remarkable architectural qualities: a complex open-air staircase leads to the first floor, and the principal rooms, all with unusual shapes, are arranged around a curved axis. A later prince adorned the perimeter wall with the grotesque stone monsters that amused the 18th-century traveler Patrick Brydone, and horrified Goethe, who also traveled here and called this the "Palagonian madhouse." Across the piazza are **Villa Valguarnera** (begun in 1713 by Napoli), set in its own park, and **Villa Trabia** (mid-18th century), but neither is open to the public. **Museo Guttuso** (18th century) houses a modern art gallery.

Stone figure on Villa Palagonia

Fishing and pleasure boats moored in the harbor of Trapani

Villa Palagonia
Piazza Garibaldi 3.
Tel 091 93 20 88.
Open daily (except during functions).

Museo Guttuso
Via Rammacca 9. **Tel** 091 94 39 02.
Open daily.

Open-air staircase of the eccentric Villa Palagonia in Bagheria

❹ Trapani

70,000. FS Piazza Scarlatti 1 (0923 290 00). daily.
W **apt.trapani.it**

Old Trapani occupies a narrow peninsula. The best buildings in this lively quarter are the churches, such as the **Cathedral of San Lorenzo** (1635) and the **Chiesa del Collegio dei Gesuiti** (*c.* 1614–40). The facades of both, and that of the **Palazzo d'Ali** (17th century) on Via Garibaldi, display magnificently the ebullience of west Sicilian Baroque architecture.

The 17th-century **Purgatorio** on Via San Francesco d'Assisi contains 18th-century *Misteri* – realistic, life-sized wooden statues used annually in the Good Friday procession. **Santa Maria del Gesù** on Via Sant' Agostino should be visited for the *Madonna degli Angeli* by Andrea della Robbia (1435–1525) and Antonello Gagini's canopy (1521). In the Jewish quarter, west of Via XXX Gennaio, the **Palazzo della Giudecca** (16th century) has a strangely textured facade.

The **Museo Pepoli** has a collection of local antiquities. Of interest are the coral objects and the Nativity scene figures *(presepi)*, modern versions of which are made here. Next to the museum, the **Santuario di Maria Santissima Annunziata** contains the *Madonna di Trapani*, a statue revered by fishermen and sailors for its legendary miraculous powers.

Museo Pepoli
Via Conte Agostino Pepoli. **Tel** 0923 55 32 69. **Open** 9am–1:30pm Mon–Sat, 9am–12:30pm Sun & hols (also 3–5:30pm Tue & Thu).

For hotels and restaurants in this region see pp562–77 and pp580–605

5 Erice

Trapani. 29,000. Via Conte a Repoli 11 (0923 50 21 11). Mon.

Poised on a crag overlooking Trapani, the medieval town of Erice was once the seat of the cult of the fertility goddess Venus Erycina. Her temple stood on the present site of the Norman castle (**Castello di Venere**), beyond the **Villa Balio** public gardens. On a clear day, you can see all the way to Tunisia from the castle. The ancient town of Eryx was renamed Gebel-Hamed by the Arabs, Monte San Giuliano by the Normans, and finally Erice in 1934 by Mussolini.

The **Duomo** (14th century) has a battlemented campanile and a 15th-century porch. Inside is a *Madonna and Child* (*c*. 1469), attributed to either Francesco Laurana or Domenico Gagini. The deconsecrated 13th-century **San Giovanni Battista** on Viale Nunzio Nasi (now a hotel) contains Antonello Gagini's *St. John the Evangelist* (1531) and Antonino Gagini's *St. John the Baptist* (1539). **San Cataldo**, a plain 14th-century building on Via San Cataldo, houses a holy water stoup (*c*. 1474) from Domenico Gagini's workshop. In the **Museo Cordici** are Antonello Gagini's *Annunciation* (1525), a variety of Classical remains, and an old library.

Museo Cordici
Piazza Umberto I. **Open** 8:30am–1:30pm, 2:30–5:30pm Mon & Thu; 8am–1:30pm Tue, Wed & Fri.

A typical medieval street in the small hill-town of Erice

Sicilian Islands

Surrounding Sicily are several island groups. The Isole Eolie (Aeolian Islands), to which Panarea, Lipari, Vulcano, and Stromboli belong, are a mass of volcanoes (most of them nearly extinct) poking out of the sea off the coast of Milazzo. The Isole Egadi (Egadi Islands), off the coast of Trapani, have a distinctly Arabic flavor. They include Favignana, Levanzo (which has Palaeolithic and Neolithic paintings and drawings), and Marettimo – the smallest and most unspoiled. Ustica, renowned for its marine life and popular among divers, lies north of Palermo. To the south are the remarkably tourist-free Isole Pelagie (Pelagic Islands), Lampedusa and Linosa, which are North African in character. Remote Pantelleria lies closer to Tunisia than to Sicily.

The biggest and most popular of the Isole Eolie is Lipari, which has a pretty port and a good range of bars, restaurants, and hotels. Nearby sulfur-smelling Vulcano offers hot mud baths and black beaches.

Favignana, the largest and most populous of the Isole Egadi, is the scene of the traditional tuna slaughter – *la mattanza*. This takes place, as it has for centuries, in May. These fishermen are bringing in the nets following the slaughter.

Part of the Isole Pelagie, Lampedusa was once owned by the family of Giuseppe Tomasi di Lampedusa, author of *The Leopard*, Sicily's most famous novel. The island is nearer to Malta than Sicily and has limpid water and white beaches.

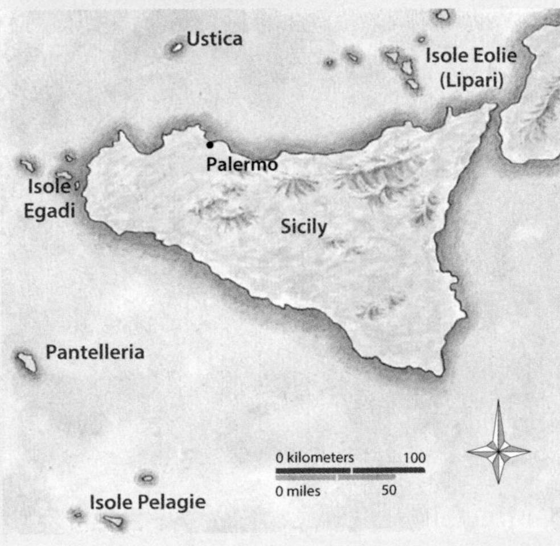

6 Marsala

Trapani. 83,000. FS Via XI Maggio 100 (0923 71 40 97). Tue. consorziovinomarsala.it

The port of Marsala is the home of a thick, strong, sweet wine that has been in production here since the 18th century. In 1798 Admiral Nelson ordered vast quantities of it following the Battle of the Nile. Its early manufacture was presided over by three British families living in Sicily. One of the old warehouses where the wine was produced is now the **Museo Archeologico di Baglio Anselmi**, housing important Phoenician artifacts.

The ruins of **Lilybaeum** are another attraction. Founded in 397 BC, this outpost of the Phoenician Empire was peopled by the survivors of the massacre by Dionysius I of Siracusa at Mozia (ancient Motya) – the island used by the Phoenicians as a commercial center. Best of all are the reconstructed remains of a Punic ship thought to have been active in the First Punic War (263–241 BC). The **Museo di Mozia** in the Whitaker villa contains a remarkable early 5th-century BC statue of a Greek youth.

The excavations here are important; what we know of the Phoenicians today comes mostly from the Bible, and from Mozia. The **Duomo**, begun in the 17th century, was built on the site of an earlier church; both were dedicated to Marsala's patron saint, Thomas Becket of Canterbury. Its interior is full of sculptural works by members of the Gagini family. The small **Museo degli Arazzi**, behind the Duomo, contains several magnificent 16th-century Brussels tapestries.

Statue of a Greek youth in Museo di Mozia

Museo Archeologico di Baglio Anselmi
Via Lungomare. **Tel** 0923 95 25 35. **Open** 9am–6pm daily.

Museo degli Arazzi
Via Garaffa 57. **Tel** 0923 71 13 27. **Open** 9:30am–1pm daily (and 4:30–6pm Tue–Sat).

Museo di Mozia
Isola di Mozia. **Tel** 0923 71 25 98. **Open** 9am–1pm, 3–6pm daily.

7 Segesta

Trapani. 7,500. from Trapani & Palermo. **Tel** 0924 95 58 41. **Open** 9:30am–6pm daily (to 4pm in winter).

According to legend, the ancient town of Segesta – still largely unexcavated – was founded by Trojan followers of Aeneas. It presents one of the most spectacular sights on the island: a massive unfinished **temple** stranded on a remote hillside. Its construction was started between 426 and 416 BC, and it was left incomplete following the devastation of Selinunte by the Carthaginians in 409 BC. Archaeologists regard the temple as a good example of "work in progress." Nearby, close to the summit of Monte Barbaro, the ruins of an ancient theater (3rd century BC) can be visited. Summer concerts are now held here.

The spectacularly situated, unfinished Doric temple at Segesta

8 Selinunte

Trapani. **Tel** 0924 462 77. FS Castelvetrano then bus. **Open** 9am–6pm daily (to 4pm in winter). **Closed** Sun pm.

Founded in 651 BC, Selinunte became one of the great cities of Magna Graecia – the part of southern Italy that was colonized by ancient Greece – and its toppled ruins are among Sicily's most important historic sites. Its ancient name, Selinus, derives from the wild celery that still grows here. The city was an important port, and its wall defenses can still be seen around the Acropolis. The Carthaginians, under Hannibal, completely destroyed the city in 409 BC in a battle famous for its epic and spectacularly savage proportions.

While the city itself has virtually disappeared, eight of its temples are distinguishable, particularly the so-called **Eastern Temples** (E, F, and G). Of these, the columns of huge Doric **Temple E** (490 – 480 BC) have been partially re-erected. **Temple F** (*c.* 560–540 BC) is in ruins. **Temple G** (late 6th century BC), which had 17 massive side columns, was one of the greatest Greek temples ever built.

Higher on the Acropolis lie the remains of **Temples A, B, C, D,** and **O**. Metope sculpture from **Temple C** (early 6th century), originally located on the frieze between the triglyphs, can be seen in the Museo Archeologico Regionale in Palermo *(see p532)*, along with ceramics, jewelry, and other artifacts excavated here. A small **museum** on site houses less important finds, as does one in Castelvetrano, 8.5 miles (14 km) north of Selinunte. The ancient city is still being excavated; its **North Gate** entrance is well preserved and farther north there is also a **necropolis**.

9 Cefalù

Palermo. 14,000. FS i Corso Ruggero 77 (0921 42 10 50). Sat.
cefalu.it

This pretty seaside town, with sandy beaches, restaurants, and hotels, is dominated by a huge rock known as **La Rocca** – once the site of a Temple of Diana – and by one of the finest Norman cathedrals in Sicily. Begun in 1131 by Roger II, the **Duomo** was intended as the main religious seat in Sicily. Though it failed to fulfill this function, the building's magnificence has never been eclipsed. Its splendid mosaics (1148), which feature an image of Christ Pantocrator in the apse, are remarkable and often celebrated as purely Byzantine works of art on Sicilian soil.

The **Museo Mandralisca** houses a fine *Portrait of a Man* (*c.* 1465) by Antonello da Messina and a collection of coins, ceramics, vases, and minerals.

Museo Mandralisca
Via Mandralisca. **Tel** 0921 42 15 47. **Open** 9am–1pm, 3–7pm daily (later in summer).

The twin-towered facade of the Norman Duomo in Cefalù

The lavish apse of Cefalù's Duomo

10 Agrigento

59,000. FS i Via Empedocle 73 (0922 203 91); Piazzale Aldo Moro (0922 204 54). Fri.
comune.agrigento.it

Modern Agrigento occupies the site of Akragas, an important city of the ancient Greek world. Founded by Daedalus, according to legend, it was famed for the luxurious lifestyle of its inhabitants, and was a great power and rival to Siracusa. In 406 BC it fell to the Carthaginians, who sacked and burned it.

The historic core of the city, with its medieval streets, focuses on the Via Atenea. **Santo Spirito** (13th century) houses stuccoes by Giacomo Serpotta (1695). **Santa Maria dei Greci** was built on the remains of a 5th-century BC temple – see the flattened columns in the nave. The **Duomo**, founded in the 14th century and altered in the 16th and 17th centuries, exhibits a unique mixture of Arab, Norman, and Catalan detailing.

Environs

The chief reason to visit Agrigento is to see the archaeological zone known as the Valley of the Temples *(see p540)*. The **Museo Regionale Archeologico** houses an interesting display of artifacts from the temples and the city, including a collection of vases, coins, and Greek and Roman sculpture.

Museo Regionale Archeologico
Contrada San Nicola, Viale Panoramica. **Tel** 0922 40 15 65. **Open** 9am–7:30pm daily (to 1:30pm Mon, Sun).

The Mafia

An international organization founded in Sicily, the Mafia developed as a result of the cruel State and severe poverty. By the late 19th century it had become a criminal organization thriving on property speculation and drug trafficking. Since the "singing" of Tommaso Buscetta and the capture of Toto Riina, the Mafia has been on the defensive against a State that has doubled its efforts against it. The "Boss of Bosses," Bernardo Provenzano, was arrested in 2006 after 43 years on the run. Violence is common in Sicily, but it is not directed at tourists.

Mafia assassination depicted in this scene from the film *The Godfather Part III* (1990)

Valley of the Temples

Straddling a low ridge to the south of Agrigento, the Valley of the Temples (Valle dei Templi) is one of the most impressive complexes of ancient Greek buildings outside Greece. Its Doric temples, dating from the 5th century BC, were destroyed in part by the Carthaginians in 406 BC, and in part by Christians, who believed the temples to be pagan, in the 6th century. Earthquakes wreaked further havoc. Nine of the original ten temples are still visible, and the whole area can be covered in a day. To avoid crowds, visit early in the morning (some temples open as early as 8:30am) or late afternoon.

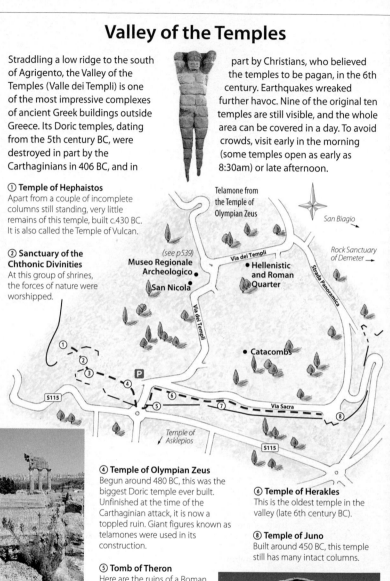

Telamone from the Temple of Olympian Zeus

① Temple of Hephaistos
Apart from a couple of incomplete columns still standing, very little remains of this temple, built c.430 BC. It is also called the Temple of Vulcan.

② Sanctuary of the Chthonic Divinities
At this group of shrines, the forces of nature were worshipped.

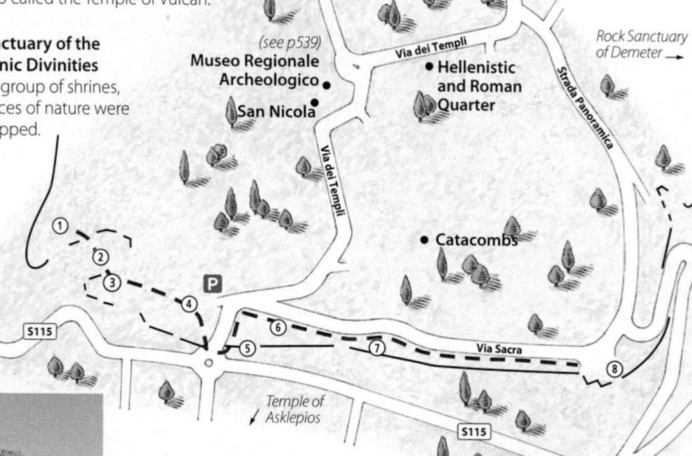

③ Temple of Castor and Pollux
This is a controversial assemblage of pieces from other buildings, erected in the 19th century. Modern Agrigento *(see p539)* is in the background.

④ Temple of Olympian Zeus
Begun around 480 BC, this was the biggest Doric temple ever built. Unfinished at the time of the Carthaginian attack, it is now a toppled ruin. Giant figures known as telamones were used in its construction.

⑤ Tomb of Theron
Here are the ruins of a Roman tomb (1st century AD).

⑥ Temple of Herakles
This is the oldest temple in the valley (late 6th century BC).

⑧ Temple of Juno
Built around 450 BC, this temple still has many intact columns.

⑦ Temple of Concord
This beautifully preserved temple (c.430 BC) was converted into a Christian church in the 4th century AD, thus saved from destruction.

Key

- Suggested route
- Ancient walls

0 meters 500
0 yards 500

⓫ Piazza Armerina

Enna. 21,000. *i* Via Generale Muscara (0935 68 02 01). Thu.
W piazzaarmerina.org

This active town is half medieval and half Baroque. The 17th-century **Duomo**, at its highest point, is the most interesting of the Baroque buildings.

In August, the lively *Palio dei Normanni* festival attracts many visitors, but the real draw are the mosaics in the UNESCO-listed **Villa Romana del Casale**, 3 miles (5 km) southwest of the town. The mosaics were only excavated in the 20th century.

It is thought that this huge, once sumptuous villa with its public halls, private quarters, baths, and courtyards, belonged to Maximianus Herculeus, Diocletian's co-emperor, from AD 286 to 305. His son and successor, Maxentius, probably continued its decoration, with Constantine taking over on Maxentius's death in 312.

Although little remains of the building fabric, the floors have some of the finest surviving mosaics from Roman antiquity. The hunting, mythological, and domestic scenes, and exotic landscapes, all exhibit realistic attention to detail.

Villa Romana del Casale
Contrada Casale. **Tel** 0935 68 00 36.
Open 9am–4:30pm Fri–Sun.

Roman *Girls in Bikinis* mosaic from the Villa Romana del Casale

⓬ Enna

28,000. FS *i* Piazza Colaianni 6 (0935 50 08 75). Tue.
W apt-enna.com

Impregnable on a crag above a fertile landscape where Persephone, mythological daughter of Demeter, once played, Sicily's highest town (3,090 ft /942 m) has been coveted by successive invaders since its earliest days. The venerated seat of the Cult of Demeter (goddess of fertility) was at Enna. Her temple stood on the **Rocca Cerere**, not far from the huge **Castello di Lombardia** (13th century) built by Frederick II.

Most of Enna's sights are clustered in the old town, among the ancient streets that open out of the Via Roma. The church of **San Francesco** has a 16th-century tower. **Piazza Crispi**, with its fine views to nearby Calascibetta, is dominated by a copy of Bernini's *Rape of Persephone*. The 14th-century **Duomo**, altered in later centuries, contains parts of Demeter's temple.

The **Museo Alessi** houses the Cathedral Treasury and an interesting coin collection. The **Museo Varisano** has exhibits on the area's history, from Neolithic to Roman. Away from the center, the octagonal **Torre di Federico II** (13th century) is a former watchtower.

Environs

The ancient hill town of **Nicosia**, northeast of Enna, was damaged in the 1967 earthquake, but still contains a smattering of churches. San Nicola, built in the 14th century, has a magnificent, carved entrance portal. Inside there is a much venerated wooden crucifix (17th century) by Fra Umile di Petralia. Santa Maria Maggiore houses a 16th-century marble polyptych by Antonello Gagini and a throne reputedly used by Charles V in 1535. Farther east is **Troina**. It was captured in 1062 by the Normans, whose work survives in the Chiesa Matrice. Southeast of Enna, **Vizzini** commands fine views of the countryside.

Museo Alessi
Via Roma 475. **Open** 8am–8pm daily.

Museo Varisano
Piazza Mazzini. **Tel** 0935 52 81 00.
Open 9am–6:30pm daily.

View from the hills overlooking Vizzini, southeast of Enna

Taormina's magnificently situated Greek theater, with Mount Etna in the distance

⓭ Tindari

Messina. Tel 0941 24 11 36. FS Patti or Oliveri, then bus. **Open** 9am–7pm daily (to 4pm in winter).

Poised on the edge of a cliff overlooking the Golfo di Patti are the ruins of **Tyndaris**, one of the last Greek cities to have been founded in Sicily (395 BC). Apart from the city walls, the ruins are mostly Roman, including the **basilica** and **theater**. An **antiquarium** houses artifacts from the site. A combined ticket allows entry at the massive 2nd-century **Villa Romana** in Patti Marina.

Tindari is also known for its shrine to a Byzantine icon, the **Black Madonna** on Piazzale Belvedere.

⓮ Messina

250,000. FS Piazza Cairoli 45 (090 293 52 92). daily.
azienturismomessina.it

Messina has been the victim of earthquakes and World War II bombing. The **Museo Regionale** houses treasures that include works by Antonello da Messina and Caravaggio. **Santissima Annunziata dei Catalani** in Piazza Catalani displays the eclecticism of 12th-century Norman architecture, with rich decoration. To visit the church, ask at the tourist office.

Outside, GA Montorsoli's **Fontana d'Orione** (1547) is the finest fountain of its kind from 16th-century Sicily. His **Fontana di Nettuno** (1557) celebrates Messina's foundation and position in the world as a principal commercial port.

Museo Regionale
Via Libertà 465. **Tel** 090 36 12 92.
Open 9am–7pm Tue–Sat, 9am–1pm Sun.

Antonello da Messina's *Madonna and Child* (1473), Museo Regionale

⓯ Taormina

Messina. 10,000. FS
Palazzo Corvaja, Piazza Santa Caterina (0942 232 43). Wed.

Splendidly situated, Taormina is Sicily's best-known resort. It retains an air of exclusivity while being on the tourist trail, with sandy beaches and a wide range of restaurants and hotels.

The most illustrious relic of the past is the **theater**. Begun in the 3rd century BC by the Greeks, it was subsequently rebuilt by the Romans. Among other Classical remains are the ruins of the **odeon** (for musical performances) and the **naumachia** (an artificial lake for mock battles). On Piazza Vittorio Emanuele (site of the Roman Forum), **Palazzo Corvaia** (14th century) was built using stone from a temple that once stood here. The 13th-century **Duomo** (renovated in 1636) is a fortresslike building.

Environs
Taormina's main beach, **Mazzarò**, boasts clear waters and is easily reached from the town. South of Taormina at **Capo Schisò** are the ruins of ancient **Naxos**. To the west is **Gole dell'Alcantara**, a 66-ft- (20-m-) deep gorge of basalt rock, a river, and waterfalls.

16 Mount Etna

Catania. FS Linguaglossa or Randazzo; Circumetnea train from Catania to Riposto. to Nicolosi. Via G. Garibaldi 63, Nicolosi (095 91 15 05). To hire a guide: 095 791 47 55. **W http://turismo.provincia.ct.it**

Europe's highest (11,050 ft/ 3,370 m) and most active volcano, Mount Etna was thought by the Romans to have been the forge of Vulcan (god of fire). The climb to the summit should be made only with an experienced guide. The Circumetnea train runs around the base, offering an alternative to hiking and good views.

17 Catania

315,000. FS Via Cimarosa 10 (095 73 06 211). Mon–Sat (general); Sun (antique & bric-a-brac). **W apt.catania.it**

Having been decimated by the earthquake of 1693, Catania was comprehensively rebuilt. While it is not immediately beautiful, it

The facade of Catania's Duomo

contains some of the most imaginative lava-built Baroque buildings in Sicily. **Piazza del Duomo**, featuring a lava elephant (Catania's symbol) carrying an Egyptian obelisk, offers a dramatic vista to Mount Etna. In 1736 the Norman **Duomo** was given a new facade by Vaccarini, who also worked on the **Municipio** (finished 1741), on the facade of **Sant'Agata** (1748), on the designs of **Collegio Cutelli**, built around 1779, and on **Palazzo Valle** (*c.* 1740–50).

Carrying on the Vaccarini tradition is Stefano Ittar's **San Placido** (around 1768). The frenzied stone carving on the **Palazzo Biscari** (early 18th century) is exceeded by Antonino Amato's unrestrained decoration of the vast Benedictine **convent** (1704) and the adjacent huge church of **San Niccolò** (1730)

On Via Vittorio Emanuele is the **Museo Belliniano**, birthplace of composer Vincenzo Bellini (1801–35). The lava ruins of the **Teatro Romano** (21 BC) are at Piazza Stesicono. **Verga's House**, home of the great Sicilian novelist Giovanni Verga (1840–1922), is on Via Sant' Anna. Via Crociferi is home to 18th-century churches **San Francesco Borgia**, **San Benedetto**, and **San Giuliano**, whose interior is Vaccarini's masterpiece (1760). Farther along Via Crociferi, the church of **Santo Carcere** contains the prison of St. Agatha, who was martyred in AD 253.

Influences on Traditional Sicilian Cuisine

Sicily has one of Italy's most varied cuisines. The island's unique location – marooned between North Africa, Europe, and the eastern Mediterranean – and the invaders it attracted are responsible for this culinary diversity. The earliest Western cookbook, the now lost *Art of Cooking* (5th century BC), was written by Mithaecus, a Siracusan Greek. Sicily's fertility attracted Greek colonists, who exported oil, wheat, honey, cheese, fruit, and vegetables to their homeland. The Arabs introduced oranges, lemons, eggplant, and sugar cane. Their love of sweet confections inspired *granita*, a form of flavored ice, and *cassata*, an elaborate sponge cake with ricotta and candied fruit. The Sicilians love to claim an Arabic origin for their ice cream, but the Greeks and Romans had created an earlier version by chilling their wine with snow from Mount Etna. Traditionally, the peasants existed on a subsistence diet while the aristocracy enjoyed extravagant fare, and one of the peculiarities of Sicilian food today is that it can be both frugal and handsomely ornate. All of the usual Italian dishes are available, but the more interesting meals are those that use local ingredients like swordfish, sardines, ricotta cheese, red chili peppers, eggplant, capers, olives, and almond paste to create unusual taste combinations.

A colorful selection of vegetables at a Sicilian market stand

Marzipan fruits made from almond paste

A picturesque beach at Capo Tindari, Sicily ▶

Shorefront in Siracusa, one of the most beautiful cities of the ancient Greek world

⓲ Pantalica

Siracusa. 🚌 from Siracusa to Sortino then 3-mile (5-km) walk to entrance (partial access), or bus from Siracusa to Ferla then 6-mile (10-km) walk to entrance. Necropolis ℹ Pro Loco, Ferla. **Tel** 0931 79 06 81.

Remote in the desolate Monti Iblei and overlooking the Anapo River is the prehistoric **necropolis** of Pantalica – a pleasant place to walk and picnic. The dead of a large, unexcavated village (occupied 13th–8th centuries BC) were buried here in cavelike tombs cut into the rock. More than 5,000 of these tombs were arranged in tiers, with a single flat stone sealing each opening.

The inhabitants of Pantalica are thought to have come from coastal **Thapsos**, which was abandoned after raids by warlike tribes from mainland Italy. The site was reinhabited in the Byzantine period, when some tombs were made into cave dwellings and chapels.

Rock-cut tombs in the prehistoric necropolis of Pantalica

Artifacts from the necropolis are displayed in Siracusa's Museo Archeologico Regionale.

Interior of Duomo in Siracusa

⓳ Siracusa

125,000. FS 🚌 ⛴ ℹ Via Maestranza (0931 46 42 55). Wed.

Siracusa (Syracuse) was the most important and powerful Greek city from the 5th to the 3rd centuries BC, and, according to the Roman consul Cicero, the most beautiful. The peninsula **Ortigia** is the hub of the old city. On the mainland, **Achradina, Tyche** and **Neapolis** have been occupied almost without a break since the expansion of the city in 480 BC. These were the years of Gelon, tyrant of Gela, when Siracusa was enriched with new temples, theaters, and dockyards. The city was a powerful force until 211 BC, when it fell to the Romans in a battle that also killed the mathematician Archimedes, its most famous inhabitant.

The highlight of Ortigia is the extraordinary **Duomo**, begun in 1728 by architect Andrea Palma. Its Baroque facade masks the **Temple of Athena** (5th century BC), which has been absorbed into the Duomo. Facing the Ponte Nuovo are the ruins of Sicily's earliest Doric temple, the **Temple of Apollo**, which had monolithic columns.

Across from the Duomo is the **Palazzo Beneventano del Bosco** (1778–88), a bold example of Siracusan Baroque, as is **Santa Lucia alla Badia** (1695–1703). In the Municipio, a small museum records the history of Ionic temples, and the coin collection of the Galleria Numismatica records Siracusa's past wealth. The delightful **Fonte Aretusa** is frequently referred to by Classical writers as the point where Aretusa emerged from the ground, having been changed into a spring by Artemis to help her escape her lover Alpheus.

At Ortigia's farthest point is the **Castello Maniace**, built by Frederick II around 1239. Here too is the **Gallerie Regionale di Palazzo Bellomo**, with sculpture and paintings including the *Burial of St. Lucy* (1608) by Caravaggio.

The painting comes from the church of **Santa Lucia** in the Achradina quarter. This area was flattened during World War II, but the church survived. It is mostly 17th century with a

Norman campanile, and occupies the site where St. Lucy, patron saint of Siracusa, was martyred in AD 304. Achradina is now the center of modern Siracusa.

To the north, in Tyche, is the **Museo Archeologico Regionale Paolo Orsi**, with its important collection of artifacts from the Palaeolithic to the Byzantine era, taken from southeastern sites in Sicily. Included are vases, coins, bronzes, sculpture, and fragments from Siracusan temples.

The Neapolis quarter and its **Parco Archeologico** feature the Teatro Romano, the Altar of Hieron II, and the spectacular Teatro Greco, carved from the hillside. Beyond the Nymphaeum is the 2nd-century AD Roman amphitheater and the stone quarries – the Latomia del Paradiso, featuring the **Ear of Dionysius**. It is thought that 7,000 Athenians were incarcerated here and left to die after their calamitous defeat in 413 BC, in a battle described by Thucydides as "the greatest action in Hellenic history."

Environs

At **Epipolae**, 5 miles (8 km) north of Neapolis is the **Castle of Euryalus** – the most important ancient Greek fortification to have survived.

Gallerie Regionale di Palazzo Bellomo
Palazzo Bellomo, Via Capodieci 14. **Tel** 0931 695 11. **Open** 9am–6:30pm Tue–Sun (to 1pm public hols).

Museo Archeologico Regionale Paolo Orsi
Viale Teocrito 66. **Tel** 0931 46 40 22. **Open** 9am–6:30pm Tue–Sun (to 1pm Sun). Last adm: 1 hr before closing.

Noto

Siracusa. 24,000. FS Piazza XVI Maggio (0931 83 67 44). Mon 1st & 3rd Tue of the month.
comune.noto.sr.it

Noto was built from scratch in the early 18th century to replace Noto Antica, which was devastated by an earthquake in 1693. The town was comprehensively designed in Baroque style, using the local white tufa, a limestone that has turned a honey-brown color from the sun. Noto is a UNESCO World Heritage site, but unfortunately much of its beauty is behind scaffolding due to ongoing restoration.

The facade of the Duomo in Noto rises above a huge staircase

The twin-towered **Duomo** (completed 1770s) that dominates Noto is by architect Rosario Gagliardi, who also designed the eccentric tower facade of the seminary of **San Salvatore** (18th century) in Piazza Municipio, the convex facade of **San Domenico** (1730s) in Piazza XVI Maggio, and the oval interior of **Santa Chiara** (1730) on Corso Vittorio Emanuele. The magnificent **Palazzo Trigona** (1781) stands on Via Cavour behind the Duomo. On Via Nicolaci, the **Palazzo Villadorata** (1730s) features a splendid facade adorned with elaborate stone carvings. At the north end of Via Nicolaci, the **Monastery of Montevergine** has a striking curved facade. In mid-May, Via Nicolaci is the site of the Infiorata flower festival. Gagliardi's church of the **Crocifisso** (1728) stands on the town's summit. It contains a sculpture of the Madonna by Francesco Laurana (1471). The **Municipio** (1740s), facing the Duomo, has a fine "billowing" ground floor design.

Environs

The earthquake of 1693 also devastated the towns of **Modica**, around 19 miles (30 km) to the west, and **Ragusa**, a short distance farther. Like Noto, they were rebuilt in the region's rich Baroque style. Gagliardi worked on Modica's **San Giorgio** (early 18th century), Ragusa's **San Giorgio** (begun around 1746, and one of his masterpieces), and **San Giuseppe** (mid-18th century).

Boisterous carving on the facade of the Palazzo Villadorata in Noto

SARDINIA

In his travelogue, *Sea and Sardinia*, D.H. Lawrence wrote that Sardinia was "left outside of time and history." Indeed, the march of time has been slow here, and traditions from ancient Europe have survived – the legacy of invasion by Phoenicians, Carthaginians, Romans, Arabs, Byzantines, Spaniards, and Savoyards.

These traditions are displayed in Sardinia's many festivals – some soberly Christian, others with pagan roots. Several different dialects and languages are spoken in Sardinia. Catalan can be heard in Alghero, and on the island of San Pietro, there is a Ligurian dialect. Even remnants of Phoenician survive. In the south, the traditional influences are Spanish, while pure native strains of people and language survive in the Gennargentu mountains. Peopled by shepherds in isolated communities, this region is so impenetrable that invaders have never bothered it.

Of particular interest are the prehistoric *nuraghe* castles, villages, temples, and tombs dotted around the countryside – most notably around Barumini, north of Cagliari, and in the Valle dei Nuraghe, south of Sassari. The *nuraghe* were built by a people whose origins constitute one of the Mediterranean's great mysteries. In Cagliari, the capital of Sardinia, there is a museum with an excellent archaeological collection that offers insight into this enigmatic people.

Sassari, Oristano, Alghero, and Olbia are all centers of areas marked by their individuality. Some remarkable Pisan-Romanesque churches are located around Sassari, and here too dialects reveal close links with the languages of Tuscany. Olbia is a boom town made rich by tourism and the proximity of the jet-setting Costa Smeralda. Sober Nuoro with its province in the shadow of the Gennargentu mountains, by contrast, has little in common with the Sardinia of tourist brochures.

Relaxing during the day in the tiny resort of Carloforte on the Isola di San Pietro, next to Sant'Antioco

◀ The gorgeous turquoise waters of Costa Paradiso, Sardinia

Exploring Sardinia

This island, called Sardegna in Italian, is characterized by an interior of dramatic, rolling uplands covered in *macchia* – grassland mingled with myrtle, wild thyme, prickly pears, and dwarf oaks – and a coastline of beguiling, translucent sea, isolated coves, long sandy beaches, and caves. The Gennargentu mountains, with the highest peak at 6,017 ft (1,834 m), shield a nearly impenetrable area of rural villages. In the northeast, mountains fall away dramatically to the Costa Smeralda, Sardinia's most exclusive coastal area. Farther south, the shoreline around the Golfo di Orosei is fairly unspoiled. Around Oristano in the west, the land is flat, leading to the plain of Campidano, where the island's corn, fruit, and vegetables grow.

A typical scene of clothes hanging out to dry in Alghero

Sights at a Glance

1. Costa Smeralda
2. Sassari
3. Alghero
4. Bosa
5. Nuoro
6. Cala Gonone
7. Nuoro Oristano
8. Sant'Antioco
9. Cagliari

Getting Around

Ferries from a wide range of ports on the Italian mainland dock at Cagliari, Olbia, and Porto Torres. International and domestic flights use the airports at Cagliari, Olbia, and Alghero. The island is neatly cut by the S131. It skirts the Gennargentu Mountains, which are accessible only by tortuously winding passes. Branches of the S131 reach Olbia and Nuoro. Express bus services connect the major cities, while the smaller towns are linked by slow and infrequent public transportation.

For additional map symbols *see back flap*

Key

Major road
Secondary road
Minor road
Scenic route
Main railroad
Minor railroad
Summit

0 kilometers 50
0 miles 25

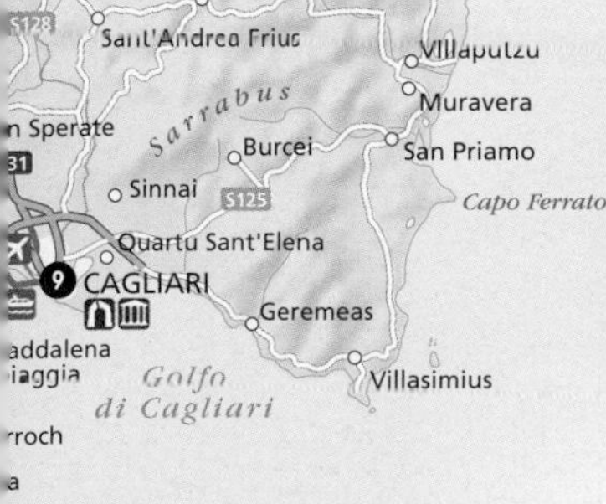

Waves lapping at the rocks on Isola di San Pietro, northwest of Sant'Antioco

Southernmost reach of the Gennargentu Mountains

The extravagantly beautiful, macchia-scented Costa Smeralda

❶ Costa Smeralda

Sassari. FS ⛴ Olbia. 🚌 Porto Cervo. ℹ AAST La Maddalena, Cava Civetta (0789 73 63 21); AAST Palau, Via Nazionale 94 (0789 70 95 70). **W quicostasmeralda.it**

Stretching from the Golfo di Cugnana to the Golfo di Arzachena, the Costa Smeralda was developed by a consortium of magnates in the 1950s. One of the world's most opulent holiday resorts, it is kept immaculate by strict controls.

In **Porto Cervo**, the main town, boutiques jostle with nightclubs, fine restaurants, and luxury hotels. It caters to the seriously rich – billionaires, crowned heads, and rock stars.

Environs
Head north to rural **Baia Sardinia** and **Cannigione**. From Palau, ferries leave for **La Maddalena** and **Isola Caprera**, the home of Garibaldi and the **Museo Nazionale Garibaldino**.

Museo Nazionale Garibaldino
Frazione Caprera, La Maddalena. **Tel** 0789 72 71 62. **Open** 9am–1:30pm, 2–7:15pm Tue–Sun. **Closed** Jan 1, May 1, Dec 25.

❷ Cassari

130,000. ✈ FS 🚌 ℹ Viale Caprera 36 (079 27 99 54). Mon. **W comune.sassari.it**

Founded by Genoese and Pisan merchants early in the 13th century, Sassari is known for its spectacular *Cavalcata Sarda* festival on Ascension Day, and for being the site of Sardinia's first university. There is a raucous, tight, church-filled medieval quarter around the **Duomo** (11th century, with later, mostly Baroque, additions), and to the north is the huge **Fonte Rosello**, a late-Renaissance fountain. The **Museo Archeologico Nazionale "GA Sanna"** is a good starting point for an investigation of the region's nuraghic history.

Facade of Santissima Trinità di Saccargia

Environs
To the southeast along the S131 is the Pisan-Romanesque church of **Santissima Trinità di Saccargia** (1116), with the only extant 13th-century fresco cycle in Sardinia. Farther on is the 12th-century church of **San Michele di Salvenero**, and at **Ardara** the basalt-built Romanesque **Santa Maria del Regno**, or "Black Cathedral."

Museo Archeologico Nazionale "GA Sanna"
Via Roma 64. **Tel** 079 27 22 03. **Open** 9am–7:30pm Tue–Sun (to 7pm Sun).

❸ Alghero

Sassari. 41,000. ✈ FS 🚌 ⛴ ℹ Lungomare Dante 1 (079 97 59 96). Wed. **W comune.alghero.ss.it**

Founded on a peninsula facing the Bay of Alghero early in the 12th century, and taken from the Genoese Dorias by the Aragonese in 1353, Alghero was peopled by settlers from Barcelona and Valencia. Its original occupants – Ligurians and Sardinians – were expelled with such thoroughness that today the Catalan language and culture is enjoying a revival and the look of old Alghero is consistently Spanish.

Filled with labyrinthine alleys and cobbled streets, the lively port of old Alghero is flanked by battlemented walls and defensive towers on all but the landward section. Facing the Giardino Pubblico is the massive 16th-century **Torre di Porta Terra**, also known as the Jewish Tower after its builders. Around the periphery of the old town are more towers, including **Torre dell'Espero Reial** and **Torre San Giacomo** on Lungomare Colombo, and **Torre della Maddalena** on Piazza Porta Terra.

The 16th-century **Duomo** at the bottom of Via Umberto is predominantly Catalan-Gothic with an Aragonese portal. Off Via Carlo Alberto, **San Francesco** (14th century) has a pretty

A typical house in Alghero

The waterfront at Bosa

cloister and octagonal campanile towering over Alghero, and Baroque **San Michele** has a bright tiled dome. In Via Principe Umberto is the **Casa Doria**, the house where the pre-Hispanic rulers of Alghero lived. It has a beautiful Renaissance portal and Gothic-arched window.

Environs

Take a boat or car trip (the latter involves much climbing down) to the spectacular **Grotta di Nettuno**, a deep natural cave around the point of Capo Caccia, or the nearby **Grotta Verde**.

4 Bosa

Nuoro. 8,500. FS Pro Loco, Via Azuni 5 (0785 37 61 07). Tue.
W **comune.bosa.nu.it**

Bosa is a small, picturesque seaside town at the mouth of Sardinia's only navigable river, the Temo. The historic **Sa Costa** district struggles up the side of a low hill capped by the **Castello di Serravalle**, built in 1122 by the Malaspina family. The narrow passages and alleys here have changed little since the Middle Ages. By the Temo are **Sas Conzas** – the former dyers' houses and workshops.

Languishing on the riverside, the cosmopolitan **Sa Piatta** district houses the Aragonese-Gothic **Duomo** (15th century) and Romanesque **San Pietro Extramuros** (11th century), with a Gothic facade added by Cistercian monks in the 13th century.

Nuraghe in Sardinia

The dominant feature of Sardinia is the 7,000 or so *nuraghe* dotted around the island. Dating from 1800 to 300 BC, these strange, truncated cone structures were built without any bonding from huge basalt blocks taken from extinct volcanoes. To this day, little is known about the identity of the nuraghic people. They must have been well organized and possessed remarkable engineering skills, judging by their buildings, but appear to have left no written word. The mystery of these enigmatic people has intrigued Sardinians for years.

The individual *nuraghe* are fairly small. A few of these structures were fortresses, equipped with wells and other defensive features.

Su Nuraxi at Barumini *(above)*, Serra Orrios, near Dorgali, and Santu Antine at Torralba are among the most important *nuraghe* complexes. Houses, temples, tombs, and even a theater have been identified.

This bronze figure of a hero with four eyes and four arms is among the many objects and statues discovered on nuraghic sites and associated with the nuraghic people.

Nobel Prize–winning novelist Grazia Deledda from Nuoro

5 Nuoro

38,000. FS Piazza d'Italia 19 (0784 300 83). Fri & Sat. 29 Aug: Sagra del Redentore. **comune.nuoro.it**

This town, in a spectacular setting beneath Monte Ortobene and the dramatic Supramonte, was the home of Grazia Deledda, who won the Nobel Prize for Literature in 1926 for her portrayal of the power and passions in the primitive communities around her. A comprehensive collection of ethnic items, such as traditional Sardinian costumes and jewelry, can be seen in the excellent **Museo Etnografico Sardo**. Attending the *Sagra del Redentore* festival is the best way to witness the region's dancing and dialects.

Environs
Nuoro is on the edge of the Barbagia region, which has isolated villages of shepherds who have never experienced the hand of any overlord, so impenetrable are the **Gennargentu** mountains. This region was known to the Romans as Barbaria; it was an area they were never able to subdue. Traces of the traditional lawlessness of the Barbagia can be seen in **Orgosolo**, with its wall murals calling for Sardinia's independence. Rival clans were locked in bloody vendetta for almost 50 years, and the deeds of native bandits form part of local folklore.

In **Mamoiada**'s *Feast of the Mamuthones*, men in sinister masks and traditional costume perform a ritual dance ending with a symbolic "killing" of a scapegoat. The fervor of the event is indicative of the fierce folkloric tradition and deep resistance to change.

Museo Etnografico Sardo
Via Mereu 56. **Tel** 0784 25 70 35. **Open** 9am–1pm Tue–Sun (to 8pm Jun–Sep). **isresardegna.it**

6 Cala Gonone

Nuoro. 800. Pro Loco, via Lamormara 108, Dorgali (0784 962 43). daily. from Dorgali to grottoes (Apr–mid-Oct). **Tel** 0784 933 05.

East of Nuoro, between the sea and the mountains, is the hamlet of Cala Gonone – a bustling seaside resort and fishing port, with magnificent beaches. Along the unspoiled coast are the isolated coves of **Cala Luna**, linked with Cala Gonone by a well-marked two-hour trail, and **Cala Sisine**. The famous **Grotta del Bue Marino**, adorned with weird rock formations, can only be reached by boat.

Entrance to the Grotta del Bue Marino, south of Cala Gonone

Environs
To the south, the villages of **Urzulei, Baunei**, and **Santa Maria Navarrese**, along the spectacular SS125 road to Tortolì, feature breathtaking landscapes.

Ruins of Tharros near Oristano

7 Oristano

Cagliari. 32,000. FS EPT, Piazza Eleonora 1 (0783 79 13 06); Pro Loco, Via Vittorio Emanuele 8 (0783 706 21). Tue & Fri.

The province of Oristano corresponds roughly with historical Arborea, over which Eleonora ruled *(see opposite)*. She is commemorated by an 18th-century statue in **Piazza Eleonora**. On Corso Vittorio Emanuele is the 16th-century **Casa di Eleonora**, and nearby the **Antiquarium Arborense**, which has Neolithic, nuraghic, Punic, and Roman artifacts. The **Torre di San Cristoforo** (1291) in Piazza Roma once formed part of Oristano's fortifications. The **Duomo** (13th century) was later rebuilt in the Baroque style. More interesting are the churches of **Santa Chiara** (1343) on Via Garibaldi and 14th-century **San Martino** on Via Cagliari.

Environs
The 12th-century Pisan-Romanesque **Cathedral** at Santa Giusta has columns probably taken from Tharros, an 8th-century BC Punic

The tiny resort of Carloforte, the capital of Isola di San Pietro

settlement, 12 miles (20 km) west of Oristano on the Sinis peninsula.

Antiquarium Arborense
Palazzo Parpaglia. **Tel** 0783 79 12 62. **Open** 9am–2pm, 5–8pm Tue, Thu, Sun.

8 Sant'Antioco

Cagliari. FS Pro Loco, Piazza Repubblica 31a (0781 84 05 92).

The main town on this unspoiled island off Sardinia's southern coast is **Sant'Antioco**, once a Phoenician port and an important Roman base. Proof of almost continuous occupation is clear from the **catacombs**, a Phoenician burial place later used by Christians, under the 12th-century basilica of **Sant'Antioco Martire**. The **Museo Archeologico** contains Phoenician artifacts. The Punic **Tophet** (sanctuary of the goddess Tanit) and the **necropolis** are nearby. The small **Isola di San Pietro** can be reached by ferry from Calasetta.

Catacombs
Piazza Parrocchia.
Tel 0781 830 44. **Open** 9am–noon, 3:30–6pm daily. only.

Museo Archeologico
Via Regina Margherita 113.
Tel 0783 744 33.
Open 9am–2pm, 3–8pm daily. **Closed** Jan 1, Easter, Dec 8, 25 & 26. (& Tophet & necropolis).

9 Cagliari

165,000. FS Piazza Matteotti (070 66 92 55). daily; also Sun (flea) and 2nd Sun of month (antiques). **visit-cagliari.it**

The capital of Sardinia, this site was occupied by the Phoenicians, Carthaginians, and Romans, and extensive ruins of the Phoenician city of Nora lie to the southwest of Cagliari. A 2nd-century **amphitheater** survives from the Roman era, cut from rock. Discover the town's earlier history in the **Cittadella dei Musei**, the former royal arsenal. It houses several museums, including the **Museo Archeologico Nazionale**. The nuraghic items are the most interesting in the collection, especially the bronze votive statuettes. Also in the Cittadella dei Musei is the **Pinacoteca**, an art gallery.

The old core of Cagliari has an appealing North African character. In the high **Castello** district, the Romans and, later, Pisans built defenses. The gracious **Bastione San Remy** on Piazza Costituzione offers magnificent views over the city and surrounding countryside. The **Duomo** is a 20th-century rehash of a Romanesque building. Flanking the entrance are two 12th-century pulpits originally destined for the cathedral in Pisa.

Nearby is the Pisan tower **Torre San Pancrazio** (14th century). From the partially ruined **Torre dell'Elefante** on Via dell'Università to the port lies the **Marina** quarter, which expanded from the old town in the 16th to 17th centuries. In Piazza San Cosimo, the 6th-century church of **San Saturnino** is a rare monument to Byzantine occupation.

The 6th-century church of San Saturnino in Cagliari, built on a Greek cross plan

Amphitheater
Viale Sant'Ignazio. **Tel** 070 677 64 70. **Open** 9am–5pm Tue–Sun (summer: 9am–1pm, 3:30–7:30pm).

Cittadella dei Musei
Piazza Arsenale. **Tel** 070 675 76 27.
Museo Archeologico Nazionale
Open 9am–8pm Tue–Sun.
Pinacoteca Tel 070 66 24 96.
Open 9am–8pm Tue–Sun. **Closed** Jan 1, May 1, Dec 25.

Eleonora of Arborea

A champion against rule from abroad, Eleonora was governing *giudicessa* (judge) of Arborea, one of four administrative divisions of Sardinia, from 1383–1404. Her marriage to Brancaleone Doria consolidated Genoese interests in Sardinia. She rallied the island to keep out Spanish invaders who tried to claim land that had been given to the Aragonese King James II. Her greatest legacy was the completion of the codifying of laws begun by her father. Written in Sardinian, they called for community of property in marriage and the right of women to seek redress for rape.

TRAVELERS' NEEDS

WHERE TO STAY

People come from all over the world to visit Italy, and most Italians spend their vacations here as well, particularly in the mountains or by the sea. This means that there is a dazzling range of accommodation options, from splendid hotels in old palazzi and historic residences, to simple family-run *pensioni* and hostels. Most major cities also offer upscale guest houses. Those who want accommodations with cooking facilities are well served too, with everything from stately villas in Tuscany to purpose-built vacation flats in, or near, seaside resorts. Italian hotels can have a reputation for being expensive and short on services, but this is not always the case, and you can find excellent value in all price ranges. The hotels listed on pages 562–77 have been selected from every price category as among the best value in each area for style, comfort, or location.

The Gritti Palace, one of Venice's historic palazzi *(see p562)*

Ratings

Hotels in Italy are classified with a rating system of one to five stars. The grading depends on the facilities offered, and each region awards stars according to slightly different criteria.

Sometimes a hotel has a lower rating than it deserves. This may be because the local tourist office has not upgraded the rating or because the hotel itself has opted to stay in a lower category to avoid higher taxes.

Alberghi

Albergo is Italian for hotel, but the term tends to refer to establishments classified as three-star or above. Room sizes vary considerably: in city centers even expensive hotels can have small rooms, especially if the hotel is located in a historic building, whereas you get far more space for your money in rural areas. *Alberghi* will have private baths or showers in all rooms. Many high-end and boutique hotels also offer spa and fitness facilities.

Pensioni

Although the term *pensione* is no longer in official use, one- and two-star hotels still use the term to describe their status. On the whole you will find immaculate standards of cleanliness and friendly, helpful service with basic, although perfectly functional, rooms. Be aware that while your *pensioni* may be in an old building full of historic charm, this can also mean noisy, erratic plumbing and dark rooms. Many *pensioni* do not have public rooms other than a sparsely furnished breakfast room. Most will offer at least some bedrooms with a private shower although rarely a bath. If you intend to be out late, check that you'll be able to get back into the *pensione*. Not all of them are staffed after midnight or 1am, but most will at least be able to provide a key to the main door.

A *locanda* was traditionally an inn, offering cheap food and a place to sleep for the traveler. The word is still in use, particularly in central and northern Italy, but is now synonymous with *pensione* and may be more of an affectation for the benefit of the tourist.

Street sign showing the direction and location of hotels

Chain Hotels

There are various Italian chain hotels, including **Atahotels** and **Una Hotels and Resorts**, as well as the usual big internationals. **NH Hoteles** hotels appeal to the business traveler, and there are one or two in most large cities; **Marriott**, **Hyatt**, and **Best Western** are international luxury chains, while **Italia Lodging** caters to the more modest budget. **Relais et Châteaux** run charming hotels in historic castles, villas, and monasteries, with facilities to match.

Meals and Facilities

There has been a general improvement in the facilities offered by Italian hotels, especially in the more modern four- and five-star hotels. However, in some older establishments there may not

◀ The popular San Carlo cafe on Piazza San Carlo, Turin

Romantic Hotel Villa Pagoda in Nervi, Genoa *(see p568)*

always be air-conditioning or 24-hour room service, so it's best to check before you book.

Some hotels may insist on full board *(pensione completa)* or half board *(mezza pensione)* in peak season. Most hotel rates include breakfast, which in many establishments will consist of a large buffet, although smaller hotels and *pensioni* may offer a simple continental breakfast.

For a double room, state if you want twin beds *(letti singoli)* or a double bed *(matrimoniale)*. Bathrooms in most hotels will have showers rather than baths.

Most hotels offer Internet access, but it is not always free, and charges will vary. If a city center hotel does not have its own parking spaces, it may have an arrangement with a nearby garage. Check the availability and cost of parking with the hotel before making a reservation.

Children

Italians love children, and although most hotels may not offer special facilities for families, kids are always welcome.

Some of the cheaper hotels may not be able to provide cots. However, virtually all hotels will be happy to put a small bed into a double room for families traveling together. The price of this is usually an extra 30–40 percent of the double room rate per bed. Many large hotels also offer babysitting services.

Prices

As a rule hotels in Italy are not cheap, although prices vary considerably between regions. Hotels in major cities and resorts are likely to be more expensive. Booking online is one way to secure a better rate, as hotel websites may offer special deals. Or you can save money by booking your hotel and flight together on most travel websites.

Prices, which include tax and service and are quoted per room, start from around €60 for a double room without a bathroom, and can rise to at least €80 with a bath, even for a very basic hotel. A single room will cost about two thirds of a double. Outside the big cities, €100 should get you something comfortable and often picturesque, although not particularly luxurious. For €210 and upward you can expect a good range of facilities, a pleasant or central location, and often a hotel with local or historic charm. In Rome, all campsites, guest houses and hotels must add a city tax *(contributo di soggiorno)* to the bill. At present, these rates are fixed at €1 per day per person for campsites, €2 for establishments up to and including three-star hotels, and €3 for four- and five-star hotels.

In larger hotels there is often a considerable difference in quality and price between standard and more luxurious, deluxe rooms. If you would like a view or a terrace, this is also likely to be more expensive, though for those who prefer peaceful nights, it is generally best to avoid rooms facing the street in busy cities.

Also, beware of extra charges: the minibar can be very expensive as can the cost of parking, laundry, or making telephone calls directly from your hotel bedroom.

Reservations

Book as soon as possible, particularly if you have special requests such as a room with a view, off the street, or with a bath. August tends to be very busy at beach resorts, and February is peak season at mountain resorts. Peak times for cities and towns depend on their particular cultural calendars *(see pp70–73)*.

You will be asked for a deposit when you book; this can usually be paid for by credit card (even in hotels that do not accept credit cards for final payment); otherwise you can use PayPal for online transactions, or transfer the money via EFT from your bank account.

Under Italian law the hotel must issue you with a receipt *(ricevuta fiscale)* for final payment, which you must keep until you leave Italy.

The Italian State Tourist Office (**ENIT**) has accommodation lists for every region, although this might not be the most up-to-date resource. Rooms can also be booked via the **APT** (Azienda Provinciale per il Turismo).

A traditional Florentine hotel interior

The multilevel terrace of the Raphael in Rome *(see p573)*

Checking In and Out

Italian hotels are legally obliged to register you with the police, which is why you'll always be asked for your passport when checking in. This is a mere formality, and your passport should be returned to you within an hour or two.

Checking-out time is usually before noon, although some larger hotels may extend your checking-out time upon request, but only if your room is not already reserved for another guest. All rooms must be vacated on time, but most hotels will allow you to leave your luggage in a safe place to be collected later in the day.

Al Sole, Venice *(see p563)*

Self-Catering and Agriturismo

Across rural Italy, there are more than 2,000 farms, villas, and mountain chalets offering reasonably priced apartment- or hotel-style accommodations with cooking facilities as part of the **Agriturismo** scheme. Options range from beautifully kept villas or ancient castles with first-class facilities, to simple rooms in the family home on a working farm. Some places have excellent restaurants that serve farm and local produce, while others can arrange riding, fishing, or other sporting activities *(see p610)*. Note that there may be a minimum stay requirement at some of these establishments, especially during peak season. The annual *Agriturist* publication can be found in the central tourist office in Rome, in regional offices, and in bookstores. Other self-catering options can be arranged through specialized agencies such as **Villas4you** and **Simply Travel** before you leave for Italy, but again, make sure you do this well in advance, as accommodations can be booked up months ahead.

There are also so-called *residenze*, found in the ENIT accommodation lists. These are halfway between hotels and apartments and normally offer cooking facilities and some sort of restaurant service.

For stays of several months or more, accommodation agencies for apartments in the city center, as well as the nearby countryside, can be found under *Immobiliari* in the *Pagine Gialle* (Yellow Pages).

Budget Accommodations

As well as the International Youth Hostels Association (**AIG** in Italy), tourist offices in the major cities have lists of hostels. Prices start at around €12 per person per night (€15 during peak season), and are much lower than even the cheapest *pensione*. Accommodation may be in single- or mixed-sex dormitories, though many hostels also have small private rooms. A room in a private house is another cheap option, often offering small but clean rooms. Guest house accommodations are available but are of variable quality.

The **Centro Turistico Studentesco** can help students find rooms in university accommodations across Italy. This is not limited to students, however, particularly in the summer when resident students are on vacation.

A peaceful alternative is to stay in a convent or monastery with guest accommodations. The rooms are clean, if a little spartan, and they are usually in a secluded area. Note that strict rules may be the price for a cheap room: most have early curfews and many will not admit members of the opposite sex even when with their spouses. There is no central agency dealing with these, but they are included in the ENIT accommodation lists for each region.

Mountain Refuges and Campsites

Basic accommodation in huts and refuges is available in mountainous areas where there are hiking trails. Most of these huts are owned and run by the **Club Alpino Italiano**, whose headquarters are in Milan.

Campsites abound in the mountains and around the

A boat carrying visitors' luggage to a hotel in Venice

coastal regions. Many of them offer basic accommodations in family-sized cabins *(bungalow)* as well as spaces for tents, RVs, and trailers, along with facilities such as water, electricity, and laundry. There is usually a restaurant, and, especially in campsites by the sea, there may also be sports facilities such as swimming pools, boat and water sports equipment rental, and tennis courts. The **Touring Club Italiano** publishes a good list of campsites with details of facilities for each one, as does **Federcampeggio**.

A Park Spa Suite bedroom in the Park Hyatt Milano *(see p566)*

A high-altitude refuge in the Valsesia Alps

Disabled Travelers

In general, only newer hotels in Italy have special facilities for disabled travelers, although in many cases, older hotels will do all they can to accommodate people in wheelchairs by giving them downstairs rooms (when available) and help with elevators or stairs. It is best to contact the hotel of your choice directly before making a reservation, to check whether they are wheelchair accessible and what facilities they have *(for more information see pp616–17)*.

Recommended Hotels

The hotels listed in this guidebook have been chosen because they represent the best Italy has to offer in hospitality, service, value, or location. A huge variety of accommodation options are covered, from simple farmhouses and alpine chalets to family-run guest houses and luxury palaces.

Entries labeled DK Choice are outstanding in some way. They may be set in beautiful surroundings or in a historically important building, offer excellent service, have a romantic atmosphere, be particularly charming or environmentally friendly, or have a great spa. Whatever the reason it is a guarantee of a memorable stay.

DIRECTORY

Chain Hotels

Atahotels
Tel 066 964 69 64.
W atahotels.com

Best Western Hotels
Tel 800 820 080.
W bestwestern.it

Hyatt
Tel 02 88 21 12 34.
W hyatt.com

Marriott
Tel 800 22 89 29 00.
W marriott.com

NH Hoteles
Tel 848 390 227.
W nh-hotels.com

Relais & Châteaux
Tel 02 62 69 00 64.
W relaischateaux.com

Una Hotels and Resorts
Tel 800 60 61 62.
W unahotels.it

Reservations

ENIT
Via Marghera 2–6, 00185 Rome. **Tel** 06 497 11.
W enit.it

Italian State Tourist Board
1 Princes Street, London W1B 2AY. **Tel** 020 7408 1254. **W italiantourist board.co.uk**

Self-Catering and Agriturismo

Agriturismo
Corso Vittorio Emanuele II 101, 00186 Rome.
Tel 06 685 23 37.
W agriturist.it

Simply Travel
Tel 0871 231 40 50.
W simplytravel.co.uk

Villas4you
PO Box 1310, Maidstone ME14 9QH.
Tel 0800 096 3439.
W villas4you.co.uk

Budget Accommodations

AIG (Associazione Italiana Alberghi per la Gioventù)
Via Cavour 44, 00184 Rome. **Tel** 06 487 11 52.
W aighostels.com

Bed and Breakfast
W bed-and-breakfast.it

Centro Turistico Studentesco
Tel 06 462 04 31.
W cts.it

Italia Lodging
Tel 06 77 25 05 43.
W italialodging.com

Mountain Refuges and Campsites

Club Alpino Italiano
Via E. Petrella 19, Milan.
Tel 02 205 72 31. **W cai.it**

Federcampeggio
Via Vittorio Emanuele 11, 50041 Calenzano, Firenze.
Tel 055 88 23 91.
W federcampeggio.it

Touring Club Italiano
Corso Italia 10, 20122 Milano. **Tel** 02 852 61.
W touringclub.it

Where to Stay

Venice

CANNAREGIO: Al Saor €
B&B **Map** 3 A4
Calle Zotti 3904/A, 30121
Tel *041 296 06 54*
W alsaor.com
Simple and elegant, this guesthouse offers cozy rooms and a friendly atmosphere.

CANNAREGIO: Hotel Giorgione €€
Luxury **Map** 3 B5
Calle dei Proverbi 4587, 30121
Tel *041 522 58 10*
W hotelgiorgione.com
Lovely old building, completely and charmingly refurbished.

CANNAREGIO: Palazzo Abadessa €€
Historic **Map** 3 A4
Calle Priuli 4011, 30131
Tel *041 24 137 84*
W abadessa.com
Charming 16th-century palace furnished with antiques and rich colors. Spacious rooms.

CANNAREGIO: Ca' Sagredo €€€
Historic **Map** 3 A5
Campo Santa Sofia 4198, 30121
Tel *041 241 31 11*
W casagredohotel.com
Just across from Rialto market, this modernized 13th-century palazzo offers superb views.

CASTELLO: Locanda La Corte €€
Historic **Map** 3 C5
Calle Bressana 6317, 30122
Tel *041 241 13 00*
W locandalacorte.it
Inviting rooms in a converted 16th-century palace with a charming courtyard.

CASTELLO: Metropole €€
Luxury **Map** 8 D2
Riva degli Schiavoni 4149, 30122
Tel *041 520 50 44*
W hotelmetropole.com
The somewhat nondescript exterior belies the comforts within.

CASTELLO: Pensione Wildner €€
Pensione **Map** 8 D2
Riva degli Schiavoni 4161, 30122
Tel *041 522 74 63*
W hotelwildner.com
Family-run establishment with wonderful views from the terrace.

CASTELLO: Londra Palace €€€
Boutique **Map** 8 D2
Riva degli Schiavoni 4171, 30122
Tel *041 520 05 33*
W londrapalace.com
Excellent service and spacious, luxurious rooms. Splendid views of the lagoon and city.

DORSODURO: Locanda Ca' Zose €
B&B **Map** 6 F4
Calle del Bastion 193/B, 30123
Tel *041 522 66 35*
W hotelcazose.com
Charming guesthouse run by two sisters with an eye for quality.

DORSODURO: Agli Alboretti €€
Pensione **Map** 6 E4
Rio Terrà Foscarini 884, 30123
Tel *041 523 00 58*
W aglialboretti.com
Simple, comfortable rooms equipped with free minibar.

DORSODURO: Hotel Pausania €€
Historic **Map** 6 D3
Fondamenta Gerardini 2824, 30123
Tel *041 522 20 83*
W hotelpausania.it
Elegant light-filled rooms and a lovely veranda for breakfast.

DORSODURO: Instituto Artigianelli €€
Historic **Map** 6 E4
Rio Terrà Foscarini 909/A, 30123
Tel *041 522 40 77*
W donorione-venezia.it
Religious institution offering simple, modern rooms with en suite bathrooms. Nice, quiet courtyard.

DORSODURO: Locanda San Barnaba €€
Rooms with a view **Map** 6 D3
Calle del Traghetto 2785–2786, 30123
Tel *041 241 12 33*
W locanda-sanbarnaba.com
The perfect place to return to after a hard day's sightseeing. Spacious foyer and spotless rooms, most overlooking the canal.

Elegant interiors and great views at the Cipriani hotel, Giudecca

Price Guide
Prices are based on one night's stay in peak season for a standard double room, inclusive of service charges and taxes.

€	under €120
€€	€120 to 300
€€€	over €300

GIUDECCA: Cipriani €€€
Luxury **Map** 7 C5
Giudecca 10, 30133
Tel *041 520 77 44*
W hotelcipriani.com
Exquisite rooms in this Venice institution. There's a private launch to and from Piazza San Marco.

LIDO: Villa Mabapa €€
Rooms with a view
Riviera San Nicolò 16, 30126
Tel *041 526 05 90*
W villamabapa.com
Attractive period villas overlooking the Venice lagoon.

DK Choice

MAZZORBO: Venissa €€
Pensione **Map** 3 B4
Fondamenta Santa Caterina 3, 30170
Tel *041 527 22 81*
W venissa.it
A stylish option on a little known island for those who want a more exclusive Venetian experience. Rooms are modern and spacious. Delicious meals are served in the restaurant.

SAN MARCO: Saturnia and International €€
Luxury **Map** 7 A3
Via XXII Marzo 2398, 30124
Tel *041 520 83 77*
W hotelsaturnia.it
Opulence wrapped in a simple setting. Antique furnishings and a pretty courtyard.

SAN MARCO: Splendid Venice €€
Luxury **Map** 7 B7
Mercerie 760, 30124
Tel *041 520 07 55*
W splendidvenice.starhotels.com
This hotel is comfortable and quiet, with a well-stocked library and peaceful reading areas.

SAN MARCO: Bauer €€€
Luxury **Map** 7 A3
Campo San Moisè 1459, 30124
Tel *041 520 70 22*
W bauerhotels.com

Beautifully decorated rooms and stunning views of the Grand Canal.

SAN MARCO: Europa & Regina €€€
Luxury **Map** 7 A3
Calle Larga XXII Marzo 2159, 30124
Tel *041 240 00 01*
W westineuropareginavenice.com
Panoramic terraces with magnificent views. Impeccable service.

SAN MARCO: Gritti Palace €€€
Luxury **Map** 7 A3
Santa Maria del Giglio 2467, 30124
Tel *041 79 46 11*
W thegrittipalace.com
Iconic palazzo, dating back to 1475, with modern comforts.

SAN MARCO: Luna Hotel Baglioni €€€
Luxury **Map** 7 B3
Calle Large dell'Ascension 1243, 30124
Tel *041 528 98 40*
W baglionihotels.com
Spacious rooms in a historic palazzo. Arrive by water taxi at the private jetty.

SAN POLO: Al Campaniel €
B&B **Map** 6 E2
Calle del Campaniel 2889, 30125
Tel *041 275 07 49*
W alcampaniel.com
Clean and cozy guesthouse in a quiet street. The small apartment is great for families.

DK Choice

SANTA CROCE: Al Sole €€
Historic **Map** 5 C1
Fondamenta Minotto 136, 30135
Tel *041 244 03 28*
W alsolehotels.com
Housed in Palazzo Marcello, a 15th-century palace with a beautiful facade and marble-floored reception area, this hotel offers well-appointed rooms. Enjoy the rich breakfast spread served in a patio garden.

SANTA CROCE: Hotel Falier €€
Charming **Map** 5 C1
Salizzada San Pantalon 130, 30135
Tel *041 71 08 82*
W hotelfalier.com
This hotel is full of light, airy rooms and has a pretty wisteria-filled garden and helpful staff.

TORCELLO: Locanda Cipriani €€
Rooms with a view
Piazza Santa Fosca 29, 30012
Tel *041 73 01 50*
W locandacipriani.com
Comfortable old-world inn located far from the madding crowd. Famed for its discerning guests and quiet elegance.

Romantic natural setting of Hotel Cappella in Colfosco

The Veneto and Friuli

ASOLO: Albergo al Sole €€
Rooms with a view
Via Collegio 33, 31011
Tel *0423 95 13 32*
W albergoalsoleasolo.com
Pleasant, spacious rooms looking out over the town square.

ASOLO: Villa Cipriani €€
Historic
Via Canova 298, 31011
Tel *0423 52 34 11*
W villaciprianiasolo.com
Comfortable hotel in a 16th-century villa once home to poet Robert Browning.

CASTELROTTO: Cavallino d'Oro €
Spa hotel
Piazza Kraus 2, 39040
Tel *0471 70 63 37*
W cavallino.it
Charming hotel in a pretty setting with a cozy atmosphere.

CIVIDALE DEL FRIULI: La Cjase dai Toscans €
B&B
Corso Mazzini 15/1, 33043
Tel *349 076 52 88*
W lacjasedaitoscans.it
Friendly, well-positioned B&B with a terrace for summer breakfasts.

CIVIDALE DEL FRIULI: Locanda al Pomo d'Oro €
Historic
Piazzetta San Giovanni 20, 33043
Tel *0432 73 14 89*
W alpomodoro.it
Traditional family inn set in a quiet square in the historic center.

COLFOSCO: Hotel Cappella €€
Rooms with a view
Strada Pecei 17, 39033
Tel *0471 83 61 83*
W hotelcappella.com
A chalet in the Dolomites opened by the present owner's grandfather. Various styles of suite to choose from.

CONEGLIANO: Il Faè €
Rooms with a view
Via Faè 1, San Pietro di Feletto, 31020
Tel *0438 78 71 17*
W ilfae.com
Pleasant guesthouse surrounded by vineyards. Good views over the foothills of the Alps.

CORNO DI ROSAZZO: Villa Butussi €
Rooms with a view
Via San Martino 29, Visinale dello Judrio, 33040
Tel *0432 75 99 22*
W butussi.it
A 17th-century villa tastefully converted into a guesthouse that offers both rooms and apartments.

CORTINA D'AMPEZZO: Cristallo Hotel €€€
Luxury
Via R. Menardi 42, 32043
Tel *0436 88 11 11*
W cristallo.it
Beautifully presented rooms, some with balconies that have views of the Alps. Excellent facilities include a spa and a nine-hole golf course.

CORTINA D'AMPEZZO: Montana €€€
Pensione
Corso Italia 94, 32043
Tel *0436 86 21 26*
W cortina-hotel.com
Quiet hotel with simple, tasteful rooms and a hearty breakfast.

FOLLINA: Villa Abbazia €€
Historic
Piazza IV Novembre 3, 31051
Tel *0438 97 12 77*
W hotelabbazia.it
Delightful 17th-century villa with spacious rooms decorated in English country-house style.

For more information on types of hotels *see p561*

GARDA: Locanda San Vigilio €€
Rooms with a view
Località San Vigilio 17, 37016
Tel *045 725 66 88*
W locanda-sanvigilio.it
Exuding old-world charm, this is one of the loveliest, most exclusive hotels on Lake Garda.

MALCESINE: Sailing Center Hotel €€
Rooms with a view
Via Gardesana 187, 37018
Tel *045 740 00 55*
W hotelsailing.com
Located on the shores of Lake Garda, this hotel has comfortable rooms and its own private beach.

PADUA: Augustus Terme €€
Spa Hotel
Viale Stazione 150, 35036
Tel *049 79 32 00*
W hotelaugustus.com
Comfortable hotel with opulent rooms, thermal swimming pools, and a reputable restaurant.

PADUA: Belludi 37 €€
Boutique
Via L. Beato Belludi 37, 35124
Tel *049 66 56 33*
W belludi37.it
Steps from the Basilica del Santo, this hotel is decorated with a flair of contemporary design.

PESCHIERA DEL GARDA: Active Hotel Paradiso & Golf €
Boutique
Via Coppo 2/b, 37014
Tel *045 640 58 11*
W golfhotelparadiso.it
A stylish hotel with pleasant, airy rooms. Amenities include an 18-hole golf course.

POVOLETTO: La Faula €€
Agriturismo
Via Faula 5, 33040
Tel *334 399 67 34*
W faula.com
Lovingly restored farmhouse surrounded by vineyards and farmland. The rooms are spacious.

Comfortable furnishings at Hotel Laurin in Bolzano

Key to prices *see p562*

TORRI DEL BENACO: Hotel Gardesana €€
Historic
Piazza Calderini 5, 37010
Tel *045 722 54 11*
W gardesana.eu
A 15th-century former harbor-master's house converted into a friendly, comfortable hotel.

TREVISO: Locanda da Renzo B&B €
Via Terraglio 108, 31100
Tel *0422 40 20 68*
W locandadarenzo.it
A small family-run guesthouse with a home-cooked evening meal available on request.

TRIESTE: Le Corderie €€
Boutique
Via di Calvola 43, 34143
Tel *040 322 92 77*
W lecorderiehotel.it
You're assured of a warm welcome at this comfortable, modern hotel. Great breakfast spread.

UDINE: Hotel Clocchiatti & Next €€
Boutique
Via Cividale 29, 33100
Tel *0432 50 50 47*
W hotelclocchiatti.it
Choose between rooms with traditional period decor or modern fittings.

DK Choice

VALDOBBIADENE: Villa Barberina €€
Historic
Via Roma 2, 31049
Tel *0423 97 24 79*
W villabarberina.it
In past centuries, wealthy Venetians would live part of the year in their country estates. This hotel gives guests an idea of the opulence of such residences. This handsome 18th-century villa has elegantly decorated rooms, magnificent grounds, and a well-stocked library.

VERONA: Giulietta e Romeo €€
Charming
Vicolo Tre Marchetti 3, 37121
Tel *045 800 35 54*
W giuliettaeromeo.com
The rooms are comfortable and bright. The breakfast is hearty.

VERONA: Il Torcolo €€
Charming
Vicolo Listone 3, 37121
Tel *045 800 75 12*
W hoteltorcolo.it
Small, family-run hotel with simple rooms and a pleasant terrace where breakfast is served.

VICENZA: Glam Boutique Hotel €€
Boutique
Via A. Giuriolo 10, 36100
Tel *0444 32 64 58*
W gboutiquehotel.com
Stylish hotel with a perfect blend of traditional and modern decor.

Trentino–Alto Adige

BOLZANO: Hotel Laurin €€
Historic
Via Laurin 4, 39100
Tel *0471 31 10 00*
W laurin.it
Marvel at the original Art Nouveau features in this charming hotel.

BOLZANO: Luna-Mondschein €€
Spa hotel
Via Piave 15, 39100
Tel *0471 97 56 42*
W hotel-luna.it
This stylish hotel in the city center has fabulous grounds.

BRESSANONE: Hotel Dominik €
Rooms with a view
Via Terzo di Sotto 13, 39042
Tel *0472 83 01 44*
W hoteldominik.com
Furnished with antiques, most rooms boast views of the river.

FIE ALLO SCILIAR: Edelansitz Zimmerlehen €
Agriturismo
Via Kühbach 15, Obervöls, 39050
Tel *0471 72 50 53*
W zimmerlehen.it
A 13th-century manor farm with four towerlike buildings converted into simple apartments. Enjoy a breakfast of farm produce.

MERANO: Hotel Castel Fragsburg €€
Rooms with a view
Via Fragsburg 3, 39012
Tel *0473 24 40 71*
W fragsburg.com
This hotel boasts fine views of the mountains and the town below.

DK Choice

MERANO: Ottmanngut €€
Boutique
Via Verdi 18, 39012
Tel *0473 44 96 56*
W ottmanngut.it
Surrounded by lush greenery, this family-run guesthouse is within walking distance of the spa town. The suites are elegantly decorated with period furnishings and modern conveniences. There is also a lovely garden to relax in.

ORTISEI: Adler Dolomiti Spa & Sport Resort €€
Spa hotel
Via Rezia 7, 39046
Tel *0471 77 50 01*
W adler-dolomiti.com
A good choice for all seasons. Excellent service and facilities, including vast gardens.

REDAGNO: Berghotel Zirmerhof €€
Agriturismo
Oberradein 59, 39040
Tel *0471 88 72 15*
W zirmerhof.com
Simple accommodations in a beautiful mountain setting.

TRENTO: Accademia €€
Historic
Vicolo Colico 4-6, 38122
Tel *0461 23 36 00*
W accademiahotel.eu
Restored medieval building with a pleasant courtyard.

Lombardy

APRICA: Relais Volla Brioschi €€
Boutique
Via Valeriana 187, 25040
Tel *0342 74 56 81*
W relaisvillabrioschi.com
A luxury Art Nouveau–style country house with a garden, parking, and its own restaurant.

BELLAGIO: Hotel Florence €€
Spa hotel
Piazza Mazzini 46, 22021
Tel *031 95 03 42*
W hotelflorencebellagio.it
This lakeside hotel offers stylish decor, canopy beds, claw-foot tubs, and a gourmet restaurant.

BELLAGIO: Hotel Suisse €€
Historic
Piazza Mazzini 8/10, 22021
Tel *031 95 17 55*
W hotelsuissebellagio.com
This lakeside hotel has an excellent restaurant.

BELLAGIO: Grand Hotel Villa Serbelloni €€€
Luxury
Via Roma 1, 22021
Tel *031 95 02 16*
W villaserbelloni.com
The hotel boasts frescoed ceilings and views of Lake Como.

BERGAMO: Hotel Gombit €€€
Design
Via Mario Lupo 6, 24129
Tel *035 24 70 09*
W gombithotel.it
A concept hotel with distinctive architecture and interior design.

The stately Grand Hotel Villa Serbelloni in Bellagio

BORMIO: Hotel Cristallo €€
Spa hotel
Via Milano 44, 23032
Tel *0342 90 27 00*
W cristallohotelresidence.it
A short stroll from ski lifts and thermal baths, this hotel offers a large garden, a ski room, and a games room.

BRATTO: Hotel Milano €€
Spa hotel
Via Silvio Pellico 3, 24020
Tel *0346 31 211*
W hotelmilano.com
Large Alpine resort hotel and spa. Plenty of comfort and style.

BRESCIA: Park Hotel Cà Noa €
Rooms with a view
Via Triumplina 66, 25123
Tel *030 39 87 62*
W hotelcanoa.it
Situated in a quiet park, this hotel has an outdoor pool.

BRESCIA: AC Hotel Brescia €€
Design
Via Giulio Quinto Stefana 3, 25126
Tel *030 24 05 511*
W hotelacbrescia.com
This minimalist design hotel with modern facilities has a fitness center and a gourmet restaurant.

CERNOBBIO: Villa d'Este €€€
Luxury
Via Regina 40, 22012
Tel *031 34 81*
W villadeste.it
An elegant and sumptuous hotel set in 25 acres (10 ha) of lush parkland.

CERVESINA: Hotel Castello di San Gaudenzio €€
Historic
Via Mulino 1, 27050
Tel *0383 33 31*
W castellosangaudenzio.com
A 15th-century castle boasting romantic rooms, a gym, and a pool, plus a top-class restaurant.

COLOGNE: Cappuccini €€
Historic
Via Cappuccini 54, 25033
Tel *030 715 72 54*
W cappuccini.it
This former monastery has a wellness center, an outdoor pool, and a restaurant.

COMO: Hotel Firenze €
Rooms with a view
Piazza Volta 16, 22100
Tel *031 30 03 33*
W albergofirenze.it
A renovated Neo-Classical hotel situated in a pedestrianized square in the town center.

COMO: In Riva al Lago €
B&B
Via Crespi 4, 22100
Tel *031 30 23 33*
W inrivaallago.com
Basic, spotless hotel that also offers self-contained apartments.

CREMONA: Dellearti Design Hotel €€
Boutique
Via Bonomelli 8, 26100
Tel *0372 231 31*
W dellearti.com
Accommodations with artsy touches. Close to the cathedral and the medieval bell tower.

DESENZANO DEL GARDA: Park Hotel €€
Luxury
Lungolago Cesare Battisti 17, 25015
Tel *030 914 34 95*
W parkhotelonline.it
Elegant hotel with well-furnished rooms, some with lake views.

GARDONE RIVIERA: Villa del Sogno €€€
Historic
Via Zanardelli 107, 25083
Tel *0365 29 01 81*
W villadelsogno.it
A Neo-Classical villa with tennis courts and an outdoor pool.

For more information on types of hotels *see p561*

Stylish minimalist decor at Nhow Milano in Milan

GARDONE RIVIERA: Villa Fiordaliso €€€
Luxury
Corso Zanardelli 132, 25083
Tel *0365 201 58*
W villafiordaliso.it
Beautiful three-story villa overlooking Lake Garda. Furnished with eclectic decor with a floral theme.

GARGNANO: Villa Sostaga €€€
Boutique
Via Sostaga 19, 25084
Tel *0365 79 12 18*
W villasostaga.it
This family-run hotel offers large rooms with modern facilities and an Art Nouveau dining room.

ISEO: Iseolago €€
Spa hotel
Via Colombera 2, 25049
Tel *030 98 891*
W iseolagohotel.it
Extensive gardens with swimming pools, a tennis court, and a children's playground.

DK Choice

LIMONE SUL GARDA: Hotel Capo Reamol €
Budget
Via IV Novembre 92, 25010
Tel *0365 95 40 40*
W hotelcaporeamol.it
This hotel's idyllic location offers breathtaking views of Lake Garda. Rooms are compact but clean and the staff are friendly. A fitness room and spa services are available to guests, along with a private beach and a swimming pool. Excellent value for money.

LIVIGNO: Hotel Capriolo €
Pensione
Via Borch 96, 23030
Tel *0342 99 67 23*
W capriololivigno.com
Family-run hotel located close to ski lifts and hiking paths. Offers traditional *Valtellina* cuisine.

MANTUA: Casa Poli €€
Boutique
Corso Giuseppe Garibaldi 32, 46100
Tel *0376 28 81 70*
W hotelcasapoli.it
Near the harbor, this hotel has cozy rooms and minimalist decor.

MANTUA: Hotel La Favorita €€
Business
Via S. Cognetti De Martiis 1, 46100
Tel *0376 25 47 11*
W hotellafavorita.it
A modern and elegant hotel with an excellent restaurant.

DK Choice

MILAN: Antica Locanda Leonardo €€
Boutique
Corso Magenta 78, 20123
Tel *02 48 01 41 97*
W anticalocandaleonardo.com
Peacefully located in an elegant 19th-century palazzo, this family-run hotel has well-decorated rooms overlooking a charming and picturesque inner garden. The staff are helpful and friendly.

MILAN: Antica Locanda Solferino €€
Boutique
Via Castelfidardo 2, 20121
Tel *02 65 70 12 9*
W anticalocandasolferino.it
A welcoming guesthouse with eclectic old-world charm.

MILAN: Ata Hotel Executive €€
Business
Viale Sturzo 45, 20154
Tel *02 62 941*
W atahotels.it/executive
Rooms are spacious, and facilities include a gym and sun terrace.

MILAN: Nhow Milano €€
Design
Via Tortona 35, 20144
Tel *02 48 98 861*
W nh-hotels.it
This hotel boasts an interesting collection of contemporary art.

MILAN: Una Hotel Century €€
Business
Via Fabio Filzi 25/B, 20124
Tel *02 67 50 41*
W unahotels.it
Modern facilities are available in this contemporary hotel.

MILAN: Hotel Manzoni €€€
Luxury
Via Santo Spirito 20, 20121
Tel *02 76 00 57 00*
W hotelmanzoni.com
Beautiful hotel set in a quiet, yet central location.

MILAN: Park Hyatt Milano €€€
Luxury
Via Tommaso Grossi 1, 20121
Tel *02 88 21 12 34*
W milan.park.hyatt.com
Housed in a former bank, this elegant hotel has a spa and gym.

PAVIA: Hotel Italia €
Pensione
Corso Partigiani 48, 27012
Tel *0382 92 56 56*
W italiacertosa.pavia.it
Family-run hotel in an 18th-century farmhouse. Rooms are simply but tastefully decorated with antique pieces.

RANCO: Il Sole di Ranco €€
Rooms with a view
Piazza Venezia 5, 21020
Tel *0331 97 65 07*
W ilsolediranco.it
Overlooking Lake Maggiore, this hotel boasts a private garden and an infinity pool.

RIVA DI SOLTO: Albergo Ristorante Miranda €
Pensione
Via Cornello 8, 24060
Tel *035 98 60 21*
W albergomiranda.it
This family-run guesthouse has views over Lake Iseo and comfortable rooms with balconies.

RODIGO: Hotel Villa dei Tigli €€
Historic
Via Cantarana 20/I, 46040
Tel *0376 65 06 91*
W hotelvilladeitigli.it
A 20th-century former aristocratic villa with an outdoor pool and a high-class terrace restaurant.

SALÒ: Hotel Laurin €€
Boutique
Viale Landi 9, 25087
Tel *0365 22 022*
W laurinhotelsalo.com
A romantic lakeside villa with a restaurant and an outdoor pool.

Key to prices *see p562*

SIRMIONE: Hotel Catullo €€
Historic
Piazza Flaminia 7, 25019
Tel *030 990 58 11*
W hotelcatullo.it
This hotel offers rooms with balconies and a rooftop terrace.

TREMEZZO: Hotel la Darsena €€
Rooms with a view
Via Regina 3, 22019
Tel *0344 431 66*
W hotelladarsena.it
A lakeside hotel-cum-restaurant in a great location for visiting nearby villas and other sights.

TREMEZZO: Grand Hotel Tremezzo €€€
Historic
Via Regina 8, 22019
Tel *0344 424 91*
W grandhoteltremezzo.com
A prestigious lakeside hotel, in Art Nouveau style; great facilities.

VARENNA: Hotel Du Lac €€
Rooms with a view
Via del Prestino 11, 23829
Tel *0341 83 02 38*
W albergodulac.com
A peaceful hotel at the water's edge with enchanting views.

Valle d'Aosta and Piedmont

ACQUI TERME: Hotel Rondò €
Spa hotel
Viale Acquedotto Romano 44, 15011
Tel *0144 32 28 89*
W albergorondo.it
Rooms are bright and basic, and the staff friendly and helpful.

ACQUI TERME: Hotel Talice Radicati €€
Historic
Piazza Conciliazione 12, 15011
Tel *0144 32 86 11*
W taliceradicati.com
The rooms in this 15th-century palazzo are elegant and refined.

DK Choice

ALBA: Villa La Meridiana Cascina Reinè €
Agriturismo
Località Altavilla 9, 12051
Tel *0173 44 01 12*
W villalameridianaalba.it
This 18th-century villa benefits from enchanting views over the surrounding vineyards. Rooms are comfortable and furnished with the family's antique collection, and there are three cozy apartments with small kitchens. Guests can participate in harvesting the crop from the estate's vineyards and hunt for truffles in the woods.

ALESSANDRIA: Hotel Alli Due Buoi Rossi €€
Historic
Via Cavour 32, 15121
Tel *0131 51 71 71*
W hotelalliduebuoirossi.com
A welcoming and friendly hotel with a renowned *trattoria*.

AOSTA: Hotel Village Aosta €€
Resort
Località Torrent de Maillod 1, 11020
Tel *0165 77 49 11*
W hotelvillageaosta.it
This small but charming hotel offers both rooms and chalets.

ARONA: Hotel Giardino €
Pensione
Corso Repubblica 1, 28041
Tel *0322 459 94*
W giardinoarona.com
A comfortable hotel with splendid views across Lake Maggiore from the large terrace and grounds.

BARDONECCHIA: Hotel Jafferau €€
Resort
Località Fregiusia, 10052
Tel *0122 998 99*
W hoteljafferau.it
High-altitude hotel with a pool, a sauna, and hydromassage.

DK Choice

BAVENO: Hotel Splendid €€
Resort
Via Sempione 12, 28831
Tel *0323 92 45 83*
W zaccherahotels.com
This elegant hotel has its own private beach (which has sun beds and a private jetty), and an outdoor pool. The rooms are comfortable and well appointed – most have balconies with lakeside views. Helpful and attentive staff provide excellent service.

Stone steps leading to the charming Villa La Meridiana Cascina Reinè in Alba

CANNOBIO: Residenza Patrizia €
Pensione
Viale Vittorio Veneto 9, 28822
Tel *0323 73 97 13*
W residenzapatrizia.com
Inviting rooms and self-contained apartments as well, plus amenities such as a sauna and a pool.

ORTO SAN GIULIO: Hotel San Rocco €€
Historic
Via Gippini 11, 28016
Tel *0322 91 19 77*
W hotelsanrocco.it
Unwind at the lakeside pool or enjoy the excellent restaurant, and views of San Giulio Island.

STRESA: Hotel La Palma €€
Resort
Lungolago Umberto I 33, 28838
Tel *0323 324 01*
W hlapalma.it
This hotel offers a private beach, an outdoor pool, spa facilities, and a terrace bar. There is also a well-regarded restaurant.

TORTONA: Villa Giulia €
Boutique
Corso Alessandria 7/A, 15057
Tel *0131 86 23 96*
W villagiulia-hotel.com
Former private villa, with elegant decor. Homey atmosphere and an ample breakfast.

TURIN: Albergo Serenella €
Pensione
Via Tarino 4, 10124
Tel *011 83 70 31*
W albergoserenella.com
This family-run establishment has clean and basic rooms at unbeatable prices for the city center.

TURIN: Hotel Conte Biancamano €
Pensione
Corso Vittorio Emanuele 73, 10128
Tel *011 562 32 81*
W hotelcontebiancamano.it
An intimate hotel with elegant decor located on the third floor of a 19th century palazzo.

TURIN: Grand Hotel Sitea €€
Luxury
Via Carlo Alberto 35, 10123
Tel *011 517 01 71*
W grandhotelsitea.it
Set in a Neo-Classical palazzo, this place offers elegant suites and a top-class restaurant.

For more information on types of hotels *see p561*

TURIN: NH Lingotto Tech €€
Design
Via Nizza 230, 10126
Tel *011 664 20 00*
W **nh-hotels.com**
A contemporary hotel located in the Lingotto Building, once a huge Fiat factory.

TURIN: Turin Golden Palace €€€
Luxury
Via dell'Arcivescovado 18, 10121
Tel *011 551 21 11*
W **goldenpalace.it**
This hotel, set in a 19th-century palazzo, offers a spa with a pool, sauna, and fitness center.

VARALLO SESIA: Vecchio Albergo Sacro Monte €
Pensione
Località Sacro Monte 14, 13019
Tel *0163 542 54*
W **sacromontealbergo.it**
A comfortable hotel with simple rooms and a small private garden.

Liguria

DK Choice

CAMOGLI: Locanda I Tre Merli €€
Rooms with a view
Via Scalo 5, 6032
Tel *0185 77 67 52*
W **locandaitremerli.com**
Located right on the enchanting fishing port of Camogli, this cozy hotel offers wonderful views and personalized service. Room amenities include basic cooking facilities. A small spa area offers a Jacuzzi and a steam bath. Ferries to Portofino and the Cinque Terre are nearby. Parking is available upon request.

CAMOGLI: Villa Rosmarino €€
Rooms with a view
Via Figari 38, 16032
Tel *0185 77 15 80*
W **villarosmarino.com**
At the foot of Monte di Portofino, this villa has an outdoor pool.

CAMOGLI: Cenobio dei Dogi €€€
Luxury
Via Nicolò Cuneo 34, 16032
Tel *0185 72 41*
W **cenobio.it**
Built for the Doges of Genoa, this 17th-century villa houses a vast hotel with a private beach.

FINALE LIGURE: Punta Est €€€
Luxury
Via Aurelia 1, 17024
Tel *019 60 06 11*
W **puntaest.com**
An 18th-century villa with superb views over the Ligurian bay.

GARLENDA: La Meridiana Resort €€
Via ai Castelli, 17033
Tel *0182 58 02 71*
W **lameridianaresort.com**
This relaxing country house–style hotel is perfect for walking vacations and outdoor activities.

GENOA: Hotel Villa Pagoda €€
Rooms with a view
Via Capolungo 15, 16167
Tel *010 372 61 61*
W **villapagoda.it**
This luxurious 19th-century villa is only steps from the coast.

GENOA: NH Marina €€
Rooms with a view
Molo Ponte Calvi 5, 16124
Tel *0848 39 02 27*
W **nh-hotels.com**
An international hotel overlooking the harbor and close to the Aquarium, old town, and markets.

ISOLA PALMARIA: Locanda Lorena €€
Rooms with a view
Via Cavour 4, 19025
Tel *0187 79 23 70*
W **locandalorena.com**
A small beach hotel accessible by stylish Venetian motorboats.

LEVANTO: Hotel Stella Maris €€
Boutique
Via Marconi 4, 19015
Tel *0187 80 82 58*
W **hotelstellamaris.it**
Close to the beach, this place is exquisitely decorated.

MANAROLA: Ca' d'Andrean €
Pensione
Via Discovolo 101, 19017
Tel *0187 92 00 40*
W **cadandrean.it**
This family-run guesthouse serves breakfast alfresco in summer.

Charming views from the vibrant Locanda I Tre Merli, Camogli

MONTEROSSO: Hotel Marina €
Pensione
Via Buranco 40, 19016
Tel *0187 81 76 13*
W **hotelmarina5terre.com**
Cooking lessons are available on request from this quiet hotel.

OSPEDALETTI: Hotel Firenze €
Rooms with a view
Corso Regina Margherita 97, 18014
Tel *0184 68 92 21*
W **firenze.azurline.com**
A small hillside hotel with basic but cheerful rooms, most of which have balconies.

PORTO VENERE: Hotel della Baia €
Rooms with a view
Via Lungomare 111, 19025
Tel *0187 79 07 97*
W **baiahotel.com**
All rooms have balconies and views over the bay. There's an outdoor pool and a restaurant.

PORTOFINO: Splendido €€€
Luxury
Salita Baratta 16, 16034
Tel *0185 26 78 01*
W **hotelsplendido.com**
Housed in a former monastery, this hotel has elegantly furnished rooms, many with private terraces.

RAPALLO: Hotel Stella €
Rooms with a view
Via Aurelia Ponente 6, 16035
Tel *0185 503 67*
W **hotelstella-riviera.com**
This small hotel lies in the center of Rapallo, close to the beach and seafront promenade.

RAPALLO: Hotel Italia e Lido €€
Rooms with a view
Lungomare Castello 1, 16035
Tel *0185 504 94*
W **italiaelido.com**
Overlooking the Gulf of Tigullio, this hotel has bright, airy rooms.

SANREMO: Hotel Nazionale €€
Rooms with a view
Corso Matteotti 3, 18038
Tel *0184 57 75 77*
W **hotelnazionalesanremo.com**
A high level of service and classically furnished rooms.

SANREMO: Royal Hotel €€€
Luxury
Corso Imperatrice 80, 18038
Tel *0184 53 91*
W **royalhotelsanremo.com**
Located on the seafront, this place is renowned for its restaurants.

Key to prices *see p562*

SESTRI LEVANTE: Hotel Helvetia €€
Boutique
Via Cappuccini 43, 16039
Tel *0185 411 75*
W hotelhelvetia.it/
This hotel boasts its own private beach, garden, and solarium.

VENTIMIGLIA: La Riserva di Castel d'Appio €€
Rooms with a view
Via Peidaigo 71, 18039
Tel *0184 22 95 33*
W lariserva.it
Enjoy panoramic views over the Italian Riviera and the Côte d'Azur at this hotel. Excellent service.

Outdoor swimming pool at La Riserva di Castel d'Appio in Ventimiglia

Emilia-Romagna

BOLOGNA: Delle Drapperie €
Pensione
Via Drapperie 5, 40124
Tel *051 223 955*
W albergodrapperie.com
Decoratively painted ceilings and luxurious bathrooms characterize this well-priced option.

BOLOGNA: Il Guercino €
Boutique
Via Luigi Serra 7, 40129
Tel *051 369 893*
W guercino.it
An Indian flavor prevails at this charming hotel, which has two solariums and a relaxation area.

BOLOGNA: Indipendenza Suite €
Pensione
Via dell'Indipendenza 30, 40121
Tel *331 4575 920*
Four independent apartments decorated in simple, classic style.

BOLOGNA: Panorama Hotel €
Budget
Via Giovanni Livraghi 1, 40121
Tel *051 221 802*
W hotelpanoramabologna.it
A clean and central option; some rooms have a private bath.

BOLOGNA: Commercianti €€
Historic
Via De' Pignattari 11, 40124
Tel *051 745 75 11*
W commercianti.hotelsbologna.it
Located next to the Bologna Cathedral, this 13th-century building is bursting with romantic details.

BOLOGNA: Corona d'Oro €€
Romantic
Via Guglielmo Oberdan 12, 40126
Tel *051 7457 611*
W hco.it
Historic hotel with an eclectic style: from medieval to Art Deco.

BOLOGNA: Il Convento dei Fiori di Seta €€
Historic
Via Orfeo 34, 40124
Tel *051 272 039*
W silkflowersnunnery.com
Ten well-appointed rooms in this converted medieval convent.

BOLOGNA: Roma €€
Pensione
Via Massimo D'Azeglio 9, 40123
Tel *051 226 322*
W hotelroma.biz
Quaint rooms, ask for one of the few with balconies.

DK Choice

BOLOGNA: Grand Hotel Majestic €€€
Luxury
Via Indipendenza 8, 40121
Tel *051 225 445*
W grandhotelmajestic.hotelsbologna.com
This legendary hotel expertly combines opulent old-world elegance with modern comfort and hospitality. Each room is individually decorated with lush fabrics and antique furniture. Breakfast is served on the romantic rooftop terrace with sweeping views of the city. The dining room boasts beautiful frescoes.

BOLOGNA: Royal Hotel Carlton €€€
Luxury
Via Montebello 8, 40121
Tel *051 249 361*
W monrifhotels.it/RoyalCarltonHotel
Elegant, grand hotel with a fully-equipped wellness center.

FERRARA: Principessa Leonora €€
Boutique
Via Mascheraio 39, 44121
Tel *0532 20 60 20*
W principessaleonora.it
A 16th-century residence exquisitely decorated with antique French tapestries and traditional furniture.

FERRARA: Duchessa Isabella €€€
Historic
Via Palestro 70, 44121
Tel *0532 20 21 21*
W duchessaisabella.it
Minute attention to detail in both decor and service. Rooms are sumptuously furnished.

MODENA: Daunia €
Pensione
Via del Pozzo 158, 41125
Tel *059 37 11 82*
W hoteldaunia.it
A simple, modern building with restaurant. Breakfast is served in the garden, weather permitting.

MODENA: Canalgrande €€€
Historic
Corso Canal Grande 6, 41100
Tel *059 21 71 60*
W canalgrandehotel.it
Housed in a former convent and with fresh, Neo-Classical decor.

PARMA: Button €
Budget
Borgo della Salina 7, 43121
Tel *0521 20 80 39*
W hotelbutton.it
Courteous service makes up for the basic accommodations.

PARMA: Stendhal €€
Romantic
Via Giambattista Bodoni 3, 43121
Tel *0521 20 80 57*
W hotelstendhal.it
Eclectically decorated rooms in a centrally located old palazzo.

PIACENZA: San Francesco €
Pensione
Galleria San Francesco 2, 29121
Tel *0523 32 66 88*
Excellent location and prices for spotlessly clean accommodations.

For more information on types of hotels *see p561*

PIACENZA GENEPRETO: La Pobiella €€
Agriturismo
Località Pobiella 16, 29010
Tel *0523 99 75 14*
This rustic stone villa is ideal for a relaxed hillside vacation.

RAVENNA: Sant'Andrea €
Boutique
Via Carlo Cattaneo 33, 48121
Tel *0544 21 55 64*
W santandreahotel.com
A converted convent with a tranquil cloister-garden.

RAVENNA: Cappello €€
Romantic
Via IV Novembre 41, 48121
Tel *0544 21 98 13*
W albergocappello.it
The rooms in this exquisite hotel have coffered ceilings.

RIMINI: Acasamia €
Budget
Viale Renato Parisano 34, 47921
Tel *0541 39 13 70*
W hotelacasamia.com
Colorful rooms, and located a short stroll from the beach.

RIMINI: Grand Hotel Rimini €€€
Luxury
Parco Federico Fellini 1, 47900
Tel *0541 560 00*
W grandhotelrimini.com
Deluxe seaside establishment made famous by Federico Fellini.

Florence

Antica Dimora Firenze €
B&B **Map** 2 D3/4
Via San Gallo 72/r, 50129
Tel *055 462 72 96*
W johanna.it
Canopy beds and antique furniture set this B&B apart.

Pleasantly bright, large rooms at the Relais Uffizi in Florence

Palazzo Guadagni €
Historic **Map** 5 B5
Piazza di Santo Spirito 9, 50125
Tel *055 265 83 76*
W palazzoguadagni.com
Fantastic service, a great location, and reasonable prices.

Relais Il Campanile €
B&B **Map** 6 E1
Via Ricasoli 10, 50125
Tel *055 21 16 88*
W relaiscampanile.it
Quaint rooms with wrought iron accents in a 17th-century palazzo.

Residenza Johanna €
Pensione **Map** 2 D3
Via Bonifacio Lupo 14, 50129
Tel *055 48 18 96*
W johanna.it
This tiny and charming hotel is fantastic value. Free parking.

Brunelleschi €€
Historic **Map** 6 D2
Piazza Sant'Elisabetta 3, 50122
Tel *055 273 70*
W hotelbrunelleschi.it
Located in a Byzantine tower, this place offers classy, opulent rooms.

David €€
Pensione **Map** 4 E3
Viale Michelangiolo 1, 50125
Tel *055 681 16 95*
W davidhotel.com
Some rooms have balconies that look out over leafy Oltrarno in this family-owned guesthouse.

Grifone €€
Business
Via Gaetano Pilati 20, 50136
Tel *055 62 33 00*
W hotelgrifonefirenze.com
Comfortable and spacious rooms, some with a kitchenette.

Hotel Home €€
Boutique **Map** 4 F2
Piazza Piave 3, 50122
Tel *055 24 36 68*
W hhflorence.it
All white and extremely elegant decor in this stylish hotel.

DK Choice

Relais Uffizi €€
Romantic **Map** 6 D4
Chiasso del Buco 16, 50122
Tel *055 267 62 39*
W relaisuffizi.it
Located behind the Piazza della Sugnoria, this hotel is a fantastic buy. All rooms are charmingly decorated, and the breakfast room looks out onto the Piazza.

Four Seasons Hotel Firenze €€€
Luxury **Map** 2 E4
Borgo Pinti 99, 50121
Tel *055 262 61*
W fourseasons.com/florence
The epitome of elegance, with silk wall hangings, frescoes, and bas-reliefs. Service is impeccable, and the restaurant is worth visiting even if you are not staying here. The hotel runs a frequent shuttle bus into the center of Florence.

Grand Hotel Minerva €€€
Historic **Map** 5 B2
Piazza di Santa Maria Novella 16, 50123
Tel *055 272 30*
W grandhotelminerva.com
A panoramic terrace with a pool gives a modern touch to one of the city's oldest hotels. Its convenient location near the train station means many sights are in walking distance.

The Westin Excelsior €€€
Luxury **Map** 5 A2
Piazza d'Ognissanti 3, 50123
Tel *055 271 51*
W westinflorence.com
Opulent rooms, some with balconies that have views of the Arno. The roof terrace is exquisitely presented.

Tuscany

DK Choice

AREZZO: Badia di Pomaio €€
Boutique
Loc. Pomaio 4, 52100
Tel *0575 37 14 07*
W badiadipomaio.it
This superbly converted 17th-century abbey is situated in a picturesque spot amidst lush gardens with a swimming pool and panoramic views of the medieval town below. Comfortable and quiet rooms with elegant furnishings. The staff are warm and hospitable.

AREZZO: Graziella Patio Hotel €€
Boutique
Via Cavour 23, 52100
Tel *0575 40 19 62*
W hotelpatio.it
Charming hotel with rooms in African and Far Eastern styles.

CORTONA: Italia €
Budget
Via Ghibellina 5/7, 52044
Tel *0575 63 02 54*
W hotelitaliacortona.com
Excellent value at this lovely central spot full of character.

CORTONA: San Michele €€
Historic
Via Guelfa 15, 52044
Tel *0575 60 43 48*
hotelsanmichele.net
Modern comfort in Renaissance setting. Very classy decor.

DK Choice

ELBA MARCIANA: Cernia Isola Botanica €€
Rooms with a view
Via San Gaetano 23, 57030
Tel *0565 90 82 10*
hotelcernia.it
A lush, flower-filled park and botanical garden surround this charming hotel. Rooms are spacious and minimalist, with interesting design elements. There is a freshwater swimming pool and wellness center. Situated a short walk from Capo Sant'Andra, the location is hard to beat.

ELBA SPARTAIA: Desiree €€
Rooms with a view
Spartaia, Procchio, 57030
Tel *0565 90 73 11*
htdesiree.it
Clean rooms and private beach access at this comfortable hotel.

LUCCA: Piccolo Hotel Puccini €
Pensione
Via di Poggio 9, 55100
Tel *0583 554 21*
hotelpuccini.com
The prices may be low but you get warm service and charming rooms.

LUCCA: Alla Corte degli Angeli €€
Boutique
Via degli Angeli 23, 55100
Tel *0583 46 92 04*
allacortedegliangeli.it
A jewel of a hotel with distinctively personalized rooms.

MONTEPULCIANO: San Biagio €
Budget
Via San Bartolomeo 2, 53045
Tel *0578 71 72 33*
albergosanbiagio.it
Located just outside of the town with glorious views, this hotel has comfortable and clean rooms, and a heated swimming pool.

MONTERIGGIONI: Borgo Gallinaio €€
Agriturismo
Strada del Gallinaio 5, 53035
Tel *0577 30 47 51*
gallinaio.it
This converted 15th-century stone-built farmhouse is surrounded by cypress and olive trees. There is an outdoor pool.

Dining area with medieval details in the Antica Residenza Cicogna, Siena

PISA: Guerrazzi €
B&B
Via Francesco da Buti 4, 56125
Tel *3389 32 81 69*
bbguerrazzi.hostel.com
Simple but quaint, with comfortable and clean rooms.

PISA: Royal Victoria Hotel €€
Historic
Lungarno Antonio Pacinotti 12, 56126
Tel *050 94 01 11*
royalvictoria.it
Housed in a 10th-century tower, Pisa's very first hotel has stately decor and spacious rooms.

PISA: Relais dell'Orologio €€€
Historic
Via della Faggiola 12, 56126
Tel *050 83 03 61*
hotelrelaisorologio.com
Built into a 14th-century tower, this hotel has elegant rooms and a delightful reading room. Enjoy breakfast on the veranda.

SAN GIMIGNANO: Bel Soggiorno €
Budget
Via San Giovanni 91, 53037
Tel *0577 94 03 75*
hotelbelsoggiorno.it
Comfortable and well-priced hotel run by the same family since 1886. Excellent restaurant.

SAN GIMIGNANO: Leon Bianco €€
Rooms with a view
Piazza Cisterna 13, 53037
Tel *0577 94 12 94*
leonbianco.com
Elegant rooms with spectacular views of the hillside piazza.

SIENA: Antica Residenza Cicogna €
Pensione
Via Termini 67, 53100
Tel *0577 28 56 13*
anticaresidenzacicogna.it
Romantic location set in a medieval building full of charming details.

SIENA: Palazzo Ravizza €€
Romantic
Piano dei Mantellini 34, 53100
Tel *0577 28 04 62*
palazzoravizza.it
Lovely rooms with original period furniture. Some rooms overlook a picturesque garden.

SIENA: Grand Hotel Continental €€€
Luxury
Via Banchi di Sopra 85, 53100
Tel *0577 560 11*
grandhotelcontinentalsiena.com
The most prestigious address in Siena. This 17th-century building has impressive frescoes and luxurious rooms.

VIAREGGIO: London €€
Rooms with a view
Viale Daniele Manin 16, 55049
Tel *0584 498 41*
hotellondon.it
Simple, comfortable rooms and an elegant lobby. Located a short walk from the sea.

VOLTERRA: Villa Rioddi €
Historic
Strada Provinciale del Monte Volterrano 71, 56048
Tel *0588 880 53*
hotelvillarioddi.it
Experience ultimate relaxation in this medieval 15th-century villa.

VOLTERRA: Marcampo €€
Agriturismo
Località San Cipriano, Podere Marcampo 30, 56048
Tel *0588 853 93*
agriturismo-marcampo.com
There are just six rooms in this tranquil slice of Tuscan paradise. Enjoy the pool with views of the surrounding vineyards.

Umbria

ASSISI: Sole €
Budget
Corso Giuseppe Mazzini 35, 06081
Tel *075 81 23 73*
assisihotelsole.com
Basic but spacious rooms in a 15th-century medieval building.

ASSISI: Subasio €€
Romantic
Via Elia Frate 2c, 06081
Tel *075 81 22 06*
hotelsubasio.com
Located beside the famous basilica: atmospheric and spacious rooms, some with a terrace.

For more information on types of hotels *see p561*

GUBBIO: Le Cinciallegre €
Agriturismo
Fraz. Pisciano, 06024
Tel *075 925 59 57*
W lecinciallegre.it
This is a jewel hidden in the countryside. Small but cozy rooms.

GUBBIO: Relais Ducale €€
Romantic
Via Galeotti 19, 06024
Tel *075 922 01 57*
W mencarelligroup.com
Beautiful rooms in a converted manor house. Panoramic views.

NORCIA: Casale nel Parco dei Monti Sibillini €
Agriturismo
Vocabolo Fontevena 8, 06046
Tel *0743 81 64 81*
W casalenelparco.com
Canopy beds and wood-beamed ceilings; some rooms also have kitchenettes. Great service.

ORVIETO: Filippeschi €
Budget
Via Filippeschi 19, 05018
Tel *0763 34 32 75*
W albergofilippeschi.it
Basic but comfortable rooms in the historic center. Spacious lobby.

ORVIETO: La Badia €€
Historic
Località la Badia 8, 05018
Tel *0763 30 19 59*
W labadiahotel.it
Breathtaking hotel built into the ruins of an 8th-century monastery.

ORVIETO: Locanda Pallazone €€
Agriturismo
Località Rocca Ripesena 66, 05018
Tel *0763 39 36 14*
W locandapalazzone.it
Elegant accommodations in a former cardinal's residence; surrounded by vineyards.

PERUGIA: Fortuna €
Historic
Via Luigi Bonazzi 19, 06121
Tel *075 572 28 45*
W hotelfortunaperugia.com
Restoration work revealed over-300-year-old frescoes at this hotel.

PERUGIA: Castello di Monterone €€
Historic
Strada Montevile 3, 06126
Tel *075 572 42 14*
W castellomonterone.com
Luxurious rooms and two stellar restaurants are available here.

PERUGIA: La Rosetta €€
Boutique
Piazza Italia 19, 06121
Tel *075 572 08 41*
W larosetta.eu
Fantastic rooms, decorated either in 1920s or Baroque style.

PERUGIA: Brufani Palace €€€
Luxury
Piazza Italia 12, 06121
Tel *075 573 25 41*
W brufanipalace.com
Sumptuous accommodations plus a roof garden with views of the town and countryside.

SPOLETO: Hotel Aurora €
Budget
Via dell'Apollinare 3, 06049
Tel *0743 22 03 15*
W hotelauroraspoleto.it
Great value at this central but quiet family-run hotel.

SPOLETO: San Luca €€
Boutique
Via Interna delle Mura 21, 06049
Tel *0743 22 33 99*
W hotelsanluca.com
Sophisticated elegance in one of the loveliest palaces in Spoleto.

TODI CANONICA: Tenuta di Canonica €€
Agriturismo
Vocabolo Casalzetta 75, 06059
Tel *075 894 75 45*
W tenutadicanonica.com
Sublime country residence on the site of a 9th-century farm. Superb location.

Le Marche

ANCONA: Grand Hotel Palace €€
Historic
Lungomare Luigi Vanvitelli 24, 60121
Tel *071 20 18 13*
W hotelancona.it
Old-world elegance at this grand 17th-century portside palazzo.

Luxuriously decorated room in the Locanda Pallazone in Orvieto

ANCONA: NH Ancona €€
Rooms with a view
Via XXIX Settembre 14, 60122
Tel *071 20 11 71*
W nh-hotels.it
Stylish, contemporary hilltop hotel with simple rooms.

ASCOLI PICENO: Pennile €
Budget
Via Gaetano Spalvieri 1, 63100
Tel *0736 41 64 5*
W hotelpennile.it
Reasonable prices for simple and well-kept rooms.

DK Choice

ASCOLI PICENO: Villa Cicchi €€
Agriturismo
Via Salaria Superiore 137, 63100
Tel *0736 25 22 72*
W villacicchi.it
An exquisite, meticulously presented villa is at the heart of this agriturismo that combines luxury accommodations with rustic hospitality. There are magnificent grounds, a large pool, period furniture, and frescoed ceilings. Available activities include trekking, wine tasting, cooking and photography courses, and yoga.

PESARO: Bellevue €
Resort
Viale Trieste 88, 61121
Tel *0721 690 18*
W bellevuehotel.net
Great value for this simple but accommodating beach resort.

DK Choice

PESARO: Alexander Museum Palace Hotel €€
Historic
Viale Trieste 20, 61121
Tel *0721 344 41*
W alexandermuseum.it
As the name implies, this unique accommodation is part museum, part hotel. Both established and emerging Italian artists have collaborated to transform this elegant hotel into a literal work of art. Each room is different, and every single design element from the colors to the chairs and floors is one of a kind. The sea views are a bonus.

SAN MARINO: Villa Giardi €
B&B
Via Palamede Ferri 22, 47890
Tel *0549 99 10 74*
Warm atmosphere and a handful of simple rooms.

Key to prices *see p562*

SAN MARINO: Cesare €€
Boutique
Sallta alla Rocca 7, 47890
Tel *0549 99 23 55*
W hotelcesare.com
This hotel blends convenience with refined elegance. Rooms are clean and bright. The staff are very attentive.

URBINO: Cà Andreana €
Agriturismo
Via Gadana 119, 61029
Tel *0722 32 78 45*
W caandreana.it
This farm stay is located in a magnificent country setting with stunning views. Rooms are quaint and well-presented.

URBINO: Raffaello €
Rooms with a view
Via Santa Margherita 38, 61029
Tel *0722 47 84*
W albergoraffaello.com
Situated near the famous artist's childhood home. Rooms are simple but inviting.

Rome

The Ancient Center

Nicolas Inn €€
B&B **Map** 3 B5
Via Cavour 295, 00184
Tel *06 97 61 84 83*
W nicolasinn.com
Basic service, but the rooms are pleasant and cozy, and all have en suite bathrooms. The hosts are warm and friendly.

Fortyseven €€€
Rooms with a view **Map** 6 E1
Via Luigi Petroselli 47, 00186
Tel *06 678 78 16*
W fortysevenhotel.com
Stellar views of the ancient city from this retro-styled hotel. Elegant rooms, including two suites, both with private terraces.

Hotel Forum €€€
Rooms with a view **Map** 3 B5
Via Tor de' Conti 25, 00184
Tel *06 679 24 46*
W hotelforum.com
Enjoy magnificent views of ancient Rome from a charming terrace. Graceful interiors and plenty of old-world charm.

Palazzo Manfredi €€€
Rooms with a view **Map** 7 A1
Via Labicana 125, 00184
Tel *06 77 59 13 80*
W palazzomanfredi.com
The Colosseum seems close enough to touch at this hotel. Elegantly decorated rooms and excellent service.

Glass walls of the Alexander Museum Palace Hotel in Pesaro

Around Piazza Navona

Albergo Santa Chiara €€
Boutique **Map** 10 D3
Via di Santa Chiara 21, 00186
Tel *06 687 29 79*
W albergosantachiara.com
The lobby is the most impressive part of this hotel; the rooms are pleasant but don't compare. Enjoy a drink in the alfresco bar.

Sole al Biscione €
Historic **Map** 9 C4
Via del Biscione 76, 00186
Tel *06 68 80 68 73*
W solealbiscione.it
This basic but charming hotel claims to be the oldest in Rome.

Campo de'Fiori Hotel €€
Rooms with a view **Map** 9 C4
Via del Biscione 6, 00186
Tel *06 68 80 68 65*
W hotelcampodefiori.com
Romantically decorated rooms with refined furnishings, and views of rooftops and domes.

Casa di Santa Brigida €€
Religious institution **Map** 9 B4
Via Monserato 54, 00186
Tel *06 68 89 25 96*
W brigidine.org
Not the cheapest convent in town, but the location is worth the price. Clean and spacious rooms.

Due Torri €€
Historic **Map** 9 C1
Vicolo del Leonetto 23, 00186
Tel *06 68 80 69 56*
W hotelduetorriroma.com
Small but lovely rooms in a converted Renaissance palace.

Portoghesi €€
Charming **Map** 10 D2
Via dei Portoghesi 1, 00186
Tel *06 686 42 31*
W hotelportoghesiroma.it
Nestled in a quiet cobbled alley, this hotel has a charming breakfast terrace.

Teatro di Pompeo €€
Historic **Map** 9 C4
Largo del Pallaro 8, 00186
Tel *06 68 30 01 70*
W hotelteatrodipompeo.it
Built on the ruins of Pompey's ancient theater, this hotel has simple rooms and friendly staff.

Teatropace33 €€
Rooms with a view **Map** 9 C3
Via del Teatro Pace 33, 00186
Tel *06 687 90 75*
W hotelteatropace.com
Excellent price-quality ratio at this charming Baroque-style hotel with elegant decor.

Albergo del Sole al Pantheon €€€
Rooms with a view **Map** 9 C4
Piazza della Rotonda 63, 00186
Tel *06 678 04 41*
W solealpantheonrome.com
Unparalleled views of the bustling Piazza Navona, if you don't mind the noise.

Grand Hotel de La Minerve €€€
Luxury **Map** 10 D3
Piazza della Minerva 69, 00186
Tel *06 69 52 01*
W grandhoteldelaminerve.com
Excellent views from nearly every room. The decor is luxurious and the service is excellent.

Locanda Cairoli €€€
Boutique **Map** 10 D4
Piazza Benedetto Cairoli 2, 00186
Tel *06 68 80 92 78*
W hotelcairoliroma.com
Centrally located hotel with comfortable rooms. Spacious family-style breakfast room.

Raphael €€€
Romantic **Map** 9 C2
Largo Febo 2, 00186
Tel *06 68 28 31*
W raphaelhotel.com
World-class service, gorgeous decor, and a terrace with views.

For more information on types of hotels *see p561*

Charming outdoor garden area at Beehive, Northeast Rome

St. George Hotel €€€
Luxury **Map** 9 A3
Via Giulia 62, 00186
Tel *06 68 66 11*
W stgeorgehotel.it
This elegant five-star hotel offers rooms with contemporary design.

Northeast Rome

DK Choice

Beehive €
Budget **Map** 4 E3
Via Marghera 8, 00185
Tel *06 44 70 45 53*
W the-beehive.com
A gem of a hotel with both private rooms and small dormitories. Some rooms have private bathrooms. Extras include yoga lessons, massage and a café serving organic food and drinks.

Blue Hostel €
Budget **Map** 4 D4
Via Carlo Alberto 13, 00185
Tel *34 09 25 85 03*
W bluehostel.it
A charming hotel with clean and spacious rooms.

Hostel des Artistes €
Budget **Map** 4 E2
Via Villafranca 20, 00185
Tel *06 445 43 65*
W hostelrome.com
Friendly and clean, with private rooms and dorm accommodations.

DK Choice

Casa Howard €€
B&B **Map** 3 A3
Via di Capo le Case 18, 00187 & Via Sistina 149, 00187
Tel *06 69 92 45 55*
W casahoward.com
This funky B&B, inspired by E. M. Forster's novel *Howard's End*, comprises 10 uniquely decorated rooms in two adjacent locations.

Daphne Inn €€
B&B **Map** 3 B2
Via di San Basilio 55, 00187
Tel *06 87 45 00 86*
W daphne-rome.com
Top-notch B&B with personal service and a modern look.

Deko Rome €€
Pensione **Map** 3 C1
Via Toscana 1, 00187
Tel *06 42 02 00 32*
W dekorome.com
Small rooms in minimalist style; surprisingly luxurious bathrooms.

Hotel Suisse €€
Pensione **Map** 3 A2
Via Gregoriana 54, 00187
Tel *06 678 36 49*
W hotelsuisserome.com
Great value at this elegantly appointed hotel.

Locarno €€
Historic **Map** 2 F1
Via della Penna 22, 00186
Tel *06 361 08 41*
W hotellocarno.com
A masterpiece of Art Deco and the location for many classic films.

Piranesi €€
Boutique **Map** 2 F1
Via del Babuino 196, 00187
Tel *06 32 80 41*
W hotelpiranesi.com
Quiet elegance in an ideal location. There's a roof garden, sauna, and a solarium. It also has a small gym.

Residenza Cellini €€
Pensione **Map** 3 C3
Via Modena 5, 00184
Tel *06 47 82 52 04*
W residenzacellini.it
Large, simply furnished rooms; some bathrooms have Jacuzzi tubs.

Aldrovandi Palace €€€
Luxury
Via Ulisse Aldrovandi 15, 00197
Tel *06 322 39 93*
W aldrovandi.com
A spectacular five-star hotel with airy rooms rooms, a swimming pool, and views of the park.

Aleph €€€
Luxury **Map** 3 B2
Via di San Basilio 15, 00185
Tel *06 42 29 01*
W aleph-roma.boscolohotels.com
Experience modern opulence at this relaxing, luxurious spa.

Babuino181 €€€
Boutique **Map** 2 F1
Via del Babuino 181, 00187
Tel *06 32 29 52 95*
W romeluxurysuites.com
Splendid modern hotel with luxurious details. Set in a Renaissance palace with a leafy roof terrace.

Eden €€€
Luxury **Map** 3 B2
Via Ludovisi 49, 00187
Tel *06 47 81 21*
W edenroma.com
A grand hotel with elegantly furnished rooms and a rooftop dining area. Service is exceptional.

es Hotel €€€
Rooms with a view **Map** 4 E4
Via Filippo Turati 171, 00185
Tel *06 44 48 41*
W radissonblu.com/eshotel-rome
Splendid five-star hotel with sleek modern design and all white rooms.

Exedra €€€
Luxury **Map** 3 C3
Piazza della Repubblica 47, 00185
Tel *06 48 93 81*
W exedra-roma.boscolohotels.com
Lavish five-star hotel with plush rooms, a rooftop pool, and an award-winning spa.

DK Choice

Hassler €€€
Luxury **Map** 3 A2
Piazza Trinità dei Monti 6, 00187
Tel *06 69 93 40*
W hotelhasslerroma.com
The discreet service, plush furnishings, and stunning bedrooms make this a firm favorite with celebrities. Guests can also take advantage of the Michelin-stared Imàgora restaurant or enjoy a signature Venschuas cocktail in the Hassler Bar.

Hotel d'Inghilterra €€€
Romantic **Map** 3 A
Via Bocca di Leone 14, 00187
Tel *06 69 98 11*
W hoteldinghilterrarome.com

Key to prices *see p562*

Spacious accommodations in an enviable location near the Spanish Steps. All the rooms and suites are individually styled.

Portrait Suites €€€
Boutique **Map** 3 A2
Via Bocca di Leone 23, 00187
Tel *06 69 38 07 42*
W lungarnocollection.com
Accommodations with style; this hotel is owned by famed shoe designer Salvatore Ferragamo's family, and it shows.

Westin Excelsior €€€
Romantic **Map** 3 B2
Via Veneto 125, 00187
Tel *06 470 81*
W westinrome.com
This favorite with honeymooners is the perfect place to enact *la dolce vita*.

The Vatican and Trastevere

Arco del Lauro €
B&B **Map** 6 D1
Via dell'Arco de' Tolomei 27, 00153
Tel *06 97 84 03 50*
W arcodellauro.it
Tiny hotel in a picturesque medieval location with simple but lovely rooms.

Casa Internazionale delle Donne €
Budget **Map** 2 D5
Vicolo di San Francesco di Sales 47, 00165
Tel *06 68 89 24 65*
W casainternazionaledelledonne.org
Basic accommodations in a quiet but central area; women only.

Centro Diffusione Spiritualità €
Religious institution **Map** 2 D5
Via dei Riari 44, 00153
Tel *06 68 80 61 22*
Budget accommodations including breakfast and dinner. There is an 11pm curfew.

Domus Tiberina €
Budget **Map** 6 D1
Via in Piscinula 37, 00153
Tel *06 581 36 48*
W hoteldomustiberina.it
This tiny, quaint hotel is just steps from the Tiber. Offers simple rooms and continental breakfast.

Hotel Ottaviano €
Budget **Map** 1 C2
Via Ottaviano 6, 00192
Tel *06 39 73 81 38*
W pensioneottaviano.com
A few steps from the Vatican Museums, this hotel is a back-packer's paradise. Great views of St. Peter's square.

Hotel Trastevere €
Budget **Map** 5 C1
Via Luciano Manara 24, 00153
Tel *06 581 47 13*
W hoteltrastevere.net
Simple, clean, and large rooms at this hotel, which offers good value for money. Good breakfast spread.

Bramante €€
Historic **Map** 1 C3
Vicolo delle Palline 24, 00193
Tel *06 68 80 64 26*
W hotelbramante.com
In the shadow of St. Peter's, this family-run accommodation has quiet and tasteful rooms.

Relais Casa della Fornarina €€
Historic **Map** 2 D5
Via di Porta Settimiana 7, 00153
Tel *06 64 56 22 68*
W casadellafornarina.com
Guesthouse where Raphael's muse once lived. Spacious rooms and good service.

Sant'Anna €€
Boutique **Map** 1 C3
Borgo Pio 134, 00193
Tel *06 68 80 16 02*
W santannahotel.net
Modern convenience with an old-world feel. Rooms are spacious, and there is an exquisite courtyard.

DK Choice

Donna Camilla Savelli €€€
Romantic **Map** 5 B1
Via Garibaldi 27, 00153
Tel *06 58 88 61*
W hoteldonnacamillasavelli.com
Designed by Baroque genius Borromini, this meticulously restored monastery still belongs to the nuns of the original order, but is now a four-star hotel. The cloister is an oasis in the heart of the bustling city.

Chic and comfortable sitting area at Portrait Suites, Northeast Rome

Aventine and Lateran

Domus Aventina €
Budget **Map** 5 E2
Via di Santa Prisca 11b, 00153
Tel *06 574 61 35*
W hoteldomusaventina.com
Simple but elegant rooms opening onto a lush courtyard. Rooms are quiet, and a number of attractions are in easy walking distance. Staff are welcoming and helpful.

Sant'Anselmo €€
Romantic **Map** 6 E3
Via Santa Melania 19, 00153
Tel *06 57 00 57*
W aventinohotels.com
Four-poster beds and claw-foot tubs are available at this simple and graceful hotel, on a residential street and close to many restaurants and sights. There is a lovely courtyard. Parking is free.

Villa San Pio €€
Romantic **Map** 6 E3
Via Santa Melania 19, 00153
Tel *06 57 00 57*
W aventinohotels.com
Quiet and secluded, but located conveniently in the city center. Good breakfasts and drinks are served in the lovely garden.

Lazio

BRACCIANO: Villa Clementina Spa & Resort €€
Spa hotel
Traversa Quarto del Lago 12, 00062
Tel *06 998 62 68*
W hotelvillaclementina.it
Beautifully frescoed rooms in lush surroundings with a large pool.

CERVETERI: L'Isola di Rosa €€
Spa hotel
Via del Grano 20, 00052
Tel *06 99552819*
W isoladirosa.com
Old manor house with well-appointed rooms.

FRASCATI: Poggio Regillo €
Agriturismo
Via Pietra Porzia 30, 00044
Tel *06 941 78 00*
W poggioregillo.it
An environmentally friendly hotel that offers excellent value. Pets welcome.

SPERLONGA: Grotta di Tiberio €€
Rooms with a view
Via Flacca km 15, 700, 04029
Tel *0771 54 81 37/0771 54 89 44*
W hotelgrottaditiberio.it
Charming beachside hotel with a large pool. Rooms are spacious.

For more information on types of hotels *see p561*

TARQUINIA: Casale Poggio Nebbia €
Agriturismo
S.S. Aurelia km 84, 100, Loc. Farnesiana, 01016
Tel *0766 84 12 68*
W poggionebbia.it
Relaxing farm stay nestled in a valley and popular with Italians. Ideal for families.

TARQUINIA: Hotel all'Olivo €
Budget
Via Palmiro Togliatti 15, 01016
Tel *0766 85 73 18*
W allolivo.it
Old-fashioned hotel in the countryside with an excellent traditional restaurant.

TIVOLI: Palazzo Maggiore €
B&B
Via Domenico Giuliani 89, 00019
Tel *393 104 49 37*
W palazzomaggiore.com
This sweet hotel provides the perfect base to explore Tivoli.

TIVOLI: Grand Hotel Duca d'Este €€
Business
Via Tiburtina Valeria 330, 00019
Tel *0774 38 83*
W ducadeste.com
Large, comfortable hotel with fully equipped wellness center.

VITERBO: Hotel Viterbo Best Western €
Budget
Via San Camillo de Lellis 6, 01100
Tel *0761 27 01 00*
W hotelviterbo.com
Comfortable hotel with good service and an abundant breakfast.

VITERBO: Niccolò V €€
Spa hotel
Strada Bagni 12, 01100
Tel *0761 35 01*
W termedeipapi.it
Historic thermal baths and wellness center in an elegant four-star hotel.

Naples and Campania

AMALFI COAST: Hotel Desirée €
Rooms with a view
Via Capo 31, 80067
Tel *081 878 15 63*
W desireehotelsorrento.com
This simple, cliff-side hotel offers excellent value. There's an elevator to a small private beach.

AMALFI COAST: Antica Repubblica €€
Boutique
Vico dei Pastai 2, 84011
Tel *089 873 63 10*
W anticarepubblica.it
A charming hotel with elegantly furnished rooms and a terrace.

AMALFI COAST: Miramare €€
Rooms with a view
Via Trara Genoino, 84017
Tel *089 87 50 02*
W miramarepositano.it
Rooms are brightly decorated and have views looking out over Positano and the ocean beyond.

AMALFI COAST: Bellevue Syrene €€€
Luxury
Piazza della Vittoria 5, 80067
Tel *081 878 10 24*
W bellevue.it
A dreamy 18th-century villa with a flowering terrace and private beach access.

AMALFI COAST: La Sirenuse €€€
Luxury
Via Cristoforo Colombo 30, 84017
Tel *089 87 50 66*
W sirenuse.it
World-class hotel with spectacular views of Sorrento and the coast.

CAPRI: Bellavista €€
Boutique
Via Giuseppe Orlandi 10, 80071
Tel *081 837 14 63/081 837 18 21*
W bellavistacapri.com
Enjoy the spectacular views from this sweet 1960s-style hotel.

CAPRI: Grand Hotel Quisisana €€€
Luxury
Via Camerelle 2, 80073
Tel *081 837 07 88*
W quisisana.com
Deluxe accommodations in an extraordinary setting.

CASERTA: Amadeus €
Boutique
Via Giuseppe Verdi 72/76, 81100
Tel *0823 35 26 63*
W hotelamadeuscaserta.it
A centrally located, comfortable hotel with spacious rooms.

DK Choice

ISCHIA AND PROCIDA: Miramare €€
Spa hotel
Via Maddalena Comandante 29, Sant'Angelo, 80070
Tel *081 99 92 19*
W hotelmiramare.it
This gorgeous old-world hotel is perched on the rocks right over the Tyrrhenian Sea. The lovely rooms, most with canopy beds and balconies, all face the sea. A short walk leads to the spa complex with thermal pools and a private beach. The ample breakfast is served on a flowering terrace with spectacular views.

NAPLES: Decumani €€
Historic
Piazzetta Giustino Fortunato 8, 80100
Tel *081 420 13 79/081 410 91 44*
W palazzodecumani.com
Tasteful furnishings and elegant bathrooms in a Baroque palace.

NAPLES: Grand Hotel Vesuvio €€€
Rooms with a view
Via Partenope 45, 80121
Tel *081 764 00 44*
W vesuvio.it
Sumptuous lodgings with views of the gulf and Castel dell'Ovo.

SALERNO: Hotel dei Templi €€
B&B
Via Tavernelle 64, 84063
Tel *082 881 17 47*
W www.hoteldeitempli.it
Stylish hotel located minutes from the ruined temples at Paestum.

SALERNO: Lloyd's Baia €€
Rooms with a view
Via Enrico de Marinis 2, 84013
Tel *089 763 31 11*
W lloydsbaiahotel.it
Lovely hotel hanging over a cliff and offering remarkable views.

Outdoor pool beside the beach at Grotta di Tiberio hotel in Lazio

Key to prices *see p562*

Abruzzo, Molise, and Puglia

DK Choice

ALBEROBELLO: B&B Fascino Antico €
Historic
Strada Statale 172, 74015
Tel *080 432 50 89*
W fascinoantico.eu
At this charming B&B, you can lodge in one of the five 19th-century huts without losing the comforts of a modern vacation. Surrounded by centuries-old olive trees, the apartments face a large courtyard, and there is an outdoor pool.

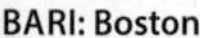

BARI: Boston €
Business
Via Niccolò Piccinni 155, 70122
Tel *080 521 66 33*
W bostonbari.it
Functional and comfortable rooms in a convenient location.

ISOLE TREMITI: Baely Resort €€
Resort
Via Matteotti, 71040
Tel *0882 46 37 67*
W baely.it
Intimate hotel with comfortable, distinctively decorated rooms.

L'AQUILA: Magione Papale €€
Boutique
Via Porta Napoli 67, 67100
Tel *0862 41 49 83/0862 42 21 94*
W magionepapale.it
Set in a restored mill, this quaint country inn has plenty of character.

Basilicata and Calabria

MARATEA: La Locanda delle Donne Monache €€
Romantic
Via Carlo Mazzei 4, 85046
Tel *0973 87 61 39*
W locandamonache.com
Spacious, bright rooms at this lovely former convent.

DK Choice

MATERA: Sassi Hotel €
Historic
Via San Giovanni Vecchio 89, 75100
Tel *0835 33 10 09*
W hotelsassi.it
Matera's famous rock dwellings make an evocative setting for this one-of-a-kind hotel. Each

Ultramodern lounge area in Riva del Sole in Cefalù

room is carved into the mountain, with distinctive vaulted stone ceilings and panoramic views of the medieval town below. Furnishings are simple and classic, letting the natural elements of the 18th-century building shine.

MELFI: Relais la Fattoria €
Agriturismo
Località la Cavallerizza, 85025
Tel *0972 247 76*
W relaislafattoria.it
A country inn set amid olive trees and vineyards. Charming rooms.

TROPEA: Cala di Volpe €€
Resort
Località Torre Marino, 89865
Tel *0963 66 92 22/0963 66 96 99*
W caladivolpe.it
A beautiful seaside resort surrounded by a lush tropical garden. A short walk to the beach.

Sicily

AGRIGENTO: Camere a Sud €
B&B
Via Ficani, 92100
Tel *349 638 44 24*
W camereasud.it
Warm, simple rooms in this sunny B&B. Friendly, helpful owners.

CEFALÙ: Riva del Sole €€
Rooms with a view
Lungomare Giardina 25, 90015
Tel *0921 42 12 30*
W rivadelsole.com
A modern hotel ideally located between the sea and city center.

ERICE: Elimo €€
Rooms with a view
Via Vittorio Emanuele 73, 91016
Tel *0923 86 93 77*
W hotelelimo.it
Small but lovely rooms with panoramic views of the countryside.

PALERMO: Principe di Villafranca €€€
Luxury
Via Giuseppina Turrisi Colonna 4, 90141
Tel *091 611 85 23*
W principedivillafranca.it
Elegant hotel full of intricate details and antique art and furnishings.

Sardinia

ALGHERO: Villa Las Tronas €€€
Spa hotel
Lungomare Valencia 1, 07041
Tel *079 98 18 18*
W hotelvillalastronas.it
Scenic views at this elegant hotel, with indoor and outdoor pools.

CAGLIARI: T Hotel €€
Design
Via dei Giudicati 66, 09131
Tel *070 474 00*
W thotel.it
Modern design hotel with large rooms and a fitness center.

COSTA SMERALDA: Nibaru €€
Resort
Località Cala di Volpe
Tel *0789 960 38*
W hotelnibaru.it
A tranquil oasis a short walk from the sea. Comfortable and clean rooms, and a lovely pool.

COSTA SMERALDA: Pitrizza €€€
Luxury
Via Nazionale 35, 07020
Tel *0789 93 01 11*
W pitrizzahotel.com
A grand hotel with fabulous amenities and breathtaking views.

SASSARI: Grazie Deledda €
Business
Viale Dante 47, 07100
Tel *079 27 12 35*
W hotelgraziadeledda.it
Remarkable low prices for this large and comfortable hotel.

For more information on types of hotels *see p561*

WHERE TO EAT AND DRINK

Food is a serious subject in Italy. The Italians are justly proud of their fine cuisine and wines, and many sociable hours are spent around the table. One of the great pleasures of traveling in Italy is sampling regional variations in pasta, breads, and cheeses. You don't have to head to the most expensive places for good food; a simple *trattoria*, which serves the local clientele, will often produce a better meal than the nearby international restaurant. However, whether it is a crowded *osteria*, a local *pizzeria*, or a terrace with sea views, this introduction gives plenty of practical tips on types of restaurants, ordering, and service to help you enjoy eating out in Italy.

Places to Eat

Traditionally a *trattoria* and an *osteria* are cheaper and more casual alternatives to the more upscale *ristorante*.

A *pizzeria* is usually a cheap place to eat (as little as €18 with beer) and many serve pasta, meat, and fish dishes as well as pizzas. *Pizzerie* are often open in the evening only, especially those with wood-fired ovens *(forno a legna)*.

A *birreria* is another cheap option, serving pasta and snacks such as sausages and burgers. An *enoteca*, or *vineria*, will offer a selection of wines to try, along with a range of light dishes. Prices vary and tend to be relatively expensive for the quantities served.

At lunchtime and in the early evening, *rosticcerie* sell roast chicken, slices of pizza *(pizza al taglio)*, and other snacks to take out. *Pizza al taglio* can also be bought straight from the baker. Many bars offer filled rolls *(panini)* and sandwiches *(tramezzini)*, and some also serve simple hot dishes from the *tavola calda* counter for around €8.

Stop at a *gelateria* for ice cream, with a sometimes bewildering choice of different flavors, or a *pasticceria* for one of a dazzling variety of sweet and savory pastries, cakes, and cookies.

A restaurant in Chioggia offering a cozy environment in a vaulted room

Villa Crespi in Piedmont, inspired by the Arabian Nights *(see p588)*

Opening Times

Lunch is generally served between 12:30pm and 2:30pm and, particularly in the south, all other activity stops between these hours. Dinner is at about 7:30pm and goes on until 11pm or later (in the south, eating hours tend to be later). It is not unusual to see tables still full from lunch at 4pm or diners sipping *digestivi* well after midnight.

Reservations

Good restaurants in Italy are likely to be popular, so reserve a table in advance if you can *(prenotazione)*. Otherwise, get there early to avoid having to wait. Many restaurants close one day a week and for a few weeks in either winter or the summer vacation season; this information will be included in the list of restaurants on the pages that follow, but call first if in doubt.

The Menu

Italian meals consist of three or four courses, and restaurants generally expect patrons to order at least two, though you should not feel obligated to do so. The *antipasto* (appetizer) is followed by the *primo*, of pasta, rice, or soup. The *secondo* is the main meat or fish course, for which you will need to order vegetables *(contorni)* separately. Fruit *(frutta)*, cheese *(formaggi)*, or dessert *(dolce)* follow, with coffee and the preferred *digestivo* of the region to finish the meal.

Menus usually change with the season to make use of the freshest local produce, and the day's specials may be recited to you by the waiter rather than written down. Persevere, if you don't immediately understand, using the menu information at the beginning of each section. Try to avoid restaurants that do not state prices on their menus.

Vegetarians

Italian restaurants offer plenty of choices for vegetarians, as the menu will always feature a selection of seasonal vegetables and beans. Many pasta and *antipasto* dishes use no meat at all and for a main course you can ask for an omelet *(frittata)* with a side dish of vegetables from the *contorni*. Most menus are adaptable because dishes are prepared to order – tell your waiter that you are *vegetariano* (female *vegetariana*) and they will advise you accordingly.

Wine and Drinks

Many regions have their own *aperitivo* served before the meal and a *digestivo* for afterward. Universal alternatives are *prosecco* (dry, fizzy white wine) or an *analcolico* (nonalcoholic) aperitif, and *grappa* as a digestive. House wine (red or white) will be a simple local wine served by the liter or by the glass and will generally be perfectly palatable. In addition, all but the cheapest eateries have a range of other local and regional wines specially selected to accompany the food on the menu, with more upscale establishments also offering foregin vintages.

Tap water *(acqua del rubinetto)* is always drinkable and often very good, but Italy has a large range of mineral waters. Fizzy ones *(frizzante)* may contain carbon dioxide, while *naturale* can mean still or naturally sparkling. If you particularly want a still water, ask for *non gassata*. Espresso bars usually charge more for table service.

Paying

Tax and service are usually included in the menu prices, but it is normal to leave a tip of around 10 percent. Note that many restaurants include a cover charge *(coperto)*, on the bill *(il conto)*, which covers bread (whether you eat it or not) and is charged per person.

Credit cards are not always accepted in Italy, particularly in smaller towns, so it is wise to check before you order.

Diners enjoying a meal *al fresco* in Chianti, Tuscany

Dress

Italians generally tend to look chic but don't necessarily expect visitors to do the same. However, very scruffy or dirty clothes are unlikely to get you good, efficient, or particularly friendly service.

Children

Children are welcome in all but high-end establishments, and restaurants are likely to be filled with extensive Italian families for Sunday lunch. Facilities such as high chairs or special menus are rare, but most places will provide a small or half portion *(mezza porzione)*.

Smoking

Smoking is still popular in Italy. However, smoking laws now mean that all restaurants in the country are nonsmoking establishments. Unless a smokers' room is provided, you should step outside if you want to light up.

Outdoor tables at the seafood restaurant Il Riccio on Capri *(see p600)*

Wheelchair Access

Few restaurants have special facilities for people in wheelchairs, but if you make reservations in advance, the establishment can prepare a suitable table and be ready to help when you arrive.

The charming interior of U'Giancu in Rapallo, Liguria *(see p590)*

Recommended Restaurants

The restaurants listed in this guidebook cover a wide range of eateries, from the simple *pizzeria* and *tavola calda* (cafeteria) to family-run *trattoria* and elegant *ristorante*. Each restaurant has a cuisine type listed beneath the name of the establishment. Most of these descriptions are self explanatory, but the *Places to Eat* section will provide more information on what you can expect from the menu.

The DK Choice label means the restaurant has outstanding qualities and is highly recommended. It may serve delicious local dishes, offer excellent value for money, be in a beautiful location, have a romantic atmosphere, or be particularly charming. Whatever the reason, it is a guarantee of a great meal.

Where to Eat and Drink

Venice

BURANO: Da Romano €€
Seafood
Via Piazza Galuppi 221, 30012
Tel *041 73 00 30* **Closed** *Sun dinner; mid-Dec–Jan: Tue*
A wide range of fish dishes served in the traditional Venetian fashion. Advance reservations advised.

DK Choice

BURANO-MAZZORBO: Venissa €€€
Modern Italian
Fondamenta Santa Caterina 3, 30170
Tel *041 527 22 81* **Closed** *Mon; Nov: Mon, Tue, Wed; Dec–Mar*
Dine at the elegant Venissa restaurant for an extraspecial gastronomic experience. The menu features a wide selection of seafood, meat, and vegetarian options using fresh, seasonal ingredients grown in the restaurant's own garden. The menu changes daily.

CANNAREGIO: Osteria al Timon €
Regional Italian **Map** 2 E3
Fondamenta Ormesini 2754, 30121
Tel *041 524 60 66* **Closed** *Wed; 2 wks Oct*
Fantastic range of *cicchetti* (finger food) to accompany a glass of wine, but also good meat dishes.

CANNAREGIO: Trattoria da Gigio €
Regional Italian **Map** 2 D3
Rio Terrà San Leonardo 1594, 30121
Tel *041 71 75 74* **Closed** *Sun, Mon dinner*
Seafood is a popular option here, as are the generous hors d'oeuvres.

DK Choice

CANNAREGIO: Osteria da Rioba €€
Seafood
Fondamenta della Misericordia 2553, 30121
Tel *041 524 43 79* **Closed** *Mon*
Charming canal-side restaurant specializing in fish. Friendly and knowledgeable staff. Try the seafood mosaic. Reservations are recommended

CANNAREGIO: Osteria l'Orto dei Mori €€
Regional Italian **Map** 2 F3
Campo dei Mori 3386, 30121
Tel *041 524 36 77* **Closed** *Tue*
This off-the-beaten-track *osteria* has a refined take on local cuisine. Elegant Modernist interiors.

CANNAREGIO: Vini da Gigio €€
Regional Italian **Map** 3 A4
Fondamenta San Felice 3628A, 30121
Tel *041 528 51 40* **Closed** *Mon, Tue; mid-Jan–1st wk Feb, 2 wks Aug*
The menu largely depends on what Rialto market has to offer that morning. Reservations advised.

CANNAREGIO: Fiaschetteria Toscana €€€
Seafood **Map** 3 B5
Salizzada San Giovanni Grisostomo 5719, 30121
Tel *041 528 52 81* **Closed** *Tue, Wed lunch; end Jul–mid-Aug, 1 wk Dec*
Try the delectable warm octopus salad and the turbot in caper sauce. Book ahead.

CASTELLO: Enoteca La Mascareta €
Enoteca **Map** 7 C1
Calle Santa Maria Formosa 5183, 30122
Tel *041 523 07 44* **Closed** *lunch*
Wine expert Mauro Lorenzon provides some delicious food to accompany the excellent drinks.

CASTELLO: Al Covo €€
Seafood **Map** 8 E2
Campiello della Pescaria 3968, 30122
Tel *041 522 38 12* **Closed** *Wed, Thu; 2 wks Jan, 1 wk Aug*
Tucked away behind the Arsenale boat strip, Al Cova has interesting tasting menus.

CASTELLO: Da Remigio €€
Seafood **Map** 8 D2
Salizzada dei Greci 3416, 30122
Tel *041 523 00 89* **Closed** *Mon dinner, Tue; 2 wks Jul–Aug, 3 wks Dec–Jan*
Book early as space is limited. Specials include the fish and shellfish risotto.

CASTELLO: Ristorante Giorgione €€
Regional Italian **Map** 8 F3
Via Garibaldi 1533, 30122
Tel *041 522 87 27* **Closed** *Wed; 2 wks Nov*
Great neighborhood *trattoria* serving flavorsome fish dishes, including lasagna and risotto.

CASTELLO: Ristorante Wildner €€
Regional Italian **Map** 8 D2
Riva degli Schiavoni 4161, 30122
Tel *041 522 74 63* **Closed** *Tue; 3 wks Jan*
Fresh fish, locally grown organic vegetables, and an interesting wine list at this restaurant.

Price Guide
Prices are based on a three-course meal per person, with a half-bottle of house wine, including tax and service.

€	up to €40
€€	€40 to 75
€€€	over €75

CASTELLO: Osteria di Santa Marina €€€
Regional Italian **Map** 3 B5
Campo Santa Marina 5911, 30122
Tel *041 528 52 39* **Closed** *Sun, Mon lunch; 2 wks Jan, 2 wks Aug*
A restaurant with a reputation for its creative take on local cuisine.

DORSODURO: La Rivista €
Vegetarian **Map** 6 E4
Rio Terrà Foscarini 979/A, 30123
Tel *041 240 14 25* **Closed** *Mon; 2 wks Jan*
A welcoming restaurant offering salads and cold platters for lunch.

DORSODURO: Ai Gondolieri €€
Regional Italian **Map** 6 F4
San Vio 366, 30123
Tel *041 528 63 96* **Closed** *Tue; 1 wk Aug: lunch; Dec 25.*
Here, regional meat and vegetable dishes are served with flair.

GIUDECCA: Trattoria Altanella €€
Regional Italian
Rio del Ponte Lungo 268, 33035
Tel *041 522 7780* **Closed** *Mon, Tue.*
A charming canalside restaurant run by the same family for four generations.

GIUDECCA: Cipriani €€€
Fine Dining
Giudecca 10, 30133
Tel *041 520 77 44* **Closed** *Nov–Mar*
Guests are ferried from the San Marco waterfront to these exclusive island hotel restaurants.

Spectacular setting of one of the waterfront restaurants at Cipriani, Giudecca

SAN MARCO: Acqua Pazza €€
Seafood **Map** 7 A2
Campo Sant'Angelo 3808, 30124
Tel *041 277 06 88* **Closed** *Mon; Jan–Feb*
This is where the Amalfi Coast meets Venice. A different take on fish, with wines to match.

SAN MARCO: Gran Caffè e Ristorante Quadri €€€
Fine Dining **Map** 7 B2
Piazza San Marco 121, 30124
Tel *041 522 21 05* **Closed** *Mon*
Fantastic historic site now in the capable, creative hands of star chef Massimiliano Alajmo.

SAN MARCO: Trattoria Do Forni €€€
Fine Dining **Map** 7 B2
Calle dei Specchieri 468, 30124
Tel *041 523 21 48*
Two dining areas with different decors serve careful interpretations of classic Venetian cuisine.

SAN POLO: Muro €
Pizzeria **Map** 6 E1
Rio Terà dei Frari 2604, 30125
Tel *041 524 53 10* **Closed** *Thu*
A branch of the Muro pizza restaurants, popular with young locals. Mega salads also available available, along with a wide selection of beer on tap.

SAN POLO: Osteria da Fiore €€€
Fine Dining **Map** 6 D1
Calle del Scaleter 2202, 30125
Tel *041 72 13 08* **Closed** *Sun, Mon; Jan 8–22, 3 wks Aug*
Many deem this the city's best restaurant. Seasonal produce is the rule. Leave room for dessert.

SANTA CROCE: Enoteca al Prosecco €
Enoteca **Map** 2 E3
Campo San Giacomo dell'Orio 1503, 30135
Tel *041 524 02 22* **Closed** *Sun; Jan, Aug*
Enjoy light meals indoors or outside in the square, with a glass of excellent wine.

SANTA CROCE: Il Rèfolo €
Pizzeria **Map** 2 E5
Campo del Piovan 1459, 30135
Tel *041 524 00 16* **Closed** *Mon, Tue lunch; Jan*
Set in a picturesque square, this modern establishment serves innovative gourmet pizzas.

SANTA CROCE: Osteria La Zucca €
Regional Italian **Map** 2 E5
Ponte del Megio 1762, 30135
Tel *041 524 15 70* **Closed** *Sun*
Pretty canalside restaurant popular with Venetians as well as visitors.

Tasteful interiors and charming garden at Villa Cipriani, Asolo

SANTA CROCE: Antiche Carampane €€€
Seafood **Map** 2 F5
Rio Terà Carampane 1911, 30125
Tel *041 524 01 65* **Closed** *Sun, Mon; 10 days Jan, 3 wks Aug*
Seek out this local favorite, for great fish and pasta dishes.

TORCELLO: Locanda Cipriani €€€
Fine Dining
Piazza Santa Fosca 29, 30012
Tel *041 73 01 50* **Closed** *Tue; Jan–Feb*
Charming and exclusive island restaurant with a shady courtyard.

The Veneto and Friuli

ARCO: Alla Lega €
Regional Italian
Via Vergolano 8, 38062
Tel *046 451 62 05* **Closed** *Nov: Wed*
Lively restaurant serving traditional regional fare. Housed in a rustic 18th-century building with a lovely courtyard.

ASOLO: Locanda Baggio €€
Regional Italian
Via Bassane 1, Località Casonetto, 31011
Tel *0423 52 96 48* **Closed** *Mon*
Changing seasonal menu with innovative interpretations of traditional fare. Cooking classes are also available.

ASOLO: Villa Cipriani €€€
Fine Dining
Via Canova 298, 31011
Tel *0423 52 34 11*
A hotel restaurant offering creative cuisine and overlooking a glorious garden, with breathtaking views of the hills below.

BASSANO DEL GRAPPA: Osteria Trinità €
Regional Italian
Contrà San Giorgio 17, 36061
Tel *0424 50 37 00* **Closed** *Wed, Sat lunch*
Traditional eatery serving Venetian classics such as *pasta e fagioli* (bean and pasta soup) and *baccalà* (cod) in various forms.

BASSANO DEL GRAPPA: Pulierin Enotavola €
Enoteca
Strada Soarda 26, San Michele, 36061
Tel *042 450 55 62* **Closed** *Sat lunch, Sun*
A wine-tasting facility in a lovely rural setting serving food based on local products.

BELLUNO: Ristorante Terracotta €
Regional Italian
Borgo Garibaldi 61, 32100
Tel *043 729 16 92* **Closed** *Tue, Wed lunch; Aug*
Friendly family-run restaurant specializing in regional seasonal dishes. Delicious selection of desserts and extensive wine list.

CASTELFRANCO: Barbesin €€
Regional Italian
Via Montebelluna di Salva Rosa 41, 31033
Tel *042 349 04 46* **Closed** *Sun dinner; 2 wks Jan, 2 wks Aug*
Dishes based on local radicchio predominate, but there are also mixed grills and salted cod in the Vicenza tradition.

CHIOGGIA: Osteria Penzo €
Seafood
Calle Larga Bersaglio 525, 30015
Tel *041 400992* **Closed** *Mon dinner, Tue*
The place for traditional fare such as squid with peas or gnocchi with onions, mussels, and radicchio.

CHIOGGIA: La Taverna €€
Seafood
Via Felice Cavallotti 348, 30015
Tel *041 40 18 06* **Closed** *Wed; mid-Jan–mid-Feb*
Classic seafood dishes in an elegant setting. The outdoor tables look over the main square.

For more information on types of restaurants *see p579*

CIVIDALE DEL FRIULI: Al Castello €
Regional Italian
Via del Castello 12, 33043
Tel *043 273 32 42* **Closed** *Wed; 2 wks Aug*
Set in a magnificent castle. The menu boasts traditional dishes and fine local wines.

CONEGLIANO: Al Salisa €€
Regional Italian
Via XX Settembre 2–4, 31015
Tel *0438 242 88* **Closed** *Tue dinner, Wed; last 2 wks Jun*
An elegant restaurant housed in a medieval building. Serving fresh fish, game, and even sushi.

CORMONS: Ristorante al Cacciatore – La Subida €€€
Regional Italian
Via Subida 52, 34071
Tel *048 16 05 31* **Closed** *lunch: Mon, Thu, Fri; Tue, Wed; 2 wks Feb*
Inventive Friulian and Slovenian menu that changes with the seasons. Beautiful country setting.

CORTINA D'AMPEZZO: Baita Fraina €
Regional Italian
Località Fraina 1, 32043
Tel *0436 36 34* **Closed** *off-season: Mon; after Easter–Jun, Oct–Nov*
Attractive wood-paneled B&B with an on-site restaurant, panoramic terrace, and spacious play area for kids.

CORTINA D'AMPEZZO: Ristorante El Zoco €€
Regional Italian
Località Cademai 18, 32043
Tel *043 686 00 41* **Closed** *Mon; May, Nov*
Small but cozy restaurant on the outskirts of trendy Cortina. Good grilled meats and fresh vegetables.

FUMANE: Ristorante Scamperle alla Rosa €
Regional Italian
Via Incisa 8, 37022
Tel *045 770 10 06* **Closed** *off-season: Mon; 1st wk Jul, 2nd wk Jan*
One of the oldest restaurants in the Valpolicella. All pasta, bread, and pastries are made on-site.

GARDA: Locanda San Vigilio €€
Traditional Italian
Punta San Vigilio, 37016
Tel *045 725 66 88* **Closed** *mid-Nov–end Mar*
Five centuries of experience in delighting guests with excellent food, wine, and gorgeous views.

GRADO: Trattoria de Toni €€
Seafood
Piazza Duca d'Aosta 37, 34073
Tel *043 18 01 04* **Closed** *Wed; Dec–Feb*
The house specialty here is *boreto alla gradese*, a delicious fish stew cooked in vinegar.

GRANCONA: Isetta €
Regional Italian
Via Pederiva 96, 36040
Tel *044 488 99 92* **Closed** *Tue dinner, Wed; 1 wk Jan*
Pretty restaurant in a hilly area outside Vicenza. Regional food, with emphasis on grilled meats.

LONIGO: La Peca €€€
Fine Dining
Via Giovanelli 2, 36045
Tel *044 483 02 14* **Closed** *Sun, Mon; 1 wk mid-Aug*
Traditional ingredients revisited with inventive flair. Similar mixture of classic and creative in the decor.

MESTRE: La Vivanderia €
Regional Italian
Via Pasqualigo 59/H, 30175
Tel *041 61 07 42* **Closed** *Sat lunch; Jun–Aug: Sun; Sep–May: Thu*
Dishes based on seasonal ingredients are the focus at this *osteria*. Limited but excellent wine selection.

MIANE: Da Gigetto €
Regional Italian
Via De Gasperi 5, 31050
Tel *043 896 00 20* **Closed** *Mon dinner, Tue; 2 wks Jan, 3 wks Aug*
An elegant take on traditional dishes made with seasonal ingredients, including pumpkin and mushrooms in fall.

MONTECCHIA DI CROSARA: Ristorante Cassandra €€
Regional Italian
Via Cabalao 11, 37030
Tel *045 745 02 22* **Closed** *Sun dinner, Mon*
A refined country restaurant with a modern, interesting menu and an oustanding wine list.

NOVENTA PADOVANA: Boccadoro €€
Regional Italian
Via della Resistenza 49, 35027
Tel *049 62 50 29* **Closed** *Wed; 3 wks Aug, Dec 27–Jan 6*
Quietly elegant family-run restaurant offering well-balanced fish and meat dishes.

PADUA: Da Giovanni €
Regional Italian
Via Pietro Maroncelli 22, 35129
Tel *049 77 26 20* **Closed** *Sat lunch, Sun; Aug, 1 wk Christmas*
Time-honored *trattoria* offering classics such as homemade pasta, risotto, and meat stews.

PADUA: Trattoria San Pietro €
Regional Italian
Via San Pietro 95, 35139
Tel *049 876 03 30* **Closed** *Sun, Jul*
The perfect place for regional dishes cooked with fresh local ingredients. Informal atmosphere.

RUBANO: Le Calandre €€€
Fine Dining
Via Liguria 1, 35030
Tel *049 630303* **Closed** *Sun, Mon; 2 wks Jan, 2 wks Aug*
The cuisine at this three-Michelin-starred restaurant will enchant the senses.

DK Choice

SAN GIORGIO DI VALPOLICELLA: Trattoria Dalla Rosa Alda €
Regional Italian
Strada Garibaldi 4, 37015
Tel *045 770 10 18* **Closed** *Sun dinner, Mon; Jan–Feb*
Nestled in a charming village surrounded by vineyards, this family-run *trattoria* has been serving excellent traditional fare for several generations. The ingredients are carefully sourced from local producers. The cellars are full of carefully chosen wines, from the Valpolicella region, to accompany your meal. Guests can eat alfresco on a beautiful terrace, weather permitting.

Guests relaxing under the shade of umbrellas at Locanda San Vigilio in Garda

SANTA MARIA DI SALA: Trattoria Barison €
Regional Italian
Via Ronchi 14, Borgoricco, 35010
Tel *049 579 80 63* **Closed** *Mon dinner, Tue; 2 wks Jan, 3 wks Aug*
Serves not only the traditional *baccalà*, but also grilled meats, cooked vegetables, and wild salads.

SOLIGHETTO: Locanda da Lino €
Regional Italian
Via Roma 19, 31053
Tel *043 88 21 50* **Closed** *Mon; last 2 wks Jul*
This restaurant is part of an inn overlooking the Prosecco hillsides. Offers homemade pasta and good grilled meats.

TREVISO: Antico Ristorante Beccherie €€
Regional Italian
Piazza Ancilotto 11, 31100
Tel *0422 54 08 71* **Closed** *Sun dinner, Mon; last 2 wks Jul*
The name is derived from a word in the local dialect that means "butcher's," so not surprisingly, meat is the specialty here.

TRIESTE: Antica Ghiacceretta €€
Regional Italian
Via dei Fornellli 2, 34121
Tel *040 322 03 07* **Closed** *Sun; 1 wk Feb, 1 wk Aug*
Enjoy fish dishes revisited with an inventive, light touch in a modern setting. Wines to match.

UDINE: Da Raffaele €
Pizzeria
Via Leonardo da Vinci 56, 33100
Tel *043 229 58 31* **Closed** *Wed lunch; 3 wks Jul-Aug*
More than just a classic pizzeria, this place boasts a traditional wood-fired oven and beer on tap.

DK Choice

UDINE: Agli Amici €€€
Fine Dining
Via Liguria 252, 33100
Tel *043 256 54 11*
Closed *summer: Sun, Mon, Tue lunch, first 3 wks Aug; winter: Sun dinner, Tue lunch*
Agli Amici whips up a cuisine that draws on local influences, traditions, and ingredients and is served with elegance. Sample one of the tasting menus for a chance to taste a few dishes.

VALEGGIO SUL MINCIO: Antica Locanda Mincio €
Traditional Italian
Via Michelangelo Buonarroti 12, 37067
Tel *045 795 00 59* **Closed** *Wed, Thu; 2 wks Feb, 2 wks Nov*
Frescoed walls, open fireplaces, and an outdoor terrace. Specials include trout from Lake Garda.

VERONA: Al Bersagliere €
Regional Italian
Via Dietro Pallone 1, 37121
Tel *045 820 48 24* **Closed** *Sun, Mon*
This pleasantly informal, yet chic restaurant offers great risotto with Amarone and pasta dishes.

VERONA: Arche €€
Regional Italian
Via Arche Scaligere 6, 37121
Tel *045 800 74 15* **Closed** *Sun, Mon lunch; 2 wks Jan*
Established in 1879, this seafood restaurant serves unmatched marinated rock lobster.

VERONA: Il Desco €€€
Fine Dining
Via Dietro San Sebastiano 5–7, 37121
Tel *045 59 53 58* **Closed** *Sun, Mon; 2 wks Jun & Dec; Jul–Aug & Dec: Mon lunch*
This elegant Michelin-starred restaurant offers a creative take on traditional dishes.

VICENZA: Antica Casa della Malvasia €
Regional Italian
Contrà delle Morette 5, 36100
Tel *044 454 37 04* **Closed** *Mon; 2 wks Jul*
Osteria serving pumpkin pancakes, local cheeses, and cold cuts, and pork fillet with truffles.

VICENZA: Locanda Veneta €
Regional Italian
Via Battaglione Valtellina 138, 36100
Tel *044 456 80 07* **Closed** *Mon dinner, Sat lunch*
A wide range of fish and meat dishes is served at this family restaurant with a kids' play area.

Trentino–Alto Adige

DK Choice

BOLZANO: Cavallino Bianco €
Regional Italian
Via dei Bottai 6, 39100
Tel *0471 97 32 67* **Closed** *Sat dinner, Sun*
Also known by its German name, Weisses Rössl, this busy family restaurant serves traditional South Tyrol fare. A breakfast buffet is followed by good lunch options and a waiter-service dinner at this hotel restaurant. The gastronomic theme evenings are popular with the locals. Good value and speedy service.

Wood-beamed ceilings and soft lighting at the informal Al Bersagliere, Verona

BOLZANO: Forst €
Birreria
Goethestrasse 6, 39042
Tel *0471 97 72 43* **Closed** *Sun*
Popular restaurant serving not only the hallmark beer, but also good wines and excellent food.

BOLZANO: Hopfen & Co €
Birreria
Obstplatz 17, 39100
Tel *0471 30 07 88*
A sought-after brewery serving cold cuts, sausages, and desserts.

BRESSANONE: Fink €
Regional Italian
Via Portici Minori 4, 39042
Tel *0472 83 48 83* **Closed** *Tue dinner, Wed; 3 wks May*
Dining areas comprise elegant seating upstairs, and more casual rooms on the ground floor. Classic local cuisine revisited with flair.

BRUNICO: Oberraut €
Regional Italian
Via Ameto 1, Località Amaten, 39031
Tel *0474 55 99 77* **Closed** *Thu; 2 wks Jan*
Nestled in the countryside, this Tyrolean-style guesthouse specializes in game and seasonal dishes.

CALDARO: Ristorante Ritterhof €
Regional Italian
Weinstrasse 1A, 39052
Tel *0471 96 33 30* **Closed** *Sun dinner; Mon*
Set in a charming chalet with views over the lake. Fine fare and seasonally changing menu.

CERMES: Restaurant Miil €€
Fine Dining
Gampenstrasse 1, 39010
Tel *0473 56 37 33* **Closed** *Sun, Mon; 2 wks Jan*
Head to the Kränzelhof wine estate for a modern take on classic fare.

For more information on types of restaurants *see p579*

GUDON: Unterwirt €€
Regional Italian
Chiusa (Klausen), 39043
Tel *0472 84 40 00* **Closed** *Sun, Mon; 2 wks mid-Jun*
Chef Thomas Haselwanter's homemade breads are a tasty introduction to the seasonal menu.

LEVICO TERME: Boivin €
Regional Italian
Via Garibaldi 9, 38056
Tel *0461 70 16 70* **Closed** *lunch (except Sun, Jul, Aug), Mon; 2 wks Jan*
Cozy *trattoria* serving classic dishes such as potato dumplings stuffed with cheese and walnuts.

ROVERETO: Novecento €
Regional Italian
Corso Rosmini 82d, 38068
Tel *0464 43 54 54* **Closed** *Sun*
Run by the Zani family, this restaurant is renowned for its homemade pasta and pizza.

TRENTO: Happy Hour €
Seafood
Via Perini 57, 38122
Tel *0461 39 23 94* **Closed** *Sun dinner, Mon*
Pleasantly informal, with a menu that changes daily, according to the top picks from the fish market.

TRENTO: Osteria Alle Due Spade €€
Regional Italian
Via Don Rizzi 11, 38122
Tel *0461 23 43 43* **Closed** *Sun, Mon lunch; last 2 wks Jun*
Welcoming cellar restaurant serving traditional fare including game and freshwater fish.

VAL SENALES: Zur Goldenen Rose €€
Regional Italian
Kartaus 29, 39020
Tel *0473 67 91 30* **Closed** *Apr 20–May 25; Nov 10–Dec 5*
Explore the surrounding countryside and then unwind at this excellent hotel restaurant.

Lombardy

BELLAGIO: Albergo Ristorante Silvio €
Regional Italian
Via Carcano 12, 22021
Tel *031 95 03 22* **Closed** *Nov–mid-Mar*
Enjoy freshwater fish on a vine-clad terrace. Offers fishing trips.

BELLAGIO: Barchetta €€
Regional Italian
Salita Mella 13, 22021
Tel *031 95 13 89* **Closed** *Tue; Nov–Easter*
A creative Mediterranean menu, including fresh fish and homemade desserts.

BERGAMO: Colleoni dell'Angelo €€
Modern Italian
Piazza Vecchia 7, 24129
Tel *035 23 25 96* **Closed** *Mon*
Offers excellent service and imaginative cuisine.

BERGAMO: Vineria Cozzi €€
Enoteca
Via Colleoni 22, 24129
Tel *035 23 88 36* **Closed** *1 wk end Jan, 1 wk Jun*
A century-old Bergamo favorite serving local dishes.

BERGAMO: Roof Garden €€€
Mediterranean
Piazzale della Repubblica 6, 24122
Tel *035 36 61 59* **Closed** *Sat lunch, Sun*
This rooftop restaurant offers great views, a fusion of world flavors, and Mediterranean dishes.

BORMIO: Al Filò €
Regional Italian
Via Dante 6, 23032
Tel *0342 90 17 32* **Closed** *Mon & Tue lunch; 3 wks Jun, 3 wks Nov*
Dishes based on game, cured meats, and mushrooms are served in a converted barn.

BRESCIA: Osteria Delle Streghe €
International
Via Sorbana 72, 25125
Tel *030 32 12 15* **Closed** *Sat lunch, Sun; 2 wks Aug, 2 wks Dec*
Serves grilled meats, including kangaroo. Reservations required.

BRESCIA: Trattoria Mezzeria €
Regional Italian
Via Trieste 66, 25121
Tel *030 40 306* **Closed** *Sun, Aug*
Try the homemade *gnocchi di zucca* (pumpkin dumplings) in this busy little *trattoria.*

The welcoming entrance to Barchetta, in Bellagio, which specializes in local cuisine

CANTÙ: Le Querce €
Modern Italian
Via Marche 27, 22063
Tel *031 73 13 36* **Closed** *Mon, Tue; 3 wks Aug; Dec 27–Jan 6*
Set amid oak and rhododendron, Le Querce serves local dishes and offers a rich selection of wines.

CASTELVECCANA: Sant'Antonio €
Traditional Italian
Località Sant'Antonio, 21010
Tel *334 276 65 85* **Closed** *Sep–May (except weekends & public hols)*
Trattoria set in an old farmhouse overlooking Lake Maggiore. Try the local cheeses and cured meats.

COMO: Al Giardino €
Regional Italian
Via Monte Grappa 52, 22100
Tel *031 26 50 16* **Closed** *Sun dinner, Mon; 2 wks Aug*
Child-friendly restaurant serving local and regional specialties.

DK Choice

COMO: L'Angolo del Silenzio €
Regional Italian
Viale Lecco 25, 22100
Tel *031 377 21 57* **Closed** *Mon & Tue lunch, 2 wks Aug*
This reasonably priced *osteria*, just a few steps from the cathedral and lake, offers homemade pasta, meat, game, and fish dishes in a friendly atmosphere. Try the wild boar with red currant sauce and Roquefort. An inexpensive one-dish lunch is available on weekdays, and gluten-free dishes are available upon request. Book ahead.

COMO: Sant'Anna 1907 €
Regional Italian
Via Turati 3, 22100
Tel *031 50 52 66* **Closed** *Sat lunch, Sun*
Creative local cuisine, including seafood and vegetarian options.

CREMONA: Il Violino €€
Traditional Italian
Via Sicardo 3, 26100
Tel *0372 46 10 10* **Closed** *Tue*
Traditional local cuisine is served in this elegant restaurant.

GARGNANO DEL GARDA: La Tortuga €€
Modern Italian
Via XXIV Maggio 5, 25084
Tel *0365 712 51* **Closed** *Tue; Mar–Oct: lunch*
Light, imaginative cuisine in this renowned lakeside restaurant.

ISEO: Trattoria Al Castello €€
Modern Italian
Via Mirolte 53, 25049
Tel *030 98 12 85* **Closed** *Mon–Fri lunch, Wed; 2 wks Jan; 10 days Nov*
Classic and creative dishes in a restored 17th-century wine cellar in the historic center of Iseo.

LAKE COMO:
Locanda dell'Isola Comacina €€
Seafood
Isola Comacina, 22010
Tel *034 455 083* **Closed** *Tue; Nov–Mar*
A unique experience on this wonderful island, deserted except for this spot serving fresh fish.

LECCO: Osteria del Filet €
Regional Italian
Corso Matteotti 71, 23900
Tel *0341 28 30 17* **Closed** *Jun–Sep: Sun; Oct–May: Thu*
Offers grilled meat, fish, and local salami. A fixed-price two-course lunch is offered on weekdays.

LECCO:
Antica Osteria Casa di Lucia €€
Fine Dining
Via Lucia 27, Località Acquate, 23900
Tel *0341 49 45 94* **Closed** *Sat lunch, Sun; 2 wks Aug*
A superb gourmet restaurant set in a 17th-century house.

LEGNANO: Al Vintun Osteria €
Modern Italian
Via Bramante 95, 20025
Tel *0331 45 49 59* **Closed** *lunch, Sun*
Serves Italian fish and meat dishes. A fixed-price menu is offered every Thursday evening.

MANERBA DEL GARDA:
Capriccio €€€
Regional Italian
Piazza San Bernardo 6, Località Montinelle, 25080
Tel *0365 55 11 24* **Closed** *Tue; Jan–Feb*
Refined dining in an elegant setting with a breathtaking view of Lake Garda from all tables.

MANTUA:
Antica Osteria Ai Ranari €
Regional Italian
Via Trieste 11, 46100
Tel *0376 32 84 31* **Closed** *Mon*
Traditional Mantuan dishes, including the famous *tortelli di zucca* (pumpkin-filled pasta).

MANTUA: L'Ochina Bianca €
Regional Italian
Via Finzi 2, 46100
Tel *0376 32 37 00* **Closed** *Mon–Thu lunch; Jul–Aug: Fri–Sun lunch*
Regional dishes with a modern touch; try the local *torta sbrisolona*, a classic Mantuan sweet cake.

Casual dining at Pasta Madre, near Porta Romana, Milan

MANTUA: Il Cigno Trattoria dei Martini €€
Modern Italian
Piazza Carlo D'Arco 1, 46100
Tel *0376 32 71 01* **Closed** *Mon, Tue; Aug*
Fine fare complemented by an impeccable wine list.

MILAN: Be Bop Ristorante €
Pizzeria
Viale Col di Lana 4, 20136
Tel *02 83 76 972* **Closed** *Aug*
This restaurant offers gluten-free and vegetarian pizzas.

MILAN: Bianco Latte €
Mediterranean
Via Turati 30, 20121
Tel *02 60 08 61 77* **Closed** *Mon dinner; 2 wks Aug*
Stop here for a hearty brunch or light dinner. Great bread selection and excellent coffee.

MILAN: Erba Brusca €
Mediterranean
Alzaia Naviglio Pavese 286, 20144
Tel *02 87 38 07 11* **Closed** *Mon, Tue*
This small restaurant has its own kitchen garden, where the creative cuisine can be enjoyed alfresco.

MILAN: Omelette e Baguette €
Bistro
Via Pollaiuolo 9, 20159
Tel *02 688 46 87* **Closed** *Mon; Aug*
Burgers, sandwiches, quiches, and salads to eat in or take out.

MILAN: Osteria Brunello €
Regional Italian
Corso Garibaldi 117, 20121
Tel *02 659 29 73* **Closed** *lunch; 2 wks Aug*
Dishes based on Tuscan traditions; try the *pappardelle* (broad, flat pasta) with wild boar.

MILAN: Pasta Madre €
Modern Italian
Via Bernardino Corio 8, 20135
Tel *02 55 19 00 20* **Closed** *Sun; Aug*
Contemporary decor with a relaxed atmosphere and creative Italian cuisine. Gluten-free desserts available.

MILAN: Premiata Pizzeria €
Pizzeria
Via Alzaia Naviglio Grande 2, 20144
Tel *02 89 40 06 48*
A great pizzeria with delicious toppings like salami, gorgonzola cheese, and truffle oil. Casual dining on shared tables.

MILAN: Trattoria Aurora €
Traditional Italian
Via Savona 23, 20144
Tel *02 89 40 49 78* **Closed** *Mon*
This upscale brasserie near the Navigli district offers hearty Piedmontese food. Finish your meal with a slice of *tiramisù*.

MILAN: U Barba €
Regional Italian
Via Decembrio 33, 20137
Tel *02 45 48 70 32* **Closed** *Mon, Tue–Fri lunch*
Friendly traditional Genoese *osteria* with a bocce ball court. Great fish and game dishes. Try the freshly made gnocchi.

MILAN:
Alla Cucina delle Langhe €€
Traditional Italian
Corso Como 6, 20144
Tel *02 65 54 279* **Closed** *Sun; last 3 wks Aug*
Delectable interpretations of classic Piedmontese fare, just a few steps from the outlet store 10 Corso Como.

MILAN: Da Giacomo €€
Regional Italian
Via Sottocorno 6, corner of Via B. Cellini, 20129
Tel *02 76 02 33 13* **Closed** *2 wks Aug, 2 wks Dec*
An insider Milanese address offering simply cooked fish and seafood in a friendly atmosphere.

For more information on types of restaurants *see p579*

Exquisite grounds of the lovely Locanda del Pilone di Alba, Alba

MILAN: Giglio Rosso €€
Fine Dining
Piazza Luigi di Savoia 2, 20124
Tel *02 669 41 74* **Closed** *Sat & Sun lunch; Aug, Dec 23–Jan 6*
This elegant restaurant offers innovative Tuscan dishes, staples such as variations of risotto, gnocchi, and ravioli.

DK Choice

MILAN:
Nobile Bistrò de Milan €€
Regional Italian
Corso Venezia 45, 20121
Tel *02 49 52 65 92* **Closed** *2 wks Aug*
This reasonably priced restaurant is a short walk from the Montenapoleone shopping area. Well-known Milanese chef Claudio Sadler offers traditional regional meat and fish dishes with a modern twist. Continental breakfast, lunch, afternoon tea, *aperitivo*, and dinner are all served in an informal atmosphere, with tables both indoors and in a private courtyard.

MILAN: Victoria €€
Pizzeria
Via Clerici 1, 20121
Tel *02 869 07 92*
A few steps behind La Scala, Victoria offers traditional fare and pizza in an Art Nouveau setting.

MILAN:
Il Ristorante Bulgari Hotel €€€
Fine Dining
Via Privata Fratelli Gabba 7/B, 20122
Tel *02 80 50 52 33*
A luxury dining experience a few steps from Via Montenapoleone.

MONTE ISOLA: La Foresta €€
Regional Italian
Via Peschiera 174, Maraglio, 25050
Tel *030 988 62 10* **Closed** *Wed; 10 days Dec*
Family-run lakeside restaurant serving fresh Lake Iseo fish; sun-dried salted fish is a specialty.

PAVIA: Le Tre Torri €
Pizzeria
Via Lazzaro Spallanzani 6, 27100
Tel *0382 30 28 20* **Closed** *Sun, Mon, Sat lunch; Aug*
This restaurant offers a varied selection of pizza and pasta dishes.

PAVIA: La Locanda Vecchia Pavia al Mulino €€
Regional Italian
Via al Monumento 5, Località Certosa, 27012
Tel *0382 92 58 94* **Closed** *Mon; Apr–Oct: Tue lunch; Nov–Mar: Sun dinner*
Located on the grounds of the Certosa di Pavia, this restaurant offers local specialties.

SALÒ: Osteria dell'Orologio €
Traditional Italian
Via Butturini 26, 25087
Tel *0365 29 01 58* **Closed** *Wed; 1 wk end Jan, 1 wk end Nov*
This bistro offers great-value, traditional, local cuisine and a reasonably priced wine list.

SALÒ:
Antica Trattoria alle Rose €€
Regional Italian
Via Gasparo da Salò 33, 25087
Tel *0365 432 20* **Closed** *Wed; Nov*
A traditional *trattoria* offering lake fish, local dishes, and homemade pasta. There is a delicious selection of desserts.

SALÒ: La Campagnola €€
Modern Italian
Via Brunati 11, 25087
Tel *0365 22 153* **Closed** *Mon, Tue lunch*
One of the oldest establishments around Lake Garda, La Campagnola has a extensive selection of dishes, with a separate steak menu and an extensive wine list. Book ahead.

Valle d'Aosta and Piedmont

ACQUI TERME: La Schiavia €
Regional Italian
Vicolo della Schiavia, Acqui Terme, 15011
Tel *0144 559 39* **Closed** *Sun; 3 wks Aug*
Piedmontese and Ligurian cuisine in a renovated ancient palace. Extensive wine list. Reservations required.

ALBA:
Ristorante Madonna di Como €
Regional Italian
Frazione Madonna di Como 31, 12051
Tel *017 336 33 21* **Closed** *Tue*
Set in the hills above Alba and with panoramic views, this restaurant offers regional dishes.

DK Choice

ALBA:
Locanda del Pilone di Alba €€
Regional Italian
Strada della Cicchetta Frazione Madonna di Como 34, 12051
Tel *0173 36 66 16* **Closed** *Tue, Wed (Oct–Nov: Tue, Wed lunch); Jan–Feb*
Set in a stunning location, this converted *cascina* (barn) has views over the Alps. The menu features classic Piedmontese cuisine with Neapolitan touches. Each dish is served with a carefully selected wine. The wide range of desserts are delicious. Cooking classes and wine tasting are also offered.

ALBA: Piazza Duomo €€€
Regional Italian
Piazza Risorgimento 4, 12050
Tel *0173 36 61 67* **Closed** *Sun dinner, Mon; 2 wks Aug, 3 wks Dec–Jan*
Gourmet fare and impeccable service on offer near the main square of Alba.

ALESSANDRIA: Il Grappolo €€
Regional Italian
Via Casale 28, 15121
Tel *0131 25 32 17* **Closed** *Mon dinner, Tue*
Located in a 17th-century palace. Offers Piedmontese food with a modern twist; there's also a very good wine list.

AOSTA: Grotta Azzurra €
Pizzeria
Via Croce di Citta' 97, 11100
Tel *0165 26 24 74* **Closed** *Wed; Jul*
Reasonably priced pizzeria in the town center. Varied menu features a delicious fish soup.

Key to prices *see p580*

AOSTA: Trattoria degli Artisti €€
Regional Italian
Via Maillet 5–7, 11100
Tel *0165 40 96 04* **Closed** *Sun, Mon; 15 days Jan, 15 days Nov*
On a cobbled street in the town center, this *trattoria* offers a regional menu and great home-made cakes and desserts.

AOSTA: Il Vecchio Ristoro €€€
Regional Italian
Via Tourneuve 4, 11100
Tel *0165 332 38* **Closed** *Wed*
This restaurant in an old water mill uses local ingredients to make creative dishes.

ARONA: Il Calicanto €€
Mediterranean
Piazza Nazario Sauro 6, 28041
Tel *0322 24 33 50* **Closed** *Mon*
A well-chosen wine list accompanies fish and meat dishes of high quality.

DK Choice

ARONA: La Taverna del Pittore €€
Fine Dining
Piazza del Popolo 39, 28041
Tel *0322 24 33 66* **Closed** *Mon*
With a veranda offering stunning views of the Rocca di Angera, this restaurant whips up creative Italian cuisine using seafood, fish, and meat. Dishes include ravioli with truffles, tagliolini with lobster sauce, and grilled beef fillet with porcini mushrooms. The menu is presented on an artist's palette, owing to the restaurant's past as a meeting place for painters.

ASTI: L'Angolo del Beato €
Regional Italian
Vicolo Cavalleri 2, 14100
Tel *0141 53 16 68* **Closed** *Sun*
Family-run spot in a medieval setting offering Piedmontese dishes; try the varied antipasti.

ASTI: Gener Neuv €€
Traditional Italian
Lungo Tanaro dei Pescatori 4, 14100
Tel *0141 55 72 70* **Closed** *Sun, Mon dinner*
Family-run restaurant near the river with excellent local cuisine; reservations required.

ASTI: Osteria da Marisa al Castello €€
Regional Italian
Piazza Castello 1, 14100
Tel *0141 20 41 15* **Closed** *Mon, Tue*
Set in an 18th-century castle overlooking the Monferrato hills. Excellent Piedmontese cuisine.

BRA: Battaglino €
Regional Italian
Piazza Roma 18, 12042
Tel *0172 41 25 09* **Closed** *Sun dinner, Mon; 2 wks Jan, 3 wks Aug*
Traditional Piedmontese meat dishes offered in this convivial restaurant in the heart of Bra.

BRA: Guido Ristorante €€
Regional Italian
Via Fossano 19, 12042
Tel *0172 45 84 22* **Closed** *Mon, Tue–Fri: lunch; 2 wks Jan, 1st wk Aug*
Located inside the castle of Pollenzo. Refined regional meat and fish dishes à la carte, or a high-price tasting menu.

BREUIL-CERVINIA: Al Solito Posto €
Regional Italian
Via Meynet 10 11021
Tel *0166 94 91 26*
Charming, rustic restaurant with a good fixed-price menu.

BREUIL-CERVINIA: Les Neiges d'Antan €€
French
Cretes Perreres
Tel *0166 94 87 75* **Closed** *May–mid-Jun, mid-Sep–end Oct*
This restaurant-cum-hotel serves refined rustic and rich mountain fare accompanied by great wines.

CANNOBIO: Del Lago €
Traditional Italian
Via Nazionale 2, Località Carmine Inferiore, 28822
Tel *0323 705 95* **Closed** *Tue, Wed lunch; Nov*
Simple yet imaginative dishes and views of Lake Maggiore.

CANNOBIO: Osteria Vino Divino €
Modern Italian
Strada Valle Cannobina 1, 28822
Tel *0323 719 19* **Closed** *Wed; Jan–Feb*

Stunning views of the Rocca di Angera from La Taverna del Pittore, Arona

Traditional dishes reinvented with a twist in a converted 19th-century stable block. Good wine.

CANNOBIO: Lo Scalo €€
Seafood
Piazza Vittorio Emanuele 32, 28822
Tel *0323 714 80* **Closed** *Apr & Oct: Wed; Nov–Easter*
Daily catch of lake fish baked in foil, plus an array of shellfish and local produce.

CASALE MONFERRATO: La Torre €€
Modern Italian
Via Candiani d'Olivola 36,15033
Tel *0142 702 95* **Closed** *Tue, Wed lunch; 3 wks Aug*
La Torre offers creative regional cuisine and has a good wine list.

CHIUSA SAN MICHELE: Ristorante della Sacra €
Mediterranean
Piazzale della Sacra di San Michele, 10057
Tel *011 93 98 43* **Closed** *Apr–mid-Oct: Mon; mid-Oct–end Mar: Mon, Tue, Wed*
Good-quality café, hotel, and restaurant next to the famous Sacra San Michele monastery.

COGNE: Lou Rossignon €
Traditional Italian
Rue Mines de Cogne 22, 11012
Tel *0165 740 34* **Closed** *Mon dinner, Tue (except Aug, Dec–Feb); May, Nov*
Traditional Alpine and local fare in a cozy mountain taverna.

COSSANO BELBO: Trattoria della Posta da Camulin €
Regional Italian
Corsi Fratelli Negro 3, 12054
Tel *0141 881 26* **Closed** *Sun dinner, Mon; mid-Jul–mid-Aug*
Friendly, century-old *trattoria* serving regional dishes and homemade pasta.

COSTIGLIOLE D'ASTI: Caffè Roma €
Traditional Italian
Piazza Umberto I 14, 14037
Tel *0141 96 65 44* **Closed** *Mon; 1 wk end Feb, 1 wk Jun*
A wine bar at the foot of the castle with light dishes in a cozy atmosphere.

COSTIGLIOLE D'ASTI: Cascina Collavini €
Traditional Italian
Strada Traniera 24, 14037
Tel *0141 96 64 40* **Closed** *Tue dinner, Wed; 2 wks Jan, 2 wks Aug*
Simple, elegant restaurant located in an old farmhouse. The menu features traditional regional fare. Wines come from the local vineyard.

For more information on types of restaurants *see p579*

COURMAYEUR: Du Tunnel €
Pizzeria
Via Circonvallazione 80, 11013
Tel *0165 84 17 05* **Closed** *winter: Wed lunch*
A simple snack bar–pizzeria offering wood-fired pizzas and a convivial atmosphere.

COURMAYEUR: Cadran Solaire €€
Traditional Italian
Via Roma 122,11013
Tel *0166 84 46 09* **Closed** *Tue; May, 2 wks Nov*
Local dishes including *risotto alla Valdostana* (made with Fontina cheese) served in a cozy setting.

CUNEO: Osteria della Chiocciola €
Regional Italian
Via Fossano 1, 12100
Tel *0171 662 77* **Closed** *Sun*
Top-quality regional cuisine. Homemade classics such as gnocchi, ravioli, and risotto are served with excellent wine.

CUNEO: La Ciau del Tornavento €€
Regional/Modern Italian
Piazza Baracco 7, 12050
Tel *0173 63 83 33* **Closed** *Wed, Thu lunch; Feb*
Piedmontese dishes are served in a dining room with wonderful views of rolling vineyards..

DOMODOSSOLA: Antica Ristorante Piemonte da Sciolla €
Regional Italian
Piazza della Convenzione 4, 28845
Tel *0324 24 26 33* **Closed** *Sun dinner, Wed; 10 days Jan, 1 wk Aug, 1 wk Sep*
Known for its local mountain fare of hearty meat and game dishes.

IVREA: Trattoria Boccon Divino €
Regional Italian
Via Aosta 47,10015
Tel *0125 489 98* **Closed** *Thu*
A small *trattoria* in the historic center of Ivrea serving traditional regional cuisine.

NOVARA: I Due Ladroni €
Traditional Italian
Corso Cavallotti 15, 28100
Tel *0321 62 45 81* **Closed** *Sun*
Classic cuisine in a 16th-century palazzo in the heart of town. Excellent food with great flavors.

NOVARA: Osteria Del Laghetto €€
Regional Italian
Via Case Sparse 11, 28100
Tel *0321 47 29 62* **Closed** *Sun; 10 days Aug, Dec 24–Jan 7*
Truffles, mushrooms, and fish are offered at this restaurant set in its own grounds. Book ahead.

Rustic and charming entrance of the popular Al Sorriso, Soriso

ORTA SAN GIULIO: Ristoro Olina €
Traditional Italian
Via Olina 40, 28016
Tel *0322 90 56 56* **Closed** *Wed; mid-Nov–mid-Dec*
Serves homemade pasta. Local mushrooms and truffles feature on the menu, as do fish dishes.

ORTA SAN GIULIO: Villa Crespi €€€
Modern Italian
Via Fava 18, 28016
Tel *0322 91 19 02* **Closed** *Mar–Dec: Mon, Tue (except Apr–Oct: Tue dinner)*
Set in a 19th-century folly, this restaurant offers high-level gastronomy and a vast wine list.

RIVOLI: Combal.Zero €€€
Modern Italian
Il Castello, Piazza Mafalda di Savoia 62, 10098
Tel *010 956 52 25* **Closed** *Sun, Mon, Sat lunch; Aug*
Located in the grounds of the Castello di Rivoli, this restaurant offers a creative Italian menu.

DK Choice

SAINT VINCENT: Le Grenier €€
Modern Italian
Piazza Monte Zerbion 1, 11010
Tel *0166 51 01 38* **Closed** *Mon–Fri lunch, Wed; Jul*
Housed in an old barn, where soft lighting and a copper fireplace create a warm ambience. Try the *carpaccio di filetto* (thin slices of raw beef) with curry sauce, the venison, or the *ravioli di carciofi e robiola con gamberi rossi* (pasta filled with artichokes, robiola cheese, and shrimp). Ample choice of Italian and French wines and a good cheese selection.

SESTRIERE: La Vineria del Colle €€
Enoteca
Via Assietta 1, 10058
Tel *0122 764 76* **Closed** *Mon; May, Oct*
Housed in an old wine cellar next to the ski slopes, this *enoteca* combines traditional flavors with contemporary tastes.

SORISO: Al Sorriso €€€
Regional Italian
Via Roma 18, 28016
Tel *0322 98 32 28* **Closed** *Mon, Tue; 1 wk Jan, 10 days Aug*
Renowned for its good, creative cuisine with a range of seasonal specialties. Book ahead.

STRESA: Il Vicoletto €€
Modern Italian
Vicolo del Poncivo 3, 28838
Tel *0323 93 21 02* **Closed** *Nov–Mar: Thu*
Piedmontese cuisine including classic dishes with a touch of creativity. Good wine cellar.

STRESA: Piemontese €€
Regional Italian
Via Mazzini 25, 28838
Tel *0323 30 235* **Closed** *Mon; Dec–Jan*
Intimate family-run restaurant with interesting versions of local fare. There is also a pretty alfresco terrace for summer dining.

TORTONA: Aurora Girarrosto €
Regional Italian
Strada Statale per Genova 13, 15057
Tel *0131 86 30 33* **Closed** *2 wks Aug*
The specialty here is barbecued meats, with all produce coming from local organic farmers.

TURIN: Birilli €€
Modern Italian
Strada Val San Martino 6, 10131
Tel *011 819 05 67* **Closed** *1st wk Jan; Oct–May: Sun*
Hearty home cooking offering a good variety of pasta, grilled fish, and meat dishes.

TURIN: Dai Saletta €€
Regional Italian
Via Belfiore 37, 10126
Tel *011 668 78 67* **Closed** *Sun; 1st week Jan, Aug*
Typical *trattoria* ambience. Has a classic Piedmontese menu and a good wine list. Good selection of homemade desserts.

TURIN: La Porta Rossa €€
Seafood
Via Passalacqua 3/B, 10122
Tel *011 53 08 16* **Closed** *Sat lunch, Sun; Aug 7, Dec 25–Jan 6*
Serving fresh fish accompanied by fine wines.

Key to prices *see p580*

TURIN: Neuv Caval' Brons €€€
Fine Dining
Piazza San Carlo 155, 10123
Tel *011 53 90 30*
Set in a beautiful square, this restaurant offers Piedmontese dishes with an international twist.

VENARIA REALE: Il Convito della Venaria €
Regional Italian
Via Andrea Mensa 37G, 10078
Tel *011 459 83 92* **Closed** *Sun dinner, Mon*
A menu of meat and fish dishes, pizza cooked in a wood-fired oven, and homemade desserts.

VERBANIA PALLANZA: Osteria del Castello €
Enoteca
Piazza Castello 9, 28921
Tel *0323 51 65 79* **Closed** *Sun; 1 wk Dec*
A local favorite serving pasta and Piedmontese beef. Good wine list.

VERBANIA PALLANZA: Osteria dell 'Angolo €
Regional Italian
Piazza Garibaldi 35, 28048
Tel *0323 55 63 62* **Closed** *Mon; Nov*
Typical regional taverna offering fish dishes and Piedmontese and Lombardy cuisine. Book ahead.

VERBANIA PALLANZA: Milano €€
Regional Italian
Corso Zanitello 2, 28922
Tel *0323 55 68 16* **Closed** *Tue; Nov–Easter*
Choose from a selection of fish served with organic vegetables.

VERCELLI: Acqua Pazza €
Pizzeria
Corso Gastaldi 25, 13100
Tel *0161 21 74 20* **Closed** *Wed*
In addition to a range of pizzas, this centrally located restaurant also offers Vercellese dishes.

VERCELLI: Il Giardinetto €
Regional Italian
Via Sereno 3, 13100
Tel *0161 25 72 30* **Closed** *Mon; 1 wk Jan, 3 wks Aug*
Housed in a 19th-century villa, this restaurant serves delicious fare using Piedmontese delicacies.

VERCELLI: Il Paiolo €
Regional Italian
Viale Garibaldi 72, 13100
Tel *0161 25 05 77* **Closed** *Thu; mid-Jul–mid-Aug*
A *trattoria* set in the rice-growing country. Serves excellent risotto.

Liguria

DK Choice

CAMOGLI: La Cucina di Nonna Nina €€
Regional Italian
Via Molfino 126, 16032
Tel *0185 77 38 35* **Closed** *Wed; 10 days Jan, Nov*
This restaurant is nestled on a picturesque hill and encircled by citrus and olive trees. The chef produces excellent dishes, using top-quality local products including olive oil from the Ligurian coast, fish bought from local fishermen, and organic vegetables grown in its own garden. The focaccia, among other breads, cakes, and Ligurian pasta, are all homemade on the day of serving.

CAMOGLI: Rosa €€
Seafood
Via Jacopo Ruffini 13, 16032
Tel *0185 77 34 11* **Closed** *Tue, Wed lunch; Jun–Aug: Tue lunch*
Try the seafood and pasta in this Art Nouveau–style restaurant.

Spacious terrace with spectacular views, perfect for alfresco dining at Rosa in Camogli

CERVO: San Giorgio €€
Seafood
Via Volta 19, 18010
Tel *0183 40 01 75* **Closed** *Sep–Jun: Tue lunch; Oct–Easter: Mon dinner*
Popular, charming restaurant offering simple dishes. Book ahead.

GENOA: Da Genio €
Regional Italian
Salita San Leonardo 61r, 16128
Tel *010 58 84 63* **Closed** *Sun; Aug*
Sample the classic *trenette al pesto* (local pasta with pesto sauce) and fish dishes.

GENOA: Da O' Colla €
Regional Italian
Via alla Chiesa di Murta 10, 16162
Tel *010 740 85 79* **Closed** *Mon, Sun dinner*
Excellent home-cooked Ligurian cuisine. Located away from the city center, but worth the taxi fare.

GENOA: Cantine Squarciafico €€
Regional Italian
Piazza Invrea 3r, 16123
Tel *010 24 70 82 3* **Closed** *1 wk Jan, 2 wks Aug*
Ligurian wine bar offering local specialties including *stracci* (a type of lasagna).

LEVANTO: Cavour €€
Regional Italian
Piazza Cavour 1, 19015
Tel *0187 80 77 86* **Closed** *Mon; Dec–Jan*
Traditional *trattoria* specializing in local seafood dishes.

MANAROLA: La Scogliera €€
Regional Italian
Via Birolli 103, 19017
Tel *0187 92 07 47* **Closed** *Thu*
A pretty, family-run restaurant renowned for seafood specialties.

NERVI: Astor €
Regional Italian
Viale delle Palme 16, 16167
Tel *010 32 90 11*
Steps away from the seashore, Astor offers local cuisine in a simple and elegant setting.

PORTOFINO: Da U Batti €€
Seafood
Vico Nuovo 18, 16034
Tel *0185 26 93 79* **Closed** *Mon; Nov–mid-Jan*
A chic, intimate restaurant, in Liguria's most elegant town, offers exceptional fish cuisine.

PORTOVENERE: Da Iseo €€
Regional Italian
Calata Doria 9, 19025
Tel *0187 79 06 10* **Closed** *Wed; 20 days Nov*
This *trattoria* on the waterfront serves typical fish dishes.

For more information on types of restaurants *see p579*

PORTOVENERE: Le Bocche €€
Regional Italian
Calata Doria 102, 19025
Tel *0187 79 06 22* **Closed** *Jan; Sep–Apr: Tue*
Delicate Ligurian fish dishes served alfresco overlooking Portovenere.

RAPALLO: U'Giancu €
Regional Italian
Via San Massimo 78, 16035
Tel *0185 26 05 05* **Closed** *lunch, Thu; last 2 wks Dec*
Ligurian specialties are served here, and the walls are full of drawings by comic masters.

RAPALLO: Hostaria Vecchia Rapallo €€
Seafood
Via Cairoli 10, 16035
Tel *0185 500 53* **Closed** *Mon; Dec–1st wk Feb*
This elegant restaurant offers creative seafood dishes and a good selection of wine.

RAPALLO: La Nave €€
Seafood
Via Pomaro 15, 16035
Tel *0185 66 95 02* **Closed** *Wed*
Excellent location on the beach. Sample the *frittura di pesce* (fried fish) and homemade pesto.

DK Choice

SANREMO: Da Paolo e Barbara €€
Seafood
Via Roma 47, 18038
Tel *0184 53 16 53* **Closed** *Mon–Fri lunch, Wed, Thu; 1 wk Jan, 2 wks mid-Jun, Dec 17–28*
This small family-run restaurant serves local fresh fish, meat sourced from the nearby Langhe region, vegetables from its own farm, and homemade focaccia. Try the pasta with *gambero rosso di Sanremo* (local red prawn) or *trofie al Marò* (pasta with bean and mint sauce). A special "Saturday shopping" menu is offered to shoppers.

SANREMO: Da Vittorio €€
Seafood
Piazza Bresca 16, 18038
Tel *0184 50 19 24* **Closed** *2 wks Nov*
A traditional favorite close to the shore. Daily caught fish and seafood are the main draw.

SANTA MARGHERITA: Cinzia e Mario €
Seafood
Via Palestro 6, 16038
Tel *0185 28 75 05* **Closed** *Thu*
Good choice of four different tasting menus, together with à la carte dishes and a range of pizzas.

SANTA MARGHERITA: L'Insolita Zuppa €
Traditional Italian
Via Romana 7, 16038
Tel *0185 28 95 94* **Closed** *Wed; 2 wks Feb, Nov*
A cozy place offering traditional meat and fish dishes.

SESTRI LEVANTE: Ristorante Olimpo €€
Mediterranean
Via Della Chiusa 28, 16039
Tel *0185 426 61* **Closed** *Jan 7–Mar 22, Nov 4–Dec 26*
Overlooking the Baia del Silenzio, this restaurant serves fine cuisine with an emphasis on fish.

VERNAZZA: Gambero Rosso €€
Seafood
Piazza Marconi 7, 19018
Tel *0187 81 22 65* **Closed** *Thu; mid-Jan–Feb*
Inventive modern interpretations of Ligurian seafood dishes.

Emilia-Romagna

BOLOGNA: Antica Trattoria della Gigina €
Regional Italian
Via Stendhal 1, 40128
Tel *051 32 23 00*
Delivers a modern take on regional cuisine without compromising the flavors.

BOLOGNA: Battibecco €
Regional Italian
Via Battibecco 4, 40123
Tel *051 22 32 98*
Classic Bolognese cuisine and seafood dishes in this centrally located, elegant restaurant.

BOLOGNA: Pepperoni €
Pizzeria
Via di Barbiano 7, 40136
Tel *051 33 36 58*
Minimalist decor in this trendy spot serving high-quality pizza.

BOLOGNA: Pino €
Pizzeria
Via Goito 2, 40126
Tel *051 22 72 91*
Boisterous spot in the heart of town offering first-rate pizzas topped with quality ingredients.

BOLOGNA: Posta €
Regional Italian
Via della Grada 21, 41022
Tel *051 649 21 06* **Closed** *Mon, Sat lunch; last 2 wks Aug*
Enjoy Tuscan cuisine at this rustic spot with wood-beamed ceilings and terracotta-tiled floors.

BOLOGNA: Cesarina €€
Regional Italian
Via Santo Stefano 19, 40125
Tel *051 23 20 37* **Closed** *Mon, Tue lunch*
This over 100-year-old restaurant, situated beside an exquisite church, offers regional dishes.

BOLOGNA: Il Cantuccio €€
Seafood
Via Volturno 4, 40121
Tel *051 23 34 24* **Closed** *Mon, Tue; Sun lunch; Aug*
Fresh Mediterranean cuisine in an intimate setting. Family-run, with courteous service.

BOLOGNA: Marco Fadiga €€
Bistro
Via Rialto 23/C, 40124
Tel *051 22 01 18* **Closed** *Mon, Sun; 1 wk Aug*
Part bistro, part *osteria* offering local cuisine with a creative spin; classic French dishes are available too.

BOLOGNA: Pappagallo €€
Fine Dining
Piazza della Mercanzia 3, 40125
Tel *051 23 28 07*
Excellent traditional cuisine is served here, under dramatically high ceilings. The desserts are delicious and the cellar is well stocked.

Elegant seating at Sanremo's noted Da Paolo e Barbara restaurant

Key to prices *see p580*

BOLOGNA: Bitone €€€
Fine Dining
Via Emilia Levante 111, 40134
Tel *051 54 61 10* **Closed** *Mon, Tue; Aug*
Just outside the city center, this find is more than worth the trek. Fantastic Bolognese dishes and attentive service.

BOLOGNA: I Portici €€€
Fine Dining
Via dell'Indipendenza 69, 40121
Tel *051 421 85* **Closed** *Mon, Sun*
The Michelin-starred chef here creates traditional Bolognese and modern Italian cuisine. Romantic setting in a former theater.

CASTELL'ARQUATO: Da Faccini €€
Regional Italian
Località S. Antonio, 29014
Tel *0523 89 63 40* **Closed** *Wed; Jun, Jul*
In-season local ingredients decide the daily changing menu at this warm, family-run eatery.

FAENZA: La Pavona €
Regional Italian
Via Santa Lucia 45, 48018
Tel *0546 310 75* **Closed** *Tue, Sat lunch; 3 wks Jul*
Just outside the historic center, this rustic and cozy spot serves the favorites of Emilian cooking.

FERRARA: Ca d'Frara €
Regional Italian
Via del Gambero 4, 44121
Tel *0532 20 50 57* **Closed** *Tue, Wed*
A slightly sterile atmosphere does not detract from the quality of the Emilian cuisine; low prices.

FERRARA: Big Night-da Giovanni €€
Regional Italian
Largo Castello 38, 44121
Tel *0532 24 23 67* **Closed** *winter*
Large windows afford castle views at this restaurant serving traditional dishes from land and sea.

FIDENZA FORNIO: Osteria di Fornio €
Regional Italian
Via Fornio 78, 43036
Tel *0524 601 18* **Closed** *Mon dinner, Tue*
Tucked away in the countryside, this restaurant has a changing menu of regional delicacies.

MODENA: Al Boschetto da Loris €
Regional Italian
Via Due Canali Nord 218, 41122
Tel *059 25 17 59*
Housed in a 16th-century hunting lodge, this place serves home-cooked style meals.

DK Choice

MODENA: Osteria Francescana €€€
Fine Dining
Via Stella 22, 41121
Tel *059 21 01 18* **Closed** *Jan & Aug: Sat lunch, Sun*
This two-Michelin-starred restaurant is avant-garde and experimental. The regional specialty – Parmigiano Reggiano – is available in five different stages of aging, and the most notable dishes include ravioli with veal offal, chlorophyll, and black truffles. Sample the marinated suckling pig with cream of fennel, and the famous Modena balsamic vinegar.

PARMA: I Tri Siochètt €
Regional Italian
Strada Farnese-Vigheffio 74/A, 43125
Tel *0521 96 88 70* **Closed** *2 wks in Dec*
Named for the three "mad" siblings who opened this *trattoria* years ago. Hearty local cuisine.

PARMA: Parizzi €€
Fine Dining
Strada della Repubblica 71, 43100
Tel *0521 28 59 52* **Closed** *Mon; last 3 wks Aug*
Modern decor with spotlights and gold floors and a menu of contemporary and classic dishes.

PARMA: Le Viole €
Modern Italian
Strada Nuova di Castelnuovo, 60
Tel *0521 60 10 00* **Closed** *Jan 15; Jul & Aug: Mon, Sun (Aug 15–30); Dec–Feb: Wed, Thu (Feb 10)*
Seasonal produce inspires gastronomic inventions by the two sisters who run this friendly spot.

PIACENZA: Vecchia Piacenza €€
Modern Italian
Via Taverna/C.ne S. Bernardo 1, 29100
Tel *0523 30 54 62* **Closed** *Sun*
A husband and wife team combine innovative cuisine with original interior artwork.

PIACENZA: Antica Osteria del Teatro €€€
Fine Dining
Via Giuseppe Verdi 16, 29121
Tel *0523 32 37 77*
French-inspired choices include *foie gras* marinated in port and Armagnac.

RAVENNA: Antica Trattoria al Gallo 1909 €
Regional Italian
Via Maggiore 87, 48123
Tel *0544 21 37 75* **Closed** *Sun dinner, Mon, Tue*
The rustic exterior of this historic *trattoria* hides an Art Deco interior. Ample Emilian specialties.

Sophisticated at the Michelin-starred Osteria Francescana, Modena

RAVENNA: Ca de Ven €
Regional Italian
Via Corrado Ricci 24, 48121
Tel *0544 301 63* **Closed** *Mon*
Authentic eatery popular with locals. Shared tables available for a more casual dining experience.

RAVENNA: Bella Venezia €€
Regional Italian
Via 4 Novembre 16, 48121
Tel *0544 21 27 46* **Closed** *Sun; 3 wks Jan, 1 wk Jun*
Excellent pasta and fresh fish in a romantic, intimate setting. Great service and a central location.

RIMINI: Osteria de Borg €
Regional Italian
Via Forzieri 12, 47921
Tel *0541 560 74*
A rustic setting in which to sample meat specialties, local cheeses, and cured meats.

RIMINI: Dallo Zio €€
Seafood
Via Santa Chiara 16, 47921
Tel *0541 78 67 47*
The cuisine at this fresh, modern spot is inspired from the classic flavors of the Adriatic.

RIMINI: Europa €€
Seafood
Via Roma 51, 47922
Tel *0541 287 61*
Traditional yet inventive restaurant serving fresh fish and meat dishes.

RIMINI: Guido €€
Seafood
Lungomare Guido Spadazzi 12, 47924
Tel *0541 37 46 12* **Closed** *Mon; 1 wk Dec*
Cuttlefish, oysters, and calamari are just a few of the specialties served at this spot on the beach.

For more information on types of restaurants *see p579*

Florence

Bar 53 Bottega €
Enoteca **Map** 2 D3
Via di Santa Caterina d'Alesssandria 3, 50129
Tel *055 463 38 95* **Closed** *Sat*
There's a chilled vibe at this wine bar that's also a popular spot for breakfast and lunch. Free Wi-Fi.

Il Pizzaiuolo €
Pizzeria **Map** 4 E1
Via de' Macci 113, 50122
Tel *055 24 11 71* **Closed** *3 wks Aug, 1 wk Dec*
Treat yourself to a thick-crusted Neapolitan-style pizza.

Il Vegetariano €
Vegetarian **Map** 2 D3
Via delle Ruote 30, 50129
Tel *055 47 50 30* **Closed** *Mon, Sat & Sun lunch; 3 wks Aug, Christmas*
There is excellent value is to be had at this long-established restaurant. Service is meager, portions are not.

La Bussola €
Pizzeria **Map** 5 C3
Via Porta Rossa, 58 50123
Tel *055 293376*
Charming, low-key pizzeria with a wood-burning oven. The service is excellent, and the wine list surprisingly ample.

Ruth's €
Kosher/Vegetarian **Map** 2 E5
Via Luigi Carlo Farini 2, 50121
Tel *055 248 08 88* **Closed** *Fri dinner, Sat lunch, Jewish festivities*
Located beside the synagogue, this kosher restaurant serves Jewish-inspired recipes; many vegetarian and seafood options.

Tarocchi €
Pizzeria **Map** 6 E5
Via dei Renai 12, 50125
Tel *055 234 39 12* **Closed** *Mon*
Great prices at this off-the-beaten-path pizzeria. Pasta dishes are available, too.

Trattoria Zàzà €
Regional Italian **Map** 1 C4
Piazza del Mercato Centrale 26, 50123
Tel *055 21 54 11*
Traditional Florentine favorites from land and sea, as well as, vegetarian and gluten-free fare.

Da Kou €€
Japanese **Map** 5 C1
Via del Melarancio 19/r, 50123
Tel *055 28 29 22* **Closed** *Tue*
Fresh and authentic sushi prepared with skill; portions are generous. The decor is modern and informal.

DK Choice

Alle Murate €€
Regional Italian **Map** 6 E2
Via del Proconsolo 16/r, 50122
Tel *055 24 06 18* **Closed** *Sun lunch, Mon*
This unique restaurant offers a one-of-a-kind opportunity to combine Florentine art and food. Housed in a 14th-century palace, it boasts original frescoes on the walls and vaulted ceilings, hidden for centuries and uncovered in a painstaking restoration process. The excellent, understated local cuisine is a perfect companion to the stunning early-Renaissance art.

Dei Frescobaldi €€
Enoteca **Map** 6 D3
Via dei Magazzini 2, 50122
Tel *055 28 47 24* **Closed** *Mon lunch; 1 wk Jan, 3 wks Aug*
Sample top fine wines and meticulously matched dishes in a setting of frescoed walls and exposed stonework.

Ora d'Aria €€
Modern Italian **Map** 6 D4
Via dei Georgofili11/r, 50100
Tel *055 200 16 99* **Closed** *Sun, Mon lunch; 2 wks Jan, 2 wks Aug*
Tucked away in an alley, this place is well worth the hunt for its authentic specialty dishes.

Osteria Santo Spirito €€
Regional Italian **Map** 5 A5
Piazza Santo Spirito 16, 50125
Tel *055 238 23 83* **Closed** *Mon, public hols*
Tuscan specialties with a twist at this cozy eatery.

Pane e Vino €€
Modern Italian **Map** 3 A1
Piazza di Cestello 37/r, 50124
Tel *055 247 69 56*
Cozy and familial restaurant offering traditional Florentine dishes and more modern ones.

Bistrò Del Mare €€€
Fine Dining **Map** 5 C3
Lungarno Corsini 4/r, 50123
Tel *055 239 92 24* **Closed** *Mon; 1 wk Aug*
Steps away from Ponte Vecchio, this refined restaurant serves dishes inspired by old Tuscan recipes but brought up to date.

Cibrèo €€€
Modern Italian **Map** 4 E1
Via Andrea del Verrocchio 8/r, 50122
Tel *055 234 11 00* **Closed** *Mon; 3 wks Aug*
This trendy place delights diners with its take on local cuisine.

Interior of Pane e Vino, popular for traditional Florentine dishes, Florence

DK Choice

Enoteca Pinchiorri €€€
Fine Dining **Map** 4 E1
Via Ghibellina 87, 50122
Tel *055 24 27 57* **Closed** *Sun, Mon; Aug, public hols*
This triple Michelin-starred restaurant is considered by some to be the finest in Italy. Its modern, understated interior and soft lighting provide the ideal setting to indulge in any of the exquisite gastronomic creations. Specials include the ravioli with *taggiasche* olives and burrata cheese, and the roast pigeon with honey, spices, and breaded eggplant. The wine cellar is legendary. A private dining room is available.

Tuscany

AREZZO:
La Lancia d'Oro €€
Regional Italian
Piazza Grande 18, 52100
Tel *0575 210 33* **Closed** *Mon; 2 wks Feb, 2 wks Nov*
Hearty Tuscan meals served in a stunning setting with outdoor seating under *Vasari's Loggias* (Vasari's Corridor).

AREZZO:
Le Chiavi d'Oro €€
Modern Italian
Piazza San Francesco 7, 52100
Tel *0575 403 313* **Closed** *Mon; 1 wk Feb, 1 wk Aug*
This stylish Danish-designed restaurant is elegantly decorated with 1960s swivel stools and blond wood floors. The kitchen specializes in contemporary, regionally inspired cuisine.

Key to prices *see p580*

ARTIMINO: Da Delfina €€
Regional Italian
Via della Chiesa 1, 59015
Tel *055 871 80 74* **Closed** *Mon, Tue; 1 wk Jan, 1 wk Feb*
The chef's creations are inspired by his mother's cooking. Hidden away in a delightful walled town.

CORTONA: Hostaria la Bucaccia €
Regional Italian
Via Ghibellina 17, 52044
Tel *0575 606 039* **Closed** *Jan 15–30; Dec–Feb: Mon*
This restaurant has original features, built over a Roman road. Home cooking is served.

CORTONA: Il Falconiere €€€
Fine Dining
Località San Martino 370, 52044
Tel *0575 612 679* **Closed** *Jan 7–30*
Nestled among olive and cypress trees, this restaurant is out of a fantasy. Great place to sample exalted Tuscan cuisine.

ELBA: La Lucciola €€
Seafood
Lungomare Pino Nomellini 64, 57034
Tel *0565 976 395* **Closed** *Nov–Apr*
The catch of the day is served directly on the beach at this romantic and intimate spot.

ELBA: Publius €
Regional Italian
Piazza del Castagneto 11, 57030
Tel *0565 992 08* **Closed** *Mon; Nov–Mar*
A wide variety of dishes and an impressive wine cellar at this charming restaurant boasting fantastic sea views.

ELBA: Stella Marina €€
Seafood
Via Vittorio Emanuele II 1, 57037
Tel *0565 915 983* **Closed** *Mon*
Fish doesn't get much fresher than at this tiny restaurant on the edge of the port; excellent wine list.

LUCCA: Da Giulio in Pelleria €
Regional Italian
Via delle Conce 47, 55100
Tel *0583 559 48* **Closed** *3 wks Jan*
Prices are reasonable at this popular *trattoria* serving Tuscan fare such as polenta and *zuppa di farro* (bean and spelt soup).

LUCCA: La Tana dell'Orco €
Pizzeria
Viale Regina Margherita 225, 55100
Tel *389 023 32 34* **Closed** *Tue*
The concept is simple at this pizzeria just outside the city walls: minimal service and low prices.

LUCCA: Buca di Sant'Antonio €€
Regional Italian
Via della Cervia 3, 55100
Tel *0583 558 81* **Closed** *Sun dinner, Mon; 1 wk Jan, 1 wk Jun*
Ancient local recipes are lovingly prepared at this historic eatery in a medieval stable.

MONTALCINO: Il Boccon Divino €€
Regional Italian
Strada Provinciale Traversa dei Monti 201, 53024
Tel *0577 848 233* **Closed** *Tue*
Enjoy classic Tuscan dishes and admire the sweeping views of the countryside. Fantastic wines.

MONTE ARGENTARIO: Osteria dei Nobili Santi €€
Seafood
Le Piane, 58019
Tel *0564 833 015* **Closed** *Mon*
Good prices at this intimate restaurant serving plenty of delectable fish dishes.

MONTEPULCIANO: Osteria Acquacheta €
Regional Italian
Via del Teatro 22, 53045
Tel *0578 717 086* **Closed** *Tue*
This tiny, popular restaurant is always packed. The Tuscan meat dishes are a specialty.

The well-stocked wine cellar at Da Delfina in Artimino

MONTEPULCIANO: La Grotta €€
Regional Italian
Via di San Biagio 15, 53045
Tel *0578 757 479* **Closed** *Wed; Jan, Feb*
A restaurant set in a 16th-century building. The menu features expertly revisited Tuscan classics.

MONTERIGGIONI: Il Pozzo €€
Regional Italian
Piazza Roma 20, 53035
Tel *0577 304 127* **Closed** *Sun dinner, Mon; 2 wks Jan, 2 wks Feb*
Well located in the center of the walled town, this rustic *osteria* serves traditional fare.

PIENZA: Latte di Luna €
Regional Italian
Via San Carlo 2, 53026
Tel *0578 748 606* **Closed** *Tue*
Classic Tuscan dishes at this quaint, family-friendly eatery. Dont forget to try the locally produced Pecorino cheese.

PISA: La Taverna di Emma €
Modern Italian
Carlo Salomone Cammeo 50, 56122
Tel *050 555 003* **Closed** *Sun; 1 wk Feb, last wk Aug*
Simple local eatery with a talented chef who whips up imaginative yet tradition-inspired recipes. Gorgeous desserts.

PISA: Osteria del Porton Rosso €
Regional Italian
Via Porton Rosso 11, 56126
Tel *050 580 566* **Closed** *Mon*
The menu of classic Tuscan meat and seafood are scrawled on a blackboard at this eatery hidden in the backstreets.

PISA: V. Beni €€
Seafood
Piazza Chiara Gambacorti 22, 56125
Tel *050 250 67* **Closed** *Sun; 2 wks Aug*
Slightly off the tourist track, this favorite with the locals is housed in a rustic 600-year-old building.

PISA: A Casa Mia €
Regional Italian
Via Provinciale Calcesana 10, 56010
Tel *050 879 265* **Closed** *Sun; 1 wk Jan, Aug*
Traditional recipes are served with familial warmth in the one-time home of the owners.

PISTOIA: La Bottegaia €
Enoteca
Via Del Lastrone 17, 51100
Tel *0573 365 602* **Closed** *Mon; 2 wks Aug*
Cheeses, cured meats, tempting desserts, and, of course, plenty of fantastic bottles at this friendly, unpretentious wine bar.

For more information on types of restaurants *see p579*

The traditionally decorated dining area of Osterie le Logge in Siena

PRATO: Osteria Cibbè €
Regional Italian
Piazza Mercatale 49, 59100
Tel *0574 607 509* **Closed** *Sun; 3 wks Aug*
Try the traditional Tuscan recipes and comforting homemade desserts at this charming eatery.

SAN GIMIGNANO: Antica Macelleria €
Regional Italian
Via Dei Marsili 1/3, 53037
Tel *0577 942 228*
Pick your meat from the old-style butcher's counter and the chef will prepare it to your liking.

SAN GIMIGNANO: Dorandò €€
Regional Italian
Vicolo dell'Oro 2, 53037
Tel *0577 941 862* **Closed** *Dec–Feb*
Enjoy the Slow Food dining experience at Dorandò.

SAN SEPOLCRO: Ristorante da Ventura €
Regional Italian
Via Aggiunti Niccolò 30, 52037
Tel *0575 742 560* **Closed** *Sun dinner, Mon; 2 wks Aug*
Enjoy homemade delights at this family-run eatery. Try the slow-cooked veal, or truffle-filled ravioli.

DK Choice

SIENA: 53 Cento €
Enoteca
Viale Pietro Toselli 19, 53100
Tel *0577 050 169* **Closed** *Sun; 2 wks Aug*
This eclectic wine bar is open from breakfast to the early hours. The well-stocked cellar and the capable staff are happy to make suggestions. The cuisine is pan-Mediterranean with imaginative takes on Italian staples, including many vegetarian options. There is also an oyster bar.

SIENA: Enoteca i Terzi €
Enoteca
Via dei Termini 7, 53100
Tel *0577 443 29* **Closed** *Sun*
Airy, spacious wine bar with copious varieties of cheeses and smoked and cured meats.

SIENA: Grotta Santa Caterina da Bagoga €
Regional Italian
Via della Galluzza 26, 53100
Tel *0577 282 208* **Closed** *Sun dinner, Mon; 2 wks Jan, 1 wk Jul*
Tucked in a narrow backstreet, this authentic restaurant offers good food and great service.

SIENA: La Taverna di San Giuseppe €
Regional Italian
Via Giovanni Duprè 132, 53100
Tel *0577 422 86* **Closed** *Sun; 2 wks Jul, 2 wks Dec*
Rustic eatery with local flavors. Check out the wine cellar, carved from an ancient Etruscan dwelling.

SIENA: Trattoria Papei €
Regional Italian
Piazza del Mercato 6, 53100
Tel *0577 280 894*
This informal spot is run by an entire family, with mama preparing Tuscan specialties.

SIENA: Osteria le Logge €€
Modern Italian
Via del Porrione 33, 53100
Tel *0577 480 13* **Closed** *Sun; 1 wk Jan*
This lovely restaurant with traditional furnishings presents a novel interpretation of classic cuisine and has a fine wine list.

SIENA: Il Canto €€€
Modern Italian
Strada di Certosa 82, 53100
Tel *0577 288 180* **Closed** *Nov–Feb*
Siena's most experimental and creative restaurant offers a gastronomic adventure.

VIAREGGIO: Cabreo €€
Seafood
Via Firenze 14, 55049
Tel *0584 546 43* **Closed** *Sun; Nov*
Whatever is caught on any given day ends up on the plate at this authentic fish eatery. Meat dishes are available.

VIAREGGIO: Piccolo Principe €€€
Fine Dining
Piazza Giacomo Puccini 1, 55049
Tel *0584 40 11* **Closed** *Nov–May*
Creative and sophisticated cuisine served in a rooftop garden with magnificent sea views. Its Michelin star is well earned.

VOLTERRA: Enoteca del Duca €
Enoteca
Via di Castello 2, 56048
Tel *0588 815 10* **Closed** *Tue; Jan, Feb*
Cozy wine bar serving rustic snacks. There's also an elegant restaurant for full meals in the typical Tuscan tradition.

VOLTERRA: Il Sacco Fiorentino €
Regional Italian
Via Turazza 13, 56048
Tel *0588 885 37* **Closed** *Tue; 1 wk Jan*
An intriguing tasting menu, as well as numerous à la carte options, offering traditional Tuscan with international touches.

Umbria

ASSISI: I Monaci €
Pizzeria
Via Scalette 10, 06081
Tel *075 81 25 12*
A warm and rustic pizzeria in the heart of the medieval center.

ASSISI: La Fortezza €
Regional Italian
Vicolo della Fortezza 2b, 06081
Tel *075 81 29 93* **Closed** *Thu; Jul*
Mostly traditional cuisine, with some creative touches. Friendly but professional service and good price-quality ratio.

GUBBIO: Grotta dell'Angelo €€
Enoteca
Via Gioia 47, 06024
Tel *075 9271 747* **Closed** *Tue; Jan 7, Feb 7*
This rustic wine bar is carved into a 13th-century cave. Enjoy dining in the garden in summer.

GUBBIO: Taverna del Lupo €€
Regional Italian
Via Ansidei 6, 06024
Tel *075 92743 68* **Closed** *Mon*
Succulent local cuisine at this centrally located spot run by a husband and wife team.

Key to prices *see p580*

MONTEFALCO: Coccorone €
Regional Italian
Largo Tempestivi 11, 06036
Tel *074 2379 535* **Closed** *Wed*
Traditional seasonal ingredients, including truffles and porcini mushrooms, make for a fresh and authentic dining experience.

NORCIA: Beccofino €
Regional Italian
Piazza San Benedetto 12, 06046
Tel *0743 81 60 86* **Closed** *Wed; Dec 25*
Traditional Umbrian cuisine served in a simple setting. Ample wine cellar with over 250 labels.

NORCIA: Taverna de' Massari €€
Regional Italian
Via Roma 13, 06046
Tel *0743 81 62 18* **Closed** *Tue; 2 wks Jan, 1 wk Jul*
Intimate spot offering the time-honored cured meats and dishes that make this tiny town famous.

ORVIETO: Del Moro-Aronne €
Regional Italian
Via San Leonardo 7, 05018
Tel *0763 34 27 63* **Closed** *Tue*
Simple, home-style cooking is served up enthusiastically at this restaurant with low prices.

ORVIETO: La Volpe e l'Uva €
Regional Italian
Via Ripa Corsica 2, 05018
Tel *0763 34 16 12*
A wide variety of tempting options – even for vegetarians – at this bustling restaurant in town.

ORVIETO: Duca di Orvieto €€
Regional Italian
Via della Pace 5, 05018
Tel *0763 34 46 63* **Closed** *Wed*
A family-run restaurant using centuries-old local recipes. Patient servers will explain the day's specials in detail.

Traditional rustic charm at the cozy Duca di Orvieto, Orvieto

ORVIETO: I Sette Consoli €€
Modern Italian
Piazza Sant'Angelo 1A, 05018
Tel *0763 343 911* **Closed** *Sun dinner, Wed*
Original and imaginative cuisine in a rustic yet dignified setting. Dine in the garden in summer, weather permitting.

PASSIGNANO SUL TRASIMENO: Cacciatori da Luciano €€€
Seafood
Lungolago Aganor Pompilj 3, 06061
Tel *075 827 210* **Closed** *Wed; Jan 6–30*
Fresh fish from the adjacent lake and delicacies from the sea are cooked using authentic recipes. Extensive wine list.

PERUGIA: Il Falchetto €
Modern Italian
Via Bartolo 20, 06123
Tel *075 5731 775* **Closed** *Mon*
Gorgeous little restaurant inside a medieval building, with seating on the piazza in summer. Classic Umbrian dishes fill the menu.

PERUGIA: La Botte €
Pizzeria
Via Volte della Pace 31, 06122
Tel *075 5722 679* **Closed** *Sun*
Simple, no-frills pizzeria serving time-honored family recipes.

PERUGIA: Antica Trattoria San Lorenzo €€
Modern Italian
Piazza Danti 19/a, 06122
Tel *075 5721 956*
Creative Umbrian-inspired cuisine at a cozy spot just behind the Duomo.

PERUGIA: Il Gradale €€
Modern Italian
Strada Montevile, 06126
Tel *075 5717 402*
A branch of Castello di Monterone's restaurants delights diners with a choice of light and sophisticated dishes.

PERUGIA: Il Postale €€€
Fine Dining
Strada Montevile 3, 06126
Tel *075 5724 214* **Closed** *Sun dinner, Mon, Tue; Jan 15–Feb 15*
Set within a wonderful castle location, this award-winning restaurant serves meals rich with local ingredients.

SPOLETO: Il Tempio del Gusto €
Modern Italian
Via Arco di Druso 11, 06049
Tel *0743 471 21* **Closed** *Thu*
Stone floors and small tables create an intimate atmosphere in this restaurant serving creative and top-notch cuisine.

DK Choice

SPOLETO: Il Tartufo €
Regional Italian
Piazza Giuseppe Garibaldi 24, 06049
Tel *0743 40 236* **Closed** *Sun dinner, Mon*
The decor may be simple and old-fashioned, but the local truffles that this restaurant is proudly named for make it worth a special trip. The owners, members of the family who opened the restaurant in 1927, are dedicated to creating dishes based on traditional local recipes. Look out for the ancient Roman paving tiles in one of the dining rooms. In good weather, it's possible to eat outside on the bustling piazza.

TODI: Antica Hostaria della Valle €
Modern Italian
Via Augusto Ciuffelli 19, 06059
Tel *075 894 48 48* **Closed** *Mon*
Imaginative gastronomic delights at this cozy and welcoming *osteria*. The homemade pasta is the star of the show.

TODI: Umbria €€
Regional Italian
Via San Bonaventura 13, 06059
Tel *075 894 27 37* **Closed** *Tue*
Traditional cuisine is carefully prepared at this legendary restaurant. There is a dining terrace with picturesque views.

Le Marche

ANCONA: Boccon Divino €
Regional Italian
Via Giacomo Matteotti 13, 60121
Tel *071 572 69* **Closed** *Sun; Aug*
Classic Marchegiana cuisine is served up here by a young but capable staff.

ANCONA: La Moretta €
Regional Italian
Piazza Plebiscito 52, 60121
Tel *071 20 23 17* **Closed** *Sun; Jan 1–6*
This traditional restaurant has been in the same family for over 100 years. Sample the excellent *stoccafisso* (dried cod) in broth.

ANCONA: Sale Grosso €€
Modern Italian
Via Guglielmo Marconi 3, 60125
Tel *071 207 52 79*
Imaginative reinvention of Italian cuisine using local ingredients from land and sea. The decor is fresh and minimalist.

For more information on types of restaurants *see p579*

ASCOLI PICENO: Gallo d'Oro €
Regional Italian
Corso Vittorio Emanuele 54, 63100
Tel *0736 25 35 20* **Closed** *Sun dinner, Mon*
Despite the sophisticated interior, prices are reasonable at this spot serving regional fare.

ASCOLI PICENO: Del Corso €€
Seafood
Corso Giuseppe Mazzini 277, 63100
Tel *0736 25 67 60* **Closed** *3 wks Jan, Dec 2*
Tiny stone-walled restaurant located in a historic palazzo. Most dishes on the changing menu are fish-based.

LORETO: Andreina €
Regional Italian
Via Buffolareccia 14, 60025
Tel *071 97 01 24* **Closed** *Tue, Wed*
Rustic with a few modern touches. Tuscan specialties reign, with tempting options from the grill.

LORETO: Vecchia Fattoria €
Regional Italian
Via Manzoni 19, 60025
Tel *071 97 89 76*
This converted farmhouse offers classic regional dishes in a welcoming family atmosphere.

PESARO: Da Gennaro €
Seafood
Via Santa Marina Alta 30/1, 61100
Tel *0721 273 21* **Closed** *Sun dinner, Mon; Sep 1–20*
Perched in the mountains 4 miles (7 km) west of the sea, this is one of the most authentic eateries in town.

PESARO: Il Commodoro €€
Enoteca
Viale Trieste 269, 61121
Tel *0721 326 80* **Closed** *Mon*
This inviting modern spot serves up fresh fish and much more. Cozy wine bar attached.

PESARO: Da Alceo €€€
Seafood
Strada Panoramica Ardizio 101, 61100
Tel *0721 513 60*
A panoramic seaside terrace provides an exquisite setting in which to sample some of the best seafood in the area.

SAN MARINO: Righi la Taverna €€€
Fine Dining
Piazzale della Libertà 10, 47825
Tel *0549 99 11 96* **Closed** *Sun dinner, Mon; Jan, Feb*
The most famous restaurant in this republic serves a mix of age-old and modern Italian cuisine.

URBANIA: Big Ben €
Regional Italian
Corso V. Emanuele 61, 61049
Tel *0722 31 97 95*
Marchegiana specialties such as truffles, snails, and wild fennel are offered at this restaurant.

URBINO: Guanábana €
Modern Italian
Via Giuseppe Mazzini 65, 61029
Tel *366 726 55 51*
This quirky little restaurant offers an interesting fusion of local and Venezuelan cuisines. The flavors are surprisingly complementary.

URBINO: Taverna degli Artisti €
Regional Italian
Via Donato Bramante 52, 61029
Tel *0722 26 76*
Opulent frescoed ceilings make a dramatic contrast to the simple home-style cooking.

URBINO: Antica Osteria da la Stella €€
Regional Italian
Via Santa Margherita 1, 61029
Tel *0722 320228*
This historic restaurant counts famous painters Raphael and Piero della Francesca among its one-time clientele. Elegant interior with a cozy fireplace.

Rome

The Ancient Center

Enoteca Provincia Romana €€
Enoteca **Map** 3 A4
Largo di Foro Traiano 82-84, 00187
Tel *06 69 94 02 73* **Closed** *Sun & Mon dinner*
Both the wine list and the menu ingredients are refreshingly local at this *enoteca*.

Aroma €€€
Fine Dining **Map** 7 1A
Via Labicana 125, 00184
Tel *06 77 59 13 80*
A sleek interior and unequaled views of the Colosseum. Seasonal menu of regional favorites.

Around Piazza Navona

Acchiappafantasmi €
Pizzeria **Map** 9 B3
Via dei Cappellari 66, 00186
Tel *06 687 34 62* **Closed** *Mon*
The name means "Ghostbusters," and the ghost-shaped pizzas are as tasty as they are amusing.

Angolo Divino €
Enoteca **Map** 9 C4
Via dei Balestrari 12, 00186
Tel *06 686 44 13* **Closed** *Mon & Tue lunch; Aug 10–20*
Intimate and romantic spot. The warm chocolate cake is almost as divine as the wine list.

Baffetto €
Pizzeria **Map** 9 B3
Via del Governo Vecchio 114, 00186
Tel *06 686 16 17* **Closed** *Tue*
The crunchy Roman-style pizza is considered by those in the know to be the best in Rome, but be prepared to wait for a long time and share a table when you're finally seated.

Capricci Siciliani €
Regional Italian **Map** 9 B2
Via di Panico 83, 00186
Tel *06 45 43 38 23* **Closed** *Aug*
Elegant Sicilian dining in the heart of the historic center; specialties include swordfish medallions and anchovy rolls.

Cul de Sac €
Enoteca **Map** 9 C3
Piazza di Pasquino 73, 00186
Tel *06 68 80 10 94* **Closed** *Dec 24, 25, & 31*
This narrow wine bar boasts hundreds of labels as well as a wide variety of tasty eats.

Nonna Betta €
Regional Italian **Map** 10 D5
Via del Portico d'Ottavia 16, 00186
Tel *06 68 80 62 63* **Closed** *Tue*
An authentic Jewish eatery. Don't expect an English translation on the handwritten menu, but the food is glorious.

Old Bear €
Regional Italian **Map** 9 C2
Via dei Gigli d'Oro 3, 00186
Tel *06 68 21 00 09* **Closed** *Apr; Nov: Mon, Tue*
Dark wood beams and low ceilings create a warm and inviting ambience. Don't miss the Tuscan soup with truffle oil.

Diners at the well-known Jewish-Roman eatery Nonna Betta

Key to prices *see p580*

Open Baladin €
Birreria **Map** 10 D5
Via degli Specchi 6, 00186
Tel *06 683 89 89* **Closed** *2 wks Aug, Dec 24, 25, & 31*
Over 120 labels of craft beers, as well as original, all-natural sodas. Staple snack food is served.

Camponeschi €€
Fine Dining **Map** 9 C4
Piazza Farnese, 50/50a, 00186
Tel *06 687 49 27*
World-class dining in the heart of town. Try tagliolini with lobster and black truffles; wild game is the house specialty.

Da Giggetto €€
Regional Italian **Map** 10 E5
Via del Portico d'Ottavia 21/22, 00186
Tel *06 686 11 05* **Closed** *Mon; last 2 wks Aug, Dec 24 & 31*
Dine in the shadow of ancient ruins at this famous Jewish-Roman eatery. Don't miss the deep-fried artichokes.

Il Bacaro €€
Modern Italian **Map** 10 D2
Via degli Spagnoli 27, 00186
Tel *06 687 25 54*
Romantic with specialties such as *trofie* with asparagus and beef *carpaccio* with endive and truffles.

Il Pagliaccio €€
Fine Dining **Map** 9 B2
Via dei Banchi Vecchi 129, 00186
Tel *06 68 80 95 95* **Closed** *Tue lunch; Aug*
Surprising blend of pan-Asian and Mediterranean fare. Try one of the tasting menus, some of which have up to 12 courses.

Roscioli €€
Enoteca **Map** 9 C4
Via dei Giubbonari 21, 00186
Tel *06 687 52 87* **Closed** *Sun*
Part wine bar, part *salumeria*, with drool-worthy meats and cheeses and a dizzying selection of labels.

Terra di Siena €€
Regional Italian **Map** 9 C3
Piazza di Pasquino 77, 00186
Tel *06 68 30 77 04* **Closed** *Sun in summer*
Hearty Tuscan dishes such as Florentine steak and *ribollita* soup; seating in a cheerful dining room or on the buzzing piazza.

Al Bric €€€
Enoteca **Map** 9 C4
Via del Pellegrino 51, 00186
Tel *06 687 95 33* **Closed** *Mon; 2 wks Aug*
The impeccable wine list at cozy Al Bric is matched with tempting creations from the kitchen.

Bright and inviting interior of Al Bric, around Piazza Navona

Hostaria dell'Orso €€€
Fine Dining **Map** 9 C2
Via dei Soldati 25c, 00186
Tel *06 68 30 11 92* **Closed** *Aug*
This legendary restaurant and nightclub, located in a beautiful old house, has been welcoming guests since the start of the 16th century.

Northeast Rome

Ai Tre Scalini €
Enoteca **Map** 3 C4
Via Panisperna 251, 00184
Tel *06 48 90 74 95*
One of the hippest wine bars in town, with excellent wines, beers, and savory delicacies.

Antica Birreria Peroni €
Birreria **Map** 10 F3
Via di San Marcello 19, 00187
Tel *06 679 53 10* **Closed** *Sun; Aug 2 & 5; Dec 24, 25, & 31*
Casual spot that's been serving beer for over 100 years (wine is also available). All-Italian grilled beef and pork is on the menu.

Cavour 313 €
Enoteca **Map** 3 C5
Via Cavour 313, 00184
Tel *06 678 54 96* **Closed** *Sun in Aug*
Highly trained staff help guests select a memorable vintage in this wood-lined wine bar.

'Gusto €
Pizzeria **Map** 2 E2
Piazza Augusto Imperatore 9, 00186
Tel *06 322 62 73* **Closed** *Jan 1, Dec 24*
Factory-like setting with exposed brick and iron. The Neapolitan-style pizzas are thick-crusted.

Hang Zhou €
Chinese **Map** 9 E5
Via Principe Eugenio 82, 00184
Tel *06 487 27 32* **Closed** *Aug*
Unanimously touted as the best Chinese food in town. The all-you-can eat buffet is a steal; other meals are higher than average.

La Carbonara €
Regional Italian **Map** 3 C4
Via Panisperna 214, 00184
Tel *06 482 51 76* **Closed** *Sun; Aug*
This busy, inexpensive *osteria* serves hearty local fare and of course a delicious Carbonara. The pistachio pasta is also popular.

San Marco €
Pizzeria **Map** 3 C1
Via Sardegna 38, 00187
Tel *06 42 01 26 20* **Closed** *1 wk Aug, Dec 24*
A wine bar and grill noted for its pizzas and warm service. Blackboard-covered walls list the day's specials.

Trattoria Monti €
Regional Italian **Map** 4 D4
Via di San Vito 13, 00185
Tel *06 446 65 73* **Closed** *Sun dinner, Mon; Aug, Dec 24–Jan 3*
The day's specials, featuring local seasonal ingredients, are explained by the brothers who own this heavenly spot.

Trimani il Wine Bar €
Enoteca **Map** 4 D2
Via Cernaia 37b, 00185
Tel *06 446 96 30* **Closed** *Sun; Jan 1, 2 wks Aug, Dec 25 & 26*
Modern wine bar with labels that pair perfectly with cold and hot dishes, as well as Italian cheeses.

Urbana 47 €
Modern Italian **Map** 3 C4
Via Urbana 47, 00184
Tel *06 47 88 40 06* **Closed** *2 wks Aug*
Eclectic place offering creative and delicious dining. Great range of desserts and exceptional value.

Ambasciata d'Abruzzo €€
Regional Italian
Via Pietro Tacchini, 26
Tel *06 807 82 56* **Closed** *Aug 2–4*
Traditional Abruzzese dishes such as *maccheroni* with lamb *ragu* mingle with Roman favorites in a convivial setting.

For more information on types of restaurants *see p579*

Cuoco e Camicia €€
Modern Italian **Map** 3 C5
Via Monte Polacco 2/4, 00184
Tel *06 88 92 29 87* **Closed** *Sun, Sat lunch; 2 wks Aug, Dec 24 & 25*
Cheerful eatery that prides itself on using only the freshest local ingredients. Good tasting menu.

Hamasei €€
Japanese **Map** 10 F1
Via della Mercede 35/36, 00187
Tel *06 679 21 34* **Closed** *Mon; Aug*
Inventive sushi and sashimi dishes are served in a minimalist setting, with low tables for authentic Nipponese dining.

La Campana €€
Regional Italian **Map** 10 D1
Vicolo della Campana 18, 00186
Tel *06 687 52 73* **Closed** *Mon; Aug*
Packed any night of the week, this is the oldest restaurant in Rome, dating back to 1518. Traditional favorites are served.

Doozo €€€
Japanese **Map** 3 C4
Via Palermo 51, 00184
Tel *06 481 56 55* **Closed** *Sun lunch, Mon; 1 wk Aug, Dec 22–Jan 15*
Excellent sushi, and origami courses, at this restaurant and Japanese cultural center.

Imàgo €€€
Fine Dining **Map** 3 A2
Piazza Trinità dei Monti 6, 00187
Tel *06 69 93 47 26* **Closed** *lunch*
Creative Italian cuisine and exceptional views from the top of the Spanish Steps. The desserts are divine and the wine list is expertly chosen.

L'Olimpo €€€
Fine Dining **Map** 3 B2
Piazza Barberini 23, 00187
Tel *06 48 89 31*
Dine with sweeping views of the entire city. Considerable savings at lunchtime; a more expensive menu in the evenings.

Oliver Glowig €€€
Fine Dining
Via Ulisse Aldrovandi, 15 00197
Tel *06 321 61 26* **Closed** *Sun & Mon in winter*
Try Mediterranean delicacies such as scampi with artichoke heart and burrata cheese at this exquisite poolside restaurant.

Osteria Margutta €€€
Modern Italian **Map** 3 A2
Via Margutta 82b, 00187
Tel *06 323 10 25* **Closed** *Sun dinner, Mon lunch; 1 wk Aug*
Historic restaurant on a vine-covered street serving classic Roman fare with a modern twist.

Sleek interiors at the Japanese restaurant Doozo, Northeast Rome

The Vatican and Trastevere

Arian €
Persian **Map** 2 D2
Via Tacito 54a, 00193
Tel *06 45 44 11 22* **Closed** *Sun & Mon lunch; 1 wk Aug*
Iranian cuisine in a vibrant atmosphere. Live belly dancing on Friday and Saturday nights.

Arlù €
Regional Italian **Map** 1 C3
Borgo Pio 135, 00193
Tel *06 686 89 36* **Closed** *Sun; Jan 1, 2 wks Aug, Dec 25 & 26*
The most authentic restaurant in the area. A husband and wife team serve up delectable cuisine. Great choice of beverages.

Bir and Fud €
Birreria **Map** 2 E5
Via Benedetta 23, 00153
Tel *06 589 40 16* **Closed** *Dec 25 & 31*
Boutique beers and microbrews accompany crusty pizzas and gourmet chips.

BRASSERIE 4:20 €
Birreria **Map** 5 C3
Via Portuense 82, 00153
Tel *06 58 31 07 37*
Craft beers from around the world are paired with snacks such as burgers, fries, and hot dogs as well as a selection of desserts.

Da Gildo €
Regional Italian **Map** 2 D5
Via della Scala 31/A, 00153
Tel *06 580 07 33* **Closed** *Thu*
Quirky decoration and a cozy outdoor seating area. Try the divine *gnocchi alla romana* (baked *gnocchi* with cheese on top).

Da Lucia €
Regional Italian **Map** 5 B1
Vicolo del Mattonato 2b, 00153
Tel *06 580 36 01* **Closed** *Mon; 2 wks Aug; Dec 24, 25, & 31*
Simple pasta dishes as well as more hearty meals and delicious homemade desserts are served on a beautifully lit street.

Dar Poeta €
Pizzeria **Map** 2 E5
Vicolo del Bologna 45, 00153
Tel *06 588 05 16* **Closed** *Dec 24 & 31*
Perfect balance between thick- and thin-crusted pizza; the buffalo mozzarella topping is unmatched.

Fish Market €
Seafood **Map** 5 C2
Vicolo della Luce 2/3, 00153
Tel *06 914 41 57*
This restaurant has no frills; choose your fish, state how you would like it cooked, and pick it up from the counter when it's ready.

In Vino Veritas €
Enoteca **Map** 2 D5
Via Garibaldi 2a, 00153
Tel *06 583 320 12*
Cozy and informal wine bar with over 200 varieties of wine. Food is simple and made for sharing.

Ivo a Trastevere €
Pizzeria **Map** 5 C1
Via di San Francesco a Ripa 158, 00153
Tel *06 581 70 82*
Snacks and thin-crusted pizza have this eatery bustling with locals.

Panattoni L'Obitorio €
Pizzeria **Map** 5 C1
Viale di Trastevere 53, 00153
Tel *06 580 09 19* **Closed** *Wed; Aug 10 & 28*
Nicknamed "the morgue" for its long marble-top tables. Try the *supplì al telefono* (fried rice balls).

Rajdhani €
Indian **Map** 6 D1
Via di Santa Cecilia 8, 00153
Tel *06 581 85 08* **Closed** *Mon*
Tandoori chicken is the specialty at this friendly spot.

Key to prices *see p580*

DK Choice

Isole di Sicilia €€
Regional Italian **Map** 5 B1
Via Garibaldi 68, 00153
Tel *06 58 33 42 12* **Closed** *Wed*
This cheerful restaurant dishes up some of the best Sicilian food in town. The elaborate dishes are inspired by the native cuisine of the tiny islands around Sicily. A vast antipasto spread kicks off a memorable meal. In good weather, dine on the tree-lined street.

Spirito Divino €€
Modern Italian **Map** 6 D1
Via dei Genovesi 31, 00153
Tel *06 589 66 89* **Closed** *Sun*
Fine dishes served in a converted medieval synagogue; take a peek in the 2,000-year-old wine cellar.

Taverna Trilussa €€
Regional Italian **Map** 2 E5
Via del Politeama 23, 00153
Tel *06 581 89 18* **Closed** *Sun, lunch daily; 3 days mid-Aug; Dec 24, 25 & 31*
A bustling yet elegant spot. Some pasta dishes are served in the pan they were cooked in.

Antica Pesa €€€
Fine Dining **Map** 5 B1
Via Garibaldi 18, 00153
Tel *06 580 92 36* **Closed** *Sun; Jan 1, Dec 26*
Eat exquisite cuisine in a beautifully decorated restaurant with murals covering the walls. Dine alfresco in warm weather.

Antico Arco €€€
Fine Dining **Map** 5 A1
Piazzale Aurelio 7, 00152
Tel *06 581 52 74* **Closed** *Jan 1*
Truffles, wild strawberries, and other such delights are available. The vast wine list is as tantalizing.

Settembrini €€€
Modern Italian
Via Luigi Settembrini 25, 00195
Tel *06 323 26 17* **Closed** *Sun, Sat lunch; 2 wks Aug*
Renowned chef Gigi Nastri serves creative Italian cuisine that is as beautiful as it is tasty.

Aventine and Lateran

Angelina a Testaccio €
Regional Italian **Map** 6 D3
Via Galvani 24, 00153
Tel *06 57 28 38 40* **Closed** *Sat lunch, Sun*
The gem of Testaccio, this shabby-chic bistro offers a tempting Sunday brunch. The desserts are scrumptious.

Oasi della Birra €
Birreria **Map** 6 D3
Piazza Testaccio 39, 00153
Tel *06 574 61 22* **Closed** *1 wk Aug, Dec 24 & 25*
This oasis of beer starts serving in the early afternoon and no one leaves thirsty.

Checchino dal 1887 €€
Regional Italian **Map** 6 D4
Via di Monte Testaccio 30, 00153
Tel *06 574 38 16* **Closed** *Sun, Mon; Aug*
Lovingly prepared hearty Roman dishes make this restaurant a favorite with discerning diners.

Farther Afield

La Gatta Mangiona €
Pizzeria
Via Federico Ozanam 30, Monteverde Nuovo, 00152
Tel *06 534 67 02* **Closed** *Mon; Aug 10–25, Dec 24–26 & 31*
Creative toppings and daily specials make this spot popular with locals and in-the-know visitors.

DK Choice

Momò Republic €€
Pizzeria
Piazza Forlanini 10, Monteverde Nuovo, 00151
Tel *06 537 30 87*
A 19th-century mansion in a garden is the setting for this trendy pizzeria. Huge chandeliers and parquet floors add to the ambience. In summer, start with *aperitivo* on the lawn. Pasta, meat, and fish are also available.

Osteria Flaminio €€
Modern Italian
Via Flaminia 297, 00196
Tel *06 323 69 00* **Closed** *lunch*
Trek north of the center to try the innovative and original Italian cuisine available here.

Bastianelli al Molo €€€
Fine Dining
Via Torre Clementina 312, 00054
Tel *06 650 53 58*
A terrace overlooking the Tyrrhenian Sea is the setting for a meal of ultra-fresh seafood.

DK Choice

La Pergola €€€
Fine Dining
Via Alberto Cadlolo 101, 00136
Tel *06 350 91* **Closed** *Sun, Mon*
Rome's finest restaurant, La Pergola is also the only one to earn the coveted three Michelin stars. Chef Heinz Beck dazzles with exquisite Mediterranean creations. Perched atop Monte Mario hill, it offers great views of St. Peter's Basilica. The award-winning wine cellar boasts more than 53,000 bottles, the oldest dating from 1888.

Lazio

BRACCIANO: Quattro Castagni €
Regional Italian
Via Olmata Tre Cancelli, 7
Tel *06 99 84 91 55* **Closed** *Tue*
Traditional cuisine, specializing in wild game, served in a rustic setting with exposed stonework.

BRACCIANO: Trattoria La Tavernetta €
Modern Italian
Via Giuseppe Garibaldi 73, 00062
Tel *06 999 90 26*
Welcoming atmosphere and regional cuisine. The patio offers spectacular views of the lake.

CASTELLI ROMANI FRASCATI: Pezzafina €
Modern Italian
Vicolo Manara 2, 00044
Tel *06 60 65 17 80* **Closed** *lunch, Sun*
The menu features daring ingredient combinations, while maintaining traditional flavors.

CERVETERI: Trattoria Zi Maria €
Regional Italian
Via Sasso Manziana 2, 00050
Tel *06 99 07 90 29* **Closed** *Tue*
Typical regional cuisine at good prices. Hearty specialties include venison with wild berries.

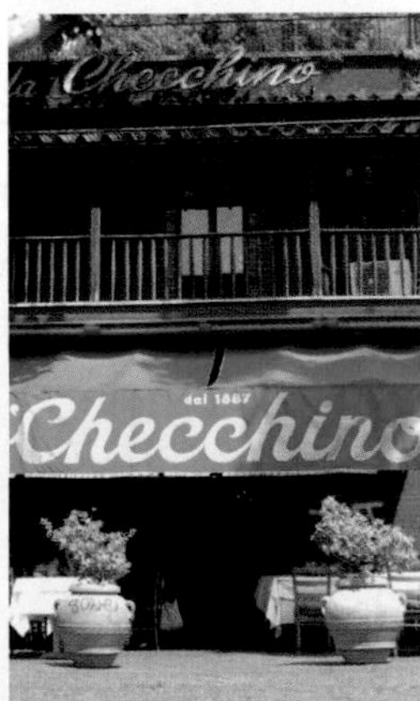

Exterior of the friendly Checchino dal 1887, known for its filling Roman dishes

CERVETERI: Rendez-vous Bistrot €€
Regional Italian
Piazza Risorgimento 16, 00052
Tel *06 90 20 97 50*
A romantic getaway on a pedestrian piazza. Creative cuisine, modern decor, and attentive service.

GAETA: Narì €
Seafood
Via Duomo 15, 04024
Tel *0771 46 30 94* **Closed** *Mon*
Excellent fish and pasta dishes in the medieval center of Gaeta.

OSTIA: La Bussola €€
Seafood
Lungomare A. Vespucci 72, 00122
Tel *06 56 47 08 67* **Closed** *Mon*
Inspired by the recipes of the owners' great aunt. Try the gnocchi with octopus and the fish stew.

SERMONETA: Il Giardino del Simposio €
Modern Italian
Corso Garibaldi 33, 04010
Tel *339 284 69 05* **Closed** *Mon; Jan–Feb: Sat & Sun*
Innovative dishes such as pasta with fresh ricotta and wild fennel.

SPERLONGA: Gli Archi €€
Traditional Italian
Via Ottaviano 17, 04029
Tel *0771 54 83 00* **Closed** *Wed; Jan*
Simple traditional cuisine in the heart of this seaside village. Outdoor seating in warm weather.

TARQUINIA: La Cantinetta €
Regional Italian
Via XX Settembre 27, 01016
Tel *0766 85 68 10* **Closed** *Tue; summer*
Simple spot offering staples from land and sea. Try the spaghetti with octopus and clams.

TIVOLI: Avec 55 €€
Modern Italian
Via Domenico Giuliani 55, 00019
Tel *0774 31 72 43* **Closed** *Mon*
Gastronomic feats paired with excellent wine. Divine desserts.

TIVOLI: La Sibilla €€
Regional Italian
Via della Sibilla 42, 00019
Tel *0774 33 52 81* **Closed** *Mon*
Fine views of the Roman ruins provide a great setting to indulge in high-quality regional cuisine.

DK Choice

VITERBO: Il Labirinto €
Pizzeria
Via di San Lorenzo 46, 00100
Tel *0761 30 70 26* **Closed** *Mon*
This charming restaurant prepares a variety of bruschetta, pizza, pasta, and main courses in traditional style. The outdoor seating area is next to a quaint fountain and a medieval church. Service is friendly and prices low.

VITERBO: Ristorantino La Torre €€
Fine Dining
Via della Torre 5, 01100
Tel *0761 22 64 67* **Closed** *Sun dinner, Mon lunch; 3 wks Aug*
The chef and sommelier create an unforgettable dining experience at this vibrant spot.

VITERBO: Villa San Michele €€€
Fine Dining
Via Pian di Quercia, 01030
Tel *338 501 03 87* **Closed** *Mon, Tue*
Icelandic *baccalà* (salt cod) in coconut milk, cinnamon, and orange zest is a menu highlight.

Naples and Campania

AMALFI: Da Ciccio Cielo Mare Terra €€
Regional Italian
Via Nazionale per Sorrento, 84011
Tel *089 83 12 65* **Closed** *Tue; Jan, Nov*
Great views of the coastline are matched by the delicious food.

AMALFI: La Caravella €€€
Fine Dining
Via Matteo Camera 12, 84011
Tel *089 87 10 29* **Closed** *Tue; Jan, Nov*
The award-winning chef here uses local flavors to exalt the regional cuisine.

BENEVENTO: Pascalucci €€
Regional Italian
Via Appia 1, 82010
Tel *0824 77 84 00* **Closed** *winter*
Simple recipes prepared with fresh local ingredients.

CAPRI: Da Gelsomina €€
Regional Italian
Via Migliara 72, 80071
Tel *081 837 14 99* **Closed** *Tue; Jan–Feb*
Much of the produce is grown on-site at this delightful restaurant.

CAPRI: Da Paolino €€
Regional Italian
Via Palazzo a Mare 11, 80073
Tel *081 837 61 02* **Closed** *Oct–Apr*
Rustic country restaurant with rich regional cuisine.

CAPRI: L'Olivo €€
Fine Dining
Via Capodimonte 14, 80071
Tel *081 978 01 11* **Closed** *mid-Oct–mid-Apr*
Uses saffron, bergamot, fava beans, and asparagus to make gorgeous flavor combinations.

CAPRI: Il Riccio €€€
Seafood
Via Grotta Azzurra 11, 80071
Tel *081 837 13 80* **Closed** *Nov–Mar*
Pleasant atmosphere in which to enjoy exceptional seafood dishes.

CASERTA: Antica Locanda €
Regional Italian
Piazza della Seta 7, 81100
Tel *0823 30 54 44* **Closed** *Sun dinner, Mon; Aug, Dec 24 & 31*
Simple, characterful *osteria* with rustic details. Southern Italian cooking and excellent risotto.

CASERTA: Leucio €
Seafood
Via Giardini Reali 86, 81100
Tel *0823 30 12 41* **Closed** *Sun dinner, Mon; 1 wk Aug*
Exceptional prices at this simple fish restaurant run by a father and son. Also serves great pasta.

CASERTA: Le Colonne €€
Fine Dining
Viale Giulio Douhet 7, 81100
Tel *0823 46 74 94* **Closed** *Tue*
Indulge in superbly reinterpreted local cuisine in a luxurious setting.

Romantic dining amid lemon trees at Da Paolino, Capri

Key to prices *see p580*

Sunny patio of the Neapolitan gem, Il Comandante, Naples

ISCHIA AND PROCIDA: La Stadera €
Enoteca
Via C. Maddalena 15, Sant'Angelo, 80070
Tel *081 99 98 93*
Narrow alleys lead to this *enoteca* where the owners delight with unusual wines and liqueurs. The food here is also delicious.

ISCHIA AND PROCIDA: La Tinaia €
Pizzeria
Via Matteo Verde 39, Forio, 80075
Tel *081 99 84 48* **Closed** *Dec 24*
Fantastic thick-crusted pizza, as well as pasta and seafood. Basic but friendly service.

ISCHIA AND PROCIDA: Lo Scoglio €
Seafood
Via Cava Ruffano 58, Sant'Angelo, 80077
Tel *081 999529*
Stunningly located on a rock jutting over the sea, this simple restaurant serves quality fish. There is also a good selection of wine.

ISCHIA AND PROCIDA: Alberto €€
Modern Italian
Via Cristoforo Colombo 8, Ischia, 80077
Tel *081 98 12 59* **Closed** *Nov–Mar*
Sample traditional Italian seafood specialties with creative reinterpretation at this lovely beach-front restaurant.

ISCHIA AND PROCIDA: Gorgonia €€
Seafood
Via Marina di Corricella 50, Procida, 80079
Tel *081 810 10 60*
Set high above a picturesque bay, Gorgonia serves the catch of the day.

ISCHIA AND PROCIDA: Il Mosaico €€€
Fine Dining
Piazza Bagni, Casamicciola Terme, 80074
Tel *081 99 47 22* **Closed** *Tue; mid-Oct–Mar*
Rich Neapolitan cuisine inspires this multitalented chef's innovative and exquisite menu. The wine list is excellent and the desserts are divine.

DK Choice

ISCHIA AND PROCIDA: Umberto a Mare €€€
Fine Dining
Via del Soccorso 2, Forio, 80075
Tel *081 99 71 71* **Closed** *Nov–Mar*
Time seems to stand still as you take a seat on the tiny terrace that juts out over the sea in the shadow of the evocative Santa Maria del Sorrorso church. The tasting menus feature the gastronomic delights of the Mediterranean. The wine selection is outstanding, and the staff attend to every need.

DK Choice

NAPLES: Da Michele €
Pizzeria
Via Cesare Sersale 1, 80139
Tel *081 553 92 04* **Closed** *Sun*
A trip to Naples wouldn't be complete without tasting a Margherita at this institution, probably the most famous pizzeria in the world. Only Margherita and Marinara pizzas are served here.

NAPLES: Di Matteo €
Pizzeria
Via dei Tribunali 94, 80138
Tel *081 455 262* **Closed** *Sun*
A Naples institution serving classic chewy pizza and tasty *fritti* (fried food). Popular with locals and celebrities.

NAPLES: La Notizia €
Pizzeria
Via Michelangelo da Caravaggio 53, 80126
Tel *081 714 21 55* **Closed** *Mon; Aug, Dec 25*
Tiny pizzas with intense flavors at this popular spot, considered one of the world's best pizzerias.

NAPLES: La Piazzetta €
Regional Italian
Via Nazario Sauro 21, 80132
Tel *081 764 61 95* **Closed** *Mon*
Traditional local fare and pizzeria at this quaint restaurant designed to look like a small-town piazza.

NAPLES: Sorbillo €
Pizzeria
Via dei Tribunali 38, 80138
Tel *081 033 10 09* **Closed** *Sun; 1 wk Feb*
A comfortable setting, good pizza, and attentive service for a great price.

NAPLES: Kukai Nibu €€
Japanese
Via Carlo de Cesare 52, 80132
Tel *081 42 58 88*
Generous portions of sushi and sashimi; a glass kitchen allows diners a great view of the action.

NAPLES: La Cantinella €€
Fine Dining
Via Cuma 42, 80132
Tel *081 764 86 84* **Closed** *Sun dinner*
A bamboo forest is re-created in this award-winning restaurant with an imaginative chef.

NAPLES: La Scialuppa €€
Seafood
Piazzetta Marinari 4, 80132
Tel *081 764 53 33* **Closed** *Mon; Jan*
Right on the gulf, this traditional restaurant serves fresh fish, as well as pasta and pizza.

NAPLES: Palazzo Petrucci €€
Modern Italian
Piazza San Domenico Maggiore 4, 80134
Tel *081 552 40 68* **Closed** *Sun dinner, Mon lunch; Aug 2–4, Dec 25*
This Michelin-starred restaurant in an ancient setting serves modern fare made with local ingredients.

NAPLES: Il Comandante €€€
Fine Dining
Via Cristoforo Colombo, 80133
Tel *081 01 75* **Closed** *Tue*
The chef creates exquisite dishes from a few basic ingredients.

POSITANO: Chez Black €€
Seafood
Via del Brigantino, 84017
Tel *089 87 57 96* **Closed** *mid-Jan–mid-Feb*
Idyllic beachfront location. Serves traditional fish recipes.

POSITANO: Le Terrazze €€
Regional
Via Grotte Dell'Incanto 51, 84017
Tel *089 87 58 74* **Closed** *Oct–Apr*
Wine bar with panoramic sea views. The wine cellar is carved right into the hillside rock.

POSITANO: Zass €€€
Fine Dining
Via Laurito 2, 84017
Tel *089 87 54 55*
Mouthwateringly delicious elevation of regional cuisine. Desserts to die for.

For more information on types of restaurants *see p579*

SALERNO: Addor I Pizza €
Pizzeria
Piazza San Francesco d'Assisi, 84122
Tel *089 24 18 76* **Closed** *Mon, Sun*
Courteous service in this tiny pizzeria that also serves pasta.

SALERNO: Il Timone €€
Seafood
Via Generale Allende 29/35, 84122
Tel *089 33 51 11* **Closed** *Mon; Aug 15–31*
Friendly, bright fish restaurant with fast, courteous service.

SALERNO: Osteria Dedicato a mio Padre €€
Seafood
Vicolo Giudaica 8, 84100
Tel *089 23 15 55* **Closed** *Sun*
Numerous varieties of fresh fish, served up in a cozy setting in the heart of the historic center.

SORRENTO: La Basilica €
Regional Italian
Via Sant'Antonino 28, 80067
Tel *081 877 47 90* **Closed** *Mon*
It's possible to dine until 1am at this restaurant. Fish, meat and vegeatrian options in classic regional style.

SORRENTO: Zi'ntonio €
Regional Italian
Via Luigi De Maio 11, 80067
Tel *081 878 16 23*
Local favorites served in a room with exposed tufa blocks and wood-beamed ceilings.

SORRENTO: Il Buco €€
Modern Italian
II Rampa Marina Piccola 5, 80067
Tel *081 878 23 54* **Closed** *Wed; Jan*
Elegant yet informal restaurant housed in the cellar of an ancient monastery. A perfect blend of tradition and more daring cuisine.

Abruzzo, Molise, and Puglia

ALBEROBELLO: Trullo d'Oro €
Regional Italian
Via Felice Cavallotti 27, 70011
Tel *080 432 18 20* **Closed** *Mon*
Local cuisine in the characterful setting of an authentic *trullo*. Great antipasto spread.

ALBEROBELLO: Il Poeta Contadino €€
Fine Dining
Via Indipendenza 21, 70011
Tel *080 432 19 17* **Closed** *Mon; Jan (except for group reservations)*
Awarded a Michelin star for its delectable regional cuisine and a stunning location. The desserts are heavenly.

Homey setting for regional cuisine at Il Cortiletto, Lucera

BARI: Osteria delle Travi "Il Buco" €
Regional Italian
Largo Ignazio Chiurlia 12, 70122
Tel *339 157 88 48* **Closed** *Sun dinner, Mon*
Authentic home-style cooking in the old Pugliese style *osteria*.

BARI: Bacco €€
Modern Italian
Corso Vittorio Emanuele II 126, 70122
Tel *080 527 58 71* **Closed** *Sun dinner, Mon; Aug*
Both meat and fish are on the menu at this award-winning restaurant. Ample wine list.

GARGANO PENINSULA: Medioevo €
Regional Italian
Via Castello 21, 71037
Tel *0884 56 53 56* **Closed** *Nov: dinner; Dec–Feb: Mon*
This simple *osteria* uses the best seasonal produce available. Meat and soup specialties.

GARGANO PENINSULA: Porta di Basso €€
Seafood
Via Cristoforo Colombo 38, 71010
Tel *0884 91 53 64* **Closed** *Thu*
Creative reinterpretations of Pugliese fish recipes. Located on a cliff above the sea.

GARGANO PENINSULA: Al Dragone €€
Regional Italian
Via Duomo 8, 71019
Tel *0884 70 12 12* **Closed** *Apr–Nov: Tue; Dec–Mar*
Dining in this restaurant built into a natural cave is an experience in itself. Delicious regional dishes and a good wine list.

ISOLE TREMITI: La Nassa €
Seafood
Via Aldo Moro 24, 71040
Tel *0882 46 33 45* **Closed** *Easter; Apr–Oct*
Nestled in a lush garden, this restaurant offers fresh fish served in the simple but rich local tradition.

L'AQUILA: Le Rocce dell'Aquila €
Regional Italian
Viale della Croce Rossa 40, 67100
Tel *0862 41 90 12*
Creativity meets local produce at this small restaurant.

L'AQUILA: Elodia €€
Fine Dining
Via Valle Perchiana 22, 67100
Tel *0862 60 68 30* **Closed** *Mon, Tue*
Gourmet interpretations of great local recipes; delicious desserts.

LECCE: Osteria degli Spiriti €
Regional Italian
Via Cesare Battisti 4, 73100
Tel *0832 24 62 74*
Local cuisine served in a high-ceilinged *trattoria* that was once a warehouse.

LUCERA: Il Cortiletto €
Regional Italian
Via Famiglia de Nicastri 26, 71036
Tel *0881 54 25 54* **Closed** *Sun dinner*
The short weekly menu is described by the staff. Regional favorites with original touches.

DK Choice

LUCERA: Osteria Utz €
Modern Italian
Corso Garibaldi 103, 71036
Tel *0881 61 82 34* **Closed** *Sun*
This warm, cozy restaurant selects only the freshest local ingredients – from cured meats and cheeses to native herbs – and uses them to craft innovative dishes inspired by the area's cuisine. The atmosphere is informal but romantic. The specialty is numerous varieties of fresh homemade bread.

OSTUNI: Osteria Piazzetta Cattedrale €
Modern Italian
Largo Arcidiacono T. Trinchera 7, 72017
Tel *0831 33 50 26* **Closed** *Tue*
This elegant restaurant serves local cuisine with a modern touch.

Key to prices *see p580*

OSTUNI:
Osteria del Tempo Perso €€
Modern Italian
Via Gaetano Tanzarella Vitale 47, 72017
Tel *0831 30 48 19* **Closed** *Mon; Jan 15–20*
Set in an antique mill, the dishes are reinventions of classic recipes.

OSTUNI: Porta Nova €€
Seafood
Via Gaspare Petrarolo 28, 72017
Tel *0831 33 89 83*
This fish restaurant boasts fine food and views of the surrounding area from its large terrace.

OTRANTO: Peccato di Vino €€
Modern Italian
Via Rondachi 7, 73028
Tel *0836 80 14 88* **Closed** *Tue*
One of the finest restaurants in town, serving creative Pugliese cuisine in a jovial atmosphere.

SULMONA: Rigoletto €
Regional Italian
Via Stazione Introdacqua 46, 67039
Tel *086 45 55 29*
Homemade dishes with local ingredients such as rabbit, truffles, and scamorza cheese.

TARANTO: Al Canale €€
Seafood
Scesa Vasto, 74100
Tel *099 476 42 01* **Closed** *Sun dinner; Nov 1–15*
Seafood specialties are prepared at this luminous restaurant.

TARANTO:
Trattoria al Gatto Rosso €€
Regional Italian
Via Cavour 2, 74123
Tel *099 452 98 75* **Closed** *Sun lunch, Mon*
Innovative contemporary cuisine based on local recipes.

TRANI: Torrente Antico €€€
Fine Dining
Via Edoardo Fusco 3, 70059
Tel *0883 48 79 11* **Closed** *Mon*
Light and modern versions of Puglia's traditional recipes at the finest restaurant in the area.

Basilicata and Calabria

MARATEA:
Il Giardino di Epicuro €
Regional Italian
Contrada Massa Piano, 85046
Tel *0973 87 01 30* **Closed** *Jan, Feb, Nov*
The owner's mother creates heavenly traditional meals.

MARATEA: Zà Mariuccia €€
Seafood
Via Grotte 2, 85040
Tel *0973 87 61 63* **Closed** *Mon; mid-Oct–Mar*
Call ahead to secure one of the few terrace tables with splendid sea views. Top-notch local seafood with an excellent wine list.

MARATEA: Taverna Rovita €€€
Regional Italian
Via Rovita 12, 85046
Tel *0973 87 65 88*
Serves tempting meat and fish dishes and homemade pasta with seasonal ingredients.

MATERA: Alle Fornaci €
Seafood
Piazza Cesare Firrao 5/7, 75100
Tel *0835 33 50 37* **Closed** *Mon*
Fresh fish from the Ionian and Tyrrhenian seas is brought in daily for the no-fuss dishes.

MATERA: Don Matteo €€
Modern Italian
Via San Potito 12, 75100
Tel *0835 34 41 45* **Closed** *lunch*
Dine inside a *sassi* (characteristic stone dwelling). A modern take on traditional local recipes.

DK Choice

MELFI: La Villa €
Regional Italian
Contrada Cavallerizza, 85025
Tel *0972 23 60 08* **Closed** *Sun dinner, Fri; 2 wks mid-Jul*
Set in the heart of the countryside, this rustic restaurant mills its own flour and grows its own grapes. Every ingredient used is local, and the traditional recipes are executed with attention to detail. The family who run the estate treat guests like family members.

The warmly lit entrance to seafood restaurant Porta Nova in Ostuni

MELFI: Novecento €
Regional Italian
Contrada Incoronata, 85025
Tel *0972 23 74 70*
Authentic local cuisine served in a welcoming restaurant. Worth the trek outside town.

MELFI: La Grotta Azzurra €€
Regional Italian
Via Carmine 13, 85025
Tel *0972 23 81 34*
Bring a big appetite to this excellent restaurant with hearty Lucano specialties. Heavenly desserts and a good wine list.

REGGIO DI CALABRIA:
Il Fiore del Cappero €
Seafood
Via Zaleuco 7, 89125
Tel *0965 209 55* **Closed** *Sun, 1st wk Jan*
Sicilian cuisine, based mostly on fish, in this welcoming restaurant with ample Calabrian wines.

REGGIO DI CALABRIA:
Bistrot 15 €€
Bistro
Via Nazionale Pellaro 15, 89134
Tel *0965 35 03 41* **Closed** *May–Sep; Dec–Feb: Mon*
Innovative and artistic seafood served in a modern setting. Worth the small journey out of the center.

ROSSANO: Bella Napoli €
Pizzeria
Via Capri 5, 87067
Tel *0983 51 01 53*
Authentic Neapolitan-style pizzas are served in generous portions. Pasta and meat dishes also on the menu.

ROSSANO: Paridò €
Modern Italian
Via dei Normanni, 87067
Tel *0983 29 07 31*
Regional staple ingredients such as cuttlefish, swordfish, citrus fruits, and eggplant are reinterpreted in modern Mediterranean style.

TROPEA: Al Pinturicchio €
Pizzeria
Via Dardano, 89861
Tel *0963 60 34 52*
Come early to this popular pizzeria with tables that spill out onto the narrow street.

TROPEA: La Lamia €
Modern Italian
Largo Vulcano, 89861
Tel *0963 612 74*
Both meat and fish dishes feature heavily on the menu at this characteristic and popular neighborhood *osteria*.

For more information on types of restaurants *see p579*

TROPEA: Pimm's €€
Seafood
Largo Migliarese 10, 89861
Tel *0963 66 61 05* **Closed** *Mon*
Elegant and quiet restaurant in the heart of town.

VENOSA: Locanda Accademia dei Piacevoli €€
Modern Italian
Via Discesa Capovalle 1, 85029
Tel *0972 360 82* **Closed** *Mon; first 2 wks Nov*
Small gourmet restaurant built into a tiny stone house.

Sicily

AGRIGENTO: Trattoria dei Templi €
Seafood
Via Panoramica Valle dei Templi 15, 92100
Tel *0922 40 31 10*
This inviting restaurant overlooking the temples offers expertly prepared seafood specialties.

AGRIGENTO: Kokalos €€
Regional Italian
Via Cavaleri Magazzeni 3
Tel *0922 60 64 27*
Traditional Sicilian cuisine using local ingredients such as oranges, almonds, and sun-dried tomatoes.

CATANIA: La Siciliana €
Regional Italian
Viale Marco Polo 52, 95126
Tel *095 37 64 00* **Closed** *Sun dinner*
Classic Sicilian recipes, including dishes specific to the town. One of Catania's best restaurants.

CATANIA: Il Cuciniere €€
Modern Italian
Via Finocchiaro Aprile 110, 95129
Tel *095 747 07 02* **Closed** *Sun*

Erice's Monte San Giuliano restaurant, serving local dishes

The chef uses traditional Sicilian ingredients in unique ways, such as fish with Modica chocolate.

CEFALÙ: La Brace €
Bistro
Via 25 Novembre 10, 90015
Tel *0921 42 35 70* **Closed** *Mon, Tue; Dec 15–Jan 15*
Hints of the Orient mingle with local flavors at this bistro hidden away in the historic center.

ENNA: Ariston €
Regional Italian
Piazza Napoleone Colajanni 6, 94100
Tel *0935 260 38*
Fresh local ingredients from land and sea served with enthusiasm at this friendly spot.

ERICE: Monte San Giuliano €
Regional Italian
Vicolo San Rocco 7, 91016
Tel *0923 86 95 95* **Closed** *Mon; Nov 15*
The remarkable terrace garden here is an ideal setting to enjoy some authentic local cuisine.

ERICE: Osteria di Venere €€
Regional Italian
Via Roma 6, 91016
Tel *0923 86 93 62*
Sample diverse Mediterranean cuisine including homemade pasta and grilled catch of the day.

MARSALA: Garibaldi €
Regional Italian
Piazza dell'Addolorata 1, 91025
Tel *0923 95 30 06* **Closed** *Sat lunch, Sun dinner*
Dizzying selection of regional favorites, as well as fish cooked any way you please.

MESSINA: La Durlindana €
Regional Italian
Via Nicola Fabrizi 143, 98123
Tel *090 641 31 56*
This modern restaurant with an open kitchen offers regional dishes and wines

MESSINA: Piero €€
Regional Italian
Via Ghibellina 119, 98123
Tel *090 640 93 54* **Closed** *Aug*
This restaurant has been serving large plates of fish, big salads, and hearty meat dishes since its opening in 1962.

MONREALE: Taverna del Pavone €
Regional Italian
Vicolo Pensato 18, 90046
Tel *091 640 62 09* **Closed** *Mon; 2 wks Jan, 2 wks Jul*
Sample authentic, no-frills Sicilian specialties served in a cozy and friendly setting.

PALERMO: Antico Caffè Spinnato €
Enoteca
Via Principe di Belmonte 111, 90139
Tel *091 749 51 04* **Closed** *Christmas*
Come for the wines, liqueurs, and espresso, but stay for the *cassata* (traditional Sicilian dessert), *cannoli* (fried pastry with a creamy filling), and gelato.

PALERMO: Santandrea €
Regional Italian
Piazza Sant'Andrea 4, 90133
Tel *091 33 49 99*
In a tranquil oasis of exposed wood and stone, this eatery dishes up time-honored regional fare.

PALERMO: Bye Bye Blues €€
Fine Dining
Via del Garofalo 23, 90149
Tel *091 684 14 15* **Closed** *Mon; 2 wks Jan*
Fantastic prices for a Michelin-starred restaurant. Diners can watch their dishes being prepared at this restaurant.

PALERMO: Lo Scudiero €€
Seafood
Via Filippo Turati 7, 90139
Tel *091 58 16 28* **Closed** *Sun; 2 wks Aug*
The impeccable and attentive service is almost as refreshing as the delectable fish.

PALERMO: Sapori Perduti €€
Modern Italian
Via Principe di Belmonte 32, 90139
Tel *091 32 73 87* **Closed** *Mon; Aug*
Modern design goes hand-in-hand with expertly prepared modern Italian cuisine.

SIRACUSA: Enoteca Solaria €
Enoteca
Via Roma 86, 96100
Tel *0931 46 30 07*
The oldest wine bar in the city, with labels from Italy and France.

SIRACUSA: Oinos €€
Modern Italian
Via della Giudecca 69/75, 96100
Tel *0931 46 49 00*
Intimate and informal setting for a variety of modern dishes based on recipes from across Italy. There is also a good range of beverages to accompany meals.

SIRACUSA: Porta Marina €€
Regional Italian
Via dei Candelai 35, 96100
Tel *0931 225 53* **Closed** *Mon; 2 wks Feb*
A lovely restaurant set in a crumbling early Renaissance palazzo. It offers good value for the quality of food it serves.

Key to prices *see p580*

DK Choice

TAORMINA: Al Duomo €€
Seafood
Vico Ebrei (Piazza Duomo), 98039
Tel *0942 62 56 56* **Closed** *Mon*
The picturesque location for this restaurant is on a terrace in Taormina's most beautiful piazza, with the backdrop of a 12th-century cathedral. Classic and modern fish dishes are whipped up by the chefs with enthusiasm. The kitchen is open well past midnight.

TAORMINA: Principe Cerami €€€
Fine Dining
Piazza San Domenico 5, 98039
Tel *0942 61 31 11* **Closed** *lunch, Mon*
Heavenly terrace overlooking crystal waters offering uber-refined Sicilian fare. Book early.

TRAPANI: Taverna Paradiso €€
Seafood
Lungomare Dante Alighieri 22, 91100
Tel *0923 223 03*
Ask the friendly staff for their recommendations at this lovely eatery with super-fresh fish.

Sardinia

ALGHERO: Al Tuguri €€
Seafood
Via Maiorca 113, 07041
Tel *079 97 67 72* **Closed** *Sun; mid-Dec–Mar*
Just a few tables are available in this cozy seafood restaurant.

ALGHERO: Andreini €€€
Modern Italian
Via Ardoino 45, 07041
Tel *079 98 20 98* **Closed** *Dec–Apr*
A romantic, family-run place offering Mediterranean cuisine.

BOSA: Mannu da Giancarlo e Rita €€
Seafood
Viale Alghero 14, 08013
Tel *0785 37 53 07* **Closed** *winter*
A modern restaurant where lobster dominates the menu.

CAGLIARI: La Stella Marina di Montecristo €
Seafood
Via Sardegna 140, 09124
Tel *347 578 89 64* **Closed** *Sun*
This is a simple *osteria* with cordial service. Wild game on Thursdays.

CAGLIARI: Dal Corsaro €€
Modern Italian
Viale Regina Margherita 28, 09124
Tel *070 66 43 18* **Closed** *Sun; 3 wks Jan*

Buzzing atmosphere at Hivaoa, Costa Smeralda

Sardinian classics are re-created with a contemporary twist.

CALA GONONE: Il Pescatore €€
Seafood
Lungomare Acqua Dolce 1, 08022
Tel *0784 931 74*
A seaside spot serving classic Sardinian fish dishes.

COSTA SMERALDA: Corbezzolo €€
Seafood
Piazzetta della Fontana, Baia Sardinia, 07021
Tel *0789 998 93* **Closed** *Dec–May*
Tasty classic seafood dishes served on a sea-view terrace.

COSTA SMERALDA: Hivaoa €€
Pizzeria
Via della Marina, Porto Cervo, 07021
Tel *0789 914 51*
Dine on a breezy terrace. Pizza, pasta, and excellent seafood.

COSTA SMERALDA: Spinnaker €€€
Seafood
Res. Alba Ruja, Porto Cervo, 07020
Tel *0789 912 26* **Closed** *winter*
One of the Emerald Coast's best-known restaurants. Excellent fish.

DK Choice

COSTA SMERALDA: Pedristellas €€
Regional Italian
Via Monte Ladu, Porto Rotondo, 07026
Tel *377 236 92 01* **Closed** *winter*
Literally "rocks and stars" in the Sardinian dialect, this restaurant is set in a rock garden dotted with centuries-old pine trees. The tables, lighting, and meandering paths complement the natural setting. It offers an abundant menu of seafood and meat in the Sardinian tradition.

COSTA SMERALDA: Stella di Gallura €€
Regional Italian
Loc. Monte Ladu, Porto Rotondo, 07026
Tel *0789 344 02* **Closed** *winter*
Dine by the poolside and sample typical Sardinian dishes from both land and sea.

COSTA SMERALDA: Da Giovannino €€€
Fine Dining
Piazza Quadra 10, Porto Rotondo, 07026
Tel *0789 352 80* **Closed** *winter*
High-profile restaurant with a pretty garden. Excellent Mediterranean cuisine.

NUORO: Il Rifugio €€
Regional Italian
Via Antonio Mereu 28, 08100
Tel *0784 23 23 55* **Closed** *winter*
An ample variety of classic Sardinian dishes. Excellent pizza.

ORISTANO: Craf da Banana €€
Regional Italian
Via De Castro S. A. 34, 09170
Tel *0783 42 01 82* **Closed** *winter*
Wild game is the house specialty. Try the mixed grill for a range.

SANT'ANTIOCO: Moderno-da Achille €€
Regional Italian
Via Nazionale 82, 09017
Tel *0781 831 05* **Closed** *winter*
Tasty Sardinian fare expertly prepared by a talented chef who makes each dish his own, served in an elegant setting.

SASSARI: Liberty €€
Seafood
Piazza Nazario Sauro, 07100
Tel *079 23 63 61* **Closed** *winter*
The look is distinctly Art Deco at this sophisticated spot serving super-fresh fish. Long list of Sardinian wines.

For more information on types of restaurants *see p579*

SHOPPING IN ITALY

Italy is known for its quality designer goods, ranging from chic clothing and sleek cars to stylish household items. There is a strong tradition of craftsmanship, often from family-run businesses, and there are numerous markets selling regional specialties. Apart from the town markets, it is not a country for bargains, but the joys of window shopping will offer plenty of compensation. If you come from outside the European Union, you may be able to claim back the 21 percent IVA tax (VAT). Make sure you leave time at your departure airport to fulfill all administrative requirements.

Fresh vegetables on display at a Venetian market stall

Opening Hours

Open hours for shops are usually 9:30am–1pm and around 3:30–8pm, Tuesday to Saturday and Monday afternoons. However, shopkeepers are increasingly using more flexible hours. There are few department stores, but most large towns will have a Standa, Upim, Coin, or Rinascente. These stores are often open nonstop *(orario continuato)* from 9am–8pm, Monday to Saturday. Music stores and bookstores sometimes stay open after 8pm and on Sundays.

Food Shops

Even though there are supermarkets throughout Italy, the specialist shops, although more expensive, are still the most interesting way to shop. A *forno* has the best bread and a *macellaio* has the finest meat (go to a *norcineria* for pork products). Vegetables are freshest from market stalls or the *fruttivendolo*. You can buy cakes at the *pasticceria*, milk at the *latteria*, and pasta, ham, cheese, and general foods at the often impressively stocked *alimentari*. Here you can also buy wine, but for a wider choice, head for the *enoteca*, *vineria*, or *vinaio*, where you can sometimes taste the wine before purchasing.

Markets

All towns have regional weekly markets. Large towns will have several small daily markets followed by a weekly flea market, usually on Sunday. In this guide the main market days are listed under each town. Traders set up at 5am and start to clear away at about 1:30pm. Food is sold by the *etto* (100 grams, or 3.5 oz) and the *chilo* (kilo, or 2.2 pounds) *(see p665)*, or in numbers (two onions, etc.). Food stands selling seasonal products generally have fresher and cheaper produce than the shops. Bargaining is not customary when buying food, but it is worth asking for a discount *(sconto)* for clothes.

Seasonal Produce

To make the most of Italian food, try to buy and eat what is in season. Grapes and mushrooms are best in fall, while spring is the season for asparagus and strawberries. In winter, vegetables such as Roman artichokes, cauliflower, and broccoli are at their best, as are lemons from Amalfi and Sicilian blood oranges. Summer is the time for plums, pears, and cherries, as well as zucchini, eggplant, tomatoes, and melons.

Clothes and Designer Shops

Italy is renowned worldwide for its fashion industry. Milan is the fashion capital and Via Monte Napoleone, in the city center, is lined with designer boutiques. All large towns will have a selection of designer shops, usually situated near each other. Less expensive clothes are

Souvenir shop in Ostuni, near Brindisi, Puglia

An elegant designer clothing boutique in Treviso

available in markets and many department stores, where the styles tend to be more conventional. Italy is also famous for leather shoes and bags, the prices of which tend to be reasonable.

Sales *(saldi)* are held in summer and winter. Second-hand shops can be expensive, but the quality and condition of the clothes are usually very good. Larger markets have stalls piled high with used clothes. Rummage through and you will often find bargains.

Colorful shop display of leather handbags in Florence

Jewelry and Antique Shops

Glitzy gold jewelry is very popular in Italy and every *gioielleria* (jewelry shop) will have a wide selection. For more unusual items, try the *bigiotteria* or artisan shops *(oreficeria)*. Antique stores like *Antichità* and *Antiquariato* sell furniture and ornaments of varying quality and prices. You will rarely find bargains in Italy, except perhaps at the *Fiere dell'Antiquariato* (antique fairs), held throughout the year all over the country.

Interior Design and Housewares

Interior design is another Italian sector where top names demand extravagant prices, with many shops concentrating on modern, high-tech styles. There are household stores in cities and towns throughout the country. Italian kitchenware is particularly striking, with its stainless steel and copper pots, pans, and utensils. For the lowest prices, avoid the tourist shops and, if possible, buy directly from the manufacturer. Less expensive items include the characteristic brown espresso and cappuccino cups sold in all markets.

Regional Specialties

Many of Italy's regional specialties are world famous: Parma ham, Chianti wine, olive oil, and *grappa*. Regional sweets, including the Sienese *panforte* and Sicilian marzipan, are also well-known, as are cheeses such as Gorgonzola from Lombardy and Parmesan from Emilia-Romagna. Traditional crafts are still practiced in Italy and range from delicate lacework and glassware in the Veneto to leatherwork, jewelry, and marbled paper in Florence. Italian ceramics include elaborate Tuscan pottery, hand-painted dishes around Amalfi and De Simone's stylized designer plates from Sicily.

Display of decorative glazed pottery from Tuscany

Size Chart

For Australian sizes follow the British and American conversions.

Women's dresses, coats, and skirts

Italian	38	40	42	44	46	48	50
British	8	10	12	14	16	18	20
American	6	8	10	12	14	16	18

Women's shoes

Italian	36	37	38	39	40	41
British	3	4	5	6	7	8
American	5	6	7	8	9	10

Men's suits

Italian	44	46	48	50	52	54	56	58 (size)
British	34	36	38	40	42	44	46	48 (inches)
American	34	36	38	40	42	44	46	48 (inches)

Men's shirts (collar size)

Italian	36	38	39	41	42	43	44	45 (cm)
British	14	15	15½	16	16½	17	17½	18 (inches)
American	14	15	15½	16	16½	17	17½	18 (inches)

Men's shoes

Italian	39	40	41	42	43	44	45	46
British	6	7	7½	8	9	10	11	12
American	7	7½	8	8½	9½	10½	11	11½

ENTERTAINMENT IN ITALY

Italians exude strong national pride and passion about every aspect of their cultural heritage. One of Europe's key centers of culture since Roman times, Italy was the cradle of the Renaissance, and it is known today as the home of opera and a mixed bag of regional styles of folk music. The country holds one of the most acclaimed international film festivals and every town boasts a *teatro*, an elaborate classical venue with mixed programs incorporating every aspect of classic and traditional culture. Add to this the many street festivals and fairs, often in celebration of food, wine, and *la dolce vita*, and you will never have a dull moment.

Practical Information

Most venues have booking facilities online or a reservations line to call. However, major events and most opera performances tend to sell out well in advance, so it is wise to reserve tickets through ticket companies such as **Liaisons Abroad** that may still have availability when the venue itself has sold out.

If you wish to find out what's happening in Italy during your stay, check the Italian tourism website (www.italiantourism.com) or pick up a copy of *Dove*, a monthly publication about culture, travel, and gastronomy that also highlights the month's events in Rome and Milan.

Il Corriere della Sera, Italy's oldest daily, contains sections on events and culture; its ViviMilano website (www.corriere.it/vivimilano) is a mine of information on events taking place in the fashion capital. Another website (www.romaturismo.it) offers excellent service for Rome.

Tourist information offices *(see p617)* will also provide information on programs, events, and venues, as will the **Italian State Tourist Board**. Few Italian venues provide easy access for people with restricted mobility. The situation improves a little in the summer, when many events are held outside.

Opera and Classical Music

Italy has some of the world's most beautiful and historic opera houses. Venice's **La Fenice**, destroyed by fire in 1996, has been restored to its former splendor, and **Teatro alla Scala** *(see p197)* in Milan also underwent a major renovation. In addition to the original building, there is also an extra theater, **Teatro degli Arcimboldi**, allowing the Scala to host more performances.

Verona hosts a summer season of opera and classical music in the outdoor **Arena di Verona** *(see p151)*, while Rome's venues include the open-air **Baths of Caracalla** *(see p441)*, the breathtaking Renzo Piano–designed auditorium **Parco della Musica**, and the **Teatro dell'Opera**.

In May and June, Florence's **Maggio Musicale** *(see p70)* is packed with opera, ballet, and classical performances.

The opera festival in Verona attracts huge crowds to the Roman arena

Poster advertising the Venice Film Festival

Rock, Jazz, and Contemporary Music

Large concerts tend to be held in classic theaters or in sports stadiums. The **Arena di Verona** hosts big names in summer, as does the **Stadio Olimpico** in Rome. In Milan, the **Forum di Assago** sports stadium is a popular venue. Tickets for concerts are sometimes sold in record stores.

World-class jazz performers gather annually in Perugia for the **Umbria Jazz** festival in July. The website provides booking details and information.

Theater and Ballet

Italy has the highest concentration of traditional theaters in Europe, offering a mixture of theater, ballet, and classical music all under one roof. All theaters also hold ballet performances, mainly by international touring troupes. The **Scala**'s ballet company has gained international renown. Both tradition and innovation can be seen at the international festival of ballet that takes place at Genoa's **Teatro Carlo Felice** in July.

Cinema

One of the highlights of the cinema year is the **Venice Film Festival** *(see p71)*, which takes place from August to September. The Rome International Festival of Cinema *(see p72)* also draws major film stars. A smaller International Film Festival *(see p71)* is held in Taormina, Sicily, while Florence has the Festa dei Popoli *(see p72)* in winter.

A thrilling moment in the Sienese Palio race held in Piazza del Campo

Regional Dance, Music, and Festivals

Seasonal festivals are either religious, relating to patron saints, or food-oriented. The best known is *Carnevale* (literally "farewell to meat") *(see p73)*, which celebrates the end of winter and introduces Lent. Venice holds the most opulent and the oldest masquerade party, while Viareggio, in Tuscany, is famous for its lively themed floats.

Another festival highlight is the Palio of Siena *(see pp71* and *345)*, a bareback horse race that takes place twice a year in one of Italy's most beautiful squares. For further details on festivals throughout Italy, see pp70–73.

An elaborate Carnival mask

Every region in Italy has its own ancient music and dance, but the best known is the *tarantella*, a lively dance and rhythmic song from Puglia *(see p515)*. Legends trace the origins of the name to the tarantula spider, since victims of a tarantula bite would perform a frenzied dance in order to sweat out the poison.

Culture

Spectating, whether at sporting events, rural festivals, or even grand events, is what entertainment is all about. And part of this, of course, involves that very Italian pastime – seeing and being seen. You can witness this in daily life in the café culture – visit any of the large cities' popular squares, such as Piazza di Spagna or Piazza Navona in Rome, Piazza del Duomo in Milan, or Piazza San Marco in Venice, and you will see people of all ages parading around in their best clothes. This is referred to as *la passeggiata*, a walk around that becomes a ritual at weekends, along the seafront and lakeside promenades in summer and in city and town centers.

Another aspect of daily life is *l'aperitivo*. This ritual of joining friends for an early evening drink after work or before going on to dinner or to a nightclub is back in fashion. Bars provide abundant finger-food buffets to accompany the drinks, which are generally priced higher than at other times of day. This trend has spawned lounge clubs in the major cities.

DIRECTORY

Practical Information

Italian State Tourist Board
1 Princes Street, London W1B 2AY.
Tel 020 7408 1254.
W italiantouristboard.co.uk

Liaisons Abroad
Tel 020 7808 7330.
W liaisonsabroad.com

Opera and Classical Music

Arena di Verona
Piazza Brà, Verona.
Tel 045 800 51 51.
W arena.it

Baths of Caracalla
Via delle Terme di Caracalla 52, Rome.
Map 7 A3.

La Fenice
Campo San Fantin, Venice.
Map 7 A2. **Tel** 041 786 511. **W teatrolafenice.it**

Maggio Musicale
Florence.
W maggiofiorentino.it

Parco della Musica
Viale de Coubertin 30, Rome. **Tel** 06 80 24 12 81.
W auditorium.com

Teatro alla Scala
Via Filodrammatici 2, Milan. **Tel** 02 72 00 37 44.
W teatroallascala.org

Teatro degli Arcimboldi
Viale dell'Innovazione 20, Milan.
Tel 02 641 142 212.
W teatroarcimboldi.it

Teatro dell'Opera
Piazza B. Gigli 7, Rome.
Map 3 C3.
Tel 06 48 16 01.
W operaroma.it

Rock, Jazz, and Contemporary Music

Forum di Assago
Via G. Di Vittorio 6, Assago, Milan.
Tel 02 48 85 71.
W mediolanumforum.it

Stadio Olimpico
Viale dei Gladiatori, Rome.

Umbria Jazz
Tel 075 573 24 32.
W umbriajazz.com

Theater and Ballet

Teatro Carlo Felice
Passo E. Montale 4, Genova.
Tel 010 58 93 29.
W carlofelicegenova.it

Cinema

Venice Film Festival
Tel 041 521 87 11.
W labiennale.org

Specialty Vacations and Outdoor Activities

Italy offers an amazing variety of cultural, sporting, and leisure activities. However, many schools and groups require annual membership and short-term activities are often expensive and difficult to find. Information on current leisure and sporting events in a specific region is available from the tourist office listed for each town in this guide. For details on annual festivals, see *Italy Through the Year* on pages 70–73. The following suggestions include some of the most popular as well as some more unusual pursuits.

Cycling on the tree-lined flatlands of the Po Delta

Walking, Cycling, and Horseback Riding

Some Italian branches of the **World Wide Fund for Nature (WWF)** organize walks and treks. **Club Alpino Italiano (CAI)** runs trekking and climbing excursions and the **Italian Birds Protection League (LIPU)** arranges nature walks and bird-watching trips. The military *IGM* maps are the most detailed but unfortunately are only available from specialty map shops.

Cycling is popular despite Italy's mountainous landscape. Travel bookshops stock publications with suggested routes, such as the Po Delta, which has miles of scenic flatlands.

Many riding schools organize trips and outings, which are also advertised in the local press. For general information, contact the **Federazione Italiana Sport Equestri**.

Mountain Sports

The most well-equipped and famous ski resorts are in the Dolomites, in the Italian Alps, and around Turin, the city chosen to host the 2006 Winter Olympics. There are also smaller and less expensive resorts in the Apennines and in Sicily. Package ski vacations, arranged from outside Italy, offer the best deals.

Group hiking tour in the Dolomites of Trentino-Alto Adige *(see p82)*

The **Federazione Arrampicata Sportiva Italiana** has a list of mountain climbing schools that arrange climbs for all levels.

Ski lift near the desolate Falzarego Pass, in the heart of the Dolomites

Archaeological Digs

The British monthly magazine *Archaeology Abroad*, available in the UK, gives a comprehensive list of archaeology groups and digs worldwide. In Italy, the **Gruppo Archeologico Romano** runs two-week digs in various regions. There are summer and winter digs, for both adults and children. The group has contacts with local archaeological organizations as well.

Italian Language and Culture

For a wide selection of material on courses and schools in Italy, contact the Italian consulate in your home country. The **Società Dante Alighieri** provides courses in the Italian language, history of art, literature, and culture. There are both full- and part-time courses available, for every level. Language schools abound in Italy's main cities and are advertised in the Yellow Pages *(Pagine Gialle)* or foreign-language bookshops and newspapers. For young students, **Intercultura** will organize weekly, monthly, and year-long exchanges including language courses, accommodation with Italian families, and enrollment in Italian schools. Cooking vacations run

A lesson in Italian cookery in Sicily

by English-speaking experts in Italian cooking have become very popular. **Tasting Places**, for example, has wine tours and week-long courses in Italian cuisine, and provides beautiful accommodations. The course locations include the Veneto, Sicily, Tuscany, and Umbria. Wine-tasting tours are organized by local tourist boards. The Università per Stranieri in Perugia runs courses in Italian, art history, and literature (www.unistrapg.it).

Water Sports

Most lakes and many seaside resorts rent out sailboats, canoes, and windsurfing equipment. Lessons and courses are organized by clubs, which usually require membership. For a list of authorized associations, contact the **Federazione Italiana Canoa Kayak** and the **Federazione Italiana Vela**. Weekend and weekly sailing vacations and courses are featured in the magazine *Avventure nel Mondo*, and most travel agents have a selection of sailing vacations.

Swimming pools are expensive in Italy and many do not accept people on a daily basis. You often have to pay a membership fee and a monthly tariff. Some of the luxurious hotels open their pools to the public in summer, but at pricey rates. Water parks are popular and provide pools, slides, wave machines, and games. Before diving into any lakes or rivers (and even the sea near main towns) it is best to check that the water is not polluted. The **Federazione Italiana di Attività Subacquee** runs underwater diving courses, and can give information on all local centers.

Air Sports

There are schools nationwide that offer hang-gliding and flying courses, but the minimum duration of each course is one month. For information and a list of schools contact the **AeroClub Italia**. You must be licensed before you can fly and all crafts must be registered with AeroClub.

Other Sports

Golf is a popular sport in Italy, and there are plenty of courses to choose from. Home membership and handicap are often required for daily access to a club. Italian tennis clubs usually operate on a membership basis, unless you are invited as a member's guest. The national **Federazione Italiana di Tennis** has a list of all the tennis clubs in Italy. The opportunity to watch a professional soccer game should not be missed. Seats can be scarce, so buy tickets in advance from the stadium. Most Serie A matches are played on Sundays, with international games taking place on Tuesdays and Wednesdays.

Playing golf

Sailing in Italy, a popular leisure activity and competitive sport

DIRECTORY

AeroClub Italia
Via Cesare Beccaria 35a, 00196 Rome. **Tel** 06 36 08 46 00.
W aeci.it

Club Alpino Italiano
Via E Petrella 19, Milan.
Tel 02 205 72 31. **W cai.it**

Federazione Arrampicata Sportiva Italiana
Via del Terrapieno 27, 40127 Bologna. **Tel** 051 601 48 90.
W federclimb.it

Federazione Italiana Attività Subacquee
Via A Doria 8, Milan.
Tel 02 670 50 05. **W fias.it**

Federazione Italiana Canoa Kayak
Viale Tiziano 70, 00196 Rome.
Tel 06 36 85 81 88.
W federcanoa.it

Federazione Italiana Sport Equestri
Viale Tiziano 74, 00196 Rome.
Tel 06 836 68 41. **W fise.it**

Federazione Italiana di Tennis
Stadio Olimpico, Rome.
Tel 06 36 85 82 18.
W federtennis.it

Federazione Italiana Vela
Piazza Borgo Pila 40, Genova.
Tel 010 54 45 41. **W federvela.it**

Gruppo Archeologico Romano
Via Baldi degli Ubaldi 168, 00167 Rome. **Tel** 06 638 52 56.
W gruppoarcheologico.it

Intercultura
Via Venezia 25, 00184 Rome.
Tel 06 48 88 24 01.
W intercultura.it

Italian Birds Protection League (LIPU)
Via Udine 3A, 43122 Parma.
Tel 0521 27 30 43. **W lipu.it**

Società Dante Alighieri
Piazza Firenze 27, 00186 Rome.
Tel 06 687 36 94. **W ladante.it**

Tasting Places Cookery and Wine Tours
PO Box 38174, London W10 5ZP.
Tel 020 8964 5333.
W tastingplaces.com

World Wide Fund for Nature
Via Po 25c, 00198 Rome.
Tel 06 84 49 71. **W wwf.it**

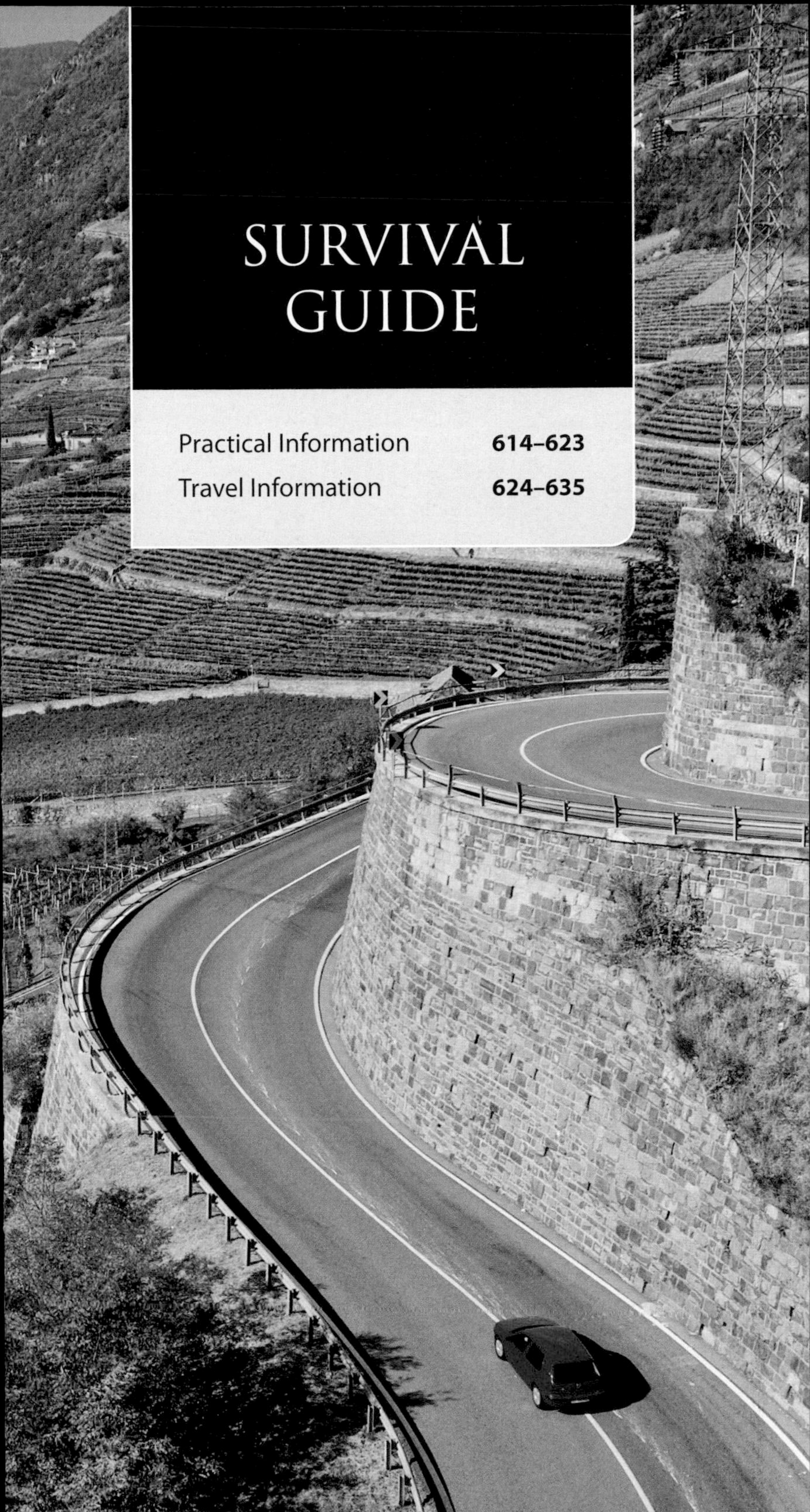

SURVIVAL GUIDE

PRACTICAL INFORMATION

Ask any Italian and they will almost certainly tell you that Italy is the most beautiful country in the world. They may not be far wrong. However, the charm and allure of Italy may help to veil some of her numerous practical problems. Getting information is rarely straightforward; public offices and banks are nearly always crippled by long lines and bureaucracy; and the postal service is renowned for its inefficiency. This section, together with some forward planning and a little patience, should help you cope with some of Italy's idiosyncrasies.

Tourists crossing the Ponte della Paglia in Venice *(see p113)*

When to Visit

The northern part of Italy is generally more temperate than the south, which has a Mediterranean climate. From June to September the weather is hot throughout the country and, in peak summer, also humid. Seaside resorts tend to get very busy. Spring and autumn are ideal for visiting cities as temperatures are milder, making sightseeing much more comfortable, although you should be prepared for the unexpected downpour.

Italy's towns and historic sites are extremely popular attractions and it is worth considering this when planning your trip. Most sights are open all year, except on some public holidays *(see p73)*, and most close one day a week. Rome, Florence, and Venice are all crowded from spring to October and it is a good idea to reserve a hotel room well in advance. In August the cities are generally slightly less busy, seemingly abandoned by their inhabitants for summer vacations.

In February, Venice triples its population during Carnevale *(see p73)*, and at Easter, Rome is overrun by pilgrims and tourists. Winter can be bitterly cold, especially in the north, and December to March is the time of year for skiing in the high-altitude resorts of the Italian Alps. *The Climate of Italy* on pages 76–7 takes a detailed look at the country's regional weather.

Visas and Permesso di Soggiorno

European Union nationals and citizens of the United States, Canada, Australia, and New Zealand do not need visas for stays of up to three months. Most European Union (EU) visitors need only a valid passport, including a photograph.

All visitors should check requirements with the Italian embassy before traveling and officially declare themselves to the Italian police within eight days of arrival. If you are staying in a hotel or campsite, this will be done for you by the staff, otherwise you will need to contact the local *Questura* (police station) yourself.

Anyone wishing to stay in Italy for more than three months will have to obtain a *permesso di soggiorno* (permit to stay or residence permit). Non-EU citizens must apply for one within eight days of arrival. You can apply for a residence permit at any main police station (*Questura*). In some cases you can obtain a kit containing the necessary application form from main post offices. You must apply for the correct permit, either a permit to work *(lavoro)* or a permit to study *(studio)*. The necessary documentation is listed on the *Questura* website *(see p617)*.

To apply for a study permit, it is necessary to get a letter from the relevant school or university at which you intend to study, giving details of your course of study. This then has to be sent to the Italian consulate in your own country of origin to obtain an official cover letter, or declaration.

You will also need some form of guarantee that your medical bills will be paid if you become ill or have an accident where you require medical treatment. A comprehensive insurance policy for the length of your stay *(see p619)* will usually be sufficient.

Rome's renowned Tazza d'Oro café, an ideal rest stop after sightseeing

◀ The wonderful view from the A22 road that carves through the mountains and vineyards that surround Bolzano

Customs

On June 30, 1999, the intra-EU Duty and Tax Free Allowances, better known as Duty-free and mainly affecting such high-tax items as alcohol, perfumes, and tobacco, were abolished. However, for EU residents the amount of these goods that can be imported for personal use has increased.

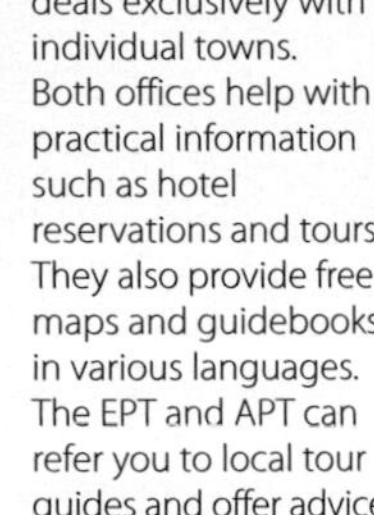

Sign for tourist information

Consulates can generally provide up-to-date information on particular customs regulations. To find out what you can take back from Italy to non-EU countries, contact that particular country's customs department, which will be able to advise you.

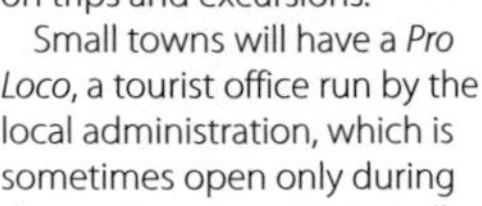

Tax Exemption

Value Added Tax (IVA in Italy) ranges from about 21 percent, with a reduced rate of 4–10 percent on some items. Non-European Union citizens making purchases in Italy can claim an IVA rebate, provided that total purchases in the one shop are over €155. It is a long process, and it is easier to get a refund if you shop where you see the "Euro Free Tax" sign, rather than from a market stall. In this instance, show your passport to the shop assistant, complete a form, and the IVA will be deducted from your bill. Alternatively, present a customs officer with your purchases and their receipts on your departure from Italy. He or she will stamp the receipts, which you then send to the vendor. A refund should eventually be sent to you.

Tourist Information

The national tourist board, **ENIT**, has a good website as well as branches in capital cities worldwide, and offers general information on Italy. For specific requests, contact the local tourist office. The addresses and telephone numbers are listed under each town or city, directly under the title, and they are plotted on the town and city maps. An EPT *(Ente Provinciale di Turismo)* has information on its town and surrounding province, whereas an APT *(Azienda di Promozione Turistica)* deals exclusively with individual towns. Both offices help with practical information such as hotel reservations and tours. They also provide free maps and guidebooks in various languages. The EPT and APT can refer you to local tour guides and offer advice on trips and excursions.

Small towns will have a *Pro Loco*, a tourist office run by the local administration, which is sometimes open only during the tourist season. It is usually located in the town hall.

Tours

Many tour companies organize bus tours, with English-speaking guides, that include all the main tourist attractions in Italy. Companies such as the UK-based **Leger Holidays** offer bus tours that go all over the country. If you are looking for something a little more personal and off the beaten track, check the local pages of national newspapers for tour groups or organizations. Local tourist boards will also be able to advise you. Always employ official guides and be sure to establish the fee in advance. For information on theme vacations, including sporting and cultural activities, turn to pages 610–11.

A guided group tour through the streets of Florence

Daytime sightseeing on a tranquil canal in Venice

Sightseeing Opening Hours

Italian museums are gradually conforming to regulations, particularly in the northern and central regions of the country, opening from 9am–7pm daily, except for Mondays. In winter, however, many museums revert to slightly earlier closing times, particularly on Sundays, but it is best to check.

Privately run and smaller museums set their own opening times, so it is a good idea to phone in advance to avoid disappointment. Archaeological sites are generally open from 9am to one hour before sunset, Tuesday to Sunday. Churches are usually open from about 7am–12:30pm and 4–7pm. However, they often prefer not to let tourists in during services, so Sunday is not the best day to visit.

Admission Charges

Sightseeing fees range from €2 to €12. Churches are usually free, but some expect a donation, and you will need coins to illuminate some works of art. Discounts for students are not always offered but many state-run museums and archaeological sites allow free entry for EU residents under 18 and over 60 or 65 years of age. Large groups are often entitled to a discount as well. If discounts are available, you will need to show a valid form of identification.

Etiquette and Tipping

People in Italy are friendly toward foreign visitors. On entering a shop or bar it is customary to greet people with a general *buon giorno* (good morning) or *buona sera* (good evening), and the same applies when leaving. They will also try to be helpful when asked directions in the street. If your Italian is slight, simply saying *scusi*, followed by the name of the place you wish to go to, will often suffice. *Grazie* (thank you) is replied to with *prego* (you're welcome).

Tipping in restaurants is expected when the 10–15 percent service is not included. However, as much as 10 percent would be considered generous, and a tip is often not expected at all in more basic restaurants. Taxi drivers and hotel porters expect a few euros if they have been helpful. You could simply round the bill up to the nearest €2.

Italians are very dress-conscious and unusual clothes do get noticed. Be aware that in places of worship you should cover your torso and upper arms; shorts and skirts must reach below the knee.

Smoking is forbidden in all buildings open to the public (including offices, shops, bars, and restaurants). However, it is tolerated in outdoor public places, whereas drunkenness is definitely frowned upon.

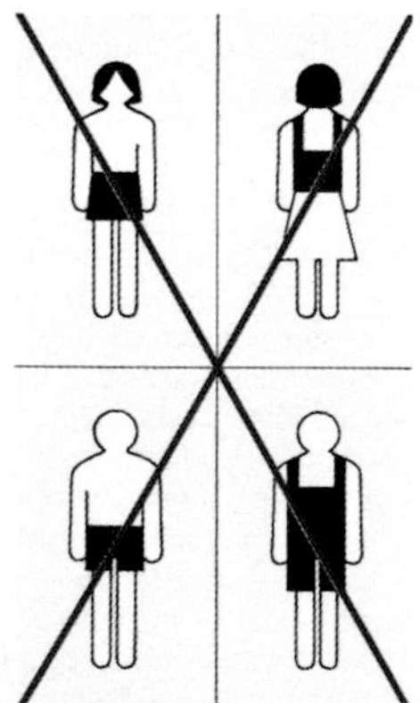

Unacceptable dress in church: both sexes are required to cover torsos and upper arms

A student relaxing in the sun in Gaiole in Chianti

Religious Services

Around 35 percent of the population is practicing Catholic. Sunday mass is celebrated throughout the country, while in the principal churches, services are also held during the week. In major cities some churches, such as the church of Santa Susanna (Via XX Settembre 14) in Rome, offer services and confession in English. For some visitors, a trip to Rome will include an audience with the pope *(see p423)*.

With increasing numbers of foreigners making their home in Italy, all the main religious beliefs are also represented. For details contact the main centers in Rome.

Student Information

The national student travel organization, **CTS** (Centro Turistico Studentesco), has branches throughout Italy and Europe. They issue the International Student Identity Card (ISIC) and the Youth International Educational Exchange Card (YIEE). Both can be used, along with a passport, for discounts at museums and other tourist attractions. The ISIC card also gives holders access to a free 24-hour telephone helpline in cases of emergency. As well as issuing youth cards, CTS offers cut-rate car rental and will organize vacations and courses. For details about youth hostels, contact the **Associazione Italiana Alberghi per la Gioventù** (the Italian YHA), providing that you are a current member.

ISIC card

Traveling with Children

On the whole, Italians love children, to an extent that sometimes seems over-indulgent. Most trattorias and pizzerias welcome them and there are no rules excluding children from bars; however, high chairs are unusual. Hotels also welcome children, but smaller establishments may have limited facilities. Some of the more upscale hotels will arrange a babysitting service. Very few museums, on the other hand, provide special child-oriented activities. It is common to see children playing outside fairly late at night, especially in summer. Most towns have city parks with playgrounds, and many have summer amusement parks. Regular stops for *gelato* are guaranteed to go down well with youngsters. For young swimmers, the calm Mediterranean is ideal, though care should always be taken.

Disabled Travelers

Awareness of the needs of the disabled is improving in Italy, especially in major cities, with ramps being added to museums and some churches. Trains and buses are also becoming more disabled-friendly. In Milan **AIAS**

(Associazione Italiana Assistenza Spastici) and in Rome **CO.IN. Sociale** and **Roma per Tutti** provide information and general assistance. Train travelers with **Trenitalia** on both international and domestic routes receive help with reservations and assistance at stations.

Public Conveniences

Gabinetto means public restroom, though signs often say WC. Tourist cities have well-marked public conveniences that charge around €1. Some have cleaning staff on hand and a tip may be left. Italian cafés usually have a restroom for their customers, but it is worth checking first. Old-style "crouch" toilets are still common.

Electrical Adapters

The voltage in Italy is 220 volts, with two-pin round-pronged plugs, so it is a good idea to bring a universal adapter with you or buy one in the country. Most hotels with three or more stars have hair-dryer points in all bedrooms, but check the voltage first, to be safe.

Italian Time

Italy is one hour ahead of Greenwich Mean Time (GMT). The clocks are put forward one hour in March and back in October. For example: London is 1 hour behind Italy; Sydney is 9 hours ahead; while Ottawa is 6 hours behind.

Responsible Travel

Local attitudes toward environmental issues are developing rather slowly in Italy, despite the efforts of many concerned groups such as the Verdi political party. However, there are opportunities for low-impact travel and alternative green options available.

Staying at family run guest-houses instead of international hotel chains helps support local economies. National and regional parks award eco labels to hotels and guesthouses that adhere to EU rules governing sustainable tourism, which cover issues such as energy and water saving, waste disposal, and use of local products. The **National Association for Agritourism and Agriturismo** *(see p560)* offers countrywide farm stays. These are a great way of enjoying the countryside and experiencing local traditions, as well as helping supplement the income of small farm owners. Facilities vary and some farms offer visitors the opportunity to help out.

Farmers' markets and growers who sell their produce direct to the public are now more common, guaranteeing fresh, seasonal produce. Look for the label *biologico* when searching for organic produce.

Conversion Chart

Imperial to Metric
1 inch = 2.54 centimeters
1 foot = 30 centimeters
1 mile = 1.6 kilometers
1 ounce = 28 grams
1 pound = 454 grams
1 pint = 0.57 liter
1 gallon = 4.6 liters

Metric to Imperial
1 centimeter = 0.4 inch
1 meter = 3 feet 3 inches
1 kilometer = 0.6 mile
1 gram = 0.04 ounce
1 kilogram = 2.2 pounds
1 liter = 1.8 pints

DIRECTORY

Questura and Permits

W **poliziadistato.it**

W **portale immigrazione.it**

W **esteri.it/visti**

Italian Customs and Tax

W **agenziadogane.it**

Tourist Information and Tours

APT Florence
Via Cavour 1r. **Map** 2 D4.
Tel 055 29 08 32.
W **firenzeturismo.it**

APT Siena
Piazza del Campo 56.
Tel 0577 28 05 51.
W **terresiena.it**

APT Venice
Piazza San Marco 71f.
Map 7 B2.
Tel 041 529 87 11.
W **turismovenezia.it**

ENIT
W **italia.it**

IAT Milan
Piazza Castello 1.
Tel 02 77 40 43 43.
W **visitamilano.it**

Leger Holidays
Tel 0844 504 62 51.
W **leger.co.uk**

Rome Tourist Office
Termini Station, Platform 24. **Map** 4 D3. **Tel** 06 06 08. W **060608.it**

Religious Organizations

Catholic
Ufficio Informazioni Vaticano, Piazza San Pietro, Vaticano, Rome.
Map 1 B3.
Tel 06 69 88 16 62.

Jewish
Unione delle Comunità Ebraiche Italiane, Lungotevere Sanzio 9, Rome. **Map** 6 D1.
Tel 06 45 54 22 00.
W **ucei.it**

Muslim
Centro Islamico Culturale d'Italia, Viale della Moschea 85, Rome.
Tel 06 808 22 58.

Student Information

Associazione Italiana Alberghi per la Gioventù
Via Cavour 44 (3rd floor), Rome. **Map** 3 C5.
Tel 06 487 11 52.
W **aighostels.com**

CTS
Via Solferino 6A, Rome.
Map 4 D3.
Tel 06 462 04 31.
W **cts.it**

Disabled Tours

AIAS
Via P. Mantegazza 10, Milan. **Tel** 02 330 20 21.
W **aiasmilano.it**

CO.IN.Sociale
Via E. Giglioli 54A, Rome.
W **coinsociale.it**

Roma per Tutti
Tel 06 57 17 70 94.
W **romapertutti.it**

Responsible Travel

National Association for Agritourism
W **agriturist.it**

Personal Security and Health

Although Italy is generally a safe place for visitors, it is wise to keep a watchful eye on your personal belongings, especially in the larger towns and cities. There is a conspicuous police presence throughout the country, and in the event of an emergency or crime, any of the police officers described in this section will be able to assist you and tell you where to go to report an incident. If you fall ill, pharmacies are a good first stop where medically trained staff can give advice or tell you where to find further help. In an emergency, the Emergency Department (*Pronto Soccorso*) of any hospital will treat you and it is likely that you will encounter English-speaking staff, especially in large towns.

Commissariato di Polizia – a police station

Police car

Green Cross ambulance in Venice

Roman fire engine

Personal Property

Petty theft such as pickpocketing, bag snatching, and car theft is common in Italian cities. In the event of a theft you must report it within 24 hours to the nearest *questura* or *commissariato di polizia* (police station). If possible, show them some ID.

Avoid leaving anything visible in an unattended car, including a car radio. If you have to leave luggage in a car, find a hotel that has private parking. When making a purchase, always check your change, and do not keep wallets in back pockets, especially on buses or in other crowded places. "Fanny packs" and money belts are a favorite target for pickpockets, so try to keep them hidden. When walking, hold bags and cameras in front of you and on the inside of the sidewalk so as not to tempt motorized snatchers, and do not show expensive cameras and video equipment in areas off tourist routes.

If attacked, never attempt to hang on to your things, as you could be seriously injured and dragged along the street.

Avoid carrying large sums of money – take out only what you need for the day.

It is recommended to get comprehensive travel insurance that covers theft of personal possessions in addition to covering cancellation/delay of flights; loss/damage of luggage, money, and other valuables; and personal liability and accidents. It should include coverage for legal assistance and advice.

If you do need to make an insurance claim for stolen or lost property, you must get a copy of the report (*denuncia*) from the police station when you report the incident. In case of lost passports, go to your embassy or consulate; for lost credit cards or travelers' checks, contact the issuing company's nearest office.

If you do not have insurance coverage, contact your embassy as soon as possible after an incident, such as an accident, occurs. The embassy can offer advice and should provide you with a list of English- and Italian-speaking lawyers who are knowledgeable about both the Italian and other legal systems.

Personal Security

Although petty crime in cities is frequent, violent crime in Italy is rare. However, it is common for people to raise their voices aggressively during an argument. Usually, remaining calm and being polite will help to defuse the situation.

Always be wary of unofficial tour guides, taxi drivers, or strangers who wish to assist you or advise you on accommodations, restaurants, or shops, as they may expect something in return. Decline their offers politely but firmly.

A team of *carabinieri* in their usual police uniform

Women Travelers

Women traveling on their own in Italy are likely to meet with a lot of attention. This is often more of an irritation than a danger, but it is best to keep away from lonely, unlit streets and areas near train stations at night, and to carry an alarm or whistle and be equipped with the telephone numbers of your hotel and a local taxi service. Walking quickly and purposefully is a good way to avoid any unwanted attention. The staff at hotels and restaurants generally treat their single female guests and customers with extra care and attention.

The Police

There are several different police forces in Italy and each one fulfills a particular role. The state police, *la polizia*, wear blue uniforms and drive blue cars. They deal with most crimes.

The *carabinieri* are militarily trained and wear dark blue and black uniforms with red striped trousers. These officers deal with a variety of offenses from organized crime to speeding and can also conduct random security checks.

The *guardia di finanza* are the financial police force (the fraud squad), and wear gray uniforms with yellow striped trousers. The *vigili urbani*, or the municipal traffic police, wear blue and white uniforms in winter and white during the summer.

Municipal policeman

Even though they are not official police officers, the *vigili urbani* can issue heavy fines for traffic and parking offenses. They can usually be spotted patrolling the streets, enforcing laws, or directing traffic. Officers from any of the forces will be able to help in an emergency.

Outside a Florentine pharmacy with a green cross sign

Medical Treatment

Emergency medical care in Italy is free for all EU and Australian citizens, thanks to reciprocal agreements. The EHIC European Health Insurance Card, which Is available from the UK Department of Health offices and website, or from a main post office, covers emergencies only; private medical insurance is needed for all other types of treatment. The card comes with a booklet that contains general health advice and information about how to claim free medical treatment when traveling abroad. You may find you have to pay and reclaim the money later. Australians need to apply to Medicare.

Non-EU citizens should try to arrive in Italy with comprehensive private medical insurance to cover all eventualities. If you do need emergency treatment, go to the *Pronto Soccorso* (Emergency Department) of the nearest hospital. If necessary, you will be referred to the appropriate specialist or department within the same structure. As an alternative, ask your hotel to call the night doctor – *guardia medica* – who can be consulted on the phone.

No inoculations are needed for Italy, but mosquito repellent is recommended in summer. Repellent creams and sprays are found in pharmacies, as are electric insect repellers, which burn pellets to deter the bugs.

Pharmacies

Various medical products, including homeopathic medicines, are available in any pharmacy (*farmacia*), but a prescription is often required. Qualified staff will offer advice for minor ailments and common illnesses and provide appropriate medicines. Thanks to a night duty roster (*servizio notturno*), there is always a pharmacy open in all cities and most towns. Those that are open at night are listed in the local pages of daily newspapers and on all pharmacy doors.

Pharmacies also sell toiletries and beauty items. Common nonprescription pharmaceutical products such as aspirin are also sold at lower prices in many large supermarkets.

DIRECTORY

Embassies and Consulates

Australia
Via A. Bosio 5, Rome. **Tel** 06 85 27 21. **W italy.embassy.gov.au**

Canada
Via Zara 30, Rome. **Tel** 06 8544 429 11. **W canada.it**

United Kingdom
Via XX Settembre 80a, Rome. **Map** 4 D2. **Tel** 06 42 20 00 01. **W ukinitaly.fco.gov.uk**

United States
Via Veneto 119a, Rome. **Map** 3 C1. **Tel** 06 467 41. **W italy.usembassy.gov**

Emergency Numbers

General Emergency
Tel 113.

Fire Service
Tel 115.

Medical Emergencies
Tel 118.

Police (Carabinieri)
Tel 112.

Medical Treatment

Medicare Australia
Information for individuals and families
W medicareaustralia.gov.au

UK Department of Health
Information for travelers
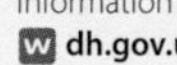
W dh.gov.uk

Banking and Local Currency

Virtually all Italian hotels, many shops, large restaurants, and gas stations accept major credit cards. Only in the more off-the-beaten-track locations will you have difficulties without euros, and some establishments will offer a discount for payments made in cash, especially in the off-season. When you pay with a credit card, you might be asked to show identification, such as your passport. Foreign currency can be changed in banks, although these are often crowded and service tends to be slow. All banks will cash travelers' checks, and cash machines *(bancomat)* will accept cards with a PIN. Most machines also accept MasterCard, VISA, and American Express cards. Although banks often have the best exchange rates, bureaux de change and foreign exchange machines can be more convenient.

ATM, which also accepts VISA and MasterCard (Access)

Changing money

Banking hours are somewhat restrictive and can also be slightly erratic, so it is safest to acquire a small amount of local currency before you arrive in Italy. Exchange rates will vary from place to place.

Travelers' checks are still a safe way to carry money, though commission charges can be hefty. Choose a well-known name such as Thomas Cook or American Express. Once you arrive, the most convenient way to change money is to use the electronic exchange machines, which are located at all major airports, train stations, and some banks. The machines have multilingual instructions and the exchange rate is clearly displayed on the screen. Simply feed in bills of the same foreign currency and you will receive euros in return.

Bureaux de change can be found in all main towns. Although they are easier to use, they usually have worse exchange rates and charge more commission than banks.

Regional differences in cost of living

The north is generally more expensive than the south, but there are many exceptions. Restaurants and hotels off the beaten track are usually better value, and buying locally made produce is cost effective if you avoid obvious tourist traps.

Banking hours

Banks are usually open between 8:30am and 1:30pm, Monday to Friday. Most also open for an hour in the afternoon, from about 2:15pm to 3pm or 2:30pm until 3:30pm, depending on the bank. All banks close on week-ends and for public holidays, and they also close early the day before a major holiday.

Metal-detecting security doors found at most banks

Bureaux de change, however, are often open all day, and in some places they also stay open until late at night.

Using banks

For security purposes, most banks have electronic double doors with metal detectors, allowing one person in at a time. Metal objects and bags should first be deposited in lockers situated in the foyer. Press the button to open the outer door, then wait for it to close behind you. The inner door then opens automatically. Do not be alarmed by the heavily armed guards who patrol most banks in Italy.

Changing money at a bank can be a frustrating process involving endless form-filling and standing in line. First you have to go to the window that displays the *cambio* sign and then to the *cassa* to obtain your money. If in doubt, ask someone in order to avoid waiting in the wrong line.

If you need to have money sent to you in Italy, banks at home can transfer money to an Italian bank, but it can take up to a week. American Express, Thomas Cook, and Western Union all provide swifter money transfer services, with a charge to the sender.

Cash machines

Withdrawing cash from an ATM (automatic teller machine) with a credit card is a straightforward process. Choose your language on the screen and follow the instructions. You will need to type in your PIN, so have it handy. Should your card be swallowed up by a cash machine for some reason (for example if you typed an incorrect number), it may be sent back to the issuing bank. However, if the bank is open do ask inside. Costs for cash withdrawals are set by your bank so check before you travel. It may be a good idea to take out a largish amount of money in one go, but bear in mind that ATMs may run out of bills on weekends.

The euro

The euro (€) is the common currency of the European Union. It came into general circulation on January 1, 2002, initially for twelve participating countries. Italy was one of those twelve countries, and the lire was phased out by March 2002.

EU members using the Euro as sole official currency are known as the Eurozone. Several EU members have opted out of joining this common currency. Euro bills are identical throughout the Eurozone countries, each one including designs of fictional architectural structures. The coins, however, have one side identical (the value side) and one side with an image unique to each country. Bills and coins are exchangeable in each participating country.

Euro Bills

The EU prints euro bills in seven denominations. The €5 bill (gray in color) is the smallest, followed by the €10 bill (pink), €20 bill (blue), €50 bill (orange), €100 bill (green), €200 bill (yellow), and €500 bill (purple). All euro bills show the 12 stars of the European Union.

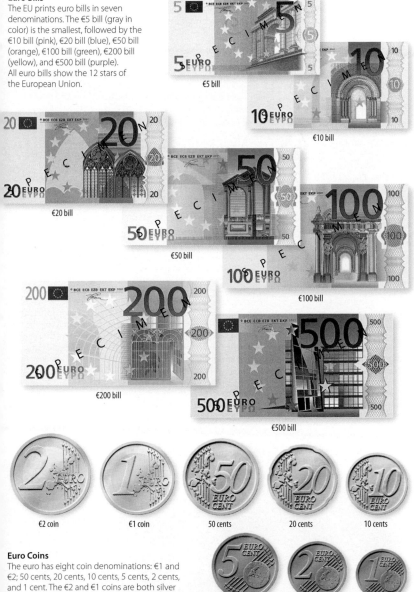

€5 bill

€10 bill

€20 bill

€50 bill

€100 bill

€200 bill

€500 bill

€2 coin

€1 coin

50 cents

20 cents

10 cents

Euro Coins

The euro has eight coin denominations: €1 and €2; 50 cents, 20 cents, 10 cents, 5 cents, 2 cents, and 1 cent. The €2 and €1 coins are both silver and gold in color. The 50-, 20-, and 10-cent coins are gold. The 5-, 2-, and 1-cent coins are bronze.

5 cents

2 cents

1 cent

Communications and Media

Although the Italian postal service is known for being very slow, Italy's other forms of communication, at least in the cities, are more efficient. Fax machines, courier services, and telephones are all widespread, and Internet access is available throughout Italy. Foreign-language newspapers and magazines are on sale in all cities and most large towns. Both state-run and privately owned television stations exist, but only satellite television and radio stations broadcast foreign-language programs.

Telephone company logo

Public Telephones

The Italian national telephone company is Telecom Italia. Coin-operated telephones have been phased out and replaced by card-operated machines. Most public telephones have instructions in five languages (Italian, English, French, Spanish, and German). To select a language, push the top right-hand button. To use a public telephone you will need a Telecom Italia phone card. Phone cards (*carta* or *scheda telefonica*) can be purchased from bars, newspaper kiosks, post offices, and *tabacchi* displaying the black-and-white T sign.

International phone cards, on sale at *tabacchi* and newsstands, are still a very cheap way to call abroad. Some cards offer as many as 3 hours of calls for about €10, depending on the country being called. Dial the toll-free number on the card and then enter the secret code found by scratching off the silver strip on the back of the card. You will be told the amount of credit available and then asked to dial the number you wish to call. Rates are slightly higher when calling from a mobile or public phone. Check with your hotel before using a card from your room as extra charges may be applied.

Telephone sign

Email and Internet

Internet and email services are widely available throughout Italy, particularly in urban areas, so it should not be difficult to access email accounts or connect to the web. Telecom Italia, the Italian national phone company, has set up Internet service in the country's major train stations and public phone centers. Internet time can be purchased using a regular phone card.

Some major chains of Internet providers sell magnetic cards with credit that can be used in any of their stores throughout Italy. **Internet Train**, with branches in over 40 towns, is the most visible. Visit its website for a full list of stores. In addition, small Internet shops are very common. These are usually clustered around train stations, cheap hotels, and university areas and can range from the back room of a café or bar to the corner of a launderette. Users can buy computer time in blocks as short as 15 minutes. There are usually student discounts available, and cost per minute decreases as the amount of time purchased increases.

Many hotels have Wi-Fi so travelers with their own laptop can have easy access. You'll probably need a plug adapter too. Remember that with **Skype** or **Voip Stunt** installed it's possible to make phone calls over the Internet with the help of a small microphone. Calls are free between Skype users.

Using a public Telecom Italia telephone

Cell Phones

There are four main GSM frequencies (Global System for Mobile Communications) in use around the world, so to guarantee that your phone will work, make sure you have a quad-band phone. Tri-band phones from outside the United States are also usually compatible, but because the United States uses two frequency bands itself, a U.S. tri-band phone may only have limited global coverage. Contact your service provider for clarification.

To use your mobile phone abroad you may need to get "permission" from your network operator, as often they need to enable "roaming" for your phone. At the moment, you are charged for the calls you receive as well as the calls you make, and you have to pay a substantial premium for the international leg of the call.

Another option is to purchase a local SIM card – the electronic chip that links your phone to a particular network – that can be topped up with credit and uses the local mobile phone networks. You can only do this if your handset is "unlocked" – some operators lock their phones to specific networks.

It is worth checking your insurance policy in case your phone gets stolen. You should also keep your network operator's helpline number handy for emergencies.

TV and Radio

Television channels in Italy include the state-owned RAI (Uno, Due, and Tre) and Mediaset (Retequattro, Canale Cinque, and Italia Uno). There are also many local channels. Most foreign programs are dubbed into Italian, although satellite channels, such as BBC World News, Sky, and CNN, show news and sports programs in English. There are three national radio stations and hundreds of local stations.

A selection of newspapers available at a newsstand

Newspapers

There are several national daily newspapers, including *La Stampa*, *Il Corriere della Sera*, and *La Repubblica*. Papers with the most detailed news of Italy's major cities include *Il Mattino* for Naples, *Il Messaggero* for Rome, *La Nazione* for Florence, and *Il Giornale* for Milan.

All newspapers will have local pages and listings for movies, theaters, main concerts, and other cultural events. In Rome and Milan, *La Repubblica* also publishes regular "what's happening and where to go" supplements called *TrovaRoma* and *ViviMilano* respectively. Florence's *Firenze Spettacolo* has weekly magazines with entertainment listings. The latter also has a useful restaurant section and a summary of listings in English at the back.

British and American papers, such as the *International Herald Tribune*, *The Guardian*, and *USA Today*, are readily available and tend to arrive in the main cities at around midday on the day of publication.

Post Offices

Local post offices open from 8:25am–1:50pm weekdays, and from 8:25am–noon on Saturday. Main city post offices are open from 8:25am–7pm nonstop. Many tobacconists also sell stamps.

The Vatican City and the state of San Marino have their own postal systems and stamps. Bear in mind that letters bearing San Marino or Vatican stamps can only be posted in San Marino and Vatican mailboxes.

The red mailboxes (blue in the Vatican) usually have two slots labeled *per la città* (for the city only) and *tutte le altre destinazioni* (for all other destinations).

The Italian postal service is notorious for its unreliability, and letters can take between four days and two weeks to arrive.

For faster service it is best to send letters by express mail services such as Postacelere (for letters) and Paccocelere (for larger packages). Both services are available at all main post offices and guarantee delivery within 24–72 hours. They are far cheaper than private couriers. Another reliable option is recorded delivery *(raccomandata)*. Anything of value should be sent by insured mail *(assicurata)*.

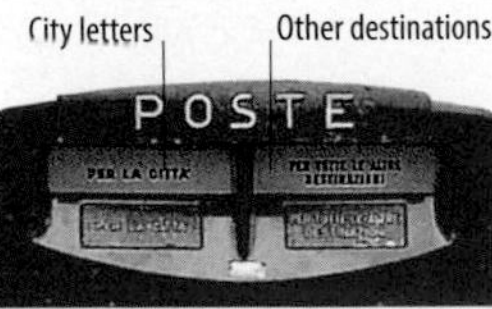

Italian mailbox

DIRECTORY

Remember to always use the full area code (including the first zero), even when making a call within a city.

Useful Numbers

Directory Assistance
Tel 1254 (Option 1).

Multilingual Directory Assistance
Tel 1254 (Option 2).

Operator Services
Tel 170 (also for collect and calling card calls).

American Operators
Tel 800 17 24 44 (AT&T).
Tel 800 17 24 01 (Verizon).
Tel 800 17 24 05 (Sprint).

Australian Operators
Tel 800 17 26 10 (Telstra).
Tel 800 17 26 11 (Optus).

Country Codes

To call Italy from these countries, dial the code and then the full area code (including the 0) and the number.

Tel 00 39 – UK

Tel 0 1139 – U.S. & Canada

Tel 00 39 – Ireland

Tel 00 1139 – Australia

Email and Internet

Internet Train
W internettrain.it

Skype
W skype.com

Voip Stunt
W voipstunt.com

Mail and Couriers

Italian Post Office
W poste.it

Private Couriers

DHL
Tel 199 199 345.
W dhl.it

FedEx
Tel 199 151 119.
W fedex.com

UPS
Tel 02 30 30 30 39.
W ups.com

TRAVEL INFORMATION

Italy has transportation systems of varying efficiency, from the modern road, bus, and railroad networks of the north to the slower systems of the south. Numerous airlines operate flights to several of the country's major airports, while within Italy itself the national carrier Alitalia, and several smaller companies, provide an extensive network of internal flights. Connections by road to the rest of Europe are good, though Alpine roads can be adversely affected by the weather in winter. Highways and other roads within the country are generally good, but can be busy on weekends and during peak periods. Italy also has an efficient system of ferries connecting Sicily, Sardinia, and many of the smaller off-shore islands. Many of these are car ferries, and are busy in summer.

Green Travel

Traveling in Italy without using high-impact flights or long car drives is straightforward, thanks to an excellent public transportation network. Train and bus systems both offer regular and reliable services and are reasonably priced. Connections with major European cities are good and travelers can often choose between day services on the Eurocity trains and overnight services on the EuroNight trains. There are also high-speed trains, known as the *Alta Velocità* (*see pp628–9*).

Where only a few people use a particular route (such as to outlying hamlets in the Alps and Apennines), some authorities have set up a *servizio a chiamata* (demand-responsive service), whereby passengers phone a toll-free number to reserve a vehicle. This results in cost savings for the council and a reduction in carbon emissions, plus passengers get a personalized taxi for the price of a single bus ticket. Within cities, less polluting vehicles such as battery- or methane-powered buses and *vaporetti* have been introduced.

Bicycle routes and rentals are increasing in number, and many cities such as Milan and Rome have plenty of rental shops and marked safe bicycle lanes. The Trentino–Alto Adige regions are especially well organized with long-distance cycle routes. For a small charge bicycles can be transported on many regional and international trains.

Arriving by Air

Rome's Leonardo da Vinci (Fiumicino) and Milan's Malpensa are the key airports for long-distance flights into Italy. Milan's Linate airport handles some European flights, and most European airlines also fly to Venice, Turin, Naples, and Pisa (for Florence). Many airlines are now flying regularly to smaller cities such as Florence, Genoa, Bologna, Verona, and Bergamo, while charter flights serve summer destinations such as Catania, Olbia, and Rimini in peak season.

Part of the extension to Fiumicino airport, Rome

Long-Distance Flights

If you are flying from the United States, **Delta** and **United Airlines** operate regular direct scheduled flights to Rome and Milan, with service from New York, Philadelphia, Los Angeles, Boston, and Chicago. **Air Canada** flies from Montreal and Toronto, and **Qantas** flies from Sydney and Melbourne.

Regular service between Rome and Milan and New York, Boston, Chicago, Miami, and Toronto is also offered by the Italian state airline, **Alitalia**.

It may, however, be more convenient and cheaper for long-distance passengers to take a budget flight to London, Frankfurt, Paris, Athens, or Amsterdam and then continue to Italy from there.

European Low-Cost Flights

It has never been so easy to get to Italy by air. **British Airways** and **Alitalia** and its partners fly to major destinations in Italy from large European cities. However, low-cost, "no-frills" airlines offer many more destinations.

Ryanair flies to more than 20 airports (including Genoa, Rome-Ciampino, Turin, and Venice-Treviso) from Stansted; while **easyJet**, from Gatwick or Stansted, serves Rome-Ciampino, Milan, Venice, Pisa, Palermo, and Naples, and also Rome, Olbia, and Pisa from Bristol. **Meridiana** flies to Florence and Olbia from Gatwick and, like **Blu-Express**, also offers a number of domestic flights.

The entrance hall at Pisa airport

Tickets and Fares

Fares vary enormously according to season and supply and demand. You can usually get the best deals by booking online well in advance.

Consult a good travel agent or check availability on the Internet. If you are based in the UK, it may be worthwhile to scour the small ads of newspapers for charter and discounted scheduled flights on major routes. Most charters leave from Gatwick or Luton, and may land at a city's second (and often less convenient) airport. Fares tend to vary greatly during the year, but the most expensive periods are during the summer months and over the Christmas and Easter holidays. Where possible, ask for available student discounts.

Package Vacations

Package vacations to Italy are usually cheaper than traveling independently, unless you are traveling on a tight budget and are prepared to make use of youth hostels and campsites. Rome, Florence, and Venice are often offered as separate or linked package deals, and many operators have packages to the Tuscan and Umbrian countryside, Sicily, the Italian Lakes, the Italian Riviera, Naples, and the Amalfi coast. In winter, ski packages are available to many Alpine resorts. Themed vacation packages, such as cooking, walking, and art tours, are also common.

In cities, different tour operators may use different hotels, so it is worth researching the most pleasant (and centrally located) accommodation options. Many operators include transfers from the airport to your hotel. Some include tour guides.

DIRECTORY

Green Travel

Cycling in Trentino
W **visittrentino.it**

Airlines

Air Canada
W **aircanada.com**

Alitalia
Tel 89 20 10. W **alitalia.com**

Blu-Express
W **blu-express.com**

British Airways
Tel 02 69 63 36 02.
W **britishairways.com**

Delta
W **delta.com**

easyJet
W **easyjet.com**

Meridiana
W **meridiana.it**

Qantas
W **qantas.com**

Ryanair
W **ryanair.com**

United Airlines
W **united.com**

Airport	Information	Distance to city center	Taxi fare to city center	Public transportation to city center
Rome (Fiumicino)	06 659 51 W **adr.it**	22 miles (35 km)	€48	FS 30 mins
Rome (Ciampino)	06 659 51 W **adr.it**	9 miles (15 km)	€35	[bus] [metro] 45 mins
Milan (Linate)	02 23 23 23 W **seamilano.eu**	5 miles (8 km)	€20	[bus] 15 mins
Milan (Malpensa)	02 23 23 23 W **seamilano.eu**	31 miles (50 km)	€90	FS [metro] 60 mins
Pisa (Galileo Galilei)	050 84 91 11 W **pisa-airport.com**	1 mile (2 km)	€10	FS to Pisa: 10 mins FS to Florence: 80 mins
Venice (Marco Polo)	041 260 111 W **veniceairport.it**	8 miles (13 km)	€35 (€100 water taxi)	[water bus] 60 mins [bus] 20 mins
Venice (Treviso)	0422 31 51 11 W **trevisoairport.it**	15 miles (25 km)	€70 to Venice	[bus] to Treviso: 20 mins [bus] to Venice: 70 mins
Verona	045 809 56 66 W **aeroportoverona.it**	7 miles (12 km)	€25	[bus] 15 mins
Bergamo	035 32 63 23 W **orioaeroporto.it**	3 miles (5 km)	€18	[bus] 25 mins
Turin	011 567 63 61 W **turin-airport.com**	9 miles (15 km)	€30	[bus] 20 mins
Naples	081 789 61 11 W **portal.gesac.it**	4 miles (7 km)	€20	[bus] 30 mins
Palermo	091 702 02 73 W **gesap.it**	21 miles (35 km)	€40–€45	[bus] 50 mins [bus] 1 hr

Arriving by Sea, Rail, and Road

Italy is served by an extensive network of roads, railroads, and international ferry lines. Road and railroad links cross into the country from France, Switzerland, Austria, and Slovenia, and there are through train services from as far afield as Budapest, London, and Barcelona. Road connections into the country are generally of highway standard, though delays can occur at some of the many Alpine passes and tunnels during bad weather or peak summer vacation periods.

Ticket windows at Florence's Santa Maria Novella station

Do-it-yourself help kiosks with train information on screens

Arriving by Car

Most roads into Italy from the rest of Europe involve Alpine crossings by tunnel or mountain passes. The notable exceptions are the approach from Slovenia in the northeast (on the A4 highway) and the route along the French Riviera that enters Italy as the A10 highway at Ventimiglia.

The most popular route from Geneva and southeast France is via the Mont Blanc tunnel and A5 highway, entering Italy close to Aosta and Turin. Another busy approach (from Switzerland) uses the St. Bernard Pass and tunnel.

Further east, the main route from Austria and southern Germany crosses the Brenner Pass and goes down to Verona on the A22 highway via Trento and the Adige valley. Weather conditions rarely close the passes, but snow and fog can make progress slow on the winding roads through the mountains. Most highways are toll roads; you pay as you exit the highway.

Arriving by Train

After air travel, arriving by train is the least painful way to reach Italy. Countless through services (including many sleepers) link Italian towns and cities with places as far afield as Brussels, Budapest, and Barcelona. Connections from Paris (and London, via Eurostar) run to Turin, Milan, Venice, Bologna, Florence, or along Italy's west coast, via Genoa and Pisa, to Rome and Naples. Train services also operate from German, Swiss, and other northern European cities to Milan, Turin, Venice, and Verona. There are also direct services from Vienna, Spain, and the south of France. Motorail connections exist from several centers in northern Europe and the Channel ports.

The popularity of low-cost airlines has forced international train travel to be a little more competitive – if booked online. Special discount fares, however, are often available for senior travelers and for travelers under 26.

Trains can be extremely busy during peak periods, particularly on Friday and Sunday evenings, and during the Christmas and Easter holiday periods. July and August can also be frantically busy, especially on routes from Germany and ports connecting with Greek ferries in the south. Reservations are recommended on most routes.

BINARIO 17

Platform sign

← uscita

Exit sign

The sleeping car on an international Eurocity train

Arriving by Boat

Most people arriving in Italy by boat do so from Greece, using services from Corfu and Patras to Brindisi and other south-eastern ports. Boats are crowded in summer, as are connecting train services from Brindisi to the rest of Italy.

Other international connections include ferries from Malta and North African ports to Palermo, Naples, and various southern Italian ports. Boats also run from towns in the south of France to Genoa, Livorno, and ports on the Italian Riviera, and from the Croatian coast across the Adriatic to Venice.

Arriving by Bus

Bus travel to Italy is relatively cheap, but long travel times make it one of the least comfortable ways to travel. The travel time from London to Milan is about 24 hours, and it is about 33 hours from London to Rome. A night on the road is thus unavoidable. **Eurolines** runs buses from London's Victoria Coach Station to most of Italy's major cities as far as Rome and Naples (a change at Milan or Paris is often necessary). Buses travel via Dover, Calais, Paris, and Dijon and it is useful to have some euros with you for stops en route. Travel around Italy by long-distance bus is feasible with SITA.

SITA bus arriving at the station in Florence

Traveling Around by Ferry

Italy's large number of off-shore islands mean that it has a large and well-developed network of ferries, as well as services to the rest of Europe and North Africa.

One of the Moby Lines car ferries that sail the Mediterranean

Ferries

Car ferries are a convenient link with the beautiful islands scattered off the Italian mainland. Boats for Sardinia leave from Civitavecchia (north of Rome), Livorno, and Genoa, and depart for Sicily from Naples and Reggio di Calabria. Ferries run from the major Sicilian ports to the Egadi and the Aeolian archipelagoes, as well as to countless other small islands around Sicily (although be aware that ferries to the smaller islands do not always carry cars).

Boats also ply between Elba and Piombino, as well as the smaller islands of the Tuscan archipelago such as Capraia. Ferries run from ports close to Rome to Ponza and its surrounding islands, and from Naples to Capri and Ischia. On the east coast the Tremiti islands are linked to ports on the Gargano peninsula.

Hydrofoils are increasingly complementing conventional ferries, particularly on busy routes to Capri and Ischia. Hydrofoils, and ferries, also run on some of Italy's lakes, such as Como and Garda.

Lines for ferries are common in summer, so make reservations well in advance if you wish to travel in July or August, especially if taking a vehicle. Ferry services are more frequent and reliable in summer than in winter.

Reservations can be made online, through travel agents, or at a ferry line's agents in your own country. Ticket prices can vary according to the time of year but are generally reasonable. To check schedules and fares, visit the relevant website.

DIRECTORY

Arriving by Train

Ferrovie dello Stato
Tel 89 20 21 (in Italy).
W trenitalia.com

Arriving by Bus

Eurolines
Tel 0861 199 19 00.
W eurolines.co.uk

SITA
W sitabus.it

Ferries

Corsica Sardinia Ferries
Tel 199 400 500.
W corsicaferries.com
Civitavecchia/Livorno – Golfo Aranci

Grandi Navi Veloci
Tel 010 209 45 91.
W gnv.it Genoa/Civitavecchia – Palermo
Genoa – Porto Torres/Olbia

Moby Lines
Tel 199 303 040; 02 76 02 81 32.
W moby.it
Piombino – Elba
Genoa/Livorno – Olbia

SNAV
Tel 081 428 55 55.
W snav.it
Ancona – Split
Naples/Sorrento – Capri/Ischia
Naples – Aeolian Islands

Tirrenia
Tel 892 123; 02 26 30 28 03. **W tirrenia.it**
Bari – Durazzo
Genoa – Porto Torres
Civitavecchia – Olbia
Naples – Palermo/Cagliari
Cagliari – Palermo

Venezia Lines
Tel 041 882 11 01.
W venezialines.com
Venice – Rabac
Venice – Porec/Rovinj/Pula
Bari – Durazzo

Traveling Around by Train

Train travel is one of the best ways to explore Italy. Tickets are inexpensive, services frequent, and rolling stock some of the most modern in Europe. Services can be busy, but the days of rampant overcrowding are mostly over. Lines often run through lovely countryside, from mountain lakes to rolling plateaus, and they provide more convenient links between cities than roads or air travel. Only in the south, or deeply rural areas, are services slow and infrequent.

The Network

The bulk of Italy's rail network is an integrated state-run system operated by Trenitalia of the Ferrovie dello Stato (FS), which has introduced super-fast services reducing travel times between major cities. In this, it competes with the NTV consortium, whose trains are known as Italo by most people. Smaller privately run lines also fill crucial gaps left by the FS, but through tickets are generally available where travel involves both networks. State and private lines often share the same main station *(stazione)*, and also charge similar fares.

Trains

Trenitalia and NTV (Italo) take advantage of the *Alta Velocità* (AV) network between major cities in the north and southward as far as Naples. These, the fast Eurostar (ES) and a handful of other special high-speed trains always require pre-booking of seats. Intercity (IC) trains and Eurocity (EC) trains only stop at major stations and require the payment of a supplement *(un supplemento)* on top of the standard ticket (supplements can be bought on the train, but are more expensive). *Regionali* and *Interregionali* trains make more stops and require no supplement.

All AV, ES, EC, and Intercity trains are usually air-conditioned. Branch line cars can still be ancient.

Facilities for the disabled, including assistance at stations, exist on all fast trains and international services. For assistance, ask at the special *Sale Blu* (Blue Halls) in mainline stations.

Tickets and Fares

Tickets *(biglietti)* are available as one-way *(andata)* or round-trip *(andata e ritorno)* in first *(prima)* or second class *(seconda classe)*. They can be bought at some travel agents or at any station ticket office *(biglietteria)*.

Major stations have automatic ticket machines and you can also buy tickets for journeys of up to 155 miles (250 km) from newsstands or station tobacconists (such a ticket is called *biglietto a fascia chilometrica*). Be sure to validate all tickets on both outbound and return journeys, or you will be fined. A ticket's validity usually starts on the day of purchase, so be sure to specify the day of travel when buying tickets. Fares are calculated on a kilometric basis and are among the cheapest in western Europe. Many discounted fares are offered, including special family tickets. Some online ticket purchases also carry discounts.

Refunds involve a complicated process – inquire at the *Assistenza* counter at major stations. It is important, therefore, to buy the correct ticket before traveling.

The concourse at Stazione Termini, Rome

A Eurostar – one of Italy's fastest trains

Passes

The most useful pass for visitors is the **Interrail Pass**, which gives unlimited travel for consecutive or nonconsecutive days over varying periods, with special rates for those under 26. It can be purchased online or at most mainline stations and various agencies outside Italy. An Interrail One Country Pass allows travel on any five or ten days within a specific period.

Timetables

If you plan to use trains often, it is a good idea to pick up an official Trenitalia timetable *(un orario)* at the train station or a newsstand. It is updated yearly. Alternatively, visit www.trenitalia.com for the online timetable.

Validity and Reservations

One-way or round-trip tickets are valid for up to two months from the date of purchase. If a seat reservation is made with the ticket, however, the date you wish to travel will be stamped on the ticket. Reservations are automatic on AV and Eurostar services, and they are a good idea on all trains on and around public holidays. Reservations can be made at most main stations or online.

Discounts

The Smart Price deal offers discounts on international trains between Italy and various European countries. One-way prices range from €19 to €70, though there are additions for couchettes and sleeper cars. Tickets can be bought at major stations or on the Trenitalia website, though only a fixed number are available so book ahead.

Luggage Storage

Main city stations usually have luggage storage. Most are manned (but the smaller stations have self-service lockers), and you may need to present identification when depositing or picking up bags. Fees are calculated per bag and by the number of hours they are left.

Scenic Rail Routes

Italy's varied geography makes for some memorable train trips across the length and breadth of the country. The glacially shaped Adige Valley between Bolzano and Verona in the north is thick with apple orchards and surrounded by soaring alpine peaks, with the pretty Trento-Male line branching off it. The Tuscan countryside south of Florence boasts views of hill towns and rolling wheat fields, while close by in Lazio the Roma Nord-Viterbo line winds its way through beautiful rural scenery. Farther south, trains cross the Straits of Messina to Sicily on a special ferry, while a narrow-gauge line circles Mount Etna. For steam train enthusiasts, there are trips run by the **FTI (Ferrovie Turistiche Italiane)** groups in the north through alpine foothills and past picturesque lakes, as well as in the countryside outside Siena.

DIRECTORY

Trains

Erail Travel Ltd
Tel 020 7619 1083 (UK).
W **erail.co.uk**

FTI (Ferrovie Turistiche Italiane)
W **ferrovieturistiche.it**

Interrail Pass
W **interrail.eu**

NTV
W **ntvspa.it**

Trenitalia
Information for travel all over Italy. **Tel** 89 20 21.
W **trenitalia.com**

Machines for Trenitalia Rail Tickets

These machines are easy to use, and most have instructions on screen in a choice of six languages. They accept coins, bills, and credit cards.

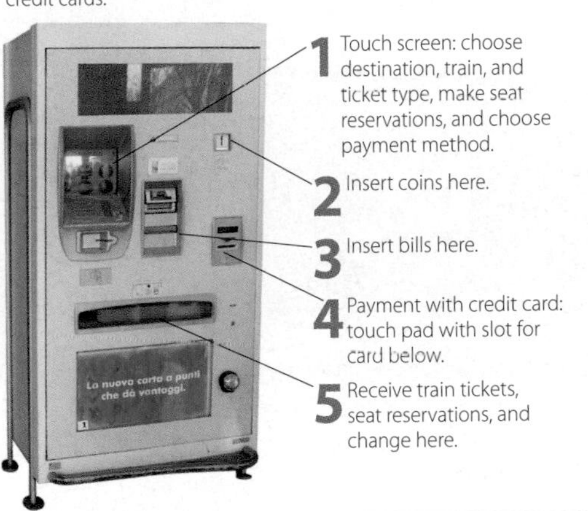

Italy's Principal FS Network

The Italian state rail network operates various types of services. Check what is available before buying your ticket.

Traveling Around by Car

A road trip is a practical way of exploring the country, though you should take into account high gas prices, difficulties parking, driving restrictions in cities, and the Italians' occasionally erratic approach to driving. A car is invaluable in the countryside and for extensive touring, but less useful in major towns and cities, due to congestion and the fact that most city centers are off-limits to nonresidents' cars.

Automatic tollbooths on the highway outside Florence

What to Take

Drivers from outside Italy who bring their own foreign-registered cars into the country must carry a Green Card (for insurance purposes), all the vehicle's registration documents, and a full, valid driver's license (*patente* in Italian). Any EU nationals who do not have the standard EU "pink" license and are planning to stay for more than six months will need an Italian translation of their license, obtainable from most automobile organizations or from the Italian state tourist office in your home country. A red warning triangle and fluorescent vests must also be carried at all times, for use in the event of a breakdown or emergency.

Gas

Gas *(benzina)* in Italy is some of the most expensive in Europe (diesel, or *gasolio*, is a little cheaper). Although many gas stations are now self-service, it is still common to be served by an attendant. Most gas stations follow normal business hours, so make sure you have a full tank before lunchtime or public holidays. On highways gas stations tend to be open 24 hours a day. Credit cards are usually accepted.

Roads

Italy has a good network of highways, though many have a total of only four lanes, often leading to congestion. Busy routes include the A1 from Bologna to Florence and between Bologna, Parma, and Milan. Tolls must be paid on most highways *(autostrade)*, again leading to congestion at tollbooths *(Alt Stazione)* during busy periods. Payment is made at the end of the journey in cash, credit card, or prepaid magnetic VIA cards, available from tobacconists and the **ACI**. There is a congestion charge in Milan (7:30am–7:30pm Mon–Fri); call 800 437 437 or visit www.comunemilano.it/ecopass before entering the city.

Secondary roads are known as *Nazionali* (N) or as *Strade Statali* (SS), and vary enormously in quality. Mountain roads are usually good, but distances can be deceptive. In winter, snow chains are obligatory on many higher routes. Some back roads (known as *strade bianche*, or "white roads") have only a gravel surface. These are slow, but usually passable for cars.

Rules and Regulations

Drive on the right and yield to traffic from the right. Seat belts are required for all passengers. Heavy fines are levied for using a mobile phone while driving. Headlights must be turned on even during the day on highways and outside built-up areas. The speed limit in urban areas is 30 mph (50 km/h); outside urban areas it is 70 mph (110 km/h) on divided highways and 55 mph (90 km/h) on other secondary roads. On highways the limit is 80 mph (130 km/h) for vehicles over 1100cc, 70 mph (110 km/h) for those under 1100cc.

One-way street

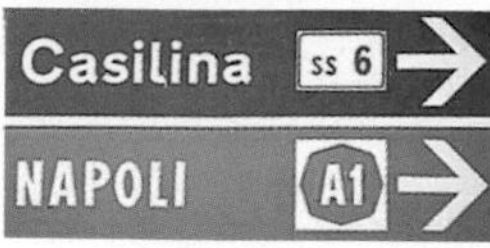

Blue signs showing main roads and green signs showing highways

No stopping

End of speed restriction

Pedestrianized street – no traffic

Yield to oncoming traffic

No parking

Danger (often with description)

Europcar

Logo for international car rental company

Car Rental

Car rentals *(autonoleggio)* in Italy are expensive, and should be organized beforehand through package airfare-plus-rental deals or advance reservations with rental agencies that have branches in Italy. For on-the-ground rentals, Italian firms may be cheaper than big international names. Agencies are listed in the Yellow Pages *(Pagine Gialle)* under Autonoleggio. Most airports have car rental offices on site.

To rent a car in Italy you must generally be over 21 (sometimes older) and have held a valid driver's license for at least a year. Visitors from outside the EU must have an international license, though in practice not all rental agencies insist on this. Check the fine print of the agreement for insurance coverage.

Accidents and Breakdowns

If you have an accident or a breakdown, switch on your hazard warning lights and place a warning triangle 164 ft (50 m) behind your car. Then (for breakdowns) call the **ACI** emergency number (803 116) or emergency services (112 or 113). The ACI will tow any foreign-registered car free to the nearest ACI-affiliated garage. They also do free repairs for members of affiliated automobile associations, such as the AA and RAC in Britain.

If you have an accident, stay calm, and do not admit liability or make any statements that might incriminate you later. Simply exchange car and insurance details, names, and addresses.

Parking

Parking in most Italian cities and large towns is a problem. Many historic centers have restricted daytime access and baffling one-way systems. Other areas may be reserved for residents' parking (marked *riservato ai residenti*). Most towns have metered parking areas that charge an hourly fee paid with coins, cards, or coupons bought from *tabacchi*. Cars can be towed away or have their wheels clamped, especially in areas marked *zona rimozione*, particularly on street-cleaning days. Call the Municipal Police *(Vigili)* to retrieve your car.

Official parking area patrolled by attendant

Safety

Car theft is rife in Italy. Never leave anything in your car, and (if possible) always remove radio-CD players and GPS devices.

Leave your car in a guarded parking lot whenever you can. Be especially careful driving at night, when Italian driving is more cavalier than usual, and when many traffic lights switch to flashing amber. Hitchhiking *(autostop)* is not a good idea (and is not common), certainly never for women on their own.

DIRECTORY

Car Rental

Avis
Tel 06 452 10 83 91.
W avisautonoleggio.it

Europcar
Tel 199 307 030.
W europcar.it

Hertz
Tel 06 65 01 15 53 (Rome airport).
W hertz.it

Maggiore
Tel 199 151 120.
W maggiore.it

Sixt
Tel 06 65 21 11 (Rome).
W sixt.it

Emergencies

ACI emergency
Tel 803 116. **W aci.it**

Police
Tel 112 or 113.

Ambulance
Tel 118.

Distance Chart

10 Distance in kilometers
10 Distance in miles

	Rome	Ancona	Aosta	Bologna	Bolzano	Florence	Genoa	Lecce	Milan	Naples	Turin
Ancona	**286** 178										
Aosta	**748** 465	**617** 383									
Bologna	**383** 238	**219** 136	**401** 249								
Bolzano	**645** 401	**494** 307	**449** 279	**280** 174							
Florence	**278** 173	**262** 163	**470** 292	**106** 66	**367** 228						
Genoa	**510** 317	**506** 315	**245** 152	**291** 181	**422** 262	**225** 140					
Lecce	**601** 373	**614** 382	**1220** 758	**822** 511	**1097** 682	**871** 541	**1103** 685				
Milan	**575** 357	**426** 265	**181** 113	**210** 130	**295** 183	**299** 186	**145** 90	**1029** 639			
Naples	**219** 136	**409** 254	**959** 596	**594** 369	**856** 532	**489** 304	**714** 444	**393** 244	**786** 488		
Turin	**673** 418	**547** 340	**110** 68	**332** 206	**410** 255	**395** 245	**170** 106	**1150** 715	**138** 86	**884** 549	
Venice	**530** 329	**364** 226	**442** 275	**154** 96	**214** 133	**255** 158	**397** 247	**967** 601	**273** 170	**741** 460	**402** 250

Traveling within Cities

The best ways of getting around Italian cities differ from place to place. In Rome buses are most useful, in Milan the metro is more efficient, and in Venice you will need to take a boat to get about. Streetcars still run in some cities, such as Milan and Rome. Cars are a liability almost everywhere, unlike walking, which in many cases is the easiest way to negotiate the tight historic cores of Italian towns and cities. Florence and Rome have a large limited-traffic zone, and most towns now have a pedestrian area in the center.

A Roman bus in the red and gray livery of ATAC

One of the distinctive orange city buses, central Verona

Buses and Streetcars

Virtually every Italian city and large town has a bus system. Most are cheap, comprehensive, and as efficient as traffic and narrow streets will allow, and systems vary only slightly from city to city. Bus stops are known as *fermate*, and increasingly (notably in Rome) list full details of the routes they serve. Buses *(autobus)* usually run from about 6am to midnight, and there are night buses *(servizio notturno)* in larger cities. If you arrive in a town by train, stations are invariably linked to the center by shuttle buses from the front of the station (tickets are usually available from the station bar or tobacconist).

Tickets

Tickets *(biglietti)* must be bought before boarding the bus, and can be found at kiosks belonging to the bus company (ATAF in Florence, ATAC in Rome), bars, newsstands, or tobacconists displaying the bus company's sticker. A few cities also have on-street vending machines around main transportation hubs. It is worth buying more than one ticket at a time, as outlets often close in the afternoon or early evening. Discounted tickets *(un blocchetto)*, or day- or weeklong visitors' tickets and passes *(una tessera* or *tesserino)* are also available. In some cities tickets are valid for any number of trips within a given time. The ATAC website has more details on buses in Rome.

ATAC
W atac.roma.it

Using Buses and Streetcars

Board buses via the front and rear doors, and exit via the central doors. Buses usually have a driver and no conductor (night buses may have a conductor from whom tickets can be bought).

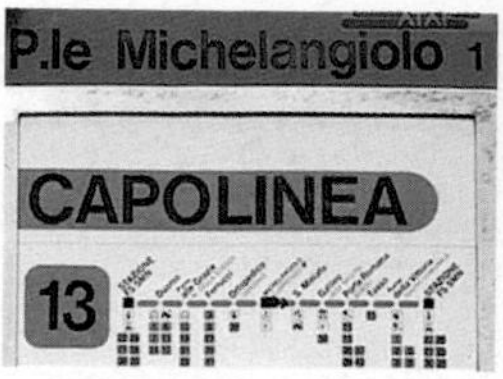

Bus stop displaying the route

Tickets must be validated by punching them in machines at the front or rear of the bus. There are large on-the-spot fines if you are caught without a properly validated ticket. The front, low seats on buses are for people with children, the elderly, and the disabled.

Most larger cities have transportation information offices at the main train station or piazza that provide free maps, timetables, and tickets.

The majority of city buses are painted bright orange and display the final destination *(capolinea)* on the front.

Metropolitana

Underground systems, known as *metropolitana* (*la metro* for short), are found in Rome and Milan. Rome's network amounts to just two lines, A and B, which converge at Stazione Termini, the city's central train station. Several stations are useful for key sights, and at peak times the lines provide the best way of crossing the city quickly. Stations are fairly dingy – though rarely dangerous – and train cars can be stiflingly hot in summer. In Milan the network is more extensive, with three principal lines – MM1 (the red line), MM2 (green), and MM3 (yellow) – that meet at the hub stations of Stazione Centrale, Duomo, Cadorna, and Loreto. These

Metro sign

Termini metro station, Rome

An official taxi waiting at a pedestrian crossing

three lines give easy access to the majority of the city's main sights.

Metro tickets in both cities are available from the same sources as bus and streetcar tickets, and from machines and ticket offices in underground stations. Tickets in Rome are valid for 75 minutes for one metro journey only, but can be used on any number of bus and streetcar trips. One-day, three-day, and seven-day tickets are also available and offer unlimited metro, bus, and streetcar travel. In Milan, by contrast, ordinary metro tickets are valid for 90 minutes for one metro journey and can also be used on the buses and streetcars.

Walking

Walking can be a wonderful way to explore Italy's historic towns and cities, most of whose historic centers are smaller than you might expect. Traffic can be a curse, however, especially in narrow streets (Rome is worst in this respect), but many cities are introducing pedestrianized areas or cutting down on car access around key tourist sights. On certain Sundays *(Domenica a Piedi)*, entire town centers may be designated traffic-free zones.

Italian towns have plenty of shady squares and cafés to escape the heat of the summer sun, and churches and cathedrals also provide cool retreats from the rigors of sightseeing. Most sights are well marked (churches, museums, and other places of interest are often indicated by yellow signs). Always carry your valuables well out of sight. The best times to walk are in the cool of the morning, or in the early evening, when you can join in the pre-dinner stroll known as the *passeggiata*.

Stay on the sidewalk at all costs

Marginally less dangerous to cross

Taxis

Only accept rides in official taxis. Most drivers are honest but there are many supplements that can be legitimately levied. Generally an extra charge is made for each piece of luggage placed in the trunk, for rides between 10pm and 7am, on Sundays and public holidays, and for travel to and from airports.

In theory, taxis cannot be hailed. Take one at an official taxi stand (usually found at the train station or main piazza, or close to key tourist sights) or reserve one by phone. When you order a taxi by phone, take the driver's code name, e.g., Napoli 18. If you call a cab, the meter will start at the time of your call.

Bicycle Rental

Many towns and cities, especially those popular with visitors, have stands and shops offering bikes and scooters for rent. You can usually rent hourly or by the day, and you may have to leave your passport with the shop as a deposit. Be very careful, however, if riding a bike in the busy traffic of the larger towns and cities.

BikeMi in Milan provides access to bikes at various places in the city. The initial fee is €2.50 a day (€6 a week), which covers the first 30 minutes' rental. Rates are then €0.50 for 30 minutes, rising to €2 per hour after the first two hours. You can register by phone (800 80 81 81) or via the website (www.bikemi.it).

Intercity Transportation: Buses

Long-haul buses *(pullman* or *corriere)* between towns operate in a similar way to local buses, though you can usually buy tickets on board, and services are often run by different companies in different-colored buses (blue is the most common color for *pullman*, orange for city buses). Buses in some areas may be run by several companies (notably around Florence and in Tuscany), and not all operate from the same terminals. Intercity bus routes often depart from outside train stations, or from a town's main piazza. If in doubt, ask at a local tourist office. Reduced schedules may be offered on weekends, when offices are closed.

Rome to Gubbio bus

Rome
COTRAL
Tel 800 174 471
or 06 72 05 72 05.
W **cotralspa.it**
Appian
Tel 06 48 78 66 01.
W **appianline.it**

Tuscany
Lazzi **Tel** 0573 193 79 00. **W** **lazzi.it**
Sita **Tel** 800 37 37 60. **W** **sitabus.it**
Tra-In **Tel** 0577 20 41 11. **W** **trainspa.it**

National & International
Eurolines
Tel 0861 199 19 00.
W **eurolines.it**

Traveling Around Venice

For visitors to Venice, the *vaporetti* or waterbuses *(see pp140–41)* provide an entertaining form of public transportation, although most journeys within the city can usually be covered more quickly on foot. The main route through the city for the *vaporetti* is the Grand Canal. Waterbuses also supply a useful service connecting outlying points on the periphery of Venice, and linking the city to the islands in the lagoon. The most important service from a visitor's point of view is the No. 1. This operates from one end of the Grand Canal to the other and travels slowly enough for you to admire the parade of palaces at the waterside *(see pp92–95)*.

A *vaporetto* or waterbus

The smaller, sleeker *motoscafo*

The Boats

The original *vaporetti* were steam-powered (*vaporetto* means little steamer); today they are mostly diesel-run motorboats, with a handful of electric, battery-powered prototypes. Although all the boats tend to be called *vaporetti*, the word only really applies to the large, wide boats used on slow routes, such as No. 1. These boats provide the best views. *Motoscafi* are the slimmer, smaller boats that look old but go at a fair pace, while *motonavi* are two-tier boats that run to the islands. To visit the islands of Murano, Burano, or Torcello, take the LN Line, which departs from San Zaccaria and Fondamenta Nuove.

Types of Ticket

If booths at landing stages are closed, single tickets can be purchased on board at no extra charge – the tickets are valid for 1 hour from purchase. A good way to save money, however, is by buying a travel card, available for 12, 24, 36, 48, or 72 hours. Such a card entitles the holder to unlimited travel on most lines. Discounts on advance tickets are also available, especially if you reserve seven days in advance. A single- or round-trip supplement to/from Marco Polo airport can also be added to the price of the card (see www.veniceconnected.com).

If you are staying more than a few days, it is worth buying a weekly season ticket *(abbonamento)*, available from ticket offices, though non-residents are charged €50 for the privilege. Holders of Rolling Venice cards (with information packs and discounts for 14–29-year-olds) can buy a three-day youth pass. Tickets include transporting one piece of luggage: be prepared to buy another ticket for extra items.

Vaporetto stop at the Giardini Pubblici, Venice

Hours of Service

The main routes run every 10 to 20 minutes until the early evening. Services are less frequent after midnight, but run all night. From June to September the services are more frequent and certain routes are extended. Timetables are available at main landing stages. Be warned: from May to September the main routes and island boats are very crowded.

Vaporetto Information

ACTV (Hello Venezia Office) Piazzale Roma, Venice. **Map** 5 B1. **Tel** 041 2424.
W actv.it

Traghetti

Traghetti are gondola ferries that cross the Grand Canal at seven different points, providing a useful service for pedestrians. Few tourists make use of this cheap (about 50 euro cents per trip) and constant service. Points where *traghetti* cross the Grand Canal are marked on the Street Finder maps *(see pp130–39)*. A gondola on yellow street signs points to *traghetti* stops.

A two-tier *motonave* boat

Gondolas

Gondolas are a luxury form of transportation used only by visitors and Venetians at weddings. Before boarding, check the official tariffs and agree on a price with the gondolier. Official costs are around €80 for 40 minutes, increasing to €100 after 7pm. During the off-season, you may be able to negotiate a lower fee, and a journey shorter than the usual 40 minutes.

Water Taxis

For those with little time and sufficient funds, the fastest and most practical means of getting from A to B in Venice is by water taxi. The craft are sleek, white or polished wood motorboats, and all are equipped with a cabin.

They zip efficiently to and from the airport in only 20 minutes. There are 16 water taxi ranks, including one at the airport and one at the Lido.

A water taxi

Beware of extra charges for transporting luggage, waiting, night service, and for calling a taxi. When the *vaporetti* go on strike, taxis are scarce.

Water Taxi Stands

Radio Taxi (all of Venice)
Tel 041 522 23 03.

Piazzale Roma
Map 5 B1. **Tel** 041 71 69 22.

Crossing the Grand Canal by *traghetto*

The Main Routes

① This is the slow boat down the Grand Canal, stopping at every landing stage. The route starts at Piazzale Roma, travels the length of the Grand Canal, then from San Marco it heads east to the Lido.

② The No. 2 is the faster route down the Grand Canal. With an extension to the Lido during the summer months, the route serves San Zaccaria, continuing westward along the Giudecca Canal to Tronchetto and Piazzale Roma, then down the Grand Canal back to San Zaccaria.

(41)(42)(51)(52)(6) These lines all sail around the central islands. The circular *Giracittà* routes 4.1–4.2 provide a scenic tour of Venice and Murano, while lines 5.1–5.2 and 6 also extend to the Lido.

(12)(14) The 12 departs from the Fondamenta Nuove and runs to the main islands in the northern lagoon – Murano, Mazzorbo, and Burano (with a connection to Torcello) – then calls at Punta Sabbioni. The 14 takes you to the Lido, before concluding at San Zaccaria.

Using the Vaporetti

1 Tickets are available at most landing stages, some bars, and at shops and tobacconists displaying the ACTV sign. It is also possible to buy tickets on board. The price of a ticket remains the same whether you are going one stop or traveling the whole line.

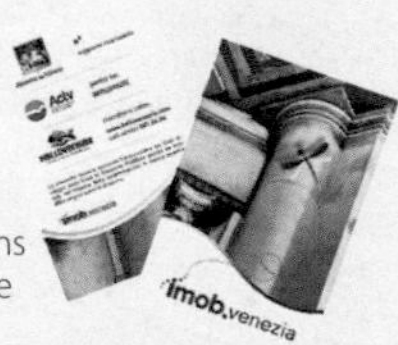

2 Signs on the landing stage tell you the direction of the boats stopping there.

3 Imob electronic chip tickets are in use and should be validated before each journey at the electronic machines on the landing stages. Inspectors rarely board the boats, and this makes it surprisingly easy to hop on and off the boats without a validated ticket. However, there are steep fines for any passengers caught without tickets.

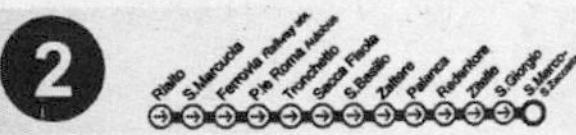

4 An indicator board at the front of each boat gives the line number and main stops. (Ignore the black numbers on the boat's side.)

5 Each landing stage has its name clearly marked on a board. Most stops have two landing stages and it is quite easy, particularly if it is crowded and you can't see which way the boat is facing, to board a boat traveling in the wrong direction. It is helpful to watch which direction the boat is approaching from; if in doubt, check with the boatman.

General Index

Page numbers in **bold** type refer to main entries

B

C

D

G

H

I

N

O

Q

R